PRAISE FOR THE FIRST EDITION OF *A PRACTICAL GUIDE TO UBUNTU LINUX*®

"I am so impressed by how Mark Sobell can approach a complex topic in such an understandable manner. His command examples are especially useful in providing a novice (or even an advanced) administrator with a cookbook on how to accomplish real-world tasks on Linux. He is truly an inspired technical writer!"

—*George Vish II*
Senior Education Consultant
Hewlett-Packard Company

"Overall, I think it's a great, comprehensive Ubuntu book that'll be a valuable resource for people of all technical levels."

—*John Dong*
Ubuntu Forum Council Member
Backports Team Leader

"The JumpStart sections really offer a quick way to get things up and running, allowing you to dig into the details of the book later."

—*Scott Mann*
Aztek Networks

"Ubuntu is gaining popularity at the rate alcohol did during Prohibition, and it's great to see a well-known author write a book on the latest and greatest version. Not only does it contain Ubuntu-specific information, but it also touches on general computer-related topics, which will help the average computer user to better understand what's going on in the background. Great work, Mark!"

—*Daniel R. Arfsten*
Pro/ENGINEER Drafter/Designer

"The author has done a very good job at clarifying such a detail-oriented operating system. I have extensive Unix and Windows experience and this text does an excellent job at bridging the gaps between Linux, Windows, and Unix. I highly recommend this book to both 'newbs' and experienced users. Great job!"

—Mark Polczynski
Information Technology Consultant

"When I first started working with Linux just a short 10 years or so ago, it was a little more difficult than now to get going. . . . Now, someone new to the community has a vast array of resources available on the web, or if they are inclined to begin with Ubuntu, they can literally find almost every single thing they will need in the single volume of Mark Sobell's *A Practical Guide to Ubuntu Linux*®.

"I'm sure this sounds a bit like hyperbole. Everything a person would need to know? Obviously not everything, but this book, weighing in at just under 1200 pages, covers so much so thoroughly that there won't be much left out. From install to admin, networking, security, shell scripting, package management, and a host of other topics, it is all there. GUI and command line tools are covered. There is not really any wasted space or fluff, just a huge amount of information. There are screen shots when appropriate but they do not take up an inordinate amount of space. This book is information-dense."

—JR Peck
Editor
GeekBook.org

PRAISE FOR OTHER BOOKS BY MARK G. SOBELL

"I currently own one of your books, *A Practical Guide to Linux*®. I believe this book is one of the most comprehensive and, as the title says, practical guides to Linux I have ever read. I consider myself a novice and I come back to this book over and over again."

—Albert J. Nguyen

"Thank you for writing a book to help me get away from Windows XP and to never touch Windows Vista. The book is great; I am learning a lot of new concepts and commands. Linux is definitely getting easier to use."

—*James Moritz*

"I have been wanting to make the jump to Linux but did not have the guts to do so—until I saw your familiarly titled *A Practical Guide to Red Hat® Linux®* at the bookstore. I picked up a copy and am eagerly looking forward to regaining my freedom."

—*Carmine Stoffo*
Machine and Process Designer
to pharmaceutical industry

"I am currently reading *A Practical Guide to Red Hat® Linux®* and am finally understanding the true power of the command line. I am new to Linux and your book is a treasure."

—*Juan Gonzalez*

A Practical Guide to Ubuntu Linux®

SECOND EDITION

A PRACTICAL GUIDE TO UBUNTU LINUX®

SECOND EDITION

MARK G. SOBELL

PRENTICE
HALL

Upper Saddle River, NJ • Boston • Indianapolis • San Francisco
New York • Toronto • Montreal • London • Munich • Paris • Madrid
Capetown • Sydney • Tokyo • Singapore • Mexico City

Many of the designations used by manufacturers and sellers to distinguish their products are claimed as trademarks. Where those designations appear in this book, and the publisher was aware of a trademark claim, the designations have been printed with initial capital letters or in all capitals.

Ubuntu is a registered trademark of Canonical Limited.

The author and publisher have taken care in the preparation of this book, but make no expressed or implied warranty of any kind and assume no responsibility for errors or omissions. No liability is assumed for incidental or consequential damages in connection with or arising out of the use of the information or programs contained herein.

The publisher offers excellent discounts on this book when ordered in quantity for bulk purchases or special sales, which may include electronic versions and/or custom covers and content particular to your business, training goals, marketing focus, and branding interests. For more information, please contact:

U.S. Corporate and Government Sales
(800) 382-3419
corpsales@pearsontechgroup.com

For sales outside the United States, please contact:

International Sales
international@pearsoned.com

Visit us on the Web: informit.com/ph

Library of Congress Cataloging-in-Publication Data
Sobell, Mark G.
  A practical guide to Ubuntu Linux / Mark G. Sobell. — 2nd ed.
    p. cm.
  Includes index.
  ISBN 978-0-13-700388-4 (pbk.)
  1. Ubuntu (Electronic resource) 2. Linux. 3. Operating systems (Computers) I. Title.
  QA76.76.O63S59497 2009
  005.4'32—dc22

                                                      2008045136

ISBN-13: 978-0-13-700388-4
ISBN-10:   0-13-700388-9

Printed in the United States of America at Edwards Brothers in Ann Arbor, Michigan.
Second printing, February 2009

For my sons,
Sam, Zach, and Max,
each of whom is blooming
and bringing light into the world.

Brief Contents

CONTENTS

PART II   GETTING STARTED WITH UBUNTU LINUX   83

CHAPTER 4: INTRODUCTION TO UBUNTU LINUX   85

CHAPTER 5: THE LINUX UTILITIES   145

CHAPTER 7: THE SHELL   223

CHAPTER 10: NETWORKING AND THE INTERNET   355

PART IV   SYSTEM ADMINISTRATION   399

CHAPTER 11: SYSTEM ADMINISTRATION: CORE CONCEPTS   401

CHAPTER 15: BUILDING A LINUX KERNEL   555

CHAPTER 16: ADMINISTRATION TASKS   577

CHAPTER 17: CONFIGURING A LAN   613

PART V   USING CLIENTS AND SETTING UP SERVERS   625

CHAPTER 20: **exim4**: SETTING UP MAIL SERVERS, CLIENTS, AND MORE   677

CHAPTER 21: NIS AND LDAP   705

CHAPTER 22: NFS: SHARING FILESYSTEMS   737

CHAPTER 25: firestarter, ufw, AND iptables: SETTING UP A FIREWALL   823

CHAPTER 26: APACHE: SETTING UP A WEB SERVER   855

PART VI   PROGRAMMING TOOLS   907

CHAPTER 27: PROGRAMMING THE BOURNE AGAIN SHELL   909

PART VII   APPENDIXES   1041

APPENDIX A: REGULAR EXPRESSIONS   1043

APPENDIX B: HELP   1053

APPENDIX C: SECURITY   1063

APPENDIX D: THE FREE SOFTWARE DEFINITION   1083

APPENDIX E: THE LINUX 2.6 KERNEL   1087

JumpStarts

JumpStarts get you off to a quick start when you need to use a client or set up a server. Once you have the client or server up and running, you can refine its configuration using the information presented in the sections following each JumpStart.

APT

CUPS

OpenSSH

FTP

PREFACE

The book   Whether you are an end user, a system administrator, or a little of both, this book explains with step-by-step examples how to get the most out of an Ubuntu Linux system. In 28 chapters, this book takes you from installing an Ubuntu system through understanding its inner workings to setting up secure servers that run on the system.

The audience   This book is designed for a wide range of readers. It does not require you to have programming experience, although having some experience using a general-purpose computer, such as a Windows, Macintosh, UNIX, or another Linux system is certainly helpful. This book is appropriate for

- **Students** who are taking a class in which they use Linux
- **Home users** who want to set up and/or run Linux
- **Professionals** who use Linux at work
- **System administrators** who need an understanding of Linux and the tools that are available to them including the bash and Perl scripting languages
- **Computer science students** who are studying the Linux operating system
- **Technical executives** who want to get a grounding in Linux

Benefits   *A Practical Guide to Ubuntu Linux®, Second Edition,* gives you a broad understanding of many facets of Linux, from installing Ubuntu Linux through using and customizing it. No matter what your background, this book provides the knowledge you need to get on with your work. You will come away from this book understanding how to use Linux, and this book will remain a valuable reference for years to come.

New in this edition This edition includes

- An all-new chapter on the Perl programming language (Chapter 28; page 997).

- Coverage of LDAP, which has been added to Chapter 21 (page 722).

- Coverage of the ufw firewall, which has been added to Chapter 25 (page 834).

- Updated chapters to reflect the Ubuntu 8.04 LTS (Hardy Heron; maintained until 2011) and Ubuntu 8.10 (Intrepid Ibex) releases.

- Four indexes to make it easier to find what you are looking for quickly. These indexes locate tables (page numbers followed by the letter **t**, definitions (italic page numbers), and differentiate between light and comprehensive coverage (light and standard fonts).

  - The JumpStart index (page 1143) lists all the JumpStart sections in this book. These sections help you set up servers and clients as quickly as possible.

  - The File Tree index (page 1145) lists, in hierarchical fashion, most files mentioned in this book. These files are also listed in the main index.

  - The Utility index (page 1149) locates all utilities mentioned in this book. A page number in a light font indicates a brief mention of the utility while the regular font indicates more substantial coverage.

  - The completely revised main index (page 1155) is designed for ease of use.

Overlap If you have read the first edition of *A Practical Guide to Linux® Commands, Editors, and Shell Programming,* you will notice some overlap between that book and the one you are reading now. The first chapter, the chapters on the utilities and the filesystem, the appendix on regular expressions, and the Glossary are very similar in the two books, as are the three chapters on the Bourne Again Shell (bash). Chapters that appear in this book but do not appear in *A Practical Guide to Linux® Commands, Editors, and Shell Programming* include Chapters 2 and 3 (installation), Chapters 4 and 8 (Ubuntu Linux and the GUI), Chapter 10 (networking), all of the chapters in Part IV (system administration) and Part V (servers), Chapter 28 (Perl), and Appendix C (security).

Differences While this book explains how to use Linux from a graphical interface and from the command line (a textual interface), *A Practical Guide to Linux® Commands, Editors, and Shell Programming* works exclusively with the command line. It includes full chapters on the vi and emacs editors, as well as chapters on the gawk pattern processing language and the sed stream editor. In addition, it has a command reference section that provides extensive examples of the use of more than 80 of the most important Linux utilities. You can use these utilities to solve problems without resorting to programming in C.

THIS BOOK INCLUDES UBUNTU INTREPID IBEX (8.10) ON A LIVE/INSTALL DVD

This book includes a live/install DVD that holds the Intrepid Ibex (8.10) release of Ubuntu Linux. You can use this DVD to run a live Ubuntu session that displays the GNOME desktop without making any changes to your computer: Boot from the DVD, run an Ubuntu live session, and log off. Your system remains untouched: When you reboot, it is exactly as it was before you ran the Ubuntu live session. Alternatively, you can install Ubuntu from the live session. Chapter 2 helps you get ready to install Ubuntu. Chapter 3 provides step-by-step instructions for installing Ubuntu from this DVD. This book guides you through learning about, using, and administrating an Ubuntu Linux system.

DVD features   The included DVD incorporates all the features of the live/install Desktop CD as well as the Alternate and Server CDs. It also includes all software packages supported by Ubuntu. You can use it to perform a graphical or textual (command line) installation of either a graphical or a textual Ubuntu system. If you do not have an Internet connection, you can use the DVD as a software repository and install any supported software packages from it.

FEATURES OF THIS BOOK

This book is designed and organized so you can get the most out of it in the shortest amount of time. You do not have to read this book straight through in page order. Instead, once you are comfortable using Linux, you can use this book as a reference: Look up a topic of interest in the table of contents or in an index and read about it. Or think of the book as a catalog of Linux topics: Flip through the pages until a topic catches your eye. The book includes many pointers to Web sites where you can get additional information: Consider the Internet an extension of this book.

A Practical Guide to Ubuntu Linux®, Second Edition, is structured with the following features:

- **Optional sections** enable you to read the book at different levels, returning to more difficult material when you are ready to delve into it.

- **Caution boxes** highlight procedures that can easily go wrong, giving you guidance *before* you run into trouble.

- **Tip boxes** highlight ways you can save time by doing something differently or situations when it may be useful or just interesting to have additional information.

- **Security boxes** point out places where you can make a system more secure. The **security appendix** presents a quick background in system security issues.

- Concepts are illustrated by **practical examples** throughout the book.

- **Chapter summaries** review the important points covered in each chapter.

- **Review exercises** are included at the end of each chapter for readers who want to further hone their skills. Answers to even-numbered exercises are available at www.sobell.com.

- The **glossary** defines more than 500 common terms.

- The chapters that cover servers include **JumpStart** sections that get you off to a quick start using clients and setting up servers. Once a server is up and running, you can test and modify its configuration as explained in the rest of each of these chapters.

- This book provides resources for **finding software** on the Internet. It also explains how to **download** and **install** software using Synaptic, aptitude, the GNOME Add/Remove Applications window, and BitTorrent. It details controlling automatic updates using the Update Notifier and the Update Manager window.

- This book describes in detail many important **GNU tools**, including the GNOME desktop, the Nautilus File Browser, the parted and gparted partition editors, the gzip compression utility, and many command-line utilities that come from the GNU project.

- Pointers throughout the text provide help in obtaining **online documentation** from many sources, including the local system, the Ubuntu Web site, and other locations on the Internet.

- Many **useful URLs** point to Web sites where you can obtain software, security programs and information, and more.

- The multiple **comprehensive indexes** help you locate topics quickly and easily.

KEY TOPICS COVERED IN THIS BOOK

This book contains a lot of information. This section distills and summarizes its contents. In addition, "Details" (starting on page xlv) describes what each chapter covers. Finally, the table of contents provides more detail. This book:

Installation
- Describes how to download Ubuntu Linux ISO images from the Internet and burn the Ubuntu live/install Desktop CD, the DVD, or the Ubuntu Alternate or Server installation CD.

- Helps you plan the layout of the system's hard disk. It includes a discussion of partitions, partition tables, and mount points, and assists you in using the ubiquity or gparted graphical partitioner or the Ubuntu textual partitioner to partition the hard disk.

- Explains how to set up a dual-boot system so you can install Ubuntu Linux on a Windows system and boot either operating system.

- Describes in detail how to install Ubuntu Linux from a live/install Desktop CD or the live/install DVD using the ubiquity graphical installer. It also explains how to use the textual installer found on the Alternate CD, the Server CD, and the DVD. The graphical installer is fast and easy to use. The textual installer gives you more options and works on systems with less RAM (system memory).

- Covers testing an Ubuntu CD/DVD for defects, setting boot command-line parameters (boot options), and creating a RAID array.

- Covers the details of customizing the X.org version of the X Window System using the Screen and Graphics Preferences window.

Working with Ubuntu Linux

- Introduces the GNOME desktop (GUI) and explains how to use desktop tools, including the Top and Bottom panels, panel objects, the Main menu, object context menus, the Workspace Switcher, the Nautilus File Browser, and the GNOME terminal emulator.

- Explains how to use the Appearance Preferences window to add and modify themes to customize your desktop to please your senses and help you work more efficiently.

- Details how to set up 3D desktop visual effects that take advantage of Compiz Fusion.

- Covers the Bourne Again Shell (bash) in three chapters, including an entire chapter on shell programming that includes many sample shell scripts. These chapters provide clear explanations and extensive examples of how bash works both from the command line in day-to-day work and as a programming language to write shell scripts.

- Explains the textual (command-line) interface and introduces more than 30 command-line utilities.

- Presents a tutorial on the vim textual editor.

- Covers types of networks, network protocols, and network utilities.

- Explains hostnames, IP addresses, and subnets, and explores how to use host and dig to look up domain names and IP addresses on the Internet.

- Covers distributed computing and the client/server model.

- Explains how to use ACLs (Access Control Lists) to fine-tune user access permissions.

System administration

- Explains how to use the Ubuntu graphical and textual (command-line) tools to configure the display, DNS, NFS, Samba, Apache, a firewall, a network interface, and more. You can also use these tools to add users and manage local and remote printers.

- Goes into detail about using sudo to allow specific users to work with **root** privileges (become Superuser) and customizing the way sudo works by editing the **sudoers** configuration file. It also explains how you can unlock the **root** account if necessary.

- Describes how to use the following tools to download and install software to keep a system up-to-date and to install new software:

  - The **Software Sources** window controls which Ubuntu and third-party software repositories Ubuntu downloads software packages from and whether Ubuntu downloads updates automatically. You can also use this window to cause Ubuntu to download and install security updates automatically.

  - If you do not have an Internet connection, you can use the **Software Sources** window to set up the DVD included with this book as a software repository. You can then install any software packages that Ubuntu supports from this repository.

  - Based on how you set up updates in the Software Sources window, the **Update Notifier** pops up on the desktop to let you know when software updates are available. Click the Update Notifier to open the Update Manager window, from which you can download and install updates.

  - The **Add/Remove Applications** window provides an easy way to select, download, and install a wide range of software packages.

  - **Synaptic** allows you to search for, install, and remove software packages. It gives you more ways to search for packages than does the Add/Remove Applications window.

  - **APT** downloads and installs software packages from the Internet (or the included DVD), keeping a system up-to-date and resolving dependencies as it processes the packages. You can use APT from a graphical interface (Synaptic) or from several textual interfaces (e.g., aptitude and apt-get).

  - **BitTorrent** is a good choice for distributing large amounts of data such as the Ubuntu installation DVD and CDs. The more people who use BitTorrent to download a file, the faster it works.

- Covers graphical system administration tools, including the many tools available from the GNOME Main menu.

- Explains system operation, including the boot process, init scripts, recovery (single-user) and multiuser modes, and steps to take if the system crashes.

- Describes how to use and program the new Upstart **init** daemon, which replaces the System V **init** daemon.

- Describes files, directories, and filesystems, including types of files and filesystems, **fstab** (the filesystem table), and automatically mounted filesystems, and explains how to fine-tune and check the integrity of filesystems.

- Covers backup utilities, including tar, cpio, dump, and restore.

- Describes compression/archive utilities, including gzip, bzip2, compress, and zip.

- Explains how to customize and build a Linux kernel.

Security
- Helps you manage basic system security issues using ssh (secure shell), **vsftpd** (secure FTP server), Apache (Web server), iptables (firewalls), and more.

- Describes how to use the uncomplicated firewall (ufw) to protect the system.

- Covers using firestarter to share an Internet connection over a LAN, run a DHCP server, and set up a basic firewall to protect the system.

- Provides instructions on using iptables to share an Internet connection over a LAN and to build advanced firewalls.

- Describes how to set up a chroot jail to help protect a server system.

- Explains how to use TCP wrappers to control who can access a server.

Clients and servers
- Explains how to set up and use the most popular Linux servers, providing a chapter on each: Apache, Samba, OpenSSH, **exim4**, DNS, NFS, FTP, firestarter and iptables, and NIS/LDAP (all of which are supported by Ubuntu Linux).

- Describes how to set up a CUPS printer server.

- Describes how to set up and use a DHCP server either by itself or from firestarter.

Programming
- Provides an all-new chapter explaining the Perl programming language and a full chapter covering shell programming using bash, including many examples.

DETAILS

Chapter 1 **Chapter 1** presents a brief history of Linux and explains some of the features that make it a cutting-edge operating system. The "Conventions Used in This Book" (page 19) section details the typefaces and terminology this book uses.

Part I Part I, "Installing Ubuntu Linux," discusses how to install Ubuntu Linux. **Chapter 2** presents an overview of the process of installing Ubuntu Linux, including hardware requirements, downloading and burning a CD or DVD, and planning the layout of the hard disk. **Chapter 3** is a step-by-step guide to installing Ubuntu Linux from a CD or DVD, using the graphical or textual installer. It also shows how to customize your desktop (GUI).

Part II   Part II, "Getting Started with Ubuntu Linux," familiarizes you with Ubuntu Linux, covering logging in, the GUI, utilities, the filesystem, and the shell. **Chapter 4** introduces desktop features, including the Top and Bottom panels and the Main menu; explains how to use the Nautilus File Browser to manage files, run programs, and connect to FTP and HTTP servers; covers finding documentation, dealing with login problems, and using the window manager; and presents some suggestions on where to find documentation, including manuals, tutorials, software notes, and HOWTOs. **Chapter 5** introduces the shell command-line interface, describes more than 30 useful utilities, and presents a tutorial on the vim text editor. **Chapter 6** discusses the Linux hierarchical filesystem, covering files, filenames, pathnames, working with directories, access permissions, and hard and symbolic links. **Chapter 7** introduces the Bourne Again Shell (bash) and discusses command-line arguments and options, redirecting input to and output from commands, running programs in the background, and using the shell to generate and expand filenames.

Experienced users may want to skim Part II

tip   If you have used a UNIX or Linux system before, you may want to skim or skip some or all of the chapters in Part II. Two sections that all readers should take a look at are: "Conventions Used in This Book" (page 19), which explains the typographic and layout conventions used in this book, and "Where to Find Documentation" (page 121), which points out both local and remote sources of Linux and Ubuntu documentation.

Part III   Part III, "Digging into Ubuntu Linux," goes into more detail about working with the system. **Chapter 8** discusses the GUI (desktop) and includes a section on how to run a graphical program on a remote system and have the display appear locally. The section on GNOME describes several GNOME utilities and goes into more depth about the Nautilus File Browser. **Chapter 9** extends the bash coverage from Chapter 7, explaining how to redirect error output, avoid overwriting files, and work with job control, processes, startup files, important shell builtin commands, parameters, shell variables, and aliases. **Chapter 10** explains networks, network security, and the Internet and discusses types of networks, subnets, protocols, addresses, hostnames, and various network utilities. The section on distributed computing describes the client/server model and some of the servers you can use on a network. Details of setting up and using clients and servers are reserved until Part V.

Part IV   Part IV covers system administration. **Chapter 11** discusses core concepts such as the use of sudo, working with **root** privileges, system operation, chroot jails, TCP wrappers, general information about how to set up a server, DHCP, and PAM. **Chapter 12** explains the Linux filesystem, going into detail about types of files, including special and device files; the use of fsck to verify the integrity of and repair filesystems; and the use of tune2fs to change filesystem parameters. **Chapter 13** explains how to keep a system up-to-date by downloading software from the Internet and installing it, including examples of using APT programs such as aptitude, apt-get, and apt-cache. It also covers the **dpkg** software packaging system and the use of some **dpkg** utilities. Finally, it explains how to use BitTorrent from the command line to download files. **Chapter 14** explains how to set up the CUPS printing system so you can print on both local and remote systems. **Chapter 15** details customizing and building a Linux kernel. **Chapter 16** covers additional administration tasks, including setting up user accounts, backing up files, scheduling automated tasks, tracking disk usage, and solving general problems. **Chapter 17** explains how to set up a local area network (LAN), including both hardware (including wireless) and software configuration.

Part V   Part V goes into detail about setting up and running servers and connecting to them using clients. Where appropriate, these chapters include JumpStart sections that get you off to a quick start in using clients and setting up servers. The chapters in Part V cover the following clients/servers:

- **OpenSSH**—Set up an OpenSSH server and use ssh, scp, and sftp to communicate securely over the Internet.

- **FTP**—Set up a **vsftpd** secure FTP server and use any of several FTP clients to exchange files with the server.

- **Mail**—Configure **exim4** and use Webmail, POP3, or IMAP to retrieve email; use SpamAssassin to combat spam.

- **NIS and LDAP**—Set up NIS to facilitate system administration of a LAN and LDAP to maintain databases.

- **NFS**—Share filesystems between systems on a network.

- **Samba**—Share filesystems and printers between Windows and Linux systems.

- **DNS/BIND**—Set up a domain nameserver to let other systems on the Internet know the names and IP addresses of local systems they may need to contact.

- firestarter, ufw, and iptables—Share a single Internet connection between systems on a LAN, run a DHCP server, and set up a firewall to protect local systems.

- **Apache**—Set up an HTTP server that serves Web pages that browsers can display. This chapter includes many suggestions for increasing Apache security.

Part VI   Part VI covers two important programming tools that are used extensively in Ubuntu system administration and general-purpose programming. **Chapter 27** continues where Chapter 9 left off, going into greater depth about shell programming using bash, with the discussion enhanced by extensive examples. **Chapter 28** introduces the popular, feature-rich Perl programming language, including coverage of regular expressions and file handling.

Part VII   Part VII includes appendixes on regular expressions, helpful Web sites, system security, and free software. This part also includes an extensive glossary with more than 500 entries plus the JumpStart index, the File Tree index, the Utility index, and a comprehensive traditional index.

SUPPLEMENTS

The author's home page (www.sobell.com) contains downloadable listings of the longer programs from this book as well as pointers to many interesting and useful Linux sites on the World Wide Web, a list of corrections to the book, answers to even-numbered exercises, and a solicitation for corrections, comments, and suggestions.

THANKS

First and foremost, I want to thank Mark L. Taub, Editor-in-Chief, Prentice Hall, who provided encouragement and support through the hard parts of this project. Mark is unique in my 26 years of book writing experience: an editor who works with the tools I write about. Because Mark runs Ubuntu on his home computer, we shared experiences as I wrote this book. Mark, your comments and direction are invaluable; this book would not exist without your help. Thank you, Mark T.

Molly Sharp of ContentWorks worked with me day-by-day during production of this book providing help, listening to my rants, and keeping everything on track. Thanks to Jill Hobbs, Copyeditor, who made the book readable, understandable, and consistent; and Andrea Fox, Proofreader, who made each page sparkle and found the mistakes that the author left behind.

Thanks also to the folks at Prentice Hall who helped bring this book to life, especially Julie Nahil, Full-Service Production Manager, who oversaw production of the book; John Fuller, Managing Editor, who kept the large view in check; Brandon Prebynski, Marketing Manager; Kim Boedigheimer, Editorial Assistant, who attended to the many details involved in publishing this book; Heather Fox, Publicist; Dan Scherf, Media Developer; Cheryl Lenser, Senior Indexer; Sandra Schroeder, Design Manager; Chuti Prasertsith, Cover Designer; and everyone else who worked behind the scenes to make this book come into being.

I am also indebted to Denis Howe, Editor of *The Free On-Line Dictionary of Computing* (FOLDOC). Denis has graciously permitted me to use entries from his compilation. Be sure to look at this dictionary (www.foldoc.org).

A big "thank you" to the folks who read through the drafts of the book and made comments that caused me to refocus parts of the book where things were not clear or were left out altogether: John Dong, Ubuntu Developer, Forums Council Member; Andy Lester, author of *Land the Tech Job You Love: Why Skill and Luck Are Not Enough,* who helped extensively with the Perl chapter; Mike Basinger, Ubuntu Community and Forums Council Member; Joe Barker, Ubuntu Forums Staff Member; Max Sobell, New York University; Matthew Miller, Senior Systems Analyst/Administrator, BU Linux Project, Boston University Office of Information Technology; George Vish II, Senior Education Consultant, Hewlett-Packard; James Stockford, Systemateka, Inc.; Stephanie Troeth, Book

Oven; Doug Sheppard; Bryan Helvey, IT Director, OpenGeoSolutions; and Vann Scott, Baker College of Flint.

Thanks also to the people who helped with the first edition of this book: David Chisnall, Swansea University; Scott Mann, Aztek Networks; Thomas Achtemichuk, Mansueto Ventures; Scott James Remnant, Ubuntu Development Manager and Desktop Team Leader; Daniel R. Arfsten, Pro/Engineer Drafter/Designer; Chris Cooper, Senior Education Consultant, Hewlett-Packard Education Services; Sameer Verma, Associate Professor of Information Systems, San Francisco State University; Valerie Chau, Palomar College and Programmers Guild; James Kratzer; Sean McAllister; Nathan Eckenrode, New York Ubuntu Local Community Team; Christer Edwards; Nicolas Merline; and Michael Price.

Thanks also to the following people who helped with my previous Linux books, which provided a foundation for this book: Chris Karr, Northwestern University; Jesse Keating, Fedora Project; Carsten Pfeiffer, Software Engineer and KDE Developer; Aaron Weber, Ximian; Cristof Falk, Software Developer at CritterDesign; Steve Elgersma, Computer Science Department, Princeton University; Scott Dier, University of Minnesota; Robert Haskins, Computer Net Works; Lars Kellogg-Stedman, Harvard University; Jim A. Lola, Principal Systems Consultant, Privateer Systems; Eric S. Raymond, Cofounder, Open Source Initiative; Scott Mann; Randall Lechlitner, Independent Computer Consultant; Jason Wertz, Computer Science Instructor, Montgomery County Community College; Justin Howell, Solano Community College; Ed Sawicki, The Accelerated Learning Center; David Mercer; Jeffrey Bianchine, Advocate, Author, Journalist; John Kennedy; and Jim Dennis, Starshine Technical Services.

Thanks also to Dustin Puryear, Puryear Information Technology; Gabor Liptak, Independent Consultant; Bart Schaefer, Chief Technical Officer, iPost; Michael J. Jordan, Web Developer, Linux Online; Steven Gibson, Owner, SuperAnt.com; John Viega, Founder and Chief Scientist, Secure Software; K. Rachael Treu, Internet Security Analyst, Global Crossing; Kara Pritchard, K & S Pritchard Enterprises; Glen Wiley, Capital One Finances; Karel Baloun, Senior Software Engineer, Looksmart; Matthew Whitworth; Dameon D. Welch-Abernathy, Nokia Systems; Josh Simon, Consultant; Stan Isaacs; and Dr. Eric H. Herrin II, Vice President, Herrin Software Development. And thanks to Doug Hughes, long-time system designer and administrator, who gave me a big hand with the sections on system administration, networks, the Internet, and programming.

More thanks go to consultants Lorraine Callahan and Steve Wampler; Ronald Hiller, Graburn Technology; Charles A. Plater, Wayne State University; Bob Palowoda; Tom Bialaski, Sun Microsystems; Roger Hartmuller, TIS Labs at Network Associates; Kaowen Liu; Andy Spitzer; Rik Schneider; Jesse St. Laurent; Steve Bellenot; Ray W. Hiltbrand; Jennifer Witham; Gert-Jan Hagenaars; and Casper Dik.

A Practical Guide to Ubuntu Linux®, Second Edition, is based in part on two of my previous UNIX books: *UNIX System V: A Practical Guide* and *A Practical Guide to the UNIX System.* Many people helped me with those books, and thanks here go to

Pat Parseghian; Dr. Kathleen Hemenway; Brian LaRose; Byron A. Jeff, Clark Atlanta University; Charles Stross; Jeff Gitlin, Lucent Technologies; Kurt Hockenbury; Maury Bach, Intel Israel; Peter H. Salus; Rahul Dave, University of Pennsylvania; Sean Walton, Intelligent Algorithmic Solutions; Tim Segall, Computer Sciences Corporation; Behrouz Forouzan, DeAnza College; Mike Keenan, Virginia Polytechnic Institute and State University; Mike Johnson, Oregon State University; Jandelyn Plane, University of Maryland; Arnold Robbins and Sathis Menon, Georgia Institute of Technology; Cliff Shaffer, Virginia Polytechnic Institute and State University; and Steven Stepanek, California State University, Northridge, for reviewing the book.

I continue to be grateful to the many people who helped with the early editions of my UNIX books. Special thanks are due to Roger Sippl, Laura King, and Roy Harrington for introducing me to the UNIX system. My mother, Dr. Helen Sobell, provided invaluable comments on the original manuscript at several junctures. Also, thanks go to Isaac Rabinovitch, Professor Raphael Finkel, Professor Randolph Bentson, Bob Greenberg, Professor Udo Pooch, Judy Ross, Dr. Robert Veroff, Dr. Mike Denny, Joe DiMartino, Dr. John Mashey, Diane Schulz, Robert Jung, Charles Whitaker, Don Cragun, Brian Dougherty, Dr. Robert Fish, Guy Harris, Ping Liao, Gary Lindgren, Dr. Jarrett Rosenberg, Dr. Peter Smith, Bill Weber, Mike Bianchi, Scooter Morris, Clarke Echols, Oliver Grillmeyer, Dr. David Korn, Dr. Scott Weikart, and Dr. Richard Curtis.

Finally, thanks to Peter and his family for providing nourishment and a very comfortable place to work. I spent many hours reading the manuscript at JumpStart, Peter's neighborhood coffee and sandwich shop. If you are in the neighborhood (24th & Guerrero in San Francisco), stop by and say "Hi."

I take responsibility for any errors and omissions in this book. If you find one or just have a comment, let me know (mgs@sobell.com) and I will fix it in the next printing. My home page (www.sobell.com) contains a list of errors and credits those who found them. It also offers copies of the longer scripts from the book and pointers to interesting Linux pages on the Internet.

Mark G. Sobell
San Francisco, California

1

WELCOME TO LINUX

An operating system is the low-level software that schedules tasks, allocates storage, and handles the interfaces to peripheral hardware, such as printers, disk drives, the screen, keyboard, and mouse. An operating system has two main parts: the *kernel* and the *system programs*. The kernel allocates machine resources—including memory, disk space, and *CPU* (page 1103) cycles—to all other programs that run on the computer. The system programs include device drivers, libraries, utility programs, shells (command interpreters), configuration scripts and files, application programs, servers, and documentation. They perform higher-level housekeeping tasks, often acting as servers in a client/server relationship. Many of the libraries, servers, and utility programs were written by the GNU Project, which is discussed shortly.

1

Linux kernel The Linux *kernel* was developed by Finnish undergraduate student Linus Torvalds, who used the Internet to make the source code immediately available to others for free. Torvalds released Linux version 0.01 in September 1991.

The new operating system came together through a lot of hard work. Programmers around the world were quick to extend the kernel and develop other tools, adding functionality to match that already found in both BSD UNIX and System V UNIX (SVR4) as well as new functionality. The name *Linux* is a combination of *Linus* and *UNIX*.

The Linux operating system, which was developed through the cooperation of many, many people around the world, is a *product of the Internet* and is a *free* operating system. In other words, all the source code is free. You are free to study it, redistribute it, and modify it. As a result, the code is available free of cost—no charge for the software, source, documentation, or support (via newsgroups, mailing lists, and other Internet resources). As the GNU Free Software Definition (reproduced in Appendix D) puts it:

Free beer   "Free software" is a matter of liberty, not price. To understand the concept, you should think of "free" as in "free speech," not as in "free beer."

UBUNTU LINUX

Distributions Various organizations package the Linux kernel and system programs as *Linux distributions* (visit distrowatch.com for more information). Some of the most popular distributions are SUSE, Fedora, Ubuntu, Red Hat, Debian, and Mandriva. One of the biggest differences between distributions typically is how the user installs the operating system. Other differences include which graphical configuration tools are installed by default and which tools are used to keep the system up-to-date.

Canonical Under the leadership of Mark Shuttleworth, Canonical Ltd. (www.canonical.com), the sponsor of Ubuntu Linux, supports many, similar Linux distributions: Ubuntu runs the GNOME desktop manager, Kubuntu (www.kubuntu.org) runs the KDE desktop manager, Edubuntu (www.edubuntu.org) includes many school-related applications, and Xubuntu (www.xubuntu.org) runs the lightweight Xfce desktop, which makes it ideal for older, slower machines.

From its first release in October 2004, Ubuntu has been a community-oriented project. Ubuntu maintains several structures that keep it functioning effectively, with community members invited to participate in all structures. For more information about Ubuntu governance, see www.ubuntu.com/community/processes/governance.

Ubuntu Linux is based on Debian Linux and focuses on enhancing usability, accessibility, and internationalization. Although Ubuntu initially targeted the desktop user, recent releases have put increasing emphasis on the server market. With a new release scheduled every six months, Ubuntu provides cutting-edge software.

An Ubuntu system uses the GNOME desktop manager (www.gnome.org) and includes the OpenOffice.org suite of productivity tools, the Firefox Web browser, the Pidgin (formerly Gaim) IM client, and an assortment of tools and games. To keep software on a system up-to-date, Ubuntu uses Debian's **deb** package format and various APT-based tools.

The Ubuntu governance structure follows a benevolent dictator model: Mark Shuttleworth is the Self-Appointed Benevolent Dictator for Life (SABDFL). The structure includes the Technical Board, Ubuntu Community Council, Local Communities (LoCos), and Masters of the Universe (MOTU; wiki.ubuntu.com/MOTU). For more information about Ubuntu, see www.ubuntu.com/aboutus/faq.

THE LINUX 2.6 KERNEL

The Linux 2.6 kernel was released on December 17, 2003. This kernel has many features that offer increased security and speed. Some of these features benefit end users directly; others help developers produce better code and find problems more quickly. See Appendix E for a description of the features introduced in the Linux 2.6 kernel.

THE HISTORY OF UNIX AND GNU–LINUX

This section presents some background on the relationships between UNIX and Linux and between GNU and Linux.

THE HERITAGE OF LINUX: UNIX

The UNIX system was developed by researchers who needed a set of modern computing tools to help them with their projects. The system allowed a group of people working together on a project to share selected data and programs while keeping other information private.

Universities and colleges played a major role in furthering the popularity of the UNIX operating system through the "four-year effect." When the UNIX operating system became widely available in 1975, Bell Labs offered it to educational institutions at nominal cost. The schools, in turn, used it in their computer science programs, ensuring that computer science students became familiar with it. Because UNIX was such an advanced development system, the students became acclimated to a sophisticated programming environment. As these students graduated and went into industry, they expected to work in a similarly advanced environment. As more of them worked their way up the ladder in the commercial world, the UNIX operating system found its way into industry.

In addition to introducing students to the UNIX operating system, the Computer Systems Research Group (CSRG) at the University of California at Berkeley made significant additions and changes to it. In fact, it made so many popular changes that one version of the system is called the Berkeley Software Distribution (BSD) of the UNIX system (or just Berkeley UNIX). The other major version is UNIX System V (SVR4), which descended from versions developed and maintained by AT&T and UNIX System Laboratories.

FADE TO 1983

Richard Stallman (www.stallman.org) announced[1] the GNU Project for creating an operating system, both kernel and system programs, and presented the GNU Manifesto,[2] which begins as follows:

> GNU, which stands for Gnu's Not UNIX, is the name for the complete UNIX-compatible software system which I am writing so that I can give it away free to everyone who can use it.

Some years later, Stallman added a footnote to the preceding sentence when he realized that it was creating confusion:

> The wording here was careless. The intention was that nobody would have to pay for *permission* to use the GNU system. But the words don't make this clear, and people often interpret them as saying that copies of GNU should always be distributed at little or no charge. That was never the intent; later on, the manifesto mentions the possibility of companies providing the service of distribution for a profit. Subsequently I have learned to distinguish carefully between "free" in the sense of freedom and "free" in the sense of price. Free software is software that users have the freedom to distribute and change. Some users may obtain copies at no charge, while others pay to obtain copies—and if the funds help support improving the software, so much the better. The important thing is that everyone who has a copy has the freedom to cooperate with others in using it.

In the manifesto, after explaining a little about the project and what has been accomplished so far, Stallman continues:

> **Why I Must Write GNU**
> I consider that the golden rule requires that if I like a program I must share it with other people who like it. Software sellers want to divide the users and conquer them, making each user agree not to share with others. I refuse to break solidarity with other users in this way. I cannot in good conscience sign a nondisclosure agreement or a

---

1. www.gnu.org/gnu/initial-announcement.html

2. www.gnu.org/gnu/manifesto.html

software license agreement. For years I worked within the Artificial Intelligence Lab to resist such tendencies and other inhospitalities, but eventually they had gone too far: I could not remain in an institution where such things are done for me against my will.

So that I can continue to use computers without dishonor, I have decided to put together a sufficient body of free software so that I will be able to get along without any software that is not free. I have resigned from the AI Lab to deny MIT any legal excuse to prevent me from giving GNU away.

NEXT SCENE, 1991

The GNU Project has moved well along toward its goal. Much of the GNU operating system, except for the kernel, is complete. Richard Stallman later writes:

> By the early '90s we had put together the whole system aside from the kernel (and we were also working on a kernel, the GNU Hurd,[3] which runs on top of Mach[4]). Developing this kernel has been a lot harder than we expected, and we are still working on finishing it.[5]

> ...[M]any believe that once Linus Torvalds finished writing the kernel, his friends looked around for other free software, and for no particular reason most everything necessary to make a UNIX-like system was already available.

> What they found was no accident—it was the GNU system. The available free software[6] added up to a complete system because the GNU Project had been working since 1984 to make one. The GNU Manifesto had set forth the goal of developing a free UNIX-like system, called GNU. The Initial Announcement of the GNU Project also outlines some of the original plans for the GNU system. By the time Linux was written, the [GNU] system was almost finished.[7]

Today the GNU "operating system" runs on top of the FreeBSD (www.freebsd.org) and NetBSD (www.netbsd.org) kernels with complete Linux binary compatibility and on top of Hurd pre-releases and Darwin (developer.apple.com/opensource) without this compatibility.

---

3. www.gnu.org/software/hurd/hurd.html

4. www.gnu.org/software/hurd/gnumach.html

5. www.gnu.org/software/hurd/hurd-and-linux.html

6. See Appendix D or www.gnu.org/philosophy/free-sw.html.

7. www.gnu.org/gnu/linux-and-gnu.html

THE CODE IS FREE

The tradition of free software dates back to the days when UNIX was released to universities at nominal cost, which contributed to its portability and success. This tradition eventually died as UNIX was commercialized and manufacturers came to regard the source code as proprietary, making it effectively unavailable. Another problem with the commercial versions of UNIX related to their complexity. As each manufacturer tuned UNIX for a specific architecture, the operating system became less portable and too unwieldy for teaching and experimentation.

MINIX   Two professors created their own stripped-down UNIX look-alikes for educational purposes: Doug Comer created XINU and Andrew Tanenbaum created MINIX. Linus Torvalds created Linux to counteract the shortcomings in MINIX. Every time there was a choice between code simplicity and efficiency/features, Tanenbaum chose simplicity (to make it easy to teach with MINIX), which meant this system lacked many features people wanted. Linux went in the opposite direction.

You can obtain Linux at no cost over the Internet (page 42). You can also obtain the GNU code via the U.S. mail at a modest cost for materials and shipping. You can support the Free Software Foundation (www.fsf.org) by buying the same (GNU) code in higher-priced packages, and you can buy commercial packaged releases of Linux (called *distributions*), such as Ubuntu Linux, that include installation instructions, software, and support.

GPL   Linux and GNU software are distributed under the terms of the GNU General Public License (GPL, www.gnu.org/licenses/licenses.html). The GPL says you have the right to copy, modify, and redistribute the code covered by the agreement. When you redistribute the code, however, you must also distribute the same license with the code, thereby making the code and the license inseparable. If you get source code off the Internet for an accounting program that is under the GPL and then modify that code and redistribute an executable version of the program, you must also distribute the modified source code and the GPL agreement with it. Because this arrangement is the reverse of the way a normal copyright works (it *gives* rights instead of *limiting* them), it has been termed a *copyleft*. (This paragraph is not a legal interpretation of the GPL; it is intended merely to give you an idea of how it works. Refer to the GPL itself when you want to make use of it.)

HAVE FUN!

Two key words for Linux are "Have Fun!" These words pop up in prompts and documentation. The UNIX—now Linux—culture is steeped in humor that can be seen throughout the system. For example, less is more—GNU has replaced the UNIX paging utility named more with an improved utility named less. The utility to view PostScript documents is named ghostscript, and one of several replacements for the vi editor is named elvis. While machines with Intel processors have "Intel Inside" logos on their outside, some Linux machines sport "Linux Inside" logos. And Torvalds himself has been seen wearing a T-shirt bearing a "Linus Inside" logo.

WHAT IS SO GOOD ABOUT LINUX?

In recent years Linux has emerged as a powerful and innovative UNIX work-alike. Its popularity has surpassed that of its UNIX predecessors. Although it mimics UNIX in many ways, the Linux operating system departs from UNIX in several significant ways: The Linux kernel is implemented independently of both BSD and System V, the continuing development of Linux is taking place through the combined efforts of many capable individuals throughout the world, and Linux puts the power of UNIX within easy reach of both business and personal computer users. Using the Internet, today's skilled programmers submit additions and improvements to the operating system to Linus Torvalds, GNU, or one of the other authors of Linux.

Standards   In 1985, individuals from companies throughout the computer industry joined together to develop the POSIX (Portable Operating System Interface for Computer Environments) standard, which is based largely on the UNIX System V Interface Definition (SVID) and other earlier standardization efforts. These efforts were spurred by the U.S. government, which needed a standard computing environment to minimize its training and procurement costs. Released in 1988, POSIX is a group of IEEE standards that define the API (application programming interface), shell, and utility interfaces for an operating system. Although aimed at UNIX-like systems, the standards can apply to any compatible operating system. Now that these standards have gained acceptance, software developers are able to develop applications that run on all conforming versions of UNIX, Linux, and other operating systems.

Applications   A rich selection of applications is available for Linux—both free and commercial—as well as a wide variety of tools: graphical, word processing, networking, security, administration, Web server, and many others. Large software companies have recently seen the benefit in supporting Linux and now have on-staff programmers whose job it is to design and code the Linux kernel, GNU, KDE, or other software that runs on Linux. For example, IBM (www.ibm.com/linux) is a major Linux supporter. Linux conforms increasingly more closely to POSIX standards, and some distributions and parts of others meet this standard. These developments indicate that Linux is becoming mainstream and is respected as an attractive alternative to other popular operating systems.

Peripherals   Another aspect of Linux that appeals to users is the amazing range of peripherals that is supported and the speed with which support for new peripherals emerges. Linux often supports a peripheral or interface card before any company does. Unfortunately some types of peripherals—particularly proprietary graphics cards—lag in their support because the manufacturers do not release specifications or source code for drivers in a timely manner, if at all.

Software   Also important to users is the amount of software that is available—not just source code (which needs to be compiled) but also prebuilt binaries that are easy to install and ready to run. These programs include more than free software. Netscape, for example, has been available for Linux from the start and included Java support before it was available from many commercial vendors. Its sibling Mozilla/Thunderbird/Firefox is also a viable browser, mail client, and newsreader, performing many other functions as well.

Platforms   Linux is not just for Intel-based platforms (which now include Apple computers): It has been ported to and runs on the Power PC—including older Apple computers (ppclinux), Compaq's (née Digital Equipment Corporation) Alpha-based machines, MIPS-based machines, Motorola's 68K-based machines, various 64-bit systems, and IBM's S/390. Nor is Linux just for single-processor machines: As of version 2.0, it runs on multiple-processor machines (*SMPs;* page 1132). It also includes an O(1) scheduler, which dramatically increases scalability on SMP systems.

Emulators   Linux supports programs, called *emulators,* that run code intended for other operating systems. By using emulators you can run some DOS, Windows, and Macintosh programs under Linux. For example, Wine (www.winehq.com) is an open-source implementation of the Windows API that runs on top of the X Window System and UNIX/Linux.

Virtual machines   A virtual machine (VM or guest) appears to the user and to the software running on it as a complete physical machine. It is, however, one of potentially many such VMs running on a single physical machine (the host). The software that provides the virtualization is called a virtual machine monitor (VMM) or hypervisor. Each VM can run a different operating system from the other VMs. For example, on a single host you could have VMs running Windows, Ubuntu 7.10, Ubuntu 8.04, and Fedora 9.

A multitasking operating system allows you to run many programs on a single physical system. Similarly, a hypervisor allows you to run many operating systems (VMs) on a single physical system.

VMs provide many advantages over single, dedicated machines:

• **Isolation**—Each VM is isolated from the other VMs running on the same host: Thus, if one VM crashes or is compromised, the others are not affected.

• **Security**—When a single server system running several servers is compromised, all servers are compromised. If each server is running on its own VM, only the compromised server is affected; other servers remain secure.

• **Power consumption**—Using VMs, a single powerful machine can replace many less powerful machines, thereby cutting power consumption.

• **Development and support**—Multiple VMs, each running a different version of an operating system and/or different operating systems, can facilitate development and support of software designed to run in many environments. With this organization you can easily test a product in different environments before releasing it. Similarly, when a user submits a bug, you can reproduce the bug in the same environment it occurred in.

- **Servers**—In some cases, different servers require different versions of system libraries. In this instance, you can run each server on its own VM, all on a single piece of hardware.

- **Testing**—Using VMs, you can experiment with cutting-edge releases of operating systems and applications without concern for the base (stable) system, all on a single machine.

- **Networks**—You can set up and test networks of systems on a single machine.

- **Sandboxes**—A VM presents a sandbox—an area (system) that you can work in without regard for the results of your work or for the need to clean up.

- **Snapshots**—You can take snapshots of a VM and return the VM to the state it was in when you took the snapshot simply by reloading the VM from the snapshot.

Xen
Xen, which was created at the University of Cambridge and is now being developed in the open-source community, is an open-source VMM. Xen introduces minimal performance overhead when compared with running each of the operating systems natively.

The Intrepid release of Ubuntu supports Xen 3.3. This book does not cover the installation or use of Xen. See help.ubuntu.com/community/Xen for information on running Xen under Ubuntu. For more information on Xen, refer to the Xen home page at www.cl.cam.ac.uk/research/srg/netos/xen and to wiki.xensource.com/xenwiki

VMware
VMware, Inc. (www.vmware.com) offers VMware Server, a free, downloadable, proprietary product you can install and run as an application under Ubuntu. VMware Server enables you to install several VMs, each running a different operating system, including Windows and Linux. VMware also offers a free VMware player that enables you to run VMs you create with the VMware Server.

KVM
The Kernel-based Virtual Machine (KVM; kvm.qumranet.com and libvirt.org) is an open-source VM and runs as part of the Linux kernel. It works only on systems based on the Intel VT (VMX) CPU or the AMD SVM CPU; it is implemented as the **kvm**, **libvirt-bin**, and **ubuntu-vm-builder** packages. For more information refer to help.ubuntu.com/community/KVM.

Qemu
Qemu (bellard.org/qemu), written by Fabrice Bellard, is an open-source VMM that runs as a user application with no CPU requirements. It can run code written for a different CPU than that of the host machine. For more information refer to https://help.ubuntu.com/community/Installation/QemuEmulator.

VirtualBox
VirtualBox (www.virtualbox.org) is a VM developed by Sun Microsystems. If you want to run a virtual instance of Windows, you may want to investigate KVM (help.ubuntu.com/community/KVM) and VirtualBox.

Why Linux Is Popular with Hardware Companies and Developers

Two trends in the computer industry set the stage for the growing popularity of UNIX and Linux. First, advances in hardware technology created the need for an operating system that could take advantage of available hardware power. In the mid-1970s, minicomputers began challenging the large mainframe computers because, in many applications, minicomputers could perform the same functions less expensively. More recently, powerful 64-bit processor chips, plentiful and inexpensive memory, and lower-priced hard disk storage have allowed hardware companies to install multiuser operating systems on desktop computers.

Proprietary operating systems Second, with the cost of hardware continually dropping, hardware manufacturers could no longer afford to develop and support proprietary operating systems. A *proprietary* operating system is one that is written and owned by the manufacturer of the hardware (for example, DEC/Compaq owns VMS). Today's manufacturers need a generic operating system that they can easily adapt to their machines.

Generic operating systems A *generic* operating system is written outside of the company manufacturing the hardware and is sold (UNIX, Windows) or given (Linux) to the manufacturer. Linux is a generic operating system because it runs on different types of hardware produced by different manufacturers. Of course, if manufacturers can pay only for development and avoid per-unit costs (which they have to pay to Microsoft for each copy of Windows they sell), they are much better off. In turn, software developers need to keep the prices of their products down; they cannot afford to create new versions of their products to run under many different proprietary operating systems. Like hardware manufacturers, software developers need a generic operating system.

Although the UNIX system once met the needs of hardware companies and researchers for a generic operating system, over time it has become more proprietary as manufacturers added support for their own specialized features and introduced new software libraries and utilities. Linux emerged to serve both needs: It is a generic operating system that takes advantage of available hardware power.

Linux Is Portable

A *portable* operating system is one that can run on many different machines. More than 95 percent of the Linux operating system is written in the C programming language, and C is portable because it is written in a higher-level, machine-independent language. (The C compiler is written in C.)

Because Linux is portable, it can be adapted (ported) to different machines and can meet special requirements. For example, Linux is used in embedded computers, such as the ones found in cellphones, PDAs, and the cable boxes on top of many TVs. The file structure takes full advantage of large, fast hard disks. Equally important, Linux was originally designed as a multiuser operating system—it was not modified to serve several users as an afterthought. Sharing the computer's power among many users and giving them the ability to share data and programs are central features of the system.

Because it is adaptable and takes advantage of available hardware, Linux runs on many different microprocessor-based systems as well as mainframes. The popularity of the microprocessor-based hardware drives Linux; these microcomputers are getting faster all the time, at about the same price point. Linux on a fast microcomputer has become good enough to displace workstations on many desktops. This widespread acceptance benefits both users, who do not like having to learn a new operating system for each vendor's hardware, and system administrators, who like having a consistent software environment.

The advent of a standard operating system has given a boost to the development of the software industry. Now software manufacturers can afford to make one version of a product available on machines from different manufacturers.

THE C PROGRAMMING LANGUAGE

Ken Thompson wrote the UNIX operating system in 1969 in PDP-7 assembly language. Assembly language is machine dependent: Programs written in assembly language work on only one machine or, at best, on one family of machines. For this reason, the original UNIX operating system could not easily be transported to run on other machines (it was not portable).

To make UNIX portable, Thompson developed the B programming language, a machine-independent language, from the BCPL language. Dennis Ritchie developed the C programming language by modifying B and, with Thompson, rewrote UNIX in C in 1973. Originally, C was touted as a "portable assembler." The revised operating system could be transported more easily to run on other machines.

That development marked the start of C. Its roots reveal some of the reasons why it is such a powerful tool. C can be used to write machine-independent programs. A programmer who designs a program to be portable can easily move it to any computer that has a C compiler. C is also designed to compile into very efficient code. With the advent of C, a programmer no longer had to resort to assembly language to get code that would run well (that is, quickly—although an assembler will always generate more efficient code than a high-level language).

C is a good systems language. You can write a compiler or an operating system in C. It is a highly structured but is not necessarily a high-level language. C allows a programmer to manipulate bits and bytes, as is necessary when writing an operating system. At the same time, it has high-level constructs that allow for efficient, modular programming.

In the late 1980s the American National Standards Institute (ANSI) defined a standard version of the C language, commonly referred to as *ANSI C* or *C89* (for the

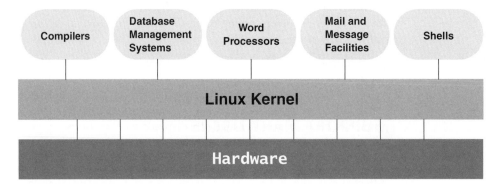

Figure 1-1   A layered view of the Linux operating system

year the standard was published). Ten years later the C99 standard was published; it is mostly supported by the GNU Project's C compiler (named gcc). The original version of the language is often referred to as *Kernighan & Ritchie* (or *K&R*) C, named for the authors of the book that first described the C language.

Another researcher at Bell Labs, Bjarne Stroustrup, created an object-oriented programming language named C++, which is built on the foundation of C. Because object-oriented programming is desired by many employers today, C++ is preferred over C in many environments. Another language of choice is Objective-C, which was used to write the first Web browser. The GNU Project's C compiler supports C, C++, and Objective-C.

OVERVIEW OF LINUX

The Linux operating system has many unique and powerful features. Like other operating systems, it is a control program for computers. But like UNIX, it is also a well-thought-out family of utility programs (Figure 1-1) and a set of tools that allow users to connect and use these utilities to build systems and applications.

LINUX HAS A KERNEL PROGRAMMING INTERFACE

The Linux kernel—the heart of the Linux operating system—is responsible for allocating the computer's resources and scheduling user jobs so each one gets its fair share of system resources, including access to the CPU; peripheral devices, such as hard disk, DVD, and CD-ROM storage; printers; and tape drives. Programs interact with the kernel through *system calls,* special functions with well-known names. A programmer can use a single system call to interact with many kinds of devices. For example, there is one **write**() system call, rather than many device-specific ones.

When a program issues a **write**() request, the kernel interprets the context and passes the request to the appropriate device. This flexibility allows old utilities to work with devices that did not exist when the utilities were written. It also makes it possible to move programs to new versions of the operating system without rewriting them (provided the new version recognizes the same system calls). See page 1087 for information on the Linux 2.6 kernel.

LINUX CAN SUPPORT MANY USERS

Depending on the hardware and the types of tasks the computer performs, a Linux system can support from 1 to more than 1,000 users, each concurrently running a different set of programs. The per-user cost of a computer that can be used by many people at the same time is less than that of a computer that can be used by only a single person at a time. It is less because one person cannot generally take advantage of all the resources a computer has to offer. That is, no one can keep all the printers going constantly, keep all the system memory in use, keep all the disks busy reading and writing, keep the Internet connection in use, and keep all the terminals busy at the same time. By contrast, a multiuser operating system allows many people to use all of the system resources almost simultaneously. The use of costly resources can be maximized and the cost per user can be minimized—the primary objectives of a multiuser operating system.

LINUX CAN RUN MANY TASKS

Linux is a fully protected multitasking operating system, allowing each user to run more than one job at a time. Processes can communicate with one another but remain fully protected from one another, just as the kernel remains protected from all processes. You can run several jobs in the background while giving all your attention to the job being displayed on the screen, and you can switch back and forth between jobs. If you are running the X Window System (page 17), you can run different programs in different windows on the same screen and watch all of them. This capability helps users be more productive.

LINUX PROVIDES A SECURE HIERARCHICAL FILESYSTEM

A *file* is a collection of information, such as text for a memo or report, an accumulation of sales figures, an image, a song, or an executable program. Each file is stored under a unique identifier on a storage device, such as a hard disk. The Linux filesystem provides a structure whereby files are arranged under *directories*, which are like folders or boxes. Each directory has a name and can hold other files and directories. Directories, in turn, are arranged under other directories, and so forth, in a treelike organization. This structure helps users keep track of large numbers of

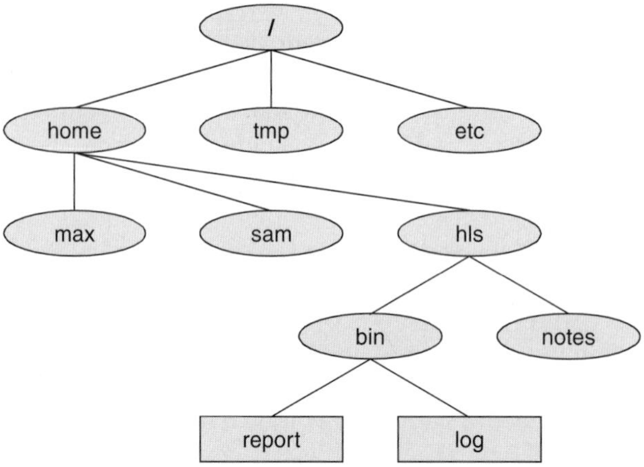

Figure 1-2   The Linux filesystem structure

files by grouping related files in directories. Each user has one primary directory and as many subdirectories as required (Figure 1-2).

Standards   With the idea of making life easier for system administrators and software developers, a group got together over the Internet and developed the Linux Filesystem Standard (FSSTND), which has since evolved into the Linux Filesystem Hierarchy Standard (FHS). Before this standard was adopted, key programs were located in different places in different Linux distributions. Today you can sit down at a Linux system and expect to find any given standard program at a consistent location (page 199).

Links   A *link* allows a given file to be accessed by means of two or more names. The alternative names can be located in the same directory as the original file or in another directory. Links can make the same file appear in several users' directories, enabling those users to share the file easily. Windows uses the term *shortcut* in place of *link* to describe this capability. Macintosh users will be more familiar with the term *alias.* Under Linux, an *alias* is different from a *link;* it is a command macro feature provided by the shell (page 330).

Security   Like most multiuser operating systems, Linux allows users to protect their data from access by other users. It also allows users to share selected data and programs with certain other users by means of a simple but effective protection scheme. This level of security is provided by file access permissions, which limit the users who can read from, write to, or execute a file. More recently, Linux has implemented Access Control Lists (ACLs), which give users and administrators finer-grained control over file access permissions.

THE SHELL: COMMAND INTERPRETER AND PROGRAMMING LANGUAGE

In a textual environment, the shell—the command interpreter—acts as an interface between you and the operating system. When you enter a command on the screen, the shell interprets the command and calls the program you want. A number of shells are available for Linux. The four most popular shells are

- The Bourne Again Shell (bash), an enhanced version of the original Bourne Shell (the original UNIX shell).

- The Debian Almquist Shell (dash), a smaller version of bash, with fewer features. Most startup shell scripts call dash in place of bash to speed the boot process.

- The TC Shell (tcsh), an enhanced version of the C Shell, developed as part of BSD UNIX.

- The Z Shell (zsh), which incorporates features from a number of shells, including the Korn Shell.

Because different users may prefer different shells, multiuser systems can have several different shells in use at any given time. The choice of shells demonstrates one of the advantages of the Linux operating system: the ability to provide a customized interface for each user.

Shell scripts Besides performing its function of interpreting commands from a keyboard and sending those commands to the operating system, the shell is a high-level programming language. Shell commands can be arranged in a file for later execution (Linux calls these files *shell scripts;* Windows calls them *batch files*). This flexibility allows users to perform complex operations with relative ease, often by issuing short commands, or to build with surprisingly little effort elaborate programs that perform highly complex operations.

FILENAME GENERATION

Wildcards and ambiguous file references When you type commands to be processed by the shell, you can construct patterns using characters that have special meanings to the shell. These characters are called *wildcard* characters. The patterns, which are called *ambiguous file references,* are a kind of shorthand: Rather than typing in complete filenames, you can type patterns; the shell expands these patterns into matching filenames. An ambiguous file reference can save you the effort of typing in a long filename or a long series of similar filenames. For example, the shell might expand the pattern **mak✳** to **make-3.80.tar.gz**. Patterns can also be useful when you know only part of a filename or cannot remember the exact spelling of a filename.

COMPLETION

In conjunction with the Readline library, the shell performs command, filename, pathname, and variable completion: You type a prefix and press ESCAPE, and the shell lists the items that begin with that prefix or completes the item if the prefix specifies a unique item.

DEVICE-INDEPENDENT INPUT AND OUTPUT

Redirection Devices (such as a printer or a terminal) and disk files appear as files to Linux programs. When you give a command to the Linux operating system, you can instruct it to send the output to any one of several devices or files. This diversion is called output *redirection.*

Device
independence

In a similar manner, a program's input, which normally comes from a keyboard, can be redirected so that it comes from a disk file instead. Input and output are *device independent;* that is, they can be redirected to or from any appropriate device.

As an example, the cat utility normally displays the contents of a file on the screen. When you run a cat command, you can easily cause its output to go to a disk file instead of the screen.

SHELL FUNCTIONS

One of the most important features of the shell is that users can use it as a programming language. Because the shell is an interpreter, it does not compile programs written for it but rather interprets programs each time they are loaded from the disk. Loading and interpreting programs can be time-consuming.

Many shells, including the Bourne Again Shell, support shell functions that the shell holds in memory so it does not have to read them from the disk each time you execute them. The shell also keeps functions in an internal format so it does not have to spend as much time interpreting them.

JOB CONTROL

Job control is a shell feature that allows users to work on several jobs at once, switching back and forth between them as desired. When you start a job, it is frequently run in the foreground so it is connected to the terminal. Using job control, you can move the job you are working with to the background and continue running it there while working on or observing another job in the foreground. If a background job then needs your attention, you can move it to the foreground so it is once again attached to the terminal. (The concept of job control originated with BSD UNIX, where it appeared in the C Shell.)

A LARGE COLLECTION OF USEFUL UTILITIES

Linux includes a family of several hundred utility programs, often referred to as *commands*. These utilities perform functions that are universally required by users. The sort utility, for example, puts lists (or groups of lists) in alphabetical or numerical order and can be used to sort lists by part number, last name, city, ZIP code, telephone number, age, size, cost, and so forth. The sort utility is an important programming tool that is part of the standard Linux system. Other utilities allow users to create, display, print, copy, search, and delete files as well as to edit, format, and typeset text. The man (for manual) and info utilities provide online documentation for Linux.

INTERPROCESS COMMUNICATION

Pipes and filters

Linux enables users to establish both pipes and filters on the command line. A *pipe* sends the output of one program to another program as input. A *filter* is a special kind of pipe that processes a stream of input data to yield a stream of output data.

A filter processes another program's output, altering it as a result. The filter's output then becomes input to another program.

Pipes and filters frequently join utilities to perform a specific task. For example, you can use a pipe to send the output of the sort utility to head (a filter that lists the first ten lines of its input); you can then use another pipe to send the output of head to a third utility, lpr, that sends the data to a printer. Thus, in one command line, you can use three utilities together to sort and print part of a file.

SYSTEM ADMINISTRATION

On a Linux system the system administrator is frequently the owner and only user of the system. This person has many responsibilities. The first responsibility may be to set up the system, install the software, and possibly edit configuration files. Once the system is up and running, the system administrator is responsible for downloading and installing software (including upgrading the operating system), backing up and restoring files, and managing such system facilities as printers, terminals, servers, and a local network. The system administrator is also responsible for setting up accounts for new users on a multiuser system, bringing the system up and down as needed, monitoring the system, and taking care of any problems that arise.

ADDITIONAL FEATURES OF LINUX

The developers of Linux included features from BSD, System V, and Sun Microsystems' Solaris, as well as new features, in their operating system. Although most of the tools found on UNIX exist for Linux, in some cases these tools have been replaced by more modern counterparts. This section describes some of the popular tools and features available under Linux.

GUIs: GRAPHICAL USER INTERFACES

The X Window System (also called X or X11) was developed in part by researchers at MIT (Massachusetts Institute of Technology) and provides the foundation for the GUIs available with Linux. Given a terminal or workstation screen that supports X, a user can interact with the computer through multiple windows on the screen, display graphical information, or use special-purpose applications to draw pictures, monitor processes, or preview formatted output. X is an across-the-network protocol that allows a user to open a window on a workstation or computer system that is remote from the CPU generating the window.

Desktop manager   Usually two layers run on top of X: a desktop manager and a window manager. A *desktop manager* is a picture-oriented user interface that enables you to interact with system programs by manipulating icons instead of typing the corresponding commands to a shell.

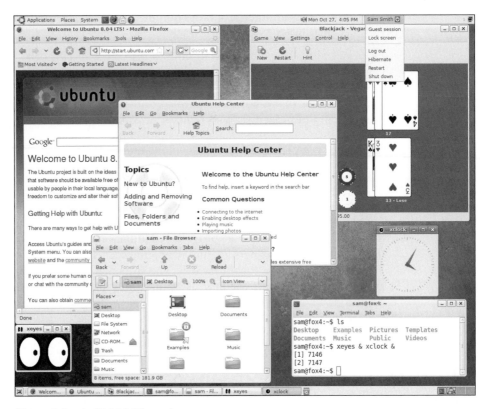

Figure 1-3   A GNOME workspace

Ubuntu runs the GNOME desktop manager (Figure 1-3; www.gnome.org) by default, but it can also run KDE (www.kde.org) and a number of other desktop managers.

Window manager   A *window manager* is a program that runs under the desktop manager and allows you to open and close windows, run programs, and set up a mouse so it has different effects depending on how and where you click. The window manager also gives the screen its personality. Whereas Microsoft Windows allows you to change the color of key elements in a window, a window manager under X allows you to customize the overall look and feel of the screen: You can change the way a window looks and works (by giving it different borders, buttons, and scrollbars), set up virtual desktops, create menus, and more.

Several popular window managers run under X and Linux. Ubuntu Linux provides both Metacity (the default under GNOME) and kwin (the default under KDE). Other window managers, such as Sawfish and WindowMaker, are also available. Chapters 4 and 8 present information on GUIs.

(INTER)NETWORKING UTILITIES

Linux network support includes many utilities that enable you to access remote systems over a variety of networks. In addition to sending email to users on other systems, you can access files on disks mounted on other computers as if they were located on the local system, make your files available to other systems in a similar manner, copy files back and forth, run programs on remote systems while displaying the results on the local system, and perform many other operations across local area networks (LANs) and wide area networks (WANs), including the Internet.

Layered on top of this network access is a wide range of application programs that extend the computer's resources around the globe. You can carry on conversations with people throughout the world, gather information on a wide variety of subjects, and download new software over the Internet quickly and reliably. Chapter 10 discusses networks, the Internet, and the Linux network facilities.

Software Development

One of Linux's most impressive strengths is its rich software development environment. Linux supports compilers and interpreters for many computer languages. Besides C and C++, languages available for Linux include Ada, Fortran, Java, Lisp, Pascal, Perl, and Python. The bison utility generates parsing code that makes it easier to write programs to build compilers (tools that parse files containing structured information). The flex utility generates scanners (code that recognizes lexical patterns in text). The make utility and the GNU Configure and Build System make it easier to manage complex development projects. Source code management systems, such as CVS, simplify version control. Several debuggers, including ups and gdb, can help you track down and repair software defects. The GNU C compiler (gcc) works with the gprof profiling utility to help programmers identify potential bottlenecks in a program's performance. The C compiler includes options to perform extensive checking of C code, thereby making the code more portable and reducing debugging time. Table B-4 on page 1058 lists some sites you can download software from.

Conventions Used in This Book

This book uses conventions to make its explanations shorter and clearer. The following paragraphs describe these conventions.

Widgets A widget is a simple graphical element that a user interacts with, such as a text box, radio button, or combo box. When referring to a widget, this book specifies the type of widget and its label. The term "tick" refers to the mark you put in a check box, sometimes called a check mark. For example, "put a tick in the check box labeled **Run in terminal**." See the glossary for definitions of various widgets.

Tabs and frames Tabs allow windows to display sets of related information, one set at a time. For example, Figure 4-11 on page 100 shows the Appearance Preferences window, which has five tabs; the Theme tab is highlighted. A frame isolates a set of information within a window. See Figure 14-3 on page 533 for an example.

Menu selection path The menu selection path is the name of the menu or the location of the menu, followed by a colon, a SPACE, and the menu selections separated by ⇨ markers. The entire menu selection path appears in **bold** type. You can read **Main menu: System⇨ Preferences⇨Appearance** as "From the Main menu, select **System**; from **System**, select **Preferences**; and then select **Appearance**."

Text and examples   The text is set in this type, whereas examples are shown in a monospaced font (also called a *fixed-width* font):

```
$ cat practice
This is a small file I created
with a text editor.
```

Items you enter   Everything you enter at the keyboard is shown in a bold typeface. Within the text, **this bold typeface** is used; within examples and screens, `this one` is used. In the previous example, the dollar sign ($) on the first line is a prompt that Linux displays, so it is not bold; the remainder of the first line is entered by a user, so it is bold.

Utility names   Names of utilities are printed in this bold sans serif typeface. This book references the emacs text editor and the ls utility or ls command (or just ls) but instructs you to enter ls –a on the command line. In this way the text distinguishes between utilities, which are programs, and the instructions you give on the command line to invoke the utilities.

Filenames   Filenames appear in a bold typeface. Examples are **memo5**, **letter.1283**, and **reports**. Filenames may include uppercase and lowercase letters; however, Linux is *case sensitive* (page 1099), so **memo5**, **MEMO5**, and **Memo5** name three different files.

Character strings   Within the text, characters and character strings are marked by putting them in a bold typeface. This convention avoids the need for quotation marks or other delimiters before and after a string. An example is the following string, which is displayed by the passwd utility: **Sorry, passwords do not match.**

Buttons and labels   Words appear in a bold typeface in the sections of the book that describe a GUI. This font indicates you can click a mouse button when the mouse pointer is over these words on the screen or over a button with this name: Click **Next**.

Keys and characters   This book uses SMALL CAPS for three kinds of items:

- Keyboard keys, such as the SPACE bar and the RETURN,[8] ESCAPE, and TAB keys.

- The characters that keys generate, such as the SPACEs generated by the SPACE bar.

- Keyboard keys that you press with the CONTROL key, such as CONTROL-D. (Even though D is shown as an uppercase letter, you do not have to press the SHIFT key; enter CONTROL-D by holding the CONTROL key down and pressing **d**.)

Prompts and RETURNS   Most examples include the *shell prompt*—the signal that Linux is waiting for a command—as a dollar sign ($), a pound sign (#), or sometimes a percent sign (%). The prompt does not appear in a bold typeface in this book because you do not enter it. Do not type the prompt on the keyboard when you are experimenting with examples from this book. If you do, the examples will not work.

Examples *omit* the RETURN keystroke that you must use to execute them. An example of a command line is

```
$ vim memo.1204
```

---

8. Different keyboards use different keys to move the *cursor* (page 1103) to the beginning of the next line. This book always refers to the key that ends a line as the RETURN key. Your keyboard may have a RET, NEWLINE, ENTER, RETURN, or other key. Use the corresponding key on your keyboard each time this book asks you to press RETURN.

To use this example as a model for running the vim text editor, give the command **vim memo.1204** and press the RETURN key. (Press ESCAPE ZZ to exit from vim; see page 172 for a vim tutorial.) This method of entering commands makes the examples in the book correspond to what appears on the screen.

Definitions   All glossary entries marked with ᶠᴼᴸᴰᴼᶜ are courtesy of Denis Howe, editor of the Free Online Dictionary of Computing (foldoc.org), and are used with permission. This site is an ongoing work containing definitions, anecdotes, and trivia.

---

optional OPTIONAL INFORMATION

Passages marked as optional appear in a gray box. This material is not central to the ideas presented in the chapter but often involves more challenging concepts. A good strategy when reading a chapter is to skip the optional sections and then return to them when you are comfortable with the main ideas presented in the chapter. This is an optional paragraph.

URLs (Web addresses)   Web addresses, or URLs, have an implicit **http://** prefix, unless **ftp://** or **https://** is shown. You do not normally need to specify a prefix when the prefix is **http://**, but you must use a prefix from a browser when you specify an FTP or secure HTTP site. Thus you can specify a URL in a browser exactly as shown in this book.

Tip, caution, and security boxes   The following boxes highlight information that may be helpful while you are using or administrating a Linux system.

This is a tip box

tip   A tip box may help you avoid repeating a common mistake or may point toward additional information.

This box warns you about something

caution   A caution box warns you about a potential pitfall.

This box marks a security note

security   A security box highlights a potential security issue. These notes are usually for system administrators, but some apply to all users.

CHAPTER SUMMARY

The Linux operating system grew out of the UNIX heritage to become a popular alternative to traditional systems (that is, Windows) available for microcomputer (PC) hardware. UNIX users will find a familiar environment in Linux. Distributions of Linux contain the expected complement of UNIX utilities, contributed by programmers around the world, including the set of tools developed as part of the GNU Project. The Linux community is committed to the continued development of this system. Support for new microcomputer devices and features is added soon after the hardware becomes available, and the tools available on Linux continue to be refined. Given the many commercial software packages available to run on

Linux platforms and the many hardware manufacturers offering Linux on their systems, it is clear that the system has evolved well beyond its origin as an undergraduate project to become an operating system of choice for academic, commercial, professional, and personal use.

EXERCISES

1. What is free software? List three characteristics of free software.

2. Why is Linux popular? Why is it popular in academia?

3. What are multiuser systems? Why are they successful?

4. What is the Free Software Foundation/GNU? What is Linux? Which parts of the Linux operating system did each provide? Who else has helped build and refine this operating system?

5. In which language is Linux written? What does the language have to do with the success of Linux?

6. What is a utility program?

7. What is a shell? How does it work with the kernel? With the user?

8. How can you use utility programs and a shell to create your own applications?

9. Why is the Linux filesystem referred to as *hierarchical*?

10. What is the difference between a multiprocessor and a multiprocessing system?

11. Give an example of when you would want to use a multiprocessing system.

12. Approximately how many people wrote Linux? Why is this project unique?

13. What are the key terms of the GNU General Public License?

PART I
INSTALLING UBUNTU LINUX

2

INSTALLATION
OVERVIEW

Installing Ubuntu Linux is the process of copying operating system files from a CD or DVD to hard drive(s) on a system and setting up configuration files so that Linux runs properly on the hardware. Several types of installations are possible, including fresh installations, upgrades from older releases of Ubuntu Linux, and dual-boot installations.

This chapter discusses the installation process in general: planning, partitioning the hard disk, obtaining the files for the installation, burning a CD or a DVD, and collecting information about the hardware that may be helpful for installation and administration. Chapter 3 covers the process of installing Ubuntu.

The ubiquity utility is a user-friendly, graphical tool that installs Ubuntu. To install Ubuntu Linux on standard hardware, you can typically insert the live/install Desktop CD or DVD, boot the system, and double-click **Install**. After you answer a few questions, you are done. Of course, sometimes you may want to customize the system or you may be installing on nonstandard hardware: The installer gives you choices as the installation process unfolds. Ubuntu also provides a textual installer that gives you more control over the installation. Refer to "Basic Installation from the Live/Install Desktop CD/DVD" (page 50) and "Advanced Installation" (page 67) for information about installing and customizing Ubuntu Linux.

THE LIVE/INSTALL DESKTOP CD/DVD

A live/install Desktop CD/DVD runs Ubuntu without installing it on the system. To boot from a live/install Desktop CD/DVD, make sure the computer is set up to boot from a CD/DVD; see "BIOS setup" and "CMOS" on page 28 for more information. When you boot a live/install Desktop CD/DVD, it brings up a GNOME desktop: You are running a live session. When you exit from the live session, the system is as it was before you booted from the CD/DVD. If the system has a Linux swap partition (most Linux systems have one; see page 37), the live session uses it to improve its performance but does not otherwise write to the hard disk. You can also install Ubuntu from a live session.

Booting a live/install Desktop CD/DVD is a good way to test hardware and fix a system that will not boot from the hard disk. A live session is ideal for people who are new to Ubuntu or Linux and want to experiment with Ubuntu but are not ready to install Ubuntu on their system.

Saving files during a live session

tip   You cannot save a file to a live/install CD/DVD as these are readonly media. During a live session, even though you may appear to save a file, it will not be there after you exit from the live session. To save data from a live session, save to a network share or a flash drive, or mail it to yourself.

MORE INFORMATION

In addition to the following references, see "Where to Find Documentation" on page 121 and refer to Appendix B for additional resources.

Web   memtest86+: www.memtest.org
gparted (GNOME Partition Editor): gparted.sourceforge.net
Hardware compatibility: wiki.ubuntu.com/HardwareSupport
Swap space: help.ubuntu.com/community/SwapFaq
Partition HOWTO: tldp.org/HOWTO/Partition
Upgrading: www.ubuntu.com/getubuntu/upgrading
Boot command-line parameters: help.ubuntu.com/community/BootOptions and www.tldp.org/HOWTO/BootPrompt-HOWTO.html
RAID: en.wikipedia.org/wiki/RAID and tldp.org/HOWTO/Software-RAID-HOWTO.html
LVM Resource Page (includes many links): sourceware.org/lvm2
LVM HOWTO: www.tldp.org/HOWTO/LVM-HOWTO

BitTorrent: help.ubuntu.com/community/BitTorrent
BitTorrent: azureus.sourceforge.net
X.org release information: wiki.x.org

Download Ubuntu
Easiest download: www.ubuntu.com/getubuntu
Released versions: releases.ubuntu.com
Older versions: old-releases.ubuntu.com/releases
Development images and unsupported releases: cdimage.ubuntu.com
Mac (PowerPC): wiki.ubuntu.com/PowerPCDownloads
BitTorrent torrent files: torrent.ubuntu.com/releases

PLANNING THE INSTALLATION

The major decision when planning an installation is determining how to divide the hard disk into partitions or, in the case of a dual-boot system, where to put the Linux partitions. Once you have installed Ubuntu, you can decide which software packages you want to add to the base system (or whether you want to remove some). In addition to these topics, this section discusses hardware requirements for Ubuntu Linux and fresh installations versus upgrades.

CONSIDERATIONS

GUI On most systems, except for servers, you probably want to install a graphical user interface (a desktop). Ubuntu installs GNOME by default. See page 65 for information about installing KDE.

Software and services As you install more software packages on a system, the number of updates and the interactions between the packages increase. Server packages that listen for network connections make the system more vulnerable by increasing the number of ways the system can be attacked. Including additional services can also slow the system down.

For a system to learn on, or for a development system, additional packages and services may be useful. For a more secure production system, it is best to install and maintain the minimum number of packages required and enable only needed services. See page 423 for information on starting and stopping system services.

REQUIREMENTS

Hardware This chapter and Chapter 3 cover installing Ubuntu on 32-bit Intel and compatible processor architectures such as AMD as well as 64-bit processor architectures such as AMD64 processors and Intel processors with Intel EM64T technology. Within these processor architectures, Ubuntu Linux runs on much of the available hardware. You can view Ubuntu's list of compatible and supported hardware at wiki.ubuntu.com/HardwareSupport. Many Internet sites discuss Linux hardware; use Google (www.google.com/linux) to search for **linux hardware**, **ubuntu hardware**, or **linux** and the specific hardware you want more information on (for example, **linux sata** or **linux a8n**). In addition, many HOWTOs cover specific hardware. The *Linux Hardware Compatibility HOWTO* is also available, although it may not be up-to-date at the time you read it. Ubuntu Linux usually runs on systems that Windows runs on, unless the system includes a very new or unusual component.

The hardware required to run Ubuntu depends on which kind of system you want to set up. A very minimal system that runs a textual (command-line) interface and has very few software packages installed requires very different hardware from a system that runs a GUI, has many installed packages, and supports visual effects (page 101). Use the Alternate CD (page 32) if you are installing Ubuntu on a system with less than 320 megabytes of RAM. If you want to run visual effects on the system, look up **visual effects** on help.ubuntu.com.

A network connection is invaluable for keeping Ubuntu up-to-date. A sound card is nice to have for multimedia applications. If you are installing Ubuntu on old or minimal hardware and want to run a GUI, consider installing Xubuntu (www.xubuntu.org), as it provides a lightweight desktop and uses system resources more efficiently than Ubuntu does.

RAM (memory)   An extremely minimal textual (command-line) system requires 32 megabytes of RAM. A standard desktop system requires 320 megabytes, although you may be able to use less if you install Xubuntu. Installing Ubuntu from a live session requires 256 megabytes, although it will run slowly if the system has less than 512 megabytes. Use the textual installer (page 73) if the system has less than 256 megabytes of RAM.

Linux makes good use of extra memory: The more memory a system has, the faster it runs. Adding memory is one of the most cost-effective ways you can speed up a Linux system.

CPU   Ubuntu Linux requires a minimum of a 200-megahertz Pentium-class processor or the equivalent AMD or other processor for textual mode and at least a 400-megahertz Pentium II processor or the equivalent for graphical mode.

Hard disk space   The amount of hard disk space Ubuntu requires depends on which edition of Ubuntu Linux you install, which packages you install, how many languages you install, and how much space you need for user data (your files). The operating system typically requires 2–8 gigabytes, although a minimal system can make do with much less space. Installing Ubuntu from a live session requires 4 gigabytes of space on a hard disk.

BIOS setup   Modern computers can be set up to boot from a CD/DVD or hard disk. The BIOS determines the order in which the system tries to boot from each device. You may need to change this order: Make sure the BIOS is set up to try booting from the CD/DVD before it tries to boot from the hard disk.

CMOS   CMOS is the persistent memory that stores hardware configuration information. To change the BIOS setup, you need to edit the information stored in CMOS. When the system boots, it displays a brief message about how to enter System Setup or CMOS Setup mode. Usually you need to press DEL or F2 while the system is booting. Press the key that is called for and move the cursor to the screen and line that deal with booting the system. Generally there is a list of three or four devices that the system tries to boot from; if the first attempt fails, the system tries the second device, and so on. Manipulate the list so that the CD/DVD is the first choice, save the list, and reboot. Refer to the hardware/BIOS manual for more information.

PROCESSOR ARCHITECTURE

Ubuntu CDs and DVDs hold programs compiled to run on a specific processor architecture (class of processors, or CPUs). The following list describes each of the architectures Ubuntu is compiled for. See help.ubuntu.com/community/ProcessorArch for a detailed list of processors in each architecture. Because Linux source code is available to everyone, a knowledgeable user can compile Ubuntu Linux to run on other processor architectures.

Should I install 32-bit or 64-bit Ubuntu on a 64-bit capable processor?

tip   The following list may help you decide whether to install 32-bit or 64-bit Ubuntu on a 64-bit capable processor.

- EM64T/AMD64 processors can run either version of Ubuntu equally well.
- A 64-bit distribution allows each process to address more than 4 gigabytes of RAM. Larger address space is the biggest advantage of a 64-bit distribution and is typically useful only for certain engineering/scientific computational work and when you are running multiple virtual machines.
- A 64-bit processor is not faster than a 32-bit processor in general. Most benchmarks show more or less similar performance. In some cases the performance is better and in some cases it is worse: There is no clear performance advantage for either type of processor.
- The memory model for 64-bit Linux makes pointers twice as big as for 32-bit Linux. This size difference translates to a more than 5 percent RAM usage increase depending on the application. If a system is low on RAM, this overhead may make performance worse.
- Because more people are using 32-bit Linux, bugs in 32-bit Linux tend to be discovered and fixed faster than those in 64-bit Linux.
- Ubuntu can set up Flashplayer and Java with a single click on 64-bit systems just as it can on 32-bit systems. However, for some applications, such as Skype, you must apply ugly workarounds to run them on 64-bit systems.
- There is no simple way to go back and forth between 32-bit and 64-bit versions of Ubuntu without reinstalling Ubuntu.
- If you are not sure which distribution to use, install the 32-bit version of Ubuntu.

PC (Intel x86)   Software on an Ubuntu PC (Intel x86) CD/DVD is compiled to run on Intel x86-compatible processors, including most machines with Intel and AMD processors, almost all machines that run Microsoft Windows, and newer Apple Macintosh machines that use Intel processors. If you are not sure which type of processor a machine has, assume it has this type of processor.

64-bit PC (AMD64) Software on an Ubuntu 64-bit PC (AMD64) CD/DVD is compiled to run on AMD64 processors, including the Athlon64, Opteron, and Intel 64-bit processors that incorporate EM64T technology, such as the EMT64 Xeon. Because some features of proprietary third-party applications are not available for 64-bit architecture, you may want to run Ubuntu compiled for a 32-bit (Intel x86) processor on a system with a 64-bit processor.

SPARC Software on an Ubuntu SPARC CD (there is no DVD for this architecture) is compiled to run on UltraSPARC machines, including those based on the multicore UltraSPARC T1 (Niagara) processors.

Mac (PowerPC) Ubuntu does not officially support the PowerPC, but there is extensive community support for this processor architecture. See wiki.ubuntu.com/PowerPCFAQ for more information about running Ubuntu on a PowerPC. You can download PowerPC versions of Ubuntu from wiki.ubuntu.com/PowerPCDownloads.

INTERFACES: INSTALLER AND INSTALLED SYSTEM

When you install Ubuntu, you have a choice of interfaces to use while you install it (to work with the installer). You also have a choice of interfaces to use to work with the installed system. This section describes the two basic interfaces: textual and graphical.

Textual (CLI) A textual interface, also called a command-line interface (CLI) or character-based interface, displays characters and some simple graphical symbols. It is line oriented; you give it instructions using a keyboard only.

Graphical (GUI) A graphical user interface (GUI) typically displays a desktop (such as GNOME) and windows; you give it instructions using a mouse and keyboard. You can run a textual interface within a GUI by opening a terminal emulator window (page 111). A GUI uses more computer resources (CPU time and memory) than a textual interface does.

Pseudographical A pseudographical interface is a textual interface that takes advantage of graphical elements on a text-based display device such as a terminal. It may also use color. This interface uses text elements, including simple graphical symbols, to draw rudimentary boxes that emulate GUI windows and buttons. The TAB key frequently moves the cursor from one element to the next and the RETURN key selects the element the cursor is on.

Advantages A GUI is user friendly, whereas the textual interface is compact, uses fewer system resources, and can work on a text-only terminal or over a text-only connection. Because it is more efficient, a textual interface is useful for older, slower systems and systems with minimal amounts of RAM. Server systems frequently use a textual interface because it allows the system to dedicate more resources to the job it is set up to do and fewer resources to pleasing the system administrator. Not running a GUI can also improve system security.

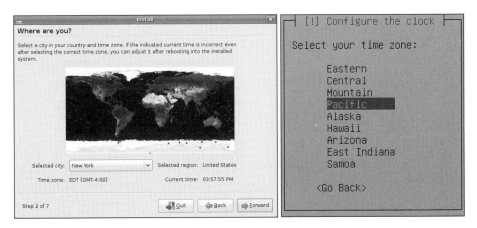

Figure 2-1   Graphical (left) and textual (pseudographical, right) installers

Installer interfaces   Ubuntu provides a user-friendly, graphical installer (ubiquity) and an efficient, pseudographical installer that offers more options and gives you greater control over the installation (Figure 2-1). Both interfaces accomplish the same task: They enable you to tell the installer how you want it to configure Ubuntu.

UBUNTU RELEASES

Canonical, the company that releases Ubuntu, distributes a new release about every six months. Each release has both a number and a name. The number comprises the last digit of the year and the two digits of the month of the release. For example, the 8.10 release was released in October 2008. In sequence, recent releases are 6.06 (Dapper Drake), 6.10 (Edgy Eft), 7.04 (Feisty Fawn), 7.10 (Gutsy Gibbon), 8.04 (Hardy Heron), and 8.10 (Intrepid Ibex). Ubuntu supports (i.e., provides updates for, including security updates) each release for at least 18 months.

LTS releases   Some releases of Ubuntu are marked LTS (long-term support); for example, Hardy Heron is an LTS release. Canonical supports LTS releases for three years for a desktop system and for five years for a server system. LTS releases are designed for people who are more interested in having a stable, unchanging operating system rather than the latest, fastest version. Large and corporate installations, servers, and highly customized distributions frequently fall into this category. You can install and upgrade an LTS release just as you would any other release.

UBUNTU EDITIONS

Desktop CD   The Desktop CD is a live/install CD (page 26); you can use it to boot into a live session. You can install Ubuntu from a live session (page 53). This CD is available for PC and 64-bit PC architectures (page 29), uses the graphical installer, and installs a graphical (desktop) Ubuntu system.

Alternate CD   The Alternate Install CD is not a live CD; it is intended for special installations only. It presents more advanced installation options than the Desktop CD does. This CD is available for PC and 64-bit PC architectures (page 29), uses the textual installer, and installs an Ubuntu system that displays either a graphical or a textual interface. You can use this CD to

- Upgrade from older releases of Ubuntu on systems without an Internet connection.
- Rescue a broken system (page 70).
- Set up encrypted partitions.
- Install Ubuntu on systems with less than 320 megabytes of RAM. These systems may work best from a textual interface, as they may not be able to run a graphical interface fast enough to be usable.
- Set up RAID (page 39) and/or LVM (page 40) partitions.
- Create preconfigured OEM systems.
- Set up automated deployments (having the installer answer installation questions automatically; also called preseeding).

Server CD   The Server CD is not a live CD; it is intended for installation purposes only. This CD is available for PC, 64-bit PC, and SPARC architectures (page 29). It uses the textual installer and installs an Ubuntu system that displays a textual interface (no desktop). During installation, the Server CD gives you the option of installing DNS and/or LAMP (Linux, Apache, MySQL, and PHP). A system installed using this CD has no open ports (page 385) and includes only software essential to a server.

DVD   The DVD is a live/install DVD (page 26); you can use it to boot into a live session. You can install Ubuntu from a live session (page 53). The DVD is available for PC and 64-bit PC architectures (page 29), uses the graphical or textual installer, and installs an Ubuntu system that displays either a graphical or a textual interface. The DVD includes all software packages supported by Ubuntu, not just those installed by default. It is an excellent resource for someone with a system that has no Internet connection.

INSTALLING A FRESH COPY OR UPGRADING AN EXISTING UBUNTU SYSTEM?

Clean install   An *installation*, sometimes referred to as a *clean install*, writes all fresh data to a disk. The installation program overwrites all system programs and data as well as the kernel. You can preserve some user data during an installation depending on where it is located and how you format/partition the disk. Alternatively, you can perform a clean install on an existing system without overwriting data by setting up a dual-boot system (page 66).

Upgrade   An *upgrade* replaces all installed software packages with the most recent version available on the new release. During an upgrade, the installation program preserves both system configuration and user data files. An upgrade brings utilities that are present in the old release up-to-date and installs new utilities. Before you upgrade a system, back up all files on the system.

Because an upgrade preserves the desktop, an upgraded system may not display or take advantage of new features that a clean install would display. For example, if you upgrade from Hardy to Intrepid, you will not see the fast-user-switching applet (the new logout/switch user button). An upgraded desktop will maintain the old logout button. See page 64 for instructions on upgrading an Ubuntu system to a new release.

SETTING UP THE HARD DISK

A hard disk must be prepared in several ways so Linux can write to and read from it. Low-level formatting is the first step in preparing a disk for use. You do not need to perform this task, as it is done at the factory. The next steps in preparing a hard disk for use are to write a partition table to it and to create partitions on the disk. Finally, you need to create a filesystem on the partition. The area of the disk not occupied by partitions is called *free space*. A new disk has no partition table and no partitions. Under DOS/Windows, the term *formatting* means creating a filesystem on a partition; see "Filesystems" below.

Partitions   A *partition,* or *slice,* is a logical section of a hard disk that has a device name, such as **/dev/sda1**, so you can refer to it separately from other sections. For normal use, you must create at least one partition on a hard disk (pages 34 and following). From a live session, and after you install Ubuntu, you can use the GNOME Partition Editor (page 58) to view, resize, and create partitions on an existing system. During installation, you can use the ubiquity partitioner (pages 54 and 61) to create partitions. After installation, you can use parted (page 593) or fdisk to manipulate partitions. See **/dev** on page 470 for more information on device names.

Partition table   A partition table holds information about the partitions on a hard disk. Before the first partition can be created on a disk, the program creating the partition must set up an empty partition table on the disk. As partitions are added, removed, and modified, information about these changes is recorded in the partition table. If you remove the partition table, you can no longer access information on the disk except by extraordinary means.

Filesystems   Before most programs can write to a partition, a *data structure* (page 1104), called a *filesystem,* needs to be written to the partition. This data structure holds inodes (page 483) that map locations on the disk that store files to the names of the files. At the top of the data structure is a single unamed directory. As will be explained shortly, this directory joins the system directory structure when the filesystem is mounted.

When the Ubuntu installer creates a partition, it also automatically writes a filesystem to the partition. You can use the mkfs (make filesystem; page 441) utility, which is similar to the DOS/Windows format utility, to manually create a filesystem on a partition. Table 12-1 on page 487 lists some common types of filesystems. Ubuntu

Linux typically creates **ext3** filesystems for data; unless you have reason to use another filesystem type, use **ext3**. Windows uses FAT16, FAT32, and NTFS filesystems. Apple uses HFS (Hierarchical Filesystem) and HFS+. OS X uses either HFS+ or UFS. Different types of filesystems can coexist in different partitions on a single hard disk, including both Windows and Linux filesystems.

PRIMARY, EXTENDED, AND LOGICAL PARTITIONS

You can divide an IDE/ATA/SATA disk into a maximum of 63 partitions and a SCSI disk into a maximum of 15 partitions. You can use each partition independently for swap devices, filesystems, databases, other resources, and even other operating systems.

Primary and extended partitions Unfortunately, disk partitions follow the template established for DOS machines a long time ago. At most, a disk can hold four *primary partitions*. You can divide one (and only one) of these primary partitions into multiple *logical partitions;* this divided primary partition is called an *extended partition*. If you want more than four partitions on a drive—and you frequently do—you must set up an extended partition.

A typical disk is divided into three primary partitions (frequently numbered 1, 2, and 3) and one extended partition (frequently numbered 4). The three primary partitions are the sizes you want the final partitions to be. The extended partition occupies the rest of the disk. Once you establish the extended partition, you can subdivide it into additional logical partitions (numbered 5 or greater), each of which is the size you want. You cannot use the extended partition (number 4)—only the logical partitions it holds. Figure 16-5 on page 594 illustrates the disk described in this paragraph. See the *Linux Partition HOWTO* (tldp.org/HOWTO/Partition) for more information.

THE LINUX DIRECTORY HIERARCHY

Skip this section for a basic installation

tip This section briefly describes the Linux directory hierarchy so you may better understand some of the decisions you may need to make when you divide the hard disk into partitions while installing Linux. You do not have to read this section to install Linux. You can use guided partitioning (pages 54 and 61) to set up the disk and return to this section when and if you want to. See the beginning of Chapter 6 for a more thorough explanation of the Linux directory hierarchy.

Namespace A *namespace* is a set of names (identifiers) in which each name is unique.

Windows versus Linux As differentiated from a Windows machine, a Linux system presents a single namespace that holds all files, including directories, on the local system. The Linux system namespace is called the *directory hierarchy* or *directory tree*. Under Windows, **C:** is a separate namespace from **D:**. The directory hierarchy rooted at **C:** is separate from the directory hierarchy rooted at **D:** and there is no path or connection between them. Under Linux, the single system namespace is rooted at **/**, which is the *root directory*. Under the root directory are top-level subdirectories such as **bin, boot, etc, home,** and **usr.**

Absolute pathnames   All files on a Linux system, including directories, have a unique identifier called an *absolute pathname*. An absolute pathname traces a path through the directory hierarchy starting at the root directory and ending at the file or directory identified by the pathname. Thus the absolute pathname of the top-level directory named **home** is **/home**. See page 191 for more information.

Slashes (/) in pathnames   Within a pathname, a slash (**/**) follows (appears to the left of) the name of a directory. Thus **/home/sam** specifies that the ordinary or directory file named **sam** is located in the directory named **home**, which is a subdirectory of the root directory (**/**). The pathname **/home/sam/** specifies that **sam** is a directory file. In most instances this distinction is not important. The root directory is implied when a slash appears at the left end of a pathname or when it stands alone.

Linux system namespace   The Linux system namespace comprises the set of absolute pathnames of all files, including directories, in the directory hierarchy of a system.

MOUNT POINTS

A filesystem on a partition holds no information about where it will be mounted in the directory hierarchy (the top-level directory of a filesystem does not have a name). When you use the installer to create most partitions, you specify the type of filesystem to be written to the partition and the name of a directory that Ubuntu associates with the partition.

Mounting a filesystem associates the filesystem with a directory in the directory hierarchy. You can mount a filesystem on any directory in the directory hierarchy. The directory that you mount a filesystem on is called a *mount point*. The directory you specify when you use the installer to create a partition is the mount point for the partition. Most mount points are top-level subdirectories, although there are exceptions (such as **/usr/local**, which is frequently used as a mount point).

Do not create files on mount points before mounting a filesystem

caution   Do not put any files in a directory that is a mount point while a filesystem is not mounted on that mount point. Any files in a directory that is used as a mount point are covered up while the filesystem is mounted on that directory; you will not be able to access them. They reappear when the filesystem is unmounted.

For example, if on the second partition on the first hard disk, which has the device name **/dev/sda2**, you create an **ext3** filesystem that you want to appear as **/home** in the directory hierarchy, you must instruct Linux to mount the **/dev/sda2** partition on **/home** when the system boots. With this filesystem mounted on its normal mount point, you can access it as the **/home** directory.

Filesystem independence   The state of one filesystem does not affect other filesystems: One filesystem on a drive may be corrupt and unreadable, while other filesystems function normally. One filesystem may be full so you cannot write to it, while others have plenty of room for more data.

/etc/fstab   The file that holds the information relating partitions to mount points is **/etc/fstab** (filesystem table; page 492). The associations stored in the **fstab** file are normal for the system, but you can easily override them. When you work in recovery mode, you may mount a filesystem on the **/target** directory so you can repair the filesystem. For example, if you mount on **/target** the partition holding the filesystem normally mounted on **/home**, the directory you would normally find at **/home/sam** will be found at **/target/sam**.

Naming partitions and filesystems

A partition and any filesystem it holds have no name or identification other than a device name (and a related UUID value—see page 492). The partition and the filesystem are frequently referred to by the name of the partition's normal mount point. Thus "the **/home** partition" and "the **/home** filesystem" refer to the partition that holds the filesystem normally mounted on the **/home** directory. See page 488 for more information on mounting filesystems.

PARTITIONING A DISK

During installation, the installer calls a partitioner to set up disk partitions. This section discusses how to plan partition sizes. Although this section uses the term *partition*, planning and sizing LVs (logical volumes; page 40) works the same way. For more information refer to pages 58 and 61 and to the *Linux Partition HOWTO* at www.tldp.org/HOWTO/Partition.

GiB versus GB

tip   Historically a *gigabyte* (GB) meant either 2^{30} (1,073,741,824) or 10^9 (1,000,000,000) bytes. Recently the term *gibibyte* (giga binary byte; abbreviated as GiB) has been used to mean 2^{30} bytes; in turn, gigabyte is used more frequently to mean 10^9 bytes. Similarly, a *mebibyte* (MiB) is 2^{20} (1,048,576) bytes. The Ubuntu partitioner uses mebibytes and gibibytes for specifying the size of partitions.

GUIDED PARTITIONING

It can be difficult to plan partition sizes appropriately if you are not familiar with Linux. During installation, Ubuntu provides *guided partitioning*. Without asking any questions, guided partitioning divides the portion of the disk allotted to Ubuntu into two partitions. One partition is the swap partition, which can be any size from 512 megabytes to 2 or more gigabytes. The other partition is designated as **/** (root) and contains the remainder of the disk space. See the next section for a discussion of the advantages of manual partitioning.

MANUAL PARTITIONING: PLANNING PARTITIONS

If you decide to manually partition the hard disk and set up partitions other than a root partition (**/**) and a swap partition, consider which kinds of activities occur under each top-level subdirectory. Then decide whether it is appropriate to isolate that subdirectory by creating a filesystem and mounting it on its own partition. Advantages of creating additional filesystems include these points:

- Separating data that changes frequently (e.g., **/var** and **/home**) from data that rarely changes (e.g., **/usr** and **/boot**) can reduce fragmentation on the less frequently changing filesystems, helping to maintain optimal system performance.

- Isolating filesystems (e.g., **/home**) can preserve data when you reinstall Linux.

- Additional filesystems can simplify backing up data on a system.

- If all directories are part of a single filesystem and a program runs amok or if the system is the target of a *DoS attack* (page 1106), the entire disk can fill up. System accounting and logging information, which may contain data that can tell you what went wrong, may be lost. On a system with multiple filesystems, such problems typically fill a single filesystem and do not affect other filesystems. Data that may help determine what went wrong will likely be preserved and the system is less likely to crash.

/ (root) The following paragraphs discuss the advantages of making each of the major top-level subdirectories a separate, mountable filesystem. Any directories you do not create filesystems for automatically become part of the root (**/**) filesystem. For example, if you do not create a **/home** filesystem, **/home** is part of the root (**/**) filesystem.

(swap) Linux temporarily stores programs and data on a swap partition when it does not have enough RAM to hold all the information it is processing. The swap partition is also used when you hibernate (suspend to disk) a system. The size of the swap partition should be between one and two times the size of the RAM in the system, with a minimum size of 256 megabytes and a maximum around 2 gigabytes. The worst-case hibernation requires a swap size that is one and a half times the size of RAM. For example, a system with 1 gigabyte of RAM should have a 1- to 2-gigabyte swap partition. Although a swap partition is not required, most systems perform better when one is present. On a system with more than one drive, swap partitions on each drive can further improve performance. A swap partition is not mounted, so it is not associated with a mount point. See **swap** on page 480 for more information.

/boot The **/boot** partition holds the kernel and other data the system needs when it boots. This partition is typically about 100 megabytes, although the amount of space required depends on how many kernel images you want to keep on hand. It can be as small as 50 megabytes. Although you can omit the **/boot** partition, it is useful in many cases. Many administrators put an **ext2** filesystem on this partition because the data on it does not change frequently enough to justify the overhead of the **ext3** journal. Some older BIOSs require the **/boot** partition [or the **/** (root) partition if there is no **/boot** partition] to appear near the beginning of the disk.

Where to put the /boot partition

caution On older systems, the **/boot** partition must reside *completely below cylinder 1023* of the hard disk. An easy way to ensure compliance with this restriction is to make the **/boot** partition one of the first partitions on the disk. When a system has more than one hard disk, the **/boot** partition must also reside on a drive on the following locations:

- Multiple IDE or EIDE drives: the primary controller
- Multiple SCSI drives: ID 0 or ID 1
- Multiple IDE and SCSI drives: the primary IDE controller or SCSI ID 0

/var   The name **var** is short for *variable:* The data in this partition changes frequently. Because it holds the bulk of system logs, package information, and accounting data, making **/var** a separate partition is a good idea. In this way, if a user runs a job that consumes all of the users' disk space, system log files in **/var/log** will not be affected. The **/var** partition can occupy from 500 megabytes up to several gigabytes for extremely active systems with many verbose daemons and a lot of printer and mail activity (the print queues reside in **/var/spool/cups** and incoming mail is stored in **/var/mail**). For example, software license servers are often extremely active systems. By default, Apache content (Web pages it serves) is stored on **/var** under Ubuntu; you may want to change the location Apache uses.

Although such a scenario is unlikely, many files or a few large files may be created under the **/var** directory. Creating a separate filesystem to hold the files in **/var** will prevent these files from overrunning the entire directory structure, bringing the system to a halt, and possibly creating a difficult recovery problem.

/var/log   Some administrators choose to put the log directory in a separate partition to isolate system logs from other files in the **/var** directory.

/home   It is a common strategy to put user home directories on their own filesystem. This filesystem is usually mounted on **/home**. Having **/home** as a separate filesystem allows you to perform a clean install without risking damage to or loss of user files. Also, a separate **/home** filesystem prevents a user from filling the directory structure with her data; at most she can fill the **/home** filesystem, which will affect other users but not bring the system down.

Set up partitions to aid in making backups

tip   Plan partitions based on which data you want to back up and how often you want to back it up. One very large partition can be more difficult to back up than several smaller ones.

/usr   Separating the **/usr** partition can be useful if you plan to export **/usr** to another system and want the security that a separate partition can give. Many administrators put an **ext2** filesystem on this partition because the data on it does not change frequently enough to justify the overhead of the **ext3** journal. The size of **/usr** depends on the number of packages you install. On a default system, it is typically 2–4 gigabytes.

/usr/local   Both **/usr/local** and **/opt** are candidates for separation. If you plan to install many
and /opt   packages in addition to Ubuntu Linux, such as on an enterprise system, you may want to keep them on a separate partition. If you install the additional software in the same partition as the users' home directories, for example, it may encroach on the users' disk space. Many sites keep all **/usr/local** or **/opt** software on one server and export it to other systems. If you choose to create a **/usr/local** or **/opt** partition, its size should be appropriate to the software you plan to install.

Table 2-1 gives guidelines for minimum sizes for partitions used by Linux. Set the sizes of other partitions, such as those for **/home, /opt,** and **/usr/local,** according to need and the size of the hard disk. If you are not sure how you will use additional disk space, you can create extra partitions using whatever names you like (for example, **/b01,**

/b02, and so on). Of course, you do not have to partition the entire drive when you install Linux. You can wait until later to divide the additional space into partitions.

Table 2-1 Example minimum partition sizes[a]

Partition	Example size
/boot	50–100 megabytes
/ (root)	1 gigabyte
(swap)	One to two times the amount of RAM in the system with a minimum of 256 megabytes
/home	As large as necessary; depends on the number of users and the type of work they do
/tmp	Minimum of 500 megabytes
/usr	Minimum of 2–16 gigabytes; depends on which and how many software packages you install
/var	Minimum of 500 megabytes—much larger if you are running a server

a. The sizes in this table assume you create all partitions separately. For example, if you create a 1-gigabyte / (root) partition and do not create a **/usr** partition, in most cases you will not have enough room to store all the system programs.

RAID

RAID (Redundant Array of Inexpensive/Independent Disks) employs two or more hard disk drives or partitions in combination to improve fault tolerance and/or performance. Applications and utilities see these multiple drives/partitions as a single logical device. RAID, which can be implemented in hardware or software (Ubuntu gives you this option), spreads data across multiple disks. Depending on which level you choose, RAID can provide data redundancy to protect data in the case of hardware failure. Although it can improve disk performance by increasing read/write speed, software RAID uses quite a bit of CPU time, which may be a consideration. True hardware RAID requires hardware designed to implement RAID and is not covered in this book (but see "Fake RAID" on the next page).

RAID does not replace backups

caution The purposes of RAID are to improve performance and/or to minimize downtime in the case of a disk failure. RAID does not replace backups.

Do not use RAID as a replacement for regular backups. If the system undergoes a catastrophic failure, RAID is useless. Earthquake, fire, theft, and other disasters may leave the entire system inaccessible (if the hard disks are destroyed or missing). RAID also does not take care of the simple case of replacing a file when a user deletes it by accident. In these situations, a backup on a removable medium (which has been removed) is the only way you will be able to restore a filesystem.

RAID can be an effective *addition* to a backup. Ubuntu offers RAID software that you can install either when you install an Ubuntu system or as an afterthought. The Linux kernel automatically detects RAID arrays (sets of partitions) at boot time if the partition ID is set to 0xfd (**raid autodetect**).

Software RAID, as implemented in the kernel, is much cheaper than hardware RAID. Not only does this approach avoid the need for specialized RAID disk controllers, but it also works with the less expensive ATA disks as well as SCSI disks.

Fake RAID   Ubuntu provides support for motherboard-based RAID (known as *fake RAID*) through the **dmraid** driver set. Linux software RAID is almost always better than fake RAID. For more information see help.ubuntu.com/community/FakeRaidHowto.

The partitioner on the Alternate CD gives you the choice of implementing RAID level 0, 1, or 5. For levels 1 and 5, be sure to put member partitions on different drives. That way, if one drive fails, your data is preserved.

- **RAID level 0 (striping)**—Improves performance but offers no redundancy. The storage capacity of the RAID device is equal to that of the member partitions or disks.

- **RAID level 1 (mirroring)**—Provides simple redundancy, improving data reliability, and can improve the performance of read-intensive applications. The storage capacity of the RAID device is equal to one of the member partitions or disks.

- **RAID level 5 (disk striping with parity)**—Provides redundancy and improves (most notably, read) performance. The storage capacity of the RAID device is equal to that of the member partitions or disks, minus one of the partitions or disks (assuming they are all the same size).

For more information refer to the *Software-RAID HOWTO*.

LVM: LOGICAL VOLUME MANAGER

The Logical Volume Manager (LVM2, which this book refers to as LVM) allows you to change the size of *logical volumes* (LVs, the LVM equivalent of partitions) on the fly. With LVM, if you make a mistake in setting up LVs or your needs change, you can make LVs smaller or larger without affecting user data. You must choose to use LVM at the time you install the system or add a hard disk; you cannot retroactively apply it to a disk full of data. LVM supports IDE and SCSI drives as well as multiple devices such as those found in RAID arrays.

LVM groups disk components (partitions, hard disks, or storage device arrays), called *physical volumes* (PVs), into a storage pool, or virtual disk, called a *volume group* (VG). See Figure 2-2. You allocate a portion of a VG to create a *logical volume*.

An LV is similar in function to a traditional disk partition in that you can create a filesystem on an LV. It is much easier, however, to change and move LVs than partitions: When you run out of space on a filesystem on an LV, you can grow (expand) the LV and its filesystem into empty or new disk space, or you can move the filesystem to a

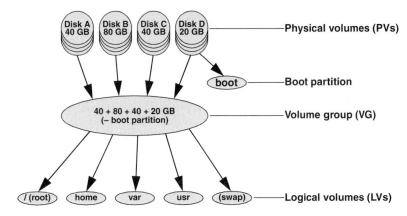

Figure 2-2 LVM: Logical Volume Manager

larger LV. For example, you can add a hard drive to a system and incorporate it into an LV to expand the capacity of that LV. LVM's disk space manipulation is transparent to users; service is not interrupted.

LVM also eases the burden of storage migration. When you outgrow or need to upgrade PVs, LVM can move data to new PVs. To read more about LVM, refer to the resources listed on page 26.

THE INSTALLATION PROCESS

The following steps outline the process of installing Ubuntu Linux from a CD/DVD. See Chapter 3 for installation specifics.

1. Make sure the BIOS is set to boot from the CD/DVD (page 28). Insert the installation CD/DVD in and reset the computer. The computer boots from the CD/DVD and displays the initial install screen (Figure 3-2, page 51).

2. You can press function keys to display options, select an item from the initial install screen menu, and begin bringing up a live session or installing Ubuntu when you are ready. Or you can do nothing. A live/install Desktop CD/DVD starts to bring up the system after 30 seconds; an installation-only CD waits for you to select an item from the menu. One of the menu items checks the installation medium.

3. As part of the process of bringing up a live session or installing Ubuntu, Ubuntu Linux creates *RAM disks* (page 1128) that it uses in place of the hard disk used for a normal boot operation. The installer copies tools required for the installation or to bring up a system from a live/install Desktop CD/DVD to the RAM disks. The use of RAM disks allows the installation process to run through the specification and design phases without writing to the hard disk and enables you to opt out of the installation at

any point before the system warns you it is about to write to the hard disk (or you complete the installation). If you opt out before this point, the system is left in its original state. The RAM disks also allow a system booted from a live/install Desktop CD to leave the hard disk untouched.

4. The installer prompts you with questions about how you want to configure Ubuntu Linux.

5. When the installer is finished collecting information, it displays the Ready to install screen (Figure 3-8, page 57). When you click **Install**, it writes the operating system files to the hard disk.

6. The installer prompts you to remove the CD/DVD and press RETURN; it then reboots the system.

7. The Ubuntu Linux system is ready for you to log in and use.

DOWNLOADING AND BURNING A CD/DVD

There are several ways to obtain an Ubuntu CD/DVD. Ubuntu makes available releases of Linux as CD and DVD *ISO image* files (named after the ISO9660 standard that defines the CD filesystem). This section describes how to download one of these images and burn a CD/DVD. You can also point a browser at shipit.ubuntu.com to display a Web page with links that enable you to request a free CD from Ubuntu or purchase a CD/DVD from a Web site.

THE EASY WAY TO DOWNLOAD A CD ISO IMAGE FILE

This section explains the easiest way to download a CD ISO image file. This technique works in most situations; it is straightforward but limited. For example, it does not allow you to use BitTorrent to download the file nor does it download a DVD image.

To begin, point a browser at www.ubuntu.com and click **Download Now** or **Get Ubuntu**. Select the release (page 31) and edition (page 31) you want to download. Then select the type of system you want to install it on (see "Processor Architecture" on page 29). Finally select a location from the drop-down list labeled **Choose a location near you** and click **Start Download**. If the browser gives you a choice of what to do with the file, save it to the hard disk. The browser saves the ISO image file to the hard disk. Continue reading at "Burning the CD/DVD" on page 46.

OTHER WAYS TO DOWNLOAD A CD/DVD ISO IMAGE FILE

This section explains how to download a release that is not listed on the Ubuntu download page or a DVD image, and how to download a torrent that enables you

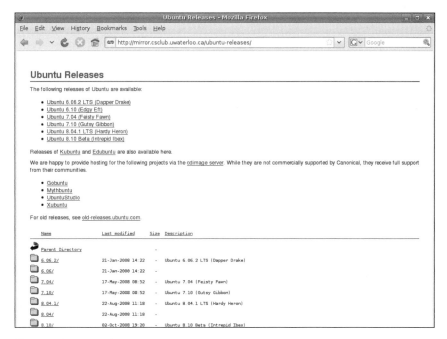

Figure 2-3 An Ubuntu mirror I

to use BitTorrent to download the ISO image file. See "Download Ubuntu" on page 27 for other locations you can download Ubuntu from.

Browser When you use a Web browser to download a file, the browser contacts a Web (HTTP) or FTP server and downloads the file from that server. If too many people download files from a server at the same time, the downloads become slower.

BitTorrent BitTorrent efficiently distributes large amounts of static data, such as ISO image files. Unlike using a browser to download a file from a single server, BitTorrent distributes the functions of a server over its clients. As each client downloads a file, it becomes a server for the parts of the file it has downloaded. To use BitTorrent, you must download a small file called a *torrent* (or have a Web browser do it for you). This file, which holds information that allows clients to communicate with one another, has a filename extension of **.torrent**. As more people use a torrent to download a file at the same time, the downloads become faster. Downloading an ISO image file using BitTorrent is covered later in this section.

Mirrors Many sites mirror (hold copies of) the Ubuntu ISO image files and BitTorrent torrents. Some mirrors use HTTP while others use FTP; you can use a browser to download files from either type of site. FTP and HTTP appear slightly different. Point a browser at www.ubuntu.com/getubuntu/downloadmirrors to locate a mirror site. Scroll through the list of mirror sites, find a site near you, and click that site's URL. The browser displays a page similar to the one shown in Figure 2-3.

Figure 2-4   An Ubuntu mirror II

Click any link on the page that includes the name or release number of the version of Ubuntu you want to install. The browser displays a page similar to the one shown in Figure 2-4.

Downloading an ISO image file

You can click the links at the top of the page, although there is usually a better selection of versions in the list of files at the bottom of the page. Click the number or name of the release you want to download (e.g., **intrepid** or **8.10**). At this point, some sites display a page with two links: **Parent Directory** and **release**. If the browser displays this page, click **release**. The browser displays a page with the name and number of the release at the top, followed by a description of the different types of CDs. At the bottom of the page is a list of files, with each line showing the name of the file, the date it was created, its size, and a short description. Each filename is a link. The following two lines describe the Intel x86 desktop ISO image file for Intrepid (8.10) and the torrent file that enables you to use BitTorrent to download the same ISO image file. The ISO image file is almost 700 *mega*bytes; the torrent file is 27 *kilo*bytes.

```
ubuntu-8.10-desktop-i386.iso   ...   695M Desktop CD for PC (Intel x86) computers (standard download)
ubuntu-8.10-desktop-i386.iso.torrent..27k Desktop CD for PC (Intel x86) computers (BitTorrent download)
```

Click the filename/link that specifies the release, edition, and architecture you want. For example, clicking **ubuntu-8.10-desktop-i386.iso** downloads the CD ISO image for Intrepid (release 8.10) desktop (edition) for the i386 architecture. Save the file to the hard disk. Next download the file named **MD5SUMS** (at the top of the list) to the same directory. An easy way to save a file is to right-click it, select **Save Link/Target As**, and save the file to a directory with enough space for the file. See the next section for an explanation of how to use the **MD5SUMS** file to verify the ISO image file you download.

Downloading a DVD   To download a DVD ISO image file, go to cdimage.ubuntu.com/releases and follow the instructions under "Downloading an ISO image file." You can identify DVD ISO image files by the string **dvd** in their names. Make sure you have room for the file on the hard disk: A DVD ISO image file occupies about 4 gigabytes. A DVD image takes about five times as long to download as a CD image.

Using BitTorrent   You can use BitTorrent to obtain an ISO image file. Because BitTorrent is available for both Windows and Mac OS X (www.bittorrent.com), you can download and burn the Ubuntu CD/DVD under either of these operating systems. To download a torrent, point a browser at releases.ubuntu.com and click the filename of the torrent. You can identify a torrent file by its filename extension of **.torrent**. A BitTorrent client should start automatically and ask where to put the downloaded file. You can also download the torrent manually; follow the instructions under "Downloading an ISO image file" on page 44. You can then start downloading the file from the command line (page 521) or by clicking it in a file browser such as Nautilus (page 94).

You can download and burn the CD/DVD on any operating system

tip   You can download and burn the CD/DVD on any computer that is connected to the Internet, has a browser, has enough space on the hard disk to hold the ISO image file (about 700 megabytes for a CD and 4 gigabytes for a DVD), and can burn a CD/DVD. You can frequently use ftp (page 654) or, on a Linux system, **Nautilus menubar: File⇨Places⇨Connect to Server** (page 265) in place of a browser to download the file.

VERIFYING AN ISO IMAGE FILE

This section assumes you have an ISO image file and a **MD5SUMS.htm** file saved on the hard disk and explains how to verify that the ISO IMAGE file is correct. The **MD5SUMS.htm** file contains the *MD5* (page 1119) sums for each of the available ISO image files. When you process a file using the md5sum utility, md5sum generates a number based on the file. If that number matches the corresponding number in the **MD5SUMS** file, the downloaded file is correct. You can run the following commands from a terminal emulator:

```
$ grep desktop-i386 MD5SUMS;md5sum ubuntu-8.10-desktop-i386.iso
574c9b48dbb5cf471b05ff18a9adc082 *ubuntu-8.10-desktop-i386.iso
574c9b48dbb5cf471b05ff18a9adc082  ubuntu-8.10-desktop-i386.iso
```

Computing an MD5 sum for a large file takes a while. The two long strings that the preceding command displays must be identical: If they are not, you must download the file again.

Make sure the software is set up to burn an ISO image

tip   Burning an ISO image is not the same as copying files to a CD/DVD. Make sure the CD/DVD burning software is set up to burn an ISO image. If you simply copy the ISO file to a CD/DVD, it will not work when you try to install Ubuntu Linux.

BURNING THE CD/DVD

An ISO image file is an exact image of what needs to be on the CD/DVD. Putting that image on a CD/DVD involves a different process than copying files to a CD/DVD. The CD/DVD burning software you use has a special selection for burning an ISO image. It has a label similar to **Record CD from CD Image** or **Burn CD Image**. Refer to the instructions for the software you are using for information on how to burn an ISO image file to a CD/DVD.

You must use 700-megabyte CD-ROM blanks

tip   When you burn an Ubuntu Linux CD from an ISO image, you must use a 700-megabyte blank. A 650-megabyte blank will not work because there is too much data to fit on it.

GATHERING INFORMATION ABOUT THE SYSTEM

It is not difficult to install and bring up an Ubuntu Linux system. Nevertheless, the more you know about the process before you start, the easier it will be. The installation software collects information about the system and can help you make decisions during the installation process. However, the system will work better when you know how you want your disk partitioned rather than letting the installation program create partitions without your input. There are many details, and the more details you take control of, the more pleased you are likely to be with the finished product. Finding the information that this section asks for will help ensure you end up with a system you understand and know how to change when necessary. To an increasing extent, the installation software probes the hardware and figures out what you have. Newer equipment is more likely to report on itself than older equipment is.

Test the ISO file and test the CD/DVD

tip   It is a good idea to test the ISO image file and the burned CD/DVD before you use it to install Ubuntu Linux. When you boot the system from the CD/DVD, Ubuntu gives you the option of checking the CD/DVD for defects (page 51). A bad file on a CD may not show up until you finish installing Ubuntu Linux and have it running. At that point, it may be difficult and time-consuming to figure out where the problem lies. Testing the file and CD/DVD takes a few minutes, but can save you hours of trouble if something is not right. If you decide to perform one test only, test the CD/DVD.

It is critical to have certain pieces of information before you start. One thing Linux can never figure out is all the relevant names and IP addresses (unless you are using DHCP, in which case the addresses are set up for you).

Following is a list of items you may need information about. Get as much information on each item as you can: manufacturer, model number, size (megabytes, gigabytes, and so forth), number of buttons, chipset (for cards), and so on. Some items, such as the network interface card, may be built into the motherboard.

- Hard disks.
- Memory. You don't need it for installation, but it is good to know.
- SCSI interface card.
- Network interface card (NIC).
- Video interface card (including the amount of video RAM/memory).
- Sound card and compatibility with standards, such as SoundBlaster.
- Mouse (PS/2, USB, AT, and number of buttons).
- Monitor (size and maximum resolution).
- IP addresses and names, unless you are using DHCP (page 454; most routers are set up as DHCP servers), in which case the IP addresses are automatically assigned to the system. Most of this information comes from the system administrator or ISP.
  - System hostname (anything you like).
  - System address.
  - Network mask (netmask).
  - Gateway address (the connecting point to the network or Internet) or a phone number when you use a dial-up connection.
  - Addresses for nameservers, also called DNS addresses.
  - Domain name (not required).

CHAPTER SUMMARY

A live/install Desktop CD runs a live Ubuntu session without installing Ubuntu on the system. You can install Ubuntu from a live session. Booting a live/install Desktop CD is a good way to test hardware and fix a system that will not boot from the hard disk.

Before you download or otherwise obtain an Ubuntu CD or DVD, make sure you are using a medium that is appropriate to the hardware you are installing it on and to the purposes the system will be used for. Ubuntu has three editions: Desktop (the most common), Alternate (for special cases), and Server. The Ubuntu live DVD combines features of all three of these editions.

When you install Ubuntu Linux, you copy operating system files from a CD or DVD to hard disk(s) on a system and set up configuration files so that Linux runs properly on the hardware. Operating system files are stored as CD or DVD ISO image files. You can use a Web browser or BitTorrent to download an ISO image file. It is a good idea to test the ISO image file when it is downloaded and the burned CD/DVD before you use it to install Ubuntu Linux.

When you install Ubuntu, you can let the installer decide how to partition the hard disk (guided partitioning) or you can manually specify how you want to partition it.

EXERCISES

1. Briefly, what does the process of installing an operating system such as Ubuntu Linux involve?

2. What is an installer?

3. Would you set up a GUI on a server system? Why or why not?

4. A system boots from the hard disk. To install Linux, you need it to boot from a CD/DVD. How can you make the system boot from a CD/DVD?

5. What is free space on a hard disk? What is a filesystem?

6. What is an ISO image? How do you burn an ISO image to a CD/DVD?

ADVANCED EXERCISES

7. List two reasons why RAID cannot replace backups.

8. What are RAM disks? How are they used during installation?

9. What is MD5? How does it work to ensure that an ISO image file you download is correct?

3

STEP-BY-STEP
INSTALLATION

Chapter 2 covered planning the installation of Ubuntu Linux: determining the requirements; performing an upgrade versus a clean installation; planning the layout of the hard disk; obtaining the files you need for the installation, including how to download and burn CD/DVD ISO images; and collecting information about the system. This chapter focuses on installing Ubuntu. Frequently the installation is quite simple, especially if you have done a good job of planning. Sometimes you may run into a problem or have a special circumstance; this chapter gives you tools to use in these cases. Read as much of this chapter as you need to; once you have installed Ubuntu Linux, continue with Chapter 4, which covers getting started using the Ubuntu desktop. If you install a textual (command-line) system, continue with Chapter 5.

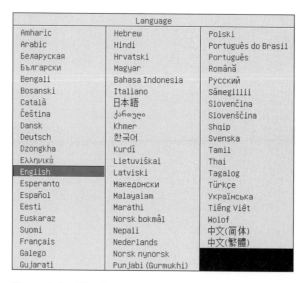

Language		
Amharic	Hebrew	Polski
Arabic	Hindi	Português do Brasil
Беларуская	Hrvatski	Português
Български	Magyar	Română
Bengali	Bahasa Indonesia	Русский
Bosanski	Italiano	Sámegillii
Català	日本語	Slovenčina
Čeština	ქართული	Slovenščina
Dansk	Khmer	Shqip
Deutsch	한국어	Svenska
Dzongkha	Kurdî	Tamil
Ελληνικά	Lietuviškai	Thai
English	Latviski	Tagalog
Esperanto	Македонски	Türkçe
Español	Malayalam	Українська
Eesti	Marathi	Tiếng Việt
Euskaraz	Norsk bokmål	Wolof
Suomi	Nepali	中文(简体)
Français	Nederlands	中文(繁體)
Galego	Norsk nynorsk	
Gujarati	Punjabi (Gurmukhi)	

Figure 3-1 The Language menu

BASIC INSTALLATION FROM THE LIVE/INSTALL DESKTOP CD/DVD

To begin installing Ubuntu from a live/install Desktop CD/DVD, insert the disk in the computer and boot the system. The system displays the Language menu (Figure 3-1). If you do nothing, after 30 seconds the system boots to a live session using the highlighted language. If you press any key before the 30 seconds is up, the system stops its countdown.

From the Language menu, press RETURN to select this highlighted language and display the initial install screen (Figure 3-2). Before you press RETURN, you can use the ARROW keys to select the language you want Ubuntu to use during a live session. Refer to "BIOS setup" on page 28 if the system does not boot from the CD/DVD. See "The Function Keys" on page 67 for information about changing the language, keyboard layout, and accessibility features used by the live session.

The menu on the initial install screen differs depending on which edition of Ubuntu (page 31) you are installing; along the bottom of the screen, the labels for the function keys remain the same. This section describes how to boot into a live session and how to install Ubuntu from that session.

BOOTING THE SYSTEM

Before Ubuntu can display a desktop from a live/install Desktop CD/DVD or install itself on a hard disk, the Ubuntu operating system must be read into memory

Try Ubuntu without any change to your computer
Install Ubuntu
Check CD for defects
Test memory
Boot from first hard disk

Press F4 to select alternative start-up and installation modes.

F1 Help   F2 Language   F3 Keymap   F4 Modes   F5 Accessibility   F6 Other Options

Figure 3-2   The initial install screen for the live/install Desktop CD

(booted). This process can take a few minutes on older, slower systems or systems with minimal RAM (memory). Each of the menu selections on the initial install screen, except the memory test, boots the system.

CHECKING THE CD/DVD FOR DEFECTS

Whether you burned your own CD/DVD, purchased it, or are using the disk included with this book, it is a good idea to verify that the contents of the CD/DVD is correct. On the initial install screen, use the ARROW keys to highlight **Check CD for Defects** (this selection checks DVDs, too) and press RETURN. Checking the CD/DVD takes a few minutes—Ubuntu keeps you apprised of its progress. When Ubuntu finishes checking the CD/DVD, it displays the result of its testing. Press RETURN to redisplay the initial install screen.

Test the CD/DVD

tip   Testing the CD/DVD takes a few minutes but can save you much aggravation if the installation fails or you run into problems after installing Ubuntu owing to bad media.

LIVE SESSION

In most cases, you can boot Ubuntu to run a live session that displays a desktop without doing anything after you boot from the live/install Desktop CD/DVD: Ubuntu displays the Language menu, counts down from 30, boots the system, displays the Ubuntu logo while an orange cursor moves back and forth on the progress

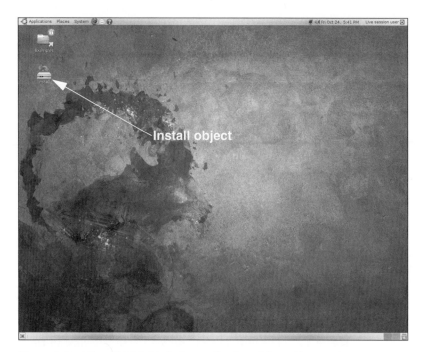

Install object

Figure 3-3 The GNOME desktop displayed by a live session

bar, and finally displays the GNOME desktop (Figure 3-3). To speed up this process, you can press RETURN when Ubuntu displays the Language menu. The first time you use a CD/DVD, it is a good idea to check it for defects (see the previous page).

If you encounter problems with the display while you are bringing up the desktop from a live/install Desktop CD/DVD or during installation, reboot the system and use the F4 Modes menu to bring it up in safe graphics mode, as explained on page 68. If that tactic does not work, install Ubuntu using the textual installer on the Alternate CD (page 70) or the DVD.

The live/install Desktop CD/DVD gives you a chance to preview Ubuntu without installing it. Boot the live/install Desktop CD/DVD to begin a live session and work with Ubuntu as explained in Chapter 4. When you are finished, remove the CD/DVD and reboot the system. The system boots as it did before the live session.

Because a live session does not write to the hard disk (other than using a Linux swap partition if one is available), none of the work you save will be available once you reboot. You can use Webmail or another method, such as a USB flash drive, to transfer files you want to preserve to another system.

optional SEEING WHAT IS GOING ON

If you are curious and want to see what Ubuntu is doing as it boots, remove **quiet** and **splash** from the boot command line (Figure 3-18, page 69): With the initial install screen displayed, press F6 to display the boot command line. Press BACKSPACE or

DEL to back up and erase **quiet** and **splash** from the boot command line. If you have not added anything to this line, you can remove the two hyphens at the end of the line. If you have added to this line, use the LEFT ARROW key to back up over—but not remove—whatever you added, the hyphens, and the SPACE on each side of them. Then remove **quiet** and **splash**. As Ubuntu boots, it displays information about what it is doing. Text scrolls on the screen, although sometimes too rapidly to read.

THE UBUNTU GRAPHICAL INSTALLER

ubiquity   The ubiquity utility is a graphical installer, written mostly in Python, that installs Ubuntu from a live session. You can use the Alternate or Server CD or the DVD to install Ubuntu using the textual installer (page 73).

Before you start, see what is on the hard disk

tip   Unless you are certain you are working with a new disk, or you are sure the data on the disk is of no value, it is a good idea to see what is on the disk before you start installing Ubuntu. You can use the GNOME Partition Editor to examine the organization of a hard disk. See page 58 for more information.

Welcome screen   To install Ubuntu from the live/install Desktop CD/DVD, start a live session and double-click (use the left mouse button) the object on the desktop labeled **Install** (Figure 3-3).

After a few moments Ubuntu displays the Welcome screen of the Install window (Figure 3-4). This screen contains a welcome message and a query about which language you would like ubiquity to use. The language you choose will be the default language for the installed system; you can change this default once the system is installed (page 130).

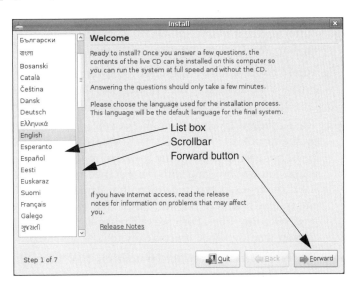

Figure 3-4   The Install window, Welcome screen

USING THE MOUSE TO WORK WITH THE INSTALL WINDOW

You can use either the mouse or the keyboard to make selections from the Install window screens. To select a language from the Welcome screen using the mouse, left-click the language you want to use in the list box at the left. If the language you want does not appear on the displayed portion of the list, click or drag the scrollbar (Figure 3-4) to display more languages; then click the language of your choice. Ubuntu highlights the language you click. Once you select a language, you are finished working with the Welcome screen; click the **Forward** button to display the next screen.

USING THE KEYBOARD TO WORK WITH THE INSTALL WINDOW

To use the keyboard to make selections, first use the TAB key to move the highlight to the object you want to work with. On the Welcome screen, the objects are the selected item in the list box, the release notes link, and the buttons labeled **Quit**, **Back**, and **Forward**. With a language in the list box highlighted, use the UP ARROW and DOWN ARROW keys to move the highlight to the language you want to use. The list scrolls automatically when you move the highlight to the next, undisplayed entry in the list. See "F3 Keymap" on page 68 if you want to change the layout of the keyboard ubiquity uses during installation.

Once you select a language, you are finished working with the Welcome screen; use the TAB key to highlight the Forward button. The border of a button becomes thicker and darker when it is highlighted. With the Forward button highlighted, press RETURN to display the next screen.

This book describes using the mouse to make selections from a graphical interface; you can use the keyboard if you prefer.

Where are you?   Next ubiquity displays the Where are you? screen. This screen allows you to specify the time zone the computer is in. You can use the map or the drop-down list labeled **Selected city** to specify the time zone. Allow the mouse pointer to hover over the area of the map near a city that is in the same time zone as the computer; the map zooms in on that area. Click a city; the name of the city appears in the box labeled **Selected city**.

To use the drop-down list, click anywhere in the box labeled **Selected city**; ubiquity expands the box into a list of cities. Use the mouse or ARROW keys to select a city and then either click the city or press RETURN. Click **Forward**.

Keyboard layout   The Keyboard layout screen allows you to specify the type of keyboard to be used by the installed system. (See "F3 Keymap" on page 68 to change the layout of the keyboard ubiquity uses during installation.) Select the country you are in or the language you will be using with the installed system from the list box on the left. Then select the type of keyboard you will be using from the list box on the right. Click the empty text box near the bottom of the window and enter some characters to test your selection. Click **Forward**. The installer briefly displays the Starting Up the Partitioner window while it gets ready for the next step.

Prepare disk space   The Prepare disk space screen controls how ubiquity partitions the hard disk. See page 36 for a discussion of the issues involved in partitioning a hard disk.

Figure 3-5   The ubiquity partitioner showing one empty hard disk

With a single, clean hard disk—a hard disk with nothing installed on it, as it comes from the factory (i.e., no partition table)—the ubiquity partitioner displays a Prepare disk space screen similar to the one shown in Figure 3-5. In this case, the simplest way to partition the disk is to allow ubiquity do it for you. By default, the radio button labeled **Guided – use entire disk** and the radio button next to the name of the only hard disk in the system are selected. If the system has two or more clean hard disks, the ubiquity partitioner displays a line for each hard disk; click the radio button next to the one where you want to install Ubuntu. Click **Forward** and ubiquity creates two partitions on the hard disk: a small swap partition (page 37) and a root partition (**/**, page 37) that occupies the rest of the disk. The installer displays the Guided Partitioning window while it gets ready for the next step.

If the Prepare disk space screen includes **Guided - resize...** and **Guided - use the largest continuous free space** selections, the hard disk probably contains at least one partition (there could just be an empty partition table). If you are sure you do not want to keep any of the information on the hard disk, you can select **Guided - use entire disk**. To find out more about what is on the disk, see the section on the Partition Editor on page 58. For more information on guided partitioning, see page 61. For information on manual partitioning, see page 62.

The ubiquity partitioner displays a warning window (Figure 3-6) if it is going to write to the hard disk before it displays the Ready to install screen (Figure 3-8, page 57). If you click **Continue**, ubiquity writes to the hard disk immediately. If it does not display this window, ubiquity will not make changes to the hard disk until you click **Install** on the Ready to install screen.

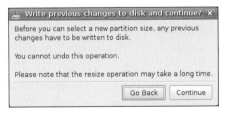

Figure 3-6   Write to disk warning window

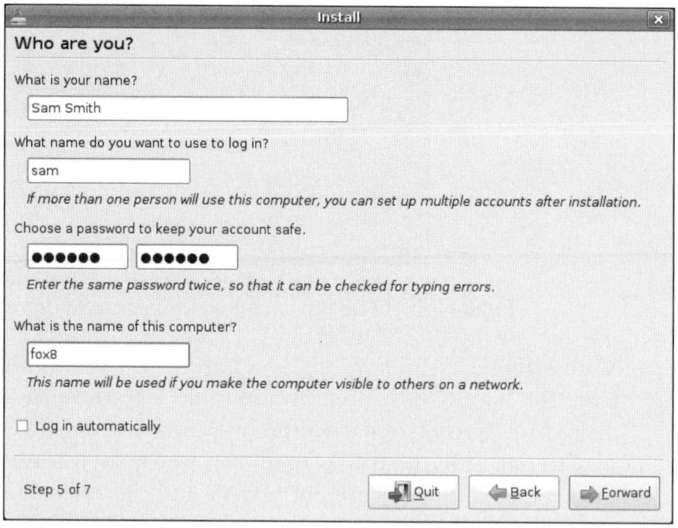

Figure 3-7   The Install window, Who are you? screen

Migrate documents and settings
If you are installing Ubuntu on a system that already has one or more operating systems installed on it, and you are not overwriting those operating systems, the Migrate documents and settings screen displays a list of accounts and settings from the existing operating systems. For example, if you are creating a dual-boot system on a system that already has Windows installed on it, this screen shows the accounts from the Windows system and a list of programs and settings. It might show your name from the Windows system and, under that, Internet Explorer and My Documents. Put ticks in the check boxes adjacent to those items you want to migrate to the Ubuntu system. On the lower portion of the screen, enter the information necessary to create an Ubuntu user to receive the migrated information.

Who are you?
The Who are you? screen (Figure 3-7) sets up the first Ubuntu user. This user can use sudo (page 86) to administer the system, including setting up additional users (page 578). Enter the full name of the user in the text box labeled **What is your name?**. As you type, ubiquity enters the first name from the name you just entered in the box labeled **What name do you want to use to log in?**. Press TAB to move the cursor to this box. If you want to use a different username, press BACKSPACE (page 136) to erase the username and enter a new one. Press TAB. Enter the same password in the two (adjacent) boxes labeled **Choose a password to keep your account safe.** Although ubiquity accepts any password, it is a good idea to choose a more secure password if the system is connected to the Internet. See "Changing Your Password" on page 133 for a discussion of password security.

The final text box specifies the name of the computer. For use on a local network and to connect to the Internet with a Web browser or other client, you can use a simple name such as **fox8**. If you are setting up a server system, see "FQDN" on page 785 for information on names that are valid on the Internet. Put a tick in the

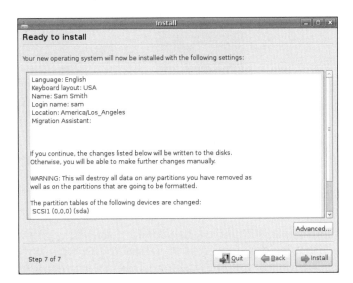

Figure 3-8   The Install window, Ready to install screen

check box labeled **Log in automatically** if you want Ubuntu to log you in automatically when the system boots—select this option only if you trust everyone who has physical access to the system. Click **Forward.**

Ready to install   The final screen ubiquity displays is the Ready to install screen (Figure 3-8). Unless ubiquity asked your permission to write to the hard disk during the partitioning phase of the installation, it has not written to the disk yet. If you click **Quit** at this point, the hard disk will remain untouched. This screen summarizes your answers to the questions ubiquity asked in the previous screens. Click **Advanced** to display the Advanced Options window, which allows you to choose whether to install a boot loader (normally you want to), whether the system should participate in an automatic, informal package usage survey, and whether to set up a network proxy (page 389). Click **OK** to close the Advanced Options window. If everything looks right in the summary in the Ready to install screen, click **Install**. The installer begins installing Ubuntu on the hard disk.

When ubiquity writes to the hard disk

caution   You can abort the installation by clicking the **Quit** button at any point up to and including the Ready to install screen (Figure 3-8) without making any changes to the system. Once you click **Install** in this screen, ubiquity writes to the hard disk. However, if ubiquity displayed the warning window shown in Figure 3-6 on page 55 and you clicked **Continue**, it wrote to the hard disk at that time.

The ubiquity installer displays a series of windows to keep you informed of its progress. When the new system is installed, Ubuntu displays the Installation Complete window, which gives you the choice of continuing the live session or rebooting the system so you can use the newly installed copy of Ubuntu. Click **Restart now** to reboot the system.

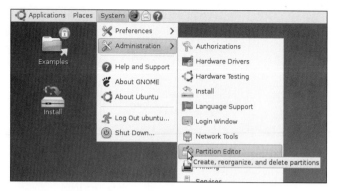

Figure 3-9   Selecting the Partition Editor from the Main menu

The installer displays the Ubuntu logo and a progress bar. When it has finished shutting down the system, it asks you to remove the disk (so you do not reboot from the live/install Desktop CD/DVD) and press RETURN. After you complete these steps, Ubuntu reboots the system and displays the Ubuntu GNOME login screen (Figure 4-1, page 88).

GRAPHICAL PARTITIONERS

A partitioner displays and can add, delete, and modify partitions on a hard disk. This section describes two graphical partitioners you can use to configure a hard disk so you can install Ubuntu Linux. The first partitioner, gparted, is available on the live/install Desktop CD desktop. The other partitioner is part of the ubiquity installer and is not available by itself. See page 75 for information on using the textual partitioner, which is available when you use the textual installer. After you install Ubuntu Linux, you can use parted (page 593) to manipulate partitions. If you want a basic set of partitions, you can allow ubiquity to partition the hard disk automatically using guided partitioning.

See "Setting Up the Hard Disk" on page 33 for a discussion of free space, partitions, partition tables, and filesystems. "Manual Partitioning: Planning Partitions" on page 36 discusses some of the filesystems for which you may want to set up partitions if you manually partition the hard disk.

gparted: THE GNOME PARTITION EDITOR

Unless you know the hard disk you are installing Ubuntu Linux on has nothing on it (it is a new disk) or you are sure the disk holds no information of value, it is a good idea to examine the organization of the disk before you start the installation. The GNOME Partition Editor (gparted), which is available from a live session, is a good tool for this job. Open the Partition Editor window by selecting **Main menu: System⇨Administration⇨Partition Editor** as shown in Figure 3-9.

The Partition Editor displays the layout of a hard disk and can resize partitions, such as when you are setting up a dual-boot system by adding Ubuntu to a Windows system

Figure 3-10   The Partition Editor displaying an empty disk drive

(page 66). Although you can create partitions using the Partition Editor, you cannot specify the mount point (page 35) for a partition—this step must wait until you are installing Ubuntu and using the ubiquity partitioner.

AN EMPTY HARD DISK

The gparted Partition Editor shows one large unallocated space for a new hard disk (empty, with no partition table). If you have more than one hard disk, use the list box in the upper-right corner of the screen to select which disk the Partition Editor displays information about. Figure 3-10 shows an empty 200-gigabyte hard disk on the device named **/dev/sda**. Figure 3-5 on page 55 shows the ubiquity partitioner ready to partition an empty drive similar to the one shown in Figure 3-10.

DELETING A PARTITION

Before deleting a partition, make sure it does not contain any data you need. To use the Partition Editor to delete a partition, highlight the partition you want to delete and click **Delete** and then **Apply** on the toolbar.

RESIZING A PARTITION

HARDY Although you can resize a partition using the ubiquity partitioner while you are installing Ubuntu, you may find it easier to see what you are doing when you use the gparted Partition Editor from a live session for this task. This section explains how to use gparted to resize a partition.

INTREPID Intrepid introduced Before and After graphics in the ubiquity partitioner, as shown in Figure 3-12 on page 61. These graphics show relative partition sizes and free space before and after your proposed changes. "Advanced Guided Partitioning" on page 61 explains how to use the ubiquity partitioner to resize a partition.

Always back up the data on a hard disk

caution If you are installing Ubuntu on a disk that holds important data, always back up the data before you start the installation. Things can and do go wrong. The power may go out in the middle of an installation, corrupting the data on the hard disk. There may be a bug in the partitioning software that destroys a filesystem. Although it is unlikely, you might make a mistake and format a partition holding data you want to keep.

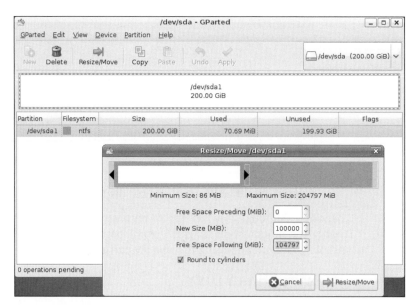

Figure 3-11   The gparted Partition Editor displaying a disk drive holding a Windows system

Figure 3-11 shows the Partition Editor displaying information about a hard disk with a single partition that occupies the entire disk. This partition holds a single 200-gigabyte NTFS filesystem. The process of resizing a partition is the same regardless of the type of partition: You can use the following technique to resize Windows, Linux, or other types of partitions.

To install Ubuntu on this system, you must resize (shrink) the partition to make room for Ubuntu. Before you resize a Windows partition, you must boot Windows and defragment the partition using the Windows defragmenter; see the tip on page 66. To resize the partition, right-click to highlight the line that describes the partition and select **Resize/Move** on the toolbar. The Partition Editor opens a small Resize/Move window, as shown in Figure 3-11.

At the top of the Resize/Move window is a graphical representation of the partition. Initially the partition occupies the whole disk. The spin box labeled **New Size (MiB)** shows the number of mebibytes occupied by the partition—in this case, the whole disk. The two spin boxes labeled **Free Space** show no free space.

You can specify how you want to resize the partition by (right-clicking and) dragging one of the triangles at the ends of the graphical representation of the partition or by entering the number of mebibytes you want to shrink the Windows partition to in the spin box labeled **New Size**. The value in one of the spin boxes labeled **Free Space** increases when you make this change. Click **Resize/Move** to add the resize operation to the list of pending operations at the bottom of the window. Click **Apply** on the toolbar to resize the partition.

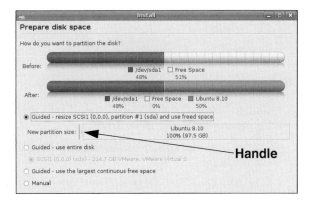

Figure 3-12   The Prepare disk space screen showing a hard disk
with one partition and some free space

Although you can use the Partition Editor to create partitions to install Ubuntu on, the ubiquity partitioner allows you to specify mount points for the partitions; the gparted Partition Editor does not.

ubiquity: SETTING UP PARTITIONS

While you are installing Ubuntu, ubiquity offers two ways to partition a disk: guided and manual. Guided partitioning sets up two partitions—one for swap space (page 37) and one for / (root, where the entire Ubuntu filesystem gets mounted; page 37). The amount of space occupied by root depends on which guided option you select. Manual partitioning enables you to set up partitions of any type and size, and to specify the mount point for each partition.

ADVANCED GUIDED PARTITIONING

"Prepare disk space" on page 54 explained how to use guided partitioning to partition an empty disk. This section explains how guided partitioning works on a disk that is already partitioned.

Depending on what is on the hard disk you are installing Ubuntu on, the ubiquity partitioner presents different choices. Figure 3-12 shows the Prepare disk space screen for a hard disk with one partition and some free space. This screen shows all possible choices. In some cases, not all of these choices appear. Click the radio button adjacent to the choice you want to select:

- **Guided (resize and use freed space)**—Allows you to shrink a partition and use the space freed up by this operation to install Ubuntu. This choice is typically the one you use for setting up a dual-boot system. Under Hardy, it may be easier to see what you are doing if you use the gparted Partition Editor from a live session to resize a partition before you begin installing Ubuntu. See "Resizing a Partition" on page 59. This section describes how to use the ubiquity partitioner to resize a partition.

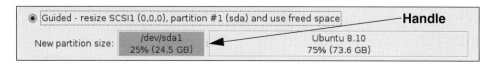

Figure 3-13   Part of the Prepare disk space screen showing the resizing slider

- **Guided (use entire disk)**—Deletes all information on the disk and installs Ubuntu on the entire disk.
- **Guided (use free space)**—Uses the largest chunk of existing free space to install Ubuntu.
- **Manual**—Gives you total control over the size, placement, and naming of partitions that Ubuntu is installed on.

When you are done working with the Prepare disk space screen, click **Forward**.

RESIZING TO CREATE FREE SPACE

The **Guided – resize ...** choice includes a slider that allows you to specify how you want to resize the partition. Click and drag the handle (Figures 3-12 and 3-13) to specify the new size of the partition you are resizing and, by default, the size of the new partition that Ubuntu will be installed on. If you are resizing a Windows partition, defragment it before resizing it (page 66).

USING THE ENTIRE DISK

Using the whole disk for Ubuntu is easy. Before you start, make certain the disk does not contain any information you need. Once you rewrite the partition table, the data will be gone for good. If you are not sure what is on the disk, use the Nautilus File Browser to take a look. (See page 94; select **Main menu: Places ▷ Computer** and double-click one or more of the Filesystem objects.)

USING EXISTING FREE SPACE

If a large enough chunk of free space exists on the disk, you can use that space to install Ubuntu. Because free space holds no data, this technique does not change any data on the disk.

MANUAL PARTITIONING

This section explains how to use the ubiquity partitioner to create a partition on an empty hard disk. Figure 3-5 on page 55 shows the Prepare disk space screen for an empty hard disk. To create partitions manually, click the radio button labeled

Figure 3-14   An empty hard disk with a partition table

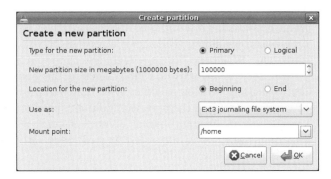

Figure 3-15   The Create Partition window

Manual and click **Forward**. The ubiquity partitioner displays a Prepare partitions screen that shows a device without any partitions—only free space. Before you can create partitions, you must set up a partition table (page 33). To do so, highlight the device name (e.g., **/dev/sda**) and click **New partition table**. The partitioner asks you to confirm you want to create a new empty partition table. Click **Continue** to create a partition table that contains only free space. Now ubiquity displays a screen that looks similar to the one in Figure 3-14. (Note: 214,748 MiB [*mebibytes*; page 1119] equals 200 GB [gigabytes; page 1110]—Figure 3-14 should show MiB in place of MB.) The device (hard disk) at **/dev/sda** has a partition table without any partitions; in other words, it contains only free space.

To create a partition, highlight the line with **free space** in the Device column and click **New partition**. The ubiquity partitioner displays a Create Partition window (Figure 3-15), which asks you to specify whether you want to create a primary or a logical partition (page 34), what size you want to make the partition (in megabytes), whether you want the partition to appear at the beginning or end of the free space, what type you want to make the partition (**Use as**), and the name of the mount point (page 35) for the partition. Because Linux does not mount a swap partition, you cannot specify a mount point for a type swap partition. If you are unsure of which type a partition should be, choose **ext3** (page 487). Click **OK**.

After a few moments the Prepare partitions screen displays the new partition (Figure 3-16). To create another partition, highlight **free space** and repeat the preceding steps. Remember to create a swap partition (page 37). When you have finished creating partitions, click **Forward**.

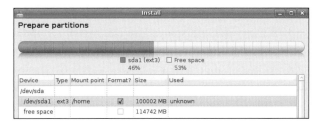

Figure 3-16   The Prepare partitions screen displays a new partition

The Prepare partitions screen displays two or three buttons immediately below the frame that lists the disks and partitions. The labels on these buttons change depending on what is highlighted. This screen always displays a button labeled **Undo changes to partitions**. When the device is highlighted, the Prepare partitions screen displays a button labeled **New partition table**. Clicking this button creates a new partition table, destroying any existing partition table. Highlighting a partition gives you the choice of editing or deleting the partition. Editing a partition you just created allows you to change only its type and mount point. You must delete and re-create a partition to change any of its other attributes. As mentioned earlier, highlighting **free space** allows you to create a new partition.

UPGRADING TO A NEW RELEASE

Upgrading a system is the process of installing a new release of Ubuntu over an older one. All user and configuration files are preserved and all software is upgraded to the most recent version consistent with the new release of Ubuntu. Ubuntu advises against upgrading systems that have had packages installed from repositories (page 504) that it does not control. These packages may corrupt the software package database, causing the upgrade to fail.

Use a standard upgrade procedure

caution   Do not use procedures for upgrading to a new release of Ubuntu other than the ones specified in this section or at www.ubuntu.com/getubuntu/upgrading. Specifically, do not use **apt-get dist-upgrade**, **aptitude full-upgrade**, or any Debian tools.

Before you upgrade a system, it is a good idea to back up all user files on the system. Also make sure the drop-down list labeled **Show new distribution releases** in the Updates tab of the Software Sources window (page 117) displays the type of release you want to upgrade to. The following procedure assumes that you have a desktop system that is connected to the Internet. Even with a fast Internet connection, this process takes a long time. Follow these steps to upgrade a system:

1. Open the Update Manager window (Figure 4-10, page 99) by selecting **Main menu: System⇨Administration⇨Update Manager**.

2. Regardless of whether the window says **You can install *nn* updates** or not, click **Check**. This step ensures the software package database is up-to-date.

3. If the window displays **You can install *nn* updates**, click **Install Updates**. This step ensures all software packages on the system are up-to-date.

4. At this point, if a new release is available, the window displays the message **New distribution release 'X.XX' is available**. Click **Upgrade**.

5. The utility displays the Release Notes window. Read the release notes and then click **Upgrade**.

6. The utility downloads the upgrade tool and updates some files.

7. You are asked if you want to start the upgrade. Click **Start Upgrade**.

8. When the upgrade is complete, reboot the system.

See www.ubuntu.com/getubuntu/upgrading for more detailed instructions on upgrading Ubuntu.

INSTALLING KDE

You can install KDE in one of two ways. The first approach installs KDE only: Follow the instructions in Chapter 2 and this chapter but instead of downloading and burning an Ubuntu CD/DVD, download a Kubuntu CD/DVD from www.kubuntu.org, burn it, and use that disk to install Linux.

The second approach requires the system to be connected to the Internet and installs KDE plus a host of other programs (e.g., Amarok, Kate) in addition to GNOME. After you install Ubuntu as explained in this chapter, use Synaptic (page 118) or aptitude (page 508) to perform the following steps. This process takes a while; you will be downloading and installing more than 200 software packages.

1. Ensure the software package database is up-to-date: From Synaptic, click **Reload**. To use aptitude, give the command **sudo aptitude update** from a command line, terminal emulator, or Run Application window (ALT-F2).

2. Ensure all software packages on the system are up-to-date: From Synaptic, click **Mark All Upgrades** and then click **Apply**. To use aptitude, give the command **sudo aptitude safe-upgrade** from a command line, terminal emulator, or Run Application window (ALT-F2).

3. Install the KDE software: From Synaptic, search for and install the **kubuntu-desktop** virtual package (page 508). To use aptitude, give the command **sudo aptitude install kubuntu-desktop** from a command line, terminal emulator, or Run Application window (ALT-F2).

After the software is downloaded, while it is being installed, debconf asks if you want to use the gdm (GNOME) or kdm (KDE) display manager. Either one works with either desktop. One way to choose which display manager to use is to select the one associated with the desktop you will be using most often.

Once KDE is installed, reboot the system. From the Login screen, follow the instructions on page 130 to display the Actions menu and select the session you want to run (GNOME or KDE).

SETTING UP A DUAL-BOOT SYSTEM

A *dual-boot* system is one that can boot one of two (or more) operating systems. This section describes how to add Ubuntu to a system that can boot Windows, thereby creating a system that can boot Windows or Linux. You can use the same technique for adding Ubuntu to a system that runs a different version or distribution of Linux. One issue in setting up a dual-boot system is finding disk space for the new Ubuntu system. The next section discusses several ways to create the needed space.

CREATING FREE SPACE ON A WINDOWS SYSTEM

Typically you install Ubuntu Linux in free space on a hard disk. To add Ubuntu Linux to a Windows system, you must have enough free space on a hard disk that already holds Windows. There are several ways to provide or create this free space. The following paragraphs discuss these options in order from easiest to most difficult.

Add a new disk drive   Add another disk drive to the system and install Linux on the new disk, which contains only free space. This technique is very easy and clean but requires a new disk drive.

Use existing free space   If there is sufficient free space on the Windows disk, you can install Linux there. This technique is the optimal choice, but there is rarely enough free space on an installed hard disk.

Always defragment before resizing

caution   You must boot Windows and defragment a Windows partition before you resize it. Sometimes you may need to run the Windows defragmenter several times to consolidate most file fragments. Not only will defragmenting give you more space for a Linux partition, but it may also keep the process of setting up a dual-boot system from failing.

Resize Windows partitions   Windows partitions typically occupy the entire disk, making resizing a Windows partition the technique most commonly used to free up space. Windows systems typically use NTFS, FAT32, and/or FAT16 filesystems. You can use the gparted Partition Editor to examine and resize an existing Windows partition to open up free space in which to install Linux (page 59). You can also use the ubiquity partitioner while you are installing Ubuntu for the same purpose (page 61).

Remove a Windows partition   If you can delete a big enough Windows partition, you can install Linux in its place. To delete a Windows partition, you must have multiple partitions under Windows and be willing to lose the data in the partition you delete. In many cases, you can move the data from the partition you will delete to another Windows partition.

Once you are sure a partition contains no useful information, you can use the Partition Editor to delete it (page 59). After deleting the partition, you can install Ubuntu Linux in the free space left by the partition you removed.

INSTALLING UBUNTU LINUX AS THE SECOND OPERATING SYSTEM

After creating enough free space on a Windows system (see the previous section), you can install Ubuntu Linux. On the ubiquity Prepare disk space screen, select **Guided - use the largest continuous free space**. Or, if you are installing Ubuntu on its own hard disk, select **Guided - use entire disk** and click the radio button next to the disk you want to install Ubuntu on. Click **Forward**. After the installation is complete, when you boot from the hard disk, you will be able to choose which operating system you want to run.

ADVANCED INSTALLATION

This section discusses the live/install Desktop CD initial install screen, using the Alternate and Server CDs as well as the live/install DVD to install Ubuntu, and the Ubuntu textual installer.

THE LIVE/INSTALL DESKTOP CD: THE INITIAL INSTALL SCREEN

This section covers some of the things you can do from the initial install screen (Figure 3-2, page 51) other than simply booting to a live session.

MENU SELECTIONS

Try Ubuntu without any change to your computer
Boots to a live session (page 51). You can install Ubuntu from a live session.

Install Ubuntu
Boots an X session with the Metacity window manager and Ubiquity installer, rather than launching a full GNOME desktop. For systems with minimal RAM, this selection installs Ubuntu more quickly than installing from a live session.

Check CD for defects
Verifies the contents of the CD/DVD you are booting from (page 51).

Test memory
Runs memtest86+, a GPL-licensed, stand-alone memory test utility for x86-based computers. Press **C** to configure the test; press ESCAPE to exit and reboot. For more information see www.memtest.org.

Boot from first hard disk
Boots the system from the first hard disk. This selection frequently has the same effect as booting the system without the CD/DVD (depending on how the BIOS [page 28] is set up).

THE FUNCTION KEYS

Along the bottom of the initial install screen is a row of labeled function key names (Figure 3-2, page 51). Pressing these function keys displays information that may be helpful if you experience a problem while booting Ubuntu or working in a live session. Some of the keys allow you to change boot parameters.

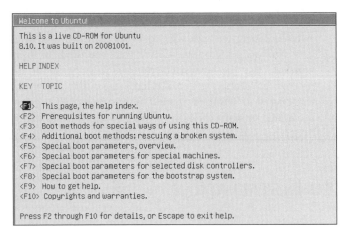

Figure 3-17   Initial install screen, F1 help window

F1 Help   The F1 key displays the help window shown in Figure 3-17. Pressing a function key while this window is visible displays yet another help window. Pressing a function key when this window is not displayed has the effect described in the following paragraphs. Press ESCAPE to close the help window.

F2 Language   The F2 key displays a menu of languages. Use the ARROW keys to highlight the language you want the live session to use and then press RETURN. This language is not necessarily the language the installed system displays. This menu is the same one Ubuntu displays when you boot from a CD/DVD.

F3 Keymap   The F3 key displays a menu of countries and languages. Use the ARROW keys to highlight the country/language of the keyboard layout you want the live session to use and then press RETURN. This keyboard layout is not necessarily the keyboard layout the installed system uses.

F4 Modes   The F4 key displays the following list of startup modes:

• Normal—Starts Ubuntu in normal mode, as though you had not pressed F4.

• Safe graphics mode—If you encounter problems with the display while you are bringing up a live session or during installation, choose this menu selection. It adds **xforcevesa** to the boot parameters, causing Ubuntu to use the generic vesa driver in place of the driver for the graphics chip in the system. The vesa driver is slow and does not support high resolutions, but it works with almost any graphics chip.

• Use driver update CD—Installs Ubuntu with an updated driver.

• OEM install (for manufacturers)—Allows a manufacturer or reseller to preinstall Ubuntu but leave some configuration details, such as creating a user account, to the purchaser.

F5 Accessibility   The F5 key displays a list of features, such as a high-contrast display and a Braille terminal, that can make Ubuntu more accessible for some people. Use the ARROW keys to highlight the feature you want the live session to use and then press RETURN.

Figure 3-18 Initial install screen, F6 boot command line

F6 Other Options   The F6 key displays the boot command line (Figure 3-18). Type the parameters you want to add to the boot command line (discussed in the next section) after the double hyphen and press RETURN to boot the system. If you remove **quiet** and **splash** from this line, Ubuntu displays information about what it is doing while it boots (page 52).

BOOT COMMAND-LINE PARAMETERS (BOOT OPTIONS)

Following are some of the parameters you can add to the boot command line (see "F6 Other Options" above). You can specify multiple parameters separated by SPACEs. See help.ubuntu.com/community/BootOptions and *The Linux BootPrompt-HowTo* for more information.

noacpi   Disables ACPI (Advanced Configuration and Power Interface). Useful for systems that do not support ACPI or that have problems with their ACPI implementation. Also **acpi=off**. The default is to enable ACPI.

noapic   Disables APIC (Advanced Programmable Interrupt Controller). The default is to enable APIC.

noapm   Disables APM (Advanced Power Management). Also **apm=off**. The default is to enable APM.

irqpoll   Changes the way the kernel handles interrupts.

nolapic   Disables local APIC. The default is to enable local APIC.

VIRTUAL CONSOLES

While it is running, ubiquity opens a shell on each of the six virtual consoles (also called virtual terminals; page 134). You can display a virtual console by pressing

CONTROL-ALT-F*x*, where *x* is the virtual console number and F*x* is the function key that corresponds to the virtual console number.

At any time during the installation, you can switch to a virtual console and give shell commands to display information about processes and files. Do not give commands that change any part of the installation process. To switch back to the graphical installation screen, press CONTROL-ALT-F7. To switch back to the textual (pseudographical) installation screen, press CONTROL-ALT-F1.

THE ALTERNATE CD INITIAL INSTALL SCREEN MENU

The Alternate CD uses the textual installer (page 73) to install a system that uses a graphical interface or one that uses a textual interface. It is not a live CD (i.e., it does not bring up a desktop to install from), does not require as much RAM to install Ubuntu, and presents more installation options. The Alternate CD starts with the Language menu (Figure 3-1, page 50). Its initial install screen takes advantage of the function keys described on page 67 (except for F4) and accepts the boot parameters described on page 69. This screen differs from that presented by the live/install Desktop CD/DVD (page 67) in several ways: It does not include a live session choice, it includes a choice to rescue a broken system, and the F4 key displays different modes.

F4 Modes   The F4 key displays the following list of startup modes:

- Normal—Starts Ubuntu in normal mode, as though you had not pressed F4.

- OEM install (for manufacturers)—Allows a manufacturer or reseller to preinstall Ubuntu but leave some configuration details, such as creating a user account, to the purchaser.

- Install a command-line system—Installs a textual Ubuntu system (no graphical interface [GUI] or desktop; only a textual interface [page 30]).

- Install an LTSP server—Installs a Linux Terminal Server Project server. For more information refer to "Diskless systems" on page 738.

RESCUE A BROKEN SYSTEM

This selection brings up Ubuntu but does not install it. After detecting the system's disks and partitions, the system enters recovery mode and allows you to select the device you want to mount as the root filesystem. Once you select a device, recovery mode displays a list of rescue operations (Figure 3-19):

- **Execute a shell in /dev/*xxx*—Mounts the device you selected (/dev/*xxx*) as / (root) and spawns a **root** shell (e.g., dash or bash; Chapter 7) *if a shell is available on the mounted device.* You are working with **root** privileges (page 86) and can make changes to the filesystem on the device you selected. You have access only to the shell and utilities on the mounted filesystem, although you may be able to mount other filesystems. If the mounted filesystem does not include a shell, you must use the next selection. Give an **exit** command to return to the list of rescue operations.

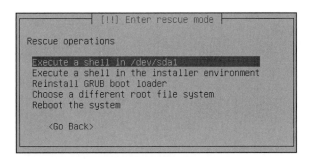

Figure 3-19   The list of rescue operations

- **Execute a shell in the installer environment**—Mounts the device you selected as **/target** and spawns a **root** dash shell (Chapter 7). You are working in the installer environment with **root** privileges (page 86). You have access to dash and the many utilities available in the installer environment. The root filesystem is on a *RAM disk* (page 1128) and you can use nano to edit files. You can make changes to the filesystem on the device you selected, which is mounted on **/target**. You can mount other filesystems. Give an **exit** command to return to the list of rescue operations.

- **Choose a different root file system**—Returns to the previous step where you can select a filesystem to work with.

- **Reboot the system**—Reboots the system. Remove the CD if you want to boot from the hard disk.

THE SERVER CD INITIAL INSTALL SCREEN MENU

The Server CD uses the textual installer (page 73) to install a minimal system with a textual interface and no open ports. The installed system is appropriate for a server. The Server CD starts with the Language menu (Figure 3-1, page 50). Its initial install screen takes advantage of the functions keys described on page 67 (except for F4) and accepts the boot parameters described on page 69. This screen differs from that presented by the live/install Desktop CD/DVD (page 67) in several ways: It does not include a live session choice, it includes choices to rescue a broken system and install a server, and the F4 key displays different modes. The Rescue a broken system choice is explained on page 70.

Install Ubuntu Server — Installs a textual Ubuntu server system using the textual installer. For more information refer to "The Ubuntu Textual Installer" on page 73. During the installation, the installer displays the Software selection screen, which asks if you want to install various servers including a DNS server (Chapter 24), a LAMP server (includes Apache [Chapter 26], MySQL, and PHP), an OpenSSH server (Chapter 18), a Samba server (Chapter 23), and others. Use the ARROW keys to move the highlight to the space between the brackets ([ ]) and press the SPACE bar to select a choice.

```
              Try Ubuntu without any change to your computer
                             Install Ubuntu
                        Install Ubuntu in text mode
                          Check CD for defects
                              Test memory
                        Boot from first hard disk




   Press F4 to select alternative start-up and installation modes.

   F1 Help  F2 Language  F3 Keymap  F4 Modes  F5 Accessibility  F6 Other Options
```

Figure 3-20   The DVD initial install screen

F4 Modes   The F4 key displays the following list of startup modes:

- Normal—Starts Ubuntu in normal mode, as though you had not pressed F4.

- Install a minimal system—Installs the absolute minimum set of packages required for a working Ubuntu system as specified by the **ubuntu-minimal** virtual package (page 508). This setup used to be called JeOS and is useful for routers and other systems that must occupy minimal disk space. Contrast a minimal system with the default server system, which installs additional packages such as Python and rsync.

THE DVD

The Ubuntu DVD does everything each of the CDs does and includes all software packages supported by Ubuntu, not just those installed by default. If the system you are installing is not connected to the Internet, you can install software packages from the DVD but you will have no way to update the system. The initial install screen takes advantage of the function keys described on page 67 and accepts the boot parameters described on page 69. Figure 3-20 shows the DVD initial install screen. See the descriptions of the CD initial install screens on pages 67, 70, and 71 for information on the selections on this screen.

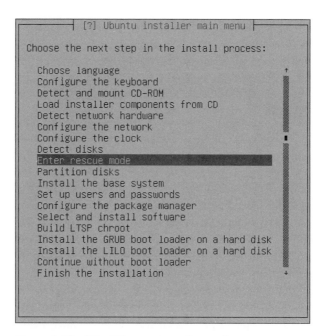

Figure 3-21   The Ubuntu installer main menu

THE UBUNTU TEXTUAL INSTALLER

The Ubuntu textual installer gives you more control over the installation process than the Ubuntu graphical installer does (page 53). The textual installer displays a pseudographical (page 30) interface and uses fewer system resources, including less RAM, than the graphical installer does. You can install either a graphical (desktop) or textual (command-line) system using the textual installer, depending on which CD/DVD you use and which selection you make from the initial install screen and the F4 menu.

Many of the screens that the textual installer displays parallel the screens displayed by the graphical installer. Within the textual installer's screens, TAB moves between items, ARROW keys move between selections on a list, and RETURN activates the highlighted selection and causes the installer to display the next screen. A few screens include brackets ([ ]) that function similarly to check boxes; they use an asterisk in place of a tick. Use the ARROW keys to move the highlight to the space between the brackets. Press the SPACE bar to place an asterisk between the brackets and select the adjacent choice. Press the SPACE bar again to remove the asterisk.

The Ubuntu installer main menu (the contents of this menu varies—Figure 3-21 shows an example) allows you to go directly to any step of the installation process or enter recovery mode (see "Rescue a Broken System" on page 70). At the lower-left

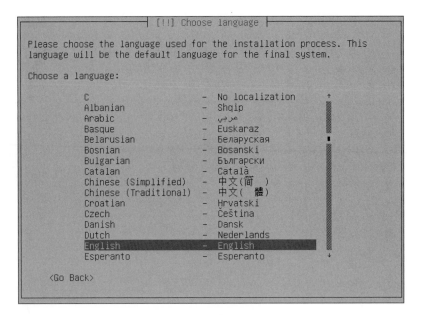

```
┌──────────────────────┤ [!!] Choose language ├──────────────────────┐
│                                                                     │
│  Please choose the language used for the installation process. This │
│  language will be the default language for the final system.        │
│                                                                     │
│  Choose a language:                                                 │
│                                                                     │
│           C                         -  No localization         ↑    │
│           Albanian                  -  Shqip                        │
│           Arabic                    -  عربي                         │
│           Basque                    -  Euskaraz                     │
│           Belarusian                -  Беларуская               ▮   │
│           Bosnian                   -  Bosanski                     │
│           Bulgarian                 -  Български                    │
│           Catalan                   -  Català                       │
│           Chinese (Simplified)      -  中文(简  )                   │
│           Chinese (Traditional)     -  中文(  體)                   │
│           Croatian                  -  Hrvatski                     │
│           Czech                     -  Čeština                      │
│           Danish                    -  Dansk                        │
│           Dutch                     -  Nederlands                   │
│           English                   -  English                      │
│           Esperanto                 -  Esperanto               ↓    │
│                                                                     │
│    <Go Back>                                                        │
│                                                                     │
└─────────────────────────────────────────────────────────────────────┘
```

Figure 3-22   The Choose a language screen

corner of most textual installer screens is **<Go Back>**. See Figure 3-22 for an example. Use the TAB key to highlight this item and press RETURN to display the Ubuntu installer main menu. You may have to back up through several screens to display this menu.

The first screen the textual installer displays is Choose a language (Figure 3-22). Use the UP and DOWN arrow keys to select the language you want the installer to use. You can type the first letter of the language to move the highlight to the vicinity of the language you want to choose. This language will be the default language for the installed system; you can change the default once the system is installed (page 130). Press RETURN to select the highlighted language and display the next screen.

The installer steps through a series of screens, each of which has an explanation and asks a question. Use the ARROW keys and/or TAB key to highlight an answer or selection and press RETURN to make a selection on each of the screens. After a few screens, the installer detects and installs programs from the CD/DVD, detects the network hardware, and configures it with DHCP (if available).

As it is configuring the network, the installer asks you for the hostname of the system you are installing. For use on a local network and to connect to the Internet with a Web browser or other client, you can make up a simple name. If you are setting up a server, see "FQDN" on page 785 for information on names that are valid on the Internet.

After this step, the installer asks which time zone the computer is in, continues detecting hardware, starts the partitioner, and displays the Partitioning method screen (Figure 3-23). Many of the selections available from the textual partitioner

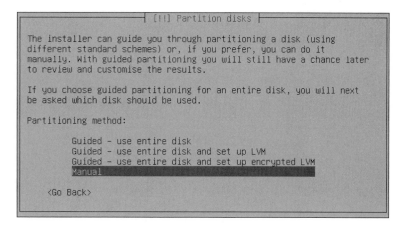

Figure 3-23   The Partitioning method screen

parallel those available from the graphical partitioner. This section describes how to use the textual partitioner to partition a hard disk manually. Page 61 describes guided partitioning using the graphical partitioner. Guided partitioning using the textual installer is similar but offers more options.

MANUAL PARTITIONING

When you select **Manual** from the Partitioning method screen (Figure 3-23), the textual partitioner displays the Partition overview screen, which lists the hard disks in the system and partitions on those disks. If a hard disk has no partitions, the partitioner displays only information about the hard disk. Figure 3-24 shows a single 200-gigabyte hard disk (highlighted) that has no partition table (and no partitions). (Note: 214.7 GB [*gigabytes*; page 1110] equals 200 GiB [*gibibytes*; page 1110].)

If you want to set up RAID, see page 78 before continuing.

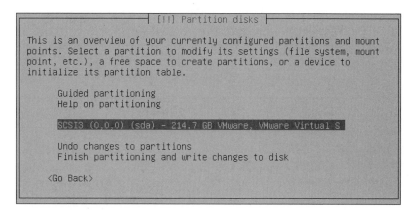

Figure 3-24   The Partition overview screen I

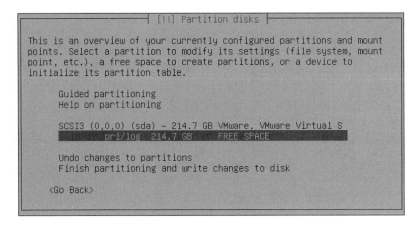

Figure 3-25   The Partition overview screen II

Creating a partition table   If the Partition overview screen shows no partitions and no free space on a hard disk, as it does in Figure 3-24, the hard disk does not have a partition table: You need to create one. If this screen shows at least one partition or some free space, the disk has a partition table and you can skip this step and continue with "Creating a partition" below.

To create a partition table, highlight the disk you want to create a partition table on and press RETURN. The installer asks if you want to create a new partition table on the device and warns that doing so will destroy all data on the disk. Highlight **Yes** and press RETURN. The installer displays the Partition disks screen showing the disk with a single block of free space as large as the disk (Figure 3-25).

Creating a partition   To create a partition, highlight the line with **FREE SPACE** on it and press RETURN. The partitioner asks how you want to use the free space; highlight **Create a new partition** and press RETURN. Next the partitioner asks you to specify the size of the new partition. You can enter either a percentage (e.g., **50%**) or a number of gigabytes followed by **GB** (e.g., **30 GB**). Press RETURN. The partitioner then asks you to specify the type of the new partition (primary or logical; page 34) and asks whether you want to create the partition at the beginning or the end of the free space. It does not usually matter where you create the partition. After answering each of these questions, press RETURN. The partitioner then displays the Partition settings screen (Figure 3-26).

To change a setting on the Partition settings screen, use the ARROW keys to move the highlight to the setting you want to change and press RETURN. The partitioner displays a screen that allows you to change the setting.

Specifying a partition type (Use as)   The first line, labeled **Use as**, allows you to specify the type of filesystem the installer creates on the partition. This setting defaults to **ext3**, which is a good choice for most normal filesystems. If you want to change the filesystem type, move the highlight to this line and press RETURN; the installer displays the How to use this partition screen (Figure 3-27). You can select swap area (page 37), RAID (page 78), LVM (page 40), or another type of filesystem. Table 12-1 on page 487 lists some

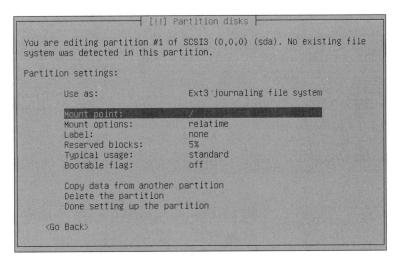

Figure 3-26   The Partition settings screen

common types of filesystems. Move the highlight to the selection you want and press RETURN. The partitioner returns to the Partition settings screen, which now reflects the selection you made. For a swap area, there is nothing else to set up; skip to "Done setting up the partition" on the next page.

Ubuntu officially supports ext3 filesystems only

caution   The **ext3** filesystem is the only type of filesystem officially supported by Ubuntu (other than swap). Set up other types of filesystems—such as JFS, XFS, or reiserfs—only if you know what you are doing. Filesystems other than **ext3** may be more likely to become corrupted when the system crashes and may exhibit unusual performance characteristics (e.g., XFS runs slowly with small files and may take a long time to upgrade).

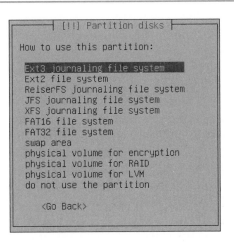

Figure 3-27   How to use this partition screen

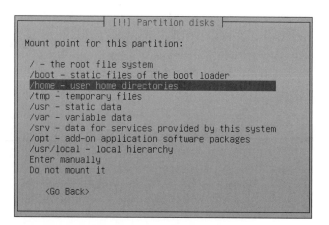

Figure 3-28 Mount point screen

Specifying a mount point · The mount point defaults to **/** (root). To change the mount point for the filesystem, highlight the line labeled **Mount point** and press RETURN. The partitioner displays a screen that allows you to specify a mount point (Figure 3-28). Select a mount point; if the mount point you want to use is not listed, select **Enter manually**. Press RETURN.

The bootable flag · Typically the only other setting you need to change is the bootable flag. Turn this flag on for the **/boot** partition if the system has one; otherwise, turn it on for the **/** (root) partition. To change the state of the bootable flag, highlight the line labeled **Bootable flag** on the Partition settings screen and press RETURN. After a moment, the partitioner redisplays the screen, now showing the changed state of this flag.

Done setting up the partition · When you are satisfied with the partition settings, highlight **Done setting up the partition** and press RETURN. The partitioner displays the Partition overview screen showing the new partition setup. To create another partition, repeat the steps starting with "Creating a partition" on page 76. To modify a partition, highlight the partition and press RETURN.

Write the partitions to disk · When you are satisfied with the design of the partition table(s), highlight **Finish partitioning and write changes to disk** and press RETURN. After giving you another chance to back out, the partitioner writes the partitions to the hard disk.

Finishing the installation · The installer continues by installing the base system and asking you to set up a user account. It gives you the option of setting up an encrypted directory named **Private** as a subdirectory of your home directory and specifying an HTTP proxy and continues installing the system. Finally it asks if the system clock is set to *UTC* (page 1139). When the installer displays the Installation Complete window, remove the CD/DVD and click **Continue** to reboot the system.

SETTING UP A RAID ARRAY

To set up a RAID array (page 39), you must first create two or more partitions of the same size. Usually these partitions will be on different hard disks. You create RAID partitions as explained in the preceding section, except instead of making the

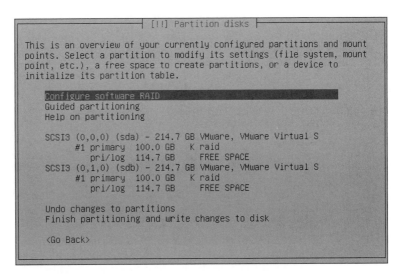

```
                    ┤ [!!] Partition disks ├
  This is an overview of your currently configured partitions and mount
  points. Select a partition to modify its settings (file system, mount
  point, etc.), a free space to create partitions, or a device to
  initialize its partition table.

      Configure software RAID
      Guided partitioning
      Help on partitioning

      SCSI3 (0,0,0) (sda) - 214.7 GB VMware, VMware Virtual S
          #1 primary  100.0 GB    K raid
             pri/log  114.7 GB       FREE SPACE
      SCSI3 (0,1,0) (sdb) - 214.7 GB VMware, VMware Virtual S
          #1 primary  100.0 GB    K raid
             pri/log  114.7 GB       FREE SPACE

      Undo changes to partitions
      Finish partitioning and write changes to disk

      <Go Back>
```

Figure 3-29   The partitioner ready to set up RAID

partitions type **ext3** or **swap**, you declare each to be a RAID volume. (RAID partitions are referred to as *volumes*.) Once you have two or more RAID volumes, the partitioner allows you to combine these volumes into a RAID array that looks and acts like a single partition.

The following example uses 100 gigabytes from each of two new hard disks to set up a 100-gigabyte RAID 1 array that is mounted on **/home**. Follow the instructions on page 76 to create a new partition table on each hard disk. Then create two 100-gigabyte partitions, one on each disk. When the partitioner displays the How to use this partition screen (Figure 3-27, page 77), follow the instructions on page 76 and specify a partition type of **physical volume for RAID**.

Figure 3-29 shows the partitioner screen after setting up the RAID volumes. Once you have at least two RAID volumes, the partitioner adds the Configure software RAID selection as the top line of its menu (this line is highlighted in Figure 3-29).

Highlight **Configure software RAID**, press RETURN, and confirm you want to write changes to the hard disk. From the next screen, select **Create MD device** (MD stands for *multidisk*) and press RETURN. Then select RAID 0, 1, or 5 and press RETURN. The different types of RAID arrays are described on page 40. The partitioner then asks you to specify the number of active devices (2) and the number of spares (0) in the RAID array. The values the partitioner enters in these fields are based on your previous input and are usually correct. Next select the active devices for the RAID array (use the SPACE bar to put an asterisk before each device; Figure 3-30, next page) and press RETURN.

Select **Finish** from the next screen (the one that asks if you want to create an MD device again) and press RETURN. Now you need to tell the installer where to mount the RAID array. Highlight the RAID array. In the example, this line contains **#1 100.0**

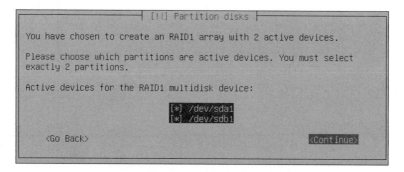

Figure 3-30   Specifying the active devices in the RAID array

GB FREE SPACE (this line is highlighted in Figure 3-31, but is shown after the partition is created). Press RETURN. (If the RAID array line does not include the words **FREE SPACE** and does not show a partition, highlight the RAID array line, press RETURN, highlight **Delete the Partition**, and press RETURN. The RAID array line should now include **FREE SPACE**.) Set up this partition as you would any other partition by following the instructions under "Creating a partition" on page 76. In the example, the full 100 gigabytes is used for an **ext3** filesystem mounted on **/home**.

To complete this example, create a bootable **/** (root) partition using the rest of the free space on the first drive and a 4-gigabyte swap partition on the second drive. Figure 3-31 shows the Partition overview screen that includes these changes. Highlight **Finish partitioning and write changes to disk** and press RETURN.

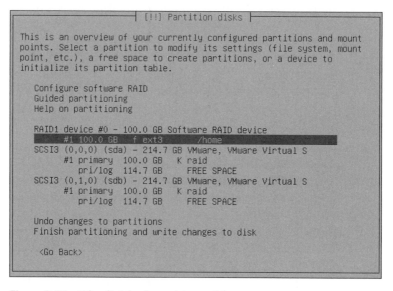

Figure 3-31   The finished partition tables

CHAPTER SUMMARY

Most installations of Ubuntu Linux begin by booting from the live/install Desktop CD/DVD and running a live session that displays a GNOME desktop. To start the installation, double-click the object on the desktop labeled **Install**.

Ubuntu provides a graphical installer (ubiquity) on the live/install Desktop CD/DVD; it offers a textual installer on the Alternate and Server CDs and the DVD. Both installers identify the hardware, build the filesystems, and install the Ubuntu Linux operating system. The ubiquity installer does not write to the hard disk until it displays the Ready to install screen or warns you it is about to write to the disk. Until that point, you can back out of the installation without making any changes to the hard disk.

A dual-boot system can boot one of two operating systems—frequently either Windows or Linux. You can use the GNOME Partition Editor from a live session to examine the contents of a hard disk and to resize partitions to make room for Ubuntu when setting up a dual-boot system. During installation from a live session, you can use the ubiquity partitioner to add, delete, and modify partitions.

EXERCISES

1. How do you start a live session? List two problems you could encounter and explain what you would do to fix them.

2. What should you do before the first time you start a live session or install Ubuntu with a new CD/DVD? How would you do it?

3. What is guided partitioning?

4. What is ubiquity?

5. Describe the ubiquity partitioner. How does it differ from the partitioner on the Alternate and Server CDs?

6. When is it beneficial to use an **ext2** filesystem instead of an **ext3** filesystem?

ADVANCED EXERCISES

7. What is a virtual console? During installation, what can you use a virtual console for? If the system is displaying a virtual console, how do you display the graphical installation screen instead?

8. What steps would you take to have the system display all the things it is doing as it boots from a live/install Desktop CD/DVD?

PART II
GETTING STARTED WITH UBUNTU LINUX

INTRODUCTION TO UBUNTU LINUX

One way or another you are sitting in front of a computer that is running Ubuntu Linux. After describing **root** privileges, this chapter takes you on a tour of the system to give you some ideas about what you can do with it. The tour does not go into depth about choices, options, menus, and so on; that is left for you to experiment with and to explore in greater detail in Chapter 8 and throughout later chapters. Instead, this chapter presents a cook's tour of the Linux kitchen: As you read it, you will have a chance to sample the dishes that you will enjoy more fully as you read the rest of this book.

Following the tour are sections that describe where to find Linux documentation (page 121) and offer more about logging in on the system, including information about passwords (page 130). The chapter concludes with a more advanced, optional section about working with Linux windows (page 138).

Be sure to read the warning about the dangers of misusing the powers of **root** (sudo) in the next section. Heed that warning, but feel free to experiment with the system: Give commands, create files, click objects, choose items from menus, follow the examples in this book, and have fun.

root account

tip   Most Linux systems include an account for a user named **root**. This user has special privileges and is sometimes referred to as Superuser. On a classic Linux system a user can log in and work as **root** by providing the **root** password.

As installed, Ubuntu has a **root** account but no password for the account: The **root** account is locked. The next section explains how you can use sudo and provide *your* password to run a command with **root** privileges. This book uses the phrase "working with **root** privileges" to distinguish this temporary escalation of privileges from the classic scenario wherein a user can work with **root** privileges for an entire session. See page 403 for more information on **root** privileges.

CURBING YOUR POWER: root PRIVILEGES/sudo

When you enter your password to run a program (not when you log in on the system), or when you use sudo from the command line, you are working with **root** privileges and have extraordinary systemwide powers. A person working with **root** privileges is sometimes referred to as *Superuser* or *administrator*. When working with **root** privileges, you can read from or write to any file on the system, execute programs that ordinary users cannot, and more. On a multiuser system you may not be permitted to run certain programs, but someone—the *system administrator*—can and that person maintains the system. When you are running Linux on your own computer, the first user you set up, usually when you install Ubuntu, is able to use sudo and its graphical counterpart, gksudo, to run programs with **root** privileges.

Who is allowed to run sudo?

security   The first user you set up when you install Ubuntu can administer the system: This user can use sudo to execute any command. When you add user accounts, you can specify whether they are allowed to administer the system. See page 578 and Figure 16-2 on page 579 for more information.

In this chapter and in Chapter 8, when this book says you have to enter your password, it assumes you have permission to administer the system. If not, you must get an administrator to perform the task.

There are two primary ways to gain **root** privileges. First, when you start a program that requires **root** privileges, a dialog box pops up asking you to **Enter your password to perform administrative tasks**. After you enter your password, the program runs with **root** privileges. Second, if you use the sudo utility (for textual applications; page 406) or gksudo utility (for graphical applications; page 407) from the command line (such as from a terminal emulator; page 111) and provide your password, the command you enter runs with **root** privileges. In both cases you cease working with **root** privileges when the command finishes or when you exit from the program you started with **root** privileges. For more information refer to "Running Commands with **root** Privileges" on page 403.

Do not experiment while you are working with root privileges

caution   Feel free to experiment when you are *not* working with **root** privileges. When you *are* working with **root** privileges, do only what you have to do and make sure you know exactly what you are doing. After you have completed the task at hand, revert to working as yourself. When working with **root** privileges, you can damage the system to such an extent that you will need to reinstall Ubuntu Linux to get it working again.

If you bought your system with Ubuntu installed at the factory

security   When a manufacturer installs Ubuntu, it cannot set up an account for you (it does not know your name). Typically, these systems come with the **root** account unlocked. Ubuntu suggests you not unlock the **root** account. To set the system up the way Ubuntu suggests, use **users-admin** as explained on page 578 to add a user who will be the system administrator. Make sure to put a tick in the check box labeled **Administer the system** in the User Privileges tab (page 578). Then relock the **root** account (page 415).

A TOUR OF THE UBUNTU LINUX DESKTOP

This section presents new words (for some readers) in a context that explains the terms well enough to get you started with the Ubuntu desktop. If you would like exact definitions as you read this section, refer to "GNOME Desktop Terminology" on page 104 and to the Glossary. The Glossary also describes the data entry *widgets* (page 1140), such as the *combo box* (page 1101), *drop-down list* (page 1106), *list box* (page 1117), and *text box* (page 1136).

GNOME   GNOME (www.gnome.org), a product of the GNU project (page 6), is the user-friendly default desktop manager under Ubuntu Linux. KDE, the K Desktop Environment, is a powerful desktop manager and complete set of tools you can use in place of GNOME. The version of Ubuntu that runs KDE is named Kubuntu. See page 65 for instructions on installing KDE.

This tour describes GNOME, a full-featured, mature desktop environment that boasts a rich assortment of configurable tools. After discussing logging in, this section covers desktop features—including panels, objects, and workspaces—and explains how to move easily from one workspace to another. It describes several ways to launch objects (run programs) from the desktop, how to set up the desktop to meet your needs and please your senses, and how to manipulate windows. As the tour continues, it explains how to work with files and folders using the Nautilus File Browser window, one of the most important GNOME tools. The tour concludes with a discussion of the Update Notifier, the object that allows you to keep a system up-to-date with the click of a button; getting help; and logging out.

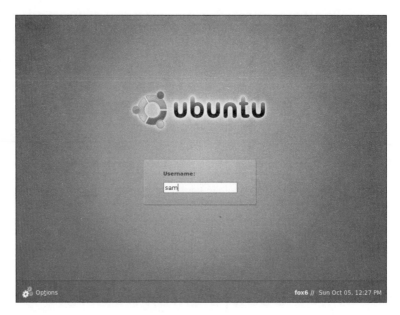

Figure 4-1   The Ubuntu GNOME Login screen

LOGGING IN ON THE SYSTEM

When you boot a standard Ubuntu Linux system, it displays a Login screen (Figure 4-1) on the system console. At the lower-left corner of the screen is a small object labeled **Options**. Click this object or press F10 to display the Actions menu. The selections on this menu allow you to work in a different language (**Select Language**), specify a desktop manager (**Select Session**), log in remotely, reboot the system (**Restart**), turn the system off (**Shut Down**), suspend the system, or have the system hibernate. For more information refer to "The Login Screen" on page 130.

To log in, enter your username in the text box labeled **Username** and press RETURN. The label changes to **Password**. Enter your password and press RETURN. If Ubuntu displays an error message, try entering your username and password again. Make sure the CAPS LOCK key is not on (Ubuntu displays a message if it is); the routine that verifies your entries is case sensitive. See page 131 if you need help with logging in and page 133 if you want to change your password. The system takes a moment to set things up and then displays a workspace (Figure 4-2).

INTRODUCTION

You can use the desktop as is or you can customize it until it looks and functions nothing like the initial desktop. If you have a computer of your own, you may want to add a user and work as that user while you experiment with the desktop. When you figure out which features you like, you can log in as yourself and implement those features. That way you need not concern yourself with "ruining" your desktop and not being able to get it back to a satisfactory configuration.

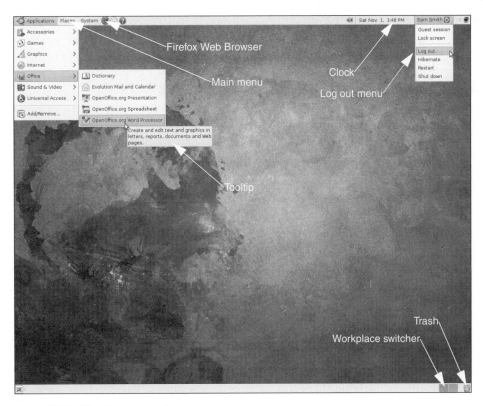

Figure 4-2   The initial workspace

Panels and objects When you log in, GNOME displays a workspace that includes Top and Bottom panels (bars) that are essential to getting your work done easily and efficiently (Figure 4-2). Each of the bars holds several icons and words called objects. (Buttons, applets, and menus are all types of objects.) When you click an object, something happens.

A panel does not allow you to do anything you could not do otherwise, but rather collects objects in one place and makes your work with the system easier. Because the panels are easy to configure, you can set them up to hold tools you use frequently. You can create additional panels to hold different groups of tools.

Workspaces and the Desktop What you see displayed on the screen is a *workspace*. Initially Ubuntu configures GNOME with two workspaces. The desktop, which is not displayed all at once, is the collection of all workspaces. "Switching Workspaces" on page 91 describes some of the things you can do with workspaces.

Do not remove objects or panels yet

caution You can add and remove panels and objects as you please. Until you are comfortable working with the desktop and have finished reading this section, however, it is best not to remove any panels or objects from the desktop.

Click and right-click

tip   This book uses the term **click** when you need to click the *left* mouse button and **right-click** when you need to click the *right* mouse button. See page 93 to adapt the mouse for left-handed use.

LAUNCHING PROGRAMS FROM THE DESKTOP

This section describes three of the many ways you can start a program running from the desktop.

Click an object   The effect of clicking an object depends on what the object is designed to do. Clicking an object may, for example, start a program; display a menu or a folder; or open a file, a window, or a dialog box.

For example, to start the Firefox Web browser, (left) click the Firefox object (the blue and orange globe on the Top panel; see Figure 4-2 on page 89). GNOME opens a window running Firefox. When you are done using Firefox, click the small **x** at the right end of the titlebar at the top of the window. GNOME closes the window.

When you (left) click the date and time near the right end of the Top panel, the Clock applet displays a calendar for the current month. (If you double-click a date on the calendar, the object opens the Evolution calendar to the date you clicked—but first you have to set up Evolution.) Click the date and time again to close the calendar.

Select from the   The second way to start a program is by selecting it from a menu. The Main menu is
Main menu   the object at the left end of the Top panel that includes the words **Applications**, **Places**, and **System**. Click one of these words to display the corresponding menu. Each menu selection that holds a submenu displays a small triangle (pointing to the right) to the right of the name of the menu (Figure 4-3). When you move the mouse pointer over one of these selections and leave it there for a moment (this action is called *hovering*), the menu displays the submenu. When you allow the mouse cursor to hover over one of the submenu selections, GNOME displays a *tooltip* (page 104).

Experiment with the Main menu. Start Solitaire (**Main menu: Applications⇨Games⇨ Free Cell Solitaire**), a terminal emulator (**Main menu: Applications⇨Accessories⇨ Terminal**), and other programs from the Applications menu. The Places and System menus are discussed on page 108.

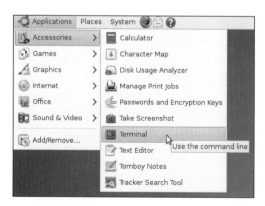

Figure 4-3   The Applications menu⇨Accessories⇨Terminal

Figure 4-4   Run Application window

Use the Run
Application window
Finally, you can start a program by pressing ALT-F2 to display the Run Application window (Figure 4-4). As you start to type **firefox** in the text box at the top of the window, the window recognizes what you are typing and displays the Firefox logo and the rest of the word **firefox**. Click **Run** to start Firefox.

optional

Running textual
applications
You can run command-line utilities, which are textual (not graphical), from the Run Applications window. When you run a textual utility from this window, you must put a tick in the check box labeled **Run in terminal** (click the box to put a tick in it; click it again to remove the tick). The tick tells GNOME to run the command in a terminal emulator window. When the utility finishes running, GNOME closes the window.

For example, type **vim** (a text-based editor) in the text box, put a tick in the box labeled **Run in terminal**, and click **Run**. GNOME opens a Terminal (emulator) window and runs the vim text editor in that window. When you exit from vim (press ESCAPE:**q!** sequentially to do so), GNOME closes the Terminal window.

You can run a command-line utility that only displays output and then terminates. Because the window closes as soon as the utility is finished running, and because most utilities run quickly, you will probably not see the output. Type the following command in the text box to run the df (disk free; page 738) utility and keep the window open until you press RETURN:

```
bash -c "df -h ; read"
```

This command starts a bash shell (Chapter 7) that executes the command line following the **–c** option. The command line holds two commands separated by a semicolon. The second command, read (page 959), waits for you to press RETURN before terminating. Thus the output from the **df –h** command remains on the screen until you press RETURN. Replace **read** with **sleep 10** to have the window remain open for ten seconds.

SWITCHING WORKSPACES

Workplace Switcher
Each rectangle in the *Workplace Switcher applet* (or just *Switcher*)—the group of rectangles near the right end of the Bottom panel—represents a workspace (Figure 4-2, page 89). When you click a rectangle, the Switcher displays the corresponding workspace and highlights the rectangle to indicate which workspace is displayed.

Click the rightmost rectangle in the Switcher. Next, select **Main menu: System⇨ Preferences⇨Mouse**. GNOME opens the Mouse Preferences window. The Switcher rectangle that corresponds to the workspace you are working in displays a small colored rectangle. This small rectangle corresponds in size and location within the

Switcher rectangle to the window within the workspace. Click and hold the left mouse button with the mouse pointer on the titlebar at the top of the window and drag the window to the edge of the desktop. When you release the mouse button, the small rectangle within the Switcher moves to the corresponding location within the Switcher rectangle.

Now click a different rectangle in the Switcher and open another application—for example, the Ubuntu Help Center (click the blue question mark on the Top panel). With the Ubuntu Help Center window in one workspace and the Mouse Preferences window in another, you can click the corresponding rectangles in the Switcher to switch back and forth between the workspaces (and applications).

Right-click to display an Object context menu

tip   A *context menu* is one that is appropriate to its context. When you right-click an object, it displays an Object context menu. Each object displays its own context menu, although similar objects have similar context menus. Most Object context menus have either a Preferences or Properties selection. See the adjacent section, "Setting Personal Preferences," and page 112 for more information on Object context menus.

SETTING PERSONAL PREFERENCES

You can set preferences for many objects on the desktop, including those on the panels.

Workspace Switcher   To display the Workspace Switcher Preferences window (Figure 4-5), first *right*-click anywhere on the Switcher to display the Switcher menu and then select **Preferences**. Specify the number of workspaces you want in the spin box labeled **Number of workspaces**. (The window looks different if you have Visual Effects [page 101] enabled and the spin box is labeled **Columns**.) The number of workspaces the Switcher displays changes as you change the number in the spin box—you can see the result of your actions before you close the Preferences window. Four workspaces is typically a good number to start with. Click **Close**.

Figure 4-5   The Workspace Switcher Preferences window

Clock applet   The Clock applet has an interesting preferences window. Right-click the Clock applet (Figure 4-2, page 89) and select **Preferences**. GNOME displays the General tab of the Clock Preferences window. This tab enables you to customize the date and time the Clock applet displays on the Top panel. The clock immediately reflects the changes you make in this window. Click the **Location** tab and then the **Add** button and enter the name of the city you are in or near to cause the Clock applet to display weather information.

Different objects display different Preferences windows. Objects that launch programs display Properties windows and do not have Preferences windows. Experiment with different Preferences and Properties windows and see what happens.

MOUSE PREFERENCES

The Mouse Preferences window (Figure 4-6) enables you to change the characteristics of the mouse to suit your needs. To display this window, select **Main menu: System⇨ Preferences⇨Mouse** or give the command **gnome-mouse-properties** from a terminal emulator or Run Application window (ALT-F2). The Mouse Preferences window has two tabs: General and Accessibility (and a third, Touchpad, on a laptop).

Left-handed mouse   Select the General tab. To change the orientation of the mouse buttons for use by a left-handed person, click the radio button labeled **Left-handed**. If you change the

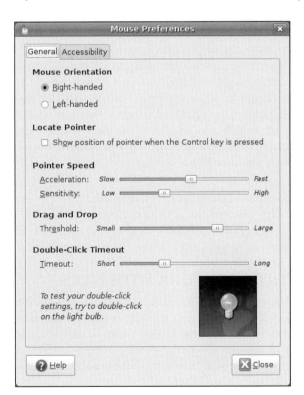

Figure 4-6   The Mouse Preferences window, General tab

setup of the mouse buttons, remember to reinterpret the descriptions in this book accordingly. When this book asks you to click the left button or does not specify a button to click, click the right button, and vice versa. See "Remapping Mouse Buttons" on page 260 if you want to change the orientation of the mouse buttons from the command line.

Double-click timeout — Use the Double-Click Timeout slider to change the speed with which you must double-click a mouse button to have the system recognize your action as a double-click rather than as two single clicks. You can also control the acceleration and sensitivity of the mouse. The Drag and Drop Threshold specifies how far you must drag an object before the system considers the action the drag part of a drag and drop.

From the Accessibility tab, you can control different aspects of mouse clicks.

WORKING WITH WINDOWS

To resize a window, move the mouse pointer over an edge of the window; the pointer turns into an arrow. When the pointer is an arrow, you can click and drag the side of a window. When you position the mouse pointer over a corner of the window, you can resize both the height and the width of the window at the same time.

To move a window, click and drag the titlebar (the bar across the top of the window with the name of the window in it). For fun, try moving the window past either side of the workspace. What happens? The result depends on how Visual Effects (page 101) is set.

Titlebar — At the right of the titlebar are three icons that control the window (Figure 4-16, page 109). Clicking the underscore, usually at the left of the set of icons, minimizes (iconifies) the window so the only indication of the window is the object with the window's name in it on the Bottom panel (a Window List applet; page 107). Click this object to toggle the window between visible and minimized. Clicking the box icon, usually the middle of the three icons, toggles the window between its maximum size (maximizes the window) and its normal size. Double-clicking the titlebar does the same thing.

Terminating a program — Clicking the **x** closes the window and usually terminates the program running in the window. In some cases you may need to click several times. Some programs, such as Pidgin Internet Messenger, do not terminate. These programs continue to run in the background and display an icon near the right end of the Top panel. Right-click the icon and select **Quit** from the drop-down menu to terminate the program.

USING NAUTILUS TO WORK WITH FILES

Nautilus, the GNOME file manager, is a simple, powerful file manager. You can use it to create, open, view, move, and copy files and folders as well as to execute programs and scripts. One of its most basic and important functions is to create and manage the desktop. This section introduces Nautilus and demonstrates the correspondence between Nautilus and the desktop. See page 262 for more detailed information on Nautilus.

Terms: folder and directory   Nautilus displays the File Browser window, which displays the contents of a folder. The terms *folder* and *directory* are synonymous; "folder" is frequently used in graphical contexts whereas "directory" may be used in textual or command-line contexts. This book uses these terms interchangeably.

Term: File Browser   This book sometimes uses the terms *File Browser window* and *File Browser* when referring to the Nautilus File Browser window.

Double-clicking an object in a File Browser window has the same effect as double-clicking an object on the desktop: Nautilus takes an action appropriate to the object. For example, when you double-click a text file, Nautilus opens the file with a text editor. When you double-click an OpenOffice.org document, Nautilus opens the file with OpenOffice.org. If the file is executable, Nautilus runs it. If the file is a folder, Nautilus opens the folder and displays its contents in place of what had previously been in the window.

INTREPID   From within a Nautilus File Browser window, you can open a folder in a new tab. To do so, middle-click the folder or right-click the folder and select **Open in New Tab** from the drop-down menu; Nautilus displays a new tab named for the directory you clicked. Click the tab to display contents of the directory.

THE Desktop DIRECTORY

The files on the desktop are held in a directory that has a pathname (page 191) of **/home/*username*/Desktop**, where **username** is your login name. The simple directory name is **Desktop**. When you select **Main menu: Places⇨Desktop**, GNOME opens a File Browser window showing the files on the desktop (Figure 4-7). Initially there are no files. If you click the pencil and paper object at the left edge near the top of the File Browser window, Nautilus displays in the Location text box the pathname of the directory it is displaying.

To see the correspondence between the graphical desktop and the **Desktop** directory, right-click anywhere within the large clear area of the Desktop File Browser window. Select **Create Document⇨Empty File**. Nautilus creates a new file on the desktop and displays its object in this window. When you create this file, GNOME highlights the name **new file** under the file: You can type any name you like at this

Figure 4-7   The desktop with a Nautilus File Browser window

point. Press RETURN when you are finished entering a name. If you double-click the new file, Nautilus assumes it is a text file and opens the file in a gedit window. (The gedit utility is a simple text editor.) Type some text and click **Save** on the toolbar. Close the window from the File menu or by clicking the **x** at the right end of the titlebar. You have created a text document on the desktop. You can double-click the document object on the desktop or in the File Browser window to open and edit it.

Next, create a folder by right-clicking the root window (any empty part of the workspace) and selecting **Create Folder**. You can name this folder in the same way that you named the file you created. The folder object appears on the desktop and within the Desktop File Browser window.

On the desktop, drag the file until it is over the folder; the folder opens. Release the mouse button to drop the file into the folder; GNOME moves the file to the folder. Again on the desktop, double-click the folder you just moved the file to. GNOME opens another File Browser window, this one displaying the contents of the folder you clicked on. The file you moved to the folder appears in the new window. Now drag the file from the window to the previously opened Desktop File Browser window. The file is back on the desktop, although it may be hidden by one of the File Browser windows.

Next, open a word processing document by selecting **Main menu: Applications⇨Office⇨OpenOffice.org Word Processor**. Type some text and click the floppy disk icon or select **menubar: File⇨Save** to save the document. OpenOffice.org displays a Save window (Figure 4-8). Type the name you want to save the document as (use **memo** for now) in the text box labeled **Name**. You can specify the directory in which you want to save the document in one of two ways: by using the drop-down list labeled **Save in folder** or by using the **Browse for other folders** section of the Save window.

Click the triangle to the left of **Browse for other folders** to open and close this section of the window. Figure 4-8 shows the Save window with this section closed. With the **Browse for other folders** section closed, you can select a directory from the drop-down list labeled **Save in folder**. This technique is quick and easy, but presents a limited number of choices of folders. By default, it saves the document in **Documents** (**/home/*username*/Documents**). If you want to save the document to the desktop, click **Desktop** in this drop-down list and then click **Save**. OpenOffice.org

Figure 4-8   The Save window

saves the document with a filename extension of **.odt**, which indicates it is an Open-Office.org word processing document. The object for this type of file has some text and a picture in it.

optional
Browse/Save
window With the **Browse for other folders** section opened, the Save window grays out the drop-down list labeled **Save in folder** and expands the **Browse for other folders** section, as shown in Figure 4-9. This expanded section holds two large side-by-side list boxes: Places and Name. The list box labeled **Places** displays directories and locations on the system, including File System. The list box labeled **Name** lists the files within the directory highlighted in Places.

The **Browse for other folders** section of the Browse/Save window allows you to look through the filesystem and select a directory or file. GNOME utilities and many applications use this window, although sometimes applications call it a Browse window. In this example, OpenOffice.org calls it a Save window and uses it to locate the directory to save a document in.

Assume you want to save a file in the **/tmp** directory. Click **File System** in the list box on the left; the list box on the right displays the files and directories in the root directory (represented by **/**; see "Absolute Pathnames" on page 191 for more information). Next, double-click **tmp** in the list box on the right. The button(s) above the list box on the left change to reflect the directory the list box on the right is displaying. Click **Save**.

The buttons above the list box on the left represent directories. The list box on the right displays the directories found within the directory named in the highlighted (darker) button. This directory is the one you would save the file to if you clicked **Save**. Click one of these buttons to display the corresponding directory in the list box on the right and then click **Save** to save the file in that directory.

Figure 4-9   A Save window with Browse for other folders open

When you have finished editing the document, close the window. If you have made any changes since you last saved it, OpenOffice.org asks if you want to save the document. If you choose to save it, OpenOffice.org saves the revised version over (in the same file as) the version you saved previously. Now the **memo.odt** object appears on the desktop and in the Desktop File Browser window. Double-click either object to open it in OpenOffice.org.

The **Desktop** directory is special

In summary, the **Desktop** directory is like any other directory, except that GNOME displays its contents on the desktop (in every workspace). It is as though the desktop is a large, plain Desktop File Browser window. You can work with the **Desktop** directory because it is always displayed. Within the GUI, you must use a utility, such as Nautilus, to display and work with the contents of any other directory.

SELECTING OBJECTS

The same techniques select one or more objects in a File Browser window or on the desktop. Select an object by clicking it once; GNOME highlights the object. Select additional objects by holding down the CONTROL key while you click each object. You can select a group of adjacent objects by highlighting the first object and then, while holding down the SHIFT key, clicking the last object; GNOME highlights all objects between the two objects you clicked. Or, you can use the mouse pointer to drag a box around a group of objects.

To experiment with these techniques, open a File Browser window displaying your home folder. Display the **Examples** folder by double-clicking it. Select a few objects, right-click, and select **Copy**. Now move the mouse pointer over an empty part of the desktop, right-click, and select **Paste**. You have copied the selected objects from the **Examples** folder to the desktop. You can drag and drop objects to move them, although you do not have permission to move the objects from the **Examples** folder.

EMPTYING THE TRASH

Selecting **File Browser menubar: File⇨Move to Trash** moves the selected (highlighted) object to the **.Trash** directory. Like the **Desktop** directory, **.Trash** is a directory in **/home/***username*. Because its name starts with a period however, it is not usually displayed. Press CONTROL-H or select **File Browser menubar: View⇨Show Hidden Files** to display hidden files. For more information refer to "Hidden Filenames" on page 190.

Because files in the trash take up space on the hard disk (just as any files do), it is a good idea to remove them periodically. All File Browser windows allow you to permanently delete all files in the **.Trash** directory by selecting **File Browser menubar: File⇨Empty Trash**. To view the files in the trash, click the Trash applet (Figure 4-2, page 89). Nautilus displays the Trash File Browser window. Select **Empty Trash** from the Trash applet context menu to permanently remove all files from the trash. (This selection does not appear if there are no files in the trash.) Or you can open the **.Trash** directory, right-click an object, and select **Delete from Trash** to remove only that object (file). You can drag and drop files to and from the trash just as you can with any other folder.

THE UPDATE NOTIFIER

On systems connected to the Internet, Ubuntu is initially set up to automatically search for and notify you when software updates are available. GNOME displays the message **Software updates available** in a yellow notification popup (balloon) and places the Update Notifier (Figure 4-10) toward the right end of the Top panel when updates are available. Clicking this object opens the Update Manager window (Figure 4-10). You can also open this window by selecting **Main menu: System⇨ Administration⇨Update Manager** or by giving the command **update-manager** from a terminal emulator or Run Application window (ALT-F2).

Update Manager window | When the Update Manager window opens, it displays the message **Starting Update Manager**; after a moment it displays the number of available updates. If no updates are available, this window displays the message **Your system is up-to-date**. If you have reason to believe the system is not aware of available updates, click **Check**. The update-manager asks for your password, reloads its database, and checks for updates again.

If updates are available, click **Install Updates**. The Update Manager asks for your password, displays the Downloading Package Files window, and counts the packages as it downloads them. Next the Update Manager displays the Applying Changes window with the message **Installing software** and describes the steps it is taking to install the packages. When it is finished, the Update Manager displays the Changes Applied window, which displays the message **Update is complete**. After you click **Close**, the Update Manager again checks for updates and usually displays

Figure 4-10   The Update Notifier and the Update Manager window

the message **Your system is up-to-date**. Click **Close**. If the updates require you to reboot the system or restart a program, an object appears on the Top panel. Click this object and take the required action as soon as you are ready. For more information refer to "Updating, Installing, and Removing Software Packages" on page 116.

CHANGING APPEARANCE (THEMES)

One of the most exciting aspects of a Linux desktop is the ability it gives you to change its appearance. You can change not only the backgrounds, but also window borders (including the titlebar), icons, the buttons that applications use, and more. To see some examples of what you can do, visit art.gnome.org.

Themes   In a GUI, a *theme* is a recurring pattern and overall look that (ideally) pleases the eye and is easy to interpret and use. You can work with desktop themes at several levels. First and easiest is to leave well enough alone. Ubuntu comes with a good-looking theme named Human. If you are not interested in changing the way the desktop looks, continue with the next section.

The next choice, which is almost as easy, is to select one of the alternative themes that comes with Ubuntu. You can also modify one of these themes, changing the background, fonts, or interface. In addition, you can download themes from many sites on the Internet and change them in the same ways.

The next level is customizing a theme, which changes the way the theme looks—for example, changing the icons a theme uses. At an even higher level, you can design and code your own theme. For more information see the tutorials at art.gnome.org.

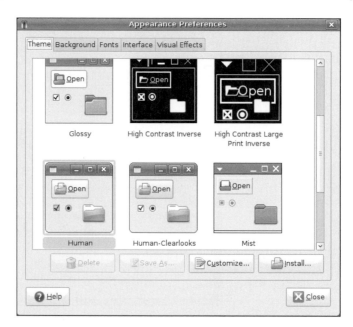

Figure 4-11   The Appearance Preferences window, Theme tab

Appearance
Preferences window

The key to changing the appearance of your desktop is the Appearance Preferences window. Display this window by choosing **Main menu: System⇨Preferences⇨ Appearance** or by right-clicking the root window (any empty space on a workspace) and selecting **Change Desktop Background**. The Appearance Preferences window has five tabs:

- The **Theme** tab (Figure 4-11) enables you to select one of several themes. Click a theme and the workspace immediately reflects the use of that theme. The Human theme is the default Ubuntu theme; select this theme to make the workspace appear as it did when you installed the system. Once you select a theme, you can click **Close** or you can click the other tabs to modify the theme.

- The **Background** tab enables you to specify a wallpaper or color for the desktop background. To specify a wallpaper, click one of the samples in the Wallpaper frame or click **Add** and choose a file—perhaps a picture—you want to use as wallpaper. (Clicking **Add** displays the Add Wallpaper window; see "Browse/Save window" on page 97 for instructions on selecting a file using this window.) Then choose the style you want GNOME to use to apply the wallpaper. For example, Zoom makes the picture you chose fit the workspace.

  You can also specify a color for the background: either solid or a gradient between two colors. To use a color, you must first select **No Wallpaper** from the Wallpaper frame: Allow the mouse pointer to hover over each of the wallpapers displayed in the Wallpaper frame until you find one that displays the tooltip **No Wallpaper**. Select that (non)wallpaper. Next, select **Solid color** from the drop-down list labeled **Colors** and click the colored box to the right of this list. GNOME displays the Pick a Color window. Click a color you like from the ring and adjust the color by dragging the little circle within the triangle. Click **OK** when you are done. The color you chose becomes the background color of the desktop. See page 270 for more information on the Pick a Color window.

- The **Fonts** tab (Figure 8-7, page 268) enables you to specify which fonts you want GNOME to use in different places on the desktop. You can also change how GNOME renders the fonts (page 269).

- The **Interface** tab enables you to modify the appearance of window menus and toolbars and presents a Preview pane that shows what your choices will look like.

Visual effects

- The **Visual Effects** tab enables you to select one of three levels of visual effects: None, Normal, and Extra. Normal and Extra effects replace the Metacity window manager with Compiz Fusion (compiz-fusion.org), which implements 3D desktop visual effects. (Compiz is the name of the core; the plugins are called Compiz Fusion.) When you install Ubuntu, Ubuntu determines what the hardware is capable of running and sets the proper level of effects. One of the most dramatic visual effects is wiggly windows: To see this effect, select **Normal** or **Extra** and drag a window around using its title-bar. If you experience problems with the system, select **None**.

Visual effects can cause problems

caution   Setting Visual Effects to **Normal** or **Extra** can cause unexpected graphical artifacts, shorten battery life, and reduce performance in 3D applications and video playback. If you are having problems with an Ubuntu system, try setting Visual Effects to **None** and see if the problem goes away.

The changes you make in the Background, Fonts, Interface, and Visual Effects tabs are used by any theme you select, including ones you customize. When you are through making changes in the Appearance Preferences window tabs, you can click **Close** to use the theme as you have modified it or return to the Theme tab to customize the theme.

Customizing a theme   From the Theme tab of the Appearance Preferences window, select the theme you want to customize or continue with the theme you modified in the preceding section. Click **Customize** to open the Customize Theme window. Go through each tab in this window; choose entries and watch the change each choice makes in the workspace. Not all tabs work with all themes. When you are satisfied with the result, click **Close**.

After you customize a theme, it is named Custom. When you customize another theme, those changes overwrite the Custom theme. For this reason it is best to save a customized theme by clicking **Save As** and specifying a name for the theme. After saving a theme, it appears among the themes in the Theme tab.

SESSION MANAGEMENT

A session starts when you log in and ends when you log out or reset the session. With fully GNOME-compliant applications, GNOME can manage sessions so the desktop looks the same when you log in as it did when you saved a session or logged out: The same windows will be positioned as they were on the same workspaces and programs will be as you left them.

To save a session, first make sure you have only the windows open that you want to appear the next time you log in. Then select **Main menu: System⇨Preferences⇨ Sessions** to display the Sessions window. Click the **Session Options** tab and then click **Remember currently running applications**. The window displays **Your session has been saved**. Each time you log in, the same windows will appear. If you want GNOME to remember what you were doing each time you log off, put a tick in the check box labeled **Automatically remember running applications when logging out**.

GETTING HELP

Ubuntu provides help in many forms. Clicking the question mark object on the Top panel displays the Ubuntu Help Center window, which provides information on the desktop. To display other information, click a topic in the list on the left side of this window. You can also enter text to search for in the text box labeled **Search** and press RETURN. In addition, most windows provide a Help object or menu. See "Where to Find Documentation" on page 121 for more resources.

Feel Free to Experiment

Try selecting different items from the Main menu and see what you discover. Following are some applications you may want to explore:

- OpenOffice.org's Writer is a full-featured word processor that can import and export MS Word documents. Select **Main menu: Applications⇨Office⇨OpenOffice.org Word Processor**. The **Office** menu also offers a database, presentation manager, and spreadsheet.

- Firefox is a powerful, full-featured Web browser. Click the blue and orange globe object on the Top panel to start Firefox. You can also select **Main menu: Applications⇨Internet⇨Firefox Web Browser**.

- Pidgin is a graphical IM (instant messenger) client, formerly called Gaim, that allows you to chat on the Internet with people who are using IM clients such as AOL, MSN, and Yahoo! To start Pidgin, select **Main menu: Applications⇨Internet⇨Pidgin Internet Messenger**.

  The first time you start Pidgin, it opens the Accounts window; click **Add** to open the Add Account window. In the Add Account window, select a protocol (such as AIM or MSN), enter your screen name and password, and put a tick in the check box labeled **Remember password** if you want Pidgin to remember your password. Click **Save**. Visit pidgin.im for more information, including Pidgin documentation and plugins that add features to Pidgin.

Logging Out

To log out, click the Logout button (Figure 4-2, page 89) at the upper-right corner of the workspace.

HARDY GNOME displays the Logout window. This window looks different from other windows because it has no decorations (page 139). Or, you can select **Main Menu: System⇨Quit** and click **Logout**.

INTREPID GNOME displays a drop-down menu; select **Logout**. Or, you can select **Main Menu: System⇨Logout** *username*. If you are running Pidgin, the Logout button changes appearance to indicate your IM status (online, busy, away, or offline).

You can also choose to shut down or restart the system, among other options. From a textual environment, press CONTROL-D or give the command **exit** in response to the shell prompt.

GETTING THE MOST OUT OF THE DESKTOP

The GNOME desktop is a powerful tool with many features. This section covers many aspects of panels, the Main menu, windows, terminal emulation, and ways to update, install, and remove software. Chapter 8 continues where this chapter leaves off, discussing the X Window System, covering Nautilus in more detail, and describing a few of the GNOME utilities.

GNOME DESKTOP TERMINOLOGY

The following terminology, from the GNOME Users Guide, establishes a foundation for discussing the GNOME desktop. Figure 4-2 on page 89 shows the initial Ubuntu GNOME desktop.

Desktop   The *desktop* comprises all aspects of the GNOME GUI. While you are working with GNOME, you are working on the desktop. There is always exactly one desktop.

Panels   Panels are bars that appear on the desktop and hold (panel) objects. Initially there are two gray panels: one along the top of the screen (the Top Edge panel, or just Top panel) and one along the bottom (the Bottom Edge panel, or just Bottom panel). You can add and remove panels. You can place panels at the top, bottom, and both sides of the desktop, and you can stack more than one panel at any of these locations. The desktop can have no panels, one panel, or several panels. See page 105 for more information on panels.

Panel objects   Panel objects appear as words or icons on panels. You can click these objects to display menus, run applets, or launch programs. The five types of panel objects are applets, launchers, buttons, menus, and drawers. See page 107 for more information on panel objects.

Windows   A graphical application typically runs within and displays a window. At the top of most windows is a titlebar that you can use to move, resize, and close the window. The *root window* is the unoccupied area of the workspace and is frequently obscured. The desktop can have no windows, one window, or many windows. Most windows have decorations (page 139) but some, such as the Logout window, do not.

Workspaces   Workspaces divide the desktop into one or more areas, with one such area filling the screen at any given time. Initially there are two workspaces. Because panels and objects on the desktop are features of the desktop, all workspaces display the same panels and objects. By default, a window appears in a single workspace. The Switcher (page 91) enables you to display any one of several workspaces.

Tooltips   Tooltips (Figure 4-2, page 89) is a minicontext help system that you activate by moving the mouse pointer over a button, icon, window border, or applet (such as those on a panel) and allowing it to hover there. When the mouse pointer hovers over an object, GNOME displays a brief explanation of the object.

OPENING FILES

By default, you double-click an object to open it; or you can right-click the object and select **Open** from the drop-down menu. When you open a file, GNOME figures out the appropriate tool to use by determining the file's *MIME* (page 1120) type. GNOME associates each filename extension with a MIME type and each MIME type with a program. Initially GNOME uses the filename extension to try to determine a file's MIME type. If GNOME does not recognize the filename extension, it examines the file's *magic number* (page 1118).

For example, when you open a file with a filename extension of **ps**, GNOME calls the Evince document viewer, which displays the PostScript file in a readable format. When you open a text file, GNOME uses gedit to display and allow you to edit the file. When you open a directory, GNOME displays its contents in a File Browser window. When you open an executable file such as Firefox, GNOME runs the executable. When GNOME uses the wrong tool to open a file, the tool generally issues an error message. See "Open With" on page 115 for information on how to use a tool other than the default tool to open a file.

PANELS

As explained earlier, panels are the bars that initially appear at the top and bottom of the desktop. They are part of the desktop and therefore are consistent across workspaces.

THE PANEL (CONTEXT) MENU

Right-clicking an empty part of a panel displays the Panel (Context) menu. Aside from help and informational selections, this menu has four selections.

Add to Panel   Selecting **Add to Panel** displays the Add to Panel window (Figure 4-12). You can drag an object from this window to a panel, giving you the choice of which panel the object appears on. You can also highlight an object and click **Add** to add the object to the panel whose menu you used to display this window. Many objects in this window are whimsical: Try Eyes and select Bloodshot from its preferences window, or try Fish. One of the more useful objects is Search for Files. When you click this object on the panel, it displays the Search for Files window (page 270).

Figure 4-12   The Add to Panel window

Figure 4-13   The Panel Properties window, General tab

Properties   Selecting **Properties** displays the Panel Properties window (Figure 4-13). This window has two tabs: General and Background.

In the General tab, Orientation selects which side of the desktop the panel appears on; Size adjusts the width of the panel. Expand causes the panel to span the width or height of the workspace; without a tick in this check box the panel is centered and just wide enough to hold its objects. Autohide causes the panel to disappear until you bump the mouse pointer against the side of the workspace. Hide buttons work differently from autohide: Show hide buttons displays buttons at each end of the panel. When you click one of these buttons, the panel slides out of view, leaving only a button remaining. When you click that button, the panel slides back into place.

If you want to see what stacked panels look like, use the Orientation drop-down list to change the location of the panel you are working with. If you are working with the Top panel, select **Bottom** and vice versa. As with Preferences windows, Properties windows have no Apply and Cancel buttons; they implement changes immediately. Use the same procedure to put the panel back where it was.

The Background tab of the Panel Properties window enables you to specify a color and transparency or an image for the panel. See "Pick a Color Window" on page 270 for instructions on how to change the color of the panel. Once you have changed the color, move the slider labeled **Style** to make the color of the panel more or less transparent. If you do not like the effect, click the radio button labeled **None** (**use system theme**) to return the panel to its default appearance. Click **Close**.

Delete This Panel   Selecting **Delete This Panel** does what you might expect. Be careful with this selection: When it removes a panel, it removes all the objects on the panel and you will need to reconstruct the panel if you want it back as it was.

INTREPID: Allow   By default, you can move a panel to any edge of the workspace. Selecting **Allow**
Panel to be Moved   **Panel to be Moved** toggles a lock that prevents the panel from being moved.

New Panel   Selecting **New Panel** adds a new panel to the desktop. GNOME decides where it goes; you can move the panel to somewhere else.

Figure 4-14   Window List applets

MOVING A PANEL

You can drag any panel to any of the four sides of the desktop: Left-click any empty space on a panel; the mouse pointer turns into a small hand. Drag the panel to the side you want to move it to. Unlike dragging an object across a workspace, the panel does not move until you have dragged the mouse pointer all the way to the new location of the panel; it then snaps into place. If you have stacked panels and are having trouble restacking them in the order you want, try dragging a panel first to an empty side of the workspace and then to its final location.

PANEL OBJECTS

The icons and words on a panel, called *panel objects,* display menus, launch programs, and present information. The panel object with the blue and orange globe starts Firefox. The email button (the open envelope icon) starts Evolution, an email and calendaring application (www.gnome.org/projects/evolution). You can start almost any utility or program on the system using a panel object. This section describes the different types of panel objects.

Applets   An applet is a small program that displays its user interface on or adjacent to the panel. You interact with the applet using its Applet panel object. The Mixer (volume control), Clock (date and time; Figure 4-2, page 89), and Workspace Switcher (Figure 4-2, page 89) are applets.

Window List applet   Although not a distinct type of object, the Window List applet is a unique and important tool. One Window List applet (Figure 4-14) appears on the Bottom panel for each open or iconified window on the displayed workspace. Left-clicking this object minimizes its window or restores the window if it is minimized. Right-click to display the Window Operations menu (page 110). If a window is buried under other windows, click its Window List applet to make it visible.

Launchers   When you open a launcher, it can execute a command, start an application, display the contents of a folder or file, open a URI in a Web browser, and so on. In addition to appearing on panels, launchers can appear on the desktop. The Firefox object is a launcher: It starts the Firefox application. Under **Main menu: Applications,** you can find launchers that start applications. Under **Main menu: Places,** the Home Folder, Documents, Desktop, and Computer objects are launchers that open File Browser windows to display folders.

Buttons   A button performs a single, simple action. The Logout button (Figure 4-2, page 89) displays a window that enables you to log off, shut down, or reboot the system. The Show Desktop button at the left of the Bottom panel minimizes all windows on the workspace.

Menus   A menu displays a list of selections you can choose from. Some of the selections can be submenus with more selections. All other selections are launchers. The next section discusses the Main menu.

Drawers   A drawer is an extension of a panel. You can put the same objects in a drawer that you can put on a panel, including another drawer. When you click a drawer object, the drawer opens; you can then click an object in the drawer the same way you click an object on a panel.

THE PANEL OBJECT CONTEXT MENUS

Three selections are unique to Panel Object context menus (right-click a panel object). The Remove from Panel selection does just that. The Move selection allows you to move the object within the panel and to other panels; you can also move an object by dragging it with the middle mouse button. The Lock to Panel selection locks the object in position so it cannot be moved. When you move an object on a panel, it can move through other objects. If the other object is not locked, it can displace the object if necessary. The Move selection is grayed out when the object is locked.

THE MAIN MENU

The Main menu appears at the left of the Top panel and includes **Applications**, **Places**, and **System**. Click one of these words to display the corresponding menu.

Applications   The **Applications** menu holds several submenus, each named for a category of applications (e.g., Games, Graphics, Internet, Office). The last selection, Add/Remove, is discussed on page 118. Selections from the submenus launch applications—peruse these selections, hovering over those you are unsure of to display tooltips.

Places   The **Places** menu holds a variety of launchers, most of which open a File Browser window. The Home Folder, Desktop, and Documents objects display your directories with corresponding names. The Computer, CD/DVD Creator, and Network objects display special locations. Each of these locations enables you to access file manager functions. A special *URI* (page 1139) specifies each of these locations. For example, the CD/DVD Creator selection displays the **burn:///** URI which enables you to create a CD or DVD. The Connect to Server selection opens a window that allows you to connect to various types of servers, including SSH and FTP (see "File" on page 265). Below these selections are mounted filesystems; click one of these to display the top-level directory of that filesystem. The Search for Files selection enables you to search for files (page 270).

System   The **System** menu holds two submenus as well as selections that can provide support and allow you to log out. The two submenus are key to configuring your account and setting up and maintaining the system.

The Preferences submenu establishes the characteristics of your account; each user can establish her own preferences. Click some of these selections to become familiar with the ways you can customize your account on an Ubuntu system.

The Administration submenu controls the way the system works. For example, **Administration⇨Printing** sets up and configures printers you can use from the system and **Administration⇨Software Sources** controls which repositories you can download software from and how often the system checks for updated software. Most of these selections require you to be a system administrator and enter your password to make changes. These menu selections are discussed throughout this book.

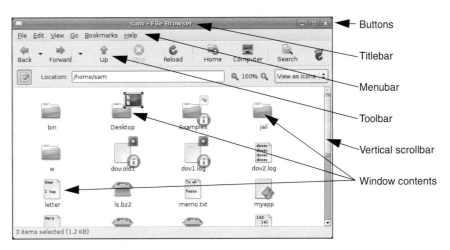

Figure 4-15 A typical window

Copying launchers
to a panel

You can copy any launcher from the Main menu to the Top panel or the desktop. Instead of left-clicking the menu selection, right-click it. GNOME displays a small menu that enables you to add the launcher to the Top panel or desktop.

WINDOWS

In a workspace, a *window* is a region that runs, or is controlled by, a particular program (Figure 4-15). Because you can control the look and feel of windows—even the buttons they display—your windows may not look like the ones shown in this book. Each window in a workspace has a Window List applet (page 107) on the Bottom panel.

Titlebar

A titlebar (Figures 4-15 and 4-16) appears at the top of most windows and controls the window it is attached to. You can change the appearance and function of a titlebar, but it will usually have at least the functionality of the buttons shown in Figure 4-16.

The minimize (iconify) button collapses the window so that the only indication of the window is its Window List applet on the Bottom panel; click this applet to restore the window. Click the maximize button to expand the window so that it occupies the whole workspace; click the same button on the titlebar of a maximized window to

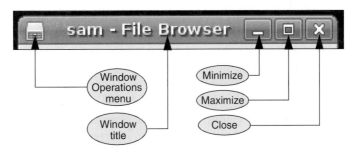

Figure 4-16 A window titlebar

restore the window to its former size. You can also double-click the titlebar to maximize and restore a window. Clicking the maximize button with the middle mouse button expands the window vertically; using the left button expands it horizontally. Use the same or a different mouse button to click the maximize button again and see what happens. Clicking the close button closes the window and terminates the program that is running in it. Left-click the titlebar and drag the window to reposition it.

Window Operations menu   The Window Operations menu contains most common operations you need to perform on any window. Click the Window Operations menu button or right-click either the titlebar or the Window List applet (page 107) to display this menu.

Toolbar   A *toolbar* (Figure 4-15) usually appears near the top of a window and contains icons, text, applets, menus, and more. Many kinds of toolbars exist. The titlebar is not a toolbar; rather, it is part of the window decorations placed there by the window manager (page 139).

CHANGING THE INPUT FOCUS (WINDOW CYCLING)

The window with the input focus is the one that receives keyboard characters and commands you type. In addition to using the Window List applet (page 107), you can change which window on the current workspace has the input focus by using the keyboard; this process is called *window cycling*. When you press ALT-TAB, GNOME displays in the center of the workspace a box that holds the icons representing the programs running in the windows in the workspace. It also shifts the input focus to the window that was active just before the currently active window, making it easy to switch back and forth between two windows. When you hold ALT and press TAB multiple times, the focus moves from window to window. Holding ALT and SHIFT and repeatedly pressing TAB cycles in the other direction. See page 138 for more information on input focus.

CUTTING AND PASTING OBJECTS USING THE CLIPBOARD

There are two similar ways to cut/copy and paste objects and text on the desktop and both within and between windows. First you can use the clipboard, technically called the *copy buffer,* to copy or move objects or text: You explicitly copy an object or text to the buffer and then paste it somewhere else. Applications that follow the user interface guidelines use CONTROL-X to cut, CONTROL-C to copy, and CONTROL-V to paste. Application context menus frequently have these same selections.

You may be less familiar with the second method—using the *selection* or *primary* buffer, which always contains the text you most recently selected (highlighted). You cannot use this method to copy objects. Clicking the middle mouse button (click the scroll wheel on a mouse that has one) pastes the contents of the selection buffer at the location of the mouse pointer (if you are using a two-button mouse, click both buttons at the same time to simulate clicking the middle button).

With both these techniques, start by highlighting the object or text to select it. You can drag a box around multiple objects to select them or drag the mouse pointer over text to select it. Double-click to select a word or triple-click to select a line. Next, to use the clipboard, explicitly copy (CONTROL-C) or cut (CONTROL-X) the objects or text.[1] If you want to use the selection buffer, skip this step.

To paste the selected objects or text, position the mouse pointer where you want to put it and then either press CONTROL-V (clipboard method) or press the middle mouse button (selection buffer method).

Using the clipboard, you can give as many commands as you like between the CONTROL-C or CONTROL-X and CONTROL-V, as long as you do not press CONTROL-C or CONTROL-X again. Using the selection buffer, you can give other commands after selecting text and before pasting it, as long as you do not select (highlight) other text.

USING THE ROOT WINDOW

The *root window* is any part of a workspace that is not occupied by a window, panel, or object. It is the part of the workspace where you can see the background. To view the root window when it is obscured, click the Show Desktop button at the left end of the Bottom panel to minimize the windows in the workspace.

Desktop menu   Right-click the root window to display the Desktop menu, which enables you to create a folder, launcher, or document. The Change Desktop Background selection opens the Appearance Preferences window (page 101) to the Background tab.

RUNNING COMMANDS FROM A TERMINAL EMULATOR/SHELL

A *terminal emulator* is a window that presents a command-line interface (CLI); it functions as a textual (character-based) terminal and is displayed in a graphical environment.

To display the GNOME terminal emulator named Terminal (Figure 4-17, next page), select **Main menu: Applications⇨Accessories⇨Terminal** or enter the command **gnome-terminal** from a Run Application window (ALT-F2). Because you are already logged in and are creating a subshell in a desktop environment, you do not need to log in again. Once you have opened a terminal emulator window, try giving the command **man man** to read about the man utility (page 122), which displays Linux manual pages. Chapter 5 describes utilities that you can run from a terminal emulator.

You can run character-based programs that would normally run on a terminal or from the console in a terminal emulator window. You can also start graphical programs, such as xeyes, from this window. A graphical program opens its own window.

When you are typing in a terminal emulator window, several characters, including *, ?, |, [, and], have special meanings. Avoid using these characters until you have read "Special Characters" on page 146.

The shell   Once you open a terminal emulator window, you are communicating with the command interpreter called the *shell*. The shell plays an important part in much of your communication with Linux. When you enter a command at the keyboard in response to the shell prompt on the screen, the shell interprets the command and

---

1. These control characters do not work in a terminal emulator window because the shell running in the window intercepts them before the terminal emulator can receive them. You must either use the selection buffer in this environment or use copy/paste from the **Edit** selection on the menubar or from the context menu (right-click).

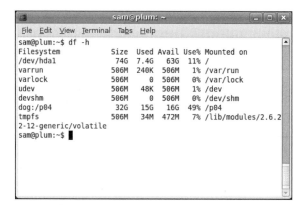

Figure 4-17   A Terminal terminal emulator window

initiates the appropriate action—for example, executing a program; calling a compiler, a Linux utility, or another standard program; or displaying an error message indicating that you entered a command incorrectly. When you are working on a GUI, you bypass the shell and execute a program by clicking an object or name. Refer to Chapter 7 for more information on the shell.

THE OBJECT CONTEXT MENU

When you right-click an object or group of objects either on the desktop or in a File Browser window, GNOME displays an Object context menu. Different types of objects display different context menus, but most context menus share common selections. Figure 4-18 shows context menus for an OpenOffice.org spreadsheet file and for a plain text file. Table 4-1 lists some common Object context menu selections.

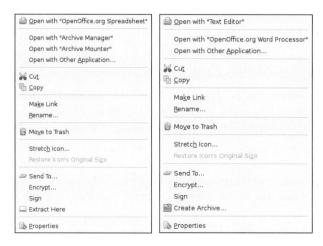

Figure 4-18   The Object context menus for a spreadsheet (left) and a text file (right)

Table 4-1   Common Object context menu selections

Open	Runs an executable file. Opens a file with an appropriate application. Opens a folder in a File Browser window. Same as double-clicking the object.
Open in New Window	(From a File Browser window only.) Opens a folder in a new File Browser window instead of replacing the contents of the current window. Same as holding SHIFT while double-clicking a folder in a Browser window.
Open with "*App*"	Opens the file using the application named *App*. When this selection appears as the first selection in the menu, *App* is the default application that GNOME uses to open this type of file. See page 115 for information on changing this default.
Open with ➤	A triangle appearing to the right of a selection indicates the selection is a menu. Allow the mouse pointer to hover over the selection to display the submenu. Each submenu selection is an Open with "*App*" selection (above). The last selection in the submenu is Open with Other Application (below).
Browse Folder	(On the desktop only.) Opens a folder in a File Browser window. Same as double-clicking a folder on the desktop.
Open with Other Application	Displays the Open With menu. This menu allows you to select an application to open this type of file; the next time you use the Object context menu to open this type of file, the application you selected appears as an Open with "*App*" selection (above). Does not change the default application for this type of file. See page 115 for information on changing the default application.
Cut	Removes the object and places it on the clipboard (page 110).
Copy	Copies the object to the clipboard (page 110).
Extract Here	Extracts the contents of an archive and some other types of files, such as some documents, to a directory with the same name as the original file plus **_FILES**.
Make Link	Creates a link to the object in the same directory as the object. You can then move the link to a different directory where it may be more useful.
Move to Trash	Moves the object to the trash (page 98).
Send to	Opens a Send To window that allows you to email the object.
Create Archive	Opens the Create Archive window, which allows you to specify a format and a name for an archive of one or more objects (page 266).
Share Folder	Opens the Share Folder window, which allows you to share a folder using NFS (Chapter 22) or Samba (Chapter 23), depending on which is installed on the local system. Select **Main menu: System⇨Administration⇨Shared Folders** to display the Shared Folders window, which lists folders that are shared from the local system. Requires **root** privileges.
Properties	Displays the Object Properties window.

The Object Properties Window

The Object Properties window displays information about a file, such as who owns it, permissions, size, location, MIME type, ways to work with it, and so on. This window is titled *filename* **Properties**, where *filename* is the name of the file you clicked to open the window. Display this window by right-clicking an object and selecting **Properties** from the drop-down menu. The Properties window initially displays some basic information. Click the tabs at the top of the window to display additional information. Different types of files display different sets of tabs. You can modify the settings in this window only if you have permission to do so. This section describes the five tabs common to most Object Properties windows.

Basic   The Basic tab displays information about the file, including its MIME type, and enables you to select a custom icon for the file and change its name. Change the name of the file in the text box labeled **Name**. If the filename is not listed in a text box, you do not have permission to change it. An easy way to change the icon is to open a File Browser window at **/usr/share/icons**. Work your way down through the directories until you find an icon you like, and then drag and drop it on the icon to the left of **Name** in the Basic tab of the Object Properties window. This technique does not work for files that are links (indicated by the arrow emblem at the upper right of the object).

Emblems   The Emblems tab (Figure 4-19, left) allows you to add and remove emblems associated with the file by placing (removing) a tick in the check box next to an emblem. Figure 4-15 on page 109 shows some emblems on file objects. Nautilus displays emblems in both its Icon and List views, although there may not be room for more than one emblem in the List view. Emblems are displayed on the desktop as well. You can also place an emblem on an object by dragging the emblem from the Side pane/Emblems and dropping it on an object in the View pane (page 263) of a File Browser window. Drag the Erase emblem to an object to remove most emblems from the object.

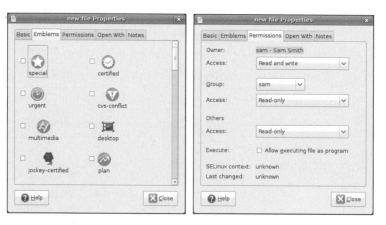

Figure 4-19 The Object Properties window: Emblems tab (left); Permissions tab (right)

Permissions   The Permissions tab (Figure 4-19, right) allows the owner of a file to change the file's permissions (page 201) and to change the group (see **/etc/group** on page 474) that the file is associated with to any group the owner is associated with. When running with **root** privileges, you can also change the owner of the file. The command **gksudo nautilus** opens a File Browser window running with **root** privileges (but read the caution on page 86). Nautilus grays out items you are not allowed to change.

Using the drop-down lists, you can give the owner (called *user* elsewhere; see the tip about chmod on page 203), group, and others read or read and write permission for a file. You can prohibit the group and others from accessing the file by specifying permissions as **None**. Put a tick in the check box labeled **Execute** to give all users permission to execute the file. This tab does not give you as fine-grained control over assigning permissions as chmod (page 202) does.

Permissions for a directory work as explained on page 206. Owner, group, and others can be allowed to list files in a directory, access (read and—with the proper permissions—execute) files, or create and delete files. Group and others permissions can be set to **None**. The tri-state check box labeled **Execute** does not apply to the directory; it applies to the files in the directory. A tick in this check box gives everyone execute access to these files; a hyphen does not change execute permissions of the files; and an empty check box removes execute access for everyone from these files.

Open With   When you ask GNOME to open a file that is not executable (by double-clicking its icon or right-clicking and selecting the first **Open with** selection), GNOME determines which application or utility it will use to open the file. GNOME uses several techniques to determine the *MIME* (page 1120) type of a file and selects the default application based on that determination.

The Open With tab (Figure 4-20) enables you to change which applications GNOME can use to open the file and other files of the same MIME type (typically

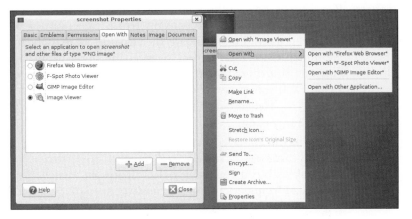

Figure 4-20   The Object Properties window, Open With tab, and the Object context menu, Open With submenu for the same file

files with the same filename extension). Click the **Add** button to add to the list of applications. Highlight an application and click **Remove** to remove an application from the list. You cannot remove the default application.

When you add an application, GNOME adds that application to the Open With list, but does not change the default application it uses to open that type of file. Click the radio button next to an application to cause that application to become the default application that GNOME uses to open this type of file.

When a file has fewer than four applications in the Open With tab, the Object context menu displays all applications in that menu. With four or more applications, the Object context menu uses an Open With submenu (Figure 4-20).

Notes   The Notes tab provides a place to keep notes about the file.

UPDATING, INSTALLING, AND REMOVING SOFTWARE PACKAGES

Ubuntu software comes in packages that include all necessary files, instructions so that a program can automatically install and remove the software, and a list of other packages that the package depends on. There are many ways to search for and install software packages. The Update Notifier (page 99) prompts you each time updates are available for software on the system. The Software Sources window (discussed next) is an easy way to install popular software. synaptic (page 118) is more complex and gives you a wider selection of software. Chapter 13 explains how to work with software packages from the command line.

SOFTWARE SOURCES WINDOW

Repositories   Repositories hold collections of software packages and related information. The Software Sources window controls which categories of packages Ubuntu installs, which repositories it downloads the packages from, how automatic updating works, and more. Open this window by selecting **Main menu: System⇨Administration⇨Software Sources** (you will need to supply your password) or by giving the command **gksudo software-properties-gtk** from a terminal emulator or Run Application window (ALT-F2). The Software Sources window has five tabs, which are discussed next.

Ubuntu Software   The Ubuntu Software tab controls which categories of packages (page 504) APT (page 504) and synaptic install and the Update Manager updates automatically. Typically all categories have ticks in their check boxes except for **Source code**. Put a tick in this check box if you want to download source code. If the drop-down list labeled **Download from** does not specify a server near you, use the list to specify one.

If the system does not have an Internet connection, put a tick in one of the check boxes in the frame labeled **Installable from CD-ROM/DVD**; APT will then install software from that source. If you do have an Internet connection, remove the tick from that check box. You can specify a new CD/DVD in the Third-Party Software tab.

Add only repositories you know to be trustworthy

security   Adding software from other than the Ubuntu repositories can cause the system to not work properly and cause updates to fail. Even worse, it can make the system vulnerable to attack.

The package installation process runs with **root** privileges. Regard adding a repository as giving the person in control of that repository the sudo password. Do not add a third-party repository unless you trust it implicitly.

Third-Party Software   You can add, edit, and remove repositories from the Third-Party Software tab. (See the adjacent security box concerning adding repositories.) Unless you are working with software that is not distributed by Ubuntu, you do not need to add any repositories. To add a CD/DVD as a repository, click **Add CD-ROM.**

Updates   The top part of the Updates tab (Figure 4-21) specifies which types of updates you want the Update Manager to download. Typically you will want to download important security updates and recommended updates. In the middle section of this tab you can specify if and how often the Update Manager will check for updates and what to do when it finds updates. The drop-down list labeled **Show new distribution releases** allows you to specify whether you want the Update Manager to inform you when you can upgrade the system to a new release of Ubuntu and whether you are interested in all releases or just LTS (page 31) releases.

Authentication   The Authentication tab holds keys for trusted software providers. Ubuntu uses keys to authenticate software, which protects the system against malicious software. Typically Ubuntu provides these keys automatically.

Statistics   The Statistics tab allows you to participate in a software popularity contest.

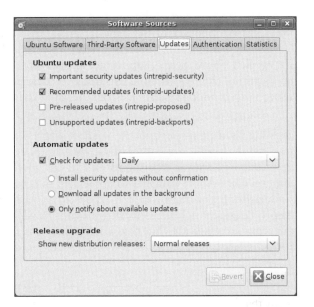

Figure 4-21   The Software Sources window, Updates tab

Figure 4-22   The Add/Remove Applications window

ADD/REMOVE APPLICATIONS

The Add/Remove Applications window (Figure 4-22) adds and removes applications from the system. It is simpler and has fewer selections than synaptic (described next). Open this window by selecting **Main menu: Applications⇨Add/Remove** or by giving the command **gnome-app-install** from a terminal emulator or Run Application window (ALT-F2). Maximizing this window may make it easier to use.

Enter the name or part of the name of an application in the text box labeled **Search** at the upper-right corner of the window and press RETURN to search for an application. Unless you want to limit selections, select **All available applications** in the drop-down list labeled **Show**. Select **Supported applications** (HARDY) or **Canonical-maintained applications** (INTREPID) to limit selections to packages supported by Ubuntu. You can select a category of applications from the list at the left of the window.

Scroll through the applications displayed at the right of the window. When you click/highlight an application, the window displays a summary of the application in the frame at the lower-right corner of the window. Put a tick in the check box next to each application you want to install. Remove tick marks from applications you want to remove. Click **Apply Changes** to implement the changes you have marked. This utility summarizes the changes you have requested and asks if you want to apply them. Click **Apply**. Because you need to work with **root** privileges to install and remove software, the utility may ask for your password. When it is finished it tells you it has been successful. Click **Close**. Packages you installed should be available on the Main menu.

optional
synaptic: FINDS, INSTALLS, AND REMOVES SOFTWARE

This section describes how to use synaptic to find, download, install, and remove software packages. Open the Synaptic Package Manager window by selecting **System⇨ Administration⇨Synaptic Package Manager** from the Main menu or by giving the

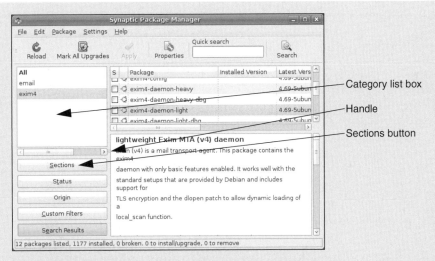

Figure 4-23   The Synaptic Package Manager window

command **gksudo synaptic** from a terminal emulator or Run Application window (ALT-F2). Figure 4-23 shows the initial window. The first time you run synaptic, it reminds you to reload package information regularly. You can do so by clicking **Reload** on the toolbar.

The Synaptic Package Manager window displays a lot of information. Maximizing this window and widening the left column (by dragging the handle) may make it easier to use. When the **Sections** button is highlighted in the left column, the top of the left column holds a list box containing categories of software. Initially **All** is selected in this list box, causing the window to display all software packages in the list box at the top of the right column. You can shorten the list of packages in the list box by selecting a category in the category list box or by searching for a package.

To search for a package, display the Find window by clicking **Search** on the toolbar. Enter the name or part of the name of the package you are looking for in the text box labeled **Search**. (*INTREPID*: You can also search using the text box labeled **Quick search** on the main Synaptic window.) For example, to display all packages related to **exim4**, enter **exim4** in the text box labeled **Search** and select **Description and Name** from the drop-down list labeled **Look in** (Figure 4-24). Click **Search**. The Synaptic Package Manager window displays the list of packages meeting the search criteria specified in the list box at the top of the right column. When you click a package name in this list, synaptic displays a description of the package in the frame below the list.

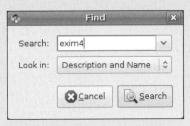

Figure 4-24   The Find window

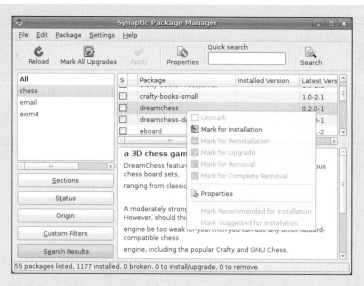

Figure 4-25   The Synaptic Package Manager window displaying chess programs

The following example explains how to use synaptic to locate, download, and install a chess program. With the Synaptic Package Manager window open, search for **chess**. The synaptic utility displays a list of chess-related packages in the righthand list box. Click several packages, one at a time, reading the descriptions in the frame at the lower right of the window. Assume you decide to install Dream Chess (the **dreamchess** package, www.dreamchess.org). When you click the check box to the left of **dreamchess**, synaptic displays a list of options. Because this package is not installed, all selections except **Mark for Installation** are grayed out (Figure 4-25). Click this selection. Because the **dreamchess** package is dependent on other packages that are not installed, synaptic displays a window asking if you want to mark additional required changes (Figure 4-26). This window lists additional packages synaptic needs to install so that Dream Chess will run. Click **Mark** to mark the additional packages. All packages marked for installation are highlighted in green.

To apply the changes you have marked, click **Apply** on the toolbar. synaptic displays a Summary window. If you were installing and/or removing several packages, this

Figure 4-26   Mark additional required changes screen

summary would be longer. Click **Apply**. synaptic keeps you informed of its progress. When it is done, it displays the Changes Applied window. Click **Close** and then close the Synaptic Package Manager window. Now Dream Chess appears on the **Main menu: Applications⇨Games** menu.

WHERE TO FIND DOCUMENTATION

Distributions of Linux, including Ubuntu, typically do not come with hardcopy reference manuals. However, its online documentation has always been one of Linux's strengths. The man (or manual) and info pages have been available via the man and info utilities since early releases of the operating system. Ubuntu provides a graphical help center. Not surprisingly, with the growth of Linux and the Internet, the sources of documentation have expanded as well. This section discusses some of the places you can look for information on Linux in general and Ubuntu Linux in particular. See also Appendix B.

UBUNTU HELP CENTER

To display the Ubuntu Help Center window (Figure 4-27), click the blue object with a question mark in it on the Top panel or select **Main menu: System⇨Help and Support**. Click topics in this window until you find the information you are looking for. You can also search for a topic using the text box labeled **Search**.

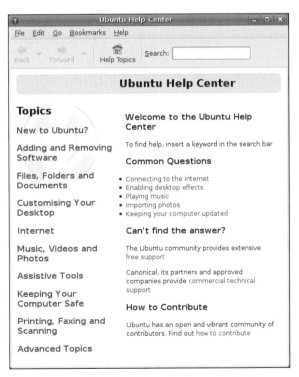

Figure 4-27   The Ubuntu Help Center window

man: DISPLAYS THE SYSTEM MANUAL

In addition to the graphical Ubuntu Help Center, the textual man utility displays (man) pages from the system documentation. This documentation is helpful when you know which utility you want to use but have forgotten exactly how to use it. You can also refer to the man pages to get more information about specific topics or to determine which features are available with Linux. Because the descriptions in the system documentation are often terse, they are most helpful if you already understand the basic functions of a utility.

Online man pages

tip   The new Ubuntu manpages.ubuntu.com site holds dynamically generated copies of man pages from every package of every supported Ubuntu release. In addition to presenting man pages in easy-to-read HTML format, this site does not require you to install the package holding a utility to read its man page. In addition, it allows you to read man pages for a release you do not have installed.

Because man is a character-based utility, you need to open a terminal emulator window (page 111) to run it. You can also log in on a virtual terminal (page 134) and run man from there.

To find out more about a utility, give the command **man,** followed by the name of the utility. Figure 4-28 shows man displaying information about itself; the user entered a **man man** command.

less (pager)   The man utility automatically sends its output through a *pager*—usually less (page 148), which displays one screen at a time. When you access a manual page in this manner, less displays a prompt [e.g., **Manual page man(1) line 1**] at the bottom of the screen after it displays each screen of text and waits for you to request another screen of text by pressing the SPACE bar. Pressing **h** (help) displays a list of

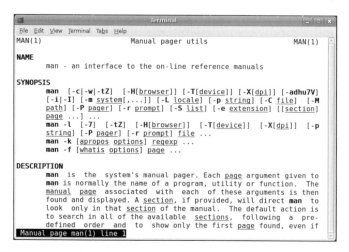

Figure 4-28   The man utility displaying information about itself

less commands. Pressing **q** (quit) stops less and causes the shell to display a prompt. You can search for topics covered by man pages using the apropos utility (page 124).

Based on the FHS (Filesystem Hierarchy Standard, page 199), the Linux system manual and the man pages are divided into ten sections, where each section describes related tools:

1. User Commands
2. System Calls
3. Subroutines
4. Devices
5. File Formats
6. Games
7. Miscellaneous
8. System Administration
9. Kernel
10. New

This layout closely mimics the way the set of UNIX manuals has always been divided. Unless you specify a manual section, man displays the earliest occurrence in the manual of the word you specify on the command line. Most users find the information they need in sections 1, 6, and 7; programmers and system administrators frequently need to consult the other sections.

In some cases the manual contains entries for different tools with the same name. For example, the following command displays the man page for the passwd utility from section 1 of the system manual:

```
$ man passwd
```

To see the man page for the **passwd** file from section 5, enter

```
$ man 5 passwd
```

The preceding command instructs man to look only in section 5 for the man page. In documentation you may see this man page referred to as **passwd(5)**. Use the **–a** option (see the adjacent tip) to view all man pages for a given subject (press **q**RETURN to display the next man page). For example, give the command **man –a passwd** to view all man pages for **passwd**.

Options

tip An option modifies the way a utility or command works. Options are usually specified as one or more letters that are preceded by one or two hyphens. An option typically appears following the name of the utility you are calling and a SPACE. Other *arguments* (page 1095) to the command follow the option and a SPACE. For more information refer to "Options" on page 225.

apropos: Searches for a Keyword

When you do not know the name of the command you need to carry out a particular task, you can use apropos with a keyword to search for it. This utility searches for the keyword in the short description line (the top line) of all man pages and displays those that contain a match. The man utility, when called with the –k (keyword) option, gives you the same output as apropos (it is the same command).

The database apropos uses, named **whatis**, is not on Ubuntu Linux systems when they are first installed, but is built automatically by cron (page 588) using mandb. If apropos does not produce any output, run the command **sudo mandb**.

The following example shows the output of apropos when you call it with the **who** keyword. The output includes the name of each command, the section of the manual that contains it, and the brief description from the top of the man page. This list includes the utility that you need (who) and identifies other, related tools that you might find useful:

```
$ apropos who
at.allow (5)        - determine who can submit jobs via at or batch
at.deny (5)         - determine who can submit jobs via at or batch
from (1)            - print names of those who have sent mail
w (1)               - Show who is logged on and what they are doing.
w.procps (1)        - Show who is logged on and what they are doing.
who (1)             - show who is logged on
whoami (1)          - print effective userid
whois (1)           - client for the whois directory service
```

whatis   The whatis utility is similar to apropos but finds only complete word matches for the name of the utility:

```
$ whatis who
who                 (1)   - show who is logged on
```

info: Displays Information About Utilities

The textual info utility is a menu-based hypertext system developed by the GNU project (page 4) and distributed with Ubuntu Linux. The info utility includes a tutorial on itself (www.gnu.org/software/texinfo/manual/info) and documentation on many Linux shells, utilities, and programs developed by the GNU project. Figure 4-29 shows the screen that info displays when you give the command **info coreutils** (the **coreutils** software package holds the Linux core utilities).

man and info display different information

tip   The info utility displays more complete and up-to-date information on GNU utilities than does man. When a man page displays abbreviated information on a utility that is covered by info, the man page refers to info. The man utility frequently displays the only information available on non-GNU utilities. When info displays information on non-GNU utilities, it is frequently a copy of the man page.

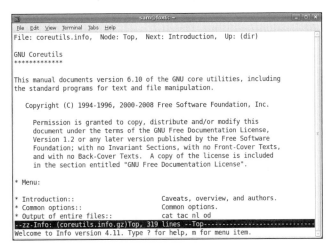

Figure 4-29   The initial screen **info coreutils** displays

Because the information on this screen is drawn from an editable file, your display may differ from the screens shown in this section. When you see the initial info screen, you can press any of the following keys or key combinations:

- **h** to go through an interactive tutorial on info
- **?** to list info commands
- SPACE to scroll through the menu of items for which information is available
- **m** followed by the name of the menu you want to display or a SPACE to display a list of menus
- **q** or CONTROL-C to quit

The notation info uses to describe keyboard keys may not be familiar to you. The notation **C-h** is the same as CONTROL-H. Similarly **M-x** means hold down the META or ALT key and press **x**. (On some systems you need to press ESCAPE and then **x** to duplicate the function of META-X.)

You may find pinfo **easier to use than** info

tip   The pinfo utility is similar to info but is more intuitive if you are not familiar with the emacs editor. This utility runs in a textual environment, as does info. When it is available, pinfo uses color to make its interface easier to use. Use synaptic to install the **pinfo** package if you want to experiment with it. Run pinfo from a terminal emulator or Run Application window (ALT-F2) and select **Run in terminal**).

After giving the command **info coreutils**, press the SPACE bar a few times to scroll through the display. Type **/sleep**RETURN to search for the string **sleep**. When you type **/**, the cursor moves to the bottom line of the window and displays **Search for string** [*string*]: where *string* is the last string you searched for. Press RETURN to search for

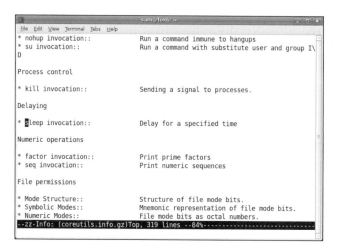

Figure 4-30   The screen **info coreutils** displays after you type **/sleep**RETURN twice

string or enter the string you want to search for. Typing **sleep** displays **sleep** on that line, and pressing RETURN displays the next occurrence of **sleep**.

Next, type **/**RETURN (or **/sleep**RETURN) to search for the next occurrence of **sleep** as shown in Figure 4-30. The asterisk at the left end of the line indicates that this entry is a menu item. Following the asterisk is the name of the menu item and a description of the item.

Each menu item is a link to the info page that describes the item. To jump to that page, use the ARROW keys to move the cursor to the line containing the menu item and press RETURN. Alternatively, you can type the name of the menu item in a menu command to view the information. To display information on **sleep**, for example, you can give the command **m sleep**, followed by RETURN. When you type **m** (for *menu*), the cursor moves to the bottom line of the window (as it did when you typed **/**) and displays **Menu item:**. Typing **sleep** displays **sleep** on that line, and pressing RETURN displays information about the menu item you have chosen.

Figure 4-31 shows the *top node* of information on **sleep**. A node groups a set of information you can scroll through with the SPACE bar. To display the next node, press **n**. Press **p** to display the previous node.

As you read through this book and learn about new utilities, you can use man or info to find out more about those utilities. If you can print PostScript documents, you can print a manual page with the man utility using the **–t** option (for example, **man –t cat | lpr** prints information about the cat utility). You can also use a Web browser to display the documentation at www.tldp.org, help.ubuntu.com, help.ubuntu.com/community, or answers.launchpad.net/ubuntu and print the desired information from the browser.

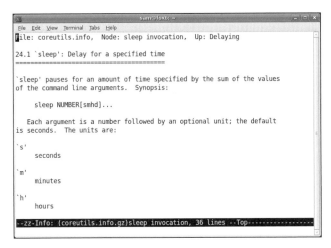

Figure 4-31   The info page on the sleep utility

THE ––help OPTION

Another tool you can use in a textual environment is the **––help** option. Most GNU utilities provide a **––help** option that displays information about the utility. Non-GNU utilities may use a **–h** or **–help** option to display help information.

```
$ cat --help
Usage: cat [OPTION] [FILE]...
Concatenate FILE(s), or standard input, to standard output.

  -A, --show-all             equivalent to -vET
  -b, --number-nonblank      number nonblank output lines
  -e                         equivalent to -vE
  -E, --show-ends            display $ at end of each line
  ...
```

If the information that **––help** displays runs off the screen, send the output through the less pager (page 122) using a pipe (page 156):

```
$ ls --help | less
```

HOWTOs: FINDING OUT HOW THINGS WORK

A HOWTO document explains in detail how to do something related to Linux—from setting up a specialized piece of hardware to performing a system administration task to setting up specific networking software. Mini-HOWTOs offer shorter explanations. As with Linux software, one person or a few people generally are responsible for writing and maintaining a HOWTO document, but many people may contribute to it.

Figure 4-32   Google reporting on an error message

The Linux Documentation Project (LDP, page 129) site houses most HOWTO and mini-HOWTO documents. Use a Web browser to visit www.tldp.org, click **HOWTOs**, and pick the index you want to use to find a HOWTO or mini-HOWTO. You can also use the LDP search feature on its home page to find HOWTOs and other documents.

GETTING HELP WITH THE SYSTEM

GNOME provides tooltips (page 104), a context-sensitive Help system, and Ubuntu provides the help center discussed on page 121.

FINDING HELP LOCALLY

/usr/share/doc   The **/usr/src/linux/Documentation** (present only if you installed the kernel source code as explained in Chapter 15) and **/usr/share/doc** directories often contain more detailed and different information about a utility than man or info provides. Frequently this information is meant for people who will be compiling and modifying the utility, not just using it. These directories hold thousands of files, each containing information on a separate topic.

USING THE INTERNET TO GET HELP

The Internet provides many helpful sites related to Linux. Aside from sites that carry various forms of documentation, you can enter an error message from a program you are having a problem with in a search engine such as Google (www.google.com, or its Linux-specific version at www.google.com/linux). Enclose the error message within double quotation marks to improve the quality of the results. The search will likely yield a post concerning your problem and suggestions about how to solve it. See Figure 4-32.

Ubuntu Web sites   The Ubuntu Web site is a rich source of information. The following list identifies some locations that may be of interest:

- Ubuntu documentation is available at help.ubuntu.com.

- Ubuntu community documentation is available at help.ubuntu.com/community.

- You can find answers to many questions at answers.launchpad.net/ubuntu.

- The Ubuntu forums (ubuntuforums.org) is a good place to find answers to questions.

- You can talk with other Ubuntu users using IRC (Internet relay chat). See help.ubuntu.com/community/InternetRelayChat for a list of Ubuntu IRC channels available via the Freenode IRC service.

- You can subscribe to Ubuntu mailing lists. See lists.ubuntu.com.

- You can search for information about packages and find out which package contains a specific file at packages.ubuntu.com.

GNU GNU manuals are available at www.gnu.org/manual. In addition, you can visit the GNU home page (www.gnu.org) for more documentation and other GNU resources. Many of the GNU pages and resources are available in a variety of languages.

The Linux Documentation Project The Linux Documentation Project (www.tldp.org), which has been around for almost as long as Linux, houses a complete collection of guides, HOWTOs, FAQs, man pages, and Linux magazines. The home page is available in English, Portuguese, Spanish, Italian, Korean, and French. It is easy to use and supports local text searches. It also provides a complete set of links (Figure 4-33) you can use to find almost anything you want related to Linux (click **Links** in the Search box or go to www.tldp.org/links). The links page includes sections on general information, events, getting started, user groups, mailing lists, and newsgroups, with each section containing many subsections.

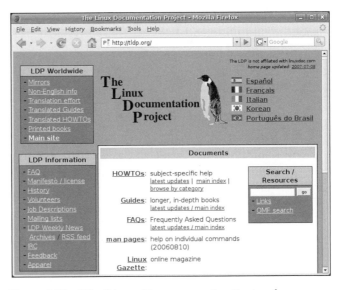

Figure 4-33   The Linux Documentation Project home page

MORE ABOUT LOGGING IN

Refer to "Logging In on the System" on page 88 for information about logging in. This section covers options you can choose from the Login screen and solutions to common login problems. It also describes how to log in from a terminal and from a remote system.

Always use a password

security   Unless you are the only user of a system; the system is not connected to any other systems, the Internet, or a modem; and you are the only one with physical access to the system, it is poor practice to maintain a user account without a password.

THE LOGIN SCREEN

At the lower-left corner of the Login screen is a small object labeled **Options** (Figure 4-1, page 88). Click this object or press F10 to display the Actions menu, which has the following selections:

- **Select Language**—Displays a window from which you can select the language for the session you are about to start. This change affects window titles, prompts, error messages, and other textual items displayed by GNOME and many applications. Just after you log in, the system asks whether you want to make the language you specified the default language or just use it for this session.

- **Select Session**—Displays the Sessions dialog box, which presents several choices concerning the session you are about to start. Choose one of the following, click **Change Session**, and continue logging in:

  - **Last Session**—Brings up the same desktop environment you used the last time you logged in. This choice is the default.

  - **Run Xclient script**—Brings up the default desktop environment.

  - **GNOME**—Brings up the GNOME desktop environment.

  - **KDE**—Brings up the KDE desktop environment (if you have installed Kubuntu or KDE, see page 65).

  - **Failsafe GNOME**—Brings up a default GNOME session without running any startup scripts. Use this choice to fix problems that prevent you from logging in normally.

  - **Failsafe Terminal**—Brings up an xterm terminal emulator window without a desktop manager and without running any startup scripts. This setup allows you to log in on a minimal desktop when your standard login does not work well enough to allow you to log in to fix a problem. Give the command **exit** from the xterm window to log out and display the Login screen.

Just after you log in, the system asks whether to use your selection from the Sessions dialog box just for this session or permanently. The failsafe logins do not ask this question.

• **Restart**—Shuts down and reboots the system.

• **Shut Down**—Shuts down the system and turns off the power.

• **Suspend**—Puts the system in power-saving mode. Exactly what this selection does is hardware dependent.

• **Hibernate**—Saves the system state to the hard disk and turns off the system. When you boot the system it returns to the state it was in before it hibernated.

WHAT TO DO IF YOU CANNOT LOG IN

If you enter either your username or password incorrectly, the system displays an error message after you enter *both* your username *and* your password. This message indicates you have entered either the username or the password incorrectly or they are not valid. It does not differentiate between an unacceptable username and an unacceptable password—a strategy meant to discourage unauthorized people from guessing names and passwords to gain access to the system. Following are some common reasons why logins fail:

• **The username and password are case sensitive.** Make sure the CAPS LOCK key is off and enter your username and password exactly as specified or as you set them up.

• **You are not logging in on the right machine.** The login/password combination may not be valid if you are trying to log in on the wrong machine. On a larger, networked system, you may have to specify the machine you want to connect to before you can log in.

• **Your username is not valid.** The login/password combination may not be valid if you have not been set up as a user. If you are the system administrator, refer to "Configuring User and Group Accounts" on page 578. Otherwise, check with the system administrator.

• **A filesystem is full.** When a filesystem critical to the login process is full, it may appear as though you have logged in successfully, but after a moment the Login screen reappears. You must log in using one of the failsafe logins and delete some files.

Refer to "Changing Your Password" on page 133 if you want to change your password.

LOGGING IN REMOTELY: TERMINAL EMULATORS, ssh, AND DIAL-UP CONNECTIONS

When you are not using a console, terminal, or other device connected directly to the Linux system you are logging in on, you are probably connected to the Linux system using terminal emulation software on another system. Running on the local system, this software connects to the remote Linux system via a network (Ethernet, asynchronous phone line, PPP, or other type) and allows you to log in.

Make sure **TERM** is set correctly

tip   No matter how you connect, make sure you have the **TERM** variable set to the type of terminal your emulator is emulating. For more information refer to "Specifying a Terminal" on page 1060.

When you log in via a dial-up line, the connection is straightforward: You instruct the local emulator program to contact the remote Linux system, it dials the phone, and the remote system displays a login prompt. When you log in via a directly connected network, you use ssh (secure, page 634) or telnet (not secure, page 375) to connect to the remote system. The ssh program has been implemented on many operating systems, not just Linux. Many user interfaces to ssh include a terminal emulator. From an Apple, PC, or UNIX machine, open the program that runs ssh and give it the name or IP address (refer to "Host Address" on page 365) of the system you want to log in on. For examples and more details on working with a terminal emulator, refer to "Running Commands from a Terminal Emulator/Shell" on page 111. The next section provides more information about logging in from a terminal emulator.

LOGGING IN FROM A TERMINAL (EMULATOR)

Before you log in on a terminal, terminal emulator, or other textual device, the system displays a message called *issue* (stored in the **/etc/issue** file) that identifies the version of Ubuntu Linux running on the system. A sample issue message follows:

```
Ubuntu 8.10 tiny tty1
```

This message is followed by a prompt to log in. Enter your username and password in response to the system prompts. If you are using a *terminal* (page 1136) and the screen does not display the **login:** prompt, check whether the terminal is plugged in and turned on, and then press the RETURN key a few times. If **login:** still does not appear, try pressing CONTROL-Q (Xoff). If you are using a *workstation* (page 1141), run ssh (page 634), telnet (page 375), or whatever communications/emulation software you use to log in on the system. Log in.

Next the *shell prompt* (or just *prompt*) appears, indicating you have successfully logged in; it indicates the system is ready for you to give a command. The first shell prompt line may be preceded by a short message called the *message of the day,* or **motd** (page 475), which is stored in the **/etc/motd** file. Ubuntu Linux establishes a prompt of *[user@host: directory]$*, where **user** is your username, *host* is the name of the local system, and **directory** is the name of the directory you are working in. A tilde (~) represents your home directory. For information on how to change the prompt, refer to page 305.

Did you log in last?

security   As you are logging in to a textual environment, after you enter your username and password, the system displays information about the last login on this account, showing when it took place and where it originated. You can use this information to determine whether anyone else has accessed the account since you last used it. If someone has, perhaps an unauthorized user has learned your password and logged on as you. In the interest of maintaining security, advise the system administrator of any circumstances that make you suspicious and change your password.

INTREPID: In addition to the above, Intrepid displays information on disk usage as well as RAM and CPU availability. It also provides connectivity to Landscape (www.canonical.com/projects/landscape), a for-cost service Canonical provides for logging system statistics.

CHANGING YOUR PASSWORD

If someone else assigned you a password, it is a good idea to give yourself a new one. For security reasons none of the passwords you enter is displayed by any utility.

Protect your password

security   Do not allow someone to find out your password: *Do not* put your password in a file that is not encrypted, allow someone to watch you type your password, or give your password to someone you do not know (a system administrator never needs to know your password). You can always write your password down and keep it in a safe, private place.

Choose a password that is difficult to guess

security   Do not use phone numbers, names of pets or kids, birthdays, words from a dictionary (not even a foreign language), and so forth. Do not use permutations of these items or a l33t-speak variation of a word as modern dictionary crackers may also try these permutations.

Differentiate between important and less important passwords

security   It is a good idea to differentiate between important and less important passwords. For example, Web site passwords for blogs or download access are not very important; it is acceptable to use the same password for these types of sites. However, your login, mail server, and bank account Web site passwords are critical: Never use these passwords for an unimportant Web site.

To change your password, select **Main menu: System⇨Preferences⇨About Me** and click **Change Password**. From a command line, give the command **passwd**.

The first item the system asks for is your current (old) password. This password is verified to ensure that an unauthorized user is not trying to alter your password. Then the system requests a new password.

A password should contain a combination of numbers, uppercase and lowercase letters, and punctuation characters and meet the following criteria to be relatively secure:

- Must be at least four characters long (or longer if the system administrator sets it up that way). Seven or eight characters is a good compromise between length and security.

- Should not be a word in a dictionary of any language, no matter how seemingly obscure.

- Should not be the name of a person, place, pet, or other thing that might be discovered easily.

- Should contain at least two letters and one digit or punctuation character.

- Should not be your username, the reverse of your username, or your username shifted by one or more characters.

Only the first item is mandatory. Avoid using control characters (such as CONTROL-H) because they may have a special meaning to the system, making it impossible for you to log in. If you are changing your password, the new password should differ from the old one by at least three characters. Changing the case of a character does not make it count as a different character. Refer to "Keeping the System Secure" on page 602 for more information about choosing a password.

pwgen **helps you pick a password**

security   The pwgen utility (install the pwgen package) generates a list of almost random passwords. With a little imagination, you can pronounce, and therefor remember, some of these passwords.

After you enter your new password, the system asks you to retype it to make sure you did not make a mistake when you entered it the first time. If the new password is the same both times you enter it, your password is changed. If the passwords differ, you made an error in one of them. In this situation the system displays an error message or does not allow you to click the **OK** button. If the password you enter is not long enough, the system displays a message similar to **The password is too short**.

When you successfully change your password, you change the way you log in. If you forget your password, a user running with **root** privileges can change it and tell you the new password.

USING VIRTUAL CONSOLES

When running Linux on a personal computer, you frequently work with the display and keyboard attached to the computer. Using this physical console, you can access as many as 63 *virtual consoles* (also called *virtual terminals*). Some are set up to allow logins; others act as graphical displays. To switch between virtual consoles, hold the CONTROL and ALT keys down and press the function key that corresponds to the console you want to view. For example, CONTROL-ALT-F5 displays the fifth virtual console. This book refers to the console you see when you press CONTROL-ALT-F1 as the *system console*, or just *console*.

By default, six virtual consoles are active and have textual login sessions running. When you want to use both textual and graphical interfaces, you can set up a textual session on one virtual console and a graphical session on another. No matter which virtual console you start a graphical session from, the graphical session runs on the first unused virtual console (number seven by default).

WORKING FROM THE COMMAND LINE

Before the introduction of the graphical user interface (GUI), UNIX and then Linux provided only a command-line (textual) interface (CLI). Today, a CLI is available when you log in from a terminal, a terminal emulator, a textual virtual console, or when you use ssh (page 631) or telnet (insecure, page 375) to log in on a system.

This section introduces the Linux CLI. Chapter 5 describes some of the more important utilities you can use from the command line. Most of the examples in Parts IV and V of this book use the CLI, adding examples of graphical tools where available.

Advantages of the CLI
Although the concept may seem antiquated, the CLI has a place in modern computing. In some cases an administrator may use a command-line tool either because a graphical equivalent does not exist or because the graphical tool is not as powerful or flexible as the textual one. Frequently, on a server system, a graphical interface may not even be installed. The first reason for this omission is that a GUI consumes a lot of system resources; on a server, those resources are better dedicated to the main task of the server. Additionally, security mandates that a server system run as few tasks as possible because each additional task can make the system more vulnerable to attack.

Pseudographical interface
Before the introduction of GUIs, resourceful programmers created textual interfaces that included graphical elements such as boxes, borders outlining rudimentary windows, highlights, and, more recently, color. These textual interfaces, called pseudographical interfaces, bridge the gap between textual and graphical interfaces.

One example of a modern utility that uses a pseudographical interface is the dpkg-reconfigure utility, which reconfigures an installed software package.

CORRECTING MISTAKES

This section explains how to correct typographical and other errors you may make while you are logged in on a textual display. Because the shell and most other utilities do not interpret the command line or other text until after you press RETURN, you can readily correct typing mistakes before you press RETURN.

You can correct typing mistakes in several ways: erase one character at a time, back up a word at a time, or back up to the beginning of the command line in one step.

After you press RETURN, it is too late to correct a mistake: You must either wait for the command to run to completion or abort execution of the program (page 136).

ERASING A CHARACTER

While entering characters from the keyboard, you can back up and erase a mistake by pressing the *erase key* once for each character you want to delete. The erase key backs over as many characters as you wish. It does not, in general, back up past the beginning of the line.

The default erase key is BACKSPACE. If this key does not work, try DELETE or CONTROL-H. If these keys do not work, give the following stty[2] command to set the erase and line kill (see "Deleting a Line") keys to their default values:

```
$ stty ek
```

DELETING A WORD

You can delete a word you entered by pressing CONTROL-W. A *word* is any sequence of characters that does not contain a SPACE or TAB. When you press CONTROL-W, the cursor moves left to the beginning of the current word (as you are entering a word) or the previous word (when you have just entered a SPACE or TAB), removing the word.

CONTROL-Z **suspends a program**

tip   Although it is not a way of correcting a mistake, you may press the suspend key (typically CONTROL-Z) by mistake and wonder what happened (you will see a message containing the word **Stopped**). You have just stopped your job, using job control (page 241). Give the command **fg** to continue your job in the foreground, and you should return to where you were before you pressed the suspend key. For more information refer to "bg: Sends a Job to the Background" on page 293.

DELETING A LINE

Any time before you press RETURN, you can delete the line you are entering by pressing the *(line) kill key*. When you press this key, the cursor moves to the left, erasing characters as it goes, back to the beginning of the line. The default line kill key is CONTROL-U. If this key does not work, try CONTROL-X. If these keys do not work, give the stty command described under "Erasing a Character."

ABORTING EXECUTION

Sometimes you may want to terminate a running program. For example, you may want to stop a program that is performing a lengthy task such as displaying the

---

2. The command stty is an abbreviation for *set teletypewriter*, the first terminal that UNIX was run on. Today stty is commonly thought of as *set terminal*.

contents of a file that is several hundred pages long or copying a file that is not the one you meant to copy.

To terminate a program from a textual display, press the *interrupt key* (CONTROL-C or sometimes DELETE or DEL). When you press this key, the Linux operating system sends a terminal interrupt signal to the program you are running and to the shell. Exactly what effect this signal has depends on the program. Some programs stop execution immediately, some ignore the signal, and some take other actions. When it receives a terminal interrupt signal, the shell displays a prompt and waits for another command.

If these methods do not terminate the program, try stopping the program with the suspend key (typically CONTROL-Z), giving a **jobs** command to verify the number of the job running the program, and using kill to abort the job. The job number is the number within the brackets at the left end of the line that **jobs** displays ([**1**]). The **kill** command (page 438) uses **–TERM** to send a termination signal[3] to the job specified by the job number, which is preceded by a percent sign (**%1**):

```
$ bigjob
^Z
[1]+  Stopped                 bigjob
$ jobs
[1]+  Stopped                 bigjob
$ kill -TERM %1
$ RETURN
[1]+  Killed                  bigjob
```

The **kill** command returns a prompt; press RETURN again to see the confirmation message. For more information refer to "Running a Command in the Background" on page 240.

REPEATING/EDITING COMMAND LINES

To repeat a previous command, press the UP ARROW key. Each time you press this key, the shell displays an earlier command line. To reexecute the displayed command line, press RETURN. Press the DOWN ARROW key to browse through the command lines in the other direction.

The RIGHT and LEFT ARROW keys move the cursor back and forth along the displayed command line. At any point along the command line, you can add characters by typing them. Use the erase key to remove characters from the command line. For information about more complex command-line editing, see page 316.

---

3. When the terminal interrupt signal does not work, use the kill (**–KILL**) signal. A running program cannot ignore a kill signal; it is sure to abort the program (page 438).

optional

CONTROLLING WINDOWS: ADVANCED OPERATIONS

Refer to "Windows" on page 109 for an introduction to working with windows under Ubuntu Linux. This section explores changing the input focus on the workspace, changing the resolution of the display, and understanding more about the window manager.

CHANGING THE INPUT FOCUS

When you type on the keyboard, the window manager (page 139) directs the characters you type somewhere, usually to a window. The *active window* (the window accepting input from the keyboard) is said to have the *input focus*. Depending on how you set up your account, you can use the mouse in one of three ways to change the input focus (you can also use the keyboard; see page 110):

- Click-to-focus (*explicit focus*)—Gives the input focus to a window when you click the window. That window continues to accept input from the keyboard regardless of the location of the mouse pointer. The window loses the focus when you click another window. Although clicking the middle or the right mouse button also activates a window, use only the left mouse button for this purpose; other buttons may have unexpected effects when you use them to activate a window.

- Focus-follows-mouse (*sloppy focus, enter-only*, or *focus-under-mouse*)—Gives the input focus to a window when you move the mouse pointer onto the window. That window maintains the input focus until you move the mouse pointer onto another window, at which point the new window gets the focus. Specifically, when you move the mouse pointer off a window and onto the root window, the window that had the input focus does not lose it.

- Focus-strictly-under-mouse (*enter-exit focus*)—Gives the input focus to a window when you move the mouse pointer onto the window. That window maintains the input focus until you move the mouse pointer off the window, at which point no window has the focus. Specifically, when you move the mouse pointer off a window and onto the root window, the window that had the input focus loses it, and input from the keyboard is lost.

GNOME   The Window Preferences window changes the focus policy. To display this window, select **Main menu: System⇨Preferences⇨Windows** or give the command **gnome-window-properties** from a terminal emulator or Run Application window (ALT-F2). Put a tick in the check box next to **Select windows when the mouse moves over them** to select the focus-follows-mouse policy. When there is no tick in this check box, click-to-focus is in effect. Click **Close**. Focus-strictly-under-mouse is not available from this window.

To determine which window has the input focus, compare the window borders. The border color of the active window is different from the others or, on a monochrome display, is darker. Another indication that a window is active is that the keyboard cursor is a solid rectangle; in windows that are not active, the cursor is an outline of a rectangle.

Use the following tests to determine which keyboard focus method you are using. If you position the mouse pointer in a window and that window does not get the input focus, your window manager is configured to use the click-to-focus method. If the border of the window changes, you are using the focus-follows-mouse or focus-strictly-under-mouse method. To determine which of the latter methods you are using, start typing something, with the mouse pointer positioned on the active window. Then move the mouse pointer over the root window and continue typing. If characters continue to appear within the window, you are using focus-follows-mouse. Otherwise, you are using focus-strictly-under-mouse.

CHANGING THE RESOLUTION OF THE DISPLAY

The X server (the basis for the Linux graphical interface; see page 254) starts at a specific display resolution and *color depth* (page 1101). Although you can change the color depth only when you start an X server, you can change the resolution while the X server is running. The number of resolutions available depends both on the display hardware and on the configuration of the X server. Many users prefer to do most of their work at a higher resolution but might want to switch to a lower resolution for some tasks, such as playing games. You can switch between display resolutions by pressing either CONTROL-ALT-KEYPAD-+ or CONTROL-ALT-KEYPAD--, using the + and – on the keyboard's numeric keypad. You can also use the Monitor Resolution Settings window (**Main menu: System⇨Preferences⇨Screen Resolution**) to change the resolution of the display.

Changing to a lower resolution has the effect of zooming in on the display; as a result, you may no longer be able to view the entire workspace at once. You can scroll the display by pushing the mouse pointer against the edge of the screen.

THE WINDOW MANAGER

A *window manager*—the program that controls the look and feel of the basic GUI—runs under a desktop manager (such as GNOME or KDE) and controls all aspects of the windows in the X Window System environment. The window manager defines the appearance of the windows on the desktop and controls how you operate and position them: open, close, move, resize, minimize, and so on. It may also handle some session management functions, such as how a session is paused, resumed, restarted, or ended (page 102).

Window decorations   A window manager controls *window decorations*—that is, the titlebar and border of a window. Aside from the aesthetic aspects of changing window decorations, you can alter their functionality by modifying the number and placement of buttons on the titlebar.

The window manager takes care of window manipulation so client programs do not need to. This setup is very different from that of many other operating systems, and the way that GNOME deals with window managers is different from how other desktop environments work. Window managers do more than simply manage windows—they provide a useful, good-looking, graphical shell to work from. Their open design allows users to define their own policy down to the fine details.

Theoretically GNOME is not dependent on any particular window manager and can work with any of several window managers. Because of their flexibility, you would not see major parts of the desktop environment change if you were to switch from one window manager to another. A desktop manager collaborates with the window manager to make your work environment intuitive and easy to use. Although the desktop manager does not control window placement, it does get information from the window manager about window placement.

UBUNTU LINUX WINDOW MANAGERS

Metacity and Compiz—the default window managers for Ubuntu GNOME—provide window management and start many components through GNOME panel objects. They also communicate with and facilitate access to other components in the environment. The Visual Effects tab of the Appearance Preferences window (page 101) allows you to switch between Metacity and Compiz.

Using the standard X libraries, programmers have created other window managers, including **blackbox**, **fluxbox**, and **WindowMaker**. You can use synaptic (page 118) to install any of these packages.

USING A WINDOW MANAGER WITHOUT A DESKTOP MANAGER

It is interesting to see exactly where the line that separates the window manager and the desktop manager falls. Toward this end, you can run the Failsafe Terminal from the Login screen: Specify **Options: Select Session**⇨**Failsafe Terminal**, click **Change Session**, and log in. GNOME displays a message; click **OK** to display a clean screen with an undecorated window running xterm. You can give commands from this window to open other windows. Try xeyes, xterm, and xclock. Give the command **exit** to return to the Login screen.

CHAPTER SUMMARY

As with many operating systems, your access to a Linux system is authorized when you log in. You enter your username and password on the Login screen. You can change your password at any time while you are logged in. Choose a password that is difficult to guess and that conforms to the criteria imposed by the utility that changes your password.

The system administrator is responsible for maintaining the system. On a single-user system, you are the system administrator. On a small, multiuser system, you or another user may act as the system administrator, or this job may be shared. On a large, multiuser system or a network of systems, there is frequently a full-time system administrator. When extra privileges are required to perform certain system tasks, the system administrator uses sudo to obtain extra privileges, called **root** privileges. An administrator working with **root** privileges is sometimes referred to as Superuser.

Do not work with **root** privileges as a matter of course. When you have to do something that requires **root** privileges, work with **root** privileges for only as long as absolutely necessary; revert to working as yourself as soon as possible.

Understanding the desktop and its components is essential to getting the most out of the Ubuntu GUI. The panels offer a convenient way to launch applications, either by clicking objects or by using the Main menu. The Main menu is a multilevel menu you can use to customize and maintain the system and to start many common applications. A window is the graphical manifestation of an application. You can control its size, location, and appearance by clicking buttons on the window's titlebar. A terminal emulator allows you to use the Linux command-line interface from a graphical environment. You can use a terminal emulator to launch both textual and graphical programs.

Panels and menus enable you to select an object (which can be just about anything on the system). On a panel, you generally click an object; on a menu, you typically click text in a list.

The GNOME environment provides the casual user, the office worker, the power user, and the programmer/system designer a space to work in and a set of tools to work with. GNOME also provides off-the-shelf productivity and many ways to customize its look, feel, and response.

Nautilus is GNOME's simple, yet powerful file manager. It can create, open, display, move, and copy files and directories as well as execute programs and scripts. One of its most basic and important functions is to create and manage the desktop.

The man utility provides online documentation for system utilities. This utility is helpful both to new Linux users and to experienced users who must often delve into system documentation for information on the finer points of a utility's behavior. The info utility also helps the beginner and the expert alike. It provides a tutorial on its use and documentation on many Linux utilities.

The textual or command-line interface (CLI) continues to have a place in modern computing. For example, sometimes a graphical tool does not exist or may not be as powerful or flexible as its textual counterpart. Security concerns on a server system mandate that the system run as few tasks as possible. Because each additional task can make a server more vulnerable to attack, frequently these systems do not have GUIs installed.

EXERCISES

1. The system displays the following message when you attempt to log in with an incorrect username *or* an incorrect password:

   ```
   Incorrect username or password. Letters must be typed in the
   correct case.
   ```

   a. This message does not indicate whether your username, your password, or both are invalid. Why does it not reveal this information?

   b. Why does the system wait for a couple of seconds after you supply an incorrect username or password?

2. Give three examples of poor password choices. What is wrong with each?

3. Is **fido** an acceptable password? Give several reasons why or why not.

4. What is a context menu? How does a context menu differ from other menus?

5. What appears when you right-click the root window? How can you use this object?

6. How would you swap the effects of the right and left buttons on a mouse? What is the drag and drop threshold? How would you change it?

7. What are the primary functions of the Main menu?

8. What is the input focus? When no window has the input focus, what happens to the letters you type on the keyboard? Which type of input focus would you prefer to work with? Why?

9. What are the functions of a Window Operations menu? How do you display this menu?

10. What is a panel? Name a few objects on the panels and explain what you can use them for. What do the Workspace Switcher applet and the Window List applet do?

11. What are tooltips? How are they useful?

ADVANCED EXERCISES

12. What change does the mouse pointer undergo when you move it to the edge of a window? What happens when you right-click and drag the mouse pointer when it looks like this? Repeat this experiment with the mouse pointer at the corner of a window.

13. Try the experiment described in "Using a Window Manager Without a Desktop Manager" on page 140. What is missing from the screen? Based

only on what you see, describe what a window manager does. How does a desktop manager make it easier to work with a GUI?

14. When the characters you type do not appear on the screen, what might be wrong? How can you fix this problem?

15. What happens when you run vim from the Run Application window without specifying that it be run in a terminal? Where does the output go?

16. The example on page 123 shows that the man pages for passwd appear in sections 1 and 5 of the system manual. Explain how you can use man to determine which sections of the system manual contain a manual page with a given name.

17. How many man pages are in the Devices subsection of the system manual? (*Hint:* Devices is a subsection of Special Files.)

5

THE LINUX UTILITIES

When Linus Torvalds introduced Linux and for a long time there-after, Linux did not have a graphical user interface (GUI): It ran on character-based terminals only, using a command-line interface (CLI), also referred to as a textual interface. All the tools ran from a command line. Today the Linux GUI is important but many people—especially system administrators—run many command-line utilities. Command-line utilities are often faster, more power-ful, or more complete than their GUI counterparts. Sometimes there is no GUI counterpart to a textual utility; some people just prefer the hands-on feeling of the command line.

When you work with a command-line interface, you are working with a shell (Chapters 7, 9, and 27). Before you start working with a shell, it is important that you understand something about the characters that are special to the shell, so this chapter starts with a discussion of special characters. The chapter then describes five basic utilities: ls, cat, rm, less, and hostname. It continues by describing several other file manipulation utilities as well as utili-ties that display who is logged in; that communicate with other users; that print, compress, and decompress files; and that pack and unpack archive files.

SPECIAL CHARACTERS

Special characters, which have a special meaning to the shell, are discussed in "File-name Generation/Pathname Expansion" on page 242. These characters are mentioned here so that you can avoid accidentally using them as regular characters until you understand how the shell interprets them. For example, it is best to avoid using any of the following characters in a filename (even though emacs and some other programs do) because they make the file harder to reference on the command line:

$$\& \; ; \; | \; * \; ? \; ' \; " \; ` \; [\;] \; (\;) \; \$ \; < \; > \; \{ \; \} \; \# \; / \; \backslash \; ! \; \sim$$

Whitespace Although not considered special characters, RETURN, SPACE, and TAB have special meanings to the shell. RETURN usually ends a command line and initiates execution of a command. The SPACE and TAB characters separate elements on the command line and are collectively known as *whitespace* or *blanks.*

Quoting special characters If you need to use a character that has a special meaning to the shell as a regular character, you can *quote* (or *escape*) it. When you quote a special character, you keep the shell from giving it special meaning. The shell treats a quoted special character as a regular character. However, a slash (/) is always a separator in a pathname, even when you quote it.

Backslash To quote a character, precede it with a backslash (\). When two or more special characters appear together, you must precede each with a backslash (for example, you would enter ** as **). You can quote a backslash just as you would quote any other special character—by preceding it with a backslash (\\).

Single quotation marks Another way of quoting special characters is to enclose them between single quotation marks: '**'. You can quote many special and regular characters between a pair of single quotation marks: '**This is a special character: >**'. The regular characters are interpreted as usual, and the shell also interprets the special characters as regular characters.

The only way to quote the erase character (CONTROL-H), the line kill character (CONTROL-U), and other control characters (try CONTROL-M) is by preceding each with a CONTROL-V. Single quotation marks and backslashes do not work. Try the following:

```
$ echo 'xxxxxxCONTROL-U'
$ echo xxxxxxCONTROL-V CONTROL-U
```

optional Although you cannot see the CONTROL-U displayed by the second of the preceding pair of commands, it is there. The following command sends the output of echo (page 157) through a pipe (page 156) to od (octal display, see the od man page) to display CONTROL-U as octal 25 (025):

```
$ echo xxxxxxCONTROL-V CONTROL-U | od -c
0000000   x   x   x   x   x   x 025  \n
0000010
```

The \n is the NEWLINE character that echo sends at the end of its output.

BASIC UTILITIES

One of the important advantages of Linux is that it comes with thousands of utilities that perform myriad functions. You will use utilities whenever you work with Linux, whether you use them directly by name from the command line or indirectly from a menu or icon. The following sections discuss some of the most basic and important utilities; these utilities are available from a CLI. Some of the more important utilities are also available from a GUI; others are available only from a GUI.

Run these utilities from a command line

tip   This chapter describes command-line, or textual, utilities. You can experiment with these utilities from a terminal, a terminal emulator within a GUI (page 111), or a virtual console (page 134).

Folder/directory   The term *directory* is used extensively in the next sections. A directory is a resource that can hold files. On other operating systems, including Windows and Macintosh, and frequently when speaking about a Linux GUI, a directory is referred to as a *folder*. That is a good analogy: A traditional manila folder holds files just as a directory does.

In this chapter you work in your home directory

tip   When you log in on the system, you are working in your *home directory*. In this chapter that is the only directory you use: All the files you create in this chapter are in your home directory. Chapter 6 goes into more detail about directories.

ls: LISTS THE NAMES OF FILES

Using the editor of your choice, create a small file named **practice**. (A tutorial on the vim editor appears on page 172.) After exiting from the editor, you can use the ls (list) utility to display a list of the names of the files in your home directory. In the first command in Figure 5-1, ls lists the name of the **practice** file. (You may also see files that the system or a program created automatically.) Subsequent commands in Figure 5-1 display the contents of the file and remove the file. These commands are described next.

```
$ ls
practice
$ cat practice
This is a small file that I created
with a text editor.
$ rm practice
$ ls
$ cat practice
cat: practice: No such file or directory
$
```

Figure 5-1   Using ls, cat, and rm on the file named **practice**

cat: DISPLAYS A TEXT FILE

The cat utility displays the contents of a text file. The name of the command is derived from *catenate*, which means to join together, one after the other. (Figure 7-8 on page 233 shows how to use cat to string together the contents of three files.)

A convenient way to display the contents of a file to the screen is by giving the command **cat**, followed by a SPACE and the name of the file. Figure 5-1 shows cat displaying the contents of **practice**. This figure shows the difference between the ls and cat utilities: The ls utility displays the *name* of a file, whereas cat displays the *contents* of a file.

rm: DELETES A FILE

The rm (remove) utility deletes a file. Figure 5-1 shows rm deleting the file named **practice**. After rm deletes the file, ls and cat show that **practice** is no longer in the directory. The ls utility does not list its filename, and cat says that no such file exists. Use rm carefully.

A safer way of removing files

tip   You can use the interactive form of rm to make sure that you delete only the file(s) you intend to delete. When you follow rm with the **−i** option (see page 123 for a tip on options) and the name of the file you want to delete, rm displays the name of the file and then waits for you to respond with **y** (yes) before it deletes the file. It does not delete the file if you respond with a string that begins with a character other than **y**.

```
$ rm -i toollist
rm: remove regular file 'toollist'? y
```

Optional: You can create an alias (page 330) for **rm −i** and put it in your startup file (page 190) so that rm always runs in interactive mode.

less Is more: DISPLAY A TEXT FILE ONE SCREEN AT A TIME

Pagers   When you want to view a file that is longer than one screen, you can use either the less utility or the more utility. Each of these utilities pauses after displaying a screen of text; press the SPACE bar to display the next screen of text. Because these utilities show one page at a time, they are called *pagers*. Although less and more are very similar, they have subtle differences. At the end of the file, for example, less displays an **END** message and waits for you to press **q** before returning you to the shell. In contrast, more returns you directly to the shell. While using both utilities you can press **h** to display a Help screen that lists commands you can use while paging through a file. Give the commands **less practice** and **more practice** in place of the **cat** command in Figure 5-1 to see how these commands work. Use the command **less /etc/adduser.conf** instead if you want to experiment with a longer file. Refer to the less and more man pages for more information.

hostname: DISPLAYS THE SYSTEM NAME

The hostname utility displays the name of the system you are working on. Use this utility if you are not sure that you are logged in on the right machine.

```
$ hostname
bravo.example.com
```

WORKING WITH FILES

This section describes utilities that copy, move, print, search through, display, sort, and compare files.

Filename completion

tip After you enter one or more letters of a filename (following a command) on a command line, press TAB and the Bourne Again Shell will complete as much of the filename as it can. When only one filename starts with the characters you entered, the shell completes the filename and places a SPACE after it. You can keep typing or you can press RETURN to execute the command at this point. When the characters you entered do not uniquely identify a filename, the shell completes what it can and waits for more input. When pressing TAB does not change the display, press TAB again to display a list of possible completions. For more information refer to "Pathname Completion" on page 326.

cp: COPIES A FILE

The cp (copy) utility (Figure 5-2) makes a copy of a file. This utility can copy any file, including text and executable program (binary) files. You can use cp to make a backup copy of a file or a copy to experiment with.

The cp command line uses the following syntax to specify source and destination files:

cp source-file destination-file

The *source-file* is the name of the file that cp will copy. The *destination-file* is the name that cp assigns to the resulting (new) copy of the file.

```
$ ls
memo
$ cp memo memo.copy
$ ls
memo memo.copy
```

Figure 5-2   cp copies a file

The cp command line in Figure 5-2 copies the file named **memo** to **memo.copy**. The period is part of the filename—just another character. The initial ls command shows that **memo** is the only file in the directory. After the cp command, a second ls shows two files in the directory, **memo** and **memo.copy**.

Sometimes it is useful to incorporate the date in the name of a copy of a file. The following example includes the date January 30 (**0130**) in the copied file:

```
$ cp memo memo.0130
```

Although it has no significance to Linux, the date can help you find a version of a file you created on a certain date. Including the date can also help you avoid overwriting existing files by providing a unique filename each day. For more information refer to "Filenames" on page 187.

Use scp (page 631) or ftp (page 651) when you need to copy a file from one system to another on a common network.

cp can destroy a file

caution   If the **destination-file** exists *before* you give a cp command, cp overwrites it. Because cp overwrites (and destroys the contents of) an existing **destination-file** without warning, you must take care not to cause cp to overwrite a file that you need. The cp **–i** (interactive) option prompts you before it overwrites a file. See page 123 for a tip on options.

The following example assumes that the file named **orange.2** exists before you give the cp command. The user answers **y** to overwrite the file:

```
$ cp -i orange orange.2
cp: overwrite 'orange.2'? y
```

mv: CHANGES THE NAME OF A FILE

The mv (move) utility can rename a file without making a copy of it. The mv command line specifies an existing file and a new filename using the same syntax as cp:

mv existing-filename new-filename

The command line in Figure 5-3 changes the name of the file **memo** to **memo.0130**. The initial ls command shows that **memo** is the only file in the directory. After you give the mv command, **memo.0130** is the only file in the directory. Compare this result to that of the cp example in Figure 5-2.

The mv utility can be used for more than changing the name of a file. Refer to "mv, cp: Move or Copy Files" on page 198. See the mv info page for more information.

mv can destroy a file

caution   Just as cp can destroy a file, so can mv. Also like cp, mv has a **–i** (interactive) option. See the caution box labeled "cp can destroy a file."

```
$ ls
memo
$ mv memo memo.0130
$ ls
memo.0130
```

Figure 5-3   mv renames a file

lpr: PRINTS A FILE

The lpr (line printer) utility places one or more files in a print queue for printing. Linux provides print queues so that only one job is printed on a given printer at a time. A queue allows several people or jobs to send output simultaneously to a single printer with the expected results. On systems that have access to more than one printer, you can use **lpstat –p** to display a list of available printers. Use the **–P** option to instruct lpr to place the file in the queue for a specific printer—even one that is connected to another system on the network. The following command prints the file named **report**:

```
$ lpr report
```

Because this command does not specify a printer, the output goes to the default printer, which is *the* printer when you have only one printer.

The next command line prints the same file on the printer named **mailroom**:

```
$ lpr -P mailroom report
```

You can see which jobs are in the print queue by giving an **lpstat –o** command or by using the lpq utility:

```
$ lpq
lp is ready and printing
Rank  Owner   Job Files              Total Size
active max      86 (standard input)     954061 bytes
```

In this example, Max has one job that is being printed; no other jobs are in the queue. You can use the job number (86 in this case) with the lprm utility to remove the job from the print queue and stop it from printing:

```
$ lprm 86
```

You can send more than one file to the printer with a single command. The following command line prints three files on the printer named **laser1**:

```
$ lpr -P laser1 05.txt 108.txt 12.txt
```

Refer to Chapter 14 for information on setting up a printer and defining the default printer.

```
$ cat memo
Helen:

In our meeting on June 6 we
discussed the issue of credit.
Have you had any further thoughts
about it?

            Max

$ grep 'credit' memo
discussed the issue of credit.
```

Figure 5-4   grep searches for a string

grep: SEARCHES FOR A STRING

The grep[1] utility searches through one or more files to see whether any contain a specified string of characters. This utility does not change the file it searches but simply displays each line that contains the string.

The grep command in Figure 5-4 searches through the file **memo** for lines that contain the string **credit** and displays the single line that meets this criterion. If **memo** contained such words as **discredit, creditor,** or **accreditation,** grep would have displayed those lines as well because they contain the string it was searching for. The **–w** (words) option causes grep to match only whole words. Although you do not need to enclose the string you are searching for in single quotation marks, doing so allows you to put SPACEs and special characters in the search string.

The grep utility can do much more than search for a simple string in a single file. Refer to the grep info page and Appendix A, "Regular Expressions," for more information.

head: DISPLAYS THE BEGINNING OF A FILE

By default the head utility displays the first ten lines of a file. You can use head to help you remember what a particular file contains. For example, if you have a file named **months** that lists the 12 months of the year in calendar order, one to a line, then head displays **Jan** through **Oct** (Figure 5-5).

This utility can display any number of lines, so you can use it to look at only the first line of a file, at a full screen, or even more. To specify the number of lines

---

1. Originally the name grep was a play on an ed—an original UNIX editor, available on Ubuntu Linux—command: **g/re/p**. In this command **g** stands for global, **re** is a regular expression delimited by slashes, and **p** means print.

```
$ head months
Jan
Feb
Mar
Apr
May
Jun
Jul
Aug
Sep
Oct

$ tail -5 months
Aug
Sep
Oct
Nov
Dec
```

Figure 5-5   head displays the first ten lines of a file

displayed, include a hyphen followed by the number of lines you want head to display. For example, the following command displays only the first line of **months**:

```
$ head -1 months
Jan
```

The head utility can also display parts of a file based on a count of blocks or characters rather than lines. Refer to the head info page for more information.

tail: DISPLAYS THE END OF A FILE

The tail utility is similar to head but by default displays the *last* ten lines of a file. Depending on how you invoke it, this utility can display fewer or more than ten lines, use a count of blocks or characters rather than lines to display parts of a file, and display lines being added to a file that is changing. The tail command in Figure 5-5 displays the last five lines (**Aug** through **Dec**) of the **months** file.

You can monitor lines as they are added to the end of the growing file named **logfile** with the following command:

```
$ tail -f logfile
```

Press the interrupt key (usually CONTROL-C) to stop tail and display the shell prompt. Refer to the tail info page for more information.

```
$ cat days
Monday
Tuesday
Wednesday
Thursday
Friday
Saturday
Sunday

$ sort days
Friday
Monday
Saturday
Sunday
Thursday
Tuesday
Wednesday
```

Figure 5-6   sort displays the lines of a file in order

sort: DISPLAYS A FILE IN ORDER

The sort utility displays the contents of a file in order by lines but does not change the original file.

Figure 5-6 shows cat displaying the file named **days,** which contains the name of each day of the week on a separate line in calendar order. The sort utility then displays the file in alphabetical order.

The sort utility is useful for putting lists in order. The **–u** option generates a sorted list in which each line is unique (no duplicates). The **–n** option puts a list of numbers in numerical order. Refer to the sort info page for more information.

uniq: REMOVES DUPLICATE LINES FROM A FILE

The uniq (unique) utility displays a file, skipping adjacent duplicate lines, but does not change the original file. If a file contains a list of names and has two successive entries for the same person, uniq skips the extra line (Figure 5-7).

If a file is sorted before it is processed by uniq, this utility ensures that no two lines in the file are the same. (Of course, sort can do that all by itself with the **–u** option.) Refer to the uniq info page for more information.

diff: COMPARES TWO FILES

The diff (difference) utility compares two files and displays a list of the differences between them. This utility does not change either file; it is useful when you want to compare two versions of a letter or a report or two versions of the source code for a program.

The diff utility with the **–u** (unified output format) option first displays two lines indicating which of the files you are comparing will be denoted by a plus sign (**+**)

```
$ cat dups
Cathy
Fred
Joe
John
Mary
Mary
Paula

$ uniq dups
Cathy
Fred
Joe
John
Mary
Paula
```

Figure 5-7   uniq removes duplicate lines

and which by a minus sign (–). In Figure 5-8, a minus sign indicates the **colors.1** file; a plus sign indicates the **colors.2** file.

The **diff –u** command breaks long, multiline text into *hunks*. Each hunk is preceded by a line starting and ending with two at signs (**@@**). This hunk identifier indicates the starting line number and the number of lines from each file for this hunk. In Figure 5-8, the hunk covers the section of the **colors.1** file (indicated by a minus sign) from the first line through the sixth line. The **+1,5** then indicates that the hunk covers **colors.2** from the first line through the fifth line.

Following these header lines, **diff –u** displays each line of text with a leading minus sign, a leading plus sign, or a SPACE. A leading minus sign indicates that the line occurs only in the file denoted by the minus sign. A leading plus sign indicates that the line occurs only in the file denoted by the plus sign. A line that begins with a SPACE (neither a plus sign nor a minus sign) occurs in both files in the same location. Refer to the diff info page for more information.

```
$ diff -u colors.1 colors.2
--- colors.1   2008-07-29 16:41:11.000000000 -0700
+++ colors.2   2008-07-29 16:41:17.000000000 -0700
@@ -1,6 +1,5 @@
red
+blue
green
yellow
-pink
-purple
orange
```

Figure 5-8   diff displaying the unified output format

file: IDENTIFIES THE CONTENTS OF A FILE

You can use the file utility to learn about the contents of any file on a Linux system without having to open and examine the file yourself. In the following example, file reports that **letter_e.bz2** contains data that was compressed by the bzip2 utility (page 160):

```
$ file letter_e.bz2
letter_e.bz2: bzip2 compressed data, block size = 900k
```

Next file reports on two more files:

```
$ file memo zach.jpg
memo:     ASCII text
zach.jpg: JPEG image data, ... resolution (DPI), 72 x 72
```

Refer to the file man page for more information.

| (PIPE): COMMUNICATES BETWEEN PROCESSES

Because pipes are integral to the functioning of a Linux system, this chapter introduces them for use in examples. Pipes are covered in detail beginning on page 237.

A *process* is the execution of a command by Linux (page 312). Communication between processes is one of the hallmarks of both UNIX and Linux. A *pipe* (written as a vertical bar, |, on the command line and appearing as a solid or broken vertical line on a keyboard) provides the simplest form of this kind of communication. Simply put, a pipe takes the output of one utility and sends that output as input to another utility. Using UNIX/Linux terminology, a pipe takes standard output of one process and redirects it to become standard input of another process. (For more information refer to "Standard Input and Standard Output" on page 229.) Most of what a process displays on the screen is sent to standard output. If you do not redirect it, this output appears on the screen. Using a pipe, you can redirect the output so that it becomes instead standard input of another utility. For example, a utility such as head can take its input from a file whose name you specify on the command line following the word **head**, or it can take its input from standard input. The following command line sorts the lines of the **months** file (Figure 5-5, page 153) and uses head to display the first four months of the sorted list:

```
$ sort months | head -4
Apr
Aug
Dec
Feb
```

The next command line displays the number of files in a directory. The wc (word count) utility with the **–w** (words) option displays the number of words in its standard input or in a file you specify on the command line:

```
$ ls | wc -w
14
```

You can use a pipe to send output of a program to the printer:

```
$ tail months | lpr
```

FOUR MORE UTILITIES

The echo and date utilities are two of the most frequently used members of the large collection of Linux utilities. The script utility records part of a session in a file, and todos makes a copy of a text file that can be read on either a Windows or a Macintosh machine.

echo: DISPLAYS TEXT

The echo utility copies the characters you type on the command line after **echo** to the screen. Figure 5-9 shows some examples. The last example shows what the shell does with an unquoted asterisk (*) on the command line: It expands the asterisk into a list of filenames in the directory.

The echo utility is a good tool for learning about the shell and other Linux utilities. Some examples on page 243 use echo to illustrate how special characters, such as the asterisk, work. Throughout Chapters 7, 9, and 27, echo helps explain how shell variables work and how you can send messages from shell scripts to the screen. Refer to the echo info page for more information.

optional   You can use echo to create a simple file by redirecting its output to a file:

```
$ echo 'My new file.' > myfile
$ cat myfile
My new file.
```

The greater than (>) sign tells the shell to send the output of echo to the file named **myfile** instead of to the screen. For more information refer to "Redirecting Standard Output" on page 232.

```
$ ls
memo   memo.0714   practice
$ echo Hi
Hi
$ echo This is a sentence.
This is a sentence.
$ echo star: *
star: memo memo.0714 practice
$
```

Figure 5-9   echo copies the command line (but not the word **echo**) to the screen

date: DISPLAYS THE TIME AND DATE

The date utility displays the current date and time:

```
$ date
Thu Jan 24 10:24:00 PST 2008
```

The following example shows how you can choose the format and select the contents of the output of date:

```
$ date +"%A %B %d"
Thursday January 24
```

Refer to the date info page for more information.

script: RECORDS A SHELL SESSION

The script utility records all or part of a login session, including your input and the system's responses. This utility is useful only from character-based devices, such as a terminal or a terminal emulator. It does capture a session with vim; however, because vim uses control characters to position the cursor and display different typefaces, such as bold, the output will be difficult to read and may not be useful. When you cat a file that has captured a vim session, the session quickly passes before your eyes.

By default script captures the session in a file named **typescript**. To specify a different filename, follow the script command with a SPACE and the filename. To append to a file, use the **–a** option after **script** but before the filename; otherwise script overwrites an existing file. Following is a session being recorded by script:

```
$ script
Script started, file is typescript
$ whoami
sam
$ ls -l /bin | head -5
total 5024
-rwxr-xr-x 1 root root    2928 Sep 21 21:42 archdetect
-rwxr-xr-x 1 root root    1054 Apr 26 15:37 autopartition
-rwxr-xr-x 1 root root    7168 Sep 21 19:18 autopartition-loop
-rwxr-xr-x 1 root root  701008 Aug 27 02:41 bash
$ exit
exit
Script done, file is typescript
```

Use the exit command to terminate a script session. You can then view the file you created using cat, less, more, or an editor. Following is the file that was created by the preceding script command:

```
$ cat typescript
Script started on Mon Sep 24 20:54:59 2007
$ whoami
sam
```

```
$ ls -l /bin | head -5
total 5024
-rwxr-xr-x 1 root root     2928 Sep 21 21:42 archdetect
-rwxr-xr-x 1 root root     1054 Apr 26 15:37 autopartition
-rwxr-xr-x 1 root root     7168 Sep 21 19:18 autopartition-loop
-rwxr-xr-x 1 root root   701008 Aug 27 02:41 bash
$ exit
exit

Script done on Mon Sep 24 20:55:29 2007
```

If you will be editing the file with vim, emacs, or another editor, you can use fromdos (below) to eliminate from the **typescript** file the ^M characters that appear at the ends of the lines. Refer to the script man page for more information.

todos: CONVERTS LINUX AND MACINTOSH FILES TO WINDOWS FORMAT

If you want to share a text file you created on a Linux system with someone on a Windows or Macintosh system, you need to convert the file before the person on the other system can read it easily. The todos (to DOS) utility converts a Linux text file so it can be read on a Windows or Macintosh system. This utility is part of the **tofrodos** software package; give the command **sudo aptitude install tofrodos** to install this package. Give the following command to convert a file named **memo.txt** (created with a text editor) to a DOS-format file:

```
$ todos memo.txt
```

You can now email the file as an attachment to someone on a Windows or Macintosh system. Without any options, todos overwrites the original file. Use the **–b** (backup) option to cause todos to make a copy of the file with a **.bak** filename extension before modifying it.

fromdos You can use the fromdos utility to convert Windows or Macintosh files so they can be read on a Linux system:

```
$ fromdos memo.txt
```

See the todos and fromdos man pages for more information.

tr You can also use tr (translate) to change a Windows or Macintosh text file into a Linux text file. In the following example, the **–d** (delete) option causes tr to remove RETURNs (represented by **\r**) as it makes a copy of the file:

```
$ cat memo | tr -d '\r' > memo.txt
```

The greater than (**>**) symbol redirects the standard output of tr to the file named **memo.txt**. For more information refer to "Redirecting Standard Output" on page 232. Converting a file the other way without using todos is not as easy.

COMPRESSING AND ARCHIVING FILES

Large files use a lot of disk space and take longer than smaller files to transfer from one system to another over a network. If you do not need to look at the contents of a large file often, you may want to save it on a CD, DVD, or another medium and remove it from the hard disk. If you have a continuing need for the file, retrieving a copy from another medium may be inconvenient. To reduce the amount of disk space you use without removing the file entirely, you can compress the file without losing any of the information it holds. Similarly a single archive of several files packed into a larger file is easier to manipulate, upload, download, and email than multiple files. You may frequently download compressed, archived files from the Internet. The utilities described in this section compress and decompress files and pack and unpack archives.

bzip2: COMPRESSES A FILE

The bzip2 utility compresses a file by analyzing it and recoding it more efficiently. The new version of the file looks completely different. In fact, because the new file contains many nonprinting characters, you cannot view it directly. The bzip2 utility works particularly well on files that contain a lot of repeated information, such as text and image data, although most image data is already in a compressed format.

The following example shows a boring file. Each of the 8,000 lines of the **letter_e** file contains 72 e's and a NEWLINE character that marks the end of the line. The file occupies more than half a megabyte of disk storage.

```
$ ls -l
-rw-rw-r-- 1 sam sam 584000 Mar  1 22:31 letter_e
```

The –l (long) option causes ls to display more information about a file. Here it shows that **letter_e** is 584,000 bytes long. The **–v** (verbose) option causes bzip2 to report how much it was able to reduce the size of the file. In this case, it shrank the file by 99.99 percent:

```
$ bzip2 -v letter_e
letter_e: 11680.00:1, 0.001 bits/byte, 99.99% saved, 584000 in, 50 out.
$ ls -l
-rw-rw-r-- 1 sam sam 50 Mar  1 22:31 letter_e.bz2
```

.bz2 filename
extension

Now the file is only 50 bytes long. The bzip2 utility also renamed the file, appending **.bz2** to its name. This naming convention reminds you that the file is compressed; you would not want to display or print it, for example, without first decompressing it. The bzip2 utility does not change the modification date associated with the file, even though it completely changes the file's contents.

Keep the original file by using the –k option

tip   The bzip2 utility (and its counterpart, bunzip2) remove the original file when they compress or decompress a file. Use the **–k** (keep) option to keep the original file.

In the following, more realistic example, the file **zach.jpg** contains a computer graphics image:

```
$ ls -l
-rw-r--r--  1 sam sam 33287 Mar  1 22:40 zach.jpg
```

The bzip2 utility can reduce the size of the file by only 28 percent because the image is already in a compressed format:

```
$ bzip2 -v zach.jpg
zach.jpg:  1.391:1,  5.749 bits/byte, 28.13% saved, 33287 in, 23922 out.

$ ls -l
-rw-r--r--  1 sam sam 23922 Mar  1 22:40 zach.jpg.bz2
```

Refer to the bzip2 man page, www.bzip.org, and the *Bzip2 mini-HOWTO* (see page 127 for instructions on obtaining this document) for more information.

bunzip2 AND bzcat: DECOMPRESS A FILE

You can use the bunzip2 utility to restore a file that has been compressed with bzip2:

```
$ bunzip2 letter_e.bz2
$ ls -l
-rw-rw-r--  1 sam sam 584000 Mar  1 22:31 letter_e
$ bunzip2 zach.jpg.bz2
$ ls -l
-rw-r--r--  1 sam sam  33287 Mar  1 22:40 zach.jpg
```

The bzcat utility displays a file that has been compressed with bzip2. The equivalent of cat for **.bz2** files, bzcat decompresses the compressed data and displays the decompressed data. Like cat, bzcat does not change the source file. The pipe in the following example redirects the output of bzcat so instead of being displayed on the screen it becomes the input to head, which displays the first two lines of the file:

```
$ bzcat letter_e.bz2 | head -2
eeeeeeeeeeeeeeeeeeeeeeeeeeeeeeeeeeeeeeeeeeeeeeeeeeeeeeeeeeeeeeeeeeeeeee
eeeeeeeeeeeeeeeeeeeeeeeeeeeeeeeeeeeeeeeeeeeeeeeeeeeeeeeeeeeeeeeeeeeeeee
```

After bzcat is run, the contents of **letter_e.bz** is unchanged; the file is still stored on the disk in compressed form.

bzip2recover   The bzip2recover utility supports limited data recovery from media errors. Give the command **bzip2recover** followed by the name of the compressed, corrupted file from which you want to try to recover data.

gzip: COMPRESSES A FILE

gunzip and zcat   The gzip (GNU zip) utility is older and less efficient than bzip2. Its flags and operation are very similar to those of bzip2. A file compressed by gzip is marked by a **.gz** filename extension. Linux stores manual pages in gzip format to save disk space; likewise, files you download from the Internet are frequently in gzip format. Use gzip, gunzip, and zcat just as you would use bzip2, bunzip2, and bzcat, respectively. Refer to the gzip info page for more information.

compress   The compress utility can also compress files, albeit not as well as gzip. This utility marks a file it has compressed by adding .Z to its name.

gzip **versus** zip

tip   Do not confuse gzip and gunzip with the zip and unzip utilities. These last two are used to pack and unpack zip archives containing several files compressed into a single file that has been imported from or is being exported to a system running Windows. The zip utility constructs a zip archive, whereas unzip unpacks zip archives. The zip and unzip utilities are compatible with PKZIP, a Windows program that compresses and archives files.

tar: PACKS AND UNPACKS ARCHIVES

The tar utility performs many functions. Its name is short for *tape archive,* as its original function was to create and read archive and backup tapes. Today it is used to create a single file (called a *tar file, archive,* or *tarball*) from multiple files or directory hierarchies and to extract files from a tar file. The cpio utility (page 584) performs a similar function.

In the following example, the first ls shows the sizes of the files **g**, **b**, and **d**. Next tar uses the –c (create), –v (verbose), and –f (write to or read from a file) options to create an archive named **all.tar** from these files. Each line of output displays the name of the file tar is appending to the archive it is creating.

The tar utility adds overhead when it creates an archive. The next command shows that the archive file **all.tar** occupies about 9,700 bytes, whereas the sum of the sizes of the three files is about 6,000 bytes. This overhead is more appreciable on smaller files, such as the ones in this example.

```
$ ls -l g b d
-rw-r--r--   1 zach   other  1178 Aug 20 14:16 b
-rw-r--r--   1 zach   zach   3783 Aug 20 14:17 d
-rw-r--r--   1 zach   zach   1302 Aug 20 14:16 g

$ tar -cvf all.tar g b d
g
b
d
$ ls -l all.tar
-rw-r--r--   1 zach        zach          9728 Aug 20 14:17 all.tar

$ tar -tvf all.tar
-rw-r--r-- zach /zach    1302 2007-08-20 14:16 g
-rw-r--r-- zach /other   1178 2007-08-20 14:16 b
-rw-r--r-- zach /zach    3783 2007-08-20 14:17 d
```

The final command in the preceding example uses the –t option to display a table of contents for the archive. Use –x instead of –t to extract files from a tar archive. Omit the –v option if you want tar to do its work silently.[2]

---

2. Although the original UNIX tar did not use a leading hyphen to indicate an option on the command line, the GNU/Linux version accepts hyphens, but works as well without them. This book precedes tar options with a hyphen for consistency with most other utilities.

You can use bzip2, compress, or gzip to compress tar files, making them easier to store and handle. Many files you download from the Internet will already be in one of these formats. Files that have been processed by tar and compressed by bzip2 frequently have a filename extension of **.tar.bz2** or **.tbz**. Those processed by tar and gzip have an extension of **.tar.gz** or **.tz**, whereas files processed by tar and compress use **.tar.Z** as the extension.

You can unpack a tarred and gzipped file in two steps. (Follow the same procedure if the file was compressed by bzip2, but use bunzip2 instead of gunzip.) The next example shows how to unpack the GNU make utility after it has been downloaded (ftp.gnu.org/pub/gnu/make/make-3.80.tar.gz):

```
$ ls -l mak*
-rw-rw-r--  1 sam sam 1211924 Jan 20 11:49 make-3.80.tar.gz

$ gunzip mak*
$ ls -l mak*
-rw-rw-r--  1 sam sam 4823040 Jan 20 11:49 make-3.80.tar

$ tar -xvf mak*
make-3.80/
make-3.80/po/
make-3.80/po/Makefile.in.in
...
make-3.80/tests/run_make_tests.pl
make-3.80/tests/test_driver.pl
```

The first command lists the downloaded tarred and gzipped file: **make-3.80.tar.gz** (about 1.2 megabytes). The asterisk (*****) in the filename matches any characters in any filenames (page 243), so ls displays a list of files whose names begin with **mak**; in this case there is only one. Using an asterisk saves typing and can improve accuracy with long filenames. The gunzip command decompresses the file and yields **make-3.80.tar** (no **.gz** extension), which is about 4.8 megabytes. The tar command creates the **make-3.80** directory in the working directory and unpacks the files into it.

```
$ ls -ld mak*
drwxrwxr-x  8 sam sam    4096 Oct  3  2002 make-3.80
-rw-rw-r--  1 sam sam 4823040 Jan 20 11:49 make-3.80.tar
$ ls -l make-3.80
total 1816
-rw-r--r--  1 sam sam   24687 Oct  3  2002 ABOUT-NLS
-rw-r--r--  1 sam sam    1554 Jul  8  2002 AUTHORS
-rw-r--r--  1 sam sam   18043 Dec 10  1996 COPYING
-rw-r--r--  1 sam sam   32922 Oct  3  2002 ChangeLog
...
-rw-r--r--  1 sam sam   16520 Jan 21  2000 vmsify.c
-rw-r--r--  1 sam sam   16409 Aug  9  2002 vpath.c
drwxrwxr-x  5 sam sam    4096 Oct  3  2002 w32
```

After tar extracts the files from the archive, the working directory contains two files whose names start with **mak: make-3.80.tar** and **make-3.80**. The **–d** (directory) option causes ls to display only file and directory names, not the contents of directories as it normally does. The final ls command shows the files and directories in the **make-3.80** directory. Refer to the tar info page for more information.

tar: the –x option may extract a lot of files

caution   Some tar archives contain many files. To list the files in the archive without unpacking them, run tar with the **–t** option and the name of the tar file. In some cases you may want to create a new directory (mkdir [page 194]), move the tar file into that directory, and expand it there. That way the unpacked files will not mingle with existing files, and no confusion will occur. This strategy also makes it easier to delete the extracted files. Depending on how they were created, some tar files automatically create a new directory and put the files into it; the **–t** option indicates where tar will place the files you extract.

tar: the –x option can overwrite files

caution   The **–x** option to tar overwrites a file that has the same filename as a file you are extracting. Follow the suggestion in the preceding caution box to avoid overwriting files.

---

optional   You can combine the gunzip and tar commands on one command line with a pipe (|), which redirects the output of gunzip so that it becomes the input to tar:

```
$ gunzip -c make-3.80.tar.gz | tar -xvf -
```

The **–c** option causes gunzip to send its output through the pipe instead of creating a file. The final hyphen (–) causes tar to read from standard input. Refer to "Pipes" (page 237) and gzip (page 161) for more information about how this command line works.

A simpler solution is to use the **–z** option to tar. This option causes tar to call gunzip (or gzip when you are creating an archive) directly and simplifies the preceding command line to

```
$ tar -xvzf make-3.80.tar.gz
```

In a similar manner, the **–j** option calls bzip2 or bunzip2.

LOCATING COMMANDS

The whereis and slocate utilities can help you find a command whose name you have forgotten or whose location you do not know. When multiple copies of a utility or program are present, which tells you which copy you will run. The slocate utility searches for files on the local system.

which AND whereis: LOCATE A UTILITY

When you give Linux a command, the shell searches a list of directories for a program with that name and runs the first one it finds. This list of directories is called a *search path*. For information on how to change the search path, refer to "PATH: Where the Shell Looks for Programs" on page 303. If you do not change the search path, the shell searches only a standard set of directories and then stops searching. However, other directories on the system may also contain useful utilities.

which   The which utility locates utilities by displaying the full pathname of the file for the utility. (Chapter 6 contains more information on pathnames and the structure of the

Linux filesystem.) The local system may include several utilities that have the same name. When you type the name of a utility, the shell searches for the utility in your search path and runs the first one it finds. You can find out which copy of the utility the shell will run by using which. In the following example, which reports the location of the tar utility:

```
$ which tar
/bin/tar
```

The which utility can be helpful when a utility seems to be working in unexpected ways. By running which, you may discover that you are running a nonstandard version of a tool or a different one from the one you expected. ("Important Standard Directories and Files" on page 199 provides a list of standard locations for executable files.) For example, if tar is not working properly and you find that you are running **/usr/local/bin/tar** instead of **/bin/tar**, you might suspect that the local version is broken.

whereis   The whereis utility searches for files related to a utility by looking in standard locations instead of using your search path. For example, you can find the locations for files related to tar:

```
$ whereis tar
tar: /bin/tar /usr/include/tar.h /usr/share/man/man1/tar.1.gz
```

In this example whereis finds three references to tar: the tar utility file, a tar header file, and the tar man page.

which **versus** whereis

tip   Given the name of a utility, which looks through the directories in your *search path* (page 303), in order, and locates the utility. If your search path includes more than one utility with the specified name, which displays the name of only the first one (the one you would run).

The whereis utility looks through a list of *standard directories* and works independently of your search path. Use whereis to locate a binary (executable) file, any manual pages, and source code for a program you specify; whereis displays all the files it finds.

which, whereis, **and builtin commands**

caution   Both the which and whereis utilities report only the names for utilities as they are found on the disk; they do not report shell builtins (utilities that are built into a shell; see page 247). When you use whereis to try to find where the echo command (which exists as both a utility program and a shell builtin) is kept, you get the following result:

```
$ whereis echo
echo: /bin/echo /usr/share/man/man1/echo.1.gz
```

The whereis utility does not display the echo builtin. Even the which utility reports the wrong information:

```
$ which echo
/bin/echo
```

Under bash you can use the type builtin (page 959) to determine whether a command is a builtin:

```
$ type echo
echo is a shell builtin
```

slocate: SEARCHES FOR A FILE

The slocate (secure locate) utility searches for files on the local system:

```
$ slocate motd
/usr/share/app-install/icons/xmotd.xpm
/usr/share/app-install/desktop/motd-editor.desktop
/usr/share/app-install/desktop/xmotd.desktop
/usr/share/base-files/motd.md5sums
/usr/share/base-files/motd
...
```

This utility is part of the **slocate** software package; give the command **sudo aptitude install slocate** to install this package. Before you can use slocate the updatedb utility must build or update the slocate database. Typically the database is updated once a day by a cron script (page 588).

If you are not on a network, skip to the vim tutorial

tip   If you are the only user on a system that is not connected to a network, you may want to skip to the tutorial on the vim editor on (page 172). If you are not on a network but are set up to send and receive email, read "Email" on page 171.

OBTAINING USER AND SYSTEM INFORMATION

This section covers utilities that provide information about who is using the system, what those users are doing, and how the system is running.

To find out who is using the local system, you can employ one of several utilities that vary in the details they provide and the options they support. The oldest utility, who, produces a list of users who are logged in on the local system, the device each person is using, and the time each person logged in.

The w and finger utilities show more detail, such as each user's full name and the command line each user is running. You can use the finger utility to retrieve information about users on remote systems if the local system is attached to a network. Table 5-1 on page 169 summarizes the output of these utilities.

who: LISTS USERS ON THE SYSTEM

The who utility displays a list of users who are logged in on the local system. In Figure 5-10 the first column who displays shows that Sam, Max, and Zach are logged in. (Max is logged in from two locations.) The second column shows the device that each user's terminal, workstation, or terminal emulator is connected to. The third column shows the date and time the user logged in. An optional fourth column shows (in parentheses) the name of the system that a remote user logged in from.

```
$ who
sam        tty4          2008-07-25 17:18
max        tty2          2008-07-25 16:42
zach       tty1          2008-07-25 16:39
max        pts/4         2008-07-25 17:27 (coffee)
```

Figure 5-10   who lists who is logged in

The information that who displays is useful when you want to communicate with a user on the local system. When the user is logged in, you can use write (page 170) to establish communication immediately. If who does not list the user or if you do not need to communicate immediately, you can send email to that person (page 171).

If the output of who scrolls off the screen, you can redirect the output through a pipe (l, page 156) so that it becomes the input to less, which displays the output one screen at a time. You can also use a pipe to redirect the output through grep to look for a specific name.

If you need to find out which terminal you are using or what time you logged in, you can use the command **who am i**:

```
$ who am i
max        tty2          2008-07-25 16:42
```

finger: LISTS USERS ON THE SYSTEM

You can use finger to display a list of users who are logged in on the local system. In addition to usernames, finger supplies each user's full name along with information about which device the user's terminal is connected to, how recently the user typed something on the keyboard, when the user logged in, and what contact information is available. If the user has logged in over the network, the name of the remote system is shown as the user's location. For example, in Figure 5-11 Max is logged in from the remote system named **coffee**. The asterisks (✶) in front of the device names in the **Tty** column indicate that the user has blocked messages sent directly to his terminal (refer to "mesg: Denies or Accepts Messages" on page 171).

```
$ finger
Login      Name            Tty      Idle  Login Time   Office ...
max        Max Wild        ✶tty2          Jul 25 16:42
max        Max Wild         pts/4      3  Jul 25 17:27 (coffee)
sam        Sam the Great   ✶tty4      29  Jul 25 17:18
zach       Zach Brill      ✶tty1    1:07  Jul 25 16:39
```

Figure 5-11   finger I: lists who is logged in

```
$ finger max
Login: max                               Name: Max Wild
Directory: /home/max                     Shell: /bin/bash
On since Fri Jul 25 16:42 (PDT) on tty2 (messages off)
On since Fri Jul 25 17:27 (PDT) on pts/4 from coffee
   3 minutes 7 seconds idle
New mail received Fri Jul 25 17:16 2008 (PDT)
     Unread since Fri Jul 25 16:44 2008 (PDT)
Plan:
I will be at a conference in Hawaii all next week.
If you need to see me, contact Zach Brill, x1693.
```

Figure 5-12 finger II: lists details about one user

finger **can be a security risk**

security On systems where security is a concern, the system administrator may disable finger. This utility can reveal information that can help a malicious user break into a system.

You can also use finger to learn more about an individual by specifying a username on the command line. In Figure 5-12, finger displays detailed information about Max. Max is logged in and actively using one of his terminals (**tty2**); he has not used his other terminal (**pts/4**) for 3 minutes and 7 seconds. You also learn from finger that if you want to set up a meeting with Max, you should contact Zach at extension 1693.

.plan and .project Most of the information in Figure 5-12 was collected by finger from system files. The information shown after the heading **Plan:**, however, was supplied by Max. The finger utility searched for a file named **.plan** in Max's home directory and displayed its contents.

(Filenames that begin with a period, such as **.plan**, are not normally listed by ls and are called hidden filenames [page 190].) You may find it helpful to create a **.plan** file for yourself; it can contain any information you choose, such as your schedule, interests, phone number, or address. In a similar manner, finger displays the contents of the **.project** and **.pgpkey** files in your home directory. If Max had not been logged in, finger would have reported only his user information, the last time he logged in, the last time he read his email, and his plan.

```
$ w
 17:47:35 up 1 day,  8:10,  6 users,  load average: 0.34, 0.23, 0.26
 USER     TTY      FROM           LOGIN@   IDLE   JCPU    PCPU WHAT
 sam      tty4     -              17:18   29:14m  0.20s  0.00s vi memo
 max      tty2     -              16:42    0.00s  0.20s  0.07s w
 zach     tty1     -              16:39    1:07   0.05s  0.00s run_bdgt
 max      pts/4    coffee         17:27    3:10m  0.24s  0.24s -bash
```

Figure 5-13 The w utility

You can also use finger to display a user's username. For example, on a system with a user named Helen Simpson, you might know that Helen's last name is Simpson but might not guess her username is **hls**. The finger utility, which is not case sensitive, can search for information on Helen using her first or last name. The following commands find the information you seek as well as information on other users whose names are Helen or Simpson:

```
$ finger HELEN
Login: hls                                    Name: Helen Simpson.
...
$ finger simpson
Login: hls                                    Name: Helen Simpson.
...
```

See page 373 for information about using finger over a network.

w: LISTS USERS ON THE SYSTEM

The w utility displays a list of the users who are logged in. As discussed in the section on who, the information that w displays is useful when you want to communicate with someone at your installation.

The first column in Figure 5-13 shows that Max, Zach, and Sam are logged in. The second column shows the name of the device file each user's terminal is connected to. The third column shows the system that a remote user is logged in from. The fourth column shows the time each user logged in. The fifth column indicates how long each user has been idle (how much time has elapsed since the user pressed a key on the keyboard). The next two columns identify how much computer processor time each user has used during this login session and on the task that user is running. The last column shows the command each user is running.

The first line that the w utility displays includes the time of day, the period of time the computer has been running (in days, hours, and minutes), the number of users logged in, and the load average (how busy the system is). The three load average numbers represent the number of jobs waiting to run, averaged over the past 1, 5, and 15 minutes. Use the uptime utility to display just this line. Table 5-1 compares the w, who, and finger utilities.

Table 5-1 Comparison of w, who, and finger

Information displayed	w	who	finger
Username	X	X	X
Terminal-line identification (tty)	X	X	X
Login time (and day for old logins)	X		
Login date and time		X	X
Idle time	X		X

Table 5-1   Comparison of w, who, and finger (continued)

Information displayed	w	who	finger
Program the user is executing	X		
Location the user logged in from			X
CPU time used	X		
Full name (or other information from **/etc/passwd**)			X
User-supplied vanity information			X
System uptime and load average	X		

COMMUNICATING WITH OTHER USERS

You can use the utilities discussed in this section to exchange messages and files with other users either interactively or through email.

write: SENDS A MESSAGE

The write utility sends a message to another user who is logged in. When you and another user use write to send messages to each other, you establish two-way communication. Initially a write command (Figure 5-14) displays a banner on the other user's terminal, saying that you are about to send a message.

The syntax of a write command line is

write *username [terminal]*

The *username* is the username of the user you want to communicate with. The *terminal* is an optional device name that is useful if the user is logged in more than once. You can display the usernames and device names of all users who are logged in on the local system by using who, w, or finger.

To establish two-way communication with another user, you and the other user must each execute write, specifying the other's username as the *username.* The write utility then copies text, line by line, from one keyboard/display to the other (Figure 5-15). Sometimes it helps to establish a convention, such as typing o (for "over") when you are ready for the other person to type and typing oo (for "over and out") when you are ready to end the conversation. When you want to stop communicating with the other user, press CONTROL-D at the beginning of a line. Pressing CONTROL-D tells write to

```
$ write max
Hi Max, are you there? o
```

Figure 5-14   The write utility I

```
$ write max
Hi Max, are you there? o

Message from max@bravo.example.com on pts/0 at 16:23 ...
Yes Zach, I'm here. o
```

Figure 5-15   The write utility II

quit, displays **EOF** (end of file) on the other user's terminal, and returns you to the shell. The other user must do the same.

If the **Message from** banner appears on your screen and obscures something you are working on, press CONTROL-L or CONTROL-R to refresh the screen and remove the banner. Then you can clean up, exit from your work, and respond to the person who is writing to you. You have to remember who is writing to you, however, because the banner will no longer appear on the screen.

mesg: DENIES OR ACCEPTS MESSAGES

By default, messages to your screen are blocked. Give the following mesg command to allow other users to send you messages:

```
$ mesg y
```

If Max had given this command before Zach tried to send him a message, Zach would have seen the following message:

```
$ write max
write: max has messages disabled
```

You can block messages again by entering **mesg n**. Give the command **mesg** by itself to display **is y** (for "yes, messages are allowed") or **is n** (for "no, messages are not allowed").

If you have messages blocked and you write to another user, write displays the following message because, even if you are allowed to write to another user, the user will not be able to respond to you:

```
$ write max
write: write: you have write permission turned off.
```

EMAIL

Email enables you to communicate with users on the local system and, if the installation is part of a network, with other users on the network. If you are connected to the Internet, you can communicate electronically with users around the world.

Email utilities differ from write in that email utilities can send a message when the recipient is not logged in. In this case the email is stored until the recipient reads it. These utilities can also send the same message to more than one user at a time.

Many email programs are available for Linux, including the original character-based mail program, Mozilla/Thunderbird, pine, mail through emacs, KMail, and evolution. Another popular graphical email program is sylpheed (sylpheed.good-day.net).

Two programs are available that can make any email program easier to use and more secure. The procmail program (www.procmail.org) creates and maintains email servers and mailing lists; preprocesses email by sorting it into appropriate files and directories; starts various programs depending on the characteristics of incoming email; forwards email; and so on. The GNU Privacy Guard (GPG or GNUpg, page 1067) encrypts and decrypts email and makes it almost impossible for an unauthorized person to read.

Refer to Chapter 20 for more information on setting email clients and servers.

Network addresses   If the local system is part of a LAN, you can generally send email to and receive email from users on other systems on the LAN by using their usernames. Someone sending Max email on the Internet would need to specify his *domain name* (page 1106) along with his username. Use this address to send email to the author of this book: **mgs@sobell.com**.

TUTORIAL: USING vim TO CREATE AND EDIT A FILE

This section explains how to start vim, enter text, move the cursor, correct text, save the file to the disk, and exit from vim. The tutorial discusses three of the modes of operation of vim and explains how to switch from one mode to another.

vimtutor   In addition to working with this tutorial, you may want to try vim's instructional program, named vimtutor. Give its name as a command to run it.

vimtutor and vim help files are not installed by default

tip   To run vimtutor and to get help as described on page 176, you must install the **vim-runtime** package; give the command **sudo aptitude install vim-runtime** to install this package.

Specifying a terminal   Because vim takes advantage of features that are specific to various kinds of terminals, you must tell it what type of terminal or terminal emulator you are using. On many systems, and usually when you work on a terminal emulator, your terminal type is set automatically. If you need to specify your terminal type explicitly, refer to "Specifying a Terminal" on page 1060.

STARTING vim

Start vim with the following command to create and edit a file named **practice**:

```
$ vim practice
```

When you press RETURN, the command line disappears, and the screen looks similar to the one shown in Figure 5-16.

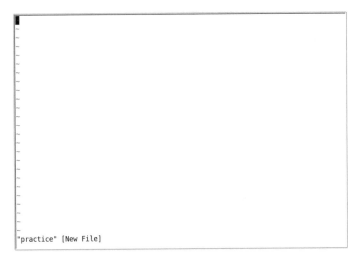

Figure 5-16   Starting vim

The tildes (~) at the left of the screen indicate that the file is empty. They disappear as you add lines of text to the file. If your screen looks like a distorted version of the one shown in Figure 5-16, your terminal type is probably not set correctly.

The vi command runs vim

tip   On Ubuntu Linux systems the command **vi** runs vim in vi-compatible mode (page 179).

If you start vim with a terminal type that is not in the **terminfo** database, vim displays an error message and the terminal type defaults to **ansi**, which works on many terminals. In the following example, the user mistyped **vt100** and set the terminal type to **vg100**:

```
E558: Terminal entry not found in terminfo
'vg100' not known. Available builtin terminals are:
    builtin_ansi
    builtin_xterm
    builtin_iris-ansi
    builtin_dumb
defaulting to 'ansi'
```

Emergency exit   To reset the terminal type, press ESCAPE and then give the following command to exit from vim and display the shell prompt:

```
:q!
```

When you enter the colon (:), vim moves the cursor to the bottom line of the screen. The characters **q!** tell vim to quit without saving your work. (You will not ordinarily exit from vim this way because you typically want to save your work.) You must

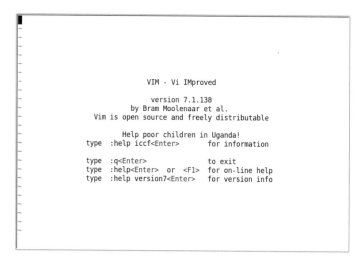

```
                    VIM - Vi IMproved

                       version 7.1.138
                     by Bram Moolenaar et al.
              Vim is open source and freely distributable

                    Help poor children in Uganda!
           type  :help iccf<Enter>         for information

           type  :q<Enter>                 to exit
           type  :help<Enter>  or  <F1> for on-line help
           type  :help version7<Enter>     for version info
```

Figure 5-17   Starting vim without a filename

press RETURN after you give this command. Once you get the shell prompt back, refer to "Specifying a Terminal" on page 1060, and then start vim again.

If you start this editor without a filename, vim assumes that you are a novice and tells you how to get started (Figure 5-17).

The **practice** file is new so it does not contain any text. The vim editor displays a message similar to the one shown in Figure 5-16 on the status (bottom) line of the terminal to indicate that you are creating and editing a new file. When you edit an existing file, vim displays the first few lines of the file and gives status information about the file on the status line.

COMMAND AND INPUT MODES

Two of vim's modes of operation are *Command mode* (also called *Normal mode*) and *Input mode* (Figure 5-18). While vim is in Command mode, you can give vim commands. For example, you can delete text or exit from vim. You can also command vim to enter Input mode. In Input mode, vim accepts anything you enter as text and displays it on the screen. Press ESCAPE to return vim to Command mode. By default the vim editor keeps you informed about which mode it is in: It displays **INSERT** at the lower-left corner of the screen while it is in Insert mode.

The following command causes vim to display line numbers next to the text you are editing:

:set number RETURN

Last Line mode   The colon (:) in the preceding command puts vim into another mode, *Last Line mode*. While in this mode, vim keeps the cursor on the bottom line of the screen. When you finish entering the command by pressing RETURN, vim restores the cursor to its place in the text. Give the command **:set nonumber** RETURN to turn off line numbers.

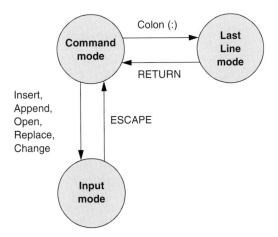

Figure 5-18   Modes in vim

vim is case
sensitive
When you give vim a command, remember that the editor is case sensitive. In other words, vim interprets the same letter as two different commands, depending on whether you enter an uppercase or lowercase character. Beware of the CAPS LOCK (SHIFTLOCK) key. If you set this key to enter uppercase text while you are in Input mode and then exit to Command mode, vim interprets your commands as uppercase letters. It can be confusing when this happens because vim does not appear to be executing the commands you are entering.

ENTERING TEXT

i/a (Input mode)
When you start vim, you must put it in Input mode before you can enter text. To put vim in Input mode, press the **i** (insert before cursor) key or the **a** (append after cursor) key.

If you are not sure whether vim is in Input mode, press the ESCAPE key; vim returns to Command mode if it was in Input mode or beeps, flashes, or does nothing if it is already in Command mode. You can put vim back in Input mode by pressing the **i** or **a** key again.

While vim is in Input mode, you can enter text by typing on the keyboard. If the text does not appear on the screen as you type, vim is not in Input mode.

To continue with this tutorial, enter the sample paragraph shown in Figure 5-19 (next page), pressing the RETURN key at the end of each line. If you do not press RETURN before the cursor reaches the right side of the screen or window, vim wraps the text so that it appears to start a new line. Physical lines will not correspond to programmatic (logical) lines in this situation, so editing will be more difficult. While you are using vim, you can always correct any typing mistakes you make. If you notice a mistake on the line you are entering, you can correct it before you continue (page 176). You can correct other mistakes later. When you finish entering the paragraph, press ESCAPE to return vim to Command mode.

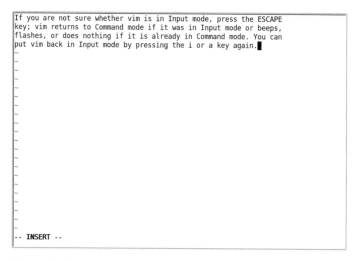

Figure 5-19 Entering text with vim

GETTING HELP

You must have the **vim-runtime** package installed to use vim's help system; see the tip on page 172.

To get help while you are using vim, give the command **:help** [*feature*] followed by RETURN (you must be in Command mode when you give this command). The colon moves the cursor to the last line of the screen. If you type **:help**, vim displays an introduction to vim Help (Figure 5-20). Each dark band near the bottom of the screen names the file that is displayed above it. (Each area of the screen that displays a file, such as the two areas shown in Figure 5-20, is a vim "window.") The **help.txt** file occupies most of the screen (the upper window) in Figure 5-20. The file that is being edited (**practice**) occupies a few lines in the lower portion of the screen (the lower window).

Read through the introduction to Help by scrolling the text as you read. Press **j** or the DOWN ARROW key to move the cursor down one line at a time; press CONTROL-D or CONTROL-U to scroll the cursor down or up half a window at a time. Give the command **:q** to close the Help window.

You can display information about the insert commands by giving the command **:help insert** while vim is in Command mode (Figure 5-21).

CORRECTING TEXT AS YOU INSERT IT

The keys that back up and correct a shell command line serve the same functions when vim is in Input mode. These keys include the erase, line kill, and word kill keys (usually CONTROL-H, CONTROL-U, and CONTROL-W, respectively). Although vim may not remove deleted text from the screen as you back up over it using one of these keys, the editor does remove it when you type over the text or press RETURN.

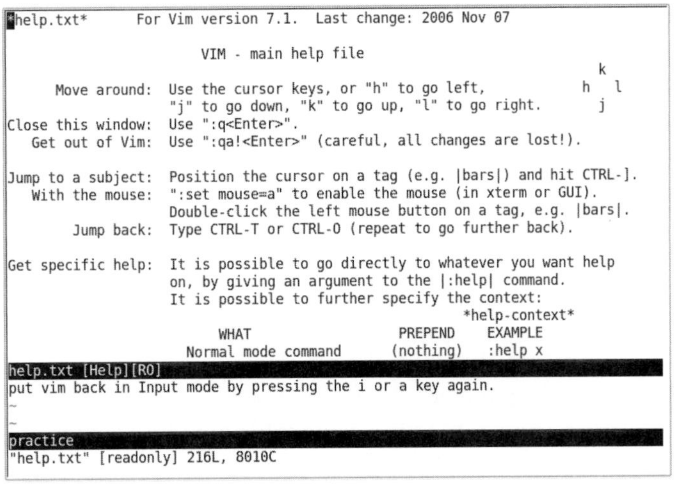

```
help.txt*      For Vim version 7.1.  Last change: 2006 Nov 07

                    VIM - main help file
                                                              k
       Move around:  Use the cursor keys, or "h" to go left,    h   l
                     "j" to go down, "k" to go up, "l" to go right.  j
Close this window:  Use ":q<Enter>".
  Get out of Vim:  Use ":qa!<Enter>" (careful, all changes are lost!).

Jump to a subject:  Position the cursor on a tag (e.g. |bars|) and hit CTRL-].
  With the mouse:  ":set mouse=a" to enable the mouse (in xterm or GUI).
                     Double-click the left mouse button on a tag, e.g. |bars|.
        Jump back:  Type CTRL-T or CTRL-O (repeat to go further back).

Get specific help:  It is possible to go directly to whatever you want help
                     on, by giving an argument to the |:help| command.
                     It is possible to further specify the context:
                                                       *help-context*
                          WHAT             PREPEND    EXAMPLE
                     Normal mode command   (nothing)  :help x
help.txt [Help][RO]
put vim back in Input mode by pressing the i or a key again.
~

practice
"help.txt" [readonly] 216L, 8010C
```

Figure 5-20   The main vim Help screen

MOVING THE CURSOR

You need to be able to move the cursor on the screen so that you can delete, insert, and correct text. While vim is in Command mode, you can use the RETURN key, the SPACE bar, and the ARROW keys to move the cursor. If you prefer to keep your hand closer to the center of the keyboard, if your terminal does not have ARROW keys, or if the emulator you are using does not support them, you can use the **h**, **j**, **k**, and **l** (lowercase "l") keys to move the cursor left, down, up, and right, respectively.

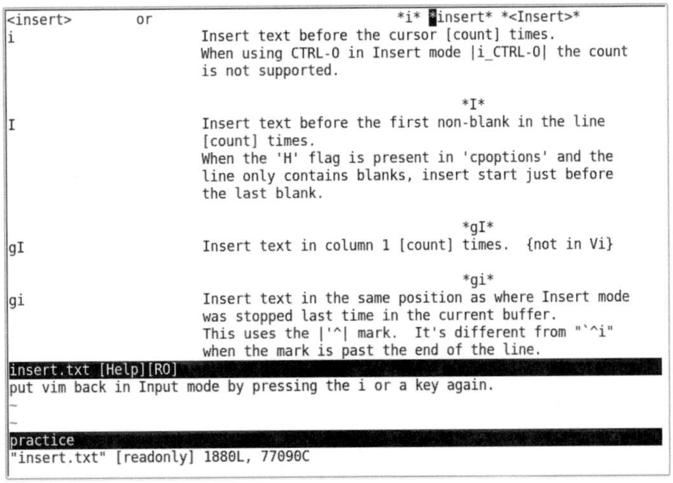

```
<insert>      or                           *i* insert* *<Insert>*
i                     Insert text before the cursor [count] times.
                      When using CTRL-O in Insert mode |i_CTRL-O| the count
                      is not supported.

                                                 *I*
I                     Insert text before the first non-blank in the line
                      [count] times.
                      When the 'H' flag is present in 'cpoptions' and the
                      line only contains blanks, insert start just before
                      the last blank.

                                                 *gI*
gI                    Insert text in column 1 [count] times.  {not in Vi}

                                                 *gi*
gi                    Insert text in the same position as where Insert mode
                      was stopped last time in the current buffer.
                      This uses the |'^| mark.  It's different from "`^i"
                      when the mark is past the end of the line.
insert.txt [Help][RO]
put vim back in Input mode by pressing the i or a key again.
~

practice
"insert.txt" [readonly] 1880L, 77090C
```

Figure 5-21   Help with insert commands

DELETING TEXT

x (Delete character)
dw (Delete word)
dd (Delete line)

You can delete a single character by moving the cursor until it is over the character you want to delete and then giving the command **x**. You can delete a word by positioning the cursor on the first letter of the word and then giving the command **dw** (Delete word). You can delete a line of text by moving the cursor until it is anywhere on the line and then giving the command **dd**.

UNDOING MISTAKES

u (Undo)

If you delete a character, line, or word by mistake or give any command you want to reverse, give the command **u** (Undo) immediately after the command you want to undo. The vim editor will restore the text to the way it was before you gave the last command. If you give the **u** command again, vim will undo the command you gave before the one it just undid. You can use this technique to back up over many of your actions. With the **compatible** parameter (page 179) set, however, vim can undo only the most recent change.

:redo (Redo)

If you undo a command you did not mean to undo, give a Redo command: CONTROL-R or **:redo** (followed by a RETURN). The vim editor will redo the undone command. As with the Undo command, you can give the Redo command many times in a row.

ENTERING ADDITIONAL TEXT

i (Insert)
a (Append)

When you want to insert new text within existing text, move the cursor so it is on the character that follows the new text you plan to enter. Then give the **i** (Insert) command to put vim in Input mode, enter the new text, and press ESCAPE to return vim to Command mode. Alternatively, you can position the cursor on the character that precedes the new text and use the **a** (Append) command.

o/O (Open)

To enter one or more lines, position the cursor on the line above where you want the new text to go. Give the command **o** (Open). The vim editor opens a blank line below the line the cursor was on, puts the cursor on the new, empty line, and goes into Input mode. Enter the new text, ending each line with a RETURN. When you are finished entering text, press ESCAPE to return vim to Command mode. The **O** command works in the same way **o** works, except it opens a blank line *above* the line the cursor is on.

CORRECTING TEXT

To correct text, use **dd**, **dw**, or **x** to remove the incorrect text. Then use **i**, **a**, **o**, or **O** to insert the correct text.

For example, to change the word **pressing** to **hitting** in Figure 5-19 on page 176, you might use the ARROW keys to move the cursor until it is on top of the **p** in **pressing**. Then give the command **dw** to delete the word **pressing**. Put vim in Input mode by giving an **i** command, enter the word **hitting** followed by a SPACE, and press ESCAPE. The word is changed and vim is in Command mode, waiting for another command. A shorthand for the two commands **dw** followed by the **i** command is **cw** (Change word). The command **cw** puts vim into Input mode.

Page breaks for the printer

tip   CONTROL-L tells the printer to skip to the top of the next page. You can enter this character anywhere in a document by pressing CONTROL-L while you are in Input mode. If **^L** does not appear, press CONTROL-V before CONTROL-L.

ENDING THE EDITING SESSION

While you are editing, vim keeps the edited text in an area named the *Work buffer*. When you finish editing, you must write out the contents of the Work buffer to a disk file so that the edited text is saved and available when you next want it.

Make sure vim is in Command mode, and use the **ZZ** command (you must use uppercase **Z**s) to write your newly entered text to the disk and end the editing session. After you give the **ZZ** command, vim returns control to the shell. You can exit with **:q!** if you do not want to save your work.

Do not confuse ZZ with CONTROL-Z

caution   When you exit from vim with **ZZ**, make sure that you type **ZZ** and not CONTROL-Z (typically the suspend key). When you press CONTROL-Z, vim disappears from your screen, almost as though you had exited from it. In fact, vim will continue running in the background with your work unsaved. Refer to "Job Control" on page 291. If you try to start editing the same file with a new **vim** command, vim displays a message about a swap file.

THE compatible PARAMETER

The **compatible** parameter makes vim more compatible with vi. By default this parameter is not set. From the command line use the **–C** option to set the **compatible** parameter and use the **–N** option to unset it. To get started with vim you can ignore this parameter.

Setting the **compatible** parameter changes many aspects of how vim works. For example, when the **compatible** parameter is set, the Undo command (page 178) can undo only your most recent change; in contrast, with the **compatible** parameter unset, you can call Undo repeatedly to undo many changes. To obtain more details on the **compatible** parameter, give the command **:help compatible** RETURN. To display a complete list of vim's differences from the original vi, use **:help vi-diff** RETURN. See page 176 for a discussion of the **help** command.

CHAPTER SUMMARY

The utilities introduced in this chapter are a small but powerful subset of the many utilities available on an Ubuntu Linux system. Because you will use them frequently and because they are integral to the following chapters, it is important that you become comfortable using them.

The utilities listed in Table 5-2 manipulate, display, compare, and print files.

Table 5-2   File utilities

Utility	Function
cp	Copies one or more files (page 149)
diff	Displays the differences between two files (page 154)
file	Displays information about the contents of a file (page 156)
grep	Searches file(s) for a string (page 152)
head	Displays the lines at the beginning of a file (page 152)
lpq	Displays a list of jobs in the print queue (page 151)
lpr	Places file(s) in the print queue (page 151)
lprm	Removes a job from the print queue (page 151)
mv	Renames a file or moves file(s) to another directory (page 150)
sort	Puts a file in order by lines (page 154)
tail	Displays the lines at the end of a file (page 153)
uniq	Displays the contents of a file, skipping adjacent duplicate lines (page 154)

To reduce the amount of disk space a file occupies, you can compress it with the bzip2 utility. Compression works especially well on files that contain patterns, as do most text files, but reduces the size of almost all files. The inverse of bzip2—bunzip2—restores a file to its original, decompressed form. Table 5-3 lists utilities that compress and decompress files. The bzip2 utility is the most efficient of these.

Table 5-3   (De)compression utilities

Utility	Function
bunzip2	Returns a file compressed with bzip2 to its original size and format (page 161)
bzcat	Displays a file compressed with bzip2 (page 161)
bzip2	Compresses a file (page 160)
compress	Compresses a file (not as well as bzip2 or gzip; page 162)
gunzip	Returns a file compressed with gzip or compress to its original size and format (page 161)
gzip	Compresses a file (not as well as bzip2; page 161)
zcat	Displays a file compressed with gzip (page 161)

An archive is a file, frequently compressed, that contains a group of files. The tar utility (Table 5-4) packs and unpacks archives. The filename extensions **.tar.bz2,**

.tar.gz, and **.tgz** identify compressed tar archive files and are often seen on software packages obtained over the Internet.

Table 5-4   Archive utility

Utility	Function
tar	Creates or extracts files from an archive file (page 162)

The utilities listed in Table 5-5 determine the location of a utility on the local system. For example, they can display the pathname of a utility or a list of C++ compilers available on the local system.

Table 5-5   Location utilities

Utility	Function
locate	Searches for files on the local system (page 166)
whereis	Displays the full pathnames of a utility, source code, or man page (page 164)
which	Displays the full pathname of a command you can run (page 164)

Table 5-6 lists utilities that display information about other users. You can easily learn a user's full name, the user's login status, the login shell of the user, and other items of information maintained by the system.

Table 5-6   User and system information utilities

Utility	Function
finger	Displays detailed information about users, including their full names (page 167)
hostname	Displays the name of the local system (page 149)
w	Displays detailed information about users who are logged in on the local system (page 169)
who	Displays information about users who are logged in on the local system (page 166)

The utilities shown in Table 5-7 can help you stay in touch with other users on the local network.

Table 5-7   User communication utilities

Utility	Function
mesg	Permits or denies messages sent by write (page 171)
write	Sends a message to another user who is logged in (page 170)

Table 5-8 lists miscellaneous utilities.

Table 5-8   Miscellaneous utilities

Utility	Function
date	Displays the current date and time (page 158)
echo	Copies its *arguments* (page 1095) to the screen (page 157)
vim	Edits text (page 172)

EXERCISES

1. Which commands can you use to determine who is logged in on a specific terminal?

2. How can you keep other users from using write to communicate with you? Why would you want to?

3. What happens when you give the following commands if the file named **done** already exists?

   ```
   $ cp to_do done
   $ mv to_do done
   ```

4. How can you find out which utilities are available on your system for editing files? Which utilities are available for editing on your system?

5. How can you find the phone number for **Ace Electronics** in a file named **phone** that contains a list of names and phone numbers? Which command can you use to display the entire file in alphabetical order? How can you display the file without any adjacent duplicate lines? How can you display the file without any duplicate lines?

6. What happens when you use diff to compare two binary files that are not identical? (You can use gzip to create the binary files.) Explain why the diff output for binary files is different from the diff output for ASCII files.

7. Create a **.plan** file in your home directory. Does finger display the contents of your **.plan** file?

8. What is the result of giving the which utility the name of a command that resides in a directory that is *not* in your search path?

9. Are any of the utilities discussed in this chapter located in more than one directory on the local system? If so, which ones?

10. Experiment by calling the file utility with the names of files in **/usr/bin**. How many different types of files are there?

11. Which command can you use to look at the first few lines of a file named **status.report**? Which command can you use to look at the end of the file?

ADVANCED EXERCISES

12. Re-create the **colors.1** and **colors.2** files used in Figure 5-8 on page 155. Test your files by running **diff –u** on them. Do you get the same results as in the figure?

13. Try giving these two commands:

    ```
    $ echo cat
    $ cat echo
    ```

    Explain the differences between the output of each command.

14. Repeat exercise 5 using the file **phone.gz**, a compressed version of the list of names and phone numbers. Consider more than one approach to answer each question, and explain how you made your choices.

15. Find existing files or create files that

    a. gzip compresses by more than 80 percent.

    b. gzip compresses by less than 10 percent.

    c. Get larger when compressed with gzip.

    d. Use **ls –l** to determine the sizes of the files in question. Can you characterize the files in a, b, and c?

16. Older email programs were not able to handle binary files. Suppose that you are emailing a file that has been compressed with gzip, which produces a binary file, and the recipient is using an old email program. Refer to the man page on uuencode, which converts a binary file to ASCII. Learn about the utility and how to use it.

    a. Convert a compressed file to ASCII using uuencode. Is the encoded file larger or smaller than the compressed file? Explain. (If uuencode is not on the local system, you can install it using aptitude [page 501]; it is part of the **sharutils** package.)

    b. Would it ever make sense to use uuencode on a file before compressing it? Explain.

6

THE LINUX FILESYSTEM

A *filesystem* is a set of *data structures* (page 1104) that usually resides on part of a disk and that holds directories of files. Filesystems store user and system data that are the basis of users' work on the system and the system's existence. This chapter discusses the organization and terminology of the Linux filesystem, defines ordinary and directory files, and explains the rules for naming them. It also shows how to create and delete directories, move through the filesystem, and use absolute and relative pathnames to access files in various directories. It includes a discussion of important files and directories as well as file access permissions and Access Control Lists (ACLs), which allow you to share selected files with other users. It concludes with a discussion of hard and symbolic links, which can make a single file appear in more than one directory.

In addition to reading this chapter, you may want to refer to the df info page and to the fsck, mkfs, and tune2fs man pages for more information on filesystems.

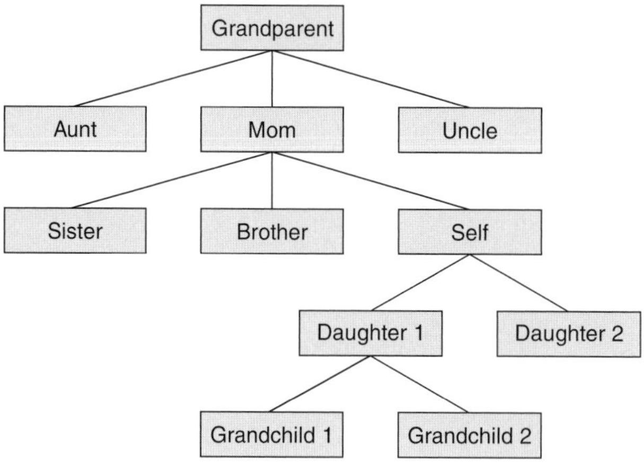

Figure 6-1   A family tree

THE HIERARCHICAL FILESYSTEM

Family tree   A *hierarchical* structure (page 1111) frequently takes the shape of a pyramid. One example of this type of structure is found by tracing a family's lineage: A couple has a child, who may in turn have several children, each of whom may have more children. This hierarchical structure is called a *family tree* (Figure 6-1).

Directory tree   Like the family tree it resembles, the Linux filesystem is called a *tree*. It consists of a set of connected files. This structure allows you to organize files so you can easily find any particular one. On a standard Linux system, each user starts with one directory, to which the user can add subdirectories to any desired level. By creating multiple levels of subdirectories, a user can expand the structure as needed.

Subdirectories   Typically each subdirectory is dedicated to a single subject, such as a person, project, or event. The subject dictates whether a subdirectory should be subdivided further. For example, Figure 6-2 shows a secretary's subdirectory named **correspond**. This directory contains three subdirectories: **business, memos,** and **personal**. The **business** directory contains files that store each letter the secretary types. If you expect many letters to go to one client, as is the case with **milk_co**, you can dedicate a subdirectory to that client.

One major strength of the Linux filesystem is its ability to adapt to users' needs. You can take advantage of this strength by strategically organizing your files so they are most convenient and useful for you.

DIRECTORY FILES AND ORDINARY FILES

Like a family tree, the tree representing the filesystem is usually pictured upside down, with its *root* at the top. Figures 6-2 and 6-3 show that the tree "grows"

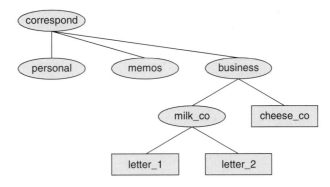

Figure 6-2   A secretary's directories

downward from the root, with paths connecting the root to each of the other files. At the end of each path is either an ordinary file or a directory file. Special files, which can also appear at the ends of paths, are described on page 483. *Ordinary files*, or simply *files*, appear at the ends of paths that cannot support other paths. *Directory files*, also referred to as *directories* or *folders*, are the points that other paths can branch off from. (Figures 6-2 and 6-3 show some empty directories.) When you refer to the tree, *up* is toward the root and *down* is away from the root. Directories directly connected by a path are called *parents* (closer to the root) and *children* (farther from the root). A *pathname* is a series of names that trace a path along branches from one file to another. See page 191 for more information about pathnames.

FILENAMES

Every file has a *filename*. The maximum length of a filename varies with the type of filesystem; Linux supports several types of filesystems. Although most of today's filesystems allow files with names up to 255 characters long, some filesystems

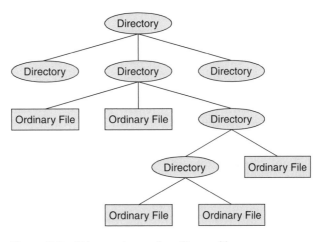

Figure 6-3   Directories and ordinary files

restrict filenames to fewer characters. While you can use almost any character in a filename, you will avoid confusion if you choose characters from the following list:

- Uppercase letters (A–Z)
- Lowercase letters (a–z)
- Numbers (0–9)
- Underscore (_)
- Period (.)
- Comma (,)

Like the children of one parent, no two files in the same directory can have the same name. (Parents give their children different names because it makes good sense, but Linux requires it.) Files in different directories, like the children of different parents, can have the same name.

The filenames you choose should mean something. Too often a directory is filled with important files with such unhelpful names as **hold1**, **wombat**, and **junk**, not to mention **foo** and **foobar**. Such names are poor choices because they do not help you recall what you stored in a file. The following filenames conform to the suggested syntax *and* convey information about the contents of the file:

- **correspond**
- **january**
- **davis**
- **reports**
- **2001**
- **acct_payable**

Filename length When you share your files with users on other systems, you may need to make long filenames differ within the first few characters. Systems running DOS or older versions of Windows have an 8-character filename body length limit and a 3-character filename extension length limit. Some UNIX systems have a 14-character limit and older Macintosh systems have a 31-character limit. If you keep the filenames short, they are easy to type; later you can add extensions to them without exceeding the shorter limits imposed by some filesystems. The disadvantage of short filenames is that they are typically less descriptive than long filenames. See stat on page 442 for a way to determine the maximum length of a filename on the local system.

Long filenames enable you to assign descriptive names to files. To help you select among files without typing entire filenames, shells support filename completion. For more information about this feature, see the "Filename completion" tip on page 149.

Case sensitivity You can use uppercase and/or lowercase letters within filenames. Linux is case sensitive, so files named **JANUARY**, **January**, and **january** represent three distinct files.

Do not use SPACEs within filenames

caution   Although you can use SPACEs within filenames, it is a poor idea. Because a SPACE is a special character, you must quote it on a command line. Quoting a character on a command line can be difficult for a novice user and cumbersome for an experienced user. Use periods or underscores instead of SPACEs: **joe.05.04.26**, **new_stuff**.

If you are working with a filename that includes a SPACE, such as a file from another operating system, you must quote the SPACE on the command line by preceding it with a backslash or by placing quotation marks on either side of the filename. The two following commands send the file named **my file** to the printer.

```
$ lpr my\ file
$ lpr "my file"
```

FILENAME EXTENSIONS

A *filename extension* is the part of the filename following an embedded period. In the filenames listed in Table 6-1, filename extensions help describe the contents of the file. Some programs, such as the C programming language compiler, default to specific filename extensions; in most cases, however, filename extensions are optional. Use extensions freely to make filenames easy to understand. If you like, you can use several periods within the same filename—for example, **notes.4.10.01** or **files.tar.gz**.

Table 6-1   Filename extensions

Filename with extension	Meaning of extension
compute.c	A C programming language source file
compute.o	The object code file for **compute.c**
compute	The executable file for **compute.c**
memo.0410.txt	A text file
memo.pdf	A PDF file; view with xpdf or kpdf under a GUI
memo.ps	A PostScript file; view with gs or kpdf under a GUI
memo.Z	A file compressed with compress (page 162); use uncompress or gunzip (page 161) to decompress
memo.tgz or **memo.tar.gz**	A tar (page 162) archive of files compressed with gzip (page 161)
memo.gz	A file compressed with gzip (page 161); view with zcat or decompress with gunzip (both on page 161)
memo.bz2	A file compressed with bzip2 (page 160); view with bzcat or decompress with bunzip2 (both on page 161)
memo.html	A file meant to be viewed using a Web browser, such as Firefox
photo.gif, **photo.jpg**, **photo.jpeg**, **photo.bmp**, **photo.tif**, or **photo.tiff**	A file containing graphical information, such as a picture

```
login: max
Password:
Last login: Wed Oct 20 11:14:21 from bravo
$ pwd
/home/max
```

Figure 6-4   Logging in and displaying the pathname of your home directory

Hidden Filenames

A filename that begins with a period is called a *hidden filename* (or a *hidden file* or sometimes an *invisible file*) because ls does not normally display it. The command ls –a displays *all* filenames, even hidden ones. Names of startup files (page 190) usually begin with a period so that they are hidden and do not clutter a directory listing. The .plan file (page 168) is also hidden. Two special hidden entries—a single and double period (. and ..)—appear in every directory (page 196).

The Working Directory

pwd   While you are logged in on a character-based interface to a Linux system, you are always associated with a directory. The directory you are associated with is called the *working directory* or *current directory*. Sometimes this association is referred to in a physical sense: "You are *in* (or *working in*) the **zach** directory." The pwd (print working directory) builtin displays the pathname of the working directory.

Your Home Directory

When you first log in on a Linux system or start a terminal emulator window, the working directory is your *home directory*. To display the pathname of your home directory, use pwd just after you log in (Figure 6-4).

When used without any arguments, the ls utility displays a list of the files in the working directory. Because your home directory has been the only working directory you have used so far, ls has always displayed a list of files in your home directory. (All the files you have created up to this point were created in your home directory.)

Startup Files

Startup files, which appear in your home directory, give the shell and other programs information about you and your preferences. Frequently one of these files tells the shell what kind of terminal you are using (page 1060) and executes the stty (set terminal) utility to establish the erase (page 136) and line kill (page 136) keys.

Either you or the system administrator can put a shell startup file containing shell commands in your home directory. The shell executes the commands in this file each time you log in. Because the startup files have hidden filenames, you must use the ls –a command to see whether one is in your home directory. A GUI has many startup files. Usually you do not need to work with these files directly but can control startup sequences using icons on the desktop. See page 277 for more information about startup files.

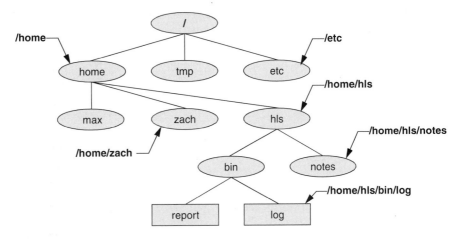

Figure 6-5 Absolute pathnames

PATHNAMES

Every file has a *pathname*, which is a trail from a directory through part of the directory hierarchy to an ordinary file or a directory. Within a pathname, a slash (*/*) following (to the right of) a filename indicates that the file is a directory file. The file following (to the right of) the slash can be a ordinary file or a directory file. The simplest pathname is a simple filename, which points to a file in the working directory. This section discusses absolute and relative pathnames and explains how to use each.

ABSOLUTE PATHNAMES

/ (root) The root directory of the filesystem hierarchy does not have a name; it is referred to as the *root directory* and is represented by a */* (slash) standing alone or at the left end of a pathname.

An *absolute pathname* starts with a slash (*/*), which represents the root directory. The slash is followed by the name of a file located in the root directory. An absolute pathname can continue, tracing a path through all intermediate directories, to the file identified by the pathname. String all the filenames in the path together, following each directory with a slash (*/*). This string of filenames is called an absolute pathname because it locates a file absolutely by tracing a path from the root directory to the file. Typically the absolute pathname of a directory does not include the trailing slash, although that format may be used to empathize that the pathname specifies a directory (e.g., **/home/zach/**). The part of a pathname following the final slash is called a *simple filename*, *filename*, or *basename*. Figure 6-5 shows the absolute pathnames of directories and ordinary files in part of a filesystem hierarchy.

Using an absolute pathname, you can list or otherwise work with any file on the local system, assuming you have permission to do so, regardless of the working directory at the time you give the command. For example, Sam can give the following command while working in his home directory to list the files in the **/etc/apt** directory:

```
$ pwd
/home/sam
$ ls /etc/apt
apt.conf.d    sources.list      sources.list.save  trusted.gpg
secring.gpg   sources.list.d  trustdb.gpg         trusted.gpg~
```

~ (TILDE) IN PATHNAMES

In another form of absolute pathname, the shell expands the characters **~/** (a tilde followed by a slash) at the start of a pathname into the pathname of your home directory. Using this shortcut, you can display your **.bashrc** startup file (page 278) with the following command, no matter which directory is the working directory:

```
$ less ~/.bashrc
```

A tilde quickly references paths that start with your or someone else's home directory. The shell expands a tilde followed by a username at the beginning of a pathname into the pathname of that user's home directory. For example, assuming he has permission to do so, Max can examine Sam's **.bashrc** file with the following command:

```
$ less ~sam/.bashrc
```

Refer to "Tilde Expansion" on page 343 for more information.

RELATIVE PATHNAMES

A *relative pathname* traces a path from the working directory to a file. The pathname is *relative* to the working directory. Any pathname that does not begin with the root directory (represented by **/**) or a tilde (**~**) is a relative pathname. Like absolute pathnames, relative pathnames can trace a path through many directories. The simplest relative pathname is a simple filename, which identifies a file in the working directory. The examples in the next sections use absolute and relative pathnames.

SIGNIFICANCE OF THE WORKING DIRECTORY

To access any file in the working directory, you need only a simple filename. To access a file in another directory, you *must* use a pathname. Typing a long pathname is tedious and increases the chance of making a mistake. This possibility is less likely under a GUI, where you click filenames or icons. You can choose a working directory for any particular task to reduce the need for long pathnames. Your choice of a working directory does not allow you to do anything you could not do otherwise—it just makes some operations easier.

When using a relative pathname, know which directory is the working directory

caution   The location of the file that you are accessing with a relative pathname is dependent on (is relative to) the working directory. Always make sure you know which directory is the working directory before you use a relative pathname. Use pwd to verify the directory. If you are creating a file using vim and you are not where you think you are in the file hierarchy, the new file will end up in an unexpected location.

It does not matter which directory is the working directory when you use an absolute pathname. Thus, the following command always edits a file named **goals** in your home directory:

```
$ vim ~/goals
```

Refer to Figure 6-6 as you read this paragraph. Files that are children of the working directory can be referenced by simple filenames. Grandchildren of the working directory can be referenced by short relative pathnames: two filenames separated by a slash. When you manipulate files in a large directory structure, using short relative pathnames can save you time and aggravation. If you choose a working directory that contains the files used most often for a particular task, you need use fewer long, cumbersome pathnames.

WORKING WITH DIRECTORIES

This section discusses how to create directories (mkdir), switch between directories (cd), remove directories (rmdir), use pathnames to make your work easier, and move and copy files and directories between directories. It concludes with a section that lists and describes briefly important standard directories and files in the Ubuntu filesystem.

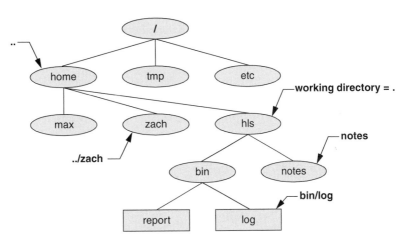

Figure 6-6   Relative pathnames

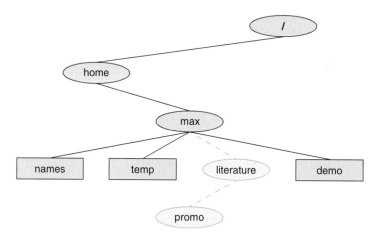

Figure 6-7   The file structure developed in the examples

mkdir: CREATES A DIRECTORY

The mkdir utility creates a directory. The *argument* (page 1095) to mkdir becomes the pathname of the new directory. The following examples develop the directory structure shown in Figure 6-7. In the figure, the directories that are added appear in a lighter shade than the others and are connected by dashes.

In Figure 6-8, pwd shows that Max is working in his home directory (**/home/max**) and ls shows the names of the files in his home directory: **demo, names,** and **temp.** Using mkdir, Max creates a directory named **literature** as a child of his home directory. He uses a relative pathname (a simple filename) because he wants the **literature** directory to be a child of the working directory. Max could have used an absolute pathname to create the same directory: **mkdir /home/max/literature.**

The second ls in Figure 6-8 verifies the presence of the new directory. The **–F** option to ls displays a slash after the name of each directory and an asterisk after each executable file (shell script, utility, or application). When you call it with an argument

```
$ pwd
/home/max
$ ls
demo  names  temp
$ mkdir literature
$ ls
demo  literature  names  temp
$ ls -F
demo  literature/  names  temp
$ ls literature
$
```

Figure 6-8   The mkdir utility

that is the name of a directory, ls lists the contents of that directory. The final ls does not display anything because there are no files in the **literature** directory.

The following commands show two ways to create the **promo** directory as a child of the newly created **literature** directory. The first way checks that **/home/max** is the working directory and uses a relative pathname:

```
$ pwd
/home/max
$ mkdir literature/promo
```

The second way uses an absolute pathname:

```
$ mkdir /home/max/literature/promo
```

Use the **–p** (parents) option to mkdir to create both the **literature** and **promo** directories with one command:

```
$ pwd
/home/max
$ ls
demo   names   temp
$ mkdir -p literature/promo
```

or

```
$ mkdir -p /home/max/literature/promo
```

cd: CHANGES TO ANOTHER WORKING DIRECTORY

The cd (change directory) utility makes another directory the working directory but does *not* change the contents of the working directory. Figure 6-9 shows two ways to make the **/home/max/literature** directory the working directory, as verified by pwd. First Max uses cd with an absolute pathname to make **literature** his working directory—it does not matter which is the working directory when you give a command with an absolute pathname.

A pwd command confirms the change made by Max. When used without an argument, cd makes your home directory the working directory, as it was when you logged in. The second cd command in Figure 6-9 does not have an argument so it

```
$ cd /home/max/literature
$ pwd
/home/max/literature
$ cd
$ pwd
/home/max
$ cd literature
$ pwd
/home/max/literature
```

Figure 6-9   cd changes the working directory

makes Max's home directory the working directory. Finally, knowing that he is working in his home directory, Max uses a simple filename to make the **literature** directory his working directory (**cd literature**) and confirms the change using pwd.

The working directory versus your home directory

tip   The working directory is not the same as your home directory. Your home directory remains the same for the duration of your session and usually from session to session. Immediately after you log in, you are always working in the same directory: your home directory.

Unlike your home directory, the working directory can change as often as you like. You have no set working directory, which explains why some people refer to it as the *current directory.* When you log in and until you change directories using cd, your home directory is the working directory. If you were to change directories to Sam's home directory, then Sam's home directory would be the working directory.

THE . AND .. DIRECTORY ENTRIES

The mkdir utility automatically puts two entries in each directory it creates: a single period (.) and a double period (..). The . is synonymous with the pathname of the working directory and can be used in its place; the .. is synonymous with the pathname of the parent of the working directory. These entries are hidden because their filenames begin with a period.

With the **literature** directory as the working directory, the following example uses .. three times: first to list the contents of the parent directory (**/home/max**), second to copy the **memoA** file to the parent directory, and third to list the contents of the parent directory again.

```
$ pwd
/home/max/literature
$ ls ..
demo  literature  names  temp
$ cp memoA ..
$ ls ..
demo  literature  memoA  names  temp
```

After using cd to make **promo** (a subdirectory of **literature**) his working directory, Max can use a relative pathname to call vim to edit a file in his home directory.

```
$ cd promo
$ vim ../../names
```

You can use an absolute or relative pathname or a simple filename virtually anywhere a utility or program requires a filename or pathname. This usage holds true for ls, vim, mkdir, rm, and most other Linux utilities.

rmdir: DELETES A DIRECTORY

The rmdir (remove directory) utility deletes a directory. You cannot delete the working directory or a directory that contains files other than the . and .. entries. If you need to delete a directory that has files in it, first use rm to delete the files and then delete the directory. You do not have to (nor can you) delete the . and .. entries; rmdir removes them automatically. The following command deletes the **promo** directory:

```
$ rmdir /home/max/literature/promo
```

The rm utility has a –r option (**rm –r** *filename*) that recursively deletes files, including directories, within a directory and also deletes the directory itself.

Use rm –r carefully, if at all

caution Although **rm –r** is a handy command, you must use it carefully. Do not use it with an ambiguous file reference such as ∗. It is frighteningly easy to wipe out your entire home directory with a single short command.

USING PATHNAMES

touch Use a text editor to create a file named **letter** if you want to experiment with the examples that follow. Alternatively you can use touch to create an empty file:

```
$ cd
$ pwd
/home/max
$ touch letter
```

With **/home/max** as the working directory, the following example uses cp with a relative pathname to copy the file **letter** to the **/home/max/literature/promo** directory. (You will need to create **promo** again if you deleted it earlier.) The copy of the file has the simple filename **letter.0610**:

```
$ cp letter literature/promo/letter.0610
```

If Max does not change to another directory, he can use vim as shown to edit the copy of the file he just made:

```
$ vim literature/promo/letter.0610
```

If Max does not want to use a long pathname to specify the file, he can use cd to make **promo** the working directory before using vim:

```
$ cd literature/promo
$ pwd
/home/max/literature/promo
$ vim letter.0610
```

To make the parent of the working directory (named **/home/max/literature**) the new working directory, Max can give the following command, which takes advantage of the .. directory entry:

```
$ cd ..
$ pwd
/home/max/literature
```

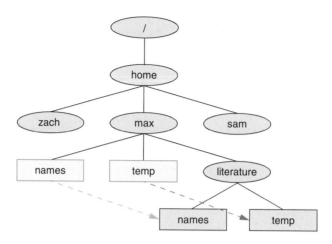

Figure 6-10   Using mv to move **names** and **temp**

mv, cp: MOVE OR COPY FILES

Chapter 5 discussed the use of mv to rename files. However, mv works even more generally: You can use this utility to move files from one directory to another (change the pathname of a file) as well as to change a simple filename. When used to move one or more files to a new directory, the mv command has this syntax:

   mv existing-file-list directory

If the working directory is **/home/max**, Max can use the following command to move the files **names** and **temp** from the working directory to the **literature** directory:

```
$ mv names temp literature
```

This command changes the absolute pathnames of the **names** and **temp** files from **/home/max/names** and **/home/max/temp** to **/home/max/literature/names** and **/home/max/literature/temp**, respectively (Figure 6-10). Like most Linux commands, mv accepts either absolute or relative pathnames.

As you work with Linux and create more files, you will need to create new directories using mkdir to keep the files organized. The mv utility is a useful tool for moving files from one directory to another as you extend your directory hierarchy.

The cp utility works in the same way as mv does, except that it makes copies of the *existing-file-list* in the specified *directory*.

mv: MOVES A DIRECTORY

Just as it moves ordinary files from one directory to another, so mv can move directories. The syntax is similar except that you specify one or more directories, not ordinary files, to move:

   mv existing-directory-list new-directory

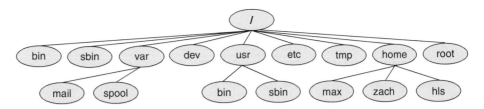

Figure 6-11   A typical FHS-based Linux filesystem structure

If *new-directory* does not exist, the *existing-directory-list* must contain just one directory name, which mv changes to *new-directory* (mv renames the directory). Although you can rename directories using mv, you cannot copy their contents with cp unless you use the **–r** (recursive) option. Refer to the tar and cpio man pages for other ways to copy and move directories.

IMPORTANT STANDARD DIRECTORIES AND FILES

Originally files on a Linux system were not located in standard places within the directory hierarchy. The scattered files made it difficult to document and maintain a Linux system and just about impossible for someone to release a software package that would compile and run on all Linux systems. The first standard for the Linux filesystem, the FSSTND (Linux Filesystem Standard), was released early in 1994. In early 1995 work was started on a broader standard covering many UNIX-like systems: FHS (Linux Filesystem Hierarchy Standard; proton.pathname.com/fhs). More recently FHS has been incorporated in LSB (Linux Standard Base; www.linuxfoundation.org/en/LSB), a workgroup of FSG (Free Standards Group). Finally, FSG combined with Open Source Development Labs (OSDL) to form the Linux Foundation (www.linuxfoundation.org). Figure 6-11 shows the locations of some important directories and files as specified by FHS. The significance of many of these directories will become clear as you continue reading.

The following list describes the directories shown in Figure 6-11, some of the directories specified by FHS, and some other directories. Ubuntu Linux, however, does not use all the directories specified by FHS. Be aware that you cannot always determine the function of a directory by its name. For example, although **/opt** stores add-on software, **/etc/opt** stores configuration files for the software in **/opt**. See also "Important Files and Directories" on page 470.

/ **Root**   The root directory, present in all Linux filesystem structures, is the ancestor of all files in the filesystem.

/bin **Essential command binaries** Holds the files needed to bring the system up and run it when it first comes up in recovery mode (page 428).

/boot **Static files of the boot loader** Contains all the files needed to boot the system.

/dev **Device files** Contains all files that represent peripheral devices, such as disk drives, terminals, and printers. Previously this directory was filled with all possible devices. The udev utility (page 484) provides a dynamic device directory that enables **/dev** to contain only devices that are present on the system.

/etc	**Machine–local system configuration files** Holds administrative, configuration, and other system files. One of the most important is **/etc/passwd**, which contains a list of all users who have permission to use the system.
/etc/opt	**Configuration files for add-on software packages kept in /opt**
/etc/X11	**Machine–local configuration files for the X Window System**
/home	**User home directories** Each user's home directory is typically one of many sub-directories of the **/home** directory. As an example, assuming that users' directories are under **/home**, the absolute pathname of Zach's home directory is **/home/zach**. On some systems the users' directories may not be found under **/home** but instead might be spread among other directories such as **/inhouse** and **/clients**.
/lib	**Shared libraries**
/lib/modules	**Loadable kernel modules**
/mnt	**Mount point for temporarily mounting filesystems**
/opt	**Add-on (optional) software packages**
/proc	**Kernel and process information virtual filesystem**
/root	**Home directory for the root account**
/sbin	**Essential system binaries** Utilities used for system administration are stored in **/sbin** and **/usr/sbin**. The **/sbin** directory includes utilities needed during the booting process, and **/usr/sbin** holds utilities used after the system is up and running. In older versions of Linux, many system administration utilities were scattered through several directories that often included other system files (**/etc**, **/usr/bin**, **/usr/adm**, **/usr/include**).
/sys	**Device pseudofilesystem** See udev on page 484 for more information.
/tmp	**Temporary files**
/usr	**Second major hierarchy** Traditionally includes subdirectories that contain information used by the system. Files in **/usr** subdirectories do not change often and may be shared by several systems.
/usr/bin	**Most user commands** Contains the standard Linux utility programs—that is, binaries that are not needed in recovery mode (page 428).
/usr/games	**Games and educational programs**
/usr/include	**Header files included by C programs**
/usr/lib	**Libraries**
/usr/local	**Local hierarchy** Holds locally important files and directories that are added to the system. Subdirectories can include **bin, games, include, lib, sbin, share**, and src.
/usr/sbin	**Nonvital system administration binaries** See **/sbin**.
/usr/share	**Architecture-independent data** Subdirectories can include **dict, doc, games, info, locale, man, misc, terminfo**, and **zoneinfo**.

/usr/share/doc   Documentation

/usr/share/info   GNU info system's primary directory

/usr/share/man   Online manuals

/usr/src   Source code

/var   **Variable data** Files with contents that vary as the system runs are kept in sub-directories under **/var**. The most common examples are temporary files, system log files, spooled files, and user mailbox files. Subdirectories can include **cache, lib, lock, log, opt, run, spool, tmp,** and **yp.** Older versions of Linux scattered such files through several subdirectories of **/usr** (**/usr/adm, /usr/mail, /usr/spool, /usr/tmp**).

/var/log   **Log files** Contains **lastlog** (a record of the last login by each user), **messages** (system messages from **syslogd**), and **wtmp** (a record of all logins/logouts), among other log files.

/var/spool   **Spooled application data** Contains **anacron, at, cron, lpd, mail, mqueue, samba,** and other directories. The file **/var/spool/mail** typically has a symbolic link in **/var**.

ACCESS PERMISSIONS

Ubuntu Linux supports two methods of controlling who can access a file and how they can access it: traditional Linux access permissions and Access Control Lists (ACLs). This section describes traditional Linux access permissions. See page 207 for a discussion of ACLs, which provide finer-grained control of access permissions than do traditional access permissions.

Three types of users can access a file: the owner of the file (*owner*), a member of a group that the file is associated with (*group*; see page 474 for more information on groups), and everyone else (*other*). A user can attempt to access an ordinary file in three ways: by trying to *read from, write to,* or *execute* it.

ls –l: DISPLAYS PERMISSIONS

When you call ls with the –l option and the name of one or more ordinary files, ls displays a line of information about the file. The following example displays information for two files. The file **letter.0610** contains the text of a letter, and

Figure 6-12   The columns displayed by the ls –l command

check_spell contains a shell script, a program written in a high-level shell programming language:

```
$ ls -l letter.0610 check_spell
-rwxr-xr-x 1 max pubs  852 Jul 31 13:47 check_spell
-rw------- 1 max pubs 3355 Jun 22 12:44 letter.0610
```

From left to right, the lines that an **ls –l** command displays contain the following information (refer to Figure 6-12):

- The type of file (first character)
- The file's access permissions (the next nine characters)
- The ACL flag (present if the file has an ACL, page 207)
- The number of links to the file (page 212)
- The name of the owner of the file (usually the person who created the file)
- The name of the group the file is associated with
- The size of the file in characters (bytes)
- The date and time the file was created or last modified
- The name of the file

The type of file (first column) for **letter.0610** is a hyphen (–) because it is an ordinary file (directory files have a **d** in this column).

The next three characters specify the access permissions for the *owner* of the file: **r** indicates read permission, **w** indicates write permission, and **x** indicates execute permission. A – in a column indicates that the owner does *not* have the permission that could have appeared in that position.

In a similar manner the next three characters represent permissions for the *group*, and the final three characters represent permissions for *other* (everyone else). In the preceding example, the owner of **letter.0610** can read from and write to the file, whereas the group and others can only read from the file and no one is allowed to execute it. Although execute permission can be allowed for any file, it does not make sense to assign execute permission to a file that contains a document, such as a letter. The **check_spell** file is an executable shell script, so execute permission is appropriate for it. (The owner, group, and others have execute permission.)

chmod: CHANGES ACCESS PERMISSIONS

The Linux file access permission scheme lets you give other users access to the files you want to share yet keep your private files confidential. You can allow other users to read from *and* write to a file (handy if you are one of several people working on a joint project). You can allow others only to read from a file (perhaps a project specification you are proposing). Or you can allow others only to write to a file (similar to an inbox or mailbox, where you want others to be able to send you mail but do not want them to read your mail). Similarly you can protect entire directories from being scanned (covered shortly).

A user with **root** privileges can access any file on the system

There is an exception to the access permissions described in this section. Anyone who can gain **root** privileges has full access to *all* files, regardless of the file's owner or access permissions.

The owner of a file controls which users have permission to access the file and how those users can access it. When you own a file, you can use the chmod (change mode) utility to change access permissions for that file. You can specify symbolic (relative) or numeric (absolute) arguments to chmod.

SYMBOLIC ARGUMENTS TO chmod

The following example, which uses symbolic arguments to chmod, adds (**+**) read and write permissions (**rw**) for all (**a**) users:

```
$ ls -l letter.0610
-rw------- 1 max pubs 3355 Jun 22 12:44 letter.0610
$ chmod a+rw letter.0610
$ ls -l letter.0610
-rw-rw-rw- 1 max pubs 3355 Jun 22 12:44 letter.0610
```

You must have read permission to execute a shell script

Because a shell needs to read a shell script (a text file containing shell commands) before it can execute the commands within that script, you must have read permission for the file containing the script to execute it. You also need execute permission to execute a shell script directly from the command line. In contrast, binary (program) files do not need to be read; they are executed directly. You need only execute permission to run a binary program.

Using symbolic arguments with chmod modifies existing permissions; the change a given argument makes depends on (is relative to) the existing permissions. In the next example, chmod removes (**–**) read (**r**) and execute (**x**) permissions for other (**o**) users. The owner and group permissions are not affected.

```
$ ls -l check_spell
-rwxr-xr-x 1 max pubs 852 Jul 31 13:47 check_spell
$ chmod o-rx check_spell
$ ls -l check_spell
-rwxr-x--- 1 max pubs 852 Jul 31 13:47 check_spell
```

In addition to **a** (all) and **o** (other), you can use **g** (group) and **u** (user, although *user* refers to the *owner* of the file who may or may not be the user of the file at any given time) in the argument to chmod. For example, **chmod a+x** adds execute permission for all users (other, group, and owner) and **chmod go–rwx** removes all permissions for all but the owner of the file.

chmod: **o** for other, **u** for owner

When using chmod, many people assume that the **o** stands for *owner;* it does not. The **o** stands for *other,* whereas **u** stands for *owner* (*user*). The acronym UGO (user-group-other) may help you remember how permissions are named.

NUMERIC ARGUMENTS TO chmod

You can also use numeric arguments to specify permissions with chmod. In place of the letters and symbols specifying permissions used in the previous examples, numeric arguments comprise three octal digits. (A fourth, leading digit controls setuid and setgid permissions and is discussed next.) The first digit specifies permissions for the owner, the second for the group, and the third for other users. A **1** gives the specified user(s) execute permission, a **2** gives write permission, and a **4** gives read permission. Construct the digit representing the permissions for the owner, group, or others by ORing (adding) the appropriate values as shown in the following examples. Using numeric arguments sets file permissions absolutely; it does not modify existing permissions as symbolic arguments do.

In the following example, chmod changes permissions so only the owner of the file can read from and write to the file, regardless of how permissions were previously set. The **6** in the first position gives the owner read (**4**) and write (**2**) permissions. The 0s remove all permissions for the group and other users.

```
$ chmod 600 letter.0610
$ ls -l letter.0610
-rw------- 1 max pubs 3355 Jun 22 12:44 letter.0610
```

Next, **7** (**4** + **2** + **1**) gives the owner read, write, and execute permissions. The **5** (**4** + **1**) gives the group and other users read and write permissions:

```
$ chmod 755 check_spell
$ ls -l check_spell
-rwxr-xr-x 1 max pubs 852 Jul 31 13:47 check_spell
```

Refer to Table 6-2 for more examples of numeric permissions.

Table 6-2   Examples of numeric permission specifications

Mode	Meaning
777	Owner, group, and others can read, write, and execute file
755	Owner can read, write, and execute file; group and others can read and execute file
711	Owner can read, write, and execute file; group and others can execute file
644	Owner can read and write file; group and others can read file
640	Owner can read and write file, group can read file, and others cannot access file

Refer to page 284 for more information on using chmod to make a file executable and to the chmod man page for information on absolute arguments and chmod in general. Refer to page 474 for more information on groups.

SETUID AND SETGID PERMISSIONS

When you execute a file that has setuid (set user ID) permission, the process executing the file takes on the privileges of the file's owner. For example, if you run a setuid program that removes all files in a directory, you can remove files in any of the file owner's directories, even if you do not normally have permission to do so. In a similar manner, setgid (set group ID) permission gives the process executing the file the privileges of the group the file is associated with.

Minimize use of setuid and setgid programs owned by root

security   Executable files that are setuid and owned by **root** have **root** privileges when they run, even if they are not run by **root**. This type of program is very powerful because it can do anything that **root** can do (and that the program is designed to do). Similarly executable files that are setgid and belong to the group **root** have extensive privileges.

Because of the power they hold and their potential for destruction, it is wise to avoid indiscriminately creating and using setuid programs owned by **root** and setgid programs belonging to the group **root**. Because of their inherent dangers, many sites minimize the use of these programs on their systems. One necessary setuid program is passwd. See page 405 for a tip on setuid files owned by **root** and page 437 for a command that lists setuid files on the local system.

The following example shows a user working with **root** privileges and using symbolic arguments to chmod to give one program setuid privileges and another program setgid privileges. The ls –l output (page 201) shows setuid permission by displaying an **s** in the owner's executable position and setgid permission by displaying an **s** in the group's executable position:

```
$ ls -l myprog*
-rwxr-xr-x 1 root pubs 19704 Jul 31 14:30 myprog1
-rwxr-xr-x 1 root pubs 19704 Jul 31 14:30 myprog2

$ sudo chmod u+s myprog1
$ sudo chmod g+s myprog2

$ ls -l myprog*
-rwsr-xr-x 1 root pubs 19704 Jul 31 14:30 myprog1
-rwxr-sr-x 1 root pubs 19704 Jul 31 14:30 myprog2
```

The next example uses numeric arguments to chmod to make the same changes. When you use four digits to specify permissions, setting the first digit to **1** sets the *sticky bit* (page 1134), setting it to **2** specifies setgid permissions, and setting it to **4** specifies setuid permissions:

```
$ ls -l myprog*
-rwxr-xr-x 1 root pubs 19704 Jul 31 14:30 myprog1
-rwxr-xr-x 1 root pubs 19704 Jul 31 14:30 myprog2

$ sudo chmod 4755 myprog1
$ sudo chmod 2755 myprog2

$ ls -l myprog*
-rwsr-xr-x 1 root pubs 19704 Jul 31 14:30 myprog1
-rwxr-sr-x 1 root pubs 19704 Jul 31 14:30 myprog2
```

Do not write setuid shell scripts

security   Never give shell scripts setuid permission. Several techniques for subverting them are well known.

DIRECTORY ACCESS PERMISSIONS

Access permissions have slightly different meanings when they are used with directories. Although the three types of users can read from or write to a directory, the directory cannot be executed. Execute permission is redefined for a directory: It means that you can cd into the directory and/or examine files that you have permission to read from in the directory. It has nothing to do with executing a file.

When you have only execute permission for a directory, you can use ls to list a file in the directory if you know its name. You cannot use ls without an argument to list the entire contents of the directory. In the following exchange, Zach first verifies that he is logged in as himself. He then checks the permissions on Max's **info** directory. You can view the access permissions associated with a directory by running ls with the **–d** (directory) and **–l** (long) options:

```
$ who am i
zach       pts/7   Aug 21 10:02
$ ls -ld /home/max/info
drwx-----x  2 max pubs 512 Aug 21 09:31 /home/max/info
$ ls -l /home/max/info
ls: /home/max/info: Permission denied
```

The **d** at the left end of the line that ls displays indicates that **/home/max/info** is a directory. Max has read, write, and execute permissions; members of the pubs group have no access permissions; and other users have execute permission only, indicated by the **x** at the right end of the permissions. Because Zach does not have read permission for the directory, the **ls –l** command returns an error.

When Zach specifies the names of the files he wants information about, he is not reading new directory information but rather searching for specific information, which he is allowed to do with execute access to the directory. He has read permission for **notes** so he has no problem using cat to display the file. He cannot display **financial** because he does not have read permission for it:

```
$ ls -l /home/max/info/financial /home/max/info/notes
-rw-------  1 max pubs 34 Aug 21 09:31 /home/max/info/financial
-rw-r--r--  1 max pubs 30 Aug 21 09:32 /home/max/info/notes
$ cat /home/max/info/notes
This is the file named notes.
$ cat /home/max/info/financial
cat: /home/max/info/financial: Permission denied
```

Next Max gives others read access to his **info** directory:

```
$ chmod o+r /home/max/info
```

When Zach checks his access permissions on **info**, he finds that he has both read and execute access to the directory. Now **ls –l** works just fine without arguments, but he still cannot read **financial**. (This restriction is an issue of file permissions, not directory permissions.) Finally, Zach tries to create a file named **newfile** using touch.

If Max were to give him write permission to the **info** directory, Zach would be able to create new files in it:

```
$ ls -ld /home/max/info
drwx---r-x   2 max pubs 512 Aug 21 09:31 /home/max/info
$ ls -l /home/max/info
total 8
-rw-------   1 max pubs 34 Aug 21 09:31 financial
-rw-r--r--   1 max pubs 30 Aug 21 09:32 notes
$ cat /home/max/info/financial
cat: financial: Permission denied
$ touch /home/max/info/newfile
touch: cannot touch '/home/max/info/newfile': Permission denied
```

ACLs: Access Control Lists

Access Control Lists (ACLs) provide finer-grained control over which users can access specific directories and files than do traditional Linux permissions (page 201). Using ACLs you can specify the ways in which each of several users can access a directory or file. Because ACLs can reduce performance, do not enable them on filesystems that hold system files, where the traditional Linux permissions are sufficient. Also be careful when moving, copying, or archiving files: Not all utilities preserve ACLs. In addition, you cannot copy ACLs to filesystems that do not support ACLs.

An ACL comprises a set of rules. A rule specifies how a specific user or group can access the file that the ACL is associated with. There are two kinds of rules: *access rules* and *default rules*. (The documentation refers to *access ACLs* and *default ACLs*, even though there is only one type of ACL: There is one type of list [ACL] and there are two types of rules that an ACL can contain.)

An access rule specifies access information for a single file or directory. A default ACL pertains to a directory only; it specifies default access information (an ACL) for any file in the directory that is not given an explicit ACL.

Most utilities do not preserve ACLs

caution   When used with the **–p** (preserve) or **–a** (archive) option, cp preserves ACLs when it copies files. The mv utility also preserves ACLs. When you use cp with the **–p** or **–a** option and it is not able to copy ACLs, and in the case where mv is unable to preserve ACLs, the utility performs the operation and issues an error message:

```
$ mv report /tmp
mv: preserving permissions for '/tmp/report': Operation not supported
```

Other utilities, such as tar, cpio, and dump, do not support ACLs. You can use cp with the **–a** option to copy directory hierarchies, including ACLs.

You can never copy ACLs to a filesystem that does not support ACLs or to a filesystem that does not have ACL support turned on.

Enabling ACLs

Before you can use ACLs you must install the **acl** software package:

```
$ sudo aptitude install acl
```

Ubuntu Linux officially supports ACLs on **ext2** and **ext3** filesystems only, although informal support for ACLs is available on other filesystems. To use ACLs on an **ext2** or **ext3** filesystem, you must mount the device with the **acl** option (**no_acl** is the default). For example, if you want to mount the device represented by **/home** so that you can use ACLs on files in **/home**, you can add **acl** to its options list in **/etc/fstab**:

```
$ grep home /etc/fstab
LABEL=/home              /home             ext3    defaults,acl       1 2
```

After changing **fstab**, you need to remount **/home** before you can use ACLs. If no one else is using the system, you can unmount it and mount it again (working with **root** privileges) as long as the working directory is not in the **/home** hierarchy. Alternatively you can use the **remount** option to mount to remount **/home** while the device is in use:

```
$ sudo mount -v -o remount /home
/dev/hda3 on /home type ext3 (rw,acl)
```

See page 492 for information on **fstab** and page 488 for information on mount.

Working with Access Rules

The setfacl utility modifies a file's ACL and getfacl displays a file's ACL. When you use getfacl to obtain information about a file that does not have an ACL, it displays the same information as an **ls –l** command, albeit in a different format:

```
$ ls -l report
-rw-r--r--  1 max max 9537 Jan 12 23:17 report

$ getfacl report
# file: report
# owner: max
# group: max
user::rw-
group::r--
other::r--
```

The first three lines of the getfacl output comprise the header; they specify the name of the file, the owner of the file, and the group the file is associated with. For more information refer to "**ls –l**: Displays Permissions" on page 201. The **––omit-header** (or just **––omit**) option causes getfacl not to display the header:

```
$ getfacl --omit-header report
user::rw-
group::r--
other::r--
```

In the line that starts with **user**, the two colons (**::**) with no name between them indicate that the line specifies the permissions for the owner of the file. Similarly, the two colons in the **group** line indicate that the line specifies permissions for the group the file is associated with. The two colons following **other** are there for consistency: No name can be associated with **other**.

The setfacl **––modify** (or **–m**) option adds or modifies one or more rules in a file's ACL using the following format:

> setfacl ––modify *ugo:name:permissions file-list*

where *ugo* can be either **u**, **g**, or **o** to indicate that the command sets file permissions for a user, a group, or all other users, respectively; *name* is the name of the user or group that permissions are being set for; *permissions* is the permissions in either symbolic or absolute format; and *file-list* is the list of files the permissions are to be applied to. You must omit *name* when you specify permissions for other users (**o**). Symbolic permissions use letters to represent file permissions (**rwx**, **r–x**, and so on), whereas absolute permissions use an octal number. While chmod uses three sets of permissions or three octal numbers (one each for the owner, group, and other users), setfacl uses a single set of permissions or a single octal number to represent the permissions being granted to the user or group represented by *ugo* and *name*. See the discussion of chmod on page 202 for more information about symbolic and absolute representations of file permissions.

For example, both of the following commands add a rule to the ACL for the **report** file that gives Sam read and write permission to that file:

```
$ setfacl --modify u:sam:rw- report
```

or

```
$ setfacl --modify u:sam:6 report
$ getfacl report
# file: report
# owner: max
# group: max
user::rw-
user:sam:rw-
group::r--
mask::rw-
other::r--
```

The line containing **user:sam:rw–** shows that the user named **sam** has read and write access (**rw–**) to the file. See page 201 for an explanation of how to read access permissions. See the following optional section for a description of the line that starts with **mask**.

When a file has an ACL, **ls –l** displays a plus sign (**+**) following the permissions, even if the ACL is empty:

```
$ ls -l report
-rw-rw-r--+ 1 max max 9537 Jan 12 23:17 report
```

optional EFFECTIVE RIGHTS MASK

The line that starts with **mask** specifies the *effective rights mask*. This mask limits the effective permissions granted to ACL groups and users. It does not affect the owner of the file or the group the file is associated with. In other words, it does not affect traditional Linux permissions. However, because setfacl always sets the effective rights mask to the least restrictive ACL permissions for the file, the mask has no effect unless you set it explicitly after you set up an ACL for the file. You can set the mask by specifying **mask** in place of *ugo* and by not specifying a *name* in a setfacl command.

The following example sets the effective rights mask to **read** for the **report** file:

```
$ setfacl -m mask::r-- report
```

The **mask** line in the following getfacl output shows the effective rights mask set to read (**r--**). The line that displays Sam's file access permissions shows them still set to read and write. However, the comment at the right end of the line shows that his effective permission is read.

```
$ getfacl report
# file: report
# owner: max
# group: max
user::rw-
user:sam:rw-                              #effective:r--
group::r--
mask::r--
other::r--
```

As the next example shows, setfacl can modify ACL rules and can set more than one ACL rule at a time:

```
$ setfacl -m u:sam:r--,u:zach:rw- report

$ getfacl --omit-header report
user::rw-
user:sam:r--
user:zach:rw-
group::r--
mask::rw-
other::r--
```

The **–x** option removes ACL rules for a user or a group. It has no effect on permissions for the owner of the file or the group that the file is associated with. The next example shows setfacl removing the rule that gives Sam permission to access the file:

```
$ setfacl -x u:sam report

$ getfacl --omit-header report
user::rw-
user:zach:rw-
group::r--
mask::rw-
other::r--
```

You must not specify *permissions* when you use the **–x** option. Instead, specify only the *ugo* and *name*. The **–b** option, followed by a filename only, removes all ACL rules and the ACL itself from the file or directory you specify.

Both setfacl and getfacl have many options. Use the **––help** option to display brief lists of options or refer to the man pages for details.

Setting Default Rules for a Directory

The following example shows that the **dir** directory initially has no ACL. The setfacl command uses the **–d** (default) option to add two default rules to the ACL for **dir**. These rules apply to all files in the **dir** directory that do not have explicit ACLs. The rules give members of the **pubs** group read and execute permissions and give members of the **admin** group read, write, and execute permissions.

```
$ ls -ld dir
drwx------ 2 max max 4096 Feb 12 23:15 dir
$ getfacl dir
# file: dir
# owner: max
# group: max
user::rwx
group::---
other::---

$ setfacl -d -m g:pubs:r-x,g:admin:rwx dir
```

The following ls command shows that the **dir** directory now has an ACL, as indicated by the **+** to the right of the permissions. Each of the default rules that getfacl displays starts with **default:**. The first two default rules and the last default rule specify the permissions for the owner of the file, the group that the file is associated with, and all other users. These three rules specify the traditional Linux permissions and take precedence over other ACL rules. The third and fourth rules specify the permissions for the **pubs** and **admin** groups. Next is the default effective rights mask.

```
$ ls -ld dir
drwx------+ 2 max max 4096 Feb 12 23:15 dir
$ getfacl dir
# file: dir
# owner: max
# group: max
user::rwx
group::---
other::---
default:user::rwx
default:group::---
default:group:pubs:r-x
default:group:admin:rwx
default:mask::rwx
default:other::---
```

Remember that the default rules pertain to files held in the directory that are not assigned ACLs explicitly. You can also specify access rules for the directory itself.

When you create a file within a directory that has default rules in its ACL, the effective rights mask for that file is created based on the file's permissions. In some cases the mask may override default ACL rules.

In the next example, touch creates a file named **new** in the **dir** directory. The ls command shows that this file has an ACL. Based on the value of umask (page 442), both the owner and the group that the file is associated with have read and write permissions for the file. The effective rights mask is set to read and write so that the effective permission for **pubs** is read and the effective permissions for **admin** are read and write. Neither group has execute permission.

```
$ cd dir
$ touch new
$ ls -l new
-rw-rw----+ 1 max max 0 Feb 13 00:39 new
$ getfacl --omit new
user::rw-
group::---
group:pubs:r-x                    #effective:r--
group:admin:rwx                   #effective:rw-
mask::rw-
other::---
```

If you change the file's traditional permissions to read, write, and execute for the owner and the group, the effective rights mask changes to read, write, and execute and the groups specified by the default rules gain execute access to the file.

```
$ chmod 770 new
$ ls -l new
-rwxrwx---+ 1 max max 0 Feb 13 00:39 new
$ getfacl --omit new
user::rwx
group::---
group:pubs:r-x
group:admin:rwx
mask::rwx
other::---
```

LINKS

A *link* is a pointer to a file. Each time you create a file using vim, touch, cp, or by another other means, you are putting a pointer in a directory. This pointer associates a filename with a place on the disk. When you specify a filename in a command, you are indirectly pointing to the place on the disk that holds the information you want.

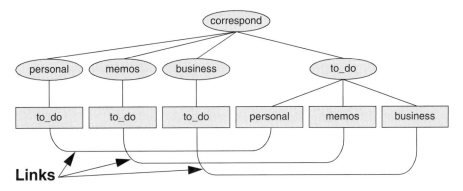

Figure 6-13   Using links to cross-classify files

Sharing files can be useful when two or more people are working on the same project and need to share some information. You can make it easy for other users to access one of your files by creating additional links to the file.

To share a file with another user, first give the user permission to read from and write to the file (page 202). You may also have to change the access permissions of the parent directory of the file to give the user read, write, or execute permission (page 206). Once the permissions are appropriately set, the user can create a link to the file so that each of you can access the file from your separate directory hierarchies.

A link can also be useful to a single user with a large directory hierarchy. You can create links to cross-classify files in your directory hierarchy, using different classifications for different tasks. For example, if you have the file layout depicted in Figure 6-2 on page 187, a file named **to_do** might appear in each subdirectory of the **correspond** directory—that is, in **personal**, **memos**, and **business**. If you find it difficult to keep track of everything you need to do, you can create a separate directory named **to_do** in the **correspond** directory. You can then link each subdirectory's to-do list into that directory. For example, you could link the file named **to_do** in the **memos** directory to a file named **memos** in the **to_do** directory. This set of links is shown in Figure 6-13.

Although it may sound complicated, this technique keeps all your to-do lists conveniently in one place. The appropriate list is easily accessible in the task-related directory when you are busy composing letters, writing memos, or handling personal business.

About the discussion of hard links

tip Two kinds of links exist: hard links and symbolic (soft) links. Hard links are older and becoming outdated. The section on hard links is marked as optional; you can skip it, although it discusses inodes and gives you insight into the structure of the filesystem.

optional

HARD LINKS

A hard link to a file appears as another file. If the file appears in the same directory as the linked-to file, the links must have different filenames because two files in the same directory cannot have the same name. You can create a hard link to a file only from within the filesystem that holds the file.

ln: CREATES A HARD LINK

The ln (link) utility (without the –s or ––symbolic option) creates a hard link to an existing file using the following syntax:

ln existing-file new-link

The next command shows Zach making the link shown in Figure 6-14 by creating a new link named **/home/max/letter** to an existing file named **draft** in Zach's home directory:

```
$ pwd
/home/zach
$ ln draft /home/max/letter
```

The new link appears in the **/home/max** directory with the filename **letter**. In practice, Max may need to change directory permissions so Zach will be able to create the link. Even though **/home/max/letter** appears in Max's directory, Zach is the owner of the file because he created it.

The ln utility creates an additional pointer to an existing file but it does *not* make another copy of the file. Because there is only one file, the file status information—such as access permissions, owner, and the time the file was last modified—is the same for all links; only the filenames differ. When Zach modifies **/home/zach/draft**, for example, Max sees the changes in **/home/max/letter**.

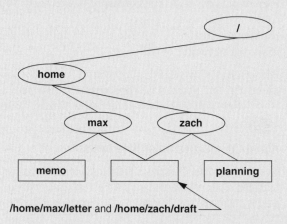

Figure 6-14   Two links to the same file: **/home/max/letter** and **/home/zach/draft**

cp VERSUS ln

The following commands verify that ln does not make an additional copy of a file.
Create a file, use ln to make an additional link to the file, change the contents of the
file through one link, and verify the change through the other link:

```
$ cat file_a
This is file A.
$ ln file_a file_b
$ cat file_b
This is file A.
$ vim file_b
...
$ cat file_b
This is file B after the change.
$ cat file_a
This is file B after the change.
```

If you try the same experiment using cp instead of ln and change a *copy* of the file,
the difference between the two utilities will become clearer. Once you change a *copy*
of a file, the two files are different:

```
$ cat file_c
This is file C.
$ cp file_c file_d
$ cat file_d
This is file C.
$ vim file_d
...
$ cat file_d
This is file D after the change.
$ cat file_c
This is file C.
```

ls and link counts   You can use ls with the –l option, followed by the names of the files you want to
compare, to confirm that the status information is the same for two links to the
same file and is different for files that are not linked. In the following example, the
2 in the links field (just to the left of **max**) shows there are two links to **file_a** and
file_b (from the previous example):

```
$ ls -l file_a file_b file_c file_d
-rw-r--r-- 2 max pubs 33  May 24 10:52 file_a
-rw-r--r-- 2 max pubs 33  May 24 10:52 file_b
-rw-r--r-- 1 max pubs 16  May 24 10:55 file_c
-rw-r--r-- 1 max pubs 33  May 24 10:57 file_d
```

Although it is easy to guess which files are linked to one another in this example, ls
does not explicitly tell you.

ls and inodes   Use ls with the –i option to determine without a doubt which files are linked. The –i
option lists the *inode* (page 1113) number for each file. An inode is the control
structure for a file. If the two filenames have the same inode number, they share the
same control structure and are links to the same file. Conversely, when two filenames have different inode numbers, they are different files. The following example

shows that **file_a** and **file_b** have the same inode number and that **file_c** and **file_d** have different inode numbers:

```
$ ls -i file_a file_b file_c file_d
3534 file_a    3534 file_b    5800 file_c    7328 file_d
```

All links to a file are of equal value: The operating system cannot distinguish the order in which multiple links were created. When a file has two links, you can remove either one and still access the file through the remaining link. You can remove the link used to create the file, for example, and, as long as one link remains, still access the file through that link.

SYMBOLIC LINKS

In addition to hard links, Linux supports *symbolic links,* also called *soft links* or *symlinks*. A hard link is a pointer to a file (the directory entry points to the inode), whereas a symbolic link is an *indirect* pointer to a file (the directory entry contains the pathname of the pointed-to file—a pointer to the hard link to the file).

Advantages of symbolic links
Symbolic links were developed because of the limitations inherent in hard links. You cannot create a hard link to a directory, but you can create a symbolic link to a directory.

In many cases the Linux file hierarchy encompasses several filesystems. Because each filesystem keeps separate control information (that is, separate inode tables or filesystem structures) for the files it holds, it is not possible to create hard links between files in different filesystems. A symbolic link can point to any file, regardless of where it is located in the file structure, but a hard link to a file must be in the same filesystem as the other hard link(s) to the file. When you create links only among files in your home directory, you will not notice this limitation.

A major advantage of a symbolic link is that it can point to a nonexistent file. This ability is useful if you need a link to a file that is periodically removed and re-created. A hard link keeps pointing to a "removed" file, which the link keeps alive even after a new file is created. In contrast, a symbolic link always points to the newly created file and does not interfere when you delete the old file. For example, a symbolic link could point to a file that gets checked in and out under a source code control system, a **.o** file that is re-created by the C compiler each time you run **make**, or a log file that is repeatedly archived.

Although they are more general than hard links, symbolic links have some disadvantages. Whereas all hard links to a file have equal status, symbolic links do not have the same status as hard links. When a file has multiple hard links, it is analogous to a person having multiple full legal names, as many married women do. In contrast, symbolic links are analogous to nicknames. Anyone can have one or more nicknames, but these nicknames have a lesser status than legal names. The following sections describe some of the peculiarities of symbolic links.

ln: CREATES SYMBOLIC LINKS

The ln utility with the **--symbolic** (or **-s**) option creates a symbolic link. The following example creates a symbolic link **/tmp/s3** to the file **sum** in Max's home directory. When you use an **ls –l** command to look at the symbolic link, ls displays the name of the link and the name of the file it points to. The first character of the listing is l (for link).

```
$ ln --symbolic /home/max/sum /tmp/s3
$ ls -l /home/max/sum /tmp/s3
-rw-rw-r--   1 max max 38 Jun 12 09:51 /home/max/sum
lrwxrwxrwx   1 max max 14 Jun 12 09:52 /tmp/s3 -> /home/max/sum
$ cat /tmp/s3
This is sum.
```

The sizes and times of the last modifications of the two files are different. Unlike a hard link, a symbolic link to a file does not have the same status information as the file itself.

You can also use **ln** to create a symbolic link to a directory. When you use the **--symbolic** option, ln works as expected whether the file you are creating a link to is an ordinary file or a directory.

Use absolute pathnames with symbolic links

tip Symbolic links are literal and are not aware of directories. A link that points to a relative pathname, which includes simple filenames, assumes the relative pathname is relative to the directory that the link was created *in* (not the directory the link was created *from*). In the following example, the link points to the file named **sum** in the **/tmp** directory. Because no such file exists, cat gives an error message:

```
$ pwd
/home/max
$ ln --symbolic sum /tmp/s4
$ ls -l sum /tmp/s4
lrwxrwxrwx   1 max     max          3 Jun 12 10:13 /tmp/s4 -> sum
-rw-rw-r--   1 max     max         38 Jun 12 09:51 sum
$ cat /tmp/s4
cat: /tmp/s4: No such file or directory
```

optional cd AND SYMBOLIC LINKS

When you use a symbolic link as an argument to **cd** to change directories, the results can be confusing, particularly if you did not realize that you were using a symbolic link.

If you use **cd** to change to a directory that is represented by a symbolic link, the pwd shell builtin (page 247) lists the name of the symbolic link. The pwd utility (**/bin/pwd**) lists the name of the linked-to directory, not the link, regardless of how you got there.

```
$ ln -s /home/max/grades /tmp/grades.old
$ pwd
/home/max
$ cd /tmp/grades.old
$ pwd
/tmp/grades.old
$ /bin/pwd
/home/max/grades
```

When you change directories back to the parent, you end up in the directory holding the symbolic link:

```
$ cd ..
$ pwd
/tmp
$ /bin/pwd
/tmp
```

rm: REMOVES A LINK

When you create a file, there is one hard link to it. You can then delete the file or, using Linux terminology, remove the link with the rm utility. When you remove the last hard link to a file, you can no longer access the information stored there and the operating system releases the space the file occupied on the disk for use by other files. This space is released even if symbolic links to the file remain. When there is more than one hard link to a file, you can remove a hard link and still access the file from any remaining link. Unlike DOS and Windows, Linux does not provide an easy way to undelete a file once you have removed it. A skilled hacker, however, can sometimes piece the file together with time and effort.

When you remove all hard links to a file, you will not be able to access the file through a symbolic link. In the following example, cat reports that the file **total** does not exist because it is a symbolic link to a file that has been removed:

```
$ ls -l sum
-rw-r--r-- 1 max pubs 981  May 24 11:05 sum
$ ln -s sum total
$ rm sum
$ cat total
cat: total: No such file or directory
$ ls -l total
lrwxrwxrwx 1 max pubs 6  May 24 11:09 total -> sum
```

When you remove a file, be sure to remove all symbolic links to it. Remove a symbolic link in the same way you remove other files:

```
$ rm total
```

CHAPTER SUMMARY

Linux has a hierarchical, or treelike, file structure that makes it possible to organize files so you can find them quickly and easily. The file structure contains directory files and ordinary files. Directories contain other files, including other directories; ordinary files generally contain text, programs, or images. The ancestor of all files is the root directory and is represented by / standing alone or at the left end of a pathname.

Most Linux filesystems support 255-character filenames. Nonetheless, it is a good idea to keep filenames simple and intuitive. Filename extensions can help make filenames more meaningful.

When you are logged in, you are always associated with a working directory. Your home directory is the working directory from the time you log in until you use cd to change directories.

An absolute pathname starts with the root directory and contains all the filenames that trace a path to a given file. The pathname starts with a slash, representing the root directory, and contains additional slashes following all the directories in the path, except for the last directory in the case of a path that points to a directory file.

A relative pathname is similar to an absolute pathname but traces the path starting from the working directory. A simple filename is the last element of a pathname and is a form of a relative pathname; it represents a file in the working directory.

A Linux filesystem contains many important directories, including **/usr/bin**, which stores most of the Linux utility commands, and **/dev**, which stores device files, many of which represent physical pieces of hardware. An important standard file is **/etc/passwd**; it contains information about users, such as each user's ID and full name.

Among the attributes associated with each file are access permissions. They determine who can access the file and how the file may be accessed. Three groups of users can potentially access the file: the owner, the members of a group, and all other users. An ordinary file can be accessed in three ways: read, write, and execute. The ls utility with the –l option displays these permissions. For directories, execute access is redefined to mean that the directory can be searched.

The owner of a file or a user working with **root** privileges can use the chmod utility to change the access permissions of a file. This utility specifies read, write, and execute permissions for the file's owner, the group, and all other users on the system.

Access Control Lists (ACLs) provide finer-grained control over which users can access specific directories and files than do traditional Linux permissions. Using ACLs you can specify the ways in which each of several users can access a directory or file. Few utilities preserve ACLs when working with files.

An ordinary file stores user data, such as textual information, programs, or images. A directory is a standard-format disk file that stores information, including names, about ordinary files and other directory files. An inode is a data structure, stored on disk, that defines a file's existence and is identified by an inode number. A directory relates each of the filenames it stores to an inode.

A link is a pointer to a file. You can have several links to a file so you can share the file with other users or have the file appear in more than one directory. Because only one copy of a file with multiple links exists, changing the file through any one link causes the changes to appear in all the links. Hard links cannot link directories or span filesystems, whereas symbolic links can.

Table 6-3 summarizes the utilities introduced in this chapter.

Table 6-3   Utilities introduced in Chapter 6

Utility	Function
cd	Associates you with another working directory (page 195)
chmod	Changes access permissions on a file (page 202)
getfacl	Displays a file's ACL (page 208)
ln	Makes a link to an existing file (page 214)
mkdir	Creates a directory (page 194)
pwd	Displays the pathname of the working directory (page 190)
rmdir	Deletes a directory (page 196)
setfacl	Modifies a file's ACL (page 208)

EXERCISES

1. Is each of the following an absolute pathname, a relative pathname, or a simple filename?

   a. **milk_co**

   b. **correspond/business/milk_co**

   c. **/home/max**

   d. **/home/max/literature/promo**

   e. **..**

   f. **letter.0610**

2. List the commands you can use to perform these operations:

   a. Make your home directory the working directory

   b. Identify the working directory

3. If the working directory is **/home/max** with a subdirectory named **literature**, give three sets of commands that you can use to create a subdirectory named **classics** under **literature**. Also give several sets of commands you can use to remove the **classics** directory and its contents.

4. The df utility displays all mounted filesystems along with information about each. Use the df utility with the **–h** (human-readable) option to answer the following questions.

   a. How many filesystems are mounted on your Linux system?

   b. Which filesystem stores your home directory?

   c. Assuming that your answer to exercise 4a is two or more, attempt to create a hard link to a file on another filesystem. What error message do you get? What happens when you attempt to create a symbolic link to the file instead?

5. Suppose you have a file that is linked to a file owned by another user. How can you ensure that changes to the file are no longer shared?

6. You should have read permission for the **/etc/passwd** file. To answer the following questions, use cat or less to display **/etc/passwd**. Look at the fields of information in **/etc/passwd** for the users on your system.

   a. Which character is used to separate fields in **/etc/passwd**?

   b. How many fields are used to describe each user?

   c. How many users are on the local system?

   d. How many different login shells are in use on your system? (*Hint:* Look at the last field.)

   e. The second field of **/etc/passwd** stores user passwords in encoded form. If the password field contains an **x**, your system uses shadow passwords and stores the encoded passwords elsewhere. Does your system use shadow passwords?

7. If **/home/zach/draft** and **/home/max/letter** are links to the same file and the following sequence of events occurs, what will be the date in the opening of the letter?

   a. Max gives the command **vim letter**.

   b. Zach gives the command **vim draft**.

   c. Zach changes the date in the opening of the letter to January 31, 2009, writes the file, and exits from vim.

   d. Max changes the date to February 1, 2009, writes the file, and exits from vim.

8. Suppose a user belongs to a group that has all permissions on a file named **jobs_list**, but the user, as the owner of the file, has no permissions. Describe which operations, if any, the user/owner can perform on **jobs_list**. Which command can the user/owner give that will grant the user/owner all permissions on the file?

9. Does the root directory have any subdirectories you cannot search as an ordinary user? Does the root directory have any subdirectories you cannot read as a regular user? Explain.

10. Assume you are given the directory structure shown in Figure 6-2 on page 187 and the following directory permissions:

```
d--x--x---   3 zach pubs 512 Mar 10 15:16 business
drwxr-xr-x   2 zach pubs 512 Mar 10 15:16 business/milk_co
```

For each category of permissions—owner, group, and other—what happens when you run each of the following commands? Assume the working directory is the parent of **correspond** and that the file **cheese_co** is readable by everyone.

a. cd correspond/business/milk_co

b. ls –l correspond/business

c. cat correspond/business/cheese_co

ADVANCED EXERCISES

11. What is an inode? What happens to the inode when you move a file within a filesystem?

12. What does the **..** entry in a directory point to? What does this entry point to in the root (**/**) directory?

13. How can you create a file named **–i**? Which techniques do not work, and why do they not work? How can you remove the file named **–i**?

14. Suppose the working directory contains a single file named **andor**. What error message do you get when you run the following command line?

```
$ mv andor and\/or
```

Under what circumstances is it possible to run the command without producing an error?

15. The **ls –i** command displays a filename preceded by the inode number of the file (page 215). Write a command to output inode/filename pairs for the files in the working directory, sorted by inode number. (*Hint:* Use a pipe.)

16. Do you think the system administrator has access to a program that can decode user passwords? Why or why not? (See exercise 6.)

17. Is it possible to distinguish a file from a hard link to a file? That is, given a filename, can you tell whether it was created using an **ln** command? Explain.

18. Explain the error messages displayed in the following sequence of commands:

```
$ ls -l
total 1
drwxrwxr-x   2 max pubs 1024 Mar  2 17:57 dirtmp
$ ls dirtmp
$ rmdir dirtmp
rmdir: dirtmp: Directory not empty
$ rm dirtmp/*
rm: No match.
```

THE SHELL

This chapter takes a close look at the shell and explains how to use some of its features. For example, it discusses command-line syntax. It also describes how the shell processes a command line and initiates execution of a program. In addition the chapter explains how to redirect input to and output from a command, construct pipes and filters on the command line, and run a command in the background. The final section covers filename expansion and explains how you can use this feature in your everyday work.

The exact wording of the shell output differs from shell to shell: What your shell displays may differ slightly from what appears in this book. Refer to Chapter 9 for more information on bash and to Chapter 27 for information on writing and executing bash shell scripts.

THE COMMAND LINE

The shell executes a program when you give it a command in response to its prompt. For example, when you give the ls command, the shell executes the utility program named ls. You can cause the shell to execute other types of programs—such as shell scripts, application programs, and programs you have written—in the same way. The line that contains the command, including any arguments, is called the *command line*. This book uses the term *command* to refer to both the characters you type on the command line and the program that action invokes.

SYNTAX

Command-line syntax dictates the ordering and separation of the elements on a command line. When you press the RETURN key after entering a command, the shell scans the command line for proper syntax. The syntax for a basic command line is

command [arg1] [arg2] ... [argn] RETURN

One or more SPACEs must separate elements on the command line. The **command** is the name of the command, **arg1** through **argn** are arguments, and RETURN is the keystroke that terminates all command lines. The brackets in the command-line syntax indicate that the arguments they enclose are optional. Not all commands require arguments: Some commands do not allow arguments; other commands allow a variable number of arguments; and still others require a specific number of arguments. Options, a special kind of argument, are usually preceded by one or two hyphens (also called a dash or minus sign: –).

COMMAND NAME

Usage message   Some useful Linux command lines consist of only the name of the command without any arguments. For example, ls by itself lists the contents of the working directory. Commands that require arguments typically give a short error message, called a *usage message*, when you use them without arguments, with incorrect arguments, or with the wrong number of arguments.

ARGUMENTS

On the command line each sequence of nonblank characters is called a *token* or *word*. An *argument* is a token, such as a filename, string of text, number, or other object that a command acts on. For example, the argument to a vim or emacs command is the name of the file you want to edit.

The following command line shows cp copying the file named **temp** to **tempcopy**:

```
$ cp temp tempcopy
```

Arguments are numbered starting with the command itself, which is argument zero. In this example, **cp** is argument zero, **temp** is argument one, and **tempcopy** is argument two. The cp utility requires at least two arguments on the command line. Argument one is the name of an existing file. Argument two is the name of the file that cp is creating or overwriting. Here the arguments are not optional; both arguments must be

```
$ ls
hold    mark    names    oldstuff  temp  zach
house   max     office   personal  test
$ ls -r
zach  temp         oldstuff  names  mark   hold
test  personal  office    max    house
$ ls -x
hold        house     mark    max    names  office
oldstuff  personal  temp    test   zach
$ ls -rx
zach    test    temp    personal  oldstuff  office
names   max     mark    house     hold
```

Figure 7-1 Using options

present for the command to work. When you do not supply the right number or kind of arguments, cp displays a usage message. Try typing **cp** and then pressing RETURN.

OPTIONS

An *option* is an argument that modifies the effects of a command. You can frequently specify more than one option, modifying the command in several different ways. Options are specific to and interpreted by the program that the command line calls, not by the shell.

By convention options are separate arguments that follow the name of the command and usually precede other arguments, such as filenames. Most utilities require you to prefix options with a single hyphen. However, this requirement is specific to the utility and not the shell. GNU program options are frequently preceded by two hyphens in a row. For example, **--help** generates a (sometimes extensive) usage message.

Figure 7-1 first shows the output of an ls command without any options. By default ls lists the contents of the working directory in alphabetical order, vertically sorted in columns. Next the –r (reverse order; because this is a GNU utility, you can also use **--reverse**) option causes the ls utility to display the list of files in reverse alphabetical order, still sorted in columns. The –x option causes ls to display the list of files in horizontally sorted rows.

Combining options   When you need to use several options, you can usually group multiple single-letter options into one argument that starts with a single hyphen; do not put SPACEs between the options. You cannot combine options that are preceded by two hyphens in this way. Specific rules for combining options depend on the program you are running. Figure 7-1 shows both the –r and –x options with the ls utility. Together these options generate a list of filenames in horizontally sorted columns, in reverse alphabetical order. Most utilities allow you to list options in any order; thus **ls –xr** produces the same results as **ls –rx**. The command **ls –x –r** also generates the same list.

Option arguments   Some utilities have options that themselves require arguments. For example, the gcc utility has a –o option that must be followed by the name you want to give the executable file that gcc generates. Typically an argument to an option is separated from its option letter by a SPACE:

```
$ gcc -o prog prog.c
```

Displaying readable file sizes: the –h option

tip   Most utilities that report on file sizes specify the size of a file in bytes. Bytes work well when you are dealing with smaller files, but the numbers can be difficult to read when you are working with file sizes that are measured in megabytes or gigabytes. Use the **–h** (or **––human-readable**) option to display file sizes in kilo-, mega-, and gigabytes. Experiment with the **df –h** (disk free) and **ls –lh** commands.

Arguments that start with a hyphen   Another convention allows utilities to work with arguments, such as filenames, that start with a hyphen. If a file's name is –l, the following command is ambiguous:

```
$ ls -l
```

This command could mean a long listing of all files in the working directory or a listing of the file named –l. It is interpreted as the former. Avoid creating files whose names begin with hyphens. If you do create them, many utilities follow the convention that a –– argument (two consecutive hyphens) indicates the end of the options (and the beginning of the arguments). To disambiguate the command, you can type

```
$ ls -- -l
```

You can use an alternative format in which the period refers to the working directory and the slash indicates that the name refers to a file in the working directory:

```
$ ls ./-l
```

Assuming that you are working in the **/home/max** directory, the preceding command is functionally equivalent to

```
$ ls /home/max/-l
```

The following command displays a long listing of this file:

```
$ ls -l -- -l
```

These are conventions, not hard-and-fast rules, and a number of utilities do not follow them (e.g., find). Following such conventions is a good idea; it becomes much easier for users to work with your program. When you write shell programs that require options, follow the Linux option conventions.

PROCESSING THE COMMAND LINE

As you enter a command line, the Linux tty device driver (part of the Linux kernel) examines each character to see whether it must take immediate action. When you press CONTROL-H (to erase a character) or CONTROL-U (to kill a line), the device driver immediately adjusts the command line as required; the shell never sees the character(s) you erased or the line you killed. Often a similar adjustment occurs when you press CONTROL-W (to erase a word). When the character you entered does not require immediate action, the device driver stores the character in a buffer and waits for additional characters. When you press RETURN, the device driver passes the command line to the shell for processing.

Parsing the command line   When the shell processes a command line, it looks at the line as a whole and *parses* (breaks) it into its component parts (Figure 7-2). Next the shell looks for the name of the command. Usually the name of the command is the first item on the command

The --help option

tip   Many utilities display a (sometimes extensive) help message when you call them with an argument of **--help**. All utilities developed by the GNU Project (page 4) accept this option. An example follows.

```
$ bzip2 --help
bzip2, a block-sorting file compressor.  Version 1.0.5, 10-Dec-2007.

   usage: bunzip2 [flags and input files in any order]

   -h --help           print this message
   -d --decompress     force decompression
   -z --compress       force compression
   -k --keep           keep (don't delete) input files
   -f --force          overwrite existing output files
...
   If invoked as 'bzip2', default action is to compress.
            as 'bunzip2',  default action is to decompress.
            as 'bzcat', default action is to decompress to stdout.
...
```

line after the prompt (argument zero). The shell takes the first characters on the command line up to the first blank (TAB or SPACE) and then looks for a command with that name. The command name (the first token) can be specified on the command line

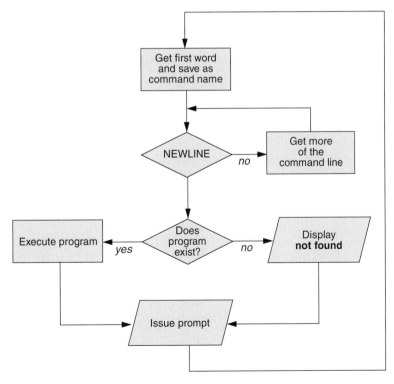

Figure 7-2   Processing the command line

either as a simple filename or as a pathname. For example, you can call the ls command in either of the following ways:

```
$ ls
$ /bin/ls
```

optional   The shell does not require that the name of the program appear first on the command line. Thus you can structure a command line as follows:

```
$ >bb <aa cat
```

This command runs cat with standard input coming from the file named **aa** and standard output going to the file named **bb**. When the shell recognizes the redirect symbols (page 231), it recognizes and processes them and their arguments before finding the name of the program that the command line is calling. This is a properly structured—albeit rarely encountered and possibly confusing—command line.

Absolute versus relative pathnames   When you give an absolute pathname on the command line or a relative pathname that is not a simple filename (i.e., any pathname that includes at least one slash), the shell looks in the specified directory (**/bin** in the case of the **/bin/ls** command) for a file that has the name **ls** and that you have permission to execute. When you give a simple filename, the shell searches through a list of directories for a filename that matches the specified name and for which you have execute permission. The shell does not look through all directories but only the ones specified by the variable named **PATH**. Refer to page 303 for more information on **PATH**. Also refer to the discussion of the which and whereis utilities on page 164.

When it cannot find the executable file, the Bourne Again Shell (bash) displays a message such as the following:

```
$ abc
bash: abc: command not found
```

One reason the shell may not be able to find the executable file is that it is not in a directory in your **PATH**. Under bash the following command temporarily adds the working directory (.) to **PATH**:

```
$ PATH=$PATH:.
```

For security reasons, you may not want to add the working directory to **PATH** permanently; see the tip on the next page and the one on page 304.

When the shell finds the program but cannot execute it (i.e., because you do not have execute permission for the file that contains the program), it displays a message similar to

```
$ def
bash: ./def: Permission denied
```

See "ls –l: Displays Permissions" on page 201 for information on displaying access permissions for a file and "chmod: Changes Access Permissions" on page 202 for instructions on how to change file access permissions.

Figure 7-3   The command does not know where standard input comes from or where standard output and standard error go

Try giving a command as *./command*

tip You can always execute an executable file in the working directory by prepending ./ to the name of the file. For example, if **myprog** is an executable file in the working directory, you can execute it with the following command, regardless of how **PATH** is set:

```
$ ./myprog
```

EXECUTING THE COMMAND LINE

Process If it finds an executable file with the same name as the command, the shell starts a new process. A *process* is the execution of a command by Linux (page 312). The shell makes each command-line argument, including options and the name of the command, available to the called program. While the command is executing, the shell waits for the process to finish. At this point the shell is in an inactive state called *sleep*. When the program finishes execution, it passes its exit status (page 952) to the shell. The shell then returns to an active state (wakes up), issues a prompt, and waits for another command.

The shell does not process arguments Because the shell does not process command-line arguments but merely passes them to the called program, the shell has no way of knowing whether a particular option or other argument is valid for a given program. Any error or usage messages about options or arguments come from the program itself. Some utilities ignore bad options.

EDITING THE COMMAND LINE

You can repeat and edit previous commands and edit the current command line. See pages 137 and 316 for more information.

STANDARD INPUT AND STANDARD OUTPUT

Standard output is a place that a program can send information, such as text. The program never "knows" where the information it sends to standard output is going (Figure 7-3). The information can go to a printer, an ordinary file, or the screen. The following sections show that by default the shell directs standard output from a command to the screen[1] and describe how you can cause the shell to redirect this output to another file.

---

1. This book uses the term *screen* to refer to a screen, terminal emulator window, or workstation—in other words, to the device that the shell displays its prompt and messages on.

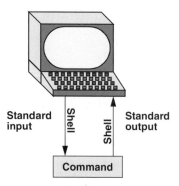

Figure 7-4   By default, standard input comes from the keyboard and standard output goes to the screen

Standard input is a place that a program gets information from. As with standard output the program never "knows" where the information comes from. The following sections explain how to redirect standard input to a command so that it comes from an ordinary file instead of from the keyboard (the default).

In addition to standard input and standard output, a running program normally has a place to send error messages: *standard error*. Refer to page 281 for more information on working with standard error.

THE SCREEN AS A FILE

Chapter 6 introduced ordinary files, directory files, and hard and soft links. Linux has an additional type of file: a *device file*. A device file resides in the Linux file structure, usually in the **/dev** directory, and represents a peripheral device, such as a screen, printer, or disk drive.

The device name that the who utility displays after your username is the filename of your screen. For example, when who displays the device name **pts/4**, the pathname of your screen is **/dev/pts/4**. When you work with multiple windows, each window has its own device name. You can also use the tty utility to display the name of the device that you give the command from. Although you would not normally have occasion to do so, you can read from and write to this file as though it were a text file. Writing to it displays what you write on the screen; reading from it reads what you enter on the keyboard.

THE KEYBOARD AND SCREEN AS STANDARD INPUT AND STANDARD OUTPUT

When you first log in, the shell directs standard output of your commands to the device file that represents the screen (Figure 7-4). Directing output in this manner causes it to appear on the screen. The shell also directs standard input to come from the same file, so that your commands receive as input anything you type on the keyboard.

```
$ cat
This is a line of text.
This is a line of text.
Cat keeps copying lines of text
Cat keeps copying lines of text
until you press CONTROL-D at the beginning
until you press CONTROL-D at the beginning
of a line.
of a line.
CONTROL-D
$
```

Figure 7-5   The cat utility copies standard input to standard output

cat   The cat utility provides a good example of the way the keyboard and screen function as standard input and standard output, respectively. When you use cat, it copies a file to standard output. Because the shell directs standard output to the screen, cat displays the file on the screen.

Up to this point cat has taken its input from the filename (argument) you specify on the command line. When you do not give cat an argument (that is, when you give the command cat followed immediately by RETURN), cat takes its input from standard input. Thus, when called without an argument, cat copies standard input to standard output, one line at a time.

To see how cat works, type **cat** and press RETURN in response to the shell prompt. Nothing happens. Enter a line of text and press RETURN. The same line appears just under the one you entered. The cat utility is working. Because the shell associates cat's standard input with the keyboard and cat's standard output with the screen, when you type a line of text cat copies the text from standard input (the keyboard) to standard output (the screen). Figure 7-5 shows this exchange.

CONTROL-D   The cat utility keeps copying text until you enter CONTROL-D on a line by itself.
signals EOF   Pressing CONTROL-D sends an EOF (end of file) signal to cat to indicate that it has reached the end of standard input and there is no more text for it to copy. The cat utility then finishes execution and returns control to the shell, which displays a prompt.

REDIRECTION

The term *redirection* encompasses the various ways you can cause the shell to alter where standard input of a command comes from and where standard output goes to. By default the shell associates standard input and standard output of a command with the keyboard and the screen. You can cause the shell to redirect standard input or standard output of any command by associating the input or output with a command or file other than the device file representing the keyboard or the screen. This section demonstrates how to redirect input from and output to ordinary text files and utilities.

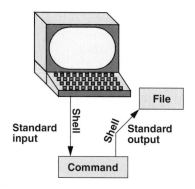

Figure 7-6   Redirecting standard output

REDIRECTING STANDARD OUTPUT

The *redirect output symbol* (**>**) instructs the shell to redirect the output of a command to the specified file instead of to the screen (Figure 7-6). The format of a command line that redirects output is

command [arguments] > filename

where ***command*** is any executable program (such as an application program or a utility), ***arguments*** are optional arguments, and ***filename*** is the name of the ordinary file the shell redirects the output to.

Figure 7-7 uses cat to demonstrate output redirection. This figure contrasts with Figure 7-5, where standard input *and* standard output are associated with the keyboard and screen. The input in Figure 7-7 comes from the keyboard. The redirect output symbol on the command line causes the shell to associate cat's standard output with the **sample.txt** file specified on the command line.

Redirecting output can destroy a file I

caution   Use caution when you redirect output to a file. If the file exists, the shell will overwrite it and destroy its contents. For more information see the tip "Redirecting output can destroy a file II" on page 235.

After giving the command and typing the text shown in Figure 7-7, the **sample.txt** file contains the text you entered. You can use cat with an argument of **sample.txt** to display this file. The next section shows another way to use cat to display the file.

Figure 7-7 shows that redirecting standard output from cat is a handy way to create a file without using an editor. The drawback is that once you enter a line and press RETURN, you cannot edit the text. While you are entering a line, the erase and kill keys work to delete text. This procedure is useful for creating short, simple files.

Figure 7-8 shows how to use cat and the redirect output symbol to *catenate* (join one after the other—the derivation of the name of the cat utility) several files into one

```
$ cat > sample.txt
This text is being entered at the keyboard and
cat is copying it to a file.
Press CONTROL-D to indicate the
end of file.
CONTROL-D
$
```

Figure 7-7   cat with its output redirected

larger file. The first three commands display the contents of three files: **stationery**, **tape**, and **pens**. The next command shows cat with three filenames as arguments. When you call it with more than one filename, cat copies the files, one at a time, to standard output. This command redirects standard output to the file **supply_orders**. The final cat command shows that **supply_orders** contains the contents of all three of the original files.

REDIRECTING STANDARD INPUT

Just as you can redirect standard output, so you can redirect standard input. The *redirect input symbol* (<) instructs the shell to redirect a command's input to come from the specified file instead of from the keyboard (Figure 7-9, next page). The format of a command line that redirects input is

> *command [arguments] < filename*

where *command* is any executable program (such as an application program or a utility), *arguments* are optional arguments, and *filename* is the name of the ordinary file the shell redirects the input from.

```
$ cat stationery
2,000 sheets letterhead ordered:     10/7/08
$ cat tape
1 box masking tape ordered:          10/14/08
5 boxes filament tape ordered:       10/28/08
$ cat pens
12 doz. black pens ordered:          10/4/08

$ cat stationery tape pens > supply_orders

$ cat supply_orders
2,000 sheets letterhead ordered:     10/7/08
1 box masking tape ordered:          10/14/08
5 boxes filament tape ordered:       10/28/08
12 doz. black pens ordered:          10/4/08
$
```

Figure 7-8   Using cat to catenate files

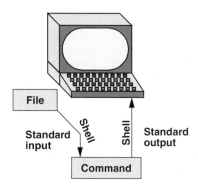

Figure 7-9   Redirecting standard input

Figure 7-10 shows cat with its input redirected from the **supply_orders** file created in Figure 7-8 and standard output going to the screen. This setup causes cat to display the sample file on the screen. The system automatically supplies an EOF signal at the end of an ordinary file.

Utilities that take input from a file or standard input

Giving a cat command with input redirected from a file yields the same result as giving a cat command with the filename as an argument. The cat utility is a member of a class of Linux utilities that function in this manner. Other members of this class of utilities include lpr, sort, grep, and Perl. These utilities first examine the command line that you call them with. If you include a filename on the command line, the utility takes its input from the file you specify. If you do not specify a filename, the utility takes its input from standard input. It is the utility or program—not the shell or operating system—that functions in this manner.

noclobber: AVOIDS OVERWRITING FILES

The shell provides the **noclobber** feature that prevents overwriting a file using redirection. Enable this feature by setting **noclobber** using the command **set −o noclobber**. The same command with **+o** unsets **noclobber**. With **noclobber** set, if you redirect output to an existing file, the shell displays an error message and does not execute the command. The following example creates a file using touch, sets **noclobber**, attempts to redirect the output from echo to the newly created file, unsets **noclobber**, and performs the same redirection:

```
$ touch tmp
$ set -o noclobber
$ echo "hi there" > tmp
bash: tmp: cannot overwrite existing file
$ set +o noclobber
$ echo "hi there" > tmp
```

You can override **noclobber** by putting a pipe symbol after the redirect symbol (>|). In the following example, the user creates a file by redirecting the output of date.

```
$ cat < supply_orders
2,000 sheets letterhead ordered:    10/7/08
1 box masking tape ordered:         10/14/08
5 boxes filament tape ordered:      10/28/08
12 doz. black pens ordered:         10/4/08
```

Figure 7-10   cat with its input redirected

Next the user sets the **noclobber** variable and redirects output to the same file again. The shell displays an error message. Then the user places a pipe symbol after the redirect symbol and the shell allows the user to overwrite the file.

```
$ date > tmp2
$ set -o noclobber
$ date > tmp2
bash: a: cannot overwrite existing file
$ date >| tmp2
```

Redirecting output can destroy a file II

caution   Depending on which shell you are using and how the environment is set up, a command such as the following may yield undesired results:

```
$ cat orange pear > orange
cat: orange: input file is output file
```

Although cat displays an error message, the shell destroys the contents of the existing **orange** file. The new **orange** file will have the same contents as **pear** because the first action the shell takes when it sees the redirection symbol (**>**) is to remove the contents of the original **orange** file. If you want to catenate two files into one, use cat to put the two files into a temporary file and then use mv to rename this third file:

```
$ cat orange pear > temp
$ mv temp orange
```

What happens in the next example can be even worse. The user giving the command wants to search through files **a**, **b**, and **c** for the word **apple** and redirect the output from grep (page 152) to the file **a.output**. Unfortunately the user enters the filename as **a output**, omitting the period and inserting a SPACE in its place:

```
$ grep apple a b c > a output
grep: output: No such file or directory
```

The shell obediently removes the contents of **a** and then calls grep. The error message may take a moment to appear, giving you a sense that the command is running correctly. Even after you see the error message, it may take a while to realize that you have destroyed the contents of **a**.

APPENDING STANDARD OUTPUT TO A FILE

The *append output symbol* (**>>**) causes the shell to add new information to the end of a file, leaving existing information intact. This symbol provides a convenient way of catenating two files into one. The following commands demonstrate the action of

```
$ date > whoson
$ cat whoson
Fri Mar 27 14:31:18 PST 2009
$ who >> whoson
$ cat whoson
Fri Mar 27 14:31:18 PST 2009
sam        console      Mar 27 05:00(:0)
max        pts/4        Mar 27 12:23(:0.0)
max        pts/5        Mar 27 12:33(:0.0)
zach       pts/7        Mar 26 08:45 (bravo.example.com)
```

Figure 7-11   Redirecting and appending output

the append output symbol. The second command accomplishes the catenation described in the preceding caution box:

```
$ cat orange
this is orange
$ cat pear >> orange
$ cat orange
this is orange
this is pear
```

The first command displays the contents of the **orange** file. The second command appends the contents of the **pear** file to the **orange** file. The final cat displays the result.

Do not trust **noclobber**

caution   Appending output is simpler than the two-step procedure described in the preceding caution box but you must be careful to include both greater than signs. If you accidentally use only one and the **noclobber** feature is not set, the shell will overwrite the **orange** file. Even if you have the **noclobber** feature turned on, it is a good idea to keep backup copies of the files you are manipulating in case you make a mistake.

Although it protects you from overwriting a file using redirection, **noclobber** does not stop you from overwriting a file using cp or mv. These utilities include the **–i** (interactive) option that helps protect you from this type of mistake by verifying your intentions when you try to overwrite a file. For more information see the tip "cp can destroy a file" on page 150.

The next example shows how to create a file that contains the date and time (the output from date), followed by a list of who is logged in (the output from who). The first line in Figure 7-11 redirects the output from date to the file named **whoson**. Then cat displays the file. Next the example appends the output from who to the **whoson** file. Finally cat displays the file containing the output of both utilities.

/dev/null: MAKING DATA DISAPPEAR

The **/dev/null** device is a *data sink*, commonly referred to as a *bit bucket*. You can redirect output that you do not want to keep or see to **/dev/null** and the output will disappear without a trace:

```
$ echo "hi there" > /dev/null
$
```

When you read from **/dev/null**, you get a null string. Give the following cat command to truncate a file named **messages** to zero length while preserving the ownership and permissions of the file:

```
$ ls -l messages
-rw-r--r--   1 max pubs 25315 Oct 24 10:55 messages
$ cat /dev/null > messages
$ ls -l messages
-rw-r--r--   1 max pubs 0 Oct 24 11:02 messages
```

PIPES

The shell uses a *pipe* to connect standard output of one command to standard input of another command. A pipe (sometimes referred to as a *pipeline*) has the same effect as redirecting standard output of one command to a file and then using that file as standard input to another command. A pipe does away with separate commands and the intermediate file. The symbol for a pipe is a vertical bar (l). The syntax of a command line using a pipe is

command_a [arguments] l *command_b [arguments]*

The preceding command line uses a pipe on a single command line to generate the same result as the following three command lines:

command_a [arguments] > *temp*
command_b [arguments] < *temp*
rm temp

In the preceding sequence of commands, the first line redirects standard output from *command_a* to an intermediate file named *temp*. The second line redirects standard input for *command_b* to come from *temp*. The final line deletes *temp*. The command using a pipe is not only easier to type, but is generally more efficient because it does not create a temporary file.

tr You can use a pipe with any of the Linux utilities that accept input either from a file specified on the command line or from standard input. You can also use pipes with commands that accept input only from standard input. For example, the tr (translate) utility takes its input from standard input only. In its simplest usage tr has the following format:

tr string1 string2

The tr utility accepts input from standard input and looks for characters that match one of the characters in **string1**. Upon finding a match, it translates the matched character in **string1** to the corresponding character in **string2**. (The first character in **string1** translates into the first character in **string2**, and so forth.) The tr utility sends its output to standard output. In both of the following examples, tr displays

```
$ ls > temp
$ lpr temp
$ rm temp
```

or

```
$ ls | lpr
```

Figure 7-12   A pipe

the contents of the **abstract** file with the letters **a**, **b**, and **c** translated into **A**, **B**, and **C**, respectively:

```
$ cat abstract | tr abc ABC
$ tr abc ABC < abstract
```

The tr utility does not change the contents of the original file; it cannot change the original file because it does not "know" the source of its input.

lpr   The lpr (line printer) utility also accepts input from either a file or standard input. When you type the name of a file following lpr on the command line, it places that file in the print queue. When you do not specify a filename on the command line, lpr takes input from standard input. This feature enables you to use a pipe to redirect input to lpr. The first set of commands in Figure 7-12 shows how you can use ls and lpr with an intermediate file (**temp**) to send a list of the files in the working directory to the printer. If the **temp** file exists, the first command overwrites its contents. The second set of commands uses a pipe to send the same list (with the exception of **temp**) to the printer.

The commands in Figure 7-13 redirect the output from the who utility to **temp** and then display this file in sorted order. The sort utility (page 154) takes its input from the file specified on the command line or, when a file is not specified, from standard input; it sends its output to standard output. The sort command line in Figure 7-13 takes its input from standard input, which is redirected (<) to come from **temp**. The output that sort sends to the screen lists the users in sorted (alphabetical) order.

Because sort can take its input from standard input or from a filename on the command line, omitting the < symbol from Figure 7-13 yields the same result.

Figure 7-14 achieves the same result without creating the **temp** file. Using a pipe, the shell redirects the output from who to the input of sort. The sort utility takes input from standard input because no filename follows it on the command line.

When many people are using the system and you want information about only one of them, you can send the output from who to grep (page 152) using a pipe. The grep utility displays the line containing the string you specify—**sam** in the following example:

```
$ who | grep 'sam'
sam        console     Mar 24 05:00
```

```
$ who > temp
$ sort < temp
max          pts/4        Mar 24 12:23
max          pts/5        Mar 24 12:33
zach         pts/7        Mar 23 08:45
sam          console      Mar 24 05:00
$ rm temp
```

Figure 7-13   Using a temporary file to store intermediate results

Another way of handling output that is too long to fit on the screen, such as a list of files in a crowded directory, is to use a pipe to send the output through less or more (both on page 148).

```
$ ls | less
```

The less utility displays text one screen at a time. To view another screen, press the SPACE bar. To view one more line, press RETURN. Press **h** for help and **q** to quit.

Some utilities change the format of their output when you redirect it. Compare the output of ls by itself and when you send it through a pipe to less.

FILTERS

A *filter* is a command that processes an input stream of data to produce an output stream of data. A command line that includes a filter uses a pipe to connect standard output of one command to the filter's standard input. Another pipe connects the filter's standard output to standard input of another command. Not all utilities can be used as filters.

In the following example, sort is a filter, taking standard input from standard output of who and using a pipe to redirect standard output to standard input of lpr. This command line sends the sorted output of who to the printer:

```
$ who | sort | lpr
```

The preceding example demonstrates the power of the shell combined with the versatility of Linux utilities. The three utilities who, sort, and lpr were not specifically designed to work with each other, but they all use standard input and standard output in the conventional way. By using the shell to handle input and output, you can piece standard utilities together on the command line to achieve the results you want.

```
$ who | sort
max          pts/4        Mar 24 12:23
max          pts/5        Mar 24 12:33
zach         pts/7        Mar 23 08:45
sam          console      Mar 24 05:00
```

Figure 7-14   A pipe doing the work of a temporary file

```
$ who | tee who.out | grep sam
sam            console      Mar 24 05:00
$ cat who.out
sam            console      Mar 24 05:00
max            pts/4        Mar 24 12:23
max            pts/5        Mar 24 12:33
zach           pts/7        Mar 23 08:45
```

Figure 7-15   Using tee

tee: SENDS OUTPUT IN TWO DIRECTIONS

The tee utility copies its standard input both to a file and to standard output. This utility is aptly named: It takes a single stream of input and sends the output in two directions. In Figure 7-15 the output of who is sent via a pipe to standard input of tee. The tee utility saves a copy of standard input in a file named **who.out** and also sends a copy to standard output. Standard output of tee goes via a pipe to standard input of grep, which displays only those lines containing the string **sam**. Use the **–a** (append) option to cause tee to append to a file instead of overwriting it.

RUNNING A COMMAND IN THE BACKGROUND

Foreground   All commands up to this point have been run in the foreground. When you run a command in the *foreground,* the shell waits for it to finish before displaying another prompt and allowing you to continue. When you run a command in the *background,* you do not have to wait for the command to finish before running another command.

Jobs   A *job* is a series of one or more commands that can be connected by pipes. You can have only one foreground job in a window or on a screen, but you can have many background jobs. By running more than one job at a time, you are using one of Linux's important features: multitasking. Running a command in the background can be useful when the command will run for a long time and does not need supervision. It leaves the screen free so you can use it for other work. Of course, when you are using a GUI, you can open another window to run another job.

Job number,   To run a command in the background, type an ampersand (**&**) just before the RETURN
PID number   that ends the command line. The shell assigns a small number to the job and displays this *job number* between brackets. Following the job number, the shell displays the *process identification (PID) number*—a larger number assigned by the operating system. Each of these numbers identifies the command running in the background. The shell then displays another prompt and you can enter another command. When the background job finishes, the shell displays a message giving both the job number and the command line used to run the command.

The next example runs in the background; it sends the output of ls through a pipe to lpr, which sends it to the printer.

```
$ ls -l | lpr &
[1] 22092
$
```

The [1] following the command line indicates that the shell has assigned job number 1 to this job. The 22092 is the PID number of the first command in the job. When this background job completes execution, you see the message

```
[1]+ Done              ls -l | lpr
```

(In place of ls –l, the shell may display something similar to ls ––color=always –l. This difference is due to the fact that ls is aliased [page 330] to ls ––color=always.)

MOVING A JOB FROM THE FOREGROUND TO THE BACKGROUND

CONTROL-Z You can suspend a foreground job (stop it from running) by pressing the suspend key, usually CONTROL-Z. The shell then stops the process and disconnects standard input from the keyboard. You can put a suspended job in the background and restart it by using the bg command followed by the job number. You do not need to specify the job number when there is only one stopped job.

Only the foreground job can take input from the keyboard. To connect the keyboard to a program running in the background, you must bring it to the foreground. To do so, type fg without any arguments when only one job is in the background. When more than one job is in the background, type fg, or a percent sign (%), followed by the number of the job you want to bring into the foreground. The shell displays the command you used to start the job (promptme in the following example), and you can enter any input the program requires to continue:

```
bash $ fg 1
promptme
```

Redirect the output of a job you run in the background to keep it from interfering with whatever you are working on in the foreground (on the screen). Refer to "Separating and Grouping Commands" on page 287 for more detail about background tasks.

kill: ABORTING A BACKGROUND JOB

The interrupt key (usually CONTROL-C) cannot abort a background process; you must use kill (page 438) for this purpose. Follow kill on the command line with either the PID number of the process you want to abort or a percent sign (%) followed by the job number.

Determining the PID of a process using ps If you forget a PID number, you can use the ps (process status) utility (page 312) to display it. The following example runs a tail –f outfile command (the –f [follow] option causes tail to watch outfile and display new lines as they are written to the file) as a background job, uses ps to display the PID number of the process, and aborts the job with kill:

```
$ tail -f outfile &
[1] 18228
$ ps | grep tail
18228 pts/4    00:00:00 tail
$ kill 18228
[1]+ Terminated            tail -f outfile
$
```

Determining the number of a job using jobs

If you forget a job number, you can use the jobs command to display a list of job numbers. The next example is similar to the previous one except it uses the job number instead of the PID number to identify the job to be killed. Sometimes the message saying the job is terminated does not appear until you press RETURN after the RETURN that executes the kill command.

```
$ tail -f outfile &
[1] 18236
$ bigjob &
[2] 18237
$ jobs
[1]-  Running                 tail -f outfile &
[2]+  Running                 bigjob &
$ kill %1
$ RETURN
[1]-  Terminated              tail -f outfile
$
```

FILENAME GENERATION/PATHNAME EXPANSION

Wildcards, globbing

When you give the shell abbreviated filenames that contain *special characters*, also called *metacharacters*, the shell can generate filenames that match the names of existing files. These special characters are also referred to as *wildcards* because they act much as the jokers do in a deck of cards. When one of these characters appears in an argument on the command line, the shell expands that argument in sorted order into a list of filenames and passes the list to the program called by the command line. Filenames that contain these special characters are called *ambiguous file references* because they do not refer to any one specific file. The process that the shell performs on these filenames is called *pathname expansion* or *globbing*.

Ambiguous file references refer to a group of files with similar names quickly, saving the effort of typing the names individually. They can also help find a file whose name you do not remember in its entirety. If no filename matches the ambiguous file reference, the shell generally passes the unexpanded reference—special characters and all—to the command.

THE ? SPECIAL CHARACTER

The question mark (?) is a special character that causes the shell to generate filenames. It matches any single character in the name of an existing file. The following command uses this special character in an argument to the lpr utility:

```
$ lpr memo?
```

The shell expands the **memo?** argument and generates a list of files in the working directory that have names composed of **memo** followed by any single character. The shell then passes this list to lpr. The lpr utility never "knows" the shell generated the filenames it was called with. If no filename matches the ambiguous file reference, the shell passes the string itself (**memo?**) to lpr or, if it is set up to do so, passes a null string (see **nullglob** on page 339).

The following example uses ls first to display the names of all files in the working directory and then to display the filenames that **memo?** matches:

```
$ ls
mem    memo12  memo9  memomax    newmemo5
memo   memo5   memoa  memos
$ ls memo?
memo5  memo9  memoa  memos
```

The **memo?** ambiguous file reference does not match **mem, memo, memo12, memomax,** or **newmemo5.** You can also use a question mark in the middle of an ambiguous file reference:

```
$ ls
7may4report  may4report      mayqreport  may_report
may14report  may4report.79   mayreport   may.report
$ ls may?report
may.report  may4report  may_report  mayqreport
```

You can use echo and ls to practice generating filenames. The echo utility displays the arguments that the shell passes to it:

```
$ echo may?report
may.report may4report may_report mayqreport
```

The shell first expands the ambiguous file reference into a list of all files in the working directory that match the string **may?report.** It then passes this list to echo, just as though you had entered the list of filenames as arguments to echo. The echo utility displays the list of filenames.

A question mark does not match a leading period (one that indicates a hidden filename; see page 190). When you want to match filenames that begin with a period, you must explicitly include the period in the ambiguous file reference.

THE * SPECIAL CHARACTER

The asterisk (*) performs a function similar to that of the question mark but matches any number of characters, *including zero characters,* in a filename. The following example first shows all files in the working directory and then shows three commands that display all the filenames that begin with the string **memo,** end with the string **mo,** and contain the string **alx:**

```
$ ls
amemo    memo         memoalx.0620  memosally  user.memo
mem      memo.0612    memoalx.keep  sallymemo
memalx   memoa        memorandum    typescript
$ echo memo*
memo memo.0612 memoa memoalx.0620 memoalx.keep memorandum memosally
$ echo *mo
amemo memo sallymemo user.memo
$ echo *alx*
memalx memoalx.0620 memoalx.keep
```

The ambiguous file reference **memo*** does not match **amemo, mem, sallymemo,** or **user.memo**. Like the question mark, an asterisk does *not* match a leading period in a filename.

The **–a** option causes ls to display hidden filenames. The command **echo** * does not display . (the working directory), .. (the parent of the working directory), **.aaa**, or **.profile**. In contrast, the command **echo .*** displays only those four names:

```
$ ls
aaa         memo.sally  sally.0612  thurs
memo.0612   report      saturday
$ ls -a
.   .aaa       aaa         memo.sally  sally.0612  thurs
..  .profile   memo.0612   report      saturday
$ echo *
aaa memo.0612 memo.sally report sally.0612 saturday thurs
$ echo .*
. .. .aaa .profile
```

In the following example, **.p*** does not match **memo.0612, private, reminder,** or **report**. The ls **.*** command causes ls to list **.private** and **.profile** in addition to the contents of the . directory (the working directory) and the .. directory (the parent of the working directory). When called with the same argument, echo displays the names of files (including directories) in the working directory that begin with a dot (.), but not the contents of directories.

```
$ ls -a
.       .private    memo.0612   reminder
..      .profile    private     report
$ echo .p*
.private .profile
$ ls .*
.private .profile

.:
memo.0612   private    reminder    report

..:
.
.
$ echo .*
. .. .private .profile
```

You can plan to take advantage of ambiguous file references when you establish conventions for naming files. For example, when you end all text filenames with **.txt**, you can reference that group of files with *.txt. The next command uses this convention to send all text files in the working directory to the printer. The ampersand causes lpr to run in the background.

```
$ lpr *.txt &
```

THE [ ] SPECIAL CHARACTERS

A pair of brackets surrounding a list of characters causes the shell to match filenames containing the individual characters. Whereas **memo?** matches **memo** followed by any character, **memo[17a]** is more restrictive: It matches only **memo1**, **memo7**, and **memoa**. The brackets define a *character class* that includes all the characters within the brackets. (GNU calls this a *character list*; a GNU *character class* is something different.) The shell expands an argument that includes a character-class definition, by substituting each member of the character class, *one at a time*, in place of the brackets and their contents. The shell then passes the list of matching filenames to the program it is calling.

Each character-class definition can replace only a single character within a filename. The brackets and their contents are like a question mark that substitutes only the members of the character class.

The first of the following commands lists the names of all files in the working directory that begin with **a**, **e**, **i**, **o**, or **u**. The second command displays the contents of the files named **page2.txt**, **page4.txt**, **page6.txt**, and **page8.txt**.

```
$ echo [aeiou]*
...
$ less page[2468].txt
...
```

A hyphen within brackets defines a range of characters within a character-class definition. For example, **[6–9]** represents **[6789]**, **[a–z]** represents all lowercase letters in English, and **[a–zA–Z]** represents all letters, both uppercase and lowercase, in English.

The following command lines show three ways to print the files named **part0**, **part1**, **part2**, **part3**, and **part5**. Each of these command lines causes the shell to call lpr with five filenames:

```
$ lpr part0 part1 part2 part3 part5

$ lpr part[01235]

$ lpr part[0-35]
```

The first command line explicitly specifies the five filenames. The second and third command lines use ambiguous file references, incorporating character-class definitions. The shell expands the argument on the second command line to include all files that have names beginning with **part** and ending with any of the characters in the character class. The character class is explicitly defined as 0, 1, 2, 3, and 5. The third command line also uses a character-class definition but defines the character class to be all characters in the range 0–3 plus 5.

The following command line prints 39 files, **part0** through **part38**:

```
$ lpr part[0-9] part[12][0-9] part3[0-8]
```

The first of the following commands lists the files in the working directory whose names start with **a** through **m**. The second lists files whose names end with **x**, **y**, or **z**.

```
$ echo [a-m]*
...
$ echo *[x-z]
...
```

optional   When an exclamation point (!) or a caret (^) immediately follows the opening bracket ([) that defines a character class, the string enclosed by the brackets matches any character *not* between the brackets. Thus [^tsq]* matches any filename that does *not* begin with **t**, **s**, or **q**.

The following examples show that *[^ab] matches filenames that do not end with the letters **a** or **b** and that [^b-d]* matches filenames that do not begin with **b**, **c**, or **d**.

```
$ ls
aa  ab  ac  ad  ba  bb  bc  bd  cc  dd
$ ls *[^ab]
ac  ad  bc  bd  cc  dd
$ ls [^b-d]*
aa  ab  ac  ad
```

You can cause a character class to match a hyphen (–) or a closing bracket (]) by placing it immediately before the final closing bracket.

The next example demonstrates that the ls utility cannot interpret ambiguous file references. First ls is called with an argument of ?old. The shell expands ?old into a matching filename, **hold**, and passes that name to ls. The second command is the same as the first, except the ? is quoted (refer to "Special Characters" on page 146). The shell does not recognize this question mark as a special character and passes it to ls. The ls utility generates an error message saying that it cannot find a file named ?old (because there is no file named ?old).

```
$ ls ?old
hold
$ ls \?old
ls: ?old: No such file or directory
```

Like most utilities and programs, ls cannot interpret ambiguous file references; that work is left to the shell.

The shell expands ambiguous file references

tip   *The shell does the expansion* when it processes an ambiguous file reference, not the program that the shell runs. In the examples in this section, *the utilities* (ls, cat, echo, lpr) *never see the ambiguous file references.* The shell expands the ambiguous file references and passes a list of ordinary filenames to the utility. In the previous examples, echo shows this to be true because it simply displays its arguments; it never displays the ambiguous file reference.

BUILTINS

A *builtin* is a utility (also called a *command*) that is built into a shell. Each of the shells has its own set of builtins. When it runs a builtin, the shell does not fork a new process. Consequently builtins run more quickly and can affect the environment of the current shell. Because builtins are used in the same way as utilities, you will not typically be aware of whether a utility is built into the shell or is a stand-alone utility.

The echo utility, for example, is a shell builtin. The shell always executes a shell builtin before trying to find a command or utility with the same name. See page 958 for an in-depth discussion of builtin commands and page 971 for a list of bash built-ins.

Listing bash builtins
To display a list of bash builtins, give the command **info bash builtin**. To display a page with more information on each builtin, move the cursor to one of the lines listing a builtin command and press RETURN. Alternatively, after typing **info bash**, give the command **/builtin** to search the bash documentation for the string **builtin**. The cursor will rest on the word **Builtin** in a menu; press RETURN to display the builtins menu.

Because bash was written by GNU, the info page has better information than does the man page. If you want to read about builtins in the man page, give the command **man bash** and search for the section on builtins with the command **/^SHELL BUIL-TIN COMMANDS** (search for a line that begins with **SHELL . . .**).

CHAPTER SUMMARY

The shell is the Linux command interpreter. It scans the command line for proper syntax, picking out the command name and any arguments. The first argument is argument one, the second is argument two, and so on. The name of the command itself is argument zero. Many programs use options to modify the effects of a command. Most Linux utilities identify an option by its leading one or two hyphens.

When you give it a command, the shell tries to find an executable program with the same name as the command. When it does, the shell executes the program. When it does not, the shell tells you that it cannot find or execute the program. If the command is a simple filename, the shell searches the directories given in the variable **PATH** in an attempt to locate the command.

When it executes a command, the shell assigns one file to the command's standard input and another file to its standard output. By default the shell causes a command's standard input to come from the keyboard and its standard output to go to the screen. You can instruct the shell to redirect a command's standard input from or standard output to any file or device. You can also connect standard output of one command to standard input of another command using a pipe. A filter is a command that reads its standard input from standard output of one command and writes its standard output to standard input of another command.

When a command runs in the foreground, the shell waits for it to finish before it displays a prompt and allows you to continue. When you put an ampersand (&) at the end of a command line, the shell executes the command in the background and displays another prompt immediately. Run slow commands in the background when you want to enter other commands at the shell prompt. The jobs builtin displays a list of suspended jobs and jobs running in the background; it includes the job number of each.

The shell interprets special characters on a command line to generate filenames. A question mark represents any single character, and an asterisk represents zero or more characters. A single character may also be represented by a character class: a list of characters within brackets. A reference that uses special characters (wildcards) to abbreviate a list of one or more filenames is called an ambiguous file reference.

A builtin is a utility that is built into a shell. Each shell has its own set of builtins. When it runs a builtin, the shell does not fork a new process. Consequently builtins run more quickly and can affect the environment of the current shell.

UTILITIES AND BUILTINS INTRODUCED IN THIS CHAPTER

Table 7-1 lists the utilities introduced in this chapter.

Table 7-1   New utilities

Utility	Function
tr	Maps one string of characters to another (page 237)
tee	Sends standard input to both a file and standard output (page 240)
bg	Moves a process to the background (page 241)
fg	Moves a process to the foreground (page 241)
jobs	Displays a list of suspended jobs and jobs running in the background (page 242)

EXERCISES

1. What does the shell ordinarily do while a command is executing? What should you do if you do not want to wait for a command to finish before running another command?

2. Using sort as a filter, rewrite the following sequence of commands:

```
$ sort list > temp
$ lpr temp
$ rm temp
```

3. What is a PID number? Why are these numbers useful when you run processes in the background? Which utility displays the PID numbers of the commands you are running?

4. Assume that the following files are in the working directory:

```
$ ls
intro     notesb    ref2      section1   section3   section4b
notesa    ref1      ref3      section2   section4a  sentrev
```

Give commands for each of the following, using wildcards to express filenames with as few characters as possible.

a. List all files that begin with **section**.

b. List the **section1**, **section2**, and **section3** files only.

c. List the **intro** file only.

d. List the **section1**, **section3**, **ref1**, and **ref3** files.

5. Refer to the man pages to determine which command will

a. Output the number of lines in the standard input that contain the *word* **a** or **A**.

b. Output only the names of the files in the working directory that contain the pattern **$(**.

c. List the files in the working directory in reverse alphabetical order.

d. Send a list of files in the working directory to the printer, sorted by size.

6. Give a command to

a. Redirect standard output from a sort command to a file named **phone_list**. Assume the input file is named **numbers**.

b. Translate all occurrences of the characters [and { to the character (, and all occurrences of the characters] and } to the character) in the file **permdemos.c**. (*Hint:* Refer to the tr man page.)

c. Create a file named **book** that contains the contents of two other files: **part1** and **part2**.

7. The lpr and sort utilities accept input either from a file named on the command line or from standard input.

a. Name two other utilities that function in a similar manner.

b. Name a utility that accepts its input only from standard input.

8. Give an example of a command that uses grep

a. With both input and output redirected.

b. With only input redirected.

c. With only output redirected.

d. Within a pipe.

In which of the preceding cases is grep used as a filter?

9. Explain the following error message. Which filenames would a subsequent ls display?

```
$ ls
abc  abd  abe  abf  abg  abh
$ rm abc ab*
rm: cannot remove 'abc': No such file or directory
```

ADVANCED EXERCISES

10. When you use the redirect output symbol (>) with a command, the shell creates the output file immediately, before the command is executed. Demonstrate that this is true.

11. In experimenting with shell variables, Max accidentally deletes his **PATH** variable. He decides he does not need the **PATH** variable. Discuss some of the problems he may soon encounter and explain the reasons for these problems. How could he *easily* return **PATH** to its original value?

12. Assume your permissions allow you to write to a file but not to delete it.

a. Give a command to empty the file without invoking an editor.

b. Explain how you might have permission to modify a file that you cannot delete.

13. If you accidentally create a filename that contains a nonprinting character, such as a CONTROL character, how can you remove the file?

14. Why does the **noclobber** variable *not* protect you from overwriting an existing file with cp or mv?

15. Why do command names and filenames usually not have embedded SPACEs? How would you create a filename containing a SPACE? How would you remove it? (This is a thought exercise, not recommended practice. If you want to experiment, create and work in a directory that contains only your experimental file.)

16. Create a file named **answer** and give the following command:

```
$ > answers.0102 < answer cat
```

Explain what the command does and why. What is a more conventional way of expressing this command?

PART III
DIGGING INTO UBUNTU LINUX

8

LINUX GUIs: X AND GNOME

This chapter covers the Linux graphical user interface (GUI). It continues where Chapter 4 left off, going into more detail about the X Window System, the basis for the Linux GUI. It presents a brief history of GNOME and KDE and discusses some of the problems and benefits of having two major Linux desktop environments. The section on the Nautilus File Browser covers the View and Side panes, the control bars, and the menubar. The final section explores some GNOME utilities, including the new Deskbar applet and Terminal, the GNOME terminal emulator.

X WINDOW SYSTEM

History of X   The X Window System (www.x.org) was created in 1984 at the Massachusetts Institute of Technology (MIT) by researchers working on a distributed computing project and a campuswide distributed environment, called Project Athena. This system was not the first windowing software to run on a UNIX system, but it was the first to become widely available and accepted. In 1985, MIT released X (version 9) to the public, for use without a license. Three years later, a group of vendors formed the X Consortium to support the continued development of X, under the leadership of MIT. By 1998, the X Consortium had become part of the Open Group. In 2001, the Open Group released X version 11, release 6.6 (X11R6.6).

The X Window System was inspired by the ideas and features found in earlier proprietary window systems but is written to be portable and flexible. X is designed to run on a workstation, typically attached to a LAN. The designers built X with the network in mind. If you can communicate with a remote computer over a network, running an X application on that computer and sending the results to a local display is straightforward.

Although the X protocol has remained stable for a long time, additions to it in the form of extensions are quite common. One of the most interesting—albeit one that has not yet made its way into production—is the Media Application Server, which aims to provide the same level of network transparency for sound and video that X does for simple windowing applications.

XFree86 and X.org   Many distributions of Linux used the XFree86 X server, which inherited its license from the original MIT X server, through release 4.3. In early 2004, just before the release of XFree86 4.4, the XFree86 license was changed to one that is more restrictive and not compatible with the GPL (page 6). In the wake of this change, a number of distributions abandoned XFree86 and replaced it with an X.org X server that is based on a pre-release version of XFree86 4.4, which predates the change in the XFree86 license. Ubuntu uses the X.org X server, named X; it is functionally equivalent to the one distributed by XFree86 because most of the code is the same so modules designed to work with one server work with the other. Intrepid uses X.org release 7.4.

The X stack   The Linux GUI is built in layers (Figure 8-1). The bottom layer is the kernel, which provides the basic interfaces to the hardware. On top of the kernel is the X server, which is responsible for managing windows and drawing basic graphical primitives such as lines and bitmaps. Rather than directly generating X commands, most programs use Xlib, the next layer, which is a standard library for interfacing with an X server. Xlib is complicated and does not provide high-level abstractions, such as buttons and text boxes. Rather than using Xlib directly, most programs rely on a toolkit that provides high-level abstractions. Using a library not only makes programming easier, but also brings consistency to applications.

In recent years, the popularity of X has grown outside the UNIX community and extended beyond the workstation class of computers it was originally conceived for. Today X is available for Macintosh computers as well as for PCs running Windows.

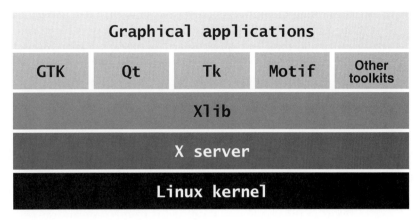

Figure 8-1   The X stack

Client/server
environment

Computer networks are central to the design of X. It is possible to run an application on one computer and display the results on a screen attached to a different computer; the ease with which this can be done distinguishes X from other window systems available today. Thanks to this capability, a scientist can run and manipulate a program on a powerful supercomputer in another building or another country and view the results on a personal workstation or laptop computer. For more information refer to "Remote Computing and Local Displays" on page 256.

When you start an X Window System session, you set up a *client/server environment*. One process, called the *X server*, displays a desktop and windows under X. Each application program and utility that makes a request of the X server is a *client* of that server. Examples of X clients include xterm, Compiz, xclock, and such general applications as word processing and spreadsheet programs. A typical request from a client is to display an image or open a window.

The roles of X client and server may be counterintuitive

tip   The terms *client* and *server,* when referring to X, have the opposite meanings of how you might think of them intuitively: The server runs the mouse, keyboard, and display; the application program is the client.

This disparity becomes even more apparent when you run an application program on a remote system. You might think of the system running the program as the server and the system providing the display as the client, but in fact it is the other way around. With X, the system providing the display is the server, and the system running the program is the client.

Events   The server also monitors keyboard and mouse actions (*events*) and passes them to the appropriate clients. For example, when you click the border of a window, the server sends this event to the window manager (client). Characters you type into a terminal emulation window are sent to that terminal emulator (client). The client takes appropriate action when it receives an event—for example, making a window active or displaying the typed character on the server.

Separating the physical control of the display (the server) from the processes need-ing access to the display (the client) makes it possible to run the server on one com-puter and the client on another computer. In general, this book discusses running the X server and client applications on a single system. "Remote Computing and Local Displays" describes using X in a distributed environment.

optional   You can run xev (X event) by giving the command **xev** from a terminal emulator window and then watch the information flow from the client to the server and back again. This utility opens the Event Tester window, which has a box in it, and asks the X server to send it events each time anything happens, such as moving the mouse pointer, clicking a mouse button, moving the mouse pointer into the box, typing, or resizing the window. The xev utility displays information about each event in the window you opened it from. You can use xev as an educational tool: Start it and see how much information is processed each time you move the mouse. Close the Event Tester window to exit from xev.

USING X

This section provides basic information about starting and configuring X from the command line. For more information see the Xserver man page and the man pages listed at the bottom of the Xserver man page.

STARTING X FROM A CHARACTER-BASED DISPLAY

Once you have logged in on a virtual console (page 134), you can start an X Win-dow System server by using startx. See page 422 for information on creating a **/etc/inittab** file that causes Linux to boot into recovery (single-user) mode, where it displays a textual interface. When you run startx, the X server displays an X screen, using the first available virtual console. The following command causes startx to run in the background so you can switch back to this virtual console and give other commands:

```
$ startx &
```

REMOTE COMPUTING AND LOCAL DISPLAYS

Typically the X server and the X client run on the same machine. To identify a remote X server (display) an X application (client) is to use, you can either set a glo-bal shell variable or use a command-line option. Before you can connect to a remote X server, you must turn off two security features: You must run xhost on the server to give the client permission to connect to the X server and you must turn off the **X –nolisten tcp** option on the server. Unless you have a reason to leave these features off, turn them back on when you finish with the examples in this section—leaving them off lessens system security. Both of these tasks must be performed on the X server because the features protect the server. You do not have to prepare the client. The examples in this section assume a server named **tiny** and a client named **dog**.

Security and the X –nolisten tcp option

security In a production environment, if you need to place an X server and the clients on different systems, it is best to forward (tunnel) X over ssh. This setup provides a secure, encrypted connection. The method described in this section is useful on local, secure networks and for understanding how X works. See "Forwarding X11" on page 645 for information on setting up ssh so it forwards X.

THE X –nolisten tcp OPTION

As Ubuntu is installed, the X server starts with the **–nolisten tcp** option, which protects the X server by preventing TCP connections to the X server. To connect to a remote X server, you must turn this option off on the server. To turn it off, select **Main menu: System⇨Administration⇨Login Window**, Security tab, and remove the tick from the check box labeled **Deny TCP connections to Xserver**. You must restart the X server (log off and log in again) to make this change take effect.

xhost GRANTS ACCESS TO A DISPLAY

As Ubuntu is installed, xhost protects each user's X server. A user who wants to grant access to his X server needs to run xhost. Assume Max is logged in on the system named **tiny** and wants to allow a user on **dog** to use his display (X server). Max runs the following command:

```
max@tiny:~$ xhost +dog
dog being added to access control list
max@tiny:~$ xhost
access control enabled, only authorized clients can connect
INET:dog
```

Without any arguments, xhost describes its state. In the preceding example, **INET** indicates an IPv4 connection. If Max wants to allow all systems to access his display, he can give the following command:

```
$ xhost +
access control disabled, clients can connect from any host
```

If you frequently work with other users via a network, you may find it convenient to add an xhost line to your **.bash_profile** file (page 277), but see the adjacent tip regarding security and xhost. Be selective in granting access to your X display with xhost, however; if another system has access to your display, you may find your work frequently interrupted.

Security and xhost

security Giving a remote system access to your display using xhost means any user on the remote system can watch everything you type in a terminal emulation window, including passwords. For this reason, some software packages, such as the Tcl/Tk development system (www.tcl.tk), restrict their own capabilities when xhost permits remote access to the X server. If you are concerned about security or want to take full advantage of systems such as Tcl/Tk, you should use a safer means of granting remote access to your X session. See the xauth man page for information about a more secure replacement for xhost.

THE DISPLAY VARIABLE

The most common method of identifying a display is to use the **DISPLAY** shell environment variable to hold the X server ID string. This locally unique identification string is automatically set up when the X server starts. The **DISPLAY** variable holds the screen number of a display:

```
$ echo $DISPLAY
:0.0
```

The format of the complete (globally unique) ID string for a display is

[hostname]:display-number[.screen-number]

where *hostname* is the name of the system running the X server, *display-number* is the number of the logical (physical) display (0 unless multiple monitors or graphical terminals are attached to the system, or if you are running X over ssh), and *screen-number* is the logical number of the (virtual) terminal (0 unless you are running multiple instances of X). When you are working with a single physical screen, you can shorten the identification string. For example, you can use **tiny:0.0** or **tiny:0** to identify the only physical display on the system named **tiny**. When the X server and the X clients are running on the same system, you can shorten this identification string even further to **:0.0** or **:0**. An ssh connection shows **DISPLAY** as **localhost:10.0**. See "X11 forwarding" on page 628 for information on setting up ssh so that it forwards X.

If **DISPLAY** is empty or not set, the screen you are working from is not running X. An application (the X client) uses the value of the **DISPLAY** variable to determine which display, keyboard, and mouse (collectively, the X server) to use. One way to run an X application, such as xclock, on the local system but have it use the X display on a remote system is to change the value of the **DISPLAY** variable on the client system so that it identifies the remote X server.

```
sam@dog:~$ export DISPLAY=tiny:0.0
sam@dog:~$ xclock &
```

The preceding example shows Sam running xclock with the default X server running on the system named **tiny**. After setting the **DISPLAY** variable to the ID of the **tiny** server, all X programs (clients) Sam starts use **tiny** as their server (i.e., output appears on **tiny**'s display and input comes from **tiny**'s keyboard and mouse). Try running xterm in place of xclock and see which keyboard it accepts input from. If this example generates an error, refer back to the two preceding sections, which explain how to set up the server to allow a remote system to connect to it.

When you change the value of DISPLAY

tip   When you change the value of the **DISPLAY** variable, all X programs send their output to the display named by **DISPLAY**.

THE −display OPTION

For a single command, you can specify the X server on the command line:

```
sam@dog:~$ xclock -display tiny:0.0
```

Many X programs accept the **–display** option. Those that do not accept this option send their output to the display specified by the **DISPLAY** variable.

RUNNING MULTIPLE X SERVERS

You can run multiple X servers on a single system. The most common reason for running a second X server is to use a second display that allocates a different number of bits to each screen pixel (uses a different *color depth* [page 1101]). The possible values are 8, 16, 24, and 32 bits per pixel. Most X servers available for Linux default to 24 or 32 bits per pixel, permitting the use of millions of colors simultaneously. Starting an X server with 8 bits per pixel permits the use of any combination of 256 colors at the same time. The maximum number of bits per pixel allowed depends on the computer graphics hardware and X server. With fewer bits per pixel, the system has to transfer less data, possibly making it more responsive. In addition, many games work with only 256 colors.

When you start multiple X servers, each must have a different ID string. The following command starts a second X server:

```
$ startx -- :1
```

The – – option marks the end of the startx options and arguments. The startx script uses the arguments to the left of this option and passes arguments to the right of this option to the X server. When you give the preceding command in a graphical environment, such as from a terminal emulator, you must work with **root** privileges; you will initiate a privileged X session. The following command starts an X server running at 16 bits per pixel:

```
$ startx -- -depth 16 &
```

Refer to "Using Virtual Consoles" on page 134 for information on how to switch to a virtual console to start a second server where you do not have to work with **root** privileges.

Guest Session When you click the Logout object (Figure 4-2, page 89), select Guest Session and Ubuntu starts a second X server to accommodate the guest user. When the guest user logs off, the original X server displays the first user's desktop. You can switch between the X servers (and users) by selecting the virtual console (page 134) that displays the X server you want to work with.

X over ssh See "Tunneling/Port Forwarding" on page 645 for information about running X over an ssh connection.

STOPPING THE X SERVER

How you terminate a window manager depends on which window manager you are running and how it is configured. If X stops responding, switch to a virtual terminal, log in from another terminal or a remote system, or use ssh to access the system. Then kill (page 438) the process running X. You can also press CONTROL-ALT-BACKSPACE to quit the X server. This method may not shut down the X session cleanly; use it only as a last resort.

REMAPPING MOUSE BUTTONS

Throughout this book, each description of a mouse click refers to the button by its position (left, middle, or right, with left implied when no button is specified) because the position of a mouse button is more intuitive than an arbitrary name or number. X numbers buttons starting at the left and continuing with the mouse wheel. The buttons on a three-button mouse are numbered 1 (left), 2 (middle), and 3 (right). A mouse wheel, if present, is numbered 4 (rolling it up) and 5 (rolling it down). Clicking the wheel is equivalent to clicking the middle mouse button. The buttons on a two-button mouse are 1 (left) and 2 (right).

If you are right-handed, you can conveniently press the left mouse button with your index finger; X programs take advantage of this fact by relying on button 1 for the most common operations. If you are left-handed, your index finger rests most conveniently on button 2 or 3 (the right button on a two- or three-button mouse).

"Mouse Preferences" on page 93 describes how to use a GUI to change a mouse between right-handed and left-handed. You can also change how X interprets the mouse buttons using xmodmap. If you are left-handed and using a three-button mouse with a wheel, the following command causes X to interpret the right button as button 1 and the left button as button 3:

```
$ xmodmap -e 'pointer = 3 2 1 4 5'
```

Omit the 4 and 5 if the mouse does not have a wheel. The following command works for a two-button mouse without a wheel:

```
$ xmodmap -e 'pointer = 2 1'
```

If xmodmap displays a message complaining about the number of buttons, use the xmodmap –pp option to display the number of buttons X has defined for the mouse:

```
$ xmodmap -pp
There are 9 pointer buttons defined.
```

Physical Button	Button Code
1	1
2	2
3	3
4	4
5	5
6	6
7	7
8	8
9	9

Then expand the previous command, adding numbers to complete the list. If the –pp option shows nine buttons, give the following command:

```
$ xmodmap -e 'pointer = 3 2 1 4 5 6 7 8 9'
```

Changing the order of the first three buttons is critical to making the mouse suitable for a left-handed user. When you remap the mouse buttons, remember to reinterpret the descriptions in this book accordingly. When this book asks you to click the left button or does not specify which button to click, use the right button, and vice versa.

DESKTOP ENVIRONMENTS/MANAGERS

Conceptually X is very simple and does not provide some of the more common features found in GUIs, such as the ability to drag windows. The UNIX/Linux philosophy is one of modularity: X relies on a window manager, such as Metacity or Compiz, to draw window borders and handle moving and resizing operations.

Unlike a window manager, which has a clearly defined task, a desktop environment (manager) does many things. In general, a desktop environment, such as KDE or GNOME, provides a means of launching applications and utilities, such as a file manager, that work with a window manager.

KDE AND GNOME

The KDE project began in 1996, with the aim of creating a consistent, user-friendly desktop environment for free UNIX-like operating systems. KDE is based on the Qt toolkit made by Trolltech. When KDE development began, the Qt license was not compatible with the GPL (page 6). For this reason the Free Software Foundation decided to support a different project, the GNU Network Object Model Environment (GNOME). More recently Qt has been released under the terms of the GPL, eliminating part of the rationale for GNOME's existence.

GNOME   GNOME is the default desktop environment for Ubuntu Linux. It provides a simple, coherent user interface that is suitable for corporate use. GNOME uses GTK for drawing widgets. GTK, developed for the GNU Image Manipulation Program (gimp), is written in C, although bindings for C++ and other languages are available.

GNOME does not take much advantage of its component architecture. Instead, it continues to support the traditional UNIX philosophy of relying on many small programs, each of which is good at doing a specific task.

KDE   KDE is written in C++ on top of the Qt framework. KDE tries to use existing technology, if it can be reused, but creates its own if nothing else is available or a superior solution is needed. For example, KDE implemented an HTML rendering engine long before the Mozilla project was born. Similarly, work on KOffice began a long time before StarOffice became the open-source OpenOffice.org. In contrast, the GNOME office applications are stand-alone programs that originated outside the GNOME project. KDE's portability is demonstrated by the use of most of its core components, including Konqueror and KOffice, under Mac OS X.

Interoperability   Since version 2, GNOME has focused on simplifying its user interface, removing options where they are deemed unnecessary, and aiming for a set of default settings that the end user will not wish to change. KDE has moved in the opposite direction, emphasizing configurability.

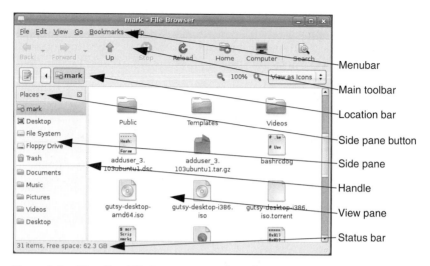

Menubar
Main toolbar
Location bar
Side pane button
Side pane
Handle
View pane
Status bar

Figure 8-2   Nautilus File Browser window displaying icons

The freedesktop.org group (freedesktop.org), whose members are drawn from the GNOME and KDE projects, is improving interoperability and aims to produce standards that will allow the two environments to work together. One standard released by freedesktop.org allows applications to use the notification area of either the GNOME or KDE panel without being aware of which desktop environment they are running in.

GNUStep

The GNUStep project (www.gnustep.org), which began before both the KDE and GNOME projects, is creating an open-source implementation of the OPENSTEP API and desktop environment. The result is a very clean and fast user interface.

The default look of WindowMaker, the GNUStep window manager is somewhat dated, but it supports themes so you can customize its appearance. The user interface is widely regarded as one of the most intuitive found on a UNIX platform. GNUStep has less overhead than KDE and GNOME, so it runs better on older hardware. If you are running Linux on hardware that struggles with GNOME and KDE or you would prefer a user interface that does not attempt to mimic Windows, try GNUStep. WindowMaker is provided in the **wmaker** package.

THE NAUTILUS FILE BROWSER WINDOW

"Using Nautilus to Work with Files" on page 94 presented an introduction to using Nautilus. This section discusses the Nautilus File Browser window in more depth. Figure 8-2 shows a File Browser window with a Side pane (sometimes called a *sidebar*), View pane, menubar, toolbar, location bar, and status bar. To display your home folder in a File Browser window, select **Main menu: Places⇨Home Folder**.

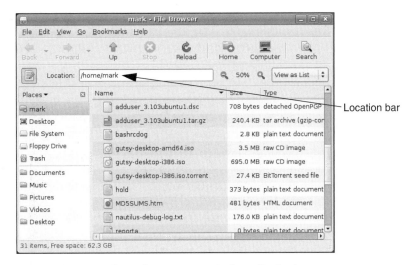

Figure 8-3 Nautilus File Browser window displaying a List view and a textual location bar

THE VIEW PANE

The View pane displays icons or a list of filenames. Select the view you prefer from the drop-down list at the right end of the location bar. Figure 8-2 shows **View as Icons** (*HARDY*) and Figure 8-3 shows **View as List**(*HARDY*). *INTREPID* uses the terms **Icon View** and **List View,** respectively, and also provides a **Compact View.** Objects in the View pane behave exactly as objects on the desktop do. See the sections starting on page 89 for information on working with objects.

You can cut/copy and paste objects within a single View pane, between View panes, or between a View pane and the desktop. The Object context menu (right-click) has cut, copy, and paste selections. Or, you can use the clipboard (page 110) to cut/copy and paste objects.

Nautilus can open a terminal emulator

tip When you install the **nautilus-open-terminal** package and log out and log back in, Nautilus presents an Open in Terminal selection in context menus where appropriate. For example, with this package installed, when you right-click a folder (directory) object and select **Open in Terminal**, Nautilus opens a terminal emulator with that directory as the working directory (page 190).

THE SIDE PANE

The Side pane augments the information Nautilus displays in the View pane. Press F9 or click the small **x** at the top of the Side pane to close it. You can display the Side pane by pressing F9 or selecting **File Browser menubar: View⇨Side Pane.** To change the horizontal size of the Side pane and its contents, drag the handle (Figure 8-2) on its right side.

The Side pane can display six types of information. The button at its top controls which type it displays. This button is initially labeled **Places**; click it to display the Side pane drop-down list, which has the following selections:

Places   Places lists folders. Double-click one of these folders to display that folder in the View pane. You can open a directory in a new File Browser window by right-clicking the directory in Places and selecting **Open in New Window**. INTREPID: Right-click and select **Open New Tab** to open the directory in a new tab.

Places contains two parts: The list above the divider is static and holds your home directory, your desktop, the filesystem, a CD-ROM drive (when there is media in it) and unmounted filesystems (if present), and the trash. The list below the divider holds bookmarks. Add a bookmark by displaying the directory you want to book-mark in the View pane and pressing CONTROL-D or by selecting **File Browser menubar: Bookmarks⇨Add Bookmark**. Remove a bookmark by selecting **File Browser menubar: Bookmarks⇨Edit Bookmarks** or by right-clicking the bookmark and selecting **Remove**. You can also use **Edit Bookmarks** to reorder bookmarks.

Information   Information presents information about the folder displayed by the View pane.

Tree   Tree presents an expandable tree view of your home folder, and each mounted file-system. Each directory in the tree has a triangle to its left. Click a triangle that points right to expand a directory; click a triangle that points down to close a directory. Click a directory in the tree to display that directory in the View pane. Double-click a directory to expand it in the Side pane and display it in the View pane.

History   History displays a chronological list of the folders that have been displayed in the View pane, with the most recently displayed folder at the top. Double-click a folder in this list to display it in the View pane.

Notes   Notes provides a place to keep notes about the folder displayed in the View pane.

Emblems   Similar to the Emblems tab in the Object Properties window (page 114), Emblems allows you to drag emblems from the Side pane and drop them on objects in the View pane. Drag and drop the **Erase** emblem to erase emblems associated with an object. You cannot erase emblems that Ubuntu places on objects, such as locked and link emblems.

CONTROL BARS

This section discusses the four control bars that initially appear in a File Browser window: the status bar, menubar, Main toolbar, and location bar (Figure 8-2). From **File Browser menubar: View**, you can choose which of these bars to display, except for the menubar, which Nautilus always displays.

Menubar   The menubar appears at the top of the File Browser window and displays a menu when you click one of its selections. Which menu selections Nautilus displays depend on what the View pane is displaying and which object(s) are selected. The next section describes the menubar in detail.

Main toolbar The Main toolbar appears below the menubar and holds navigation tool icons: Back, Forward, Up, Stop, Reload, Home, Computer, and Search. If the Main toolbar is too short to hold all icons, Nautilus displays a button with a triangle pointing down at the right end of the toolbar. Click this button to display a drop-down list of the remaining icons.

Location bar Below the Main toolbar is the location bar, which displays the name of the directory that appears in the View pane. It can display this name in two formats: iconic (using buttons) and textual (using a text box). Press CONTROL-L to switch to textual format, click the pencil and paper icon at the left of this bar to switch between iconic and textual formats.

In iconic format, each button represents a directory in a pathname (page 191). The View pane displays the directory of the depressed (darker) button. Click one of these buttons to display that directory. If the leftmost button holds a triangle that points to the left, Nautilus is not displaying buttons for all the directories in the absolute (full) pathname; click the button with a triangle in it to display more directory buttons.

In textual format, the text box displays the absolute pathname of the displayed directory. To have Nautilus display another directory, enter the pathname of the directory and press RETURN.

The location bar also holds the magnification selector and the View drop-down list. To change the magnification of the display in the View pane, click the plus or minus sign in a magnifying glass on either side of the magnification percentage. Right-click the magnification percentage itself to return to the default magnification. Left-click the magnification percentage to display a drop-down list of magnifications. Click **View as** (to the right of the right-hand magnifying glass) to choose whether to view files as icons, a list, or, under *INTREPID*, in compact format.

Status bar The status bar, at the bottom of the window, indicates how many items are displayed in the View pane. If the directory you are viewing is on the local system, it also tells you how much free space is on the device that holds the directory displayed by the View pane.

MENUBAR

The Nautilus File Browser menubar controls what information the File Browser displays and how it displays that information. Many of the menu selections duplicate controls found elsewhere in the File Browser window. This section highlights some of the selections on the menubar; click **Help** on the menubar and select **Contents** or **Get Help Online** for more information. This section describes the six parts of the menubar.

File The several Open selections and the Property selection of File work with the highlighted object(s) in the View pane. If no objects are highlighted, these selections

Figure 8-4   Connect to Server window

are grayed out or absent. Selecting **Connect to Server** displays the Connect to Server window (Figure 8-4). This window presents a **Service type** drop-down list that allows you to select FTP, SSH, Windows, or other types of servers. Enter the URL of the server in the text box labeled **Server**. For an FTP connection, do not enter the **ftp://** part of the URL. Fill in the optional information as appropriate. Click **Connect**. If the server requires authentication, Nautilus displays a window so you can enter your username and password. Nautilus opens a window displaying a directory on the server and an object, named for the URL you specified, on the desktop. After you close the window, you can open the object to connect to and display a directory on the server.

Edit   Many of the Edit selections work with highlighted object(s) in the View pane; if no objects are highlighted, these selections are grayed out or absent. This section discusses three selections from Edit: Create Archive, Backgrounds and Emblems, and Preferences.

The **Edit⇨Create Archive** selection creates a single archive file comprising the selected objects. This selection opens a Create Archive window (Figure 8-5) that allows you to specify the name and location of the archive. The drop-down list to the right of the Archive text box allows you to specify a filename extension that determines the type of archive this tool creates. For example, **.tar.gz** creates a tar (page 162) file compressed by gzip (page 161) and **.tar.bz2** creates a tar file compressed by bzip2 (page 160). *INTREPID*: Click the triangle to the left of Other Objects to specify a password for the archive (available only with certain types of archives).

The **Edit⇨Backgrounds and Emblems** selection has three buttons on the left: Patterns, Colors, and Emblems. Click **Patterns** to display many pattern objects on the right side of the window. Drag and drop one of these objects on the View pane of a File Browser window to change the background of all File Browser View panes. Drag and drop the Reset object to reset the background to its default color and pattern (usually white). The Colors button works the same way as the Patterns button. The Emblems button works the same way as the Emblems tab in the Side pane (page 264).

Figure 8-5   Create Archive window

The **Edit⇨Preferences** selection displays the File Management Preferences window (Figure 8-6). This window has six tabs that control the appearance and behavior of File Browser windows.

The **Views** tab sets several defaults, including which view the File Browser displays (Icon, List, or, under *INTREPID*, Compact view), the arrangement of the objects, and the default zoom level. *INTREPID* has a Compact View Defaults section.

Delete Versus Move to Trash   The **Behavior** tab controls how many clicks it takes to open an object and what Nautilus does when it opens an executable text object (script). For more confident users, this tab has an option that includes a Delete selection in addition to the Move to Trash

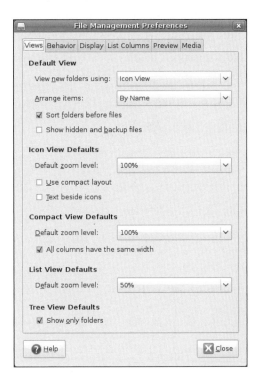

Figure 8-6   File Management Preferences window, Views tab

selection on several menus. The Delete selection immediately removes the selected object instead of moving it to the **Trash** folder.

The **Display** tab specifies which information Nautilus includes in object (icon) captions. The three drop-down lists specify the order in which Nautilus displays information as you increase the zoom level of the View pane. This tab also specifies the date format Nautilus uses.

The **List Columns** tab specifies which columns Nautilus displays, and in what order it displays them, in the View pane when you select **View as List** (*HARDY*) or **List View** (*INTREPID*).

The **Preview** tab controls when Nautilus displays or plays previews of files (Always, Local Files Only, Never).

The **Media** tab specifies what action Nautilus takes when you insert media such as a CD, or connect devices such as a flash drive, to the system.

View   Click the **Main Toolbar, Side Pane, Location Bar,** and **Statusbar** selections in View to display or remove these elements from the window. The **Show Hidden Files** selection displays in the View pane files with hidden filenames (page 190).

Go   The Go selections display various folders in the View pane.

Bookmarks   Bookmarks appear at the bottom of this menu and in the Side pane under Places. The Bookmarks selections are explained under "Places" on page 264.

INTREPID Tabs   The Tabs selections work with tabs in the Nautilus window.

Help   The Help selections display local and online information about Nautilus.

Figure 8-7   Appearance Preferences window, Fonts tab

GNOME UTILITIES

GNOME comes with numerous utilities that can make your work with the desktop easier and more productive. This section covers several tools that are integral to the use of GNOME.

FONT PREFERENCES

The Fonts tab of the Appearance Preferences window (Figure 8-7) enables you to change the font that GNOME uses for applications, documents, the desktop, window titles, and terminal emulators (fixed width). To display this window, select **Main menu: System⇨Preferences⇨Appearance** or enter **gnome-appearance-properties** on a command line. Click the **Fonts** tab. Click one of the five font bars in the upper part of the window to display the Pick a Font window (discussed next).

Examine the four sample boxes in the lower part of the window and select the one in which the letters look the best. Subpixel smoothing is usually best for LCD monitors. Click **Details** to refine the font rendering further, again picking the box in each section in which the letters look the best.

PICK A FONT WINDOW

The Pick a Font window (Figure 8-8) appears when you need to choose a font (see "Font Preferences"). From this window you can select a font family, a style, and a size. A preview of your choice appears in the Preview box in the lower part of the window. Click **OK** when you are satisfied with your choice.

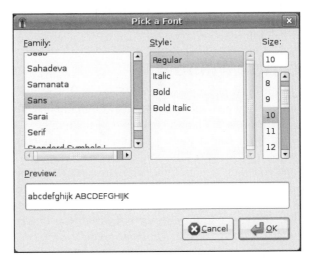

Figure 8-8   The Pick a Font window

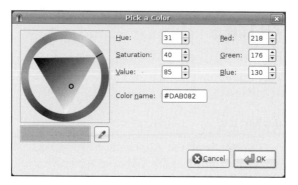

Figure 8-9   Pick a Color window

PICK A COLOR WINDOW

The Pick a Color window (Figure 8-9) appears when you need to specify a color, such as when you specify a solid color for the desktop background (page 101) or a panel. To specify a color for a panel, right-click the panel to display its context menu, select **Properties**, click the **Background** tab, click the radio button labeled **Solid color**, and click within the box labeled **Color**. GNOME displays the Pick a Color window.

When the Pick a Color window opens, the bar below the color circle displays the current color. Click the desired color on the color ring, and click/drag the lightness of that color in the triangle. As you change the color, the right end of the bar below the color circle previews the color you are selecting, while the left end continues to display the current color. You can also use the eyedropper to pick up a color from the workspace: Click the eyedropper, and then click the resulting eyedropper mouse pointer on the color you want to select. The color you choose appears in the bar. Click **OK** when you are satisfied with the color you have specified.

RUN APPLICATION WINDOW

The Run Application window (Figure 4-4, page 91) enables you to run a program as though you had initiated it from a command line. To display the Run Application window, press Alt-F2. Enter a command in the text box. As soon as GNOME can uniquely identify the command you are entering, it completes the command and may display an object that identifies the application. Keep typing if the displayed command is not the one you want to run. Otherwise, press RETURN to run the command or TAB to accept the command in the text box. You can then continue entering information in the window. Click **Run with file** to specify a file to use as an argument to the command in the text box. Put a tick in the check box labeled **Run in terminal** to run a textual application, such as vim, in a terminal emulator window.

SEARCHING FOR FILES

The Search for Files window (Figure 8-10) can help you find files whose locations or names you do not know or have forgotten. Open this window by selecting **Main menu: Places⇨Search for Files** or enter **gnome-search-tool** on a command

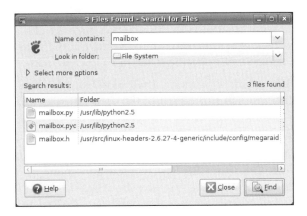

Figure 8-10   The Search for Files window

line from a terminal emulator or Run Application window (ALT-F2). To search by filename or partial filename, enter the (partial) filename in the combo box labeled **Name contains** and then select the folder you want to search in from the drop-down list labeled **Look in folder**. When GNOME searches in a folder, it searches subfolders to any level (it searches the directory hierarchy). To search all directories in all mounted filesystems, select **File System** from the drop-down list labeled **Look in folder**. Select **Other** to search a folder not included in the drop-down list; GNOME opens the Browse window (page 97). Once you have entered the search criteria, click **Find**. GNOME displays the list of files matching the criteria in the list box labeled **Search results**. Double-click a file in this list box to open it.

You can refine the search by entering more search criteria. Click the triangle to the left of **Select more options** to expand the window and display more search criteria. GNOME initially displays one search criterion and a line for adding criteria as shown in Figure 8-11. With this part of the window expanded, GNOME incorporates all visible search criteria when you click **Find**.

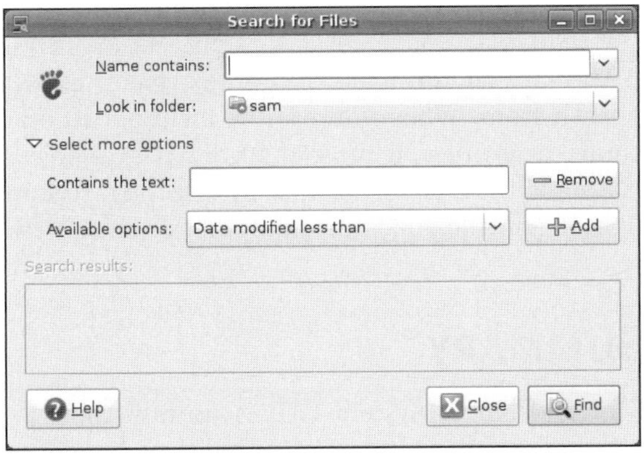

Figure 8-11   The Search for Files window with Select more options expanded

The first line below **Select more options** holds a text box labeled **Contains the text.** Absence of an entry in this text box matches all files. You can leave this text box as is or remove the line by clicking **Remove** at the right end of the line. To search for a file that contains a specific string of characters (text), enter the string in this text box.

Add criteria by making a selection from the list box labeled **Available options** and clicking **Add** to the right of the drop-down list. Remove criteria by clicking **Remove** at the right end of the line that holds the criterion you want to remove.

To select files that were modified fewer than a specified number of days ago, select **Date modified less than** from the drop-down list labeled **Available options** and click **Add.** The Search for Files window adds a line with a spin box labeled **Date modified less than.** With this spin box showing **0** (zero), as it does initially, no file matches the search criteria. Change this number as desired and click **Find** to begin the search.

GNOME Terminal Emulator/Shell

The GNOME terminal emulator (Figure 4-17, page 112) displays a window that mimics a character-based terminal (page 111). To display a terminal emulator window, select **Main menu: Applications⇨Accessories⇨Terminal** or enter **gnome-terminal** on a command line or from a Run Application window (ALT-F2). When the GNOME terminal emulator is already displayed, select **Terminal menubar: File⇨Open Terminal** or right-click within the Terminal window and select **Open Terminal** to display a new terminal emulator window.

GNOME terminal emulator shortcuts

tip   While using the GNOME terminal emulator, CONTROL-SHIFT-N opens a new window and CONTROL-SHIFT-T opens a new tab. New windows and tabs open to the working directory. In addition, you can use CONTROL-PAGE UP and CONTROL-PAGE DOWN to switch between tabs.

To open an additional terminal session within the same Terminal window, right-click the window and select **Open Tab** from the context menu or select **Terminal menubar: File⇨Open Tab.** A row of tabs appears below the menubar as gnome-terminal opens another terminal session on top of the existing one. Add as many terminal sessions as you like; click the tabs to switch between sessions.

A session you add from the context menu uses the same profile as the session you open it from. When you use the menubar to open a session, GNOME gives you a choice of profiles, if more than one is available. You can add and modify profiles, including the Default profile, by selecting **Terminal menubar: Edit⇨Profiles.** Highlight the profile you want to modify or click **New** to design a new profile.

Chapter Summary

The X Window System GUI is portable and flexible and makes it easy to write applications that work on many different types of systems without having to know low-level details for the individual systems. This GUI can operate in a networked environment, allowing a user to run a program on a remote system and send the results to a local display. The client/server concept is integral to the operation of the X Window System, in which the X server is responsible for fulfilling requests made of X Window System applications or clients. Hundreds of clients are available that can run under X. Programmers can also write their own clients, using tools such as the Qt and KDE libraries to write KDE programs and the GTK+ and GTK+2 GNOME libraries to write GNOME programs.

The window managers, and virtually all X applications, are designed to help users tailor their work environments in simple or complex ways. You can designate applications that start automatically, set such attributes as colors and fonts, and even alter the way keyboard strokes and mouse clicks are interpreted.

Built on top of the X Window System, the GNOME desktop manager can be used as is or customized to better suit your needs. It is a graphical user interface to system services (commands), the filesystem, applications, and more. Although not part of GNOME, the Metacity and Compiz window managers work closely with GNOME and are the default window managers for GNOME under Ubuntu Linux. A window manager controls all aspects of the windows, including placement, decoration, grouping, minimizing and maximizing, sizing, and moving.

The Nautilus File Browser window is a critical part of GNOME; the desktop is a modified File Browser window. The File Browser View pane displays icons or a list of filenames that you can work with. The Side pane, which can display six types of information, augments the information Nautilus displays in the View pane.

GNOME also provides many graphical utilities you can use to customize and work with the desktop. It supports MIME types so when you double-click an object, GNOME generally knows which tool to use to display the data represented by the object. In sum, GNOME is a powerful desktop manager that can make your job both easier and more fun.

EXERCISES

1. a. What is Nautilus?

   b. List four things you can do with Nautilus.

   c. How do you use Nautilus to search for a file?

2. What is a terminal emulator? What does it allow you to do from a GUI that you would not be able to do without one?

3. How would you search the entire filesystem for a file named **today.odt**?

4. a. List two ways you can open a file using Nautilus.

   b. How does Nautilus "know" which program to use to open different types of files?

c. Which are the three common Nautilus control bars? What kinds of tools do you find on each?

d. Discuss the use of the Nautilus location bar in textual mode.

ADVANCED EXERCISES

5. Assume a mouse with nine pointer buttons defined. How would you reverse the effects of using the mouse wheel?

6. a. How would you use Nautilus to connect to the FTP server at ftp.ubuntu.com?

   b. Open the following folders: **ubuntu, dists,** and **intrepid.** How would you copy the file named **Contents-i386.gz** to the desktop? What type of file is **Contents-i386.gz**?

   c. How would you open the **Contents-i386.gz** file on the desktop? How would you open the **Contents-i386.gz** file on the FTP server? Which file opens more quickly? Why? Which file can you modify?

7. Discuss the client/server environment the X Window System sets up. How does the X server work? List three X clients. Where is the client and where is the server when you log in on a local system? What is an advantage of this setup?

8. Run xwininfo from a terminal emulator window and answer these questions:

   a. What does xwininfo do?

   b. What does xwininfo give as the name of the window you clicked? Does that agree with the name in the window's titlebar?

   c. What is the size of the window? What units does xwininfo display? What is the depth of a window?

   d. How can you get xwininfo to display the same information without having to click the window?

9. Write an xeyes command to display a window that is 600 pixels wide and 400 pixels tall, is located 200 pixels from the right edge of the screen and 300 pixels from the top of the screen, and contains orange eyes outlined in blue with red pupils. (*Hint:* Refer to the xeyes man page.)

THE BOURNE AGAIN SHELL

This chapter picks up where Chapter 7 left off. Chapter 27 expands on this chapter, exploring control flow commands and more advanced aspects of programming the Bourne Again Shell (bash). The bash home page is at www.gnu.org/software/bash. The bash info page is a complete Bourne Again Shell reference.

The Bourne Again Shell is a command interpreter and high-level programming language. As a command interpreter, it processes commands you enter on the command line in response to a prompt. When you use the shell as a programming language, it processes commands stored in files called *shell scripts*. Like other languages, shells have variables and control flow commands (for example, **for** loops and **if** statements).

When you use a shell as a command interpreter, you can customize the environment you work in. You can make your prompt display the name of the working directory, create a function or alias for cp that keeps it from overwriting certain kinds of files, take advantage of keyword variables to change aspects of how the shell works, and so on. You can also write shell scripts that do your bidding—anything from a one-line script that stores a long, complex command to a longer script that runs a set of reports, prints them, and mails you a reminder when the job is done. More complex shell scripts are themselves programs; they do not just run other programs. Chapter 27 has some examples of these types of scripts.

Most system shell scripts are written to run under bash (or dash; see below). If you will ever work in recovery mode—when you boot the system or perform system maintenance, administration, or repair work, for example—it is a good idea to become familiar with this shell.

This chapter expands on the interactive features of the shell described in Chapter 7, explains how to create and run simple shell scripts, discusses job control, introduces the basic aspects of shell programming, talks about history and aliases, and describes command-line expansion. Chapter 27 presents some more challenging shell programming problems.

BACKGROUND

The Bourne Again Shell is based on the Bourne Shell (the early UNIX shell; this book refers to it as the *original Bourne Shell* to avoid confusion), which was written by Steve Bourne of AT&T's Bell Laboratories. Over the years the original Bourne Shell has been expanded but it remains the basic shell provided with many commercial versions of UNIX.

sh Shell   Because of its long and successful history, the original Bourne Shell has been used to write many of the shell scripts that help manage UNIX systems. Some of these scripts appear in Linux as Bourne Again Shell scripts. Although the Bourne Again Shell includes many extensions and features not found in the original Bourne Shell, bash maintains compatibility with the original Bourne Shell so you can run Bourne Shell scripts under bash. On UNIX systems the original Bourne Shell is named sh.

dash Shell   The bash executable file is about 800 kilobytes, has many features, and is well suited as a user login shell. The dash (Debian Almquist) shell is about 100 kilobytes, offers Bourne Shell compatibility for shell scripts (noninteractive use), and, because of its size, can load and execute shell scripts much more quickly than bash. Most system scripts are set up to run sh, which under Ubuntu is a symbolic link to dash. This setup allows the system to boot and run system shell scripts quickly.

On many Linux systems sh is a symbolic link to bash, ensuring scripts that require the presence of the Bourne Shell still run. When called as sh, bash does its best to emulate the original Bourne Shell.

Korn Shell   System V UNIX introduced the Korn Shell (ksh), written by David Korn. This shell extended many features of the original Bourne Shell and added many new features. Some features of the Bourne Again Shell, such as command aliases and command-line editing, are based on similar features from the Korn Shell.

POSIX   The POSIX (Portable Operating System Interface) family of related standards is being developed by PASC (IEEE's Portable Application Standards Committee, www.pasc.org). A comprehensive FAQ on POSIX, including many links, appears at www.opengroup.org/austin/papers/posix_faq.html.

POSIX standard 1003.2 describes shell functionality. The Bourne Again Shell provides the features that match the requirements of this standard. Efforts are under way to make the Bourne Again Shell fully comply with the POSIX standard. In the meantime, if you invoke bash with the --posix option, the behavior of the Bourne Again Shell will closely match the POSIX requirements.

SHELL BASICS

This section covers writing and using startup files, redirecting standard error, writing and executing simple shell scripts, separating and grouping commands, implementing job control, and manipulating the directory stack.

chsh: **changes your login shell**

tip   The person who sets up your account determines which shell you use when you first log in on the system or when you open a terminal emulator window in a GUI environment. Under Ubuntu, **bash** is the default shell. You can run any shell you like once you are logged in. Enter the name of the shell you want to use (**bash**, **tcsh**, or another shell) and press RETURN; the next prompt will be that of the new shell. Give an **exit** command to return to the previous shell. Because shells you call in this manner are nested (one runs on top of the other), you will be able to log out only from your original shell. When you have nested several shells, keep giving **exit** commands until you reach your original shell. You will then be able to log out.

Use the chsh utility to change your login shell permanently. First give the command **chsh**. In response to the prompts, enter your password and the absolute pathname of the shell you want to use (**/bin/bash**, **/bin/tcsh**, or the pathname of another shell). When you change your login shell in this manner using a terminal emulator (page 111) under a GUI, subsequent terminal emulator windows will not reflect the change until you log out of the system and log back in. See page 441 for an example of how to use chsh.

STARTUP FILES

When a shell starts, it runs startup files to initialize itself. Which files the shell runs depends on whether it is a login shell, an interactive shell that is not a login shell (such as you get by giving the command **bash**), or a noninteractive shell (one used to execute a shell script). You must have read access to a startup file to execute the commands in it. Ubuntu Linux puts appropriate commands in some of these files. This section covers bash startup files.

LOGIN SHELLS

The files covered in this section are executed by login shells and shells that you start with the bash **--login** option. Login shells are, by their nature, interactive.

/etc/profile   The shell first executes the commands in **/etc/profile**. A user working with **root** privileges can set up this file to establish systemwide default characteristics for users running bash.

.bash_profile
.bash_login
.profile   Next the shell looks for ~/.bash_profile, ~/.bash_login, and ~/.profile (~/ is short-hand for your home directory), in that order, executing the commands in the first of these files it finds. You can put commands in one of these files to override the defaults set in **/etc/profile**. A shell running on a virtual terminal does not execute commands in these files.

.bash_logout   When you log out, bash executes commands in the ~/.bash_logout file. This file often holds commands that clean up after a session, such as those that remove temporary files.

INTERACTIVE NONLOGIN SHELLS

The commands in the preceding startup files are not executed by interactive, non-login shells. However, these shells inherit values from the login shell variables that are set by these startup files.

/etc/bashrc   Although not called by bash directly, many ~/.bashrc files call **/etc/bashrc**. This setup allows a user working with **root** privileges to establish systemwide default characteristics for nonlogin bash shells.

.bashrc   An interactive nonlogin shell executes commands in the ~/.bashrc file. Typically a startup file for a login shell, such as **.bash_profile**, runs this file, so both login and nonlogin shells run the commands in **.bashrc**.

NONINTERACTIVE SHELLS

The commands in the previously described startup files are not executed by nonin-teractive shells, such as those that runs shell scripts. However, these shells inherit login shell variables that are set by these startup files.

BASH_ENV   Noninteractive shells look for the environment variable **BASH_ENV** (or **ENV** if the shell is called as sh) and execute commands in the file named by this variable.

SETTING UP STARTUP FILES

Although many startup files and types of shells exist, usually all you need are the **.bash_profile** and **.bashrc** files in your home directory. Commands similar to the following in **.bash_profile** run commands from **.bashrc** for login shells (when **.bashrc** exists). With this setup, the commands in **.bashrc** are executed by login and nonlogin shells.

```
if [ -f ~/.bashrc ]; then . ~/.bashrc; fi
```

The [**–f ~/.bashrc**] tests whether the file named **.bashrc** in your home directory exists. See pages 911 and 913 for more information on test and its synonym [ ]. See page 280 for information on the . (dot) builtin.

Use .bash_profile to set PATH

tip Because commands in **.bashrc** may be executed many times, and because subshells inherit exported variables, it is a good idea to put commands that add to existing variables in the **.bash_profile** file. For example, the following command adds the **bin** subdirectory of the **home** directory to **PATH** (page 303) and should go in **.bash_profile**:

```
PATH=$PATH:$HOME/bin
```

When you put this command in **.bash_profile** and not in **.bashrc**, the string is added to the **PATH** variable only once, when you log in.

Modifying a variable in **.bash_profile** causes changes you make in an interactive session to propagate to subshells. In contrast, modifying a variable in **.bashrc** overrides changes inherited from a parent shell.

Sample **.bash_profile** and **.bashrc** files follow. Some commands used in these files are not covered until later in this chapter. In any startup file, you must export variables and functions that you want to be available to child processes. For more information refer to "Locality of Variables" on page 948.

```
$ cat ~/.bash_profile
if [ -f ~/.bashrc ]; then
    . ~/.bashrc               # Read local startup file if it exists
fi
PATH=$PATH:.                  # Add the working directory to PATH
export PS1='[\h \W \!]\$ '    # Set prompt
```

The first command in the preceding **.bash_profile** file executes the commands in the user's **.bashrc** file if it exists. The next command adds to the **PATH** variable (page 303). Typically **PATH** is set and exported in **/etc/profile** so it does not need to be exported in a user's startup file. The final command sets and exports **PS1** (page 305), which controls the user's prompt.

A sample **.bashrc** file is shown on the next page. The first command executes the commands in the **/etc/bashrc** file if it exists. Next the file sets and exports the **LANG** (page 310) and **VIMINIT** (for vim initialization) variables and defines several aliases. The final command defines a function (page 333) that swaps the names of two files.

```
$ cat ~/.bashrc
if [ -f /etc/bashrc ]; then
    source /etc/bashrc             # read global startup file if it exists
fi

set -o noclobber                   # prevent overwriting files
unset MAILCHECK                    # turn off "you have new mail" notice
export LANG=C                      # set LANG variable
export VIMINIT='set ai aw'         # set vim options
alias df='df -h'                   # set up aliases
alias rm='rm -i'                   # always do interactive rm's
alias lt='ls -ltrh | tail'
alias h='history | tail'
alias ch='chmod 755 '

function switch()                  # a function to exchange the names
{                                  # of two files
    local tmp=$$switch
    mv "$1" $tmp
    mv "$2" "$1"
    mv $tmp "$2"
}
```

. (DOT) OR source: RUNS A STARTUP FILE IN THE CURRENT SHELL

After you edit a startup file such as .bashrc, you do not have to log out and log in again to put the changes into effect. Instead, you can run the startup file using the . (dot) or source builtin (they are the same command). As with all other commands, the . must be followed by a SPACE on the command line. Using . or source is similar to running a shell script, except these commands run the script as part of the current process. Consequently, when you use . or source to run a script, changes you make to variables from within the script affect the shell you run the script from. If you ran a startup file as a regular shell script and did not use the . or source builtin, the variables created in the startup file would remain in effect only in the subshell running the script—not in the shell you ran the script from. You can use the . or source command to run any shell script—not just a startup file—but undesirable side effects (such as changes in the values of shell variables you rely on) may occur. For more information refer to "Locality of Variables" on page 948.

In the following example, .bashrc sets several variables and sets **PS1**, the prompt, to the name of the host. The . builtin puts the new values into effect.

```
$ cat ~/.bashrc
export TERM=vt100                  # set the terminal type
export PS1="$(hostname -f): "      # set the prompt string
export CDPATH=:$HOME               # add HOME to CDPATH string
stty kill '^u'                     # set kill line to control-u

$ . ~/.bashrc
bravo.example.com:
```

COMMANDS THAT ARE SYMBOLS

The Bourne Again Shell uses the symbols (,), [,], and $ in a variety of ways. To minimize confusion, Table 9-1 lists the most common use of each of these symbols, even though some of them are not introduced until later in this book.

Table 9-1   Builtin commands that are symbols

Symbol	Command
( )	Subshell (page 290)
$( )	Command substitution (page 346)
(( ))	Arithmetic evaluation; a synonym for **let** (use when the enclosed value contains an equal sign; page 972)
$(( ))	Arithmetic expansion (not for use with an enclosed equal sign; page 344)
[ ]	The **test** command (pages 911 and 913)
[[ ]]	Conditional expression; similar to [ ] but adds string comparisons (page 973)

REDIRECTING STANDARD ERROR

Chapter 7 covered the concept of standard output and explained how to redirect standard output of a command. In addition to standard output, commands can send output to *standard error*. A command can send error messages to standard error to keep them from getting mixed up with the information it sends to standard output.

Just as it does with standard output, by default the shell directs standard error to the screen. Unless you redirect one or the other, you may not know the difference between the output a command sends to standard output and the output it sends to standard error. This section describes the syntax used by the Bourne Again Shell to redirect standard error and to distinguish between standard output and standard error.

File descriptors A *file descriptor* is the place a program sends its output to and gets its input from. When you execute a program, Linux opens three file descriptors for the program: 0 (standard input), 1 (standard output), and 2 (standard error). The redirect output symbol (> [page 232]) is shorthand for **1>**, which tells the shell to redirect standard output. Similarly < (page 233) is short for **0<**, which redirects standard input. The symbols **2>** redirect standard error. For more information refer to "File Descriptors" on page 943.

The following examples demonstrate how to redirect standard output and standard error to different files and to the same file. When you run the cat utility with the name of a file that does not exist and the name of a file that does exist, cat sends an error message to standard error and copies the file that does exist to standard output. Unless you redirect them, both messages appear on the screen.

```
$ cat y
This is y.
$ cat x
cat: x: No such file or directory

$ cat x y
cat: x: No such file or directory
This is y.
```

When you redirect standard output of a command, output sent to standard error is not affected and still appears on the screen.

```
$ cat x y > hold
cat: x: No such file or directory
$ cat hold
This is y.
```

Similarly, when you send standard output through a pipe, standard error is not affected. The following example sends standard output of cat through a pipe to tr, which in this example converts lowercase characters to uppercase. (See the tr info page for more information.) The text that cat sends to standard error is not translated because it goes directly to the screen rather than through the pipe.

```
$ cat x y | tr "[a-z]" "[A-Z]"
cat: x: No such file or directory
THIS IS Y.
```

The following example redirects standard output and standard error to different files. The token following **2>** tells the shell where to redirect standard error (file descriptor 2). The token following **1>** tells the shell where to redirect standard output (file descriptor 1). You can use **>** in place of **1>**.

```
$ cat x y 1> hold1 2> hold2
$ cat hold1
This is y.
$ cat hold2
cat: x: No such file or directory
```

Combining standard output and standard error
In the next example, the **&>** token redirects standard output and standard error to a single file:

```
$ cat x y &> hold
$ cat hold
cat: x: No such file or directory
This is y.
```

Duplicating a file descriptor
In the next example, first **1>** redirects standard output to **hold** and then **2>&1** declares file descriptor 2 to be a duplicate of file descriptor 1. As a result, both standard output and standard error are redirected to **hold**.

```
$ cat x y 1> hold 2>&1
$ cat hold
cat: x: No such file or directory
This is y.
```

In this case, **1> hold** precedes **2>&1**. If they had been listed in the opposite order, standard error would have been made a duplicate of standard output before standard output was redirected to **hold**. Only standard output would have been redirected to **hold** in that scenario.

The next example declares file descriptor 2 to be a duplicate of file descriptor 1 and sends the output for file descriptor 1 through a pipe to the tr command.

```
$ cat x y 2>&1 | tr "[a-z]" "[A-Z]"
CAT: X: NO SUCH FILE OR DIRECTORY
THIS IS Y.
```

Sending errors to standard error
You can use **1>&2** to redirect standard output of a command to standard error. Shell scripts use this technique to send the output of echo to standard error. In the following script, standard output of the first echo is redirected to standard error:

```
$ cat message_demo
echo This is an error message. 1>&2
echo This is not an error message.
```

If you redirect standard output of **message_demo**, error messages such as the one produced by the first echo appear on the screen because you have not redirected standard error. Because standard output of a shell script is frequently redirected to another file, you can use this technique to display on the screen any error messages generated by the script. The **lnks** script (page 918) uses this technique. You can also use the exec builtin to create additional file descriptors and to redirect standard input, standard output, and standard error of a shell script from within the script (page 963).

The Bourne Again Shell supports the redirection operators shown in Table 9-2.

Table 9-2   Redirection operators

Operator	Meaning
< *filename*	Redirects standard input from *filename*.
> *filename*	Redirects standard output to *filename* unless *filename* exists and **noclobber** (page 234) is set. If **noclobber** is not set, this redirection creates *filename* if it does not exist and overwrites it if it does exist.
>| *filename*	Redirects standard output to *filename*, even if the file exists and **noclobber** (page 234) is set.
>> *filename*	Redirects and appends standard output to *filename* unless *filename* exists and **noclobber** (page 234) is set. If **noclobber** is not set, this redirection creates *filename* if it does not exist.
&> *filename*	Redirects standard output and standard error to *filename*.
<&*m*	Duplicates standard input from file descriptor *m* (page 944).
[n]>&*m*	Duplicates standard output or file descriptor *n* if specified from file descriptor *m* (page 944).
[n]<&–	Closes standard input or file descriptor *n* if specified (page 944).
[n]>&–	Closes standard output or file descriptor *n* if specified.

WRITING A SIMPLE SHELL SCRIPT

A *shell script* is a file that holds commands that the shell can execute. The commands in a shell script can be any commands you can enter in response to a shell prompt. For example, a command in a shell script might run a Linux utility, a compiled program, or another shell script. Like the commands you give on the command line, a command in a shell script can use ambiguous file references and can have its input or output redirected from or to a file or sent through a pipe. You can also use pipes and redirection with the input and output of the script itself.

In addition to the commands you would ordinarily use on the command line, *control flow* commands (also called *control structures*) find most of their use in shell scripts. This group of commands enables you to alter the order of execution of commands in a script in the same way you would alter the order of execution of statements using a structured programming language. Refer to "Control Structures" on page 910 for specifics.

The shell interprets and executes the commands in a shell script, one after another. Thus a shell script enables you to simply and quickly initiate a complex series of tasks or a repetitive procedure.

chmod: MAKES A FILE EXECUTABLE

To execute a shell script by giving its name as a command, you must have permission to read and execute the file that contains the script (refer to "Access Permissions" on page 201). Read permission enables you to read the file that holds the script. Execute permission tells the shell and the system that the owner, group, and/or public has permission to execute the file; it implies that the content of the file is executable.

When you create a shell script using an editor, the file does not typically have its execute permission set. The following example shows a file named **whoson** that contains a shell script:

```
$ cat whoson
date
echo "Users Currently Logged In"
who

$ ./whoson
bash: ./whoson: Permission denied
```

You cannot execute **whoson** by giving its name as a command because you do not have execute permission for the file. The shell does not recognize **whoson** as an executable file and issues the error message **Permission denied** when you try to execute it. (See the tip on the next page if you get a **command not found** error message.) When you give the filename as an argument to bash (**bash whoson**), bash takes the argument to be a shell script and executes it. In this case **bash** is executable and **whoson** is an argument that bash executes so you do not need to have execute permission to **whoson**. You must have read permission.

```
$ ls -l whoson
-rw-rw-r--   1 max group 40 May 24 11:30 whoson

$ chmod u+x whoson
$ ls -l whoson
-rwxrw-r--   1 max group 40 May 24 11:30 whoson

$ ./whoson
Fri May 22 11:40:49 PDT 2009
Users Currently Logged In
zach      pts/7     May 21 18:17
hls       pts/1     May 22 09:59
sam       pts/12    May 22 06:29 (bravo.example.com)
max       pts/4     May 22 09:08
```

Figure 9-1   Using chmod to make a shell script executable

The chmod utility changes the access privileges associated with a file. Figure 9-1 shows ls with the –l option displaying the access privileges of **whoson** before and after chmod gives execute permission to the file's owner.

The first ls displays a hyphen (–) as the fourth character, indicating that the owner does not have permission to execute the file. Next chmod gives the owner execute permission: **u+x** causes chmod to add (**+**) execute permission (**x**) for the owner (**u**). (The **u** stands for *user*, although it means the owner of the file.) The second argument is the name of the file. The second ls shows an **x** in the fourth position, indicating that the owner has execute permission.

Command not found?

tip   If you give the name of a shell script as a command without including the leading ./, the shell typically displays the following error message:

```
$ whoson
bash: whoson: command not found
```

This message indicates the shell is not set up to search for executable files in the working directory. Give this command instead:

```
$ ./whoson
```

The ./ tells the shell explicitly to look for an executable file in the working directory. To change the environment so the shell searches the working directory automatically, see the section about **PATH** on page 303.

If other users will execute the file, you must also change group and/or public access permissions for the file. Any user must have execute access to use the file's name as a command. If the file is a shell script, the user trying to execute the file must have read access to the file as well. You do not need read access to execute a binary executable (compiled program).

The final command in Figure 9-1 shows the shell executing the file when its name is given as a command. For more information refer to "Access Permissions" on page 201 as well as the discussions of ls (page 201) and chmod (page 202).

#! SPECIFIES A SHELL

You can put a special sequence of characters on the first line of a shell script to tell the operating system which shell (or other program) should execute the file. Because the operating system checks the initial characters of a program before attempting to execute it using **exec**, these characters save the system from making an unsuccessful attempt. If **#!** are the first two characters of a script, the system interprets the characters that follow as the absolute pathname of the utility that should execute the script. This can be the pathname of any program, not just a shell. The following example specifies that bash should run the script:

```
$ cat bash_script
#!/bin/bash
echo "This is a Bourne Again Shell script."
```

The **#!** characters are useful if you have a script that you want to run with a shell other than the shell you are running the script from. The next example shows a script that should be executed by tcsh (part of the **tcsh** package):

```
$ cat tcsh_script
#!/bin/tcsh
echo "This is a tcsh script."
set person = zach
echo "person is $person"
```

Because of the **#!** line, the operating system ensures that tcsh executes the script no matter which shell you run it from.

You can use **ps –f** within a shell script to display the name of the shell that is executing the script. The three lines that ps displays in the following example show the process running the parent bash shell, the process running the tcsh script, and the process running the ps command:

```
$ cat tcsh_script2
#!/bin/tcsh
ps -f
```

```
$ ./tcsh_script2
UID        PID  PPID  C STIME TTY          TIME CMD
max       3031  3030  0 Nov16 pts/4    00:00:00 -bash
max       9358  3031  0 21:13 pts/4    00:00:00 /bin/tcsh ./tcsh_script2
max       9375  9358  0 21:13 pts/4    00:00:00 ps -f
```

If you do not follow **#!** with the name of an executable program, the shell reports that it cannot find the command that you asked it to run. You can optionally follow **#!** with SPACEs. If you omit the **#!** line and try to run, for example, a tcsh script from bash, the script will run under bash and may generate error messages or not run properly.

BEGINS A COMMENT

Comments make shell scripts and all code easier to read and maintain by you and others. If a pound sign (#) in the first character position of the first line of a script is not immediately followed by an exclamation point (!) or if a pound sign occurs in any other location in a script, the shell interprets it as the beginning of a comment. The shell then ignores everything between the pound sign and the end of the line (the next NEWLINE character).

EXECUTING A SHELL SCRIPT

fork and **exec**
system calls

A command on the command line causes the shell to **fork** a new process, creating a duplicate of the shell process (a subshell). The new process attempts to **exec** (execute) the command. Like **fork**, the **exec** routine is executed by the operating system (a system call). If the command is a binary executable program, such as a compiled C program, **exec** succeeds and the system overlays the newly created subshell with the executable program. If the command is a shell script, **exec** fails. When **exec** fails, the command is assumed to be a shell script, and the subshell runs the commands in the script. Unlike a login shell, which expects input from the command line, the subshell takes its input from a file—namely, the shell script.

As discussed earlier, you can run commands in a shell script file that you do not have execute permission for by using a bash command to **exec** a shell that runs the script directly. In the following example, bash creates a new shell that takes its input from the file named **whoson**:

```
$ bash whoson
```

Because the bash command expects to read a file containing commands, you do not need execute permission for **whoson**. (You do need read permission.) Even though bash reads and executes the commands in **whoson**, standard input, standard output, and standard error remain directed from/to the terminal.

Although you can use bash to execute a shell script, this technique causes the script to run more slowly than giving yourself execute permission and directly invoking the script. Users typically prefer to make the file executable and run the script by typing its name on the command line. It is also easier to type the name, and this practice is consistent with the way other kinds of programs are invoked (so you do not need to know whether you are running a shell script or an executable file). However, if bash is not your interactive shell or if you want to see how the script runs with different shells, you may want to run a script as an argument to **bash** or **tcsh**.

SEPARATING AND GROUPING COMMANDS

Whether you give the shell commands interactively or write a shell script, you must separate commands from one another. This section reviews the ways to separate commands that were covered in Chapter 7 and introduces a few new ones.

; AND NEWLINE SEPARATE COMMANDS

The NEWLINE character is a unique command separator because it initiates execution of the command preceding it. You have seen this behavior throughout this book each time you press the RETURN key at the end of a command line.

The semicolon (;) is a command separator that *does not* initiate execution of a command and *does not* change any aspect of how the command functions. You can execute a series of commands sequentially by entering them on a single command line and separating each from the next with a semicolon (;). You initiate execution of the sequence of commands by pressing RETURN:

```
$ x ; y ; z
```

If **x**, **y**, and **z** are commands, the preceding command line yields the same results as the next three commands. The difference is that in the next example the shell issues a prompt after each of the commands (**x**, **y**, and **z**) finishes executing, whereas the preceding command line causes the shell to issue a prompt only after **z** is complete:

```
$ x
$ y
$ z
```

Whitespace   Although the whitespace around the semicolons in the earlier example makes the command line easier to read, it is not necessary. None of the command separators needs to be surrounded by SPACEs or TABs.

\ CONTINUES A COMMAND

When you enter a long command line and the cursor reaches the right side of the screen, you can use a backslash (\) character to continue the command on the next line. The backslash quotes, or escapes, the NEWLINE character that follows it so the shell does not treat the NEWLINE as a command terminator. Enclosing a backslash within single quotation marks or preceding it with another backslash turns off the power of a backslash to quote special characters such as NEWLINE. Enclosing a backslash within double quotation marks has no effect on the power of the backslash.

Although you can break a line in the middle of a word (token), it is typically simpler to break a line immediately before or after whitespace.

optional   You can enter a RETURN in the middle of a quoted string on a command line without using a backslash. The NEWLINE (RETURN) you enter will then be part of the string:

```
$ echo "Please enter the three values
> required to complete the transaction."
Please enter the three values
required to complete the transaction.
```

In the three examples in this section, the shell does not interpret RETURN as a command terminator because it occurs within a quoted string. The greater than (>) sign is a secondary prompt (**PS2**; page 306) indicating the shell is waiting for you to continue the unfinished command. In the next example, the first RETURN is quoted (escaped) so the shell treats it as a separator and does not interpret it literally.

```
$ echo "Please enter the three values \
> required to complete the transaction."
Please enter the three values required to complete the transaction.
```

Single quotation marks cause the shell to interpret a backslash literally:

```
$ echo 'Please enter the three values \
> required to complete the transaction.'
Please enter the three values \
required to complete the transaction.
```

| AND & SEPARATE COMMANDS AND DO SOMETHING ELSE

The pipe symbol (|) and the background task symbol (&) are also command separators. They *do not* start execution of a command but *do* change some aspect of how the command functions. The pipe symbol alters the source of standard input or the destination of standard output. The background task symbol causes the shell to execute the task in the background and display a prompt immediately; you can continue working on other tasks.

Each of the following command lines initiates a single job comprising three tasks:

```
$ x | y | z
$ ls -l | grep tmp | less
```

In the first job, the shell redirects standard output of task **x** to standard input of task **y** and redirects **y**'s standard output to **z**'s standard input. Because it runs the entire job in the foreground, the shell does not display a prompt until task **z** runs to completion: Task **z** does not finish until task **y** finishes, and task **y** does not finish until task **x** finishes. In the second job, task **x** is an **ls –l** command, task **y** is **grep tmp**, and task **z** is the pager **less**. The shell displays a long (wide) listing of the files in the working directory that contain the string **tmp**, piped through less.

The next command line executes tasks **d** and **e** in the background and task **f** in the foreground:

```
$ d & e & f
[1] 14271
[2] 14272
```

The shell displays the job number between brackets and the PID number for each process running in the background. It displays a prompt as soon as **f** finishes, which may be before **d** or **e** finishes.

Before displaying a prompt for a new command, the shell checks whether any background jobs have completed. For each completed job, the shell displays its job number, the word **Done**, and the command line that invoked the job; the shell then displays a prompt. When the job numbers are listed, the number of the last job started is followed by a **+** character and the job number of the previous job is followed by a – character. Other jobs are followed by a SPACE character. After running the last command, the shell displays the following lines before issuing a prompt:

```
[1]-  Done                    d
[2]+  Done                    e
```

The next command line executes all three tasks as background jobs. The shell displays a shell prompt immediately:

```
$ d & e & f &
[1] 14290
[2] 14291
[3] 14292
```

You can use pipes to send the output from one task to the next task and an ampersand (&) to run the entire job as a background task. Again the shell displays the prompt immediately. The shell regards the commands joined by a pipe as a single job. That is, it treats all pipes as single jobs, no matter how many tasks are connected with the pipe (|) symbol or how complex they are. The Bourne Again Shell reports only one process in the background (although there are three):

```
$ d | e | f &
[1] 14295
```

optional () GROUPS COMMANDS

You can use parentheses to group commands. The shell creates a copy of itself, called a *subshell,* for each group. It treats each group of commands as a job and creates a new process to execute each command (refer to "Process Structure" on page 312 for more information on creating subshells). Each subshell (job) has its own environment, meaning that it has its own set of variables whose values can differ from those found in other subshells.

The following command line executes commands **a** and **b** sequentially in the background while executing **c** in the background. The shell displays a prompt immediately.

```
$ (a ; b) & c &
[1] 15520
[2] 15521
```

The preceding example differs from the earlier example **d & e & f &** in that tasks **a** and **b** are initiated sequentially, not concurrently.

Similarly the following command line executes **a** and **b** sequentially in the background and, at the same time, executes **c** and **d** sequentially in the background. The subshell running **a** and **b** and the subshell running **c** and **d** run concurrently. The shell displays a prompt immediately.

```
$ (a ; b) & (c ; d) &
[1] 15528
[2] 15529
```

The next script copies one directory to another. The second pair of parentheses creates a subshell to run the commands following the pipe. Because of these parentheses, the output of the first tar command is available for the second tar command despite the intervening cd command. Without the parentheses, the output of the first tar command would be sent to cd and lost because cd does not process input from standard input. The shell variables **$1** and **$2** represent the first and second command-line arguments (page 953), respectively. The first pair of parentheses, which creates a subshell to run the first two commands, allows users to call **cpdir** with relative pathnames. Without them, the first cd command would change the working directory of the script (and consequently the working directory of the second cd command). With them, only the working directory of the subshell is changed.

```
$ cat cpdir
(cd $1 ; tar -cf - . ) | (cd $2 ; tar -xvf - )
$ ./cpdir /home/max/sources /home/max/memo/biblio
```

The **cpdir** command line copies the files and directories in the **/home/max/sources** directory to the directory named **/home/max/memo/biblio**. This shell script is almost the same as using cp with the **–r** option. Refer to the cp and tar man pages for more information.

JOB CONTROL

A *job* is a command pipeline. You run a simple job whenever you give the shell a command. For example, if you type **date** on the command line and press RETURN, you have run a job. You can also create several jobs with multiple commands on a single command line:

```
$ find . -print | sort | lpr & grep -l max /tmp/* > maxfiles &
[1] 18839
[2] 18876
```

The portion of the command line up to the first & is one job consisting of three processes connected by pipes: find, sort (page 154), and lpr (page 151). The second job is a single process running grep. The trailing & characters put each job in the background, so bash does not wait for them to complete before displaying a prompt.

Using job control you can move commands from the foreground to the background (and vice versa), stop commands temporarily, and list all commands that are running in the background or stopped.

jobs: LISTS JOBS

The jobs builtin lists all background jobs. Following, the sleep command runs in the background and creates a background job that jobs reports on:

```
$ sleep 60 &
[1] 7809
$ jobs
[1] + Running                    sleep 60 &
```

fg: BRINGS A JOB TO THE FOREGROUND

The shell assigns a job number to each command you run in the background. For each job run in the background, the shell lists the job number and PID number immediately, just before it issues a prompt:

```
$ xclock &
[1] 1246
$ date &
[2] 1247
$ Tue Dec 2 11:44:40 PST 2008
[2]+ Done            date
$ find /usr -name ace -print > findout &
[2] 1269
$ jobs
[1]- Running         xclock &
[2]+ Running         find /usr -name ace -print > findout &
```

Job numbers, which are discarded when a job is finished, can be reused. When you start or put a job in the background, the shell assigns a job number that is one more than the highest job number in use.

In the preceding example, the jobs command lists the first job, xclock, as job 1. The date command does not appear in the jobs list because it finished before jobs was run. Because the date command was completed before find was run, the find command became job 2.

To move a background job to the foreground, use the fg builtin followed by the job number. Alternatively, you can give a percent sign (%) followed by the job number as a command. Either of the following commands moves job 2 to the foreground. When you move a job to the foreground, the shell displays the command it is now executing in the foregound.

```
$ fg 2
find /usr -name ace -print > findout
```

or

```
$ %2
find /usr -name ace -print > findout
```

You can also refer to a job by following the percent sign with a string that uniquely identifies the beginning of the command line used to start the job. Instead of the preceding command, you could have used either **fg %find** or **fg %f** because both uniquely identify job 2. If you follow the percent sign with a question mark and a string, the string can match any part of the command line. In the preceding example, **fg %?ace** also brings job 2 to the foreground.

Often the job you wish to bring to the foreground is the only job running in the background or is the job that jobs lists with a plus (**+**). In these cases fg without an argument brings the job to the foreground.

SUSPENDING A JOB

Pressing the suspend key (usually CONTROL-Z) immediately suspends (temporarily stops) the job in the foreground and displays a message that includes the word **Stopped**.

```
CONTROL-Z
[2]+  Stopped                         find /usr -name ace -print > findout
```

For more information refer to "Moving a Job from the Foreground to the Background" on page 241.

bg: SENDS A JOB TO THE BACKGROUND

To move the foreground job to the background, you must first suspend the job (above). You can then use the bg builtin to resume execution of the job in the background.

```
$ bg
[2]+ find /usr -name ace -print > findout &
```

If a background job attempts to read from the terminal, the shell stops the program and displays a message saying the job has been stopped. You must then move the job to the foreground so it can read from the terminal.

```
$ (sleep 5; cat > mytext) &
[1] 1343
$ date
Tue Dec  2 11:58:20 PST 2008
[1]+ Stopped                     ( sleep 5; cat >mytext )
$ fg
( sleep 5; cat >mytext )
Remember to let the cat out!
CONTROL-D
$
```

In the preceding example, the shell displays the job number and PID number of the background job as soon as it starts, followed by a prompt. Demonstrating that you can give a command at this point, the user gives the command date and its output appears on the screen. The shell waits until just before it issues a prompt (after date has finished) to notify you that job 1 is stopped. When you give an **fg** command, the shell puts the job in the foreground and you can enter the data the command is waiting for. In this case the input needs to be terminated with CONTROL-D, which sends an EOF (end of file) signal to the shell. The shell then displays another prompt.

The shell keeps you informed about changes in the status of a job, notifying you when a background job starts, completes, or stops, perhaps because it is waiting for input from the terminal. The shell also lets you know when a foreground job is suspended. Because notices about a job being run in the background can disrupt your work, the shell delays displaying these notices until just before it displays a prompt. You can set **notify** (page 339) to cause the shell to display these notices without delay.

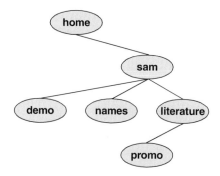

Figure 9-2   The directory structure in the examples

If you try to exit from a shell while jobs are stopped, the shell issues a warning and does not allow you to exit. If you then use jobs to review the list of jobs or you immediately try to exit from the shell again, the shell allows you to exit. If **huponexit** (page 339) is not set (the default), stopped and background jobs keep running in the background. If it is set, the shell terminates the jobs.

MANIPULATING THE DIRECTORY STACK

The Bourne Again Shell allows you to store a list of directories you are working with, enabling you to move easily among them. This list is referred to as a *stack*. It is analogous to a stack of dinner plates: You typically add plates to and remove plates from the top of the stack, so this type of stack is named a last in, first out (LIFO) stack.

dirs: DISPLAYS THE STACK

The dirs builtin displays the contents of the directory stack. If you call dirs when the directory stack is empty, it displays the name of the working directory:

```
$ dirs
~/literature
```

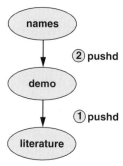

Figure 9-3   Creating a directory stack

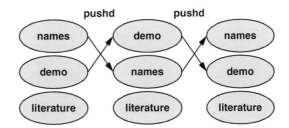

Figure 9-4   Using pushd to change working directories

The dirs builtin uses a tilde (~) to represent the name of a user's home directory. The examples in the next several sections assume that you are referring to the directory structure shown in Figure 9-2.

pushd: PUSHES A DIRECTORY ON THE STACK

When you supply the pushd (push directory) builtin with one argument, it pushes the directory specified by the argument on the stack, changes directories to the specified directory, and displays the stack. The following example is illustrated in Figure 9-3:

```
$ pushd ../demo
~/demo ~/literature
$ pwd
/home/sam/demo
$ pushd ../names
~/names ~/demo ~/literature
$ pwd
/home/sam/names
```

When you use pushd without an argument, it swaps the top two directories on the stack, makes the new top directory (which was the second directory) the new working directory, and displays the stack (Figure 9-4):

```
$ pushd
~/demo ~/names ~/literature
$ pwd
/home/sam/demo
```

Using pushd in this way, you can easily move back and forth between two directories. You can also use cd – to change to the previous directory, whether or not you have explicitly created a directory stack. To access another directory in the stack, call pushd with a numeric argument preceded by a plus sign. The directories in the stack are numbered starting with the top directory, which is number 0. The following pushd command continues with the previous example, changing the working directory to **literature** and moving **literature** to the top of the stack:

```
$ pushd +2
~/literature ~/demo ~/names
$ pwd
/home/sam/literature
```

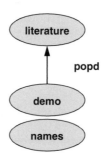

Figure 9-5   Using popd to remove a directory from the stack

popd: POPS A DIRECTORY OFF THE STACK

To remove a directory from the stack, use the popd (pop directory) builtin. As the following example and Figure 9-5 show, without an argument, popd removes the top directory from the stack and changes the working directory to the new top directory:

```
$ dirs
~/literature ~/demo ~/names
$ popd
~/demo ~/names
$ pwd
/home/sam/demo
```

To remove a directory other than the top one from the stack, use popd with a numeric argument preceded by a plus sign. The following example removes directory number 1, **demo**. Removing a directory other than directory number 0 does not change the working directory.

```
$ dirs
~/literature ~/demo ~/names
$ popd +1
~/literature ~/names
```

PARAMETERS AND VARIABLES

Variables   Within a shell, a *shell parameter* is associated with a value that is accessible to the user. There are several kinds of shell parameters. Parameters whose names consist of letters, digits, and underscores are often referred to as *shell variables,* or simply *variables*. A variable name must start with a letter or underscore, not with a number. Thus **A76**, **MY_CAT**, and **___X___** are valid variable names, whereas **69TH_STREET** (starts with a digit) and **MY-NAME** (contains a hyphen) are not.

User-created   Shell variables that you name and assign values to are *user-created variables*. You
variables   can change the values of user-created variables at any time, or you can make them *readonly* so that their values cannot be changed. You can also make user-created variables *global*. A global variable (also called an *environment variable*) is available

to all shells and other programs you fork from the original shell. One naming convention is to use only uppercase letters for global variables and to use mixed-case or lowercase letters for other variables. Refer to "Locality of Variables" on page 948 for more information on global variables.

To assign a value to a variable in the Bourne Again Shell, use the following syntax:

VARIABLE=value

There can be no whitespace on either side of the equal sign (=). An example assignment follows:

```
$ myvar=abc
```

The Bourne Again Shell permits you to put variable assignments on a command line. This type of assignment creates a variable that is local to the command shell—that is, the variable is accessible only from the program the command runs. The **my_script** shell script displays the value of **TEMPDIR**. The following command runs **my_script** with **TEMPDIR** set to */home/sam/temp*. The echo builtin shows that the interactive shell has no value for **TEMPDIR** after running **my_script**. If **TEMPDIR** had been set in the interactive shell, running **my_script** in this manner would have had no effect on its value.

```
$ cat my_script
echo $TEMPDIR
$ TEMPDIR=/home/sam/temp ./my_script
/home/sam/temp
$ echo $TEMPDIR

$
```

Keyword variables *Keyword shell variables* (or simply *keyword variables*) have special meaning to the shell and usually have short, mnemonic names. When you start a shell (by logging in, for example), the shell inherits several keyword variables from the environment. Among these variables are **HOME**, which identifies your home directory, and **PATH**, which determines which directories the shell searches and in what order to locate commands that you give the shell. The shell creates and initializes (with default values) other keyword variables when you start it. Still other variables do not exist until you set them.

You can change the values of most keyword shell variables. It is usually not necessary to change the values of keyword variables initialized in the */etc/profile* or */etc/csh.cshrc* systemwide startup files. If you need to change the value of a bash keyword variable, do so in one of your startup files (page 277). Just as you can make user-created variables global, so you can make keyword variables global—a task usually done automatically in startup files. You can also make a keyword variable readonly.

Positional and special parameters The names of positional and special parameters do not resemble variable names. Most of these parameters have one-character names (for example, **1**, **?**, and **#**) and are referenced (as are all variables) by preceding the name with a dollar sign ($1, $?, and $#). The values of these parameters reflect different aspects of your ongoing interaction with the shell.

Whenever you give a command, each argument on the command line becomes the value of a *positional parameter* (page 952). Positional parameters enable you to access command-line arguments, a capability that you will often require when you write shell scripts. The set builtin (page 954) enables you to assign values to positional parameters.

Other frequently needed shell script values, such as the name of the last command executed, the number of command-line arguments, and the status of the most recently executed command, are available as *special parameters* (page 950). You cannot assign values to special parameters.

USER-CREATED VARIABLES

The first line in the following example declares the variable named **person** and initializes it with the value **max**:

```
$ person=max
$ echo person
person
$ echo $person
max
```

Parameter substitution   Because the echo builtin copies its arguments to standard output, you can use it to display the values of variables. The second line of the preceding example shows that **person** does not represent **max**. Instead, the string **person** is echoed as **person**. The shell substitutes the value of a variable only when you precede the name of the variable with a dollar sign ($). Thus the command **echo $person** displays the value of the variable **person**; it does not display $person because the shell does not pass $person to echo as an argument. Because of the leading $, the shell recognizes that $person is the name of a variable, *substitutes* the value of the variable, and passes that value to echo. The echo builtin displays the value of the variable—not its name—never "knowing" that you called it with a variable.

Quoting the $ You can prevent the shell from substituting the value of a variable by quoting the leading $. Double quotation marks do not prevent the substitution; single quotation marks or a backslash (\) do.

```
$ echo $person
max
$ echo "$person"
max
$ echo '$person'
$person
$ echo \$person
$person
```

SPACES   Because they do not prevent variable substitution but do turn off the special meanings of most other characters, double quotation marks are useful when you assign values to variables and when you use those values. To assign a value that contains SPACEs or TABs to a variable, use double quotation marks around the value. Although double quotation marks are not required in all cases, using them is a good habit.

```
$ person="max and zach"
$ echo $person
max and zach
$ person=max and zach
bash: and: command not found
```

When you reference a variable whose value contains TABs or multiple adjacent SPACEs, you need to use quotation marks to preserve the spacing. If you do not quote the variable, the shell collapses each string of blank characters into a single SPACE before passing the variable to the utility:

```
$ person="max    and    zach"
$ echo $person
max and zach
$ echo "$person"
max    and    zach
```

Pathname expansion in assignments   When you execute a command with a variable as an argument, the shell replaces the name of the variable with the value of the variable and passes that value to the program being executed. If the value of the variable contains a special character, such as * or ?, the shell *may* expand that variable.

The first line in the following sequence of commands assigns the string **max*** to the variable **memo**. The Bourne Again Shell does *not expand the string* because bash does not perform pathname expansion (page 242) when it assigns a value to a variable. All shells process a command line in a specific order. Within this order bash expands variables before it interprets commands. In the following echo command line, the double quotation marks quote the asterisk (*) in the expanded value of **$memo** and prevent bash from performing pathname expansion on the expanded **memo** variable before passing its value to the echo command:

```
$ memo=max*
$ echo "$memo"
max*
```

All shells interpret special characters as special when you reference a variable that contains an unquoted special character. In the following example, the shell expands the value of the **memo** variable because it is not quoted:

```
$ ls
max.report
max.summary
$ echo $memo
max.report max.summary
```

Here the shell expands the **$memo** variable to **max***, expands **max*** to **max.report** and **max.summary**, and passes these two values to echo.

optional

Braces   The *$VARIABLE* syntax is a special case of the more general syntax *${VARIABLE}*, in which the variable name is enclosed by **${}**. The braces insulate the variable name from adjacent characters. Braces are necessary when catenating a variable value with a string:

```
$ PREF=counter
$ WAY=$PREFclockwise
$ FAKE=$PREFfeit
$ echo $WAY $FAKE

$
```

The preceding example does not work as planned. Only a blank line is output because, although the symbols **PREFclockwise** and **PREFfeit** are valid variable names, they are not set. By default bash evaluates an unset variable as an empty (null) string and displays this value. To achieve the intent of these statements, refer to the **PREF** variable using braces:

```
$ PREF=counter
$ WAY=${PREF}clockwise
$ FAKE=${PREF}feit
$ echo $WAY $FAKE
counterclockwise counterfeit
```

The Bourne Again Shell refers to the arguments on its command line by position, using the special variables **$1, $2, $3**, and so forth up to **$9**. If you wish to refer to arguments past the ninth argument, you must use braces: **${10}**. The name of the command is held in **$0** (page 953).

unset: REMOVES A VARIABLE

Unless you remove a variable, it exists as long as the shell in which it was created exists. To remove the *value* of a variable but not the variable itself, assign a null value to the variable:

```
$ person=
$ echo $person

$
```

You can remove a variable using the unset builtin. The following command removes the variable **person**:

```
$ unset person
```

VARIABLE ATTRIBUTES

This section discusses attributes and explains how to assign them to variables.

readonly: MAKES THE VALUE OF A VARIABLE PERMANENT

You can use the readonly builtin to ensure that the value of a variable cannot be changed. The next example declares the variable **person** to be readonly. You must assign a value to a variable *before* you declare it to be readonly; you cannot change its value after the declaration. When you attempt to unset or change the value of a readonly variable, the shell displays an error message:

```
$ person=zach
$ echo $person
zach
$ readonly person
$ person=helen
bash: person: readonly variable
```

If you use the readonly builtin without an argument, it displays a list of all readonly shell variables. This list includes keyword variables that are automatically set as readonly as well as keyword or user-created variables that you have declared as readonly. See page 302 for an example (**readonly** and **declare –r** produce the same output).

declare AND typeset: ASSIGN ATTRIBUTES TO VARIABLES

The declare and typeset builtins (two names for the same command) set attributes and values for shell variables. Table 9-3 lists five of these attributes.

Table 9-3 Variable attributes (typeset or declare)

Attribute	Meaning
–a	Declares a variable as an array (page 946)
–f	Declares a variable to be a function name (page 333)
–i	Declares a variable to be of type integer (page 302)
–r	Makes a variable readonly; also readonly (page 301)
–x	Exports a variable (makes it global); also export (page 948)

The following commands declare several variables and set some attributes. The first line declares **person1** and assigns it a value of **max**. This command has the same effect with or without the word **declare**.

```
$ declare person1=max
$ declare -r person2=zach
$ declare -rx person3=helen
$ declare -x person4
```

The readonly and export builtins are synonyms for the commands **declare –r** and **declare –x**, respectively. You can declare a variable without assigning a value to it, as the preceding declaration of the variable **person4** illustrates. This declaration makes **person4** available to all subshells (i.e., makes it global). Until an assignment is made to the variable, it has a null value.

You can list the options to declare separately in any order. The following is equivalent to the preceding declaration of **person3**:

```
$ declare -x -r person3=helen
```

Use the **+** character in place of **–** when you want to remove an attribute from a variable. You cannot remove the readonly attribute. After the following command is given, the variable **person3** is no longer exported but it is still readonly.

```
$ declare +x person3
```

You can use typeset instead of declare.

Listing variable attributes
Without any arguments or options, declare lists all shell variables. The same list is output when you run set (page 954) without any arguments.

If you use a declare builtin with options but no variable names as arguments, the command lists all shell variables that have the indicated attributes set. For example, the command **declare –r** displays a list of all readonly shell variables. This list is the same as that produced by the **readonly** command without any arguments. After the declarations in the preceding example have been given, the results are as follows:

```
$ declare -r
declare -ar BASH_VERSINFO='([0]="3" [1]="2" [2]="39" [3]="1" ... )'
declare -ir EUID="500"
declare -ir PPID="936"
declare -r SHELLOPTS="braceexpand:emacs:hashall:histexpand:history:..."
declare -ir UID="500"
declare -r person2="zach"
declare -rx person3="helen"
```

The first five entries are keyword variables that are automatically declared as read-only. Some of these variables are stored as integers (**–i**). The **–a** option indicates that **BASH_VERSINFO** is an array variable; the value of each element of the array is listed to the right of an equal sign.

Integer
By default the values of variables are stored as strings. When you perform arithmetic on a string variable, the shell converts the variable into a number, manipulates it, and then converts it back to a string. A variable with the integer attribute is stored as an integer. Assign the integer attribute as follows:

```
$ declare -i COUNT
```

KEYWORD VARIABLES

Keyword variables either are inherited or are declared and initialized by the shell when it starts. You can assign values to these variables from the command line or from a startup file. Typically you want these variables to apply to all subshells you start as well as to your login shell. For those variables not automatically exported by the shell, you must use export (page 948) to make them available to child shells.

HOME: YOUR HOME DIRECTORY

By default your home directory is the working directory when you log in. Your home directory is established when your account is set up; its name is stored in the **/etc/passwd** file.

```
$ grep sam /etc/passwd
sam:x:501:501:Sam S. x301:/home/sam:/bin/bash
```

When you log in, the shell inherits the pathname of your home directory and assigns it to the variable **HOME**. When you give a **cd** command without an argument, cd makes the directory whose name is stored in **HOME** the working directory:

```
$ pwd
/home/max/laptop
$ echo $HOME
/home/max
$ cd
$ pwd
/home/max
```

This example shows the value of the **HOME** variable and the effect of the cd builtin. After you execute cd without an argument, the pathname of the working directory is the same as the value of **HOME**: your home directory.

Tilde (~) The shell uses the value of **HOME** to expand pathnames that use the shorthand tilde (~) notation (page 192) to denote a user's home directory. The following example uses echo to display the value of this shortcut and then uses ls to list the files in Max's **laptop** directory, which is a subdirectory of his home directory:

```
$ echo ~
/home/max
$ ls ~/laptop
tester       count       lineup
```

PATH: WHERE THE SHELL LOOKS FOR PROGRAMS

When you give the shell an absolute or relative pathname rather than a simple filename as a command, it looks in the specified directory for an executable file with the specified filename. If the file with the pathname you specified does not exist, the shell reports **command not found**. If the file exists as specified but you do not have execute permission for it, or in the case of a shell script you do not have read and execute permission for it, the shell reports **Permission denied.**

If you give a simple filename as a command, the shell searches through certain directories (your search path) for the program you want to execute. It looks in several directories for a file that has the same name as the command and that you have execute permission for (a compiled program) or read and execute permission for (a shell script). The **PATH** shell variable controls this search.

The default value of **PATH** is determined when bash is compiled. It is not set in a startup file, although it may be modified there. Normally the default specifies that the shell search several system directories used to hold common commands. These system directories include **/bin** and **/usr/bin** and other directories appropriate to the local system. When you give a command, if the shell does not find the executable—and, in the case of a shell script, readable—file named by the command in any of the directories listed in **PATH**, the shell generates one of the aforementioned error messages.

Working directory   The **PATH** variable specifies the directories in the order the shell should search them. Each directory must be separated from the next by a colon. The following command sets **PATH** so that a search for an executable file starts with the **/usr/local/bin** directory. If it does not find the file in this directory, the shell looks next in **/bin**, and then in **/usr/bin**. If the search fails in those directories, the shell looks in the **~/bin** directory, a subdirectory of the user's home directory. Finally the shell looks in the working directory. Exporting **PATH** makes its value accessible to subshells:

```
$ export PATH=/usr/local/bin:/bin:/usr/bin:~/bin:
```

A null value in the string indicates the working directory. In the preceding example, a null value (nothing between the colon and the end of the line) appears as the last element of the string. The working directory is represented by a leading colon (not recommended; see the following security tip), a trailing colon (as in the example), or two colons next to each other anywhere in the string. You can also represent the working directory explicitly with a period (.).

Because Linux stores many executable files in directories named **bin** (*binary*), users typically put their own executable files in their own **~/bin** directories. If you put your own **bin** directory at the end of your **PATH**, as in the preceding example, the shell looks there for any commands that it cannot find in directories listed earlier in **PATH**.

PATH and security

security   Do not put the working directory first in **PATH** when security is a concern. If you are working as **root**, you should *never* put the working directory first in **PATH**. It is common for **root**'s **PATH** to omit the working directory entirely. You can always execute a file in the working directory by prepending ./ to the name: **./myprog**.

Putting the working directory first in **PATH** can create a security hole. Most people type **ls** as the first command when entering a directory. If the owner of a directory places an executable file named **ls** in the directory, and the working directory appears first in a user's **PATH**, the user giving an **ls** command from the directory executes the ls program in the working directory instead of the system ls utility, possibly with undesirable results.

If you want to add directories to **PATH**, you can reference the old value of the **PATH** variable in setting **PATH** to a new value (but see the preceding security tip). The following command adds **/usr/local/bin** to the beginning of the current **PATH** and the **bin** directory in the user's home directory (**~/bin**) to the end:

```
$ PATH=/usr/local/bin:$PATH:~/bin
```

MAIL: WHERE YOUR MAIL IS KEPT

The **MAIL** variable contains the pathname of the file that holds your mail (your *mailbox*, usually */var/mail/name*, where *name* is your username). If **MAIL** is set and **MAILPATH** (next) is not set, the shell informs you when mail arrives in the file specified by **MAIL**. In a graphical environment you can unset **MAIL** so the shell does not display mail reminders in a terminal emulator window (assuming you are using a graphical mail program).

The **MAILPATH** variable contains a list of filenames separated by colons. If this variable is set, the shell informs you when any one of the files is modified (for example, when mail arrives). You can follow any of the filenames in the list with a question mark (?), followed by a message. The message replaces the **you have mail** message when you receive mail while you are logged in.

The **MAILCHECK** variable specifies how often, in seconds, the shell checks for new mail. The default is 60 seconds. If you set this variable to zero, the shell checks before each prompt.

PS1: USER PROMPT (PRIMARY)

The default Bourne Again Shell prompt is a dollar sign ($). When you run bash with **root** privileges, bash typically displays a pound sign (#) prompt. The **PS1** variable holds the prompt string that the shell uses to let you know that it is waiting for a command. When you change the value of **PS1**, you change the appearance of your prompt.

You can customize the prompt displayed by **PS1**. For example, the assignment

```
$ PS1="[\u@\h \W \!]$ "
```

displays the following prompt:

[user@host directory event]$

where *user* is the username, *host* is the hostname up to the first period, *directory* is the basename of the working directory, and *event* is the event number (page 315) of the current command.

If you are working on more than one system, it can be helpful to incorporate the system name into your prompt. For example, you might change the prompt to the name of the system you are using, followed by a colon and a SPACE (a SPACE at the end of the prompt makes the commands you enter after the prompt easier to read). This command uses command substitution (page 346) in the string assigned to **PS1**:

```
$ PS1="$(hostname): "
bravo.example.com: echo test
test
bravo.example.com:
```

The first example that follows changes the prompt to the name of the local host, a SPACE, and a dollar sign (or, if the user is running with **root** privileges, a pound sign). The second example changes the prompt to the time followed by the name of the user. The third example changes the prompt to the one used in this book (a pound sign for **root** and a dollar sign otherwise):

```
$ PS1='\h \$ '
bravo $

$ PS1='\@ \u $ '
09:44 PM max $

$ PS1='\$ '
$
```

Table 9-4 describes some of the symbols you can use in **PS1**. For a complete list of special characters you can use in the prompt strings, open the bash man page and search for the second occurrence of **PROMPTING** (give the command **/PROMPTING** and then press **n**).

Table 9-4   PS1 symbols

Symbol	Display in prompt
\$	# if the user is running with **root** privileges; otherwise, **$**
\w	Pathname of the working directory
\W	Basename of the working directory
\!	Current event (history) number (page 319)
\d	Date in Weekday Month Date format
\h	Machine hostname, without the domain
\H	Full machine hostname, including the domain
\u	Username of the current user
\@	Current time of day in 12-hour, AM/PM format
\T	Current time of day in 12-hour HH:MM:SS format
\A	Current time of day in 24-hour HH:MM format
\t	Current time of day in 24-hour HH:MM:SS format

PS2: USER PROMPT (SECONDARY)

The **PS2** variable holds the secondary prompt. On the first line of the next example, an unclosed quoted string follows echo. The shell assumes the command is not finished and, on the second line, gives the default secondary prompt (>). This prompt indicates the shell is waiting for the user to continue the command line. The shell waits until it receives the quotation mark that closes the string. Only then does it execute the command:

```
$ echo "demonstration of prompt string
> 2"
demonstration of prompt string
2
$ PS2="secondary prompt: "
$ echo "this demonstrates
secondary prompt: prompt string 2"
this demonstrates
prompt string 2
```

The second command changes the secondary prompt to **secondary prompt:** followed by a SPACE. A multiline echo demonstrates the new prompt.

PS3: MENU PROMPT

The **PS3** variable holds the menu prompt for the **select** control structure (page 940).

PS4: DEBUGGING PROMPT

The **PS4** variable holds the bash debugging symbol (page 922).

IFS: SEPARATES INPUT FIELDS (WORD SPLITTING)

The **IFS** (Internal Field Separator) shell variable specifies the characters you can use to separate arguments on a command line. It has the default value of SPACE TAB NEWLINE. Regardless of the value of **IFS**, you can always use one or more SPACE or TAB characters to separate arguments on the command line, provided these characters are not quoted or escaped. When you assign **IFS** character values, these characters can also separate fields—but only if they undergo expansion. This type of interpretation of the command line is called *word splitting*.

Be careful when changing IFS

caution   Changing **IFS** has a variety of side effects, so work cautiously. You may find it useful to save the value of **IFS** before changing it. Then you can easily restore the original value if you get unexpected results. Alternatively, you can fork a new shell with a **bash** command before experimenting with **IFS**; if you get into trouble, you can **exit** back to the old shell, where **IFS** is working properly.

The following example demonstrates how setting IFS can affect the interpretation of a command line:

```
$ a=w:x:y:z

$ cat $a
cat: w:x:y:z: No such file or directory
$ IFS=":"

$ cat $a
cat: w: No such file or directory
cat: x: No such file or directory
cat: y: No such file or directory
cat: z: No such file or directory
```

The first time cat is called, the shell expands the variable **a**, interpreting the string **w:x:y:z** as a single word to be used as the argument to cat. The cat utility cannot find a file named **w:x:y:z** and reports an error for that filename. After **IFS** is set to a colon (:), the shell expands the variable **a** into four words, each of which is an argument to cat. Now cat reports errors for four files: **w**, **x**, **y**, and **z**. Word splitting based on the colon (:) takes place only *after* the variable **a** is expanded.

The shell splits all *expanded* words on a command line according to the separating characters found in **IFS**. When there is no expansion, there is no splitting. Consider the following commands:

```
$ IFS="p"
$ export VAR
```

Although **IFS** is set to **p**, the **p** on the **export** command line is not expanded, so the word **export** is not split.

The following example uses variable expansion in an attempt to produce an **export** command:

```
$ IFS="p"
$ aa=export
$ echo $aa
ex ort
```

This time expansion occurs, so the character **p** in the token **export** is interpreted as a separator (as the echo command shows). Now when you try to use the value of the **aa** variable to export the **VAR** variable, the shell parses the **$aa VAR** command line as **ex ort VAR**. The effect is that the command line starts the **ex** editor with two filenames: **ort** and **VAR**.

```
$ $aa VAR
2 files to edit
"ort" [New File]
Entering Ex mode.  Type "visual" to go to Normal mode.
:q
E173: 1 more file to edit
:q
$
```

If you unset **IFS**, only SPACEs and TABs work as field separators.

Multiple separator characters

tip   Although the shell treats sequences of multiple SPACE or TAB characters as a single separator, it treats *each occurrence* of another field-separator character as a separator.

CDPATH: BROADENS THE SCOPE OF cd

The **CDPATH** variable allows you to use a simple filename as an argument to the cd builtin to change the working directory to a directory other than a child of the working directory. If you have several directories you typically work out of, this variable can speed things up and save you the tedium of using cd with longer path-names to switch among them.

When **CDPATH** is not set and you specify a simple filename as an argument to cd, cd searches the working directory for a subdirectory with the same name as the argument. If the subdirectory does not exist, cd displays an error message. When **CDPATH** is set, cd searches for an appropriately named subdirectory in the directories in the **CDPATH** list. If it finds one, that directory becomes the working directory. With **CDPATH** set, you can use cd and a simple filename to change the working directory to a child of any of the directories listed in **CDPATH**.

The **CDPATH** variable takes on the value of a colon-separated list of directory pathnames (similar to the **PATH** variable). It is usually set in the ~/.bash_profile startup file with a command line such as the following:

```
export CDPATH=$HOME:$HOME/literature
```

This command causes cd to search your home directory, the **literature** directory, and then the working directory when you give a cd command. If you do not include the working directory in **CDPATH**, cd searches the working directory if the search of all the other directories in **CDPATH** fails. If you want cd to search the working directory first, include a null string, represented by two colons (::), as the first entry in **CDPATH**:

```
export CDPATH=::$HOME:$HOME/literature
```

If the argument to the cd builtin is an absolute pathname—one starting with a slash (/)—the shell does not consult **CDPATH**.

KEYWORD VARIABLES: A SUMMARY

Table 9-5 presents a list of bash keyword variables.

Table 9-5   bash keyword variables

Variable	Value
BASH_ENV	The pathname of the startup file for noninteractive shells (page 278)
CDPATH	The cd search path (page 308)
COLUMNS	The width of the display used by **select** (page 939)
FCEDIT	The name of the editor that fc uses by default (page 318)
HISTFILE	The pathname of the file that holds the history list (default: ~/.bash_history; page 314)
HISTFILESIZE	The maximum number of entries saved in **HISTFILE** (default: 500; page 314)
HISTSIZE	The maximum number of entries saved in the history list (default: 500; page 314)

Table 9-5   bash keyword variables (continued)

Variable	Value
HOME	The pathname of the user's home directory (page 303); used as the default argument for cd and in tilde expansion (page 192)
IFS	Internal Field Separator (page 307); used for word splitting (page 347)
INPUTRC	The pathname of the Readline startup file (default: ~/.inputrc; page 327)
LANG	The locale category when that category is not specifically set with an **LC_*** variable
LC_*	A group of variables that specify locale categories including **LC_COLLATE**, **LC_CTYPE**, **LC_MESSAGES**, and **LC_NUMERIC**; use the locale builtin to display a complete list with values
LINES	The height of the display used by **select** (page 939)
MAIL	The pathname of the file that holds a user's mail (page 305)
MAILCHECK	How often, in seconds, bash checks for mail (page 305)
MAILPATH	A colon-separated list of file pathnames that bash checks for mail in (page 305)
PATH	A colon-separated list of directory pathnames that bash looks for commands in (page 303)
PROMPT_COMMAND	A command that bash executes just before it displays the primary prompt
PS1	Prompt String 1; the primary prompt (page 305)
PS2	Prompt String 2; the secondary prompt (default: '> '; page 306)
PS3	The prompt issued by **select** (page 939)
PS4	The bash debugging symbol (page 922)
REPLY	Holds the line that read accepts (page 960); also used by **select** (page 939)

SPECIAL CHARACTERS

Table 9-6 lists most of the characters that are special to the bash shell.

Table 9-6   Shell special characters

Character	Use
NEWLINE	Initiates execution of a command (page 288)
;	Separates commands (page 288)

Table 9-6   Shell special characters (continued)

Character	Use
( )	Groups commands (page 290) for execution by a subshell or identifies a function (page 333)
(( ))	Expands an arithmetic expression (page 344)
&	Executes a command in the background (pages 240 and 289)
|	Sends standard output of the preceding command to standard input of the following command (pipe; page 289)
>	Redirects standard output (page 232)
>>	Appends standard output (page 235)
<	Redirects standard input (page 233)
<<	Here document (page 941)
*	Any string of zero or more characters in an ambiguous file reference (page 243)
?	Any single character in an ambiguous file reference (page 242)
\	Quotes the following character (page 146)
'	Quotes a string, preventing all substitution (page 146)
"	Quotes a string, allowing only variable and command substitution (pages 146 and 298)
` ... `	Performs command substitution (page 346)
[ ]	Character class in an ambiguous file reference (page 245)
$	References a variable (page 296)
. (dot builtin)	Executes a command (page 280)
#	Begins a comment (page 287)
{ }	Surrounds the contents of a function (page 333)
: (null builtin)	Returns *true* (page 967)
&& (Boolean AND)	Executes command on right only if command on left succeeds (returns a zero exit status; page 978)
|| (Boolean OR)	Executes command on right only if command on left fails (returns a nonzero exit status; page 978)
! (Boolean NOT)	Reverses exit status of a command
$()	Performs command substitution (preferred form; page 346)
[ ]	Evaluates an arithmetic expression (page 344)

PROCESSES

A *process* is the execution of a command by the Linux kernel. The shell that starts when you log in is a command, or a process, like any other. When you give the name of a Linux utility on the command line, you initiate a process. When you run a shell script, another shell process is started and additional processes are created for each command in the script. Depending on how you invoke the shell script, the script is run either by the current shell or, more typically, by a subshell (child) of the current shell. A process is not started when you run a shell builtin, such as cd.

PROCESS STRUCTURE

fork system call   Like the file structure, the process structure is hierarchical, with parents, children, and even a *root*. A parent process *forks* a child process, which in turn can fork other processes. (The term *fork* indicates that, as with a fork in the road, one process turns into two. Initially the two forks are identical except that one is identified as the parent and one as the child. You can also use the term *spawn;* the words are interchangeable.) The operating system routine, or *system call,* that creates a new process is named **fork**().

When Linux begins execution when a system is started, it starts init, a single process called a *spontaneous process,* with PID number 1. This process holds the same position in the process structure as the root directory does in the file structure: It is the ancestor of all processes the system and users work with. When a command-line system is in multiuser mode, init runs getty or mingetty processes, which display **login:** prompts on terminals. When a user responds to the prompt and presses RETURN, getty hands control over to a utility named login, which checks the username and password combination. After the user logs in, the login process becomes the user's shell process.

PROCESS IDENTIFICATION

PID numbers   Linux assigns a unique PID (process identification) number at the inception of each process. As long as a process exists, it keeps the same PID number. During one session the same process is always executing the login shell. When you fork a new process—for example, when you use an editor—the PID number of the new (child) process is different from that of its parent process. When you return to the login shell, it is still being executed by the same process and has the same PID number as when you logged in.

The following example shows that the process running the shell forked (is the parent of) the process running ps. When you call it with the –f option, ps displays a full listing of information about each process. The line of the ps display with **bash** in the **CMD** column refers to the process running the shell. The column headed by **PID** identifies the PID number. The column headed **PPID** identifies the PID number of the *parent* of the process. From the PID and PPID columns you can see that the process running the shell (PID 21341) is the parent of the process running sleep

(PID 22789). The parent PID number of sleep is the same as the PID number of the shell (21341).

```
$ sleep 10 &
[1] 22789
$ ps -f
UID        PID  PPID  C STIME TTY         TIME CMD
max      21341 21340  0 10:42 pts/16   00:00:00 bash
max      22789 21341  0 17:30 pts/16   00:00:00 sleep 10
max      22790 21341  0 17:30 pts/16   00:00:00 ps -f
```

Refer to the ps man page for more information on ps and the columns it displays with the –f option. A second pair of **sleep** and **ps –f** commands shows that the shell is still being run by the same process but that it forked another process to run sleep:

```
$ sleep 10 &
[1] 22791
$ ps -f
UID        PID  PPID  C STIME TTY         TIME CMD
max      21341 21340  0 10:42 pts/16   00:00:00 bash
max      22791 21341  0 17:31 pts/16   00:00:00 sleep 10
max      22792 21341  0 17:31 pts/16   00:00:00 ps -f
```

You can also use pstree (or **ps ––forest**, with or without the **–e** option) to see the parent–child relationship of processes. The next example shows the **–p** option to pstree, which causes it to display PID numbers:

```
$ pstree -p
init(1)-+-acpid(1395)
        |-atd(1758)
        |-crond(1702)
        ...
        |-kdeinit(2223)-+-firefox(8914)---run-mozilla.sh(8920)---firefox-bin(8925)
        |               |-gaim(2306)
        |               |-gqview(14062)
        |               |-kdeinit(2228)
        |               |-kdeinit(2294)
        |               |-kdeinit(2314)-+-bash(2329)---ssh(2561)
        |               |               |-bash(2339)
        |               |               '-bash(15821)---bash(16778)
        |               |-kdeinit(16448)
        |               |-kdeinit(20888)
        |               |-oclock(2317)
        |               '-pam-panel-icon(2305)---pam_timestamp_c(2307)
        ...
        |-login(1823)---bash(20986)-+-pstree(21028)
        |                           '-sleep(21026)
        ...
```

The preceding output is abbreviated. The line that starts with **–kdeinit** shows a graphical user running many processes, including **firefox, gaim,** and **oclock.** The line that starts with **–login** shows a textual user running sleep in the background and running pstree in the foreground. Refer to "$$: PID Number" on page 951 for a description of how to instruct the shell to report on PID numbers.

EXECUTING A COMMAND

fork and **sleep**   When you give the shell a command, it usually forks [spawns using the **fork**() system call] a child process to execute the command. While the child process is executing the command, the parent process *sleeps* [implemented as the **sleep**() system call]. While a process is sleeping, it does not use any computer time; it remains inactive, waiting to wake up. When the child process finishes executing the command, it tells its parent of its success or failure via its exit status and then dies. The parent process (which is running the shell) wakes up and prompts for another command.

Background process   When you run a process in the background by ending a command with an ampersand (&), the shell forks a child process without going to sleep and without waiting for the child process to run to completion. The parent process, which is executing the shell, reports the job number and PID number of the child process and prompts for another command. The child process runs in the background, independent of its parent.

Builtins   Although the shell forks a process to run most of the commands you give it, some commands are built into the shell. The shell does not need to fork a process to run builtins. For more information refer to "Builtins" on page 247.

Variables   Within a given process, such as your login shell or a subshell, you can declare, initialize, read, and change variables. By default, however, a variable is local to a process. When a process forks a child process, the parent does not pass the value of a variable to the child. You can make the value of a variable available to child processes (global) by using the export builtin (page 948).

HISTORY

The history mechanism, a feature adapted from the C Shell, maintains a list of recently issued command lines, also called *events*, that provides a quick way to reexecute any of the events in the list. This mechanism also enables you to execute variations of previous commands and to reuse arguments from them. You can use the history list to replicate complicated commands and arguments that you used earlier in this login session or in a previous one and enter a series of commands that differ from one another in minor ways. The history list also serves as a record of what you have done. It can prove helpful when you have made a mistake and are not sure what you did or when you want to keep a record of a procedure that involved a series of commands.

The history builtin displays the history list. If it does not, read the next section, which describes the variables you need to set.

VARIABLES THAT CONTROL HISTORY

The value of the **HISTSIZE** variable determines the number of events preserved in the history list during a session. A value in the range of 100 to 1,000 is normal.

When you exit from the shell, the most recently executed commands are saved in the file whose name is stored in the **HISTFILE** variable (the default is **~/.bash_history**).

The next time you start the shell, this file initializes the history list. The value of the **HISTFILESIZE** variable determines the number of lines of history saved in **HISTFILE**. See Table 9-7.

history **can help track down mistakes**

tip   When you have made a mistake on a command line (not an error within a script or program) and are not sure what you did wrong, look at the history list to review your recent commands. Sometimes this list can help you figure out what went wrong and how to fix things.

Table 9-7   History variables

Variable	Default	Function
HISTSIZE	500 events	Maximum number of events saved during a session
HISTFILE	~/.bash_history	Location of the history file
HISTFILESIZE	500 events	Maximum number of events saved between sessions

Event number   The Bourne Again Shell assigns a sequential *event number* to each command line. You can display this event number as part of the bash prompt by including \! in **PS1** (page 305). Examples in this section show numbered prompts when they help to illustrate the behavior of a command.

Give the following command manually, or place it in ~/**.bash_profile** to affect future sessions, to establish a history list of the 100 most recent events:

```
$ HISTSIZE=100
```

The following command causes bash to save the 100 most recent events across login sessions:

```
$ HISTFILESIZE=100
```

After you set **HISTFILESIZE**, you can log out and log in again, and the 100 most recent events from the previous login session will appear in your history list.

Give the command **history** to display the events in the history list. This list is ordered so that the oldest events appear at the top. The following history list includes a command to modify the bash prompt so it displays the history event number. The last event in the history list is the **history** command that displayed the list.

```
32 $ history | tail
   23   PS1="\! bash$ "
   24   ls -l
   25   cat temp
   26   rm temp
   27   vim memo
   28   lpr memo
   29   vim memo
   30   lpr memo
   31   rm memo
   32   history | tail
```

As you run commands and your history list becomes longer, it may run off the top of the screen when you use the history builtin. Pipe the output of history through less to browse through it, or give the command **history 10** or **history | tail** to look at the ten most recent commands.

A handy history alias

tip   Creating the following aliases makes working with history easier. The first allows you to give the command **h** to display the ten most recent events. The second alias causes the command **hg** *string* to display all events in the history list that contain *string*. Put these aliases in your ~/.**bashrc** file to make them available each time you log in. See page 330 for more information.

```
$ alias 'h=history | tail'
$ alias 'hg=history | grep'
```

REEXECUTING AND EDITING COMMANDS

You can reexecute any event in the history list. This feature can save you time, effort, and aggravation. Not having to reenter long command lines allows you to reexecute events more easily, quickly, and accurately than you could if you had to retype the command line in its entirety. You can recall, modify, and reexecute previously executed events in three ways: You can use the fc builtin (covered next), the exclamation point commands (page 319), or the Readline Library, which uses a one-line vi- or emacs-like editor to edit and execute events (page 324).

Which method to use?

tip   If you are more familiar with vi or emacs and less familiar with the C or TC Shell, use fc or the Readline Library. If you are more familiar with the C or TC Shell, use the exclamation point commands. If it is a toss-up, try the Readline Library; it will benefit you in other areas of Linux more than learning the exclamation point commands will.

fc: DISPLAYS, EDITS, AND REEXECUTES COMMANDS

The fc (fix command) builtin enables you to display the history list and to edit and reexecute previous commands. It provides many of the same capabilities as the command-line editors.

VIEWING THE HISTORY LIST

When you call fc with the –l option, it displays commands from the history list. Without any arguments, fc –l lists the 16 most recent commands in a numbered list, with the oldest appearing first:

```
$ fc -l
1024    cd
1025    view calendar
1026    vim letter.adams01
1027    aspell -c letter.adams01
1028    vim letter.adams01
1029    lpr letter.adams01
1030    cd ../memos
```

```
1031    ls
1032    rm *0405
1033    fc -l
1034    cd
1035    whereis aspell
1036    man aspell
1037    cd /usr/share/doc/*aspell*
1038    pwd
1039    ls
1040    ls man-html
```

The fc builtin can take zero, one, or two arguments with the –l option. The arguments specify the part of the history list to be displayed:

fc –l [first [last]]

The fc builtin lists commands beginning with the most recent event that matches *first*. The argument can be an event number, the first few characters of the command line, or a negative number, which is taken to be the *n*th previous command. Without *last*, fc displays events through the most recent. If you include *last*, fc displays commands from the most recent event that matches *first* through the most recent event that matches *last*.

The next command displays the history list from event 1030 through event 1035:

```
$ fc -l 1030 1035
1030    cd ../memos
1031    ls
1032    rm *0405
1033    fc -l
1034    cd
1035    whereis aspell
```

The following command lists the most recent event that begins with **view** through the most recent command line that begins with **whereis**:

```
$ fc -l view whereis
1025    view calendar
1026    vim letter.adams01
1027    aspell -c letter.adams01
1028    vim letter.adams01
1029    lpr letter.adams01
1030    cd ../memos
1031    ls
1032    rm *0405
1033    fc -l
1034    cd
1035    whereis aspell
```

To list a single command from the history list, use the same identifier for the first and second arguments. The following command lists event 1027:

```
$ fc -l 1027 1027
1027    aspell -c letter.adams01
```

EDITING AND REEXECUTING PREVIOUS COMMANDS

You can use fc to edit and reexecute previous commands.

fc [–e editor] [first [last]]

When you call fc with the –e option followed by the name of an editor, fc calls the editor with event(s) in the Work buffer, assuming the editor you specify is installed. By default, fc invokes the nano editor. Without *first* and *last,* it defaults to the most recent command. The next example invokes the vim editor to edit the most recent command:

```
$ fc -e vi
```

The fc builtin uses the stand-alone vim editor. If you set the **FCEDIT** variable, you do not need to use the –e option to specify an editor on the command line. Because the value of **FCEDIT** has been changed to **/usr/bin/emacs** and fc has no arguments, the following command edits the most recent command using the emacs editor (part of the **emacs** package; not installed by default):

```
$ export FCEDIT=/usr/bin/emacs
$ fc
```

If you call it with a single argument, fc invokes the editor on the specified command. The following example starts the editor with event 1029 in the Work buffer. When you exit from the editor, the shell executes the command:

```
$ fc 1029
```

As described earlier, you can identify commands with numbers or by specifying the first few characters of the command name. The following example calls the editor to work on events from the most recent event that begins with the letters **vim** through event 1030:

```
$ fc vim 1030
```

Clean up the fc buffer

caution   When you execute an fc command, the shell executes whatever you leave in the editor buffer, possibly with unwanted results. If you decide you do not want to execute a command, delete everything from the buffer before you exit from the editor.

REEXECUTING COMMANDS WITHOUT CALLING THE EDITOR

You can reexecute previous commands without using an editor. If you call fc with the –s option, it skips the editing phase and reexecutes the command. The following example reexecutes event 1029:

```
$ fc -s 1029
lpr letter.adams01
```

The next example reexecutes the previous command:

```
$ fc -s
```

When you reexecute a command, you can tell fc to substitute one string for another. The next example substitutes the string **john** for the string **adams** in event 1029 and executes the modified event:

```
$ fc -s adams=john 1029
lpr letter.john01
```

USING AN EXCLAMATION POINT (!) TO REFERENCE EVENTS

The C Shell history mechanism uses an exclamation point to reference events. This technique, which is available under bash, is frequently more cumbersome to use than fc but nevertheless has some useful features. For example, the !! command reexecutes the previous event, and the shell replaces the !$ token with the last word on the previous command line.

You can reference an event by using its absolute event number, its relative event number, or the text it contains. All references to events, called event designators, begin with an exclamation point (!). One or more characters follow the exclamation point to specify an event.

You can put history events anywhere on a command line. To escape an exclamation point so that the shell interprets it literally instead of as the start of a history event, precede the exclamation point with a backslash (\) or enclose it within single quotation marks.

EVENT DESIGNATORS

An event designator specifies a command in the history list. See Table 9-8 on the next page for a list of event designators.

!! reexecutes the previous event You can reexecute the previous event by giving a !! command. In the following example, event 45 reexecutes event 44:

```
44 $ ls -l text
-rw-rw-r--  1 max group 45 Apr 30 14:53 text
45 $ !!
ls -l text
-rw-rw-r--  1 max group 45 Apr 30 14:53 text
```

The !! command works whether or not your prompt displays an event number. As this example shows, when you use the history mechanism to reexecute an event, the shell displays the command it is reexecuting.

!n event number A number following an exclamation point refers to an event. If that event is in the history list, the shell executes it. Otherwise, the shell displays an error message. A negative number following an exclamation point references an event relative to the current event. For example, the command !-3 refers to the third preceding event. After you issue a command, the relative event number of a given event changes (event -3 becomes event -4). Both of the following commands reexecute event 44:

```
51 $ !44
ls -l text
-rw-rw-r--  1 max group 45 Apr 30 14:53 text
52 $ !-8
ls -l text
-rw-rw-r--  1 max group 45 Apr 30 14:53 text
```

!string event text   When a string of text follows an exclamation point, the shell searches for and executes the most recent event that *began* with that string. If you enclose the string within question marks, the shell executes the most recent event that *contained* that string. The final question mark is optional if a RETURN would immediately follow it.

```
68 $ history 10
   59  ls -l text*
   60  tail text5
   61  cat text1 text5 > letter
   62  vim letter
   63  cat letter
   64  cat memo
   65  lpr memo
   66  pine zach
   67  ls -l
   68  history
69 $ !l
ls -l
...
70 $ !lpr
lpr memo
71 $ !?letter?
cat letter
...
```

Table 9-8 Event designators

Designator	Meaning
!	Starts a history event unless followed immediately by SPACE, NEWLINE, **=**, or **(**.
!!	The previous command.
!*n*	Command number ***n*** in the history list.
!−*n*	The ***n***th preceding command.
!*string*	The most recent command line that started with ***string***.
!?*string*[?]	The most recent command that contained ***string***. The last **?** is optional.
!#	The current command (as you have it typed so far).
!{*event*}	The ***event*** is an event designator. The braces isolate ***event*** from the surrounding text. For example, **!{−3}3** is the third most recently executed command followed by a **3**.

optional WORD DESIGNATORS

A *word designator* specifies a word (token) or series of words from an event. (Table 9-9 on page 322 lists word designators.) The words are numbered starting with 0 (the first word on the line—usually the command), continuing with 1 (the first word following the command), and ending with ***n*** (the last word on the line).

To specify a particular word from a previous event, follow the event designator (such as !14) with a colon and the number of the word in the previous event. For example, !14:3 specifies the third word following the command from event 14. You can specify the first word following the command (word number 1) using a caret (^) and the last word using a dollar sign ($). You can specify a range of words by separating two word designators with a hyphen.

```
72 $ echo apple grape orange pear
apple grape orange pear
73 $ echo !72:2
echo grape
grape
74 $ echo !72:^
echo apple
apple
75 $ !72:0 !72:$
echo pear
pear
76 $ echo !72:2-4
echo grape orange pear
grape orange pear
77 $ !72:0-$
echo apple grape orange pear
apple grape orange pear
```

As the next example shows, !$ refers to the last word of the previous event. You can use this shorthand to edit, for example, a file you just displayed with cat:

```
$ cat report.718
...
$ vim !$
vim report.718
...
```

If an event contains a single command, the word numbers correspond to the argument numbers. If an event contains more than one command, this correspondence does not hold true for commands after the first. In the following example, event 78 contains two commands separated by a semicolon so the shell executes them sequentially; the semicolon is word number 5.

```
78 $ !72 ; echo helen zach barbara
echo apple grape orange pear ; echo helen zach barbara
apple grape orange pear
helen zach barbara
79 $ echo !78:7
echo helen
helen
80 $ echo !78:4-7
echo pear ; echo helen
pear
helen
```

Table 9-9   Word designators

Designator	Meaning
n	The *nth* word. Word 0 is normally the command name.
^	The first word (after the command name).
$	The last word.
m–n	All words from word number *m* through word number *n*; *m* defaults to 0 if you omit it (0–*n*).
n∗	All words from word number *n* through the last word.
∗	All words except the command name. The same as **1**∗.
%	The word matched by the most recent **?** *string* **?** search.

MODIFIERS

On occasion you may want to change an aspect of an event you are reexecuting. Perhaps you entered a complex command line with a typo or incorrect pathname or you want to specify a different argument. You can modify an event or a word of an event by putting one or more modifiers after the word designator, or after the event designator if there is no word designator. Each modifier must be preceded by a colon (:).

Substitute modifier   The following example shows the *substitute modifier* correcting a typo in the previous event:

```
$ car /home/zach/memo.0507 /home/max/letter.0507
bash: car: command not found
$ !!:s/car/cat
cat /home/zach/memo.0507 /home/max/letter.0507
...
```

The substitute modifier has the following syntax:

[g]s/*old*/*new*/

where *old* is the original string (not a regular expression) and *new* is the string that replaces *old*. The substitute modifier substitutes the first occurrence of *old* with *new*. Placing a g before the s (as in gs/*old*/*new*/) causes a global substitution, replacing all occurrences of *old*. Although / is the delimiter in the examples, you can use any character that is not in either *old* or *new*. The final delimiter is optional if a RETURN would immediately follow it. As with the vim Substitute command, the history mechanism replaces an ampersand (&) in *new* with *old*. The shell replaces a null old string (s//*new*/) with the previous old string or string within a command that you searched for with **?** *string* **?**.

Quick substitution   An abbreviated form of the substitute modifier is *quick substitution*. Use it to reexecute the most recent event while changing some of the event text. The quick substitution character is the caret (^). For example, the command

```
$ ^old^new^
```

produces the same results as

```
$ !!:s/old/new/
```

Thus substituting **cat** for **car** in the previous event could have been entered as

```
$ ^car^cat
cat /home/zach/memo.0507 /home/max/letter.0507
...
```

You can omit the final caret if it would be followed immediately by a RETURN. As with other command-line substitutions, the shell displays the command line as it appears after the substitution.

Other modifiers   Modifiers (other than the substitute modifier) perform simple edits on the part of the event that has been selected by the event designator and the optional word designators. You can use multiple modifiers, each preceded by a colon (:).

The following series of commands uses **ls** to list the name of a file, repeats the command without executing it (**p** modifier), and repeats the last command, removing the last part of the pathname (**h** modifier) again without executing it:

```
$ ls /etc/default/locale
/etc/default/locale
$ !!:p
ls /etc/default/locale
$ !!:h:p
ls /etc/default
$
```

Table 9-10 lists event modifiers other than the substitute modifier.

Table 9-10   Event modifiers

Modifier		Function
e	(extension)	Removes all but the filename extension
h	(head)	Removes the last part of a pathname
p	(print-not)	Displays the command, but does not execute it
q	(quote)	Quotes the substitution to prevent further substitutions on it
r	(root)	Removes the filename extension
t	(tail)	Removes all elements of a pathname except the last
x		Like **q** but quotes each word in the substitution individually

THE READLINE LIBRARY

Command-line editing under the Bourne Again Shell is implemented through the *Readline Library*, which is available to any application written in C. Any application that uses the Readline Library supports line editing that is consistent with that provided by bash. Programs that use the Readline Library, including bash, read ~/.inputrc (page 327) for key binding information and configuration settings. The ——noediting command-line option turns off command-line editing in bash.

vi mode   You can choose one of two editing modes when using the Readline Library in bash: emacs or vi(m). Both modes provide many of the commands available in the stand-alone versions of the emacs and vim editors. You can also use the ARROW keys to move around. Up and down movements move you backward and forward through the history list. In addition, Readline provides several types of interactive word completion (page 326). The default mode is emacs; you can switch to vi mode with the following command:

```
$ set -o vi
```

emacs mode   The next command switches back to emacs mode:

```
$ set -o emacs
```

vi EDITING MODE

Before you start, make sure the shell is in vi mode.

When you enter bash commands while in vi editing mode, you are in Input mode (page 174). As you enter a command, if you discover an error before you press RETURN, you can press ESCAPE to switch to vim Command mode. This setup is different from the stand-alone vim editor's initial mode. While in Command mode you can use many vim commands to edit the command line. It is as though you were using vim to edit a copy of the history file with a screen that has room for only one command. When you use the **k** command or the UP ARROW to move up a line, you access the previous command. If you then use the **j** command or the DOWN ARROW to move down a line, you return to the original command. To use the **k** and **j** keys to move between commands, you must be in Command mode; you can use the ARROW keys in both Command and Input modes.

The stand-alone editor starts in Command mode

tip   The stand-alone vim editor starts in Command mode, whereas the command-line vim editor starts in Input mode. If commands display characters and do not work properly, you are in Input mode. Press ESCAPE and enter the command again.

In addition to cursor-positioning commands, you can use the search-backward (**?**) command followed by a search string to look *back* through your history list for the most recent command containing that string. If you have moved back in your history list, use a forward slash (**/**) to search *forward* toward your most recent command. Unlike the search strings in the stand-alone vim editor, these search strings cannot contain regular expressions. You can, however, start the search string with a caret (^) to force the shell to locate commands that start with the search string. As in vim, pressing **n** after a successful search looks for the next occurrence of the same string.

You can also use event numbers to access events in the history list. While you are in Command mode (press ESCAPE), enter the event number followed by a **G** to go to the command with that event number.

When you use **/**, **?**, or **G** to move to a command line, you are in Command mode, not Input mode: You can edit the command or press RETURN to execute it.

Once the command you want to edit is displayed, you can modify the command line using vim Command mode editing commands such as **x** (delete character), **r** (replace character), **~** (change case), and **.** (repeat last change). To change to Input mode, use an Insert (**i**, **I**), Append (**a**, **A**), Replace (**R**), or Change (**c**, **C**) command. You do not have to return to Command mode to execute a command; simply press RETURN, even if the cursor is in the middle of the command line.

emacs EDITING MODE

Unlike the vim editor, emacs is modeless. You need not switch between Command mode and Input mode because most emacs commands are control characters, allowing emacs to distinguish between input and commands. Like vim, the emacs command-line editor provides commands for moving the cursor on the command line and through the command history list and for modifying part or all of a command. However, in a few cases, the emacs command-line editor commands differ from those in the stand-alone emacs editor.

In emacs you perform cursor movement by using both CONTROL and ESCAPE commands. To move the cursor one character backward on the command line, press CONTROL-B. Press CONTROL-F to move one character forward. As in vim, you may precede these movements with counts. To use a count you must first press ESCAPE; otherwise, the numbers you type will appear on the command line.

Like vim, emacs provides word and line movement commands. To move backward or forward one word on the command line, press ESCAPE **b** or ESCAPE **f**. To move several words using a count, press ESCAPE followed by the number and the appropriate escape sequence. To move to the beginning of the line, press CONTROL-A; to the end of the line, press CONTROL-E; and to the next instance of the character *c*, press CONTROL-X CONTROL-F followed by *c*.

You can add text to the command line by moving the cursor to the position you want to enter text and typing the desired text. To delete text, move the cursor just to the right of the characters that you want to delete and press the erase key (page 136) once for each character you want to delete.

CONTROL-D **can terminate your screen session**

tip If you want to delete the character directly under the cursor, press CONTROL-D. If you enter CONTROL-D at the beginning of the line, it may terminate your shell session.

If you want to delete the entire command line, type the line kill character (page 136). You can type this character while the cursor is anywhere in the command line. If you want to delete from the cursor to the end of the line, press CONTROL-K.

READLINE COMPLETION COMMANDS

You can use the TAB key to complete words you are entering on the command line. This facility, called *completion*, works in both vi and emacs editing modes. Several types of completion are possible, and which one you use depends on which part of a command line you are typing when you press TAB.

COMMAND COMPLETION

If you are typing the name of a command (usually the first word on the command line), pressing TAB initiates *command completion,* in which bash looks for a command whose name starts with the part of the word you have typed. If no command starts with the characters you entered, bash beeps. If there is one such command, bash completes the command name. If there is more than one choice, bash does nothing in vi mode and beeps in emacs mode. Pressing TAB a second time causes bash to display a list of commands whose names start with the prefix you typed and allows you to continue typing the command name.

In the following example, the user types **bz** and presses TAB. The shell beeps (the user is in emacs mode) to indicate that several commands start with the letters **bz**. The user enters another TAB to cause the shell to display a list of commands that start with **bz** followed by the command line as the user had entered it so far:

```
$ bz  ⟶TAB (beep)  ⟶TAB
bzcat        bzdiff        bzip2         bzless
bzcmp        bzgrep        bzip2recover  bzmore
$ bz█
```

Next the user types **c** and presses TAB twice. The shell displays the two commands that start with **bzc**. The user types **a** followed by TAB. At this point the shell completes the command because only one command starts with **bzca**.

```
$ bzc  ⟶TAB (beep)  ⟶TAB
bzcat  bzcmp
$ bzca  ⟶TAB  ⟶ t █
```

PATHNAME COMPLETION

Pathname completion, which also uses TABs, allows you to type a portion of a pathname and have bash supply the rest. If the portion of the pathname you have typed is sufficient to determine a unique pathname, bash displays that pathname. If more than one pathname would match it, bash completes the pathname up to the point where there are choices so that you can type more.

When you are entering a pathname, including a simple filename, and press TAB, the shell beeps (if the shell is in emacs mode—in vi mode there is no beep). It then extends the command line as far as it can.

```
$ cat films/dar  →TAB (beep) cat films/dark_■
```

In the **films** directory every file that starts with **dar** has **k_** as the next characters, so bash cannot extend the line further without making a choice among files. The shell leaves the cursor just past the _ character. At this point you can continue typing the pathname or press TAB twice. In the latter case bash beeps, displays your choices, redisplays the command line, and again leaves the cursor just after the _ character.

```
$ cat films/dark_  →TAB (beep)  →TAB
dark_passage   dark_victory
$ cat films/dark_■
```

When you add enough information to distinguish between the two possible files and press TAB, bash displays the unique pathname. If you enter **p** followed by TAB after the _ character, the shell completes the command line:

```
$ cat films/dark_p  →TAB  →assage
```

Because there is no further ambiguity, the shell appends a SPACE so you can finish typing the command line or just press RETURN to execute the command. If the complete pathname is that of a directory, bash appends a slash (/) in place of a SPACE.

VARIABLE COMPLETION

When you are typing a variable name, pressing TAB results in *variable completion*, wherein bash attempts to complete the name of the variable. In case of an ambiguity, pressing TAB twice displays a list of choices:

```
$ echo $HO  →TAB  →TAB
$HOME       $HOSTNAME  $HOSTTYPE
$ echo $HOM  →TAB  →E
```

Pressing RETURN executes the command

caution   Pressing RETURN causes the shell to execute the command regardless of where the cursor is on the command line.

.inputrc: CONFIGURING THE READLINE LIBRARY

The Bourne Again Shell and other programs that use the Readline Library read the file specified by the **INPUTRC** environment variable to obtain initialization information. If **INPUTRC** is not set, these programs read the **~/.inputrc** file. They ignore lines of **.inputrc** that are blank or that start with a pound sign (#).

VARIABLES

You can set variables in **.inputrc** to control the behavior of the Readline Library using the following syntax:

> set *variable value*

Table 9-11 lists some variables and values you can use. See **Readline Variables** in the bash man or info page for a complete list.

Table 9-11   Readline variables

Variable	Effect
editing-mode	Set to **vi** to start Readline in vi mode. Set to **emacs** to start Readline in emacs mode (the default). Similar to the **set −o vi** and **set −o emacs** shell commands (page 324).
horizontal-scroll-mode	Set to **on** to cause long lines to extend off the right edge of the display area. Moving the cursor to the right when it is at the right edge of the display area shifts the line to the left so you can see more of the line. You can shift the line back by moving the cursor back past the left edge. The default value is **off**, which causes long lines to wrap onto multiple lines of the display.
mark-directories	Set to **off** to cause Readline not to place a slash (/) at the end of directory names it completes. The default value is **on**.
mark-modified-lines	Set to **on** to cause Readline to precede modified history lines with an asterisk. The default value is **off**.

KEY BINDINGS

You can specify bindings that map keystroke sequences to Readline commands, allowing you to change or extend the default bindings. Like the emacs editor, the Readline Library includes many commands that are not bound to a keystroke sequence. To use an unbound command, you must map it using one of the following forms:

> *keyname: command_name*
> *" keystroke_sequence" : command_name*

In the first form, you spell out the name for a single key. For example, CONTROL-U would be written as **control-u**. This form is useful for binding commands to single keys.

In the second form, you specify a string that describes a sequence of keys that will be bound to the command. You can use the emacs-style backslash escape sequences to represent the special keys CONTROL (**\C**), META (**\M**), and ESCAPE (**\e**). Specify a backslash by escaping it with another backslash: ****. Similarly, a double or single quotation mark can be escaped with a backslash: **\"** or **\'**.

The **kill-whole-line** command, available in emacs mode only, deletes the current line. Put the following command in **.inputrc** to bind the **kill-whole-line** command (which is unbound by default) to the keystroke sequence CONTROL-R:

```
control-r: kill-whole-line
```

bind Give the command **bind −P** to display a list of all Readline commands. If a command is bound to a key sequence, that sequence is shown. Commands you can use in vi mode start with **vi**. For example, **vi-next-word** and **vi-prev-word** move the cursor to the beginning of the next and previous words, respectively. Commands that do not begin with **vi** are generally available in emacs mode.

Use **bind −q** to determine which key sequence is bound to a command:

```
$ bind -q kill-whole-line
kill-whole-line can be invoked via "\C-r".
```

You can also bind text by enclosing it within double quotation marks (emacs mode only):

```
"QQ": "The Linux Operating System"
```

This command causes bash to insert the string **The Linux Operating System** when you type **QQ**.

CONDITIONAL CONSTRUCTS

You can conditionally select parts of the **.inputrc** file using the **$if** directive. The syntax of the conditional construct is

$if test[=value]
        commands
   [$else
        commands]
$endif

where *test* is **mode**, **term**, or **bash**. If *test* equals *value* (or if *test* is *true* when *value* is not specified), this structure executes the first set of *commands*. If *test* does not equal *value* (or if *test* is *false* when *value* is not specified), this construct executes the second set of *commands* if they are present or exits from the structure if they are not present.

The power of the **$if** directive lies in the three types of tests it can perform.

1. You can test to see which mode is currently set.

   ```
   $if mode=vi
   ```

   The preceding test is *true* if the current Readline mode is **vi** and *false* otherwise. You can test for **vi** or **emacs**.

2. You can test the type of terminal.

   ```
   $if term=xterm
   ```

   The preceding test is *true* if the **TERM** variable is set to **xterm**. You can test for any value of **TERM**.

3. You can test the application name.

   ```
   $if bash
   ```

   The preceding test is *true* when you are running bash and not another program that uses the Readline Library. You can test for any application name.

These tests can customize the Readline Library based on the current mode, the type of terminal, and the application you are using. They give you a great deal of power and flexibility when you are using the Readline Library with bash and other programs.

The following commands in **.inputrc** cause CONTROL-Y to move the cursor to the beginning of the next word regardless of whether bash is in vi or emacs mode:

```
$ cat ~/.inputrc
set editing-mode vi
$if mode=vi
        "\C-y": vi-next-word
    $else
        "\C-y": forward-word
$endif
```

Because bash reads the preceding conditional construct when it is started, you must set the editing mode in **.inputrc**. Changing modes interactively using set will not change the binding of CONTROL-Y.

For more information on the Readline Library, open the bash man page and give the command **/^READLINE**, which searches for the word **READLINE** at the beginning of a line.

If Readline commands do not work, log out and log in again

tip   The Bourne Again Shell reads **~/.inputrc** when you log in. After you make changes to this file, you must log out and log in again before the changes will take effect.

ALIASES

An *alias* is a (usually short) name that the shell translates into another (usually longer) name or (complex) command. Aliases allow you to define new commands by substituting a string for the first token of a simple command. They are typically placed in the **~/.bashrc** startup files so that they are available to interactive subshells.

The syntax of the alias builtin is

alias [name[=value]]

No SPACEs are permitted around the equal sign. If *value* contains SPACEs or TABs, you must enclose *value* within quotation marks. An alias does not accept an argument from the command line in *value*. Use a function (page 333) when you need to use an argument.

An alias does not replace itself, which avoids the possibility of infinite recursion in handling an alias such as the following:

```
$ alias ls='ls -F'
```

You can nest aliases. Aliases are disabled for noninteractive shells (that is, shell scripts). To see a list of the current aliases, give the command **alias**. To view the alias for a particular name, give the command **alias** followed by the name of the alias. You can use the unalias builtin to remove an alias.

When you give an alias builtin command without any arguments, the shell displays a list of all defined aliases:

```
$ alias
alias ll='ls -l'
alias l='ls -ltr'
alias ls='ls -F'
alias zap='rm -i'
```

Ubuntu Linux defines some aliases. Give an **alias** command to see which aliases are in effect. You can delete the aliases you do not want from the appropriate startup file.

SINGLE VERSUS DOUBLE QUOTATION MARKS IN ALIASES

The choice of single or double quotation marks is significant in the alias syntax when the alias includes variables. If you enclose *value* within double quotation marks, any variables that appear in *value* are expanded when the alias is created. If you enclose *value* within single quotation marks, variables are not expanded until the alias is used. The following example illustrates the difference.

The **PWD** keyword variable holds the pathname of the working directory. Max creates two aliases while he is working in his home directory. Because he uses double quotation marks when he creates the **dirA** alias, the shell substitutes the value of the working directory when he creates this alias. The **alias dirA** command displays the **dirA** alias and shows that the substitution has already taken place:

```
$ echo $PWD
/home/max
$ alias dirA="echo Working directory is $PWD"
$ alias dirA
alias dirA='echo Working directory is /home/max'
```

When Max creates the **dirB** alias, he uses single quotation marks, which prevent the shell from expanding the **$PWD** variable. The **alias dirB** command shows that the **dirB** alias still holds the unexpanded **$PWD** variable:

```
$ alias dirB='echo Working directory is $PWD'
$ alias dirB
alias dirB='echo Working directory is $PWD'
```

After creating the **dirA** and **dirB** aliases, Max uses cd to make **cars** his working directory and gives each of the aliases as commands. The alias he created using double quotation marks displays the name of the directory he created the alias in as the working directory (which is wrong). In contrast, the **dirB** alias displays the proper name of the working directory:

```
$ cd cars
$ dirA
Working directory is /home/max
$ dirB
Working directory is /home/max/cars
```

How to prevent the shell from invoking an alias

tip   The shell checks only simple, unquoted commands to see if they are aliases. Commands given as relative or absolute pathnames and quoted commands are not checked. When you want to give a command that has an alias but do not want to use the alias, precede the command with a back-slash, specify the command's absolute pathname, or give the command as *./command*.

Examples of Aliases

The following alias allows you to type **r** to repeat the previous command or **r abc** to repeat the last command line that began with **abc**:

```
$ alias r='fc -s'
```

If you use the command **ls –ltr** frequently, you can create an alias that substitutes **ls –ltr** when you give the command **l**:

```
$ alias l='ls -ltr'
$ l
total 41
-rw-r--r--  1 max     group     30015 Mar  1 2008 flute.ps
-rw-r-----  1 max     group      3089 Feb 11 2009 XTerm.ad
-rw-r--r--  1 max     group       641 Apr  1 2009 fixtax.icn
-rw-r--r--  1 max     group       484 Apr  9 2009 maptax.icn
drwxrwxr-x  2 max     group      1024 Aug  9 17:41 Tiger
drwxrwxr-x  2 max     group      1024 Sep 10 11:32 testdir
-rwxr-xr-x  1 max     group       485 Oct 21 08:03 floor
drwxrwxr-x  2 max     group      1024 Oct 27 20:19 Test_Emacs
```

Another common use of aliases is to protect yourself from mistakes. The following example substitutes the interactive version of the rm utility when you give the command **zap**:

```
$ alias zap='rm -i'
$ zap f*
rm: remove 'fixtax.icn'? n
rm: remove 'flute.ps'? n
rm: remove 'floor'? n
```

The **–i** option causes rm to ask you to verify each file that would be deleted, thereby helping you avoid deleting the wrong file. You can also alias rm with the **rm –i** command: **alias rm='rm –i'**.

The aliases in the next example cause the shell to substitute **ls –l** each time you give an **ll** command and **ls –F** each time you use **ls**:

```
$ alias ls='ls -F'
$ alias ll='ls -l'
$ ll
total 41
drwxrwxr-x  2 max     group      1024 Oct 27 20:19 Test_Emacs/
drwxrwxr-x  2 max     group      1024 Aug 9 17:41 Tiger/
-rw-r-----  1 max     group      3089 Feb 11 2009 XTerm.ad
-rw-r--r--  1 max     group       641 Apr 1 2009 fixtax.icn
-rw-r--r--  1 max     group     30015 Mar 1 2008 flute.ps
-rwxr-xr-x  1 max     group       485 Oct 21 08:03 floor*
-rw-r--r--  1 max     group       484 Apr 9 2009 maptax.icn
drwxrwxr-x  2 max     group      1024 Sep 10 11:32 testdir/
```

The **–F** option causes ls to print a slash (/) at the end of directory names and an asterisk (✻) at the end of the names of executable files. In this example, the string that replaces the alias **ll** (ls **–l**) itself contains an alias (ls). When it replaces an alias with its value, the shell looks at the first word of the replacement string to see whether it is an alias. In the preceding example, the replacement string contains the alias **ls**, so a second substitution occurs to produce the final command **ls –F –l**. (To avoid a *recursive plunge*, the ls in the replacement text, although an alias, is not expanded a second time.)

When given a list of aliases without the *=value* or *value* field, the alias builtin responds by displaying the value of each defined alias. The alias builtin reports an error if an alias has not been defined:

```
$ alias ll l ls zap wx
alias ll='ls -l'
alias l='ls -ltr'
alias ls='ls -F'
alias zap='rm -i'
bash: alias: wx: not found
```

You can avoid alias substitution by preceding the aliased command with a backslash (\):

```
$ \ls
Test_Emacs XTerm.ad  flute.ps  maptax.icn
Tiger      fixtax.icn floor     testdir
```

Because the replacement of an alias name with the alias value does not change the rest of the command line, any arguments are still received by the command that gets executed:

```
$ ll f✻
-rw-r--r--  1 max    group      641 Apr  1 2009 fixtax.icn
-rw-r--r--  1 max    group    30015 Mar  1 2008 flute.ps
-rwxr-xr-x  1 max    group      485 Oct 21 08:03 floor✻
```

You can remove an alias with the unalias builtin. When the **zap** alias is removed, it is no longer displayed with the alias builtin and its subsequent use results in an error message:

```
$ unalias zap
$ alias
alias ll='ls -l'
alias l='ls -ltr'
alias ls='ls -F'
$ zap maptax.icn
bash: zap: command not found
```

FUNCTIONS

A shell function is similar to a shell script in that it stores a series of commands for execution at a later time. However, because the shell stores a function in the computer's main memory (RAM) instead of in a file on the disk, the shell can access it more quickly than the shell can access a script. The shell also preprocesses (parses) a function so that it starts up more quickly than a script. Finally the shell executes a shell function in the same shell that called it. If you define too many functions, the overhead of starting a subshell (as when you run a script) can become unacceptable.

You can declare a shell function in the ~/.bash_profile startup file, in the script that uses it, or directly from the command line. You can remove functions with the unset builtin. The shell does not retain functions after you log out.

Removing variables and functions

tip If you have a shell variable and a function with the same name, using unset removes the shell variable. If you then use unset again with the same name, it removes the function.

The syntax that declares a shell function is

[function] **function-name ()**
{
    commands
}

where the word *function* is optional, *function-name* is the name you use to call the function, and *commands* comprise the list of commands the function executes when you call it. The *commands* can be anything you would include in a shell script, including calls to other functions.

The opening brace ({) can appear on the same line as the function name. Aliases and variables are expanded when a function is read, not when it is executed. You can use the **break** statement (page 932) within a function to terminate its execution.

Shell functions are useful as a shorthand as well as to define special commands. The following function starts a process named **process** in the background, with the output normally displayed by **process** being saved in **.process.out**:

```
start_process() {
process > .process.out 2>&1 &
}
```

The next example creates a simple function that displays the date, a header, and a list of the people who are logged in on the system. This function runs the same commands as the **whoson** script described on page 284. In this example the function is being entered from the keyboard. The greater than (>) signs are secondary shell prompts (**PS2**); do not enter them.

```
$ function whoson ()
> {
>     date
>     echo "Users Currently Logged On"
>     who
> }

$ whoson
Sun Aug 9 15:44:58 PDT 2009
Users Currently Logged On
hls       console     Aug  8 08:59   (:0)
max       pts/4       Aug  8 09:33   (0.0)
zach      pts/7       Aug  8 09:23   (bravo.example.com)
```

Functions in startup files If you want to have the **whoson** function always be available without having to enter it each time you log in, put its definition in **~/.bash_profile**. Then run **.bash_profile**, using the **.** (dot) command to put the changes into effect immediately:

```
$ cat ~/.bash_profile
export TERM=vt100
stty kill '^u'
whoson ()
{
    date
    echo "Users Currently Logged On"
    who
}
$ . ~/.bash_profile
```

You can specify arguments when you call a function. Within the function these arguments are available as positional parameters (page 952). The following example shows the **arg1** function entered from the keyboard:

```
$ arg1 ( ) {
> echo "$1"
> }

$ arg1 first_arg
first_arg
```

See the function **switch** () on page 280 for another example of a function. "Functions" on page 949 discusses the use of local and global variables within a function.

optional The following function allows you to export variables using tcsh syntax. The env builtin lists all environment variables and their values and verifies that **setenv** worked correctly:

```
$ cat .bash_profile
...
# setenv - keep tcsh users happy
function setenv()
{
    if [ $# -eq 2 ]
        then
                eval $1=$2
                export $1
        else
                echo "Usage: setenv NAME VALUE" 1>&2
    fi
}
$ . ~/.bash_profile
$ setenv TCL_LIBRARY /usr/local/lib/tcl
$ env | grep TCL_LIBRARY
TCL_LIBRARY=/usr/local/lib/tcl
```

eval The $# special parameter (page 953) takes on the value of the number of command-line arguments. This function uses the eval builtin to force bash to scan the command $1=$2 *twice*. Because $1=$2 begins with a dollar sign ($), the shell treats the entire string as a single token—a command. With variable substitution performed, the command name becomes **TCL_LIBRARY=/usr/local/lib/tcl**, which results in an error. Using **eval**, a second scanning splits the string into the three desired tokens, and the correct assignment occurs.

CONTROLLING bash: FEATURES AND OPTIONS

This section explains how to control bash features and options using command-line options and the set and shopt builtins.

COMMAND-LINE OPTIONS

Two kinds of command-line options are available: short and long. Short options consist of a hyphen followed by a letter; long options have two hyphens followed by multiple characters. Long options must appear before short options on a command line that calls bash. Table 9-12 lists some commonly used command-line options.

Table 9-12   Command-line options

Option	Explanation	Syntax
Help	Displays a usage message.	**––help**
No edit	Prevents users from using the Readline Library (page 324) to edit command lines in an interactive shell.	**––noediting**
No profile	Prevents reading these startup files (page 277): **/etc/profile**, **~/.bash_profile**, **~/.bash_login**, and **~/.profile**.	**––noprofile**
No rc	Prevents reading the **~/.bashrc** startup file (page 278). This option is on by default if the shell is called as **sh**.	**––norc**
POSIX	Runs bash in POSIX mode.	**––posix**
Version	Displays bash version information and exits.	**––version**
Login	Causes bash to run as though it were a login shell.	**–l** (lowercase "l")
shopt	Runs a shell with the *opt* shopt option (next page). A **–O** (uppercase "O") sets the option; **+O** unsets it.	**[±]O [*opt*]**
End of options	On the command line, signals the end of options. Subsequent tokens are treated as arguments even if they begin with a hyphen (**–**).	**––**

SHELL FEATURES

You can control the behavior of the Bourne Again Shell by turning features on and off. Different features use different methods to turn features on and off. The set builtin controls one group of features, while the shopt builtin controls another group. You can also control many features from the command line you use to call bash.

Features, options, variables?

> **tip** To avoid confusing terminology, this book refers to the various shell behaviors that you can control as *features*. The bash info page refers to them as "options" and "values of variables controlling optional shell behavior."

set ±o: Turns Shell Features On and Off

The set builtin, when used with the **−o** or **+o** option, enables, disables, and lists certain bash features. For example, the following command turns on the **noclobber** feature (page 234):

```
$ set -o noclobber
```

You can turn this feature off (the default) by giving the command

```
$ set +o noclobber
```

The command **set −o** without an option lists each of the features controlled by set, followed by its state (on or off). The command **set +o** without an option lists the same features in a form you can use as input to the shell. Table 9-13 (next page) lists bash features.

shopt: Turns Shell Features On and Off

The shopt (shell option) builtin enables, disables, and lists certain bash features that control the behavior of the shell. For example, the following command causes bash to include filenames that begin with a period (.) when it expands ambiguous file references (the **−s** stands for *set*):

```
$ shopt -s dotglob
```

You can turn this feature off (the default) by giving the following command (the **−u** stands for *unset*):

```
$ shopt -u dotglob
```

The shell displays how a feature is set if you give the name of the feature as the only argument to shopt:

```
$ shopt dotglob
dotglob         off
```

The command **shopt** without any options or arguments lists the features controlled by shopt and their state. The command **shopt −s** without an argument lists the features controlled by shopt that are set or on. The command **shopt −u** lists the features that are unset or off. Table 9-13 lists bash features.

Setting set ±o features using shopt

> **tip** You can use shopt to set/unset features that are otherwise controlled by **set ±o**. Use the regular shopt syntax with **−s** or **−u** and include the **−o** option. For example, the following command turns on the **noclobber** feature:
>
> ```
> $ shopt -o -s noclobber
> ```

Table 9-13   bash features

Feature	Description	Syntax	Alternate syntax
allexport	Automatically exports all variables and functions you create or modify after giving this command.	**set −o allexport**	**set −a**
braceexpand	Causes bash to perform brace expansion (the default; page 342).	**set −o braceexpand**	**set −B**
cdspell	Corrects minor spelling errors in directory names used as arguments to cd.	**shopt −s cdspell**	
cmdhist	Saves all lines of a multiline command in the same history entry, adding semicolons as needed.	**shopt −s cmdhist**	
dotglob	Causes shell special characters (wildcards; page 242) in an ambiguous file reference to match a leading period in a filename. By default special characters do not to match a leading period. You must always specify the filenames . and .. explicitly because no pattern ever matches them.	**shopt −s dotglob**	
emacs	Specifies emacs editing mode for command-line editing (the default; page 325).	**set −o emacs**	
errexit	Causes bash to exit when a simple command (not a control structure) fails.	**set −o errexit**	**set −e**
execfail	Causes a shell script to continue running when it cannot find the file that is given as an argument to exec. By default a script terminates when exec cannot find the file that is given as its argument.	**shopt −s execfail**	
expand_aliases	Causes aliases (page 330) to be expanded (by default it is on for interactive shells and off for noninteractive shells).	**shopt −s expand_alias**	
hashall	Causes bash to remember where commands it has found using **PATH** (page 303) are located (default).	**set −o hashall**	**set −h**
histappend	Causes bash to append the history list to the file named by **HISTFILE** (page 314) when the shell exits. By default bash overwrites this file.	**shopt −s histappend**	
histexpand	Turns on the history mechanism (which uses exclamation points by default; page 319). Turn this feature off to turn off history expansion.	**set −o histexpand**	**set −H**

Table 9-13 bash features (continued)

Feature	Description	Syntax	Alternate syntax
history	Enables command history (on by default; page 314).	**set −o history**	
huponexit	Specifies that bash send a SIGHUP signal to all jobs when an interactive login shell exits.	**shopt −s huponexit**	
ignoreeof	Specifies that bash must receive ten EOF characters before it exits. Useful on noisy dial-up lines.	**set −o ignoreeof**	
monitor	Enables job control (on by default, page 291).	**set −o monitor**	**set −m**
nocaseglob	Causes ambiguous file references (page 242) to match filenames without regard to case (off by default).	**shopt −s nocaseglob**	
noclobber	Helps prevent overwriting files (off by default; page 234).	**set −o noclobber**	**set −C**
noglob	Disables pathname expansion (off by default; page 242).	**set −o noglob**	**set −f**
notify	With job control (page 291) enabled, reports the termination status of background jobs immediately. The default behavior is to display the status just before the next prompt.	**set −o notify**	**set −b**
nounset	Displays an error and exits from a shell script when you use an unset variable in an interactive shell. The default is to display a null value for an unset variable.	**set −o nounset**	**set −u**
nullglob	Causes bash to expand ambiguous file references (page 242) that do not match a filename to a null string. By default bash passes these file references without expanding them.	**shopt −s nullglob**	
posix	Runs bash in POSIX mode.	**set −o posix**	
verbose	Displays command lines as bash reads them.	**set −o verbose**	**set −v**
vi	Specifies vi editing mode for command-line editing (page 324).	**set −o vi**	
xpg_echo	Causes the echo builtin to expand backslash escape sequences without the need for the −e option (page 936).	**shopt −s xpg_echo**	
xtrace	Turns on shell debugging (page 922).	**set −o xtrace**	**set −x**

PROCESSING THE COMMAND LINE

Whether you are working interactively or running a shell script, bash needs to read a command line before it can start processing it—bash always reads at least one line before processing a command. Some bash builtins, such as **if** and **case**, as well as functions and quoted strings, span multiple lines. When bash recognizes a command that covers more than one line, it reads the entire command before processing it. In interactive sessions, bash prompts you with the secondary prompt (**PS2, >** by default; page 306) as you type each line of a multiline command until it recognizes the end of the command:

```
$ echo 'hi
> end'
hi
end
$ function hello () {
> echo hello there
> }
$
```

After reading a command line, bash applies history expansion and alias substitution to the line.

HISTORY EXPANSION

"Reexecuting and Editing Commands" on page 316 discusses the commands you can give to modify and reexecute command lines from the history list. History expansion is the process that bash uses to turn a history command into an executable command line. For example, when you give the command **!!**, history expansion changes that command line so it is the same as the previous one. History expansion is turned on by default for interactive shells; **set +o histexpand** turns it off. History expansion does not apply to noninteractive shells (shell scripts).

ALIAS SUBSTITUTION

Aliases (page 330) substitute a string for the first word of a simple command. By default aliases are turned on for interactive shells and off for noninteractive shells. Give the command **shopt –u expand_aliases** to turn aliases off.

PARSING AND SCANNING THE COMMAND LINE

After processing history commands and aliases, bash does not execute the command immediately. One of the first things the shell does is to *parse* (isolate strings of characters in) the command line into tokens or words. The shell then scans each token for special characters and patterns that instruct the shell to take certain actions. These actions can involve substituting one word or words for another. When the shell parses the following command line, it breaks it into three tokens (**cp**, **~/letter**, and **.**):

```
$ cp ~/letter .
```

After separating tokens and before executing the command, the shell scans the tokens and performs *command-line expansion*.

COMMAND-LINE EXPANSION

Both interactive and noninteractive shells transform the command line using *command-line expansion* before passing the command line to the program being called. You can use a shell without knowing much about command-line expansion, but you can use what a shell has to offer to a better advantage with an understanding of this topic. This section covers Bourne Again Shell command-line expansion.

The Bourne Again Shell scans each token for the various types of expansion and substitution in the following order. Most of these processes expand a word into a single word. Only brace expansion, word splitting, and pathname expansion can change the number of words in a command (except for the expansion of the variable "$@"—see page 956).

1. Brace expansion (page 342)

2. Tilde expansion (page 343)

3. Parameter and variable expansion (page 344)

4. Arithmetic expansion (page 344)

5. Command substitution (page 346)

6. Word splitting (page 347)

7. Pathname expansion (page 347)

8. Process substitution (page 349)

Quote removal   After bash finishes with the preceding list, it removes from the command line single quotation marks, double quotation marks, and backslashes that are not a result of an expansion. This process is called *quote removal*.

ORDER OF EXPANSION

The order in which bash carries out these steps affects the interpretation of commands. For example, if you set a variable to a value that looks like the instruction for output redirection and then enter a command that uses the variable's value to perform redirection, you might expect bash to redirect the output.

```
$ SENDIT="> /tmp/saveit"
$ echo xxx $SENDIT
xxx > /tmp/saveit
$ cat /tmp/saveit
cat: /tmp/saveit: No such file or directory
```

In fact, the shell does *not* redirect the output—it recognizes input and output redirection before it evaluates variables. When it executes the command line, the shell checks for redirection and, finding none, evaluates the **SENDIT** variable. After replacing the variable with **> /tmp/saveit**, bash passes the arguments to echo, which dutifully copies its arguments to standard output. No **/tmp/saveit** file is created.

The following sections provide more detailed descriptions of the steps involved in command processing. Keep in mind that double and single quotation marks cause the shell to behave differently when performing expansions. Double quotation marks permit parameter and variable expansion but suppress other types of expansion. Single quotation marks suppress all types of expansion.

BRACE EXPANSION

Brace expansion, which originated in the C Shell, provides a convenient way to specify filenames when pathname expansion does not apply. Although brace expansion is almost always used to specify filenames, the mechanism can be used to generate arbitrary strings; the shell does not attempt to match the brace notation with the names of existing files.

Brace expansion is turned on in interactive and noninteractive shells by default; you can turn it off with **set +o braceexpand**. The shell also uses braces to isolate variable names (page 300).

The following example illustrates how brace expansion works. The ls command does not display any output because there are no files in the working directory. The echo builtin displays the strings that the shell generates with brace expansion. In this case the strings do not match filenames (because there are no files in the working directory).

```
$ ls
$ echo chap_{one,two,three}.txt
chap_one.txt chap_two.txt chap_three.txt
```

The shell expands the comma-separated strings inside the braces in the echo command into a SPACE-separated list of strings. Each string from the list is prepended with the string **chap_**, called the *preamble,* and appended with the string **.txt**, called the *postscript.* Both the preamble and the postscript are optional. The left-to-right order of the strings within the braces is preserved in the expansion. For the shell to treat the left and right braces specially and for brace expansion to occur, at least one comma and no unquoted whitespace characters must be inside the braces. You can nest brace expansions.

Brace expansion is useful when there is a long preamble or postscript. The following example copies four files—**main.c**, **f1.c**, **f2.c**, and **tmp.c**—located in the **/usr/local/src/C** directory to the working directory:

```
$ cp /usr/local/src/C/{main,f1,f2,tmp}.c .
```

You can also use brace expansion to create directories with related names:

```
$ ls -F
file1  file2  file3
$ mkdir vrs{A,B,C,D,E}
$ ls -F
file1  file2  file3  vrsA/  vrsB/  vrsC/  vrsD/  vrsE/
```

The **–F** option causes ls to display a slash (/) after a directory and an asterisk (*) after an executable file.

If you tried to use an ambiguous file reference instead of braces to specify the directories, the result would be different (and not what you wanted):

```
$ rmdir vrs*
$ mkdir vrs[A-E]
$ ls -F
file1  file2  file3  vrs[A-E]/
```

An ambiguous file reference matches the names of existing files. In the preceding example, because it found no filenames matching **vrs[A–E]**, bash passed the ambiguous file reference to mkdir, which created a directory with that name. Brackets in ambiguous file references are discussed on page 245.

TILDE EXPANSION

Chapter 6 introduced a shorthand notation to specify your home directory or the home directory of another user. This section provides a more detailed explanation of *tilde expansion*.

The tilde (~) is a special character when it appears at the start of a token on a command line. When it sees a tilde in this position, bash looks at the following string of characters—up to the first slash (/) or to the end of the word if there is no slash—as a possible username. If this possible username is null (that is, if the tilde appears as a word by itself or if it is immediately followed by a slash), the shell substitutes the value of the **HOME** variable for the tilde. The following example demonstrates this expansion, where the last command copies the file named **letter** from Max's home directory to the working directory:

```
$ echo $HOME
/home/max
$ echo ~
/home/max
$ echo ~/letter
/home/max/letter
$ cp ~/letter .
```

If the string of characters following the tilde forms a valid username, the shell substitutes the path of the home directory associated with that username for the tilde and name. If the string is not null and not a valid username, the shell does not make any substitution:

```
$ echo ~zach
/home/zach
$ echo ~root
/root
$ echo ~xx
~xx
```

Tildes are also used in directory stack manipulation (page 294). In addition, **~+** is a synonym for **PWD** (the name of the working directory), and **~−** is a synonym for **OLDPWD** (the name of the previous working directory).

PARAMETER AND VARIABLE EXPANSION

On a command line, a dollar sign ($) that is not followed by an open parenthesis introduces parameter or variable expansion. *Parameters* include both command-line, or positional, parameters (page 952) and special parameters (page 950). *Variables* include both user-created variables (page 298) and keyword variables (page 302). The bash man and info pages do not make this distinction.

Parameters and variables are not expanded if they are enclosed within single quotation marks or if the leading dollar sign is escaped (i.e., preceded with a backslash). If they are enclosed within double quotation marks, the shell expands parameters and variables.

ARITHMETIC EXPANSION

The shell performs *arithmetic expansion* by evaluating an arithmetic expression and replacing it with the result. Under bash the syntax for arithmetic expansion is

> *$((expression))*

The shell evaluates *expression* and replaces *$((expression))* with the result of the evaluation. This syntax is similar to the syntax used for command substitution [*$(...)*] and performs a parallel function. You can use *$((expression))* as an argument to a command or in place of any numeric value on a command line.

The rules for forming *expression* are the same as those found in the C programming language; all standard C arithmetic operators are available (see Table 27-8 on page 975). Arithmetic in bash is done using integers. Unless you use variables of type integer (page 302) or actual integers, however, the shell must convert string-valued variables to integers for the purpose of the arithmetic evaluation.

You do not need to precede variable names within *expression* with a dollar sign ($). In the following example, after read (page 959) assigns the user's response to **age**, an arithmetic expression determines how many years are left until age 60:

```
$ cat age_check
#!/bin/bash
echo -n "How old are you? "
read age
echo "Wow, in $((60-age)) years, you'll be 60!"

$ ./age_check
How old are you? 55
Wow, in 5 years, you'll be 60!
```

You do not need to enclose the *expression* within quotation marks because bash does not perform filename expansion on it. This feature makes it easier for you to use an asterisk (✻) for multiplication, as the following example shows:

```
$ echo There are $((60*60*24*365)) seconds in a non-leap year.
There are 31536000 seconds in a non-leap year.
```

The next example uses wc, cut, arithmetic expansion, and command substitution (page 346) to estimate the number of pages required to print the contents of the file **letter.txt**. The output of the wc (word count) utility used with the –l option is the number of lines in the file, in columns (character positions) 1 through 4, followed by a SPACE and the name of the file (the first command following). The cut utility with the –c1–4 option extracts the first four columns.

```
$ wc -l letter.txt
351 letter.txt
$ wc -l letter.txt | cut -c1-4
351
```

The dollar sign and single parenthesis instruct the shell to perform command substitution; the dollar sign and double parentheses indicate arithmetic expansion:

```
$ echo $(( $(wc -l letter.txt | cut -c1-4)/66 + 1))
6
```

The preceding example sends standard output from wc to standard input of cut via a pipe. Because of command substitution, the output of both commands replaces the commands between the $(and the matching) on the command line. Arithmetic expansion then divides this number by 66, the number of lines on a page. A 1 is added because the integer division results in any remainder being discarded.

Fewer dollar signs ($)

tip   When you use variables within **$((** and **))**, the dollar signs that precede individual variable references are optional:

```
$ x=23 y=37
$ echo $((2*$x + 3*$y))
157
$ echo $((2*x + 3*y))
157
```

Another way to get the same result without using cut is to redirect the input to wc instead of having wc get its input from a file you name on the command line. When you redirect its input, wc does not display the name of the file:

```
$ wc -l < letter.txt
    351
```

It is common practice to assign the result of arithmetic expansion to a variable:

```
$ numpages=$(( $(wc -l < letter.txt)/66 + 1))
```

let builtin   The let builtin evaluates arithmetic expressions just as the $(( )) syntax does. The following command is equivalent to the preceding one:

```
$ let "numpages=$(wc -l < letter.txt)/66 + 1"
```

The double quotation marks keep the SPACEs (both those you can see and those that result from the command substitution) from separating the expression into separate arguments to let. The value of the last expression determines the exit status of let. If the value of the last expression is 0, the exit status of let is 1; otherwise, its exit status is 0.

You can supply let with multiple arguments on a single command line:

```
$ let a=5+3 b=7+2
$ echo $a $b
8 9
```

When you refer to variables when doing arithmetic expansion with let or $(( )), the shell does not require a variable name to begin with a dollar sign ($). Nevertheless, it is a good practice to do so for consistency, as in most places you must precede a variable name with a dollar sign.

COMMAND SUBSTITUTION

Command substitution replaces a command with the output of that command. The preferred syntax for command substitution under bash follows:

$(command)

Under bash you can also use the following, older syntax:

` command `

The shell executes *command* within a subshell and replaces *command,* along with the surrounding punctuation, with standard output of *command.*

In the following example, the shell executes pwd and substitutes the output of the command for the command and surrounding punctuation. Then the shell passes the output of the command, which is now an argument, to echo, which displays it.

```
$ echo $(pwd)
/home/max
```

The next script assigns the output of the pwd builtin to the variable **where** and displays a message containing the value of this variable:

```
$ cat where
where=$(pwd)
echo "You are using the $where directory."
$ ./where
You are using the /home/zach directory.
```

Although it illustrates how to assign the output of a command to a variable, this example is not realistic. You can more directly display the output of pwd without using a variable:

```
$ cat where2
echo "You are using the $(pwd) directory."
$ ./where2
You are using the /home/zach directory.
```

The following command uses find to locate files with the name **README** in the directory tree rooted at the working directory. This list of files is standard output of find and becomes the list of arguments to ls.

```
$ ls -l $(find . -name README -print)
```

The next command line shows the older `command` syntax:

```
$ ls -l `find . -name README -print`
```

One advantage of the newer syntax is that it avoids the rather arcane rules for token handling, quotation mark handling, and escaped back ticks within the old syntax. Another advantage of the new syntax is that it can be nested, unlike the old syntax. For example, you can produce a long listing of all **README** files whose size exceeds the size of **./README** with the following command:

```
$ ls -l $(find . -name README -size +$(echo $(cat ./README | wc -c)c ) -print )
```

Try giving this command after giving a **set –x** command (page 922) to see how bash expands it. If there is no **README** file, you just get the output of ls –l.

For additional scripts that use command substitution, see pages 918, 937, and 967.

$((Versus $(

tip   The symbols **$((** constitute a single token. They introduce an arithmetic expression, not a command substitution. Thus, if you want to use a parenthesized subshell (page 290) within **$()**, you must insert a SPACE between the **$(** and the following **(**.

Word Splitting

The results of parameter and variable expansion, command substitution, and arithmetic expansion are candidates for word splitting. Using each character of **IFS** (page 307) as a possible delimiter, bash splits these candidates into words or tokens. If **IFS** is unset, bash uses its default value (SPACE-TAB-NEWLINE). If **IFS** is null, bash does not split words.

Pathname Expansion

Pathname expansion (page 242), also called *filename generation* or *globbing*, is the process of interpreting ambiguous file references and substituting the appropriate list of filenames. Unless **noglob** (page 339) is set, the shell performs this function when it encounters an ambiguous file reference—a token containing any of the unquoted characters *, ?, [, or]. If bash cannot locate any files that match the specified pattern, the token with the ambiguous file reference is left alone. The shell does not delete the token or replace it with a null string but rather passes it to the program as is (except see **nullglob** on page 339).

In the first echo command in the following example, the shell expands the ambiguous file reference **tmp*** and passes three tokens (**tmp1**, **tmp2**, and **tmp3**) to echo. The echo builtin displays the three filenames it was passed by the shell. After rm removes the three **tmp*** files, the shell finds no filenames that match **tmp*** when it tries to expand it. It then passes the unexpanded string to the echo builtin, which displays the string it was passed.

```
$ ls
tmp1 tmp2 tmp3
$ echo tmp*
tmp1 tmp2 tmp3
$ rm tmp*
$ echo tmp*
tmp*
```

A period that either starts a pathname or follows a slash (/) in a pathname must be matched explicitly unless you have set **dotglob** (page 338). The option **nocaseglob** (page 339) causes ambiguous file references to match filenames without regard to case.

Quotation marks   Putting double quotation marks around an argument causes the shell to suppress pathname and all other kinds of expansion except parameter and variable expansion. Putting single quotation marks around an argument suppresses all types of expansion. The second echo command in the following example shows the variable **$max** between double quotation marks, which allow variable expansion. As a result the shell expands the variable to its value: **sonar**. This expansion does not occur in the third echo command, which uses single quotation marks. Because neither single nor double quotation marks allow pathname expansion, the last two commands display the unexpanded argument **tmp***.

```
$ echo tmp* $max
tmp1 tmp2 tmp3 sonar
$ echo "tmp* $max"
tmp* sonar
$ echo 'tmp* $max'
tmp* $max
```

The shell distinguishes between the value of a variable and a reference to the variable and does not expand ambiguous file references if they occur in the value of a variable. As a consequence you can assign to a variable a value that includes special characters, such as an asterisk (*****).

Levels of expansion   In the next example, the working directory has three files whose names begin with **letter**. When you assign the value **letter*** to the variable **var**, the shell does not expand the ambiguous file reference because it occurs in the value of a variable (in the assignment statement for the variable). No quotation marks surround the string **letter***; context alone prevents the expansion. After the assignment the set builtin (with the help of grep) shows the value of **var** to be **letter***.

```
$ ls letter*
letter1  letter2  letter3
$ var=letter*
$ set | grep var
var='letter*'
```

```
$ echo '$var'
$var
$ echo "$var"
letter*
$ echo $var
letter1 letter2 letter3
```

The three **echo** commands demonstrate three levels of expansion. When **$var** is quoted with single quotation marks, the shell performs no expansion and passes the character string **$var** to echo, which displays it. With double quotation marks, the shell performs variable expansion only and substitutes the value of the **var** variable for its name, preceded by a dollar sign. No pathname expansion is performed on this command because double quotation marks suppress it. In the final command, the shell, without the limitations of quotation marks, performs variable substitution and then pathname expansion before passing the arguments to echo.

PROCESS SUBSTITUTION

A special feature of the Bourne Again Shell is the ability to replace filename arguments with processes. An argument with the syntax <*(command)* causes *command* to be executed and the output written to a named pipe (FIFO). The shell replaces that argument with the name of the pipe. If that argument is then used as the name of an input file during processing, the output of *command* is read. Similarly an argument with the syntax >*(command)* is replaced by the name of a pipe that *command* reads as standard input.

The following example uses sort (page 154) with the –**m** (merge, which works correctly only if the input files are already sorted) option to combine two word lists into a single list. Each word list is generated by a pipe that extracts words matching a pattern from a file and sorts the words in that list.

```
$ sort -m -f <(grep "[^A-Z]..$" memo1 | sort) <(grep ".*aba.*" memo2 |sort)
```

CHAPTER SUMMARY

The shell is both a command interpreter and a programming language. As a command interpreter, it executes commands you enter in response to its prompt. As a programming language, the shell executes commands from files called shell scripts. When you start a shell, it typically runs one or more startup files.

Running a shell script Assuming the file holding a shell script is in the working directory, there are three basic ways to execute the shell script from the command line.

1. Type the simple filename of the file that holds the script.

2. Type a relative pathname, including the simple filename preceded by *./*.

3. Type **bash** followed by the name of the file.

Technique 1 requires that the working directory be in the **PATH** variable. Techniques 1 and 2 require that you have execute and read permission for the file holding the script. Technique 3 requires that you have read permission for the file holding the script.

Job control   A job is one or more commands connected by pipes. You can bring a job running in the background into the foreground using the fg builtin. You can put a foreground job into the background using the bg builtin, provided that you first suspend the job by pressing the suspend key (typically CONTROL-Z). Use the jobs builtin to see which jobs are running or suspended.

Variables   The shell allows you to define variables. You can declare and initialize a variable by assigning a value to it; you can remove a variable declaration using unset. Variables are local to a process unless they are exported using the export builtin to make them available to child processes. Variables you declare are called *user-created* variables. The shell defines *keyword* variables. Within a shell script you can work with the command-line (*positional*) parameters the script was called with.

Process   Each process has a unique identification (PID) number and is the execution of a single Linux command. When you give it a command, the shell forks a new (child) process to execute the command, unless the command is built into the shell. While the child process is running, the shell is in a state called sleep. By ending a command line with an ampersand (&), you can run a child process in the background and bypass the sleep state so that the shell prompt returns immediately after you press RETURN. Each command in a shell script forks a separate process, each of which may in turn fork other processes. When a process terminates, it returns its exit status to its parent process. An exit status of zero signifies success; nonzero signifies failure.

History   The history mechanism, a feature adapted from the C Shell, maintains a list of recently issued command lines, also called *events*, that provides a way to reexecute previous commands quickly. There are several ways to work with the history list; one of the easiest is to use a command-line editor.

Command-line editors   When using an interactive Bourne Again Shell, you can edit a command line and commands from the history file, using either of the Bourne Again Shell's command-line editors (vim or emacs). When you use the vim command-line editor, you start in Input mode, unlike vim. You can switch between Command and Input modes. The emacs editor is modeless and distinguishes commands from editor input by recognizing control characters as commands.

Aliases   An alias is a name that the shell translates into another name or (complex) command. Aliases allow you to define new commands by substituting a string for the first token of a simple command.

Functions   A shell function is a series of commands that, unlike a shell script, is parsed prior to being stored in memory. As a consequence shell functions run faster than shell scripts. Shell scripts are parsed at runtime and are stored on disk. A function can be defined on the command line or within a shell script. If you want the function definition to remain in effect across login sessions, you can define it in a startup file. Like functions in many programming languages, a shell function is called by giving its name followed by any arguments.

Shell features   There are several ways to customize the shell's behavior. You can use options on the command line when you call bash. You can use the bash set and shopt builtins to turn features on and off.

Command-line   When it processes a command line, the Bourne Again Shell may replace some
expansion   words with expanded text. Most types of command-line expansion are invoked by the appearance of a special character within a word (for example, a leading dollar sign denotes a variable). Table 9-6 on page 310 lists these special characters. The expansions take place in a specific order. Following the history and alias expansions, the common expansions are parameter and variable expansion, command substitution, and pathname expansion. Surrounding a word with double quotation marks suppresses all types of expansion except parameter and variable expansion. Single quotation marks suppress all types of expansion, as does quoting (escaping) a special character by preceding it with a backslash.

EXERCISES

1. Explain the following unexpected result:

   ```
   $ whereis date
   date: /bin/date ...
   $ echo $PATH
   .:/usr/local/bin:/usr/bin:/bin
   $ cat > date
   echo "This is my own version of date."
   $ ./date
   Fri May 22 11:45:49 PDT 2009
   ```

2. What are two ways you can execute a shell script when you do not have execute permission for the file containing the script? Can you execute a shell script if you do not have read permission for the file containing the script?

3. What is the purpose of the PATH variable?

   a. Set the PATH variable so that it causes the shell to search the following directories in order:

   - /usr/local/bin

   - /usr/bin

   - /bin

   - /usr/kerberos/bin

   - The bin directory in your home directory

   - The working directory

b. If there is a file named **doit** in **/usr/bin** and another file with the same name in your **~/bin** directory, which one will be executed? (Assume that you have execute permission for both files.)

c. If your **PATH** variable is not set to search the working directory, how can you execute a program located there?

d. Which command can you use to add the directory **/usr/games** to the end of the list of directories in **PATH**?

4. Assume you have made the following assignment:

```
$ person=zach
```

Give the output of each of the following commands:

a. echo $person

b. echo '$person'

c. echo "$person"

5. The following shell script adds entries to a file named **journal-file** in your home directory. This script helps you keep track of phone conversations and meetings.

```
$ cat journal
# journal: add journal entries to the file
# $HOME/journal-file

file=$HOME/journal-file
date >> $file
echo -n "Enter name of person or group: "
read name
echo "$name" >> $file
echo >> $file
cat >> $file
echo "-----------------------------------------------" >> $file
echo >> $file
```

a. What do you have to do to the script to be able to execute it?

b. Why does the script use the read builtin the first time it accepts input from the terminal and the cat utility the second time?

6. Assume the **/home/zach/grants/biblios** and **/home/zach/biblios** directories exist. Give Zach's working directory after he executes each sequence of commands given. Explain what happens in each case.

a.
```
$ pwd
/home/zach/grants
$ CDPATH=$(pwd)
$ cd
$ cd biblios
```

b.

```
$ pwd
/home/zach/grants
$ CDPATH=$(pwd)
$ cd $HOME/biblios
```

7. Name two ways you can identify the PID number of the login shell.

8. Give the following command:

```
$ sleep 30 | cat /etc/inittab
```

Is there any output from sleep? Where does cat get its input from? What has to happen before the shell displays another prompt?

ADVANCED EXERCISES

9. Write a sequence of commands or a script that demonstrates variable expansion occurs before pathname expansion.

10. Write a shell script that outputs the name of the shell executing it.

11. Explain the behavior of the following shell script:

```
$ cat quote_demo
twoliner="This is line 1.
This is line 2."
echo "$twoliner"
echo $twoliner
```

a. How many arguments does each echo command see in this script? Explain.

b. Redefine the **IFS** shell variable so that the output of the second echo is the same as the first.

12. Add the exit status of the previous command to your prompt so that it behaves similarly to the following:

```
$ [0] ls xxx
ls: xxx: No such file or directory
$ [1]
```

13. The dirname utility treats its argument as a pathname and writes to standard output the path prefix—that is, everything up to but not including the last component:

```
$ dirname a/b/c/d
a/b/c
```

If you give **dirname** a simple filename (no / characters) as an argument, **dirname** writes a . to standard output:

```
$ dirname simple
.
```

Implement dirname as a bash function. Make sure that it behaves sensibly when given such arguments as /.

14. Implement the basename utility, which writes the last component of its pathname argument to standard output, as a bash function. For example, given the pathname **a/b/c/d**, basename writes **d** to standard output:

```
$ basename a/b/c/d
d
```

15. The Linux basename utility has an optional second argument. If you give the command **basename** *path suffix*, basename removes the *suffix* and the prefix from *path*:

```
$ basename src/shellfiles/prog.bash .bash
prog
$ basename src/shellfiles/prog.bash .c
prog.bash
```

Add this feature to the function you wrote for exercise 14.

10

NETWORKING AND THE INTERNET

The communications facilities linking computers are continually improving, allowing faster and more economical connections. The earliest computers were unconnected stand-alone systems. To transfer information from one system to another, you had to store it in some form (usually magnetic tape, paper tape, or punch cards—called IBM or Hollerith cards), carry it to a compatible system, and read it back in. A notable advance occurred when computers began to exchange data over serial lines, although the transfer rate was slow (hundreds of bits per second). People quickly invented new ways to take advantage of this computing power, such as email, news retrieval, and bulletin board services. With the speed of today's networks, a piece of email can cross the country or even travel halfway around the world in a few seconds.

Today it would be difficult to find a computer facility that does not include a LAN to link its systems. Linux systems are typically attached to an *Ethernet* (page 1107) network. Wireless networks are also prevalent. Large computer facilities usually maintain several networks, often of different types, and almost certainly have connections to larger networks (companywide or campuswide and beyond).

Internet   The Internet is a loosely administered network of networks (an *internetwork*) that links computers on diverse LANs around the globe. An internet (small *i*) is a generic network of networks that may share some parts in common with the public Internet. It is the Internet that makes it possible to send an email message to a colleague thousands of miles away and receive a reply within minutes. A related term, *intranet*, refers to the networking infrastructure within a company or other institution. Intranets are usually private; access to them from external networks may be limited and carefully controlled, typically using firewalls (page 363).

Network services   Over the past decade many network services have emerged and become standardized. On Linux and UNIX systems, special processes called *daemons* (page 1104) support such services by exchanging specialized messages with other systems over the network. Several software systems have been created to allow computers to share filesystems with one another, making it appear as though remote files are stored on local disks. Sharing remote filesystems allows users to share information without knowing where the files physically reside, without making unnecessary copies, and without learning a new set of utilities to manipulate them. Because the files appear to be stored locally, you can use standard utilities (such as cat, vim, lpr, mv, or their graphical counterparts) to work with them.

Developers have created new tools and extended existing ones to take advantage of higher network speeds and to work within more crowded networks. The rlogin, rsh, and telnet utilities, which were designed long ago, have largely been supplanted by ssh (secure shell, page 627) in recent years. The ssh utility allows a user to log in on or execute commands securely on a remote computer. Users rely on such utilities as scp and ftp to transfer files from one system to another across the network. Communication utilities, including email utilities and chat programs (e.g., talk, Internet Relay Chat [IRC], ICQ, and instant messenger [IM] programs, such as AOL's AIM and Pidgin) have become so prevalent that many people with very little computer expertise use them on a daily basis to keep in touch with friends, family, and colleagues.

Intranet   An *intranet* is a network that connects computing resources at a school, company, or other organization but, unlike the Internet, typically restricts access to internal users. An intranet is very similar to a LAN (local area network) but is based on Internet technology. An intranet can provide database, email, and Web page access to a limited group of people, regardless of their geographic location.

The ability of an intranet to connect dissimilar machines is one of its strengths. Think of all the machines you can find on the Internet: Macintosh systems, PCs running different versions of Windows, machines running UNIX and Linux, and so on. Each of these machines can communicate via IP (page 363), a common protocol. So it is with an intranet: Dissimilar machines can all talk to one another.

Another key difference between the Internet and an intranet is that the Internet transmits only one protocol suite: IP. In contrast, an intranet can be set up to use a number of protocols, such as IP, IPX, AppleTalk, DECnet, XNS, or other protocols developed by vendors over the years. Although these protocols cannot be transmitted directly over the Internet, you can set up special gateway boxes at remote sites that tunnel or encapsulate these protocols into IP packets and then use the Internet to pass them.

You can use an *extranet* (also called a *partner net*) or a virtual private network (VPN) to improve security. These terms describe ways to connect remote sites securely to a local site, typically by using the public Internet as a carrier and employing encryption as a means of protecting data in transit.

Following are some terms you may want to become familiar with before you read the rest of this chapter:

ASP (page 1095)	*hub* (page 1112)	*packet* (page 1123)
bridge (page 1098)	*internet* (page 1114)	*router* (page 1130)
extranet (page 1107)	*Internet* (page 1114)	*sneakernet* (page 1132)
firewall (page 1108)	*intranet* (page 1114)	*switch* (page 1135)
gateway (page 1109)	*ISP* (page 1115)	*VPN* (page 1140)

TYPES OF NETWORKS AND HOW THEY WORK

Computers communicate over networks using unique addresses assigned by system software. A computer message, called a *packet, frame,* or *datagram,* includes the address of the destination computer and the sender's return address. The three most common types of networks are *broadcast, point-to-point,* and *switched.* Once popular, token-based networks (such as FDDI and token ring) are rarely seen anymore.

Speed is critical to the proper functioning of the Internet. Newer specifications (cat 6 and cat 7) are being standardized for 1000BaseT (1 gigabit per second, called gigabit Ethernet, or GIG-E) and faster networking. Some of the networks that form the backbone of the Internet run at speeds of almost 40 gigabits per second (OC768) to accommodate the ever-increasing demand for network services. Table 10-1 lists some of the specifications in use today.

Table 10-1   Network specifications

Specification	Speed
DS0	64 kilobits per second
ISDN	Two DS0 lines plus signaling (16 kilobits per second) or 128 kilobits per second
T-1	1.544 megabits per second (24 DS0 lines)
T-3	43.232 megabits per second (28 T-1s)
OC3	155 megabits per second (100 T-1s)
OC12	622 megabits per second (4 OC3s)
OC48	2.5 gigabits per seconds (4 OC12s)
OC192	9.6 gigabits per second (4 OC48s)
OC768	38.4 gigabits per second (4 OC192s)

BROADCAST NETWORKS

On a *broadcast network,* such as Ethernet, any of the many systems attached to the network cable can send a message at any time; each system examines the address in each message and responds only to messages addressed to it. A problem occurs on a broadcast network when multiple systems send data at the same time, resulting in a collision of the messages on the cable. When messages collide, they can become garbled. The sending system notices the garbled message and resends it after waiting a short but random amount of time. Waiting a random amount of time helps prevent those same systems from resending the data at the same moment and experiencing yet another collision. The extra traffic that results from collisions can strain the network; if the collision rate gets too high, retransmissions may result in more collisions. Ultimately the network may become unusable.

POINT-TO-POINT NETWORKS

A point-to-point link does not seem like much of a network because only two end-points are involved. However, most connections to WANs (wide area networks) go through point-to-point links, using wire cable, radio, or satellite links. The advantage of a point-to-point link is its simplicity: Because only two systems are involved, the traffic on the link is limited and well understood. A disadvantage is that each system can typically be equipped for only a small number of such links; it is impractical and costly to establish point-to-point links that connect each computer to all the rest.

Point-to-point links often use serial lines and modems. The combination of a modem with a point-to-point link allows an isolated system to connect inexpensively to a larger network.

The most common types of point-to-point links are the ones used to connect to the Internet. When you use DSL[1] (digital subscriber line), you are using a point-to-point link to connect to the Internet. Serial lines, such as T-1, T-3, ATM links, and ISDN, are all point-to-point. Although it might seem like a point-to-point link, a cable modem is based on broadcast technology and in that way is similar to Ethernet.

SWITCHED NETWORKS

A *switch* is a device that establishes a virtual path between source and destination hosts in such a way that each path appears to be a point-to-point link, much like a railroad roundhouse. The switch creates and tears down virtual paths as hosts seek to communicate with each other. Each host thinks it has a direct point-to-point path to the host it is talking to. Contrast this approach with a broadcast network, where each host also sees traffic bound for other hosts. The advantage of a switched network over a pure point-to-point network is that each host requires only one connection: the connection to the switch. Using pure point-to-point connections, each host must have a connection to every other host. Scalability is provided by further linking switches.

---

1. The term *DSL* incorporates the xDSL suite of technologies, which includes ADSL, XDSL, SDSL, and HDSL.

LAN: LOCAL AREA NETWORK

Local area networks (LANs) are confined to a relatively small area—a single computer facility, building, or campus. Today most LANs run over copper or fiberoptic (glass or plastic) cable, but other wireless technologies, such as infrared (similar to most television remote control devices) and radio wave (wireless, or Wi-Fi), are becoming more popular.

If its destination address is not on the local network, a packet must be passed on to another network by a router (page 360). A router may be a general-purpose computer or a special-purpose device attached to multiple networks to act as a gateway among them.

ETHERNET

A Linux system connected to a LAN usually connects to a network using Ethernet. A typical Ethernet connection can support data transfer rates from 10 megabits per second to 1 gigabit per second, with further speed enhancements planned for the future. As a result of computer load, competing network traffic, and network overhead, file transfer rates on an Ethernet are always slower than the maximum, theoretical transfer rate.

Cables   An Ethernet network transfers data using copper or fiberoptic cable or wireless transmitters and receivers. Originally, each computer was attached to a thick coaxial cable (called *thicknet*) at tap points spaced at six-foot intervals along the cable. The thick cable was awkward to deal with, so other solutions, including a thinner coaxial cable called *thinnet,* or 10Base2,[2] were developed. Today most Ethernet connections are either wireless or made over unshielded twisted pair (referred to as UTP, Category 5 [cat 5], Category 5e [cat 5e], Category 6 [cat 6], 10BaseT, or 100BaseT) wire—similar to the type of wire used for telephone lines and serial data communications.

Segment   A network *segment* is a part of a network in which all systems communicate using the same physical layer (layer 1) of the IP and OSI models (page 364).

Duplex   In *half-duplex* mode, packets travel in one direction at a time over the cable. In *full-duplex* mode, packets travel in both directions.

Hub   A *hub* (sometimes called a *concentrator*) is a device that connects systems so they are all part of one network segment and share the network bandwidth. Hubs work at the physical layer of the IP and OSI models (layer 1, page 364).

Switch   A *switch* connects network segments. A switch inspects each data packet and learns which devices are connected to which of its ports. The switch sorts packets and sends each packet only to the device it is intended for. Because a switch sends packets only to their destination devices, it can conserve network bandwidth and perform better than a hub. A switch may have buffers for holding and queuing packets. Switches work at the data link layer of the IP and OSI models (layer 2, page 364).

---

2. Versions of Ethernet are classified as **X**Base**Y**, where **X** is the data rate in megabits per second, **Base** means baseband (as opposed to radio frequency), and **Y** is the category of cabling.

Some Ethernet switches have enough bandwidth to communicate simultaneously, in full-duplex mode, with all connected devices. A nonswitched (hub-based) broadcast network can run in only half-duplex mode. Full-duplex Ethernet further improves things by eliminating collisions. Theoretically, each host on a switched network can transmit and receive simultaneously at the speed of the network (e.g., 100 megabits per second) for an effective bandwidth between hosts of twice the speed of the network (e.g., 200 megabits per second), depending on the capacity of the switch.

Router A *router* connects networks. For example, a router can connect a LAN to a WAN (such as the Internet). A router determines which path packets should take to travel to a different network and forwards the packets. Routers work at the network layer of the IP and OSI models (layer 3, page 364). The next page covers routers in more depth.

WIRELESS

Wireless networks are becoming increasingly common. They are found in offices, homes, and public places, such as universities, coffee shops, and airports. Wireless access points provide functionality similar to an Ethernet hub. They allow multiple users to interact via a common radio frequency spectrum. A wireless, point-to-point connection allows you to wander about your home or office with a laptop, using an antenna to link to a LAN or to the Internet via an in-house base station. Linux includes drivers for many of the common wireless boards. A wireless access point, or base station, connects a wireless network to a wired network so that no special protocol is required for a wireless connection. Refer to page 620 and to the *Linux Wireless LAN HOWTO* at www.hpl.hp.com/personal/Jean_Tourrilhes/Linux.

WAN: WIDE AREA NETWORK

A *wide area network* (WAN) covers a large geographic area. In contrast, the technologies (such as Ethernet) used for LANs were designed to work over limited distances and for a certain number of host connections. A WAN may span long distances over dedicated data lines (leased from a telephone company) or radio or satellite links. Such networks are often used to interconnect LANs. Major Internet service providers rely on WANs to connect to their customers within a country and around the globe.

MAN Some networks do not fit into either the LAN or the WAN designation. A *metropolitan area network* (MAN) is a network that is contained in a smaller geographic area, such as a city. Like WANs, MANs are typically used to interconnect LANs.

INTERNETWORKING THROUGH GATEWAYS AND ROUTERS

Gateway A LAN connects to a WAN through a *gateway,* a generic term for a computer or a special device with multiple network connections that passes data from one network to another. A gateway converts the data traffic from the format used on the LAN to that used on the WAN. Data that crosses the country from one Ethernet to another over a WAN, for example, is repackaged from the Ethernet format to a different format that can be processed by the communications equipment that makes up the WAN backbone. When it reaches the end of its journey over the WAN, the data is converted by another gateway to a format appropriate for the receiving network. For the most part, these details are of concern only to the network administrators; the end user does not need to know anything about how the data transfer takes place.

Router A *router* is the most popular form of gateway. Routers play an important role in internetworking. Just as you might study a map to plan your route when you need to drive to an unfamiliar place, so a computer needs to know how to deliver a message to a system attached to a distant network by passing through intermediary systems and networks along the way. Although you might envision using a giant network road map to choose the route that your data should follow, a static map of computer routes is usually a poor choice for a large network. Computers and networks along the route you choose may be overloaded or down, without providing a detour for your message.

Routers instead communicate dynamically, keeping each other informed about which routes are open for use. To extend the analogy, this situation would be like heading out on a car trip without consulting a map to find a route to your destination; instead you head for a nearby gas station and ask directions. Throughout the journey you continue to stop at one gas station after another, getting directions at each to find the next one. Although it would take a while to make the stops, the owner of each gas station would advise you of bad traffic, closed roads, alternative routes, and shortcuts.

The stops made by the data are much quicker than those you would make in your car, but each message leaves each router on a path chosen based on the most current information. Think of this system as a GPS (global positioning system) setup that automatically gets updates at each intersection and tells you where to go next, based on traffic and highway conditions.

Figure 10-1 (next page) shows an example of how LANs might be set up at three sites interconnected by a WAN (the Internet). In this type of network diagram, Ethernet LANs are drawn as straight lines, with devices attached at right angles; WANs are represented as clouds, indicating that the details have been left out; and wireless connections are drawn as zigzag lines with breaks, indicating that the connection may be intermittent.

In Figure 10-1, a gateway or a router relays messages between each LAN and the Internet. Three of the routers in the Internet are shown (for example, the one closest to each site). Site A has a server, a workstation, a network computer, and a PC sharing a single Ethernet LAN. Site B has an Ethernet LAN that serves a printer and four Linux workstations. A firewall permits only certain traffic to pass between the Internet router and the site's local router. Site C has three LANs linked by a single router, perhaps to reduce the traffic load that would result if the LANs were combined or to keep workgroups or locations on separate networks. Site C also includes a wireless access point that enables wireless communication with nearby computers.

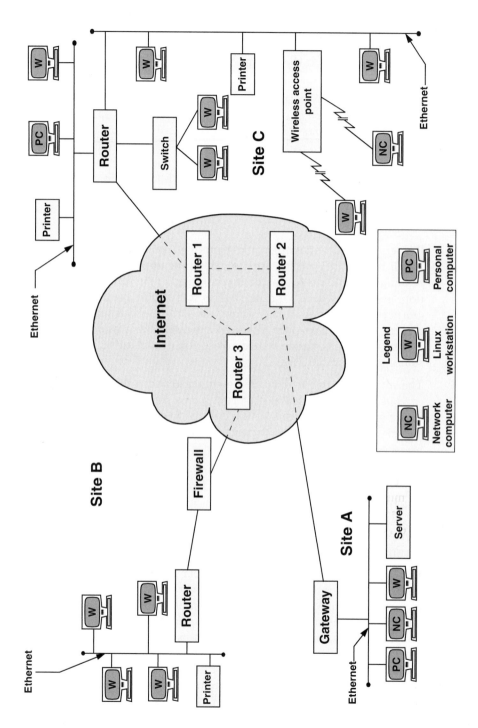

Figure 10-1   A slice of the Internet

Firewall

A firewall in a car separates the engine compartment from the passenger compartment, protecting the driver and passengers from engine fires, noise, and fumes. In much the same way, computer firewalls separate computers from malicious and unwanted users.

A *firewall* prevents certain types of traffic from entering or leaving a network. For example, a firewall might prevent traffic from your IP address from leaving the network and prevent anyone except users from selected domains from using FTP to retrieve data from the network. The implementations of firewalls vary widely—from Linux machines with two *interfaces* (page 1114) running custom software to a router (preceding section) with simple access lists to esoteric, vendor-supplied firewall appliances. Most larger installations have at least one kind of firewall in place. A firewall is often accompanied by a proxy server/gateway (page 389) that provides an intermediate point between you and the host you are communicating with.

In addition to the firewalls found in multipurpose computers, firewalls are becoming increasingly common in consumer appliances. For example, they are built into cable modems, wireless gateways, routers, and stand-alone devices.

Typically a single Linux machine will include a minimal firewall. A small group of Linux systems may have an inexpensive Linux machine with two network interfaces and packet-filtering software functioning as a dedicated firewall. One of the interfaces connects to the Internet, modems, and other outside data sources. The other connects, normally through a hub or switch, to the local network. Refer to Chapter 25 for information on firestarter, iptables, and setting up a firewall and to Appendix C for a discussion of security.

Network Protocols

To exchange information over a network, computers must communicate using a common language, or *protocol* (page 1126). The protocol determines the format of message packets. The predominant network protocols used by Linux systems are TCP and IP,[3] collectively referred to as TCP/IP (Transmission Control Protocol and Internet Protocol). Network services that need highly reliable connections, such as ssh and scp, tend to use TCP/IP. Another protocol used for some system services is UDP (User Datagram Protocol). Network services that do not require guaranteed delivery, such as RealAudio and RealVideo, operate satisfactorily with the simpler UDP.[4]

---

3. All references to IP imply *IPv4* (page 1115).

4. Voice and video protocols are delay sensitive, not integrity sensitive. The human ear and eye accept and interpolate loss in an audio or video stream but cannot deal with variable delay. The guaranteed delivery that TCP provides introduces a delay on a busy network when packets get retransmitted. This delay is not acceptable for video and audio transmissions, whereas less than 100 percent integrity is acceptable.

IP: INTERNET PROTOCOL

Layering was introduced to facilitate protocol design: Layers distinguish functional differences between adjacent protocols. A grouping of layers can be standardized into a protocol model. IP has a model that distinguishes protocol layers. The IP model differs from the ISO seven-layer protocol model (also called the OSI model) that is often illustrated in networking textbooks. Specifically IP uses the following simplified five-layer model:

1. The first layer of the IP protocol, called the *physical layer,* describes the physical medium (copper, fiber, wireless) and the data encoding used to transmit signals on that medium (pulses of light, electrical waves, or radio waves, for instance).

2. The second layer, called the *data link layer,* covers media access by network devices and describes how to put data into packets, transmit the data, and check it for errors. Ethernet is found at this layer, as is *802.11* (page 1094) wireless.

3. The third layer, called the *network layer,* frequently uses IP and addresses and routes packets.

4. The fourth layer, called the *transport layer,* is where TCP and UDP exist. This layer provides a means for applications to communicate with each other. Functions commonly performed by the transport layer include guaranteed delivery, delivery of packets in the order of their transmission, flow control, error detection, and error correction. The transport layer is responsible for dividing data streams into packets. In addition, this layer performs port addressing, which allows it to distinguish among different services using the same transport protocol. Port addressing keeps the data from multiple applications using the same protocol (for example, TCP) separate.

5. Anything above the transport layer is the domain of the application and is part of the *fifth layer.* Unlike the ISO model, the Internet model does not distinguish among application, presentation, and session layers. All of the upper-layer characteristics, such as character encoding, encryption, and GUIs, are part of the application. Applications choose the transport characteristics they require as well as the corresponding transport layer protocol with which to send and receive data.

TCP: TRANSMISSION CONTROL PROTOCOL

TCP is most frequently run on top of IP in a combination referred to as TCP/IP. This protocol provides error recovery and guaranteed delivery in packet transmission order; it also works with multiple ports so that it can handle more than one application. TCP is a *connection-oriented protocol* (page 1102), also known as a *stream-based* protocol. Once established, a TCP connection looks like a stream of data, not individual IP packets. The connection is assumed to remain up and be uniquely addressable. Every piece of information you write to the connection always goes to the same destination and arrives in the order it was sent. Because

TCP is connection oriented and establishes a *virtual circuit* between two systems, this protocol is not suitable for one-to-many transmissions (see the discussion of UDP, following). TCP has builtin mechanisms for dealing with congestion (or flow) control over busy networks and throttles back (slows the speed of data flow) when it has to retransmit dropped packets. TCP can also deal with acknowledgments, wide area links, high-delay links, and other situations.

UDP: User Datagram Protocol

UDP runs at layer 4 of the IP stack, just as TCP does, but is much simpler. Like TCP, UDP works with multiple ports and multiple applications. It has checksums for error detection but does not automatically retransmit *datagrams* (page 1104) that fail the checksum test. UDP is a datagram-oriented protocol: Each datagram must carry its own address and port information. Each router along the way examines each datagram to determine the destination, one hop at a time. You can broadcast or multicast UDP datagrams to many destinations at the same time by using special addresses.

PPP: Point-to-Point Protocol

PPP provides serial line point-to-point connections that support IP. This protocol compresses data to make the most of the limited bandwidth available on serial connections. PPP, which replaces SLIP[5] (Serial Line IP), acts as a point-to-point layer 2/3 transport that many other types of protocols can ride on. It is used mostly for IP-based services and connections, such as TCP or UDP.

Xremote and LBX

Two protocols that speed up data transfer over serial lines are Xremote and LBX. Xremote compresses the X Window System protocol so that it is more efficient over slower serial lines. LBX (low-bandwidth X) is based on the Xremote technology and is part of X Window System release X11R6 and higher.

Host Address

Each computer interface has a unique identifier called a *MAC address* (page 1118). A system attached to more than one network has multiple interfaces—one for each network, each with its own MAC address.

Each packet of information that is broadcast over the network has a destination address. All hosts on the network must process each broadcast packet to see whether it is addressed to that host.[6] If the packet is addressed to a given host, that host continues to process it. If not, the host ignores the packet.

---

5. SLIP was one of the first serial line implementations of IP and has slightly less overhead than PPP. PPP supports multiple protocols (such as AppleTalk and IPX), whereas SLIP supports only IP.

6. Contrast broadcast packets with unicast packets: Ethernet hardware on a computer filters out unicast packets that are not addressed to that machine; the operating system on that machine never sees these packets.

The network address of a machine is an IP address, which, under IPv4, is represented as one number broken into four segments separated by periods (for example, 192.168.184.5). Domain names and IP addresses are assigned through a highly distributed system coordinated by ICANN (Internet Corporation for Assigned Names and Numbers—www.icann.org) via many registrars (see www.internic.net). ICANN is funded by the various domain name registries and registrars and by IP address registries, which supply globally unique identifiers for hosts and services on the Internet. Although you may not deal with any of these agencies directly, your Internet service provider most assuredly does.

How a company uses IP addresses is determined by the system or network administrator. For example, the leftmost two sets of numbers in an IP address might represent a large network (campuswide or companywide); the third set, a subnetwork (perhaps a department or a single floor in a building); and the rightmost number, an individual computer. The operating system uses the address in a different, lower-level form, converting it to its binary equivalent, a series of 1s and 0s. See the following optional section for more information. Refer to "Private address space" on page 617 for information about addresses you can use on a LAN without registering them.

STATIC VERSUS DYNAMIC IP ADDRESSES

A static IP address is one that always remains the same. A dynamic IP address is one that can change each time you connect to the network. A dynamic address remains the same during a single login session. Any server (mail, Web, and so on) must have a static address so clients can find the machine that is acting as the server. End-user systems usually work well with dynamic addresses. During a given login session, they can function as a client (your Web browser, for example) because they maintain a constant IP address. When you log out and log in again, it does not matter that you have a different IP address because your computer, acting as a client, establishes a new connection with a server. The advantage of dynamic addressing is that it allows inactive addresses to be reused, reducing the total number of IP addresses needed.

optional   IP CLASSES

To facilitate routing on the Internet, IP addresses are divided into *classes*. These classes, which are labeled class A through class E, allow the Internet address space to be broken into blocks of small, medium, and large networks that are designed to be assigned based on the number of hosts within a network.

When you need to send a message to an address outside the local network, your system looks up the address block/class in its routing table and sends the message to the next router on the way to the final destination. Every router along the way does a similar lookup and forwards the message accordingly. At the destination, local routers direct the message to the specific address. Without classes and blocks, your host would have to know every network and subnetwork address on the Internet before it could send a message. This setup would be impractical because of the huge number of addresses on the Internet.

Each of the four numbers in the IP address is in the range 0–255 because each segment of the IP address is represented by 8 bits (an *octet*), with each bit being capable of taking on two values; the total number of values is therefore $2^8 = 256$. When you start counting at 0, the range 1–256 becomes 0–255.[7] Each IP address is divided into a net address (*netid*) portion, which is part of the class, and a host address (*hostid*) portion. See Table 10-2.

Table 10-2   IP classes

Class	Start bits	Address range	All bits (including start bits)			
			0–7	8–15	16–23	24–31
Class A	0	001.000.000.000–126.000.000.000	0-netid	========hostid=========		
Class B	10	129.000.000.000–191.255.000.000	10-----netid------	=====hostid=====		
Class C	110	192.000.000.000–223.255.255.000	110----------netid-----------			=hostid=
Class D (multicast)	1110	224.000.000.000–239.255.255.000	1110			
Class E (reserved)	11110	240.000.000.000–255.255.255.000	11110			

The first set of addresses, defining class A networks, is reserved for extremely large corporations, such as General Electric (3.0.0.0) and Hewlett-Packard (15.0.0.0), and for ISPs. One start bit (0) in the first position designates a class A network, 7 bits holds the network portion of the address (netid), and 24 bits holds the host portion of the address (hostid; see Table 10-2). This setup means that GE can have 2^{24}, or approximately 16 million, hosts on its network. Unused address space and *subnets* (page 1134) lower this number quite a bit. The 127.0.0.0 subnet (page 371) is reserved, as are several others (see *private address space* on page 1126).

Two start bits (10) in the first two positions designates a class B network, 14 bits holds the network portion of the address (netid), and 16 bits holds the host portion of the address, for a potential total of 65,534 hosts.[8] A class C network uses 3 start

---

7. Internally, the IP address is represented as a set of four unsigned 8-bit fields or a 32-bit unsigned number, depending on how programs are using it. The most common format in C is to represent it as a union of an unsigned 32-bit long integer, four unsigned chars, and two unsigned short integers.

8. A 16-bit (class B) address can address $2^{16} = 65,536$ hosts, yet the potential number of hosts is two fewer than that because the first and last addresses on any network are reserved. In a similar manner, an 8-bit (class C) address can address only 254 hosts ($2^8 - 2 = 254$). The 0 host address (for example, 194.16.100.0 for a class C network or 131.204.0.0 for a class B network) is reserved as a designator for the network itself. Several older operating systems use this as a broadcast address. The 255 host address (for example, 194.16.100.255 for a class C network or 131.204.255.255 for a class B network) is reserved as the IP broadcast address. An IP packet (datagram) that is sent to this address is broadcast to all hosts on the network.

The netid portion of a subnet does not have the same limitations. Often you are given the choice of reserving the first and last networks in a range as you would a hostid, but this is rarely done in practice. More often the first and last networks in the netid range provide more usable address space. Refer to "Subnets" on page 369.

bits (100), 21 netid bits (2 million networks), and 8 hostid bits (254 hosts). Today a new large customer will not receive a class A or B network but is likely to receive a class C or several (usually contiguous) class C networks, if merited.

Several other classes of networks exist. Class D networks are reserved for *multi-cast* (page 1121) networks. When you run **netstat –nr** on a Linux system, you can see whether the machine is a member of a multicast network. A 224.0.0.0 in the Destination column that netstat displays indicates a class D, multicast address (Table 10-2). A multicast is like a broadcast, but only hosts that subscribe to the multicast group receive the message. To use Web terminology, a broadcast is like a "push." A host pushes a broadcast on the network, and every host on the network must check each packet to see whether it contains relevant data. A multicast is like a "pull." A host will see a multicast only if it registers itself as subscribed to a multicast group or service and pulls the appropriate packets from the network.

Table 10-3   Computations for IP address 131.204.027.027

	---------------Class B-----------		netid	hostid	
	131	.204	.027	.027	decimal
IP address	83	CC	1B	1B	hexadecimal
	1000 0011	1100 1100	0001 1011	0001 1011	binary
	255	.255	.255	.000	decimal
Subnet mask	FF	FF	FF	00	hexadecimal
	1111 1111	1111 1111	1111 1111	0000 0000	binary
IP address bitwise AND	1000 0011	1100 1100	0001 1011	0001 1011	
Subnet mask	1111 1111	1111 1111	1111 1111	0000 0000	binary
= Subnet number	1000 0011	1100 1100	0001 1011	0000 0000	
	131	.204	.027	.000	decimal
Subnet number	83	CC	1B	00	hexadecimal
	1000 0011	1100 1100	0001 1011	0000 0000	binary
	131	.204	.27	.255	decimal
Broadcast address	83	CC	1B	FF	hexadecimal
(set host bits to 1)	1000 0011	1100 1100	0001 1011	1111 1111	binary

Table 10-3 shows some of the computations for the IP address 131.204.027.027. Each address is shown in decimal, hexadecimal, and binary form. Binary is the easiest to work with for bitwise (binary) computations. The first three lines show the IP address. The next three lines show the *subnet mask* (page 1135) in three bases. Next the IP address and the subnet mask are ANDed together bitwise to yield the *subnet number* (page 1135), which is shown in three bases. The last three lines show the *broadcast address* (page 1098), which is computed by taking the subnet number and turning the hostid bits to 1s. The subnet number identifies the local network. The subnet number and the subnet mask determine what range the IP address of the machine must be in. They are also used by routers to segment traffic; see *network segment* (page 1122). A broadcast on this network goes to all hosts in the range 131.204.27.1 through 131.204.27.254 but will be acted on only by hosts that have a use for it.

SUBNETS

Each host on a network must process each broadcast packet to determine whether the information in the packet is useful to that host. If the network includes numerous hosts, each host must process many packets. To maintain efficiency most networks—and particularly shared media networks such as Ethernet—need to be split into subnetworks, or *subnets*.[9] The more hosts on a network, the more dramatically network performance is affected. Organizations use router and switch technology called VLANs (virtual local area networks) to group similar hosts into broadcast domains (subnets) based on function. For example, it is not uncommon to see a switch with different ports being part of different subnets. See page 445 for information on how to specify a subnet.

Subnet mask A *subnet mask* (or *address mask*) is a bit mask that identifies which parts of an IP address correspond to the network address and the subnet portion of the address. This mask has 1s in positions corresponding to the network and subnet numbers and 0s in the host number positions. When you perform a bitwise AND on an IP address and a subnet mask (Table 10-3), the resulting address contains everything except the host address (hostid) portion.

There are several ways to represent a subnet mask: A network could have a subnet mask of 255.255.255.0 (decimal), FFFFFF00 (hexadecimal), or /24 (the number of bits used for the subnet mask). If it were a class B network (of which 16 bits are already fixed), this yields 2^8 (24 total bits − 16 fixed bits = 8 bits, 2^8 = 256) networks[10] with $2^8 - 2$ (256 − 2 = 254) hosts[11] on each network.

For example, when you divide the class C address 192.25.4.0 into eight subnets, you get a subnet mask of 255.255.255.224, FFFFFFE0, or /27 (27 1s). The eight resultant networks are 192.25.4.0, 192.25.4.32, 192.25.4.64, 192.25.4.96, 192.25.4.128, 192.25.4.160, 192.25.4.192, and 192.25.4.224. You can use a Web-based subnet mask calculator to calculate subnet masks (refer to "Network Calculators" on page 1059). To use this calculator to determine the preceding subnet mask, start with an IP host address of 192.25.4.0.

For more information refer to "Specifying a Subnet" on page 445.

---

9. Splitting a network is also an issue with other protocols, particularly AppleTalk.

10. The first and last networks are reserved in a manner similar to the first and last hosts, although the standard is flexible. You can configure routers to reclaim the first and last networks in a subnet. Different routers have different techniques for reclaiming these networks.

11. Subtract 2 because the first and last host addresses on every network are reserved.

CIDR: CLASSLESS INTER-DOMAIN ROUTING

CIDR (pronounced "cider") allows groups of addresses that are smaller than a class C block to be assigned to an organization or ISP and then further subdivided and parceled out. In addition, it helps to alleviate the potential problem of routing tables on major Internet backbone and peering devices becoming too large to manage.

The pool of available IPv4 addresses has been depleted to the point that no one gets a class A address anymore. The trend is to reclaim these huge address blocks, if possible, and recycle them into groups of smaller addresses. Also, as more class C addresses are assigned, routing tables on the Internet are filling up and causing memory overflows. The solution is to aggregate[12] groups of addresses into blocks and allocate them to ISPs, which in turn subdivide these blocks and allocate them to their customers. The address class designations (A, B, and C) described in the previous section are used less often today, although you may still encounter subnets. When you request an address block, your ISP usually gives you as many addresses as you need—and no more. The ISP aggregates several contiguous smaller blocks and routes them to your location. This aggregation is CIDR. Without CIDR, the Internet as we know it would not function.

For example, you might be allocated the 192.168.5.0/22 IP address block, which could support 2^{10} hosts (32 − 22 = 10). Your ISP would set its routers so that any packets going to an address in that block would be sent to your network. Internally, your own routers might further subdivide this block of 1,024 potential hosts into subnets, perhaps into four networks. Four networks require an additional two bits of addressing (2^2 = 4). You could therefore set up your router to support four networks with this allocation: 192.168.5.0/24, 192.168.6.0/24, 192.168.7.0/24, and 192.168.8.0/24. Each of these networks could then have 254 hosts. CIDR lets you arbitrarily divide networks and subnetworks into increasingly smaller blocks along the way. Each router has enough memory to keep track of the addresses it needs to direct and aggregates the rest.

This scheme uses memory and address space efficiently. For example, you could take 192.168.8.0/24 and further divide it into 16 networks with 14 hosts each. The 16 networks require four more bits (2^4 = 16), so you would have 192.168.8.0/28, 192.168.8.16/28, 192.168.8.32/28, and so on, up through the last subnet of 192.168.8.240/16, which would have the hosts 192.168.8.241 through 192.168.8.254.

HOSTNAMES

People generally find it easier to work with names than with numbers, so Linux provides several ways to associate hostnames with IP addresses. The oldest method is to consult a list of names and addresses that are stored in the **/etc/hosts** file:

---

12. *Aggregate* means to join. In CIDR, the aggregate of 208.178.99.124 and 208.178.99.125 is 208.178.99.124/23 (the aggregation of two class C blocks).

```
$ cat /etc/hosts
127.0.0.1      localhost
130.128.52.1   gw-example.example.com   gw-example
130.128.52.2   bravo.example.com        bravo
130.128.52.3   hurrah.example.com       hurrah
130.128.52.4   kudos.example.com        kudos
```

localhost =   The address 127.0.0.1 is reserved for the special hostname **localhost**, which serves
127.0.0.1   as a hook for the system's networking software to operate on the local machine
without going onto a physical network. The names of the other systems are shown
in two forms: in a *fully qualified domain name* (FQDN) format that is unique on
the Internet and as a nickname that is locally unique.

NIS   As more hosts joined networks, storing these name-to-address mappings in a text
file proved to be inefficient and inconvenient. The **hosts** file grew increasingly larger
and became impossible to keep up-to-date. To solve this problem Linux supports
NIS (Network Information Service, page 385), which was developed for use on Sun
computers. NIS stores information in a database, making it easier to find a specific
address, but it is useful only for host information within a single administrative
domain. Hosts outside the domain cannot access the information.

DNS   The solution to this dilemma is DNS (Domain Name Service, page 383). DNS effectively addresses the efficiency and update issues by arranging the entire network
namespace (page 1121) as a hierarchy. Each domain in the DNS manages its own
namespace (addressing and name resolution), and each domain can easily query for
any host or IP address by following the tree up or down the namespace until it finds
the appropriate domain. By providing a hierarchical naming structure, DNS distributes name administration across the entire Internet.

IPv6

The explosive growth of the Internet has uncovered deficiencies in the design of the
current address plan—most notably the shortage of addresses. Over the next few
years, a revised protocol, named IPng (IP Next Generation), also known as IPv6 (IP
version 6),[13] will be phased in. (It may take longer—the phase-in is going quite
slowly.) This new scheme is designed to overcome the major limitations of the current approach and can be implemented gradually because it is compatible with the
existing address usage. IPv6 makes it possible to assign many more unique Internet
addresses (2^{128}, or 340 *undecillion* [10^{36}]). It also supports more advanced security
and performance control features:

- IPv6 enables autoconfiguration. With IPv4, autoconfiguration is available
using optional DHCP (page 454). With IPv6, autoconfiguration is mandatory, making it easy for hosts to configure their IP addresses automatically.

---

13. IPv5 referred to an experimental real-time stream protocol named ST—thus the jump from IPv4
to IPv6.

- IPv6 reserves 24 bits in the header for advanced services, such as resource reservation protocols, better backbone routing, and improved traffic engineering.

- IPv6 makes multicast protocols mandatory and uses them extensively. In IPv4, multicast, which improves scalability, is optional.

- IPv6 aggregates address blocks more efficiently because of the huge address space. This aggregation makes obsolete *NAT* (page 1121), which decreased scalability and introduced protocol issues.

- IPv6 provides a simplified packet header that allows hardware accelerators to work better.

A sample IPv6 address is fe80::a00:20ff:feff:5be2/10. Each group of four hexadecimal digits is equivalent to a number between 0 and 65,536 (16^4). A pair of adjacent colons indicates a hex value of 0x0000; leading 0s need not be shown. With eight sets of hexadecimal groupings, $65,536^8 = 2^{128}$ addresses are possible. In an IPv6 address on a host with the default autoconfiguration, the first characters in the address are always fe80. The last 64 bits hold an interface ID designation, which is often the *MAC address* (page 1118) of the system's Ethernet controller.

COMMUNICATE OVER A NETWORK

Many commands that you can use to communicate with other users on a single computer system have been extended to work over a network. Examples of extended utilities include electronic mail programs, information-gathering utilities (such as finger, page 167), and communications utilities (such as talk). These utilities are examples of the UNIX philosophy: Instead of creating a new, special-purpose tool, modify an existing one.

Many utilities understand a convention for the format of network addresses: **user@host** (spoken as "user at host"). When you use an @ sign in an argument to one of these utilities, the utility interprets the text that follows as the name of a remote host. When you omit the @ sign, a utility assumes that you are requesting information from or corresponding with someone on the local system.

The prompts shown in the examples in this chapter include the hostname of the system you are using. If you frequently use more than one system over a network, you may find it difficult to keep track of which system you are interacting with at any particular moment. If you set your prompt to include the hostname of the current system, it will always be clear which system you are using. To identify the computer you are using, run hostname or **uname –n**:

```
$ hostname
kudos
```

See page 305 for information on how you can change the prompt.

finger: DISPLAYS INFORMATION ABOUT REMOTE USERS

The finger utility displays information about one or more users on a system. This utility was designed for local use, but when networks became popular, it was obvious that finger should be enhanced to reach out and collect information remotely. In the following examples, finger displays information about all users logged in on the system named **bravo**:

```
[kudos]$ finger @bravo
[bravo.example.com]
Login      Name           Tty    Idle  Login Time   Office    Office Phone
sam        Sam the Great  *1     1:35  Oct 22  5:00
max        Max Wild       4            Oct 22 12:23 (kudos)
max        Max Wild       5      19    Oct 22 12:33 (:0)
zach       Zach Brill     7      2:24  Oct 22  8:45 (:0)
hls        Helen Simpson  11     2d    Oct 20 12:23 (:0)
```

A user's username in front of the @ sign causes finger to display information from the remote system for the specified user only. If the remote system has multiple matches for that name, finger displays the results for all of them:

```
[kudos]$ finger max@bravo
[bravo.example.com]
Login      Name           Tty    Idle  Login Time   Office    Office Phone
max        Max Wild       4            Oct 22 12:23 (kudos)
max        Max Wild       5      19    Oct 22 12:33 (:0)
```

The finger utility works by querying a standard network service, the **in.fingerd** daemon, that runs on the system being queried. Although this service is available in the **fingerd** package for Ubuntu Linux, some sites choose not to run it to minimize the load on their systems, reduce security risks, or maintain privacy. When you use finger to obtain information about someone at such a site, you will see an error message or nothing at all. The remote **in.fingerd** daemon determines how much information to share and in what format. As a result, the report displayed for any given system may differ from that shown in the preceding examples.

The in.fingerd daemon

security The finger daemon (**in.fingerd**) gives away system account information that can aid a malicious user. Some sites disable finger or randomize user account IDs to make a malicious user's job more difficult. Do not install the **fingerd** package if you do not want to run the finger daemon.

The information for remote finger looks much the same as it does when finger runs on the local system, with one difference: Before displaying the results, finger reports the name of the remote system that answered the query (**bravo**, as shown in brackets in the preceding example). The name of the host that answers may be different from the system name you specified on the command line, depending on how the finger daemon service is configured on the remote system. In some cases, several hostnames may be listed if one finger daemon contacts another to retrieve the information.

SENDING MAIL TO A REMOTE USER

Given a user's username on a remote system and the name of the remote system or its domain, you can use an email program to send a message over the network or the Internet, using the @ form of an address:

```
zach@bravo
```

or

```
zach@example.com
```

Although many Linux utilities recognize the @ form of a network address, you may find that you can reach more remote computers with email than with the other networking utilities described in this chapter. This disparity arises because the email system can deliver a message to a host that does not run IP, even though it appears to have an Internet address. The message may be routed over the network, for example, until it reaches a remote system that has a point-to-point, dial-up connection to the destination system. Other utilities, such as talk, rely on IP and operate only between networked hosts.

MAILING LIST SERVERS

A mailing list server (listserv[14]) allows you to create and manage an email list. An electronic mailing list provides a means for people interested in a particular topic to participate in an electronic discussion and for a person to disseminate information periodically to a potentially large mailing list. One of the most powerful features of most list servers is their ability to archive email postings to the list, create an archive index, and allow users to retrieve postings from the archive based on keywords or discussion threads. Typically you can subscribe and unsubscribe from the list with or without human intervention. The owner of the list can restrict who can subscribe, unsubscribe, and post messages to the list. See page 698 for instructions on configuring the Mailman list server. Other popular list servers include LISTSERV (www.lsoft.com), Lyris (www.lyris.com), and Majordomo (www.greatcircle.com/majordomo). Ubuntu maintains quite a few mailing lists and list archives for those mailing lists at lists.ubuntu.com. Use Google to search on **linux mailing list** to find other lists.

NETWORK UTILITIES

To realize the full benefits of a networked environment, it made sense to extend certain tools, some of which have already been described. The advent of networks also created a need for new utilities to control and monitor them, spurring the development of new tools that took advantage of network speed and connectivity. This section describes concepts and utilities for systems attached to a network.

---

14. Although the term *listserv* is sometimes used generically to include many different list server programs, it is a specific product and a registered trademark of L-soft International, Inc.: LISTSERV (for more information go to www.lsoft.com).

TRUSTED HOSTS

Some commands, such as rcp and rsh, work only if the remote system trusts your local computer (that is, if the remote system knows your local computer and believes that it is not pretending to be another system). The **/etc/hosts.equiv** file lists trusted systems. For reasons of security, the **root** account does not rely on this file to identify trusted privileged users from other systems.

Host-based trust is largely obsolete. Because there are many ways to circumvent trusted host security, including subverting DNS systems and *IP spoofing* (page 1115), authentication based on IP address is widely regarded as insecure and obsolete. In a small homogeneous network of machines with local DNS control, it can be "good enough." Its greater ease of use in these situations may outweigh the security concerns.

Do not share your login account

security   You can use a ~/.**rhosts** file to allow another user to log in as you from a remote system without knowing your password. *This setup is not recommended.* Do not compromise the security of your files or the entire system by sharing your login account. Use ssh and scp instead of rsh and rcp whenever possible.

OpenSSH Tools

The OpenSSH project provides a set of tools that replace rcp, rsh, and others with secure equivalents. These tools are installed by default in Ubuntu Linux and can be used as drop-in replacements for their insecure counterparts. The OpenSSH tool suite is covered in detail in Chapter 18.

telnet: LOGS IN ON A REMOTE SYSTEM

You can use the TELNET protocol to interact with a remote computer. The telnet utility, a user interface to this protocol, is older than ssh and is not secure. Nevertheless, it may work where ssh (page 634) is not available (there is more non-UNIX support for TELNET access than for ssh access). In addition, many legacy devices, such as terminal servers and network devices, do not support ssh.

```
[bravo]$ telnet kudos
Trying 172.19.52.2...
Connected to kudos.example.com
Escape character is '^]'.

Welcome to SuSE Linux 7.3 (i386) - Kernel 2.4.10-4GB (2).
kudos login: wild
Password:
You have old mail in /var/mail/wild.
Last login: Mon Feb 27 14:46:55 from bravo.example.com
wild@kudos:~>
...
wild@kudos:~> logout
Connection closed by foreign host.
[bravo]$
```

telnet versus ssh   When you connect to a remote UNIX or Linux system using telnet, you are presented with a regular, textual **login:** prompt. Unless you specify differently, the ssh utility assumes that your username on the remote system matches that on the local system. Because telnet is designed to work with non-UNIX and non-Linux systems, it makes no such assumptions.

telnet **is not secure**

security   Whenever you enter sensitive information, such as your password, while you are using telnet, it is transmitted in cleartext and can be read by someone who is listening in on the session.

Another difference between these two utilities is that telnet allows you to configure many special parameters, such as how RETURNs or interrupts are processed. When using telnet between UNIX and/or Linux systems, you rarely need to change any parameters.

When you do not specify the name of a remote host on the command line, telnet runs in an interactive mode. The following example is equivalent to the previous telnet example:

```
[bravo]$ telnet
telnet> open kudos
Trying 172.19.52.2...
Connected to kudos.example.com
Escape character is '^]'.
...
```

Before connecting you to a remote system, telnet tells you what the *escape character* is; in most cases, it is ^] (where ^ represents the CONTROL key). When you press CONTROL-], you escape to telnet's interactive mode. Continuing the preceding example:

```
[kudos]$ CONTROL-]
telnet> ?
```

(displays help information)

```
telnet> close
Connection closed.
[bravo]$
```

When you enter a question mark in response to the **telnet>** prompt, telnet lists its commands. The **close** command ends the current telnet session, returning you to the local system. To get out of telnet's interactive mode and resume communication with the remote system, press RETURN in response to a prompt.

You can use telnet to access special remote services at sites that have chosen to make such services available. However, many of these services, such as the U.S. Library of Congress Information System (LOCIS), have moved to the Web. As a consequence, you can now obtain the same information using a Web browser.

USING telnet TO CONNECT TO OTHER PORTS

By default telnet connects to port 23, which is used for remote logins. However, you can use telnet to connect to other services by specifying a port number. In addition to standard services, many of the special remote services available on the Internet use unallocated port numbers. For example, you can access some multiplayer text games, called MUDs (Multi-User Dungeons, or Dimensions), using telnet to connect to a specified port, such as 4000 or 8888. Unlike the port numbers for standard protocols, these port numbers can be picked arbitrarily by the administrator of the game.

While telnet is no longer commonly employed to log in on remote systems, it is still used extensively as a debugging tool. This utility allows you to communicate directly with a TCP server. Some standard protocols are simple enough that an experienced user can debug problems by connecting to a remote service directly using telnet. If you are having a problem with a network server, a good first step is to try to connect to it using telnet.

In the following example, a system administrator who is debugging a problem with email delivery uses telnet to connect to the SMTP port (port 25) on a the server at **example.com** to see why it is bouncing mail from the **spammer.com** domain. The first line of output indicates which IP address telnet is trying to connect to. After telnet displays the **Connected to smtpsrv.example.com** message, the user emulates an SMTP dialog, following the standard SMTP protocol. The first line, which starts with **helo**, begins the session and identifies the local system. After the SMTP server responds, the user enters a line that identifies the mail sender as **user@spammer.com**. The SMTP server's response explains why the message is bouncing, so the user ends the session with **quit**.

```
$ telnet smtpsrv 25
Trying 192.168.1.1...
Connected to smtpsrv.example.com.
Escape character is '^]'.
helo example.com
220 smtpsrv.example.com ESMTP Sendmail 8.13.1/8.13.1; Wed, 4 May 2005 00:13:43 -0500 (CDT)
250 smtpsrv.example.com Hello desktop.example.com [192.168.1.97], pleased to meet you
mail from:user@spammer.com
571 5.0.0 Domain banned for spamming
quit
221 2.0.0 smtpsrv.example.com closing connection
```

The telnet utility allows you to use any protocol you want, as long as you know it well enough to type commands manually.

ftp: TRANSFERS FILES OVER A NETWORK

The File Transfer Protocol (FTP) is a method of downloading files from and uploading files to another system using TCP/IP over a network. FTP is not a secure protocol; use it only for downloading public information from a public server. Most Web browsers can download files from FTP servers. Chapter 19 covers FTP clients and servers.

ping: TESTS A NETWORK CONNECTION

The ping[15] utility (http://ftp.arl.mil/~mike/ping.html) sends an ECHO_REQUEST packet to a remote computer. This packet causes the remote system to send back a

---

15. The name ping mimics the sound of a sonar burst used by submarines to identify and communicate with each other. The word ping also expands to packet internet groper.

reply. This exchange is a quick way to verify that a remote system is available and to check how well the network is operating, such as how fast it is or whether it is dropping data packets. The ping utility uses the ICMP (Internet Control Message Protocol) protocol. Without any options, ping tests the connection once per second until you abort execution with CONTROL-C.

```
$ ping www.slashdot.org
PING www.slashdot.org (216.34.181.48) 56(84) bytes of data.
64 bytes from star.slashdot.org (216.34.181.48): icmp_seq=1 ttl=238 time=70.2 ms
64 bytes from star.slashdot.org (216.34.181.48): icmp_seq=2 ttl=238 time=72.6 ms
64 bytes from star.slashdot.org (216.34.181.48): icmp_seq=3 ttl=238 time=57.5 ms
64 bytes from star.slashdot.org (216.34.181.48): icmp_seq=4 ttl=238 time=71.2 ms
CONTROL-C
--- www.slashdot.org ping statistics ---
4 packets transmitted, 4 received, 0% packet loss, time 3024ms
rtt min/avg/max/mdev = 57.553/67.899/72.605/6.039 ms
```

This example shows that a connection to **www.slashdot.org** is redirected to **star.slashdot.org** and that that system is up and available over the network.

By default ping sends packets containing 64 bytes (56 data bytes and 8 bytes of protocol header information). In the preceding example, four packets were sent to the system **star.slashdot.org** before the user interrupted ping by pressing CONTROL-C. The four-part number in parentheses on each line is the remote system's IP address. A packet sequence number (named **icmp_seq**) is also given. If a packet is dropped, a gap occurs in the sequence numbers. The round-trip time is listed last; it represents the time (in milliseconds) that elapsed from when the packet was sent from the local system to the remote system until the reply from the remote system was received by the local system. This time is affected by the distance between the two systems, network traffic, and the load on both computers. Before it terminates, ping summarizes the results, indicating how many packets were sent and received as well as the minimum, average, maximum, and mean deviation round-trip times it measured. Use ping6 to test IPv6 networks.

When ping **cannot connect**

tip   If it is unable to contact the remote system, ping continues trying until you interrupt it with CONTROL-C. A system may not answer for any of several reasons: The remote computer may be down, the network interface or some part of the network between the systems may be broken, a software failure may have occurred, or the remote machine may be set up, for reasons of security, not to return pings (try pinging www.microsoft.com or www.ibm.com).

traceroute: TRACES A ROUTE OVER THE INTERNET

The traceroute utility traces the route that an IP packet follows, including all intermediary points traversed (called *network hops*), to its destination (the argument to traceroute—an Internet host). It displays a numbered list of hostnames, if available, and IP addresses, together with the round-trip time it took for a packet to reach each router along the way and an acknowledgment to get back. You can put this information to good use when you are trying to identify the location of a network bottleneck.

The traceroute utility has no concept of the path from one host to the next; instead, it simply sends out packets with increasing *TTL* (time to live) values. TTL is an IP header field that indicates how many more hops the packet should be allowed to make before being discarded or returned. In the case of a traceroute packet, the packet is returned by the host that has the packet when the TTL value is zero. The result is a list of hosts that the packet traveled through to get to its destination.

The traceroute utility can help you solve routing configuration problems and locate routing path failures. When you cannot reach a host, use traceroute to discover what path the packet follows, how far it gets, and what the delay is.

The next example shows the output of traceroute when it follows a route from a local computer to **www.linux.org**. The first line indicates the IP address of the target, the maximum number of hops that will be traced, and the size of the packets that will be used. Each numbered line contains the name and IP address of the intermediate destination, followed by the time it takes a packet to make a trip to that destination and back again. The traceroute utility sends three packets to each destination; thus three times appear on each line. Line 1 shows the statistics when a packet is sent to the local gateway (less than 3 milliseconds). Lines 4–6 show the packet bouncing around Mountain View (California) before it goes to San Jose. Between hops 13 and 14 the packet travels across the United States (San Francisco to somewhere in the East). By hop 18 the packet has found **www.linux.org**. The traceroute utility displays asterisks when it does not receive a response. Each asterisk indicates that traceroute has waited three seconds. Use traceroute6 to test IPv6 networks.

```
$ /usr/sbin/traceroute www.linux.org
traceroute to www.linux.org (198.182.196.56), 30 hops max, 38 byte packets
 1  gw.localco.com. (204.94.139.65)  2.904 ms  2.425 ms  2.783 ms
 2  covad-gw2.meer.net (209.157.140.1)  19.727 ms  23.287 ms  24.783 ms
 3  gw-mv1.meer.net (140.174.164.1)  18.795 ms  24.973 ms  19.207 ms
 4  d1-4-2.a02.mtvwca01.us.ra.verio.net (206.184.210.241)  59.091 ms d1-10-0-0-200.a03.
       mtvwca01.us.ra.verio.net (206.86.28.5)  54.948 ms  39.485 ms
 5  fa-11-0-0.a01.mtvwca01.us.ra.verio.net (206.184.188.1)  40.182 ms  44.405 ms 49.362 ms
 6  p1-1-0-0.a09.mtvwca01.us.ra.verio.net (205.149.170.66)  78.688 ms  66.266 ms 28.003 ms
 7  p1-12-0-0.a01.snjsca01.us.ra.verio.net (209.157.181.166) 32.424 ms 94.337 ms 54.946 ms
 8  f4-1-0.sjc0.verio.net (129.250.31.81)  38.952 ms  63.111 ms  49.083 ms
 9  sjc0.nuq0.verio.net (129.250.3.98)  45.031 ms  43.496 ms  44.925 ms
10  mae-west1.US.CRL.NET (198.32.136.10)  48.525 ms  66.296 ms  38.996 ms
11  t3-ames.3.sfo.us.crl.net (165.113.0.249)  138.808 ms  78.579 ms  68.699 ms
12  E0-CRL-SFO-02-E0X0.US.CRL.NET (165.113.55.2)  43.023 ms  51.910 ms  42.967 ms
13  sfo2-vva1.ATM.us.crl.net (165.113.0.254)  135.551 ms  154.606 ms  178.632 ms
14  mae-east-02.ix.ai.net (192.41.177.202)  158.351 ms  201.811 ms  204.560 ms
15  oc12-3-0-0.mae-east.ix.ai.net (205.134.161.2)  202.851 ms  155.667 ms  219.116 ms
16  border-ai.invlogic.com (205.134.175.254)  214.622 ms  *  190.423 ms
17  router.invlogic.com (198.182.196.1)  224.378 ms  235.427 ms  228.856 ms
18  www.linux.org (198.182.196.56)  207.964 ms  178.683 ms  179.483 ms
```

host AND dig: Query Internet Nameservers

The host utility looks up an IP address given a name, or vice versa. The following example shows how to use host to look up the domain name of a machine, given an IP address:

```
$ host 64.13.141.6
6.141.13.64.in-addr.arpa domain name pointer ns.meer.net.
```

You can also use host to determine the IP address of a domain name:

```
$ host ns.meer.net
ns.meer.net has address 64.13.141.6
```

The dig (domain information groper) utility queries DNS servers and individual machines for information about a domain. A powerful utility, dig has many features that you may never use. It is more complex than host.

Chapter 24 on DNS has many examples of the use of host and dig.

jwhois: Looks Up Information About an Internet Site

The jwhois utility (**jwhois** package) replaces whois and queries a **whois** server for information about an Internet site. This utility returns site contact and InterNIC or other registry information that can help you track down the person who is responsible for a site: Perhaps that person is sending you or your company *spam* (page 1133). Many sites on the Internet are easier to use and faster than jwhois. Use a browser and search engine to search on **whois** or go to www.networksolutions.com/whois or www.ripe.net/perl/whois to get started.

When you do not specify a **whois** server, jwhois defaults to **whois.internic.net**. Use the **–h** option to jwhois to specify a different **whois** server. See the jwhois info page for more options and setup information.

To obtain information on a domain name, specify the complete domain name, as in the following example:

```
$ jwhois sobell.com
[Querying whois.verisign-grs.com]
[Redirected to whois.godaddy.com]
[Querying whois.godaddy.com]
[whois.godaddy.com]
The data contained in GoDaddy.com, Inc.'s WhoIs database,
...
Registrant:
    Sobell Associates Inc
    660 Market Street
    Fifth Floor
    San Francisco, California 94104
    United States
```

```
Registered through: GoDaddy.com, Inc. (http://www.godaddy.com)
Domain Name: SOBELL.COM
    Created on: 07-Apr-95
    Expires on: 08-Apr-13
    Last Updated on: 16-Jan-04

Administrative Contact:
    Sobell, Mark  sobell@meer.net
    Sobell Associates Inc
    660 Market Street
    Fifth Floor
    SAN FRANCISCO, California 94104
    United States
    18888446337       Fax -- 18888446337

Technical Contact:
    W., Tim  hostmaster@meer.net
    meer.net
    po box 390804
    Mountain View, California 94039
    United States
    18888446337       Fax -- 18888446337

Domain servers in listed order:
    NS.MEER.NET
    NS2.MEER.NET
```

Several top-level registries serve various regions of the world. You are most likely to use the following ones:

North American registry **whois.arin.net**
European registry   **www.ripe.net**
Asia-Pacific registry   **www.apnic.net**
U.S. military   **whois.nic.mil**
U.S. government   **www.nic.gov**

DISTRIBUTED COMPUTING

When many similar systems are found on the same network, it is often desirable to share common files and utilities among them. For example, a system administrator might choose to keep a copy of the system documentation on one computer's disk and to make those files available to remote systems. In this case, the system administrator configures the files so users who need to access the online documentation are not aware that the files are stored on a remote system. This type of setup, which is an example of *distributed computing*, not only conserves disk space but also allows you to update one central copy of the documentation rather than tracking down and updating copies scattered throughout the network on many different systems.

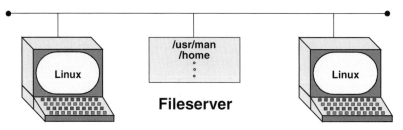

Figure 10-2   A fileserver

Figure 10-2 illustrates a *fileserver* that stores the system manual pages and users' home directories. With this arrangement, a user's files are always available to that user—no matter which system the user logs in on. Each system's disk might contain a directory to hold temporary files as well as a copy of the operating system. Chapter 22 contains instructions for setting up NFS clients and servers in networked configurations.

THE CLIENT/SERVER MODEL

Mainframe model   The client/server model was not the first computational model. First came the mainframe, which follows a one-machine-does-it-all model. That is, all the intelligence resides in one system, including the data and the program that manipulates and reports on the data. Users connect to a mainframe using terminals.

File-sharing model   With the introduction of PCs, file-sharing networks became available. In this scheme data is downloaded from a shared location to a user's PC, where a program then manipulates the data. The file-sharing model ran into problems as networks expanded and more users needed access to the data.

Client/server model   In the client/server model, a client uses a protocol, such as FTP, to request services, and a server provides the services that the client requests. Rather than providing data files as the file-sharing model does, the server in a client/server relationship is a database that provides only those pieces of information that the client needs or requests.

The client/server model dominates UNIX and Linux system networking and underlies most of the network services described in this book. FTP, NFS, DNS, email, and HTTP (the Web browsing protocol) all rely on the client/server model. Some servers, such as Web servers and browser clients, are designed to interact with specific utilities. Other servers, such as those supporting DNS, communicate with one another, in addition to answering queries from a variety of clients. Clients and servers can reside on the same or different systems running the same or different operating systems. The systems can be proximate or thousands of miles apart. A system that is a server to one system can turn around and act as a client to another. A server can reside on a single system or, as is the case with DNS, be distributed among thousands of geographically separated systems running many different operating systems.

Peer-to-peer model   The peer-to-peer (PTP) model, in which either program can initiate a transaction, stands in contrast to the client/server model. PTP protocols are common on small networks. For example, Microsoft's Network Neighborhood and Apple's Apple-Talk both rely on broadcast-based PTP protocols for browsing and automatic configuration. The Zeroconf multicast DNS protocol is a PTP alternative DNS for small networks. The highest-profile PTP networks are those used for file sharing, such as Kazaa and GNUtella. Many of these networks are not pure PTP topologies. Pure PTP networks do not scale well, so networks such as Napster and Kazaa employ a hybrid approach.

DNS: DOMAIN NAME SERVICE

DNS is a distributed service: Nameservers on thousands of machines around the world cooperate to keep the database up-to-date. The database itself, which maps hundreds of thousands of alphanumeric hostnames to numeric IP addresses, does not exist in one place. That is, no system has a complete copy of the database. Instead, each system that runs DNS knows which hosts are local to that site and understands how to contact other nameservers to learn about other, nonlocal hosts.

Like the Linux filesystem, DNS is organized hierarchically. Each country has an ISO (International Organization for Standardization) country code designation as its domain name. (For example, **AU** represents Australia, **IL** is Israel, and **JP** is Japan; see www.iana.org/cctld/cctld.htm for a complete list.) Although the United States is represented in the same way (**US**) and uses the standard two-letter Postal Service abbreviations to identify the next level of the domain, only governments and a few organizations use these codes. Schools in the **US** domain are represented by a third- (and sometimes second-) level domain: **k12**. For example, the domain name for Myschool in New York state could be www.myschool.k12.ny.us.

Following is a list of the six original top-level domains. These domains are used extensively within the United States and, to a lesser degree, by users in other countries:

COM	Commercial enterprises
EDU	Educational institutions
GOV	Nonmilitary government agencies
MIL	Military government agencies
NET	Networking organizations
ORG	Other (often nonprofit) organizations

Recently, the following additional top-level domains have been approved for use:

AERO	Air-transport industry
BIZ	Business
COOP	Cooperatives
INFO	Unrestricted use
MUSEUM	Museums
NAME	Name registries

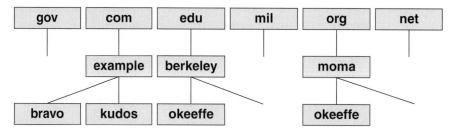

Figure 10-3 U.S. top-level domains

Like Internet addresses, domain names were once assigned by the Network Information Center (NIC, page 365); now they are assigned by several companies. A system's full name, referred to as its *fully qualified domain name* (FQDN), is unambiguous in the way that a simple hostname cannot be. The system **okeeffe.berkeley.edu** at the University of California at Berkeley (Figure 10-3) is not the same as one named **okeeffe.moma.org**, which might represent a host at the Museum of Modern Art. The domain name not only tells you something about where the system is located but also adds enough diversity to the namespace to avoid confusion when different sites choose similar names for their systems.

Unlike the filesystem hierarchy, the top-level domain name appears last (reading from left to right). Also, domain names are not case sensitive, so the names **okeeffe.berkeley.edu**, **okeeffe.Berkeley.edu**, and **okeeffe.Berkeley.EDU** refer to the same computer. Once a domain has been assigned, the local site is free to extend the hierarchy to meet local needs.

With DNS, email addressed to **user@example.com** can be delivered to the computer named **example.com** that handles the corporate mail and knows how to forward messages to user mailboxes on individual machines. As the company grows, its site administrator might decide to create organizational or geographical subdomains. The name **delta.ca.example.com** might refer to a system that supports California offices, for example, while **alpha.co.example.com** is dedicated to Colorado. Functional subdomains might be another choice, with **delta.sales.example.com** and **alpha.dev.example.com** representing the sales and development divisions, respectively.

BIND   On Linux systems, the most common interface to the DNS is BIND (Berkeley Internet Name Domain). BIND follows the client/server model. On any given local network, one or more systems may be running a nameserver, supporting all the local hosts as clients. When it wants to send a message to another host, a system queries the nearest nameserver to learn the remote host's IP address. The client, called a *resolver*, may be a process running on the same computer as the nameserver, or it may pass the request over the network to reach a server. To reduce network traffic and facilitate name lookups, the local nameserver maintains some knowledge of distant hosts. If the local server must contact a remote server to pick up an address, when the answer comes back, the local server adds that address to its internal table and reuses it for a while. The nameserver deletes the nonlocal information before it can become outdated. Refer to "TTL" on page 1138.

The system's translation of symbolic hostnames into addresses is transparent to most users; only the system administrator of a networked system needs to be concerned with the details of name resolution. Systems that use DNS for name resolution are generally capable of communicating with the greatest number of hosts—more than would be practical to maintain in a /etc/hosts file or private NIS database. Chapter 24 covers setting up and running a DNS server.

Three common sources are referenced for hostname resolution: NIS, DNS, and system files (such as /etc/hosts). Linux does not ask you to choose among these sources; rather, the nsswitch.conf file (page 458) allows you to choose any of these sources, in any combination, and in any order.

PORTS

Ports are logical channels on a network interface and are numbered from 1 to 65,535. Each network connection is uniquely identified by the IP address and port number of each endpoint.

In a system that has many network connections open simultaneously, the use of ports keeps *packets* (page 1123) flowing to and from the appropriate programs. A program that needs to receive data *binds* to a port and then uses that port for communication.

Privileged ports   Services are associated with specific ports, generally with numbers less than 1024. These ports are called *privileged* (or *reserved*) *ports*. For security reasons, only a process running with **root** privileges can bind to privileged ports. A service run on a privileged port provides assurance that the service is being provided by someone with authority over the system, with the exception that any user on Windows 98 and earlier Windows systems can bind to any port. Commonly used ports include 22 (SSH), 23 (TELNET), 80 (HTTP), 111 (Sun RPC), and 201–208 (AppleTalk).

NIS: NETWORK INFORMATION SERVICE

NIS (Network Information Service) simplifies the maintenance of frequently used administrative files by keeping them in a central database and having clients contact the database server to retrieve information from the database. Just as DNS addresses the problem of keeping multiple copies of **hosts** files up-to-date, NIS deals with the issue of keeping system-independent configuration files (such as /etc/passwd) current. Refer to Chapter 21 for coverage of NIS.

NFS: NETWORK FILESYSTEM

The NFS (Network Filesystem) protocol allows a server to share selected local directory hierarchies with client systems on a heterogeneous network. Files on the remote fileserver appear as if they are present on the local system. NFS is covered in Chapter 22.

optional

NETWORK SERVICES

Linux Internet services are provided by daemons that run continuously or by a daemon that is started automatically by the **inetd** or **xinetd** daemon (page 447) when a service request comes in. The **/etc/services** file lists network services (for example, **telnet**, **ftp**, and **ssh**) and their associated numbers. Any service that uses TCP/IP or UDP/IP has an entry in this file. IANA (Internet Assigned Numbers Authority) maintains a database of all permanent, registered services. The **/etc/services** file usually lists a small, commonly used subset of services. Visit www.rfc.net/rfc1700.html for more information and a complete list of registered services.

Most of the daemons (the executable files) are stored in **/usr/sbin**. By convention the names of many daemons end with the letter **d** to distinguish them from utilities (one common daemon whose name does not end in **d** is **sendmail**). The prefix **in.** or **rpc.** is often used for daemon names. Give the command **ls /usr/sbin/*d** to see a list of many of the daemon programs on the local system. Refer to "SysVinit (rc) Scripts: Start and Stop System Services" on page 423 for information about starting and stopping these daemons.

To see how a daemon works, consider what happens when you run **ssh**. The local system contacts the **ssh** daemon (**sshd**) on the remote system to establish a connection. The two systems negotiate the connection according to a fixed protocol. Each system identifies itself to the other, and then they take turns asking each other specific questions and waiting for valid replies. Each network service follows its own protocol.

COMMON DAEMONS

In addition to the daemons that support the utilities described up to this point, many other daemons support system-level services that you will not typically interact with. Table 10-4 lists some of these daemons.

Table 10-4   Common daemons

Daemon	Used for or by	Function
acpid	Advanced configuration and power interface	Flexible daemon for delivering ACPI events. Replaces **apmd**.
anacron	anacrontab	Used for periodic execution of tasks. This daemon looks in the **/etc/anacrontab** file. When a task comes up for execution, **anacron** executes it as the user who owns the file that describes the task.
apache2	HTTP	The Web server daemon (Apache, page 855).

Table 10-4 Common daemons (continued)

Daemon	Used for or by	Function
apmd	Advanced power management	Reports and takes action on specified changes in system power, including shutdowns. Useful with machines, such as laptops, that run on batteries.
atd	at	Executes a command once at a specific time and date. See **crond** for periodic execution of a command.
automount	Automatic mounting	Automatically mounts filesystems when they are accessed. Automatic mounting is a way of demand-mounting remote directories without having to hard-configure them into **/etc/fstab**. See page 756.
cron	crontab	Used for periodic execution of tasks. This daemon looks in the **/var/spool/cron/crontabs** directory for files with filenames that correspond to users' usernames. It also looks at the **/etc/crontab** file and at files in the **/etc/cron.d** directory. When a task comes up for execution, **cron** executes it as the user who owns the file that describes the task.
dhcpd	DHCP	Assigns Internet address, subnet mask, default gateway, DNS, and other information to hosts. This protocol answers DHCP requests and, optionally, BOOTP requests. Refer to "DHCP: Configures Network Interfaces" on page 454.
exim4	Mail programs	The **exim4** daemon came from the University of Cambridge. The the **exim4** daemon listens on port 25 for incoming mail connections and then calls a local delivery agent, such as **/bin/mail**. Mail user agents (MUAs), such as KMail and Thunderbird, typically use **exim4** to deliver mail messages.
ftpd	FTP	Handles FTP requests. Refer to "ftp: Transfers Files over a Network" on page 377. See also **vsftpd** (page 651).
gpm	General-purpose mouse or GNU paste manager	Allows you to use a mouse to cut and paste text on console applications.
in.fingerd	finger	Handles requests for user information from the finger utility.
inetd		Listens for service requests on network connections and starts up the appropriate daemon to respond to any particular request. Because of **inetd**, a system does not need the daemons running continually to handle various network requests. For more information refer to page 447. Deprecated in favor of **xinetd**.
lpd	Line printer spooler daemon	Launched by **xinetd** when printing requests come to the machine. Not used with CUPS.

Table 10-4   Common daemons (continued)

Daemon	Used for or by	Function
named	DNS	Supports DNS (page 783).
nfsd, statd, lockd, mountd, rquotad	NFS	These five daemons operate together to handle NFS (page 737) operations. The **nfsd** daemon handles file and directory requests. The **statd** and **lockd** daemons implement network file and record locking. The **mountd** daemon converts filesystem name requests from the **mount** utility into NFS handles and checks access permissions. If disk quotas are enabled, **rquotad** handles those.
ntpd	NTP	Synchronizes time on network computers. Requires a **/etc/ntp.conf** file. For more information go to www.ntp.org.
portmap	RPC	Maps incoming requests for RPC service numbers to TCP or UDP port numbers on the local system. Refer to "RPC Network Services" on page 390.
pppd	PPP	For a modem, this protocol controls the pseudointerface represented by the IP connection between the local computer and a remote computer. Refer to "PPP: Point-to-Point Protocol" on page 365.
rexecd	rexec	Allows a remote user with a valid username and password to run programs on a system. Its use is generally deprecated for security reasons; certain programs, such as PC-based X servers, may still have it as an option.
routed	Routing tables	Manages the routing tables so your system knows where to send messages that are destined for remote networks. If your system does not have a **/etc/defaultrouter** file, **routed** is started automatically to listen to incoming routing messages and to advertise outgoing routes to other systems on the local network. A newer daemon, the gateway daemon (**gated**), offers enhanced configurability and support for more routing protocols and is proportionally more complex.
sendmail	Mail programs	The **sendmail** daemon came from Berkeley UNIX and has been available for a long time. The de facto mail transfer program on the Internet, the **sendmail** daemon always listens on port 25 for incoming mail connections and then calls a local delivery agent, such as **/bin/mail**. Mail user agents (MUAs), such as KMail and Thunderbird, typically use **sendmail** to deliver mail messages.
smbd, nmbd	Samba	Allow Windows PCs to share files and printers with UNIX and Linux computers (page 761).
sshd	ssh, scp	Enables secure logins between remote systems (page 640).

Table 10-4   Common daemons (continued)

Daemon	Used for or by	Function
syslogd	System log	Transcribes important system events and stores them in files and/or forwards them to users or another host running the **syslogd** daemon. This daemon is configured with **/etc/syslog.conf** and used with the syslog utility. See page 608.
talkd	talk	Allows you to have a conversation with another user on the same or a remote machine. The **talkd** daemon handles the connections between the machines. The talk utility on each system contacts the **talkd** daemon on the other system for a bidirectional conversation.
telnetd	TELNET	One of the original Internet remote access protocols (page 375).
tftpd	TFTP	Used to boot a system or get information from a network. Examples include network computers, routers, and some printers.
timed	Time server	On a LAN synchronizes time with other computers that are also running **timed**.
xinetd	Internet superserver	Listens for service requests on network connections and starts up the appropriate daemon to respond to any particular request. Because of **xinetd**, a system does not need the daemons running continually to handle various network requests. For more information refer to page 447.

PROXY SERVERS

A *proxy* is a network service that is authorized to act for a system while not being part of that system. A proxy server or proxy gateway provides proxy services; it is a transparent intermediary, relaying communications back and forth between an application, such as a browser and a server, usually outside of a LAN and frequently on the Internet. When more than one process uses the proxy gateway/server, the proxy must keep track of which processes are connecting to which hosts/servers so that it can route the return messages to the proper process. The most commonly encountered proxies are email and Web proxies.

A proxy server/gateway insulates the local computer from all other computers or from specified domains by using at least two IP addresses: one to communicate with the local computer and one to communicate with a server. The proxy server/gateway examines and changes the header information on all packets it handles so that it can encode, route, and decode them properly. The difference between a proxy gateway and a proxy server is that the proxy server usually includes *cache* (page 1099) to store frequently used Web pages so that the next request for that page is available locally and quickly; a proxy gateway typically does not use cache. The terms "proxy server" and "proxy gateway" are frequently used interchangeably.

Proxy servers/gateways are available for such common Internet services as HTTP, HTTPS, FTP, SMTP, and SNMP. When an HTTP proxy sends queries from local systems, it presents a single organizationwide IP address (the external IP address of the proxy server/gateway) to all servers. It funnels all user requests to the appropriate servers and keeps track of them. When the responses come back, the HTTP proxy fans them out to the appropriate applications using each machine's unique IP address, thereby protecting local addresses from remote/specified servers.

Proxy servers/gateways are generally just one part of an overall firewall strategy to prevent intruders from stealing information or damaging an internal network. Other functions, which can be either combined with or kept separate from the proxy server/gateway, include packet filtering, which blocks traffic based on origin and type, and user activity reporting, which helps management learn how the Internet is being used.

RPC NETWORK SERVICES

Much of the client/server interaction over a network is implemented using the RPC (Remote Procedure Call) protocol, which is implemented as a set of library calls that make network access transparent to the client and server. RPC specifies and interprets messages but does not concern itself with transport protocols; it runs on top of TCP/IP and UDP/IP. Services that use RPC include NFS and NIS. RPC was developed by Sun as ONC RPC (Open Network Computing Remote Procedure Calls) and differs from Microsoft RPC.

In the client/server model, a client contacts a server on a specific port (page 385) to avoid any mixup between services, clients, and servers. To avoid maintaining a long list of port numbers and to enable new clients/servers to start up without registering a port number with a central registry, when a server that uses RPC starts, it specifies the port it expects to be contacted on. RPC servers typically use port numbers that have been defined by Sun. If a server does not use a predefined port number, it picks an arbitrary number.

portmap   The server then registers this port with the RPC portmapper (the **portmap** daemon) on the local system. The server tells the daemon which port number it is listening on and which RPC program numbers it serves. Through these exchanges, the **portmap** daemon learns the location of every registered port on the host and the programs that are available on each port. The **portmap** daemon, which always listens on port 111 for both TCP and UDP, must be running to make RPC calls.

Files   The **/etc/rpc** file (page 478) maps RPC services to RPC numbers. The **/etc/services** file (page 479) lists system services.

RPC client/server
communication
The sequence of events for communication between an RPC client and server occurs as follows:

1. The client program on the client system makes an RPC call to obtain data from a (remote) server system. (The client issues a "read record from a file" request.)

2. If RPC has not yet established a connection with the server system for the client program, it contacts **portmap** on port 111 of the server and asks which port the desired RPC server is listening on (for example, **rpc.nfsd**).

3. The **portmap** daemon on the remote server looks in its tables and returns a UDP or TCP port number to the local system, the client (typically 2049 for **nfs**).

4. The RPC libraries on the server system receive the call from the client and pass the request to the appropriate server program. The origin of the request is transparent to the server program. (The filesystem receives the "read record from file" request.)

5. The server responds to the request. (The filesystem reads the record.)

6. The RPC libraries on the remote server return the result over the network to the client program. (The read record is returned to the calling program.)

Under Ubuntu Linux most servers start and run their own daemons. When RPC servers are started by the **xinetd** daemon (page 447), the **portmap** daemon must be started before the **xinetd** daemon is invoked. The init scripts (page 423) make sure **portmap** starts before **xinetd**. You can confirm this sequence by looking at the numbers associated with **/etc/rc.d/*/S*portmap** and **/etc/rc.d/*/S*/xinetd**. If the **portmap** daemon stops, you must restart all RPC servers on the local system.

USENET

One of the earliest information services available on the Internet, Usenet is an electronic bulletin board that allows users with common interests to exchange information. Usenet comprises an informal, loosely connected network of systems that exchange email and news items (commonly referred to as *netnews*). It was formed in 1979 when a few sites decided to share some software and information on topics of common interest. They agreed to contact one another and to pass the information along over dial-up telephone lines (at that time running at 1,200 baud at best), using UNIX's uucp utility (UNIX-to-UNIX copy program).

The popularity of Usenet led to major changes in uucp to handle the escalating volume of messages and sites. Today much of the news flows over network links using a sophisticated protocol designed especially for this purpose: NNTP (Network News Transfer Protocol). The news messages are stored in a standard format, and the many public domain programs available let you read them. An old, simple interface is named readnews. Other interfaces, such as rn, its X Window System cousin xrn, tin, nn, and xvnews, have many features that help you browse through and reply to the articles that are available or create articles of your own. In addition, Netscape and Mozilla include an interface that you can use to read news (Netscape/Mozilla News) as part of their Web browsers. One of the easiest ways to read netnews is to go to groups.google.com. The program you select to read netnews is largely a matter of personal taste.

As programs to read netnews articles have been ported to non-UNIX and non-Linux systems, the community of netnews users has become highly diversified. In the UNIX tradition, categories of netnews groups are structured hierarchically. The top level includes such designations as **comp** (computer-related), **misc** (miscellaneous), **rec** (recreation), **sci** (science), **soc** (social issues), and **talk** (ongoing discussions). Usually at least one regional category is at the top level, such as **ba** (San Francisco Bay Area), and includes information about local events. New categories are continually being added to the more than 30,000 newsgroups. The names of newsgroups resemble domain names but are read from left to right (like Linux filenames): **comp.os.unix.misc**, **comp.lang.c**, **misc.jobs.offered**, **rec.skiing**, **sci.med**, **soc.singles**, and **talk.politics** are but a few examples.

A great deal of useful information is available on Usenet, but you need patience and perseverance to find what you are looking for. You can ask a question, and someone from halfway around the world might answer it. Before posing such a simple question and causing it to appear on thousands of systems around the world, however, first ask yourself whether you can get help in a less invasive way. Try the following:

- Refer to the man pages and info.
- Look through the files in **/usr/share/doc**.
- Ask the system administrator or another user for help.
- All of the popular newsgroups have FAQs (lists of frequently asked questions). Consult these lists and see whether your question has been answered. FAQs are periodically posted to the newsgroups; in addition, all the FAQs are archived at sites around the Internet, including Google groups (groups.google.com).
- Because someone has probably asked the same question earlier, search the netnews archives for an answer. Try looking at groups.google.com, which has a complete netnews archive.
- Use a search engine to find an answer. One good way to get help is to search on an error message.
- Review support documents at help.ubuntu.com.
- Contact an Ubuntu Linux users' group.

Post a query to the worldwide Usenet community as a last resort. If you are stuck on a Linux question and cannot find any other help, try submitting it to one of these newsgroups:

- comp.os.linux.misc
- alt.os.linux
- comp.os.linux.networking
- comp.os.linux.security
- comp.os.linux.setup

One way to find out about new tools and services is to read Usenet news. The **comp.os.linux** hierarchy is of particular interest to Linux users; for example, news about newly released software for Linux is posted to **comp.os.linux.announce**. People often announce the availability of free software there, along with instructions on how to get a copy for your own use using anonymous FTP (page 658). Other tools to help you find resources, both old and new, exist on the network; see Appendix B.

WWW: WORLD WIDE WEB

The World Wide Web (WWW, W3, or the Web) provides a unified, interconnected interface to the vast amount of information stored on computers around the world. The idea that spawned the World Wide Web came from the mind of Tim Berners-Lee (www.w3.org/People/Berners-Lee) of the European Particle Physics Laboratory (CERN) in response to a need to improve communications throughout the high-energy physics community. The first-generation solution consisted of a notebook program named Enquire, short for *Enquire Within Upon Everything* (the name of a book from Berners-Lee's childhood), which he created in 1980 on a NeXT computer and which supported links between named nodes. Not until 1989 was the concept proposed as a global hypertext project to be known as the World Wide Web. In 1990, Berners-Lee wrote a proposal for a hypertext project, which eventually produced HTML (Hypertext Markup Language), the common language of the Web. The World Wide Web program became available on the Internet in the summer of 1991. By designing the tools to work with existing protocols, such as FTP and gopher, the researchers who created the Web produced a system that is generally useful for many types of information and across many types of hardware and operating systems.

The WWW is another example of the client/server paradigm. You use a WWW client application, or *browser*, to retrieve and display information stored on a server that may be located anywhere on your local network or the Internet. WWW clients can interact with many types of servers. For example, you can use a WWW client to contact a remote FTP server and display the list of files it offers for anonymous FTP. Most commonly you use a WWW client to contact a WWW server, which offers support for the special features of the World Wide Web that are described in the remainder of this chapter.

The power of the Web derives from its use of *hypertext*, a way to navigate through information by following cross-references (called *links*) from one piece of information to another. To use the Web effectively, you need to run interactive network applications. The first GUI for browsing the Web was a tool named Mosaic, which was released in February 1993. Designed at the National Center for Supercomputer Applications at the University of Illinois, its introduction sparked a dramatic increase in the number of users of the World Wide Web. Marc Andreessen, who participated in the Mosaic project at the University of Illinois, later cofounded Netscape Communications with the founder of Silicon Graphics, Jim Clark. The pair created Netscape Navigator, a Web client program that was designed to perform better and support more features than the Mosaic browser. Netscape Navigator has enjoyed immense success and has become a popular choice for exploring the World Wide Web. Important for Linux users is the fact that from its inception Netscape has provided versions of its tools that run on Linux. Also, Netscape created Mozilla (mozilla.org) as an open-source browser project.

These browsers provide GUIs that allow you to listen to sounds, watch Web events or live news reports, and display pictures as well as text, giving you access to *hypermedia*. A picture on your screen may be a link to more detailed, nonverbal information, such as a copy of the same picture at a higher resolution or a short animation. If your system can produce audio output, you can listen to audio clips that have been linked to a document.

URL: UNIFORM RESOURCE LOCATOR

Consider the URL http://www.w3.org/Consortium/siteindex. The first component in the URL indicates the type of resource, in this case **http** (HTTP—Hypertext Transfer Protocol). Other valid resource names, such as **https** (HTTPS—secure HTTP) and **ftp** (FTP—File Transfer Protocol), represent information available on the Web using other protocols. Next come a colon and double slash (**://**). Frequently the **http://** string is omitted from a URL in print, as you seldom need to enter it to reach the URL. The next element is the full name of the host that acts as the server for the information (**www.w3.org/**). The rest of the URL consists of a relative pathname to the file that contains the information (**Consortium/siteindex**). If you enter a URL in the location bar of a Web browser, the Web server returns the page, frequently an *HTML* (page 1112) file, pointed to by this URL.

By convention many sites identify their WWW servers by prefixing a host or domain name with **www**. For example, you can reach the Web server at the New Jersey Institute of Technology at www.njit.edu. When you use a browser to explore the World Wide Web, you may never need to enter a URL. However, as more information is published in hypertext form, you cannot help but find URLs everywhere—not just online in email messages and Usenet articles, but also in newspapers, in advertisements, and on product labels.

BROWSERS

Mozilla (www.mozilla.org) is the open-source counterpart to Netscape. Mozilla, which was first released in March 1998, was based on Netscape 4 code. Since then, Mozilla has been under continuous development by employees of Netscape (now a division of AOL) and other companies and by contributors from the community. Firefox is the Web browser component of Mozilla. KDE offers Konqueror, an all-purpose file manager and Web browser. Other browsers include Epiphany (www.gnome.org/projects/epiphany) and Opera (www.opera.com). Although each Web browser is unique, all of them allow you to move about the Internet, viewing HTML documents, listening to sounds, and retrieving files. If you do not use the X Window System, try a text browser, such as lynx or links. The lynx browser works well with Braille terminals.

SEARCH ENGINES

Search engine is a name that applies to a group of hardware and software tools that help you search for World Wide Web sites that contain specific information. A search engine relies on a database of information collected by a *Web crawler,* a program that regularly looks through the millions of pages that make up the World Wide Web. A search engine must also have a way of collating the information the Web crawler collects so that you can access it quickly, easily, and in a manner that makes it most useful to you. This part of the search engine, called an *index,* allows you to search for a word, a group of words, or a concept; it returns the URLs of Web pages that pertain to what you are searching for. Many different types of search engines are available on the Internet, each with its own set of strengths and weaknesses.

CHAPTER SUMMARY

A Linux system attached to a network is probably communicating on an Ethernet, which may in turn be linked to other local area networks (LANs) and wide area networks (WANs). Communication between LANs and WANs requires the use of gateways and routers. Gateways translate the local data into a format suitable for the WAN, and routers make decisions about the optimal routing of the data along the way. The most widely used network, by far, is the Internet.

Basic networking tools allow Linux users to log in and run commands on remote systems (ssh, telnet) and copy files quickly from one system to another (scp, ftp/sftp). Many tools that were originally designed to support communication on a single-host computer (for example, finger and talk) have since been extended to recognize network addresses, thus allowing users on different systems to interact with one another. Other features, such as the Network Filesystem (NFS), were created to extend the basic UNIX model and to simplify information sharing.

Concern is growing about our ability to protect the security and privacy of machines connected to networks and of data transmitted over networks. Toward this end, many new tools and protocols have been created: ssh, scp, HTTPS, IPv6, firewall hardware and software, VPN, and so on. Many of these tools take advantage of newer, more impenetrable encryption techniques. In addition, some weaker concepts (such as that of trusted hosts) and some tools (such as finger and rwho) are being discarded in the name of security.

Computer networks offer two major advantages over other ways of connecting computers: They enable systems to communicate at high speeds and they require few physical interconnections (typically one per system, often on a shared cable). The Internet Protocol (IP), the universal language of the Internet, has made it possible for dissimilar computer systems around the world to readily communicate with one another. Technological advances continue to improve the performance of computer systems and the networks that link them.

One way to gather information on the Internet is via Usenet. Many Linux users routinely peruse Usenet news (netnews) to learn about the latest resources available for their systems. Usenet news is organized into newsgroups that cover a wide range of topics, computer-related and otherwise. To read Usenet news, you need to have access to a news server and the appropriate client software. Many modern email programs, such as Mozilla and Netscape, can display netnews.

The rapid increase of network communication speeds in recent years has encouraged the development of many new applications and services. The World Wide Web provides access to vast information stores on the Internet and makes extensive use of hypertext links to promote efficient searching through related documents. It adheres to the client/server model that is so pervasive in networking. Typically the WWW client is local to a site or is made available through an Internet service provider. WWW servers are responsible for providing the information requested by their many clients.

Mozilla/Firefox is a WWW client program that has enormous popular appeal. Firefox and other browsers use a GUI to give you access to text, picture, and audio information: Making extensive use of these hypermedia simplifies access to and enhances the presentation of information.

EXERCISES

1. Describe the similarities and differences between these utilities:

   a. scp and ftp

   b. ssh and telnet

   c. rsh and ssh

2. Assuming rwho is disabled on the systems on your LAN, describe two ways to find out who is logged in on some of the other machines attached to your network.

3. Explain the client/server model. Give three examples of services on Linux systems that take advantage of this model.

4. A software implementation of chess was developed by GNU and is available for free. How can you use the Internet to find a copy and download it?

5. What is the difference between the World Wide Web and the Internet?

6. If you have access to the World Wide Web, answer the following questions.

a. Which browser do you use?

b. What is the URL of the author of this book's home page? How many links does it have?

c. Does your browser allow you to create bookmarks? If so, how do you create a bookmark? How can you delete one?

7. Give one advantage and two disadvantages of using a wireless network.

ADVANCED EXERCISES

8. Suppose the link between routers 1 and 2 is down in the Internet shown in Figure 10-1 on page 362. What happens if someone at site C sends a message to a user on a workstation attached to the Ethernet cable at site A? What happens if the router at site A is down? What does this tell you about designing network configurations?

9. If you have a class B network and want to divide it into subnets, each with 126 hosts, which subnet mask should you use? How many networks will be available? What are the four addresses (broadcast and network number) for the network starting at 131.204.18?

10. Suppose you have 300 hosts and want to have no more than 50 hosts per subnet. What size of address block should you request from your ISP? How many class C–equivalent addresses would you need? How many subnets would you have left over from your allocation?

11. a. On your system, find two daemons running that are not listed in this chapter and explain what purpose they serve.

b. Review which services/daemons are automatically started on your system, and consider which you might turn off. Are there any services/daemons in the list in Table 10-4 on page 386 that you would consider adding?

PART IV
SYSTEM ADMINISTRATION

11

SYSTEM ADMINISTRATION: CORE CONCEPTS

The job of a system administrator is to keep one or more systems in a useful and convenient state for users. On a Linux system, the administrator and user may both be you, with you and the computer being separated by only a few feet. Alternatively, the system administrator may be halfway around the world, supporting a network of systems, with you being one of thousands of users. On one hand, a system administrator can be one person who works part-time taking care of a system and perhaps is also a user of the system. On the other hand, several administrators can work together full-time to keep many systems running.

401

A well-maintained system

- Runs quickly enough so users do not get frustrated waiting for the system to respond or complete a task.

- Has enough storage to accommodate users' reasonable needs.

- Provides a working environment appropriate to each user's abilities and requirements.

- Is secure from malicious and accidental acts altering its performance or compromising the security of the data it holds and exchanges with other systems.

- Is backed up regularly, with recently backed-up files being readily available to users.

- Has recent copies of the software that users need to get their jobs done.

- Is easier to administer than a poorly maintained system.

In addition, a system administrator should be available to help users with all types of system-related problems—from logging in to obtaining and installing software updates to tracking down and fixing obscure network issues.

Part IV of this book breaks system administration into seven chapters:

- Chapter 11 covers the core concepts of system administration, including working with **root** (Superuser) privileges, system operation, the Ubuntu configuration tools and other useful utilities, general information about setting up and securing a server (including a section on DHCP), and PAM.

- Chapter 12 covers files, directories, and filesystems from an administrator's point of view.

- Chapter 13 covers installing software on the system, including how to use APT (aptitude), the Debian package (**dpkg**) management system, BitTorrent, and wget.

- Chapter 14 discusses how to set up local and remote printers that use the CUPS printing system.

- Chapter 15 explains how to rebuild the Linux kernel.

- Chapter 16 covers additional system administrator tasks and tools, including setting up users and groups, backing up files, scheduling tasks, printing system reports, and general problem solving.

- Chapter 17 goes into detail about how to set up a LAN, including setting up and configuring network hardware and configuring software.

Because Linux is readily configurable and runs on a wide variety of platforms (Sun SPARC, DEC/Compaq Alpha, Intel x86, AMD, PowerPC, and more), this chapter cannot discuss every system configuration or every action you might potentially have to take as a system administrator. Instead, this chapter seeks to familiarize you with the concepts you need to understand and the tools you will use to maintain an Ubuntu system. Where it is not possible to go into depth about a subject, the chapter provides references to other sources.

This chapter assumes that you are familiar with the following terms:

block device (page 1097)	*filesystem* (page 1108)	*root filesystem* (page 1130)
daemon (page 1104)	*fork* (page 1109)	*runlevel* (page 1130)
device (page 1105)	*kernel* (page 1116)	*signal* (page 1132)
device filename (page 1105)	*login shell* (page 1118)	*spawn* (page 1133)
disk partition (page 1105)	*mount* (page 1120)	*system console* (page 1136)
environment (page 1107)	*process* (page 1126)	*X server* (page 1141)

Terminology: single-user mode is changing to recovery mode

tip Linux is in transition. With the advent of the Upstart **init** daemon (page 416), what was called *single-user mode* Ubuntu now refers to as *recovery mode.* However, vestiges of the old terminology remain. For example, you type **single** at the end of the **grub** kernel line to bring a system up in recovery mode. This book uses these terms interchangeably.

RUNNING COMMANDS WITH root PRIVILEGES

Some commands can damage the filesystem or crash the operating system. Other commands can invade users' privacy or make the system less secure. To keep a Linux system up and running as well as secure, Ubuntu is configured not to permit ordinary users to execute some commands and access certain files. Linux provides several ways for a trusted user to execute these commands and access these files. The default username of the trusted user with these systemwide powers is **root**; a user with these privileges is also sometimes referred to as *Superuser.* As this section explains, Ubuntu enables specified ordinary users to run commands with **root** privileges while logged in as themselves.

A user running with **root** privileges has the following powers—and more:

- Some commands, such as those that add new users, partition hard drives, and change system configuration, can be executed only by a user with **root** privileges. Such a user can configure tools, such as sudo, to give specific users permission to perform tasks that are normally reserved for a user running with **root** privileges.

- Read, write, and execute file access and directory access permissions do not affect a user with **root** privileges. A user with **root** privileges can read from, write to, and execute all files, as well as examine and work in all directories.

- Some restrictions and safeguards that are built in to some commands do not apply to a user with **root** privileges. For example, a user with **root** privileges can change any user's password without knowing the old password.

Console security

security   Ubuntu Linux is not secure from a user at the console. Additional security measures, such as setting bootloader and BIOS passwords, can help secure the console. However, when a user has physical access to the hardware, as console users typically do, it is very difficult to secure a system from that user.

Least privilege

caution   When you are working on any computer system, but especially when you are working as the system administrator (with **root** privileges), perform any task using the least privilege possible. When you can perform a task logged in as an ordinary user, do so. When you must run a command with **root** privileges, do as much as you can as an ordinary user, use sudo so that you have **root** privileges, complete the part of the task that has to be done with **root** privileges, and revert to being an ordinary user as soon as you can. Because you are more likely to make a mistake when you are rushing, this concept becomes more important when you have less time to apply it.

When you are running with **root** privileges in a command-line environment, by convention the shell displays a special prompt to remind you of your status. By default, this prompt is (or ends with) a pound sign (#). You can gain or grant **root** privileges in a number of ways:

- When you bring the system up in recovery mode (page 428), you are logged in as the user named **root**.

- The sudo utility allows specified users to run selected commands with **root** privileges while they are logged in as themselves. You can set up sudo to allow certain users to perform specific tasks that require **root** privileges without granting them systemwide **root** privileges. See page 406 for more information on sudo.

- Some programs ask for *your* password when they start. If sudo is set up to give you **root** privileges, when you provide your password, the program runs with **root** privileges. When a program requests a password when it starts, you stop running as a privileged user when you quit using the program. This setup keeps you from remaining logged in with **root** privileges when you do not need or intend to be.

- Any user can create a *setuid* (set user ID) file. Setuid programs run on behalf of the owner of the file and have all the access privileges that the owner has. While you are running as a user with **root** privileges, you can change the permissions of a file owned by **root** to setuid. When an ordinary user executes a file that is owned by **root** and has setuid permissions, the program has *effective root privileges*. In other words, the program can do anything a user with **root** privileges can do that the program normally does. The user's privileges do not change. Thus, when the program finishes running, all user privileges are as they were before the program started. Setuid programs owned by **root** are both extremely powerful and extremely dangerous to system security, which is why a system contains very few of them. Examples of setuid programs that are owned by **root** include passwd, at, and crontab. For more information refer to "Setuid and Setgid Permissions" on page 204.

root-owned setuid programs are extremely dangerous

security   Because a **root**-owned setuid program allows someone who does not know the **root** password and cannot use sudo to gain **root** privileges, it is a tempting target for a malicious user. Also, programming errors that make normal programs crash can become **root** exploits in setuid programs. A system should have as few of these programs as necessary. You can disable setuid programs at the filesystem level by mounting a filesystem with the **nosuid** option (page 490). See page 437 for a command that lists all setuid files on the local system.

optional   The following techniques for gaining **root** privileges depend on unlocking the **root** account (setting up a **root** password) as explained on page 415.

- You can give an su (substitute user) command while you are logged in as yourself. When you then provide the **root** password, you will have **root** privileges. For more information refer to "su: Gives You Another User's Privileges" on page 415.

- Once the system is up and running in multiuser mode (page 431), you can log in as **root**. When you then supply the **root** password, you will be running with **root** privileges.

Some techniques limit how someone can log in as **root**. For example, PAM (page 461) controls the who, when, and how of logging in. The /etc/securetty file controls which terminals (ttys) a user can log in on as **root**. The /etc/security/access.conf file adds another dimension to login control (see the comments in the file for details).

Do not allow root access over the Internet

security   Prohibiting **root** logins using login over a network is the default policy of Ubuntu and is implemented by the PAM **securetty** module. The /etc/security/access.conf file must contain the names of all users and terminals/workstations that you want a user to be able to log in as **root**. Initially every line in **access.conf** is commented out.

You can, however, log in as **root** over a network using ssh (page 627). As shipped by Ubuntu, ssh does not follow the instructions in **securetty** or **access.conf**. In addition, in /etc/ssh/sshd_config, Ubuntu sets **PermitRootLogin** to **yes** to permit **root** to log in using ssh (page 644).

sudo: RUNNING A COMMAND WITH root PRIVILEGES

Classically a user gained **root** privileges by logging in as **root** or by giving an su (substitute user) command and providing the **root** password. When an ordinary user executed a privileged command in a graphical environment, the system would prompt for the **root** password. More recently the use of sudo (www.sudo.ws) has taken over these classic techniques of gaining **root** privileges.

There is a **root** account, but no **root** password

tip   As installed, Ubuntu locks the **root** account by not providing a **root** password. This setup prevents anyone from logging in to the **root** account (except when you bring the system up in recovery mode [page 428]). There is, however, a **root** account (a user with the username **root**—look at the first line in **/etc/passwd**). This account/user owns files (give the command **ls –l /bin**) and runs processes (give the command **ps –ef** and look at the left column of the output). The **root** account is critical to the functioning of an Ubuntu system.

The sudo utility enables you to run a command as though it had been run by a user logged in as **root**. This book uses the phrase "working with **root** privileges" to emphasize that, although you are not logged in as **root**, when you use sudo you have the powers of the **root** user.

Ubuntu strongly encourages the use of sudo. In fact, as shipped, Ubuntu locks the **root** account (there is no password) so you cannot use the classic techniques. There are many advantages of using sudo over using the **root** account for system administration:

- When you run sudo, it requests *your* password—not the **root** password— so you have to remember only one password.

- The sudo utility logs all commands it executes. This log can be useful for retracing your steps if you make a mistake and for system auditing.

- The sudo utility allows implementation of a finer-grained security policy than does the use of su and the **root** account. Using sudo, you can enable specific users to execute specific commands—something you cannot do with the classic **root** account setup.

- Using sudo makes it harder for a malicious user to gain access to a system. When there is an unlocked **root** account, a malicious user knows the username of the account she wants to crack before she starts. When the **root** account is locked, the user has to determine the username *and* the password to break into a system.

Some users question whether sudo is less secure than su. Because both rely on passwords, they share the same strengths and weaknesses. If the password is compromised, the system is compromised. However, if the password of a user who is allowed by sudo to do one task is compromised, the entire system may not be at risk. Thus, *if used properly,* the finer granularity of sudo's permissions structure *can* make it a more secure tool than su. Also, when sudo is used to invoke a single command, it is less likely that a user will be tempted to keep working with **root** privileges than if the user opens a **root** shell with su.

Run graphical programs using gksudo **not** sudo

caution   Use gksudo (or kdesu from KDE) instead of sudo when you run a graphical program that requires **root** privileges. Although both utilities run a program with **root** privileges, sudo uses your configuration files, whereas gksudo uses **root**'s configuration files. Most of the time this difference is not important, but sometimes it is critical. Some programs will not run when you call them with sudo. Using gksudo can prevent incorrect permissions from being applied to files related to the X Window System in your home directory. In a few cases, misapplying these permissions can prevent you from logging back in. In addition, you can use gksudo in a launcher (page 107) on the desktop or on a panel.

Using sudo may not always be the best, most secure way to set up a system. On a system used by a single user, there is not much difference between using sudo and carefully using su and a **root** password. In contrast, on a system with several users, and especially on a network of systems with central administration, sudo can be set up to be more secure than su. If you are a dyed-in-the-wool UNIX/Linux user who cannot get comfortable with sudo, it is easy enough to give the **root** account a password and use su. See page 415.

When you install Ubuntu, the first user you set up is included in the **admin** group. As installed, sudo is configured to allow members of the **admin** group to run with **root** privileges. Because there is no **root** password, initially the only way to perform privileged administrative tasks from the command line is for the first user to run them using sudo. Graphical programs call other programs, such as gksudo (see the adjacent tip), which in turn call sudo for authentication.

Timestamp   By default, sudo asks for *your* password (not the **root** password) the first time you run it. At that time, sudo sets your *timestamp*. After you supply a password, sudo will not prompt you again for a password for 15 minutes, based on your timestamp.

In the following example, Sam tries to set the system clock working as the user **sam**, a nonprivileged user. The date utility displays an error message followed by the expanded version of the date he entered. When he uses sudo to run date to set the system clock, sudo prompts him for his password, and the command succeeds.

```
$ date 10151620
date: cannot set date: Operation not permitted
Wed Oct 15 16:20:00 PDT 2008

$ sudo date 10151620
[sudo] password for sam:
Wed Oct 15 16:20:00 PDT 2008
```

Next Sam uses sudo to unmount a filesystem. Because he gives this command within 15 minutes of the previous sudo command, he does not need to supply a password:

```
$ sudo umount /music
$
```

Now Sam uses the **–l** option to check which commands sudo will allow him to run. Because he was the first user registered on the system (and is therefore a member of the **admin** group), he is allowed to run any command as any user.

```
$ sudo -l
User sam may run the following commands on this host:
    (ALL) ALL
```

Spawning a **root** shell
When you have several commands you need to run with **root** privileges, it may be easier to spawn a **root** shell, give the commands without having to type **sudo** in front of each one, and exit from the shell. This technique defeats some of the safeguards built in to sudo, so use it carefully and remember to return to a non**root** shell as soon as possible. (See the tip on least privilege on page 404.) Use the sudo **–i** option to spawn a **root** shell:

```
$ pwd
/home/sam
$ sudo -i
# id
uid=0(root) gid=0(root) groups=0(root)
# pwd
/root
# exit
$
```

In this example, sudo spawns a **root** shell, which displays a **#** prompt to remind you that you are running with **root** privileges. The id utility displays the identity of the user running the shell. The exit command (you can also use CONTROL-D) terminates the **root** shell, returning the user to his normal status and his former shell and prompt.

sudo's environment
The pwd builtin in the preceding example shows one aspect of the modified environment the **–i** option (page 409) creates. This option spawns a **root** login shell (a shell with the same environment as a user logging in as **root** would have) and executes **root**'s startup files (page 277). Before issuing the **sudo –i** command, the pwd builtin shows **/home/sam** as Sam's working directory; after the command it shows **/root**, **root**'s home directory, as the working directory. Use the **–s** option (page 409) to spawn a **root** shell without modifying the environment. When you call sudo without an option, it runs the command you specify in an unmodified environment. To demonstrate, the following example has sudo run pwd without an option. The working directory of a command run in this manner does not change.

```
$ pwd
/home/sam
$ sudo pwd
/home/sam
```

Redirecting output
The following command fails because, although the shell that sudo spawns executes ls with **root** privileges, the nonprivileged shell that the user is running redirects the output. The user's shell does not have permission to write to **/root**.

```
$ sudo ls > /root/ls.sam
-bash: /root/ls.sam: Permission denied
```

There are several ways around this problem. The easiest is to pass the whole command line to a shell running under sudo:

```
$ sudo bash -c 'ls > /root/ls.sam'
```

The bash –c option spawns a shell that executes the string following the option and then terminates. The sudo utility runs the spawned shell with **root** privileges. You can quote the string to prevent the nonprivileged shell from interpreting special characters. You can also spawn a **root** shell with **sudo –i**, execute the command, and exit from the privileged shell. (See the preceding section.)

optional   Another way to deal with the problem of redirecting output of a command run by sudo is to use tee (page 240):

```
$ ls | sudo tee /root/ls.sam
...
```

This command writes the output of ls to the file but also displays it. If you do not want to display the output, you can have the nonprivileged shell redirect the output to **/dev/null** (page 471). The next example uses this technique to do away with the screen output and uses the **–a** option to tee to append to the file instead of overwriting it:

```
$ ls | sudo tee -a /root/ls.sam > /dev/null
```

OPTIONS

You can use command-line options to control how sudo runs a command. Following is the syntax of an sudo command line:

sudo [options] [command]

where *options* is one or more options and *command* is the command you want to execute. Without the **–u** option, sudo runs *command* with **root** privileges. Some of the more common *options* follow; see the sudo man page for a complete list.

–b   (**background**)   Runs *command* in the background.

–i   (**initial login environment**)   Spawns the shell that is specified for **root** (or another user specified by **–u**) in **/etc/passwd**, running **root**'s (or the other user's) startup files, with some exceptions (e.g., **TERM** is not changed). Does not take a *command*.

–k   (**kill**)   Resets the timestamp (page 407) of the user running the command, which means the user must enter a password the next time she runs sudo.

–L   (**list defaults**)   Lists the parameters that you can set on a Defaults line (page 413) in the **sudoers** file. Does not take a *command*.

–l   (**list commands**)   Lists the commands the user who is running sudo is allowed to run on the local system. Does not take a *command*.

–s   (**shell**)   Spawns a new **root** (or another user specified by **–u**) shell as specified in the **/etc/passwd** file. Similar to **–i** but does not change the environment. Does not take a *command*.

–u *user*   Runs *command* with the privileges of *user*. Without this option sudo runs *command* with **root** privileges.

sudoers: CONFIGURING sudo

As installed, sudo is not as secure and robust as it can be if you configure it carefully. The sudo configuration file is **/etc/sudoers**. The best way to edit **sudoers** is to use visudo by giving this command: **sudo visudo**. The visudo utility locks, edits, and checks the grammar of the **sudoers** file. By default, visudo calls the nano editor. You can set the **VISUAL** environment variable to cause visudo to call vi with the following command:

```
$ export VISUAL=vi
```

Replace **vi** with the textual editor of your choice. Put this command in a startup file (page 277) to set this variable each time you log in.

Always use visudo to edit the sudoers file

caution   A syntax error in the **sudoers** file can prevent you from using sudo to gain **root** privileges. If you edit this file directly (without using visudo), you will not know that you introduced a syntax error until you find you cannot use sudo. The visudo utility checks the syntax of **sudoers** before it allows you to exit. If it finds an error, it gives you the choice of fixing the error, exiting without saving the changes to the file, or saving the changes and exiting. The last is usually a poor choice, so visudo marks the last choice with **(DANGER!)**.

In the **sudoers** file, comments, which start with a pound sign (#), can appear anywhere on a line. In addition to comments, this file holds two types of entries: aliases and user privilege specifications. Each of these entries occupies a line, which can be continued by terminating it with a backslash (\).

USER PRIVILEGE SPECIFICATIONS

The format of a line that specifies user privileges is as follows (the whitespace around the equal sign is optional):

> *user_list host_list = [(runas_list)] command_list*

- The *user_list* specifies the user(s) this specification line applies to. This list can contain usernames, groups (prefixed with %), and user aliases (next section).

- The *host_list* specifies the host(s) this specification line applies to. This list can contain one or more hostnames, IP addresses, or host aliases (discussed in the next section). You can use the builtin alias ALL to cause the line to apply to all systems that refer to this **sudoers** file.

- The *runas_list* specifies the user(s) the commands in the *command_list* can be run as when sudo is called with the **–u** option (page 409). This list can contain usernames, groups (prefixed with %), and runas aliases (discussed in the next section). Must be enclosed within parentheses. Without *runas_list*, sudo assumes **root**.

- The *command_list* specifies the utilities this specification line applies to. This list can contain names of utilities, names of directories holding utilities, and command aliases (discussed in the next section). All names must be absolute pathnames; directory names must end with a slash (/).

If you follow a name with two adjacent double quotation marks (" "), the user will not be able to specify any command-line arguments, including options. Alternatively, you can specify arguments, including wildcards, to limit the arguments a user is allowed to use.

Examples   The following user privilege specification allows Sam to use sudo to mount and unmount filesystems (run mount and umount with **root** privileges) on all systems (as specified by **ALL**) that refer to the **sudoers** file containing this specification:

```
sam     ALL=(root) /bin/mount, /bin/umount
```

The (**root**) *runas_list* is optional. If you omit it, sudo allows the user to run the commands in the *command_list* with **root** privileges. In the following example, Sam takes advantage of these permissions. He cannot run umount directly; instead, he must call sudo to run it.

```
$ whoami
sam
$ umount /music
umount: only root can unmount /dev/sdb7 from /music
$ sudo umount /music
[sudo] password for sam:
$
```

If you replace the line in **sudoers** described above with the following line, Sam is not allowed to unmount **/p03**, although he can still unmount any other filesystem and can mount any filesystem:

```
sam     ALL=(root) /bin/mount, /bin/umount, !/bin/umount /p03
```

The result of the preceding line in **sudoers** is shown below. The sudo utility does not prompt for a password because Sam has entered his password within the last 15 minutes.

```
$ sudo umount /p03
Sorry, user sam is not allowed to execute '/bin/umount /p03' as root on localhost.
```

The following line limits Sam to mounting and unmounting filesystems mounted on **/p01**, **/p02**, **/p03**, and **/p04**:

```
sam     ALL= /bin/mount /p0[1-4], /bin/umount /p0[1-4]
```

The following commands show the result:

```
$ sudo umount /music
Sorry, user sam is not allowed to execute '/bin/umount /music' as root on localhost.
$ sudo umount /p03
$
```

Default privileges for **admin** group

As shipped, the **sudoers** file contains the following lines:

```
# Members of the admin group may gain root privileges
%admin ALL=(ALL) ALL
```

This user privilege specification applies to all systems (as indicated by the **ALL** to the left of the equal sign). As the comment says, this line allows members of the **admin** group (specified by preceding the name of the group with a percent sign: **%admin**) to run any command (the rightmost **ALL**) as any user (the **ALL** within parentheses). When you call it without the **–u** option, the sudo utility runs the command you specify with **root** privileges, which is what sudo is used for most of the time.

If the following line were in **sudoers**, it would allow members of the **wheel** group to run any command as any user with one exception: They would not be allowed to run passwd to change the **root** password.

```
%wheel ALL=(ALL) ALL, !/usr/bin/passwd root
```

optional In the **%admin ALL=(ALL) ALL** line, if you replaced (**ALL**) with (**root**), or if you omitted (**ALL**), you would still be able to run any command with **root** privileges. You would not, however, be able to use the **–u** option to run a command as another user. Typically, when you can have **root** privileges, this limitation is not an issue. Working as a user other than yourself or **root** allows you to use the least privilege possible to accomplish a task, which is a good idea.

For example, if you are in the **admin** group, the default entry in the **sudoers** file allows you to give the following command to create and edit a file in Sam's home directory. Because you are working as Sam, he will own the file and be able to read from and write to it.

```
$ sudo -u sam vi ~sam/reminder
$ ls -l ~sam/reminder
-rw-r--r-- 1 sam sam 15 Mar  9 15:29 /home/sam/reminder
```

ALIASES

An alias enables you to rename and/or group users, hosts, or commands. Following is the format of an alias definition:

alias_type alias_name = alias_list

where *alias_type* is the type of alias (**User_Alias**, **Runas_Alias**, **Host_Alias**, **Cmnd_Alias**), *alias_name* is the name of the alias (by convention in all uppercase letters), and *alias_list* is a comma-separated list of one or more elements that make up the alias. Preceding an element of an alias with an exclamation point (**!**) negates it.

User_Alias   The *alias_list* for a user alias is the same as the *user_list* for a user privilege specification (discussed in the previous section). The following lines from a **sudoers** file define three user aliases: OFFICE, ADMIN, and ADMIN2. The *alias_list* that defines the first alias includes the usernames **mark**, **sam**, and **sls**; the second includes two usernames and members of the **admin** group; and the third includes all members of the **admin** group except Max.

```
User_Alias      OFFICE = mark, sam, sls
User_Alias      ADMIN = max, zach, %admin
User_Alias      ADMIN2 = %admin, !max
```

Runas_Alias   The *alias_list* for a runas alias is the same as the *runas_list* for a user privilege specification (discussed in the previous section). The following SM runas alias includes the usernames **sam** and **sls**:

```
Runas_Alias     SM = sam, sls
```

Host_Alias   Host aliases are meaningful only when the **sudoers** file is referenced by sudo running on more than one system. The *alias_list* for a host alias is the same as the *host_list* for a user privilege specification (discussed in the previous section). The following line defines the LCL alias to include the systems named **dog** and **plum**:

```
Host_Alias      LCL = dog, plum
```

If you want to use fully qualified hostnames (**hosta.example.com** instead of just **hosta**) in this list, you must set the **fqdn** flag (discussed in the next section), which can slow the performance of sudo.

Cmnd_Alias   The *alias_list* for a command alias is the same as the *command_list* for a user privilege specification (discussed in the previous section). The following command alias includes three files and, by including a directory (denoted by its trailing **/**), incorporates all the files in that directory:

```
Cmnd_Alias      BASIC = /bin/cat, /usr/bin/vi, /bin/df, /usr/local/safe/
```

Defaults (Options)

You can change configuration options from their default values by using the **Defaults** keyword. Most values in this list are flags that are implicitly Boolean (can either be on or off) or strings. You turn on a flag by naming it on a Defaults line, and you turn it off by preceding it with a **!**. The following line in the **sudoers** file would turn off the **lecture** and **fqdn** flags and turn on **tty_tickets**:

```
Defaults        !lecture,tty_tickets,!fqdn
```

This section lists some common flags; see the **sudoers** man page for a complete list.

env_reset   Causes sudo to reset the environment variables to contain the **LOGNAME, SHELL, USER, USERNAME,** and **SUDO_*** variables only. The default is on. See the **sudoers** man page for more information.

fqdn   (**fully qualified domain name**) Performs DNS lookups on *FQDNs* (page 1109) in the **sudoers** file. When this flag is set, you can use FQDNs in the **sudoers** file, but doing so may negatively affect sudo's performance, especially if DNS is not working. When this flag is set, you must use the local host's official DNS name, not an alias. If hostname returns an FQDN, you do not need to set this flag. The default is on.

insults   Displays mild, humorous insults when a user enters a wrong password. The default is off. See also **passwd_tries**.

lecture=*freq* Controls when sudo displays a reminder message before the password prompt. Possible values of *freq* are **never** (default), **once**, and **always**. Specifying **!lecture** is the same as specifying a *freq* of **never**.

mailsub=*subj* (**mail subject**) Changes the default email subject for warning and error messages from the default ✱✱✱ **SECURITY information for %h** ✱✱✱ to *subj*. The sudo utility expands **%h** within *subj* to the local system's hostname. Place *subj* between quotation marks if it contains shell special characters (page 146).

mailto=*eadd* Sends sudo warning and error messages to *eadd* (an email address; the default is **root**). Place *eadd* between quotation marks if it contains shell special characters (page 146).

mail_always Sends email to the **mailto** user each time a user runs sudo. The default is off.

mail_badpass Sends email to the **mailto** user when a user enters an incorrect password while running sudo. The default is off.

mail_no_host Sends email to the **mailto** user when a user whose username is in the **sudoers** file but who does not have permission to run commands on the local host runs sudo. The default is off.

mail_no_perms Sends email to the **mailto** user when a user whose username is in the **sudoers** file but who does not have permission to run the requested command runs sudo. The default is off.

mail_no_user Sends email to the **mailto** user when a user whose username is not in the **sudoers** file runs sudo. The default is on.

passwd_tries=*num*

The *num* is the number of times the user can enter an incorrect password in response to the sudo password prompt before sudo quits. The default is 3. See also **insults** and **lecture**.

rootpw Causes sudo to accept only the **root** password in response to its prompt. Because sudo issues the same prompt whether it is asking for your password or the **root** password, turning this flag on may confuse users. ***Do not turn on this flag if you have not unlocked the root account*** (page 415) as you will not be able to use sudo. To fix this problem, bring the system up in recovery mode (page 428) and turn off (remove) this flag. The default is off, causing sudo to prompt for the password of the user running sudo. See the adjacent tip.

Using the **root** password in place of your password

tip   If you have set up a **root** password (page 415), you can cause graphical programs that require a password to require the **root** password in place of the password of the user who is running the program by turning on **rootpw**. The programs will continue to ask for *your* password, but will accept only the **root** password. Making this change causes an Ubuntu system to use the **root** password in a manner similar to the way some other distributions use this password.

shell_noargs Causes sudo, when called without any arguments, to spawn a **root** shell without changing the environment. The default is off. This option is the same as the sudo –s option.

timestamp_timeout=*mins*

The *mins* is the number of minutes that the sudo timestamp (page 407) is valid. The default is 15; set *mins* to **–1** to cause the timestamp to be valid forever.

umask=*val* The *val* is the umask (page 442) that sudo uses to run the command that the user specifies. Set *val* to 0777 to preserve the user's umask value. The default is 0022.

UNLOCKING THE root ACCOUNT (ASSIGNING A PASSWORD TO root)

Except for a few instances, there is no need to unlock the **root** account on an Ubuntu system and Ubuntu suggests that you do not do so. The following command unlocks the **root** account by assigning a password to it:

```
$ sudo passwd root
Enter new UNIX password:
Retype new UNIX password:
passwd: password updated successfully
```

Relocking the **root** account If you decide you want to lock the **root** account after unlocking it, give the command **sudo passwd –l root**. You can unlock it again with the preceding command.

su: GIVES YOU ANOTHER USER'S PRIVILEGES

To use su to gain **root** privileges, you must unlock the **root** account (as discussed in the preceding section).

The su (substitute user) utility can spawn a shell or execute a program with the identity and privileges of a specified user. Follow **su** on the command line with the name of a user; if you are working with **root** privileges or if you know the user's password, you will then take on the identity of that user. When you give an su command without an argument, su defaults to spawning a shell with **root** privileges (you have to know the **root** password).

When you give an su command to work as **root**, su spawns a new shell, which displays the # prompt. You can return to your normal status (and your former shell and prompt) by terminating this shell: Press CONTROL-D or give an exit command. Giving an su command by itself changes your user and group IDs but makes minimal changes to the environment. For example, **PATH** has the same value as it did before you gave the su command. When you give the command **su –** (you can use **–l** or **––login** in place of the hyphen), you get a **root** login shell: It is as though you logged in as **root**. Not only do the shell's user and group IDs match those of **root**, but the environment is identical to that of **root**. The login shell executes the appropriate startup files (page 277) before displaying a prompt.

The id utility displays the changes in your user and group IDs and in the groups you are associated with:

```
$ id
uid=1002(sam) gid=1002(sam) groups=117(admin),1002(sam)
$ su
Password:
# id
uid=0(root) gid=0(root) groups=0(root)
```

You can use su with the −c option to run a command line with **root** privileges, returning to the original shell when the command finishes executing. The following example first shows that a user is not permitted to kill (page 438) a process. With the use of **su −c** and the **root** password, however, the user is permitted to kill the process. The quotation marks are necessary because **su −c** takes its command as a single argument.

```
$ kill -15 4982
-bash: kill: (4982) - Operation not permitted
$ su -c "kill -15 4982"
Password:
$
```

Superuser, **PATH**, and security

security   The fewer directories you keep in **PATH** when you are working as **root**, the less likely you will be to execute an untrusted program as **root**. *Never include the working directory (as . or : : anywhere in **PATH**, or : as the last element of **PATH**).* For more information refer to "PATH: Where the Shell Looks for Programs" on page 303.

THE UPSTART EVENT-BASED init DAEMON

Because the traditional System V **init** daemon (SysVinit) does not deal well with modern hardware, including hotplug (page 484) devices, USB hard and flash drives, and network-mounted filesystems, Ubuntu replaced it with the Upstart **init** daemon (upstart.ubuntu.com and upstart.ubuntu.com/wiki).

Several other replacements for SysVinit are also available. One of the most prominent, **initng** (www.initng.org), is available for Debian and runs on Ubuntu. In addition, Solaris uses SMF (Service Management Facility) and MacOS uses **launchd**. Over time, Ubuntu will likely come to incorporate features of each of these systems into Upstart.

The runlevel-based SysVinit daemon (**sysvinit** package) uses runlevels (single-user, multiuser, and more) and links from the **/etc/rc?.d** directories to the init scripts in **/etc/init.d** to start and stop system services. The event-based Upstart **init** daemon (**upstart** package) uses events to start and stop system services. With the Feisty release, Ubuntu switched to the Upstart **init** daemon and began the transition from the SysVinit setup to the Upstart setup. This section discusses Upstart and the parts of SysVinit that remain: the **/etc/rc?.d** and **/etc/init.d** directories and the concept of runlevels. See the tip about terminology on page 403.

The Upstart **init** daemon is event-based and runs specified programs when something on the system changes. These programs, which are frequently scripts, start and stop services. This setup is similar in concept to the links to init scripts that SysVinit calls as a system enters runlevels, except Upstart is more flexible. Instead of starting and stopping services only when the runlevel changes, Upstart can start and stop services upon receiving information that something on the system has changed. Such a change is called an *event*. For example, Upstart can take action when it learns from udev (page 484) that a filesystem, printer, or other device has been added or removed from the running system. It can also start and stop services when the system is brought up, when the system is shut down, or when a job changes state.

Future of Upstart   Changing from SysVinit to Upstart involves many parts of the Linux system. To make the switch smoothly and to introduce as few errors as possible, the Upstart team elected to make the transition over several releases.

Ubuntu started using the Upstart **init** daemon in Feisty. Over time, Ubuntu will move away from the SysVinit setup and toward the cleaner, more flexible Upstart setup. As more system services are put under the control of Upstart, entries in the **/etc/event.d** directory (see the tip on page 423) will replace the contents of the **/etc/init.d** and **/etc/rc?.d** directories. Runlevels will no longer be a formal feature of Ubuntu, although they will be maintained for compatibility with third-party software. Eventually Upstart will also replace **crond**.

SOFTWARE PACKAGES

The Upstart system comprises five packages, all of which are installed by default:

- **upstart**—Provides the Upstart **init** daemon and initctl utility.

- **upstart-logd**—Provides the **logd** daemon and the job definition file for the **logd** service.

- **upstart-compat-sysv**—Provides job definition files for the rc✳ tasks as well as the reboot, runlevel, shutdown, and telinit utilities that provide compatibility with SysVinit.

- **startup-tasks**—Provides job definition files for system startup tasks.

- **system-services**—Provides job definition files for **tty** services.

DEFINITIONS

Events   An *event* is a change in state that **init** can be informed of. Almost any change in state—either internal or external to the system—can trigger an event. For example, the boot loader triggers the **startup** event, the system entering runlevel 2 triggers the **runlevel 2** event, and a filesystem being mounted triggers the **path-mounted** event. Removing and installing a hotplug (page 484) or USB device (such as a printer) can trigger an event. You can also trigger an event manually by using the initctl **emit** command (page 420).

Jobs   A *job* is a series of instructions that **init** reads. The instructions typically include a program (binary file or shell script) and the name of an event. The Upstart **init** daemon runs the program when the event is triggered. You can run and stop a job manually using the initctl **start** and **stop** commands, respectively (page 420). Jobs are divided into tasks and services.

Tasks   A *task* is a job that performs its work and returns to a waiting state when it is done.

Services   A *service* is a job that does not normally terminate by itself. For example, the **logd** daemon and the gettys (page 422) are implemented as services. The **init** daemon monitors each service, restarting the service if it fails and killing the service when it is stopped manually or by an event.

Job definition files   The **/etc/event.d** directory holds *job definition files* (files defining the jobs that the Upstart **init** daemon runs). Initially this directory is populated by Upstart software packages (page 417). With Ubuntu releases following Feisty, installing some services will add a file to this directory to control the service, replacing the files that installing a service had placed in the **/etc/rc?.d** and **/etc/init.d** directories.

init is a state machine   At its core, the Upstart **init** daemon is a state machine. It keeps track of the state of jobs and, as events are triggered, tracks jobs as they change states. When **init** tracks a job from one state to another, it may execute the job's commands or terminate the job.

Runlevel emulation   The System V **init** daemon used changes in runlevels (page 426) to determine when to start and stop processes. Ubuntu systems, which use the Upstart **init** daemon, have no concept of runlevels. To ease migration from a runlevel-based system to an event-based system, and to provide compatibility with software intended for other distributions, Ubuntu emulates runlevels using Upstart.

The **rc?** jobs, which are defined by the **/etc/event.d/rc?** files, run the **/etc/init.d/rc** script. This script runs the init scripts in **/etc/init.d** from the links in the **/etc/rc?.d** directories, emulating the functionality of these links under SysVinit. The **rc?** jobs run these scripts as the system enters a runlevel; they take no action when the system leaves a runlevel. See page 421 for a discussion of the **rc2** job and page 423 for information on init scripts. Upstart implements the runlevel (page 426) and telinit (page 426) utilities to provide compatibility with SysVinit systems.

initctl   The initctl (**init** control) utility allows a system administrator working with **root** privileges to communicate with the Upstart **init** daemon. This utility can start, stop, and report on jobs. For example, the initctl **list** command lists jobs and their state:

```
$ sudo initctl list
control-alt-delete (stop) waiting
last-good-boot (stop) waiting
logd (stop) waiting
rc-default (stop) waiting
rc0 (stop) waiting
...
tty5 (start) running, process 4720
tty6 (start) running, process 4727
```

See the initctl man page and the examples in this section for more information. You can give the command **initctl help** (no hyphens before **help**) to display a list of initctl commands. Alternatively, you can give the following command to display more information about the **list** command:

```
$ initctl list --help
Usage: initctl list [OPTION]...
List known jobs.
```

```
Options:
      --show-ids              show job ids, as well as names
  -p, --pid=PID               destination process
  -q, --quiet                 reduce output to errors only
  -v, --verbose               increase output ...
      --help                  display this help and exit
      --version               output version information and exit
```

```
Report bugs to <upstart-devel@lists.ubuntu.com>
```

Replace **list** with the initctl command you want more information about. The start, stop, and status utilities are links to initctl that run the initctl commands they are named for.

JOBS

Each file in the **/etc/event.d** directory defines a job and usually has at least an event and a command. When the event is triggered, **init** executes the command. This section describes examples of both administrator-defined jobs and jobs installed with the Upstart packages.

ADMINISTRATOR-DEFINED JOBS

mudat example The following administrator-defined job uses the **exec** keyword to execute a shell command. You can also use this keyword to execute a shell script stored in a file or a binary executable file.

```
$ cat /etc/event.d/mudat
start on runlevel 2
exec echo "Entering multiuser mode on " $(date) > /tmp/mudat.out
```

This file defines a task: It runs the echo shell command when the system enters multiuser mode (runlevel 2). This command writes a message that includes the time and date to **/tmp/mudat.out**. The shell uses command substitution (page 346) to execute the date utility. After this job runs to completion, the **mudat** task stops and enters a wait state. In the next example, the cat utility shows the contents of the **/tmp/mudat.out** file and the initctl **list** command reports on this task (the status utility displays the same information):

```
$ cat /tmp/mudat.out
Entering multiuser mode on  Tue Jul 15 17:34:39 PDT 2008
```

```
$ sudo initctl list mudat
mudat (stop) waiting
```

If the **exec** command line contains shell special characters (page 146), **init** executes **/bin/sh** (a link to dash [page 276]) and passes the command line to the shell. Otherwise, **exec** executes the command line directly. To run multiple shell commands, either use **exec** to run a shell script stored in a file or use **script...end script** (discussed next).

The Upstart **init** daemon can monitor only jobs (services) whose programs are executed using **exec**. It cannot monitor jobs run using **script...end script**. Put another way, *services* require the use of **exec** while *tasks* can use either method to run a program.

myjob example   You can also define an event and set up a job that is triggered by that event. The **myjob** job definition file defines a job that is triggered by the **hithere** event:

```
$ cat /etc/event.d/myjob
start on hithere
script
    echo "Hi there, here I am!" > /tmp/myjob.out
    date >> /tmp/myjob.out
    end script
```

The **myjob** file shows another way of executing commands: It includes two command lines between the **script** and **end script** keywords. These keywords always cause **init** to execute **/bin/sh**. These commands write a message and the date to the **/tmp/myjob.out** file. You can use the **emit** initctl command to trigger the job. Following, **init** displays the stages **myjob** goes through when you trigger it:

initctl **emit**
```
$ sudo initctl emit hithere
hithere
myjob (start) waiting
myjob (start) starting
myjob (start) pre-start
myjob (start) spawned, process 6064
myjob (start) post-start, (main) process 6064
myjob (start) running, process 6064
myjob (stop) running
myjob (stop) stopping
myjob (stop) killed
myjob (stop) post-stop
myjob (stop) waiting

$ cat /tmp/myjob.out
Hi there, here I am!
Sat Jul 12 20:19:13 PDT 2008

$ sudo initctl list myjob
myjob (stop) waiting
```

initctl **start** and **stop**   In the preceding example, cat shows the output that **myjob** generates and initctl displays the status of the job. You can run the same job with the command **initctl start myjob** (or just **start myjob**). The initctl **start** command is useful when you want to run a job without triggering an event. For example, you can use the command **initctl start mudat** to run the **mudat** job from the previous example without triggering the **runlevel 2** event.

JOB DEFINITION FILES IN /etc/event.d

As Ubuntu transitions from SysVinit to Upstart **init**, more jobs will be defined in the **/etc/event.d** directory. This section describes some of the jobs that the Upstart packages (page 417) put in this directory.

optional **SPECIFYING EVENTS WITH ARGUMENTS**

The telinit and shutdown utilities emit **runlevel** events that include arguments. For example, **shutdown** emits **runlevel 0**, and **telinit 2** emits **runlevel 2**. You can match these events within a job definition using the following syntax:

start|stop on event [arg]

where *event* is an event such as **runlevel** and *arg* is an optional argument. To stop a job when the system enters runlevel 2, specify **stop on runlevel 2**. You can also specify **runlevel [235]** to match runlevels 2, 3, and 5 or **runlevel [!2]** to match any runlevel except 2.

Event arguments Although Upstart ignores additional arguments in an event, additional arguments in an event name within a job definition file must exist in the event. For example, **runlevel** (no argument) in a job definition file matches all **runlevel** events (regardless of arguments) whereas **runlevel S arg2** does not match any **runlevel** event because the **runlevel** event takes only one argument.

rc2 task The **/etc/event.d/rc2** job definition file defines the **rc2** task, which is similar to the other **rc***n* tasks. The **rc2** task is started when the system enters multiuser mode (the event is named **runlevel 2**); it is stopped when the system enters any runlevel other than runlevel 2 (**runlevel [!2]**). The first part of the script calls the runlevel utility (page 426), which makes the system appear to be in runlevel 2 (there are no real runlevels) and assigns values to two variables. The real work is done by the **exec** command, which runs the **/etc/init.d/rc** script with an argument of **2**. This script calls the links in the **/etc/rc***n***.d** directory that correspond to its argument. Thus the **rc2** task runs the init scripts that the links in the **/etc/rc2.d** directory point to.

```
$ cat /etc/event.d/rc2
# rc2 - runlevel 2 compatibility
#
# This task runs the old sysv-rc runlevel 2 ("multi-user") scripts.  It
# is usually started by the telinit compatibility wrapper.

start on runlevel 2

stop on runlevel [!2]

console output
script
    set $(runlevel --set 2 || true)
    if [ "$1" != "unknown" ]; then
        PREVLEVEL=$1
        RUNLEVEL=$2
        export PREVLEVEL RUNLEVEL
    fi

    exec /etc/init.d/rc 2
end script
```

tty services Following is the job definition file for the service that starts and monitors the getty process on **tty1**:

```
$ cat /etc/event.d/tty1
# tty1 - getty
#
# This service maintains a getty on tty1 from the point the system is
# started until it is shut down again.

start on stopped rc2
start on stopped rc3
start on stopped rc4
start on stopped rc5

stop on runlevel 0
stop on runlevel 1
stop on runlevel 6

respawn
exec /sbin/getty 38400 tty1
```

This service starts the getty process when any of the events **runlevel 2** through **runlevel 5** are triggered (i.e., when the system enters multiuser mode) and stops when any of the events **runlevel 0**, **runlevel 1**, or **runlevel 6** is triggered (i.e., when the system is shut down, enters single-user mode, or is rebooted). The **respawn** keyword tells **init** to restart the job if it terminates, and **exec** runs a getty process on tty1 at 38,400 baud. The initctl utility reports that the **tty1** service has started and is running as process 4747; ps reports on the process:

```
$ sudo initctl list tty1
tty1 (start) running, process 4747
$ ps -ef | grep 4747
root      4747     1  0 Jul02 tty1     00:00:00 /sbin/getty 38400 tty1
```

control-alt-del task See page 434 for a discussion of the **control-alt-del** task that you can use to bring the system down.

rc-default task and inittab Under SysVinit, the **initdefault** entry in the **/etc/inittab** file tells **init** which runlevel (page 426) to bring the system to when it comes up. Ubuntu does not include an **inittab** file and, by default, the Upstart **init** daemon (using the **rc-default** task) boots the system to multiuser mode (runlevel 2, the default runlevel). If you want the system to boot to a different runlevel, create an **inittab** file. The following file causes the system to boot to single-user mode (runlevel S; see the tip on page 427):

```
$ cat /etc/inittab
:id:S:initdefault:
```

When the system comes up in single-user (recovery) mode, if the **root** account on the system is unlocked (page 415), **init** requests the **root** password before displaying the **root** prompt. Otherwise it displays the **root** prompt without requesting a password.

Never set the system to boot to runlevel 0 or 6, as it will not come up properly. To boot to multiuser mode (runlevel 2), remove the **inittab** file if it exists or create the **inittab** file shown in the example and replace the **S** with a **2**.

SYSVINIT (rc) SCRIPTS: START AND STOP SYSTEM SERVICES

rc scripts The init (initialization) scripts, also called rc (run command) scripts, are shell scripts located in the **/etc/init.d** directory. They are run via symbolic links in the **/etc/rc*n*.d** directories, where *n* is the runlevel the system is entering.

Most of the files in the /etc/rc*n*.d and /etc/init.d directories will go away

tip As explained on page 418, Ubuntu emulates runlevels using Upstart to aid migration and provide compatibility with software for other distributions. This section explains how init scripts work with (emulated) runlevels to control system services. The **/etc/rc*n*.d** and the **/etc/init.d** directories described in this section will largely be empty after a few more releases, the links in these directories having been replaced by job control files in **/etc/event.d** (page 418).

The **/etc/rc*n*.d** directories contain scripts whose names begin with **K** (**K19cupsys**, **K20dhcp**, **K74bluetooth**, and so on) and scripts whose names begin with **S** (**S15bind9**, **S18nis**, **S65firestarter**, and so on). When entering a new runlevel, each **K** (kill) script is executed with an argument of **stop**, and then each **S** (start) script is executed with an argument of **start**. Each of the **K** files is run in numerical order. The **S** files are run in similar fashion. This setup allows the person who sets up these files to control which services are stopped and which are started, and in what order, whenever the system enters a given runlevel. Using scripts with **start** and **stop** arguments promotes flexibility because it allows one script to both start and kill a process, depending on which argument it is called with.

To customize system initialization, you can add shell scripts to the **/etc/init.d** directory and place links to these files in the **/etc/rc*n*.d** directories (although in practice it is best to use **sysv-rc-conf** [discussed next] to create the links). The following example shows several links to the **samba** init script. These links are called to run the **samba** init script to start or stop the **nmbd** and **smbd** daemons at various runlevels:

```
$ ls -l /etc/rc?.d/*samba*
lrwxrwxrwx 1 root root 15 May 17 10:51 /etc/rc0.d/K19samba -> ../init.d/samba
lrwxrwxrwx 1 root root 15 May 17 10:51 /etc/rc1.d/K19samba -> ../init.d/samba
lrwxrwxrwx 1 root root 15 May 17 10:51 /etc/rc2.d/S20samba -> ../init.d/samba
lrwxrwxrwx 1 root root 15 May 17 10:51 /etc/rc3.d/S20samba -> ../init.d/samba
lrwxrwxrwx 1 root root 15 May 17 10:51 /etc/rc4.d/S20samba -> ../init.d/samba
lrwxrwxrwx 1 root root 15 May 17 10:51 /etc/rc5.d/S20samba -> ../init.d/samba
lrwxrwxrwx 1 root root 15 May 17 10:51 /etc/rc6.d/K19samba -> ../init.d/samba
```

Each link in **/etc/rc*n*.d** points to a file in **/etc/init.d**. For example, the file **/etc/rc2.d/S20samba** is a link to the file named **samba** in **/etc/init.d**. (The numbers in the filenames of the links in the **/etc/rc*n*.d** directories may change from one release of Ubuntu to the next, but the scripts in **/etc/init.d** always have the same names.) The names of files in the **init.d** directory are functional. Thus, when you want to turn NFS services on or off, you use the **nfs-kernel-server** script. When you want to turn basic network services on or off, you run the **networking** script. The **cupsys** script controls the printer daemon. Each script takes an argument of **stop** or **start**, depending on what you want to do. Some scripts also take other arguments, such as **restart, reload,** and **status**. Run a script without an argument to display a usage message indicating which arguments it accepts.

Following are three examples of calls to init scripts:

```
$ sudo /etc/init.d/nfs-kernel-server stop
$ sudo /etc/init.d/networking start
$ sudo /etc/init.d/networking restart
```

The first example stops all NFS server processes (processes related to serving filesystems over the network). The second example starts all processes related to basic network services. The third example stops and then restarts these same processes.

/etc/rc.local   The **/etc/rc.local** file is executed after the other init scripts when the system boots. Put commands that customize the system in **rc.local**. Although you can add any commands you like to **rc.local**, it is best to run them in the background; that way if they hang, they will not stop the boot process.

sysv-rc-conf: CONFIGURES SERVICES

The sysv-rc-conf utility (**sysv-rc-conf** package) makes it easier for a system administrator to maintain the **/etc/rc***n***.d** directory hierarchy. This utility can add, remove, and list startup information for system services. You might also want to try the graphical boot-up manager, bum (**bum** package), which this book does not cover.

You can run sysv-rc-conf in pseudographical or textual mode. In pseudographical mode, it makes changes to configuration files as you enter the changes and can also start and stop services. For more information on this mode, see the sysv-rc-conf man page or run sysv-rc-conf without any arguments and give the command **h**. This section discusses using sysv-rc-conf in textual mode in which it changes the configuration only—it does not change the current state of any service. Give the following command to see a the list of services:

```
$ sudo sysv-rc-conf --list
NetworkManag 2:on        3:on    4:on    5:on
acpi-support 1:off       2:on    3:on    4:on    5:on
acpid        1:off       2:on    3:on    4:on    5:on
alsa-utils   0:off       6:off
anacron      1:off       2:on    3:on    4:on    5:on
apmd         0:off       1:off   2:on    3:on    4:on    5:on    6:off
apparmor     S:on
apport       0:off       1:off   2:on    3:on    4:on    5:on    6:off
atd          1:off       2:on    3:on    4:on    5:on
...
```

All services that run their own daemons are listed, one to a line, followed by their configured state for each runlevel. If a runlevel is missing, it means that there is no entry for that service in the corresponding file in the **/etc/rcn.d** directory. You can check how a specific daemon is configured by adding its name to the previous command:

```
$ sudo sysv-rc-conf --list ssh
ssh             1:off       2:on      3:on      4:on      5:on
```

The name of the init script is not always the same as name of the daemon it runs

tip The adjacent examples show that the **ssh** init script controls the **sshd** daemon. You can find the name of the script that controls a daemon by listing the contents of the **/etc/init.d** directory and searching for a filename that is similar to the name or function of the daemon you want to work with. For example, the **/etc/init.d/networking** script controls the networking daemons.

Frequently, the first few lines of a script identify the daemon it controls. In the following example, a comment explains what the **ssh** init script does and the line that starts with **test** checks whether the **sshd** file, which runs the **sshd** daemon, exists on the system:

```
$ cat /etc/init.d/ssh
#! /bin/sh
...
set -e

# /etc/init.d/ssh: start and stop the OpenBSD "secure shell(tm)" daemon

test -x /usr/sbin/sshd || exit 0
...
```

In the next example, sysv-rc-conf configures the **/etc/rcn.d** directories so that **sshd** (the OpenSSH daemon) is off in runlevels 2, 3, 4, and 5 and then confirms the change. To make changes, you must work with **root** privileges:

```
$ sudo sysv-rc-conf --level 2345 ssh off
$ sudo sysv-rc-conf --list ssh
ssh             1:off       2:off     3:off     4:off     5:off
```

For convenience, you can omit the **--level 2345** arguments. When you specify an init script and **on** or **off**, sysv-rc-conf defaults to runlevels 2, 3, 4, and 5. The following command is equivalent to the first of the preceding commands:

```
$ sudo sysv-rc-conf ssh off
```

The ps utility confirms that even though sysv-rc-conf set things up so **sshd** would be off in all runlevels, it is still running. The sysv-rc-conf utility did not shut down **sshd**.

```
$ ps -ef | grep sshd
root      5169     1   0 Mar12 ?        00:00:00 /usr/sbin/sshd
zach     11545  5749   0 19:30 pts/2    00:00:00 grep sshd
```

With the preceding changes, when you reboot the system, **sshd** will not start. You can stop it more easily using the **ssh** init script:

```
$ sudo /etc/init.d/ssh stop
 * Stopping OpenBSD Secure Shell server...                        [ OK ]
$ ps -ef | grep sshd
root     11740  8840   0 19:33 pts/1    00:00:00 grep sshd
```

SYSTEM OPERATION

This section covers the basics of how the system functions and can help you make intelligent decisions as a system administrator. It does not examine every aspect of system administration in the depth necessary to set up or modify all system functions. Instead, it provides a guide to bringing a system up and keeping it running from day to day.

RUNLEVELS

With the introduction of Upstart in the Feisty release of Ubuntu, true runlevels disappeared from the system. As a transitional tool, runlevels were replaced with a structure that runs under Upstart and emulates runlevels (page 418). Table 11-1 lists these pseudorunlevels as they exist under Upstart.

Table 11-1   Pseudorunlevels

Number	Name/function
0	Brings the system down
1	Brings the system to single-user (**S**, recovery) mode
S	Single-user (recovery) mode, textual login, few system services running
2	Multiuser mode, graphical login, all scheduled system services running
3, **4**, **5**	Multiuser mode, graphical login, all scheduled system services running (for system customization, runlevels 2–5 are identical)
6	Reboots the system

Default runlevel   By default, Ubuntu systems boot to multiuser mode (runlevel 2). See "**rc-default task** and **inittab**" on page 422 for instructions on how to change this default.

runlevel   The runlevel utility displays the previous and current runlevels. This utility is a transitional tool; it provides compatibility with SysVinit. In the following example, the N indicates that the system does not know what the previous runlevel was and the **2** indicates that the system is in multiuser mode.

```
$ runlevel
N 2
```

telinit   The telinit utility allows a user with **root** privileges to bring the system down, reboot the system, or change between recovery (single-user) and multiuser modes. The telinit utility is a transitional tool; it provides compatibility with SysVinit. On a system running Upstart, this utility emits a runlevel event based on its argument. The format of a telinit command is

*telinit **runlevel***

where ***runlevel*** is one of the pseudorunlevels described in Table 11-1.

Recovery mode and the **root** password
When the system enters recovery (single-user) mode, if the **root** account is unlocked (page 415), **init** requests the **root** password before displaying the **root** prompt. Otherwise it displays the **root** prompt without requesting a password. When the system enters multiuser mode, it displays a graphical login screen.

Do not change runlevels directly into runlevel S

caution
Using telinit to request the system change to runlevel 1 brings the system first to runlevel 1, where appropriate system processes (running system services) are killed, and then automatically to runlevel S. Changing directly to runlevel S puts the system into runlevel S but does not kill any processes first; it is usually a poor idea.

The Upstart **init** daemon consults **/etc/inittab** (page 422) only when the system is booting. At that time there are no processes left running from a previous runlevel, so there is no issue with going directly to runlevel S.

BOOTING THE SYSTEM

Booting a system is the process of reading the Linux *kernel* (page 1116) into system memory and starting it running. Refer to "grub: The Linux Boot Loader" on page 567 for more information on the initial steps of bringing a system up.

List the kernel boot messages

tip
To save a list of kernel boot messages, run dmesg immediately after booting the system and logging in:

```
$ dmesg > dmesg.boot
```

This command saves the kernel messages in a file named **dmesg.boot**. This list can be educational. It can also be useful when you are having a problem with the boot process. For more information see page 575.

init daemon
As the last step of the boot procedure, Linux starts the Upstart **init** daemon (page 416) as PID number 1. The **init** daemon is the first genuine process to run after booting and is the parent of all system processes. (That is why when you kill process 1 while you are working with **root** privileges, the system dies.)

Once **init** is running, the **startup** event triggers the **rcS** task, which stops when the system enters any runlevel. The **rc-default** task starts when **rcS** stops. Based on the contents of **/etc/inittab** (page 422) or the absence of this file, **rc-default** either

- Executes telinit with an argument of S, which triggers **rcS-sulogin** and brings the system to recovery (single-user) mode, or

- Executes telinit with an argument of 2, which triggers **rc2** (page 421) and brings the system to multiuser mode.

Reinstalling the MBR
If the Master Boot Record (MBR) gets overwritten, the system will not boot into Linux and you need to rewrite the MBR. See page 574 for details.

RECOVERY (SINGLE-USER) MODE

When the system is in recovery (single-user) mode, only the system console is enabled. You can run programs from the console in single-user mode as you would from any terminal in multiuser mode. The differences are twofold: You are working in textual mode so you cannot run graphical programs and few of the system daemons are running. All filesystems are mounted per **/etc/fstab** (page 492).

When you boot the system to recovery mode, the **init** daemon runs the init scripts in **/etc/rcS.d** as part of single-user initialization (see the tip on page 427). See the next sections for instructions on booting a system to recovery mode. When you bring a running system down to recovery mode (page 435), the **init** daemon runs the init scripts in **/etc/rc1.d** and **/etc/rcS.d**.

With the system in recovery mode, you can perform system maintenance that requires filesystems to be unmounted or that requires just a quiet system—no one except you using it, so that no user programs interfere with disk maintenance and backup programs. The classical UNIX term for this state is *quiescent*. You can often boot to recovery mode when the system will not boot normally, allowing you to change or replace configuration files, check and repair partitions using fsck (page 494), rewrite boot information (page 574), and more.

BOOTING THE SYSTEM INTO RECOVERY (SINGLE-USER) MODE

You can bring a system up in recovery mode by booting from the hard drive or from an installation CD/DVD. The Alternate and Server CDs make this task easy. Either way, you must instruct grub to bring the system to single-user mode.

BOOTING TO RECOVERY MODE FROM A HARD DRIVE

Displaying the grub menu   The first step in bringing a system up in single-user mode from the hard disk is to display the grub menu. Boot the system normally (turn on the power or reboot it). The grub menu will be hidden or displayed.

Hidden menu   If the grub menu is hidden, grub displays

```
GRUB loading, please wait...
press 'ESC' to enter the menu... 10
```

You must press ESCAPE before the **10** counts down to 0 to display the grub menu. Otherwise grub boots the default operating system, which typically brings the system to multiuser mode.

Displayed menu   If grub displays its menu, you must press ESCAPE before the **10** counts down to 0. Otherwise grub boots the default operating system.

Selecting recovery mode   Unless you have modified **menu.lst** (page 568), the grub menu starts with a few pairs of lines similar to the following:

```
Ubuntu 8.10, kernel 2.6.27-7-generic
Ubuntu 8.10, kernel 2.6.27-7-generic (recovery mode)
```

Typically the first line is highlighted. Press the DOWN ARROW key to highlight the second line, which includes the words **recovery mode**. Press RETURN to boot the system to recovery (single-user) mode.

Editing the grub menu   If there is no line with **recovery mode** in the menu, follow these instructions:

1. Highlight the kernel you want to boot—grub highlights the default kernel when grub displays its menu.

2. Press **e** to edit the grub boot command lines (from **menu.lst**) for the kernel you selected. The lines look similar to the following:

```
root    (hd0,0)
kernel  /boot/vmlinuz-2.6.27-7-generic root=UUID=9e467f91-5240-4472-8193-1954dd1be37b ro quiet splash
initrd  /boot/initrd.img-2.6.27-7-generic
```

3. Press the UP or DOWN ARROW key to highlight the line that begins with **kernel**.

4. Press **e** to edit the highlighted line; grub displays the line in a simple editor with the cursor at the end of the line. In this editor, grub displays only part of the line. You can use the RIGHT and LEFT ARROW keys to display other parts of the line.

5. With the cursor positioned at the right end of the line (where it is if you have not moved it), enter SPACE **single** (following **splash** in the preceding example) and press RETURN to display the previous screen.

6. Press **b** to boot the system using the modified kernel line. The system comes up in recovery (single-user) mode.

root password   If the **root** account on the system is unlocked (page 415), the system requests the **root** password before displaying the **root** prompt. Otherwise it displays the **root** prompt without requesting a password.

BOOTING TO RECOVERY MODE FROM AN INSTALLATION CD

If you are booting Ubuntu from the Alternate CD or the Server CD, select **Rescue a broken system** from the initial install screen. Follow the instructions on page 70, select one of the Execute a shell... selections, and continue with the "Which is the boot disk and partition?" section on the next page.

If you are booting from the live/install Desktop CD/DVD, when Ubuntu displays the Ubuntu logo and the startup menu, press F6 (Other options—see Figure 3-18 on page 69). Ubuntu stops its countdown and displays the boot options line, which looks similar to the following:

```
Boot Options ... casper initrd=/casper/initrd.gz quiet splash --
```

Boot options   Ubuntu displays only the end of the boot options line. You can use the RIGHT and LEFT ARROW keys to display other parts of the line. With the cursor positioned to the right of the SPACE following the two hyphens at the right end of the line (where it is if you have not moved it), type **single** and press RETURN. Ubuntu boots to recovery mode from the CD/DVD; it will not request a password. At this point, you are working with **root** privileges (the system displays a # prompt) and none of the hard disk partitions are mounted. If you want to make changes to the system that resides on the hard drive, you must mount the partition(s) you want to change.

Which is the boot disk and partition? The most common reason for booting to recovery mode from a CD/DVD on an installed Ubuntu system is to repair the system when it cannot boot from the hard disk. To fix this problem, you need to make changes to the bootable partition. Once you can boot the system from the hard drive, you can boot to recovery mode from the hard disk as explained earlier and make other changes as needed.

A system typically boots from the hard disk at **/dev/hda**, **/dev/sda**, **/dev/hdb**, or **/dev/sdb**. Give the following command, substituting each of the device names until parted displays a list of partitions that includes one with a boot flag:

```
$ sudo parted /dev/hda print
Error: Error opening /dev/hda: No medium found
Retry/Cancel? c

$ sudo parted /dev/sda print

Disk /dev/sda: 150GB
Sector size (logical/physical): 512B/512B
Partition Table: msdos

Number  Start   End     Size    Type     File system  Flags
   1    32.3kB  1003MB  1003MB  primary  ext2         boot
   2    1003MB  5001MB  3997MB  primary  ext3
   3    5001MB  25.0GB  20.0GB  primary  ext3
...
```

The preceding example shows that parted cannot read **/dev/hda** and that partition 1 of **/dev/sda** has the boot flag set (it is a bootable partition). The device name for this partition is the catenation of the device name and the partition number: **/dev/sda1**. Typically the boot directory is mounted on an **ext2** or **ext3** filesystem.

Dual-boot systems *The /boot directory does not have to be on a partition with the boot flag.* On a dual-boot system, the partition with the boot flag may not be the partition that holds the **/boot** directory. Or, on a system that can boot more than one version of Linux, the partition with the boot flag may not hold the **boot** directory you need to fix. Following is the line that parted displays for the primary partition of a dual-boot system that boots both Windows and Ubuntu:

```
   1       32.3kB  42.2GB  42.2GB  primary   ntfs         boot
```

The first clue that this is not the partition you want to work with is that it is an NTFS filesystem, which is unlikely to hold a Linux boot partition.

The second clue will come after you mount the partition and look at its contents (next step). If you find filenames such as **WINDOWS**, **DRIVERS**, and **Program Files**, it is likely the C drive of a Windows system. Unmount this partition and mount another one as explained next.

Mounting the boot partition

Once you determine the device name of the boot partition, mount that partition so you can edit files on it. Frequently you will need to edit **/boot/grub/menu.lst**. If you made a change to this file and you (or the system) made a backup of the file before making the change, you may only need to copy the backup over **menu.lst**.

Continuing with the preceding example, mount **/dev/sda1** on **/mnt**. A listing of **/mnt** will look similar to the following. Use cd to make **grub** the working directory and see which menu files are available to work with.

```
# ls /mnt
bin     dev     initrd            lib          mnt   root  sys  var
boot    etc     initrd.img        lost+found   opt   sbin  tmp  vmlinuz
cdrom   home    initrd.img.old    media        proc  srv   usr  vmlinuz.old

# cd /mnt/boot/grub
# ls -ltr menu.*
-rw-r--r-- 1 root root 4649 2008-06-25 17:59 menu.lst~
-rw-r--r-- 1 root root 5097 2008-07-02 08:59 menu.lst
```

If you have mounted the wrong partition, unmount it as described below; then mount another partition and see whether it contains a **/boot/grub** directory. The preceding listing shows a backup copy of the menu file (**menu.lst~**; the **dpkg postinst** script makes a backup file with this name when it installs a new, precompiled kernel). Before preceding, make a backup of **menu.lst** by copying it to a file named **menu.list.00** or something similar. You can now copy a known-good backup over **menu.lst** or edit **menu.lst** using a text editor such as nano or vi.

When you are done making changes, give the following commands to unmount the device mounted on **/mnt** (you cannot unmount a filesystem while one of its directories is the working directory):

```
# cd
# umount /mnt
```

After unmounting **/mnt**, give the command **reboot**. Ubuntu asks you to remove the CD and press ENTER (RETURN) to boot the system. If you have fixed the problem, the system will boot normally.

GOING TO MULTIUSER MODE

Multiuser/graphical mode (runlevel 2) is the default state for an Ubuntu Linux system. In this mode all appropriate filesystems are mounted, and users can log in from all connected terminals, dial-up lines, and network connections. All support services and daemons are enabled and running. With the system in multiuser mode, Ubuntu displays a graphical login screen on the console.

If you booted to recovery mode to fix something, give a **reboot** command and allow the system to come up in multiuser mode. If the system entered recovery mode automatically to allow you to repair the filesystem, when you exit from the recovery shell, **init** brings the system to the default mode—usually multiuser. Alternatively, you can give the following command in response to the **root** prompt to bring the system to multiuser mode:

```
# telinit 2
```

The telinit utility (page 426) tells **init** which runlevel to change to.

When it goes from single-user to multiuser mode, the system executes the **K** (kill or stop) scripts and then the **S** (start) scripts in **/etc/rc.d/rc2.d**. For more information refer to "SysVinit (rc) Scripts: Start and Stop System Services" on page 423. Use sysv-rc-conf (page 424) to stop any of these scripts from running when the system enters the new runlevel.

LOGGING IN

Textual login   With a textual login, the system uses **init**, getty, and login to allow a user to log in; login uses PAM modules (page 461) to authenticate a user. Once the system is in multiuser mode, **init** is responsible for spawning a getty process on each of the lines a user can log in on.

When you enter your username, getty establishes the characteristics of the terminal. It then overlays itself with a login process and passes to the login process whatever you entered in response to the **login:** prompt. The login process uses PAM to consult the **/etc/passwd** file to see whether any username there matches the username you entered. PAM then consults the **/etc/shadow** file to see whether a password is associated with the username. If it is, login prompts you for a password; if not, it continues without requiring a password. When your username requires a password, login verifies the password you enter by checking the **/etc/shadow** file again. If either your username or your password is not correct, login displays **Login incorrect** and prompts you to log in again.

All passwords in the **/etc/shadow** file are hashed using *MD5* (page 1119). It is not feasible to recover a hashed password. When you log in, the login process hashes the password you type at the prompt and compares it to the hashed password in **/etc/shadow**. If the two passwords match, you are authenticated.

Graphical login   With a graphical login, the **init** process spawns gdm (the GNOME display manager) on the first free virtual terminal, providing features similar to getty and login. The gdm utility starts an X server and presents a login window. The gdm display manager then uses PAM to authenticate the user and runs the scripts in the **/etc/gdm/PreSession** directory. These scripts inspect the user's **~/.dmrc** file, which stores the user's default session and language, and launch the user's session. The GNOME desktop environment stores the state of the last saved session and attempts to restore it when the user logs in again.

With NIS, login compares your username and password with the information in the appropriate naming service instead of (or in addition to) the **passwd** and **shadow** files. If the system is configured to use both methods (**/etc/passwd** and

NIS), it checks the **/etc/nsswitch.conf** file (page 458) to see in which order it should consult them.

PAM (page 461), the Pluggable Authentication Module facility, gives you greater control over user logins than the **/etc/passwd** and **/etc/shadow** files do. Using PAM, you can specify multiple levels of authentication, mutually exclusive authentication methods, or parallel methods, each of which is by itself sufficient to grant access to the system. For example, you can have different authentication methods for console logins and for ssh logins. Similarly, you can require modem users to authenticate themselves using two or more methods (such as a smartcard or badge reader and a password). PAM modules also provide security technology vendors with a convenient way to interface their hardware or software products with a system.

Initializing the session   When the username and password are correct, login or the scripts in **PreSession** consult the appropriate services to initialize the user and group IDs, establish the user's home directory, and determine which shell or desktop manager the user works with.

The login utility/**PreSession** scripts assign values to variables and look in the **/etc/group** file (page 474) to identify the groups the user belongs to. When login has finished its work, it overlays itself with the login shell, which inherits the variables set by login. In a graphical environment, the **PreSession** scripts start the desktop manager.

During a textual login, the login shell assigns values to additional shell variables and executes the commands in the system startup files **/etc/profile** and **/etc/bashrc**. Some systems have additional system startup files. The actions performed by these scripts are system dependent. In most cases they display the contents of the **/etc/motd** (message of the day) and **/etc/issue** files, let you know if you have mail, and set umask (page 442), the file-creation mask.

After executing the system startup commands, the shell executes the commands from the personal startup files in the user's home directory. These scripts are described on page 277. Because the shell executes the personal startup files *after* the system startup files, a sophisticated user can override any variables or conventions that were established by the system. A new user, by contrast, can remain uninvolved in these matters.

LOGGING OUT

With a shell prompt displayed, you can either execute a program or exit from the shell. If you exit from the shell, the process running the shell dies and the parent process wakes up. When the shell is a child of another shell, the parent shell wakes up and displays a prompt. Exiting from a login shell causes the operating system to send **init** a signal that one of its children has died. Upon receiving this signal, **init** takes action based on the appropriate job (page 417). In the case of a process controlling a line for a terminal, **init** calls the appropriate tty service (page 422), which then respawns getty so another user can log in.

BRINGING THE SYSTEM DOWN

The shutdown and reboot utilities perform the tasks needed to bring the system down safely. These utilities can restart the system, prepare the system to be turned off, and, on most hardware, power down the system. The poweroff and halt utilities are links to reboot.

You must tell shutdown when you want to bring the system down. This time can be expressed as an absolute time of day, as in 19:15, which causes the shutdown to occur at 7:15 PM. Alternatively, you can give this time as the number of minutes from the present time, as in **+15**, which means 15 minutes from now. To bring the system down immediately (recommended for emergency shutdowns only or when you are the only user logged in), you can give the argument **+0** or its synonym, **now**. When the shutdown time exceeds 5 minutes, all non**root** logins are disabled for the last 5 minutes before shutdown.

Calling shutdown with the **–r** option causes the system to reboot (same as reboot, except reboot implies **now**). Using **–h** instead of **–r** forces the system to halt (same as halt, except halt implies **now**). A message appears once the system has been safely halted: **System halted.** Most ATX systems power off automatically after shutdown, in which case you will not see this message.

Because Linux is a multiuser system, shutdown warns all users before taking action. This warning gives users a chance to prepare for the shutdown, perhaps by writing out editor files or exiting from applications. You can replace the default shutdown message with one of your own by following the time specification on the command line with a message:

```
$ sudo shutdown -h 09:30 Going down 9:30 to install disk, up by 10am.
```

Do not turn the power off before bringing the system down

caution   Do not turn the power off on a Linux system without first bringing it down as described in this section. Linux speeds disk access by keeping buffers in memory that it writes out to disk periodically or when system use is momentarily low. When you turn off or reset the computer without writing the contents of these buffers to the disk, you lose any information in the buffers. Running shutdown forces these buffers to be written. You can force the buffers to be written at any time by issuing a sync command. However, sync does not unmount filesystems, nor does it bring the system down. Also, turning off or resetting a system in this manner can destroy filesystems on IDE and SATA hard disks.

CONTROL-ALT-DEL: REBOOTS THE SYSTEM

In a textual environment, pressing the key sequence CONTROL-ALT-DEL (also referred to as the *three-finger salute* or the *Vulcan death grip*) on the console causes the kernel to trigger a **control-alt-delete** event that causes **init** to run the commands in **/etc/event.d/control-alt-delete**. See page 417 for more information on Upstart events. These commands safely reboot the system by issuing a shutdown command. You can disable CONTROL-ALT-DEL by removing the **/etc/event.d/control-alt-delete** file (or by moving it to another directory for safe keeping).

In a graphical environment, the X Window System traps this key sequence but the window manager does not pass it to the kernel. As a result, CONTROL-ALT-DEL does not work in a graphical environment.

GOING TO RECOVERY (SINGLE-USER) MODE

The following steps describe a method of manually bringing the system down to recovery mode—the point where it is safe to turn the power off. Make sure you give other users enough warning before switching to recovery mode; otherwise they may lose the data they are working on. Because going from multiuser to recovery mode can affect other users, you must work with **root** privileges to perform all of these tasks except the first.

1. Use wall (page 597) to warn everyone who is using the system to log out.

2. If you are sharing files via NFS, use **exportfs –ua** to disable network access to the shared filesystems. (Use **exportfs** without an argument to see which filesystems are being shared.)

3. Confirm no critical processes are running in the background (e.g., an unattended compile).

4. Give the command **telinit 1** (page 426) to bring the system down to recovery mode. The system displays messages about the services it is shutting down followed by a **root** shell prompt (#). In runlevel 1, the system kills many system services and then brings the system to runlevel S. The runlevel utility confirms the system was at runlevel 1 and is now at runlevel S. See the tip about changing runlevels on page 427.

   ```
   $ sudo telinit 1
   ...
   # runlevel
   1 S
   ```

5. Use **umount –a** to unmount all mounted devices that are not in use. Use **mount** without an argument to make sure that no devices other than root (/) are mounted before continuing.

TURNING THE POWER OFF

Once the system is in recovery mode, give the command **telinit 0** (page 426) or **halt** to bring the system down. You can build a kernel with apm so it turns the machine off at the appropriate time. If the system is not set up this way, turn the power off when prompted to do so or when the system starts rebooting.

CRASH

A *crash* occurs when the system suddenly stops or fails when you do not intend it to. A crash may result from software or hardware problems or from a loss of power. As a running system loses power, it may behave in erratic or unpredictable ways. In a fraction of a second, some components are supplied with enough voltage; others are not. Buffers are not flushed, corrupt data may be written to hard disks, and so on. IDE and SATA drives do not behave as predictably as SCSI drives under these circumstances. After a crash, you must bring the operating system up carefully to minimize possible damage to the filesystems. Frequently little or no damage will have occurred.

Repairing a Filesystem

Although the filesystems are checked automatically during the boot process if needed, you will have to check them manually if a problem cannot be repaired automatically. By default, when fsck cannot repair a filesystem automatically at boot time, Linux enters recovery mode so you can run fsck manually. If necessary, you can boot the system to recovery mode (page 428).

With the system in recovery mode, use umount to unmount local filesystems you want to check. Then run fsck (page 494) on these filesystems, repairing them as needed. Make note of any ordinary files or directories that you repair (and can identify), and inform their owners that these files may not be complete or correct. Look in the **lost+found** directory (page 470) *in each filesystem* for missing files. After successfully running fsck, if the system entered recovery mode automatically, type **exit** to exit from the recovery shell and resume booting; otherwise give a **reboot** command.

If files are not correct or are missing altogether, you may have to re-create them from a backup copy of the filesystem. For more information refer to "Backing Up Files" on page 582.

When the System Does Not Boot

When a system will not boot from the hard disk, boot the system to recovery mode from an installation CD/DVD (page 429). If the system comes up, run fsck on the root filesystem on the hard disk and try booting from the hard disk again. If the system still does not boot, you may have to reinstall the master boot record (page 574).

Avoiding a Trojan Horse

A *Trojan horse* is a program that does something destructive or disruptive to a system while appearing to be benign. As an example, you could store the following script in an executable file named mkfs:

```
while true
    do
    echo 'Good Morning Mr. Jones. How are you? Ha Ha Ha.' > /dev/console
    done
```

If you are working with **root** privileges when you run this command, it will continuously write a message to the console. If the programmer were malicious, it could do something worse. The only thing missing in this plot is access permissions.

A malicious user could implement this Trojan horse by changing root's PATH variable to include a publicly writable directory at the start of the PATH string. (The catch is that you need to be able to write to /etc/profile—where the PATH variable is set for root—and only a user with root privileges can do that.) Then you would need to put the bogus mkfs program file in that directory. Because the fraudulent version appears in a directory mentioned earlier than the real one in PATH, the shell will run it. Thus, the next time a user working with root privileges tries to run mkfs, the fraudulent version would run.

Trojan horses that lie in wait for and take advantage of the misspellings that most people make are among the most insidious types. For example, you might type sl instead of ls. Because you do not regularly execute a utility named sl and you may not remember typing the command sl, it is more difficult to track down this type of Trojan horse than one that takes the name of a more familiar utility.

A good way to help prevent the execution of a Trojan horse is to make sure your PATH variable does not contain a single colon (:) at the beginning or end of the PATH string or a period (.) or double colon (::) anywhere in the PATH string. This precaution ensures that you will not execute a file in the working directory by accident.

To check for a possible Trojan horse, examine the filesystem periodically for files with setuid (page 404) permission. The following command lists these files:

Listing setuid files

```
$ sudo find / -perm -4000 -exec ls -lh {} \; 2> /dev/null
...
-rwsr-xr-x 1 root root 113K 2008-09-01 06:17 /usr/bin/sudoedit
-rwsr-sr-x 1 daemon daemon 43K 2008-07-10 08:01 /usr/bin/at
-rwsr-xr-x 1 root lpadmin 14K 2008-10-10 02:31 /usr/bin/lppasswd
-rwsr-xr-x 1 root root 33K 2008-06-09 11:10 /usr/bin/passwd
-rwsr-sr-x 1 root root 9.4K 2008-10-10 12:47 /usr/bin/X
-rwsr-xr-x 1 root root 27K 2008-06-09 11:10 /usr/bin/chsh
-rwsr-xr-x 1 root root 27K 2008-06-09 11:10 /usr/bin/newgrp
...
```

This command uses find to locate all files that have their setuid bit set (mode 4000). The hyphen preceding the mode causes find to report on any file that has this bit set, regardless of how the other bits are set. The output sent to standard error is redirected to /dev/null so it does not clutter the screen.

Run software only from sources you trust

Another way a Trojan horse can enter a system is via a tainted ~/.bashrc (page 470) file. A bogus sudo command or alias in this file can capture a user's password, which may then be used to gain root privileges. Because a user has write permission to this file, any program the user executes can easily modify it. The best way to prevent this type of Trojan horse from entering a system is to run software only from sources you trust.

You can set up a program, such as AIDE (Advanced Intrusion Detection Environment), that will take a snapshot of the system and check it periodically. For more information see sourceforge.net/projects/aide.

GETTING HELP

The Ubuntu Linux distribution comes with extensive documentation (page 121). For example, the Support tab on the Ubuntu home page (www.ubuntu.com/support) and the Ubuntu wiki (wiki.ubuntu.com) point to many useful sources of support that can help answer many questions. You can also find help on the System Administrators Guild site (www.sage.org). The Internet is another rich source of information on managing a Linux system; refer to Appendix B (page 1053) and to the author's home page (www.sobell.com) for pointers to useful sites.

You need not act as an Ubuntu system administrator in isolation; a large community of Linux/Ubuntu experts is willing to assist you in getting the most out of your system. Of course, you will get better help if you have already tried to solve a problem yourself by reading the available documentation. If you are unable to solve a problem by consulting the documentation, a well-thought-out question to the appropriate newsgroup, such as **comp.os.linux.misc**, or mailing list can often generate useful information. Be sure to describe the problem accurately and identify the system carefully. Include information about the version of Ubuntu running on the system and any software packages and hardware that you think relate to the problem. The newsgroup **comp.os.linux.answers** contains postings of solutions to common problems and periodic postings of the most up-to-date versions of FAQs and HOWTO documents. See www.catb.org/~esr/faqs/smart-questions.html for a good paper by Eric S. Raymond and Rick Moen titled "How to Ask Questions the Smart Way."

TEXTUAL SYSTEM ADMINISTRATION UTILITIES

Many tools can help you be an efficient and thorough system administrator. This section describes a few textual (command line) tools and utilities; others are described throughout Part IV of this book.

kill: SENDS A SIGNAL TO A PROCESS

The kill builtin sends a signal to a process. This signal may or may not terminate (kill) the process, depending on which signal it is and how the process is designed. Refer to "trap: Catches a Signal" on page 965 for a discussion of the various signals and their interaction with a process. Running kill is definitely not the first method to try when a process needs to be aborted.

Usually a user can kill a process by working in another window or by logging in on another terminal. Sometimes, however, you may have to use sudo to kill a process for a user. To kill a process, you need to know its PID. The ps utility can provide this information once you determine the name of the program the user is running and/or the username of the user. The top utility (page 592) can also be helpful in finding and killing a runaway process (use the top k command).

kill: Use the kill signal (–KILL or –9) as a method of last resort

caution   When you do need to use kill, send the termination signal (**kill –TERM** or **kill –15**) first. Only if that tactic does not work should you attempt to use the kill signal (**kill –KILL** or **kill –9**).

Because of its inherent dangers, using a kill signal is a method of last resort, especially when you are working with **root** privileges. One **kill** command issued while working with **root** privileges can bring the system down without warning.

In the following example, Sam complains that xeyes is stuck and that he cannot do anything from the xeyes window—not even close it. A more experienced user could open another window and kill the process, but in this case you kill it for Sam. First you use ps with the **–u** option, followed by the name of the user and the **–f** (full/wide) option to view all processes associated with that user:

```
$ ps -u sam -f
UID        PID   PPID  C STIME TTY        TIME CMD
sam       2294   2259  0 09:31 ?      00:00:00 /bin/sh /usr/bin/startkde
sam       2339   2294  0 09:31 ?      00:00:00 /usr/bin/ssh-agent /usr/bin/dbus-launch
sam       2342      1  0 09:31 ?      00:00:00 dbus-daemon --fork --print-pid 8 --prin
sam       2343      1  0 09:31 ?      00:00:00 /usr/bin/dbus-launch --exit-with-sessio
sam       2396      1  0 09:31 ?      00:00:00 kdeinit Running...
sam       2399      1  0 09:31 ?      00:00:00 dcopserver [kdeinit] --nosid
sam       2401   2396  0 09:31 ?      00:00:00 klauncher [kdeinit]
sam       2403      1  0 09:31 ?      00:00:00 kded [kdeinit]
sam       2405      1  0 09:31 ?      00:00:00 /usr/libexec/gam_server
sam       2413   2396  0 09:31 ?      00:00:00 /usr/bin/artsd -F 10 -S 4096 -s 60 -m a
sam       2415      1  0 09:31 ?      00:00:00 kaccess [kdeinit]
sam       2416   2294  0 09:31 ?      00:00:00 kwrapper ksmserver
sam       2418      1  0 09:31 ?      00:00:00 ksmserver [kdeinit]
sam       2421   2396  0 09:31 ?      00:00:00 kwin [kdeinit] -session 1070626e6a00011
sam       2424      1  0 09:31 ?      00:00:01 kdesktop [kdeinit]
sam       2426      1  0 09:31 ?      00:00:01 kicker [kdeinit]
sam       2429   2396  0 09:31 ?      00:00:00 kio_file [kdeinit] file /tmp/ksocket-ma
sam       2434   2396  0 09:31 ?      00:00:00 konsole [kdeinit] -session 1070626e6a00
sam       2435   2396  0 09:31 ?      00:00:00 /bin/sh /usr/lib/firefox-1.5/firefox -U
sam       2446   2435  0 09:31 ?      00:00:00 /bin/sh /usr/lib/firefox-1.5/run-mozill
sam       2451   2446  0 09:31 ?      00:00:01 /usr/lib/firefox-1.5/firefox-bin -UILoc
sam       2453   2434  0 09:31 pts/2  00:00:00 /bin/bash
sam       2474      1  0 09:31 ?      00:00:00 /usr/libexec/gconfd-2 10
sam       2482      1  0 09:32 ?      00:00:00 synergyc jam
sam       3568   3567  0 13:55 pts/3  00:00:00 -bash
sam       3726      1  0 14:07 ?      00:00:00 knotify [kdeinit]
sam       3728      1  0 14:07 ?      00:00:00 /usr/bin/artsd -F 10 -S 4096 -s 60 -m a
sam       3730   2424  0 14:07 ?      00:00:00 xeyes
sam       3731   3568  0 14:07 pts/3  00:00:00 ps -u sam -f
```

This list is fairly short, and the process running xeyes is easy to find. Another way to search for this process is to use ps to produce a long list of all processes and then use grep to find which one is running xeyes.

```
$ ps -ef | grep xeyes
sam       3730   2424  0 14:07 ?      00:00:00 xeyes
sam       3766   3568  0 14:14 pts/3  00:00:00 grep xeyes
```

If several people are running xeyes, look in the left column to find the correct user-name so you can kill the right process. You can combine the two commands as **ps −u sam −f | grep xeyes**.

Now that you know Sam's process running xeyes has a PID of 3730, you can use kill to terminate it. The safest way to do so is to log in as Sam (perhaps allow him to log in for you) and give any of the following commands (they all send a termination signal to process 3730):

```
$ kill 3730
```

or

```
$ kill -15 3730
```

or

```
$ kill -TERM 3730
```

Only if this command fails should you send the kill signal:

```
$ kill -KILL 3730
```

The **−KILL** option instructs kill to send a **SIGKILL** signal, which the process cannot ignore. Although you can give the same command while you are working with **root** privileges, a typing mistake in this situation can have much more far-reaching consequences than when you make the mistake while you are working as a nonprivileged user. A nonprivileged user can kill only her own processes, whereas a user with **root** privileges can kill any process, including system processes.

As a compromise between speed and safety, you can combine the sudo and kill utilities by using the sudo **−u** option. The following command runs the part of the command line following the **−u sam** with the identity of Sam (Sam's privileges):

```
$ sudo -u sam kill -TERM 3730
```

killall   Two useful utilities related to kill are killall and pidof. The killall utility is very similar to kill but uses a command name instead of a PID number. Give the following command to kill all your processes that are running xeyes or vi:

```
$ killall xeyes vi
```

Running this command while working with **root** privileges kills all processes running xeyes or vi.

pidof   The pidof utility displays the PID number of each process running the command you specify:

```
$ pidof apache2
567 566 565 564 563 562 561 560 553
```

If it is difficult to find the right process, try using top. Refer to the man pages for these utilities for more information, including lists of options.

OTHER TEXTUAL UTILITIES

This section describes a few textual (command line) system administration tools you may find useful. To learn more about most of these utilities, read the man pages. For umask and uname, see the info pages.

chsh Changes the login shell for a user. When you call chsh without an argument, you change your login shell. When an ordinary user changes his login shell with chsh, he must specify an installed shell that is listed in the file **/etc/shells**, exactly as it is listed there; chsh rejects other entries. When working with **root** privileges, you can change any user's shell to any value by calling chsh with the username as an argument. In the following example, a user working with **root** privileges changes Sam's shell to tcsh:

```
$ sudo chsh sam
Password:
Changing the login shell for sam
Enter the new value, or press ENTER for the default
        Login Shell [/bin/bash]: /bin/tcsh
```

See page 277 for more information.

clear Clears the screen. You can also use CONTROL-L from the bash shell to clear the screen. The value of the environment variable **TERM** (page 1060) determines how to clear the screen.

dmesg Displays recent system log messages (page 575).

e2label Displays or creates a volume label on an **ext2** or **ext3** disk partition. You must run this utility with **root** privileges. An e2label command has the following format:

e2label **device** *[newlabel]*

where **device** is the name of the device (**/dev/hda2**, **/dev/sdb1**, **/dev/fd0**, and so on) you want to work with. When you include the optional **newlabel** parameter, e2label changes the label on **device** to **newlabel**. Without this parameter, e2label displays the label. You can also create a volume label with the **–L** option of tune2fs (page 495).

lshw Lists hardware. This utility provides complete information only when run with **root** privileges. Use the **–short** option to display a brief listing. See page 616 for more information.

mkfs Creates a new filesystem on a device, destroying all data on the device as it does so. This utility is a front-end for many utilities, each of which builds a different type of filesystem. By default, mkfs builds an **ext2** filesystem and works on either a hard disk partition or a floppy diskette. Although it can take many options and arguments, you can use mkfs simply as

```
$ sudo mkfs device
```

where **device** is the name of the device (**/dev/hda2**, **/dev/sdb1**, **/dev/fd0**, and so on) you want to make a filesystem on. Use the **–t** option to specify a type of filesystem. As an example, the following command creates an **ext3** filesystem on **/dev/hda2**:

```
$ sudo mkfs -t ext3 /dev/hda2
```

Page 491 has an example of using mkfs to create a filesystem on a floppy diskette.

ping   Sends packets to a remote system. This utility determines whether you can reach a remote system through the network and determines how long it takes to exchange messages with the remote system. Refer to "ping: Tests a Network Connection" on page 377.

reset (link to tset)   Resets terminal characteristics. The value of the **TERM** environment variable (page 1060) determines how to reset the screen. The screen is cleared, the kill and interrupt characters are set to their default values, and character echo is turned on. From a graphical terminal emulator, this command also changes the size of the window to its default. The reset utility is useful for restoring the screen to a sane state after it has been corrupted. In this sense, it is similar to an **stty sane** command.

setserial   Gets and sets serial port information. When run with **root** privileges, this utility can configure a serial port. The following command sets the input address of **/dev/ttys0** to 0x100, the interrupt (IRQ) to 5, and the baud rate to 115,000 baud:

```
$ sudo setserial /dev/ttys0 port 0x100 irq 5 spd_vhi
```

You can also check the configuration of a serial port with setserial:

```
$ sudo setserial /dev/ttys0
/dev/ttyS0, UART: 16550A, Port: 0x0100, IRQ: 5, Flags: spd_vhi
```

Normally the system calls setserial as it is booting if a serial port needs custom configuration. This utility is part of the **setserial** package.

stat   Displays information about a file or filesystem. Use the **–f** (filesystem) option followed by the mount point for a filesystem to display information about the filesystem, including the maximum number of characters allowed in a filename (**Namelen** in the following example). See the stat man page for more information.

```
$ stat -f /dev/hda
  File: "/home"
    ID: f0e28c32e9cb521f Namelen: 255      Type: ext2/ext3
Block size: 4096         Fundamental block size: 4096
Blocks: Total: 4807069    Free: 3022952    Available: 2778765
Inodes: Total: 2443200    Free: 2419025
```

umask   A shell builtin that specifies the mask the system uses to set up access permissions when you create a file. A umask command has the following format:

umask [mask]

where *mask* is a three-digit octal number or a symbolic value such as you would use with chmod (page 202). The *mask* specifies the permissions that are *not* allowed. When *mask* is an octal number, the digits correspond to the permissions for the owner of the file, members of the group the file is associated with, and everyone else. Because *mask* specifies the permissions that are *not* allowed, the system subtracts each of the three digits from 7 when you create a file. The result is three octal numbers that specify the access permissions for the file (the numbers you would use with chmod). A *mask* that you specify using symbolic values specifies the permissions that *are* allowed.

Most utilities and applications do not attempt to create files with execute permissions, regardless of the value of *mask*; they assume you do not want an executable file. As a result, when a utility or application (such as touch) creates a file, the system subtracts each of the three digits in *mask* from 6. An exception is mkdir, which assumes you want the execute (access in the case of a directory) bit set.

The following commands set the file-creation mask and display the mask and its effect when you create a file and a directory. The mask of 022, when subtracted from 666 or 777, gives permissions of 644 (**rw–r––r––**) for a file and 755 (**rwxr–xr–x**) for a directory.

```
$ umask 022
$ umask
0022
$ touch afile
$ mkdir adirectory
$ ls -ld afile adirectory
drwxr-xr-x  2 sam sam 4096 May  2 23:57 adirectory
-rw-r--r--  1 sam sam    0 May  2 23:57 afile
```

The next example sets the same mask using symbolic values. The –S option displays the mask symbolically:

```
$ umask u=rwx,g=rx,o=rx
$ umask
0022
$ umask -S
u=rwx,g=rx,o=rx
```

uname   Displays information about the system. Without arguments, this utility displays the name of the operating system (**Linux**). With the –a (all) option, it displays the operating system name, hostname, version number and release date of the operating system, and type of hardware you are using:

```
$ uname -a
Linux dog 2.6.22-10-generic #2 SMP Thu Jun 7 20:19:32 UTC 2007 i686 GNU/Linux
```

SETTING UP A SERVER

This section discusses issues that you may need to address when setting up a server: how to write configuration files; how to specify hosts and subnets; how to use **portmap**, rpcinfo, and TCP wrappers (**hosts.allow** and **hosts.deny**); and how to set up a chroot jail. Chapters 14 and 18–26 cover setting up specific servers; Chapter 17 discusses setting up a LAN.

STANDARD RULES IN CONFIGURATION FILES

Most configuration files, which are typically named *.conf, rely on the following conventions:

- Blank lines are ignored.

- A # anywhere on a line starts a comment that continues to the end of the line. Comments are ignored.

- When a name contains a SPACE, you must quote the SPACE by preceding it with a backslash (\) or by enclosing the entire name within single or double quotation marks.

- To make long lines easier to read and edit, you can break them into several shorter lines. To break a line, insert a backslash (\) immediately followed by a NEWLINE (press RETURN in a text editor). When you insert the NEWLINE before or after a SPACE, you can indent the following line to make it easier to read. Do not break lines in this manner while editing on a Windows machine, as the NEWLINEs may not be properly escaped (Windows uses a RETURN-LINEFEED combination to end lines).

Configuration files that do not follow these conventions are noted in the text.

SPECIFYING CLIENTS

Table 11-2 shows some common ways to specify a host or a subnet. Most of the time you can specify multiple hosts or subnets by separating their specifications with SPACEs.

Table 11-2   Specifying a client

Client name pattern	Matches
n.n.n.n	One IP address.
name	One hostname, either local or remote.
Name that starts with .	Matches a hostname that ends with the specified string. For example, **.example.com** matches the systems named **kudos.example.com** and **speedy.example.com**, among others.
IP address that ends with .	Matches a host address that starts with the specified numbers. For example, **192.168.0.** matches **192.168.0.0–192.168.0.255**. If you omit the trailing period, this format does not work.
n.n.n.n/m.m.m.m *or* n.n.n.n/mm	An IP address and subnet mask specifying a subnet.
Starts with /	An absolute pathname of a file containing one or more names or addresses as specified in this table.

Table 11-2 Specifying a client (continued)

Wildcard	Matches
* and ?	Matches one (?) or more (*) characters in a simple hostname or IP address. These wildcards do not match periods in a domain name.
ALL	Always matches.
LOCAL	Matches any hostname that does not contain a period.

Operator	
EXCEPT	Matches anything in the preceding list that is not in the following list. For example, **a b c d EXCEPT c** matches **a**, **b**, and **d**. Thus you could use **192.168. EXCEPT 192.168.0.1** to match all IP addresses that start with **192.168.** except **192.168.0.1**.

Examples   Each of the following examples specifies one or more systems:

10.10.	Matches all systems with IP addresses that start with **10.10.**
.ubuntu.com	Matches all named hosts on the Ubuntu network
localhost	Matches the local system
127.0.0.1	The loopback address; always resolves to **localhost**
192.168.*.1	Could match all routers on a network of /24 subnets

SPECIFYING A SUBNET

When you set up a server, you frequently need to specify which clients are allowed to connect to it. Sometimes it is convenient to specify a range of IP addresses, called a subnet. The discussion on page 369 explains what a subnet is and how to use a subnet mask to specify a subnet. Usually you can specify a subnet as

n.n.n.n/m.m.m.m

or

n.n.n.n/maskbits

where *n.n.n.n* is the base IP address and the subnet is represented by *m.m.m.m* (the subnet mask) or *maskbits* (the number of bits used for the subnet mask). For example, **192.168.0.1/255.255.255.0** represents the same subnet as **192.168.0.1/24**. In binary, decimal **255.255.255.0** is represented by 24 ones followed by 8 zeros. The /24 is shorthand for a subnet mask with 24 ones. Each line in Table 11-3 (on the next page) presents two notations for the same subnet, followed by the range of IP addresses that the subnet includes.

Table 11-3 Different ways to represent a subnet

Bits	Mask	Range
10.0.0.0/8	10.0.0.0/255.0.0.0	10.0.0.0–10.255.255.255
172.16.0.0/12	172.16.0.0/255.240.0.0	172.16.0.0–172.31.255.255
192.168.0.0/16	192.168.0.0/255.255.0.0	192.168.0.0–192.168.255.255

rpcinfo: DISPLAYS INFORMATION ABOUT portmap

The rpcinfo utility displays information about programs registered with **portmap** and makes RPC calls to programs to see if they are alive. For more information on **portmap**, refer to "RPC Network Services" on page 390. The rpcinfo utility takes the following options and arguments:

rpcinfo –p [host]
rpcinfo [–n port] –u | –t host program [version]
rpcinfo –b | –d program version

–p (**probe**) Lists all RPC programs registered with **portmap** on *host* or on the local system when you do not specify *host*.

–n (**port number**) With –t or –u, uses the port numbered *port* instead of the port number specified by **portmap**.

–u (**UDP**) Makes a UDP RPC call to *version* (if specified) of *program* on *host* and reports whether it receives a response.

–t (**TCP**) Makes a TCP RPC call to *version* (if specified) of *program* on *host* and reports whether it receives a response.

–b (**broadcast**) Makes an RPC broadcast to *version* of *program* and lists those hosts that respond.

–d (**delete**) Removes local RPC registration for *version* of *program*. Available to a user running with **root** privileges only.

Give the following command to see which RPC programs are registered with the **portmap** daemon on the system named **plum**:

```
$ rpcinfo -p plum
   program vers proto   port
    100000    2   tcp    111  portmapper
    100000    2   udp    111  portmapper
    100003    2   udp   2049  nfs
    100003    3   udp   2049  nfs
    100003    4   udp   2049  nfs
    100021    1   udp  32768  nlockmgr
 ...
```

Use the **–u** option to display a list of versions of a daemon, such as **ypserv**, registered on a remote system (**plum**):

```
$ rpcinfo -u plum nfs
program 100003 version 2 ready and waiting
program 100003 version 3 ready and waiting
program 100003 version 4 ready and waiting
```

Specify **localhost** to display a list of versions of a daemon registered on the local system:

```
$ rpcinfo -u localhost ypbind
program 100007 version 1 ready and waiting
program 100007 version 2 ready and waiting
```

Locking down
portmap

Because the **portmap** daemon holds information about which servers are running on the local system and which port each server is running on, only trusted systems should have access to this information. One way to ensure that only selected systems have access to **portmap** is to lock it down in the **/etc/hosts.allow** and **/etc/hosts.deny** files (page 448). Put the following line in **hosts.deny** to prevent all systems from using portmap on the local (server) system:

```
portmap: ALL
```

You can test this setup from a remote system with the following command:

```
$ rpcinfo -p hostname
No remote programs registered.
```

Replace *hostname* with the name of the remote system that you changed the **hosts.deny** file on. The change is immediate; you do not need to kill/restart a daemon.

Next add the following line to the **hosts.allow** file on the server system:

```
portmap: host-IP
```

where *host-IP* is the IP address of the trusted, remote system that you gave the preceding rpcinfo command from. Use only IP addresses with **portmap** in **hosts.allow**; do not use system names that **portmap** could get stuck trying to resolve. If you give the same command, rpcinfo should display a list of the servers that RPC knows about, including **portmap**. See page 711 for more examples.

Set the clocks

tip   The **portmap** daemon relies on the client's and the server's clocks being synchronized. A simple *DoS attack* (page 1106) can be initiated by setting the server's clock to the wrong time.

THE inetd AND xinetd SUPERSERVERS

The **inetd** (Internet daemon) daemon, and its replacement **xinetd** (extended Internet daemon; xinetd.org), are called superservers or service dispatchers because they start other daemons, such as **smbd** (Samba) and **vsftpd** (FTP), as necessary. These superservers listen for network connections. When one is made, they identify a server daemon based on the port the connection comes in on, set the daemon's standard input and standard output file descriptors to the socket (page 485), and start the daemon.

Using these superservers offers two advantages over having several servers constantly running daemons that monitor ports. First, the superservers avoid the need for daemons to be running when not in use. Second, they allow developers to write servers that read from standard input and write to standard output; they handle all socket communication.

The **inetd** superserver, which originally shipped with 4.3BSD, was not particularly insecure. However, it typically opened a lot of ports and ran many servers, increasing the possibility that exploitable software would be exposed to the Internet. Its successor, **xinetd**, introduced access control and logging. This daemon allowed an administrator to limit the hours a service was available and the origin and number of incoming connections. When compiled with **libwrap**, **xinetd** can take advantage of TCP wrappers (discussed in the next section).

At a time when CPU power was more limited than it is today and RAM was more expensive, these superservers offered the advantage of efficient memory and CPU usage. Systems have slowly moved away from using these superservers over the past few years. Today a system can easily spare the few megabytes of memory and the minimal CPU time it takes to keep a daemon running to monitor a port: It takes fewer resources to keep a process in RAM (or swap space) than it does to restart it periodically. Also, a developer can now handle socket communications more easily using various toolkits.

SECURING A SERVER

Two ways you can secure a server are by using TCP wrappers and by setting up a chroot jail. This section describes both techniques.

TCP WRAPPERS: SECURE A SERVER (hosts.allow AND hosts.deny)

Follow these guidelines when you open a local system to access from remote systems:

- Open the local system only to systems you want to allow to access it.

- Allow each remote system to access only the data you want it to access.

- Allow each remote system to access data only in the appropriate manner (readonly, read/write, write only).

libwrap   As part of the client/server model, TCP wrappers, which can be used for any daemon that is linked against **libwrap**, rely on the **/etc/hosts.allow** and **/etc/hosts.deny** files as the basis of a simple access control language (ACL). This access control language defines rules that selectively allow clients to access server daemons on a local system based on the client's address and the daemon the client tries to access. The output of ldd shows that one of the shared library dependencies of **sshd** is **libwrap**:

```
$ ldd /usr/sbin/sshd | grep libwrap
        libwrap.so.0 => /lib/libwrap.so.0 (0xb7ec7000)
```

hosts.allow and hosts.deny Each line in the **hosts.allow** and **hosts.deny** files has the following format:

daemon_list : client_list [: command]

where *daemon_list* is a comma-separated list of one or more server daemons (such as **portmap**, **vsftpd**, or **sshd**), *client_list* is a comma-separated list of one or more clients (see Table 11-2, "Specifying a client," on page 444), and the optional *command* is the command that is executed when a client from *client_list* tries to access a server daemon from *daemon_list*.

When a client requests a connection to a server, the **hosts.allow** and **hosts.deny** files on the server system are consulted as follows until a match is found:

1. If the daemon/client pair matches a line in **hosts.allow**, access is granted.

2. If the daemon/client pair matches a line in **hosts.deny**, access is denied.

3. If there is no match in the **hosts.allow** or **hosts.deny** file, access is granted.

The first match determines whether the client is allowed to access the server. When either **hosts.allow** or **hosts.deny** does not exist, it is as though that file was empty. Although it is not recommended, you can allow access to all daemons for all clients by removing both files.

Examples For a more secure system, put the following line in **hosts.deny** to block all access:

```
$ cat /etc/hosts.deny
...
ALL : ALL : echo '%c tried to connect to %d and was blocked' >> /var/log/tcpwrappers.log
```

This line prevents any client from connecting to any service, unless specifically permitted to do so in **hosts.allow**. When this rule is matched, it adds a line to the file named **/var/log/tcpwrappers.log**. The **%c** expands to client information and the **%d** expands to the name of the daemon the client attempted to connect to.

With the preceding **hosts.deny** file in place, you can include lines in **hosts.allow** that explicitly allow access to certain services and systems. For example, the following **hosts.allow** file allows anyone to connect to the OpenSSH daemon (ssh, scp, sftp) but allows telnet connections only from the same network as the local system and users on the 192.168. subnet:

```
$ cat /etc/hosts.allow
sshd: ALL
in.telnet: LOCAL
in.telnet: 192.168.* 127.0.0.1
...
```

The first line allows connection from any system (ALL) to **sshd**. The second line allows connection from any system in the same domain as the server (LOCAL). The third line matches any system whose IP address starts **192.168.** and the local system.

SETTING UP A chroot JAIL

On early UNIX systems, the root directory was a fixed point in the filesystem. On modern UNIX variants, including Linux, you can define the root directory on a per-process basis. The chroot utility allows you to run a process with a root directory other than /.

The root directory appears at the top of the directory hierarchy and has no parent. Thus a process cannot access files above the root directory because none exists. If, for example, you run a program (process) and specify its root directory as **/tmp/jail**, the program would have no concept of any files in **/tmp** or above: **jail** is the program's root directory and is labeled **/** (not **jail**).

By creating an artificial root directory, frequently called a (chroot) jail, you prevent a program from accessing, executing, or modifying—possibly maliciously—files outside the directory hierarchy starting at its root. You must set up a chroot jail properly to increase security: If you do not set up a chroot jail correctly, you can make it easier for a malicious user to gain access to a system than if there were no chroot jail.

USING chroot

Creating a chroot jail is simple: Working with **root** privileges, give the command **/usr/sbin/chroot** *directory*. The *directory* becomes the root directory and the process attempts to run the default shell. The following command sets up a chroot jail in the (existing) **/tmp/jail** directory:

```
$ sudo /usr/sbin/chroot /tmp/jail
/usr/sbin/chroot: cannot run command '/bin/bash': No such file or directory
```

This example sets up a chroot jail, but when it attempts to run the bash shell, it fails. Once the jail is set up, the directory that was named **jail** takes on the name of the root directory, **/**. As a consequence, chroot cannot find the file identified by the pathname **/bin/bash**. In this situation the chroot jail works correctly but is not useful.

Getting a chroot jail to work the way you want is more complicated. To have the preceding example run bash in a chroot jail, create a **bin** directory in **jail** (**/tmp/jail/bin**) and copy **/bin/bash** to this directory. Because the bash binary is dynamically linked to shared libraries, you need to copy these libraries into **jail** as well. The libraries go in **lib**.

The next example creates the necessary directories, copies **bash**, uses ldd to display the shared library dependencies of bash, and copies the necessary libraries to **lib**. The **linux-gate.so.1** file is a dynamically shared object (DSO) provided by the kernel to speed system calls; you do not need to copy it.

```
$ pwd
/tmp/jail
$ mkdir bin lib
$ cp /bin/bash bin
$ ldd bin/bash
        linux-gate.so.1 =>  (0xffffe000)
        libncurses.so.5 => /lib/libncurses.so.5 (0xb7f44000)
        libdl.so.2 => /lib/tls/i686/cmov/libdl.so.2 (0xb7f40000)
        libc.so.6 => /lib/tls/i686/cmov/libc.so.6 (0xb7dff000)
        /lib/ld-linux.so.2 (0xb7f96000)
```

```
$ cp /lib/{libncurses.so.5,ld-linux.so.2} lib
$ cp /lib/tls/i686/cmov/{libdl.so.2,libc.so.6} lib
```

Now start the chroot jail again. Although all the setup can be done by an ordinary user, you must be working with **root** privileges to run chroot:

```
$ sudo /usr/sbin/chroot /tmp/jail
bash-3.2# pwd
/
bash-3.2# ls
bash: ls: command not found
bash-3.2# exit
exit
$
```

This time chroot finds and starts **bash,** which displays its default prompt (**bash-3.2#**). The pwd command works because it is a shell builtin (page 247). However, bash cannot find the ls utility because it is not in the chroot jail. You can copy **/bin/ls** and its libraries into the jail if you want users in the jail to be able to use ls. An **exit** command allows you to escape from the jail.

If you provide chroot with a second argument, it takes that argument as the name of the program to run inside the jail. The following command is equivalent to the preceding one:

```
$ sudo /usr/sbin/chroot /home/sam/jail /bin/bash
```

To set up a useful chroot jail, first determine which utilities the users of the chroot jail need. Then copy the appropriate binaries and their libraries into the jail. Alternatively, you can build static copies of the binaries and put them in the jail without installing separate libraries. (The statically linked binaries are considerably larger than their dynamic counterparts. The base system with bash and the core utilities exceeds 50 megabytes.) You can find the source code for most common utilities in the **bash** and **coreutils** source packages.

The chroot utility fails unless you run it with **root** privileges. The preceding examples used sudo to gain these privileges. The result of running chroot with **root** privileges is a **root** shell (a shell with **root** privileges) running inside a chroot jail. Because a user with **root** privileges can break out of a chroot jail, it is imperative that you run a program in the chroot jail with reduced privileges (i.e., privileges other than those of **root**).

There are several ways to reduce the privileges of a user. For example, you can put su or sudo in the jail and then start a shell or a daemon inside the jail, using one of these programs to reduce the privileges of the user working in the jail. A command such as the following starts a shell with reduced privileges inside the jail:

```
$ sudo /usr/sbin/chroot jailpath /usr/bin/sudo -u user /bin/bash &
```

where *jailpath* is the pathname of the jail directory, and *user* is the username under whose privileges the shell runs. The problem with this scenario is that sudo and su as compiled for Ubuntu, call PAM. To run one of these utilities you need to put all of PAM, including its libraries and configuration files, in the jail, along with sudo (or su) and the **/etc/passwd** file. Alternatively, you can recompile su or sudo.

The source code calls PAM, however, so you would need to modify the source so it does not call PAM. Either one of these techniques is time-consuming and introduces complexities that can lead to an insecure jail.

The following C program[1] runs a program with reduced privileges in a chroot jail. Because this program obtains the UID and GID of the user you specify on the command line before calling **chroot()**, you do not need to put **/etc/passwd** in the jail. The program reduces the privileges of the specified program to those of the specified user. This program is presented as a simple solution to the preceding issues so you can experiment with a chroot jail and better understand how it works.

```
$ cat uchroot.c

/* See svn.gna.org/viewcvs/etoile/trunk/Etoile/LiveCD/uchroot.c for terms of use. */

#include <stdio.h>
#include <stdlib.h>
#include <pwd.h>

int main(int argc, char * argv[])
{
    if(argc < 4)
    {
        printf("Usage: %s {username} {directory} {program} [arguments]\n", argv[0]);
        return 1;
    }
    /* Parse arguments */
    struct passwd * pass = getpwnam(argv[1]);
    if(pass == NULL)
    {
        printf("Unknown user %s\n", argv[1]);
        return 2;
    }
    /* Set the required UID */
    chdir(argv[2]);
    if(chroot(argv[2])
        ||
        setgid(pass->pw_gid)
        ||
        setuid(pass->pw_uid))
    {
        printf("%s must be run as root.  Current uid=%d, euid=%d\n",
                argv[0],
                (int)getuid(),
                (int)geteuid()
                );
        return 3;
    }
    char buf[100];
    return execv(argv[3], argv + 3);
}
```

---

1. Thanks to David Chisnall and the Étoilé Project (etoileos.com) for the **uchroot.c** program.

The first of the following commands compiles **uchroot.c**, creating an executable file named uchroot. Subsequent commands move uchroot to **/usr/local/bin** and give it appropriate ownership.

```
$ cc -o uchroot uchroot.c
$ sudo mv uchroot /usr/local/bin
$ sudo chown root:root /usr/local/bin/uchroot
$ ls -l /usr/local/bin/uchroot
-rwxr-xr-x 1 root root 7922 Jul 17 08:26 /usr/local/bin/uchroot
```

Using the setup from earlier in this section, give the following command to run a shell with the privileges of the user **sam** inside a chroot jail:

```
$ sudo /usr/local/bin/uchroot sam /tmp/jail /bin/bash
```

Keeping multiple chroot jails

tip   If you plan to deploy multiple chroot jails, it is a good idea to keep a clean copy of the **bin** and **lib** directories somewhere other than one of the active jails.

RUNNING A SERVICE IN A chroot JAIL

Running a shell inside a jail has limited usefulness. Instead, you are more likely to want to run a specific service inside the jail. To run a service inside a jail, make sure all files needed by that service are inside the jail. Using uchroot, the format of a command to start a service in a chroot jail is

```
$ sudo /usr/local/bin/uchroot user jailpath daemonname
```

where *jailpath* is the pathname of the jail directory, *user* is the username that runs the daemon, and *daemonname* is the pathname (inside the jail) of the daemon that provides the service.

Some servers are already set up to take advantage of chroot jails. You can set up DNS so that **named** runs in a jail (page 808), for example, and the **vsftpd** FTP server can automatically start chroot jails for clients (page 667).

SECURITY CONSIDERATIONS

Some services need to be run by a user/process with **root** privileges but release their **root** privileges once started (Apache, Procmail, and **vsftpd** are examples). If you are running such a service, you do not need to use uchroot or put su or sudo inside the jail.

A process run with **root** privileges can potentially escape from a chroot jail. For this reason, always reduce privileges before starting a program running inside the jail. Also, be careful about which setuid (page 204) binaries you allow inside a jail—a security hole in one of them could compromise the security of the jail. In addition, make sure the user cannot access executable files that he uploads to the jail.

DHCP: CONFIGURES NETWORK INTERFACES

Instead of storing network configuration information in local files on each system, DHCP (Dynamic Host Configuration Protocol) enables client systems to retrieve network configuration information from a DHCP server each time they connect to the network. A DHCP server assigns IP addresses from a pool of addresses to clients as needed. Assigned addresses are typically temporary but need not be.

This technique has several advantages over storing network configuration information in local files:

- A new user can set up an Internet connection without having to deal with IP addresses, netmasks, DNS addresses, and other technical details. An experienced user can set up a connection more quickly.

- DHCP facilitates assignment and management of IP addresses and related network information by centralizing the process on a server. A system administrator can configure new systems, including laptops that connect to the network from different locations, to use DHCP; DHCP then assigns IP addresses only when each system connects to the network. The pool of IP addresses is managed as a group on the DHCP server.

- IP addresses can be used by more than one system, reducing the total number of IP addresses needed. This conservation of addresses is important because the Internet is quickly running out of IPv4 addresses. Although a particular IP address can be used by only one system at a time, many end-user systems require addresses only occasionally, when they connect to the Internet. By reusing IP addresses, DHCP has lengthened the life of the IPv4 protocol. DHCP applies to IPv4 only, as IPv6 (page 371) forces systems to configure their IP addresses automatically (called autoconfiguration) when they connect to a network.

DHCP is particularly useful for an administrator who is responsible for maintaining a large number of systems because individual systems no longer need to store unique configuration information. With DHCP, the administrator can set up a master system and deploy new systems with a copy of the master's hard disk. In educational establishments and other open-access facilities, the hard disk image may be stored on a shared drive, with each workstation automatically restoring itself to pristine condition at the end of each day.

MORE INFORMATION

Web   www.dhcp.org
       DHCP FAQ: www.dhcp-handbook.com/dhcp_faq.html
HOWTO *DHCP Mini HOWTO*

HOW DHCP WORKS

Using dhclient, the client contacts the server daemon, **dhcpd,** to obtain the IP address, netmask, broadcast address, nameserver address, and other networking parameters. In turn, the server provides a *lease* on the IP address to the client. The client can request the specific terms of the lease, including its duration; the server can limit these terms. While connected to the network, a client typically requests extensions of its lease as necessary so its IP address remains the same. This lease may expire once the client is disconnected from the network, with the server giving the client a new IP address when it requests a new lease. You can also set up a DHCP server to provide static IP addresses for specific clients (refer to "Static Versus Dynamic IP Addresses" on page 366). DHCP is broadcast based, so both client and server must be on the same subnet (page 369).

When you install Ubuntu, the system runs a DHCP client, connects to a DHCP server if it can find one, and configures its network interface. You can use firestarter (page 824) to configure and run a DHCP server.

DHCP CLIENT

A DHCP client requests network configuration parameters from the DHCP server and uses those parameters to configure its network interface.

PREREQUISITES

Make sure the following package is installed:

- **dhcp3-client**

dhclient: THE DHCP CLIENT

When a DHCP client system connects to the network, dhclient requests a lease from the DHCP server and configures the client's network interface(s). Once a DHCP client has requested and established a lease, it stores the lease information in a file named **dhclient.*interface*.leases**, which is stored in **/var/lib/dhcp3**. The *interface* is the name of the interface that the client uses, such as eth0. The system uses this information to reestablish a lease when either the server or the client needs to reboot. You need to change the default DHCP client configuration file, **/etc/dhcp3/dhclient.conf**, only for custom configurations.

The following **/etc/dhcp3/dhclient.conf** file specifies a single interface, **eth0**:

```
$ cat /etc/dhcp3/dhclient.conf
interface "eth0"
{
send dhcp-client-identifier 1:xx:xx:xx:xx:xx:xx;
send dhcp-lease-time 86400;
}
```

In the preceding file, the 1 in the **dhcp-client-identifier** specifies an Ethernet network and **xx:xx:xx:xx:xx:xx** is the *MAC address* (page 1118) of the device controlling that interface. See page 457 for instructions on how to determine the MAC address of a device. The **dhcp-lease-time** is the duration, in seconds, of the lease on the IP address. While the client is connected to the network, dhclient automatically renews the lease each time half of the lease time is up. The lease time of 86,400 seconds (or one day) is a reasonable choice for a workstation.

DHCP SERVER

A DHCP server maintains a list of IP addresses and other configuration parameters. Clients request network configuration parameters from the server.

PREREQUISITES

Install the following package:

- dhcp3-server

dhcp3-server init script

When you install the **dhcpd3-server** package, the **dpkg postinst** script attempts to start the **dhcpd3** daemon and fails because **dhcpd3** is not configured—see **/var/log/syslog** for details. After you configure **dhcpd3**, call the **dhcp3-server** init script to restart the **dhcpd3** daemon:

```
$ sudo /etc/init.d/dhcp3-server restart
```

dhcpd: THE DHCP DAEMON

A simple DCHP server (**dhcpd**) allows you to add clients to a network without maintaining a list of assigned IP addresses. A simple network, such as a home LAN sharing an Internet connection, can use DHCP to assign a dynamic IP address to almost all nodes. The exceptions are servers and routers, which must be at known network locations to be able to receive connections. If servers and routers are configured without DHCP, you can specify a simple DHCP server configuration in **/etc/dhcp3/dhcpd.conf**:

```
$ cat /etc/dhcp3/dhcpd.conf
default-lease-time 600;
max-lease-time 86400;

option subnet-mask 255.255.255.0;
option broadcast-address 192.168.1.255;
option routers 192.168.1.1;
option domain-name-servers 192.168.1.1;
option domain-name "example.com";

subnet 192.168.1.0 netmask 255.255.255.0 {
    range 192.168.1.2 192.168.1.200;
}
```

The **/etc/default/dhcp3-server** file specifies the interfaces that **dhcpd** serves requests on. By default, **dhcpd** uses eth0. To use another interface or to use more than one interface, set the **INTERFACES** variable in this file to a SPACE-separated list of the interfaces you want to use; enclose the list within quotation marks.

The preceding configuration file specifies a LAN where both the router and DNS server are located on **192.168.1.1**. The **default-lease-time** specifies the number of seconds the dynamic IP lease will remain valid if the client does not specify a duration. The **max-lease-time** is the maximum time allowed for a lease.

The information in the **option** lines is sent to each client when it connects. The names following the word **option** specify what the following argument represents. For example, the **option broadcast-address** line specifies the broadcast address of the network. The **routers** and **domain-name-servers** options allow multiple values separated by commas.

The **subnet** section includes a **range** line that specifies the range of IP addresses the DHCP server can assign. If case of multiple subnets, you can define options, such as **subnet-mask,** inside the **subnet** section. Options defined outside all **subnet** sections are global and apply to all subnets.

The preceding configuration file assigns addresses in the range from 192.168.1.2 to 192.168.1.200. The DHCP server starts at the bottom of this range and attempts to assign a new IP address to each new client. Once the DHCP server reaches the top of the range, it starts reassigning IP addresses that have been used in the past but are not currently in use. If you have fewer systems than IP addresses, the IP address of each system should remain fairly constant. Two systems cannot use the same IP address at the same time.

Once you have configured a DHCP server, restart it using the **dhcpd** init script (page 456). When the server is running, clients configured to obtain an IP address from the server using DHCP should be able to do so.

STATIC IP ADDRESSES

As mentioned earlier, routers and servers typically require static IP addresses. Although you can manually configure IP addresses for these systems, it may be more convenient to have the DHCP server provide them with static IP addresses.

When a system that requires a specific static IP address connects to the network and contacts the DHCP server, the server needs a way to identify the system so it can assign the proper IP address to that system. The DHCP server uses the *MAC address* (page 1118) of the system's Ethernet card (NIC) as an identifier. When you set up the server, you must know the MAC address of each system that requires a static IP address.

Determining a MAC address
The ifconfig utility displays the MAC addresses of the Ethernet cards in a system. In the following example, the MAC addresses are the colon-separated series of hexadecimal number pairs following **HWaddr:**

```
$ ifconfig | grep -i hwaddr
eth0      Link encap:Ethernet  HWaddr BA:DF:00:DF:C0:FF
eth1      Link encap:Ethernet  HWaddr 00:02:B3:41:35:98
```

Run ifconfig on each system that requires a static IP address. Once you have determined the MAC addresses of these systems, you can add a **host** section to the **/etc/dhcp3/dhcpd.conf** file for each one, instructing the DHCP server to assign a specific address to that system. The following **host** section assigns the address **192.168.1.1** to the system with the MAC address of **BA:DF:00:DF:C0:FF:**

```
$ cat /etc/dhcp3/dhcpd.conf
...
host router {
   hardware ethernet BA:DF:00:DF:C0:FF;
   fixed-address 192.168.1.1;
   option host-name router;
}
```

The name following **host** is used internally by **dhcpd.** The name specified after **option host-name** is passed to the client and can be a hostname or an FQDN. After making changes to **dhcpd.conf,** restart **dhcpd** using the **dhcpd** init script (page 456).

nsswitch.conf: WHICH SERVICE TO LOOK AT FIRST

With the advent of NIS and DNS, finding user and system information was no longer a simple matter of searching a local file. Where once you looked in **/etc/passwd** to get user information and in **/etc/hosts** to find system address information, you can now use several methods to obtain this type of information. The **/etc/nsswitch.conf** (name service switch configuration) file specifies which methods to use and the order in which to use them when looking for a certain type of information. You can also specify which action the system should take based on whether a method succeeds or fails.

Format   Each line in **nsswitch.conf** specifies how to search for a piece of information, such as a user's password. A line in **nsswitch.conf** has the following format:

info: *method [[action]] [method [[action]]...]*

where *info* specifies the type of information the line describes, *method* is the method used to find the information, and *action* is the response to the return status of the preceding *method*. The action is enclosed within square brackets.

How nsswitch.conf WORKS

When called upon to supply information that **nsswitch.conf** describes, the system examines the line with the appropriate *info* field. It uses the methods specified on the line, starting with the method on the left. By default, when it finds the desired information, the system stops searching. Without an *action* specification, when a method fails to return a result, the system tries the next action. It is possible for the search to end without finding the requested information.

INFORMATION

The **nsswitch.conf** file commonly controls searches for usernames, passwords, host IP addresses, and group information. The following list describes most of the types of information (*info* in the syntax given earlier) that **nsswitch.conf** controls searches for.

automount	Automount (**/etc/auto.master** and **/etc/auto.misc**, page 756)
bootparam	Diskless and other booting options (See the **bootparam** man page.)
ethers	MAC address (page 1118)
group	Groups of users (**/etc/group**, page 474)
hosts	System information (**/etc/hosts**, page 475)
networks	Network information (**/etc/networks**)
passwd	User information (**/etc/passwd**, page 476)
protocols	Protocol information (**/etc/protocols**, page 477)
publickey	Used for NFS running in secure mode
rpc	RPC names and numbers (**/etc/rpc**, page 478)
services	Services information (**/etc/services**, page 479)
shadow	Shadow password information (**/etc/shadow**, page 479)

METHODS

Following is a list of the types of information that **nsswitch.conf** controls searches for (*method* in the format above). For each type of information, you can specify one or more of the following methods:[2]

files	Searches local files such as **/etc/passwd** and **/etc/hosts**
nis	Searches the NIS database; **yp** is an alias for **nis**
dns	Queries the DNS (**hosts** queries only)
compat	± syntax in **passwd**, **group**, and **shadow** files (page 460)

SEARCH ORDER

The information provided by two or more methods may overlap: For example, both **files** and **nis** may provide password information for the same user. With overlapping information, you need to consider which method you want to be authoritative (take precedence); place that method at the left of the list of methods.

The default **nsswitch.conf** file lists methods without actions, assuming no overlap (which is normal). In this case, the order is not critical: When one method fails, the system goes to the next one and all that is lost is a little time. Order becomes critical when you use actions between methods or when overlapping entries differ.

The first of the following lines from **nsswitch.conf** causes the system to search for password information in **/etc/passwd** and, if that fails, to use NIS to find the information. If the user you are looking for is listed in both places, the information in the local file is used and is considered authoritative. The second line uses NIS to find an IP address given a hostname; if that fails, it searches **/etc/hosts**; if that fails, it checks with DNS to find the information.

```
passwd          files nis
hosts           nis files dns
```

ACTION ITEMS

Each method can optionally be followed by an action item that specifies what to do if the method succeeds or fails. An action item has the following format:

[[!]STATUS=action]

where the opening and closing square brackets are part of the format and do not indicate that the contents are optional; *STATUS* (uppercase by convention) is the status being tested for; and *action* is the action to be taken if *STATUS* matches the status returned by the preceding method. The leading exclamation point (**!**) is optional and negates the status.

---

2. There are other, less commonly used methods. See the default **/etc/nsswitch.conf** file and the **nsswitch.conf** man page for more information. Although NIS+ belongs in this list, it is not implemented as a Linux server and is not discussed in this book.

STATUS   Values for *STATUS* are

NOTFOUND   The method worked but the value being searched for was not found. The default action is **continue**.

SUCCESS   The method worked and the value being searched for was found; no error was returned. The default action is **return**.

UNAVAIL   The method failed because it is permanently unavailable. For example, the required file may not be accessible or the required server may be down. The default action is **continue**.

TRYAGAIN   The method failed because it was temporarily unavailable. For example, a file may be locked or a server overloaded. The default action is **continue**.

action   Values for *action* are

return   Returns to the calling routine with or without a value.

continue   Continues with the next method. Any returned value is overwritten by a value found by a subsequent method.

Example   The following line from **nsswitch.conf** causes the system first to use DNS to search for the IP address of a given host. The action item following the DNS method tests whether the status returned by the method is not (!) UNAVAIL.

```
hosts          dns [!UNAVAIL=return] files
```

The system takes the action associated with the *STATUS* (**return**) if the DNS method does not return UNAVAIL (**!UNAVAIL**)—that is, if DNS returns SUCCESS, NOTFOUND, or TRYAGAIN. The result is that the following method (**files**) is used only when the DNS server is unavailable. If the DNS server is *not un*available (read the two negatives as "is available"), the search returns the domain name or reports that the domain name was not found. The search uses the **files** method (checks the local **/etc/hosts** file) only if the server is not available.

compat METHOD: ± IN passwd, group, AND shadow FILES

You can put special codes in the **/etc/passwd**, **/etc/group**, and **/etc/shadow** files that cause the system, when you specify the **compat** method in **nsswitch.conf**, to combine and modify entries in the local files and the NIS maps.

A plus sign (**+**) at the beginning of a line in one of these files adds NIS information; a minus sign (**–**) removes information. For example, to use these codes in the **passwd** file, specify **passwd: compat** in **nsswitch.conf**. The system then goes through the **passwd** file in order, adding or removing the appropriate NIS entries when it reaches each line that starts with a **+** or **–**.

Although you can put a plus sign at the end of the **passwd** file, specify **passwd: compat** in **nsswitch.conf** to search the local **passwd** file, and then go through the NIS map, it is more efficient to put **passwd: file nis** in **nsswitch.conf** and not modify the **passwd** file.

PAM

PAM (Linux-PAM, or Linux Pluggable Authentication Modules) allows a system administrator to determine how applications use *authentication* (page 1096) to verify the identity of a user. PAM provides shared libraries of modules (located in **/lib/security**) that, when called by an application, authenticate a user. The configuration files kept in the **/etc/pam.d** directory determine the method of authentication and contain a list, or stack, of calls to the modules. PAM may also use other files, such as **/etc/passwd**, when necessary. The term "Pluggable" in PAM's name refers to the ease with which you can add and remove modules from an authentication stack.

Instead of building the authentication code into each application, PAM provides shared libraries that keep the authentication code separate from the application code. The techniques of authenticating users stay the same from application to application. PAM enables a system administrator to change the authentication mechanism for a given application without modifying the application.

PAM provides authentication for a variety of system-entry services (such as login, ftp, su, and sudo). You can take advantage of its ability to stack authentication modules to integrate system-entry services with different authentication mechanisms, such as RSA, DCE, Kerberos, and smartcards.

From login through using sudo to shutting the system down, whenever you are asked for a password (or not asked for a password because the system trusts you are who you say you are), PAM makes it possible for system administrators to configure the authentication process. It also makes the configuration process essentially the same for all applications that use PAM for authentication.

The configuration files stored in **/etc/pam.d** describe the authentication procedure for each application. These files usually have names that are the same as or similar to the name of the application that they authenticate for. For example, authentication for the login utility is configured in **/etc/pam.d/login**. The name of the file is the name of the PAM service[3] that the file configures. Occasionally one file may serve two programs. PAM accepts only lowercase letters in the names of files in the **/etc/pam.d** directory.

PAM warns you about errors it encounters, logging them to **/var/log/messages** or **/var/log/secure**. Review these files if you are trying to figure out why a changed PAM file is not working properly. To prevent a malicious user from seeing information about PAM, PAM sends error messages to a file rather than to the screen.

---

3. There is no relationship between PAM services and the **/etc/services** file. The name of the PAM service is an arbitrary string that each application gives to PAM; PAM then looks up the configuration file with that name and uses it to control authentication. There is no central registry of PAM service names.

Do not lock yourself out of the system

caution   Editing PAM configuration files correctly requires paying careful attention. It is easy to lock yourself out of the system with a single mistake. To avoid this problem, keep backup copies of the PAM
configuration files you edit, test every change thoroughly, and make sure you can still log in once
the change is installed. Keep a **root** shell open (use **sudo –i**) until you have finished testing. If a
change fails and you cannot log in, use the **root** shell to replace the newly edited files with the
backup copies.

MORE INFORMATION

Local   **/usr/share/doc/libpam**✷
pam man page

Web   *Linux-PAM System Administrators' Guide:*
www.kernel.org/pub/linux/libs/pam/Linux-PAM-html/Linux-PAM_SAG.html

HOWTO   *User Authentication HOWTO*

CONFIGURATION FILES, MODULE TYPES, AND CONTROL FLAGS

Following is an example of a PAM configuration file. Comment lines, which have
been omitted, begin with a pound sign (#).

Login module
```
$ grep '^[^#]' /etc/pam.d/login
auth         requisite  pam_securetty.so
auth         requisite  pam_nologin.so
session         required    pam_env.so readenv=1
session         required    pam_env.so readenv=1 envfile=/etc/default/locale
@include common-auth
auth         optional   pam_group.so
session      required   pam_limits.so
session      optional   pam_lastlog.so
session      optional   pam_motd.so
session      optional   pam_mail.so standard
@include common-account
@include common-session
@include common-password
```

Each line tells PAM to do something as part of the authentication process. The first
word on each line is a module type indicator: **account, auth, password,** or **session**
(Table 11-4). The second is a control flag (Table 11-5) that indicates the action
PAM should take if authentication fails. The rest of the line contains the name of a
PAM module (located in **/lib/security**) and any arguments for that module. The
PAM library itself uses the **/etc/pam.d** files to determine which modules to delegate
work to. Lines that begin with **@include** include the named file.

Table 11-4   Module type indicators

Module type	Description	Controls
account	Account management	Determining whether an already authenticated user is allowed to use the service she is trying to use. (That is, has the account expired? Is the user allowed to use this service at this time of day?)

Table 11-4   Module type indicators (continued)

Module type	Description	Controls
auth	Authentication	Proving that the user is authorized to use the service; uses passwords or another mechanism.
password	Password modification	Updating authentication mechanisms such as user passwords.
session	Session management	Setting things up when the service is started (as when a user logs in) and breaking them down when the service is terminated (as when a user logs out).

You can use one of the control flag keywords listed in Table 11-5 to set the control flags.

Table 11-5   Control flag keywords

Keyword	Flag function
required	Success is required for authentication to succeed. Control and a failure result are returned after all modules in the stack have been executed. The technique of delaying the report to the calling program until all modules have been executed may keep attackers from knowing precisely what caused their authentication attempts to fail and tell them less about the system, making it more difficult for them to break in.
requisite	Success is required for authentication to succeed. Further module processing is aborted, and control is returned immediately after a module fails. This technique may expose information about the system to an attacker. However, if it prevents a user from giving a password over an insecure connection, it might keep information out of the hands of an attacker.
sufficient	Success indicates that this module type has succeeded, and no subsequent required modules of this type are executed. Failure is not fatal to the stack of this module type. This technique is generally used when one form of authentication or another is good enough: If one fails, PAM tries the other. For example, when you use rsh to connect to another computer, **pam_rhosts_auth** first checks whether your connection can be trusted without a password. If the connection can be trusted, the **pam_rhosts_auth** module reports success, and PAM immediately reports success to the rsh daemon that called it. You will not be asked for a password. If your connection is not considered trustworthy, PAM starts the authentication over and asks for a password. If this second authentication succeeds, PAM ignores the fact that the **pam_rhosts_auth** module reported failure. If both modules fail, you will not be able to log in.
optional	Result is generally ignored. An optional module is relevant only when it is the only module on the stack for a particular service.

PAM uses each of the module types as requested by the application. That is, the application asks PAM separately to authenticate, check account status, manage sessions, and change the password. PAM uses one or more modules from the **/lib/security** directory to accomplish each of these tasks.

The configuration files in **/etc/pam.d** list the set of modules to be used for each application to perform each task. Each such set of the same module types is called a *stack*. PAM calls the modules one at a time in order, going from the top of the stack (the first module listed in the configuration file) to the bottom. Each module reports success or failure back to PAM. When all stacks of modules (with some exceptions) within a configuration file have been called, the PAM library reports success or failure back to the application.

EXAMPLE

Part of a sample login service's authentication stack follows:

```
$ cat /etc/pam.d/login
auth       requsite    pam_securetty.so
@include   common-auth
account    required    pam_nologin.so
...
```

The login utility first asks for a username and then asks PAM to run this stack to authenticate the user. Refer to Table 11-4 on page 462 and Table 11-5 on page 463.

1. PAM first calls the **pam_securetty** (secure tty) module to make sure the **root** user logs in only from an allowed terminal. (By default, **root** is not allowed to run login over the network; this policy helps prevent security breaches.) The **pam_securetty** module is *required* to succeed if the authentication stack is to succeed. The **pam_securetty** module reports failure only if someone is trying to log in as **root** from an unauthorized terminal. Otherwise (if the username being authenticated is not **root** or if the username is **root** and the login attempt is being made from a secure terminal), the **pam_securetty** module reports success.

    Success and failure within PAM are opaque concepts that apply only to PAM. They do not equate to true and false as used elsewhere in the operating system.

2. The included **common-auth** file holds modules that check whether the user who is logging in is authorized to do so. As part of completing this task, they verify the username and password.

3. The **pam_nologin** module makes sure that if the **/etc/nologin.txt** file exists, only the **root** user is allowed to log in. (That is, the **pam_nologin** module reports success only if **/etc/nologin.txt** does not exist or if the **root** user is logging in.) Thus, when a shutdown has been scheduled to occur in the near future, the system keeps users from logging in only to have the system shut down moments later.

The **account** module type works like the **auth** module type but is called after the user has been authenticated; it acts as an additional security check or requirement for a user to gain access to the system. For example, **account** modules might enforce a policy that a user can log in only during business hours.

The **session** module type sets up and tears down the session (perhaps mounting and unmounting the user's home directory). One common **session** module on an Ubuntu system is **pam_mail**, which announces **you have new mail** when a user logs in to a textual environment.

The **password** module type is a bit unusual: All modules in the stack are called once and told to get all information they need to store the password to persistent memory, such as a disk, but not actually to store it. If it determines that it cannot or should not store the password, a module reports failure. If all **password** modules in the stack report success, they are called a second time and told to store to persistent memory the password they obtained on the first pass. The **password** module is responsible for updating the authentication information (that is, changing the user's password).

Any one module can act as more than one module type; many modules can act as all four module types.

MODIFYING THE PAM CONFIGURATION

Be cautious when changing PAM files

caution   Unless you understand how to configure PAM, do not change the files in **/etc/pam.d**. Mistakes in the configuration of PAM can make the system unusable.

Some UNIX systems require that a user be a member of the **wheel** group to use the su command. Although Ubuntu Linux is not configured this way by default, PAM allows you to change this behavior by editing the **/etc/pam.d/su** file:

```
$ cat /etc/pam.d/su
...
# Uncomment this to force users to be a member of group root before they can use 'su'
# auth        required    pam_wheel.so

# Uncomment this if you want wheel members to be able to su without a password.
# auth        sufficient pam_wheel.so trust
...
```

The lines of this **su** module contain comments that include the lines necessary to permit only users who are in the **wheel** group to use su (required) and to permit members of the **wheel** group to run su without supplying a password (sufficient). Uncomment one of these lines when you want the system to follow one of these rules.

Brackets ([]) in the control flags field

caution   You can set the control flags in a more complex way than described in this section. When you see brackets ([ ]) in the control flags position in a PAM configuration file, the newer, more complex method is in use. Each comma-delimited argument is a *value=action* pair. When the result returned by the function matches *value*, *action* is evaluated. For more information refer to the *PAM System Administrator's Guide* (www.kernel.org/pub/linux/libs/pam/Linux-PAM-html/Linux-PAM_SAG.html).

CHAPTER SUMMARY

A system administrator is someone who keeps the system useful and convenient for its users. Much of the work you do as the system administrator will require you to work with **root** privileges. A user with these privileges (sometimes referred to as Superuser) has extensive systemwide powers that normal users do not have. A user with **root** privileges can read from and write to any file and can execute programs that ordinary users are not permitted to execute.

The system administrator controls system operation, which includes many tasks: configuring the system; booting up; running init scripts; setting up servers; working in recovery (single-user) and multiuser modes; bringing the system down; and handling system crashes. Ubuntu Linux provides both graphical and textual configuration tools.

When you bring up the system in recovery (single-user) mode, only the system console is functional. When the system is in recovery mode, you can back up files and use fsck to check the integrity of filesystems before you mount them. The telinit utility can bring the system to its default multiuser state. With the system running in multiuser mode, you can still perform many administration tasks, such as adding users and printers.

As installed, the **root** account on an Ubuntu system is locked: It has no password. Ubuntu recommends you use sudo when you need to perform a task with **root** privileges. The sudo utility grants **root** privileges based on your password. A system that does not have a **root** password and that relies on sudo to escalate permissions can be more secure than one with a **root** password.

The Upstart **init** daemon, which replaces the traditional System V **init** daemon (SysVinit), is event-based and can start and stop services upon receiving information that something on the system has changed. This kind of change is called an *event*. Events include adding devices to and removing them from the system as well as bringing the system up and shutting it down.

You can use TCP wrappers to control who can use which system services by editing the **hosts.allow** and **hosts.deny** files in the **/etc** directory. Setting up a chroot jail limits the portion of the filesystem a user sees, so it can help control the damage a malicious user can do.

You can set up a DHCP server so you do not have to configure each system on a network manually. DHCP can provide both static and dynamic IP addresses. Whether a system uses NIS, DNS, local files, or a combination (and in what order) as a source of information is determined by **/etc/nsswitch.conf**. Linux-PAM enables you to maintain fine-grained control over who can access the system, how they can access it, and what they can do.

EXERCISES

1. How does recovery (single-user) mode differ from multiuser mode?

2. How would you communicate each of the following messages?

    a. The system is coming down tomorrow at 6:00 in the evening for periodic maintenance.

    b. The system is coming down in 5 minutes.

    c. Zach's jobs are slowing the system down drastically, and he should postpone them.

    d. Zach's wife just had a baby girl.

3. How would you run a program with Sam's privileges if you did not know his password but had permission to use sudo to run a command with **root** privileges? How would you spawn a shell with the same environment that Sam has when he first logs in?

4. How would you allow a user to execute a specific, privileged command without giving the user the **root** password or permission to use sudo to run any command with **root** privileges?

5. How do you kill process 1648? How do you kill all processes running kmail? In which instances do you need to work with **root** privileges?

6. What does the **/etc/event.d/logd** file do and what starts it? What does the **respawn** keyword in this file mean?

7. Develop a strategy for coming up with a password that an intruder would not be likely to guess but that you will be able to remember.

ADVANCED EXERCISES

8. Give the command

    ```
    $ /sbin/fuser -uv /
    ```

    What does the output list? Why is it so long? Give the same command while working with **root** privileges (or ask the system administrator to do so and email you the results). How does this list differ from the first? Why is it different?

9. When it puts files in a **lost+found** directory, fsck has lost the directory information for the files and thus has lost the names of the files. Each file is given a new name, which is the same as the inode number for the file:

    ```
    $ ls -l lost+found
    -rw-r--r-- 1 max pubs   110 Jun 10 10:55 51262
    ```

    How can you identify these files and restore them?

10. Take a look at **/usr/bin/lesspipe**. Explain its purpose and give six ways it works.

11. Why are setuid shell scripts inherently unsafe?

12. When a user logs in, you would like the system to first check the local **/etc/passwd** file for a username and then check NIS. How do you implement this strategy?

13. Some older kernels contain a vulnerability that allows a local user to gain **root** privileges. Explain how this kind of vulnerability negates the value of a chroot jail.

12

FILES, DIRECTORIES, AND FILESYSTEMS

Filesystems hold directories of files. These structures store user data and system data that are the basis of users' work on the system and the system's existence. This chapter discusses important files and directories, various types of files and ways to work with them, and the use and maintenance of filesystems.

IMPORTANT FILES AND DIRECTORIES

This section details the files most commonly used to administer the system. For more information, refer to "Important Standard Directories and Files" on page 199.

lost+found Holds pre-allocated disk blocks that fsck uses to store unlinked files (files that have lost their directory [and therefore filename] information). Having these blocks available ensures that fsck does not have to allocate data blocks during recovery, a process that could further damage a corrupted filesystem. See page 494 for more information on fsck.

Each **ext2** and **ext3** filesystem contains a **lost+found** directory in the filesystem's root directory. If, for example, a filesystem is mounted at **/home**, there will be a **/home/lost+found** directory. There is always a **/lost+found** directory. These directories are normally created by mkfs when it writes an **ext2** or **ext3** filesystem to a partition. Although rarely necessary, you can create a **lost+found** directory manually using mklost+found.

~/.bash_profile Contains an individual user's login shell initialization script. By default, Ubuntu does not create this file when it adds a user. The shell executes the commands in this file in the same environment as the shell each time a user logs in. (For information on executing a shell script in this manner, refer to the discussion of the . [dot] command on page 280.) The file must be located in a user's home directory. It is not run from terminal emulator windows because you do not log in in those windows.

You can use **.bash_profile** to specify a terminal type (for vi, terminal emulators, and other programs), run stty to establish the terminal characteristics, set up aliases, and perform other housekeeping functions when a user logs in.

A simple **.bash_profile** file specifying a vt100 terminal and CONTROL-H as the erase key follows:

```
$ cat .bash_profile
export TERM=vt100
stty erase '^h'
```

For more information refer to "Startup Files" on page 277.

~/.bashrc Contains an individual user's interactive, nonlogin shell initialization script. The shell executes the commands in this file in the same environment as the (new) shell each time a user creates a new interactive shell, including when a user opens a terminal emulator window. (For information on executing a shell script in this manner, refer to the discussion of the . [dot] command on page 280.) The **.bashrc** script differs from **.bash_profile** in that it is executed each time a new shell is spawned, not just when a user logs in. For more information refer to "Startup Files" on page 277.

/dev Contains files representing pseudodevices and physical devices that may be attached to the system. The following list explains the naming conventions for some physical devices:

- **/dev/fd0**—The first floppy disk. The second floppy disk is named **/dev/fd1**.

- **/dev/hda**—The master disk on the primary IDE controller. The slave disk on the primary IDE controller is named **/dev/hdb**. This disk may be a CD-ROM drive.

- **/dev/hdc**—The master disk on the secondary IDE controller. The slave disk on the secondary IDE controller is named **/dev/hdd**. This disk may be a CD-ROM drive.

- **/dev/sda**—Traditionally the first SCSI disk; now the first non-IDE drive, including SATA and USB drives. Other, similar drives are named **/dev/sdb**, **/dev/sdc**, etc.

These names, such as **/dev/sda**, represent the order of the devices on the bus the devices are connected to, not the device itself. For example, if you swap the data cables on the disks referred to as **/dev/sda** and **/dev/sdb**, the drive's designations will change. Similarly, if you remove the device referred to as **/dev/sda**, the device that was referred to as **/dev/sdb** will now be referred to as **/dev/sda**.

/dev/disk/by-id Holds symbolic links to local devices. The names of the devices in this directory identify the devices. Each entry points to the device in **/dev** that it refers to.

```
$ ls -l /dev/disk/by-id
lrwxrwxrwx 1 root root 9 Sep  9 08:32 ata-CR-48XGTE_3E30053332_0175 -> ../../hdb
lrwxrwxrwx 1 root root 9 Sep  9 08:32 ata-WDC_WD1600JB-00GVA0_WD-WCAL95325197 -> ../../hda
```

/dev/disk/by-uuid Holds symbolic links to local devices. The names of the devices in this directory consist of the *UUID* (page 1139) numbers of the devices. Each entry points to the device in **/dev** that it refers to. See page 492 for more information.

```
$ ls -l /dev/disk/by-uuid
lrwxrwxrwx 1 root root 10 Jun  4 11:41 39fc600f-91d5-4c9f-8559-727050b27645 -> ../../hda2
lrwxrwxrwx 1 root root 10 Jun  4 11:41 7eb0ba40-d48d-4ded-b4e4-7027cc93629f -> ../../hda5
lrwxrwxrwx 1 root root 10 Jun  4 11:41 8c2e5007-9cea-4bfb-8d26-82f8b376949b -> ../../hda6
...
```

/dev/null Also called a *bit bucket*. Output sent to this file disappears. The **/dev/null** file is a device file. Input that you redirect to come from this file appears as null values, creating an empty file. You can create an empty file named **nothing** by giving one of the following commands:

```
$ cat /dev/null > nothing
$ cp /dev/null nothing
```

or, without explicitly using **/dev/null**,

```
$ > nothing
```

The last command redirects the output of a null command to the file with the same result as the previous commands. You can use any of these commands to truncate an existing file to zero length without changing its permissions. You can also use **/dev/null** to get rid of output that you do not want:

```
$ grep portable * 2> /dev/null
```

This command displays all lines in all files in the working directory that contain the string **portable**. Any output to standard error (page 281), such as a permission or directory error, is discarded, while output to standard output appears on the screen.

/dev/pts   A hook into the Linux kernel. This pseudofilesystem is part of the pseudoterminal support. Pseudoterminals are used by remote login programs, such as ssh and telnet, as well as xterm and other graphical terminal emulators. The following sequence of commands demonstrates that Sam is logged in on **/dev/pts/2**. After using **who am i** to verify the pseudoterminal he is logged in on and using ls to show that this pseudoterminal exists, Sam redirects the output of an echo command to **/dev/pts/2**, whereupon the output appears on his screen:

```
$ who am i
sam      pts/2         2007-05-31 17:37 (dog.bogus.com)
$ ls /dev/pts
0  1  2
$ echo Hi there > /dev/pts/2
Hi there
```

/dev/random
and
/dev/urandom
Interfaces to the kernel's random number generator. You can use either file with dd to create a file filled with pseudorandom bytes.

```
$ dd if=/dev/urandom of=randfile2 bs=1 count=100
100+0 records in
100+0 records out
100 bytes (100 B) copied, 0.000884387 seconds, 113 kB/s
```

The preceding command reads from **/dev/urandom** and writes to the file named **randfile**. The block size is 1 and the count is 100; thus **randfile** is 100 bytes long. For bytes that are more random, you can read from **/dev/random**. See the **urandom** and **random** man pages for more information.

optional

Wiping a file   You can use a similar technique to wipe data from a file before deleting it, making it almost impossible to recover data from the deleted file. You might want to wipe a file for security reasons.

In the following example, ls shows the size of the file named **secret**. Using a block size of 1 and a count corresponding to the number of bytes in **secret**, dd wipes the file. The **conv=notrunc** argument ensures that dd writes over the data in the file and not another (erroneous) place on the disk.

```
$ ls -l secret
-rw-r--r-- 1 sam sam 5733 2007-05-31 17:43 secret
$ dd if=/dev/urandom of=secret bs=1 count=5733 conv=notrunc
5733+0 records in
5733+0 records out
5733 bytes (5.7 kB) copied, 0.0358146 seconds, 160 kB/s
$ rm secret
```

For added security, run sync to flush the disk buffers after running dd, and repeat the two commands several times before deleting the file. See wipe.sourceforge.net for more information about wiping files.

/dev/zero   Input you take from this file contains an infinite string of zeros (numerical zeros, not ASCII zeros). You can fill a file (such as a swap file, page 480) or overwrite a file with zeros with a command such as the following:

```
$ dd if=/dev/zero of=zeros bs=1024 count=10
10+0 records in
10+0 records out
10240 bytes (10 kB) copied, 0.000160263 seconds, 63.9 MB/s

$ od -c zeros
0000000  \0  \0  \0  \0  \0  \0  \0  \0  \0  \0  \0  \0  \0  \0  \0  \0
*
0024000
```

The od utility shows the contents of the new file.

When you try to do with **/dev/zero** what you can do with **/dev/null**, you fill the partition in which you are working:

```
$ cp /dev/zero bigzero
cp: writing 'bigzero': No space left on device
$ rm bigzero
```

/etc/aliases   Used by the mail delivery system to hold **aliases** for users. Edit this file to suit local needs. For more information refer to **/etc/aliases** on page 686.

/etc/alternatives   Holds symbolic links so that you can call a utility by a name other than that of the file that holds the utility. For example, when you give the command **btdownloadcurses**, the shell calls **btdownloadcurses.bittorrent** using the following links:

```
$ ls -l /usr/bin/btdownloadcurses
lrwxrwxrwx ... /usr/bin/btdownloadcurses -> /etc/alternatives/btdownloadcurses
$ ls -l /etc/alternatives/btdownloadcurses
lrwxrwxrwx ... /etc/alternatives/btdownloadcurses -> /usr/bin/btdownloadcurses.bittorrent
```

The **alternatives** directory also allows a utility to appear in more than one directory:

```
$ ls -l /usr/X11R6/bin/btdownloadcurses /usr/bin/X11/btdownloadcurses
lrwxrwxrwx ... /usr/X11R6/bin/btdownloadcurses -> /etc/alternatives/btdownloadcurses
lrwxrwxrwx ... /usr/bin/X11/btdownloadcurses -> /etc/alternatives/btdownloadcurses
```

In addition, this directory allows you to call one utility by several names. Although the **alternatives** directory does not allow developers to do anything they could not do without it, it provides an orderly way to keep and update these links. Use whereis (page 165) to find all links to a utility.

/etc/at.allow, /etc/at.deny, /etc/cron.allow, and /etc/cron.deny   By default, users can use the at and crontab utilities. The **at.allow** and **cron.allow** files list the users who are allowed to use at and crontab, respectively. The **at.deny** and **cron.deny** files specify users who are not permitted to use the corresponding utilities. As Ubuntu Linux is configured, the **at.deny** file holds a list of some system accounts and there is no **at.allow** file, allowing nonsystem accounts to use at; the absence of **cron.allow** and **cron.deny** files allows anyone to use crontab. To prevent anyone except a user running with **root** privileges from using at, remove the **at.allow** and **at.deny** files. To prevent anyone except a user running with **root** privileges from using crontab, create a **cron.allow** file with the single entry **root**. For more information on crontab, refer to "Scheduling Tasks" on page 588.

/etc/bash.bashrc   Contains the global interactive, nonlogin shell initialization script. The default Ubuntu **/etc/profile** (page 477) file executes the commands in this file. A user can override settings made in this file in her **~/.bashrc** (page 470) file.

/etc/default   Holds files that set default values for system services and utilities such as NFS and useradd. Look at the files in this directory for more information.

/etc/dumpdates   Contains information about the last execution of dump (part of the **dump** software package). For each filesystem, it stores the time of the last dump at a given dump level. The dump utility uses this information to determine which files to back up when executing at a particular dump level. Refer to "Backing Up Files" on page 582 and the dump man page for more information.

Following is a sample **/etc/dumpdates** file from a system with four filesystems and a backup schedule that uses three dump levels:

```
/dev/hda1           5 Thu Apr 19 03:53:55 2007
/dev/hda8           2 Sun Apr 15 08:25:24 2007
/dev/hda9           2 Sun Apr 15 08:57:32 2007
/dev/hda10          2 Sun Apr 15 08:58:06 2007
/dev/hda1           2 Sun Apr 15 09:02:27 2007
/dev/hda1           0 Sun Mar 18 22:08:35 2007
/dev/hda8           0 Sun Mar 18 22:33:40 2007
/dev/hda9           0 Sun Mar 18 22:35:22 2007
/dev/hda10          0 Sun Mar 18 22:43:45 2007
```

The first column contains the device name of the dumped filesystem. The second column contains the dump level and the date of the dump.

/etc/event.d   Holds files that define Upstart **init** jobs. See page 418 for more information.

/etc/fstab   **filesystem (mount) table**—Contains a list of all mountable devices as specified by the system administrator. Programs do not write to this file; they only read from it. See page 492 for more information.

/etc/group   Groups allow users to share files or programs without giving all system users access to those files or programs. This scheme is useful when several users are working with files that are not public. The **/etc/group** file associates one or more usernames with each group (number). Refer to "ACLs: Access Control Lists" on page 207 for a finer-grained way to control file access.

Each entry in the **/etc/group** file has four colon-separated fields that describe one group:

> *group-name:password:group-ID:login-name-list*

The *group-name* is the name of the group. The *password* is an optional hashed (page 1111) password. This field frequently contains an **x**, indicating that group passwords are not used. The *group-ID* is a number, with 1–999 reserved for system accounts. The *login-name-list* is a comma-separated list of users who belong to the group. If an entry is too long to fit on one line, end the line with a backslash (\), which quotes the following RETURN, and continue the entry on the next line. A sample entry from a **group** file follows. The group is named **pubs**, has no password, and has a group ID of 1103:

```
pubs:x:1103:max,sam,zach,mark
```

You can use the groups utility to display the groups to which a user belongs:

```
$ groups sam
sam : sam pubs
```

Each user has a primary group, which is the group that user is assigned in the **/etc/passwd** file. By default, Ubuntu Linux has user private groups: Each user's primary group has the same name as the user. In addition, a user can belong to other groups, depending on which *login-name-list*s the user appears on in the **/etc/group** file. In effect, you simultaneously belong both to your primary group and to any groups you are assigned to in **/etc/group**. When you attempt to access a file you do not own, Linux checks whether you are a member of the group that has access to the file. If you are, you are subject to the group access permissions for the file. If you are not a member of the group that has access to the file and you do not own the file, you are subject to the public access permissions for the file.

When you create a new file, Linux assigns it to the group associated with the directory the file is being written into, assuming that you belong to that group. If you do not belong to the group that has access to the directory, the file is assigned to your primary group.

Refer to page 580 for information on using users-admin to work with groups.

/etc/hosts   Stores the names, IP addresses, and optionally aliases of other systems. At the very least, this file must have the hostname and IP address that you have chosen for the local system and a special entry for **localhost**. This entry supports the *loopback service*, which allows the local system to talk to itself (for example, for RPC services). The IP address of the loopback service is always 127.0.0.1, while 127.0.1.1 names the local system. Following is a simple **/etc/hosts** file:

```
$ cat /etc/hosts
127.0.0.1       localhost
127.0.1.1       tiny
192.168.0.9     jam
192.168.0.10    plum
192.168.0.12    dog
...
```

If you are not using NIS or DNS to look up hostnames (called *hostname resolution*), you must include in **/etc/hosts** all systems that the local system should be able to contact by hostname. (A system can always contact another system by using the IP address of the system.) The **hosts** entry in the **/etc/nsswitch.conf** file (page 458) controls the order in which hostname resolution services are checked.

/etc/inittab   **initialization table**—Some distributions use this file to control the behavior of the init process. It is not present on Ubuntu systems. See **rc-default** on page 422 for more information.

/etc/motd   Contains the message of the day, which can be displayed each time someone logs in using a textual login. This file typically contains site policy and legal information. Keep this file short because users tend to see the message many times.

/etc/mtab   When you call mount without any arguments, it consults this file and displays a list of mounted devices. Each time you (or an init script) call mount or umount, these utilities make the necessary changes to **mtab**. Although this is an ASCII text file, you should not edit it. See also **/etc/fstab**.

Fixing mtab

tip   The kernel maintains its own internal mount table. You can display this table with the command **cat /proc/mounts**. Sometimes the list of files in **/etc/mtab** may not be synchronized with the partitions in this table. To bring the **mtab** file in line with the operating system's mount table, you can either reboot the system or replace **/etc/mtab** with a symbolic link to **/proc/mounts** (although some information may be lost).

```
$ sudo rm /etc/mtab
$ sudo ln -s /proc/mounts /etc/mtab
```

/etc/nsswitch.conf
Specifies whether a system uses NIS, DNS, local files, or a combination as the source of certain information, and in what order it consults these services (page 458).

/etc/pam.d   Files in this directory specify the authentication methods used by PAM (page 461) applications.

/etc/passwd   Describes users to the system. Do not edit this file directly; instead, use one of the utilities discussed in "Configuring User and Group Accounts" on page 578. Each line in **passwd** has seven colon-separated fields that describe one user:

login-name:password:user-ID:group-ID:info:directory:program

The *login-name* is the user's username—the name you enter in response to the **login:** prompt or on a GUI login screen. The value of the *password* is the character **x**. The **/etc/shadow file** (page 479) stores the real password, which is hashed (page 1111). For security reasons, every account should have a password. By convention, disabled accounts have an asterisk (*) in this field.

The *user-ID* is a number, with 0 indicating the **root** account and 1–999 being reserved for system accounts. The *group-ID* identifies the user as a member of a group. It is a number, with 0–999 being reserved for system accounts; see **/etc/group** (page 474). You can change these values and set maximum values in **/etc/login.defs**.

The *info* is information that various programs, such as accounting and email programs, use to identify the user further. Normally it contains at least the first and last names of the user. It is referred to as the *GECOS* (page 1110) field.

The *directory* is the absolute pathname of the user's home directory. The *program* is the program that runs once the user logs in to a textual session. If *program* is not present, a value of **/bin/bash** is assumed. You can put **/bin/tcsh** here to log in using the TC Shell or **/bin/zsh** to log in using the Z Shell, assuming the shell you specify is installed. The chsh utility (page 441) changes this value.

The *program* is usually a shell, but it can be any program. The following line in the **passwd** file creates a "user" whose only purpose is to execute the who utility:

```
who:x:1000:1000:execute who:/usr:/usr/bin/who
```

Logging in with **who** as a username causes the system to log you in, execute the who utility, and log you out. The output of who flashes by quickly because the new login prompt clears the screen immediately after who finishes running. This entry in the **passwd** file does not provide a shell, so you cannot stay logged in after who finishes executing.

This technique is useful for providing special accounts that may do only one thing. The **ftp** account, for example, enables anonymous FTP (page 651) access to an FTP server. Because no one logs in on this account, the shell is set to **/bin/false** (which returns a false exit status) or to **/usr/sbin/nologin** (which does not permit a nonprivileged user to log in). When you put a message in **/etc/nologin**, nologin displays that message (except it has the same problem as the output of who: It is removed so quickly that it is hard to see).

Do not replace a login shell with a shell script

security   Do not use shell scripts as replacements for shells in **/etc/passwd**. A user may be able to interrupt a shell script, giving him full shell access when you did not intend to do so. When installing a dummy shell, use a compiled program, not a shell script.

/etc/printcap   The printer capability database for LPD/LPR (page 530). It is not used with CUPS (Chapter 14), Ubuntu's default printing system. This file describes system printers and is derived from 4.3BSD UNIX.

/etc/profile   Contains a systemwide interactive shell initialization script for environment and startup programs. When you log in, the shell immediately executes the commands in this file in the same environment as the shell. (For information on executing a shell script in this manner, refer to the discussion of the **.** [dot] command on page 280.) This file allows the system administrator to establish systemwide environment parameters that individual users can override in their **~/.bash_profile** (page 470) files. For example, this file can set shell variables, execute utilities, set up aliases, and take care of other housekeeping tasks.

The default Ubuntu **/etc/profile** file sets the shell prompt and executes the commands in **/etc/bash.bashrc** (page 474).

Following is an example of a **/etc/profile** file that displays the message of the day (the **/etc/motd** file), sets the file-creation mask (umask, page 442), and sets the interrupt character to CONTROL-C:

```
# cat /etc/profile
cat /etc/motd
umask 022
stty intr '^c'
```

/etc/protocols   Provides protocol numbers, aliases, and brief definitions for DARPA Internet TCP/IP protocols. Do not modify this file.

/etc/init.d   Holds SysVinit initialization scripts. See page 423 for more information.

/etc/resolv.conf The resolver (page 786) configuration file, which is used to provide access to DNS. By default, this file is rebuilt by resolvconf when you run the **bind9** init script. See "**named** options" on page 796, "resolvconf and **resolv.conf**" on page 797, and the resolver and **resolv.conf** man pages for more information.

The following example shows the **resolv.conf** file for the **example.com** domain. A **resolv.conf** file usually contains at least two lines—a search line (optional) and a nameserver line:

```
# cat /etc/resolv.conf
search example.com
nameserver 10.0.0.50
nameserver 10.0.0.51
```

The **search** keyword may be followed by a maximum of six domain names. The first domain is interpreted as the host's local domain. These names are appended one at a time to all DNS queries, shortening the time needed to query local hosts. The domains are searched in order in the process of resolving hostnames that are not fully qualified. See *FQDN* on page 1109.

When you put **search example.com** in **resolv.conf**, any reference to a host within the **example.com** domain or a subdomain (such as **marketing.example.com**) can use the abbreviated form of the host. For example, instead of issuing the command **ping speedy.marketing.example.com**, you can use **ping speedy.marketing**. The following line in **resolv.conf** causes the **marketing** subdomain to be searched first, followed by **sales**, and finally the entire **example.com** domain:

```
search marketing.example.com sales.example.com example.com
```

It is a good idea to put the most frequently used domain names first to try to outguess possible conflicts. If both **speedy.marketing.example.com** and **speedy.example.com** exist, for example, the order of the search determines which one is selected when you invoke DNS. Do not overuse this feature: The longer the search path, the more network DNS requests generated, and the slower the response. Three or four names are typically sufficient.

The **nameserver** line(s) indicate which systems the local system should query to resolve hostnames to IP addresses, and vice versa. These machines are consulted in the order they appear, with a timeout between queries. The first timeout is a few seconds; each subsequent timeout is twice as long as the previous one. The preceding file causes this system to query 10.0.0.50, followed by 10.0.0.51 when the first system does not answer within a few seconds. The **resolv.conf** file may be automatically updated when a PPP- (Point-to-Point Protocol) or DHCP- (Dynamic Host Configuration Protocol) controlled interface is activated. Refer to the **resolv.conf** and **resolver** man pages for more information.

/etc/rpc Maps RPC services to RPC numbers. The three columns in this file show the name of the server for the RPC program, the RPC program number, and any aliases.

/etc/services   Lists system services. The three columns in this file show the informal name of the service, the port number/protocol the service uses most frequently, and any aliases for the service. This file does not specify which services are running on the local system, nor does it map services to port numbers. The **services** file is used internally to map port numbers to services for display purposes.

/etc/shadow   Contains *MD5* (page 1119) hashed user passwords. Each entry occupies one line composed of nine fields, separated by colons:

login-name:password:last-mod:min:max:warn:inactive:expire:flag

The *login-name* is the user's username—the name that the user enters in response to the **login:** prompt or on a GUI login screen. The *password* is a hashed password that passwd puts in this file. New accounts that are not set up with a password are given a value of ! or * in this field to prevent the user from logging in until you assign a password to that user (page 578).

The *last-mod* field indicates when the password was last modified. The *min* is the minimum number of days that must elapse before the password can be changed; the *max* is the maximum number of days before the password must be changed. The *warn* field specifies how much advance warning (in days) will be given to the user before the password expires. The account will be closed if the number of days between login sessions exceeds the number of days specified in the *inactive* field. The account will also be closed as of the date in the *expire* field. The last field in an entry, *flag*, is reserved for future use. You can use usermod (page 581) to modify these fields.

The **shadow** password file must be owned by **root** and must not be publicly readable or writable. Setting ownership and permissions in this way makes it more difficult for someone to break into the system by identifying accounts without passwords or by using specialized programs that try to match hashed passwords.

A number of conventions exist for creating special **shadow** entries. An entry of *LK* or **NP** in the *password* field indicates *locked* or *no password*, respectively. *No password* is different from an empty password; no password implies that this is an administrative account that no one ever logs in on directly. Occasionally programs will run with the privileges of this account for system maintenance functions. These accounts are set up under the principle of least privilege (page 404).

Entries in the **shadow** file must appear in the same order as in the **passwd** file. There must be exactly one **shadow** entry for each **passwd** entry.

/etc/hosts.deny and /etc/hosts.allow   As part of the client/server model, TCP wrappers rely on these files as the basis of a simple access control language. See page 448 for more information.

/proc   Provides a window into the Linux kernel. Through the **/proc** pseudofilesystem you can obtain information on any process running on the system, including its current state, memory usage, CPU usage, terminal association, parent, and group. You can extract information directly from the files in **/proc**. An example follows:

```
$ sleep 1000 &
[1] 22756
$ cd /proc/22756
$ ls -l
total 0
dr-xr-xr-x 2 sam sam 0 2007-06-01 15:24 attr
-r-------- 1 sam sam 0 2007-06-01 15:24 auxv
-r--r--r-- 1 sam sam 0 2007-06-01 15:24 cmdline
-r--r--r-- 1 sam sam 0 2007-06-01 15:24 cpuset
lrwxrwxrwx 1 sam sam 0 2007-06-01 15:24 cwd -> /home/sam
-r-------- 1 sam sam 0 2007-06-01 15:24 environ
lrwxrwxrwx 1 sam sam 0 2007-06-01 15:24 exe -> /bin/sleep
dr-x------ 2 sam sam 0 2007-06-01 15:24 fd
-r--r--r-- 1 sam sam 0 2007-06-01 15:24 maps
-rw------- 1 sam sam 0 2007-06-01 15:24 mem
...

$ cat status
Name:   sleep
State:  S (sleeping)
SleepAVG:       88%
Tgid:   22756
Pid:    22756
PPid:   22723
TracerPid:      0
Uid:    1002    1002    1002    1002
Gid:    1002    1002    1002    1002
FDSize: 256
Groups: 1002
VmPeak:     2800 kB
VmSize:     2800 kB
...
```

In this example, bash creates a background process (PID 22756) for sleep. Next the user changes directories to the directory in **/proc** that has the same name as the PID of the background process (**cd /proc/22756**). This directory holds information about the process it is named for—the sleep process in the example. The **ls –l** command shows that some entries in this directory are links (**cwd** is a link to the directory the process was started from, and **exe** is a link to the executable file that this process is running) and some appear to be ordinary files. All appear to be empty. However, when you use cat to display one of these pseudofiles (**status** in the example), cat displays output. Obviously it is not an ordinary file.

/sbin/shutdown   A utility that brings the system down (see page 434).

swap   Even though **swap** is not normally a file, swap space can be added and deleted from the system dynamically. Swap space is used by the virtual memory subsystem of the kernel. When it runs low on real memory (RAM), the kernel writes memory pages from RAM to the swap space on the disk. Which pages are written and when they are written are controlled by finely tuned algorithms in the Linux kernel. When needed by running programs, the kernel brings these pages back into RAM—a technique called *paging* (page 1124). When a system is running very short on memory, an entire process may be paged out to disk.

Running an application that requires a large amount of virtual memory may result in the need for additional swap space. If you run out of swap space, you can use mkswap to create a swap file and swapon to enable it. Normally you use a disk partition as swap space, but you can also use a file for this purpose. A disk partition provides much better performance than a file.

If you are creating a file as swap space, first use df to ensure that the partition you are creating it in has adequate space for the file. In the following sequence of commands, the administrator first uses dd and /dev/zero (page 473) to create an empty file (do not use cp because you may create a file with holes, which may not work) in the working directory. Next mkswap takes as an argument the name of the file created in the first step to set up the swap space. For security reasons, change the file so that it cannot be read from or written to by anyone except a user with **root** privileges. Use swapon with the same argument to turn the swap file on; then use **swapon –s** to confirm the swap space is available. The final two commands turn off the swap file and remove it. Because many of the commands in this sequence must be executed with **root** privileges, and because typing **sudo** in front of each command would be tedious, the administrator spawns a shell with **root** privileges by giving the command **sudo –i** before starting. The **exit** command at the end of the sequence closes the privileged shell:

```
$ sudo -i
# dd if=/dev/zero of=swapfile bs=1024 count=65536
65536+0 records in
65536+0 records out
67108864 bytes (67 MB) copied, 0.631809 seconds, 106 MB/s
# mkswap swapfile
Setting up swapspace version 1, size = 67104 kB
no label, UUID=e2e4ec08-77a4-47b1-bca1-59dd9a59dbf7
# chmod 600 swapfile
# swapon swapfile
# swapon -s
Filename                                Type            Size      Used
Priority
/dev/hda3                               partition       1951888   33796
-1
/root/swapfile                          file            65528     0
-2
# swapoff swapfile
# rm swapfile
# exit
$
```

/sys A pseudofilesystem that was added in the Linux 2.6 kernel to make it easy for programs running in kernelspace, such as device drivers, to exchange information with programs running in userspace. Refer to udev on page 484.

/usr/share/file/magic

Most files begin with a unique identifier called a *magic number*. This file is a text database listing all known magic numbers on the system. When you use the file utility, it consults **/usr/share/file/magic** to determine the type of a file. Occasionally you may acquire a new tool that creates a new type of file that is unrecognized by the file utility. In this situation you can add entries to the **/etc/magic** file. Refer to the **magic** and **file** man pages for more details. See also "magic number" on page 1118.

/var/log   Holds system log files, many of which are generated by **syslogd** (page 608). You can use a text display program such as less, tail, or cat, or the graphical program gnome-system-log to view the files in this directory. To run gnome-system-log, select **System: Administration⇨System Log** or enter **gnome-system-log** (use **gksudo** if you are not a member of the **adm** group) from a terminal emulator or in a Run Application window (ALT-F2).

/var/log/messages

Contains messages from daemons, the Linux kernel, and security programs. For example, you will find **filesystem full** warning messages, error messages from system daemons (NFS, **exim4**, printer daemons), SCSI and IDE disk error messages, and more in **messages**. Check **/var/log/messages** periodically to keep informed about important system events. Much of the information displayed on the system console is also sent to **messages**. If the system experiences a problem and you cannot access the console, check this file for messages about the problem. See page 608 for information on **syslogd**, which generates many of these messages.

/var/log/auth.log   Holds messages from security-related programs such as sudo and the **sshd** daemon.

FILE TYPES

Linux supports many types of files. This section discusses the following types of files:

- Ordinary files, directories, links, and inodes (next)
- Symbolic links (page 483)
- Device special files (page 483)
- FIFO special files (named pipes) (page 485)
- Sockets (page 485)
- Block and character devices (page 486)
- Raw devices (page 486)

ORDINARY FILES, DIRECTORIES, LINKS, AND INODES

Ordinary and directory files

An *ordinary* file stores user data, such as textual information, programs, or images, such as a **jpeg** or **tiff** file. A *directory* is a standard-format disk file that stores information, including names, about ordinary files and other directory files.

Inodes   An *inode* is a *data structure* (page 1104), stored on disk, that defines a file's existence and is identified by an inode number. An inode contains critical information about a file, such as the name of the owner, where it is physically located on the disk, and how many hard links point to it. Except for directory inodes, inodes do not contain filenames. An inode that describes a directory file relates each of the filenames stored in the directory to the inode that describes that file. This setup allows an inode to be associated with more than one filename and to be pointed to from more than one directory.

When you move (mv) a file, including a directory file, within a filesystem, you change the filename portion of the directory entry associated with the inode that describes the file. You do not create a new inode. If you move a file to another filesystem, mv first creates a new inode on the destination filesystem and then deletes the original inode. You can also use mv to move a directory recursively from one filesystem to another. In this case mv copies the directory and all the files in it, and deletes the original directory and its contents.

When you make an additional hard link (ln, page 214) to a file, you add a directory entry that points to the inode that describes the file. You do not create a new inode.

When you remove (rm) a file, you delete the directory entry that describes the file. When you remove the last hard link to a file, the operating system puts all blocks the inode pointed to back in the *free list* (the list of blocks that are available for use on the disk) and frees the inode to be used again.

The . and ..   Every directory contains at least two entries (. and ..). The . entry is a link to the directory entries   directory itself. The .. entry is a link to the parent directory. In the case of the root directory, there is no parent and the .. entry is a link to the root directory itself. It is not possible to create hard links to directories.

Symbolic links   Because each filesystem has a separate set of inodes, you can create hard links to a file only from within the filesystem that holds that file. To get around this limitation, Linux provides symbolic links, which are files that point to other files. Files that are linked by a symbolic link do not share an inode. As a consequence, you can create a symbolic link to a file from any filesystem. You can also create a symbolic link to a directory, device, or other special file. For more information refer to "Symbolic Links" on page 216.

DEVICE SPECIAL FILES

Device special files (also called *device files* and *special files*) represent Linux kernel routines that provide access to an operating system feature. FIFO (first in, first out) special files allow unrelated programs to exchange information. Sockets allow unrelated processes on the same or different systems to exchange information. One type of socket, the UNIX domain socket, is a special file. Symbolic links are another type of special file.

Device files   *Device files* include both block and character special files and represent device drivers that allow the system to communicate with peripheral devices, such as terminals, printers, and hard disks. By convention, device files appear in the **/dev** directory and its subdirectories. Each device file represents a device; hence, the system reads from and writes to the file to read from and write to the device it represents. The following example shows part of the output that an **ls –l** command produces for the **/dev** directory:

```
$ ls -l /dev
total 0
lrwxrwxrwx 1 root root           13 May 24 16:08 MAKEDEV -> /sbin/MAKEDEV
crw-rw---- 1 root root      10,  63 May 24 16:08 acpi
crw-rw---- 1 root audio     14,  12 May 24 16:08 adsp
crw-rw---- 1 root video     10, 175 May 24 16:08 agpgart
crw-rw---- 1 root audio     14,   4 May 24 16:08 audio
drwxr-xr-x 3 root root           60 May 24 16:08 bus
lrwxrwxrwx 1 root root            3 May 24 16:08 cdrom -> hdb
lrwxrwxrwx 1 root root            3 May 24 16:08 cdrw -> hdb
crw------- 1 root root       5,   1 Jun  1 07:36 console
...
brw-rw---- 1 root disk       3,   0 Jun  6 13:49 hda
brw-rw---- 1 root disk       3,   1 Jun  6 13:50 hda1
brw-rw---- 1 root cdrom      3,  64 Jun  6 13:49 hd
...
```

The first character of each line is always **–**, **b**, **c**, **d**, **l**, or **p**, representing the file type—ordinary (plain), block, character, directory, symbolic link, or named pipe (see the following section), respectively. The next nine characters identify the permissions for the file, followed by the number of hard links and the names of the owner and the group. Where the number of bytes in a file would appear for an ordinary or directory file, a device file shows *major* and *minor device numbers* (page 485) separated by a comma. The rest of the line is the same as for any other **ls –l** listing (page 201).

udev   The **udev** utility manages device naming dynamically. It replaces the earlier **devfs** and moves the device-naming functionality from the kernel to userspace. Because devices are added to and removed from a system infrequently, the performance penalty associated with this change is minimal. The benefit of the move is that a bug in **udev** cannot compromise or crash the kernel.

The **udev** utility is part of the hotplug system (next). When a device is added to or removed from the system, the kernel creates a device name in the **/sys** pseudofilesystem and notifies hotplug of the event, which is received by **udev**. The **udev** utility then creates the device file, usually in the **/dev** directory, or removes the device file from the system. The **udev** utility can also rename network interfaces. See www.kernel.org/pub/linux/utils/kernel/hotplug/udev.html for more information.

Hotplug   The hotplug system allows you to plug a device into a running system and use it immediately. Although hotplug was available in the Linux 2.4 kernel, the 2.6 kernel integrates hotplug with the unified device driver model framework (the *driver model core*) so that any bus can report an event when a device is added to or removed from the system. User software can be notified of the event so it can take appropriate action. See linux-hotplug.sourceforge.net for more information.

FIFO SPECIAL FILE (NAMED PIPE)

A *FIFO special* file, also called a *named pipe,* represents a pipe: You read from and write to the file to read from and write to the pipe. The term *FIFO* stands for *first in, first out*—the way any pipe works. In other words, the first information you put in one end is the first information that comes out the other end. When you use a pipe on a command line to send the output of a program to the printer, the printer outputs the information in the same order that the program produced it and sent it to the pipe.

Unless you are writing sophisticated programs, you will not be working with FIFO special files. However, programs that you use on Linux use named pipes for inter-process communication. You can create a pipe using mkfifo:

```
$ mkfifo AA
$ ls -l AA
prw-rw-r--   1 zach zach 0 Apr 26 13:11 AA
```

The **p** at the left end of the output of **ls –l** indicates the file is a pipe.

Both UNIX and Linux systems have included pipes for many generations. Without named pipes, only processes that were children of the same ancestor could use pipes to exchange information. Using named pipes, *any* two processes on a single system can exchange information. When one program writes to a FIFO special file, another program can read from the same file. The programs do not have to run at the same time or be aware of each other's activity. The operating system handles all buffering and information storage. This type of communication is termed *asynchronous* (*async*) because the programs on the opposite ends of the pipe do not have to be synchronized.

SOCKETS

Like FIFO special files, *sockets* allow asynchronous processes that are not children of the same ancestor to exchange information. Sockets are the central mechanism of the interprocess communication that forms the basis of the networking facility. When you use networking utilities, pairs of cooperating sockets manage the communication between the processes on the local system and the remote system. Sockets form the basis of such utilities as ssh and scp.

MAJOR AND MINOR DEVICE NUMBERS

A *major device number* points to a driver in the kernel that works with a class of hardware devices: terminal, printer, tape drive, hard disk, and so on. In the listing of the **/dev** directory on page 484, all the hard disk partitions have a major device number of 3.

A *minor device number* identifies a particular piece of hardware within a class. Although all hard disk partitions are grouped together by their major device number, each has a different minor device number (**hda1** is 1, **hda2** is 2, and so on). This setup allows one piece of software (the device driver) to service all similar hardware, yet still be able to distinguish among different physical units.

Block and Character Devices

This section describes typical device drivers. Because device drivers can be changed to suit a particular purpose, the descriptions in this section do not pertain to every system.

Block device A *block device* is an I/O (input/output) device that has the following characteristics:

- Able to perform random access reads

- Has a specific block size

- Handles only single blocks of data at a time

- Accepts only transactions that involve whole blocks of data

- Able to have a filesystem mounted on it

- Has the Linux kernel buffer its input and output

- Appears to the operating system as a series of blocks numbered from 0 through $n - 1$, where n is the number of blocks on the device

Block devices commonly found on a Linux system include hard disks, floppy diskettes, and CDs.

Character device A *character device* is any device that is not a block device. Examples of character devices include printers, terminals, tape drives, and modems.

The device driver for a character device determines how a program reads from and writes to that device. For example, the device driver for a terminal allows a program to read the information you type on the terminal in two ways. First, a program can read single characters from a terminal in *raw* mode—that is, without the driver doing any interpretation of the characters. (This mode has nothing to do with the raw device described in the following section.) Alternatively, a program can read one line at a time. When a program reads one line at a time, the driver handles the erase and kill characters so the program never sees typing mistakes that have been corrected. In this case, the program reads everything from the beginning of a line to the RETURN that ends a line; the number of characters in a line can vary.

Raw Devices

Device driver programs for block devices usually have two entry points so they can be used in two ways: as block devices or as character devices. The character device form of a block device is called a *raw device*. A raw device is characterized by

- Direct I/O (no buffering through the Linux kernel).

- One-to-one correspondence between system calls and hardware requests.

- Device-dependent restrictions on I/O.

fsck An example of a utility that uses a raw device is fsck. It is more efficient for fsck to operate on the disk as a raw device rather than being restricted by the fixed size of blocks in the block device interface. Because it has full knowledge of the underlying filesystem structure, fsck can operate on the raw device using the largest possible units. When a filesystem is mounted, processes normally access the disk through the block device interface, which explains why it is important to allow fsck to modify only unmounted filesystems. On a mounted filesystem, there is the danger that, while fsck is rearranging the underlying structure through the raw device, another process could change a disk block using the block device, resulting in a corrupted filesystem.

FILESYSTEMS

Table 12-1 lists some types of filesystems available under Linux.

Table 12-1   Filesystems

Filesystem	Features
adfs	Advanced Disc Filing System. Used on Acorn computers. The word *Advanced* differentiated this filesystem from its predecessor DFS, which did not support advanced features such as hierarchical filesystems.
affs	Amiga Fast Filesystem (FFS).
autofs	Automounting filesystem (page 756).
cifs	Common Internet Filesystem (page 1101). Formerly the Samba Filesystem (**smbfs**).
coda	CODA distributed filesystem (developed at Carnegie Mellon).
devpts	A pseudofilesystem for pseudoterminals (page 472).
ext2	A standard filesystem for Ubuntu systems, usually with the **ext3** extension.
ext3	A journaling (page 1115) extension to the **ext2** filesystem. It greatly improves recovery time from crashes (it takes a lot less time to run fsck), promoting increased availability. As with any filesystem, a journaling filesystem can lose data during a system crash or hardware failure.
GFS	Global Filesystem. GFS is a journaling, clustering filesystem. It enables a cluster of Linux servers to share a common storage pool.
hfs	Hierarchical Filesystem. Used by older Macintosh systems. Newer Macintosh systems use **hfs+**.
hpfs	High-Performance Filesystem. The native filesystem for IBM's OS/2.
jffs2	Journaling Flash Filesystem (**jffs**). A filesystem for flash memory.
iso9660	The standard filesystem for CDs.
minix	Very similar to Linux. The filesystem of a small operating system that was written for educational purposes by Andrew S. Tanenbaum (www.minix3.org).

Table 12-1   Filesystems (continued)

Filesystem	Features
msdos	Filesystem used by DOS and subsequent Microsoft operating systems. Do not use **msdos** for mounting Windows filesystems; it does not read VFAT attributes.
ncpfs	Novell NetWare NCP Protocol Filesystem. Used to mount remote filesystems under NetWare.
nfs	Network Filesystem. Developed by Sun Microsystems, this protocol allows a computer to access remote files over a network as if the files were local (page 737).
ntfs	NT Filesystem. The native filesystem of Windows NT. See www.linux-ntfs.org.
proc	An interface to several Linux kernel *data structures* (page 1104) that behaves like a filesystem (page 479).
qnx4	QNX 4 operating system filesystem.
reiserfs	A journaling (page 1115) filesystem, based on balanced-tree algorithms. See **ext3** for more on journaling filesystems.
romfs	A dumb, readonly filesystem used mainly for *RAM disks* (page 1128) during installation.
smbfs	Samba Filesystem (deprecated). See **cifs**.
software RAID	RAID implemented in software. Refer to "RAID" on page 39.
sysv	System V UNIX filesystem.
ufs	Default filesystem under Sun's Solaris operating system and other UNIXs.
umsdos	A full-feature UNIX-like filesystem that runs on top of a DOS FAT filesystem.
vfat	Developed by Microsoft, a standard that allows long filenames on FAT partitions.
VxFS	Veritas Extended Filesystem. The first commercial journaling (page 1115) filesystem, popular under HP-UX and Solaris.
xfs	SGI's journaling filesystem (ported from Irix).

mount: MOUNTS A FILESYSTEM

The mount utility connects directory hierarchies—typically filesystems—to the Linux directory hierarchy. These directory hierarchies can be on remote and local disks, CDs, DVDs, and floppy diskettes. Linux can also mount *virtual filesystems* that have been built inside ordinary files, filesystems built for other operating systems, and the special **/proc** filesystem (page 479), which maps useful Linux kernel information to a pseudodirectory. This section covers mounting local filesystems; refer to page 737 for information on using NFS to mount remote directory hierarchies. See **/dev** on page 470 for information on device names.

Mount point The *mount point* for the filesystem/directory hierarchy that you are mounting is a directory in the local filesystem. This directory must exist before you can mount a filesystem; its contents disappear as long as a filesystem is mounted on it and reappear when you unmount the filesystem. See page 35 for a discussion of mount points.

Without any arguments, mount lists the currently mounted filesystems, showing the physical device holding each filesystem, the mount point, the type of filesystem, and any options set when each filesystem was mounted. The mount utility gets this information from the **/etc/mtab** file (page 476).

```
$ mount
/dev/hda1 on / type ext3 (rw,errors=remount-ro)
proc on /proc type proc (rw,noexec,nosuid,nodev)
...
/dev/hda2 on /home type ext3 (rw)
/dev/hda5 on /p15 type ext3 (rw)
/dev/hda6 on /p16 type ext3 (rw)
/dev/sda1 on /p01 type ext3 (rw)
//jam/C on /jam/c type cifs (rw,mand)
dog:/p04 on /p04 type nfs (rw,addr=192.168.0.12)
/dev/hdb on /media/cdrom0 type iso9660 (ro,noexec,nosuid,nodev,user=sam)
```

The first entry in the preceding example shows the root filesystem, which is mounted on **/**. The second entry shows the **/proc** pseudofilesystem (page 479). The next four entries identify disk partitions holding standard Linux **ext3** filesystems. The directory **/jam/c** has a **cifs** (Windows) filesystem mounted on it using Samba. You can use Linux utilities and applications to access the Windows files and directories on this partition as if they were Linux files and directories. The line starting with **dog** shows a mounted, remote NFS filesystem. The last line shows the CD at **/dev/hdb** mounted on **/media/cdrom0**.

If the list of filesystems in **/etc/mtab** is not correct, see the tip on page 476.

Do not mount anything on root (/)

caution Always mount network directory hierarchies and removable devices at least one level below the root level of the filesystem. The root filesystem is mounted on /; you cannot mount two filesystems in the same place. If you were to try to mount something on /, all files, directories, and filesystems that were under the root directory would no longer be available, and the system would crash.

When you add a line for a filesystem to the **/etc/fstab** file (page 474), you can mount that filesystem by giving the associated mount point or device name as the argument to mount. For example, the CD listed earlier was mounted using the following command:

```
$ mount /media/cdrom0
```

This command worked because **/etc/fstab** contains the additional information needed to mount the file. An ordinary user was able to mount the file because of the **user** option:

```
/dev/hdb        /media/cdrom0   udf,iso9660 user,nosuid,noauto    0    0
```

You can also mount filesystems that do not appear in **/etc/fstab**. For example, when you insert a floppy diskette that holds a DOS filesystem into the floppy diskette drive, you can mount that filesystem using the following command:

```
$ sudo mount -t msdos /dev/fd0 /media/floppy0
```

The **–t msdos** option specifies a filesystem type of **msdos**. You can mount DOS filesystems only if you have configured the Linux kernel (page 555) to accept DOS filesystems. You do not need to mount a DOS filesystem to read from and write to it, such as when you use mcopy (page 159). However, you do need to mount a DOS filesystem to use Linux commands (other than Mtools commands) on files on the filesystem (which may be on a diskette).

MOUNT OPTIONS

The mount utility takes many options, which you can specify either on the command line or in the **/etc/fstab** file (page 492). For a complete list of mount options for local filesystems, see the mount man page; for remote directory hierarchies, see the nfs man page.

The **noauto** option causes Linux not to mount the filesystem automatically. The **nosuid** option forces mounted setuid executables to run with regular permissions (no effective user ID change) on the local system (the system that mounted the filesystem).

Mount removable devices with the **nosuid** option

security   Always mount removable devices with the **nosuid** option so that a malicious user cannot, for example, put a setuid copy of bash on a disk and have a shell with **root** privileges. By default, Ubuntu uses the **nosuid** option when mounting removable media.

Unless you specify the **user, users,** or **owner** option, only a user running with **root** privileges can mount and unmount a filesystem. The **user** option allows any user to mount the filesystem, but the filesystem can be unmounted only by the user who mounted it; the **users** option allows any user to mount and unmount the filesystem. These options are frequently specified for CD, DVD, and floppy drives. The **owner** option, which is used only under special circumstances, is similar to the **user** option except that the user mounting the device must own the device.

MOUNTING A LINUX FLOPPY DISKETTE

Mounting a Linux floppy diskette is similar to mounting a partition of a hard disk. If it does not already exist, put an entry similar to the following in **/etc/fstab** for a diskette in the first floppy drive:

```
/dev/fd0          /media/floppy0  auto      rw,user,nosuid,noauto  0          0
```

Specifying a filesystem type of **auto** causes the system to probe the filesystem to determine its type and allows users to mount a variety of diskettes. Create the **/media/floppy0** directory if necessary. Insert a diskette and try to mount it. The diskette must be formatted (use fdformat, which deletes all data on a diskette). In the following example, the error message following the first command usually indicates there is no filesystem on the diskette. In some cases, the **mount** command may hang. If this problem occurs, pop the diskette out to display a prompt. Use mkfs (page 441) to create a filesystem—but be careful, because mkfs destroys all data on the diskette.

```
$ mount /dev/fd0
mount: I could not determine the filesystem type, and none was specified

$ mkfs /dev/fd0
mke2fs 1.40-WIP (14-Nov-2006)
Filesystem label=
OS type: Linux
Block size=1024 (log=0)
Fragment size=1024 (log=0)
184 inodes, 1440 blocks
72 blocks (5.00%) reserved for the super user
First data block=1
Maximum filesystem blocks=1572864
1 block group
8192 blocks per group, 8192 fragments per group
184 inodes per group

Writing inode tables: done
Writing superblocks and filesystem accounting information: done

This filesystem will be automatically checked every 36 mounts or
180 days, whichever comes first.  Use tune2fs -c or -i to override.
```

Now try the mount command again:

```
$ mount /dev/fd0
$ mount
...
/dev/fd0 on /media/floppy0 type ext2 (rw,noexec,nosuid,nodev,user=sam)

$ df -h /dev/fd0
Filesystem            Size  Used Avail Use% Mounted on
/dev/fd0              1.4M   19K  1.3M   2% /media/floppy0
```

The mount command without any arguments and **df –h /dev/fd0** show that the floppy diskette is mounted and ready for use.

umount: UNMOUNTS A FILESYSTEM

The umount utility unmounts a filesystem as long as it does not contain any files or directories that are in use (open). For example, a logged-in user's working directory cannot be on the filesystem you want to unmount. The next command unmounts the CD mounted earlier:

```
$ umount /media/cdrom0
```

Unmount a floppy or a remote (NFS) directory hierarchy the same way you would unmount a partition of a hard drive.

The umount utility consults **/etc/fstab** to get the necessary information and then unmounts the appropriate filesystem from its server. When a process has a file open on the filesystem that you are trying to unmount, umount displays a message similar to the following:

```
umount: /home: device is busy
```

When you cannot unmount a device because it is in use

tip   When a process has a file open on a device you need to unmount, use fuser to determine which process has the file open and to kill it. For example, when you want to unmount a floppy diskette, give the command **fuser –ki /media/floppy0** (substitute the mount point for the diskette on the local system for **/media/floppy0**). After checking with you, this command kills the process(es) using the diskette.

Use the **–a** option to umount to unmount all mounted filesystems that are not in use. You can never unmount the filesystem mounted at **/**. You can combine **–a** with the **–t** option to unmount filesystems of a given type (**ext3**, **nfs**, or others). For example, the following command unmounts all mounted **nfs** directory hierarchies that are not in use:

```
$ sudo umount -at nfs
```

fstab: KEEPS TRACK OF FILESYSTEMS

The system administrator maintains the **/etc/fstab** file, which lists local and remote directory hierarchies, most of which the system mounts automatically when it boots. The **fstab** file has six columns, where a hyphen is a placeholder for a column that has no value:

1. **Name**   The name, label, or UUID number of a local block device (page 486) or a pointer to a remote directory hierarchy. When you install the system, Ubuntu uses UUID numbers for fixed devices. It prefaces each line in **fstab** that specifies a UUID with a comment that specifies the device name. Using UUID numbers in **fstab** during installation circumvents the need for consistent device naming. Because udev (page 484) manages device naming dynamically, the installer may not be aware, for example, that the first disk is not named **/dev/hda1** but rather **/dev/sda1**, but it always knows the UUID number of a device. Using UUID numbers to identify devices also keeps partitions and mount points correctly corre-lated when you remove or swap devices. See **/dev/disk/by-uuid** (page 471) for more information on UUID numbers. You can use the volume label of

a local filesystem by using the form **LABEL=*xx***, where *xx* is the volume label. Refer to e2label on page 441.

A remote directory hierarchy appears as ***hostname:pathname***, where ***hostname*** is the name of the remote system that houses the filesystem, and ***pathname*** is the absolute pathname (on the remote system) of the directory that is to be mounted.

2. **Mount point**   The name of the directory file that the filesystem/directory hierarchy is to be mounted on. If it does not already exist, create this directory using mkdir. See pages 35 and 489.

3. **Type**   The type of filesystem/directory hierarchy that is to be mounted. Local filesystems are generally of type **ext2**, **ext3**, or **iso9660**, and remote directory hierarchies are of type **nfs** or **cifs**. Table 12-1 on page 487 lists filesystem types.

4. **Mount options**   A comma-separated list of mount options, such as whether the filesystem is mounted for reading and writing (**rw**, the default) or readonly (**ro**). See pages 490 and 742, and refer to the mount and nfs man pages for lists of options.

5. **Dump**   Used by dump (page 586) to determine when to back up the filesystem.

6. **Fsck**   Specifies the order in which fsck checks filesystems. Root (**/**) should have a **1** in this column. Filesystems that are mounted to a directory just below the root directory should have a **2**. Filesystems that are mounted on another mounted filesystem (other than root) should have a **3**. For example, if **local** is a separate filesystem from **/usr** and is mounted on **/usr** (as **/usr/local**), then **local** should have a **3**. Filesystems and directory hierarchies that do not need to be checked (for example, remotely mounted directory hierarchies and CDs/DVDs) should have a **0**.

The following example shows a typical **fstab** file:

```
$ cat /etc/fstab
# /etc/fstab: static file system information.
#
# <file system> <mount point>    <type>   <options>         <dump>   <pass>
proc            /proc            proc     defaults          0        0
# /dev/hda1
UUID=8f3c51c2-a42c-49b1-9f03-db2140cb7eb5 /    ext3    defaults,errors=remount-ro 0         1
# /dev/hda2
UUID=39fc600f-91d5-4c9f-8559-727050b27645 /home            ext3     defaults          0        2
# /dev/hda3
UUID=a68fb957-2ae7-4ae5-8656-23a1cf8fcd14 none              swap     sw                0        0
/dev/hda5       /p15             ext3     defaults          0        2
/dev/hda6       /p16             ext3     defaults          0        2
/dev/hdb        /media/cdrom0    udf,iso9660 user,nosuid,noauto 0         0
/dev/fd0        /media/floppy0   auto     rw,user,nosuid,noauto 0        0
dog:/p04        /p04             nfs      defaults          0        0
```

In the preceding example, **/pl5** and **/pl6** do not use UUID numbers because these devices were added to **fstab** by the administrator after the system was installed.

fsck: CHECKS FILESYSTEM INTEGRITY

The fsck (filesystem check) utility verifies the integrity of filesystems and, if possible, repairs problems it finds. Because many filesystem repairs can destroy data, particularly on non*journaling filesystems* (page 1115), such as **ext2**, by default fsck asks you for confirmation before making each repair.

Do not run fsck on a mounted filesystem

caution   Do not run fsck on a mounted filesystem. When you attempt to check a mounted filesystem, fsck warns you and asks whether you want to continue. Reply **no**. You can run fsck with the **–N** option on a mounted filesystem because it will not write to the filesystem; as a result, no harm can come of running it. See page 486 for more information

When fsck repairs a damaged filesystem, it may find unlinked files: files that have lost their directory information. These files have no filenames. The fsck utility gives these files their inode numbers as names and stores them in the **lost+found** directory (page 470) in the filesystem that holds the file. You can use file (page 156) to determine the type of these files and less to view readable files. Because ls –l displays the name of the owner of these files, you can return them to their owners.

The following command checks all unmounted filesystems that are marked to be checked in **/etc/fstab** (page 492) except for the root filesystem:

```
$ sudo fsck -AR
```

The **–A** option causes fsck to check filesystems listed in **fstab**. When used with the **–A** option, the **–R** option causes fsck not to check the root filesystem. You can check a specific filesystem with a command similar to one of the following:

```
$ sudo fsck /home
```

or

```
$ sudo fsck /dev/hda2
```

Crash flag   When the system boots, it runs the **/etc/init.d/checkroot.sh** and **/etc/init.d/checkfs.sh** init scripts. With some exceptions, these scripts run fsck on the filesystems as specified by the sixth column in **/etc/fstab** (page 493). The root filesystem is checked first, as long as it is mounted readonly. All checking is skipped if the system is running on batteries.

Certain filesystem parameters (discussed in the next section) determine whether fsck reports the filesystem as clean or checks it. If the file **/forcefsck** is present on the root filesystem, fsck ignores the filesystem parameters and checks filesystems as specified by **fstab**. The **/forcefsck** file exists if filesystems were not properly unmounted, such as when the system has crashed.

tune2fs: CHANGES FILESYSTEM PARAMETERS

The tune2fs utility displays and modifies filesystem parameters on **ext2** filesystems and on **ext3** filesystems, which are modified **ext2** filesystems. This utility can also set up journaling on an **ext2** filesystem, turning it into an **ext3** filesystem. With the introduction of increasingly more reliable hardware and software, systems tend to be rebooted less frequently, so it is important to check filesystems regularly. By default, fsck is run on each partition while the system is brought up, before the partition is mounted. (The checks scheduled by tune2fs are separate and scheduled differently from the checks that are done following a system crash or hard disk error [see the previous section].)

Depending on the flags, fsck may do nothing more than display a message saying the filesystem is clean. The larger the partition, the more time it takes to check it, assuming a nonjournaling filesystem. These checks are often unnecessary. The tune2fs utility helps you to find a happy medium between checking filesystems each time you reboot the system and never checking them. It does so by scheduling when fsck checks a filesystem (these checks occur only when the system is booted).[1] You can use two scheduling patterns: time elapsed since the last check and number of mounts since the last check. The following command causes fsck to check **/dev/hda5** after it has been mounted eight times or after 15 days have elapsed since its last check, whichever happens first:

```
$ sudo tune2fs -c 8 -i 15 /dev/hda5
tune2fs 1.40-WIP (14-Nov-2006)
Setting maximal mount count to 8
Setting interval between checks to 1296000 seconds
```

The next tune2fs command is similar but works on a different partition and sets the current mount count to 4. When you do not specify a current mount count, it is set to zero:

```
$ sudo tune2fs -c 8 -i 15 -C 4 /dev/hda6
tune2fs 1.40-WIP (14-Nov-2006)
Setting maximal mount count to 8
Setting current mount count to 4
Setting interval between checks to 1296000 seconds
```

The **–l** option lists a variety of information about the partition. You can combine this option with others. A maximum mount count of –1 or 0 means fsck and the kernel will ignore the mount count information.

---

1. For systems whose purpose in life is to run continuously, this kind of scheduling does not work. You must develop a schedule that is not based on system reboots but rather on a clock. Each filesystem must be unmounted periodically, checked with fsck (preceding section), and then remounted.

```
$ sudo tune2fs -l /dev/hda6
tune2fs 1.40-WIP (14-Nov-2006)
Filesystem volume name:   <none>
Last mounted on:          <not available>
Filesystem UUID:          8c2e5007-9cea-4bfb-8d26-82f8b376949b
Filesystem magic number:  0xEF53
Filesystem revision #:    1 (dynamic)
Filesystem features:      has_journal resize_inode dir_index filetype
        needs_recovery sparse_super large_file
Filesystem flags:         signed directory hash
Default mount options:    (none)
Filesystem state:         clean
Errors behavior:          Continue
Filesystem OS type:       Linux
Inode count:              183936
Block count:              367479
...
Last mount time:          Mon Jun  4 15:02:43 2007
Last write time:          Mon Jun  4 15:25:54 2007
Mount count:              4
Maximum mount count:      8
Last checked:             Mon Jun  4 15:02:42 2007
Check interval:           1296000 (2 weeks, 1 day)
...
```

Set the filesystem parameters on the local system so they are appropriate to the way you use it. When using the mount count to control when fsck checks filesystems, use the –C option to stagger the checks to ensure all checks do not occur at the same time. Always make sure new and upgraded filesystems have checks scheduled as you desire.

ext2 to ext3   To change an ext2 filesystem to an ext3 filesystem, you must put a *journal* (page 1115) on the filesystem, and the kernel must support ext3 filesystems. Use the –j option to set up a journal on an unmounted filesystem:

```
$ sudo tune2fs -j /dev/hda5
tune2fs 1.40-WIP (14-Nov-2006)
Creating journal inode: done
This filesystem will be automatically checked every 8 mounts or
15 days, whichever comes first.  Use tune2fs -c or -i to override.
```

Before you can use **fstab** (page 474) to mount the changed filesystem, you must modify its entry in the **fstab** file to reflect its new type. To do so, change the third column to **ext3**.

ext3 to ext2   The following command changes an unmounted or readonly **ext3** filesystem to an **ext2** filesystem:

```
$ sudo tune2fs -O ^has_journal /dev/hda5
tune2fs 1.40-WIP (14-Nov-2006)
```

Speeding lookups   The **dir_index** option, which is off by default, adds a balanced-tree binary hash lookup method for directories. This feature improves scalability of directories with large numbers of files, although it means that the hash needs to be updated each time a directory changes. Turn on using **tune2fs –O dir_index** and reboot to create the hash.

Refer to the tune2fs man page for more details.

RAID FILESYSTEM

RAID (Redundant Arrays of Inexpensive/Independent Disks) spreads information across several disks so as to combine several physical disks into one larger virtual device. RAID improves performance and may create redundancy. For more information see page 39.

CHAPTER SUMMARY

Filesystems hold directories of files. These structures store user data and system data that are the basis of users' work on the system and the system's existence. Linux supports many types of files, including ordinary files, directories, links, and special files. Special files provide access to operating system features. The kernel uses major and minor device numbers to identify classes of devices and specific devices within each class. Character and block devices represent I/O devices such as hard disks and printers. Inodes, which are identified by inode numbers, are stored on disk and define a file's existence.

When the system comes up, the **/etc/fstab** file controls which filesystems are mounted and how they are mounted (readonly, read-write, and so on). After a system crash, filesystems are automatically verified and repaired if necessary by fsck. You can use tune2fs to force the system to cause fsck to verify a filesystem periodically when the system boots.

EXERCISES

1. What is the function of the **/etc/hosts** file? Which services can you use in place of, or to supplement, the **hosts** file?

2. What does the **/etc/resolv.conf** file do? What do the **nameserver** lines in this file do?

3. What is an inode? What happens to the inode when you move a file within a filesystem?

4. What does the .. entry in a directory point to? What does this entry point to in the root (/) directory?

5. What is a device file? Where are device files located?

6. What is a FIFO? What does FIFO stand for? What is another name for a FIFO? How does a FIFO work?

ADVANCED EXERCISES

7. Write a line for the **/etc/fstab** file that mounts the **/dev/hdb1 ext3** filesystem on **/extra** with the following characteristics: The filesystem will not be mounted automatically when the system boots, and anyone can mount and unmount the filesystem.

8. Without using rm, how can you delete a file? (*Hint:* How do you rename a file?)

9. After burning an ISO image file named **image.iso** to a CD on **/dev/hdc**, how can you can verify the copy from the command line?

10. Why should **/var** reside on a separate partition from **/usr**?

11. Create a FIFO. Using the shell, demonstrate that two users can use this FIFO to communicate asynchronously.

12. How would you mount an ISO image so you could copy files from it without burning it to a CD?

13

DOWNLOADING AND INSTALLING SOFTWARE

A *software package* is the collection of scripts, programs, files, and directories required to install and run applications, utilities, servers, and system software. A package also includes a list of other packages that the package depends on (dependencies). Using software packages makes it easier to transfer, install, and uninstall software. A package contains either executable files or source code files. Executable files are precompiled for a specific processor architecture and operating system, whereas source files need to be compiled but will run on a wide range of machines and operating systems.

Software package formats
Software packages come in different formats. Ubuntu uses **dpkg** (page 514), which was the first Linux packaging system to incorporate dependency information; it gets its name from the Linux distribution it was developed on (Debian). Other formats include rpm (used on Red Hat, SuSE, and other systems), yum, the GNU Configure and Build System (page 524), and compressed tar. Formats such as compressed tar, which were popular before the introduction of **dpkg**, are used less often today because they require more work on the part of the installer (you) and do not provide the dependency and compatibility checking that dpkg offers.

dpkg
The Debian package management system is referred to as the **dpkg** management system, or just **dpkg**. This system is a collection of more than 20 utilities that manage and report on **dpkg** packages, both those installed on the system and those available from online repositories. Give the command **dpkg**TABTAB (press TAB twice) or **apropos dpkg** to display a list of **dpkg** utilities.

deb files
The **dpkg** utilities work with files whose names end in **.deb** and are referred to as **deb** files (page 515) or (software) packages.

APT
APT (Advanced Package Tool) is a collection of utilities that, together with **dpkg**, work with software packages. APT downloads software packages, while **dpkg** installs, removes, maintains, manages dependencies of, and reports on software packages. Give the command **apt**TABTAB or **apropos apt** to display a list of APT utilities (and a few other things).

Kernel source code
See Chapter 15 for information on downloading, compiling, and installing kernel source code.

Graphical interfaces
Several pseudographical and graphical interfaces to **dpkg** and APT are available. Among the most popular are Synaptic (page 118), aptitude, and dselect.

Repositories
APT downloads package headers and packages from servers called *repositories* that can reside on the Internet, a CD, or a local network. See page 504 for more information.

Bug tracking
Ubuntu uses Launchpad, which belongs to a class of programs formally known as *defect tracking systems,* to track bugs (launchpad.net/+about for information about Launchpad and launchpad.net/ubuntu to use it). You can use Launchpad to read about existing bugs and to report new ones. Ubuntu uses Bazaar for source code version control (bazaar-vcs.org and wiki.ubuntu.com/Bzr). Launchpad allows you to track any project that uses Bazaar version control.

Keeping software up-to-date
Of the many reasons to keep software up-to-date, one of the most important is security. Although you may hear about software-based security breaches after the fact, you rarely hear about the fixes that were available but never installed before the breach occurred. Timely installation of software updates is critical to system security. Linux open-source software is the ideal environment to find and fix bugs and make repaired software available quickly. When you keep the system and application software up-to-date, you keep abreast of bug fixes, new features, support for new hardware, speed enhancements, and more.

As shipped, most versions of Ubuntu check for updates daily and advise you when updates are available (page 99). Use the Software Sources window (page 116), Updates tab to change these options.

JumpStart: Installing and Removing Packages Using aptitude

This section explains how to install packages on and remove packages from a system using aptitude, a versatile tool that is part of APT. The aptitude utility has two interfaces: pseudographical and textual. This chapter covers the textual interface. Give the command **aptitude** without arguments to display the pseudographical interface. Information on this interface is available in the *aptitude user's manual* (algebraicthunk.net/~dburrows/projects/aptitude/doc/en).

If you do not know the name of the package you want to install, see page 503. If you want aptitude to download packages that are not supported by Ubuntu, you must add the repositories that hold those packages to the **sources.list** file; see page 505.

Before using aptitude to install a package, give the command **sudo aptitude update** to update the local list of packages (more about this process on page 510). By default, the **apt** cron script (page 506) updates this list daily. Even so, it is a good idea to give this command periodically until you are sure the script is updating the list.

aptitude **install**   The following example calls aptitude to install the tcsh shell, which is part of the **tcsh** package:

```
$ sudo aptitude install tcsh
Reading package lists... Done
Building dependency tree
Reading state information... Done
Reading extended state information
Initializing package states... Done
Building tag database... Done
The following NEW packages will be installed:
  tcsh
0 packages upgraded, 1 newly installed, 0 to remove and 0 not upgraded.
Need to get 0B/338kB of archives. After unpacking 709kB will be used.
Writing extended state information... Done
Selecting previously deselected package tcsh.
(Reading database ... 119619 files and directories currently installed.)
Unpacking tcsh (from .../tcsh_6.14.00-7_i386.deb) ...
Setting up tcsh (6.14.00-7) ...

Reading package lists... Done
...
```

The next command installs the **apache2.2-common** package. Because this package depends on other packages, and because these packages are not installed, aptitude lists the packages it will automatically install in addition to the one you asked it to install. When aptitude is going to install more packages than you requested, it asks if you want to continue. Reply y if you want to continue or **n** if you want to quit.

```
$ sudo aptitude install apache2.2-common
...
The following NEW packages will be automatically installed:
  apache2-utils libapr1 libaprutil1 libpq5
The following NEW packages will be installed:
  apache2-utils apache2.2-common libapr1 libaprutil1 libpq5
0 packages upgraded, 5 newly installed, 0 to remove and 0 not upgraded.
Need to get 0B/1698kB of archives. After unpacking 5407kB will be used.
Do you want to continue? [Y/n/?] y
...
```

When you install some packages, aptitude lists *suggested packages*. Suggested packages may be useful but are not required with the package you are installing.

aptitude **remove** The aptitude **remove** command removes a package, but leaves its configuration files in place, allowing you to reinstall the package without having to reconfigure it. Use **purge** (discussed next) in place of **remove** to remove a package and its configuration files.

```
$ sudo aptitude remove tcsh
...
The following packages will be REMOVED:
  tcsh
0 packages upgraded, 0 newly installed, 1 to remove and 0 not upgraded.
Need to get 0B of archives. After unpacking 709kB will be freed.
Writing extended state information... Done
(Reading database ... 120025 files and directories currently installed.)
Removing tcsh ...
...
```

Automatically When aptitude removes a package, it also removes the dependent packages it auto-
removes matically installed when it installed the original package. The following example
dependencies removes **apache2-common** and its dependencies:

```
$ sudo aptitude remove apache2.2-common
...
The following packages are unused and will be REMOVED:
  apache2-utils libapr1 libaprutil1 libpq5
...
The following packages will be REMOVED:
  apache2.2-common
0 packages upgraded, 0 newly installed, 5 to remove and 0 not upgraded.
Need to get 0B of archives. After unpacking 5407kB will be freed.
Do you want to continue? [Y/n/?] y
...
```

aptitude **purge** The next example uses an alternative approach—the aptitude **purge** command—to remove **apache2-common**, its dependencies, and all configuration files. The {p} following **apache2.2-common** indicates that aptitude is removing (purging) **apache2.2-common**'s configuration files, as does the last line of the example.

```
$ sudo aptitude purge apache2.2-common
...
The following packages are unused and will be REMOVED:
  apache2-utils libapr1 libaprutil1 libpq5
...
```

```
The following packages will be REMOVED:
  apache2.2-common{p}
0 packages upgraded, 0 newly installed, 5 to remove and 0 not upgraded.
Need to get 0B of archives. After unpacking 5407kB will be freed.
Do you want to continue? [Y/n/?] y
...
Purging configuration files for apache2.2-common ...
...
```

FINDING THE PACKAGE THAT HOLDS A FILE YOU NEED

Finding a package with a name that sounds like...

tip The aptitude **search** command looks for packages with names that match a pattern. For example, the command **aptitude search vnc** displays a list packages that have **vnc** in their names. See page 511 for more information.

You may know the name of a file or utility you need but not know the name of the package that holds the file. There are several ways that you can locate a package that holds a file. The Ubuntu Web page, packages.ubuntu.com, allows you to search for packages based on several criteria. Partway down the page is a section titled **Search** that gives you two ways to search for packages. You can use the second, **Search the contents of packages,** to search for a package that holds a specific file. Enter the name of the file in the text box labeled **Keyword**, click the radio button labeled **packages that contain files named like this,** select **Case sensitive (no),** select the distribution and architecture you are working with, and click **Search.** The browser displays a list of packages that hold the file you are looking for. For example, suppose you are compiling a program and get the following error message:

```
xv.h:174:22: error: X11/Xlib.h: No such file or directory
```

You are working on an Intel x86-compatible system running Intrepid and need the file **Xlib.h** located in the **X11** directory. When you enter **X11/Xlib.h** in the text box labeled **Keyword** (on packages.ubuntu.com), the browser displays the following list:

```
usr/include/X11/Xlib.h                           libdevel/libx11-dev
usr/lib/TenDRA/lib/include/x5/lib.api/X11/Xlib.h devel/tendra [universe]
```

The [**universe**] on the second line indicates that the package comes from the **universe** repository (page 504). The most likely candidate is the first entry, which is supported by Ubuntu and is the most generic. The **libdevel/libx11-dev** on the right indicates that the **libx11-dev** package is part of the **libdevel** section of packages. You can install this package using the following command:

```
$ sudo aptitude install libx11-dev
```

apt-file You can also use the apt-file utility to search for a package containing a specified file. Before you can use this utility, you must install it and update the package list on the local system. Updating the package list takes a few minutes. Because apt-file displays multiple, sequential, identical lines, you can pipe its output through uniq (page 154) to make the job of finding the right package easier:

```
$ sudo aptitude install apt-file
...
$ sudo apt-file update
...
$ apt-file search X11/Xlib.h | uniq
ivtools-dev: usr/include/IV-X11/Xlib.h
libghc6-x11-dev: usr/lib/X11-1.2.1/ghc-6.6.1/Graphics/X11/Xlib.hi
libhugs-x11-bundled: usr/lib/hugs/packages/X11/Graphics/X11/Xlib.hs
libx11-dev: usr/include/X11/Xlib.h
tendra: usr/lib/TenDRA/lib/include/x5/lib.api/X11/Xlib.h
```

Again, the most generic package (the next-to-last one listed) is probably the one you want. While apt-cache (page 512) searches installed packages only, the aptitude search command (page 511) and apt-file search all packages from the repositories listed in /etc/apt/sources.list, including packages that have not been downloaded. See also dpkg ––search (page 520) and dpkg ––listfiles (page 520) for other ways of searching for files.

APT: KEEPS THE SYSTEM UP-TO-DATE

APT (Advanced Package Tool) is a collection of utilities that download, install, remove, upgrade, and report on software packages. APT utilities download packages and call **dpkg** (page 514) utilities to manipulate the packages once they are on the local system. For more information refer to www.debian.org/doc/manuals/apt-howto.

REPOSITORIES

Repositories hold collections of software packages and related information, including headers that describe each package and provide information on other packages the package depends on. Ubuntu maintains repositories for each of its releases.

Software package categories
Software packages from Ubuntu repositories are divided into several categories, including the following:

- **main**—Ubuntu-supported open-source software
- **universe**—Community-maintained open-source software
- **multiverse**—Software restricted by copyright or legal issues
- **restricted**—Proprietary device drivers
- **backports**—Packages from later releases of Ubuntu that are not available for an earlier release.

APT selects packages from repositories it searches based on the categories specified in the **sources.list** file (next). You do not need to reconfigure APT to install supported software. You may get the following error message when you try to install a package:

```
$ sudo aptitude install xxx
...
Couldn't find package "xxx".  However, the following
packages contain "xxx" in their name:
  mixxx mixxx-data
No packages will be installed, upgraded, or removed.
...
```

This message means that the package you requested does not exist in the repositories that APT is searching (as specified in **sources.list**). It may also mean that the package does not exist; check the spelling. If you are not running the latest version of Ubuntu, it may be available on a later version; try enabling the **backports** repository in **sources.list** (discussed next).

sources.list: SPECIFIES REPOSITORIES FOR APT TO SEARCH

The **/etc/apt/sources.list** file specifies the repositories APT searches when you ask it to find or install a package. You must modify the **sources.list** file to enable APT to download software from nondefault repositories. You can use software-properties-gtk to display the Software Sources window to modify **sources.list** (as explained on page 116) or you can use an editor to modify it (as explained in this section).

Each line in **sources.list** describes one repository and has the following format:

type URI repository category-list

where *type* is **deb** (page 515) for packages of executable files and **deb-src** for packages of source files; *URI* is the location of the repository, usually **cdrom** or an Internet address that starts with **http://**; *repository* is the name of the repository that APT is to search; and *category-list* is a SPACE-separated list of categories (see "Software package categories" in the preceding section) that APT selects packages from. When a line specifies a non-Ubuntu repository, the *repository* and *category-list* may have other values. Comments begin with a pound sign (#) anywhere on a line and end at the end of the line. The comment **#Added by software-properties** indicates that software-properties-gtk added the line to **sources.list**.

The following line from **sources.list** causes APT to search the Intrepid archive located at us.archive.ubuntu.com/ubuntu for **deb** packages that contain executable files. It accepts packages that are categorized as **main, restricted,** and **multiverse:**

```
deb http://us.archive.ubuntu.com/ubuntu/ intrepid main restricted multiverse
```

Replacing **deb** with **deb-src** causes APT to search in the same manner for packages of source files. Use the apt-get **source** command to download source packages (page 514).

```
deb-src http://us.archive.ubuntu.com/ubuntu/ intrepid main restricted multiverse
```

Default repositories   The default **sources.list** file includes repositories such as **intrepid** (Intrepid as originally released), **intrepid-updates** (major bug fixes after the release of Intrepid), **intrepid-security** (critical security-related updates), and **backports** (newer, less-tested software that is not reviewed by the Ubuntu security team). Separating security updates from other updates enables you to set up a system to automatically install security updates while allowing you to review other updates before installing them. As installed, the **sources.list** file allows you to search for and retrieve packages from the **main, universe, multiverse,** and **restricted** categories (page 504) of the **intrepid, intrepid-updates,** and **intrepid-security** repositories. Some repositories in **sources.list** are commented out. Remove the leading pound sign (#) on the lines of the repositories you want to enable. After you modify **sources.list**, give the command **aptitude update** (page 510) to update the local package indexes.

The next line, which was added to **sources.list**, enables APT to search a third-party repository (but see the following security tip):

```
deb http://download.skype.com/linux/repos/debian/ stable non-free
```

In this case, the repository is named **stable** and the category is **non-free**. Although the code is compiled for Debian, it runs on Ubuntu, as is frequently the case.

Use repositories you trust

security   There are many repositories of software packages. Search the Internet for **ubuntu repositories** to display a sampling of them. Be selective in which repositories you add to **sources.list**, however: When you add a repository, you are trusting the person who runs the repository not to put malicious software in packages you may download. In addition, packages that are not supported by Ubuntu can conflict with other packages and/or cause upgrades to fail.

THE APT LOCAL PACKAGE INDEXES AND THE APT CACHE

APT local package
indexes
The **/var/lib/apt/lists** directory holds the local package index and associated files. For each repository listed in **/etc/apt/sources.list** (page 505), this directory holds a file that lists information about the most recent version of each package in that repository. APT uses these files to determine whether the packages on the system, and those in its cache, are the most recent versions.

APT cache   The **/var/cache/apt/archives** directory holds recently downloaded **deb** files (page 515). By default, the **apt** cron script (next) limits the size of this directory and the age of the files in it.

THE apt cron SCRIPT AND APT CONFIGURATION FILES

Traditionally, APT configuration instructions are kept in a single file: **/etc/apt/apt.conf**; Ubuntu breaks this file into smaller files that it keeps in the **/etc/apt/apt.conf.d** directory. The **apt** cron script, kept in **/etc/cron.daily** so it is run daily, reads the configuration files in **apt.conf.d** and maintains the APT local package indexes and the APT cache based on the instructions in those files. APT tools, such as aptitude, also read these files as they start. This section explains a few of the many directives you can use to control APT tools. See the **apt.conf** man page and use **zless** to view the **/usr/share/doc/apt/examples/configure-index.gz** file for more information.

The software-properties-gtk utility, which is part of the software package with the same name, opens the Software Sources window (page 116), which allows you to set some APT configuration directives using a graphical interface (Updates tab, Automatic updates).

The following files, which are part of the **update-notifier** package, control how the **apt** cron script maintains the APT local package indexes and the APT cache:

```
$ cat /etc/apt/apt.conf.d/10periodic
APT::Periodic::Update-Package-Lists "1";
APT::Periodic::Download-Upgradeable-Packages "1";
APT::Periodic::AutocleanInterval "0";
APT::Periodic::Unattended-Upgrade "0";
```

```
$ cat /etc/apt/apt.conf.d/20archive
APT::Archives::MaxAge "30";
APT::Archives::MinAge "2";
APT::Archives::MaxSize "500";
```

Working with **root** privileges, you can edit these files and change the values within the quotation marks to change what the **apt** cron script does. Each line must end with a semicolon. The following list explains each of the directives in these files.

APT::Periodic::Update-Package-Lists "*days*";
Synchronizes local package indexes with their corresponding repositories (page 510) every *days* days. Set *days* to 0 to disable this directive.

APT::Periodic::Download-Upgradeable-Packages "*days*";
Downloads (but does not install) the packages necessary to upgrade all packages on the system (page 510) every *days* days. Set *days* to 0 to disable this directive.

APT::Periodic::AutocleanInterval "*days*";
Clears the APT cache (page 506) of packages that can no longer be downloaded every *days* days. Set *days* to 0 to disable this directive.

APT::Periodic::Unattended-Upgrade "*days*";
Installs upgrades that relate to system security every *days* days and writes a log to **/var/log/unattended-upgrades**. Make sure the **unattended-upgrades** package is installed; for more information see **/usr/share/doc/unattended-upgrades/README**. Set *days* to 0 to disable this directive.

APT::Archives::MaxAge "*days*";
Deletes files from the APT cache (page 506) older than *days* days. Set *days* to 0 to disable this directive.

APT::Archives::MinAge "*days*";
Causes files younger than *days* days not to be deleted from the APT (page 506). Set *days* to 0 to disable this directive.

APT::Archives::MaxSize "*MB*";
Establishes the maximum size of the APT cache (page 506). When the cache grows larger than *MB* megabytes, the **apt** cron script deletes files until the cache is smaller than this size. It deletes the largest files first. Set *MB* to 0 to disable this directive.

KDE and Adept   If you are running KDE, the **apt.conf.d** directory holds two files that work with the Adept package manager (which is not covered in this book): **15adept-periodic-update** and **25adept-archive-limits**. These files should be the same as their GNOME counterparts: **10periodic** and **20archive**. If the Adept files exist on the local system and you modify their GNOME counterparts, copy **10periodic** to **15adept-periodic-update** and **20archive** to **25adept-archive-limits**.

aptitude: WORKS WITH PACKAGES AND THE LOCAL PACKAGE INDEX

One of the most commonly used APT utilities is aptitude. The JumpStart on page 501 explains how to use the aptitude **install** and **remove** commands to add and remove packages from the local system. This section describes aptitude in more detail and explains how to use other of its commands and options.

Logs   The aptitude utility keeps very readable logs in **/var/log/aptitude**.

Virtual package   When you install certain packages, aptitude queries you and, if you agree, installs more than one package. You are either installing a package with dependencies or a *virtual package,* also called a *metapackage.* A virtual package is not a software package, but rather a metapackage that depends on other packages. Virtual packages facilitate the installation of software that requires multiple packages.

The format of an aptitude command is

    aptitude **options** *command [package-list]*

where **options** is one or more options from the list of options that begins on page 509, **command** is a command from the list of commands in the next section, and *package-list* is a SPACE-separated list of the names of one or more packages you want to work with. With the **search** command, *package-list* is a list of search patterns (page 511). With other commands, an element of *package-list* that contains a tilde (~) is treated as a search pattern. Except when aptitude is only displaying package information, you must work with **root** privileges. If you call aptitude without arguments, it displays its pseudographical interface. This section lists more common commands and options; see the aptitude man page for a complete list.

See page 503 if you need to determine the name of the package that holds a file you want to install.

aptitude COMMANDS

This section describes the more common aptitude commands. You must run all these commands, except **search** and **show**, while working with **root** privileges.

autoclean   Clears the APT cache (page 506) of packages that can no longer be downloaded. Run this command periodically to keep the local cache from becoming cluttered with useless files.

clean   Deletes all packages from the APT cache (page 506).

download   Downloads the **deb** file (page 515) for a package to **/var/cache/apt/archives**.

full-upgrade   Performs the tasks **safe-upgrade** does and also works with newer packages that have different dependencies than the ones they are replacing. This command installs new packages if necessary. It does not upgrade from one release of Ubuntu to another; see page 64 for information on upgrading Ubuntu to another release.

install Downloads, unpacks, and installs all packages in the *package-list* as well as all packages those packages depend on. See page 501 for an example.

purge Removes all packages in the *package-list*, including their configuration files. See page 502 for an example of the **remove** command.

reinstall Downloads, unpacks, and reinstalls an already installed package, upgrading to the latest version if necessary.

remove Removes all packages in the *package-list*. This command does not remove configuration files. See page 502 for an example.

safe-upgrade Installs the latest versions of most packages on the system. This command will not install a package that is not already on the system, nor will it remove an installed package. It will not install a newer version of a package that cannot be installed without changing the install status of another package. To make sure the local APT cache is up-to-date, run **aptitude update** before giving this command. See page 510 for an example. See also **full-upgrade**.

search Searches the repositories specified by **sources.list** for packages whose names are matched by any element of *package-list*. For example, a search for **apache2** will yield **apache2-dev, apache2-doc, apache2, apache2-mpm**, and so on. See page 511 for an example.

show Displays detailed information about *package-list*. See page 511 for an example.

update Synchronizes the local APT package index files with those in the repositories. See page 510 for an example.

aptitude OPTIONS

This section describes some of the options you can use with aptitude commands. Each description advises you whether the option works with only certain commands.

--show-deps –D Displays information about packages a command would automatically install or remove.

--download-only –d Does not unpack or install a package after downloading it.

 –f Attempts to fix broken dependencies.

--purge-unused Removes packages that are no longer needed because they were automatically installed to satisfy a dependency of a package that has been removed.

--help –h Displays a summary of usage, commands, and options.

--simulate –s Displays what *command* would do, without taking any action.

--assume-yes –y Assumes a **yes** response to most prompts so aptitude runs noninteractively. The aptitude utility still prompts for an extraordinary event, such as removing an essential package or attempting to install an unauthenticated package.

aptitude update: SYNCHRONIZES LOCAL PACKAGE INDEXES WITH REPOSITORIES

The aptitude **update** command synchronizes local package indexes with their corresponding repositories:

```
$ sudo aptitude update
Get:1 http://us.archive.ubuntu.com intrepid Release.gpg [189B]
Ign http://us.archive.ubuntu.com intrepid/main Translation-en_US
Ign http://us.archive.ubuntu.com intrepid/restricted Translation-en_US
Ign http://us.archive.ubuntu.com intrepid/multiverse Translation-en_US
Ign http://us.archive.ubuntu.com intrepid/universe Translation-en_US
Hit http://us.archive.ubuntu.com intrepid-updates Release.gpg
Ign http://us.archive.ubuntu.com intrepid-updates/main Translation
en_US
...
Hit http://us.archive.ubuntu.com intrepid-updates/restricted Sources
Hit http://us.archive.ubuntu.com intrepid-updates/universe Packages
Hit http://us.archive.ubuntu.com intrepid-updates/universe Sources
Fetched 8477kB in 40s (209kB/s)
Reading package lists... Done

Current status: 32 updates [+27], 1 new [+1].
```

After running this command, APT can determine, without accessing repositories, whether installed packages and those in its cache are the most recent versions available.

By default, the **apt** cron script (page 506) synchronizes local package indexes nightly. If this script is running and set to update the package index, you need not run the **update** command. However, you must run this command after you add repositories to **/etc/apt/sources.list** before APT can retrieve files from new repositories.

aptitude safe-upgrade AND aptitude full-upgrade: UPGRADE THE SYSTEM

There are two aptitude commands that upgrade all packages on the system: **safe-upgrade**, which upgrades all packages on the system that do not require new packages to be installed, and **full-upgrade**, which upgrades all packages on the system, installing new packages as needed.

aptitude safe-upgrade The following example uses the aptitude **safe-upgrade** command to upgrade all packages on the system that depend only on packages that are already installed. This command will not install new packages (packages that are not already on the system). Before running this command, run **aptitude update** (page 510) to make sure the local package indexes are up-to-date.

```
$ sudo aptitude update
...
$ sudo aptitude safe-upgrade
...
```

```
The following packages will be upgraded:
   belocs-locales-bin libpam-modules libpam-runtime libpam0g
4 packages upgraded, 0 newly installed, 0 to remove and 0 not upgraded.
Need to get 571kB of archives. After unpacking 0B will be used.
Do you want to continue? [Y/n/?] y
...
```

The aptitude utility lists the changes it will make and asks you whether you want to continue. Enter **y** to upgrade the listed packages or **n** to quit. Packages that are not upgraded because they depend on packages that are not installed are listed as kept back.

aptitude full-upgrade
Use the aptitude **full-upgrade** command to upgrade all packages, including packages that are dependent on packages that are not installed. This command installs new packages as needed to satisfy dependencies.

aptitude search: SEARCHES THE REPOSITORIES FOR PACKAGES

The **search** command interprets the *package-list* on the command line as a list of patterns; all other aptitude commands normally interpret it as a list of package names. This command searches all packages from the repositories listed in **/etc/apt/sources.list**, including packages that have not been downloaded, and displays one line about each package whose name matches one of the elements of *package-list*:

```
$ aptitude search vim
v   gvim                       -
p   jvim-canna                 - Japanized VIM (Canna version)
p   jvim-doc                   - Documentation for jvim (Japanized VIM)
i   vim                        - Vi IMproved - enhanced vi editor
i   vim-common                 - Vi IMproved - Common files
p   vim-doc                    - Vi IMproved - HTML documentation
p   vim-full                   - Vi IMproved - enhanced vi editor - full fledged version
p   vim-gnome                  - Vi IMproved - enhanced vi editor - with GNOME2 GUI
...
```

The letter in the first column of each entry indicates the status of the package on the system: **i** for installed, **c** for removed except for configuration files, **p** for purged (package and configuration files removed), and **v** for a virtual package (page 508). A second letter in the first column indicates a stored action that will be performed on the package. An **A** appearing as the third letter means the package was automatically installed.

aptitude show: DISPLAYS PACKAGE INFORMATION

The aptitude **show** command displays information about packages in the repositories, including dependency information. See also the apt-cache **show** command, which displays more information (page 513), and the dpkg **status** command (page 519). On the next page is an example.

```
$ aptitude show nfs-common
Package: nfs-common
State: installed
Automatically installed: yes
Version: 1:1.1.1~git-20070709-3ubuntu1
Priority: optional
Section: net
Maintainer: Ubuntu Core Developers <ubuntu-devel-discuss@lists.ubuntu.com>
Uncompressed Size: 504k
Depends: portmap | rpcbind, adduser, ucf, lsb-base (>= 1.3-9ubuntu3),
        netbase (>= 4.24), initscripts (>= 2.86.ds1-14.1ubuntu1), libc6 (>=
        2.6-1), libcomerr2 (>= 1.33-3), libevent1 (>= 1.3b), libgssapi2,
        libkrb53 (>= 1.6.dfsg.1), libnfsidmap2, librpcsecgss3, libwrap0
Conflicts: nfs-client
Replaces: nfs-client, nfs-kernel-server (< 1:1.0.7-5), mount (< 2.13~)
Provides: nfs-client
Description: NFS support files common to client and server.
 Use this package on any machine that uses NFS, either as client or server.
 Programs included: lockd, statd, showmount, nfsstat, gssd and idmapd.

Upstream: SourceForge project "nfs", CVS module nfs-utils.

Homepage: http://nfs.sourceforge.net/
```

apt-cache: DISPLAYS PACKAGE INFORMATION

The apt-cache utility has many commands—some that manipulate the APT package cache and others that display information about packages in the cache. This section contains examples of some of the simpler commands that display information. Use apt-file (page 503) to display information about packages that are not installed on the system.

Displaying package dependencies The apt-cache **depends** command displays the list of packages that a package depends on. These are forward (normal) dependencies. Use the **--recurse** option to display the packages that the dependencies are dependent on (the dependencies' dependencies).

```
$ apt-cache depends nfs-common
nfs-common
 |Depends: portmap
  Depends: <rpcbind>
  Depends: adduser
  ...
  Depends: libwrap0
  Conflicts: <nfs-client>
  Replaces: <nfs-client>
    nfs-common
  Replaces: nfs-kernel-server
```

Use the **rdepends** apt-cache command to display the list of packages that are dependent on a specified package. These are reverse dependencies. Use the **--recurse** option to display the packages that are dependent on the dependent packages.

```
$ apt-cache rdepends nfs-common
nfs-common
Reverse Depends:
  sfs-common
  gconf
  education-networked
  rgmanager
  openoffice.org-core
  nfs-kernel-server
  netbase
  autofs
```

Displaying package records

The apt-cache **show** command displays package records from the files in the APT local package indexes. See also the aptitude **show** command, which displays less information (page 511), and the dpkg **status** command (page 519). Following is an example:

```
$ apt-cache show nfs-common
Package: nfs-common
Priority: optional
Section: net
Installed-Size: 392
Maintainer: Ubuntu Core Developers <ubuntu-devel-discuss@lists.ubuntu.com>
Original-Maintainer: Anibal Monsalve Salazar <anibal@debian.org>
Architecture: i386
Source: nfs-utils
Version: 1:1.0.12-4
Replaces: nfs-client, nfs-kernel-server (<< 1:1.0.7-5)
Provides: nfs-client
Depends: portmap | rpcbind, adduser, ucf, lsb-base (>= 1.3-9ubuntu3),
netbase (>= 4.24), libc6 (>= 2.5-0ubuntu1), libcomerr2 (>= 1.33-3),
libevent1 (>= 1.1a), libgssapi2, libkrb53 (>= 1.4.2), libnfsidmap2,
librpcsecgss3, libwrap0
Conflicts: nfs-client
Filename: pool/main/n/nfs-utils/nfs-common_1.0.12-4_i386.deb
Size: 132236
MD5sum: c381f4f9383b6e0993daff25ba463e83
SHA1: 77654317983629d331244c39ed42a0afba859802
SHA256: d1bc0e8cc4080af90148b4bf91a178c6c74ec542677738eb8a990be3ba0fe44f
Description: NFS support files common to client and server
 Use this package on any machine that uses NFS, either as client or
 server.  Programs included: lockd, statd, showmount, nfsstat, gssd
 and idmapd.
 .
 Upstream: SourceForge project "nfs", CVS module nfs-utils.
 .
  Homepage: http://nfs.sourceforge.net/
Bugs: mailto:ubuntu-users@lists.ubuntu.com
Origin: Ubuntu
Task: edubuntu-server
```

The apt-cache **showpkg** command displays package version and location information as well as dependency lists.

apt-get source: DOWNLOADS SOURCE FILES

The apt-get **source** command downloads and unpacks in the working directory source code files from repositories specified with **deb-src** lines in **sources.list** (page 505). APT does not keep index and cache files for source files as it does for binary files. With the **––download-only** option, this command does not unpack the source code. With the **––compile** option, it unpacks and compiles the source code. You do not have to run this command with **root** privileges; it requires only write access to the working directory. Following is an example:

```
$ apt-get source adduser
...
dpkg-source: extracting adduser in adduser-3.103ubuntu1
dpkg-source: unpacking adduser_3.103ubuntu1.tar.gz

$ ls -ld adduser*
drwxr-xr-x 7 zach zach   4096 Jul 10 08:12 adduser-3.103ubuntu1
-rw-r--r-- 1 zach zach    708 Jul 10 09:03 adduser_3.103ubuntu1.dsc
-rw-r--r-- 1 zach zach 246211 Jul 10 09:03 adduser_3.103ubuntu1.tar.gz
```

dpkg: THE DEBIAN PACKAGE MANAGEMENT SYSTEM

The Debian package (**dpkg**) management system database tracks which software packages are installed on a system, where each is installed, which version is installed, and which packages each depends on.

The **dpkg** management system comprises many utilities. These utilities install, uninstall, upgrade, query, and verify software packages. The original and primary utility is dpkg (page 516). Although you can use dpkg for most tasks involving the **dpkg** management system, other tools can make your job easier. Some of the most commonly used of these tools are described here:

- apt-cache—Displays information about and manipulates the APT cache (page 512).

- apt-file—Similar to apt-cache except that it works with packages that have not been installed and packages that have not been downloaded, in addition to those that are installed on the local system (page 503).

- aptitude—Retrieves software packages and calls dpkg to install and remove them (pages 501 and 508).

- apt-get—A textual interface to APT; similar to aptitude.

- dpkg—The primary **dpkg** management system utility (page 516).

- dselect—A pseudographical front-end for dpkg.

- Synaptic—A graphical interface to APT (page 118).

deb FILES

The **dpkg** management system works with **.deb** format files, frequently referred to as **deb** files. Because **dpkg** cannot download **deb** files from repositories, aptitude (page 508) typically performs this task. By default, aptitude stores downloaded **deb** files in **/var/cache/apt/archives**. The **dpkg** management system stores available package information in **/var/lib/dpkg/available** and package installation information in **/var/lib/dpkg/status**.

You can manually locate, download, and install **deb** files. However, doing so can be tedious, especially when you find that a package is dependent on several other packages and that some of those packages are dependent on yet other packages.

You can create **deb** files, as when you build a kernel. Page 563 has an example of building a kernel **deb** file; pages 518 and 566 show dpkg installing **deb** files.

Binary files   A binary **deb** file can contain the following components, which are packed and unpacked using the ar (archive) utility. All packages contain an executable file; the other components are optional.

- **binary**—Binary executable files.
- **control**—Package information including lists of dependent, recommended, and suggested packages.
- **conffiles**—Package configuration files.
- **preinst**—Preinstall script.
- **postinst**—Postinstall script.
- **prerm**—Preremove script.
- **postrm**—Postremove script.

To unpack a **deb** file, first download it to **/var/cache/apt/archives** using the command **aptitude download** *package*. Copy the file to a directory with no other files in it and use **ar –xv** to unpack the **deb** file. You can then use tar (page 162) to unpack the tar files. The example shows how to extract the control files from the **nfs-common deb** file.

```
$ ls
nfs-common_1%3a1.1.2-4ubuntu1_i386.deb
$ ar -xv nfs*deb
x - debian-binary
x - control.tar.gz
x - data.tar.gz
$ tar xvf control.tar.gz
./
./postinst
./prerm
./postrm
./conffiles
./md5sums
./control
```

Source files   A source file package contains a description file, a source code file, and a diff file that contains Ubuntu-specific changes to the source file. See page 514 for instructions on how to use apt-get to download and unpack a source file.

Installing a **deb** file   When dpkg installs a binary package (page 518), it takes the following steps:

1. Extracts **control** files.

2. If another version of the same package is installed on the system, executes the **prerm** script of the *old* package.

3. Runs the **preinst** script.

4. Backs up the old binary files and unpacks the new binary files, allowing dpkg to revert to the existing setup if installation fails.

5. If another version of the same package is installed on the system, executes the **postrm** script of the *old* package.

6. Backs up the old configuration files and unpacks the new configuration files, allowing dpkg to revert to the existing setup if installation fails.

7. Runs the **postinst** script.

Removing a **deb** file   When dpkg removes a binary package (page 518), it runs the **prerm** script, removes the files, and runs the **postrm** script.

dpkg: THE FOUNDATION OF THE DEBIAN PACKAGE MANAGEMENT SYSTEM

The dpkg (Debian package) utility installs (unpacks and configures), queries, and removes **deb** packages. Before querying the software package database, give the **update-avail** command (discussed next) to update the list of available packages.

dpkg commands and options both start with hyphens

tip   Although command-line arguments that start with one or two hyphens are generally called options, the dpkg documentation divides these arguments into commands and options. For example, **--purge** is a command and **--simulate** is an option.

Typically you will use one of the tools that acts as a front-end for dpkg and not work with dpkg itself. In some cases you may find the following dpkg commands useful. View the dpkg man page or use the **--help** option for a complete list of commands.

dpkg --update-avail: UPDATES THE LIST OF AVAILABLE PACKAGES

The list of available packages is kept in the **/var/lib/dpkg/available** file. The **--update-avail** dpkg command updates this list from files that the APT local package indexes (page 506).

```
$ sudo dpkg --update-avail /var/lib/dpkg/available
Replacing available packages info, using /var/lib/dpkg/available.
Information about 1868 package(s) was updated.
```

dpkg --list: DISPLAYS INFORMATION ABOUT A PACKAGE

The dpkg --list (or –l) command displays a line of information about packages you name as an argument. Package names can include wildcards as described in "Filename Generation/Pathname Expansion" on page 242. You must quote wildcards on the command line.

The following command lists all packages whose names begin with **apache2**. The first two lines of the header are keys for the first two letters on each line that describes a package. The first line of the header, labeled **Desired**, lists the possible desired package selection states (Table 13-1). The second line, labeled **Status**, lists possible package statuses (Table 13-1). The Name column lists the name of the package, while the Version and Description columns describe the package.

```
$ sudo dpkg --list "apache2*"
Desired=Unknown/Install/Remove/Purge/Hold
| Status=Not/Installed/Config-files/Unpacked/Failed-config/Half-installed
|/ Err?=(none)/Hold/Reinst-required/X=both-problems (Status,Err: uppercase=bad)
||/ Name                Version             Description
+++-===================-===================-==========================================
pn  apache2             <none>              (no description available)
rc  apache2-common      2.0.55-4ubuntu4     next generation, scalable, extendable web...
ii  apache2-doc         2.0.55-4ubuntu4     documentation for apache2
un  apache2-modules     <none>              (no description available)
un  apache2-mpm-perchil <none>              (no description available)
un  apache2-mpm-prefork <none>              (no description available)
un  apache2-mpm-threadp <none>              (no description available)
pn  apache2-mpm-worker  <none>              (no description available)
pn  apache2-utils       <none>              (no description available)
```

In the preceding example, the **apache2** package has a desired state of purged (**p**) and a status of not installed (**n**), meaning the package is not installed and has no configuration files on the system. The **apache2-common** package has a desired state of removed (**r**) and currently has only its configuration files installed (**c**). For **apache2-doc**, the first **i** indicates that the desired state of the package is installed and the second **i** indicates that the current state of the package is installed (the package is installed on the system). For **apache2-modules**, the desired state of the package is unknown (**u**) and it is not installed (**n**). See page 518 for more examples of the --list command.

Table 13-1   dpkg letter codes

Letter	Means that the package is
Desired (selection state)	
u (unknown)	Unknown to dpkg
i (install)	To be installed
r (remove)	To be removed (uninstalled), except for configuration files
p (purge)	To be removed, including configuration files
h (hold)	Not handled by dpkg

Table 13-1 dpkg letter codes (continued)

Letter	Means that the package is
Status (package state)	
n (not installed)	Not installed
i (installed)	Installed
c (config-files)	Not installed; only the configuration files exist on the system
u (unpacked)	Unpacked, but not configured
f (failed-config)	Unpacked, but not configured; configuration failed
h (half-installed)	Partially installed; installation is not complete

dpkg --install: INSTALLS A PACKAGE

The dpkg **--install** (**-i**) command installs (unpacks and sets up; see page 516) a package stored in a **deb** file. It does not search for and download a package from the Internet. Use aptitude (page 508) for that purpose. The following example shows dpkg installing the ftp package:

```
$ sudo dpkg --install /var/cache/apt/archives/ftp_0.17-16_i386.deb
Selecting previously deselected package ftp.
(Reading database ... 173635 files and directories currently installed.)
Unpacking ftp (from .../archives/ftp_0.17-16_i386.deb) ...
Setting up ftp (0.17-16) ...
```

dpkg --remove AND dpkg --purge: REMOVE AN INSTALLED PACKAGE

The dpkg **--remove** (**-r**) command removes an installed package except for its configuration files. Leaving these files can be useful if you decide to reinstall the package. Use **--purge** (**-P**) to completely remove a package, including configuration files. The following command displays the status of the **ftpd** package (it is installed).

```
$ dpkg --list ftpd
Desired=Unknown/Install/Remove/Purge/Hold
| Status=Not/Installed/Config-files/Unpacked/Failed-config/Half-installed
|/ Err?=(none)/Hold/Reinst-required/X=both-problems (Status,Err: uppercase=bad)
||/ Name           Version            Description
+++-=================-==================-=========================================
ii  ftpd            0.17-24            FTP server
```

The next command removes the **ftpd** package except for its configuration files:

```
$ sudo dpkg --remove ftpd
(Reading database ... 113335 files and directories currently installed.)
Removing ftpd ...
```

Next the dpkg --list command shows a status of **rc** for the **ftpd** package, indicating that it has been removed (**r**) but the configuration files (**c**) remain.

```
$ dpkg --list ftpd
...
rc  ftpd              0.17-24              FTP server
```

Finally dpkg purges the **ftpd** package and shows a state of **pn** (purged, not installed).

```
$ sudo dpkg --purge ftpd
(Reading database ... 113325 files and directories currently installed.)
Removing ftpd ...
Purging configuration files for ftpd ...

$ dpkg --list ftpd
...
pn  ftpd              <none>              (no description available)
```

If there are packages dependent on the package you are removing, the command fails. In the next example, dpkg attempts to remove the **apache2.2-common** package but fails because the **apache2-mpm-worker** package depends on **apache2.2-common**:

```
$ sudo dpkg --remove apache2.2-common
dpkg: dependency problems prevent removal of apache2.2-common:
 apache2-mpm-worker depends on apache2.2-common (= 2.2.3-3.2build1).
dpkg: error processing apache2.2-common (--remove):
 dependency problems - not removing
Errors were encountered while processing:
 apache2.2-common
```

You can remove the dependent package and then remove **apache2.2-common**. It is frequently easier to use aptitude to remove a package and its dependencies because you can do so with a single aptitude **remove** command (page 502).

When dpkg removes a package, the **prerm** script stops any running daemons associated with the package. In the case of Apache, it stops the **apache2** server.

```
$ sudo dpkg --remove apache2-mpm-worker
(Reading database ... 113816 files and directories currently installed.)
Removing apache2-mpm-worker ...
 * Stopping web server (apache2)...                                    [ OK ]
```

dpkg --status: DISPLAYS INFORMATION ABOUT A PACKAGE

The **--status** (**-s**) dpkg command displays lengthy information about the installed package you specify as an argument. This information includes package status, installed size, architecture it is compiled for, conflicting packages, a description, and the name of the package maintainer. See also the aptitude **show** command (page 511) and the apt-cache **show** command (page 513).

```
$ dpkg --status apache2-mpm-worker
Package: apache2-mpm-worker
Status: install ok installed
Priority: optional
Section: web
Installed-Size: 684
Maintainer: Ubuntu Core Developers <ubuntu-devel@lists.ubuntu.com>
Architecture: i386
Source: apache2
Version: 2.2.3-3.2build1
Replaces: apache2-mpm-threadpool (<< 2.0.53), apache2-mpm-perchild (<< 2.2.0)
Provides: apache2-modules, apache2, httpd, httpd-cgi
Depends: libapr1, libaprutil1, libc6 (>= 2.5-0ubuntu1), libdb4.4, libexpat1 (>= 1.95.8),
libldap2 (>= 2.1.17-1), libpcre3 (>= 4.5), libpq5, libsqlite3-0 (>= 3.3.10), libuuid1,
apache2.2-common (= 2.2.3-3.2build1)
Conflicts: apache2-mpm-prefork, apache2-mpm-event, apache2-common
Description: High speed threaded model for Apache HTTPD 2.1
 The worker MPM provides a threaded implementation for Apache HTTPD 2.1. It is
 considerably faster than the traditional model, and is the recommended MPM.
 .
 Worker generally is a good choice for high-traffic servers because it
 has a smaller memory footprint than the prefork MPM.
Original-Maintainer: Debian Apache Maintainers <debian-apache@lists.debian.org>
```

Use the dpkg **––info** command to display information about a **deb** file that is on the system (for example, in the APT cache) but is not installed. The following command displays information about the **ftpd deb** file in the **archives** directory:

```
$ dpkg --info /var/cache/apt/archives/ftpd_0.17-24_i386.deb
```

dpkg ––search: DISPLAYS THE NAME OF THE PACKAGE THAT CONTAINS A SPECIFIED FILE

The **––search** (or **–S**) option to dpkg displays the name of the package that includes the file you specify as an argument:

```
$ dpkg --search /etc/ssh
openssh-client: /etc/ssh
```

dpkg ––listfiles: LISTS FILES WITHIN A PACKAGE

The dpkg **––listfiles** (or **–L**) command lists the files that are part of the package you specify as an argument. The following example lists the files in the **openssh-server** package:

```
$ dpkg --listfiles openssh-server
/.
/etc
/etc/init.d
/etc/init.d/ssh
/etc/default
...
```

Use the dpkg --**contents** command to list the files contained in a package that is on the system but not installed. The following command lists the files in the **dump deb** file in the **archives** directory:

```
$ dpkg --contents /var/cache/apt/archives/dump_0.4b41-4_i386.deb
```

BITTORRENT

The easiest way to download a BitTorrent file is to click the torrent file object in a Web browser or in the Nautilus File Browser. This section describes how BitTorrent works and explains how to download a BitTorrent file from the command line.

The BitTorrent protocol implements a hybrid client/server and *P2P* (page 1123) file transfer mechanism. BitTorrent efficiently distributes large amounts of static data, such as the Ubuntu installation ISO images. It can replace protocols such as anonymous FTP, where client authentication is not required. Each BitTorrent client that downloads a file provides additional bandwidth for uploading the file, thereby reducing the load on the initial source. In general, BitTorrent downloads proceed faster than FTP downloads. Unlike protocols such as FTP, BitTorrent groups multiple files into a single package: a BitTorrent file.

Tracker, peer, seed, and swarm
BitTorrent, like other P2P systems, does not use a dedicated server. Instead, the functions of a server are performed by the tracker, peers, and seeds. The *tracker* is a server that allows clients to communicate with each other. Each client—called a *peer* when it has downloaded part of the BitTorrent file and a *seed* once it has downloaded the entire BitTorrent file—acts as an additional source for the BitTorrent file. Peers and seeds are collectively called a *swarm*. As with a P2P network, a member of a swarm uploads to other clients the sections of the BitTorrent file it has already downloaded. There is nothing special about a seed: It can be removed at any time once the torrent is available for download from other seeds.

The torrent
The first step in downloading a BitTorrent file is to locate or acquire the *torrent,* a file with the filename extension of **.torrent**. A torrent contains pertinent information (metadata) about the BitTorrent file to be downloaded, such as its size and the location of the tracker. You can obtain a torrent by accessing its URI, or you can acquire it via the Web, an email attachment, or other means. The BitTorrent client can then connect to the tracker to learn the locations of other members of the swarm that it can download the BitTorrent file from.

Manners
Once you have downloaded a BitTorrent file (the local system has become a seed), it is good manners to allow the local BitTorrent client to continue to run so peers (clients that have not downloaded the entire BitTorrent file) can upload *at least* as much information as you have downloaded.

PREREQUISITES

If necessary, use aptitude (pages 501 and 508) to install the **bittorrent** package. With this package installed, the command **apropos bittorrent** displays a list of BitTorrent utilities. See **/usr/share/doc/bittorrent** for more information. You may want to try BitTornado, an experimental BitTorrent client with additional features (**bittornado** package; see bittornado.com)

Because the BitTorrent utilities are written in Python and run on any platform with a Python interpreter, they are not dependent on system architecture. Python is installed in **/usr/bin/python** and is available in the **python** package.

USING BITTORRENT

The btdownloadcurses utility is a textual BitTorrent client that provides a pseudo-graphical interface. Once you have a torrent, give a command such as the following, substituting the name of the torrent you want to download for the Ubuntu torrent in the example:

```
$ btdownloadcurses intrepid-desktop-i386.iso.torrent
```

In the preceding command, the torrent specifies that the BitTorrent file be saved as **intrepid-desktop-i386.iso** in the working directory. The name of the BitTorrent file is not always the same as the name of the torrent. In the case of a multifile torrent, the BitTorrent files may be stored in a directory, also named by the torrent. Figure 13-1 shows btdownloadcurses running. Depending on the speed of the Internet connection and the number of seeds, downloading a large BitTorrent file can take from hours to days.

You can abort the download by pressing **q** or CONTROL-C. The download will automatically resume from where it left off when you download the same torrent to the same location again.

Make sure you have enough room to download the torrent

caution   Some torrents are huge. Make sure the partition you are working in has enough room to hold the BitTorrent file you are downloading.

See the btdownloadcurses man page for a list of options. One of the most useful options is **--max_upload_rate**, which limits how much bandwidth the swarm can use while downloading the torrent *from you*. The default is 0, meaning there is no limit to the upload bandwidth. The following command prevents BitTorrent from using more than 10 kilobytes per second of upstream bandwidth:

```
$ btdownloadcurses --max_upload_rate 10 intrepid-desktop-i386.iso.torrent
```

BitTorrent usually allows higher download rates for members of the swarm that upload more data, so it is to your advantage to increase this value if you have spare bandwidth. You need to leave enough free upstream bandwidth for the acknowledgment packets from your download to get through or else the download will be very slow. By default, btdownloadcurses uploads to a maximum of seven other clients at

Figure 13-1 btdownloadcurses working with the Ubuntu desktop torrent

once. You can change this number by using the **--max_uploads** argument, followed by the number of concurrent uploads you wish to permit. If you are downloading over a modem, try setting **--max_upload_rate** to 3 and **--max_uploads** to 2.

The name of the file or directory that BitTorrent saves a file or files in is specified by the torrent. You can specify a different file or directory name by using the **--saveas** option. The btshowmetainfo utility displays the name the BitTorrent file will be saved as, the size of the file, the name of the torrent (**metainfo file**), and other information:

```
$ btshowmetainfo intrepid-desktop-i386.iso.torrent
btshowmetainfo 20021207 - decode BitTorrent metainfo files

metainfo file.: intrepid-desktop-i386.iso.torrent
info hash.....: 58a065449872fcad7e0f1a1e0001d8e6244b1575
file name.....: intrepid-desktop-i386.iso
file size.....: 729288704 (1391 * 524288 + 4096)
announce url..: http://torrent.ubuntu.com:6969/announce
```

INSTALLING NON-dpkg SOFTWARE

Most software that is not in **dpkg** format comes with detailed instructions on how to configure, build (if necessary), and install it. Some binary distributions (those containing prebuilt executables) require you to unpack the software from the root directory.

THE /opt AND /usr/local DIRECTORIES

Some newer application packages include scripts to install themselves automatically into a directory hierarchy under **/opt**, with files in a **/opt** subdirectory that is named after the package and executables in **/opt/bin** or **/opt/**package**/bin**.

Other software packages allow you to choose where you unpack them. Because many different people develop software for Linux, there is no consistent method for installing it. As you acquire software, install it on the local system in as consistent and predictable a manner as possible. The standard Linux file structure has a directory hierarchy under **/usr/local** for binaries (**/usr/local/bin**), manual pages (**/usr/local/man**), and so forth. Because many GNU buildtools search the **/usr/local** hierarchy by default and may find the wrong version of a utility if you install developer tools there, putting these tools in **/opt** is a good idea.

To prevent confusion later and to avoid overwriting or losing the software when you install standard software upgrades, avoid installing nonstandard software in standard system directories (such as **/usr/bin**). On a multiuser system, make sure users know where to find the local software and advise them whenever you install, change, or remove local tools.

GNU CONFIGURE AND BUILD SYSTEM

The GNU Configure and Build System makes it easy to build a program that is distributed as source code (see autoconf at developer.gnome.org/tools/build.html). This process requires a shell, make, and gcc (the GNU C compiler). You do not need to work with **root** privileges except to install the program.

The following example assumes you have downloaded the GNU chess program (www.gnu.org/software/chess/chess.html) to the working directory. First unpack and decompress the file and cd to the new directory:

```
$ tar -xvzf gnuchess-5.05.tar.gz
chess/
chess/CVS/
chess/CVS/Root
...
chess/src/util.c
chess/src/version.c
chess/src/version.h
$ cd chess
```

After reading the **README** and **INSTALL** files, run the **configure** script, which gathers information about the local system and generates the **Makefile** file:

```
$ ./configure
checking for a BSD compatible install... /usr/bin/install -c
checking whether build environment is sane... yes
checking for mawk... mawk
checking whether make sets ${MAKE}... yes
checking for gcc... gcc
checking for C compiler default output... a.out
checking whether the C compiler works... yes
...
configure: creating ./config.status
config.status: creating Makefile
config.status: creating src/Makefile
config.status: creating src/config.h
```

Refer to the **configure** info page, specifically the **--prefix** option, which causes the install phase to place the software in a directory other than **/usr/local**. Next, run make:

```
$ make
Making all in src
make[1]: Entering directory '/home/zach/chess/src'
make  all-am
make[2]: Entering directory '/home/zach/chess/src'
source='atak.c' object='atak.o' libtool=no \
        depfile='.deps/atak.Po' tmpdepfile='.deps/atak.TPo' \
        depmode=gcc3 /bin/sh ../depcomp \
        gcc -DHAVE_CONFIG_H -I. -I. -I.      -g -O2 -c 'test -f atak.c || echo './''atak.c
source='book.c' object='book.o' libtool=no \
        depfile='.deps/book.Po' tmpdepfile='.deps/book.TPo' \
        depmode=gcc3 /bin/sh ../depcomp \
        gcc -DHAVE_CONFIG_H -I. -I. -I.      -g -O2 -c 'test -f book.c || echo './''book.c
...
gcc  -g -O2   -o gnuchess  atak.o book.o cmd.o epd.o eval.o genmove.o hash.o hung.o init.o
iterate.o main.o move.o null.o output.o players.o pgn.o quiesce.o random.o repeat.o
search.o solve.o sort.o swap.o test.o ttable.o util.o version.o
make[2]: Leaving directory '/home/zach/chess/src'
make[1]: Leaving directory '/home/zach/chess/src'
make[1]: Entering directory '/home/zach/chess'
make[1]: Nothing to be done for 'all-am'.
make[1]: Leaving directory '/home/zach/chess'

$ ls src/gnuchess
src/gnuchess
```

After make finishes, the **gnuchess** executable is in the **src** directory. If you want to install it, give the following command:

```
$ sudo make install
Making install in src
make[1]: Entering directory '/home/zach/chess/chess/src'
make[2]: Entering directory '/home/zach/chess/chess/src'
/bin/sh ../mkinstalldirs /usr/local/bin
  /usr/bin/install -c gnuchess /usr/local/bin/gnuchess
...
```

You can complete the entire task with the following command line:

```
$ sudo ./configure && make && make install
```

The Boolean AND operator (&&) allows the execution of a subsequent command only if the previous step returned a successful exit status.

wget: Downloads Files Noninteractively

The wget utility is a noninteractive, command-line utility that retrieves files from the Web using HTTP, HTTPS, or FTP. In the example on the next page, wget downloads the Ubuntu home page, named **index.html**, to a file in the working directory with the same name.

```
$ wget http://www.ubuntu.com
--14:58:48--  http://www.ubuntu.com/
=> 'index.html'
Resolving www.ubuntu.com... 82.211.81.158
Connecting to www.ubuntu.com|82.211.81.158|:80... connected.
HTTP request sent, awaiting response... 200 OK
Length: 13,112 (13K) [text/html]

100%[=========================================================>] 13,112          40.60K/s

14:58:49 (40.40 KB/s) - 'index.html' saved [13112/13112]

$
```

With the **--recursive** (**-r**) option, wget downloads the directory hierarchy under the URI you specify. Be careful with this option because it can download a lot of data (which may completely fill the partition you are working in). The **--background** (**-b**) option runs wget in the background and redirects its standard error to a file named **wget-log**:

```
$ wget --recursive --background http://www.ubuntu.com
Continuing in background, pid 28839.
Output will be written to 'wget-log'.
$
```

The wget utility does not overwrite log files. When **wget-log** exists, wget writes subsequent logs to **wget-log.1**, **wget-log.2**, and so on.

Running wget in the background is useful when you need to download a large file to a remote system. You can start it running from an ssh (page 634) session and then disconnect, allowing the download to complete without any interaction.

The wget **--continue** (**-c**) option continues an interrupted download. For example, if you decide to stop a download so you can run it in the background, you can continue it from where it left off with this option.

CHAPTER SUMMARY

As a system administrator, you need to keep applications and system software current. Of the many reasons to keep the software on a system up-to-date, one of the most important is system security. The Debian package (**dpkg**) management system makes the process of adding and removing **deb** format software packages quite easy.

APT utilities, such as aptitude, download software packages and dependencies and then work with **dpkg** to install, remove, or update packages. In addition, you can use the apt-cache and dpkg utilities to query and verify **dpkg** packages. For packages distributed as source code, the GNU Configure and Build System enables you to build executable files.

BitTorrent is a handy tool for downloading large static data files such as the Ubuntu installation ISO images. It can replace protocols such as anonymous FTP, where client authentication is not required.

EXERCISES

1. Why would you use HTTP or FTP instead of BitTorrent for downloading large files?

2. Which command would you give to perform a complete upgrade?

3. Why would you build a package from its source code when a (binary) **deb** file is available?

4. Suggest two advantages that **deb** files have over source distributions.

ADVANCED EXERCISES

5. When you compile a package yourself, rather than from a **deb** file, which directory hierarchy should you put it in?

6. Which steps should you take before performing an upgrade on a mission-critical server?

14

PRINTING WITH CUPS

A *printing system* handles the tasks involved in first getting a print job from an application (or the command line) through the appropriate *filters* (page 1108) and into a queue for a suitable printer and then getting it printed. While handling a job, a printing system can keep track of billing information so the proper accounts can be charged for printer use. When a printer fails, the printing system can redirect jobs to other, similar printers.

Introduction

LPD and LPR   Traditionally, UNIX had two printing systems: the BSD Line Printer Daemon (LPD) and the System V Line Printer system (LPR). Linux adopted those systems at first, and both UNIX and Linux have seen modifications to and replacements for these systems. Today CUPS is the default printing system under Ubuntu Linux.

CUPS   CUPS (Common UNIX Printing System) is a cross-platform print server built around IPP (Internet Printing Protocol), which is itself based on HTTP. CUPS provides many printer drivers and can print different types of files, including PostScript. Because it is built on IPP and written to be portable, CUPS runs under many operating systems, including Linux and Windows. Other UNIX variants, including Mac OS X, use CUPS; recent versions of Windows include the ability to print to IPP printers. Thus CUPS is an ideal solution for printing in a heterogeneous environment. CUPS provides System V and BSD command-line interfaces and, in addition to IPP, supports LPD/LPR, HTTP, SMB, and JetDirect (socket) protocols, among others.

IPP   The IPP project (www.pwg.org/ipp) began in 1996, when Novell and several other companies designed a protocol for printing over the Internet. IPP enables users to

- Determine the capabilities of a printer.
- Submit jobs to a printer.
- Determine the status of a printer.
- Determine the status of a print job.
- Cancel a print job.

IPP is a client/server protocol in which the server side can be a print server or a network-capable stand-alone printer.

Printers and queues   On a modern computing system, when you "send a job to the printer," you actually add the job to the list of jobs waiting their turn to be printed on a printer. The list is called a *print queue* or simply a *queue*. The phrase *configuring* (or *setting up*) *a printer* is often used to mean *configuring a (print) queue*. This chapter uses these phrases interchangeably.

Prerequisites

Installation   Install the following packages (most are installed with the base system). Packages for Hardy are listed first; packages for Intrepid are enclosed in [square brackets].

- **cupsys** [**cups**]
- **cupsys-common** [**cups-common**]
- **cupsys-bsd** [**cups-bsd**] (optional; BSD printing commands)
- **cupsys-client** [**cups-client**] (optional; System V printing commands)
- **openprinting-ppds** (PPD files)

- **openprinting-ppds-extra** (optional; more PPD files)
- **system-config-printer-gnome** (optional; graphical printer tool)

To add, modify, and remove printers from the local system, you must be a member of the **lpadmin** group. For more information see the tip on page 532. To use the CUPS Web interface, you need an X server and a Web browser.

cups/cupsys init script   When you install the **cupsys/cups** package, the **dpkg postinst** script starts the **cupsd** daemon. After you configure CUPS, call the **cupsys** (Hardy) or **cups** (Intrepid) init script to restart the **cupsd** daemon:

```
$ sudo /etc/init.d/cups restart
 * Restarting Common Unix Printing System: cupsd                    [ OK ]
```

MORE INFORMATION

Local   CUPS Documentation: With the CUPS Web interface up (page 543), point a local browser at localhost:631/help.

Web   www.linux-foundation.org/en/OpenPrinting: Information on printers and printing under Linux. Hosts a support database with details about many printers, including notes and driver information; also offers forums, articles, and a HOWTO document on printing.
CUPS home page: www.cups.org
IPP information: www.pwg.org/ipp

HOWTO   *SMB HOWTO* has a section titled "Sharing a Windows Printer with Linux Machines."

NOTES

Firewall   A CUPS server normally uses TCP port 631 for an IPP connection and port 80 for an LPR/LPD connection. If the CUPS server system is running a firewall, you need to open one or both of these ports. Using firestarter (page 824), open one or both of these ports by adding a rule that allows service for port 631 and/or port 80 from the clients you want to be able to access the server.

PDF printer   *HARDY:* Ubuntu automatically creates a virtual PDF printer. You can use this printer to generate PDF output from applications that are not otherwise able to generate PDF output, such as GIMP and Firefox. *INTREPID:* You can set up a virtual PDF printer by installing the **cups-pdf** package or you can set up this printer manually.

JUMPSTART I: CONFIGURING A LOCAL PRINTER

In most cases, when you connect a printer to the local system and turn it on, Ubuntu sets up the printer and may display a **Printer Added** message. If you want to modify the new printer's configuration, click **Configure** on the message or use the Printer Configuration window (Figure 14-1), described in the next section. Both techniques bring you to the same window: Printer Configuration (*HARDY;* Figure 14-1) or Printer Properties (*INTREPID;* Figure 14-3).

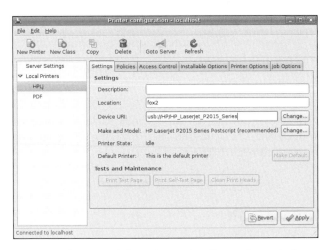

Figure 14-1   *HARDY:* The Printer Configuration window

system-config-printer: CONFIGURING A PRINTER

You must be a member of the **lpadmin** group

tip   To modify a printer using the Printer Configuration window (**system-config-printer**), you must be a member of the **lpadmin** group (the first user is a member of this group). See page 580 for instructions on how to add a user to a group.

HARDY+INTREPID   The layout of the windows that system-config-printer displays changed between the Hardy and Intrepid releases; their functionality did not change. Hardy presents configuration options for all printers in a complex, single, tabbed window, named the Printer Configuration window (Figure 14-1). Intrepid requires you to select the printer you want to configure from a simplified Printer Configuration window (Figure 14-2). Double-clicking a printer in this window displays the Printer Properties window (Figure 14-3) for that printer; you can use this window to configure the printer. Whereas Hardy's Printer Configuration window allows you to select a printer from the frame on the left and the configuration options you want to control from tabs near the top, Intrepid's Printer Properties window configures a single printer; you select the configuration options from the frame on the left.

The Printer Configuration window (*HARDY* Figure 14-1, *INTREPID* Figure 14-2) enables you to add, remove, and configure local and remote printers. To display this window, select **Main menu: System⇨Administration⇨Printing** or give the command **system-config-printer** from a terminal emulator or Run Application window (ALT-F2).

Using system-config-printer is very similar to using the CUPS Web interface, which is discussed on page 538. However, system-config-printer is a native application, not a Web interface.

Figure 14-2 *INTREPID:* The Printer Configuration window

HARDY The frame on the left side of the Printer Configuration window (Figure 14-1) lists the configured printers. Ubuntu configures a PDF printer by default. On the right side of the window, you can configure the printer highlighted on the left.

INTREPID Double-click a printer in the Printer Configuration window (Figure 14-2) to display the Printer Properties window (Figure 14-3) for that printer.

Server Settings *HARDY:* Click **Server Settings** at the top of the frame on the left of the Printer Configuration window to display Basic Server Settings on the right side of the window. *INTREPID:* Click **Server⇨Settings** from the Printer Configuration window menu to display the Basic Server Settings window. *HARDY+INTREPID:* The top two check boxes specify whether system-config-printer displays printers that are shared by other systems and whether the local system publishes printers it shares. You control whether a given printer is shared from the Policies tab/selection (next section).

CONFIGURATION TABS/SELECTIONS

This section describes the six tabs near the top of the right side of the Hardy Printer Configuration window and the six selections in the frame at the left side of the Intrepid Printer Properties window. The Hardy tabs and the Intrepid selections have the same names and similar functionality. *HARDY:* These tabs configure the printer highlighted in the frame on the left side of the window. *INTREPID:* These selections configure the printer you selected from the Printer Configuration window.

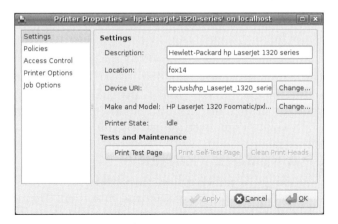

Figure 14-3 *INTREPID:* The Printer Properties window

Settings   Figure 14-3 shows the Settings selection for a Hewlett-Packard (HP) printer. The text boxes labeled **Description** and **Location** hold information for your use; the system does not use this information. The text boxes labeled **Device URI** and **Make and Model** specify the location and type of the printer.

Default printer   *HARDY:* With the Settings tab highlighted, click the button labeled **Make Default** to make the highlighted printer the default printer.

INTREPID: Highlight a printer in the Printer Configuration window and select **Printer⇨Set as Default** from the window menu to specify the highlighted printer as the default printer. The check mark on the printer in Figure 14-2 indicates the default printer.

Policies   Under the word **State** are check boxes labeled **Enabled, Accepting jobs,** and **Shared.** Table 14-1 describes the effects of putting ticks in the first two check boxes. Putting a tick in the check box labeled **Shared** shares the printer with other systems if the local system publishes shared printers (see "Server Settings," on the previous page). The Policies tab also controls whether the printer prints banners before and after jobs and what CUPS does when it encounters an error.

Table 14-1   Printer status

	Enabled	Disabled
Accepting jobs	Accepts new jobs into the queue.	Accepts new jobs into the queue.
	Prints jobs from the queue.	Does not print jobs from the queue until the printer is enabled.
Rejecting jobs	Rejects new jobs.	Rejects new jobs.
	Prints jobs from the queue.	Does not print jobs from the queue until the printer is enabled.

Access Control   The Access Control tab enables you to set the policy for printer access. By default, anyone can use the printer. You can create a blacklist of users who are not allowed to use it. Alternatively, you can prohibit anyone from using the printer and create a whitelist of users who are allowed to use it.

Installable Options   The Installable Options tab controls printer-specific options.

Printer Options   The Printer Options tab controls image quality, paper size and source (tray), and other generic printer options.

Job Options   The Job Options tab controls the number of copies, orientation (portrait or landscape), scaling, margins, and more. Options specified by an application sending a job to the printer override options you set in this tab.

SETTING UP A REMOTE PRINTER

As explained earlier, system-config-printer recognizes and sets up a printer when you connect it to the local system and turn it on. This section describes the process of setting up a printer on another system or on the local network. You can also use the same technique for setting up a printer on the local system. For more information

Figure 14-4 The New Printer window showing a verified printer

on setting up a remote printer, refer to "JumpStart II: Setting Up a Local or Remote Printer Using the CUPS Web Interface" on page 538. Because of the similarity between system-config-printer and the CUPS Web interface, many of the explanations in that section apply here.

To add a printer to the local system, click **New Printer** on the toolbar in the Printer Configuration window. The system-config-printer utility displays **Searching** as it looks for printers attached to the system or the local network and then displays the New Printer window (Figure 14-4). Click the button labeled **Verify** (if present) to make sure the printer is accessible.

To configure a printer, highlight the printer in the frame labeled **Select Connection**. The system-config-printer utility displays a description of a local printer and fills in the text boxes labeled **Host** and **Port number** or **Queue** for a remote printer.

Specifying a URI   If the printer is not listed, select **Other** from the Select Connection list; system-config-printer displays a text box labeled **Enter Device URI** on the right side of the window. The *URI* (page 1139) is the location on the network of the printer; see page 545 for more information. To specify an LPD/LPR printer, use the form **lpd://***hostname*/*printer-name;* for an IPP printer, use the form **ipp://***hostname*/**printers/***printer-name;* for an HP JetDirect-compatible network printer, use **socket://***hostname*. Replace *hostname* with the name of the host the printer is attached to (the server) or, for a network printer, the name of the printer. You can specify an IP address instead of *hostname*. Replace *printer-name* with the name of the printer on the server. Give the command **lpstat –p** on the server to display the names of all printers on that system. Click **Forward**. The system-config-printer utility displays **Searching** as it looks for a driver for the printer. See also page 545.

Figure 14-5   Selecting a printer manufacturer

In the second screen of the New Printer window (Figure 14-5), you can specify a printer manufacturer (such as HP). Typically system-config-printer selects the manufacturer automatically. Alternatively, you can specify a PPD file (page 545) or, under Intrepid, search for a driver to download. Click **Forward**.

The next screen (Figure 14-6) allows you to specify the model of the printer and select which driver you want to use (if there is more than one). Again, these selections are usually highlighted automatically.

If the model of the printer you are configuring is not listed, check whether the printer can emulate another printer (if it has an *emulation mode*). If it can, check whether the manufacturer and model of the printer it can emulate are listed and set it up that way. If all else fails, click **Back** and select **Generic** (at the top of the list) as the manufacturer. Then click **Forward** and choose a type of generic printer from the list box labeled **Models**. Choose the blank printer at the top of the list (Hardy) or **PostScript Printer** from the list (Intrepid) if the printer is PostScript capable. Then select a PostScript driver from the list box labeled **Drivers**. If the printer is not Post-Script capable, select **text-only**; you will not be able to print graphics, but you should be able to print text. If you are using a winprinter, select **GDI Printer** from the list of generic printers. Click **Forward**.

The system-config-printer utility displays a screen showing installed (printer-specific) options. Generally you do not need to make changes to this screen. Click **Forward**.

On the next screen (Figure 14-7), you must specify a name for the printer; specifying the description and location is optional. The name of the printer must start with a letter and cannot contain SPACEs. If you use only one printer, the name you choose is not important. If you use two or more printers, the name should help users distinguish between them. The printer name is the name of the print queue on the local system. Click **Apply**.

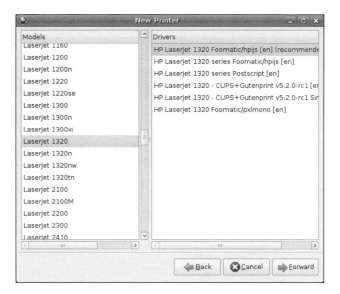

Figure 14-6   Selecting a printer model and driver

The system-config-printer utility closes the New Printer window and the new printer appears in the Printer Configuration window. If you have more than one print queue and want to set up the new print queue to be the default, highlight the printer and click **Make Default Printer** (Hardy) or select **Printer⇨Set as Default** from the window menu (Intrepid).

Figure 14-7   Specifying the name of the printer

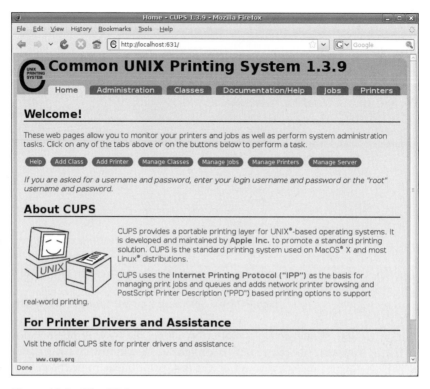

Figure 14-8   The Welcome page

JUMPSTART II: SETTING UP A LOCAL OR REMOTE PRINTER USING THE CUPS WEB INTERFACE

This JumpStart explains how to use the CUPS Web interface to set up a printer connected to the local system or connected to the local network.

If the printer you are configuring is on an older Linux system or another UNIX-like operating system that does not run CUPS, the system is probably running LPD/LPR. Newer versions of Linux and UNIX variants that support CUPS (including Mac OS X) support IPP. Most devices that connect printers directly to a network support LPR/LPD; some support IPP.

Printers connected directly to a network are functionally equivalent to printers connected to a system running a print server: They listen on the same ports as systems running print servers and queue jobs.

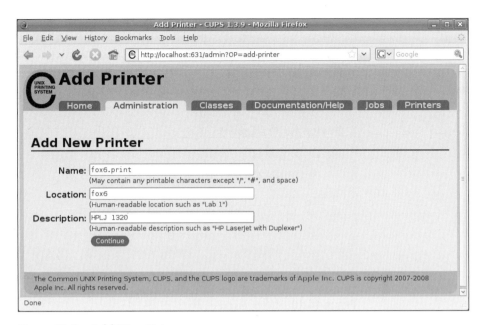

Figure 14-9   Add New Printer page

lpadmin group   At some point the CUPS Web interface will ask you for a username and password. Supply your username and password. (You must be a member of the **lpadmin** group [page 580] to change the printer configuration using the CUPS Web interface.)

Remote administration

security   When you provide your username and password to the CUPS Web interface, they are transmitted in cleartext over HTTP. The lack of encryption is a security issue when you are administrating printers over insecure networks.

Display the CUPS Web interface by pointing a Web browser at **localhost:631** on the system on which you are configuring the printer (Figure 14-8).

Clicking **Add Printer** on the row of buttons near the top of the page displays the Add New Printer page (Figure 14-9). Enter the name of the printer in the text box labeled **Name**; this name must start with a letter and not contain any SPACEs. You must supply a name—supply any name you like. Optionally, you can fill in the text boxes labeled **Location** and **Description** with text that will help users identify the printer. Click **Continue**.

Specifying a device   The next screen asks you to select the printer you want to set up (Figure 14-10, next page). Click the down arrow at the right of the list box labeled **Device** to display a list of printers. Select the printer you want to use. Click **Continue**.

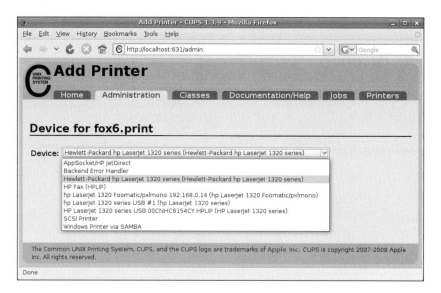

Figure 14-10   Device screen

If your selection did not specify a printer manufacturer, the CUPS Web interface displays the Make/Manufacturer page (Figure 14-11). Select and highlight the brand of printer from the list. Click **Continue**.

Figure 14-11   Make/Manufacturer page

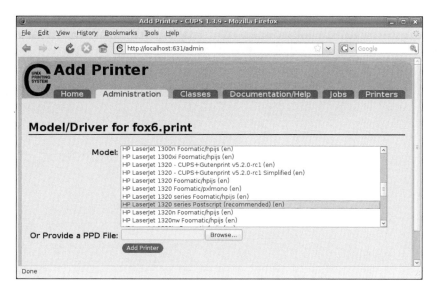

Figure 14-12   Model/Driver page

Next the Model/Driver page (Figure 14-12) allows you to choose the model and specify a driver for the printer. If the printer is PostScript capable but is not listed, select a PostScript printer such as the Apple LaserWriter 12/640ps. If the printer is not PostScript capable and is not listed, check whether the printer supports PCL; if it does, select another, similar PCL printer. If all else fails, determine which listed printer is most similar to the one you are configuring and specify that printer. You can also try configuring the printer using system-config-printer (page 532), which offers a different choice of models.

After you click **Add Printer**, the CUPS Web interface may request your password. It briefly displays a message saying that the printer has been successfully added and then displays the Set Printer Options page. This page allows you to set printer options and configuration information. Browse through the page and make any changes you like, although frequently you need change nothing. Click one of the **Set Printer Options** buttons.

After displaying another brief message, the CUPS Web interface displays the Printers page (Figure 14-13, next page) showing the new printer. Click **Print Test Page** to confirm that the new setup works. If you want to make this printer the default printer, click **Set As Default**.

The buttons at the bottom of the Printers page enable you to cancel or move jobs in the print queue. Figure 14-13 shows this page displaying information about a job the printer is printing. In addition to these tasks, the Jobs page (page 544) may enable you to reprint jobs.

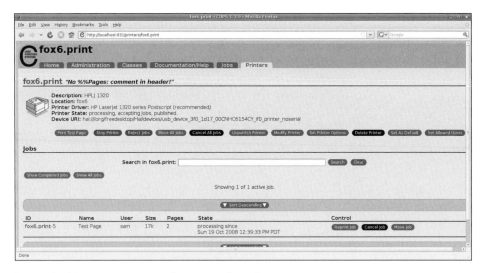

Figure 14-13   Printers page showing jobs information

TRADITIONAL UNIX PRINTING

Before the advent of GUIs and *WYSIWYG* (page 1141) word processors, UNIX users would create documents using an editor such as vi and a typesetting markup language such as TeX or nroff/troff, convert the resulting files to PostScript using an interpreter, and send the PostScript files to the printer using lpr (BSD) or lp (System V). Ubuntu Linux implements both BSD and System V command-line printing utilities for compatibility. However, these utilities are now wrappers around the equivalent functionality in CUPS rather than core components of the printing system. The corresponding utilities are functionally equivalent; use whichever you prefer (Table 14-2).

The **cupsys-bsd** (*HARDY*) and **cups-bsd** (*INTREPID*) packages hold the BSD utilities; the **cupsys-client** (*HARDY*) and **cups-client** (*INTREPID*) packages hold the System V utilities. From the command line, you can print a text, PostScript, or PDF file using lp:

```
$ lp memo.txt
request id is MainPrinter-25 (1 file(s))
```

The preceding command adds **memo.txt** to the print queue of the default printer as job 25. When this printer is available, it prints the file. You can specify a printer using the **–d** option:

```
$ lp -d ColorPtr graph.ps
request id is ColorPtr-26 (1 file(s))
```

The lpr **–P** option is equivalent to the lp **–d** option.

Without an argument, lp and lpr send their standard input to the printer:

Table 14-2   BSD and System V command-line print utilities

BSD/SysV	Purpose
lpr/lp	Sends job(s) to the printer.
lpq/lpstat	Displays the status of the print queue.
lprm/cancel	Removes job(s) from the print queue.

```
$ cat memo2.txt | lp
request id is MainPrinter-27 (1 file(s))
```

The lpq and lpstat commands display information about the print queue:

```
$ lpstat
MainPrinter-25          zach            13312   Sun Feb 22 18:28:38 2009
ColorPtr-26             zach            75776   Sun Feb 22 18:28:48 2009
MainPrinter-27          zach             8192   Sun Feb 22 18:28:57 2009
```

Use cancel or lprm to remove jobs from the print queue. By default, only the owner of a print job or a user working with **root** privileges can remove a job.

```
$ cancel 27
$ lpstat
MainPrinter-25          zach            13312   Sun Feb 22 18:28:38 2009
ColorPtr-26             zach            75776   Sun Feb 22 18:28:48 2009
```

Give the command **sudo cancel –a** or **sudo lprm –** to remove all jobs from the print queues.

CONFIGURING PRINTERS

You can use the Web interface or the command-line interface to CUPS to manage printers and queues.

THE CUPS WEB INTERFACE

To connect to the CUPS Web interface (page 538), point a Web browser running on the local system at **localhost:631**. You must be a member of the **lpadmin** group (page 580) to change the printer configuration using the CUPS Web interface.

MODIFYING A PRINTER

"JumpStart II: Setting Up a Local or Remote Printer Using the CUPS Web Interface" (page 538) discusses how to set up a printer using the CUPS Web interface. This section explains how to modify a printer that is already set up.

To modify a printer, click the **Printers** tab near the top of the page and then click the **Modify Printer** button adjacent to the printer you want to modify. The CUPS Web interface takes you through the same steps as when you are setting up a new printer.

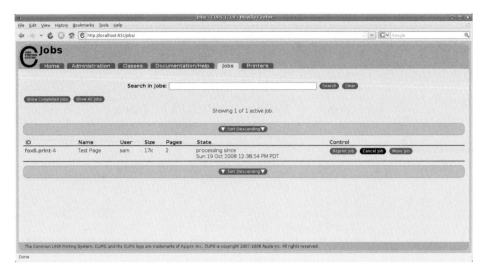

Figure 14-14   The Jobs page

Click the **Stop Printer** button to pause the printer. Click the **Reject Jobs** button to prevent jobs from being added to the print queue.

JOBS

Click the **Jobs** tab near the top of the page to display the Jobs page (Figure 14-14), which lists jobs in the print queues. From this page you can cancel print jobs and move them to other queues. Click **Show Completed Jobs** to display a list of recently completed jobs. In some cases, you can reprint completed jobs from this page.

CLASSES

CUPS allows you to put similar printers into a group called a *class*. To clients, a class of printers appears as a single printer. For each class, you must specify a name; optionally, you can specify a location and description. A printer can belong to more than one class. CUPS prints jobs sent to a class on the first available printer in the class. For example, you may be able to divide your print jobs into black-and-white jobs and color jobs. If more than one printer can fulfill each of these roles, you can allow users to select a printer manually, or you can define two printer classes (black-and-white and color) and have users send their jobs to a certain class of printers.

Plan for the future

tip   If you expect to add printers to the network, you may want to configure classes containing the existing printers when you set up the network. You can then add printers later without having to change printer configurations on client systems.

To define a class, first click the **Administration** tab near the top of the page and then click **Add Class**. At a minimum, you must enter a name for the class. You may also enter a location and description. The Members list displays the names of all CUPS printers and classes. Highlight the printers you want to be members of the class you are defining; hold SHIFT and click another printer to highlight more than one printer. To define a class that includes printers that are not adjacent in the list, define the class to have a single printer and then modify the class after you create it to add other printers. To modify existing classes, click **Manage Classes** in the Administration tab.

CUPS ON THE COMMAND LINE

In addition to using the Web interface, you can control CUPS and manage print queues from the command line. This section describes the utilities that enable you to manage printers and print queues and establish printing quotas.

lpinfo: DISPLAYS AVAILABLE DRIVERS

PPD files   The lpinfo utility provides information about the printer drivers and interfaces available to CUPS. The **–m** option displays the list of available PostScript Printer Definition (PPD) files/drivers.

```
$ lpinfo -m | headfoomatic:Alps-MD-1000-md2k.ppd Alps MD-1000 Foomatic/md2k
foomatic:Alps-MD-1300-md1xMono.ppd Alps MD-1300 Foomatic/md1xMono
foomatic:Alps-MD-1300-md2k.ppd Alps MD-1300 Foomatic/md2k
foomatic:Alps-MD-1500-md1xMono.ppd Alps MD-1500 Foomatic/md1xMono
foomatic:Alps-MD-1500-md2k.ppd Alps MD-1500 Foomatic/md2k
foomatic:Alps-MD-2000-md2k.ppd Alps MD-2000 Foomatic/md2k
foomatic:Alps-MD-4000-md2k.ppd Alps MD-4000 Foomatic/md2k
foomatic:Alps-MD-5000-md5k.ppd Alps MD-5000 Foomatic/md5k
foomatic:Alps-MD-5000-md50Eco.ppd Alps MD-5000 Foomatic/md50Eco
foomatic:Alps-MD-5000-md50Mono.ppd Alps MD-5000 Foomatic/md50Mono
```

URIs   CUPS uses URIs (page 535) to identify printer ports by type and location, just as a Web browser identifies documents by protocol and location. A parallel port has a URI with the format **parallel:/dev/lp0;** a remote LPD printer uses the format **lpd://192.168.0.101**. With the **–v** option, lpinfo provides a list of available connections:

```
$ lpinfo -v
network socket
network beh
direct hal
direct hpfax
network lpd://10.10.4.36/
network socket://10.10.4.36
direct hp
direct parallel:/dev/lp0
direct scsi
network socket://10.10.4.35
network socket://10.10.4.35
network smb
```

The **-v** option to lpinfo does not display every possible network address for the socket, HTTP, IPP, LPD, and SMB protocols because there are more than 4 billion of these addresses in the IPv4 address space.

lpadmin: Configures Printers

The lpadmin utility can add and remove printers from the system, modify printer configurations, and manage printer classes. It has three major options: **-d** (set the default printer), **-x** (remove a printer), and **-p** (add or modify a printer). The first two options are simple; examples follow the next section. Each of these three options takes an argument that is the name of a printer. The name of the printer must start with a letter and cannot contain SPACEs.

Adding or Modifying a Printer

Add a printer or modify an existing printer by giving a command in the following format:

$ *lpadmin –p printer-name options*

where ***printer-name*** is the name of the printer and ***options*** is a combination of options from the following list:

-c *class*   Adds the printer to the class ***class***, creating the class if necessary.

-D *info*   The ***info*** is a string that describes the printer for users. This string has no meaning to the system. Enclose ***info*** within quotation marks if it contains SPACEs.

-E   Enables the printer instructing CUPS to accept jobs into its print queue.

-L *loc*   The ***loc*** is a string that indicates the physical location of the printer (office, building, floor, and so on). This string has no meaning to the system. Enclose ***loc*** within quotation marks if it contains SPACEs.

-P *file*   The ***file*** is the absolute pathname of the PPD file (page 545) that describes the printer. Use **lpinfo –m** to display a list of installed PPD files. If you have a manufacturer-provided PPD file, copy it to **/usr/share/ppd/custom**.

-r *class*   Removes the printer from the class ***class***. This option removes the class if, after removing the printer, the class would be empty.

-v *URI*   The ***URI*** is the device to which the printer is attached. Use **lpinfo –v** to list possible devices.

Example lpadmin Commands

At a minimum, you need to provide a device and a model when you add a printer to the system. The following command adds an Epson Stylus Color printer to the system and enables it for use. This printer is connected locally to the first parallel port and is named **ColorPtr**.

```
$ lpadmin -p ColorPtr -E -v parallel:/dev/lp0 -P /usr/share/ppd/custom/stcolor.ppd.gz
```

The printer information generated by the preceding command is stored in the **/etc/cups/printers.conf** file:

```
$ sudo cat /etc/cups/printers.conf
# Printer configuration file for CUPS v1.3.9
# Written by cupsd on 2008-10-18 10:46
<Printer ColorPtr>
Info ColorPtr
DeviceURI parallel:/dev/lp0
State Idle
StateTime 1180495957
Accepting Yes
Shared Yes
JobSheets none none
QuotaPeriod 0
PageLimit 0
KLimit 0
OpPolicy default
ErrorPolicy retry-job
</Printer>
```

The lpadmin command decompresses and copies the printer driver information from the **/usr/share/ppd/custom/stcolor.ppd.gz** file to **/etc/cups/ppd**. The resulting file is given the printer's name: **/etc/cups/ppd/ColorPtr.ppd**.

You can modify a printer configuration with lpadmin using the same options that you used to add it. When you specify the name of an existing printer, lpadmin modifies the printer rather than creating a new one.

The next command configures an HP LaserJet-compatible printer with a JetDirect interface that is connected directly to the LAN at 192.168.1.103 and names this printer HPLJ. Specifying **socket** in the protocol part of the URI instructs CUPS to use the JetDirect protocol, a proprietary protocol developed by HP for printers connected directly to a network.

```
$ lpadmin -p HPLJ -E -v socket://192.168.1.103 -P /usr/share/ppd/custom/laserjet.ppd.gz
```

The lpstat utility with the **–d** option displays the name of the default printer:

```
$ lpstat -d
system default destination: MainPrinter
```

CUPS automatically makes the first printer you define the default printer. The following command makes HPLJ the default printer:

```
$ lpadmin -d HPLJ
```

The following command removes the configuration for the ColorPtr printer:

```
$ lpadmin -x ColorPtr
```

PRINTING QUOTAS

CUPS provides rudimentary printing quotas. You can define two forms of quotas: page count and file size. File size quotas are almost meaningless because a small PostScript file can take a long time to interpret and can require a lot more ink to print than a large one. Page quotas are more useful, although their implementation is flawed. To determine the number of pages in a document, CUPS examines the PostScript input. If a job is submitted in the printer's native language, such as PCL, CUPS bypasses this accounting mechanism. Also, if mpage is used to create a Post-Script file with multiple pages printed on each sheet, CUPS counts each page in the original document, rather than each sheet of paper it prints on.

Use **job-quota-period** and either **job-page-limit** or **job-k-limit** to establish a quota for each user on a given printer. The **job-quota-period** option specifies the number of seconds that the quota remains valid. The following command establishes a quota of 20 pages per day per user for the printer named HPLJ:

```
$ lpadmin -p HPLJ -o job-quota-period=86400 -o job-page-limit=20
```

The **job-k-limit** option works similarly but defines a file size limit in kilobytes. The limit is the total number of kilobytes that each user can print during the quota period. Once a user has exceeded her quota, she will not be allowed to print until the next quota period.

MANAGING PRINT QUEUES

When a printer is operating normally, it accepts jobs into its print queue and prints those jobs in the order they are received. You can give the command **reject** followed by the name of a printer to cause a printer to not accept jobs into its print queue; give the command **accept** to reenable it. You can also use system-config-printer to control the print queue; refer to "Settings" on page 534.

SHARING CUPS PRINTERS

IPP facilitates remote printing. The Listen directive in the CUPS configuration file, **/etc/cups/cupsd.conf**, specifies which IP address and port or which domain socket path CUPS binds to and accepts requests on. The Listen directive has the following format:

> Listen **IP:port** | *path*

where **IP** is the IP address that CUPS accepts connections on, *port* is the port number that CUPS listens on for connections on **IP**, and *path* is the pathname of the domain socket CUPS uses to communicate with printers. CUPS typically uses port 631. By default, it binds to **localhost** so it accepts connections from the loopback service of the local system only. CUPS uses **/var/run/cups/cups.sock**, a local domain socket, to communicate with local printers. It can also use a Port directive to specify the port number it listens to for HTTP requests.

```
$ cat /etc/cups/cupsd.conf
...
# Only listen for connections from the local machine.
Listen localhost:631
Listen /var/run/cups/cups.sock
...
```

To allow other systems to connect to the CUPS server on the local system, you must instruct CUPS to bind to an IP address that the other systems can reach. The following directive would be appropriate on a CUPS server running on 192.168.0.12:

```
Listen 192.168.0.12:631
```

This directive, when placed after the other Listen directives, would cause CUPS to listen on IP address 192.168.0.12, port 631. When you change **cupsd.conf**, you need to call the **cupsys** init script to restart the **cupsd** daemon (page 531).

Some directives in **cupsd.conf** use the @LOCAL macro, which is internal to CUPS and specifies the local system. This macro accepts communication from any address that resolves to the local system.

Once you restart **cupsd**, remote systems can print on the local system's printers using the IP address and port number specified by the Listen directive. If the server is running a firewall, you need to allow remote systems to connect through it; see page 531.

Alternatively, you can use CUPS's access control list to permit only selected machines to connect to local printers. An access control list is defined inside a <Location> container (see page 874 for the Apache equivalent). The following example allows only the system at IP 192.168.1.101 and the local system to print to the specified printer:

```
<Location /printers>
Order Allow,Deny
Allow from localhost
Allow from 192.168.1.101
</Location>
```

The **/printers** indicates that this container refers to all local printers. Alternatively, you can control access on a per-printer basis by specifying **/printers/***printer-name*, where *printer-name* is the printer name, or by specifying **/printers/***path*.**ppd**, where *path*.**ppd** is the full pathname of the PPD file (page 545) used by the printer.

The Order Deny,Allow directive allows access by default and denies access only to clients specified in Deny from directives. Specifying **Order Allow,Deny** denies print requests by default and allows requests from specified addresses. You can use domain names, including wildcards, and IP ranges with either wildcards or netmasks in Allow from and Deny from directives. These directives work the same way they do in Apache. For more information refer to "Order" on page 887.

With the Order Deny,Allow directive, **Deny from** specifies the only IP addresses CUPS does not accept connections from. When you use the Order Allow,Deny directive, **Allow from** specifies the only IP addresses CUPS accepts connections from.

Printing from Windows

This section explains how to use printers on Linux CUPS servers from Windows machines. CUPS is easier to manage and can be made more secure than using Samba to print from Windows.

Printing Using CUPS

Modern versions of Windows (2000 and later) support IPP and, as a result, can communicate directly with CUPS. To use this feature, you must have CUPS configured on the Linux print server to allow remote IPP printing; you also need to create a new printer on the Windows system that points to the IP address of the Linux print server.

First set up the **/etc/cups/cupsd.conf** file to allow network printing from a client, as explained under "Sharing CUPS Printers" on page 548. Setting up CUPS to allow printing from a Windows machine is exactly the same as setting it up to allow printing from a Linux client system. If necessary, open the firewall as explained on page 531.

From Windows XP, go to **Control Panel⇨Printers and Faxes** and click **Add Printer.** Click **Next** from the introductory window and select **A network printer or a printer attached to another computer.** Click **Next.** Select **Connect to a printer on the Internet or on a home or office network** and enter the following information in the text box labeled **URL:**

> *http://hostname:631/printers/printer-name*

where *hostname* is the name or IP address of the Linux CUPS server system and *printer-name* is the name of the printer on that system. For example, for the printer named **dog88** on the system named **dog** at IP address 192.168.0.12, you could enter **http://dog:631/printers/dog88** or **http://192.168.0.12:631/printers/dog88**. If you use a hostname, it must be defined in the **hosts** file on the Windows machine. Windows requests that you specify the manufacturer and model of printer or provide a driver for the printer. If you supply a printer driver, use the Windows version of the driver. After Windows copies some files, the printer appears in the Printers and Faxes window. Right-click the printer and select **Set as Default Printer** to make it the default printer. You can specify comments, a location, and other attributes of the printer by right-clicking the printer and selecting **Properties.**

Printing Using Samba

This section assumes that Samba (page 761) is installed and working on the Linux system that controls the printer you want to use from Windows. Samba must be set up so that the Windows user who will be printing is mapped to a Linux user (including mapping the Windows **guest** user to the Linux user **nobody**). Make sure these users have Samba passwords. Refer to "Samba Users, User Maps, and Passwords" on page 763.

Windows supports printer sharing via SMB, allowing a printer to be shared transparently between Windows systems using the same mechanism as file sharing. Samba allows Windows users to use printers connected to Linux systems just as they would use any other shared printers. Because all Linux printers traditionally appear to be PostScript printers, the Linux print server appears to share a PostScript printer. Windows does not include a generic PostScript printer driver. Instead, Windows users must select a printer driver for a PostScript printer. The Apple LaserWriter 12/640ps driver is a good choice.

When you install Samba, the **dpkg postinst** script creates a directory named **/var/spool/samba** that is owned by the **root** account and that anyone can read from and write to. The sticky bit (page 1134) is set for this directory, allowing a Windows user who starts a print job as a Linux user to be able to delete that job, but denying users the ability to delete the print jobs of other users. Make sure this directory is in place and has the proper ownership and permissions:

```
$ ls -ld /var/spool/samba
drwxrwxrwt 2 root root 4096 2008-10-10 12:29 /var/spool/samba
```

Put the following two lines in the [**global**] section of the **/etc/samba/smb.conf** file:

```
[global]
...
printing = cups
printcap name = cups
```

The printer's share is listed in the [**printers**] section in **smb.conf**. In the following example, the **path** is the path Samba uses as a spool directory and is not a normal share path. The settings allow anyone, including **guest**, to use the printer. Setting **use client driver** to **yes** causes Windows systems to use their own drivers. Not setting this option, or setting it to **no**, can cause printing from Windows to fail. The [**printers**] section in the default **smb.conf** file has the following entries, which are appropriate for most setups:

```
[printers]
   comment = All Printers
   browseable = no
   path = /var/spool/samba
   printable = yes
   public = no
   writable = no
   create mode = 0700
```

Ideally each user who plans to print should have an account. Otherwise, when multiple users share the same account (for example, the **nobody** account), they can delete one another's print jobs.

PRINTING TO WINDOWS

CUPS views a printer on a Windows machine exactly the same way it views any other printer. The only difference is the URI you need to specify when connecting it. To configure a printer connected to a Windows machine, go to the Printers page in the CUPS Web interface and select **Add Printer**, as you would for a local printer.

When you are asked to select the device, choose **Windows Printer via SAMBA**. Enter the URI of the printer in the following format:

    smb://windows_system/printer_name

where *windows_system* can be an IP address or a hostname. Once you have added the printer, you can use it as you would any other printer.

CHAPTER SUMMARY

A printing system such as CUPS sets up printers. It also moves print jobs from an application or the command line through the appropriate filters and into a queue for a suitable printer and then prints those jobs.

CUPS is a cross-platform print server built around IPP, the Internet Printing Protocol. CUPS handles setting up and sending jobs through print queues. The easiest way to configure printers is via the Printer Configuration window (system-config-printer). You can also configure CUPS using the Web interface, which you can access by pointing a Web browser at **localhost:631** on the system the printer is connected to. From the Web interface, you can configure print queues and modify print jobs in the queues.

You can use the traditional UNIX commands from a command line to send jobs to a printer (lpr/lp), display a print queue (lpq/lpstat), and remove jobs from a print queue (lprm/cancel). In addition, CUPS provides the lpinfo and lpadmin utilities, which allow you to configure printers from the command line.

CUPS and Samba enable you to print on a Linux printer from a Windows machine, and vice versa.

EXERCISES

1. Which commands can you use from the command line to send a file to the default printer?

2. Which command would you give to cancel all print jobs on the system?

3. Which commands list your outstanding print jobs?

4. What is the purpose of sharing a Linux printer using Samba?

5. Name three printing protocols that CUPS supports. Which is the CUPS native protocol?

ADVANCED EXERCISES

6. Which command lists the installed printer drivers available to CUPS?

7. How would you send a text file to a printer connected to the first parallel port without using a print queue? Why is doing so not a good idea?

8. Assume you have a USB printer with a manufacturer-supplied PostScript printer definition file named **newprinter.ppd**. Which command would you use to add this printer to the system on the first USB port with the name USBPrinter?

9. How would you define a quota that allows each user to print up to 50 pages per week to the printer named LaserJet?

10. Define a set of access control rules for a <Location> container inside **/etc/cups/cupsd.conf** that would allow anyone to print to all printers as long as they were either on the local system or in the **mydomain.com** domain.

15

BUILDING A LINUX KERNEL

Once you have installed Ubuntu Linux, you may want to reconfigure and build a new Linux kernel. Ubuntu Linux comes with a prebuilt kernel that simplifies the installation process. However, this kernel may not be properly configured for all system features. By configuring and building a new kernel, you can create one that is customized for a system and its unique needs. A customized kernel is typically smaller than a generic one.

Sometimes you do not need to build a new kernel. Instead, you can dynamically change many things that used to require building a new kernel. Two ways to make these changes are by using boot command-line parameters (page 69) or by modifying **/etc/sysctl.conf**, which sysctl uses when the system boots (page 556).

You can add the same parameters as you use on the boot command line to a **kernel** command in **/boot/grub/menu.lst**. For example, **acpi=off** prevents **acpid** (the advanced configuration and power interface daemon) from starting.

sysctl   The sysctl utility modifies kernel parameters while the system is running. This utility takes advantage of the facilities of **/proc/sys**, which defines the parameters that sysctl can modify.

The command **sysctl –a** displays a complete list of sysctl parameters. An example of displaying and changing the **domainname** kernel parameter follows. The quotation marks are not required in this example, but you must quote any characters that would otherwise be interpreted by the shell.

```
$ sudo /sbin/sysctl kernel.domainname
kernel.domainname = tcorp.com
$ sudo /sbin/sysctl -w kernel.domainname="testing.com"
kernel.domainname = testing.com
$ sudo /sbin/sysctl kernel.domainname
kernel.domainname = testing.com
```

Have the installation CD/DVD handy when you build a new kernel

caution   When you build a new Linux kernel to install a new version or to change the configuration of the existing version, make sure you have the installation CD/DVD handy. This disk allows you to reboot the system, even when you have destroyed the system software completely. Having this CD/DVD available can mean the difference between momentary panic and a full-scale nervous breakdown.

Before you can start building a new kernel, you must download, install, and clean the source code. You also need to build a configuration file that describes the new kernel you want to build. This chapter describes the steps involved in completing these tasks.

PREREQUISITES

Install the following packages:

- **linux-source** (the latest released Ubuntu kernel source code; not needed if you use git to download the code) Attempting to install **linux-source** displays the name of the package holding the latest kernel, which you then install; refer to the next section.

- **build-essential** (metapackage; includes the packages required to compile the code)

- **fakeroot, kernel-package** (kernel-specific)

- **git-core** (to use git to download the kernel source code)

- **ncurses-dev** (to configure the kernel using **make menuconfig**)

- **libglade2-dev** (to configure the kernel using **make gconfig**)

- **module-assistant, debhelper** (to create modules)

Compiling a kernel takes a lot of disk space

tip   Make sure you have enough disk space before you compile a kernel. Once you compile a default kernel it occupies about 3.5 gigabytes. This disk space must be available on the filesystem in which you compile the kernel.

DOWNLOADING THE KERNEL SOURCE CODE

This section describes two ways to download kernel source code on the local system: aptitude (or Synaptic, page 118) and git. If you want to download code that has not been customized (patched) by Ubuntu, visit kernel.org or see the section on git.

aptitude: DOWNLOADING AND INSTALLING THE KERNEL SOURCE CODE

The easiest way to download and install the updated kernel source code for the most recently released version of the Ubuntu kernel is to use aptitude. The following commands make sure that the package index is up-to-date and download the **linux-source** package. The **dpkg postinst** script puts the compressed source code in **/usr/src/linux-source∗**:

```
$ sudo aptitude update
...
$ sudo aptitude install linux-source
...
"linux-source" is a virtual package provided by:
  linux-source-2.6.27 linux-ports-source-2.6.25
You must choose one to install.
No packages will be installed, upgraded, or removed.
...
$ sudo aptitude install linux-source-2.6.27
...
$ ls -l /usr/src/linux-source*
-rw-r--r-- 1 root root 52842977 2008-08-23 17:46 /usr/src/linux-source-2.6.27.tar.bz2
```

Because **/usr/src** is associated with the **src** group, if you are a member of this group (page 474), you can extract and build kernels in the **/usr/src** directory. Otherwise, you can unpack the kernel in any directory you have write access to.

Do not work with root privileges

caution   You do not need to—nor should you—work as a user with **root** privileges for any portion of configuring or building the kernel except for installation (the last step). The kernel **README** file says, "Don't take the name of root in vain." As long as you are a member of the group **src**, you can download, configure, and compile the kernel in a directory under **/usr/src** without working with **root** privileges.

You can add a user to the **src** group using usermod. The following command adds Max to the **src** group so he can work in **/usr/src**. Max must log out and log in again to have the system recognize him as a member of the **src** group.

```
$ sudo usermod --append --groups src max
```

If you are not working in **/usr/src**, you must copy the **linux-source*** file to the directory you are working in; otherwise cd to **/usr/src**. Use tar to unpack the Linux source file:

```
$ tar -xjf linux-source-2.6.27.tar.bz2
```

git: OBTAINING THE LATEST KERNEL SOURCE CODE

The git utility (GNU interactive tools, git.or.cz) can download the latest versions of the source code for several different kernels and can keep that source code up-to-date. If it is not already installed, give the following command to install git:

```
$ sudo aptitude install git-core
```

Install the **git-core** package, not the **git** package

tip   Make sure to install the **git-core** package and not the **git** package. The **git** package is not useful for downloading kernel source code.

The following command uses git to download a copy of the development (not the released) kernel into the **ubuntu-2.6** subdirectory of the working directory. As a member of the **src** group, you can work in the **/usr/src** directory. Otherwise, you can work in any directory you have write access to. You can and should work as a nonprivileged user.

```
$ git-clone git://kernel.ubuntu.com/ubuntu/ubuntu-gutsy.git ubuntu-2.6
Initialized empty Git repository in /usr/src/ubuntu-2.6/.git/
remote: Counting objects: 512072, done.
remote: Compressing objects: 100% (122612/122612), done.
remote: Total 512072 (delta 407029), reused 493394 (delta 388537)
Receiving objects: 100% (512072/512072), 195.17 MiB | 389 KiB/s, done.
Resolving deltas: 100% (407029/407029), done.
Checking out files: 100% (22719/22719), done.
```

See kernel.ubuntu.com/git and git.kernel.org for a list of Ubuntu kernels you can download. Substitute the URL of the kernel you want to download for the URL in the preceding command and specify the name of an appropriate directory to hold the files you download. For example, the following command downloads the latest Intrepid kernel into the **intrepid** directory in the working directory:

```
$ git-clone git://kernel.ubuntu.com/ubuntu/ubuntu-intrepid.git intrepid
```

Once you have downloaded the kernel, cd to the directory that holds the code and give the following command to update the source code to match that available at the URL you specified in the git-clone command:

```
$ git pull
Already up-to-date.
```

The files you just downloaded should be up-to-date, as shown in the example. Give this command anytime you want to synchronize the code in the working directory with the latest source code at the URL.

Read the Documentation

The kernel package includes the latest documentation, some of which may not be available in other documents. You may wish to review the **README** file in the top level of the kernel source directory and the relevant files in the **Documentation** subdirectory. In addition, there is a lot of information in the **/usr/share/doc/kernel-package** directory. Read the *Linux Kernel-HOWTO* for a detailed, somewhat dated, generic guide to installing and configuring the Linux kernel.

Configuring and Compiling the Linux Kernel

This section describes how to configure the kernel, how to compile it, and how to download and compile kernel modules.

.config: Configures the Kernel

Before you can compile the code and create a Linux kernel, you must decide and specify which features you want the kernel to support. You can configure the kernel to support most features in one of two ways: by building the feature into the kernel or by specifying the feature as a loadable kernel module (page 564), which is loaded into the kernel only as needed. In deciding which method to use, you must weigh the size of the kernel against the time it takes to load a module. Make the kernel as small as possible while minimizing how often modules have to be loaded. Do not make the SCSI driver modular unless you have a reason to do so.

The **.config** file in the directory you downloaded the source code in controls which features the new kernel will support and how it will support them. "Customizing a Kernel" (page 561) explains how to create a default version of this file if it does not exist and how to edit the file if it does exist.

Replacing a Custom Kernel

If you have already configured a custom kernel, you may want to replace it with a similarly configured newer kernel. However, each kernel potentially has new configuration options, so it is poor practice to use an old **.config** file for compiling a new kernel. This section explains how to upgrade an existing .config file so it includes options that are new to the new kernel and maintains the existing configuration for the old options.

Work in the directory you downloaded or extracted the source code to. The system keeps a copy of the configuration file for the kernel the local system is running in **/boot**. The following command copies this file to .config in the working directory:

```
$ cp /boot/config-$(uname -r) .config
```

In this command, the shell executes **uname –r** and replaces **$(uname –r)** with the output of the command, which is the name of the release of the kernel running on the local system. For more information refer to "Command Substitution" on page 346.

Next give the command **make oldconfig** to patch the .config file with options from the new kernel that are not in the old kernel. This command displays each kernel option that is the same in the new and old kernels and automatically sets the state of the option in the new kernel the same way it was set in the old kernel. It stops when it gets to an option that is in the new kernel but not in the old kernel. It then displays a prompt, which is similar to [N/y/?] (**NEW**), showing possible responses and indicating this option is new. The prompt shows the default response as an uppercase letter; you can type this letter (uppercase or lowercase) and press RETURN, or just press RETURN to select this response. In the example, the Tickless System option is new and the default response is **Y** for *yes, include the option in the new kernel*. To select a nondefault response (**n** means *no, do not include the option* and **m** means *include the option as a module*), you must type the letter and press RETURN. Enter **?** followed by RETURN to display more information about the option.

```
$ make oldconfig
scripts/kconfig/conf -o arch/i386/Kconfig
*
* Linux Kernel Configuration
*
*
* Code maturity level options
*
Prompt for development and/or incomplete code/drivers (EXPERIMENTAL) [Y/n/?] y
*
* General setup
*
Local version - append to kernel release (LOCALVERSION) []
Automatically append version information to version string (LOCALVERSION_AUTO) [N/y/?] n
...
*
* Processor type and features
*
Tickless System (Dynamic Ticks) (NO_HZ) [Y/n/?] (NEW) ? ?
```

This option enables a tickless system: timer interrupts will
only trigger on an as-needed basis both when the system is
busy and when the system is idle.

```
Tickless System (Dynamic Ticks) (NO_HZ) [Y/n/?] (NEW) ? RETURN
High Resolution Timer Support (HIGH_RES_TIMERS) [Y/n/?] y
Symmetric multi-processing support (SMP) [Y/n/?] y
Subarchitecture Type
> 1. PC-compatible (X86_PC)
  2. AMD Elan (X86_ELAN)
...
#
# configuration written to .config
#
```

CUSTOMIZING A KERNEL

You can use one of three standard commands to build the **.config** file that configures a Linux kernel:

```
$ make config
$ make menuconfig
$ make gconfig
```

See "Prerequisites" on page 556 for a list of packages required to run all but the first of these commands.

If a **.config** file does not exist in the working directory, each of these commands except the first sets up a **.config** file that matches the kernel the local system is running and then allows you to modify that configuration. The commands can set up this **.config** file only if the configuration file for the locally running kernel is in **/boot/config-$(uname –r)**. See the preceding section if you want to build a new kernel with a configuration similar to that of an existing kernel.

The **make config** command is the simplest of the three commands, uses a textual interface, and does not require additional software. It is, however, the most unforgiving and hardest to use of the configuration interfaces. The **make menuconfig** command uses a pseudographical interface and also displays a textual interface. The **make gconfig** command uses GTK+ (www.gtk.org) and uses a graphical interface.

Each command asks the same questions and produces the same result, given the same responses. The first and second commands work in character-based environments; the third command works in graphical environments. For many administrators working with a GUI, the third method is the easiest to use.

The **make gconfig** command displays the Linux Kernel Configuration window, which you can view in three configurations: single, split, or full view. Choose a view by clicking one of the three icons to the right of the floppy diskette on the toolbar.

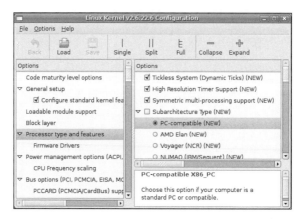

Figure 15-1   The Linux Kernel Configuration window, split view

Figure 15-1 shows the split view. In this view, the left frame shows the options and the top-right view lists the features for each option. The bottom-right view describes the highlighted option or feature. Figure 15-2 shows the full view.

In any view, you can click the boxes and circles next to the choices and subchoices. An empty box/circle indicates the feature is disabled, a tick indicates it is to be included in the kernel, and a dot means it is to be compiled as a module. With a choice or subchoice highlighted, you can also press **M** for module, **N** for not included, and **Y** for compiled into the kernel. Select **Menubar: Options⇨Show All Options** to display all options and features.

Go through the options and mark the features as you would like them to be configured in the new kernel. At any time during the configuration process, you can store the currently defined configuration to a file, load a configuration from a file, or exit with or without saving your changes. See the selections in **Menubar: File**. When you are done, select **Menubar: File⇨Save** and close the window.

CLEANING THE SOURCE TREE

After generating a **.config** file, but before compiling or recompiling the kernel, purge the source tree of all potentially stale **∗.o** files using the following command:

```
$ make-kpkg clean
exec make -f /usr/share/kernel-package/ruleset/minimal.mk clean
====== making target minimal_clean [new prereqs: ]======
Cleaning.
test ! -f .config || cp -pf .config config.precious
test ! -e stamp-building || rm -f stamp-building
test ! -f Makefile || \
        make    ARCH=i386 distclean
make[1]: Entering directory '/usr/src/linux-source-2.6.27'
  CLEAN   scripts/basic
  CLEAN   scripts/kconfig
  CLEAN   /usr/src/linux-source-2.6.27/debian/
  CLEAN   include/config
  CLEAN   .config .config.old include/linux/autoconf.h
```

```
make[1]: Leaving directory '/usr/src/linux-source-2.6.27'
test ! -f config.precious || mv -f config.precious .config
rm -f modules/modversions.h modules/ksyms.ver conf.vars scripts/cramfs/cramfsck
scripts/cramfs/mkcramfs applied_patches  stamp-build stamp-configure stamp-image stamp-
headers stamp-src stamp-diff stamp-doc stamp-manual stamp-patch stamp-buildpackage stamp-
debian
```

This command ensures that make correctly applies any numbering scheme you use when you compile the kernel. Continue to work as a nonprivileged user.

COMPILING A KERNEL IMAGE FILE AND LOADABLE MODULES

See "Prerequisites" on page 556 for a list of packages that must be installed to compile the source code. Give the following command to compile the kernel and modules. This command generates a **.deb** file in the parent of the working directory.

```
$ make-kpkg --initrd --rootcmd fakeroot --append-to-version $(date +%s) kernel_image
exec make -f /usr/share/kernel-package/ruleset/minimal.mk debian
APPEND_TO_VERSION=1219799154  INITRD=YES  ROOT_CMD=fakeroot
====== making target minimal_debian [new prereqs: ]======
This is kernel package version .
test -d debian || mkdir debian
test ! -e stamp-building || rm -f stamp-building
...
Found kernel: /boot/vmlinuz-2.6.27-rc41219799154
Found kernel: /boot/last-good-boot/vmlinuz
Found kernel: /boot/vmlinuz-2.6.26-5-generic
Found kernel: /boot/memtest86+.bin
Replacing config file /var/run/grub/menu.lst with new version
Updating /boot/grub/menu.lst ... done

Examining /etc/kernel/postinst.d.
run-parts: executing /etc/kernel/postinst.d/nvidia-common

$ ls ../*deb
linux-image-2.6.27-rc41219799154_2.6.27-rc41219799154-10.00.Custom_i386.deb
```

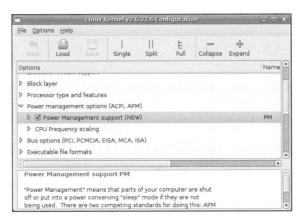

Figure 15-2   The Linux Kernel Configuration window, full view

The **--append-to-version** option allows you to specify a string that uniquely identifies the kernel you are building. This string also helps prevent overwriting existing kernels. You can specify any string you like following this option, using characters from the set of lowercase letters, numbers, – (minus), + (plus), and . (period). The value you specify is placed at the end of the kernel name and release number. You can make note of patches applied to the kernel in this string to help developers track bugs. The preceding example uses command substitution (page 346) to place the number of seconds since the UNIX epoch in the name of the kernel, making easy to tell which of several kernels is newest.

USING LOADABLE KERNEL MODULES

A *loadable kernel module* (page 1117) (sometimes called a *module* or *loadable module*) is an object file—part of the kernel—that is linked into the kernel at runtime. Modules can be inserted into and removed from a running kernel at almost any time (except when a module is being used). This ability gives the kernel the flexibility to be as small as possible at any given time. Modules are a good way to code some kernel features, including drivers that are not used continually (such as a tape driver). Module filenames end in **.ko** and are stored in subdirectories in **/lib/modules**. Under Ubuntu, kernel modules are compiled along with the kernel as explained in the preceding section.

FINDING NONSTANDARD MODULES

Many drivers that are not in the main source tree or not free are supplied as ✳-**source** packages. You can use aptitude to display a list of available ✳-**source** packages. The following example first updates APT's cache, then displays a list of ✳-**source** packages, and finally displays a list of packages that pertain to NVIDIA. The dollar sign at the end of the search string (**source$**) ensures that the string matches only the last part of a package name.

```
$ sudo aptitude update
$ aptitude search source$
p acerhk-source       - Source for the acerhk driver
p acl2-books-source   - A Computational Logic for Applicative Common Lisp: library sources
p acl2-infix-source   - A Computational Logic for Applicative Common Lisp: infix source
p acl2-source         - A Computational Logic for Applicative Common Lisp: source files
...
$ aptitude search source$ | grep -i nvidia
p nvidia-173-kernel-source  - NVIDIA binary kernel module source
p nvidia-177-kernel-source  - NVIDIA binary kernel module source
p nvidia-71-kernel-source   - NVIDIA binary kernel module source
p nvidia-96-kernel-source   - NVIDIA binary kernel module source
v nvidia-kernel-source      -
```

module-assistant: DOWNLOADING, COMPILING, AND INSTALLING NONSTANDARD MODULES

Once you determine its name, you need to download and install the module source package. Then you need to compile, build, and install the Debian module package that corresponds to the source package. Check the prerequisites listed on page 556 before starting this process. The following command uses module-assistant to perform these steps with the **nvidia-173-kernel-source** package:

```
$ module-assistant --text-mode auto-install nvidia-173-kernel-source
```

The module-assistant utility calls sudo to run apt-get and dpkg and will fail if you do not have write permission to **/usr/src** (i.e., if you are not in the **src** group); sudo may prompt you for your password. You must be a member of the **admin** group so module-assistant can call sudo successfully. Without the **−−text-mode** option, module-assistant presents a pseudographical interface that requires input.

If you run into problems, you may want to call module-assistant to perform each of the steps in turn. You must run the module-assistant **prepare** command once before running other module-assistant commands (except **auto-install**). The following commands use **m-a**, a link to **module-assistant**, and **−t** in place of **−−text-mode**:

```
$ m-a -t prepare
$ m-a -t get nvidia-kernel
$ m-a -t build nvidia-kernel
$ m-a -t install nvidia-kernel
```

The format of a module-assistant command is as follows:

*module-assistant **command** [pkg-list]*

where ***command*** is a command from the following list and *pkg-list* is a list of one or more SPACE-separated module source packages. You do not need to include the **−source** part of the package name when working with module-assistant. The **prepare** command does not accept a *pkg-list*; all other commands require it. See the module-assistant man page for a list of options, more commands, and more information.

auto-install *pkg-list*
: Combines the **prepare**, **get**, **build**, and **install** commands and processes *pkg-list*. Abbreviate this command as **a-i**.

build *pkg-list*
: Builds *pkg-list*. Error messages go to **/var/cache/modass**.

get *pkg-list*
: Downloads and installs the source code for *pkg-list*.

install *pkg-list*
: Installs *pkg-list*. Without *pkg-list*, installs the last package you built for the kernel running on the local system.

list *pkg-list*
: With arguments, lists details about *pkg-list*. Without arguments, lists all known packages. Abbreviate this command as **la** (list available).

list-installed
: Lists details about installed packages. Abbreviate this command as **li**.

prepare
: Determines the name of the kernel-header package, installs it and the **build-essential** package as needed, and creates the **/usr/src/linux** symbolic link. With the **−l** option, this command uses the kernel version you specify. Without this option, it uses the version of the kernel running on the local system. You must run this command before you run any other module-assistant commands.

LOADING A MODULE

After you install a module with module-assistant, you must load it to make it available to the running kernel. Table 15-1 lists some of the tools available to help you work with modules. Refer to the corresponding man pages for options and more information.

Table 15-1   Tools for working with modules

Tool/utility	Function
depmod	Works with dependencies for modules.
insmod	Loads modules in a running kernel.
lsmod	Lists information about all loaded modules.
modinfo	Lists information about a module.
modprobe	Loads, unloads, and reports on modules. When it loads a module, it also loads dependencies.
rmmod	Unloads modules from a running kernel.

INSTALLING THE KERNEL, MODULES, AND ASSOCIATED FILES

The next step is to copy the compiled kernel, modules, and associated files to the appropriate directories, usually **/boot** and a subdirectory of **/lib/modules**. When you have a partition mounted at **/boot**, the files are kept in the root of this partition (**/boot**). Because you have created a **deb** package, installing these files is quite easy. The following command installs the new kernel files in the proper directories:

```
$ cd ..
$ sudo dpkg -i linux-image-2.6.27-rc41219799154_2.6.27-rc41219799154-10.00.Custom_i386.deb
Selecting previously deselected package linux-image-2.6.27-rc41219799154.
(Reading database ... 105704 files and directories currently installed.)
Unpacking linux-image-2.6.27-rc41219799154 (from linux-image-2.6.27-rc41219799154_2.6.27
rc41219799154-10.00.Custom_i386.deb) ...
Done.
Setting up linux-image-2.6.27-rc41219799154 (2.6.27-rc41219799154-10.00.Custom) ...
Running depmod.
Finding valid ramdisk creators.
Using mkinitramfs-kpkg to build the ramdisk.
Running postinst hook script update-grub.
```

```
Searching for GRUB installation directory ... found: /boot/grub
Searching for default file ... found: /boot/grub/default
Testing for an existing GRUB menu.lst file ... found: /boot/grub/menu.lst
Searching for splash image ... none found, skipping ...
Found kernel: /boot/vmlinuz-2.6.27-rc41219799154
Found kernel: /boot/last-good-boot/vmlinuz
Found kernel: /boot/vmlinuz-2.6.26-5-generic
Found kernel: /boot/memtest86+.bin
Replacing config file /var/run/grub/menu.lst with new version
Updating /boot/grub/menu.lst ... done

Examining /etc/kernel/postinst.d.
run-parts: executing /etc/kernel/postinst.d/nvidia-common
```

Installing the kernel in this manner updates the **menu.lst** grub configuration file to include the new kernel. The grub bootloader is covered below.

REBOOTING

Reboot the system by selecting **Main menu: System⇨Quit** and then clicking **Restart**. If you are working at the console, press CONTROL-ALT-DEL. You can also give a **reboot** command from the console, a character-based terminal, or a terminal emulator.

grub: THE LINUX BOOT LOADER

A boot loader is a very small program that the *bootstrap* (page 1098) process uses as it brings a computer from off or reset to a fully functional state. The boot loader frequently resides on the starting sectors of a hard disk called the master boot record (MBR).

BIOS   The *BIOS* (page 1097), which is stored in an *EEPROM* (page 1107) on the system's motherboard, gains control of a system when you turn on or reset the computer. After testing the hardware, the BIOS transfers control to the MBR, which usually passes control to the partition boot record. This transfer of control starts the boot loader, which is responsible for locating the operating system kernel (kept in the **/boot** directory), loading that kernel into memory, and starting it running. The **/boot** directory, which may be mounted on a separate partition, must be present for the system to boot Linux. Refer to "Booting the System" on page 427 for more information on what happens from this point forward.

/boot   You can place the **/boot** directory on a very small filesystem that is located near the beginning of the hard drive, where the BIOS can access it. With this setup, the root

(/) filesystem can be anywhere on any hard drive that Linux can access and that perhaps the BIOS cannot. If you are using grub (discussed next), make the filesystem that holds the **/boot** directory an **ext2** filesystem.

grub   The name grub stands for Grand Unified Boot loader. A product of the GNU project, the grub loader conforms to the *multiboot specification* (page 1120), which allows it to load many free operating systems directly as well as to *chain load* (page 1100) proprietary operating systems. The grub loader can recognize various types of filesystems and kernel executable formats, allowing it to load an arbitrary operating system. You must specify the kernel's filename and location (drive and partition) so grub knows where to find the kernel. You can pass this information to grub via either the command line or the menu. When you boot the system, grub can display a menu of choices that is generated by the **/boot/grub/menu.lst** file (next). At this point you can modify a menu selection, choose which operating system or kernel to boot, or do nothing and allow grub to boot the default system.

When you install grub at the time you install Linux, the installation program configures grub automatically. See the grub info page, www.gnu.org/software/grub, and www.gnu.org/software/grub/manual/grub.html for more information on grub.

menu.lst: CONFIGURES grub

The **/boot/grub/menu.lst** file is the default grub configuration file. This file is a grub shell script that holds grub commands that tell grub which kernel and associated files and which options to use when it boots the system. It can display a menu of kernels for you to chose from when the system boots.

As generated by update-grub (which is run when you install Ubuntu or install or upgrade a kernel using APT; see page 571), **menu.lst** comprises three sections:

* The file starts with many comments and a few interspersed global commands such as **timeout**, which controls how long grub waits for you to respond to its prompt before automatically booting the default kernel.

* It continues with the Automagic Kernels List, which is divided into two sections. The first section holds default options (directives) that update-grub uses to configure **menu.lst** (page 571). (The **menu.lst** file holds directives that control the generation of a replacement **menu.lst** file.)

* The second part of the Automagic Kernels List holds update-grub-generated specifications for the grub boot-time menu (page 428). Each boot-time menu entry (boot specification) starts with a **title** keyword, which is followed by several lines that instruct grub which files to load

and which options to use when you choose that menu entry to boot the system.

Following is a single menu entry from a **menu.lst** file. Following the **title**, the **root** command tells grub which device the **/boot** directory is located on (**hd0,0** means hard disk drive 0, partition 0, typically **sda1**). Next the **kernel** command specifies the name of the file that holds the kernel that grub is to boot. The grub loader passes the arguments following this filename to the kernel. The **root=UUID=** argument tells the kernel which partition the root filesystem (**/**) is mounted on. (See page 492 for more information on identifying partitions using UUID numbers.) This partition is usually initially mounted in readonly (**ro**) mode and is remounted in read-write mode later, after being checked. The **noapic** option, which turns off the advanced programmable interrupt controllers, is required by the system this kernel is running on (you may not need to use this option). The **initrd** (initial *RAM disk;* page 1128) command specifies the name of the file that holds the initial RAM disk image. The grub boot loader loads this image and mounts it as the root filesystem as the first step in booting Linux. The **savedefault** command comes into play when the system boots and you choose a grub menu entry other than the default. If that entry includes a **savedefault** command, the menu entry becomes the default entry the next time the system boots.

```
title          Ubuntu intrepid (development branch), kernel 2.6.27-rc41219799154
root           (hd0,0)
kernel         /boot/vmlinuz-2.6.27-rc41219799154 root=UUID=8b8644... ro noapic
initrd         /boot/initrd.img-2.6.27-rc41219799154
savedefault
```

The **menu.lst** file in the next example is from a system that had its kernel replaced (there are two versions of **vmlinuz** and **initrd**). This system has a separate **boot** partition or directory, as do most systems, so all kernel and **initrd** image paths are relative to **/boot**.

The **menu.lst** file that update-grub configures when you install Ubuntu Linux starts with comments that explain many of the commands you can use in the file. Most of the comments have been removed from the following file. The first of the global commands, **default,** specifies the ordinal number of the default menu entry. Menu entries are numbered starting with 0. Although this number does not change, the default boot specification changes when you select a boot specification that includes a **savedefault** command (as explained earlier). The **timeout** command specifies the number of seconds that grub waits after it has prompted you for a boot specification before it automatically boots the system using the default boot specification. When you specify **hiddenmenu,** grub boots the default entry and does not display its menu unless you press ESCAPE while the **timeout** counter is ticking down. This option is commented out in the following listing, which causes grub to display its menu. The **color** command causes grub to display its menu in color.

```
$ cat /boot/grub/menu.lst
default        0
timeout        3
#hiddenmenu
color cyan/blue white/blue


### BEGIN AUTOMAGIC KERNELS LIST

title          Ubuntu intrepid (development branch), kernel 2.6.27-rc41219799154
root           (hd0,0)
kernel         /boot/vmlinuz-2.6.27-rc41219799154 root=UUID=8b8644... ro quiet splash
initrd         /boot/initrd.img-2.6.27-rc41219799154
quiet

title          Ubuntu intrepid (devel...), kernel 2.6.27-rc41219799154 (recovery mode)
root           (hd0,0)
kernel         /boot/vmlinuz-2.6.27-rc41219799154 root=UUID=8b8644... ro  single
initrd         /boot/initrd.img-2.6.27-rc41219799154

title          Ubuntu intrepid (development branch), kernel Last successful boot
root           (hd0,0)
kernel         /boot/last-good-boot/vmlinuz root=UUID=8b... ro quiet splash last good-boot
initrd         /boot/last-good-boot/initrd.img
quiet

title          Ubuntu intrepid (development branch), kernel 2.6.26-5-generic
root           (hd0,0)
kernel         /boot/vmlinuz-2.6.26-5-generic root=UUID=8b8644... ro quiet splash
initrd         /boot/initrd.img-2.6.26-5-generic
quiet

title          Ubuntu intrepid (development branch), kernel 2.6.26-5-generic (recovery mode)
root           (hd0,0)
kernel         /boot/vmlinuz-2.6.26-5-generic root=UUID=8b8644... ro  single
initrd         /boot/initrd.img-2.6.26-5-generic

title          Ubuntu intrepid (development branch), memtest86+
root           (hd0,0)
kernel         /boot/memtest86+.bin
quiet

### END DEBIAN AUTOMAGIC KERNELS LIST
```

Each menu entry/boot specification in the **menu.lst** file, called a *stanza*, starts with a **title** command. If you do not specify **hiddenmenu**, or if you press ESCAPE while the **timeout** counter is ticking down, grub displays a menu of these **title** strings and allows you to a select one.

The preceding **menu.lst** file includes five boot specifications: The first, numbered 0, is for the 2.6.27-rc41219799154 kernel; the second, numbered 1, is for the same kernel brought up in recovery (single-user) mode. The next two entries are for generic kernels—those installed when Ubuntu was installed. The final entry is for memtest86 (page 67) and allows you to run this memory test utility directly from the grub menu.

The menu entries that bring the system up in multiuser mode have a few more entries than those that bring the system up in recovery mode. The **quiet** option following the **kernel** command causes the kernel to produce less output so the user can more easily tell what is happening. The **splash** option causes grub to display the Ubuntu logo as it boots the system. The **single** option in the recovery mode entries brings the system up in recovery (single-user) mode.

Make sure that when you install a new kernel manually, its **title** line is different from the other **title** lines in **menu.lst**.

You must add a kernel that is not managed by update-grub before or after the Automagic Kernels List section of **menu.lst** or update-grub will replace it next time update-grub runs. The Automagic Kernels List section is delimited with the following comments: BEGIN AUTOMAGIC KERNELS LIST and END DEBIAN AUTOMAGIC KERNELS LIST.

update-grub: UPDATES THE menu.lst FILE

The update-grub utility updates the **/boot/grub/menu.lst** file if the file exists; otherwise, update-grub creates this file. This utility first looks for all files in the **/boot** directory whose names start with the string **vmlinuz–** and assumes that each of these files holds a kernel. If the **memtest86** directive (page 573) is set to **true**, it also looks for a file that holds that utility. It creates a menu entry (boot specification) in **menu.lst** for each kernel it finds (and optionally for memtest86). It also adds an **initrd** (initial RAM disk) line to **menu.lst** for each file in **/boot** whose name starts with the string **initrd–** and whose version number matches one of the kernel files it found. For example, if update-grub finds the kernel file named **vmlinuz-2.6.26-5-generic** in **/boot** and then finds **initrd.img-2.6.26-5-generic**, it creates an **initrd** line in **menu.lst** for that RAM disk image file.

After update-grub runs for the first time, such as when you install Ubuntu, and creates a **menu.lst** file, you can edit **menu.lst**. The previous section discussed some of the options, located near the beginning of **menu.lst**, that you can edit. This section discusses the portion of this file that starts and ends with the following comments:

```
### BEGIN AUTOMAGIC KERNELS LIST
## lines between the AUTOMAGIC KERNELS LIST markers will be modified
## by the debian update-grub script except for the default options below

## DO NOT UNCOMMENT THEM, Just edit them to your needs
...
## ## End Default Options ##
```

The update-grub utility uses the directives in this part of **menu.lst** to configure **menu.lst** when it updates this file. This part of the file is well commented; comments begin with two pound signs (##). Directives begin with one pound sign (#).

This section of the chapter discusses the directives you are most likely to want to change. Following is an example of three comments followed by one directive:

```
## should update-grub create memtest86 boot option
## e.g. memtest86=true
##      memtest86=false
# memtest86=true
```

The directive **memtest86=true** tells update-grub to include in **menu.lst** an entry to run a memory test (memtest86) instead of booting a kernel. If you do not want update-grub to include a memory test entry, change the **true** in the last line to **false**:

```
# memtest86=false
```

Do not remove the pound sign from the beginning of the line because a single pound sign indicates a line that holds a directive. (As mentioned earlier, comment lines start with two pound signs.)

When you run update-grub, it updates the **menu.lst** file based on the kernels in the **/boot** directory and the directives in the Automagic Kernels List. In the following example, update-grub finds three kernels and the memtest86 utility in **/boot**:

```
$ sudo update-grub
Searching for GRUB installation directory ... found: /boot/grub
Searching for default file ... found: /boot/grub/default
Testing for an existing GRUB menu.lst file ... found: /boot/grub/menu.lst
Searching for splash image ... none found, skipping ...
Found kernel: /boot/vmlinuz-2.6.27-rc41219799154
Found kernel: /boot/last-good-boot/vmlinuz
Found kernel: /boot/vmlinuz-2.6.26-5-generic
Found kernel: /boot/memtest86+.bin
Updating /boot/grub/menu.lst ... done
```

LIST OF DIRECTIVES

The following directives can appear within the Automagic Kernels List section of the **menu.lst** file.

alternative=true|false

When set to **true** (default), causes update-grub to create alternative stanzas for each kernel. This option works in conjunction with **altoption**.

altoption=(*string*) *options*

Specifies information that update-grub provides in alternative stanzas: *string*, which must be enclosed within parentheses, is appended to the **title** line, and *options* is a SPACE-separated list of options that are appended to the **kernel** line. This option has meaning only if **alternatives** is set to **true**. The default value of **(recovery mode) single** provides recovery mode menu entries for each kernel. See **kopt** and **defoptions** for more information on *options*.

defoptions=*options*

The *options* is a string that update-grub appends to the kernel line in the default stanzas but not in the alternative stanzas. See **kopt** and **altoption** for more information on *options*.

groot=(dev*X,Y***)**   Specifies the default device that update-grub places in the **root** command of each stanza. This device holds the **/boot** directory that contains the kernel file. This directive starts numbering partitions at 0, while in most other situations partitions are numbered starting at 1. For example, **groot=(hd0,0)** would generate the line **root (hd0,0)**, specifying that the **/boot** directory is located on first hard disk, first partition (hard disk drive 0, partition 1)—typically **sda1**. The string (**hd1,4**) refers to the second hard disk, first logical partition (logical partitions usually start at 5, even if there are fewer than four primary partitions; see page 34).

howmany=*num***|all**

The *num* specifies the maximum number of kernels update-grub creates stanzas for. Does not count alternative stanzas. Setting **howmany** to **all** includes all kernels.

kopt=*root=dev options*

Specifies the part of the kernel command of each stanza that tells the kernel the location of the root device (**/**). The *dev* can be the device name of a partition or a UUID (page 492), which the following example uses. The comments in the example explain how to specify kernel-specific devices and options. The *options*, such as **ro** (readonly) or **acip=off** (disables ACIP), is a SPACE-separated list that grub passes to the kernel in all stanzas. The *options* are the same as the parameters you can specify on the boot command line (page 69). See also **defoptions** and **altoption**.

```
## default kernel options for automagic boot options
## If you want special options for specific kernels use kopt_x_y_z
## where x.y.z is kernel version. Minor versions can be omitted.
## e.g. kopt=root=/dev/hda1 ro
##      kopt_2_6_8=root=/dev/hdc1 ro
##      kopt_2_6_8_2_686=root=/dev/hdc2 ro
# kopt=root=UUID=8b864434-62f5-4d84-a8a8-9a10f63d5582 ro
```

memtest86=true|false

When set to **true** (default), creates a stanza that calls the memory testing program memtest86, instead of booting a kernel.

updatedefaultentry=true|false

When set to **false** (default), update-grub sets the **default** line in **menu.lst** so that it always specifies the newest kernel. As a result, grub automatically boots the newest kernel by default. When set to **true**, update-grub sets the **default** line in **menu.lst** so that it always specifies the same kernel, even when it adds newer kernels to **menu.lst**.

grub-install: INSTALLS THE MBR AND grub FILES

The grub-install utility installs the MBR and the files, such as the ***stage*** files (the grub images), that grub needs to boot the system. This utility takes a single argument, the name of the device that is to hold the MBR. You can specify the device name as a grub device name (e.g., **hd0**) or a device filename (e.g., **/dev/sda**). The **/boot/grub/device.map** file lists both forms of the name of the device that holds the MBR. The following example shows grub-install installing files in the default location (**/boot/grub**) and the MBR on device **/dev/sda**:

```
$ sudo grub-install /dev/sda
Installation finished. No error reported.
This is the contents of the device map /boot/grub/device.map.
Check if this is correct or not. If any of the lines is incorrect,
fix it and re-run the script 'grub-install'.

$ cat /boot/grub/device.map
(hd0)    /dev/sda
```

REINSTALLING THE MBR

The following procedure reinstalls the MBR, as is necessary when it gets overwritten by a Windows installation:

1. Boot the system using an Ubuntu live (installation) CD/DVD.

2. Open a terminal emulator window (**Menubar: Applications⇨Accessories⇨ Terminal**).

3. Give the following commands, substituting the name of the device that holds the root partition (e.g., **/dev/sda2**) for **/dev/xxx**. Substitute the name of the drive that you want to install the MBR on (e.g., **/dev/sda**) for **/dev/yyy**. Do not forget to unmount **/mnt** when you are done.

   a. If the system *does not* have a separate **boot** partition, use these commands:

   ```
   $ sudo mount /dev/xxx /mnt
   $ sudo grub-install --root-directory=/mnt /dev/yyy
   Installation finished. No error reported.
   This is the contents of the device map /mnt/boot/grub/device.map.
   Check if this is correct or not. If any of the lines is incorrect,
   fix it and re-run the script 'grub-install'.
   $ cat /boot/grub/device.map
   (hd0)    /dev/sda
   $ sudo umount /mnt
   ```

   b. If the system *does* have a separate **boot** partition, use these commands, substituting the name of the device that holds the **boot** partition (e.g., **/dev/sda1**) for **/dev/zzz**:

   ```
   $ sudo mount /dev/xxx /mnt
   $ sudo mount /dev/zzz /mnt/boot
   $ sudo grub-install --root-directory=/mnt /dev/yyy
   Installation finished. No error reported.
   This is the contents of the device map /mnt/boot/grub/device.map.
   Check if this is correct or not. If any of the lines is incorrect,
   fix it and re-run the script 'grub-install'.
   ```

```
$ cat /boot/grub/device.map
(hd0)    /dev/sda
$ sudo umount /mnt
```

4. Reboot the system. Remove the CD/DVD when the system asks you to.

5. Continue to reboot the system from the hard drive you specified in place of **/dev/xxx**.

dmesg: DISPLAYS KERNEL MESSAGES

The dmesg utility displays the kernel-ring buffer, where the kernel stores messages. When the system boots, the kernel fills this buffer with messages related to hardware and module initialization. Messages in the kernel-ring buffer are often useful for diagnosing system problems.

When you run dmesg, it displays a lot of information. It is frequently easier to pipe the output of dmesg through less or grep to find what you are looking for. For example, if you find that your hard disks are performing poorly, you can use dmesg to check whether they are running in DMA mode:

```
$ dmesg | grep DMA
...
[  23.259422] ata1: SATA max UDMA/133 cmd 0x9F0 ctl 0xBF2 bmdma 0xE000 irq 5
[  23.259478] ata2: SATA max UDMA/133 cmd 0x970 ctl 0xB72 bmdma 0xE008 irq 5
...
```

The preceding lines tell you which mode each SATA device is operating in. If you are having problems with the Ethernet connection, search the dmesg log for **eth**:

```
$ dmesg | grep eth
forcedeth.c: Reverse Engineered nForce ethernet driver. Version 0.54.
eth0: forcedeth.c: subsystem: 0147b:1c00 bound to 0000:00:04.0
eth0: no IPv6 routers present
```

If everything is working properly, dmesg displays the hardware configuration information for each network interface.

Another common source of problems is the Direct Rendering Infrastructure (DRI), which allows graphics drivers direct access to the kernel. The corresponding kernel component is the Direct Rendering Module (DRM—not to be confused with Digital Rights Management).

```
$ dmesg | grep drm
[drm] AGP 0.99 Aperture @ 0xd8000000 64MB
[drm] Initialized radeon 1.7.0 20020828 on minor 0
[drm] Loading R200 Microcode
```

This output tells you that an ATi Radeon graphics card is configured correctly: Any configuration problems must be in the **/etc/X11/xorg.conf** file. The nVidia binary drivers do not use DRI. The dmesg log is a good place to start when diagnosing faults. If you have configured a system service incorrectly, this log quickly fills up with errors.

CHAPTER SUMMARY

You can build a Linux kernel from the source code. Sometimes you do not need to build a kernel; instead, you can change many aspects of the kernel by using boot options in **/boot/grub/menu.lst**. You can dynamically change options by modifying **/etc/sysctl.conf**.

Before you can build a Linux kernel, you must have the kernel source files on the system. These files are frequently located in **/usr/src/linux✷**. Once you have the source files, you need to configure the kernel, clean the source tree, compile the kernel and the loadable modules, and install the kernel and loadable modules.

The grub boot loader is a small program that controls the process of bringing the system up. The update-grub utility updates the **menu.lst** file so you can boot the new kernel.

The dmesg utility displays the kernel-ring buffer, where the kernel stores messages. You can use this utility to help diagnose boot-time problems.

EXERCISES

1. What is the purpose of the kernel?

2. How would you display a list of all loaded modules in the current kernel?

3. How would you use aptitude to download the source code for the most recently released version of the Ubuntu kernel? Where and in what form does the source code exist after you download it? How and where would you unpack the source code so that you could work with it?

4. How would you display information from the kernel about the hard disk on the first IDE channel?

5. The **acpi=off** kernel argument prevents **acpid** from starting. How would you use this argument?

6. What is a boot loader?

ADVANCED EXERCISES

7. Why would you use the **––append-to-version** option to the make-kpkg utility when compiling a kernel?

8. You have just installed an Adaptec SCSI card. How can you find out whether it has been recognized and which entry in **/dev** represents it?

9. When you install an experimental kernel for testing purposes, how do you instruct grub not to load it by default?

10. How would you obtain a list of all network-related kernel parameters?

16

ADMINISTRATION TASKS

The system administrator has many responsibilities. This chapter discusses tasks not covered in Chapter 11, including configuring user and group accounts, backing up files, scheduling tasks, general problem solving, and using the system log daemon, **syslogd**.

CONFIGURING USER AND GROUP ACCOUNTS

More than a username is required for a user to be able to log in and use a system. That is, a user must have the necessary files, directories, permissions, and usually a password to log in. At a minimum a user must have an entry in the **/etc/passwd** and **/etc/shadow** files and a home directory. This section describes several ways you can work with user accounts. Refer to Chapter 21 if you want to run NIS to manage the **passwd** database.

users-admin: MANAGES USER ACCOUNTS

The Users Settings window (Figure 16-1) enables you to add, delete, and modify system users and groups. To display this window, select **Main menu: System⇨ Administration⇨Users and Groups** or give the command **users-admin** from a terminal emulator or Run Application window (ALT-F2). If you want to add, remove, or modify user accounts, click **Unlock** and supply your password.

Modifying or adding a user
To modify the properties of an existing user, highlight the user you want to work with in the Users Settings window and click **Properties**. To create a new user, click **Add User** in the Users Settings window. The users-admin utility displays the Account tab of the Account Properties window (Figure 16-3) or New User Account window. The two windows are similar.

Account tab
Modify or enter information for the user. At a minimum you must enter a username and password. Click the **User Privileges** tab.

User Privileges tab
The User Privileges tab (Figure 16-2) enables you to add and remove privileges for a user. Place a tick in the check box next to each of the privileges you want to grant a user; remove the tick from those privileges you do not want to grant. The most important of these privileges is **Administer the system**. Putting a tick in this box adds the user to the **admin** group, which in turn allows the user to use sudo (page 406) to gain **root** privileges. Click **OK**.

Advanced tab
The Advanced tab allows you to modify the home directory, shell, group, and UID of the user. The users-admin utility fills in these values for a new user. Typically you do not need to modify these entries.

Figure 16-1   The Users Settings window

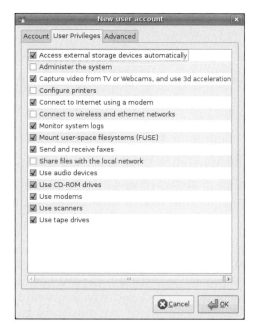

Figure 16-2   The Account Properties window, User Privileges tab

When you are finished entering information under each of the tabs for the user, click **OK**. At this point users-admin adds the user to or modifies the user on the system and closes the window, leaving the Users Settings window visible.

Figure 16-3   The Account Properties window, Account tab

Figure 16-4   The Groups Settings window

Working with groups   Click **Manage Groups** in the Users Settings window to work with groups; users-admin displays the Groups Settings window (Figure 16-4). To create a group, click **Add Group** and specify the name and number (GID) of the group. Put a tick in the check box next to each user who you want to be a member of the group and click **OK**. To change the name or number of a group or to add or remove users from a group, highlight the group in the Groups Settings window and click **Properties**. Make the changes you want, and then click **OK**. To remove a group, highlight the group and click **Delete**. See page 474 for more information on groups.

When you are finished adding and modifying users and groups, click **Close**.

useradd: ADDS A USER ACCOUNT

The useradd utility adds a new user account to the system. By default, useradd assigns the next highest unused user ID to a new account and specifies bash as the user's login shell. The following example adds entries to the **/etc/passwd** and **/etc/shadow** files, creates the user's home directory (in **/home**), specifies the user's group ID, and puts the user's full name in the comment field. The group ID you specify must exist in **/etc/group** or the command will fail. Use groupadd to add a group.

```
$ sudo useradd -g 1105 -c "Max R." max
```

The useradd utility puts a **!** in the password field of the **shadow** file (page 479) to prevent the user from logging in until you use passwd to assign a password to that user. Based on the **/etc/login.defs** file, useradd creates a home directory for the new user. When doing so, it copies the contents of **/etc/skel**, which contains bash and other startup files, to that directory. For more information on adding user information, see the useradd man page.

Under some distributions, adduser is a link to useradd. Under Ubuntu, it is a different program. See the adduser man page for more information.

userdel: REMOVES A USER ACCOUNT

The userdel utility deletes a user's account. If appropriate, back up the files belonging to the user before deleting them. The following command removes Max's account. The **--remove** (**-r**) option causes the command to remove his home directory hierarchy:

```
$ sudo userdel --remove max
```

See the userdel man page for more information.

usermod: MODIFIES A USER ACCOUNT

To turn off a user's account temporarily, you can use usermod to change the expiration date for the account. Because it specifies that his account expired in the past (December 31, 2008), the following command line prevents Max from logging in:

```
$ sudo usermod -e "12/31/08" max
```

See the usermod man page for more information.

groupadd: ADDS A GROUP

Just as useradd adds a new user to the system, so groupadd adds a new group by adding an entry to **/etc/group** (page 474). The following example creates a group named **pubs**:

```
$ sudo groupadd -g 1024 pubs
```

Unless you use the **-g** option to assign a group ID, the system picks the next available sequential number greater than 1000. The **-o** option allows the group ID to be nonunique, which allows you to assign multiple names to a group ID.

groupdel: REMOVES A GROUP

The analogue of userdel for groups is groupdel, which takes a group name as an argument. You can also use groupmod to change the name or group ID of a group, as in the following examples:

```
$ sudo groupmod -g 1025 pubs
$ sudo groupmod -n manuals pubs
```

The first example gives the previously created **pubs** group a new group ID number. The second example renames the **pubs** group to **manuals**.

Changing group ID numbers

caution | The groupmod utility does not change group numbers in **/etc/passwd** when you renumber a group. Instead, you must edit **/etc/passwd** and change the entries manually. If you change the number of a group, files that are associated with the group will no longer be associated with the group. Rather, they may be associated with no group or with another group with the old group ID number.

BACKING UP FILES

One of the most oft-neglected tasks of system administration is making backup copies of files on a regular basis. The backup copies are vital in three instances: when the system malfunctions and files are lost, when a catastrophic disaster (fire, earthquake, and so on) occurs, and when a user or the system administrator deletes or corrupts a file by accident. Even when you set up RAID (page 39), you still need to back up files. Although RAID can provide fault tolerance (helpful in the event of disk failure), it does not help when a catastrophic disaster occurs or when a file is corrupted or removed accidentally. It is a good idea to have a written backup policy and to keep copies of backups offsite (in another building, at home, or at a different facility or campus) in a fireproof vault or safe.

The time to start thinking about backups is when you partition the disk. Refer to "Partitioning a Disk" on page 36. Make sure the capacity of the backup device and your partition sizes are comparable. Although you can back up a partition onto multiple volumes, it is easier not to—and it is much easier to restore data from a single volume.

You must back up filesystems regularly. Backup files are usually kept on magnetic tape, external hard disk, or another removable medium. Alternatively, you can keep backup files on a remote system. How often and which files you back up depend on the system and your needs. Use this criterion when determining a backup schedule: If the system crashes, how much work are you willing to lose? Ideally you would back up all files on the system every few minutes so you would never lose more than a few minutes of work.

Of course, there is a tradeoff: How often are you willing to back up the files? The backup procedure typically slows the system for users, takes a certain amount of your time, and requires that you have and store the media holding the backup. Avoid backing up an active filesystem; the results may be inconsistent, and restoring from the backup may be impossible. This requirement is a function of the backup program and the filesystem you are backing up.

Another question is when to run the backup. Unless you plan to kick users off and bring the system down to single-user mode (not a user-friendly practice), you will want to perform this task when the machine is at its quietest. Depending on the use of the system, sometime in the middle of the night can work well. Then the backup is least likely to affect users, and the files are not likely to change as they are being read for backup.

A *full* backup makes copies of all files, regardless of when they were created or accessed. An *incremental* backup makes copies of those files that have been created or modified since the last (usually full) backup.

The more people using the system, the more often you should back up the filesystems. One popular schedule is to perform an incremental backup one or two times a day and a full backup one or two times a week.

CHOOSING A BACKUP MEDIUM

If the local system is connected to a network, you can write backups to a drive on another system. This technique is often used with networked computers to avoid the cost of having a backup drive on each computer in the network and to simplify management of backing up many computers in a network. Although tapes are still used for backups, system administrators are using hard disks for this purpose more frequently. Backing up to a hard disk on a remote system is cost-effective, reliable, and practical. Because hard disks hold many gigabytes of data, using them simplifies the task of backing up the system, making it more likely that you will take care of this important task regularly. Other options for holding backups are writable CDs and DVDs. These devices, although not as cost-effective or able to store as much information as hard disk or tape systems, offer the benefit of convenience.

BACKUP UTILITIES

A number of utilities are available to help you back up a system, and most work with any media. Most Linux backup utilities are based on one of the archive programs—tar or cpio—and augment these basic programs with bookkeeping support for managing backups conveniently.

You can use any of the tar, cpio, or dump/restore utilities to construct full or partial backups of a system. Each utility constructs a large file that contains, or archives, other files. In addition to file contents, an archive includes header information for each file it holds. This header information can be used when extracting files from the archive to restore file permissions and modification dates. An archive file can be saved to disk, written to tape, or shipped across the network while it is being created.

In addition to helping you back up the system, these programs offer a convenient way to bundle files for distribution to other sites. The tar program is often used for this purpose, and some software packages available on the Internet are bundled as tar archive files. A **deb** file (page 515) is an archive bundled using the ar archive utility.

amanda The amanda (Advanced Maryland Automatic Network Disk Archiver) utility (www.amanda.org), which is one of the more popular backup systems, uses dump or tar and takes advantage of Samba to back up Windows systems. The amanda utility backs up a LAN of heterogeneous hosts to a hard disk or tape. Relevant software packages are **amanda-common**, **amanda-client**, and **amanda-server**.

tar: ARCHIVES FILES

The tar (tape archive) utility writes files to and retrieves files from an archive; it can compress this archive to conserve space. If you do not specify an archive device, tar writes to standard output and reads from standard input. With the **–f** (**––file**) option, tar uses the argument to **–f** as the name of the archive device. You can use this option to refer to a device on another system on the network. Although tar has many options, you need only a few in most situations. The following command displays a complete list of options:

```
$ tar --help | less
```

Most options for tar can be given either in a short form (a single letter) or as a descriptive word. Descriptive-word options are preceded by two hyphens, as in **--help**. Single-letter options can be combined into a single command-line argument and need not be preceded by a hyphen (for consistency with other utilities, it is good practice to use the hyphen anyway).

Although the following two commands look quite different, they specify the same tar options in the same order. The first version combines single-letter options into a single command-line argument; the second version uses descriptive words for the same options:

```
$ sudo tar -ztvf /dev/st0
$ sudo tar --gzip --list --verbose --file /dev/st0
```

Both commands tell tar to generate a (**v, verbose**) table of contents (**t, list**) from the tape on **/dev/st0** (**f, file**), using gzip (**z, gzip**) to decompress the files. Unlike the original UNIX tar utility, the GNU version strips the leading **/** from absolute pathnames.

The options in Table 16-1 tell the tar program what to do. You must include exactly one of these options in a tar command.

Table 16-1   tar options

Option	Effect
--append (–r)	Appends files to an archive
--catenate (–A)	Adds one or more archives to the end of an existing archive
--create (–c)	Creates a new archive
--delete	Deletes files in an archive (not on tapes)
--dereference (–h)	Follows symbolic links
--diff (–d)	Compares files in an archive with disk files
--extract (–x)	Extracts files from an archive
--help	Displays a help list of tar options
--list (–t)	Lists the files in an archive
--update (–u)	Like the **–r** option, but the file is not appended if a newer version is already in the archive

The **–c**, **–t**, and **–x** options are used most frequently. You can use many other options to change how tar operates. The **–j** option, for example, compresses or decompresses the file by filtering it through bzip2 (page 160).

cpio: ARCHIVES FILES

The cpio (copy in/out) program is similar to tar but can read and write archive files in various formats, including the one used by tar. Normally cpio reads the names of the files to add to the archive from standard input and produces the archive file as standard output. When extracting files from an archive, it reads the archive as standard input.

As with tar, some options can be given in both a short, single-letter form and a more descriptive word form. However, unlike with tar, the syntax of the two forms in cpio differs when the option must be followed by additional information. In the short form, you must include a SPACE between the option and the additional information; with the word form, you must separate the two with an equal sign and no SPACEs.

Running cpio with the ––help option displays a complete list of options.

PERFORMING A SIMPLE BACKUP

When you prepare to make a major change to a system, such as replacing a disk drive, upgrading to a new release, or updating the Linux kernel, it is a good idea to archive some or all of the files so you can restore any that become damaged if something goes wrong. For this type of backup, tar or cpio works well. For example, if you have a SCSI tape drive as device **/dev/st0** (or it could be a hard disk at **/dev/hdb**) that is capable of holding all the files on a single tape, you can use the following commands to construct a backup tape of the entire system:

```
$ cd /
$ sudo tar -cf /dev/st0 .
```

All the commands in this section start by using cd to change to the root directory so you are sure to back up the entire system. The tar command then creates an archive (**c**) on the device **/dev/st0** (**f**). To compress the archive, replace the preceding tar command with the following command, which uses **j** to call bzip2:

```
$ sudo tar -cjf /dev/st0 .
```

You can back up a system with a combination of find and cpio. The following commands create an output file and set the I/O block size to 5120 bytes (the default is 512 bytes):

```
$ cd /
$ sudo find . -depth | cpio -oB > /dev/st0
```

The next command restores the files in the **/home** directory from the preceding backup. The options extract files from an archive (**–i**) in verbose mode, keeping the modification times and creating directories as needed.

```
$ cd /
$ sudo cpio -ivmd /home/\* < /dev/st0
```

Although all the archive programs work well for simple backups, utilities such as amanda (page 583) provide more sophisticated backup and restore systems. For example, to determine whether a file is in an archive, you must read the entire archive. If the archive is split across several tapes, this process is particularly tiresome. More sophisticated utilities, including amanda, assist you in several ways, including keeping a table of contents of the files in a backup.

Exclude some directories from a backup

tip   In practice, you will likely want to exclude some directories from the backup process. For example, not backing up **/tmp** or **/var/tmp** can save room in the archive. Also, do not back up the files in **proc**. Because the **/proc** pseudofilesystem is not a true disk filesystem but rather a way for the Linux kernel to provide information about the operating system and system memory, you need not back up **/proc**; you cannot restore it later. Similarly, you do not need to back up filesystems that are mounted from disks on other systems on the network. Do not back up FIFOs; the results are unpredictable. If you plan on using a simple backup method, similar to those just discussed, create a file naming the directories to exclude from the backup, and use the appropriate option with the archive program to read the file.

dump, restore: BACK UP AND RESTORE FILESYSTEMS

The dump utility (part of the **dump** package) first appeared in UNIX version 6. It backs up either an entire **ext2** or **ext3** filesystem or only those files that have changed since a recent dump. The restore utility can then restore an entire filesystem, a directory hierarchy, or an individual file. You will get the best results if you perform a backup on a quiescent system so that the files are not changing as you make the backup.

The next command backs up all files (including directories and special files) on the **root** (/) partition to SCSI tape 0. Frequently there is a link to the active tape drive, named **/dev/tape**, which you can use in place of the actual entry in the **/dev** directory.

```
$ sudo dump -0uf /dev/st0 /
```

The **–0** option specifies that the entire filesystem is to be backed up (a full backup). There are ten dump levels: 0–9. Zero is the highest (most complete) level and always backs up the entire filesystem. Each additional level is incremental with respect to the level above it. For example, 1 is incremental to 0 and backs up only those files that have changed since the last level 0 dump; 2 is incremental to 1 and backs up only those files that have changed since the last level 1 dump; and so on. You can construct a flexible schedule using this scheme. You do not need to use sequential numbers for backup levels, however. For example, you can perform a level 0 dump, followed by level 2 and 5 dumps.

The **–u** option updates the **/etc/dumpdates** file (page 474) with filesystem, date, and dump level information for use by the next incremental dump. The **–f** option and its argument write the backup to the device named **/dev/st0**.

The next command makes a partial backup containing all files that have changed since the last level 0 dump. The first argument (**1**) specifies a level 1 dump:

```
$ sudo dump -1uf /dev/st0 /
```

To restore an entire filesystem from a dump backup, first restore the most recent complete (level 0) backup. Perform this operation carefully because restore can overwrite the existing filesystem. Change directories to the directory the filesystem is mounted on (/**xxx** in the example) and give a **restore** command as shown following:

```
$ cd /xxx
$ sudo restore -if /dev/st0
```

The –i option invokes an interactive mode that allows you to choose which files and directories to restore. As with dump, the –f option specifies the name of the device that the backup medium is mounted on. When restore finishes, load the next lower-level (higher-number) dump tape and issue the same restore command. If multiple incremental dumps have been made at a particular level, always restore with the most recent one. You do not need to invoke restore with special arguments to restore an incremental dump; it will restore whatever appears on the tape.

You can also use restore to extract individual files from a tape by using the –x option and specifying the filenames on the command line. Whenever you restore a file, the restored file appears in the working directory. Before restoring files, make sure you are working in the correct directory.

The following commands restore the **etc/fstab** file from the tape on **/dev/st0**. The filename of the dumped file does not begin with / because all dumped pathnames are relative to the filesystem that you dumped—in this case /. Because the restore command is given from the / directory, the file will be restored to its original location of **/etc/fstab**:

```
$ cd /
$ sudo restore -xf /dev/st0 etc/fstab
```

If you use the –x option without specifying a file or directory name to extract, restore extracts the entire dumped filesystem. Use the –r option to restore an entire filesystem without using the interactive interface. The following command restores the filesystem from the tape on **/dev/st0** to the working directory without interaction:

```
$ sudo restore -rf /dev/st0
```

You can also use dump and restore to access a tape drive or hard disk on another system. Specify the file/directory as *host:file*, where *host* is the hostname of the system the tape or disk is on and *file* is the file or directory you want to dump/restore.

Occasionally, restore may prompt you with the following message:

```
You have not read any volumes yet.
Unless you know which volume your file(s) are on you should start
with the last volume and work towards the first.
Specify next volume #:
```

Enter **1** (one) in response to this prompt. If the filesystem spans more than one tape or disk, this prompt allows you to switch tapes.

At the end of the dump, you will receive another prompt:

```
set owner/mode for '.'? [yn]
```

Answer **y** to this prompt when you are restoring entire filesystems or files that have been accidentally removed. Doing so will restore the appropriate permissions to the files and directories being restored. Answer **n** if you are restoring a dump to a directory other than the one it was dumped from. The working directory permissions and owner will then be set to those of the user doing the restore (typically **root**).

A variety of device names can access the **/dev/st0** device. Each name accesses a different minor device number that controls some aspect of how the tape drive is used. After you complete a dump using **/dev/st0**, the tape drive automatically rewinds the tape. Use the nonrewinding SCSI tape device (**/dev/nst0**) to keep the tape from rewinding on completion. This feature allows you to back up multiple filesystems to the same volume.

Following is an example of backing up a system where the **/home, /usr,** and **/var** directories reside on different filesystems:

```
$ sudo dump -0uf /dev/nst0 /home
$ sudo dump -0uf /dev/nst0 /usr
$ sudo dump -0uf /dev/st0 /var
```

The preceding example uses the nonrewinding device for the first two dumps. If you use the rewinding device, the tape rewinds after each dump, and you are left with only the last dump on the tape.

You can use mt (magnetic tape), which is part of the **cpio** package, to manipulate files on a multivolume dump tape. The following mt command positions the tape (**fsf 2** instructs mt to skip forward *past* two files, leaving the tape at the start of the third file). The restore command restores the **/var** filesystem from the previous example:

```
$ sudo mt -f /dev/st0 fsf 2
$ sudo restore rf /dev/st0
```

SCHEDULING TASKS

It is a good practice to schedule certain routine tasks to run automatically. For example, you may want to remove old core files once a week, summarize accounting data daily, and rotate system log files monthly.

cron AND anacron: SCHEDULE ROUTINE TASKS

The **cron** daemon executes scheduled commands periodically. This daemon can execute commands at specific times on systems that are always running. The anacron utility executes scheduled commands when it is called. It works well on laptops and other systems that are not on all the time. The **anacron** init scrip, which calls anacron, will not run commands when a system is running on batteries (i.e., not on AC).

CRONTAB FILES

The **cron** daemon reads the commands it is to execute from crontab files. Users can use the crontab utility to set up personal crontab files in **/var/spool/cron/crontabs.** System crontab files are kept in the **/etc/cron.d** directory and in the **/etc/crontab** file. (The term *crontab* has three meanings: It refers to a text file in a specific format [a crontab file], it is the name of a utility [crontab], and it is the name of a file [/etc/crontab].)

By default, Ubuntu is set up with no restrictions on who can have **cron** run commands in their personal crontab files. See **cron.allow** and **cron.deny** on page 473 for ways of restricting this access.

System crontab files   Crontab files specify how often **cron** is to run a command. A line in a system crontab file, such as **/etc/crontab**, has the following format:

minute hour day-of-month month day-of-week user command

The first five fields indicate when **cron** will execute the *command*. The *minute* is the number of minutes after the start of the hour, the *hour* is the hour of the day based on a 24-hour clock, the *day-of-month* is a number from 1 to 31, and the *day-of-week* is a number from 0 to 7, with 0 and 7 indicating Sunday. An asterisk (*) substitutes for any value in a field. The *user* is the username or user ID of the user that the *command* will run as. Following are some examples:

```
20 1 * * *      root    /usr/local/bin/checkit
25 9 17 * *     root    /usr/local/bin/monthly.check
40 23 * * 7     root    /usr/local/bin/sunday.check
```

All three lines run as their commands with **root** privileges. The first line runs **checkit** every day at 1:20 AM. The second line runs **monthly.check** at 9:25 AM on day 17 of every month. The third line runs **sunday.check** at 11:40 PM every Sunday. Give the command **man 5 crontab** to obtain more information on crontab files.

User crontab files   A user crontab file has the same format as a system crontab file except that it does not include the *user* field because it always runs as the user who created it. Users can work with their own crontab files by giving the command **crontab** followed by –l to list the file, –r to remove the file, or –e to edit the file. This command uses the nano editor by default; if you prefer, export (page 948) and set the **VISUAL** or **EDITOR** environment variable to the textual editor of your choice. See the crontab man page for more information.

/etc/crontab   Following is the default **/etc/crontab** file. Comments begin with a pound sign (#). The file sets the **SHELL** and **PATH** (page 303) environment variables.

```
$ cat /etc/crontab
# /etc/crontab: system-wide crontab
# Unlike any other crontab you don't have to run the 'crontab'
# command to install the new version when you edit this file
# and files in /etc/cron.d. These files also have username fields,
# that none of the other crontabs do.

SHELL=/bin/sh
PATH=/usr/local/sbin:/usr/local/bin:/sbin:/bin:/usr/sbin:/usr/bin

# m h dom mon dow user   command
17 *    * * *   root    cd / && run-parts --report /etc/cron.hourly
25 6    * * *   root    test -x /usr/sbin/anacron || ( cd / && run-parts --report /etc/cron.daily )
47 6    * * 7   root    test -x /usr/sbin/anacron || ( cd / && run-parts --report /etc/cron.weekly )
52 6    1 * *   root    test -x /usr/sbin/anacron || ( cd / && run-parts --report /etc/cron.monthly )
#
```

run-parts   The run-parts utility runs all the executable files in the directory named as its argument. The **--report** option affects commands that produce output. It sends the name of the command to standard output or standard error—whichever the command sends its first output to.

The **cron** daemon runs the line that begins with **17** at 17 minutes past every hour. First the command cds to root (**/**). The AND Boolean operator (**&&**) then executes run-parts, which executes all files in the **/etc/cron.hourly** directory.

The next three lines first test whether the **/usr/sbin/anacron** file is executable. If the file is executable, the OR Boolean operator (**||**) causes the shell to ignore the rest of the line. Thus, if anacron is installed and executable, this file executes only the files in the **cron.hourly** directory. If anacron is not installed or is not executable, each of these three lines cds to root (**/**) and executes the files in the specified directory.

/etc/cron.d/anacron In addition to the **/etc/crontab** file, **cron** reads the files in **/etc/cron.d** for commands to execute. The following file causes **cron** to run the **anacron** init script once a day at 7:30 AM. This init script runs anacron if the system is up and not running on batteries):

```
$ cat /etc/cron.d/anacron
# /etc/cron.d/anacron: crontab entries for the anacron package

SHELL=/bin/sh
PATH=/usr/local/sbin:/usr/local/bin:/sbin:/bin:/usr/sbin:/usr/bin

30 7    * * *    root    test -x /etc/init.d/anacron && /usr/sbin/invoke-rc.d anacron start >/dev/null
```

/etc/anacrontab When anacron is run, it reads the commands it is to execute from the **/etc/anacrontab** file. The anacron utility keeps track of the last time it ran each of its jobs so when it is called, it can tell which jobs need to be run. This file is where the files in the **cron.daily**, **cron.weekly**, and **cron.monthly** directories get executed on a system running anacron.

```
$ cat /etc/anacrontab
# /etc/anacrontab: configuration file for anacron

# See anacron(8) and anacrontab(5) for details.

SHELL=/bin/sh
PATH=/usr/local/sbin:/usr/local/bin:/sbin:/bin:/usr/sbin:/usr/bin

# These replace cron's entries
1        5        cron.daily      nice run-parts --report /etc/cron.daily
7        10       cron.weekly     nice run-parts --report /etc/cron.weekly
@monthly          15       cron.monthly nice run-parts --report /etc/cron.monthly
```

An entry in the **anacrontab** file has the following format:

> *period delay identifier command*

where the *period* is the frequency in days (how often) that anacron executes the *command*, the *delay* is the number of minutes after anacron starts that it executes the *command*, and the *identifier* is the name of the file in **/var/spool/anacron** that anacron uses to keep track of when it last executed the *command*.

The **cron.daily** job in **anacrontab** runs the executable files in **/etc/cron.daily** every day, five minutes after anacron starts. If the system is running at 7:30 AM, **/etc/cron.d/anacron** calls the **anacron** init script, and this job runs at 7:35 AM. When Ubuntu boots, the rc scripts call the **anacron** init script. If the system is not running at 7:30 AM, the **cron.daily** job has not been run for at least a day, and the system is not running on batteries, the job runs five minutes after the system boots.

Running cron jobs at the right time

tip   As installed, if the **/usr/sbin/anacron** file is present and executable, **cron** uses anacron to run daily, weekly, and monthly cron jobs. The anacron utility always runs the jobs at 7:35 in the morning, or as soon as possible after that. Refer to "run-parts" on page 589 and the section on **/etc/anacrontab**. An easy way to get **cron** to run these jobs as scheduled in **/etc/crontab** is to change permissions on the **anacron** file so it is not executable:

```
$ sudo chmod 644 /usr/sbin/anacron
```

If you want to reenable anacron, change its permissions back to **755**.

at: RUNS OCCASIONAL TASKS

Like the cron utility, at runs a job sometime in the future. Unlike cron, at runs a job only once. For instance, you can schedule an at job that will reboot the system at 3:00 AM (when all users are probably logged off):

```
$ sudo at 3am
warning: commands will be executed using /bin/sh
at> reboot
at> CONTROL-D <EOT>
job 1 at 2008-02-01 03:00
```

It is also possible to run an at job from within an at job. For instance, an at job might check for new patches every 18 days—something that would be more difficult with cron. See the at man page for more information.

By default, Ubuntu is set up with restrictions that prevent some system accounts from running at. See **at.allow** and **at.deny** on page 473 for more information.

SYSTEM REPORTS

Many utilities report on one thing or another. The who, finger, ls, ps, and other utilities, for example, generate simple end-user reports. In some cases, these reports can help with system administration. This section describes utilities that generate more in-depth reports that can provide greater assistance with system administration tasks. Linux has many other report utilities, including (from the **sysstat** package) sar (system activity report), iostat (input/output and CPU statistics), and mpstat (processor statistics); (from the **net-tools** package) netstat (network report); and (from the **nfs-common** package) nfsstat (NFS statistics).

vmstat: REPORTS VIRTUAL MEMORY STATISTICS

The vmstat utility (**procps** package) generates virtual memory information along with (limited) disk and CPU activity data. The following example shows virtual memory statistics at three-second intervals for seven iterations (from the arguments **3 7**). The first line covers the time since the system was last booted; each subsequent line covers the period since the previous line.

```
$ vmstat 3 7
procs -----------memory---------- ---swap-- -----io---- --system-- ----cpu----
 r  b   swpd   free   buff  cache   si   so    bi    bo   in   cs us sy id wa
 0  2      0 684328  33924 219916    0    0   430   105 1052  134  2  4 86  8
 0  2      0 654632  34160 248840    0    0  4897  7683 1142  237  0  5  0 95
 0  3      0 623528  34224 279080    0    0  5056  8237 1094  178  0  4  0 95
 0  2      0 603176  34576 298936    0    0  3416   141 1161  255  0  4  0 96
 0  2      0 575912  34792 325616    0    0  4516  7267 1147  231  0  4  0 96
 1  2      0 549032  35164 351464    0    0  4429    77 1120  210  0  4  0 96
 0  2      0 523432  35448 376376    0    0  4173  6577 1135  234  0  4  0 95
```

The following list explains the column heads displayed by vmstat:

- **procs**   Process information
  - ◆ **r**   Number of waiting, runnable processes
  - ◆ **b**   Number of blocked processes (in uninterruptable sleep)
- **memory**   Memory information (in kilobytes)
  - ◆ **swpd**   Used virtual memory
  - ◆ **free**   Idle memory
  - ◆ **buff**   Memory used as buffers
  - ◆ **cache**   Memory used as cache
- **swap**   System paging activity (in kilobytes per second)
  - ◆ **si**   Memory swapped in from disk
  - ◆ **so**   Memory swapped out to disk
- **io**   System I/O activity (in blocks per second)
  - ◆ **bi**   Blocks received from a block device
  - ◆ **bo**   Blocks sent to a block device
- **system**   (Values are per second)
  - ◆ **in**   Interrupts (including the clock)
  - ◆ **cs**   Context switches
- **cpu**   Percentage of total CPU time spent in each of these states
  - ◆ **us**   User (nonkernel)
  - ◆ **sy**   System (kernel)
  - ◆ **id**   Idle
  - ◆ **wa**   Waiting for I/O

top: LISTS PROCESSES USING THE MOST RESOURCES

The top utility is a useful supplement to ps. At its simplest, top displays system information at the top and the most CPU-intensive processes below the system information. The top utility updates itself periodically; type q to quit. Although you can use command-line options, the interactive commands are often more helpful. Refer to Table 16-2 and to the top man page for more information.

Table 16-2   top: interactive commands

Command	Function
A	Sorts processes by age (newest first).
h or **?**	Displays a Help screen.

Table 16-2   top: interactive commands (continued)

Command	Function
k	(**kill**) Prompts for a PID number and type of signal and sends the process that signal. Defaults to signal 15 (SIGTERM); specify 9 (SIGKILL) only when 15 does not work.
M	Sorts processes by memory usage.
P	(**processor**) Sorts processes by CPU usage (default).
q	Quits top.
s	Prompts for time between updates in seconds. Use 0 (zero) for continuous updates; such updates can slow the system by consuming a lot of resources.
SPACE	Updates the display immediately.
T	Sorts tasks by time.
W	Writes a startup file named **~/.toprc** so that the next time you start top, it uses the same parameters it is currently using.

```
$ top
top - 17:58:53 up 3 days,  4:20,  1 user,  load average: 2.16, 1.61, 0.83
Tasks: 167 total,   5 running, 162 sleeping,   0 stopped,   0 zombie
Cpu(s):  1.5%us,  0.5%sy, 1.3%ni, 96.0%id,  0.2%wa,  0.6%hi, 0.0%si, 0.0%st
Mem:   2076092k total,  1990652k used,    85440k free,    18416k buffers
Swap:  7815580k total,    34908k used,  7780672k free,  1330008k cached

  PID USER      PR  NI  VIRT  RES  SHR S %CPU %MEM    TIME+  COMMAND
31323 zach      25   0  9020 6960  396 R   63  0.3   0:17.58 bzip2
31327 zach      18   0  2092  596  492 R   57  0.0   0:00.92 cp
31311 root      15   0     0    0    0 S   16  0.0   0:00.38 pdflush
 6870 zach      27  12  331m 190m  37m R    2  9.4 198:42.98 firefox-bin
31303 root      15   0     0    0    0 S    2  0.0   0:00.42 pdflush
    1 root      15   0  2912 1808  488 S    0  0.1   0:01.55 init
...
```

parted: REPORTS ON AND PARTITIONS A HARD DISK

The parted (partition editor) utility reports on and manipulates hard disk partitions. The following example shows how to use parted from the command line. It uses the **print** command to display information about the partitions on the **/dev/hda** drive:

```
$ sudo parted /dev/hda print
Disk geometry for /dev/hda: 0kB - 165GB
Disk label type: msdos
Number  Start   End     Size    Type      File system  Flags
1       32kB    1045MB  1045MB  primary   ext3         boot
2       1045MB  12GB    10GB    primary   ext3
3       12GB    22GB    10GB    primary   ext3
4       22GB    165GB   143GB   extended
5       22GB    23GB    1045MB  logical   linux-swap
6       23GB    41GB    18GB    logical   ext3
7       41GB    82GB    41GB    logical   ext3
```

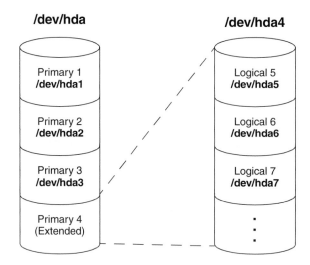

Figure 16-5   The primary and extended partitions from the example

Figure 16-5 graphically depicts the partitions shown in this example. The first line that parted displays specifies the device being reported on (**/dev/hda**) and its size (165 gigabytes). The **print** command displays the following columns:

- **Number**—The minor device number (page 485) of the device holding the partition. This number is the same as the last number in the device name. In the example, 5 corresponds to **/dev/hda5**.

- **Start**—The location on the disk where the partition starts. The parted utility specifies a location on the disk as the distance (in bytes) from the start of the disk. Thus partition 3 starts 12 gigabytes from the start of the disk.

- **End**—The location on the disk where the partition stops. Although partition 2 ends 12 gigabytes from the start of the disk and partition 3 starts at the same location, parted takes care that the partitions do not overlap at this single byte.

- **Size**—The size of the partition in kilobytes (kB), megabytes (MB), or gigabytes (GB).

- **Type**—The partition type: primary, extended, or logical. See Figure 16-5 and page 34 for information on partitions.

- **File system**—The filesystem type: **ext2, ext3, fat32, linux-swap**, and so on. See Table 12-1 on page 487 for a list of filesystem types.

- **Flags**—The flags that are turned on for the partition, including **boot, raid**, and **lvm**. In the example, partition 1 is bootable.

In the preceding example, partition 4 defines an extended partition that includes 143 gigabytes of the 165-gigabyte disk (Figure 16-5). You cannot make changes to an extended partition without affecting all logical partitions within it.

In addition to reporting on the layout and size of a hard disk, you can use parted interactively to modify the disk layout. Be *extremely* careful when using parted in this manner, and always back up the system before starting to work with this utility. Changing the partition information (the *partition table*) on a disk can destroy the information on the disk. Read the parted info page before you attempt to modify a partition table.

parted **can destroy everything**

caution Be as careful with parted as you would be with a utility that formats a hard disk. Changes you make with parted can easily result in the loss of large amounts of data. If you are using parted and have any question about what you are doing, quit with a **q** command before making any changes. Once you give parted a command, it immediately makes the change you requested.

To partition a disk, give the command **parted** followed by the name of the device you want to work with. In the following example, after starting parted, the user gives a **help** (or just **h**) command, which displays a list of parted commands:

```
$ sudo parted /dev/hdb
GNU Parted 1.8.9
Using /dev/hda
Welcome to GNU Parted! Type 'help' to view a list of commands.
(parted) help
  check NUMBER                       do a simple check on the file system
  cp [FROM-DEVICE] FROM-NUMBER TO-NUMBER   copy file system to another partition
  help [COMMAND]                     prints general help, or help on COMMAND
  mklabel LABEL-TYPE                 create a new disklabel (partition table)
  mkfs NUMBER FS-TYPE                make a FS-TYPE file system on partititon NUMBER
  mkpart PART-TYPE [FS-TYPE] START END     make a partition
  mkpartfs PART-TYPE FS-TYPE START END     make a partition with a file system
  move NUMBER START END              move partition NUMBER
  name NUMBER NAME                   name partition NUMBER as NAME
  print [devices|free|list,all|NUMBER]     display the partition table, available ...
  quit                               exit program
  rescue START END                   rescue a lost partition near START and END
  resize NUMBER START END            resize partition NUMBER and its file system
  rm NUMBER                          delete partition NUMBER
  select DEVICE                      choose the device to edit
  set NUMBER FLAG STATE              change a flag on partition NUMBER
  toggle [NUMBER [FLAG]]             toggle the state of FLAG on partition NUMBER
  unit UNIT                          set the default unit to UNIT
  version                  displays the version of GNU Parted and copyright information
(parted)
```

In response to the (**parted**) prompt, you can give the command **help** followed by the name of the command you want more information about. When you give a **print** (or just **p**) command, parted displays current partition information, just as a **print** command on the command line does.

The parted utility will not allow you to set up overlapping partitions (except for logical partitions overlapping their containing extended partition). Similarly, it will not allow you to create a partition that starts at the very beginning of the disk (cylinder 0). Both of these situations can cause loss of data.

Following are guidelines to remember when defining a partition table for a disk. For more information refer to "Partitioning a Disk" on page 36.

- Do not delete or modify the partition that defines the extended partition unless you are willing to lose all data on all the logical partitions within the extended partition.

- If you put **/boot** on a separate partition, it is a good idea to put it at the beginning of the drive (partition 1) so there is no issue of Linux having to boot from a partition located too far into the drive. When you can afford the disk space, it is desirable to put each major filesystem on a separate partition. Many people choose to combine **/** (root), **/var**, and **/usr** into a single partition, which generally results in less wasted space but can, on rare occasions, cause problems.

- Although parted can create some types of filesystems, it is typically easiest to use parted to create partitions and then use mkfs and mkswap to create filesystems on the partitions.

The following sequence of commands defines a 300-megabyte, bootable, Linux partition as partition 1 on a clean disk:

```
$ sudo /sbin/parted /dev/hdb
...
Using /dev/hdb
(parted) mkpart                              (create new partition)
Partition type?  primary/extended? primary   (select primary partition)
File system type?  [ext2]?                   (default to an ext2 filesystem)
Start? 1                                      (start at the beginning of the disk)
End? 300m                                     (specify a 300-megabyte partition)
(parted) help set                            (use help to check the syntax of the set command)
  set NUMBER FLAG STATE       change a flag on partition NUMBER

        NUMBER is the partition number used by Linux.  On msdos disk labels, the primary
        partitions number from 1 to 4, logical partitions from 5 onwards.
        FLAG is one of: boot, root, swap, hidden, raid, lvm, lba, hp-service, palo,
        prep, msftres
        STATE is one of: on, off
(parted) set 1 boot on                       (turn on the boot flag on partition 1)
(parted) print                               (verify that the partition is correct)
Disk geometry for /dev/hdb: 0kB - 250GB
Disk label type: msdos
Number  Start   End     Size    Type      File system  Flags
1       1kB     300MB   300MB   primary   ext2         boot
(parted) quit
Information: Don't forget to update /etc/fstab, if necessary.
```

When you specify a size within parted, you can use a suffix of **k** (kilobytes), **m** (megabytes), or **g** (gigabytes). After creating a partition, give a **print** command to see where the partition ends. Perform this task before defining the next contiguous partition so you do not waste space. After setting up all the partitions, exit from parted with a **quit** command.

Next make a filesystem (mkfs, page 441) on each partition that is to hold a filesystem (not swap). Make all partitions, except swap and **/boot**, of type **ext3**, unless you have a reason to do otherwise. Make the **/boot** partition of type **ext2**. Use mkswap (page 480) to set up a swap area on a partition. You can use e2label (page 441) to label a partition.

KEEPING USERS INFORMED

One of your primary responsibilities as a system administrator is communicating with system users. You need to make announcements, such as when the system will be down for maintenance, when a class on some new software will be held, and how users can access the new system printer. You can even start to fill the role of a small local newspaper, letting users know about new employees, RIFs, births, the company picnic, and so on.

Different communications have different priorities. For example, information about the company picnic in two months is not as time sensitive as the fact that you are bringing the system down in five minutes. To meet these differing needs, Linux provides different ways of communicating. The most common methods are described and contrasted in the following list. All of these methods are generally available to everyone, except for the message of the day, which is typically reserved for a user with **root** privileges.

write   Use the write utility (page 170) to communicate with a user who is logged in on the local system. You might use it, for example, to ask a user to stop running a program that is slowing the system; the user might reply that he will be done in three minutes. Users can also use write to ask the system administrator to mount a tape or restore a file. Messages sent from write may not appear in a graphical environment.

wall   The wall (write all) utility effectively communicates immediately with all users who are logged in. This utility takes its input from standard input and works much like write, except that users cannot use wall to write back to only you. Use wall when you are about to bring the system down or are in another crisis situation. Users who are not logged in will not get the message.

Run wall as a user with **root** privileges *only* in a crisis situation; it interrupts anything anyone is doing. Messages sent from wall may not appear in a graphical environment.

Email   Email is useful for communicating less urgent information to one or more systems and/or remote users. When you send mail, you have to be willing to wait for each user to read it. Email is useful for reminding users that they are forgetting to log out, their bills are past due, or they are using too much disk space.

Users can easily make permanent records of messages they receive via email, as opposed to messages received via write, so they can keep track of important details. For instance, it would be appropriate to use email to inform users about a new, complex procedure, so each user could keep a copy of the information for reference.

Message of the day   Users see the message of the day each time they log in in a textual environment, but not when they open a terminal emulator window. You can edit the **/etc/motd** file to change this message as necessary. The message of the day can alert users to upcoming periodic maintenance, new system features, or a change in procedures.

CREATING PROBLEMS

Even experienced system administrators make mistakes; new system administrators just make more mistakes. Although you can improve your odds of avoiding problems by carefully reading and following the documentation provided with software, many things can still go wrong. A comprehensive list, no matter how long, is not possible because new and exciting ways to create problems are discovered every day. This section describes a few of the more common techniques.

Failing to perform regular backups   Few feelings are more painful to a system administrator than realizing that important information is lost forever. If the local system supports multiple users, having a recent backup may be your only protection from a public lynching. If it is a single-user system, having a recent backup certainly keeps you happier when you lose a hard disk or erase a file by mistake.

Not reading and following instructions   Software developers provide documentation for a reason. Even when you have installed a software package before, carefully read the instructions again. They may have changed, or you may simply remember them incorrectly. Software changes more quickly than books are revised, so no book should be taken as offering foolproof advice. Instead, look for the latest documentation online. The **/usr/share/doc** directory has information on many utilities, libraries, and software packages.

Failing to ask for help when instructions are not clear   If something does not seem to make sense, try to find out what does make sense—do not attempt to guess. See Appendix B for a list of places you may be able to find help.

Deleting or mistyping information in a critical file   One sure way to give yourself nightmares is to execute the command

$ `sudo rm –rf /etc`   ←*do not do this*

Perhaps no other command renders a Linux system useless so quickly. The only recourse is to reboot into recovery mode using an installation CD/DVD (page 429) and restore the missing files from a recent backup. Although this example depicts an extreme case, many files are critical to proper operation of a system. Deleting one of these files or mistyping information in one of them is almost certain to cause problems. If you directly edit **/etc/passwd**, for example, entering the wrong information in a field can make it impossible for one or more users to log in. Do not use **rm –rf** with an argument that includes wildcard characters; do pause after typing the command, and read it before you press RETURN. Check everything you do carefully, and make a copy of a critical file before you edit it.

Be careful when using a wildcard character with rm

caution   When you must use a wildcard character, such as ∗, in an argument to an rm command, first use echo with the same argument to see exactly which files you will be deleting. This check is especially important when you are working with **root** privileges.

Solving Problems

As the system administrator, it is your responsibility to keep the system secure and running smoothly. When a user is having a problem, it usually falls to the administrator to help the user get back on track. This section suggests ways to keep users happy and the system functioning at peak performance.

Helping When a User Cannot Log In

When a user has trouble logging in on the system, the source may be a user error or a problem with the system software or hardware. The following steps can help determine where the problem is:

- Check the log files in **/var/log**. The **/var/log/messages** file accumulates system errors, messages from daemon processes, and other important information. It may indicate the cause or more symptoms of a problem. Also, check the system console. Occasionally messages about system problems that are not written to **/var/log/messages** (for instance, a full disk) are displayed on the system console.

- Determine whether only that one user or only that one user's terminal/workstation has a problem or whether the problem is more widespread.

- Check that the user's CAPS LOCK key is not on.

- Make sure the user's home directory exists and corresponds to that user's entry in the **/etc/passwd** file. Verify that the user owns her home directory and startup files and that they are readable (and, in the case of the user's home directory, executable). Confirm that the entry for the user's login shell in the **/etc/passwd** file is accurate and the shell exists as specified.

- Change the user's password if there is a chance that he has forgotten the correct password.

- Check the user's startup files (**.profile, .login, .bashrc,** and so on). The user may have edited one of these files and introduced a syntax error that prevents login.

- Check the terminal or monitor data cable from where it plugs into the terminal to where it plugs into the computer (or as far as you can follow it). Try turning the terminal or monitor off and then turning it back on.

- When the problem appears to be widespread, check whether you can log in from the system console. Make sure the system is not in recovery mode. If you cannot log in, the system may have crashed; reboot it and perform any necessary recovery steps (the system usually does quite a bit automatically).

- If the user is logging in over a network connection, run the appropriate init script (page 423) to restart the service the user is trying to use (e.g., ssh).

- Use df to check for full filesystems. If the **/tmp** filesystem or the user's home directory is full, login sometimes fails in unexpected ways. In some cases you may be able to log in to a textual environment but not a graphical one. When applications that start when the user logs in cannot create temporary files or cannot update files in the user's home directory, the login process itself may terminate.

SPEEDING UP THE SYSTEM

When the system is running slowly for no apparent reason, perhaps a process did not exit when a user logged out. Symptoms of this problem include poor response time and a system load, as shown by w or uptime, that is greater than 1.0. Running top (page 592) is an excellent way to find rogue processes quickly. Use **ps –ef** to list all processes. One thing to look for in **ps –ef** output is a large number in the **TIME** column. For example, if a Firefox process has a **TIME** field greater than 100.0, this process has likely run amok. However, if the user is doing a lot of Java work and has not logged out for a long time, this value may be normal. Look at the **STIME** field to see when the process was started. If the process has been running for longer than the user has been logged in, it is a good candidate to be killed.

When a user gets stuck and leaves her terminal unattended without notifying anyone, it is convenient to kill (page 438) all processes owned by that user. If the user is running a window system, such as GNOME or KDE on the console, kill the window manager process. Manager processes to look for include **startkde, x-session-manager**, or another process name that ends in **wm**. Usually the window manager is either the first or last thing to be run, and exiting from the window manager logs the user out. If killing the window manager does not work, try killing the X server process. This process is typically listed as **/usr/bin/X** or **/usr/X11R6/bin/X**. If that fails, you can kill all processes owned by a user by giving the command **kill –15 –1** or, equivalently, **kill –TERM –1** *while you are logged in as that user*. Using **–1** (one) in place of the process ID tells kill to send the signal to all processes that are owned by that user. For example, you could give the following command:

```
$ sudo -u zach kill -TERM -1
```

If this does not kill all processes (sometimes TERM does not kill a process), you can use the KILL signal (**–9**). The following line will definitely kill all processes owned by Zach and will not be friendly about it:

```
$ sudo -u zach kill -KILL -1
```

If you do not include **–u zach**, this command brings the system down.

lsof: Finds Open Files

The lsof (list open files) utility displays the names of open files. Its options display only certain processes, only certain file descriptors of a process, or only certain network connections (network connections use file descriptors just as normal files do and lsof can show these as well). Once you have identified a suspect process using ps –ef, give the following command:

```
$ sudo lsof -sp pid
```

Replace *pid* with the process ID of the suspect process; lsof displays a list of file descriptors that process *pid* has open. The –s option displays the sizes of all open files and the –p option allows you to specify the PID number of the process of interest. This size information is helpful in determining whether the process has a very large file open. If it does, contact the owner of the process or, if necessary, kill the process. The –r*n* option redisplays the output of lsof every *n* seconds.

Keeping a Machine Log

A machine log that includes the information shown in Table 16-3 can help you find and fix system problems. Note the time and date for each entry in the log. Avoid the temptation to keep the log *only* on the computer—it will be most useful to you when the system is down. Another good idea is to keep a record of all email dealing with user problems. One strategy is to save this mail to a separate file or folder as you read it. Another approach is to set up a mail alias that users can send mail to when they have problems. This alias can then forward mail to you and also store a copy in an archive file. Following is an example of an entry in the **/etc/aliases** file (page 686) that sets up this type of alias:

```
trouble: admin,/var/mail/admin.archive
```

Email sent to the **trouble** alias will be forwarded to the **admin** user as well as stored in the file **/var/mail/admin.archive**.

Table 16-3 Machine log

Entry	Function
Hardware modifications	Keep track of the system hardware configuration: which devices hold which partitions, the model of the new NIC you added, and so on.
System software modifications	Keep track of the options used when building Linux. Print such files as **/usr/src/linux/.config** (Linux kernel configuration). The file hierarchy under **/etc/default** contains valuable information about the network configuration, among other things.
Hardware malfunctions	Keep as accurate a list as possible of any problems with the system. Make note of any error messages or numbers that the system displays on the system console and identify what users were doing when the problem occurred.
User complaints	Make a list of all reasonable complaints made by knowledgeable users (for example, "Machine is abnormally slow").

KEEPING THE SYSTEM SECURE

No system with dial-in lines or public access to terminals is absolutely secure. Nevertheless, you can make a system as secure as possible by changing the passwords of users who are members of the **admin** group (these users can use sudo to gain **root** privileges) and the **root** password (if there is one) frequently and by choosing passwords that are difficult to guess. Do not tell anyone who does not *absolutely* need to know any of these passwords. You can also encourage system users to choose difficult passwords and to change them periodically.

Passwords   By default, passwords on Ubuntu Linux use *MD5* (page 1119) hashing, which makes them more difficult to break than passwords encrypted with DES (page 1066). Of course, it makes little difference how well encrypted your password is if you make it easy for someone to find out or guess what the password is.

A password that is difficult to guess is one that someone else would not be likely to think you would have chosen. Do not use words from the dictionary (spelled forward or backward); names of relatives, pets, or friends; or words from a foreign language. A good strategy is to choose a couple of short words, include some punctuation (for example, put a ^ between them), mix the case, and replace some of the letters in the words with numbers. If it were not printed in this book, an example of a good password would be **C&yGram5** (candygrams). Ideally you would use a random combination of ASCII characters, but that would be difficult to remember.

You can use one of several password-cracking programs to find users who have chosen poor passwords. These programs work by repeatedly hashing words from dictionaries, phrases, names, and other sources. If the hashed password matches the output of the program, then the program has found the password of the user. One program that cracks passwords is crack (part of the **crack** software package). It and many other programs and security tips are available from CERT (www.cert.org), which was originally called the Computer Emergency Response Team. Specifically, look at www.cert.org/tech_tips.

Setuid files   Make sure no one except a user with **root** privileges can write to files containing programs that are owned by **root** and run in setuid mode (for example, passwd and sudo). Also make sure users do not transfer programs that run in setuid mode and are owned by **root** onto the system by means of mounting tapes or disks. These programs can be used to circumvent system security. One technique that prevents users from having setuid files is to use the **–nosuid** flag to mount, which you can set in the flags section in the **fstab** file. Refer to "fstab: Keeps Track of Filesystems" on page 492.

BIOS   The BIOS in many machines gives you some degree of protection from an unauthorized person who tries to modify the BIOS or reboot the system. When you set up the BIOS, look for a section named **Security**. You can probably add a BIOS password. If you depend on the BIOS password, lock the computer case—it is usually a simple matter to reset the BIOS password by using a jumper on the motherboard.

LOG FILES AND MAIL FOR root

Users frequently email **root** and **postmaster** to communicate with the system administrator. If you do not forward **root**'s mail to yourself (**/etc/aliases** on page 686), remember to check **root**'s mail periodically. You will not receive reminders about mail that arrives for **root** when you use sudo to perform system administration tasks. However, you can give the command **sudo mail –u root** to look at **root**'s mail.

Review the system log files regularly for evidence of problems. Some important files are **/var/log/messages**, where the operating system and some applications record errors; **/var/log/mail.err** (or **/var/log/exim4/mainlog** if you are running **exim4**), which contains errors from the mail system; and **/var/log/syslog**, which contains messages from the system, including messages from **cron**.

MONITORING DISK USAGE

Sooner or later you will probably start to run out of disk space. Do not fill up a partition; Linux can write to files significantly faster if at least 5 to 30 percent of the space in a partition remains free. Using more than the maximum optimal disk space in a partition can degrade system performance.

Fragmentation   As a filesystem becomes full, it can become fragmented. This is similar to the DOS concept of fragmentation but is not nearly as pronounced and is typically rare on modern Linux filesystems; by design Linux filesystems are resistant to fragmentation. If you keep filesystems from running near full capacity, you may never need to worry about fragmentation. If there is no space on a filesystem, you cannot write to it at all.

To check for filesystem fragmentation, unmount the filesystem and run fsck (page 494) (with the –f option on **ext2** and **ext3** filesystems) on it. The output of fsck includes a percent fragmentation figure for the filesystem. You can defragment a filesystem by backing it up; using mkfs (page 441) to make a clean, empty image; and then restoring the filesystem. Which utility you use to perform the backup and restore—dump/restore, tar, cpio, or a third-party backup program—is not important.

Reports   Linux provides several programs that report on who is using how much disk space on which filesystems. Refer to the du, quota, and df man pages and the –size option in the find utility man page. In addition to these utilities, you can use the disk quota system (page 607) to manage disk space.

Four strategies to increase the amount of free space on a filesystem are to compress files, delete files, grow LVM-based filesystems, and condense directories. This section contains some ideas on ways to maintain a filesystem so that it does not become overloaded.

Files that grow quickly   Some files, such as log files and temporary files, inevitably grow over time. Core dump files, for example, take up substantial space and are rarely needed. Also, users occasionally run programs that accidentally generate huge files. As the system administrator, you must review these files periodically so they do not get out of hand.

If a filesystem is running out of space quickly (that is, over a period of an hour rather than weeks or months), first figure out why it is running out of space. Use a **ps –ef** command to determine whether a user has created a runaway process that is creating a huge file. When evaluating the output of ps, look for a process that has consumed a large amount of CPU time. If such a process is running and creating a large file, the file will continue to grow as you free up space. If you remove the huge file, the space it occupied will not be freed until the process terminates, so you need to kill the process. Try to contact the user running the process, and ask the user to kill it. If you cannot contact the user, use sudo to kill the process yourself. Refer to kill on page 438 for more information.

You can also truncate a large log file rather than removing it, although you can better deal with this recurring situation with logrotate (discussed next). For example, if the **/var/log/messages** file has become very large because a system daemon is misconfigured, you can use **/dev/null** to truncate it:

```
$ sudo cp /dev/null /var/log/messages
```

or

```
$ sudo cat /dev/null > /var/log/messages
```

or, without spawning a new process,

```
$ sudo : > /var/log/messages
```

If you remove **/var/log/messages**, you have to restart the **syslogd** daemon. If you do not restart **syslogd**, the space on the filesystem will not be released.

When no single process is consuming the disk space but capacity has instead been used up gradually, locate unneeded files and delete them. You can archive these files by using cpio, dump, or tar before you delete them. You can safely remove most files named **core** that have not been accessed for several days. The following command line performs this function without removing necessary files named **core** (such as **/dev/core**):

```
$ sudo find / -type f -name core | xargs file | grep 'B core file' | sed 's/:ELF.*//g' | xargs rm -f
```

The find command lists all ordinary files named **core** and sends its output to xargs, which runs file on each of the files in the list. The file utility displays a string that includes **B core file** for files created as the result of a core dump. These files need to be removed. The grep command filters out from file any lines that do not contain this string. Finally sed removes everything following the colon so that all that is left on the line is the pathname of the **core** file; xargs then removes the file.

To free up more disk space, look through the **/tmp** and **/var/tmp** directories for old temporary files and remove them. Keep track of disk usage in **/var/mail**, **/var/spool**, and **/var/log**.

logrotate: MANAGES LOG FILES

Rather than deleting or truncating log files, you may want to keep these files for a while in case you need to refer to them. The logrotate utility manages system log (and other) files automatically by *rotating* (page 1130), compressing, mailing, and removing each file as you specify. The logrotate utility is controlled by the **/etc/logrotate.conf** file, which sets default values and can optionally specify files to be rotated. Typically **logrotate.conf** has an **include** statement that points to utility-specific specification files in **/etc/logrotate.d**. Following is the default **logrotate.conf** file:

```
$ cat /etc/logrotate.conf
# see "man logrotate" for details
# rotate log files weekly
weekly

# keep 4 weeks worth of backlogs
rotate 4

# create new (empty) log files after rotating old ones
create

# uncomment this if you want your log files compressed
#compress

# packages drop log rotation information into this directory
include /etc/logrotate.d

# no packages own wtmp -- we'll rotate them here
/var/log/wtmp {
    missingok
    monthly
    create 0664 root utmp
    rotate 1
}

/var/log/btmp {
    missingok
    monthly
    create 0664 root utmp
    rotate 1
}

# system-specific logs may be also be configured here.
```

The **logrotate.conf** file sets default values for common parameters. Whenever logrotate reads another value for one of these parameters, it resets the default value. You have a choice of rotating files **daily, weekly,** or **monthly.** The number following the **rotate** keyword specifies the number of rotated log files you want to keep. The **create** keyword causes logrotate to create a new log file with the same name and attributes as the newly rotated log file. The **compress** keyword (commented out in the default file) causes log files to be compressed using gzip. The **include** keyword specifies the standard **/etc/logrotate.d** directory for program-specific logrotate specification files. When you install a program using dpkg (page 514) or a dpkg-based utility such as aptitude (page 508), the installation script puts the logrotate specification file in this directory.

The last sets of instructions in **logrotate.conf** take care of the **/var/log/wtmp** and **/var/log/btmp** log files (**wtmp** holds login records; you can view this file with the command **who /var/log/wtmp**). The keyword **missingok** overrides the implicit default value of **nomissingok** *for this utility only* (because the value is within brackets). This keyword causes logrotate to continue without issuing an error message if the log file is missing. The keyword **monthly** overrides the default value of **weekly**. The **create** keyword is followed by the arguments establishing the permissions, owner, and group for the new file. Finally **rotate** establishes that one rotated log file should be kept.

The **/etc/logrotate.d/cups** file is an example of a utility-specific logrotate specification file:

```
$ cat cups
/var/log/cups/*log {
        daily
        missingok
        rotate 7
        sharedscripts
        postrotate
                if [ -e /var/run/cups/cupsd.pid ]; then
                        invoke-rc.d --quiet cupsys force-reload > /dev/null
                        sleep 10
                fi
        endscript
        compress
        notifempty
        create 640 root lpadmin
}
```

This file, which is installed by the **cupsys** package install script and incorporated in **/etc/logrotate.d** because of the **include** statement in **logrotate.conf**, works with each of the files in **/var/log/cups** that has a filename ending in **log** (*log). The **sharedscripts** keyword causes logrotate to execute the command(s) in the **prerotate** and **postrotate** sections one time only—not one time for each log that is rotated. Although it does not appear in this example, the **copytruncate** keyword causes logrotate to truncate the original log file immediately after it copies it. This keyword is useful for programs that cannot be instructed to close and reopen their log files because they might continue writing to the original file even after it has been moved. The logrotate utility executes the commands between **prerotate** and **endscript** before the rotation begins. Similarly, commands between **postrotate** and **endscript** are executed after the rotation is complete. The **notifempty** keyword causes logrotate not to rotate the log file if it is empty, overriding the default action of rotating empty log files.

The logrotate utility works with a variety of keywords, many of which take arguments and have side effects. Refer to the logrotate man page for details.

REMOVING UNUSED SPACE FROM DIRECTORIES

A directory that contains too many filenames is inefficient. The point at which a directory on an **ext2** or **ext3** filesystem becomes inefficient varies, depending partly on the length of the filenames it contains. Best practice is to keep directories relatively small. Having fewer than several hundred files (or directories) in a directory is generally a good idea, and having more than several thousand is generally a bad idea. Additionally, Linux uses a caching mechanism for frequently accessed files that speeds the process of locating an inode from a filename. This caching mechanism works only on filenames of up to 30 characters in length, so avoid giving frequently accessed files extremely long filenames.

When a directory becomes too large, you can usually break it into several smaller directories by moving its contents to those new directories. Make sure you remove the original directory once you have moved all of its contents.

Because Linux directories do not shrink automatically, removing a file from a directory does not shrink the directory, even though it frees up space on the disk. To remove unused space and make a directory smaller, you must copy or move all the files to a new directory *and* remove the original directory.

The following procedure removes unused directory space. First remove all unneeded files from the large directory. Then create a new, empty directory. Next move or copy all remaining files from the old large directory to the new empty directory. Remember to copy hidden files. Finally delete the old directory and rename the new directory.

```
$ sudo mkdir /home/max/new
$ sudo mv /home/max/large/* /home/max/large/.[A-z]* /home/max/new
$ sudo rmdir /home/max/large
$ sudo mv /home/max/new /home/max/large
```

optional
DISK QUOTA SYSTEM

The disk quota system (supplied by the **quota** software package) limits the disk space and number of files owned by individual users. You can choose to limit each user's disk space, the number of files each user can own, or both. Each resource that is limited has two limits: a lower limit and an upper limit. The user can exceed the lower limit, or *quota*, although a warning is given each time the user logs in when he is above the quota. After a certain number of warnings (set by the system administrator), the system behaves as if the user had reached the upper limit. Once the upper limit is reached or the user has received the specified number of warnings, the user will not be allowed to create any more files or use any more disk space. The user's only recourse at that point is to remove some files.

Users can review their usage and limits with the quota utility. Using sudo, you can use quota to obtain information about any user.

First you must decide which filesystems to limit and how to allocate space among users. Typically only filesystems that contain users' home directories, such as **/home**, are limited. Use the edquota utility to set the quotas, and then use quotaon to start the quota system. Unmounting a filesystem automatically disables the quota system for that filesystem.

syslogd: LOGS SYSTEM MESSAGES

Traditionally UNIX programs sent log messages to standard error. If a more permanent log was required, the output was redirected to a file. Because of the limitations of this approach, 4.3BSD introduced the system log daemon (syslogd) now used by Linux. This daemon listens for log messages and stores them in the /var/log hierarchy. In addition to providing logging facilities, syslogd allows a single machine to serve as a log repository for a network and allows arbitrary programs to process specific log messages.

syslog.conf   The /etc/syslog.conf file stores configuration information for syslogd. Each line in this file contains one or more *selectors* and an *action*, separated by whitespace. The selectors define the origin and type of the messages; the action specifies how syslogd processes the message. Sample lines from syslog.conf follow (a # indicates a comment):

```
# First some standard logfiles.  Log by facility.
kern.*                          -/var/log/kern.log
lpr.*                           -/var/log/lpr.log
mail.*                          -/var/log/mail.log
#
# Some 'catch-all' logfiles.
*.=debug;\
        auth,authpriv.none;\
        news.none;mail.none     -/var/log/debug
*.=info;*.=notice;*.=warning;\
        auth,authpriv.none;\
        cron,daemon.none;\
        mail,news.none          -/var/log/messages
#
# Emergencies are sent to everybody logged in.
*.emerg                                 *
```

Selectors   A selector is split into two parts, a *facility* and a *priority*, which are separated by a period. The facility indicates the origin of the message. For example, kern messages come from the kernel and mail messages come from the mail subsystem. Following is a list of facility names used by syslogd and the systems that generate these messages:

Facilities
auth	Authorization and security systems including login
authpriv	Same as **auth**, but should be logged to a secure location
cron	cron
daemon	System and network daemons without their own categories
kern	Kernel
lpr	Printing subsystem
mail	Mail subsystem
news	Network news subsystem
user	Default facility; all user programs use this facility
uucp	The UNIX-to-UNIX copy protocol subsystem
local0 to **local7**	Reserved for local use

The priority indicates the severity of the message. The following list of the priority names and the conditions they represent appears in priority order:

Priorities	**debug**	Debugging information
	info	Information that does not require intervention
	notice	Conditions that may require intervention
	warning	Warnings
	err	Errors
	crit	Critical conditions such as hardware failures
	alert	Conditions that require immediate attention
	emerg	Emergency conditions

A selector consisting of a single facility and priority, such as **kern.info**, causes the corresponding action to be applied to every message from that facility with that priority *or higher* (more urgent). Use **.=** to specify a single priority; for example, **kern.=info** applies the action to kernel messages of **info** priority. An exclamation point specifies that a priority is not matched. Thus **kern.!info** matches kernel messages with a priority lower than **info** and **kern.!=info** matches kernel messages with a priority other than **info**.

A line with multiple selectors, separated by semicolons, applies the action if any of the selectors is matched. Each of the selectors on a line with multiple selectors constrains the match, with subsequent selectors frequently tightening the constraints. For example, the selectors **mail.info;mail.!err** match mail subsystem messages with **debug**, **info**, **notice**, or **warning** priorities.

You can replace either part of the selector with an asterisk to match anything. The keyword **none** in either part of the selector indicates no match is possible. The selector ***.crit;kern.none** matches all critical or higher-priority messages, except those from the kernel.

Actions   The action specifies how **syslogd** processes a message that matches the selector. The simplest actions are ordinary files, which are specified by their absolute pathnames; **syslogd** appends messages to these files. Specify **/dev/console** to send messages to the system console. If you want a hardcopy record of messages, specify a device file that represents a dedicated printer. Precede a filename with a hyphen (–) to keep **syslogd** from writing each message to the file as it is generated (syncing). Doing so may improve performance, but you may lose data if the system crashes after the message is generated but before it gets written to a file.

You can write important messages to users' terminals by specifying one or more usernames separated by commas. Very important messages can be written to every logged-in terminal by using an asterisk.

To forward messages to **syslogd** on a remote system, specify the name of the system preceded by @. It is a good idea to forward critical messages from the kernel to another system because these messages often precede a system crash and may not be saved to the local disk. The following line from **syslog.conf** sends critical kernel messages to **plum**:

```
kern.crit      @plum
```

Because **syslogd** is not configured by default to enable logging over the network, you must edit the **/etc/default/syslogd** file on the remote system (**plum** in this case) so that **syslogd** is started with the **–r** option. After you modify the **syslog.conf** file, restart **syslogd** using the **sysklogd** init script.

Chapter Summary

The users-admin utility adds new users and groups to the system and modifies existing users' accounts. You can also use the equivalent command-line tools (useradd, usermod, userdel, groupadd, and groupmod) to work with user accounts.

Backing up files on the system is a critical but often-overlooked part of system administration. Linux includes the tar, cpio, dump, and restore utilities to back up and restore files. You can also use more sophisticated packages such as amanda and various commercial products.

The system scheduling daemon, **cron**, periodically executes scheduled tasks. You can schedule tasks using crontab and at.

System reports present information on the health of the system. Two useful tools that generate these reports are vmstat, which details virtual memory, I/O, and CPU usage, and top, which reports on how the system is performing from moment to moment and can help you figure out what might be slowing it down.

Another aspect of system administration is solving problems. Linux includes several tools that can help track down system problems. One of the most important of these tools is **syslogd**, the system log daemon. Using **/etc/syslogd.conf**, you can control which error messages appear on the console, which are sent as email, and which go to one of several log files.

Exercises

1. How would you list all the processes running vi?

2. How would you use kill to cause a server process to reread its configuration files?

3. From the command line, how would you create a user named John Doe who has the username **jd** and who belongs to group 65535?

4. How would you notify users that you are going to reboot the system in ten minutes?

5. Give a command that creates a level 0 dump of the **/usr** filesystem on the first tape device on the system. Which command would you use to take advantage of a drive that supports compression? Which command would place a level 3 dump of the **/var** filesystem immediately after the level 0 dump on the tape?

ADVANCED EXERCISES

6. If the system is less responsive than normal, what is a good first step in figuring out where the problem is?

7. A process stores its PID number in a file named **process.pid**. Write a command line that terminates this process.

8. Working with **root** privileges, you are planning to delete some files but want to make sure that the wildcard expression you use is correct. Suggest two ways you could make sure you delete the correct files.

9. Create a crontab file that will regularly perform the following backups:

   a. Perform a level 0 backup once per month.

   b. Perform a level 2 dump one day per week.

   c. Perform a level 5 dump every day on which neither a level 0 nor a level 2 dump is performed.

   In the worst-case scenario, how many restore commands would you have to give to recover a file that was dumped using this schedule?

17

Configuring a LAN

Networks allow computers to communicate and share resources. A local area network (LAN) connects computers at one site, such as an office, home, or library, and can allow the connected computers to share an Internet connection, files, and a printer. Of course, one of the most important reasons to set up a LAN is to allow systems to communicate while users enjoy multiplayer games.

This chapter covers the two aspects of configuring a LAN: setting up the hardware and configuring the software. It is not necessarily organized in the order you will perform the tasks involved in setting up a particular LAN. Instead, read the chapter through, figure out how you will set up your LAN, and then read the parts of the chapter in the order appropriate to your setup.

SETTING UP THE HARDWARE

Each system, or *node,* on a LAN must have a network interface card (NIC). Each system must connect to a central hub or switch. If the LAN is connected to another network, such as the Internet, it must also have a router.

CONNECTING THE COMPUTERS

Computers are connected to a network using cables (wired; page 359) or radio waves (wireless or Wi-Fi, page 360). The cables can connect to a variety of devices, some of which are described in this section. See "LAN: Local Area Network" on page 359 for an explanation of cables and definitions of *hub, switch,* and *router.*

In the simple network shown in Figure 17-1, four computers are connected to a single hub or switch. Assume computers 1 and 2 are communicating at the same time as computers 3 and 4. With a hub (page 359), each conversation is limited to a maximum of half the network bandwidth. With a switch (page 359), each conversation can theoretically use the full network bandwidth.

Hubs are usually less expensive than switches, although switches are getting cheaper all the time and hubs are becoming less available. If you plan to use the network for sharing an Internet connection and light file sharing, a hub is likely to be fast enough. If systems on the network will exchange files regularly, a switch may be a better choice.

Wireless access point (WAP)   A wireless access point (WAP) connects a wireless network to a wired one. Typically a WAP acts as a transparent bridge, forwarding packets between the two networks as if they were one. If you connect multiple WAPs in different locations to the same wired network, wireless clients can roam transparently between the WAPs.

Wireless networks do not require a hub or switch, although a WAP can optionally fill the role of a hub. In a wireless network, the bandwidth is shared among all nodes within range of one another; the maximum speed is limited by the slowest node.

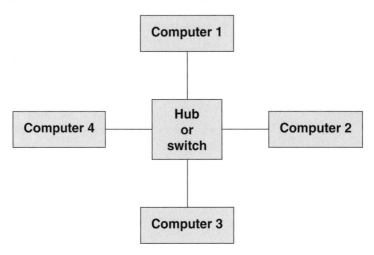

Figure 17-1   A simple network

ROUTERS

A router (page 361) connects a LAN to another network, such as the Internet. A router can perform several functions, the most common of which is allowing several systems to share a single Internet connection and IP address (NAT, page 837). When a router uses NAT, the packets from each system on the LAN appear to come from a single IP address; the router passes return packets to the correct system. A router can also act as a firewall.

You have several choices for routers:

- A simple hardware router is relatively cheap and does most of the things required by a small network.

- You can set up an Ubuntu Linux system as a router. The Linux kernel can use firestarter (page 824) or iptables (page 836) to implement a firewall to help protect a system.

- You can use a Linux distribution tailored for use as a router. For example, SmoothWall (www.smoothwall.org) provides a browser-based configuration in the style of a hardware router.

NIC: NETWORK INTERFACE CARD

Each system's NIC may be a separate Ethernet card (wired or wireless) or it may be built into the motherboard.

Supported NICs Linux supports most wired and many wireless Ethernet NICs.

Unsupported wireless NICs If a wireless network card is not supported under Linux directly, you may be able to get it to work with NdisWrapper (sourceforge.net/projects/ndiswrapper; **ndiswrapper-common, ndiswrapper-utils-1.9,** and **ndisgtk** packages), which uses Win32 drivers. NdisWrapper is a kernel module that provides a subset of the Windows network driver API. See help.ubuntu.com/community/WifiDocs/Driver/Ndiswrapper for instructions on installing a Windows driver.

Wireless bridge An alternative to a wireless NIC is a wireless bridge. A wireless bridge forwards packets between wired and wireless interfaces, eliminating the need for wireless drivers. This simple device has an Ethernet port that plugs into a NIC and an 802.11 (wireless) controller. While carrying a bridge around is usually not feasible for mobile users, a wireless bridge is an easy way to migrate a desktop computer to a wireless configuration.

Ad hoc and infrastructure modes Wireless networks operate in either ad hoc or infrastructure mode. In ad hoc mode, individual nodes in the network communicate directly with each other. In infrastructure mode, nodes communicate via a WAP (page 614). Infrastructure mode is generally more reliable if the wireless LAN must communicate with a wired LAN.

If you do not want to use a WAP, it may be possible to set up a WLAN card so it acts as a WAP. Consult the NIC/driver documentation for more information.

TOOLS

This section describes two of the tools you can use to examine system hardware.

lspci: LISTS PCI INFORMATION

The lspci utility lists PCI device information:

```
$ lspci
00:00.0 Host bridge: nVidia Corporation nForce2 AGP (different version?) (rev c1)
00:00.1 RAM memory: nVidia Corporation nForce2 Memory Controller 1 (rev c1)
00:00.2 RAM memory: nVidia Corporation nForce2 Memory Controller 4 (rev c1)
00:00.3 RAM memory: nVidia Corporation nForce2 Memory Controller 3 (rev c1)
00:00.4 RAM memory: nVidia Corporation nForce2 Memory Controller 2 (rev c1)
00:00.5 RAM memory: nVidia Corporation nForce2 Memory Controller 5 (rev c1)
00:01.0 ISA bridge: nVidia Corporation nForce2 ISA Bridge (rev a4)
00:01.1 SMBus: nVidia Corporation nForce2 SMBus (MCP) (rev a2)
00:02.0 USB Controller: nVidia Corporation nForce2 USB Controller (rev a4)
...
```

With the **–v** option, lspci is more verbose. You can use the **–vv** option to display
even more information.

```
$ lspci -v
00:00.0 Host bridge: nVidia Corporation nForce2 AGP (different version?) (rev c1)
        Subsystem: ABIT Computer Corp. Unknown device 1c00
        Flags: bus master, 66MHz, fast devsel, latency 0
        Memory at e0000000 (32-bit, prefetchable) [size=64M]
        Capabilities: <access denied>

00:00.1 RAM memory: nVidia Corporation nForce2 Memory Controller 1 (rev c1)
        Subsystem: nVidia Corporation Unknown device 0c17
        Flags: 66MHz, fast devsel

00:00.2 RAM memory: nVidia Corporation nForce2 Memory Controller 4 (rev c1)
        Subsystem: nVidia Corporation Unknown device 0c17
        Flags: 66MHz, fast devsel
...
```

lshw: LISTS HARDWARE INFORMATION

The lshw utility lists information about the hardware configuration of the local system. Run this utility with **root** privileges to display a more detailed report. The
–short option displays a brief report. Without this option lshw displays much more
information.

```
$ sudo lshw -short
H/W path         Device       Class      Description
====================================================
                              system     Desktop Computer
/0                            bus        NF7-S/NF7 (nVidia-nForce2)
/0/0                          memory     128KB BIOS
/0/4                          processor  AMD Athlon(tm) XP 2600+
/0/4/9                        memory     128KB L1 cache
/0/4/a                        memory     512KB L2 cache
/0/1b                         memory     1GB System Memory
/0/1b/0                       memory     DIMM [empty]
...
/0/100/9/0/0     /dev/hda     disk       149GB WDC WD1600JB-00GVA0
/0/100/9/0/0/1   /dev/hda1    volume     74GB Linux filesystem partition
```

```
/0/100/9/0/0/2   /dev/hda2   volume    3812MB Linux swap / Solaris partition
/0/100/9/0/1     /dev/hdb    disk      CR-48XGTE
/0/100/1e                    bridge    nForce2 AGP
/0/100/1e/0                  display   NV17 [GeForce4 MX 420]
```

You can also use lshal to display hardware information. This utility displays a report based on the HAL (hardware abstraction layer) device database. See www.freedesktop.org/wiki/Software/hal.

CONFIGURING THE SYSTEMS

Once the hardware is in place, you need to configure each system so it knows about the NIC that connects it to the network. Normally Ubuntu detects and configures new hardware automatically when you install Ubuntu or the first time you boot the system after you install a NIC.

You can use network-admin (discussed in the next section) to augment the information Ubuntu collects and to activate the NIC.

System information   In addition to information about the NIC, each system needs the following data:

- The system's IP address
- The netmask (subnet mask) for the system's address (page 445)
- The IP address of the gateway (page 615)
- The IP addresses of the nameservers (DNS addresses—specify two or three)
- The system's hostname (set when you install Ubuntu Linux)

If you set up a DHCP server (page 454) to distribute network configuration information to systems on the LAN, you do not need to specify the preceding information on each system. Instead, you just specify that the system is using DHCP to obtain this information (which Ubuntu does by default). You must specify this information when you set up the DHCP server.

Private address space   When you set up a LAN, the IP addresses of the systems on the LAN are generally not made public on the Internet. Special IP addresses, which are part of the *private address space* defined by *IANA* (page 1113), are reserved for private use and are appropriate to use on a LAN (Table 17-1). Unless you have been assigned IP addresses for the systems on the LAN, choose addresses from the private address space.

Table 17-1   Private IP ranges (defined in RFC 1918)

Range of IP addresses	From IP address	To IP address
10.0.0.0/8	10.0.0.1	10.255.255.254
172.16.0.0/12	172.16.0.1	172.31.255.254
192.168.0.0/16	192.168.0.1	192.168.255.254

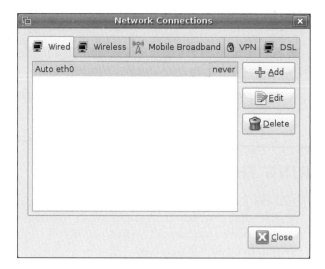

Figure 17-2   The Network Connections window

nm-connection-editor: CONFIGURES NETWORK CONNECTIONS

The Network Connections window (Figure 17-2) enables you to modify the configuration of the NICs (wired or wireless). To display this window, right-click the nm-applet icon (Figure 17-4, page 619) near the right end of the Top panel and select **Edit Connections** or give the command **nm-connection-editor** from a terminal emulator or Run Application window (ALT-F2).

The Network Connections window has tabs to configure wired, wireless, and other types of network connections. After Ubuntu identifies and configures new network hardware, you can use nm-connection-editor to modify the configuration.

To modify the configuration of a NIC, select the appropriate tab, highlight the description of the connection you want to configure, and click **Edit**; nm-connection-editor displays the Editing window (Figure 17-3). The IPv4 Settings tab allows you to select DHCP or manual configuration of the connection. When you are finished working in the Editing window, click **OK**.

Wireless settings   It is usually easier to configure a wireless connection using the nm-applet (next section). To use the Editing window to configure wireless settings, click the Wireless tab and enter the appropriate information. When you are finished entering information in the Network Connections window, click **Close**.

nm-applet: CONFIGURES NETWORK CONNECTIONS AUTOMATICALLY

The nm-applet (network manager applet) object appears toward the right end of the Top panel. Its icon appears as a double monitor when the system is using a wired connection and as a series of vertical bars when the system is using a wireless connection

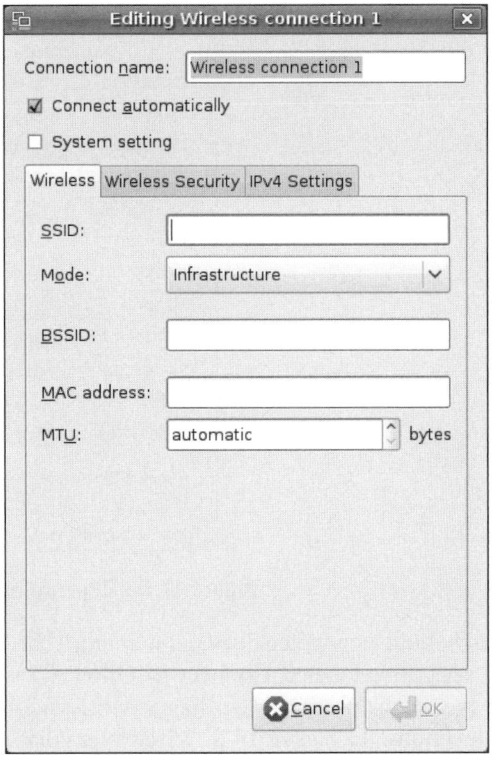

Figure 17-3   The Editing window (wireless connection)

(Figure 17-4). This applet works in conjunction with nm-connection-editor. Exactly what clicking nm-applet displays depends on system hardware and what is set up in nm-connection-editor.

Right-click nm-applet to display a menu that allows you to turn on/off networking and, if available, wireless (networking). Click either selection to place or remove a tick next to the entry. A tick indicates the service is enabled. You can also select Connection Information to display a window showing information about the active connection. Selecting Edit Connections runs nm-connection-editor (page 618) which opens the Network Connections window.

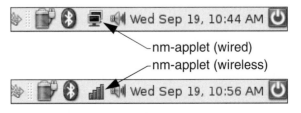

Figure 17-4   The nm-applet

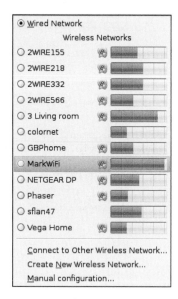

Figure 17-5   The nm-applet window

Left-clicking nm-applet displays a menu that lists the available wireless networks and selections labeled **Connect to Other Wireless Network** and **Create New Wireless Network** (if the system has a wireless connection), **Wired Network**, and **VPN Connections**. In Figure 17-5 Wired Network is selected (the adjacent radio button has a dot in it), meaning that the system is using a wired connection and is not using a wireless connection.

Click one of the wireless networks to disable the wired connection and connect to the selected wireless network. Alternatively, if the system is connected to a wireless network, click **Wired Network** to connect to the wired network. The nm-applet changes to two dots with a tail going around them in circles while it connects to the new network. It then displays the wireless or wired object, as is appropriate (Figure 17-4). Clicking **Manual Configuration** displays the Network Connections window (discussed in the previous section).

iwconfig: Configures a Wireless NIC

You can configure a wireless NIC using either nm-connection-editor, nm-applet, or iwconfig. As a last resort, you can use NdisWrapper to install a Windows driver under Ubuntu (see help.ubuntu.com/community/WifiDocs/Driver/Ndiswrapper). The iwconfig utility is based on ifconfig and configures elements of a wireless NIC not supported by ifconfig, such as setting up Master mode and binding a card to a WAP.

When you call iwconfig without any arguments, it reports on the status of the wireless interfaces:

```
$ iwconfig
lo          no wireless extensions.

eth0        no wireless extensions.

eth1    unassociated   ESSID:off/any
        Mode:Managed   Frequency=nan kHz   Access Point: Not-Associated
        Bit Rate:0 kb/s    Tx-Power:16 dBm
        Retry limit:15   RTS thr:off   Fragment thr:off
        Power Management:off
        Link Quality:0  Signal level:0  Noise level:0
        Rx invalid nwid:0  Rx invalid crypt:0  Rx invalid frag:0
        Tx excessive retries:0  Invalid misc:55   Missed beacon:0
```

The most common parameters you will change with iwconfig are the encryption key, the mode, and the name of the network. Most devices support a minimum of 40-bit Wired Equivalent Privacy (WEP) encryption. The encryption key is defined by a string of 10 hexadecimal digits. The contents of the string is arbitrary, but must be the same on all nodes:

```
$ sudo iwconfig eth1 key 19FEB47A5B
```

The algorithm used by WEP is known to be flawed; using it does not give much protection. If you require privacy, use an encrypted protocol, such as SSH or HTTPS. If you have difficulty connecting, disable encryption on all nodes:

```
$ sudo iwconfig eth1 key off
```

The **mode** defines whether you are connecting to an ad hoc or infrastructure network. Normally you can set **mode** to **Auto**, which selects the correct mode automatically:

```
$ sudo iwconfig eth1 mode Auto
```

The exception is if you want to use the NIC as a WAP, in which case you need to set **mode** to **Master**:

```
$ sudo iwconfig eth1 mode Master
```

Not all wireless NICs are capable of acting as masters.

The network name is defined by the ESSID (Extended Service Set ID), an arbitrary string. With the ESSID set (it must be the same on every node, including the WAP), you should be able to roam between any set of nodes with the same network name:

```
$ sudo iwconfig eth1 essid "My Wireless Network"
```

See the iwconfig man page for more information.

SETTING UP SERVERS

Setting up local clients and servers can make a LAN both easier to use and more useful. The following list briefly describes some of these tools and references the pages that describe them in detail.

Firewall Although not a server, a firewall—which is typically installed on the router—is an important part of a LAN. See firestarter (page 824) or iptables (page 836) for more information.

NIS NIS can provide a uniform login regardless of which system you log in on. The NIS authentication server is covered on page 714 and the client on page 708. NIS is often combined with home directories that are mounted using NFS.

NFS NFS allows you to share directory hierarchies. Sharing directories using NFS requires that the server export the directory hierarchy (page 749) and that clients mount the hierarchy (page 741).

Using NFS, you can store all home directories on one system and mount them from other systems as needed. This configuration works well with NIS login authentication. With this setup, it can be convenient to create a world-writable directory—for example, **/home/shared**—which users can use to exchange files. If you set the sticky bit (page 1134) on this directory (**chmod 1777 /home/shared**), users can delete only files they created. If you do not set the sticky bit, any user can delete any file.

OpenSSH OpenSSH tools include ssh (logs in on a remote system; page 634) and scp (copies files to and from a remote system; page 636). You can also set up automatic logins with OpenSSH: If you set up a shared home directory with NFS, each user's **~/.ssh** directory (page 630) is the same on each system; a user who sets up a personal authentication key (page 641) will be able to use OpenSSH tools between systems without entering a password. See page 641 for information on how to set up an OpenSSH server. You can just use the ssh and scp clients—you do not have to set them up.

DNS cache Setting up a local cache can reduce the traffic between the LAN and the Internet and can improve response times. For more information refer to "JumpStart: Setting Up a DNS Cache" on page 796.

DHCP DHCP enables a client system to retrieve network configuration information from a server each time it connects to a network. See page 454 for more information.

LDAP LDAP is a database server that can hold names and addresses, authentication information, and other types of data. See page 722 for more information.

Samba Samba allows Linux systems to participate in a Windows network, sharing directories and printers, and accessing those directories and printers shared by Windows systems. Samba includes a special share for accessing users' home directories. For more information refer to "The [homes] Share: Sharing Users' Home Directories" on page 776.

You can also use Samba to set up a shared directory similar to the one described under "NFS." To share a Linux directory with Windows computers, the value of **Workgroup** in **/etc/samba/smb.conf** must be the same as the Windows workgroup (frequently MSHOME or WORKGROUP by default). Place the following code in **smb.conf** (page 770):

```
[public]
    comment = Public file space
    path = /home/shared
    read only = no
    public = yes
    browseable = yes
```

Any Windows user can access this share, which can be used to exchange files between users and between Linux and Windows systems.

MORE INFORMATION

Web SmoothWall Linux distribution: www.smoothwall.org
NdisWrapper: help.ubuntu.com/community/WifiDocs/Driver/Ndiswrapper
NdisWrapper: sourceforge.net/projects/ndiswrapper

HOWTOs *Linux Wireless Lan HOWTO:* www.hpl.hp.com/personal/Jean_Tourrilhes/Linux
Wireless HOWTO
Linux Hardware Compatibility HOWTO

CHAPTER SUMMARY

A local area network (LAN) connects computers at one site and can allow the connected computers to share an Internet connection, files, and a printer. Each system, or node, on a LAN must have a network interface card (NIC). NICs can be connected to the network via cables (wired) or radio waves (wireless).

An Ethernet-based LAN has a connection between each computer and a central hub or switch. Hubs are generally slower than switches, but either is usually satisfactory for a small LAN. A wireless access point (WAP) connects a wireless network to a wired one. If the LAN you are setting up is connected to another network, such as the Internet, the LAN requires a router. A router can perform several functions, the most common of which is allowing several systems to share a single Internet connection and IP address; this function is called NAT.

Several tools are useful when you are setting up a LAN. The Network Connections window (nm-connection-editor) and the nm-applet enable you to configure NICs (wired or wireless). The iwconfig utility configures elements of a wireless NIC.

You can configure the systems on the LAN to use NIS as a login server so you do not have to set up accounts on each system. You can use NFS, which allows you to mount remote directory hierarchies, to set up a universal home directory. Samba is an important part of many LANs: It allows Linux systems to participate in a Windows network, sharing directories and printers, and accessing those directories and printers shared by Windows systems.

EXERCISES

1. What advantage does a switch have over a hub?

2. Which server would you set up to allow users to log in with the same username and password on all computers on a LAN?

3. Name two servers that allow you to share directories between systems.

4. What is a WAP and what does it do?

5. What is a common function of a router? What is this function called?

6. What does a wireless bridge do?

7. Name two tools you can use to configure a wireless NIC (rather than having it be configured automatically). What is the difference between the two?

8. What is the private address space? When would you use a private address?

ADVANCED EXERCISES

9. If you set a system's subnet mask to 255.255.255.0, how many computers can you put on the network without using a router?

10. Which file stores information about which DNS servers the system uses?

PART V

USING CLIENTS AND SETTING UP SERVERS

18

OpenSSH: Secure Network Communication

OpenSSH is a suite of secure network connectivity tools that replaces telnet/**telnetd**, rcp, rsh/**rshd**, rlogin/**rlogind**, and ftp/**ftpd**. Unlike the tools they replace, OpenSSH tools encrypt all traffic, including passwords. In this way they thwart malicious users who attempt to eavesdrop, hijack connections, and steal passwords.

This chapter covers the following OpenSSH tools:

- scp—Copies files to and from another system
- sftp—Copies files to and from other systems (a secure replacement for ftp)
- ssh—Runs a command on or logs in on another system
- **sshd**—The OpenSSH daemon (runs on the server)
- ssh-keygen—Creates, manages, and converts RSA or DSA host/user authentication keys

INTRODUCTION TO OPENSSH

Using public key encryption (page 1065), OpenSSH provides two levels of authentication: server and client/user. First the client verifies that it is connected to the correct server. Then OpenSSH encrypts communication between the systems. Once a secure, encrypted connection has been established, OpenSSH makes sure the user is authorized to log in on or copy files to and from the server. After verifying the system and user, OpenSSH allows different services to be passed through the connection. These services include interactive shell sessions (ssh), remote command execution (ssh), file copying (scp), FTP services (sftp), X11 client/server connections, and TCP/IP port tunneling.

SSH1 versus SSH2   SSH protocol version 2 (SSH2) is a complete rewrite of SSH protocol version 1 (SSH1) that offers improved security, performance, and portability. The two protocols are not compatible. Because SSH1 is being rapidly supplanted by SSH2 and because SSH1 is vulnerable to a man-in-the-middle attack (footnote 3 on page 1068), this chapter does not discuss SSH1. Because version 2 is floating-point intensive, version 1 does have a place on systems without FPUs (floating-point units or accelerators), such as old 486SX systems. As installed, the OpenSSH tools supplied with Ubuntu Linux support SSH2 only.

ssh   The ssh utility allows you to log in on a remote system over a network. You might choose to use a remote system to access a special-purpose application or to take advantage of a device that is available only on that system, or you might use a remote system because you know it is faster or less busy than the local system. While traveling, many businesspeople use ssh on a laptop to log in on a system at company headquarters. From a GUI you can use several systems simultaneously by logging in on each one from a different terminal emulator window.

X11 forwarding   Once you turn on trusted X11 forwarding, it is a simple matter to run an X11 program over an ssh connection: Run ssh from a terminal emulator running on an X11 server and give an X11 command such as **xclock**; the graphical output appears on the local display. For more information refer to "Forwarding X11" on page 645.

HOW OPENSSH WORKS

When OpenSSH starts, it first establishes an encrypted connection and then authenticates the user. Once these two tasks are completed, OpenSSH allows the two systems to send information back and forth.

keys   OpenSSH uses two key pairs to negotiate an encrypted session: a *host key* pair and a *session key* pair. The host key pair is a set of public/private keys that is established when you install the **openssh-server** package (page 640). The session key pair is a set of public/private keys that changes hourly.

The first time an OpenSSH client connects with an OpenSSH server, you are asked to verify that it is connected to the correct server (see "First-time authentication" on page 632). After verification, the client makes a copy of the server's public host key. On subsequent connections, the client compares the key provided by the server with the original key it stored. Although this test is not foolproof, the next one is quite secure.

The client then generates a random key, which it encrypts with both the server's public host key and the session key. The client sends this encrypted key to the server. The server, in turn, uses its private keys to decrypt the encrypted key. This process creates a key that is known only to the client and the server and is used to encrypt the rest of the session.

FILES

OpenSSH clients and servers rely on many files. Global files are kept in **/etc/ssh** and user files in **~/.ssh**. In this section, the first word in the description of each file indicates whether the client or the server uses the file.

rhost authentication is a security risk

caution   Although OpenSSH can get authentication information from **/etc/hosts.equiv**, **/etc/shosts.equiv**, **~/.rhosts**, and **~/.shosts**, this chapter does not cover the use of these files because they are security risks. The default settings in the **/etc/ssh/sshd_config** configuration file prevent their use.

/etc/ssh: GLOBAL FILES

Global files listed in this section appear in the **/etc/ssh** directory. They affect all users, but a user can override them with files in her **~/.ssh** directory.

moduli   client and server   Contains key exchange information that OpenSSH uses to establish a secure connection. Do not modify this file.

ssh_config   client   The global OpenSSH configuration file (page 638). Entries here can be overridden by entries in a user's **~/.ssh/config** file.

sshd_config   server   The configuration file for **sshd** (page 643).

ssh_host_dsa_key,
ssh_host_dsa_key.pub
   server   SSH protocol version 2 DSA host keys. Both files should be owned by **root**. The **ssh_host_dsa_key.pub** public file should be readable by anyone but writable only by its owner (644 permissions). The **ssh_host_dsa_key** private file should not be readable or writable by anyone except its owner (600 permissions).

ssh_host_rsa_key,
ssh_host_rsa_key.pub
   server   SSH protocol version 2 RSA host keys. Both files should be owned by **root**. The **ssh_host_rsa_key.pub** public file should be readable by anyone but writable only by its owner (644 permissions). The **ssh_host_rsa_key** private file should not be readable or writable by anyone except its owner (600 permissions).

ssh_known_hosts   client   Contains public RSA (by default) keys of hosts that users on the local system can connect to. This file contains information similar to that found in **~/.ssh/known_hosts**, but is set up by the administrator and is available to all users.

This file should be owned by **root** and should be readable by anyone but writable only by its owner (644 permissions).

sshrc   server   Contains initialization routines. When a user on a client connects to a server, if **~/.ssh/rc** is not present, OpenSSH runs this script on the server after **~/.ssh/environment** and before the user's shell starts.

~/.ssh: USER FILES

OpenSSH creates the **~/.ssh** directory and the **known_hosts** file therein automatically when a user connects to a remote system.

authorized_keys   server   Enables a user to log in on or copy files to and from another system without supplying a user login password (page 641). However, the user may need to supply a passphrase, depending on how the key was set up. No one except the owner should be able to write to this file.

config   client   A user's private OpenSSH configuration file (page 638). Entries here override those in **/etc/ssh/ssh_config**.

environment   server   Contains assignment statements that define environment variables on a server when a user logs in using ssh.

id_dsa,   client   User authentication DSA keys generated by ssh-keygen (page 641). Both
id_dsa.pub   files should be owned by the user in whose home directory they appear. The **id_dsa.pub** public file should be readable by anyone but writable only by its owner (644 permissions). The **id_dsa** private file should not be readable or writable by anyone except its owner (600 permissions).

id_rsa,   client   User authentication RSA keys generated by ssh-keygen (page 641). Both files
id_rsa.pub   should be owned by the user in whose home directory they appear. The **id_rsa.pub** public file should be readable by anyone but writable only by its owner (644 permissions). The **id_rsa** private file should not be readable or writable by anyone except its owner (600 permissions).

known_hosts   client   Contains public RSA keys (by default) of hosts the user has connected to. OpenSSH automatically adds entries each time the user connects to a new server (page 632). Refer to "HostKeyAlgorithms" (page 639) for information on using DSA keys. If **HashKnownHosts** (page 639) is set to **yes**, the hostnames and addresses in this file are hashed to improve security.

rc   server   Contains initialization routines. When a user on a client connects to a server, OpenSSH runs this script on the server after **environment** and before the user's shell starts. If this file is not present, OpenSSH runs **/etc/ssh/sshrc**; if that file does not exist, OpenSSH runs xauth.

MORE INFORMATION

Local   man pages: ssh, scp, sftp, ssh-keygen, ssh_config, sshd, sshd_config

Web   OpenSSH home page: www.openssh.com
Search on **ssh** to find various HOWTOs and other documents: tldp.org

Books *Implementing SSH: Strategies for Optimizing the Secure Shell* by Dwivedi; John Wiley & Sons (October 2003)
SSH, The Secure Shell: The Definitive Guide by Barrett, Silverman, & Byrnes; O'Reilly Media (May 2005)

RUNNING THE ssh, scp, AND sftp OPENSSH CLIENTS

This section covers setting up and using the ssh, scp, and sftp clients.

PREREQUISITES

The **openssh-client** package is installed by default. You do not need to install any packages to run an OpenSSH client. There is no init script for OpenSSH clients.

JumpStart: Using ssh AND scp TO CONNECT TO AN OpenSSH Server

The ssh and scp clients do not require setup beyond installing the requisite package, although you can create and edit files that facilitate their use. To run a secure shell on or securely copy a file to and from a remote system, the following criteria must be met: The remote system must be running the OpenSSH daemon (**sshd**), you must have an account on the remote system, and the server must positively identify itself to the client.

ssh The following example shows Zach using ssh to log in on the remote host named **plum** and giving an **exit** command to return to the shell on the local system:

```
$ ssh zach@plum
zach@plum's password:
Linux plum 2.6.27-1-generic #1 SMP Sat Aug 23 23:20:09 UTC 2008 i686
...
Last login: Mon Jan 19 21:58:22 2009 from 192.168.0.12
zach@plum:~$ exit
logout
Connection to plum closed.
```

scp You can omit *user@* (**zach@** in the preceding example) from the command line if you want to log in as yourself and you have the same username on both systems. The first time you connect to a remote OpenSSH server, ssh or scp asks you to confirm that you are connected to the right system. Refer to "First-time authentication" on page 632.

The following example uses scp to copy **ty1** from the working directory on the local system to Zach's home directory on **plum**:

```
$ scp ty1 zach@plum:
zach@plum's password:
ty1                                    100%  162     0.2KB/s   00:00
```

CONFIGURING OPENSSH CLIENTS

This section describes how to set up OpenSSH on the client side.

RECOMMENDED SETTINGS

X11 forwarding   The configuration files provided by Ubuntu establish a mostly secure system and may or may not meet your needs. One OpenSSH parameter you may want to change is ForwardX11Trusted, which is set to **yes** by default. To increase security, and in some cases reduce usability, set ForwardX11Trusted (page 639) to **no** in the Ubuntu **/etc/ssh/ssh_config** configuration file. See page 645 for more information about X11 forwarding.

SERVER AUTHENTICATION/KNOWN HOSTS

known_hosts,   Two files list the hosts the local system has connected to and positively identified:
ssh_known_hosts   **~/.ssh/known_hosts** (user) and **/etc/ssh/ssh_known_hosts** (global). No one except the owner (**root** in the case of the second file) should be able to write to either of these files. No one except the owner should have any access to a **~/.ssh** directory.

First-time   When you connect to an OpenSSH server for the first time, the OpenSSH client
authentication   prompts you to confirm that you are connected to the right system. This check can help prevent a man-in-the-middle attack (footnote 3 on page 1068):

```
The authenticity of host 'plum (192.168.0.10)' can't be established.
RSA key fingerprint is d1:9d:1b:5b:97:5c:80:e9:4b:41:9a:b7:bc:1a:ea:a1.
Are you sure you want to continue connecting (yes/no)? yes
Warning: Permanently added 'plum,192.168.0.10' (RSA) to the list of
known hosts.
```

Before you respond to the preceding query, make sure you are logging in on the correct system and not on an imposter. If you are not sure, a telephone call to someone who logs in on that system locally can help verify that you are on the intended system. When you answer **yes** (you must spell it out), the client appends the server's public host key (the single line in the **/etc/ssh/ssh_host_rsa_key.pub** or **/etc/ssh/ssh_host_dsa_key.pub** file on the server) to the user's **~/.ssh/known_hosts** file on the local system, creating the **~/.ssh** directory if necessary. So that it can keep track of which line in **known_hosts** applies to which server, OpenSSH prepends the name of the server and the server's IP address to the line.

When you subsequently use OpenSSH to connect to that server, the client verifies that it is connected to the correct server by comparing this key to the one supplied by the server. You can display the local system's RSA key fingerprint using ssh-keygen:

```
$ ssh-keygen -lf /etc/ssh/ssh_host_rsa_key.pub
2048 d1:9d:1b:5b:97:5c:80:e9:4b:41:9a:b7:bc:1a:ea:a1 /etc/ssh/ssh_host_rsa_key.pub (RSA)
```

known_hosts file   The **known_hosts** file uses one or two very long lines to identify each host it keeps track of. Each line starts with the hostname and IP address of the system the line corresponds to, followed by the type of encryption being used and the server's public host key. When **HashKnownHosts** (page 639) is set to **yes** (the default), OpenSSH hashes the system name and address for security. Because it hashes the hostname and IP address separately, OpenSSH puts two lines in **known_hosts** for each host. The following lines (they are two logical lines, each of which wraps on to several physical lines) from **known_hosts** are used to connect to a remote system using *RSA* (page 1130) encryption:

```
$ cat ~/.ssh/known_hosts
|1|PrVUqXFVnnVLrkymq1ByCnmXaZc=|TVRAtwaqi15EJ9guFR5js3f1AR8= ssh-rsa
AAAAB3NzaC1yc2EAAAABIwAAAQEA7egm4YaOOj5/JtGUlt3jqC5RfcJ8/RAUixKzDAqJ5fE
...
|1|Pnu8B9UUqe7sGIWCiCIUTl8qysc=|Ldm5/7LK6v84ds2129mzw29jqb8= ssh-rsa
AAAAB3NzaC1yc2EAAAABIwAAAQEA7egm4YaOOj5/JtGUlt3jqC5RfcJ8/RAUixKzDAqJ5fE
...
```

You can use ssh-keygen with the **–R** option followed by the hostname to remove a hashed entry. The **–F** option to ssh-keygen displays a line in a **known_hosts** file that corresponds to a specified system, even if the entry is hashed:

```
$ ssh-keygen -F plum
# Host plum found: line 1 type RSA
|1|PrVUqXFVnnVLrkymq1ByCnmXaZc=|TVRAtwaqi15EJ9guFR5js3f1AR8= ssh-rsa
AAAAB3NzaC1yc2EAAAABIwAAAQEA7egm4YaOOj5/JtGUlt3jqC5RfcJ8/RAUixKzDAqJ5fE
...
```

OpenSSH automatically stores keys from servers it has connected to in user-private files (**~/.ssh/known_hosts**). These files work only for the user whose directory they appear in. Working with **root** privileges and using a text editor, you can copy non-hashed lines from a user's private list of known hosts to the public list in **/etc/ssh/ssh_known_hosts** to make a server known globally on the local system.

The following example shows how Sam, who has administrative privileges, puts the hashed entry from his **known_hosts** file into the global **ssh_known_hosts** file. First, working as himself, Sam sends the output of ssh-keygen through tail to strip off the **Host plum found** line and redirects the output to a file named **tmp_known_hosts**. Next, working with **root** privileges, Sam appends the contents of the file he just created to **/etc/ssh/ssh_known_hosts**. This command creates this file if it does not exist. Finally, Sam removes the temporary file he created and returns to working as himself.

```
sam@dog:~$ ssh-keygen -F plum | tail -1 > tmp_known_hosts
sam@dog:~$ sudo -i
root@dog:~# cat ~sam/tmp_known_hosts >> /etc/ssh/ssh_known_hosts
root@dog:~# exit
sam@dog:~$ rm ~sam/tmp_known_hosts
```

Because the output from cat is redirected, Sam creates a shell with **root** privileges (**sudo –i**) to execute the command. See page 408 for a discussion of redirecting the output of a command run under sudo.

If, after a remote system's public key is stored in one of the known-hosts files, the remote system supplies a different fingerprint when the systems connect, OpenSSH displays the following message and does not complete the connection:

```
@@@@@@@@@@@@@@@@@@@@@@@@@@@@@@@@@@@@@@@@@@@@@@@@@@@@@@@@@@@@@@@
@    WARNING: REMOTE HOST IDENTIFICATION HAS CHANGED!     @
@@@@@@@@@@@@@@@@@@@@@@@@@@@@@@@@@@@@@@@@@@@@@@@@@@@@@@@@@@@@@@@
IT IS POSSIBLE THAT SOMEONE IS DOING SOMETHING NASTY!
Someone could be eavesdropping on you right now (man-in-the-middle attack)!
It is also possible that the RSA host key has just been changed.
The fingerprint for the RSA key sent by the remote host is
f1:6f:ea:87:bb:1b:df:cd:e3:45:24:60:d3:25:b1:0a.
Please contact your system administrator.
Add correct host key in /home/sam/.ssh/known_hosts to get rid of this message.
Offending key in /home/sam/.ssh/known_hosts:1
RSA host key for plum has changed and you have requested strict checking.
Host key verification failed.
```

If you see this message, you may be the subject of a man-in-the-middle attack. More likely, however, something on the remote system has changed, causing it to supply a new fingerprint. Check with the remote system's administrator. If all is well, remove the offending key from the specified file (the third line from the bottom in the preceding example points to the line you need to remove) and try connecting again. You can use ssh-keygen with the **–R** option followed by the name of a host to remove a hashed entry. You will be subject to first-time authentication (page 632) again as OpenSSH verifies that you are connecting to the correct system. Follow the same steps as when you initially connected to the remote host.

ssh: CONNECTS TO OR EXECUTES COMMANDS ON A REMOTE SYSTEM

The format of an ssh command line is

   ssh [options] [user@]host [command]

where *host*, the name of the OpenSSH server (the remote system) you want to connect to, is the only required argument. The *host* can be a local system name, the *FQDN* (page 1109) of a system on the Internet, or an IP address. Give the command **ssh** *host* to log in on the remote system *host* with the same username you are using on the local system. Include *user@* when you want to log in with a username other than the one you are using on the local system. Depending on how the server is set up, you may need to supply your password.

Opening a remote shell

Without *command*, ssh logs you in on *host*. The remote system displays a shell prompt and you can run commands on *host*. Give the command **exit** to close the connection to *host* and return to the local system's prompt.

In the following example, Sam, who is logged in on **dog**, uses ssh to log in on **plum**, gives a **who am i** command that shows the IP address of the system he is logged in from, and uses **exit** to close the connection to **plum** and return to the local system's prompt:

```
sam@dog:~$ ssh plum
sam@plum's password:
Linux plum 2.6.27-1-generic #1 SMP Sat Aug 23 23:20:09 UTC 2008 i686
...
Last login: Mon Jan 19 22:00:13 2009 from 192.168.0.12
sam@plum:~$ who am i
sam        pts/0        2009-01-23 14:19 (192.168.0.12)
sam@plum:~$ exit
logout
Connection to plum closed.
sam@dog:~$
```

Running commands remotely When you include *command*, ssh logs in on *host*, executes *command*, closes the connection to *host*, and returns control to the local system. The remote system never displays a shell prompt.

The following example runs ls in the **memos** directory on the remote system **plum**. The example assumes that the user running the command (Sam) has a login on **plum** and that the **memos** directory is in Sam's home directory on **plum**:

```
sam@dog:~$ ssh plum ls memos
sam@plum's password:
memo.0921
memo.draft
sam@dog:~$
```

For the next example, assume the working directory on the local system (**dog**) holds a file named **memos.new**. You cannot remember whether this file contains certain changes or whether you made these changes to the file named **memo.draft** on **plum**. You could copy **memo.draft** to the local system and run diff (page 154) on the two files, but then you would have three similar copies of the file spread across two systems. If you are not careful about removing the old copies when you are done, you may just become confused again in a few days. Instead of copying the file, you can use ssh:

```
sam@dog:~$ ssh plum cat memos/memo.draft | diff memos.new -
```

When you run ssh, standard output of the command run on the remote system is passed to the local shell as though the command had been run in place on the local system. As with all shell commands, you must quote special characters you do not want the local system to interpret. In the preceding example, the output of the cat command on **plum** is sent through a pipe on **dog** to diff (running on **dog**), which compares the local file **memos.new** to standard input (–). The following command line has the same effect but causes diff to run on the remote system:

```
sam@dog:~$ cat memos.new | ssh plum diff - memos/memo.draft
```

Standard output from diff on the remote system is sent to the local shell, which displays it on the screen (because it is not redirected).

OPTIONS

This section describes some of the options you can use with ssh.

-C (**compression**) Enables compression. (In the commercial version of ssh, –C disables compression and +C enables compression.)

-f (**not foreground**) Sends ssh to the background after asking for a password and before executing the *command.* Useful when you want to run the *command* in the background but must supply a password. Implies **–n.**

-L Forwards a port on the local system to a remote system. For more information refer to "Tunneling/Port Forwarding" on page 645.

-l *user* (**login**) Attempts to log in as *user.*

-n (**null**) Redirects standard input to ssh to come from **/dev/null.** Required when running ssh in the background (**–f** option).

-o *option* (**option**) Specifies *option* in the format used in configuration files (page 638).

-p (**port**) Specifies the port on the remote host that the connection is made to. Using the **host** declaration (page 639) in the configuration file, you can specify a different port for each system you connect to.

-R Forwards a port on the remote system to the local client. For more information refer to "Tunneling/Port Forwarding" on page 645.

-t (**tty**) Allocates a pseudo-tty (terminal) to the ssh process on the remote system. Without this option, when you run a command on a remote system, ssh does not allocate a tty (terminal) to the process. Instead, it attaches standard input and standard output of the remote process to the ssh session—which is normally, but not always, what you want. This option forces ssh to allocate a tty on the remote system so programs that require a tty will work.

-v (**verbose**) Displays debugging messages about the connection and transfer. Useful if things are not going as expected.

-X (**X11**) Turns on nontrusted X11 forwarding. This option is not necessary if you turn on X11 nontrusted forwarding in the configuration file. For more information refer to "Forwarding X11" on page 645.

-x (**X11**) Turns off X11 forwarding.

-Y (**X11trusted**) Turns on trusted X11 forwarding. This option is not necessary if you turn on trusted X11 forwarding in the configuration file. For more information refer to "Forwarding X11" on page 645.

scp: COPIES FILES TO AND FROM A REMOTE SYSTEM

The scp (secure copy) utility copies an ordinary or directory file from one system to another (including two remote systems) over a network. This utility uses ssh to transfer files and employs the same authentication mechanism as ssh; thus it provides the same security as ssh. The scp utility asks for a password when one is required. The format of an scp command is

scp [[user@]from-host:]source-file [[user@]to-host:][destination-file]

where *from-host* is the name of the system you are copying files from and *to-host* is the system you are copying to. The *from-host* and *to-host* arguments can be local system names, *FQDNs* (page 1109) of systems on the Internet, or IP addresses. When you do not specify a host, scp assumes the local system. The *user* on either system defaults to the user on the local system who is giving the command; you can specify a different user with *user@*.

The *source-file* is the file you are copying, and the *destination-file* is the resulting copy. Make sure you have read permission for the file you are copying and write permission for the directory you are copying it into. You can specify plain or directory files as relative or absolute pathnames. (A relative pathname is relative to the specified or implicit user's home directory.) When the *source-file* is a directory, you must use the **–r** option to copy its contents. When the *destination-file* is a directory, each of the source files maintains its simple filename. When the *destination-file* is missing, scp assumes the user's home directory.

Suppose Sam has an alternate username, **sls**, on **plum**. In the following example, Sam uses scp to copy **memo.txt** from the home directory of his **sls** account on **plum** to the **allmemos** directory in the working directory on the local system. If **allmemos** was not the name of a directory, **memo.txt** would be copied to a file named **allmemos** in the working directory.

```
sam@dog:~$ scp sls@plum:memo.txt allmemos
sls@plum's password:
memo.txt                              100% 4084KB    4.0MB/s    00:01
```

As the transfer progresses, the percentage and number of bytes transferred increase and the time remaining decreases.

In the next example, Sam, while working from **peach**, copies the same file as in the previous example to the directory named **old** in his home directory on **speedy**. For this example to work, Sam must be able to use ssh to log in on **speedy** from **plum** without using a password. For more information refer to "Authorized Keys: Automatic Login" on page 641.

```
sam@peach:~$ scp sls@plum:memo.txt speedy:old
sam@plum's password:
```

OPTIONS

This section describes some of the options you can use with scp.

–C (**compression**) Enables compression.

–o *option* (**option**) Specifies *option* in the format used in configuration files (discussed shortly).

–P *port*   (**port**) Connects to port *port* on the remote host. This option is given in uppercase for scp and in lowercase for ssh.

–p   (**preserve**) Preserves the modification and access times as well as the modes of the original file.

–q   (**quiet**) Does not display the progress information as scp copies a file.

–r   (**recursive**) Recursively copies a directory hierarchy.

–v   (**verbose**) Displays debugging messages about the connection and transfer. Useful if things are not going as expected.

sftp: A SECURE FTP CLIENT

As part of OpenSSH, Ubuntu Linux provides sftp, a secure alternative to ftp (page 651). Functionally the same as ftp, sftp maps ftp commands to OpenSSH commands. You can replace ftp with sftp when you are logging in on a server that is running the OpenSSH daemon, **sshd**. Once you are connected to a system with sftp, give the command ? to display a list of commands. For secure communication, use sftp or scp to perform all file transfers requiring authentication. Refer to the sftp man page for more information.

lftp   Ubuntu also offers lftp, which is more sophisticated than sftp and supports sftp. The lftp utility provides a shell-like command syntax that has many features, including support for tab completion and the ability to run jobs in the background. Use **/etc/lftp.conf** to configure lftp and see the lftp man page for more information.

~/.ssh/config AND /etc/ssh/ssh_config CONFIGURATION FILES

It is rarely necessary to modify OpenSSH client configuration files. For a given user there may be two configuration files: **~/.ssh/config** (user) and **/etc/ssh/ssh_config** (global). These files are read in this order and, for a given parameter, the first one found is the one that is used. A user can override a global parameter setting by setting the same parameter in her user configuration file. Parameters given on the ssh or scp command line take precedence over parameters set in either of these files.

A user's **~/.ssh/config** file must be owned by the user (the owner of the ~/ directory) and must not be writable by anyone except the owner; if it is, the client will exit with an error message. This file is typically set to mode 600 as there is no reason for anyone except its owner to be able to read it.

Lines in the configuration files contain declarations. Each of these declarations starts with a keyword that is not case sensitive, followed by whitespace, followed by case-sensitive arguments. You can use the **Host** keyword to cause declarations to apply to a specific system. A Host declaration applies to all the lines between it and the next Host declaration.

CheckHostIP yes | no
Identifies a remote system using the IP address in addition to a hostname from the **known_hosts** file when set to **yes** (default). Set it to **no** to use a hostname only. Setting CheckHostIP to **yes** can improve system security.

ForwardX11 yes | no

When set to **yes**, automatically forwards X11 connections over a secure channel in nontrusted mode but does not set the **DISPLAY** shell variable. If ForwardX11Trusted is also set to **yes**, the connections are made in trusted mode. Alternatively, you can use **–X** on the command line to redirect X11 connections in nontrusted mode. The default value for this parameter is **no**; set it to **yes** to enable X11 forwarding. For X11 forwarding to work, you must also set X11Forwarding to **yes** in the **/etc/sshd_config** file on the server (page 644). For more information refer to "Forwarding X11" on page 645.

ForwardX11Trusted yes | no

Works in conjunction with ForwardX11, which must be set to **yes** for this declaration to have any effect. When this declaration is set to **yes** (as it is on Ubuntu Linux systems) and ForwardX11 is set to **yes**, this declaration sets the **DISPLAY** shell variable and gives remote X11 clients full access to the original (server) X11 display. Alternatively, you can use **–Y** on the command line to redirect X11 connections in trusted mode. The default value for this declaration is **no** but Ubuntu Linux sets it to **yes**. For X11 forwarding to work, X11Forwarding must also be set to **yes** in the **/etc/sshd_config** file on the server (page 644). For more information refer to "Forwarding X11" on page 645.

HashKnownHosts

Causes OpenSSH to hash hostnames and addresses in the **~/.ssh/known_hosts** file when set to **yes**. The hostnames and addresses are written in cleartext when it is set to **no**. Ubuntu Linux sets this declaration to **yes** to improve system security. See page 632 for more information on the **known_hosts** file.

Host *hostnames*   Specifies that the following declarations, until the next Host declaration, apply only to hosts that *hostnames* matches. The *hostnames* can include **?** and ***** wildcards. A single ***** specifies all hosts. Without this keyword, all declarations apply to all hosts.

HostbasedAuthentication yes | no

Tries **rhosts** authentication when set to **yes**. For a more secure system, set to **no** (default).

HostKeyAlgorithms *algorithms*

The *algorithms* is a comma-separated list of algorithms the client uses in order of preference. Choose *algorithms* from **ssh-rsa** or **ssh-dss**. The default is **ssh-rsa,ssh-dss**.

Port *num*   Causes OpenSSH to connect to the remote system on port *num*. The default is 22.

StrictHostKeyChecking yes | no | ask

Determines whether and how OpenSSH adds host keys to a user's **known_hosts** file. Set this option to **ask** to ask whether to add a host key when connecting to a new system, set it to **no** to add a host key automatically, and set it to **yes** to require that host keys be added manually. The **yes** and **ask** arguments cause OpenSSH to refuse to connect to a system whose host key has changed. For a more secure system, set this option to **yes** or **ask**. The default is **ask**.

TCPKeepAlive yes | no

Periodically checks whether a connection is alive when set to **yes** (default). Checking causes the **ssh** or **scp** connection to be dropped when the server crashes or the connection dies for another reason, even if it is only temporary. This option tests the connection at the transport (TCP) layer (page 364). Setting this parameter to **no** causes the client not to check whether the connection is alive.

This declaration uses the TCP **keepalive** option, which is not encrypted and is susceptible to *IP spoofing* (page 1115). Refer to "ClientAliveInterval" on page 643 for a server-based nonspoofable alternative.

User *name* Specifies a username to use when logging in on a system. You can specify a system with the Host declaration. This option means that you do not have to enter a username on the command line when you are using a username that differs from your username on the local system.

VisualHostKey yes | no

(Ubuntu 8.10 and later) Displays an ASCII art representation of the key of the remote system in addition to displaying the hexadecimal representation of the key when set to **yes**. See ssh-keygen on page 641 for an example. When set to **no** (default), this declaration displays the hexadecimal key only.

SETTING UP AN OPENSSH SERVER (sshd)

This section describes how to set up an OpenSSH server.

PREREQUISITES

Installation Install the following package:

- **openssh-server**

When you install the **openssh-server** package, the **dpkg postinst** script creates the host key files in **/etc/ssh** (OpenSSH uses these files to identify the server; page 629) and starts the **sshd** daemon:

```
...
Unpacking openssh-server (from .../openssh-server_1%3a4.3p2-5ubuntu1_i386.deb) ...
Setting up openssh-server (1:5.1p1-1ubuntu1) ...
Creating SSH2 RSA key; this may take some time ...
Creating SSH2 DSA key; this may take some time ...
 * Restarting OpenBSD Secure Shell server...
```

ssh init script After you configure the OpenSSH server, call the **ssh** init script to restart the **sshd** daemon:

```
$ sudo /etc/init.d/ssh reload
 * Reloading OpenBSD Secure Shell server's configuration          [ OK ]
```

NOTE

Firewall An OpenSSH server normally uses TCP port 22. If the OpenSSH server system is running a firewall, you need to open this port. To do so, use firestarter (page 824) to set a policy that allows the SSH service.

JumpStart: Starting an OpenSSH Server

Installing the requisite package starts the OpenSSH server (**sshd**) daemon. Look in **/var/log/auth.log** to make sure everything is working properly.

Recommended Settings

The configuration files provided by Ubuntu establish a mostly secure system and may or may not meet your needs. The Ubuntu **/etc/ssh/sshd_config** file turns on X11 forwarding (page 645). It is important to set PermitRootLogin (page 644) to **no**, which prevents a known-name, privileged account from being exposed to the outside world with only password protection. If the **root** account is locked, the setting of this declaration is not an issue.

Authorized Keys: Automatic Login

You can configure OpenSSH so you do not have to enter a password each time you connect to a server (remote system). To set up this feature, you need to generate a personal authentication key on the client (local system), place the public part of the key on the server, and keep the private part of the key on the client. When you connect to the server, it issues a challenge based on the public part of the key. The private part of the key must then respond properly to this challenge. If the client provides the appropriate response, the server logs you in.

The first step in setting up an automatic login is to generate your personal authentication keys. First check whether these authentication keys already exist on the local system (client) by looking in **~/.ssh** for either **id_dsa** and **id_dsa.pub** or **id_rsa** and **id_rsa.pub**. If one of these pairs of files is present, skip the next step (do not create a new key).

On the client, the ssh-keygen utility creates the public and private parts of an RSA key. The key's randomart image is a visual representation of the public key; it is designed to be easy to recall. Display of the randomart image by a client is controlled by the **VisualHostKey** declaration (page 640) in the **ssh_config** file.

ssh-keygen

```
$ ssh-keygen -t rsa
Generating public/private rsa key pair.
Enter file in which to save the key (/home/sam/.ssh/id_rsa):RETURN
Enter passphrase (empty for no passphrase):RETURN
Enter same passphrase again:RETURN
Your identification has been saved in /home/sam/.ssh/id_rsa.
Your public key has been saved in /home/sam/.ssh/id_rsa.pub.
The key fingerprint is:
f2:eb:c8:fe:ed:fd:32:98:e8:24:5a:76:1d:0e:fd:1d sam@peach
The key's randomart image is:
+--[ RSA 2048]----+
|              oE|
|    o .      . o|
|    . o +     ..|
|    .  + o    o |
...
```

Replace **rsa** with **dsa** to generate DSA keys. In this example, the user pressed RETURN in response to each query. You have the option of specifying a passphrase (10–30 characters is a good length) to encrypt the private part of the key. There is no way to recover a lost passphrase. See the following security tip for more information about the passphrase.

When you encrypt your personal key

security   The private part of the key is kept in a file that only you can read. If a malicious user compromises your account, an account that can use sudo to gain **root** privileges, or the **root** account on the local system, that user then has access to your account on the remote system because she can read the private part of your personal key.

Encrypting the private part of your personal key protects the key and, therefore, restricts access to the remote system should someone compromise your local account. However, if you encrypt your personal key, you must supply the passphrase you used to encrypt the key each time you use the key, negating the benefit of not having to type a password when logging in on the remote system. Also, most passphrases that you can remember can be cracked quite quickly by a powerful computer.

A better idea is to store the private keys on a removable medium, such as a USB flash drive, and use your **~/.ssh** directory as the mount point for the filesystem stored on this drive. You may want to encrypt these keys with a passphrase in case you lose the flash drive.

The ssh-keygen utility generates two keys: a private key or identification in **~/.ssh/id_rsa** and a public key in **~/.ssh/id_rsa.pub**. No one except the owner should be able to write to either of these files, and only the owner should be able to read from the private key file.

authorized_keys   To enable you to log in on or copy files to and from another system without supplying a password, first create a **~/.ssh** directory with permissions set to 700 on the server (remote system). Next copy **~/.ssh/id_rsa.pub** from the client (local system) to a file named **~/.ssh/authorized_keys** on the server (remote system). Set its permissions to 600 so that no one except the owner can read from or write to this file. Now when you run ssh or scp to access the server, you do not have to supply a password. To make the server even more secure, you can disable password authentication by setting PasswordAuthentication to **no** in **/etc/ssh/sshd_config** (remove the # from the beginning of the PasswordAuthentication line and change the **yes** to **no**; page 644).

COMMAND-LINE OPTIONS

Command-line options override declarations in the configuration files. Following are descriptions of some of the more useful **sshd** options.

−d   (**debug**) Sets debug mode so that **sshd** sends debugging messages to the system log and the server stays in the foreground (implies **−D**). You can specify this option a maximum of three times to increase the verbosity of the output. See also **−e**. (The ssh client uses **−v** for debugging; see page 636.)

−e   (**error**) Sends output to standard error, not to the system log. Useful with **−d**.

−f *file*   Specifies *file* as the default configuration file instead of **/etc/ssh/sshd_config**.

–t (**test**) Checks the configuration file syntax and the sanity of the key files.

–D (**noDetach**) Keeps **sshd** in the foreground. Useful for debugging; implied by **–d**.

/etc/ssh/sshd_config Configuration File

The **/etc/ssh/sshd_config** configuration file contains one-line declarations. Each of these declarations starts with a keyword that is not case sensitive, followed by whitespace, followed by case-sensitive arguments. You must reload the **sshd** server before these changes will take effect.

AllowUsers *userlist*

The *userlist* is a SPACE-separated list of usernames that specifies which users are allowed to log in using **sshd**. This list can include * and ? wildcards. You can specify a user as *user* or *user@host*. If you use the second format, make sure you specify the host as returned by hostname. Without this declaration, any user who can log in locally can log in using an OpenSSH client.

ClientAliveCountMax *n*

The *n* specifies the number of client-alive messages that can be sent without receiving a response before **sshd** disconnects from the client. See ClientAliveInterval. The default is 3.

ClientAliveInterval *n*

Sends a message through the encrypted channel after *n* seconds of not receiving a message from the client. See ClientAliveCountMax. The default is 0, meaning that no messages are sent.

This declaration passes messages over the encrypted channel (application layer; page 364) and is not susceptible to *IP spoofing* (page 1115). It differs from TCP-KeepAlive, which uses the TCP **keepalive** option (transport layer; page 364) and is susceptible to IP spoofing.

DenyUsers *userlist*

The *userlist* is a SPACE-separated list of usernames that specifies users who are not allowed to log in using **sshd**. This list can include * and ? wildcards. You can specify a user as *user* or *user@host*. If you use the second format, make sure you specify the host as returned by hostname.

HostbasedAuthentication yes | no

Tries **rhosts** and **/etc/hosts.equiv** authentication when set to **yes**. For a more secure system, set this declaration to **no** (default).

IgnoreRhosts yes | no

Ignores **.rhosts** and **.shosts** files for authentication. Does not affect the use of **/etc/hosts.equiv** and **/etc/ssh/shosts.equiv** files for authentication. For a more secure system, set this declaration to **yes** (default).

LoginGraceTime *n*

Waits *n* seconds for a user to log in on the server before disconnecting. A value of 0 means there is no time limit. The default is 120 seconds.

LogLevel *val* Specifies how detailed the log messages are. Choose *val* from QUIET, FATAL, ERROR, INFO (default), and VERBOSE.

PasswordAuthentication
>Permits a user to use a password for authentication. For a more secure system, set up automatic login (page 641) and set this declaration to **no**. The default is **yes**.

PermitEmptyPasswords
>Permits a user to log in on an account that has an empty password. The default is **no**.

PermitRootLogin Permits **root** to log in using an OpenSSH client. Given the number of brute-force attacks on a typical system connected to the Internet, it is important to set this declaration to **no**. (How you set this declaration is not an issue if the **root** account is locked.) The default is **yes**.

Port *num* Specifies that the **sshd** server listen on port *num*. It may improve security to change *num* to a nonstandard port. The default is port 22.

StrictModes yes | no
>Checks modes and ownership of the user's home directory and files. Login fails for users other than the owner if the directories and/or files can be written to by anyone other than the owner. For a more secure system, set this declaration to **yes** (default).

TCPKeepAlive yes | no
>Periodically checks whether a connection is alive when set to **yes** (default). Checking causes the **ssh** or **scp** connection to be dropped when the client crashes or the connection dies for another reason, even if it is only temporary. This option tests the connection at the transport (TCP) layer (page 364). Setting this parameter to **no** causes the server not to check whether the connection is alive.

>This declaration uses the TCP **keepalive** option, which is not encrypted and is susceptible to *IP spoofing* (page 1115). Refer to ClientAliveInterval (page 643) for a nonspoofable alternative.

X11Forwarding yes | no
>Allows X11 forwarding when set to **yes**. The default is **no**, but Ubuntu Linux sets X11Forwarding to **yes**. For trusted X11 forwarding to work, the ForwardX11 and the ForwardX11Trusted declarations must also be set to **yes** in either the **~/.ssh/config** or **/etc/ssh/ssh_config** client configuration file (page 639). For more information refer to "Forwarding X11" on page 645.

TROUBLESHOOTING

Log files There are several places to look for clues when you have a problem connecting with **ssh** or **scp**. First look for **sshd** entries in **/var/log/auth.log** on the server. Following are messages you may see when you are using an AllowUsers declaration but have not included the user who is trying to log in (page 643). The messages that are marked (**pam_unix**) originate with PAM (page 461).

```
$ sudo grep sshd /var/log/auth.log
plum sshd[6927]: Invalid user sam from 192.168.0.12
plum sshd[6927]: Failed none for invalid user sam from 192.168.0.12 port 37134 ssh2
plum sshd[6927]: (pam_unix) check pass; user unknown
plum sshd[6927]: (pam_unix) authentication failure; logname= uid=0 euid=0 tty=ssh ruser=
rhost=192.168.0.12
plum sshd[6927]: Failed password for invalid user sam from 192.168.0.12 port 37134 ssh2
```

Debug the client   If entries in these files do not help solve the problem, try connecting with the –v option (either ssh or scp—the results should be the same). OpenSSH displays a lot of debugging messages, one of which may help you figure out what the problem is. You can use a maximum of three –v options to increase the number of messages that OpenSSH displays.

```
$ ssh -v plum
OpenSSH_5.1p1 Debian-1ubuntu1, OpenSSL 0.9.8g 19 Oct 2007
debug1: Reading configuration data /etc/ssh/ssh_config
debug1: Applying options for *
debug1: Connecting to plum [192.168.0.10] port 22.
debug1: Connection established.
debug1: identity file /home/sam/.ssh/identity type -1
debug1: identity file /home/sam/.ssh/id_rsa type 1
...
debug1: Host 'plum' is known and matches the RSA host key.
debug1: Found key in /home/sam/.ssh/known_hosts:1
debug1: ssh_rsa_verify: signature correct
...
debug1: Authentications that can continue: publickey,password
debug1: Next authentication method: publickey
debug1: Trying private key: /home/sam/.ssh/identity
debug1: Offering public key: /home/sam/.ssh/id_rsa
debug1: Authentications that can continue: publickey,password
debug1: Trying private key: /home/sam/.ssh/id_dsa
debug1: Next authentication method: password
sam@plum's password:
```

Debug the server   You can debug from the server side by running sshd with the –de options. The server will run in the foreground and its display may help you solve the problem.

TUNNELING/PORT FORWARDING

The ssh utility can forward a port (*port forwarding;* page 1125) through the encrypted connection it establishes. Because the data sent across the forwarded port uses the encrypted ssh connection as its data link layer (page 364), the term *tunneling* (page 1138) is applied to this type of connection: "The connection is tunneled through ssh." You can secure protocols—including POP, X, IMAP, VNC, and WWW—by tunneling them through ssh.

Forwarding X11   The ssh utility makes it easy to tunnel the X11 protocol. For X11 tunneling to work, you must enable it on both the server and the client, and the client must be running the X Window System. On the ssh server, enable X11 forwarding by setting the X11Forwarding declaration (page 644) to **yes** (the default) in the **/etc/ssh/sshd_config** file.

Trusted clients On a client, enable trusted X11 forwarding by setting the ForwardX11 (default is **no**; see page 639) *and* ForwardX11Trusted (default is **no**, but set to **yes** as installed; see page 639) declarations to **yes** in the **/etc/ssh/ssh_config** or **~/.ssh/ssh_config** file.

When you enable trusted X11 forwarding on a client, the client connects as a trusted client, which means that the client trusts the server and is given full access to the X11 display. With full access to the X11 display, in some situations a client may be able to modify other clients of the X11 display. Make a trusted connection only when you trust the remote system. (You do not want someone tampering with your client.) If this concept is confusing, see the tip "The roles of X client and server may be counterintuitive" on page 255.

Nontrusted clients An ssh client can connect to an ssh server as a trusted client or as a nontrusted client. A nontrusted client is given limited access to the X11 display and cannot modify other clients of the X11 display.

Few clients work properly when they are run in nontrusted mode. If you are running an X11 client in nontrusted mode and encounter problems, try running in trusted mode (assuming you trust the remote system). Ubuntu Linux sets up ssh clients to run in nontrusted mode by default.

Running ssh When you start an ssh client, you can use the **–Y** option (page 636) on the command line to start the client in trusted mode. Alternatively, you can set the ForwardX11 *and* ForwardX11trusted declarations to **yes** in a user's **~/.ssh/config** configuration file (page 639) or, working with **root** privileges, in the global **/etc/ssh/ssh_config** file (page 639) on the client to enable trusted X11 tunneling.

To use nontrusted tunneling, you can use the **–X** option (page 636) or set the ForwardX11 declaration to **yes** and set the ForwardX11trusted declaration to **no** in one of the configuration files (page 639) on the server.

With trusted X11 forwarding turned on, ssh tunnels the X11 protocol, setting the **DISPLAY** environment variable on the system it connects to and forwarding the required port. Typically you will be running from a GUI, which usually means that you are using ssh on a terminal emulator to connect to a remote system. When you give an X11 command from an ssh prompt, OpenSSH creates a new secure channel that carries the X11 data and the graphical output from the X11 program appears on the screen. Typically you will need to start the client in trusted mode.

```
sam@dog:~$ ssh plum
sam@plum's password:
...
sam@plum:~$ echo $DISPLAY
localhost:10.0
```

By default, ssh uses X Window System display numbers 10 and higher (port numbers 6010 and higher) for forwarded X sessions. Once you connect to a remote system using **ssh**, you can give a command to run an X application. The application will then run on the remote system with its display appearing on the local system, such that it appears to run locally.

Port forwarding You can forward arbitrary ports using the –L and –R options. The –L option forwards a local port to a remote system, so a program that tries to connect to the forwarded port on the local system transparently connects to the remote system. The –R option does the reverse: It forwards remote ports to the local system. The –N option, which prevents ssh from executing remote commands, is generally used with –L and –R. When you specify –N, ssh works only as a private network to forward ports. An ssh command line using the –L or –R option has the following format:

$ *ssh –N –L | –R local-port:remote-host:remote-port target*

where *local-port* is the number of the local port that is being forwarded to or from *remote-host, remote-host* is the name or IP address of the system that *local-port* gets forwarded to or from, *remote-port* is the number of the port on *remote-host* that is being forwarded from or to the local system, and *target* is the name or IP address of the system ssh connects to.

As an example, assume that there is a POP mail client on the local system and that the POP server is on a remote network, on a system named **pophost**. POP is not a secure protocol; passwords are sent in cleartext each time the client connects to the server. You can make it more secure by tunneling POP through ssh (POP-3 connects on port 110; port 1550 is an arbitrary port on the local system):

```
$ ssh -N -L 1550:pophost:110 pophost
```

After giving the preceding command, you can point the POP client at **localhost:1550**. The connection between the client and the server will then be encrypted. (When you set up an account on the POP client, specify the location of the server as **localhost, port 1550**; details vary with different mail clients.)

Firewalls In the preceding example, *remote-host* and *target* were the same system. However, the system specified for port forwarding (*remote-host*) does not have to be the same as the destination of the ssh connection (*target*). As an example, assume the POP server is behind a firewall and you cannot connect to it via ssh. If you can connect to the firewall via the Internet using ssh, you can encrypt the part of the connection over the Internet:

```
$ ssh -N -L 1550:pophost:110 firewall
```

Here *remote-host* (the system receiving the port forwarding) is **pophost**, and *target* (the system that ssh connects to) is **firewall**.

You can also use ssh when you are behind a firewall (that is running **sshd**) and want to forward a port into your system without modifying the firewall settings:

```
$ ssh -R 1678:localhost:80 firewall
```

The preceding command forwards connections from the outside to port 1678 on the firewall to the local Web server. Forwarding connections in this manner allows you to use a Web browser to connect to port 1678 on the firewall when you connect to the Web server on the local system. This setup would be useful if you ran a Web-mail program (page 695) on the local system because it would allow you to check your mail from anywhere using an Internet connection.

Compression   Compression, which is enabled with the –C option, can speed up communication over a low-bandwidth connection. This option is commonly used with port forwarding. Compression can increase latency to an extent that may not be desirable for an X session forwarded over a high-bandwidth connection.

CHAPTER SUMMARY

OpenSSH is a suite of secure network connectivity tools that encrypts all traffic, including passwords, thereby helping to thwart malicious users who might otherwise eavesdrop, hijack connections, and steal passwords. The components discussed in this chapter were **sshd** (the server daemon), **ssh** (runs a command on or logs in on another system), **scp** (copies files to and from another system), **sftp** (securely replaces **ftp**), and **ssh-keygen** (creates, manages, and converts authentication keys).

To ensure secure communications, when an OpenSSH client opens a connection, it verifies that it is connected to the correct server. Then OpenSSH encrypts communication between the systems. Finally OpenSSH makes sure that the user is authorized to log in on or copy files to and from the server. You can secure many protocols—including POP, X, IMAP, VNC, and WWW—by tunneling them through **ssh**.

OpenSSH also enables secure X11 forwarding. With this feature, you can run securely a graphical program on a remote system and have the display appear on the local system.

EXERCISES

1. What is the difference between the **scp** and **sftp** utilities?

2. How can you use **ssh** to find out who is logged in on a remote system?

3. How would you use **scp** to copy your **~/.bashrc** file from the system named **plum** to the local system?

4. How would you use **ssh** to run **xterm** on **plum** and show the display on the local system?

5. What problem can enabling compression present when you are using **ssh** to run remote X applications on a local display?

6. When you try to connect to another system using an OpenSSH client and you see a message warning you that the remote host identification has changed, what has happened? What should you do?

ADVANCED EXERCISES

7. Which scp command would you use to copy your home directory from **plum** to the local system?

8. Which single command could you give to log in as **root** on the remote system named **plum,** if **plum** has the **root** account unlocked and remote **root** logins disabled?

9. How could you use ssh to compare the contents of the ~/**memos** directories on **plum** and the local system?

19

FTP: Transferring Files Across a Network

File Transfer Protocol is a method of downloading files from and uploading files to another system using TCP/IP over a network. File Transfer Protocol is the name of a client/server protocol (FTP) and a client utility (ftp) that invokes the protocol. In addition to the original ftp utility, there are many textual and graphical FTP client programs, including most browsers, that run under many different operating systems. There are also many FTP server programs.

Introduction to FTP

This chapter starts with an introduction to FTP which discusses security, describes types of FTP connections, and presents a list of FTP clients. The first JumpStart section covers basic ftp commands and includes a tutorial on using the ftp client. Next is a section that presents more details of ftp. The final section describes how to set up a **vsftpd** FTP server.

History   First implemented under 4.2BSD, FTP has played an essential role in the propagation of Linux; this protocol/program is frequently used to distribute free software. The term *FTP site* refers to an FTP server that is connected to a network, usually the Internet. FTP sites can be public, allowing anonymous users to log in and download software and documentation. In contrast, private FTP sites require you to log in with a username and password. Some sites allow you to upload programs.

ftp and **vsftpd**   Although most FTP clients are similar, the servers differ quite a bit. This chapter describes the ftp client with references to sftp, a secure FTP client. It also covers the FTP server available under Ubuntu, which is named **vsftpd** (very secure FTP daemon).

ftp utility   The ftp utility is a user interface to FTP, the standard protocol used to transfer files between systems that communicate over a network.

Security

FTP is not a secure protocol: All usernames and passwords exchanged in setting up an FTP connection are sent in cleartext, data exchanged over an FTP connection is not encrypted, and the connection is subject to hijacking. Given these facts, FTP is best used for downloading public files. In most cases, the OpenSSH clients, ssh (page 634), scp (page 636), and sftp (page 638), offer secure alternatives to FTP.

Use FTP only to download public information

security   FTP is not secure. The sftp utility provides better security for all FTP functions other than allowing anonymous users to download information. Because sftp uses an encrypted connection, user passwords and data cannot be sniffed when you use this utility. You can replace all instances of ftp in this chapter with sftp because sftp uses the same commands as ftp. See page 638 for more information on sftp.

The **vsftpd** server does *not* make usernames, passwords, data, and connections more secure. However, it is secure in that a malicious user finds it more difficult to compromise directly the system running it, even if **vsftpd** is poorly implemented. One feature that makes **vsftpd** more secure than **ftpd** is the fact that it does not run with **root** privileges. See also "Security" on page 663.

FTP Connections

FTP uses two connections: one for control (you establish this connection when you log in on an FTP server) and one for data transfer (FTP sets up this connection when

Passive versus active connections

you ask it to transfer a file). An FTP server listens for incoming connections on port 21 by default and handles user authentication and file exchange.

A client can ask an FTP server to establish either a PASV (passive—give the command **ftp –p** or **pftp**) or a PORT (active—the default when you use **ftp**) connection for data transfer. Some servers are limited to one type of connection. The difference between a passive and an active FTP connection lies in whether the client or the server initiates the data connection. In passive mode, the client initiates the connection to the server (on port 20 by default); in active mode, the server initiates the connection (there is no default port; see "Connection Parameters" on page 672 for the parameters that determine which ports a server uses). Neither approach is inherently more secure than the other. Passive connections are more common because a client behind a NAT (page 837) can connect to a passive server and it is simpler to program a scalable passive server.

FTP CLIENTS

ftp Ubuntu supplies several FTP clients, including ftp (an older version of the BSD ftp utility). This section discusses ftp because most other FTP clients, including sftp and lftp, provide a superset of ftp commands.

sftp Part of the OpenSSH suite, sftp (**openssh-client** package) is a secure and functionally equivalent alternative to ftp. The sftp utility is not a true FTP client—it does not understand the FTP protocol. It maps ftp commands to OpenSSH commands. See page 638 for more information.

lftp The lftp utility (**lftp** package) provides the same security as sftp but offers more features. See the lftp man page for more information.

gFTP The gftp utility (**gftp** package) is a graphical client that works with FTP, SSH, and HTTP servers. This client has many useful features, including the ability to resume an interrupted file transfer. See www.gftp.org and freshmeat.net/projects/gftp for more information.

NcFTP The ncftp utility (**ncftp** package) is a textual client that offers many more features than ftp, including filename completion and command-line editing. For details see www.ncftp.com and freshmeat.net/projects/ncftp.

MORE INFORMATION

Local Type **help** or **?** at an **ftp>** prompt to display a list of commands. Follow the **?** with a SPACE and an **ftp** command to display information about that command.
Files: **/usr/share/doc/vsftpd/***
man pages: ftp, sftp, lftp, **netrc**, **vsftpd.conf**

Web **vsftpd** home page: vsftpd.beasts.org

HOWTO *FTP mini-HOWTO*

Running the ftp and sftp FTP Clients

This section describes how to use the ftp and sftp FTP clients. The commands covered here work with both utilities.

Prerequisites

The ftp and sftp utilities are installed on most Ubuntu systems. You can check for their presence by giving either of these utilities' names as commands:

```
$ ftp
ftp> quit

$ sftp
usage: sftp [-1Cv] [-B buffer_size] [-b batchfile] [-F ssh_config]
            [-o ssh_option] [-P sftp_server_path] [-R num_requests]
            [-S program] [-s subsystem | sftp_server] host
       sftp [[user@]host[:file [file]]]
       sftp [[user@]host[:dir[/]]]
       sftp -b batchfile [user@]host
```

Install the **ftp** (contains ftp and pftp) or **openssh-client** (contains sftp) package if needed.

JumpStart I: Downloading Files Using ftp

This JumpStart section is broken into two parts: a description of the basic commands and a tutorial session that shows a user working with ftp. Before you start, make sure ftp or sftp is installed on the local system as explained in the previous section.

Basic Commands

Give the command

```
$ ftp hostname
```

where *hostname* is the name of the FTP server you want to connect to. If you have an account on the server, log in with your username and password. If it is a public system, log in as the user **anonymous** (or **ftp**) and give your email address as your password. Use the **ls** and **cd** ftp commands on the server as you would use the corresponding utilities from a shell. The command **get** *file* copies *file* from the server to the local system, **put** *file* copies *file* from the local system to the server, **status** displays information about the FTP connection, and **help** displays a list of commands.

The preceding commands, except for **status**, are also available in sftp, lftp, and ncftp.

Tutorial Session

Following are two ftp sessions wherein Sam transfers files from and to a **vsftpd** server named **dog**. When Sam gives the command **pftp dog**, the local ftp client connects to the server in passive (PASV) mode, which asks for a username and password. Because he is logged in on his local system as **sam**, ftp suggests that Sam log in on **dog** as **sam**. To log in as **sam**, he could just press RETURN. Because his username on **dog** is **sls**, however, he types **sls** in response to the **Name (dog:sam):** prompt. After Sam responds to the **Password:** prompt with his normal system password, the **vsftpd** server greets him and informs him that it is **Using binary mode to transfer files**. With ftp in binary mode, Sam can transfer ASCII and binary files (page 658).

Connect and log in

```
sam@plum:~$ pftp dog
Connected to dog.bogus.com.
220 (vsFTPd 2.0.6)
Name (dog:sam): sls
331 Please specify the password.
Password:
230 Login successful.
Remote system type is UNIX.
Using binary mode to transfer files.
ftp>
```

After logging in, Sam uses the ftp **ls** command to see what is in his remote working directory, which is his home directory on **dog**. Then he cds to the **memos** directory and displays the files there.

ls and **cd**

```
ftp> ls
227 Entering Passive Mode (192,168,0,12,130,201)
150 Here comes the directory listing.
drwxr-xr-x    2 1001     1001         4096 Jan 25 04:51 expenses
drwxr-xr-x    2 1001     1001         4096 Jan 25 04:53 memos
drwxr-xr-x    2 1001     1001         4096 Jan 25 04:51 tech
226 Directory send OK.

ftp> cd memos
250 Directory successfully changed.

ftp> ls
227 Entering Passive Mode (192,168,0,12,48,84)
150 Here comes the directory listing.
-rw-r--r--    1 1001     1001         3430 Jan 25 04:52 memo.0514
-rw-r--r--    1 1001     1001         6581 Jan 25 04:52 memo.0628
-rw-r--r--    1 1001     1001         2801 Jan 25 04:52 memo.0905
-rw-r--r--    1 1001     1001         7351 Jan 25 04:53 memo.0921
-rw-r--r--    1 1001     1001        14703 Jan 25 04:53 memo.1102
226 Directory send OK.
ftp>
```

Next Sam uses the ftp **get** command to copy **memo.1102** from the server to the local system. His use of binary mode ensures that he will get a good copy of the file regardless of whether it is binary or ASCII. The server confirms that the file was copied successfully and reports on its size and the time required to copy it. Sam then copies the local file **memo.1114** to the remote system. This file is copied into his remote working directory, **memos**.

get and put

```
ftp> get memo.1102
local: memo.1102 remote: memo.1102
227 Entering Passive Mode (192,168,0,12,53,74)
150 Opening BINARY mode data connection for memo.1102 (14703 bytes).
226 File send OK.
14703 bytes received in 0.00 secs (11692.5 kB/s)

ftp> put memo.1114
local: memo.1114 remote: memo.1114
227 Entering Passive Mode (192,168,0,12,182,124)
150 Ok to send data.
226 File receive OK.
11903 bytes sent in 0.00 secs (23294.6 kB/s)
ftp>
```

Now Sam decides he wants to copy all the files in the **memo** directory on **dog** to a new directory on his local system. He gives an **ls** command to make sure he will copy the right files, but ftp has timed out. Instead of exiting from ftp and giving another ftp command from the shell, he gives ftp an **open dog** command to reconnect to the server. After logging in, he uses the ftp **cd** command to change directories to **memos** on the server.

Timeout and **open**

```
ftp> ls
No control connection for command: Success
Passive mode refused.

ftp> open dog
Connected to dog.bogus.com.
220 (vsFTPd 2.0.6)
Name (dog:sam): sls
...
ftp> cd memos
250 Directory successfully changed.
ftp>
```

Local cd (**lcd**) At this point, Sam realizes he has not created the new directory to hold the files he wants to download. Giving an ftp **mkdir** command would create a new directory on the server, but Sam wants a new directory on his local system. He uses an exclamation point (**!**) followed by a **mkdir memos.hold** command to invoke a shell and run mkdir on the local system, thereby creating a directory named **memos.hold** in his working directory on the local system. (You can display the name of the working directory on the local system with **!pwd**.) Next, because Sam wants to copy files from the server to the **memos.hold** directory on his local system, he has to change his working directory on the local system. Giving the command **!cd memos.hold** will not accomplish what Sam wants to do because the exclamation point will spawn a new shell on the local system and the **cd** command would be effective only in the new shell, which is not the shell that ftp is running under. For this situation, ftp provides the **lcd** (local cd) command, which changes the working directory for ftp and reports on the new local working directory:

```
ftp> !mkdir memos.hold
ftp> lcd memos.hold
Local directory now /home/sam/memos.hold
ftp>
```

Sam uses the ftp **mget** (multiple get) command followed by the asterisk (*****) wildcard to copy all files from the remote **memos** directory to the **memos.hold** directory on the local system. When ftp prompts him for the first file, Sam realizes that he forgot to turn off the prompts, so he responds with **n** and presses CONTROL-C to stop copying files in response to the second prompt. The server checks whether he wants to continue with his **mget** command.

Next Sam gives the ftp **prompt** command, which toggles the prompt action (turns it off if it is on and turns it on if it is off). Now when he gives a **mget *** command, ftp copies the files without prompting him. After getting the desired files, Sam gives a **quit** command to close the connection with the server, exit from ftp, and return to the local shell prompt.

mget and prompt

```
ftp> mget *
mget memo.0514? n
mget memo.0628?CONTROL-C
Continue with mget? n
ftp>
ftp> prompt
Interactive mode off.
ftp> mget *
local: memo.0514 remote: memo.0514
227 Entering Passive Mode (192,168,0,12,216,239)
150 Opening BINARY mode data connection for memo.0514 (3430 bytes).
226 File send OK.
3430 bytes received in 0.00 secs (9409.0 kB/s)
local: memo.0628 remote: memo.0628
227 Entering Passive Mode (192,168,0,12,134,149)
150 Opening BINARY mode data connection for memo.0628 (6581 bytes).
226 File send OK.
...
150 Opening BINARY mode data connection for memo.1114 (11903 bytes).
226 File send OK.
11903 bytes received in 0.00 secs (11296.4 kB/s)
ftp> quit
221 Goodbye.
sam@plum:~$
```

Notes   A Linux system running ftp can exchange files with any of the many operating systems that support FTP. Many sites offer archives of free information on an FTP server, although for many it is just an alternative to an easier-to-access Web site (see, for example, ftp://ftp.ibiblio.org/pub/Linux and http://www.ibiblio.org/pub/Linux). Most browsers can connect to and download files from FTP servers.

The ftp utility makes no assumptions about filesystem nomenclature or structure because you can use ftp to exchange files with non-UNIX/Linux systems (which may use different filenaming conventions).

This section explains how to use the ftp FTP client. Although it describes ftp, many other command-line FTP clients are based on ftp and use the same commands.

ANONYMOUS FTP

Many systems—most notably those from which you can download free software—allow you to log in as **anonymous**. Most systems that support anonymous logins accept the name **ftp** as an easier-to-spell and quicker-to-enter synonym for **anonymous**. An anonymous user is usually restricted to a portion of a filesystem set aside to hold files that are to be shared with remote users. When you log in as an anonymous user, the server prompts you to enter a password. Although any password may be accepted, by convention you are expected to supply your email address.

Many systems that permit anonymous access store interesting files in the **pub** directory. Most browsers, such as Firefox, log in on an anonymous FTP site and transfer a file when you click on the filename.

AUTOMATIC LOGIN

You can store server-specific FTP username and password information so you do not have to enter it each time you visit an FTP site. Each line of **~/.netrc** identifies a server. When you connect to an FTP server, ftp reads the **~/.netrc** file to determine whether you have an automatic login set up for that server. The format of a line in **~/.netrc** is

> machine *server* login **username** password **passwd**

where *server* is the name of the server, **username** is your username, and *passwd* is your password on *server*. Replace **machine** with *default* on the last line of the file to specify a username and password for systems not listed in **~/.netrc**. The *default* line is useful for logging in on anonymous servers. A sample **~/.netrc** file follows:

```
$ cat ~/.netrc
machine dog login sam password mypassword
default login anonymous password sam@example.com
```

To protect the account information in **.netrc**, make it readable only by the user whose home directory it appears in. Refer to the **netrc** man page for more information.

BINARY VERSUS ASCII TRANSFER MODE

The **vsftpd** FTP server can—but does not always—provide two modes to transfer files. Binary mode transfers always copy an exact, byte-for-byte image of a file and never change line endings. Transfer all binary files using binary mode. Unless you need to convert line endings, use binary mode to transfer ASCII files as well.

ASCII files, such as text or program source code, when created under Linux with a text editor such as vi, use a single NEWLINE character (CONTROL-J, written as \n) to mark the end of each line. Other operating systems mark the ends of lines differently. Windows marks the end of each such line with a RETURN (CONTROL-M, written as **\r**) followed by a NEWLINE (two characters). Macintosh uses a RETURN by itself. These descriptions do not apply to files created by word processors such as Word or OpenOffice because those programs generate binary files. The **vsftpd** server can map Linux line endings to Windows line endings as you upload files and Windows line endings to Linux line endings as you download files.

To use ASCII mode on an FTP server that allows it, give an **ascii** command (page 661) after you log in and set **cr** to ON (the default; page 661). If the server does not allow you to change line endings as you transfer a file, you can use the todos (page 159) or fromdos (page 159) utility before or after you transfer a file in binary mode.

Security When run against a very large file, the ftp **size** command, which displays the size of a file, consumes a lot of server resources and can be used to initiate a *DoS attack* (page 1106). To enhance security, by default **vsftpd** transfers every file in binary mode, even when it appears to be using ASCII mode. On the server side, you can enable *real* ASCII mode transfers by setting the **ascii_upload_enable** and **ascii_download_enable** parameters (page 670) to YES. With the server set to allow ASCII transfers, the client controls whether line endings are mapped by using the **ascii**, **binary**, and **cr** commands (page 661).

ftp SPECIFICS

This section covers the details of using ftp.

FORMAT

An ftp command line has the following format:

 ftp [options] [ftp-server]

where ***options*** is one or more options from the list in the next section and ***ftp-server*** is the name or network address of the FTP server you want to exchange files with. If you do not specify an ***ftp-server***, you will need to use the ftp **open** command to connect to a server once ftp is running.

COMMAND-LINE OPTIONS

–g (**globbing**) Turns off globbing. See **glob** (page 661).

–i (**interactive**) Turns off prompts during file transfers with **mget** (page 660) and **mput** (page 660). See also **prompt** (page 661).

–n (**no automatic login**) Disables automatic logins (page 658).

–v (**verbose**) Tells you more about how ftp is working. Responses from the remote computer are displayed, and ftp reports information on how quickly files are transferred. See also **verbose** (page 662).

ftp COMMANDS

The ftp utility is interactive: After you start ftp, it prompts you to enter commands to set parameters or transfer files. You can abbreviate commands as long as the abbreviations are unique. Enter a question mark (**?**) in response to the **ftp>** prompt to display a list of commands. Follow the question mark by a SPACE and a command to display a brief description of what the command does:

```
ftp> ? mget
mget            get multiple files
```

SHELL COMMAND

!*[command]*   Without *command*, escapes to (spawns) a shell on the local system. Use CONTROL-D or **exit** to return to ftp when you are finished using the local shell. Follow the exclamation point with *command* to execute that command only; ftp will display an **ftp>** prompt when execution of the command finishes. Because the shell that ftp spawns with this command is a child of the shell that is running ftp, no changes you make in this shell are preserved when you return to ftp. Specifically, when you want to copy files to a local directory other than the directory that you started ftp from, you need to use the ftp **lcd** command to change the local working directory: Issuing a **cd** command in the spawned shell will not make the change you desire. See "Local cd (**lcd**)" on page 656 for an example.

TRANSFER FILES

In the following descriptions, *remote-file* and *local-file* can be pathnames.

append *local-file* [*remote-file*]

Appends *local-file* to the file with the same name on the remote system or to *remote-file* if specified.

get *remote-file* [*local-file*]

Copies *remote-file* to the local system under the name *local-file*. Without *local-file*, ftp uses *remote-file* as the filename on the local system.

mget *remote-file-list*

(**multiple get**) Copies several files to the local system, with each file maintaining its original filename. You can name the remote files literally or use wildcards (see **glob**). Use **prompt** (page 661) to turn off the prompts during transfers.

mput *local-file-list*

(**multiple put**) Copies several files to the server, with each file maintaining its original filename. You can name the local files literally or use wildcards (see **glob**). Use **prompt** (page 661) to turn off the prompts during transfers.

newer *remote-file* [*local-file*]

If the modification time of *remote-file* is more recent than that of *local-file* or if *local-file* does not exist, copies *remote-file* to the local system under the name *local-file*. Without *local-file*, ftp uses *remote-file* as the filename on the local system. This command is similar to **get**, but will not overwrite a newer file with an older one.

put *local-file* [*remote-file*]

> Copies *local-file* to the remote system under the name **remote-file**. Without **remote-file**, ftp uses *local-file* as the filename on the remote system.

reget *remote-file* [*local-file*]

> If *local-file* exists and is smaller than **remote-file**, assumes that a previous **get** of *local-file* was interrupted and continues from where the previous **get** left off. Without *local-file*, ftp uses **remote-file** as the filename on the local system. This command can save time when a **get** of a large file fails partway through the transfer.

STATUS

ascii Sets the file transfer type to ASCII. The **cr** command must be ON for **ascii** to work (page 658).

binary Sets the file transfer type to binary (page 658).

bye Closes the connection to the server and terminates ftp. Same as **quit**.

case Toggles and displays the case mapping status. The default is OFF. When it is ON, for **get** and **mget** commands, this command maps filenames that are all uppercase on the server to all lowercase on the local system.

close Closes the connection to the server without exiting from ftp.

cr (**carriage** RETURN) Toggles and displays the (carriage) RETURN stripping status. Effective only when the file transfer type is **ascii**. Set **cr** to ON (default) to remove RETURN characters from RETURN/LINEFEED line termination sequences used by Windows, yielding the standard Linux line termination of LINEFEED. Set **cr** to OFF to leave line endings unmapped (page 658).

debug [*n*] Toggles/sets and displays the debugging status/level, where *n* is the debugging level. OFF or 0 (zero) is the default. When *n* > 0, this command displays each command ftp sends to the server.

glob Toggles and displays the filename expansion (page 242) status for **mdelete** (page 662), **mget** (page 660), and **mput** (page 660) commands.

hash Toggles and displays the pound sign (#, also called a hash mark) display status. When it is ON, ftp displays one pound sign for each 1024-byte data block it transfers.

open [*hostname*]

> Specifies *hostname* as the name of the server to connect to. Without *hostname*, prompts for the name of the server. This command is useful when a connection times out or otherwise fails.

passive Toggles between active (PORT—the default) and passive (PASV) transfer modes and displays the transfer mode. For more information refer to "Passive versus active connections" on page 653.

prompt Toggles and displays the prompt status. When it is ON (default), **mdelete** (page 662), **mget** (page 660), and **mput** (page 660) ask for verification before transferring each file. Set **prompt** to OFF to turn off these prompts.

quit   Closes the connection to the server and terminates ftp. Same as **bye**.

umask [*nnn*]   Changes the umask (page 442) applied to files created on the server to ***nnn***. Without ***nnn***, displays the umask.

user [*username*] [*password*]
Prompts for or accepts the ***username*** and ***password*** that enable you to log in on the server. When you call it with the **–n** option, ftp prompts you for a username and password automatically. For more information refer to "Automatic Login" on page 658.

DIRECTORIES

cd *remote-directory*
Changes the working directory on the server to ***remote-directory***.

cdup   Changes the working directory on the server to the parent of the working directory.

lcd [*local_directory*]
(**local change directory**) Changes the working directory on the local system to *local_directory*. Without an argument, this command changes the working directory on the local system to your home directory (just as the cd shell builtin does without an argument). See "Local cd (**lcd**)" on page 656 for an example.

FILES

chmod *mode remote-file*
Changes the access permissions of ***remote-file*** on the server to ***mode***. See chmod on page 202 for more information on how to specify the ***mode***.

delete *remote-file*   Removes ***remote-file*** from the server.

mdelete *remote-file-list*
(**multiple delete**) Deletes the files specified by ***remote-file-list*** from the server.

DISPLAY INFORMATION

dir [*remote-directory*] [*file*]
Displays a listing of ***remote-directory*** from the server. When you do not specify ***remote-directory***, displays the working directory. When you specify *file*, the listing is saved on the local system in a file named *file*.

help [*command*]   Displays information about ***command***. Without ***command***, displays a list of local ftp commands.

ls [*remote-directory*] [*file*]
Similar to **dir** but produces a more concise listing from some servers. When you specify *file*, the listing is saved on the local system in a file named *file*.

pwd   Displays the pathname of the working directory on the server. Use **!pwd** to display the pathname of the local working directory.

status   Displays ftp connection and status information.

verbose   Toggles and displays verbose mode, which displays responses from the server and reports how quickly files are transferred. The effect of this command is the same as specifying the **–v** option on the command line.

SETTING UP AN FTP SERVER (vsftpd)

This section explains how to set up an FTP server implemented by the **vsftpd** daemon as supplied by Ubuntu.

PREREQUISITES

Install the following package:

- **vsftpd**

vsftpd init script   When you install the **vsftpd** package, the **dpkg postinst** script starts the **vsftpd** daemon. After you configure **vsftpd**, call the **vsftpd** init script to restart the **vsftpd** daemon:

```
$ sudo /etc/init.d/vsftpd restart
 * Stopping FTP server: vsftpd                                        [ OK ]
 * Starting FTP server: vsftpd                                        [ OK ]
```

After changing the **vsftpd** configuration on an active server, use **reload** in place of **restart** to reload the **vsftpd** configuration files without disturbing clients that are connected to the server.

NOTES

The **vsftpd** server can run in normal mode (the **xinetd** daemon, which is not installed by default, calls **vsftpd** each time a client tries to make a connection) or it can run in stand-alone mode (**vsftpd** runs as a daemon and handles connections directly).

Stand-alone mode   Although by default **vsftpd** runs in normal mode, Ubuntu sets it up to run in stand-alone mode by setting the **listen** parameter (page 665) to YES in the **vsftpd.conf** file. Under Ubuntu Linux, with **vsftpd** running in stand-alone mode, you start and stop the server using the **vsftpd** init script.

Normal mode   The **xinetd** superserver (page 447) must be installed and running and you must install an **xinetd** control file to run **vsftpd** in normal mode. A sample control file is located at **/usr/share/doc/vsftpd/EXAMPLE/INTERNET_SITE/vsftpd.xinetd**. Copy the sample file to the **/etc/xinetd.d** directory, rename it **vsftpd**, edit the file to change the **no_access** and **banner_fail** parameters as appropriate, and restart **xinetd**. With the **listen** parameter in **vsftpd.conf** set to NO, **xinetd** starts **vsftpd** as needed.

Security   The safest policy is not to allow users to authenticate against FTP: Instead, use FTP for anonymous access only. When you install **vsftpd**, it allows anonymous access only; you must modify its configuration to allow users to log in by name on the **vsftpd** server. If you do allow local users to authenticate and upload files to the server, be sure to put local users in a chroot jail (page 667). Because FTP sends usernames and passwords in cleartext, a malicious user can easily *sniff* (page 1133) them. Armed with a username and password, the same user can impersonate a local user, upload a *Trojan horse* (page 1137), and compromise the system.

Firewall   An FTP server normally uses TCP port 21. If the FTP server system is running a firewall, you need to open this port. To do so, use firestarter (page 824) to set a policy that allows FTP service.

JumpStart II: Starting a vsftpd FTP Server

By default, under Ubuntu Linux **vsftpd** allows anonymous users only to log in on the server; it does not set up a guest account nor does it allow users to log in on the **vsftpd** server. When someone logs in as an anonymous user, that person works in the **/home/ftp** directory. You do not have to configure anything.

Testing the Setup

Make sure **vsftpd** is working by logging in from the system running the server. You can refer to the server as **localhost** or by using its hostname on the command line. Log in as **anonymous**; use any password.

```
$ ftp localhost
Connected to localhost.
220 (vsFTPd 2.0.6)
Name (localhost:sam): anonymous
331 Please specify the password.
Password:
230 Login successful.
Remote system type is UNIX.
Using binary mode to transfer files.
ftp> quit
221 Goodbye.
```

If you are not able to connect to the server, first make sure the server is running:

```
$ ps -ef | grep vsftpd
root      5681    1  0 12:22 ?        00:00:00 /usr/sbin/vsftpd
sam       6629 6596  0 14:49 pts/2    00:00:00 grep vsftpd
```

Next check that permissions on **/home/ftp**, or the home directory of ftp as specified in **/etc/passwd**, are set to 755 and that the directory is not owned by **ftp**. If the **ftp** user can write to **/var/ftp**, connections will fail.

```
$ ls -ld /home/ftp
drwxr-xr-x 2 root nogroup 4096 2007-01-24 08:45 /home/ftp
```

Once you are able to log in from the local system, log in from another system—either one on the LAN or another system with access to the server. On the command line, use the hostname from within the LAN or the *FQDN* (page 1109) from outside the LAN. The dialog should appear the same as in the previous example. If you cannot log in from a system that is not on the LAN, use ping (page 377) to test the connection and make sure the firewall is set up to allow FTP access. See "FTP Connections" on page 652 for a discussion of active and passive modes and the ports that each mode uses.

CONFIGURING A vsftpd SERVER

The configuration file for **vsftpd**, **/etc/vsftpd.conf**, lists Boolean, numeric, and string name-value pairs of configuration parameters, called directives. Each name-value pair is joined by an equal sign with no SPACEs on either side. Ubuntu Linux provides a well-commented **vsftpd.conf** file that changes many of the compiled-in defaults. This section covers most of the options, noting their default values and their values as specified in the **vsftpd.conf** file supplied with Ubuntu Linux.

Set Boolean options to YES or NO and numeric options to a nonnegative integer. Octal numbers, which are useful for setting umask options, must have a leading 0 (zero). Numbers without a leading zero are treated as base 10 numbers. Following are examples from **vsftpd.conf** of setting each type of option:

```
anonymous_enable=YES
local_umask=022
xferlog_file=/var/log/vsftpd.log
```

Descriptions of the directives are broken into the following groups:

- Stand-alone mode (page 665)
- Logging in (page 666)
- Working directory and the chroot jail (page 667)
- Downloading and uploading files (page 668)
- Messages (page 671)
- Display (page 671)
- Logs (page 672)
- Connection parameters (page 672)

STAND-ALONE MODE

Refer to "Notes" on page 657 for a discussion of normal and stand-alone modes. This section describes the parameters that affect stand-alone mode.

listen   YES runs **vsftpd** in stand-alone mode; NO runs it in normal mode.

Default: NO
Ubuntu: YES

listen_address   In stand-alone mode, specifies the IP address of the local interface that **vsftpd** listens on for incoming connections. When this parameter is not set, **vsftpd** uses the default network interface.

Default: none

listen_port   In stand-alone mode, specifies the port that **vsftpd** listens on for incoming connections.

Default: 21

max_clients   In stand-alone mode, specifies the maximum number of clients. Zero (0) indicates unlimited clients.

Default: 0

max_per_ip   In stand-alone mode, specifies the maximum number of clients from the same IP address. Zero (0) indicates unlimited clients from the same IP address.

Default: 0

LOGGING IN

Three classes of users can log in on a **vsftpd** server: anonymous, local, and guest. The guest user is rarely used and is not covered in this chapter. Local users log in with their system username and password. Anonymous users log in with **anonymous** or **ftp**, using their email address as a password. You can control whether each of these classes of users can log in on the server and what they can do once they log in. You can also specify what a local user can do on a per-user basis; for more information refer to **user_config_dir** on page 674.

LOCAL USERS

userlist_enable   The **/etc/vsftpd.user_list** file (page 675), or another file specified by **userlist_file**, contains a list of zero or more users. YES consults this list and takes action based on **userlist_deny**, either granting or denying users in the list permission to log in on the server. To prevent the transmission of cleartext passwords, access is denied immediately after the user enters her username. NO does not consult the list. For a more secure system, set this parameter to NO.

Default: NO
Ubuntu: YES

userlist_deny   YES prevents users listed in **/etc/vsftpd.user_list** (page 675) from logging in on the server. NO allows *only* users listed in **/etc/vsftpd.user_list** to log in on the server. Use **userlist_file** to change the name of the file that this parameter consults. This parameter is checked only when **userlist_enable** is set to YES.

Default: YES

userlist_file   The name of the file consulted when **userlist_enable** is set to YES.

Default: /etc/vsftpd.user_list

local_enable   YES permits local users (users listed in **/etc/passwd**) to log in on the server.

Default: NO

ANONYMOUS USERS

anonymous_enable

YES allows anonymous logins. NO disables anonymous logins.

Default: YES

no_anon_password

> YES skips asking anonymous users for passwords.
>
> Default: NO

deny_email_enable

> YES checks whether the password (email address) that an anonymous user enters is listed in **/etc/vsftpd.banned_emails** or another file specified by **banned_email_file**. If it is, the user is not allowed to log in on the system. NO does not perform this check. Using firestarter (page 824) or iptables (page 823) to block specific hosts is generally more productive than using this parameter.
>
> Default: NO

banned_email_file

> The name of the file consulted when **deny_email_enable** is set to YES.
>
> Default: **/etc/vsftpd.banned_emails**

THE WORKING DIRECTORY AND THE chroot JAIL

When a user logs in on a **vsftpd** server, standard filesystem access permissions control which directories and files the user can access and how the user can access them. Three basic parameters control a user who is logged in on a **vsftpd** server:

- The user ID (UID)
- The initial working directory
- The root directory

By default, the **vsftpd** server sets the user ID of a local user to that user's username and sets the user ID of an anonymous user to **ftp**. A local user starts in her home directory and an anonymous user starts in **/home/ftp**.

By default, anonymous users are placed in a chroot jail for security; local users are not. For example, when an anonymous user logs in on a **vsftpd** server, his home directory is **/home/ftp**. All that user sees, however, is that his home directory is **/**. The user sees the directory at **/home/ftp/upload** as **/upload**. The user cannot see, or work with, for example, the **/home, /usr/local**, or **/tmp** directory because the user is in a chroot jail. For more information refer to "Setting Up a chroot Jail" on page 450.

You can use the **chroot_local_user** option to put each local user in a chroot jail whose root is the user's home directory. You can use **chroot_list_enable** to put selected local users in chroot jails.

chroot_list_enable

> Upon login, YES checks whether a local user is listed in **/etc/vsftpd.chroot_list** (page 675) or another file specified by **chroot_list_file**.

When a user is in the list and **chroot_local_user** is set to NO, the user is put in a chroot jail in his home directory. Only users listed in **/etc/vsftpd.chroot_list** are put in chroot jails.

When a user is in the list and **chroot_local_user** is set to YES, that user is not put in a chroot jail. Users not listed in **/etc/vsftpd.chroot_list** are put in chroot jails.

Default: NO

chroot_local_user

See **chroot_list_enable**. Set to NO for a more open system, but remember to add new users to the **chroot_list_file** as needed when you add users to the system. Set to YES for a more secure system. New users are automatically restricted unless you add them to **chroot_list_file**.

Default: NO

chroot_list_file The name of the file consulted when **chroot_list_enable** is set to YES.

Default: **/etc/vsftpd.chroot_list**

passwd_chroot_enable

YES enables you to change the location of the chroot jail that the **chroot_list_enable** and **chroot_local_user** settings impose on a local user.

The location of the chroot jail can be moved up the directory structure by including a **/./** within the home directory string for that user in **/etc/passwd**. This change has no effect on the standard system login, just as a **cd .** command has no effect on the working directory.

For example, changing the home directory field in **/etc/passwd** (page 476) for Sam from **/home/sam** to **/home/./sam** allows Sam to cd to **/home** after logging in using **vsftpd**. Given the proper permissions, Sam can now view files and collaborate with another user.

Default: NO

secure_chroot_dir The name of an empty directory that is not writable by the user **ftp**. The **vsftpd** server uses this directory as a secure chroot jail when the user does not need access to the filesystem.

Default: **/var/run/vsftpd**

local_root After a local user logs in on the server, this directory becomes the user's working directory. No error results if the specified directory does not exist.

Default: none

DOWNLOADING AND UPLOADING FILES

By default, any user—whether local or anonymous—can download files from the **vsftpd** server, assuming proper filesystem access and permissions. You must change **write_enable** from NO (default) to YES to permit local users to upload files. By default, **local_umask** is set to 077, giving uploaded files 600 permissions (page 201). These permissions allow only the user who created a file to download and overwrite it. Change **local_umask** to 022 to allow users to download other users' files.

Security   Refer to "Security" on page 663 for information on the security hole that is created when you allow local users to upload files.

The following actions set up **vsftpd** to allow anonymous users to upload files:

1. Set **write_enable** (page 669) to YES.

2. Create a directory under **/home/ftp** that an anonymous user can write to but not read from (mode 333). You do not want a malicious user to be able to see, download, modify, and upload a file that another user originally uploaded. The following commands create a **/home/ftp/uploads** directory that anyone can write to but no one can read from:

```
$ sudo mkdir /home/ftp/uploads
$ sudo chmod 333 /home/ftp/uploads
```

Because of the security risk, **vsftpd** prevents anonymous connections when an anonymous user (**ftp**) can write to **/home/ftp**.

3. Set **anon_upload_enable** (page 670) to YES.

4. See the other options in this section.

DOWNLOAD/UPLOAD FOR LOCAL USERS

local_umask   The umask (page 442) setting for local users.

Default: 077

file_open_mode   Uploaded file permissions for local users. The umask (page 442) is applied to this value. Change to 0777 to make uploaded files executable.

Default: 0666

write_enable   YES permits users to create and delete files and directories (assuming appropriate filesystem permissions). NO prevents users from making changes to the filesystem.

Default: NO

ANONYMOUS USERS

anon_mkdir_write_enable

YES permits an anonymous user to create new directories when **write_enable=YES** and the anonymous user has permission to write to the parent directory.

Default: NO

anon_other_write_enable

YES grants an anonymous user write permission in addition to the permissions granted by **anon_mkdir_write_enable** and **anon_upload_enable**. For example, YES allows an anonymous user to delete and rename files, assuming she has permission to write to the parent directory. For a more secure site, do not set this parameter to YES.

Default: NO

anon_root   After an anonymous user logs in on the server, this directory becomes the user's working directory. No error results if the specified directory does not exist.

Default: none

anon_umask   The umask (page 442) setting for anonymous users. The default setting gives only anonymous users access to files uploaded by anonymous users; set this parameter to 022 to give everyone read access to these files.

Default: 077

anon_upload_enable

YES allows anonymous users to upload files when **write_enable**=YES and the anonymous user has permission to write to the directory.

Default: NO

anon_world_readable_only

YES limits the files that a user can download to those that are readable by the owner of the file, members of the group the file is associated with, and others. It may not be desirable to allow one anonymous user to download a file that another anonymous user uploaded. Setting this parameter to YES can avoid this scenario.

Default: YES

ascii_download_enable

YES allows a user to download files using ASCII mode. Setting this parameter to YES can create a security risk (page 659).

Default: NO

ascii_upload_enable

YES allows a user to upload files using ASCII mode (page 658).

Default: NO

chown_uploads   YES causes files uploaded by anonymous users to be owned by **root** (or another user specified by **chown_username**). To improve security, change **chown_username** to a name other than **root** if you set this parameter to YES.

Default: NO

chown_username   See **chown_uploads**.

Default: **root**

ftp_username   The username of anonymous users.

Default: **ftp**

nopriv_user   The name of the user with minimal privileges, as used by **vsftpd**. Because other programs use **nobody**, to enhance security you can replace **nobody** with the name of a dedicated user such as **ftp**.

Default: **nobody**

MESSAGES

You can replace the standard greeting banner that **vsftpd** displays when a user logs in on the system (**banner_file** and **ftpd_banner**). You can also display a message each time a user enters a directory (**dirmessage_enable** and **message_file**). When you set **dirmessage_enable**=YES, each time a user enters a directory using cd, **vsftpd** displays the contents of the file in that directory named **.message** (or another file specified by **message_file**).

dirmessage_enable

YES displays **.message** or another file specified by **message_file** as an ftp user enters a new directory by giving a **cd** command.

Default: NO
Ubuntu: YES

message_file   See **dirmessage_enable**.

Default: **.message**

banner_file   The absolute pathname of the file that is displayed when a user connects to the server. Overrides **ftpd_banner**.

Default: none

ftpd_banner   Overrides the standard **vsftpd** greeting banner displayed when a user connects to the server.

Default: none; uses standard **vsftpd** banner

DISPLAY

This section describes parameters that can improve security and performance by controlling how **vsftpd** displays information.

hide_ids   YES lists all users and groups in directory listings as **ftp**. NO lists the real owners.

Default: NO

setproctitle_enable

NO causes ps to display the process running **vsftpd** as **vsftpd**. YES causes ps to display what **vsftpd** is currently doing (uploading and so on). Set this parameter to NO for a more secure system.

Default: NO

text_userdb_names

NO improves performance by displaying numeric UIDs and GIDs in directory listings. YES displays names.

Default: NO

use_localtime   NO causes the **ls**, **mls**, and **modtime** FTP commands to display *UTC* (page 1139). YES causes these commands to display the local time.

Default: NO

ls_recurse_enable   YES permits users to give **ls –R** commands. Setting this parameter to YES may pose a security risk because giving an **ls –R** command at the top of a large directory hierarchy can consume a lot of system resources.

Default: NO

LOGS

By default, logging is turned off. However, the **vsftpd.conf** file distributed with Ubuntu Linux turns it on. This section describes parameters that control the details and locations of logs.

log_ftp_protocol   YES logs FTP requests and responses, provided that **xferlog_std_format** is set to NO.

Default: NO

xferlog_enable   YES maintains a transfer log in **/var/log/vsftpd.log** (or another file specified by **xferlog_file**). NO does not create a log.

Default: NO
Ubuntu: YES

xferlog_std_format

YES causes a transfer log (not covering connections) to be written in standard **xferlog** format, as used by wu-ftpd, as long as **xferlog_file** is explicitly set. If **xferlog_std_format** is set to YES and **xferlog_file** is not explicitly set, logging is turned off. The default **vsftpd** log format is more readable than **xferlog** format, but it cannot be processed by programs that generate statistical summaries of **xferlog** files. Search for **xferlog** on the Internet to obtain more information on this command.

Default: NO

xferlog_file   See **xferlog_enable** and **xferlog_std_format**.

Default: **/var/log/vsftpd.log**

CONNECTION PARAMETERS

You can allow clients to establish passive and/or active connections (page 653). Setting timeouts and maximum transfer rates can improve server security and performance. This section describes parameters that control the types of connections that a client can establish, the length of time **vsftpd** will wait while establishing a connection, and the speeds of connections for different types of users.

PASSIVE (PASV) CONNECTIONS

pasv_enable   NO prevents the use of PASV connections.

Default: YES

pasv_promiscuous

NO causes PASV to perform a security check that ensures that the data and control connections originate from a single IP address. YES disables this check; it is not recommended for a secure system.

Default: NO

pasv_max_port   The highest port number that **vsftpd** will allocate for a PASV data connection; useful in setting up a firewall.

Default: 0 (use any port)

pasv_min_port   The lowest port number that **vsftpd** will allocate for a PASV data connection; useful in setting up a firewall.

Default: 0 (use any port)

pasv_address   Specifies an IP address other than the one used by the client to contact the server.

Default: none; the address is the one used by the client

ACTIVE (PORT) CONNECTIONS

port_enable   NO prevents the use of PORT connections.

Default: YES

port_promiscuous

NO causes PORT to perform a security check that ensures that outgoing data connections connect only to the client. YES disables this check; it is not recommended for a secure system.

Default: NO

connect_from_port_20

YES specifies port 20 (**ftp-data**, a privileged port) on the server for PORT connections, as required by some clients. NO allows **vsftpd** to run with fewer privileges (on a nonprivileged port).

Default: NO
Ubuntu: YES

ftp_data_port   With **connect_from_port_20** set to NO, specifies the port that **vsftpd** uses for PORT connections.

Default: 20

TIMEOUTS

accept_timeout   The number of seconds the server waits for a client to establish a PASV data connection.

Default: 60

connect_timeout   The number of seconds the server waits for a client to respond to a PORT data connection.

Default: 60

data_connection_timeout

The number of seconds the server waits for a stalled data transfer to resume before disconnecting.

Default: 300

idle_session_timeout

The number of seconds the server waits between FTP commands before disconnecting.

Default: 300

local_max_rate
For local users, the maximum data transfer rate in bytes per second. Zero (0) indicates no limit.

Default: 0

anon_max_rate
For anonymous users, the maximum data transfer rate in bytes per second. Zero (0) indicates no limit.

Default: 0

one_process_model
YES establishes one process per connection, which improves performance but degrades security. NO allows multiple processes per connection. NO is recommended to maintain a more secure system.

Default: NO

MISCELLANEOUS

This section describes parameters not discussed elsewhere.

pam_service_name
The name of the PAM service used by **vsftpd**.

Default: **vsftpd**

rsa_cert_file
Specifies where the RSA certificate for SSL-encrypted connections is kept.

Default: **/usr/share/ssl/certs/vsftpd.pem**
Ubuntu: **/etc/ssl/certs/ssl-cert-snakeoil.pem**

rsa_private_key_file
Specifies where the RSA key for SSL-encrypted connections is kept.

Default: none
Ubuntu: **/etc/ssl/private/ssl-cert-snakeoil.key**

tcp_wrappers
YES causes incoming connections to use **tcp_wrappers** (page 448) if **vsftpd** was compiled with **tcp_wrappers** support. When **tcp_wrappers** sets the environment variable **VSFTPD_LOAD_CONF**, **vsftpd** loads the configuration file specified by this variable, allowing per-IP configuration.

Default: NO

user_config_dir
Specifies a directory that contains files named for local users. Each of these files, which mimic **vsftpd.conf**, contains parameters that override, on a per-user basis, default parameters and parameters specified in **vsftpd.conf**. For example, assume that **user_config_dir** is set to **/etc/vsftpd/user_conf**. Further suppose that the default configuration file, **/etc/vsftpd/vsftpd.conf**, sets **idlesession_timeout=300** and Sam's individual configuration file, **/etc/vsftpd/user_conf/sam**, sets **idlesession_timeout=1200**. Then all users' sessions except for Sam's will time out after 300 seconds of inactivity. Sam's sessions will time out after 1,200 seconds.

Default: none

OTHER CONFIGURATION FILES

In addition to **/etc/vsftpd.conf**, the following files control the functioning of **vsftpd**. The directory hierarchy that **user_config_dir** points to is not included in this list because it has no default name.

/etc/ftpusers

Lists users, one per line, who are never allowed to log in on the FTP server, regardless of how **userlist_enable** (page 666) is set and regardless of the users listed in the **user_list** file. The default file lists **root, bin, daemon**, and others.

/etc/vsftpd.user_list

Lists either the only users who can log in on the server or the only users who are not allowed to log in on the server. The **userlist_enable** (page 666) option must be set to YES for **vsftpd** to examine the list of users in this file. Setting **userlist_enable** to YES and **userlist_deny** (page 666) to YES (or not setting it) prevents listed users from logging in on the server. Setting **userlist_enable** to YES and **userlist_deny** to NO permits only the listed users to log in on the server.

/etc/vsftpd.chroot_list

Depending on the **chroot_list_enable** (page 667) and **chroot_local_user** (page 668) settings, lists either users who are forced into a chroot jail in their home directories or users who are not placed in a chroot jail.

/var/log/vsftpd.log

Log file. For more information refer to "Logs" on page 672.

CHAPTER SUMMARY

File Transfer Protocol is a protocol for downloading files from and uploading files to another system over a network. FTP is the name of both a client/server protocol (FTP) and a client utility (ftp) that invokes this protocol. Because FTP is not a secure protocol, it should be used only to download public information. You can run the **vsftpd** FTP server in the restricted environment of a chroot jail to make it significantly less likely that a malicious user can compromise the system.

Many servers and clients implement the FTP protocol. The ftp utility is the original client implementation; sftp and lftp are secure implementations that use OpenSSH facilities to encrypt the connection. Although they do not understand the FTP protocol, they map ftp commands to OpenSSH commands. The **vsftpd** daemon is a secure FTP server; it better protects the server from malicious users than do other FTP servers.

Public FTP servers allow you to log in as **anonymous** or **ftp**. By convention, you supply your email address as a password when you log in as an anonymous user. Public servers frequently have interesting files in the **pub** directory.

FTP provides two modes of transferring files: binary and ASCII. It is safe to use binary mode to transfer all types of files, including ASCII files. If you transfer a binary file using ASCII mode, the transfer will fail.

EXERCISES

1. What changes does FTP make to an ASCII file when you download it in ASCII mode to a Windows machine from a Linux server? What changes are made when you download the file to a Mac?

2. What happens if you transfer an executable program file in ASCII mode?

3. When would ftp be a better choice than sftp?

4. How would you prevent local users from logging in on a **vsftpd** server using their system username and password?

5. What advantage does sftp have over ftp?

6. What is the difference between cd and lcd in ftp?

ADVANCED EXERCISES

7. Why might you have problems connecting to an FTP server in PORT mode?

8. Why is it advantageous to run **vsftpd** in a chroot jail?

9. After downloading a file, you find that it does not match the MD5 checksum provided. Downloading the file again gives the same incorrect checksum. What have you done wrong and how would you fix it?

10. How would you configure **vsftpd** to run through **xinetd**, and what would be the main advantage of this approach?

20

exim4: SETTING UP MAIL SERVERS, CLIENTS, AND MORE

Sending and receiving email require three pieces of software. At each end, there is a client, called an MUA (mail user agent), which is a bridge between a user and the mail system. Common MUAs are mutt, Evolution, KMail, Thunderbird, and Outlook. When you send an email, the MUA hands it to an MTA (a mail transfer agent, such as **exim4** or **sendmail**), which transfers it to the destination server. At the destination, an MDA (a mail delivery agent, such as **procmail**) puts the mail in the recipient's mailbox file. On Linux systems, the MUA on the receiving system either reads the mailbox file or retrieves mail from a remote MUA or MTA, such as an ISP's SMTP (Simple Mail Transfer Protocol) server, using POP (Post Office Protocol) or IMAP (Internet Message Access Protocol).

SMTP   Most Linux MUAs expect a local MTA such as **exim4** to deliver outgoing email. On some systems, including those with a dial-up connection to the Internet, the MTA sends email to an ISP's mail server. Because most MTAs use SMTP to deliver email, they are often referred to as SMTP servers. By default, when you install **exim4** on an Ubuntu system, **exim4** uses its own builtin MDA to deliver email to the recipient's mailbox file.

You do not need to set up exim4 to send and receive email

tip   Most MUAs can use POP or IMAP to receive email from an ISP's server. These protocols do not require an MTA such as **exim4**. As a consequence, you do not need to install or configure **exim4** (or another MTA) to receive email. Although you still need SMTP to send email, the SMTP server can be at a remote location, such as your ISP. Thus you may not need to concern yourself with it, either.

INTRODUCTION TO exim4

When the network that was to evolve into the Internet was first set up, it connected a few computers, each serving a large number of users and running several services. Each computer was capable of sending and receiving email and had a unique hostname, which was used as a destination for email.

Today the Internet has a large number of transient clients. Because these clients do not have fixed IP addresses or hostnames, they cannot receive email directly. Users on these systems usually maintain an account on an email server run by their employer or an ISP, and they collect email from this account using POP or IMAP. Unless you own a domain where you want to receive email, you will not need to set up **exim4** to receive mail from nonlocal systems.

Smarthost   You can set up **exim4** on a client system so it sends mail bound for nonlocal systems to an SMTP server that relays the mail to its destination. This type of server is called a *smarthost*. Such a configuration is required by organizations that use firewalls to prevent email from being sent out on the Internet from any system other than the company's official mail servers. As a partial defense against spreading viruses, some ISPs block outbound port 25 to prevent their customers from sending email directly to a remote computer. This configuration is required by these ISPs.

You can also set up **exim4** as a server that sends mail to nonlocal systems and does not use an ISP as a relay. In this configuration, **exim4** connects directly to the SMTP servers for the domains receiving the email. An ISP set up as a smarthost is configured this way.

You can set up **exim4** to accept email for a registered domain name as specified in the domain's DNS MX record (page 790). However, most mail clients (MUAs) do not interact directly with **exim4** to receive email. Instead, they use POP or IMAP— protocols that include features for managing mail folders, leaving messages on the server, and reading only the subject of an email without downloading the entire message. If you want to collect your email from a system other than the one running the incoming mail server, you may need to set up a POP or IMAP server, as discussed on page 699.

ALTERNATIVES TO exim4

sendmail   The most popular MTA today, **sendmail** (**sendmail** package) first appeared in 4.1BSD. The **sendmail** system is complex, but its complexity allows **sendmail** to be flexible and to scale well. On the downside, because of its complexity, configuring **sendmail** can be a daunting task. See www.sendmail.org for more information.

Postfix   Postfix (**postfix** package) is an alternative MTA. Postfix is fast and easy to administer, but is compatible enough with **sendmail/exim4** to not upset **sendmail/exim4** users. Postfix has a good reputation for ease of use and security and is a drop-in replacement for **sendmail**. Point a browser at www.postfix.org/docs.html for Postfix documentation.

Qmail   Qmail is a direct competitor of Postfix and has the same objectives. By default, Qmail stores email using the **maildir** format as opposed to the **mbox** format that other MTAs use (page 684). The Qmail Web site is www.qmail.org.

MORE INFORMATION

Web   **exim4**: www.exim.org (includes the complete **exim4** specification), www.exim-new-users.co.uk, wiki.debian.org/PkgExim4
SpamAssassin: spamassassin.apache.org, wiki.apache.org/spamassassin
Spam database: razor.sourceforge.net
Mailman: www.list.org
procmail: www.procmail.org
SquirrelMail: www.squirrelmail.org
IMAP: www.imap.org
Dovecot: www.dovecot.org
Postfix: www.postfix.org/docs.html (alternative MTA)
Qmail: www.qmail.org/top.html

Local   **exim4**: **/usr/share/doc/exim4∗/∗**
SpamAssassin: **/usr/share/doc/spam∗**
Dovecot: **/usr/share/doc/dovecot∗**
man pages: **exim4 exim4_files** update-exim4.conf update-exim4defaults spamassassin spamc **spamd**
SpamAssassin: Install the **perl-doc** and **spamassassin** packages and give the following command:

```
$ perldoc Mail::SpamAssassin::Conf
```

SETTING UP A MAIL SERVER (exim4)

This section explains how to set up an **exim4** mail server.

PREREQUISITES

Install the following packages:

- **exim4** (a virtual package)
- **eximon4** (optional; monitors **exim4**)

- **mailx** (optional; installs mail, which is handy for testing **exim4** from the command line)

- **exim4-doc-html** (optional; **exim4** documentation in HTML format)

- **exim4-doc-info** (optional; **exim4** documentation in **info** format)

exim4 init script When you install the **exim4** package, the **dpkg postinst** script minimally configures **exim4** and starts the **exim4** daemon. After you configure **exim4**, call the **exim4** init script to restart **exim4**:

```
$ sudo /etc/init.d/exim4 restart
```

After changing the **exim4** configuration on an active server, use **reload** in place of **restart** to reload **exim4** configuration files without interrupting the work **exim4** is doing. The **exim4** init script accepts several nonstandard arguments:

```
$ /etc/init.d/exim4
Usage: /etc/init.d/exim4 {start|stop|restart|reload|status|what|force-stop}
```

The **status** and **what** arguments display information about **exim4**. The **force-stop** argument immediately kills all **exim4** processes.

Notes

Firewall An SMTP server normally uses TCP port 25. If an SMTP server system that receives nonlocal mail is running a firewall, you need to open this port. To do so, use **firestarter** (page 824) to set a policy that allows SMTP service.

Log files You must be a member of the **adm** group or work with **root** privileges to view the log files in **/var/log/exim4**.

sendmail and exim4 Although it does not work the same way **sendmail** does, Ubuntu configures **exim4** as a drop-in replacement for **sendmail**. The **exim4-daemon-light** package, which is part of the **exim4** virtual package, includes **/usr/sbin/sendmail**, which is a link to **exim4**. Because the **exim4** daemon accepts many of **sendmail**'s options, programs that depend on **sendmail** will work with **exim4** installed in place of **sendmail**.

Local and nonlocal systems The **exim4** daemon sends and receives email. A piece of email that **exim4** receives can originate on a local system or on a nonlocal system. Similarly, email that **exim4** sends can be destined for a local or a nonlocal system. The **exim4** daemon processes each piece of email based on its origin and destination.

The local system versus local systems *The local system* is the one **exim4** is running on. *Local systems* are systems that are on the same LAN as the local system.

As it is installed, **exim4** delivers mail to the local system only.

JumpStart I: Configuring exim4 to Use a Smarthost

This JumpStart configures an **exim4** server that sends mail from users on local systems to local and nonlocal destinations and does not accept mail from nonlocal systems. This server

- Accepts email originating on local systems for delivery to local systems.

- Accepts email originating on local systems for delivery to nonlocal systems, delivering it using an SMTP server (a smarthost)—typically an ISP—to relay email to its destination.

- Does not deliver email originating on nonlocal systems. As is frequently the case, you need to use POP or IMAP to receive email.

- Does not forward email originating on nonlocal systems to other nonlocal systems (does not relay email).

To set up this server, you need to change the values of a few configuration variables in **/etc/exim4/update-exim4.conf.conf** (page 688) and restart **exim4**. The dpkg-reconfigure utility (page 690) guides you in editing this file; this JumpStart uses a text editor. Working with **root** privileges, use a text editor to make the following changes to **update-exim4.conf.conf**:

```
dc_eximconfig_configtype='smarthost'
smarthost='mail.example.net'
```

Configuration type Set the **dc_eximconfig_configtype** configuration variable to **smarthost** to cause **exim4** to send mail bound for nonlocal systems to the system that the **smarthost** configuration variable specifies. This line should appear exactly as shown in the preceding example.

Smarthost With **dc_eximconfig_configtype** set to **smarthost**, set **smarthost** to the FQDN or IP address (preferred) of the remote SMTP server (the smarthost) that **exim4** uses to relay email to nonlocal systems. Replace *mail.example.net* with this FQDN or IP address. For Boolean variables in **update-exim4.conf.conf**, **exim4** interprets the null value (specified by '') as a value of *false*. With these changes, the file should look similar to this:

```
$ cat /etc/exim4/update-exim4.conf.conf
...
dc_eximconfig_configtype='smarthost'
dc_other_hostnames=''
dc_local_interfaces='127.0.0.1'
dc_readhost=''
dc_relay_domains=''
dc_minimaldns='false'
dc_relay_nets=''
dc_smarthost='mail.example.net'
CFILEMODE='644'
dc_use_split_config='false'
dc_hide_mailname='false'
dc_mailname_in_oh='true'
dc_localdelivery='mail_spool'
```

The **exim4** server does not use the value of the **dc_local_interfaces** variable in a smarthost configuration, so you can leave it blank. However, in other configurations, the value of 127.0.0.1 prevents **exim4** from accepting email from nonlocal systems. It is a good idea to configure **exim4** this way and change this variable only when you are ready to accept mail from other systems.

To minimize network accesses for DNS lookups, which can be helpful if you are using a dial-up line, change the value of the **dc_minimaldns** configuration variable to **true**.

/etc/mailname   The **/etc/mailname** file initially holds the node name (**uname –n**) of the server. The string stored in **/etc/mailname** appears as the name of the sending system on the envelope-from and From lines of email that originates on the local system. If you want email to appear to come from a different system, change the contents of this file. You can modify this file using a text editor; the dpkg-reconfigure utility can also change it.

The following file causes mail sent from the local system to appear to come from *username*@example.com, where *username* is the username of the user who is sending the email:

```
$ cat /etc/mailname
example.com
```

See page 688 for more information on **exim4** configuration variables. After making these changes, restart **exim4** (page 680).

Test   Test **exim4** with the following command:

```
$ echo "my exim4 test" | exim4 user@remote.host
```

Replace *user@remote.host* with an email address on *another system* where you receive email. You need to send email to a remote system to make sure that **exim4** is sending email to the remote SMTP server (the smarthost). If the mail is not delivered, check the email of the user who sent the email (on the local system) for errors. Also check the log file(s) in the **/var/log/exim4** directory.

JumpStart II: Configuring exim4 to Send and Receive Mail

To receive email sent from a nonlocal system to a registered domain (that you control), you need to configure **exim4** to accept email from nonlocal systems. This JumpStart describes how to set up a server that

- Accepts email from local and nonlocal systems.

- Delivers email that originates on local systems to a local system or directly to a nonlocal system, without using a relay.

- Delivers email that originates on nonlocal systems to a local system only.

- Does not forward email originating on nonlocal systems to other nonlocal systems (does not relay email).

This server does not relay email originating on nonlocal systems. (You must set the **dc_relay_domains** variable [page 690] for the local system to act as a relay.) For this configuration to work, you must be able to make outbound connections and receive inbound connections on port 25 (see "Firewall" on page 680).

Working with **root** privileges, use a text editor to set the following configuration variables in **/etc/exim4/update-exim4.conf.conf**:

```
dc_eximconfig_configtype='internet'
dc_other_hostnames='mydom.example.com'
dc_local_interfaces=''
```

Configuration type Set **dc_eximconfig_configtype** to **internet** to cause **exim4** to send mail directly to nonlocal systems as specified by the DNS MX record (page 790) for the domain the mail is addressed to and to accept email on the interfaces specified by **dc_local_interfaces** (next page). This line should appear exactly as shown above.

Other hostnames The **dc_other_hostnames** configuration variable specifies the FQDNs or IP addresses that the local server receives mail addressed to. Replace *mydom.example.com* with these FQDN or IP addresses. You must separate multiple entries with semicolons. These values do not necessarily include the FQDN or the IP address of the local server.

Local interfaces Set **dc_local_interfaces** to the interface you want **exim4** to listen on. Set it to the null value ('') to listen on all interfaces.

As in JumpStart I, you may need to change the value of **/etc/mailname** (page 682). For Boolean variables in this file, **exim4** interprets the null value (specified by '') as *false*. The file should look similar to this:

```
$ cat /etc/exim4/update-exim4.conf.conf
...
dc_eximconfig_configtype='internet'
dc_other_hostnames='mydom.example.com'
dc_local_interfaces=''
dc_readhost=''
dc_relay_domains=''
dc_minimaldns='false'
dc_relay_nets=''
dc_smarthost=''
CFILEMODE='644'
dc_use_split_config='false'
dc_hide_mailname=''
dc_mailname_in_oh='true'
dc_localdelivery='mail_spool'
```

See page 688 for more information on **exim4** configuration variables. Once you have restarted **exim4**, it will accept mail addressed to the local system. To receive email addressed to a domain, the DNS MX record (page 790) for that domain must point to the IP address of the local system. If you are not running a DNS server, you must ask your ISP to set up an MX record or else receive mail at the IP address of the server. If you receive email addressed to an IP address, set **dc_other_hostnames** to that IP address.

WORKING WITH exim4 MESSAGES

When **exim4** receives email, from both local and nonlocal systems, it creates in the **/var/spool/exim4/input** directory two files that hold the message while **exim4** processes it. To identify a particular message, **exim4** generates a 16-character message ID and uses that string in filenames pertaining to the email. The **exim4** daemon stores the body of the message in a file named by the message ID followed by **–D** (data). It stores the headers and envelope information in a file named by the message ID followed by **–H** (header).

Frozen messages
If **exim4** cannot deliver a message, it marks the message as *frozen* and makes no further attempt to deliver it. Once it has successfully delivered an email, **exim4** removes all files pertaining to that email from **/var/spool/exim4/input**.

Mail addressed to the local system
By default, **exim4** delivers email addressed to the local system to users' files in the mail spool directory, **/var/mail**, in **mbox** format. Within this directory, each user has a mail file named with the user's username. Mail remains in these files until it is collected, typically by an MUA. Once an MUA collects the mail from the mail spool, the MUA stores the mail as directed by the user, usually in the user's home directory.

Mail addressed to nonlocal systems
The scheme that **exim4** uses to process email addressed to a nonlocal system depends on how it is configured: It can send the email to a smarthost, it can send the email to the system pointed to by the DNS MX record of the domain the email is addressed to, or it can refuse to send the email.

mbox versus **maildir**
The **mbox** format holds all messages for a user in a single file. To prevent corruption, a process must lock this file while it is adding messages to or deleting messages from the file; thus the MUA cannot delete a message at the same time the MTA is adding messages. A competing format, **maildir**, holds each message in a separate file. This format does not use locks, allowing an MUA to delete messages from a user at the same time as mail is delivered to the same user. In addition, the **maildir** format is better able to handle larger mailboxes. The downside is that the **maildir** format adds overhead when you are using a protocol such as IMAP to check messages. The **exim4** daemon supports both **mbox** and **maildir** formats (see **dc_localdelivery** on page 689). Qmail (page 679), an alternative to **sendmail** and **exim4**, uses **maildir**-format mailboxes.

MAIL LOGS

By default, **exim4** sends normal log messages to **/var/exim4/mainlog**, with other messages going to other files in the same directory. The following lines in a **mainlog** file describe an email message sent directly to a remote system's SMTP server. The **exim4** daemon writes one line each time it receives a message and one line each time it attempts to deliver a message. The **Completed** line indicates that **exim4** has completed its part in delivering the message. Each line starts with the date and time of the entry followed by the message ID.

```
$ tail -3 /var/log/exim4/mainlog
2007-07-19 23:13:12 1IBljk-0000t8-1Z <= zachs@example.com U=sam P=local S=304
2007-07-19 23:13:17 1IBljk-0000t8-1Z => zachs@example.com R=dnslookup T=remote_smtp
   H=filter.mx.meer.net   [64.13.141.12]
2007-07-19 23:13:17 1IBljk-0000t8-1Z Completed
```

The next entry on each line except the **Completed** line is a two-character status flag that tells you which kind of event the line describes:

<=	Received a message
=>	Delivered a message normally
–>	Delivered a message normally to an additional address (same delivery)
*>	Did not deliver because of a –N command-line option
**	Did not deliver because the address bounced
==	Did not deliver because of a temporary problem

Information following the flag is preceded by one of the following letters, which indicates the type of the information, and an equal sign:

H	Name of remote system (host)
U	Username of the user who sent the message
P	Protocol used to receive the message
R	Router used to process the message
T	Transport used to process the message
S	Size of the message in bytes

The first line in the preceding example indicates that **exim4** received a 304-byte message to be delivered to **zachs@example.com** from **sam** on the **local** system. The next line indicates that **exim4** looked up the address using DNS (**dnslookup**) and delivered it to the remote SMTP server (**remote_smtp**) at **filter.mx.meer.net**, which has an IP address of 64.13.141.12.

The following log entries describe a message that **exim4** received from a remote system and delivered to the local system:

```
2007-07-19 23:13:32 1IBlk4-0000tL-8L <= zachs@gmail.com H=wx-out-0506.google.com
   [66.249.82.229]   P=esmtp S=1913 id=7154255d0707192313y304a1b27t39f...@mail.gmail.com
2007-07-19 23:13:32 1IBlk4-0000tL-8L => sam <sams@example.com> R=local_user T=mail_spool
2007-07-19 23:13:32 1IBlk4-0000tL-8L Completed
```

See the **exim4** specification for more information on log files. If you send and receive a lot of email, the mail logs can grow quite large. The logrotate (page 604) **exim4-base** file archives and rotates these files regularly.

WORKING WITH MESSAGES

You can call **exim4** with many different options to work with mail that is on the system and to generate records of mail that has passed through the system. Most of these options begin with **–M** and require the message ID (see the preceding section) of the piece of email you want to work with. The following command removes a message from the queue:

```
$ sudo exim4 -Mrm 1IEKKj-0006CQ-LM
Message 1IEKKj-0006CQ-LM has been removed
```

Following are some of the **exim4** options you can use to work with a message. Each of these options must be followed by a message ID. See the **exim4** man page for a complete list.

–Mf	Mark message as frozen
–Mrm	Remove message
–Mt	Thaw message
–Mvb	Display message body
–Mvh	Display message header

ALIASES AND FORWARDING

You can use the **aliases** and **.forward** (page 687) files to forward email.

/etc/aliases Most of the time when you send email, it goes to a specific person; the recipient, **user@system**, maps to a real user on the specified system. Sometimes, however, you may want email to go to a class of users and not to a specific recipient. Examples of classes of users include **postmaster**, **webmaster**, **root**, and **tech_support**. Different users may receive this email at different times or the email may go to a group of users. You can use the **/etc/aliases** file to map local addresses and classes to local users, files, commands, and local as well as to nonlocal addresses.

Each line in **/etc/aliases** contains the name of a local (pseudo)user, followed by a colon, whitespace, and a comma-separated list of destinations. Because email sent to the **root** account is rarely checked, the default installation includes an entry similar to the following that redirects email sent to **root** to the initial user:

```
root:   sam
```

You can set up an alias to forward email to more than one user. The following line forwards mail sent to **abuse** on the local system to **sam** and **max**:

```
abuse:  sam, max
```

You can create simple mailing lists with this type of alias. For example, the following alias sends copies of all email sent to **admin** on the local system to several users, including Zach, who is on a different system:

```
admin:  sam, helen, max, zach@example.com
```

You can direct email to a file by specifying an absolute pathname in place of a destination address. The following alias, which is quite popular among less conscientious system administrators, redirects email sent to **complaints** to **/dev/null** (page 471), where it disappears:

```
complaints:   /dev/null
```

You can also send email to standard input of a command by preceding the command with the pipe character (|). This technique is commonly used by mailing list software such as Mailman (page 697). For each list it maintains, Mailman has entries, such as the following one for **painting_class**, in the **aliases** file:

```
painting_class:    "|/var/lib/mailman/mail/mailman post painting_class"
```

See the **exim4_files** man page for information on **exim4** files, including **aliases**.

newaliases   After you edit **/etc/aliases**, you must run **newaliases** while you are working with **root** privileges. The **/usr/bin/newaliases** file is a symbolic link to **exim4**. Running **newaliases** calls **exim4**, which rebuilds the **exim4** alias database.

~/.forward   Systemwide aliases are useful in many cases, but nonroot users cannot make or change them. Sometimes you may want to forward your own mail: Maybe you want mail from several systems to go to one address or perhaps you want to forward your mail while you are working at another office. The **~/.forward** file allows ordinary users to forward their email.

Lines in a **.forward** file are the same as the right column of the **aliases** file explained earlier in this section: Destinations are listed one per line and can be a local user, a remote email address, a filename, or a command preceded by the pipe character (|).

Mail that you forward does not go to your local mailbox. If you want to forward mail and keep a copy in your local mailbox, you must specify your local username preceded by a backslash to prevent an infinite loop. The following example sends Sam's email to himself on the local system and on the system at **example.com**:

```
$cat ~sam/.forward
sams@example.com
\sam
```

RELATED PROGRAMS

exim4   The **exim4** packages include several programs. The primary program, **exim4**, reads from standard input and sends an email to the recipient specified by its argument. You can use **exim4** from the command line to check that the mail delivery system is working and to email the output of scripts. See "Test" on page 682 for an example. The command **apropos exim4** displays a list of **exim4**-related files and utilities. In addition, you can call **exim4** with options (page 685) or through links to cause it to perform various tasks.

exim4 –bp   When you call **exim4** with the **–bp** option, or when you call the **mailq** utility (which is a symbolic link to **exim4**), it displays the status of the outgoing mail queue. When there are no messages in the queue, it displays nothing. Unless they are transient, messages in the queue usually indicate a problem with the local or remote MTA configuration or a network problem.

```
$ sudo exim4 -bp
24h   262 1IBhYI-0006iT-7Q <sam@> *** frozen ***
          zachs@example.com
```

eximstats   The eximstats utility displays statistics based on **exim4** log files. Call this utility with an argument of the name of a log file, such as **/var/log/mainlog** or **/var/log/mainlog2.gz**. Without any options, eximstats sends information based on the log file in text format to standard output. When you include the **–html** option, eximstats generates output in HTML format, suitable for viewing with a browser:

```
$ eximstats -html /var/log/exim4/mainlog.2.gz  > exim.0720.html
```

If you are not a member of the **adm** group, you must run the preceding command with **root** privileges. See the eximstats man page for more information.

eximon   Part of the **eximon4** package, eximon displays a simple graphical representation of the **exim4** queue and log files.

CONFIGURING AN exim4 MAIL SERVER

The **exim4** daemon is a complex and capable MTA that is configured by **/etc/default/exim4** and the files in the **/etc/exim4** directory hierarchy. The former allows you to specify how the daemon is to be run; the latter configures all other aspects of **exim4**. You can configure **exim4** by editing its configuration files with a text editor (discussed in the next section) or by using dpkg-reconfigure (page 690).

/etc/default/exim4   The default **/etc/default/exim4** file sets QUEUERUNNER to **combined**, which starts one daemon that both runs the queue and listens for incoming email. It sets QUEUEINTERVAL to **30m**, which causes the daemon to run the queue (that is, check whether the queue contains mail to be delivered) every 30 minutes. See the comments in the file for more information.

USING A TEXT EDITOR TO CONFIGURE exim4

The files in the **/etc/exim4** directory hierarchy control how **exim4** works—which interfaces it listens on, whether it uses a smarthost or sends email directly to its destination, whether and for which systems it relays email, and so on. You can also create an **exim4.conf.localmacros** file to turn on/off **exim4** functions (see page 701 for an example). Because of its flexibility, **exim4** uses many configuration variables. You can establish the values of these variables in one of two ways: You can edit a single file, as the JumpStart sections of this chapter explain, or you can work with the approximately 40 files in the **/etc/exim4/conf.d** directory hierarchy. For many configurations, working with the single file **update-exim4.conf.conf** is sufficient. This section describes the variables in that file but does not discuss working with the files in **conf.d**. Refer to the **exim4** specification if you need to set up a more complex mail server.

THE update-exim4.conf.conf CONFIGURATION FILE

update-
exim4.conf   The update-exim4.conf utility reads the **exim4** configuration files in **/etc/exim4**, including **update-exim4.conf.conf**, and generates the **/var/lib/exim4/config.autogenerated**

file. When **exim4** starts, it reads this file for configuration information. Typically you do not need to run update-exim4.conf manually because the **exim4** init script (page 680) runs this utility before it starts, restarts, or reloads **exim4**.

Split configuration   Setting the **dc_use_split_config** variable in **update-exim4.conf.conf** to **false** specifies an unsplit configuration, wherein update-exim4.conf merges the data from **exim4.conf.localmacros**, **update-exim4.conf.conf**, and **exim4.conf.template** to create **config.autogenerated**. Setting this variable to **true** specifies a split configuration, wherein update-exim4.conf merges the data from **exim4.conf.localmacros**, **update-exim4.conf.conf**, and all the files in the **conf.d** directory hierarchy to create **config.autogenerated**.

Following is the list of configuration variables you can set in **update-exim4.conf.conf**. Enclose all values within single quotation marks. For Boolean variables, **exim4** interprets the null value (specified by '') as **false**.

CFILEMODE='*perms*'
> Sets the permissions of **config.autogenerated** to the octal value *perms,* typically 644.

dc_eximconfig_configtype='*type*'
> Specifies the type of configuration that **exim4** will run, where *type* is one of the following:
>
> **internet**   Sends and receives email locally and remotely. See "JumpStart II" on page 682 for an example.
>
> **smarthost**   Sends and receives email locally and remotely, using a smarthost to relay messages to nonlocal systems. See "JumpStart I" on page 680 for an example.
>
> **satellite**   Sends email remotely, using a smarthost to relay messages; does not receive mail locally.
>
> **local**   Sends and receives local messages only.
>
> **none**   No configuration; **exim4** will not work.

dc_hide_mailname='*bool*'
> Controls whether **exim4** displays the local mailname (from /**etc/mailname**, page 682) in the headers of email originating on local systems. Set *bool* to **true** to hide (not display) the local mailname or **false** to display it. When you set this variable to **true**, **exim4** uses the value of **dc_readhost** in headers.

dc_local_interfaces='*interface-list*'
> The *interface-list* is a semicolon-separated list of interfaces that **exim4** listens on. Set *interface-list* to the null value ('') to cause **exim4** to listen on all interfaces. Set it to 127.0.0.1 to prevent **exim4** from accepting email from other systems.

dc_localdelivery='*lcl-transport*'
> Set *lcl-transport* to **mail_spool** to cause **exim4** to store email in **mbox** format; set it to **maildir_home** for **maildir** format. See page 684 for more information.

dc_mailname_in_oh='*bool*'
> Used internally by **exim4**. Do not change this value.

dc_minimaldns='*bool*'

Set *bool* to **true** to minimize DNS lookups (useful for dial-up connections) or to **false** to perform DNS lookups as needed.

dc_other_hostnames='*host-list*'

The *host-list* is a semicolon-separated list of IP addresses and/or FQDNs the local system accepts (but does not relay) email for; **localhost** (127.0.0.1) is assumed to be in this list.

dc_readhost='*hostname*'

The *hostname* replaces the local mailname in the headers of email originating on local systems. This setting is effective only if **dc_hide_mailname** is set to **true** and **dc_eximconfig_configtype** is set to **smarthost** or **satellite**.

dc_relay_domains='*host-list*'

The *host-list* is a semicolon-separated list of IP addresses and/or FQDNs the local system accepts mail for, but does not deliver to local systems. The local system relays mail to these systems. For example, the local system may be a secondary server for these systems.

dc_relay_nets='*host-list*'

The *host-list* is a semicolon-separated list of IP addresses and/or FQDNs of systems that the local system relays mail for. The local system is a smarthost (page 681) for these systems.

dc_smarthost='*host-list*'

The *host-list* is a semicolon-separated list of IP addresses (preferred) and/or FQDNs the local system sends email to for relaying to nonlocal systems (a smarthost; page 681). See "JumpStart I" on page 680 for an example.

dc_use_split_config='*bool*'

Controls which files update-exim4.conf uses to generate the configuration file for **exim4**. See "Split configuration" (page 689) for more information.

dpkg-reconfigure: CONFIGURES exim4

The dpkg-reconfigure utility reconfigures the installed copy of a software package. It displays a pseudographical window that can be used from any character-based device, including a terminal emulator. The following command enables you to reconfigure **exim4** interactively:

```
$ sudo dpkg-reconfigure exim4-config
```

The first window this command displays briefly explains the differences between the split and unsplit configurations (page 689), tells you where you can find more information on this topic, and asks if you want to set up the split configuration (Figure 20-1). If you choose to set up a split configuration, dpkg-reconfigure assigns a value of **true** to **dc_use_split_config** (see "Split configuration" on page 689) and continues as though you had chosen to use an *unsplit* configuration: It does not modify files in the **/etc/exim4/conf.d** directory hierarchy. This setup causes update-exim4.conf to read the files in the **/etc/exim4/conf.d** directory hierarchy, incorporating any changes you make to those files.

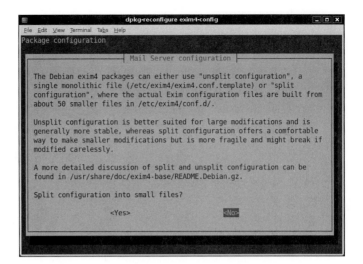

Figure 20-1   Using dpkg-reconfigure on **exim4-config**

The dpkg-reconfigure utility continues providing information, asking questions, and assigning values to the variables in **/etc/exim4/update-exim4.conf.conf** (page 688). It may also change the string in **/etc/mailname** (page 682). When it is finished, it restarts **exim4**, running update-exim4.conf in the process.

SPAMASSASSIN

Spam—or more correctly UCE (unsolicited commercial email)—accounts for more than three-fourths of all email. SpamAssassin evaluates each piece of incoming email and assigns it a number that indicates the likelihood that the email is spam. The higher the number, the more likely that the email is spam. You can filter email based on its rating. SpamAssassin is effective as installed, but you can modify its configuration files to make it better fit your needs. See page 679 for sources of more information on SpamAssassin.

HOW SPAMASSASSIN WORKS

spamc and **spamd**   SpamAssassin comprises the **spamd** daemon and the spamc client. Although it includes the spamassassin utility, the SpamAssassin documentation suggests using spamc and not spamassassin to filter mail because spamc is much quicker to load than spamassassin. While spamassassin works alone, spamc calls **spamd**. The **spamd** daemon spawns children; when **spamd** is running, ps displays several **spamd child** processes in addition to the parent **spamd** process:

```
$ ps -ef | grep spam
root      5073      1  0 10:53 ?        00:00:00 /usr/sbin/spamd --create-prefs ...
root      5106   5073  0 10:53 ?        00:00:00 spamd child
root      5107   5073  0 10:53 ?        00:00:00 spamd child
zach     16080   6225  0 12:58 pts/0    00:00:00 grep spam
```

The spamc utility is a filter. That is, it reads each piece of email from standard input, sends the email to **spamd** for processing, and writes the modified email to standard output. The **spamd** daemon uses several techniques to identify spam:

- **Header analysis**—Checks for tricks that people who send spam use to make you think email is legitimate.

- **Text analysis**—Checks the body of an email for characteristics of spam.

- **Blacklists**—Checks lists to see whether the sender is known for sending spam.

- **Database**—Checks the signature of the message against Vipul's Razor (razor.sourceforge.net), a spam-tracking database.

PREREQUISITES

Packages   Install the following packages:

- **spamassassin**

- **spamc**

- **procmail** (needed to run SpamAssassin on a mail server; page 694)

When you install the **spamassassin** package, the **dpkg postinst** script does not start the **spamd** daemon. Before you can start **spamd**, you must change the value assigned to **ENABLED** to 1 in **/etc/default/spamassassin**. Typically you do not need to make other changes to this file.

```
$ cat /etc/default/spamassassin
...
# Change to one to enable spamd
ENABLED=1
...
```

spamassassin init   After making this change, start the **spamd** daemon with the following command:
script

```
$ sudo /etc/init.d/spamassassin start
Starting SpamAssassin Mail Filter Daemon: spamd.
```

After modifying any system SpamAssassin configuration files, give the same command, but replacing **start** with **reload**, to cause **spamd** to reread its configuration files.

TESTING SPAMASSASSIN

With **spamd** running, you can see how spamc works by sending it a string:

```
$ echo "hi there" | spamc
...
X-Spam-Flag: YES
X-Spam-Checker-Version: SpamAssassin 3.2.5 (2008-06-10) on plum.bogus.com
X-Spam-Level: ********
X-Spam-Status: Yes, score=8.9 required=5.0 tests=EMPTY_MESSAGE,MISSING_DATE,
        MISSING_HB_SEP,MISSING_HEADERS,MISSING_MID,MISSING_SUBJECT,NO_HEADERS_MESSAGE,
        NO_RECEIVED,NO_RELAYS,TVD_SPACE_RATIO autolearn=no version=3.2.5
...
Content analysis details:    (8.9 points, 5.0 required)
```

```
 pts rule name              description
 ---- --------------------   -------------------------------------------------
 0.0 MISSING_MID            Missing Message-Id: header
 0.0 MISSING_DATE           Missing Date: header
-0.0 NO_RELAYS              Informational: message was not relayed via SMTP
 2.5 MISSING_HB_SEP         Missing blank line between message header and body
 1.6 MISSING_HEADERS        Missing To: header
 2.9 TVD_SPACE_RATIO        BODY: TVD_SPACE_RATIO
 1.3 MISSING_SUBJECT        Missing Subject: header
 0.6 EMPTY_MESSAGE          Message appears to have no textual parts and no
                            Subject: text
-0.0 NO_RECEIVED            Informational: message has no Received headers
 0.0 NO_HEADERS_MESSAGE     Message appears to be missing most RFC-822 headers
...
```

Of course, SpamAssassin complains because the string you gave it did not contain standard email headers. The logical line that starts with **X-Spam-Status** contains the heart of the report on the string **hi there**. First it says **Yes** (it considers the message to be spam). SpamAssassin uses a rating system that assigns a number of hits to a piece of email. If the email receives more than the required number of hits (5.0 by default), SpamAssassin marks it as spam. The string failed for many reasons that are enumerated on this status line. The reasons are detailed in the section labeled **Content analysis details**.

The following listing is from a real piece of spam processed by SpamAssassin. It received 24.5 hits, indicating that it is almost certainly spam.

```
X-Spam-Status: Yes, hits=24.5 required=5.0
    tests=DATE_IN_FUTURE_06_12,INVALID_DATE_TZ_ABSURD,
        MSGID_OE_SPAM_4ZERO,MSGID_OUTLOOK_TIME,
        MSGID_SPAMSIGN_ZEROES,RCVD_IN_DSBL,RCVD_IN_NJABL,
        RCVD_IN_UNCONFIRMED_DSBL,REMOVE_PAGE,VACATION_SCAM,
        X_NJABL_OPEN_PROXY
    version=2.55
X-Spam-Level: ************************
X-Spam-Checker-Version: SpamAssassin 2.55 (1.174.2.19-2003-05-19-exp)
X-Spam-Report:    This mail is probably spam.  The original message has been attached
  along with this report, so you can recognize or block similar unwanted
  mail in future.  See http://spamassassin.org/tag/ for more details.
  Content preview:  Paradise SEX Island Awaits! Tropical 1 week vacations
  where anything goes! We have lots of WOMEN, SEX, ALCOHOL, ETC! Every
  man's dream awaits on this island of pleasure. [...]
  Content analysis details:   (24.50 points, 5 required)
  MSGID_SPAMSIGN_ZEROES (4.3 points)  Message-Id generated by spam tool (zeroes variant)
  INVALID_DATE_TZ_ABSURD (4.3 points)  Invalid Date: header (timezone does not exist)
  MSGID_OE_SPAM_4ZERO (3.5 points)  Message-Id generated by spam tool (4-zeroes variant)
  VACATION_SCAM       (1.9 points)  BODY: Vacation Offers
  REMOVE_PAGE         (0.3 points)  URI: URL of page called "remove"
  MSGID_OUTLOOK_TIME (4.4 points)  Message-Id is fake (in Outlook Express format)
  DATE_IN_FUTURE_06_12 (1.3 points)  Date: is 6 to 12 hours after Received: date
  RCVD_IN_NJABL       (0.9 points)  RBL: Received via a relay in dnsbl.njabl.org
  [RBL check: found 94.99.190.200.dnsbl.njabl.org.]
  RCVD_IN_UNCONFIRMED_DSBL (0.5 points)  RBL: Received via a relay in unconfirmed.dsbl.org
  [RBL check: found 94.99.190.200.unconfirmed.dsbl.org.]
  X_NJABL_OPEN_PROXY (0.5 points)  RBL: NJABL: sender is proxy/relay/formmail/spam-source
  RCVD_IN_DSBL        (2.6 points)  RBL: Received via a relay in list.dsbl.org
  [RBL check: found 211.157.63.200.list.dsbl.org.]
X-Spam-Flag: YES
Subject: [SPAM] re: statement
```

CONFIGURING SPAMASSASSIN

SpamAssassin looks in many locations for configuration files; for details, refer to the spamassassin man page. The easiest configuration file to work with is **/etc/mail/spamassassin/local.cf.** You can edit this file to configure SpamAssassin globally. Users can override these global options and add their own options in the **~/.spamassassin/user_prefs** file. You can put the options discussed in this section in either of these files.

For example, you can configure SpamAssassin to rewrite the Subject line of email that it rates as spam. The **rewrite_header** keyword in the configuration files controls this behavior. The word **Subject** following this keyword tells SpamAssassin to rewrite Subject lines. Remove the # from the following line to turn on this behavior:

```
# rewrite_header Subject *****SPAM*****
```

The **required_score** keyword specifies the minimum score a piece of email must receive before SpamAssassin considers it to be spam. The default is 5.00. Set the value of this keyword to a higher number to cause SpamAssassin to mark fewer pieces of email as spam.

```
required_score 5.00
```

Sometimes mail from addresses that should be marked as spam is not, or mail from addresses that should not be marked as spam is. Use the **whitelist_from** keyword to specify addresses that should never be marked as spam and **blacklist_from** to specify addresses that should always be marked as spam:

```
whitelist_from sams@example.com
blacklist_from *@spammer.net
```

You can specify multiple addresses, separated by SPACEs, on the **whitelist_from** and **blacklist_from** lines. Each address can include wildcards. To whitelist everyone sending email from the example.com domain, use **whitelist_from *@example.com.** You can use multiple **whitelist_from** and **blacklist_from** lines.

RUNNING SPAMASSASSIN ON A MAIL SERVER

This section explains how to set up SpamAssassin on a mail server so that it will process all email being delivered to local systems before it is sent to users. It shows how to use **procmail** as the MDA and have **procmail** send email through spamc.

First make sure the **procmail** package is installed on the server system. Next, if the **/etc/procmailrc** configuration file does not exist, create it so that this file is owned by **root** and has 644 permissions and the following contents. If it does exist, append the last two lines from the following file to it:

```
$ cat /etc/procmailrc
DROPPRIVS=yes
:0 fw
| /usr/bin/spamc
```

The first line of this file ensures that **procmail** runs with the least possible privileges. The next two lines implement a rule that pipes each user's incoming email through spamc. The :0 tells **procmail** that a rule follows. The **f** flag indicates a filter; the **w** flag causes **procmail** to wait for the filter to complete and check the exit code. The last line specifies that the **/usr/bin/spamc** utility will be used as the filter.

With this file in place, all email that the server system receives for local delivery passes through SpamAssassin, which rates it according to the options in the global configuration file. Users with accounts on the server system can override the global SpamAssassin configuration settings in their **~/.spamassassin/user_prefs** files.

When you run SpamAssassin on a server, you typically want to rate the email conservatively so that fewer pieces of good email are marked as spam. Setting **required_hits** in the range of 6–10 is generally appropriate. Also, you do not want to remove any email automatically because you could prevent a user from getting a piece of nonspam email. When the server marks email as possibly being spam, users can manually or automatically filter the spam and decide what to do with it.

ADDITIONAL EMAIL TOOLS

This section covers Webmail and mailing lists. In addition, it discusses how to set up IMAP and POP3 servers.

WEBMAIL

Traditionally you read email using a dedicated email client such as mail or Evolution. Recently it has become more common to use a Web application to read email. If you have an email account with a commercial provider such as Gmail, HotMail, or Yahoo! Mail, you use a Web browser to read email. Email read in this manner is called *Webmail*. Unlike email you read on a dedicated client, you can read Webmail from anywhere you can open a browser on the Internet: You can check your email from an Internet cafe or a friend's computer, for example.

SquirrelMail SquirrelMail provides Webmail services. It is written in PHP and supports the IMAP and SMTP protocols. For maximum compatibility across browsers, SquirrelMail renders pages in HTML 4.0 without the use of JavaScript.

SquirrelMail is modular, meaning that you can easily add functionality using plugins. Plugins can allow you to share a calendar, for example, or give you the ability to change passwords using the Webmail interface. See the plugins section of the SquirrelMail Web site (www.squirrelmail.org) for more information.

To use SquirrelMail, you must run IMAP (page 699) because SquirrelMail uses IMAP to receive and authenticate email. You must also run Apache (Chapter 26) so a user can use a browser to connect to SquirrelMail. Because the **squirrelmail** package depends on several Apache packages, APT installs **apache2** when it installs **squirrelmail**. You need to install an IMAP package manually.

Installation   Install the following packages:

- **squirrelmail**
- **apache2** (page 858; installed as a dependency when you install **squirrelmail**)
- **exim4** (page 678) or **sendmail**
- **dovecot-imapd** (page 699) or another IMAP server

Startup   You do not need to start SquirrelMail, nor do you have to open any ports for it. However, you need to configure, start, and open ports (if the server is running on a system with a firewall) for **exim4** (page 682), IMAP (page 699), and Apache (page 859).

Configuration   The SquirrelMail files reside in **/usr/share/squirrelmail**. Create the following link to make SquirrelMail accessible from the Web:

```
$ sudo ln -s /usr/share/squirrelmail /var/www/mail
```

Give the following command to configure SquirrelMail:

```
$ sudo squirrelmail-configure
SquirrelMail Configuration : Read: config.php (1.4.0)
---------------------------------------------------------
Main Menu --
1.  Organization Preferences
2.  Server Settings
3.  Folder Defaults
4.  General Options
5.  Themes
6.  Address Books
7.  Message of the Day (MOTD)
8.  Plugins
9.  Database
10. Languages

D.  Set pre-defined settings for specific IMAP servers

C   Turn color on
S   Save data
Q   Quit

Command >>
```

This menu has multiple levels. When you select a setting (and not a submenu), squirrelmail-configure displays information that can help you decide how to answer the question it poses. Set the server's domain name (number **1** on the Server Settings page) and the name of the IMAP server you are using (**D** on the main menu). SquirrelMail provides several themes; if you do not like the way SquirrelMail looks, choose another theme from Themes (number **5**). When you are finished making changes, exit from squirrelmail-configure. Run squirrelmail-configure whenever you want to change the configuration of SquirrelMail.

SquirrelMail provides a Web page that tests its configuration. Point a browser on the server at **localhost/mail/src/configtest.php**. Replace **localhost** with the IP address or

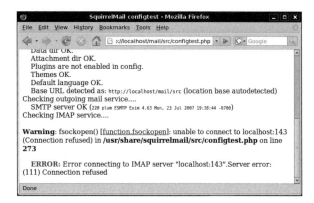

Figure 20-2   SquirrelMail running a configuration test

FQDN of the server to view the page from another system. SquirrelMail checks its configuration and displays the results on this page. Figure 20-2 shows that Squirrel-Mail cannot connect to the IMAP server on the local system, probably because IMAP has not been installed.

Logging in Point a Web browser at **localhost/mail** or **localhost/mail/src/login.php** to display the SquirrelMail login page (Figure 20-3). Replace **localhost** with the IP address or FQDN of the server to view the page from another system. Enter the username and password of a user who has an account on the server system.

MAILING LISTS

A mailing list can be an asset if you regularly send email to the same large group of people. It offers several advantages over listing numerous recipients in the To or Cc field of an email or sending the same email individually to many people:

- **Anonymity**—None of the recipients of the email can see the addresses of the other recipients.

Figure 20-3   SquirrelMail login page

- **Archiving**—Email sent to the list is stored in a central location where list members or the public, as specified by the list administrator, can browse through it.

- **Access control**—You can specify who can send email to the list.

- **Consistency**—When you send mail to a group of people using To or Cc, it is easy to forget people who want to be on the list and to erroneously include people who want to be off the list.

- **Efficiency**—A mailing list application spreads email transmissions over time so it does not overload the mail server.

Mailman   Mailman, the GNU list manager, is written mostly in Python and manages email discussions and email newsletter lists. Because it is integrated with the Web, Mailman makes it easy for users to manage their accounts and for administrators to manage lists. See the Mailman home page (www.list.org) and the files in the **/usr/share/doc/mailman** directory for more information.

Prerequisites   Install the **mailman** package and an MTA such as **exim4** (page 679). To use the Web interface you must install Apache (page 858).

Installing Mailman   When you install the **mailman** package, the **dpkg postinst** script displays a pseudo-graphical interface that asks you to specify the language you want Mailman to display and tells you that you must create a site list. Give the following newlist command to create a site list, substituting the name of your mailing site for **painting_class**:

```
$ sudo newlist painting_class
Enter the email of the person running the list: helen@example.com
Initial painting_class password:
To finish creating your mailing list, you must edit your /etc/aliases (or
equivalent) file by adding the following lines, and possibly running the
'newaliases' program:

## painting_class mailing list
painting_class:              "|/var/lib/mailman/mail/mailman post painting_class"
painting_class-admin:        "|/var/lib/mailman/mail/mailman admin painting_class"
painting_class-bounces:      "|/var/lib/mailman/mail/mailman bounces painting_class"
painting_class-confirm:      "|/var/lib/mailman/mail/mailman confirm painting_class"
painting_class-join:         "|/var/lib/mailman/mail/mailman join painting_class"
painting_class-leave:        "|/var/lib/mailman/mail/mailman leave painting_class"
painting_class-owner:        "|/var/lib/mailman/mail/mailman owner painting_class"
painting_class-request:      "|/var/lib/mailman/mail/mailman request painting_class"
painting_class-subscribe:    "|/var/lib/mailman/mail/mailman subscribe painting_class"
painting_class-unsubscribe:  "|/var/lib/mailman/mail/mailman unsubscribe painting_class"

Hit enter to notify painting_class owner...
```

Before users on the list can receive email, you need to copy the lines generated by newlist (the ones that start with the name of your mailing site) to the end of **/etc/aliases** (page 686) and run newaliases (page 687).

mailman site list   Before you can start Mailman, you must create a site list named **mailman**. Give the command **sudo newlist mailman**, copy the lines to the **aliases** file, and run newaliases.

mailman init script   After setting up the **mailman** site list and a site list of your choice, start the Mailman **qrunner** daemon with the following command:

```
$ sudo /etc/init.d/mailman start
 * Starting Mailman master qrunner mailmanctl                         [ OK ]
```

After modifying any Mailman configuration files or adding a new site list, give the same command, but replacing **start** with **reload,** to cause Mailman to reread its configuration files.

mm_cfg.py   The main Mailman configuration file is **/etc/mailman/mm_cfg.py.** When you install Mailman, it automatically assigns values to **DEFAULT_EMAIL_HOST** (the default domain for mailing lists) and **DEFAULT_URL_HOST** (the default Web server for Mailman). Change the value of these variables as needed and restart Mailman.

```
$ cat /etc/mailman/mm_cfg.py
...
# Default domain for email addresses of newly created MLs
DEFAULT_EMAIL_HOST = 'example.com'

# Default host for web interface of newly created MLs
DEFAULT_URL_HOST   = 'example.com'
...
```

Web interface   Assuming the host for the Web interface is **example.com,** anyone can point a browser at **example.com/cgi-bin/mailman/listinfo** to display a list of available mailing lists. Click the name of a mailing list to display a page that allows you to view the list's archives, send a message, or subscribe to the list. At the bottom of the page is a link to the administrative interface for the list.

SETTING UP AN IMAP OR POP3 MAIL SERVER

Dovecot   IMAP (Internet Message Access Protocol) and POP (Post Office Protocol) allow users to retrieve and manipulate email remotely. This section explains how to set up servers for these protocols. Dovecot (www.dovecot.org and wiki.dovecot.org) provides the **imap-login** and **pop3-login** daemons that implement these protocols.

Prerequisites   Install the **dovecot-pop3d** (for a POP3 server) and/or **dovecot-imapd** (for an IMAP server) packages. APT installs the **dovecot-common** package automatically when you install one of these packages. When you install either package, the **dpkg postinst** script for the **dovecot-common** package generates self-signed SSL certificates if they do not already exist.

Configuration   Dovecot will not start until you specify in the **/etc/dovecot/dovecot.conf** configuration file which servers you want to run. Near the beginning of this long file is a line that starts with **protocols =.** Put the names of the servers you want to run at the end of this line. Possible servers, depending on which packages you have installed, are **imap** (IMAP on port 143), **imaps** (IMAP over SSL on port 993), **pop3** (POP3 on port 110), and **pop3s** (POP3 over SSL on port 995). See **/usr/share/doc/dovecot**✻ for more information.

dovecot init script   After configuring Dovecot, start the Dovecot daemon(s) with the following command:

```
$ sudo /etc/init.d/dovecot start
```

After modifying a Dovecot configuration file, give the same command, but replacing **start** with **restart**, to cause Dovecot to reread its configuration files.

AUTHENTICATED RELAYING

If you travel with a portable computer such as a laptop, you may connect to the Internet through a different connection at each location where you work. Perhaps you travel for work, or maybe you just bring your laptop home at night.

This section does not apply if you always dial in to the network through your ISP. In that case, you are always connected to your ISP's network and it is as though you never moved your computer.

On a laptop you do not use a local instance of **exim4** to send email. Instead, you use SMTP to connect to an ISP or to a company's SMTP server (a smarthost), which then relays your outgoing mail. To avoid relaying email for anyone, including malicious users who would send spam, SMTP servers restrict who they relay email for, based on IP address. By implementing authenticated relaying, you can cause the SMTP server to authenticate, based on user identification. In addition, SMTP can encrypt communication when you send mail from your email client and use an SMTP server.

An authenticated relay provides several advantages over a plain connection:

- You can send email from any Internet connection.
- The secure connection makes it more difficult to intercept email as it traverses the Internet.
- The outgoing mail server requires authentication, preventing it from being used for spam.

You set up authenticated relaying by creating an SSL certificate or using an existing one, enabling SSL in **exim4**, and telling your email client to connect to the SMTP server using SSL. If you have an SSL certificate from a company such as VeriSign, you can skip the next section, in which you create a self-signed certificate.

CREATING A SELF-SIGNED CERTIFICATE FOR exim4

Typically, installing Dovecot generates self-signed certificates. If necessary, give the following command to create SSL certificates for **exim4**. The keys are stored in **exim.key** and **exim.crt** in the **/etc/exim4** directory. Apache uses a similar procedure for creating a certificate (page 899).

```
$ sudo /usr/share/doc/exim4-base/examples/exim-gencert
[*] Creating a self signed SSL certificate for Exim!
```

```
    This may be sufficient to establish encrypted connections but for
    secure identification you need to buy a real certificate!

    Please enter the hostname of your MTA at the Common Name (CN) prompt!

Generating a 1024 bit RSA private key
..............++++++
.........................................................++++++
writing new private key to '/etc/exim4/exim.key'
-----
You are about to be asked to enter information that will be incorporated
into your certificate request.
What you are about to enter is what is called a Distinguished Name or a DN.
There are quite a few fields but you can leave some blank
For some fields there will be a default value,
If you enter '.', the field will be left blank.
-----
Country Code (2 letters) [US]:
State or Province Name (full name) []:California
Locality Name (eg, city) []:San Francisco
Organization Name (eg, company; recommended) []:Sobell Associates Inc.
Organizational Unit Name (eg, section) []:
Server name (eg. ssl.domain.tld; required!!!) []:sobell.com
Email Address []:mgs@sobell.com
[*] Done generating self signed certificates for exim!
    Refer to the documentation and example configuration files
    over at /usr/share/doc/exim4-base/ for an idea on how to enable TLS
    support in your mail transfer agent.
```

You can enter any information you wish in the certificate.

ENABLING SSL IN exim4

Once you have a certificate, create a file named **exim4.conf.localmacros** in the **/etc/exim4** directory (you have to work with **root** privileges). With the following contents, this file instructs **exim4** to use SSL certificates:

```
$ cat /etc/exim4/exim4.conf.localmacros
MAIN_TLS_ENABLE = 1
```

Because **exim4** will be relaying email, you need to add the name of the system you will be sending email from to the **dc_relay_nets** variable (page 690). Restart **exim4** (page 680).

ENABLING SSL IN THE MAIL CLIENT

Enabling SSL in a mail client is usually quite simple. For example, Evolution provides the **Edit⇨Preferences⇨Mail Accounts⇨Sending Email⇨Security⇨Use Secure Connection** combo box that allows you to choose the type of encryption you want to use: **No encryption, SSL encryption,** or **TLS encryption.** Clicking the **Check for Supported Types** button (found just below this combo box) queries the server and sets Evolution to use the type of security and authentication the server supports.

CHAPTER SUMMARY

The **exim4** daemon is an MTA (mail transfer agent). When you send a message, **exim4** works with other software to get the email to the proper recipients. You can set up **exim4** to send email to an SMTP server that then relays the email to its destination or you can have **exim4** send email directly to the SMTP servers for the domains receiving the email. By default, **exim4** stores incoming messages in the mail spool directory, **/var/mail**.

The **/etc/exim4/update-exim4.conf.conf** file controls many aspects of how **exim4** works. After you edit this file, you must use the **exim4** init script to restart **exim4** so it rereads its configuration files. The system administrator can use the **/etc/aliases** file and ordinary users can use **~/.forward** files to reroute email to one or more local or remote addresses, to files, or as input to programs.

You can use a program such as SpamAssassin to grade and mark email as to the likelihood of it being spam. You can then decide what to do with the marked email: You can look at each piece of potential spam and decide where to put it, or you can have your MUA automatically put potential spam in a special mailbox for spam.

Other programs that can help with email include SquirrelMail, which provides Web-mail services, and Mailman, which provides mailing list support. IMAP (Internet Message Access Protocol) and POP (Post Office Protocol) allow users to retrieve and manipulate email remotely. The Dovecot system provides IMAP and POP servers.

EXERCISES

1. By default, email addressed to **system** goes to **root**. How would you also save a copy in **/var/logs/systemmail**?

2. How would Max store a copy of his email in **~/mbox** and send a copy to **max@example.com**?

3. If your firewall allowed only the machine with the IP address 192.168.1.1 to send email outside the network, how would you instruct the local copy of **exim4** to use this server as a relay?

4. Describe how setting the **dc_eximconfig_configtype** variable in **/etc/exim4/update-exim4.conf.conf** to **smarthost** affects **exim4** behavior. What happens when you set this variable to **internet**?

5. SpamAssassin is installed on your mail server, with the threshold set to an unusually low value of 3, resulting in a lot of false positives. What rule could you give to your mail client to allow it to identify spam with a score of 5 or higher?

6. Describe the software and protocols used when Max sends an email to Sam on a remote Linux system.

ADVANCED EXERCISES

7. Explain the differences between configuring **exim4** to use a split configuration and configuring it to use an unsplit configuration. Which files would you modify to set up each type of configuration? Name two files that are read by both configurations.

8. Assume a script stores certain information in a variable named **RESULT**. What line could you put in the script that would send the contents of **RESULT** to the email address specified by the first argument on the command line?

9. Give a simple way of reading your email that does not involve the use of an MUA.

10. Describe the relationship between spamassassin, **spamd**, and spamc. How does each work? Why not use the spamassassin utility by itself?

21

NIS AND LDAP

NIS (Network Information Service) simplifies the maintenance of common administrative files by keeping them in a central database and having clients contact the database server to retrieve information from the database. Developed by Sun Microsystems, NIS is an example of the client/server paradigm.

Just as DNS addresses the problem of keeping multiple copies of **/etc/hosts** files up-to-date, so NIS deals with the issue of keeping system-independent configuration files (such as **/etc/passwd**) current. Most networks today are *heterogeneous* (page 1111); even though they run different varieties of UNIX or Linux, they have certain common attributes, such as a **passwd** file.

An LDAP (Lightweight Directory Access Protocol) directory can hold many types of information, including names and addresses, lists of network services, and authentication data. Another example of a client/server setup, LDAP is appropriate for any kind of relatively static, structured information where fast lookups are required. Many types of clients are set up to communicate with LDAP servers, including email clients, browsers, and authentication servers.

INTRODUCTION TO NIS

A primary goal of a LAN administrator is to make the network transparent to users. One aspect of this transparency is presenting users with similar environments, including usernames and passwords, when they log in on different machines. From the administrator's perspective, the information that supports a user's environment should not be replicated but rather should be kept in a central location and distributed as required. NIS simplifies this task.

As with DNS, users need not be aware that NIS is managing system configuration files. Setting up and maintaining NIS databases are tasks for the system administrator; individual users and users on single-user Linux systems rarely need to work directly with NIS.

Yellow Pages   NIS used to be called the *Yellow Pages,* and some people still refer to it by this name. Sun renamed the service because another corporation holds the trademark to the Yellow Pages name. The names of NIS utilities and files, however, are reminiscent of the old name: ypcat displays and ypmatch searches an NIS file, and the server daemon is named **ypserv.**

HOW NIS WORKS

No encryption   NIS does not encrypt data it transfers over the network—it transfers data as plain text.

NIS domain   NIS makes a common set of information available to systems on a network. The network, referred to as an *NIS domain,* is characterized by each system having the same *NIS domain name* (different than a DNS *domain name* [page 1106]). Technically an NIS domain is a set of NIS maps (database files).

Master and slave servers   Each NIS domain must have exactly one master server; larger networks may have slave servers. Each slave server holds a copy of the NIS database from the master. The need for slave servers is based on the size of the NIS domain and the reliability of the systems and network. A system can belong to only one NIS domain at a time.

nsswitch.conf   Whether a system uses NIS, DNS, local files, or a combination of these as the source of certain information, and in what order, is determined by the **/etc/nsswitch.conf** file (page 458). When it needs information from the NIS database, a client requests the information from the NIS server. For example, when a user attempts to log in, the client system may authenticate the user with username and password information from the NIS server.

You can configure **nsswitch.conf** to cause **/etc/passwd** to override NIS password information for the local system. When you do not export the **root** account to NIS (and you should not), this setup allows you to have a unique **root** password (or no **root** password, if the **root** account is locked) for each system.

Source files   Under Ubuntu Linux, NIS derives the information it offers—such as usernames, passwords, and local system names and IP addresses—from local ASCII configuration files such as **/etc/passwd** and **/etc/hosts.** These files are called *source files* or *master files.* (Some administrators avoid confusion by using different files to hold local configuration information and NIS source information.) An NIS server can include information from as many of the following source files as is appropriate:

/etc/group	Defines groups and their members
/etc/gshadow	Provides shadow passwords for groups
/etc/hosts	Maps local systems and IP addresses
/etc/passwd	Lists user information
/etc/printcap	Lists printer information
/etc/rpc	Maps RPC program names and numbers
/etc/services	Maps system service names and port numbers
/etc/shadow	Provides shadow passwords for users

The information that NIS offers is based on files that change from time to time. NIS is responsible for making the updated information available in a timely manner to all systems in the NIS domain.

NIS maps   Before NIS can store the information contained in a source file, it must be converted to a *dbm* (page 1104) format file called a *map*. Each map is indexed on one field (column). Records (rows) from a map can be retrieved by specifying a value from the indexed field. Some files generate two maps, each indexed on a different field. For example, the **/etc/passwd** file generates two maps: one indexed by username, the other indexed by UID. These maps are named **passwd.byname** and **passwd.byuid**, respectively.

optional   NIS maps correspond to C library functions. The **getpwnam**() and **getpwuid**() functions obtain username and UID information from **/etc/passwd** on non-NIS systems. On NIS systems, these functions place RPC calls to the NIS server in a process that is transparent to the application calling the function.

Map names   The names of the maps NIS uses correspond to the files in the **/var/yp/***nisdomainname* directory on the master server, where ***nisdomainname*** is the name of the NIS domain. The examples in this chapter use the NIS domain named **mgs**:

```
$ ls /var/yp/mgs
group.bygid     netgroup.byhost   protocols.byname    services.byservicename
group.byname    netgroup.byuser   protocols.bynumber  shadow.byname
hosts.byaddr    netid.byname      rpc.byname          ypservers
hosts.byname    passwd.byname     rpc.bynumber
netgroup        passwd.byuid      services.byname
```

Map nicknames   To make it easier to refer to NIS maps, you can assign nicknames to them. The **/var/yp/nicknames** file on both clients and servers holds a list of commonly used nicknames:

```
$ cat /var/yp/nicknames
passwd          passwd.byname
group           group.byname
networks        networks.byaddr
hosts           hosts.byname
protocols       protocols.bynumber
services        services.byname
aliases         mail.aliases
ethers          ethers.byname
```

You can also use the command **ypcat –x** to display the list of nicknames. Each line in **nicknames** contains a nickname followed by whitespace and the name of the map corresponding to the nickname. You can add, remove, or modify nicknames by changing the **nicknames** file.

Displaying maps   The ypcat and ypmatch utilities display information from the NIS maps on the server. Using the nickname **passwd**, the following command, which you can run on any NIS client in the local domain, displays the information contained in the **passwd.byname** map:

```
$ ypcat passwd
sam:x:1000:1000:Sam,,,,:/home/sam:/bin/bash
sls:x:1001:1001:Sam the Great,,,,:/home/sls:/bin/bash
...
```

By default, NIS stores passwords only for users with UIDs greater than or equal to 1000 (see MINUID on page 717). Thus ypcat does not display lines for **root**, **bin**, and other system entries. You can display password information for a single user with ypmatch:

```
$ ypmatch sam passwd
sam:x:1000:1000:Sam,,,,:/home/sam:/bin/bash
```

You can retrieve the same information by filtering the output of ypcat through grep, but ypmatch is more efficient because it searches the map directly, using a single process. The ypmatch utility works on the key for the map only. To match members of the group or other fields not in a map, such as the *GECOS* (page 1110) field in **passwd**, you need to use ypcat and grep:

```
$ ypcat passwd | grep -i great
sls:x:1001:1001:Sam the Great,,,,:/home/sls:/bin/bash
```

Terminology   This chapter uses the following definitions:

NIS source files   The ASCII files that NIS obtains information from
NIS maps   The dbm-format files created from NIS source files
NIS database   The collection of NIS maps

MORE INFORMATION

Local   man pages: domainname, makedbm, **netgroup**, revnetgroup, **ypbind**, ypcat, ypinit, ypmatch, yppasswd, yppoll, yppush, ypset, **ypserv**, **ypserv.conf**, ypwhich, ypxfr, **ypxfrd**

Web   www.linux-nis.org
NIS-HOWTO

RUNNING AN NIS CLIENT

This section explains how to set up an NIS client on the local system.

PREREQUISITES

Install Install the following packages:

- **nis**

- **portmap** (installs automatically with **nis**)

When you install the **nis** package, the **dpkg postinst** script starts an NIS client. See the "**nis** init script" section below if you want to start an NIS server or do not want to start an NIS client. The **dpkg postinst** script asks you to specify the NIS domain name of the local system if it does not find one in **/etc/defaultdomain**. If necessary, the script creates this file and stores the NIS domain name in that file. If this file does not exist, the NIS client (**ypbind**) will not start. If there is a server for the domain you specify, the client quickly binds to that server.

No server If there is no NIS server for the NIS client to bind to when you install or start an NIS client or boot the system, the client spends several minutes trying to find a server, displaying the following message while doing so:

```
...
Setting up nis (3.17-14ubuntu2) ...
 * Setting NIS domainname to: mgs
 * Starting NIS services
 * binding to YP server...
 * ....
 * ....
...
```

Broadcast mode Finally the client (**ypbind**) gives up on finding a server and runs in the background in broadcast mode:

```
$ ps -ef | grep yp
root     16832     1  0 19:33 ?        00:00:00 /usr/sbin/ypbind -broadcast
sam      17390  5839  0 19:38 pts/0    00:00:00 grep yp
```

Broadcast mode is less secure than other modes because it exposes the system to rogue servers by broadcasting a request for a server to identify itself. If **ypbind** starts in this mode, it is a good idea to restart it after you set up an NIS server (page 714) and configure an NIS client as explained in the next section.

nis init script After you configure **nis**, call the **nis** init script to restart **nis**. However, as explained earlier, starting **nis** takes a while if it cannot connect to a server. The **/etc/default/nis** file specifies whether this script starts an NIS client, server, or both:

```
$ sudo /etc/init.d/nis restart
```

After changing the **nis** configuration on an active server, use **reload** in place of **restart** to reload **nis** configuration files without disturbing clients connected to the server.

NOTES

If there is no NIS server for the local system's NIS domain, you need to set one up (page 714). If there is an NIS server, you need to know the name of the NIS domain the system belongs to and (optionally) the name or IP address of one or more NIS servers for the NIS domain.

An NIS client can run on the same system as an NIS server.

/etc/default/nis   The **/etc/default/nis** file controls several aspects of NIS running on the local system, including whether the **nis** init script starts a client, a server, or both. As installed, this file causes the **nis** init script to start an NIS client (**ypbind**) and not to start an NIS server (**ypserv**). Set NISSERVER to **false** if the local system is not an NIS server or to **master** or **slave** as appropriate if it is a server. Set NISCLIENT to **true** if the local system is an NIS client; otherwise set it to **false**.

```
$ head /etc/default/nis
...
# Are we a NIS server and if so what kind (values: false, slave, master)?
NISSERVER=false

# Are we a NIS client?
NISCLIENT=true
```

In the **nis** file you can also specify which ports the NIS server uses (refer to "Firewall" on page 715) and control which values in **/etc/passwd** users can modify (refer to "Allow GECOS and Login Shell Modification" on page 721).

CONFIGURING AN NIS CLIENT

This section lists the steps involved in setting up and starting an NIS client.

/etc/defaultdomain: SPECIFIES THE NIS DOMAIN NAME

A DNS domain name is different from an NIS domain name

tip   The DNS domain name is used throughout the Internet to refer to a group of systems. DNS maps these names to IP addresses to enable systems to communicate with one another.

The NIS domain name is used strictly to identify systems that share an NIS server and is normally not seen or used by users and other programs. Although some administrators use one name as both a DNS domain name and an NIS domain name, this practice can degrade security.

The **/etc/defaultdomain** file stores the name of the NIS domain the local system belongs to. If you change this value, you need to reload the client and/or server daemon to get NIS to recognize the change. The **nis** init script reads the **defaultdomain** file and sets the name of the system's NIS domain. If the **defaultdomain** file does not exist when you install NIS, the **dpkg postinst** script prompts for it (refer to "Install" on page 709). You can use the nisdomainname utility to set or view the NIS domain name, but setting it in this manner does not maintain the name when the **nis** init script is executed (for example, when the system is rebooted):

```
$ sudo nisdomainname
(none)
$ sudo nisdomainname mgs
$ sudo nisdomainname
mgs
```

To avoid confusion, use **nisdomainname**, not **domainname**

tip   The domainname and nisdomainname utilities do the same thing: They display or set the system's NIS domain name. Use nisdomainname to avoid confusion when you are also working with DNS domain names.

You must set the local system's NIS domain name

tip   If the **/etc/defaultdomain** file is not present, the NIS server and client will not start.

/etc/yp.conf: SPECIFIES AN NIS SERVER

Edit **/etc/yp.conf** to specify one or more NIS servers (masters and/or slaves). You can use one of three formats to specify each server:

   domain **nisdomain** server **server_name**

   domain **nisdomain** broadcast (**do not use**)

   ypserver **server_name**

where **nisdomain** is the name of the NIS domain that the local (client) system belongs to and **server_name** is the hostname of the NIS server that the local system queries. It is best to specify **server_name** as an IP address or a hostname from **/etc/hosts**. If you specify a hostname that requires a DNS lookup and DNS is down, NIS will not find the server. The second format puts **ypbind** in broadcast mode and is less secure than the first and third formats because it exposes the system to rogue servers by broadcasting a request for a server to identify itself. Under Ubuntu Linux, if you do not specify an NIS server, or if the server you specify is not available, an NIS client runs in broadcast mode.

Following is a simple **yp.conf** file for a client in the **mgs** domain with a server at 192.168.0.10:

```
$ cat /etc/yp.conf
domain mgs server 192.168.0.10
```

You can use multiple lines to specify multiple servers for one or more domains. Specifying multiple servers for a single domain allows the system to change to another server when its current server is slow or down.

When you specify more than one NIS domain, you must set the system's NIS domain name before starting **ypbind** so the client queries the proper server. Specifying the NIS domain name in **/etc/defaultdomain** before running the **ypbind** init script takes care of this issue (page 710).

TESTING THE SETUP

After starting **ypbind**, use nisdomainname to make sure the correct NIS domain name is set. Refer to "/etc/defaultdomain: Specifies the NIS Domain Name" on page 710 if you need to set the NIS domain name. Next use ypwhich to check whether the system is set up to connect to the proper server; the name of this server is set in **/etc/yp.conf** (page 711):

```
$ ypwhich
plum
```

Use rpcinfo to make sure the NIS server is up and running (replace **plum** with the name of the server that ypwhich returned):

```
$ rpcinfo -u plum ypserv
program 100004 version 1 ready and waiting
program 100004 version 2 ready and waiting
```

After starting **ypbind**, check that it is registered with **portmap**:

```
$ rpcinfo -u localhost ypbind
program 100007 version 1 ready and waiting
program 100007 version 2 ready and waiting
```

If rpcinfo does not report that **ypbind** is **ready and waiting**, check that **ypbind** is running:

```
$ ps -ef | grep ypbind
root     23144    1  0 18:10 ?        00:00:00 /usr/sbin/ypbind
sam      23670 5553  0 18:31 pts/2    00:00:00 grep ypbind
```

If NIS still does not work properly, stop the NIS server and start **ypbind** with debugging turned on:

```
$ sudo /etc/init.d/nis stop
```

```
$ sudo /usr/sbin/ypbind -debug
7607: parsing config file
7607: Trying entry: domain mgs server 192.168.0.10
7607: parsed domain 'mgs' server '192.168.0.10'
7607: add_server() domain: mgs, host: 192.168.0.10, slot: 0
7607: [Welcome to ypbind-mt, version 1.20.1]

7607: ping interval is 20 seconds

7609: NetworkManager is running.

7609: Are already online
7609: interface: org.freedesktop.DBus, object path:
/org/freedesktop/DBus, method: NameAcquired
7610: ping host '192.168.0.10', domain 'mgs'
7610: Answer for domain 'mgs' from server '192.168.0.10'
7610: Pinging all active servers.
7610: Pinging all active servers.
...
```

The **–debug** option keeps **ypbind** in the foreground and causes it to send error messages and debugging output to standard error. Use CONTROL-C to stop **ypbind** when it is running in the foreground.

yppasswd: CHANGES NIS PASSWORDS

The yppasswd utility—not to be confused with the **yppasswdd** daemon (two **d**'s; see page 721) that runs on the NIS server—replaces the functionality of passwd on clients when you use NIS for passwords. Where passwd changes password information in the **/etc/shadow** file on the local system, yppasswd changes password information in the **/etc/shadow** file on the NIS master server *and* in the NIS **shadow.byname** map. Optionally, yppasswd can also change user information in the **/etc/passwd** file and the **passwd.byname** map.

The yppasswd utility changes the way you log in on all systems in the NIS domain that use NIS to authenticate passwords. It cannot change **root** and system passwords; by default, NIS does not store passwords of users with UIDs greater than or equal to 1000. You have to use passwd to change these users' passwords locally.

To use yppasswd, the **yppasswdd** daemon must be running on the NIS master server.

passwd VERSUS yppasswd

When a user who is authenticated using NIS passwords runs passwd to change her password, all appears to work properly, yet the user's password is not changed: The user needs to use yppasswd. The **root** and system accounts, in contrast, must use passwd to change their passwords. A common solution to this problem is first to rename passwd—for example, to rootpasswd—and then to change its permissions so only **root** can execute it.[1] Second, create a link to yppasswd named passwd:

```
$ ls -l /usr/bin/passwd
-rwsr-xr-x 1 root root 29104 Dec 19 12:35 /usr/bin/passwd
$ sudo -i
# mv /usr/bin/passwd /usr/bin/rootpasswd
# chmod 700 /usr/bin/rootpasswd
# ln -s /usr/bin/yppasswd /usr/bin/passwd
# exit
logout
$ ls -l /usr/bin/{yppasswd,passwd,rootpasswd}
lrwxrwxrwx 1 root root    17 May  8 18:42 /usr/bin/passwd -> /usr/bin/yppasswd
-rwx------ 1 root root 29104 Dec 19 12:35 /usr/bin/rootpasswd
-rwxr-xr-x 1 root root 20688 Mar  7 12:45 /usr/bin/yppasswd
```

The preceding example uses **sudo –i** to open a shell with **root** permissions so the administrator does not have to type **sudo** several times in a row. The administrator returns to using a normal shell as soon as possible.

With this setup, a non**root** user changing his password using passwd will run yppasswd, which is appropriate. If **root** or a system account user runs passwd (really yppasswd), yppasswd displays an error that reminds the administrator to run rootpasswd.

MODIFYING USER INFORMATION

As long as the **yppasswdd** daemon is running on the NIS master server, a user can use the yppasswd utility from an NIS client to change her NIS password while a user

---

1. The passwd utility has setuid permission with read and execute permissions for all users and read, write, and execute permissions for **root**. If, after changing its name and permissions, you want to restore its original name and permissions, first change its name and then give the command **chmod 4755 /usr/bin/passwd**. (You must work with **root** privileges to make these changes.)

running with **root** privileges can change any user's password (except that of **root** or a system account). A user can also use **yppasswd** to change his login shell and *GECOS* (page 1110) information if the **yppasswdd** daemon is set up to permit these changes. Refer to "**yppasswdd**: The NIS Password Update Daemon" on page 721 for information on how to configure **yppasswdd** to permit users to change these values. Use the **–p** option with **yppasswd** to change the password, **–f** to change GECOS information, and **–l** to change the login shell:

```
$ yppasswd -l
Changing NIS account information for sam on plum.
Please enter password:

To accept the default, simply press return. To use the
system's default shell, type the word "none".
Login shell [/bin/bash]: /bin/sh

The login shell has been changed on plum.

$ ypmatch sam passwd
sam:x:1000:1000:Sam,,,,:/home/sam:/bin/sh
```

If yppasswd does not work and the server system is running a firewall, refer to "Firewall" on page 715.

ADDING AND REMOVING USERS

There are several ways to add and remove users from the NIS **passwd** map. The simplest approach is to keep the **/etc/passwd** file on the NIS master server synchronized with the **passwd** map. You can keep these files synchronized by first making changes to the **passwd** file using standard tools such as **adduser** and **deluser**, or their graphical counterparts, and then running **ypinit** (page 719) to update the map.

SETTING UP AN NIS SERVER

This section explains how to set up an NIS server.

PREREQUISITES

Installation   Decide on an NIS domain name (page 710) and install the following packages:

- **nis**
- **portmap** (installs automatically with **nis**)

nis init script   When you install the **nis** package, the **dpkg postinst** script starts an NIS client. See "Install" on page 709 for information on how to start a server, a client, or both. The **/etc/default/nis** configuration file controls whether an NIS server starts as a master or a slave (page 710). You may also want to specify the ports for the NIS server and **yppasswdd** to run on (see "Firewall," next page). After you configure the server you can start, restart, or reload it with the **nis** init script:

```
$ sudo /etc/init.d/nis restart
```

NOTES

An NIS client can run on the same system as an NIS server.

There must be only one master server for each domain.

You can run multiple NIS domain servers (for different domains) on a single system.

An NIS server serves the NIS domains listed in **/var/yp**. For a more secure system, remove the **maps** directories from **/var/yp** when disabling an NIS server.

Firewall The NIS server (**ypserv**) and the NIS password daemon (**yppasswdd**) use **portmap** (page 446) to choose which ports they accept queries on. The **portmap** server hands out a random unused port below 1024 when a service, such as **ypserv**, requests a port. Having **ypserv** and **yppasswdd** use random port numbers makes it difficult to set up a firewall on an NIS server. You can specify ports by editing the **ypserv** and **yppasswdd** option lines in **/etc/default/nis** (choose any unused ports less than 1024):

```
YPSERVARGS='--port 114'
...
YPPASSWDDARGS='--port 112'
```

If the NIS server system is running a firewall, open the ports you specify. Using firestarter (page 824), open these ports by setting two policies: one that allows service on each of these ports. If you follow the preceding example, allow service on ports 114 and 112.

CONFIGURING THE SERVER

This section lists the steps involved in setting up and starting an NIS server.

/etc/default/nis: ALLOWS THE NIS SERVER TO START

Edit the **/etc/default/nis** file as described on page 710 so that the **nis** init script starts the NIS server. You can also specify ports for the NIS server and **yppasswdd** to listen on in this file; refer to "Firewall" above.

SPECIFY THE SYSTEM'S NIS DOMAIN NAME

Specify the system's NIS domain name as explained on page 710. This step is taken care of when you install the **nis** package.

/etc/ypserv.conf: CONFIGURES THE NIS SERVER

The **/etc/ypserv.conf** file, which holds NIS server configuration information, specifies options and access rules. Option rules specify server options and have the following format:

option: value

OPTIONS

Following is a list of *option*s and their default *value*s:

files   Specifies the maximum number of map files that **ypserv** caches. Set to 0 to turn off caching. The default is 30.

trusted_master   On a slave server, the name/IP address of the master server from which the slave accepts new maps. The default is no master server, meaning no new maps are accepted.

xfer_check_port   YES (default) requires the master server to run on a *privileged port* (page 1126). NO allows it to run on any port.

ACCESS RULES

Access rules, which specify which hosts and domains can access which maps, have the following format:

host:domain:map:security

where *host* and *domain* specify the IP address and NIS domain this rule applies to; *map* is the name of the map this rule applies to; and *security* is either **none** (always allow access), **port** (allow access from a privileged port), or **deny** (never allow access).

The following lines appear in the **ypserv.conf** file supplied with Ubuntu Linux:

```
$ cat /etc/ypserv.conf
...
# This is the default - restrict access to the shadow password file,
# allow access to all others.
*                               : *       : shadow.byname    : port
*                               : *       : passwd.adjunct.byname : port
*                               : *       : *                : none
```

These lines restrict the **shadow.byname** and **passwd.adjunct.byname** (the **passwd** map with shadow [asterisk] entries) maps to access from ports numbered less than 1024. However, anyone using a DOS or early Windows system on the network can read the maps because they can access ports numbered less than 1024. The last line allows access to the other maps from any port on any host.

The following example describes a LAN with some addresses you want to grant NIS access from and some that you do not; perhaps you have a wireless segment or some public network connections you do not want to expose to NIS. You can list the systems or an IP subnet that you want to grant access to in **ypserv.conf**. Anyone logging in on another IP address will then be denied NIS services. The following line from **ypserv.conf** grants access to anyone logging in from an IP address in the range of 192.168.0.1 to 192.168.0.255 (specified as 192.168.0.1 with a subnet mask [page 445] of /24):

```
$ cat /etc/ypserv.conf
...
  192.168.0.1/24 : * : * : none
```

/var/yp/securenets: ENHANCES SECURITY

To enhance system security, you can create the **/var/yp/securenets** file, which prevents unauthorized systems from sending RPC requests to the NIS server and retrieving NIS maps. Notably **securenets** prevents unauthorized users from retrieving the **shadow** map, which contains encrypted passwords. When **securenets** does not exist or is empty, an NIS server accepts requests from any system.

Each line of **securenets** lists a netmask and IP address. NIS accepts requests from systems whose IP addresses are specified in **securenets**; it ignores and logs requests from other addresses. You must include the (local) server system as **localhost** (127.0.0.1) in **securenets**. A simple **securenets** file follows:

```
$ cat /var/yp/securenets
# you must accept requests from localhost
255.255.255.255        127.0.0.1
#
# accept requests from IP addresses 192.168.0.1 - 192.168.0.62
255.255.255.192        192.168.0.0
#
# accept requests from IP addresses starting with 192.168.14
255.255.255.0          192.168.14.0
```

/var/yp/Makefile: CREATES MAPS

The make utility, which is controlled by **/var/yp/Makefile**, uses makedbm to create the NIS maps that hold the information distributed by NIS. When you run ypinit (page 719) on the master server, ypinit calls make: You do not need to run make manually.

Edit **/var/yp/Makefile** to set options and specify which maps to create. The following sections discuss **/var/yp/Makefile** in more detail.

VARIABLES

Following is a list of variables you can set in **/var/yp/Makefile**. The values following **Ubuntu** are the values set in the file distributed by Ubuntu.

B Do not change.

Ubuntu: not set

NOPUSH Specifies that **ypserv** is not to copy (push) maps to slave servers. Set to TRUE if you do not have any slave NIS servers; set to FALSE to cause NIS to copy maps to slave servers.

Ubuntu: TRUE

YPPUSHARGS Specifies arguments for yppush. See the yppush man page for more information.

Ubuntu: not set

MINUID, MINGID Specify the lowest UID and GID numbers, respectively, to include in NIS maps. In the **/etc/passwd** and **/etc/group** files, lower ID numbers belong to **root** and system accounts and groups. To enhance security, NIS does not distribute password and group information about these users and groups. Set **MINUID** to the lowest UID number you want to include in the NIS maps and set **MINGID** to the lowest GID number you want to include.

Ubuntu: 1000/1000

NFSNOBODYUID,
NFSNOBODYGID

Specify the UID and GID, respectively, of the user named **nfsnobody**. NIS does not export values for this user. Set to 0 to export maps for **nfsnobody**.

Ubuntu: 65534/65534

MERGE_PASSWD,
MERGE_GROUP

When set to TRUE, merge the **/etc/shadow** and **/etc/passwd** files and the **/etc/gshadow** and **/etc/group** files in the **passwd** and **group** maps, respectively, enabling shadow user passwords and group passwords.

Ubuntu: FALSE/FALSE

FILE LOCATIONS

The next sections of **/var/yp/Makefile** specify standard file locations; you do not normally need to change these entries. This part of the makefile is broken into the following groups:

Commands   Locates awk (mawk) and make and sets a value for umask (page 442)
Source directories   Locates directories that contain NIS source files
NIS source files   Locates NIS source files used to build the NIS database
Servers   Locates the file that lists NIS servers

THE ALL TARGET

The **ALL** target in **/var/yp/Makefile** specifies the maps that make is to build for NIS:

```
ALL =   passwd group hosts rpc services netid protocols netgrp
#ALL += publickey mail ethers bootparams printcap
#ALL += amd.home auto.master auto.home auto.local
#ALL += timezone locale networks netmasks
```

The first line of the **ALL** target lists the maps that make builds by default. This line starts with the word **ALL**, followed by an equal sign and a TAB. The last three lines are commented out. Uncomment lines and delete or move map names until the list matches your needs.

As your needs change, you can edit the **ALL** target in **Makefile** and run make in the **/var/yp** directory to modify the list of maps distributed by NIS.

START THE SERVERS

Restart the master server (page 709) and then the slave servers after completing the preceding steps. On a master server, the **nis** init script starts the **ypserv, yppasswdd,** and **ypxfrd** daemons. If you are running an NIS client on the local system, it also starts **ypbind**. On a slave server, the **nis** init script starts only the **ypserv** daemon and, optionally, the **ypbind** daemon.

When you start the master server before running **ypinit** (discussed in the next section), as you must do to avoid getting errors, it takes a long time to start as explained in "No server" on page 709. After running **ypinit**, you must restart the server (page 709).

ypxfrd: the map server
: The **ypxfrd** daemon speeds up the process of copying large NIS databases from the master server to slaves. It allows slaves to copy the maps, thereby avoiding the need for each slave to copy the raw data and then compile the maps. When an NIS slave receives a message from the server saying there is a new map, it starts ypxfr, which reads the map from the server.

The **ypxfrd** daemon runs on the master server only; it is not necessary to run it on slave servers. For more information refer to "Prerequisites" on page 714.

ypinit: BUILDS OR IMPORTS THE MAPS

The ypinit utility builds or imports and then installs the NIS database. On the master server, ypinit gathers information from the **passwd, group, hosts, networks, services, protocols, netgroup,** and **rpc** files in **/etc** and builds the database. On a slave server, ypinit copies the database from the master server.

You must run ypinit by giving its absolute pathname (**/usr/lib/yp/ypinit**). Use the **–m** option to create the domain subdirectory under **/var/yp** and build the maps that go in it on the master server; use the **–s** *master* option on slave servers to import maps from the master server named *master*. In the following example, ypinit asks for the name of each of the slave servers; it already has the name of the master server because this command is run on the system running the master server (**plum** in the example). Terminate the list with CONTROL-D on a line by itself. After you respond to the query about the list of servers being correct, ypinit builds the **ypservers** map and calls make with **/var/yp/Makefile**, which builds the maps specified in **Makefile**.

```
$ sudo /usr/lib/yp/ypinit -m

At this point, we have to construct a list of the hosts which will run NIS
servers.  dog is in the list of NIS server hosts.  Please continue to add
the names for the other hosts, one per line.  When you are done with the
list, type a <control D>.
next host to add:  plum
next host to add:CONTROL-D
The current list of NIS servers looks like this:

plum

Is this correct?  [y/n: y]  y
We need a few minutes to build the databases...
Building /var/yp/mgs/ypservers...
Running /var/yp/Makefile...
```

```
make[1]: Entering directory '/var/yp/mgs'
Updating passwd.byname...
Updating passwd.byuid...
Updating group.byname...
Updating group.bygid...
Updating hosts.byname...
Updating hosts.byaddr...
Updating rpc.byname...
Updating rpc.bynumber...
Updating services.byname...
Updating services.byservicename...
Updating netid.byname...
Updating protocols.bynumber...
Updating protocols.byname...
Updating netgroup...
Updating netgroup.byhost...
Updating netgroup.byuser...
Updating shadow.byname...
make[1]: Leaving directory '/var/yp/mgs'

plum has been set up as a NIS master server.

Now you can run ypinit -s plum on all slave server.
```

After running **ypinit,** you must restart the server (page 709).

If you are starting an NIS client, be sure to edit yp.conf

tip   If you are starting **ypbind** (the NIS client) on the same system on which you are running **ypserv** (the NIS server), you must edit **/etc/yp.conf** to specify a server as explained on page 711. If you do not do so, the server will start properly but the client will take a long time to come up and will start in broadcast mode. For more information refer to "No server" on page 709.

TESTING THE SERVER

From the server, check that **ypserv** is connected to **portmap:**

```
$ rpcinfo -p | grep ypserv
100004    2   udp    114   ypserv
100004    1   udp    114   ypserv
100004    2   tcp    114   ypserv
100004    1   tcp    114   ypserv
```

Again from the server system, make sure the NIS server is up and running:

```
$ rpcinfo -u localhost ypserv
program 100004 version 1 ready and waiting
program 100004 version 2 ready and waiting
```

If the server is not working properly, use the **nis** init script to stop the NIS server. Then start **ypserv** in the foreground with debugging turned on:

```
$ sudo /etc/init.d/nis stop

$ sudo /usr/sbin/ypserv --debug
[ypserv (ypserv) 2.19]
```

```
Find securenet: 255.0.0.0 127.0.0.0
Find securenet: 0.0.0.0 0.0.0.0
ypserv.conf: 0.0.0.0/0.0.0.0:*:shadow.byname:2
ypserv.conf: 0.0.0.0/0.0.0.0:*:passwd.adjunct.byname:2
ypserv.conf: 0.0.0.0/0.0.0.0:*:*:0
ypserv.conf: 192.168.0.1/192.168.0.1:*:*:0
CONTROL-C
```

The **––debug** option keeps **ypserv** in the foreground and causes it to send error messages and debugging output to standard error. Press CONTROL-C to stop **ypserv** when it is running in the foreground.

yppasswdd: THE NIS PASSWORD UPDATE DAEMON

The NIS password update daemon, **yppasswdd**, runs only on the master server; it is not necessary to run it on slave servers. (If the master server is down and you try to change your password from a client, yppasswd displays an error message.) When a user runs yppasswd (page 712) on a client, this utility exchanges information with the **yppasswdd** daemon to update the user's password (and optionally other) information in the NIS **shadow** (and optionally **passwd**) map and in the **/etc/shadow** (and optionally **/etc/passwd**) file on the NIS master server. Password change requests are sent to **syslogd** (page 608).

If the server system is running a firewall, open a port for **yppasswdd**. Refer to "Firewall" on page 715.

START yppasswdd

The **nis** init script starts **yppasswdd** (the daemon is named **rpc.yppasswdd**) on an NIS server. For more information refer to "Prerequisites" on page 714.

ALLOW GECOS AND LOGIN SHELL MODIFICATION

The **/etc/default/nis** file controls whether **yppasswdd** allows users to change *GECOS* (page 1110) information and/or the login shell when they run yppasswd. As shipped, **yppasswdd** allows users to change their login shell but not their GECOS information. You can change these settings with options on the command line when you start **yppasswdd** or, more conveniently, by modifying the **/etc/default/nis** configuration file. The **–e chfn** option to **yppasswdd** allows users to change their GECOS information; **–e chsh** allows users to change their login shell. When you set the options in **/etc/default/nis**, these values are set automatically each time **yppasswdd** is run. Set **YPCHANGEOK** as explained in the comments.

```
$ cat /etc/default/nis
...
# Do we allow the user to use ypchsh and/or ypchfn ? The YPCHANGEOK
# fields are passed with -e to yppasswdd, see it's manpage.
# Possible values: "chsh", "chfn", "chsh,chfn"
YPCHANGEOK=chsh
...
```

LDAP

LDAP (Lightweight Directory Access Protocol) is an alternative to the older X.500 DAP (Directory Access Protocol). It runs over TCP/IP and is network aware, standards based, and available on many platforms. A client queries an LDAP server, specifying the data it wants. For example, a query could ask for the first names and email addresses of all people with a last name of Smith who live in San Francisco.

Directory   Because LDAP is designed to work with data that does not change frequently, the server holds a search and read optimized database, called a *directory*. LDAP clients query and update this directory.

In addition to name and address information, an LDAP directory can hold lists of network services. Or, other services can use it for authentication. LDAP is appropriate for any kind of relatively static structured information where fast lookups are required. Many types of clients are set up to communicate with LDAP servers, including LDAP-specific clients (page 731), email clients, and authentication servers.

OpenLDAP   Ubuntu provides the OpenLDAP (www.openldap.org) implementation of LDAP. OpenLDAP uses the Sleepycat Berkeley Database (Berkeley DB, or BDB, now owned by Oracle), which meets the needs of an LDAP database. It supports distributed architecture, replication, and encryption. BDB differs from a relational database (RDBMS): Instead of holding information in rows and columns, BDB implements an LDAP directory as a hierarchical data structure that groups information with similar attributes. This section describes OpenLDAP.

In addition to BDB, Ubuntu supplies HDB, which is based on BDB but which organizes data in a true hierarchical fashion. HDB provides faster writes than does BDB. It also supports subtree renaming, which allows subtrees to be moved efficiently within a database. Under Ubuntu, HDB is the default LDAP database.

Entries and   An *entry* (a node in the LDAP directory hierarchy, or a container) is the basic unit of
attributes   information in an LDAP directory. Each entry holds one or more *attributes*. Each attribute has a name (an attribute type or description) and one or more values. Attribute names come from a standard schema that is held in files found in the **/etc/ldap/schema** directory. This schema is standard across many implementations of LDAP, enabling LDAP clients to obtain data from many LDAP servers. Although it is not usually necessary or advisable, you can augment or modify the standard schema.

DN   A Distinguished Name (DN) uniquely identifies each entry in an LDAP directory. A DN comprises a Relative Distinguished Name (RDN), which is constructed from one or more attributes in the entry, followed by the DN of the parent entry. Because a DN can change (e.g., a woman may change her last name), and because a consistent, unique identifier is sometimes required, the server assigns a UUID (an unambiguous identifier) to each entry.

DSE and DC   The DSE (DSA-Specific Entry) is the root, or top-level, entry in an LDAP directory. (DSA stands for Directory System Agent.) The DSE specifies the domain name of the server and is defined in the **/etc/ldap/slapd.d** hierarchy. LDAP defines a domain name in terms of its component parts. The following line defines the DSE comprising the Domain Component (DC) **sobell** and the DC **com**:

```
$ sudo grep -r sobell /etc/ldap/*
/etc/ldap/slapd.d/cn=config/olcDatabase={1}hdb.ldif:olcSuffix: dc=sobell,dc=com
...
```

LDIF and CN   The LDAP directory specified by the example DSE could contain the following entry, which is specified in LDAP Data Interchange Format (LDIF; see the **ldif** man page for more information):

```
dn: cn=Samuel Smith,dc=sobell,dc=com
cn: Samuel Smith
cn: Sam
cn: SLS
givenName: Samuel
sn: Smith
mail: sls@sobell.com
objectClass: inetOrgPerson
objectClass: organizationalPerson
objectClass: person
objectClass: top
```

Each line except the first specifies an attribute. The word on each line preceding the colon is the attribute name. Following the colon and a SPACE is the attribute value. The first line in this example specifies the DN of the entry. The attribute value used in the RDN is a CN (Common Name) from the entry: **Samuel Smith**. This second-level entry is a child of the top-level entry; thus the DN of the parent entry is the DN of the top-level entry (**dc=sobell,dc=com**). You can uniquely identify this entry by its DN: **cn=Samuel Smith,dc=sobell,dc=com**.

Because this entry defines three CNs, a search for **Samuel Smith, Sam,** or **SLS** will return this entry. This entry also defines a given name, a surname (**sn**), and an email address (**mail**).

objectClass   Entries inherit object class attributes from their parents. In addition, each entry
attribute   must have at least one **objectClass** attribute (the preceding entry has four). Each **objectClass** value must be a class defined in the schema. The schema specifies both mandatory and optional (allowed) attributes for an object class. For example, the following entry in the schema defines the object class named **person**. The MUST and MAY lines specify which attributes the **person** object class requires (**sn** [surname] and **cn**; attribute names are separated by a dollar sign) and which attributes are optional (**userPassword, telephoneNumber, seeAlso,** and **description**).

```
$ cat /etc/ldap/schema/core.schema
...
objectclass ( 2.5.6.6 NAME 'person'
        DESC 'RFC2256: a person'
        SUP top STRUCTURAL
        MUST ( sn $ cn )
        MAY ( userPassword $ telephoneNumber $ seeAlso $ description ) )
...
```

Abbreviations   The following list summarizes the abbreviations mentioned in this section.

CN   Common Name
DC   Domain Component
DN   Distinguished Name
DSE   DSA-Specific Entry
LDIF   LDAP Data Interchange Format
RDN   Relative Distinguished Name

MORE INFORMATION

Local   man pages: **ldap.conf**, ldapmodify, ldapsearch, **ldif, slapd, slapd.conf**, slappasswd

Web   LDAP home page: www.openldap.org
Administrator's Guide: www.openldap.org/doc/admin24
OpenLDAP Faq-O-Matic: www.openldap.org/faq
gq: gq-project.org

HOWTO   *LDAP Linux HOWTO*

Book   www.zytrax.com/books/ldap

SETTING UP AN LDAP SERVER

This section explains the steps involved in setting up an LDAP server.

PREREQUISITES

Install the following packages. When you install the **slapd** package, the **dpkg postinst** script configures a basic LDAP directory, asks for an administrative password, and starts the **slapd** daemon.

- slapd
- ldap-utils

slapd init script   After you manually configure **slapd**, call the **slapd** init script to restart **slapd**:

```
$ sudo /etc/init.d/slapd restart
Stopping OpenLDAP: slapd.
Starting OpenLDAP: slapd.
```

NOTES

slapcat   The slapcat utility, which must run as a privileged user (not the LDAP administrator), retrieves information from a **slapd** database and displays it in LDIF format (page 723). Although slapcat is a useful tool, be careful if you use it to back up a database: Other users may be changing the data as you are backing it up. Following, slapcat shows that the basic LDAP directory that the **dpkg postinst** script configures contains two entries:

```
$ sudo slapcat
dn: dc=nodomain
objectClass: top
objectClass: dcObject
objectClass: organization
o: nodomain
dc: nodomain
...

dn: cn=admin,dc=nodomain
objectClass: simpleSecurityObject
objectClass: organizationalRole
cn: admin
description: LDAP administrator
```

The first entry has a DN of **nodomain,** which itself comprises a DC of **nodomain.** The second entry sets up an administrator named **admin** with a DN of **cn=admin,dc=nodomain.** Although this setup is a functional LDAP directory, it is probably not what you want. The next section explains how to reconfigure this directory to suit your needs.

DB_CONFIG   You can modify parameters in this file to improve the performance of an LDAP server. For more information see the www.openldap.org/faq/data/cache/1072.html Web page and the **/usr/share/doc/slapd/README.DB_CONFIG.gz** file on the local system.

Firewall   The **slapd** LDAP server normally listens on TCP port 389, which is not encrypted. If you are using LDAP for authentication, use LDAP over SSL on port 636. If the LDAP server system is running a firewall, you need to open one of these ports. Using firestarter (page 824), open one of these ports by adding a rule that allows service for port 389 or port 636 from the clients you want to be able to access the server.

STEP-BY-STEP SETUP

This section lists the steps involved in setting up an LDAP server at the **sobell.com** domain. When you set up an LDAP server, substitute the domain name of the server you are setting up for **sobell.com** in the examples. The example in this section is simple; you will probably need different entries in the directory you set up.

To experiment with and learn about LDAP, set up and run locally the example server described in this section. Although the example uses **sobell.com,** when working from the server system you can refer to the LDAP server as **localhost.**

CONFIGURE THE SERVER

dpkg-reconfigure   The easiest way to reconfigure the **slapd** database is to use dpkg-reconfigure. Before running this utility, you must rename or remove two directories as shown in the following example; otherwise, the dpkg-reconfigure may fail with an error message. The **unk*ldapdb** directory is present only if you have run dpkg-reconfigure to reconfigure **slapd** previously.

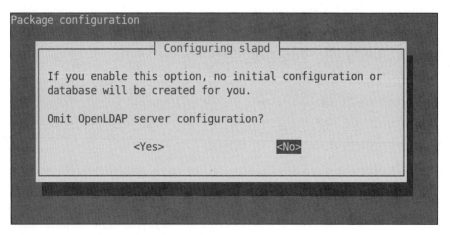

Figure 21-1   The **dpkg-reconfigure** pseudographical display

```
$ sudo mv /etc/ldap/slapd.d /etc/ldap/slapd.d.old
$ ls -ld /var/backups/unk*ldapdb
drwxr-xr-x 2 root root 4096 2008-09-25 14:24 /var/backups/unknown-2.4.11-0ubuntu3.ldapdb
$ sudo mv /var/backups/unk*ldapdb /var/backups/unknown-2.4.11-0ubuntu3.ldapdb.old
```

With these directories out of the way, give the command **sudo dpkg-reconfigure slapd**. This utility presents a pseudographical (page 30) display (Figure 21-1) that asks questions about how you want to configure **slapd**. Typically, you can accept the default answers except for the following:

- **DNS domain name**   Set to the FQDN of the LDAP server. This answer sets the DSE (page 722). For experimenting with LDAP on the local system, you can set this name to anything you like and refer to the server system as **localhost** as shown in the examples. The examples in this chapter use **sobell.com.**

- **Organization name**   Set to the name of the organization running the LDAP server. The examples in this chapter use **Sobell Associates Inc.**

- **Administrator password**   Set and confirm the password. The examples in this chapter use **porcupine.**

Following is a list of all questions **dpkg-reconfigure slapd** asks. Each question appears on a separate screen and is preceded by an explanation. If the window is small, the explanations and questions appear on sequential screens. Figure 21-1 shows the first of these screens. The answers below in brackets are the default answers; press RETURN to accept these answers. Press TAB to move the highlight and select a different answer. The answers in bold are those used in the examples in this chapter. Use these answers if you want to experiment with the local system. Alternatively, you can use answers appropriate to the LDAP server you are setting up. As its last task, dpkg-reconfigure runs the **slapd** init script; you do not have to.

```
$ sudo dpkg-reconfigure slapd
...
Omit OpenLDAP server configuration? [No]
DNS domain name: sobell.com
Organization name: Sobell Associates Inc.
Database backend to use: [HDB]
Do you want the database to be removed when slapd is purged? [No]
Administrator password: porcupine
Confirm password: porcupine
Allow LDAPv2 protocol? [No]
...
No configuration directory was found for slapd at /etc/ldap/slapd.d/.
If you have moved the slapd configuration directory please modify
/etc/default/slapd to reflect this.  If you chose to not
configure slapd during installation then you need to do so
prior to attempting to start slapd.
  Creating initial slapd configuration... done.
  Creating initial LDAP directory... done.
Reloading AppArmor profiles : done.
Starting OpenLDAP: slapd.
```

TEST THE SERVER

After running dpkg-reconfigure, test the server with the following query (you may need to reboot before this query will work):

```
$ ldapsearch -x -s base namingContexts
# extended LDIF
#
# LDAPv3
# base <> (default) with scope baseObject
# filter: (objectclass=*)
# requesting: namingContexts
#

#
dn:
namingContexts: dc=sobell,dc=com

# search result
search: 2
result: 0 Success

# numResponses: 2
# numEntries: 1
```

The **−x** on the command line specifies simple authentication, **−s base** specifies the scope of the search as the base object, and **namingContexts** is the attribute you are searching for. The output of this command should look similar to that shown in the preceding example. The **namingContexts** returned by the search should be the same as the DSE you specified in response to the dpkg-reconfigure **DNS domain name** question (page 726).

The dpkg-reconfigure utility adds a second-level entry (one below the DSE entry) and a third-level entry to the directory. After running dpkg-reconfigure, slapcat displays the two entries:

```
$ sudo slapcat
dn: dc=sobell,dc=com
objectClass: top
objectClass: dcObject
objectClass: organization
o: Sobell Associates Inc.
dc: sobell
structuralObjectClass: organization
entryUUID: 0ea9404c-2037-102d-8186-89cfe750b5e8
creatorsName:
createTimestamp: 20080926165106Z
entryCSN: 20080926165106.823966Z#000000#000#000000
modifiersName:
modifyTimestamp: 20080926165106Z

dn: cn=admin,dc=sobell,dc=com
objectClass: simpleSecurityObject
objectClass: organizationalRole
cn: admin
description: LDAP administrator
userPassword:: e2NyeXB0fTU1NUZTbEtkYnVBb0k=
...
```

The first line of each entry specifies the DN for that entry. The line that starts with **dc** specifies the DC (domain component). The **objectClass** lines specify the object classes this entry belongs to. The line that starts with **o** (short for **organization-Name**) specifies the name of the organization this entry is part of.

The server adds more information to the entry, including a UUID number that remains constant throughout the life of the entry, timestamps, and the names of the users who created and modified the entry. In this case dpkg-reconfigure set up the entry so no users are specified.

ADD ENTRIES TO THE DIRECTORY

You can use many tools, both graphical and textual, to add information to and query an LDAP directory. This section explains how to use the ldapmodify command-line utility to set up an employee LDAP directory. See page 731 for descriptions of other tools.

When you specify the following file on an ldapmodify command line, ldapmodify adds a second-level entry (one level below the DSE entry) to the LDAP directory. This file adds the object class **organizationalUnit** named **employees** (**ou=employees**). The DN is **ou=employees** followed by the DSE.

```
$ cat sa1.ldif
dn: ou=employees,dc=sobell,dc=com
changetype: add
```

```
objectClass: organizationalUnit
ou: employees
```

The first line of **sa1.ldif** specifies the DN for the entry you are adding. The **change-type** instruction tells ldapmodify to add the entry to the directory. You can omit this instruction if you use the **–a** option on the ldapmodify command line or if you use the ldapadd utility instead of ldapmodify. The **objectClass** line specifies the object classes this entry belongs to. The **ou** (short for **organizationalUnitName**) specifies the name of the organizational unit this entry is part of.

The following command modifies the LDAP directory based on the **sa1.ldif** file. The **ldif** filename extension is commonly used but is not required for files holding LDIF entries.

```
$ ldapmodify -xD "cn=admin,dc=sobell,dc=com" -w porcupine -f sa1.ldif
adding new entry "ou=employees,dc=sobell,dc=com"
```

The **–x** option causes the server to use simple authentication. The argument following **–D** specifies the DN of the LDAP administrator of the directory the command is to work with (specified by the **dpkg postinst** script when you install **slapd** [page 714] and when you run dpkg-reconfigure [page 725]). By specifying this user, this argument also specifies the DSE of the LDAP directory. (The DN of the parent of the LDAP administrator's entry specifies the DSE.) The argument following **–w** is the password for the LDAP administrator. The name of the input file follows the **–f** option. The ldapmodify utility reports the DN of the new entry.

With this object class in place, you can add employees to the LDAP directory. The following file adds an employee:

```
$ cat sa2.ldif
dn: cn=Samuel Smith,ou=employees,dc=sobell,dc=com
changetype: add
cn: Samuel Smith
cn: smith
objectClass: inetOrgPerson
mail: sls@sobell.com
givenName: Samuel
surname: Smith
displayName: Samuel L Smith
telephoneNumber: 999 999 9999
homePhone: 000 000 0000
initials: SLS
```

The following command uses **–W** to cause ldapmodify to prompt for the LDAP administrator password. Specifying a password in response to a prompt instead of on the command line can improve security by not making the password visible to a user running ps.

```
$ ldapmodify -xD "cn=admin,dc=sobell,dc=com" -W -f sa2.ldif
Enter LDAP Password:
adding new entry "cn=Samuel Smith,ou=employees,dc=sobell,dc=com"
```

Now slapcat shows the employee you just added:

```
$ sudo slapcat
dn: dc=sobell,dc=com
...
dn: cn=Samuel Smith,ou=employees,dc=sobell,dc=com
cn: Samuel Smith
cn: smith
objectClass: inetOrgPerson
mail: sls@sobell.com
givenName: Samuel
sn: Smith
displayName: Samuel L Smith
telephoneNumber: 999 999 9999
homePhone: 000 000 0000
initials: SLS
...
```

The DN shows that the new employee is at the third level of the directory structure: The first level is **dc=sobell,dc=com**; **ou=employees,dc=sobell,dc=com** is at the second level; and **cn=Samuel Smith,ou=employees,dc=sobell,dc=com**, the employee, is at the third level.

You can put as many entries in a file as you like, but each must be separated from the next by a blank line. For clarity, the examples in this section show one entry per file.

The following example adds another employee at the third level:

```
$ cat sa3.ldif
dn: cn=Helen Simpson,ou=employees,dc=sobell,dc=com
changetype: add
cn: Helen Simpson
cn: simpson
objectClass: inetOrgPerson
mail: helen@sobell.com
givenName: Helen
surname: Simpson
displayName: Helen L Simpson
telephoneNumber: 888 888 8888
homePhone: 111 111 1111
initials: HLS
$ ldapmodify -xD "cn=admin,dc=sobell,dc=com" -W -f sa3.ldif
Enter LDAP Password:
adding new entry "cn=Helen Simpson,ou=employees,dc=sobell,dc=com"
```

The next example uses the ldapmodify **modify** instruction to replace the **mail** attribute value and add a **title** attribute for the employee named Helen Simpson. Because the file specifies Helen's DN, the server knows which entry to modify.

```
$ cat sa4.ldif
dn: cn=Helen Simpson,ou=employees,dc=sobell,dc=com
changetype: modify
replace: mail
mail: hls@sobell.com
-
add: title
title: CTO
```

```
$ ldapmodify -xD "cn=admin,dc=sobell,dc=com" -W -f sa4.ldif
Enter LDAP Password:
modifying entry "cn=Helen Simpson,ou=employees,dc=sobell,dc=com"
```

You can use slapcat to verify the change. The final example deletes Helen from the LDAP directory:

```
$ cat sa5.ldif
dn: cn=Helen Simpson,ou=employees,dc=sobell,dc=com
changetype: delete
$ ldapmodify -xD "cn=admin,dc=sobell,dc=com" -W -f sa5.ldif
Enter LDAP Password:
deleting entry "cn=Helen Simpson,ou=employees,dc=sobell,dc=com"
```

OTHER TOOLS FOR WORKING WITH LDAP

You can use a variety of tools to work with LDAP. For example, most email clients are able to retrieve data from an LDAP database.

EVOLUTION MAIL

This section explains how to use Evolution (Mail) to retrieve data from the example LDAP database created earlier. It assumes you have configured Evolution on the local system. If you are running KDE, you can use KAddressBook, which is integrated into many KDE tools, including Kontact.

Open the Mail-Evolution window by selecting **Main menu: Applications⇨Internet⇨ Evolution Mail** or by giving the command **evolution** from a terminal emulator or Run Application window (ALT-F2). To query an LDAP database, select **File⇨New⇨ Address Book** from the menubar. Evolution displays the General tab of the New Address Book window (Figure 21-2).

Figure 21-2   The New Address Book window, General tab

Figure 21-3 The New Address Book window, Details tab

General tab Select **On LDAP Servers** from the drop-down list labeled **Type**. Enter the name Evolution Mail will use to refer to this LDAP directory in the text box labeled **Name**; the example uses **employees**. Enter the FQDN of the LDAP server in the text box labeled **Server**. If you are experimenting on the local system, enter **localhost** in this box. If appropriate, change the value in the text box labeled **Port**. To follow the example in this chapter, select **No encryption** from the drop-down list labeled **Use secure connection**.

In the section labeled **Authentication**, select **Using distinguished name (DN)** from the drop-down list labeled **Login method**. Enter the DN of the LDAP administrator in the text box labeled **Login** (the example uses **cn=admin,dc=sobell,dc=com**).

Details tab Next click the tab labeled **Details** (Figure 21-3). Click **Find Possible Search Bases**. If all is working properly, Evolution will display the Supported Search Bases window. Highlight the DN of the directory you want to use and click **OK**. Evolution displays the selected DN in the text box labeled **Search base**. Select **Sub** from the drop-down list labeled **Search scope** to enable searches at all levels of the directory. Click **OK**.

Next click the **Contacts** button at the lower-left corner of the Mail-Evolution window. **On this computer** and **On LDAP servers** appear at the left side of the window. If the name of the address book you specified (**employees** in the example) does not appear below **On LDAP servers**, click the triangle to the left of this label. Then click the name of the address book you want to work with. Evolution prompts for the LDAP administrator password. Enter the password and click **OK**. Evolution highlights the name of the address book; you can now search the LDAP database.

Enter the name of an entry in the **Search** text box at the upper-right corner of the window and press RETURN. Evolution displays the entry. Figure 21-4 shows the result of following the example in this chapter and entering **Sam** in the **Search** text box.

Figure 21-4   Contacts - Evolution window

KONQUEROR

If you are running KDE, you can use Konqueror to examine the contents of an LDAP directory. Enter the following string in the Konqueror location bar and press RETURN:

ldap://server-name/DN

where **server-name** is the name or IP address of the LDAP server (or **localhost** if you are running Konqueror on the server system) and **DN** is the DN of the entry you want to view. Konqueror displays all entries below the DN you specify. Double-click an entry to display it. For example, to work with the LDAP directory created earlier, enter **ldap://localhost/ou=employee,dc=sobell,dc=com** in the location bar. In response, Konqueror will display the entries with this RDN. You can then click one of these entries to display that entry in its entirety.

gq: AN LDAP CLIENT

The gq utility (gq-project.org) is a graphical (GTK+-based) LDAP client you can use to display, edit, and delete entries. It is part of the **gq** package. Figure 21-5 shows gq displaying an entry from the example LDAP directory.

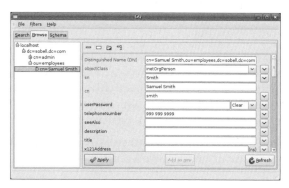

Figure 21-5   Using gq to browse an LDAP directory

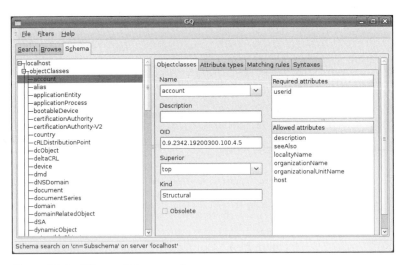

Figure 21-6   The gq Schema tab

You can also use gq for browsing the schema: Click the Schema tab and select the server from the left side of the window (**localhost** in Figure 21-6). Select **object-Classes** and then an object class to view information about that object class, including a list of required and optional attributes.

CHAPTER SUMMARY

NIS (Network Information Service) simplifies the management of common administrative files by maintaining them in a central database and having clients contact the database server to retrieve information from the database. The network that NIS serves is called an NIS domain. Each NIS domain has one master server; larger networks may have slave servers.

NIS derives the information it offers from local configuration files, such as **/etc/passwd** and **/etc/hosts**. These files are called source files or master files. Before NIS can store the information contained in a source file, it must be converted to dbm-format files, called maps. The ypcat and ypmatch utilities display information from NIS maps.

The yppasswd utility replaces the functionality of passwd on clients when you use NIS to authenticate passwords. The **/etc/ypserv.conf** file, which holds NIS server configuration information, specifies options and access rules for the NIS server. To enhance system security, you can create a **/var/yp/securenets** file, which prevents unauthorized systems from retrieving NIS maps.

An LDAP (Lightweight Directory Access Protocol) server holds a search- and read-optimized database, called a directory. LDAP clients, such as email clients, query and update this directory. In addition, authentication servers can use an LDAP directory to authenticate users.

Ubuntu provides the OpenLDAP implementation of LDAP. OpenLDAP uses the Sleepycat Berkeley Database, which supports distributed architecture, replication, and encryption.

EXERCISES

1. What is the difference between the passwd and yppasswd utilities?

2. How would you prevent NIS from exporting the **root** user and other system users to clients?

3. How would you make NIS user information override local user information on client systems?

4. Why does the **/etc/passwd** file need two NIS maps?

5. How does an LDAP directory differ from a relational database system?

6. What is the basic unit of information in an LDAP directory? What is the structure of an attribute?

ADVANCED EXERCISES

7. How can you use NIS to mirror the functionality of a private DNS server for a small network? Why should NIS not be used this way on a large network?

8. How can you determine whether the working directory is the home directory of an NIS user?

9. a. What advantage does NIS provide when you use it with NFS?

   b. Suggest a way to implement NIS maps so they can be indexed on more than one field.

10. Where is the LDAP **device** object class defined? Which of its attributes are mandatory and which are optional?

11. How would you determine the longer name for the **l** (lowercase "l") LDAP object class?

22

NFS: SHARING FILESYSTEMS

The NFS (Network Filesystem) protocol, a UNIX de facto standard developed by Sun Microsystems, allows a server to share selected local directory hierarchies with client systems on a heterogeneous network. NFS runs on UNIX, DOS, Windows, VMS, Linux, and more. Files on the remote computer (the *fileserver*) appear as if they are present on the local system (the client). Most of the time, the physical location of a file is irrelevant to an NFS user; all standard Linux utilities work with NFS remote files the same way as they operate with local files.

NFS reduces storage needs and system administration workload. As an example, each system in a company traditionally holds its own copy of an application program. To upgrade the program, the administrator needs to upgrade it on each system. NFS allows you to store a copy of a program on a single system and give other users access to it over the network. This scenario minimizes storage requirements by reducing the number of locations that need to maintain the same data. In addition to boosting efficiency, NFS gives users on the network access to the same data (not just application programs), thereby improving data consistency and reliability. By consolidating data, it reduces administrative overhead and provides a convenience to users. This chapter covers NFSv3.

737

Introduction to NFS

Figure 22-1 shows the flow of data in a typical NFS client/server setup. An NFS directory hierarchy appears to users and application programs as just another directory hierarchy. By looking at it, you cannot tell that a given directory holds a remotely mounted NFS directory hierarchy and not a local filesystem. The NFS server translates commands from the client into operations on the server's filesystem.

Diskless systems   In many computer facilities, user files are stored on a central fileserver equipped with many large-capacity disk drives and devices that quickly and easily make backup copies of the data. A *diskless* system boots from a fileserver (netboots— discussed next) or a CD/DVD and loads system software from a fileserver. The Linux Terminal Server Project (LTSP.org) Web site says it all: "Linux makes a great platform for deploying diskless workstations that boot from a network server. The LTSP is all about running thin client computers in a Linux environment." Because a diskless workstation does not require a lot of computing power, you can give older, retired computers a second life by using them as diskless systems.

Netboot/PXE   You can *netboot* (page 1121) systems that are appropriately set up. Ubuntu Linux includes the PXE (Preboot Execution Environment; **pxe** package) server package for netbooting Intel systems. Older systems sometimes use tftp (Trivial File Transfer Protocol; **tftp** and **tftpd** packages) for netbooting. Non-Intel architectures have historically included netboot capabilities, which Ubuntu Linux also supports. In addition, you can build the Linux kernel so it mounts **root** (**/**) using NFS. Given the many ways to set up a system, the one you choose depends on what you want to do. See the *Remote-Boot mini-HOWTO* for more information.

Dataless systems   Another type of Linux system is a *dataless* system, in which the client has a disk but stores no user data (only Linux and the applications are kept on the disk). Setting up this type of system is a matter of choosing which directory hierarchies are mounted remotely.

df: shows where directory hierarchies are mounted   The df utility displays a list of the directory hierarchies available on the system, along with the amount of disk space, free and used, on each. The **–h** (human) option makes the output more intelligible. Device names in the left column that are prepended with *hostname:* specify filesystems that are available through NFS.

```
zach@plum:~$ cd;pwd
/dog.home/zach
zach@plum:~$ df -h
Filesystem           Size  Used Avail Use% Mounted on
/dev/hda1             28G   8.9G   18G  35% /
...
/dev/hda2             28G   220M   26G   1% /home
/dev/hda5            9.2G   150M  8.6G   2% /pl5
/dev/hda6            1.4G    35M  1.3G   3% /pl6
dog:/home/zach        19G   6.7G   11G  39% /dog.home/zach
grape:/gc1           985M    92M  844M  10% /grape.gc1
grape:/gc5           3.9G   3.0G  738M  81% /grape.gc5
```

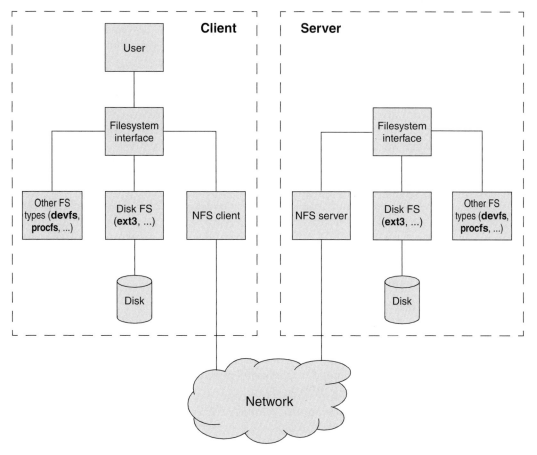

Figure 22-1 Flow of data in a typical NFS client/server setup

In the preceding example, Zach's home directory, **/home/zach**, is on the remote system **dog**. Using NFS, the **/home/zach** directory hierarchy on **dog** is mounted on **plum**; to make it easy to recognize, it is mounted as **/dog.home/zach**. The **/gc1** and **/gc5** filesystems on **grape** are mounted on **plum** as **/grape.gc1** and **/grape.gc5**, respectively.

You can use the **–T** option to df to add a Type column to the display. The following command uses **–t nfs** to display NFS filesystems only:

```
zach@plum:~$ df -ht nfs
Filesystem          Size  Used Avail Use% Mounted on
dog:/home/zach       19G  6.7G   11G  39% /dog.home/zach
grape:/gc1          985M   92M  844M  10% /grape.gc1
grape:/gc5          3.9G  3.0G  738M  81% /grape.gc5
```

Errors Sometimes a client may lose access to files on an NFS server. For example, a network problem or a remote system crash may make these files temporarily unavailable. If you try to access a remote file in these circumstances, you will get an error message, such as

NFS server dog not responding. When the local system can contact the remote server again, NFS will display another message, such as **NFS server dog OK**. A stable network and server (or not using NFS) is the best defense against this problem.

Security   NFS is based on the trusted-host paradigm (page 375), so it has all the security shortcomings that plague other services based on this paradigm. In addition, NFS is not encrypted. Because of these issues, you should implement NFS on a single LAN segment only, where you can be (reasonably) sure systems on the LAN segment are what they claim to be. Make sure a firewall blocks NFS traffic from outside the LAN and never use NFS over the Internet.

To improve security, make sure UIDs and GIDs are the same on the server and clients (page 752).

NFSv4   NFSv4 addresses many of these security issues, including the problem of users having different UIDs on different systems (NFSv4 uses usernames, not UID numbers). The new version of NFS adds Kerberos authentication, provides for encrypted file transfers, and increases WAN performance.

More Information

Web   Good information on NFS, including the *Linux NFS-HOWTO*: nfs.sourceforge.net
Running NFS behind a firewall: wiki.debian.org/?SecuringNFS
autofs tutorial: www.linuxhq.com/lg/issue24/nielsen.html

Local   man pages: autofs, **automount, auto.master**, exportfs, **exports, nfs** (provides **fstab** information), **rpc.idmapd, rpc.mountd, rpc.nfsd**, and showmount

HOWTO   *Linux NFS-HOWTO*: nfs.sourceforge.net
Netboot and PXE: *Remote-Boot mini-HOWTO*
Automount mini-HOWTO

Book   *NFS Illustrated* by Callaghan, Addison-Wesley (January 2000)

Running an NFS Client

This section describes how to set up an NFS client, mount remote directory hierarchies, and improve NFS performance.

Prerequisites

Installation   Install the following package:

- **nfs-common**

portmap   The portmap utility (which is part of the **portmap** package and is installed as a dependency when you install **nfs-common**; page 390) must be running to enable reliable file locking.

nfs-common init
script   When you install the **nfs-common** package, the **dpkg postinst** script starts the daemons that an NFS client requires (not all daemons are always required): **rpc.statd**,

rpc.lockd (does not run but starts the NFS lock manager if necessary), **rpc.idmapd**, and **rpc.gssd**. You do not normally need to restart any of these daemons.

JUMPSTART I: MOUNTING A REMOTE DIRECTORY HIERARCHY

To set up an NFS client, mount the remote directory hierarchy the same way you mount a local directory hierarchy (page 488).

The following examples show two ways to mount a remote directory hierarchy, assuming **dog** is on the same network as the local system and is sharing **/home** and **/export** with the local system. The **/export** directory on **dog** holds two directory hierarchies you want to mount: **/export/progs** and **/export/oracle**. The example mounts **dog**'s **/home** directory on **/dog.home** on the local system, **/export/progs** on **/apps**, and **/export/oracle** on **/oracle**.

First run mkdir on the local (client) system to create the directories that are the mount points for the remote directory hierarchies:

```
$ sudo mkdir /dog.home /apps /oracle
```

You can mount any directory hierarchy from an exported directory hierarchy. In this example, **dog** exports **/export** and the local system mounts **/export/progs** and **/export/oracle**. The following commands manually mount the directory hierarchies one time:

```
$ sudo mount dog:/home /dog.home
$ sudo mount -o ro,nosuid dog:/export/progs /apps
$ sudo mount -o ro dog:/export/oracle /oracle
```

If you receive the error **mount: RPC: Program not registered**, it may mean NFS is not running on the server.

By default, directory hierarchies are mounted read-write, assuming the NFS server is exporting them with read-write permissions. The first of the preceding commands mounts the **/home** directory hierarchy from **dog** on the local directory **/dog.home**. The second and third commands use the **–o ro** option to force a readonly mount. The second command adds the **nosuid** option, which forces setuid (page 204) executables in the mounted directory hierarchy to run with regular permissions on the local system.

nosuid option   If a user has the ability to run a setuid program, that user has the power of a user with **root** privileges. This ability should be limited. Unless you know a user will need to run a program with setuid permissions from a mounted directory hierarchy, always mount a directory hierarchy with the **nosuid** option. For example, you would need to mount a directory hierarchy with setuid privileges when the root partition of a diskless workstation is mounted using NFS.

nodev option   Mounting a device file creates another potential security hole. Although the best policy is not to mount untrustworthy directory hierarchies, it is not always possible to implement this policy. Unless a user needs to use a device on a mounted directory hierarchy, mount directory hierarchies with the **nodev** option, which prevents character and block special files (page 486) on the mounted directory hierarchy from being used as devices.

fstab file If you mount directory hierarchies frequently, you can add entries for the directory hierarchies to the **/etc/fstab** file (page 745). (Alternatively, you can use **automount**; see page 756.) The following **/etc/fstab** entries automatically mount the same directory hierarchies as in the previous example at the same time that the system mounts the local filesystems:

```
$ cat /etc/fstab
...
dog:/home           /dog.home      nfs    rw         0  0
dog:/export/progs   /apps          nfs    ro,nosuid  0  0
dog:/export/oracle  /oracle        nfs    ro         0  0
```

A file mounted using NFS is always of type **nfs** on the local system, regardless of what type it is on the remote system. Typically you do not run fsck on or back up an NFS directory hierarchy. The entries in the third, fifth, and sixth columns of **fstab** are usually **nfs** (filesystem type), 0 (do not back up this directory hierarchy with dump [page 586]), and 0 (do not run fsck [page 494] on this directory hierarchy). The options for mounting an NFS directory hierarchy differ from those for mounting an **ext3** or other type of filesystem. See the section on mount (below) for details.

Unmounting directory hierarchies Use umount to unmount a remote directory hierarchy the same way you unmount a local filesystem (page 491).

mount: MOUNTS A DIRECTORY HIERARCHY

The mount utility (page 488) associates a directory hierarchy with a mount point (a directory). You can use mount to mount an NFS (remote) directory hierarchy. This section describes some mount options. It lists default options first, followed by non-default options (enclosed in parentheses). You can use these options on the command line or set them in **/etc/fstab** (page 745). For a complete list of options, refer to the mount and nfs man pages.

ATTRIBUTE CACHING

A file's inode (page 483) stores file attributes that provide information about a file, such as file modification time, size, links, and owner. File attributes do not include the data stored in a file. Typically file attributes do not change very often for an ordinary file; they change even less often for a directory file. Even the size attribute does not change with every write instruction: When a client is writing to an NFS-mounted file, several write instructions may be given before the data is transferred to the server. In addition, many file accesses, such as that performed by ls, are read-only operations and, therefore, do not change the file's attributes or its contents. Thus a client can cache attributes and avoid costly network reads.

The kernel uses the modification time of the file to determine when its cache is out-of-date. If the time the attribute cache was saved is later than the modification time of the file itself, the data in the cache is current. The server must periodically refresh the attribute cache of an NFS-mounted file to determine whether another process has modified the file. This period is specified as a minimum and maximum number of seconds for ordinary and directory files. Following is a list of options that affect attribute caching:

ac (noac) (**attribute cache**) Permits attribute caching (default). The **noac** option disables attribute caching. Although **noac** slows the server, it avoids stale attributes when two NFS clients actively write to a common directory hierarchy.

acdirmax=*n* (**attribute cache directory file maximum**) The *n* is the number of seconds, at a maximum, that NFS waits before refreshing directory file attributes (default is 60 seconds).

acdirmin=*n* (**attribute cache directory file minimum**) The *n* is the number of seconds, at a minimum, that NFS waits before refreshing directory file attributes (default is 30 seconds).

acregmax=*n* (**attribute cache regular file maximum**) The *n* is the number of seconds, at a maximum, that NFS waits before refreshing regular file attributes (default is 60 seconds).

acregmin=*n* (**attribute cache regular file minimum**) The *n* is the number of seconds, at a minimum, that NFS waits before refreshing regular file attributes (default is 3 seconds).

actimeo=*n* (**attribute cache timeout**) Sets **acregmin**, **acregmax**, **acdirmin**, and **acdirmax** to *n* seconds (without this option, each individual option takes on its assigned or default value).

ERROR HANDLING

The following options control what NFS does when the server does not respond or when an I/O error occurs. To allow for a mount point located on a mounted device, a missing mount point is treated as a timeout.

fg (bg) (**foreground**) Retries failed NFS mount attempts in the foreground (default). The **bg** (background) option retries failed NFS mount attempts in the background.

hard (soft) Displays **NFS server not responding** on the console on a major timeout and keeps retrying (default). The **soft** option reports an I/O error to the calling program on a major timeout. In general, it is not advisable to use **soft**. As the mount man page says of **soft**, "Usually it just causes lots of trouble." For more information refer to "Improving Performance" on page 744.

nointr (intr) (**no interrupt**) Does not allow a signal to interrupt a file operation on a **hard**-mounted directory hierarchy when a major timeout (see **retrans**) occurs (default). The **intr** option allows this type of interrupt.

retrans=*n* (**retransmission value**) After *n* minor timeouts, NFS generates a major timeout (default is 3). A major timeout aborts the operation or displays **server not responding** on the console, depending on whether **hard** or **soft** is set.

retry=*n* (**retry value**) The number of minutes that NFS retries a mount operation before giving up (default is 10,000).

timeo=*n* (**timeout value**) The *n* is the number of tenths of a second that NFS waits before retransmitting following an RPC, or minor, timeout (default is 7). The value is increased at each timeout to a maximum of 60 seconds or until a major timeout occurs (see **retrans**). On a busy network, in case of a slow server, or when the request passes through multiple routers, increasing this value may improve performance. See "Timeouts" below for more information.

MISCELLANEOUS OPTIONS

Following are additional useful options:

lock (nolock) Permits NFS locking (default). The **nolock** option disables NFS locking (does not start the **lockd** daemon) and is useful with older servers that do not support NFS locking.

nodev (**no device**) Causes mounted device files not to function as devices (page 741).

port=*n* The port used to connect to the NFS server (defaults to 2049 if the NFS daemon is not registered with portmap). When **n** is set to 0 (default), NFS queries portmap on the server to determine the port.

rsize=*n* (**read block size**) The number of bytes read at one time from an NFS server. The default block size is 4096. Refer to "Improving Performance."

wsize=*n* (**write block size**) The number of bytes written at one time to an NFS server. The default block size is 4096. Refer to "Improving Performance."

tcp Uses TCP in place of the default UDP protocol for an NFS mount. This option may improve performance on a congested network; however, some NFS servers support UDP only.

udp Uses the default UDP protocol for an NFS mount.

IMPROVING PERFORMANCE

hard/soft Several parameters can affect the performance of NFS, especially over slow connections such as a line with a lot of traffic or a line controlled by a modem. If you have a slow connection, make sure **hard** (page 743) is set (this setting is the default) so that timeouts do not abort program execution.

Block size One of the easiest ways to improve NFS performance is to increase the block size—that is, the number of bytes NFS transfers at a time. The default of 4096 is low for a fast connection using modern hardware. Try increasing **rsize** and **wsize** (both above) to 8192 or higher. Experiment until you find the optimal block size. Unmount and mount the directory hierarchy each time you change an option. See the *Linux NFS-HOWTO* for more information on testing different block sizes.

Timeouts NFS waits the amount of time specified by the **timeo** (timeout, page 743) option for a response to a transmission. If it does not receive a response in this amount of time, NFS sends another transmission. The second transmission uses bandwidth that, over a slow connection, may slow things down even more. You may be able to increase performance by increasing **timeo**.

The default value of **timeo** is seven-tenths of a second (700 milliseconds). After a timeout, NFS doubles the time it waits to 1400 milliseconds. On each timeout it doubles the amount of time it waits to a maximum of 60 seconds. You can test the speed of a connection with the size of packets you are sending (**rsize** and **wsize**; both on page 744) by using ping with the **−s** (size) option:

```
$ ping -s 4096 dog
PING dog (192.168.0.12) 4096(4124) bytes of data.
4104 bytes from dog (192.168.0.12): icmp_seq=1 ttl=64 time=0.823 ms
4104 bytes from dog (192.168.0.12): icmp_seq=2 ttl=64 time=0.814 ms
4104 bytes from dog (192.168.0.12): icmp_seq=3 ttl=64 time=0.810 ms
...
4104 bytes from dog (192.168.0.12): icmp_seq=28 ttl=64 time=0.802 ms
4104 bytes from dog (192.168.0.12): icmp_seq=29 ttl=64 time=0.802 ms
4104 bytes from dog (192.168.0.12): icmp_seq=30 ttl=64 time=0.801 ms

--- dog.bogus.com ping statistics ---
30 packets transmitted, 30 received, 0% packet loss, time 28999ms
rtt min/avg/max/mdev = 0.797/0.803/0.823/0.020 ms
```

The preceding example uses Ubuntu Linux's default packet size of 4096 bytes and shows a fast average packet round-trip time of slightly less than 1 millisecond. Over a modem line, you can expect times of several seconds. If the connection is dealing with other traffic, the time will be even longer. Run the test during a period of heavy traffic. Try increasing **timeo** to three or four times the average round-trip time (to allow for unusually bad network conditions, such as when the connection is made) and see whether performance improves. Remember that the **timeo** value is given in tenths of a second (100 milliseconds = one-tenth of a second).

/etc/fstab: Mounts Directory Hierarchies Automatically

The **/etc/fstab** file (page 492) lists directory hierarchies that the system mounts automatically as it comes up. You can use the options discussed in the preceding sections on the command line or in the **fstab** file.

The following line from **fstab** mounts **grape**'s **/gc1** filesystem on the **/grape.gc1** mount point:

```
grape:/gc1              /grape.gc1    nfs     rsize=8192,wsize=8192   0 0
```

A mount point should be an empty, local directory. (Files in a mount point are hidden when a directory hierarchy is mounted on it.) The type of a filesystem mounted using NFS is always **nfs**, regardless of its type on its local system. You can increase the **rsize** and **wsize** options to improve performance. Refer to "Improving Performance" on page 744.

The next example from **fstab** mounts a filesystem from **dog**:

```
dog:/export             /dog.export   nfs   timeo=50,hard          0 0
```

Because the local system connects to **dog** over a slow connection, **timeo** is increased to 5 seconds (50-tenths of a second). Refer to "Timeouts" on page 744. In addition, **hard** is set to make sure NFS keeps trying to communicate with the server after a major timeout. Refer to "**hard/soft**" on page 744.

The final example from **fstab** shows a remote-mounted home directory. Because **dog** is a local server and is connected via a reliable, high-speed connection, **timeo** is decreased and **rsize** and **wsize** are increased substantially:

```
dog:/home       /dog.home           nfs     timeo=4,rsize=16384,wsize=16384 0 0
```

SETTING UP AN NFS SERVER

PREREQUISITES

Installation   Install the following package:

- **nfs-kernel-server**

portmap   The portmap utility (which is part of the **portmap** package and is installed as a dependency when you install **nfs-kernel-server**; page 390) must be running to enable reliable file locking.

nfs-kernel-server   When you install the **nfs-kernel-server** package, the **dpkg postinst** script starts the
init script   **nfsd** (the NFS kernel) daemon. After you configure NFS, call the **nfs-kernel-server** init script to reexport directory hierarchies and restart the **nfsd** daemon:

```
$ sudo /etc/init.d/nfs-kernel-server restart
 *  Stopping NFS kernel daemon                             [ OK ]
 *  Unexporting directories for NFS kernel daemon...       [ OK ]
 *  Exporting directories for NFS kernel daemon...         [ OK ]
 *  Starting NFS kernel daemon                             [ OK ]
```

After changing the NFS configuration on an active server, use **reload** in place of **restart** to reexport directory hierarchies without disturbing clients connected to the server.

NOTES

Firewall   An NFS server normally uses TCP port 111 for portmap and TCP port 2049 for **nfsd**. In addition, unless you instruct it otherwise, the NFS server uses portmap to assign (almost) random ports for the services it provides: **rpc.statd**, **rpc.mountd**, and (optionally) **rpc.quotad**. It is difficult to set up a firewall to protect a server from queries from random ports; it is much easier to specify which port each of these services uses. To specify the ports that NFS services use, modify the lines in the following files as shown:

```
$ grep STATD /etc/default/nfs-common
NEED_STATD=
STATDOPTS="--port 32765 --outgoing-port 32766"

$ grep MOUNTD /etc/default/nfs-kernel-server
RPCMOUNTDOPTS="-p 32767"

$ grep QUOTAD /etc/default/quota
RPCQUOTADOPTS="-p 32769"
```

If you are not running **rpc.quotad**, you do not need to create or modify the **quota** file. The ports used in the example are the ones suggested in the *Linux NFS-HOWTO*, but you can use any unused ports you like. See wiki.debian.org/?SecuringNFS for more information.

If the NFS server system is running a firewall, you need to open ports 111 and 2049. To do so, use firestarter (page 824) to set a policy that allows NFS service. In addition, open the ports you specified in the files in **/etc/default**, as explained earlier. Because firestarter has no defined policy for these ports, you need to specify the ports manually when you add a rule in firestarter.

Security   The **rpc.mountd** daemon uses TCP wrappers to control client access to the server. As explained on page 448, you can set up **/etc/hosts.allow** and **/etc/hosts.deny** files to specify which clients can contact **rpc.mountd** on the server and thereby use NFS. The name of the daemon to use in these files is **mountd.**

JumpStart II: Configuring an NFS Server Using shares-admin

The Shared Folders window (Figure 22-2) enables the local system to share directory hierarchies using Samba (Chapter 23) and/or NFS. To display this window, give the command **shares-admin** from a terminal emulator or Run Application window (ALT-F2). Click **Unlock**, enter your password, and click **Authenticate** to enable you to use this window to set up shares.

As part of the process of setting up an NFS server, the Shared Folders window modifies the **/etc/exports** file. If the system is running a firewall, see "Firewall" on page 746. The shares-admin utility allows you to specify which directory hierarchies you want to share and how they are shared using NFS. Each exported hierarchy is called a *share*—terminology that is borrowed from Samba.

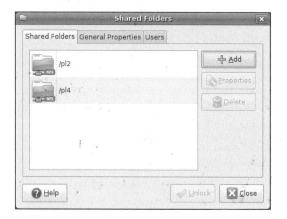

Figure 22-2   Shared Folders window

Figure 22-3   The Share Folder window

To add a share, click **Add,** which displays the Share Folder window (Figure 22-3). This window has two sections: Shared Folder and Allowed Hosts. In the first section, choose the pathname of the directory hierarchy you want to share from the list box labeled **Path**. If the directory you want is not listed, click **Other;** then double-click **File System** in the Places column and double-click the directory you want in the Name column. Continue selecting directories in the Name column until the buttons at the top of the window display the pathname of the directory hierarchy you want to share. Click **Open** to select the directory hierarchy. Then select **Unix networks (NFS)** from the list box labeled **Share through**.

In the Allowed Hosts section of the Share Folder window, click **Add** to display the Add Allowed Hosts window (Figure 22-4). Select **Specify hostname, Specify IP address,** or **Specify network** from the list box labeled **Allowed hosts** and specify the system in the text box labeled **Host name, IP address,** or **Network**. Put a tick in the check box labeled **Read only** if you do not want users on the remote system to be able to write to the mounted directory hierarchy. Click **OK**. The shares-admin utility stores this information in **/etc/exports**. Click **Add** and repeat this process for each system you want to be able to access the directory hierarchy specified in the list box labeled **Path**. Click **Share**.

To modify a share, highlight the object representing the share in the Shared Folders window and click **Properties,** or double-click the object. The shares-admin utility displays the Settings for Folder *share-name* window. To modify an existing host, you must delete it from the Allowed Hosts list and then add it again. Make the changes you want and click **OK**.

To remove a share, highlight the object representing the share in the Shared Folders window and click **Delete**.

Click **Close** when you are finished setting up shares. There is no need to restart any daemons. After running shares-admin, give the following command from a terminal emulator:

```
$ sudo exportfs -r
```

Figure 22-4   The Add Allowed Hosts window

You can ignore error messages that refer to **subtree_check**. For more information on this parameter, see page 751.

Give the command **exportfs** without any options to display a list of exported directory hierarchies and the systems each is exported to:

```
$ exportfs
/p16              192.168.0.12
```

See page 755 for more information on exportfs.

MANUALLY EXPORTING A DIRECTORY HIERARCHY

Exporting a directory hierarchy makes the directory hierarchy *available* for mounting by designated systems via a network. "Exported" does not mean "mounted": When a directory hierarchy is exported, it is placed in the list of directory hierarchies that can be mounted by other systems. An exported directory hierarchy may be mounted (or not) at any given time.

Exporting symbolic links and device files

tip   When you export a directory hierarchy that contains a symbolic link, make sure the object of the link is available on the client (remote) system. If the object of the link does not exist on a client system, you must export and mount it along with the exported link. Otherwise, the link will not point to the same file it points to on the server.

A device file refers to a Linux kernel interface. When you export a device file, you export that interface. If the client system does not have the same type of device available, the exported device will not work. To improve security on a client, you can use mount's **nodev** option (page 741) to prevent device files on mounted directory hierarchies from being used as devices.

A mounted directory hierarchy whose mount point is within an exported partition is not exported with the exported partition. You need to explicitly export each directory hierarchy you want exported, even if it resides within an already exported directory hierarchy. For example, assume two directory hierarchies, **/opt/apps** and **/opt/apps/oracle**, reside on two partitions. You must export each directory hierarchy explicitly, even though **oracle** is a subdirectory of **apps**. Most other subdirectories and files are exported automatically.

/etc/exports: HOLDS A LIST OF EXPORTED DIRECTORY HIERARCHIES

The **/etc/exports** file is the access control list for exported directory hierarchies that NFS clients can mount; it is the only file you need to edit to set up an NFS server. The exportfs utility (page 755) reads this file when it updates the files in **/var/lib/nfs** (page 753), which the kernel uses to keep its mount table current. The **exports** file controls the following NFS characteristics:

- Which clients can access the server (see also "Security" on page 740)
- Which directory hierarchies on the server each client can access
- How each client can access each directory hierarchy
- How client usernames are mapped to server usernames
- Various NFS parameters

Each line in the **exports** file has the following format:

export-point client1(option-list) [client2(option-list) ...]

where *export-point* is the absolute pathname of the root directory of the directory hierarchy to be exported. The *client1-n* are the names or IP addresses of one or more clients, separated by SPACEs, that are allowed to mount the *export-point*. The *option-list*, described in the next section, is a comma-separated list of options that applies to the preceding *client*; it must not contain any SPACEs. There must not be any SPACE between each client name and the open parenthesis that starts the *option-list*.

You can either use shares-admin (page 747) to make changes to **exports** or edit this file manually. The following **exports** file gives **grape** read and write access to **/home**, and **jam** and the system at 192.168.0.12 read and write access to **/pl6**:

```
$ cat /etc/exports
/home    grape(rw,no_subtree_check)
/pl6     192.168.0.12(rw,no_subtree_check) jam(rw,no_subtree_check)
```

The specified directories are on the local server. In each case, access is implicitly granted for the directory hierarchy rooted at the exported directory. You can specify IP addresses or hostnames and you can specify more than one client system on a line. By default, directory hierarchies are exported in readonly mode. The current version of exportfs complains when you do not specify either **subtree_check** or **no_subtree_check** (page 751).

GENERAL OPTIONS

The left column of this section lists default options, followed by nondefault options enclosed in parentheses. Refer to the **exports** man page for more information.

auth_nlm (no_auth_nlm) or secure_locks (insecure_locks)
Causes the server to require authentication of lock requests (using the NLM [NFS Lock Manager] protocol). Use **no_auth_nlm** for older clients when you find that only files that anyone can read can be locked.

mountpoint[=*path*]

Allows a directory to be exported only if it has been mounted. This option prevents a mount point that does not have a directory hierarchy mounted on it from being exported and prevents the underlying mount point from being exported. Also **mp**.

nohide (hide)

When a server exports two directory hierarchies, one of which is mounted on the other, a client has to mount both directory hierarchies explicitly to access both. When the second (child) directory hierarchy is not explicitly mounted, its mount point appears as an empty directory and the directory hierarchy is hidden. The **nohide** option causes the underlying second directory hierarchy to appear when it is not explicitly mounted, but this option does not work in all cases.

ro (rw)

(**readonly**) Permits only read requests on an NFS directory hierarchy. Use **rw** to permit read and write requests.

secure (insecure)

Requires NFS requests to originate on a *privileged port* (page 1126) so a program running without **root** privileges cannot mount a directory hierarchy. This option does not guarantee a secure connection.

no_subtree_check (subtree_check)

Checks subtrees for valid files. Assume you have an exported directory hierarchy that has its root below the root of the filesystem that holds it (that is, an exported subdirectory of a filesystem). When the NFS server receives a request for a file in that directory hierarchy, it performs a subtree check to confirm the file is in the exported directory hierarchy.

Subtree checking can cause problems with files that are renamed while opened and, when **no_root_squash** is used, files that only a process running with **root** privileges can access. The **no_subtree_check** option disables subtree checking and can improve reliability in some cases.

For example, you may need to disable subtree checking for home directories. Home directories are frequently subtrees (of **/home**), are written to often, and can have files within them frequently renamed. You would probably not need to disable subtree checking for directory hierarchies that contain files that are mostly read, such as **/usr**.

Because the default has changed (it is now **no_subtree_check**), exportfs displays a warning when you do not specify either **subtree_check** or **no_subtree_check**.

sync (async)

(**synchronize**) Specifies that the server should reply to requests only after disk changes made by the request are written to disk. The **async** option specifies that the server does not have to wait for information to be written to disk and can improve performance, albeit at the cost of possible data corruption if the server crashes or the connection is interrupted.

wdelay (no_wdelay)

(**write delay**) Causes the server to delay committing write requests when it anticipates that another, related request will follow, thereby improving performance by committing multiple write requests within a single operation. The **no_wdelay** option does not delay committing write requests and can improve performance when the server receives multiple, small, unrelated requests.

USER ID MAPPING OPTIONS

Each user has a UID number and a primary GID number on the local system. The local **/etc/passwd** and **/etc/group** files may map these numbers to names. When a user makes a request of an NFS server, the server uses these numbers to identify the user on the remote system, raising several issues:

- The user may not have the same ID numbers on both systems. As a consequence, the user may have owner access to files of another user and not have owner access to his own files (see "NIS and NFS" for a solution).

- You may not want a user with **root** privileges on the client system to have owner access to **root**-owned files on the server.

- You may not want a remote user to have owner access to some important system files that are not owned by **root** (such as those owned by **bin**).

Critical files in NFS-mounted directories should be owned by root

security   Despite the mapping done by the **root-squash** option, a user with **root** privileges on a client system can use sudo or su to assume the identity of any user on the system and then access that user's files on the server. Thus, without resorting to **all-squash**, you can protect only files owned by **root** on an NFS server. Make sure that **root**—and not **bin** or another user—owns and is the only user who can modify or delete critical files within any NFS-mounted directory hierarchy.

Taking this precaution does not completely protect the system against an attacker with **root** privileges, but it can help thwart an attack from a less experienced malicious user.

Owner access to a file means that the remote user can execute or—worse—modify the file. NFS gives you two ways to deal with these cases:

- You can use the **root_squash** option to map the ID number of the **root** account on a client to UID 65534 on the server.

- You can use the **all-squash** option to map all NFS users on the client to UID 65534 on the server.

Use the **anonuid** and **anongid** options to override these values.

NIS and NFS   When you use NIS (page 705) for user authorization, users automatically have the same UIDs on both systems. If you are using NFS on a large network, it is a good idea to use a directory service such as NIS (page 738) or LDAP (page 722) for authorization. Without such a service, you must synchronize the **passwd** files on all the systems manually.

root_squash (no_root_squash)

Maps requests from **root** on a remote system so they appear to come from the UID 65534, a nonprivileged user on the local system, or as specified by **anonuid**. This option does not affect other sensitive UIDs such as **bin**. The **no_root_squash** option turns off this mapping so that requests from **root** appear to come from **root**.

no_all_squash (all_squash) Does not change the mapping of users making requests of the NFS server. The **all_squash** option maps requests from all users—not just **root**—on remote systems to appear to come from the UID 65534, a nonprivileged user on the local system, or as specified by **anonuid**. This option is useful for controlling access to exported public FTP, news, and other directories.

anonuid=*un* and anongid=*gn* Set the UID or the GID of the anonymous account to *un* or *gn*, respectively. NFS uses these accounts when it does not recognize an incoming UID or GID and when it is instructed to do so by **root_squash** or **all_squash**.

WHERE THE SYSTEM KEEPS NFS MOUNT INFORMATION

A server holds several lists of directory hierarchies it can export. The list that you as a system administrator work with is **/etc/exports**. The following discussion assumes that the local server, **plum**, is exporting these directory hierarchies:

```
$ cat /etc/exports
/home   grape(rw,no_subtree_check)
/pl6    192.168.0.12(rw,no_subtree_check) jam(rw,no_subtree_check)
```

As explained in more detail on page 755, exportfs displays the list of exported directory hierarchies:

```
$ exportfs
/home        grape
/pl6         jam
/pl6         192.168.0.12
```

The important files and pseudofiles that NFS works with are described next.

/var/lib/nfs/etab (export table) On the server, lists the directory hierarchies that are exported (can be mounted, but are not necessarily mounted at the moment) and the options they are exported with:

```
$ cat /var/lib/nfs/etab
/home   grape(rw,sync,wdelay,hide,nocrossmnt,secure,root_squash,no_all_s
quash,no_subtree_check,secure_locks,acl,mapping=identity,anonuid=65534,
anongid=65534)
/pl6    jam(rw,sync,wdelay,hide,nocrossmnt,secure,root_squash,no_all_squa
sh,no_subtree_check,secure_locks,acl,mapping=identity,anonuid=65534,ano
ngid=65534)
/pl6    192.168.0.12(rw,sync,wdelay,hide,nocrossmnt,secure,root_squash,no
_all_squash,no_subtree_check,secure_locks,acl,mapping=identity,anonuid=
65534,anongid=65534)
```

The preceding output shows that **grape** can mount **/home** and that **jam** and 192.168.0.12 can mount **/pl6**. The **etab** file is initialized from **/etc/exports** when the system is brought up, read by **mountd** when a client asks to mount a directory hierarchy, and modified by exportfs (page 755) as the list of exported directory hierarchies changes.

/var/lib/nfs/rmtab   (remote mount table) On the server, lists the directory hierarchies that are mounted by client systems:

```
$ cat /var/lib/nfs/rmtab
192.168.0.12:/pl6:0x00000002
```

The preceding output shows **/pl6** is mounted by 192.168.0.12. The **rmtab** file is updated by **mountd** as it mounts and unmounts directory hierarchies. This file is "mostly ornamental" (from the **mountd** man page) and may not be accurate.

/proc/mounts   On the client, this pseudofile displays the kernel mount table, which lists filesystems mounted by the local system. In the following example, grep displays lines that contain the string **nfs** followed by a SPACE. The SPACE, which you must quote, eliminates lines with the string **nfs** that do not pertain to mounted filesystems.

```
$ grep nfs\  /proc/mounts
plum:/pl6 /mnt nfs rw,vers=3,rsize=131072,wsize=131072,hard,intr,proto=
tcp,timeo=600,retrans=2,sec=sys,addr=plum 0 0
```

showmount: DISPLAYS NFS STATUS INFORMATION

Without any options, the showmount utility displays a list of systems that are allowed to mount local directories. You typically use showmount to display a list of directory hierarchies that a server is exporting. To display information for a remote system, give the name of the remote system as an argument. The information showmount provides may not be complete, however, because it depends on **mountd** and trusts that remote servers are reporting accurately.

In the following example, 192.168.0.12 is allowed to mount local directories, but you do not know which ones:

```
$ showmount
Hosts on plum:
192.168.0.12
```

If showmount displays an error such as **RPC: Program not registered**, NFS is not running on the server. Start NFS on the server with the **nfs-kernel-server** init script (page 746).

–a   (**all**) Displays a list of client systems and indicates which directories each client system can mount. This information is stored in **/etc/exports**. In the following example, showmount lists the directories that 192.168.0.12 can mount from the local system:

```
$ /sbin/showmount -a
All mount points on plum:
192.168.0.12:/pl6
```

–e   (**exports**) Displays a list of exported directories and the systems that each directory is exported to.

```
$ showmount -e
Export list for plum:
/pl6  192.168.0.12
```

exportfs: Maintains the List of Exported Directory Hierarchies

The exportfs utility maintains the **/var/lib/nfs/etab** file (page 753). When **mountd** is called, it checks this file to see if it is allowed to mount the requested directory hierarchy. Typically exportfs is called with simple options and modifies the **etab** file based on changes in **/etc/exports**. When called with client and directory arguments, it can add to or remove the directory hierarchies specified by those arguments from the list kept in **etab**, without reference to the **exports** file. An exportfs command has the following format:

/usr/sbin/exportfs [options] [client:dir ...]

where *options* is one or more options (as discussed in the next section), *client* is the name of the system that *dir* is exported to, and *dir* is the absolute pathname of the directory at the root of the directory hierarchy being exported. Without any arguments, exportfs reports which directory hierarchies are exported to which systems:

```
$ exportfs
/home          grape
/p16           jam
/p16           192.168.0.12
```

The system executes the following command when it comes up (it is in the **nfs-kernel-server** init script). This command reexports the entries in **/etc/exports** and removes invalid entries from **/var/lib/nfs/etab** so **etab** is synchronized with **/etc/exports**:

```
$ sudo exportfs -r
```

Options

−a   (**all**) Exports directory hierarchies specified in **/etc/exports**. This option does not *unexport* entries you have removed from **exports** (that is, it does not remove invalid entries from **/var/lib/nfs/etab**); use **−r** to perform this task.

−f   (**flush**) Removes everything from the kernel's export table.

−i   (**ignore**) Ignores **/etc/exports**; uses what is specified on the command line only.

−o   (**options**) Specifies options. You can specify options following **−o** the same way you do in the **exports** file. For example, exportfs **−i −o ro dog:/home/sam** exports **/home/sam** on the local system to **dog** for readonly access.

−r   (**reexport**) Reexports the entries in **/etc/exports** and removes invalid entries from **/var/lib/nfs/etab** so **/var/lib/nfs/etab** is synchronized with **/etc/exports**.

−u   (**unexport**) Makes an exported directory hierarchy no longer exported. If a directory hierarchy is mounted when you unexport it, users see the message **Stale NFS file handle** when they try to access the directory hierarchy from a remote system.

−v   (**verbose**) Provides more information. Displays export options when you use exportfs to display export information.

TESTING THE SERVER SETUP

From the server, run the **nfs-kernel-server** init script with an argument of **status**. If all is well, the system displays the following:

```
$ /etc/init.d/nfs-kernel-server status
nfsd running
```

Also check that **mountd** is running:

```
$ ps -e | grep mountd
29609 ?         00:00:00 rpc.mountd
```

Next, from the server, use rpcinfo to make sure NFS is registered with portmap:

```
$ rpcinfo -p localhost | grep nfs
   100003    2   udp   2049  nfs
   100003    3   udp   2049  nfs
   100003    4   udp   2049  nfs
   100003    2   tcp   2049  nfs
   100003    3   tcp   2049  nfs
   100003    4   tcp   2049  nfs
```

Repeat the preceding command from the client, replacing **localhost** with the name of the server. The results should be the same.

Finally, try mounting directory hierarchies from remote systems and verify access.

automount: MOUNTS DIRECTORY HIERARCHIES ON DEMAND

In a distributed computing environment, when you log in on any system on the network, all your files—including startup scripts—are available. All systems are also commonly able to mount all directory hierarchies on all servers: Whichever system you log in on, your home directory is waiting for you.

As an example, assume **/home/zach** is a remote directory hierarchy that is mounted on demand. When you issue the command **ls /home/zach**, autofs goes to work: It looks in the **/etc/auto.home** map, finds **zach** is a key that says to mount **plum:/export/home/zach**, and mounts the remote directory hierarchy. Once the directory hierarchy is mounted, ls displays the list of files in that directory. If you give the command **ls /home** after this mounting sequence, ls shows that **zach** is present within the **/home** directory. The df utility shows that **zach** is mounted from **plum**.

PREREQUISITES

Installation   Install the following package:

- **autofs**

autofs init script — When you install the **autofs** package, the **dpkg postinst** script starts the **automount** daemon. After you configure **automount**, call the **autofs** init script to restart the **automount** daemon:

```
$ sudo /etc/init.d/autofs restart
```

After changing the **automount** configuration on an active server, use **reload** in place of **restart** to reload **automount** configuration files without disturbing automatically mounted filesystems. With an argument of **status**, **autofs** displays information about configured and active **autofs** mount points. See the example on page 759.

autofs: AUTOMATICALLY MOUNTED DIRECTORY HIERARCHIES

An **autofs** directory hierarchy is like any other directory hierarchy but remains unmounted until it is needed, at which time the system mounts it automatically (*demand mounting*). The system unmounts an **autofs** directory hierarchy when it is no longer needed—by default, after 5 minutes of inactivity. Automatically mounted directory hierarchies are an important part of managing a large collection of systems in a consistent way. The **automount** daemon is particularly useful when an installation includes a large number of servers or a large number of directory hierarchies. It also helps to remove server–server dependencies (discussed next).

When you boot a system that uses traditional **fstab**-based mounts and an NFS server is down, the system can take a long time to come up as it waits for the server to time out. Similarly, when you have two servers, each mounting directory hierarchies from the other, and both systems are down, both may hang as they are brought up while each tries to mount a directory hierarchy from the other. This situation is called a *server–server dependency*. The **automount** facility gets around these issues by mounting a directory hierarchy from another system only when a process tries to access it.

When a process attempts to access one of the directories within an unmounted **autofs** directory hierarchy, the kernel notifies the **automount** daemon, which mounts the directory hierarchy. You must give a command, such as **cd /home/zach**, that accesses the **autofs** mount point (in this case **/home/zach**) to create the demand that causes **automount** to mount the **autofs** directory hierarchy; only then can the system display or use the **autofs** directory hierarchy. Before you issue this **cd** command, **zach** does not appear in **/home**.

The main file that controls the behavior of **automount** is **/etc/auto.master**. A simple example follows:

```
$ cat /etc/auto.master
/free1    /etc/auto.misc   --timeout=60
/plum     /etc/auto.plum
```

The **auto.master** file has three columns. The first column names the parent of the **autofs** *mount point*—the location where the **autofs** directory hierarchy is to be mounted. (The **/free1** and **/plum** directories in the example are not mount points but will hold the mount points when the directory hierarchies are mounted.) The second column names the files, called *map files,* that store supplemental configuration information. The optional third column holds mount options for map entries. In the preceding example, the first line sets the timeout (the length of time a directory stays mounted when it is not in use) to 60 seconds; the default timeout value is 300 seconds. You can change **autofs** default values in **/etc/default/autofs.**

Although the map files can have any names, one is traditionally named **auto.misc.** Following are the two map files specified in **auto.master:**

```
$ cat /etc/auto.misc
music       -fstype=ext3          :/dev/sdb7

$ cat /etc/auto.plum
pl6         -fstype=nfs           plum:/pl6
```

The first column of a map file holds the relative **autofs** mount point (**music** and **pl6** in the preceding files). This mount point is appended to the corresponding **autofs** mount point from column 1 of the **auto.master** file to create the absolute **autofs** mount point. In this example, **music** (from **auto.misc**) is appended to **/free1** (from **auto.master**) to make **/free1/music; pl6** is appended to **/plum** to make **/plum/pl6.** The second column holds options, and the third column shows the server and directory hierarchy to be mounted. The first example shows a local drive (**/dev/sdb7**). You can tell it is local because its filesystem type is specified as **ext3** and no system name appears before the colon. The second example shows a filesystem on a remote system. It has a filesystem type of **nfs** and specifies the name of the remote system, a colon, and the name the filesystem is mounted under on the remote system.

Before the new setup can work, you must reload the **automount** daemon using the **autofs** init script (page 757). This script creates the directories that hold the mount points (**/free1** and **/plum** in the example) when you start, restart, or reload **autofs** and removes those directories when you stop it.

In the following example, the first ls command shows that the **/free1** and **/plum** directories do not exist. The next command, running with **root** privileges, runs the **autofs** init script to reload **autofs.** Now the directories exist but do not hold any files. When the user lists the contents of **/plum/pl6, autofs** mounts **pl6** and ls displays its contents:

```
$ ls /free1 /plum
ls: /free1: No such file or directory
ls: /plum: No such file or directory

$ sudo /etc/init.d/autofs reload
Reloading automounter: checking for changes ...
Reloading automounter map for: /free1
Reloading automounter map for: /plum

$ ls /free1 /plum
/free1:
/plum:

$ ls /plum/pl6
lost+found  memo
```

The following command displays information about configured and active **autofs** mount points:

```
$ /etc/init.d/autofs status
Configured Mount Points:
-----------------------
/usr/sbin/automount --timeout=60 /free1 file /etc/auto.misc
/usr/sbin/automount --timeout=300 /plum file /etc/auto.plum

Active Mount Points:
-------------------
/usr/sbin/automount --pid-file=/var/run/autofs/_free1.pid --timeout=60 /free1 file
/etc/auto.misc
/usr/sbin/automount --pid-file=/var/run/autofs/_plum.pid --timeout=300 /plum file
/etc/auto.plum
```

CHAPTER SUMMARY

NFS allows a server to share selected local directory hierarchies with client systems on a heterogeneous network, thereby reducing storage needs and administrative overhead. NFS defines a client/server relationship in which a server provides directory hierarchies that clients can mount.

On the server, the **/etc/exports** file typically lists the directory hierarchies that the system exports. Each line in **exports** specifies a directory hierarchy and the client systems that are allowed to mount it, including options for each client (readonly, read-write, and so on). An **exportfs –r** command causes NFS to reread this file.

From a client, a **mount** command mounts an exported NFS directory hierarchy. Alternatively, you can put an entry in **/etc/fstab** to have the system automatically mount the directory hierarchy when it boots.

Automatically mounted directory hierarchies help manage large groups of systems containing many servers and filesystems in a consistent way and can help remove server–server dependencies. The **automount** daemon automatically mounts **autofs** directory hierarchies when they are needed and unmounts them when they are no longer needed.

EXERCISES

1. What are three reasons to use NFS?

2. Which command would you give to mount on the local system the **/home** directory hierarchy that resides on the file server named **plum**? Assume the mounted directory hierarchy will appear as **/plum.home** on the local system. How would you mount the same directory hierarchy if it resided on the fileserver at 192.168.1.1? How would you unmount **/home**?

3. How would you list the mount points on the remote system named **plum** that the local system named **grape** can mount?

4. Which command line lists the currently mounted NFS directory hierarchies?

5. What does the **/etc/fstab** file do?

6. From a server, how would you allow readonly access to **/opt** for any system in **example.com**?

ADVANCED EXERCISES

7. When is it a good idea to disable attribute caching?

8. Describe the difference between the **root_squash** and **all_squash** options in **/etc/exports**.

9. Why does the **secure** option in **/etc/exports** not really provide any security?

10. Some diskless workstations use NFS as swap space. Why is this approach useful? What is the downside?

11. NFS maps users on the client to users on the server. Explain why this mapping is a security risk.

12. What does the mount **nosuid** option do? Why would you want to use this option?

23

SAMBA: LINUX AND WINDOWS FILE AND PRINTER SHARING

Samba is a suite of programs that enables UNIX-like operating systems, including Linux, Solaris, FreeBSD, and Mac OS X, to work with other operating systems, such as OS/2 and Windows, as both a server and a client.

As a server, Samba shares Linux files and printers with Windows systems. As a client, Samba gives Linux users access to files on Windows systems. Its ability to share files across operating systems makes Samba an ideal tool in a heterogeneous computing environment.

Refer to pages 550 and 552 for information about printing using Samba.

INTRODUCTION TO SAMBA

This chapter starts by providing a list of Samba tools followed by some basic information. The JumpStart section discusses how to set up a simple Samba server using the Shared Folders window. The section following that covers how to use swat, a Web-based advanced configuration tool, to set up a Samba server. The final server section discusses how to set up a Samba server by using a text editor to manually edit the files that control Samba. The next two sections of this chapter, "Working with Linux Shares from Windows" (page 776) and "Working with Windows Shares from Linux" (page 777), explain how to work with Linux and Windows files and printers. The final section, "Troubleshooting" (page 779), offers tips on what to do when Samba does not work properly.

Table 23-1 lists some of the utilities and daemons that make up the Samba suite of programs. See the **samba** man page for a complete list.

Table 23-1   Samba utilities and daemons

Utility or daemon	Function
net	This utility has the same syntax as the DOS net command and, over time, will eventually replace other Samba utilities such as smbpasswd.
nmbd	The *NetBIOS* (page 1121) nameserver program, run as a daemon by default. Provides NetBIOS over IP naming services for Samba clients. Also provides browsing support (as in the Windows Network Neighborhood or My Network Places view).
nmblookup	Queries the *NetBIOS* (page 1121) name; see page 780.
pdbedit	Maintains Samba user database.
smbclient	Displays shares on a Samba server such as a Windows machine; uses ftp-like commands (page 778).
smbd	The Samba program, run as a daemon by default. Provides file and print services for Samba clients.
smbpasswd	Changes Windows NT password hashes on Samba and Windows NT servers (page 766).
smbstatus	Displays information about current **smbd** connections.
smbtar	Backs up and restores data from Samba servers; similar to tar.
smbtree	Displays a hierarchical diagram of available shares (page 777).
swat	Samba Web Administration Tool. A browser-based editor for the **smb.conf** file (page 766).
testparm	Checks syntax of the **smb.conf** file (page 780).

MORE INFORMATION

Local
Documentation: Samba/swat home page has links to local Samba documentation (page 766)
/usr/share/doc/samba-doc✳

Web Samba: www.samba.org (mailing lists, documentation, downloads, and more)
CIFS: www.samba.org/cifs

HOWTO *Unofficial Samba HOWTO*: hr.uoregon.edu/davidrl/samba.html
Samba Documentation Collection: Point a browser at **/usr/share/doc/samba-doc/ htmldocs/index.html**; if you have installed the **samba-doc-pdf** package, look in **/usr/share/doc/samba-doc-pdf**.

NOTES

Firewall The Samba server normally uses UDP ports 137 and 138 and TCP ports 139 and 445. If the Samba server system is running a firewall, you need to open these ports. Using firestarter (page 824), open these ports by setting a policy that allows service for Samba.

Share Under Samba, an exported directory hierarchy is called a *share*.

Mapping a share The Samba term *mapping a share* is equivalent to the Linux term *mounting a directory hierarchy*.

Samba The name *Samba* is derived from *SMB* (page 1132), the protocol that is the native method of file and printer sharing for Windows.

swat You must set up a **root** password to use swat to change the Samba configuration; see page 415 for instructions.

SAMBA USERS, USER MAPS, AND PASSWORDS

For a Windows user to access Samba services on a Linux system, the user must provide a Windows username and a Samba password. In some cases, Windows supplies the username and password for you. It is also possible to authenticate using other methods. For example, Samba can use *LDAP* (page 1116) or PAM (page 461) instead of the default password file. Refer to the Samba documentation for more information on authentication methods.

Usernames The username supplied by Windows must be the same as a Linux username or must map to a Linux username.

User maps You can create a file, typically named **/etc/samba/smbusers**, to map Windows usernames to Linux usernames. For more information see **username map** on page 773.

Passwords By default, Samba uses Linux passwords to authenticate users. However, Ubuntu sets **passdb backend** (page 772) to **tdbsam**, causing Samba to use trivial database passwords. Change this parameter to **smbpasswd** in **smb.conf** (page 769) to cause Samba to use Linux passwords.

SETTING UP A SAMBA SERVER

This section describes how to install and configure a Samba server using both the shares-admin utility and the swat browser-based configuration tool.

PREREQUISITES

Installation Install the following packages:

- **samba**
- **smbclient**
- **smbfs** (the only package needed to mount a Windows share)
- **swat** (optional, but useful)
- **openbsd-inetd** (needed to run swat; installed as a swat dependency)
- **samba-doc** (optional documentation; installed with **swat**)
- **samba-doc-pdf** (optional; documentation in PDF format)

samba init script When you install the **samba** package, the **dpkg postinst** script configures Samba to run as a normal daemon (not from **inetd**), copies all Linux users to the list of Samba users, sets up Samba to use encrypted passwords, and starts the **smbd** and **nmbd** daemons. After you configure **samba**, call the **samba** init script to restart **smbd** and **nmbd**:

```
$ sudo /etc/init.d/samba restart
```

After changing the **samba** configuration on an active server, use **reload** in place of **restart** to reload **samba** configuration files without disturbing clients connected to the server.

Figure 23-1   Shared Folders window

Figure 23-2   The Share Folder window

JumpStart: Configuring a Samba Server Using shares-admin

The shares-admin utility can set up only basic features of a Samba server. It is, however, the best tool to use if you are not familiar with Samba and you want to set up a simple Samba server quickly. The shares-admin utility exports shares (directory hierarchies) to Windows machines.

The Shared Folders window (Figure 23-1) enables you to share directory hierarchies using NFS (Chapter 22) and/or Samba. To display this window, give the command **shares-admin** from a terminal emulator or Run Application window (ALT-F2). When you run shares-admin from the command line you will need to click **Unlock** and provide your password in order to modify the Samba configuration.

The Shared Folders window allows you to modify the **/etc/samba/smb.conf** file, which is a large part of setting up a Samba server. (If the system is running a firewall, see "Firewall" on page 763.) In this window you can specify which directory hierarchies you want to share and how they are shared.

Click the **Shared Folders** tab in the Shared Folders window and click **Add** to display the Share Folder window (Figure 23-2). Then select **Windows networks (SMB)** from the list box labeled **Share through**. Now the Share Folder window has two sections: Shared Folder and Share Properties. In the first section, choose the pathname of the directory hierarchy you want to share from the list box labeled **Path**. If the directory you want is not listed, click **Other;** then double-click **File System** in the Places column and double-click the directory you want in the Name column. Continue selecting directories in the Name column until the buttons at the top of the window display the pathname of the directory hierarchy you want to share. Click **Open** to select the directory hierarchy.

Under Share Properties, shares-admin names the share with the simple filename of the directory you selected to share. This name is the one you will use from Windows when you map (mount) the share. For example, if you select **/pl5/documents** on the host named **plum** as the directory to share, shares-admin names the share **documents**. From Windows, you would map the share as the folder named **//plum/documents**.

For more information refer to "Mapping a Share" on page 777. You can change the name of the share; doing so changes the name you use to map the share from Windows. Add a comment if you like.

The General Properties tab of the Shared Folders window allows you to change the name of the workgroup the server belongs to and to declare the server to be a WINS server. If necessary, change the workgroup name so it is the same as the workgroup name on the Windows machine. In most cases you do not need to make the system a WINS server. Add more shares if you like. When you are done adding shares, click **Close** to close the Shared Folders window.

smbpasswd   Working with **root** privileges, you can use smbpasswd to change a Linux user's Samba password.

```
$ sudo smbpasswd sam
New SMB password:
Retype new SMB password:
```

This example assumes Sam was a user on the Linux system before Samba was installed. When you install Samba, it copies all Linux users to the list of Samba users. If you add a user after you install Samba, you need to use the **–a** option to instruct smbpasswd to add the user to the list of Samba users. The following command adds a new Linux user, Max, to the list of Samba users and assigns a Samba password to Max:

```
$ sudo smbpasswd -a max
New SMB password:
Retype new SMB password:
Added user max.
```

Once a user has a Samba password, he can use smbpasswd without any arguments to change his password.

If a user has different usernames on the Linux and Windows systems, you must map the Windows username to a Linux username (see **username map** on page 773). Make sure all Linux users who will log in using Samba have Samba passwords.

You should now be able to access the new shares from a Windows machine (page 776). There is no need to restart the Samba server.

swat: Configures a Samba Server

Make a copy of smb.conf

tip   As installed, the **/etc/samba/smb.conf** file contains extensive comments (page 770). The swat utility overwrites this file, removing the comments. Make a copy of **smb.conf** for safekeeping before you run this utility for the first time.

The swat (Samba Web Administration Tool, **swat** package) utility is a browser-based graphical editor for the **/etc/samba/smb.conf** file. For each of the configurable parameters, it provides Help links, default values, and a text box to change the value. The swat utility is a well-designed tool in that it remains true to the lines in the **smb.conf** file you edit: You can use and learn from swat, so that, if you want to use a text editor to modify **smb.conf**, the transition will be straightforward.

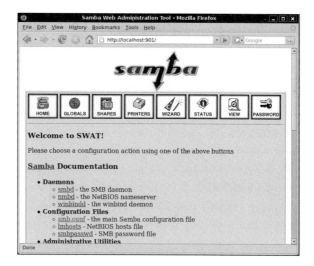

Figure 23-3 The local swat home page

The swat utility is run from **inetd** (**openbsd-inetd** package). When you install the **swat** package, it installs **openbsd-inetd** as a dependency and places the following line in **/etc/inetd.conf**:

```
swat            stream tcp  nowait.400   root /usr/sbin/tcpd /usr/sbin/swat
```

This line enables swat when **inetd** is running. If necessary, give the following command to restart **inetd** so that it rereads its configuration file:

```
$ sudo /etc/init.d/openbsd-inetd restart
 * Restarting internet superserver inetd                          [ OK ]
```

Now you should be able to run swat: From the local system, open a browser and enter either **http://127.0.0.1:901** or **http://localhost:901** in the location bar. When prompted, enter your username and password. (You must set up a **root** password to use swat to change the Samba configuration; see page 415 for instructions.) If you provide a username other than **root**, you will be able to view some configuration information but will not be able to make changes. From a remote system, replace **127.0.0.1** with the IP address of the server (but see the adjacent security tip). If a firewall is running on the local system and you want to access swat from a remote system, open TCP port 901 using firestarter (page 832).

Do not allow unencrypted remote access to swat

security   Do not allow access to swat from a remote system on an insecure network. When you do so and log in, the **root** password is sent in cleartext over whatever connection you are using and can easily be sniffed. If you want to access swat over an insecure network, use ssh to forward port 901 (page 645).

The browser displays the local Samba/swat home page (Figure 23-3). This page includes links to local Samba documentation and the buttons listed on the next page.

HOME   Links to local Samba documentation. When you click the word **Samba** (not the logo, but the one just before the word **Documentation** in the Samba/swat home page), swat displays the Samba man page, which defines each Samba program.

GLOBALS   Edits global parameters (variables) in **smb.conf**.

SHARES   Edits share information in **smb.conf**.

PRINTERS   Edits printer information in **smb.conf**.

WIZARD   Rewrites the **smb.conf** file, removing all comment lines and lines that specify default values.

STATUS   Shows the active connections, active shares, and open files. Stops and restarts the **smbd** and **nmbd** daemons.

VIEW   Displays a subset (click **Full View**) or all of the configuration parameters as determined by the default values and settings in **smb.conf** (click **Normal View**).

PASSWORD   Manages Samba passwords.

It is quite easy to establish a basic Samba setup so you can work with a Linux directory hierarchy from a Windows system. More work is required to set up a secure connection or one with special features. The following example creates a basic setup based on the sample **smb.conf** file included with Ubuntu Linux.

swat Help and defaults   Each of the parameters swat displays has a button labeled **Help** next to it. Click **Help** to open a new browser window containing an explanation of that parameter. Each parameter also has a **Set Default** button that sets the parameter to its default value (not necessarily the initial value as supplied by Ubuntu).

For this example, do not click any of the **Set Default** buttons. Make sure to click **Commit Changes** at the top of each page after you finish making changes on a page but before you click a menu button at the top of the page. Otherwise, swat will discard your changes.

GLOBALS page   To follow this example, first click **GLOBALS** at the top of the Samba/swat home page. Leave everything at its current setting with two exceptions: **hosts allow** and **hosts deny**. Setting these parameters makes the server more secure by limiting the clients that Samba responds to. Scroll to the bottom of the Security Options and set **hosts allow** to the names or IP addresses of systems you want to allow to access the local system's shares and printers. If there are any addresses in **hosts allow** or if you set **hosts deny** to ALL, you must also add 0.0.0.0 to **hosts allow** to be able to use swat. Separate the entries with SPACEs or commas. See page 771 for more information on the various ways you can set **hosts allow**. Set **hosts deny** to ALL. Click **Commit Changes** (near the top of the page) when you are done with the GLOBALS page.

SHARES page   Next click **SHARES** at the top of the page. Three buttons and two text boxes appear near the bottom of the page (Figure 23-4). In the text box adjacent to the **Create Share** button, enter the name you want to assign to the share you are setting up. You will use this share name from Windows when you map (mount) the share. Click **Create Share**. To modify an existing share, display the name of the share in the drop-down list labeled **Choose Share**, and click **Choose Share**. Either of these actions expands the Share Parameters page so it displays information about the selected share.

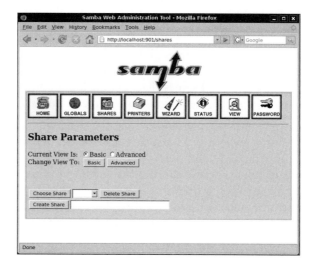

Figure 23-4 Share Parameters page

If you can no longer use swat

tip If you can no longer use swat, you probably changed the **hosts allow** setting incorrectly. In this case you need to edit **/etc/samba/smb.conf** manually and fix the line with the words **hosts allow** in it:

```
# grep hosts smb.conf
        hosts allow = 0.0.0.0, 192.168.0.8
        hosts deny = ALL
```

The preceding entries allow access from 192.168.0.8 only. They also allow swat to work. You do not need to restart Samba after changing **smb.conf**.

Set **path** to the absolute pathname on the Linux server of the share and, if you like, set **comment** to a string that will help you remember where the share is located. The values for **hosts allow** and **hosts deny,** if any, are taken from the global parameters. Make sure **read only, guest ok,** and **browseable** are set as you desire. Set **available** to YES or you will not have access to the share. Click **Commit Changes** when you are done with the SHARES page. If you want to see how many parameters there really are, click **Advanced** near the top of the page. Switching between the Basic and Advanced views removes any changes you have not committed.

From a Windows machine, you should now be able to access the share you just created (page 776).

You do not need to restart Samba when you change **smb.conf**

tip Samba rereads its configuration files each time a client connects. Unless you change the **security** parameter (page 772), you do not need to restart Samba when you change **smb.conf**.

smb.conf: MANUALLY CONFIGURING A SAMBA SERVER

The **/etc/samba/smb.conf** file controls most aspects of how Samba works and is divided into sections. Each section begins with a line that holds some text between brackets ([...]). The text within the brackets identifies the section. Typical sections are

[globals]	Defines global parameters
[printers]	Defines printers
[homes]	Defines shares in the **homes** directory
[*share name*]	Defines a share (you can have more than one of these sections)

smb.conf comments As installed on an Ubuntu Linux system, the **smb.conf** sample configuration file contains extensive comments and commented-out examples. Comment lines start with either a pound sign (#) or a semicolon (;). The sample file uses pound signs to begin lines that are intended to remain as comments. Semicolons begin lines that you may want to mimic or use as is by removing the semicolons. The following segment of **smb.conf** contains three lines of true comments and three lines beginning with semicolons that you may want to uncomment and change:

```
# Un-comment the following (and tweak the other settings below to suit)
# to enable the default home directory shares.  This will share each
# user's home directory as \\server\username
;[homes]
;    comment = Home Directories
;    browseable = no
```

As Ubuntu sets the global parameters in **smb.conf**, you need simply add a share for a Windows system to be able to access a directory on the Linux server. Add the following simple share to the end of the **smb.conf** file to enable a user on a Windows system to be able to read from and write to the local **/tmp** directory:

```
[tmp]
        comment = temporary directory
        path = /tmp
        writable = YES
        guest ok = YES
```

The name of the share under Windows is **tmp**; the path under Linux is **/tmp**. Any Windows user who can log in on Samba, including **guest**, can read from and write to this directory, assuming the user's Linux permissions allow it. To allow a user to log in on Samba, you must run smbpasswd (page 766). Because **browseable** defaults to YES, unless you specify **browseable = NO**, the share appears as a share on the server without explicitly being declared **browseable**. The Linux permissions that apply to a Windows user using Samba are the same permissions that apply to the Linux user that the Windows user maps to.

PARAMETERS IN THE smbd.conf FILE

The **smb.conf** man page and the Help feature of swat list all the parameters you can set in **smb.conf**. The following sections identify some of the parameters you are likely to want to change.

SETTING UP A SAMBA SERVER 771

GLOBAL PARAMETERS

interfaces A SPACE-separated list of networks Samba uses. Specify as interface names (such as eth0) or as IP address/net mask pairs (page 445).

Default: all active interfaces except 127.0.0.1

server string The string that the Windows machine displays in various places. Within the string, Samba replaces **%v** with the Samba version number and **%h** with the hostname.

Default: Samba %v
Ubuntu: %h server (Samba, Ubuntu)

workgroup The workgroup the server belongs to. Set to the same workgroup as the Windows clients that use the server. This parameter controls the domain name that Samba uses when **security** (page 772) is set to DOMAIN.

Default: WORKGROUP

SECURITY PARAMETERS

encrypt passwords YES accepts only encrypted passwords from clients. Windows 98 and Windows NT 4.0 Service Pack 3 and later use encrypted passwords by default. This parameter uses smbpasswd to authenticate passwords unless you set **security** to SERVER or DOMAIN, in which case Samba authenticates using another server.

Default: YES

guest account The username that is assigned to users logging in as **guest** or mapped to **guest**; applicable only when **guest ok** (page 776) is set to YES. This username should be present in **/etc/passwd** but should not be able to log in on the system. Typically **guest account** is assigned a value of **nobody** because the user **nobody** can access only files that any user can access. If you are using the **nobody** account for other purposes on the Linux system, set this parameter to a name other than **nobody**.

Default: **nobody**

hosts allow Analogous to the **/etc/hosts.allow** file (page 448); specifies hosts that are allowed to connect to the server. Overrides hosts specified in **hosts deny**. A good strategy is to specify ALL in **hosts deny** and to specify the hosts you want to grant access to in this file. Specify hosts in the same manner as in **hosts.allow**.

Default: none (all hosts permitted access)

hosts deny Analogous to the **/etc/hosts.deny** file (page 448); specifies hosts that are not allowed to connect to the server. Overridden by hosts specified in **hosts allow**. If you specify ALL in this file, remember to include the local system (127.0.0.1) in **hosts allow**. Specify hosts in the same manner as in **hosts.deny**.

Default: none (no hosts excluded)

invalid users Lists users who are not allowed to log in using Samba.

Default: none (all users are permitted to log in)
Ubuntu: *HARDY*: **root**, *INTREPID*: none (all users are permitted to log in)

map to guest   Defines when a failed login is mapped to the **guest account**. Useful only when **security** (page 772) is not set to SHARE.

Never: Allows **guest** to log in only when the user explicitly provides **guest** as the username and a blank password.

Bad User: Treats any attempt to log in as a user who does not exist as a **guest** login. This parameter is a security risk because it allows a malicious user to retrieve a list of users on the system quickly.

Bad Password: Silently logs in as **guest** any user who incorrectly enters her password. This parameter may confuse a user when she mistypes her password and is unknowingly logged in as **guest** because she will suddenly see fewer shares than she is used to.

Default: Never
Ubuntu: Bad User

passdb backend   Specifies how Samba stores passwords. Set to ldapsam for LDAP, smbpasswd for Samba, or tdbsam for TDB (trivial database) password storage. See page 766 for instructions on using smbpasswd to change Samba passwords.

Default: smbpasswd
Ubuntu: tdbsam

passwd chat   The chat script Samba uses to converse with the passwd program. If this script is not followed, Samba does not change the password. Used only when **unix password sync** (page 773) is set to YES.

Default: *new*password* %n\n*new*password* %n\n *changed*
Ubuntu: *Enter\snew\s*\spassword:* %n\n *Retype\snew\s*\spassword:*
%n\n *password\supdated\ssuccessfully* .

passwd program   The program Samba uses to set *Linux* passwords. Samba replaces **%u** with the user's username.

Default: none
Ubuntu: **/usr/bin/passwd %u**

security   Specifies if and how clients transfer user and password information to the server. Choose one of the following:

USER: Causes Samba to require a username and password from Windows users when logging in on the Samba server. With this setting you can use

- **username map** (page 773) to map Samba usernames to Linux usernames
- **encrypt passwords** (page 771) to encrypt passwords (recommended)
- **guest account** (page 771) to map users to the **guest** account

SHARE: Causes Samba not to authenticate clients on a per-user basis. Instead, Samba uses the Windows 9*x* setup, in which each share can have an individual password for either read or full access. This option is not compatible with more recent versions of Windows.

SERVER: Causes Samba to use another SMB server to validate usernames and passwords. If the remote validation fails, the local Samba server tries to validate usernames and passwords as though **security** were set to USER.

DOMAIN: Samba passes an encrypted password to a Windows NT domain controller for validation. The **workgroup** parameter (page 771) must be properly set in **smb.conf** for DOMAIN to work.

ADS: Instructs Samba to use an Active Directory server for authentication, allowing a Samba server to participate as a native Active Directory member. (Active Directory is the centralized information system that Windows 2000 and later use. It replaces Windows Domains, which was used by Windows NT and earlier.)

Default: USER

unix password sync   YES causes Samba to change a user's Linux password when the associated user changes the encrypted Samba password.

Default: NO
Ubuntu: YES

update encrypted   YES allows users to migrate from cleartext passwords to encrypted passwords without logging in on the server and using smbpasswd. To migrate users, set to YES and set **encrypt passwords** to NO. As each user logs in on the server with a cleartext Linux password, smbpasswd encrypts and stores the password. Set to NO and set **encrypt passwords** to YES after all users have been converted.

Default: NO

username map   The name of the file, typically **/etc/samba/smbusers**, that maps usernames from a Windows client to usernames on the Linux server. This parameter is effective only when **security** (page 772) is set to USER. Each line of the map file starts with a server (Linux) username, followed by a SPACE, an equal sign, another SPACE, and one or more SPACE-separated client (Windows) usernames. An asterisk (*) on the client side matches any client username.

This file frequently maps Windows usernames to Linux usernames and/or maps multiple Windows usernames to a single Linux username to facilitate file sharing. Following is a sample map file:

```
$ cat /etc/samba/smbusers
# Unix_name = SMB_name1 SMB_name2 ...
root = administrator admin
nobody = guest pcguest smbguest
```

The first entry maps the two Windows usernames (**administrator** and **admin**) to the Linux username **root** (you must change the Ubuntu value for **invalid users** [page 771] to be able to log in as **root**). The second entry maps three Windows usernames, including **guest**, to the Linux username **nobody**: When a Windows user attempts to log in on the Samba server as **guest**, Samba authenticates the Linux user named **nobody**. Each user, including **nobody**, must have a Samba password (refer to smbpasswd on page 766), even if it is blank.

Add the following line to the file this parameter points to, creating the file if necessary, to map the Windows username **sam** to the Linux username **sls**:

```
sls = sam
```

After you add a user to this file, you must give the user a password using smbpasswd. When Sam logs in as **sam**, Samba now maps **sam** to **sls** and looks up **sls** in the Samba password database. Assuming Sam provides the correct password, he logs in on the Samba server as **sls**.

Default: no map

LOGGING PARAMETERS

log file   The name of the Samba log file. Samba replaces **%m** with the name of the client system, allowing you to generate a separate log file for each client.

Default: none
Ubuntu: **/var/log/samba/log.%m**

log level   Sets the log level, with 0 (zero) being off and higher numbers being more verbose.

Default: 0 (off)

max log size   An integer specifying the maximum size of the log file in kilobytes. A 0 (zero) specifies no limit. When a file reaches this size, Samba appends **.old** to the filename and starts a new log, deleting any old log file.

Default: 5000
Ubuntu: 1000

BROWSER PARAMETERS

The *domain master browser* is the system responsible for maintaining the list of machines on a network used when browsing a Windows Network Neighborhood or My Network Places. *SMB* (page 1132) uses weighted elections every 11–15 minutes to determine which machine is the domain master browser.

Whether a Samba server wins this election depends on two parameters:

* Setting **domain master** to YES instructs the Samba server to enter the election.
* The **os level** determines how much weight the Samba server's vote receives.

Setting **os level** to 2 should cause the Samba server to win against any Windows *9x* machines. NT Server series domain controllers—including Windows 2000, XP, and 2003—use an **os level** of 32. The maximum setting for **os level** is 255, although setting it to 65 should ensure that the Samba server wins.

domain master   YES causes **nmbd** to attempt to be the domain master browser. If a domain master browser exists, then local master browsers will forward copies of their browse lists to it. If there is no domain master browser, then browse queries may not be able to cross subnet boundaries. A Windows PDC (primary domain controller) will always try to become the domain master and may behave in unexpected ways if it fails. Refer to the preceding discussion for more information.

Default: AUTO

local master   YES causes **nmbd** to enter elections for the local master browser on a subnet. A local master browser stores a cache of the *NetBIOS* (page 1121) names of entities on the local subnet, allowing browsing. Windows machines automatically enter elections; for browsing to work, the network must have at least one Windows machine or one Samba server with **local master** set to YES. It is poor practice to set local master to NO. If you do not want a computer to act as a local master, set its **os level** to a lower number, allowing it to be used as the local master if all else fails.

Default: YES

os level An integer that controls how much Samba advertises itself for browser elections and how likely **nmbd** is to become the local master browser for its workgroup. A higher number increases the chances of the local server becoming the local master browser. Refer to the discussion at the beginning of this section for more information.

Default: 20

preferred master YES forces **nmbd** to hold an election for local master and enters the local system with a slight advantage. With **domain master** set to YES, this parameter helps ensure the local Samba server becomes the domain master. Setting this parameter to YES on more than one server causes the servers to compete to become master, generating a lot of network traffic and sometimes leading to unpredictable results. A Windows PDC automatically acts as if this parameter is set.

Default: AUTO

COMMUNICATION PARAMETERS

dns proxy When acting as a *WINS server* (page 1141), YES causes **nmbd** to use DNS if *Net-BIOS* (page 1121) resolution fails.

Default: YES
Ubuntu: NO

socket options Tunes the network parameters used when exchanging data with a client. Adding **SO_RCVBUF=8192 SO_SNDBUF=8192** to this parameter may improve network performance.

Default: TCP_NODELAY

wins server The IP address of the WINS server **nmbd** should register with.

Default: not enabled

wins support YES specifies **nmbd** is to act as a WINS server.

Default: NO

SHARE PARAMETERS

Each of the following parameters can appear many times in **smb.conf**, once in each share definition.

available YES specifies the share as active. Set this parameter to NO to disable the share but continue logging requests for it.

Default: YES

browseable Determines whether the share can be browsed, for example, in Windows My Network Places.

Default: YES
Ubuntu: YES, except for printers

comment A description of the share, shown when browsing the network from Windows.

Default: none
Ubuntu: varies

guest ok Allows a user who logs in as **guest** to access this share.

Default: NO

path The path of the directory being shared.

Default: none
Ubuntu: various

read only Does not allow write access. Use **writable** to allow read-write access.

Default: YES

THE [HOMES] SHARE: SHARING USERS' HOME DIRECTORIES

Frequently users want to share their Linux home directories with a Windows machine. To make this task easier, Samba provides the [**homes**] share, which Ubuntu comments out. When you define this share, each user's home directory is shared with the specified parameters. In most cases, the following parameters are adequate:

```
[homes]
        comment = Home Directories
        browseable = NO
        writable = YES
```

These settings prevent users other than the owners from browsing home directories while allowing logged-in owners full access.

WORKING WITH LINUX SHARES FROM WINDOWS

This section describes how to access Linux directories from a Windows machine.

BROWSING SHARES

To access a share on a Samba server from Windows, open My Computer or Explorer on the Windows system and, in the text box labeled **Address**, enter \\ followed by the NetBIOS name (or just the hostname if you have not assigned a different NetBIOS name) of the Samba server. Windows then displays the directories the Linux system is sharing. To view the shares on the Linux system named **dog**, for example, enter **dog**. From this window, you can view and, if permitted, browse the shares available on the Linux system. If you set a share so it is not browseable, you need to enter the path of the share using the format *servername**sharename* to display the share.

MAPPING A SHARE

Another way to access a share on a Samba server is by mapping (mounting) a share. Open My Computer or Explorer on the Windows system and click **Map Network Drive** from one of the drop-down menus on the menubar (found on the **Tools** menu on Windows XP). Windows displays the Map Network Drive window. Select an unused Windows drive letter from the list box labeled **Drive** and enter the Windows path to the share you want to map in the text box labeled **Folder**. The format of the windows path is ***hostname**sharename*.** For example, to map **/tmp** on **dog** to Windows drive J, assuming the share is named **tmp** on the Linux system, select **J** in the list box labeled **Drive**, enter **\\dog\tmp** in the text box labeled **Folder**, and click **Finish**. After supplying a username and password, you should be able to access the **/tmp** directory from **dog** as **J** (**tmp**) on the Windows machine. If you cannot map the drive, refer to "Troubleshooting" on page 779.

WORKING WITH WINDOWS SHARES FROM LINUX

Samba enables you to view and work with files on a Windows system (client) from a Linux system (server). This section discusses several ways of accessing Windows files from Linux.

smbtree: DISPLAYS WINDOWS SHARES

The smbtree utility displays a hierarchical diagram of available shares. When you run smbtree, it prompts you for a password; do not enter a password if you want to browse shares that are visible to the **guest** user. The password allows you to view restricted shares, such as a user's home directory in the **[homes]** share. Following is sample output from smbtree:

```
$ smbtree
Password: RETURN      (do not enter a password)
MGS
        \\JAM
                \\JAM\C$                  Default share
                \\JAM\ADMIN$              Remote Admin
                \\JAM\F
                \\JAM\E
            ...
        \\DOG                             Samba 3.0.22
                \\DOG\dogprinter          HP LaserJet 1320
                \\DOG\print$              Printer Drivers
                \\DOG\home
                \\DOG\p01                 common backed-up directory
                \\DOG\p02                 common backed-up directory
```

In the preceding output, **MGS** is the name of the workgroup, **JAM** is the name of the Windows machine, and **DOG** is the name of the Samba server that the smbtree utility is run from. Workgroup and machine names are always shown in uppercase letters. If smbtree does not display output, set the **workgroup** (page 771) and **wins server** (page 775) parameters in **smb.conf**. Refer to the smbtree man page for more information.

smbclient: CONNECTS TO WINDOWS SHARES

The smbclient utility functions similarly to ftp (page 651) and connects to a Windows share. However, smbclient uses Linux-style forward slashes (/) as path separators rather than Windows-style backslashes (\). The next example connects to one of the shares displayed in the preceding example:

```
$ smbclient //JAM/D
Enter sam's password: RETURN  (do not enter a password)
Anonymous login successful
Domain=[JAM] OS=[Windows 5.1] Server=[Windows 2000 LAN Manager]
smb: \> ls
  audit                         D        0  Tue May  6 18:46:33 2008
  data                          D        0  Tue May  6 18:47:09 2008
  laptop.data                   D        0  Tue May  6 19:12:16 2008
  Linux                         D        0  Tue May  6 18:57:49 2008
  oldfonts                      D        0  Wed May  7 00:02:17 2008
  PSFONTS                       D        0  Tue May  6 18:45:36 2008
  RECYCLER                    DHS        0  Thu May  8 20:05:21 2008
  System Volume Information   DHS        0  Tue May  6 18:45:32 2008

            46547 blocks of size 1048576. 42136 blocks available
smb: \>
```

You can use most ftp commands from smbclient. Refer to "Tutorial Session" on page 654 for some examples. Alternatively, give the command **help** to display a list of commands or **help** followed by a command for information on a specific command:

```
smb: \> help history
HELP history:
        displays the command history
```

BROWSING WINDOWS NETWORKS

Browsing Windows shares using smbtree and smbclient is quite awkward compared with the ease of browsing a network from Windows; GNOME provides a more user-friendly alternative. From Nautilus, enter **smb:///** in the location bar to browse the Windows shares on the network.

Nautilus uses virtual filesystem add-ons, which are part of the desktop environment and not part of the native Linux system. As a consequence, only native GNOME applications can open files on remote shares; normal Linux programs cannot. For example, gedit can open files on remote shares, while OpenOffice, mplayer, and xedit cannot.

MOUNTING WINDOWS SHARES

The mount utility (page 488) with a **–t cifs** option mounts a Windows share as if it were a Linux directory hierarchy. See page 1101 for more information on the CIFS protocol. When you mount a Windows share, you can write to the files on the share; you cannot write to files on a share using smbclient.

A mount command that mounts a Windows share has the following syntax (you must run this command with **root** privileges):

mount -t cifs //host/share dir

where *host* is the name of the system the share is on, *share* is the name of the Windows share that you want to mount, and *dir* is the absolute pathname of the Linux directory that you are mounting the share on (the mount point).

The following command, when run with **root** privileges, mounts on the **/share** directory the share used in the preceding example:

```
$ sudo mount -t cifs //jam/d /share -o username=sam
Password:
$ ls /share
Linux     RECYCLER                         audit   laptop.data
PSFONTS   System Volume Information   data   oldfonts
```

You can omit the **username** argument and provide a blank password to mount shares that are visible to the **guest** user. Use the **uid**, **file_mode**, and **dir_mode** mount options with type **cifs** filesystems to establish ownership and permissions of mounted files.

```
$ sudo mount -t cifs //jam/d /share -o username=sam,uid=sam,file_mode=0644,dir_mode=0755
```

Permissions must be expressed as octal numbers preceded by a zero. For more information refer to the mount.cifs man page.

TROUBLESHOOTING

Samba provides two utilities that can help troubleshoot a connection: testparm checks the syntax of **/etc/samba/smb.conf** and displays its contents; smbstatus displays a report on open Samba connections.

The following steps can help you narrow down the problem when you cannot get Samba to work.

1. Restart the Samba daemons. Make sure the last line of output ends with **OK**.

```
$ sudo /etc/init.d/samba restart
 * Stopping Samba daemons...                                    [ OK ]
 * Starting Samba daemons...                                    [ OK ]
```

testparm   2. Run testparm to confirm that the **smb.conf** file is syntactically correct:

```
$ testparm
Load smb config files from /etc/samba/smb.conf
Processing section "[printers]"
Processing section "[print$]"
Processing section "[pl2]"
Loaded services file OK.
Server role: ROLE_STANDALONE
Press enter to see a dump of your service definitions
...
```

If you misspell a keyword in **smb.conf**, you get an error such as the following:

```
$ testparm
Load smb config files from /etc/samba/smb.conf
Unknown parameter encountered: "workgruop"
Ignoring unknown parameter "workgruop"
...
```

ping   3. Use ping (page 377) from both sides of the connection to make sure the network is up.

Firewall   4. Confirm the firewall on the server is not blocking the Samba connection (page 763).

Password   5. Make sure you have set up a password for the Samba user you are trying to log in as.

net view   6. From a Windows command prompt, use net view to display a list of shares available from the server (**dog** in this example):

```
C:>net view \\dog
Shared resources at \\dog

Samba 3.0.24

Share name    Type    Used as    Comment

-------------------------------------------------------------------
backup        Disk               The backup partition
dogprinter    Print              HP Laserjet 1320
homes         Disk               Home Directories
p04           Disk    O:         common backed-up directory
...
The command completed successfully.
```

net use   7. Try to map (mount) the drive from a Windows command prompt. The following command attempts to mount the share named **p04** on **dog** as drive X:

```
C:>net use x: \\dog\p04
The command completed successfully.
```

nmblookup   8. From the Samba server, query the **nmbd** server, using the special name __SAMBA__ for the server's NetBIOS name. The **–d 2** option turns the

debugger on at level 2, which generates a moderate amount of output. The
–B option specifies the server you are querying.

```
$ nmblookup -d 2 -B localhost __SAMBA__
added interface ip=192.168.0.10 bcast=192.168.0.127 nmask=255.255.255.128
querying __SAMBA__ on 127.0.0.1
Got a positive name query response from 127.0.0.1 ( 192.168.0.10 )
192.168.0.10 __SAMBA__<00>
```

The next example uses nmblookup, without setting the debug level, to
query the local system for all NetBIOS names.

```
$ nmblookup -B localhost \*
querying * on 127.0.0.1
192.168.0.10 *<00>
```

To query for the master browser from the local server, run nmblookup with
the **–A** option followed **localhost** or the name of the server:

```
$ nmblookup -A localhost
Looking up status of 127.0.0.1
        PLUM            <00> -          H <ACTIVE>
        PLUM            <03> -          H <ACTIVE>
        PLUM            <20> -          H <ACTIVE>
        ..__MSBROWSE__. <01> - <GROUP> H <ACTIVE>
        MGS             <1d> -          H <ACTIVE>
        MGS             <1e> - <GROUP> H <ACTIVE>
        MGS             <00> - <GROUP> H <ACTIVE>

        MAC Address = 00-00-00-00-00-00
```

smbclient   9. From the Samba server, use smbclient with the **–L** option followed by the
name of the server to generate a list of shares offered by the server:

```
$ smbclient -L localhost
Password: RETURN  (do not enter a password)
Anonymous login successful
Domain=[MGS] OS=[Unix] Server=[Samba 3.0.24]

        Sharename       Type        Comment
        ---------       ----        -------
        IPC$            IPC         IPC Service (plum server (Samba, Ubuntu))
        tmp             Disk        mgs comment tmp
        p15             Disk
        print$          Disk        Printer Drivers
Anonymous login successful
Domain=[MGS] OS=[Unix] Server=[Samba 3.0.24]

        Server              Comment
        ---------           -------
        PLUM                plum server (Samba, Ubuntu)

        Workgroup           Master
        ---------           -------
        MGS                 PLUM
```

CHAPTER SUMMARY

Samba is a suite of programs that enables Linux and Windows to share directory hierarchies and printers. A directory hierarchy or printer that is shared between Linux and Windows systems is called a share. To access a share on a Linux system, a Windows user must supply a username and password. Usernames must correspond to Linux usernames either directly or as mapped by the file that is pointed to by the **username map** parameter in **smb.conf**, often **/etc/samba/smbusers**. Samba passwords are generated by smbpasswd.

The main Samba configuration file is **/etc/samba/smb.conf**, which you can edit using the Shared Folders window, swat (a Web-based administration utility), or a text editor. The swat utility is a powerful configuration tool that provides integrated online documentation and clickable default values to help you set up Samba.

From a Windows machine, you can access a share on a Linux Samba server by opening My Computer or Explorer and, in the text box labeled **Address**, entering \\ followed by the name of the server. In response, Windows displays the shares on the server. You can work with these shares as though they were Windows files.

From a Linux system, you can use any of several Samba tools to access Windows shares. These tools include smbtree (displays shares), smbclient (similar to ftp), and mount with the **–t cifs** option (mounts shares). In addition, you can enter **smb:///** in the Nautilus location bar and browse the shares.

EXERCISES

1. Which two daemons are part of the Samba suite? What does each do?

2. What steps are required for mapping a Windows user to a Linux user?

3. How can a system administrator add a Samba password for a new user?

4. What is the purpose of the [**homes**] share?

ADVANCED EXERCISES

5. Describe how Samba's handling of users differs from that of NFS.

6. Which configuration changes would you need to apply to routers if you wanted to allow SMB/CIFS browsing across multiple subnets without configuring master browsers?

7. How could you use swat securely from a remote location?

8. WINS resolution allows hosts to define their own names. Suggest a way to use Samba to assign names from a centralized list.

24

DNS/BIND: TRACKING DOMAIN NAMES AND ADDRESSES

DNS (Domain Name System) maps domain names to IP addresses, and vice versa. It reduces the need for humans to work with IP addresses, which, with the introduction of IPv6, are complex. The DNS specification defines a secure, general-purpose database that holds Internet host information. It also specifies a protocol that is used to exchange this information. Further, DNS defines library routines that implement the protocol. Finally, DNS provides a means for routing email. Under DNS, *nameservers* work with clients, called *resolvers*, to distribute host information in the form of *resource records* in a timely manner as needed.

This chapter describes BIND (Berkeley Internet Name Domain) version 9, a popular open-source implementation of DNS. Part of the Ubuntu Linux distribution, BIND includes the DNS server daemon (**named**), a DNS resolver library, and tools for working with DNS. Although DNS can be used for private networks, this chapter covers DNS as used by the Internet.

INTRODUCTION TO DNS

You typically use DNS when you display a Web page. For example, to display Ubuntu's home page, you enter its name, www.ubuntu.com, in a browser; the browser then displays the page you want. You never enter or see the IP address for the displayed page. However, without the IP address, the browser could not display the page. DNS works behind the scenes to find the IP address when you enter the name in the browser. The DNS database is

- **Hierarchical**, so it provides quick responses to queries. DNS has a root, branches, and nodes.
- **Distributed**, so it offers fast access to servers. The DNS database is spread across thousands of systems worldwide; each system is referred to as a *DNS server* (or a *domain server* or *nameserver*).
- **Replicated**, to enhance reliability. Because many systems hold the same information, when some systems fail, DNS does not stop functioning.

As implemented, DNS is

- **Secure**, so your browser or email is directed to the correct location.
- **Flexible**, so it can adapt to new names, deleted names, and names whose information changes.
- **Fast**, so Internet connections are not delayed by slow DNS lookups.

History   The mapping that DNS does was originally handled statically in a **/etc/hosts** file (page 475) on each system on a network. Small LANs still make use of this file. As networks—specifically the Internet—grew, a dynamic mapping system was required. DNS was specified in 1983 and BIND became part of BSD in 1985. Today BIND is by far the most popular implementation of DNS.

Security   Historically BIND has not been very secure. Recently, however, developers have focused on improving the security of BIND. You may want to run BIND inside a chroot jail (page 808) and use transaction signatures (TSIG, page 806) to improve security.

host and dig   The host and dig utilities (page 380) query DNS servers. The host utility is simpler, is easier to use, and returns less information than dig. This chapter uses both tools to explore DNS.

NODES, DOMAINS, AND SUBDOMAINS

Node   Each node in the hierarchical DNS database is called a *domain* and is labeled with a (domain) name. As with the Linux file structure, the node at the top of the DNS hierarchy is called the *root node* or *root domain*. While the Linux file structure separates the nodes (directory and ordinary files) with slashes (/) and labels the root node (directory) with a slash, the DNS structure uses periods in place of the file structure's slashes (Figure 24-1).

You read an absolute pathname in a Linux filesystem from left to right: It starts with the root directory (represented by /) at the left and, as you read to the right,

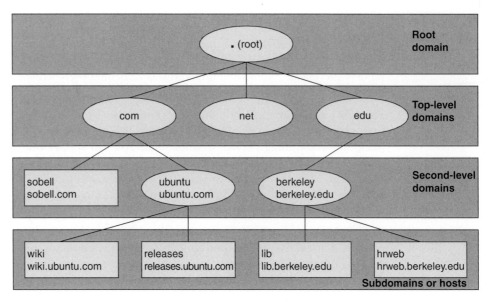

Figure 24-1 The DNS domain structure (FQDNs are shown below hostnames.)

describes the path to the file being identified (for example, **/var/spool/cups**). Unlike a Linux pathname, you read a DNS domain name from right to left: It starts with the root domain at the right (represented by a period [.]) and, as you read to the left, works its way down through the top-level and second-level domains to a subdomain or host. Frequently the name of the root domain (the period at the right) is omitted from a domain name.

Domain   The term *domain* refers both to a single node in the DNS domain structure and to a catenated, period-separated list (path) of domain names that describes the location of a domain.

FQDN   A fully qualified domain name (FQDN) is the DNS equivalent of a filesystem's absolute pathname: It is a pointer that positively locates a domain on the Internet. Just as you (and Linux) can identify an absolute pathname by its leading slash (**/**) that represents the root directory, so an FQDN can be identified by its trailing period (.) that names the root domain (Figure 24-2).

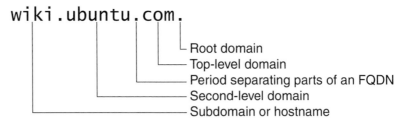

Figure 24-2 A fully qualified domain name (FQDN)

Resolver   The resolver comprises the routines that turn an unqualified domain name into an FQDN that is passed to DNS to be mapped to an IP address. The resolver can append several domains, one at a time, to an unqualified domain name, producing several FQDNs that it then passes, one at a time, to DNS. For each FQDN, DNS reports success (it found the FQDN and is returning the corresponding IP address) or failure (the FQDN does not exist).

The resolver always appends the root domain (.) to an unqualified domain name first, thereby allowing you to type **www.sobell.com** instead of **www.sobell.com.** (including the trailing period) in a browser. You can specify other domains for the resolver to try if the root domain fails. Put the domain names, in the order you want them tried, after the **search** keyword in **/etc/resolv.conf** (page 478). For example, if your search domains include **ubuntu.com.**, then the domains **wiki** and **wiki.ubuntu.com.** will resolve to the same address.

Subdomains   Each node in the domain hierarchy is a domain. Each domain that has a parent (that is, every domain except the root domain) is also a subdomain, regardless of whether it has children. All subdomains *can* resolve to hosts—even those with children. For example, the **ubuntu.com.** domain resolves to the host that serves the Ubuntu Web site, without preventing its children—domains such as **wiki.ubuntu.com**—from resolving. The leftmost part of an FQDN is often called the *hostname*.

Hostnames   In the past, hostnames could contain only characters from the set a–z, A–Z, 0–9, and –. As of March 2004, however, hostnames can include various accents, umlauts, and so on (www.switch.ch/id/idn). DNS considers uppercase and lowercase letters to be the same (it is not case sensitive), so www.sobell.com is the same as WWW.sObEll.coM.

ZONES

For administrative purposes, domains are grouped into zones that extend downward from a domain (Figure 24-3). A single DNS server is responsible for (holds the information required to resolve) all domains within a zone. The DNS server for a zone also holds pointers to DNS servers that are responsible for the zones immediately below the zone it is responsible for. Information about zones originates in zone files, one zone per file.

Root domain   The highest zone—the one containing the root domain—does not contain any hosts. Instead, this domain delegates to the DNS servers for the top-level domains (Figure 24-1, page 785).

Authority   Each zone has at least one authoritative DNS server. This server holds all information about the zone. A DNS query returns information about a domain and specifies which DNS server is authoritative for that domain.

DNS employs a hierarchical structure to keep track of names and authority. At the top or root of the structure is the root domain, which employs 13 authoritative nameservers. These are the only servers that are authoritative for the root and top-level domains.

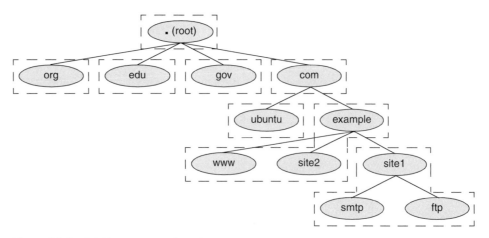

Figure 24-3   DNS structure showing zones

Delegation of authority   When referring to DNS, the term *delegation* means *delegation of authority*. ICANN (Internet Corporation for Assigned Names and Numbers, www.icann.org) delegates authority to the root and top-level domains. In other words, ICANN says which servers are authoritative for these domains. Authority is delegated to each domain below the top-level domains by the authoritative server at the next-higher-level domain. ICANN is not authoritative for most second-level domains. For example, Ubuntu is authoritative for the ubuntu.com domain. This scheme of delegating authority allows for local control over segments of the DNS database while making all segments available to the public.

QUERIES

There are two types of DNS queries: *iterative* and *recursive*.[1]

Iterative queries   An iterative query sends a domain name to a DNS server and asks the server to return either the IP address of the domain or the name of the DNS server that is authoritative for the domain or one of its parents: The server does not query other servers when seeking an answer. Nameservers typically send each other iterative queries.

Recursive queries   A recursive query sends a domain name to a DNS server and asks the server to return the IP address of the domain. The server may need to query other servers to get the answer.

Both iterative and recursive queries can fail. In this case, the server returns a message saying it is unable to locate the domain.

---

1. A third type of query is not covered in this book: *inverse*. An inverse query provides a domain name given a resource record. Reverse name resolution (page 793), not an inverse query, is used to query for a domain name given an IP address.

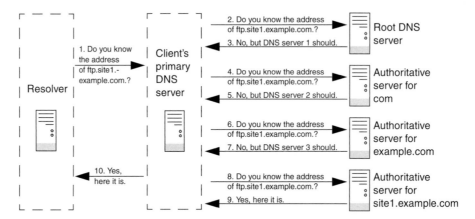

Figure 24-4   A recursive query that starts several iterative queries to find the answer

When a client, such as a browser, needs the IP address that corresponds to a domain name, the client queries a resolver. Most resolvers are quite simple and require a DNS server to do most of the work—that is, they send recursive queries. The resolver communicates with a single DNS server, which can perform multiple iterative queries in response to the resolver's recursive query.

All DNS servers must answer iterative queries. DNS servers can also be set up to answer recursive queries. A DNS server that is not set up to answer recursive queries treats a recursive query as though it is an iterative query.

In Figure 24-4, the resolver on a client system is trying to discover the IP address of the server ftp.site1.example.com. on the network with the DNS layout shown in Figure 24-3 on page 787. The resolver on the client sends a recursive query to its primary DNS server. This server interrogates the root server and one additional server for each zone until it receives an answer, which it returns to the resolver on the client. In practice, the query would not start with the root server because most servers have the location of the authoritative nameserver for the **com.** domain stored in cache (memory).

SERVERS

There are three main types of DNS servers: primary (master), secondary (slave), and caching-only.

- A *primary master server,* also called a *primary server* or *master server,* is the authoritative server that holds the master copy of zone data. It copies information from the *zone* or *master file,* a local file that the server administrator maintains. For security and efficiency, a primary master server should provide iterative answers only. A primary master server that provides recursive answers is more easily subverted by a *DoS attack* (page 1106) than one that provides iterative answers only.

- *Slave servers,* also called *secondary servers,* are authoritative and copy zone information from the primary master server or another slave server. On some systems, when information on the primary master server changes, the primary master server notifies the slave servers. When a slave receives such a message, it uses a process called *zone transfer* to copy the new zone information from the master server to itself.

- *DNS caches,* also called *caching-only servers,* are not authoritative. These servers store answers to previous queries in cache (memory). When a DNS cache receives a query, it answers it from cache if it can. If the DNS cache does not have the answer in cache, it forwards the query to an authoritative server.

It is possible—but for reasons of security not recommended—for the same server to be the primary master server (authoritative) for some zones and a DNS cache for others. When the same server acts as both a DNS cache and a master server, if a malicious local user or malfunctioning resolver on the local network floods the DNS cache with more traffic than it can handle (a DoS attack), users may be prevented from accessing the public servers handled by the primary master server. Conversely, if the authoritative server is compromised, the attacker can subvert all traffic leaving the network.

RESOURCE RECORDS

Resource records store information about nodes (domains) in the DNS database and are kept in zone files (page 800). The zone that a resource record pertains to is defined by the zone file that contains the resource record. The zone is named in the **named.conf** file (page 798) that references the zone file.

A resource record has the following fields:

- **Name**—The domain name or IP address
- **TTL**—Time to live (not in all resource records; see page 1138)
- **Class**—Always IN for Internet (the only class supported by DNS)
- **Type**—Record type (discussed in the next section)
- **Data**—Varies with record type

If the Name field is missing, the resource record inherits the name from the previous resource record in the same file. Cached resource records become out-of-date when the information in the record changes on the authoritative server. The TTL field indicates the maximum amount of time a server may keep a record in cache before checking whether a newer one is available. Typically the TTL is on the order of days. A TTL of 0 (zero) means that the resource record should not be cached.

More than 30 types of resource records exist, ranging from common types, such as address records that store the address of a host, to those that contain geographical information. The following paragraphs describe the types of resource records you are most likely to encounter.

A   IPv4 Address Maps a domain name to the IPv4 address of a host. There must be at least one address record for each domain; multiple address records can point to the same IP address. The Name field holds the domain name, which is assumed to be in the same zone as the domain. The Data field holds the IP address associated with the name. The following address resource record maps the **ns** domain in the zone to 192.168.0.1:

```
ns      IN      A       192.168.0.1
```

AAAA   IPv6 Address Maps a domain name to the IPv6 address of a host. The following address resource record maps the **ns** domain in the zone to an IPv6 address:

```
ns      IN      AAAA    2001:630:d0:131:a00:20ff:feb5:ef1e
```

CNAME   Canonical Name Maps an alias or nickname to a domain name. The Name field holds the alias or nickname; the Data field holds the official or canonical name. CNAME is useful for specifying an easy-to-remember name or multiple names for the same domain. It is also useful when a system changes names or IP addresses. In this case the alias can point to the real name that must resolve to an IP address.

When a query returns a CNAME, a client or DNS tool performs a DNS lookup on the domain name returned with the CNAME. It is acceptable to provide multiple levels of CNAME records. The following resource record maps **ftp** in the zone to www.sam.net.:

```
ftp     IN      CNAME   www.sam.net.
```

MX   Mail Exchange Specifies a destination for mail addressed to the domain. MX records must always point to A (or AAAA) records. The Name field holds the domain name, which is assumed to be in the zone; the Data field holds the name of a mail server preceded by its priority. Unlike A records, MX records contain a priority number that allows mail delivery agents to fall back to a backup server if the primary server is down. Several mail servers can be ranked in priority order, where the lowest number has the highest priority. DNS selects randomly from among mail servers with the same priority. The following resource records forward mail sent to **speedy** in the zone first to **mail** in the zone and then, if that attempt fails, to **mail.sam.net.**. The value of **speedy** in the Name field on the second line is implicit.

```
speedy IN      MX      10 mail
       IN      MX      20 mail.sam.net.
```

NS   Nameserver Specifies the name of the system that provides domain service (DNS records) for the domain. The Name field holds the domain name; the Data field holds the name of the DNS server. Each domain must have at least one NS record. DNS servers do not need to reside in the domain and, in fact, it is better if at least one does not. The system name **ns** is frequently used to specify a nameserver, but this name is not required and does not have any significance beyond assisting humans in identifying a nameserver. The following resource record specifies **ns.max.net.** as a nameserver for **peach** in the zone:

```
peach   IN      NS      ns.max.net.
```

PTR   Pointer Maps an IP address to a domain name and is used for reverse name resolution. The Name field holds the IP address; the Data field holds the domain name. Do not use PTR resource records with aliases. The following resource record maps

3 in a reverse zone (for example, 3 in the 0.168.192.in-addr.arpa zone is 192.168.0.3) to **peach** in the zone:

```
3       IN    PTR     peach
```

For more information refer to "Reverse Name Resolution" on page 793.

SOA **Start of Authority** Designates the start of a zone. Each zone must have exactly one SOA record. An authoritative server maintains the SOA record for the zone it is authoritative for.

All zone files must have one SOA resource record, which must be the first resource record in the file. The Name field holds the name of the domain at the start of the zone. The Data field holds the name of the host the data was created on, the email address of the person responsible for the zone, and the following information, which must be enclosed within parentheses if the record does not fit on one line. If this information is enclosed within parentheses (and it usually is), the opening parenthesis must appear on the first physical line of the SOA record:

serial A value in the range 1 to 2,147,483,647. A change in this number indicates the zone data has changed. By convention, this field is set to the string **yyyymmddnn** (year, month, day, change number). Along with the date, the final two digits—that is, the change number—should be incremented each time you change the SOA record.

refresh The elapsed time after which the primary master server notifies slave (secondary) servers to refresh the record; the amount of time between updates.

retry The time to wait after a refresh fails before trying to refresh again.

expiry The elapsed time after which the zone is no longer authoritative and the root servers must be queried. The expiry applies to slave servers only.

minimum The *negative caching* (page 1121) TTL, which is the amount of time that a nonexistent domain error (NXDOMAIN) can be held in a slave server's cache. A negative caching TTL is the same as a normal TTL except that it applies to domains that do not exist rather than to domains that do exist.

The $TTL directive (page 801) specifies the default zone TTL (the maximum amount of time data stays in a slave server's cache). Jointly, the default zone TTL and the negative caching TTL encompass all types of replies the server can generate. If you will be adding subdomains or modifying existing domains frequently, set the negative caching TTL to a low number. A short TTL increases traffic to DNS for clients requesting domains that do not exist, but allows new domains to propagate quickly, albeit at the expense of increased traffic.

The following two SOA resource records are equivalent (the parentheses in the first record are optional because the record fits on one physical line):

```
@ IN SOA ns.zach.net. mgs@sobell.com. ( 2007111247 8H 2H 4W 1D )

@       IN      SOA     ns.zach.net. mgs@sobell.com. (
                        2007111247      ; serial
                        8H              ; refresh
                        2H              ; retry
                        4W              ; expire
                        1D )            ; minimum
```

The second format is more readable because of its layout and the comments. The at symbol (@) at the start of the SOA resource record stands for the zone name (also called the origin) as specified in the **named.conf** file. Because the **named.conf** file specifies the zone name to be **zach.net**, you could rewrite the first line as follows:

```
zach.net.   IN  SOA    ns.zach.net. mgs@sobell.com. (
```

The host utility returns something closer to the first format with each of the times specified in seconds:

```
$ host -t soa zach.net
zach.net. SOA ns.zach.net. mgs\@sobell.com. 03111 28800 7200 2419200 86400
```

TXT   **Text** Associates a character string with a domain. The Name field holds the domain name. The data field can contain up to 256 characters and must be enclosed within quotation marks. TXT records can contain any arbitrary text value. As well as general information, they can be used for things such as public key distribution. Following is a TXT resource record that specifies a company name:

```
zach.net   IN  TXT     "Sobell Associates Inc."
```

DNS QUERIES AND RESPONSES

Queries   A DNS query has three parts:

1. Name—Domain name, FQDN, or IP address for reverse name resolution

2. Type—Type of record requested (page 789)

3. Class—Always IN for Internet class

Cache   Most DNS servers store in cache memory the query responses from other DNS servers. When a DNS server receives a query, it first tries to resolve the query from its cache. If that attempt fails, the server may query other servers to get an answer. Because DNS uses cache, when you make a change to a DNS record, the change takes time—sometimes a matter of days—to propagate throughout the DNS hierarchy.

Responses   A DNS message sent in response to a query has the following structure:

- Header record—Information about this message

- Query record—Repeats the query

- Answer records—Resource records that answer the query

- Authority records—Resource records for servers that have authority for the answers

- Additional records—Additional resource records, such as NS records

The dig utility does not consult **/etc/nsswitch.conf** (page 458) to determine which server to query. The following example uses dig to query a DNS server:

```
$ dig ubuntu.com

; <<>> DiG 9.3.2 <<>> ubuntu.com
;; global options:  printcmd
;; Got answer:
;; ->>HEADER<<- opcode: QUERY, status: NOERROR, id: 61389
;; flags: qr rd ra; QUERY: 1, ANSWER: 1, AUTHORITY: 3, ADDITIONAL: 4

;; QUESTION SECTION:
;ubuntu.com.                    IN      A

;; ANSWER SECTION:
ubuntu.com.            600      IN      A       82.211.81.166

;; AUTHORITY SECTION:
ubuntu.com.            2823     IN      NS      ns.ubuntu.com.
ubuntu.com.            2823     IN      NS      ns0.blackcatnetworks.co.uk.
ubuntu.com.            2823     IN      NS      ns1.blackcatnetworks.co.uk.

;; ADDITIONAL SECTION:
ns.ubuntu.com.            77912   IN   A      82.211.81.173
ns0.blackcatnetworks.co.uk. 39247 IN   A      193.201.200.34
ns0.blackcatnetworks.co.uk. 39247 IN   AAAA   2001:1b40:0:20::34
ns1.blackcatnetworks.co.uk. 39247 IN   A      69.55.225.40
...
```

REVERSE NAME RESOLUTION

In addition to normal or forward name resolution, DNS provides *reverse name resolution* (also referred to as *inverse mapping* or *reverse mapping*) so you can look up domain names given an IP address. Because resource records in the forward DNS database are indexed hierarchically by domain name, DNS cannot perform an efficient search by IP address on this database.

DNS implements reverse name resolution by means of special domains named **in-addr.arpa** (IPv4) and **ip6.int** (IPv6). Resource records in these domains have Name fields that hold IP addresses; the records are indexed hierarchically by IP address. The Data fields hold the FQDNs that correspond to these IP addresses.

Reverse name resolution can verify that someone is who he says he is or at least is from the domain he says he is from. In general, it allows a server to retrieve and record the domain names of the clients it provides services to. For example, legitimate mail contains the domain of the sender and the IP address of the sending machine. A mail server can verify the stated domain of a sender by checking the domain associated with the IP address. Reverse name resolution can also be used by anonymous FTP servers to verify that a domain specified in an email address used as a password is legitimate.

For example, to determine the domain name that corresponds to the IP address 82.211.81.150 in Figure 24-5, a resolver would query DNS for information about the domain named 150.81.211.82.in-addr.arpa.

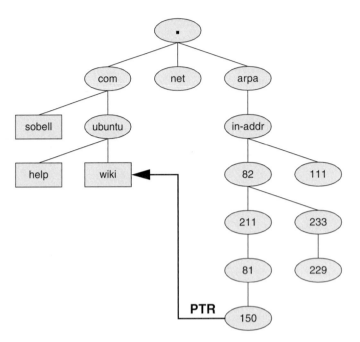

Figure 24-5   Reverse name resolution and the **in-addr.arpa** domain

The following example uses dig to query DNS for the IP address that corresponds to www.sobell.com, which is 209.157.128.22. The second command line uses the dig utility to query the same IP address, reversed and appended with **.in-addr.arpa** (22.128.157.209.in-addr.arpa) to display a PTR resource record (page 790). The data portion of the resultant resource record is the domain name from the original query: www.sobell.com.

```
$ dig www.sobell.com
...
;; QUESTION SECTION:
;www.sobell.com.                      IN      A

;; ANSWER SECTION:
www.sobell.com.         2274    IN      A       209.157.128.22
...
$ dig 22.128.157.209.in-addr.arpa PTR
...
;; QUESTION SECTION:
;22.128.157.209.in-addr.arpa.    IN      PTR

;; ANSWER SECTION:
22.128.157.209.in-addr.arpa. 2244 IN    PTR     www.sobell.com.
...
```

Instead of reformatting the IP address as in the preceding example, you can use the **–x** option to dig to perform a reverse query:

```
$ dig -x 209.157.128.22
...
```

```
;; QUESTION SECTION:
;22.128.157.209.in-addr.arpa.    IN        PTR

;; ANSWER SECTION:
22.128.157.209.in-addr.arpa. 2204 IN      PTR       www.sobell.com.
...
```

Alternatively, you can just use host:

```
$ host 209.157.128.22
22.128.157.209.in-addr.arpa domain name pointer www.sobell.com.
```

How DNS Works

Application programs do not issue DNS queries directly but rather use the **gethostbyname**() system call. How the system comes up with the corresponding IP address is transparent to the calling program. The **gethostbyname**() call examines the **hosts** line in **/etc/nsswitch.conf** (page 458) to determine which files it should examine and/or which services it should query and in what order to obtain the IP address corresponding to a domain name. When it needs to query DNS, the local system (i.e., the DNS client) queries the DNS database by calling the resolver library on the local system. This call returns the required information to the application program.

More Information

DNS for Rocket Scientists is an excellent site that makes good use of links to present information on DNS in a very digestible form. The same information is available in the *Pro DNS and BIND* book.

Local   *Bind Administrator Reference Manual:*
/usr/share/doc/bind9-doc/arm/Bv9ARM.html.

Web   DNS for Rocket Scientists: www.zytrax.com/books/dns
BIND: www.isc.org/products/BIND
DNS security: www.sans.org/reading_room/whitepapers/dns/1069.php
(downloadable PDF file)

HOWTO   *DNS HOWTO*

Book   *DNS & BIND*, fifth edition, by Albitz & Liu, O'Reilly & Associates (May 2006)
Pro DNS and BIND, first edition, by Ron Aitchison, Apress (August 2005)

Notes

Terms: The name of the DNS server is **named**. This chapter uses "DNS" and "**named**"
DNS and **named**   interchangeably.

Firewall   The **named** server normally accepts queries on TCP and UDP port 53. If the server system is running a firewall, you need to open these ports. Using firestarter (page 824), open this port by setting a policy that allows service for DNS.

chroot jail   The bind-chroot.sh script sets up **named** to run in a chroot jail. After you run this script, all files that control BIND are located within this jail. In this case the filenames used in this chapter are symbolic links to the files in the chroot jail. See page 808 for more information.

named options   When the **bind9** init script starts or restarts the **named** server, but not when it just reloads the configuration files, it reads the options in the **/etc/default/bind9** file. If the **RESOLVCONF** variable is set to **yes** (as it is by default), the script runs resolv-conf, which rebuilds **/etc/resolv.conf**. You can cause the script not to run resolvconf by setting **RESOLVCONF** to **no**.

```
$ cat /etc/default/bind9
# run resolvconf?
RESOLVCONF=yes

# startup options for the server
OPTIONS="-u bind"
```

SETTING UP A DNS SERVER

This section starts with an explanation of how to set up the simplist type of DNS server, a DNS cache.

PREREQUISITES

Installation   Install the following packages:

- **bind9** (automatically installs **bind9utils**)
- **bind9-doc** (optional; installs **bind** documentation)
- **dnsutils** (installed by default; installs dig, nslookup, and nsupdate)

bind9 init script   When you install the **bind9** package, the **dpkg postinst** script starts the **named** daemon. After you configure BIND, call the **bind9** init script to restart the **named** daemon:

```
$ sudo /etc/init.d/bind9 restart
```

After changing the BIND configuration on an active server, use **reload** in place of **restart** to reload **named** configuration files without disturbing clients connected to the server. By default, starting or restarting—but not reloading—**named** runs resolv-conf, which rebuilds the **/etc/resolv.conf** file. See "**named** options" on page 796 for more information.

JUMPSTART: SETTING UP A DNS CACHE

As explained earlier, a DNS cache is a bridge between a resolver and authoritative DNS servers: It is not authoritative, but simply stores the results of its queries in memory. Most ISPs provide a DNS cache for the use of their customers. Setting up a local cache can reduce the traffic between the LAN and the outside world, thereby improving response times. While it is possible to set up a DNS cache on each system on a LAN, setting up a single DNS cache on a LAN prevents multiple systems on the LAN from having to query a remote server for the same information.

After installing BIND, you have most of a caching-only nameserver ready to run. Refer to "Setting Up a DNS Cache" (page 801) for an explanation of which files this nameserver uses and how it works.

resolvconf and
resolv.conf

Before you start the DNS cache, you need to modify the **/etc/resolv.conf** file (page 478). How you go about modifying this file depends on whether the **resolv-conf** package is installed and set up to run on the local system. When you give the command **resolvconf**, a usage message tells you the package is installed, whereas a **command not found** message tells you it is not installed.

If resolvconf *is not* installed or you have turned it off as explained in "**named** options," put the following line in **/etc/resolv.conf**, before other nameserver lines:

```
nameserver 127.0.0.1
```

If resolvconf *is* installed and is set up to rebuild **resolv.conf** when you run the **bind9** init script (page 796), put the preceding line in **/etc/resolvconf/resolv.conf.d/head**, following the comments and before any other nameserver lines. You can ignore the comment telling you not to edit the file: This comment is intended for someone who is trying to edit **/etc/resolv.conf**. You must put this line in the **head** file so resolvconf puts it in **resolv.conf** before any other nameserver lines; otherwise the local DNS cache will never be used. Put other nameserver lines in **base** in the same directory as needed.

The nameserver line tells the resolver to use the local system (**localhost** or 127.0.0.1) as the primary nameserver. To experiment with using the local system as the only nameserver, comment out other nameserver lines in **resolv.conf** or **base** by preceding each with a pound sign (#).

Finally, run the **bind9** init script to restart the **named** daemon (page 796). When you do so, if resolvconf is installed and set up to run, the **bind9** init script will rebuild **resolv.conf**. See the resolver and **resolv.conf** man pages for more information on **resolv.conf**.

Refer to "Troubleshooting" on page 810 for ways to confirm that the DNS cache is working. Once you have restarted **named**, you can see the effect of the cache by using dig to look up the IP address of www.ubuntu.com, a remote system:

```
$ dig www.ubuntu.com

; <<>> DiG 9.3.4 <<>> www.ubuntu.com
;; global options:  printcmd
;; Got answer:
;; ->>HEADER<<- opcode: QUERY, status: NOERROR, id: 59184
;; flags: qr rd ra; QUERY: 1, ANSWER: 1, AUTHORITY: 3, ADDITIONAL: 3

;; QUESTION SECTION:
;www.ubuntu.com.                      IN      A

;; ANSWER SECTION:
www.ubuntu.com.          60     IN      A       82.211.81.199
...
;; Query time: 496 msec
;; SERVER: 127.0.0.1#53(127.0.0.1)
;; WHEN: Wed Apr 25 16:08:17 2007
;; MSG SIZE  rcvd: 183
```

The fourth line from the bottom of the example on the preceding page shows that this query took 496 milliseconds (about one-half of a second). When you run the same query again, it runs more quickly because the DNS cache has saved the information locally in memory:

```
$ dig www.ubuntu.com
...
;; Query time: 1 msec
;; SERVER: 127.0.0.1#53(127.0.0.1)
;; WHEN: Wed Apr 25 16:08:23 2007
;; MSG SIZE  rcvd: 183
```

CONFIGURING A DNS SERVER

This section discusses the **/etc/named.conf** file, zone files, implementation of a DNS cache, and running DNS inside a chroot jail.

named.conf: THE named CONFIGURATION FILE

Configuration information for **named**, including zone names and the names and locations of zone files, is kept in **/etc/bind/named.conf**. By default, the zone files reside in **/etc/bind**. If you are running **named** in a chroot jail, these files are kept in **/var/lib/named/etc/bind**, with a link in **/etc/bind** (page 808).

Try not to modify named.conf

tip   The Ubuntu **bind9** package breaks the **named.conf** file distributed with BIND into three files: **named.conf**, **named.conf.options**, and **named.conf.local**. There are two motivations for breaking this file apart. First, it makes the configuration files easier to understand. Second, it enables you to configure **named** without modifying **named.conf**. This setup allows the **bind9** package to be upgraded, including changes to **named.conf**, without requiring you to modify the local configuration.

When you configure **named**, try to put your changes in the **named.conf.options** and **named.conf.local** files. For more complex setups it may be easier to modify **named.conf** and carry those changes forward when **bind9** is upgraded.

IP-list

In the descriptions in this section, *IP-list* is a semicolon-separated list of IP addresses, where each IP address is optionally followed by a slash and a subnet mask length (page 445). Prefix an *IP-list* with an exclamation point (!) to negate it. Builtin names you can use in *IP-list* include **any**, **none**, and **localhost**. You must enclose these builtin names within double quotation marks.

COMMENTS

Within **named.conf**, specify a comment by preceding it with a pound sign (#) as in a Perl or shell program, preceding it with a double slash (//) as in a C++ program, or enclosing it between /* and */ as in a C program. Within a DNS **db.*** file, a comment starts with a semicolon (;).

INCLUDED FILES

An **include** statement within the **named.conf** file includes the file named as its argument as though its contents appeared inline in the **named.conf** file. The default Ubuntu **named.conf** file includes both the **/etc/bind/named.conf.options** and **/etc/bind/named.conf.local** files. The **named.conf.options** file holds the Options clause of **named.conf**. The **named.conf.local** file gives you a place to put local configuration information.

OPTIONS CLAUSE

Options statements can appear in two places: in the Options clause found in **named.conf.options** and in the Zone clauses found in **named.conf**. Option statements within the Options clause apply globally. When an option statement appears in a Zone clause, the option applies to the zone, and within that zone, overrides a corresponding global option.

An Options clause starts with the keyword **options** and continues with braces surrounding the statements. Following is a list of some option statements. Statements that can appear only in an Options clause and statements that cannot appear in a View clause (page 816) are so noted.

allow-query {*IP-list*}

Allows queries from *IP-list* only. Without this option, the server responds to all queries.

allow-recursion {*IP-list*}

Specifies systems for which this server will perform recursive queries (page 787). For systems not in *IP-list*, the server performs iterative queries only. Without this option, the server performs recursive queries for any system. This statement may be overridden by the **recursion** statement.

allow-transfer {*IP-list*}

Specifies systems that are allowed to perform zone transfers from this server. Specify an *IP-list* of **"none"** (include the quotation marks) to prevent zone transfers. For a more secure network, include only trusted systems in *IP-list* because systems on the list can obtain a list of all systems on the network.

directory *path*   Specifies the absolute pathname of the directory containing the zone files. Under Ubuntu Linux, this directory is initially **/var/cache/bind**. Relative pathnames specified in **named.conf** are relative to this directory. Options clause only; not in View clause.

forward ONLY|FIRST

ONLY forwards all queries and fails if it does not receive an answer. **FIRST** forwards all queries and, if a query does not receive an answer, attempts to find an answer using additional queries. Valid with the **forwarders** statement only.

forwarders {*IP* [*port*] [; ...]}

> Specifies IP addresses and optionally port numbers that queries are forwarded to. See the **forward** statement.

notify YES|NO   YES sends a message to slave servers for the zone when zone information changes. Master servers only. See page 815.

recursion YES|NO

> **YES** (default) provides recursive queries (page 787) if the client requests. **NO** provides iterative queries only (page 787). An answer is always returned if it appears in the server's cache. This statement overrides **allow-recursion** statements. Options clause only.

ZONE CLAUSE

A Zone clause defines a zone and can include any of the statements listed for the Options clause except as noted. A Zone clause is introduced by the keyword **zone**, the name of the zone enclosed within double quotation marks, and the class (always IN). The body of the Zone clause consists of a pair of braces surrounding one or more zone statements. See the listing of **named.conf** on page 801 for examples of Zone clauses. Following is a list of some zone statements:

allow-update {*IP-list*}

> Specifies systems that are allowed to update this zone dynamically. This statement may be useful when hosting a master DNS server for a domain owned by someone other than the local administrator because it allows a remote user to update the DNS entry without granting the user access to the server.

file *filename*   Specifies the *zone file*—the file that specifies the characteristics of the zone. The *filename* is relative to the directory specified by the **directory** statement in the Options clause. The **file** statement is mandatory for master and hint zones. Including it for slave zones is a good idea (see **type**).

masters (*IP-list*)   Specifies systems that a slave zone can use to update zone files. Slave zones only.

type *ztype*   Specifies the type of zone defined by this clause. Choose *ztype* from the following list:

- **forward**—Specifies a forward zone, which forwards queries directed to this zone. See the **forward** and/or **forwarders** statements in the Options clause.

- **hint**—Specifies a hint zone. A hint zone lists root servers that the local server queries when it starts and when it cannot find an answer in its cache.

- **master**—Specifies the local system as a primary master server (page 788) for this zone.

- **slave**—Specifies the local system as a slave server (page 788) for this zone.

ZONE FILES

Zone files define zone characteristics. The name of the zone is typically specified in **named.conf**. In contrast to **named.conf**, zone files use periods at the ends of domain names. See page 803 for example zone files.

TIME FORMATS

All times in BIND files are given in seconds, unless they are followed by one of these letters (uppercase or lowercase): S (seconds), M (minutes), H (hours), D (days), or W (weeks). You can combine formats. For example, the time 2h25m30s means 2 hours, 25 minutes, and 30 seconds and is the same as 8,730 seconds.

DOMAIN QUALIFICATION

An unqualified domain in a zone file is assumed to be in the current zone (the zone defined by the zone file and named by the **named.conf** file that refers to the zone file). The name **zach** in the zone file for **myzone.com**, for example, would be expanded to the FQDN **zach.myzone.com.**. Use an FQDN (include the trailing period) to specify a domain that is not in the current zone. Any name that does not end with a period is regarded as a subdomain of the current zone.

ZONE NAME

Within a zone file, an at sign (@) is replaced with the zone name as specified by the **named.conf** file that refers to the zone file. The zone name is also referred to as the *origin*. See "$ORIGIN" in the next section.

ZONE FILE DIRECTIVES

The following directives can appear within a zone file. Each directive is identified by a leading dollar sign. The $TTL directive is mandatory and must be the first entry in a zone file.

$TTL   Defines the default time to live for all resource records in the zone. This directive must appear in a zone file before any resource records that it applies to. Any resource record can include a TTL value that overrides this value, except for the resource record in the root zone (.).

$ORIGIN   Changes the zone name from that specified in the **named.conf** file. This name, or the zone name if this directive does not appear in the zone file, replaces an @ sign in the Name field of a resource record.

$INCLUDE   Includes a file as though it were part of the zone file. The scope of an $ORIGIN directive within an included file is the included file. That is, an $ORIGIN directive within an included file does not affect the file that holds the $INCLUDE directive.

SETTING UP A DNS CACHE

You install a DNS cache (also called a resolving, caching nameserver) when you install the **bind9** package. The section "JumpStart: Setting Up a DNS Cache" (page 796) explains how to run this server. This section describes how the files provided by Ubuntu Linux implement this server.

named.conf: THE named CONFIGURATION FILE

The default **/etc/bind/named.conf** file is shown on the next page.

```
$ cat /etc/bind/named.conf
// This is the primary configuration file for the BIND DNS server named.
//
// Please read /usr/share/doc/bind9/README.Debian.gz for information on the
// structure of BIND configuration files in Debian, *BEFORE* you customize
// this configuration file.
//
// If you are just adding zones, please do that in /etc/bind/named.conf.local

include "/etc/bind/named.conf.options";

// prime the server with knowledge of the root servers
zone "." {
        type hint;
        file "/etc/bind/db.root";
};

// be authoritative for the localhost forward and reverse zones, and for
// broadcast zones as per RFC 1912

zone "localhost" {
        type master;
        file "/etc/bind/db.local";
};

zone "127.in-addr.arpa" {
        type master;
        file "/etc/bind/db.127";
};

zone "0.in-addr.arpa" {
        type master;
        file "/etc/bind/db.0";
};

zone "255.in-addr.arpa" {
        type master;
        file "/etc/bind/db.255";
};

include "/etc/bind/named.conf.local";
```

Options clause   The Options clause is in **named.conf.options; named.conf** incorporates it with an include statement.

Zone clauses   The **named.conf** file holds five Zone clauses, each of which uses an absolute filename to locate its zone file. Any relative filenames appearing in this file would be relative to **/var/cache/bind,** which the directory statement in **named.conf.options** points to.

   • **.**—(The name of the zone is a period.) The hint zone. Specifies that when the server starts or does not know which server to query, it should look in the **/etc/bind/db.root** file to find the addresses of authoritative servers for the root domain.

• **localhost**—Sets up the normal server on the local system.

• **127.in-addr.arpa**—Sets up IPv4 reverse name resolution.

• **0.in-addr.arpa**—Specifies that the local server handle reverse lookup for IP addresses starting with 0, thereby preventing the local server from looking upstream for this information.

• **255.in-addr.arpa**—Specifies that the local server handle reverse lookup for IP addresses starting with 255, preventing the local server from looking upstream for this information.

named.conf.options: OPTIONS FILE

The **named.conf.options** file, which **named.conf** incorporates with an include statement, holds mostly comments with the following uncommented statements:

```
directory "/var/cache/bind";

auth-nxdomain no;    # conform to RFC1035

listen-on-v6 { any; };
```

The **directory** statement specifies the directory that all relative pathnames in this file, **named.conf**, and all other files incorporated in **named.conf** are relative to. If you are running **named** in a chroot jail, this directory is located under **/var/lib/named** (page 808). The **auth-nxdomain no** statement does not allow the server to answer authoritatively on NXDOMAIN (nonexistent domain error; see *negative caching* [page 1121]) answers. The **listen-on-v6 { any }** statement enables the server to listen for IPv6 queries on any address.

ZONE FILES

There are five zone files in **/etc/bind**, each of which corresponds to one of the Zone clauses in **named.conf**. This section describes three of these zone files.

The root zone: **db.root** The hint zone file, **db.root**, is similar to the output of a **dig @a.root-servers.net.** command, which does not change frequently (check the date on the **last update** line near the beginning of the file). It specifies authoritative servers for the root domain. The DNS server initializes its cache from this file and can determine an authoritative server for any domain from this information.

The root zone is required only for servers that answer recursive queries: If a server responds to recursive queries, it needs to perform a series of iterative queries starting at the root domain. Without the root domain hint file, it would not know where to find the root domain servers.

```
$ cat /etc/bind/db.root
;         This file holds the information on root name servers needed to
;         initialize cache of Internet domain name servers
;         (e.g. reference this file in the "cache  .  <file>"
;         configuration file of BIND domain name servers).
;
;         This file is made available by InterNIC
;         under anonymous FTP as
;              file              /domain/named.root
;              on server         FTP.INTERNIC.NET
;         -OR-                   RS.INTERNIC.NET
;
;         last update:    Feb 04, 2008
;         related version of root zone:    2008020400
;
; formerly NS.INTERNIC.NET
;
.                          3600000   IN  NS    A.ROOT-SERVERS.NET.
A.ROOT-SERVERS.NET.        3600000       A     198.41.0.4
A.ROOT-SERVERS.NET.        3600000       AAAA  2001:503:BA3E::2:30
;
; formerly NS1.ISI.EDU
;
.                          3600000       NS    B.ROOT-SERVERS.NET.
B.ROOT-SERVERS.NET.        3600000       A     192.228.79.201
;
; formerly C.PSI.NET
;
.                          3600000       NS    C.ROOT-SERVERS.NET.
C.ROOT-SERVERS.NET.        3600000       A     192.33.4.12
;
; formerly TERP.UMD.EDU
;
.                          3600000       NS    D.ROOT-SERVERS.NET.
D.ROOT-SERVERS.NET.        3600000       A     128.8.10.90
;
; formerly NS.NASA.GOV
;
.                          3600000       NS    E.ROOT-SERVERS.NET.
...
L.ROOT-SERVERS.NET.        3600000       A     199.7.83.42
;
; operated by WIDE
;
.                          3600000       NS    M.ROOT-SERVERS.NET.
M.ROOT-SERVERS.NET.        3600000       A     202.12.27.33
M.ROOT-SERVERS.NET.        3600000       AAAA  2001:dc3::35
; End of File
```

db.local   The **db.local** zone file defines the **localhost** zone, the normal server on the local system. It starts with a $TTL directive and holds three resource records: SOA, NS, and A. The $TTL directive in the following file specifies that the default time to live for the resource records specified in this file is 604,800 seconds (one week):

```
$ cat /etc/bind/db.local
;
; BIND data file for local loopback interface
;
$TTL    604800
@       IN      SOA     localhost. root.localhost. (
                                2          ; Serial
                                604800     ; Refresh
                                86400      ; Retry
                                2419200    ; Expire
                                604800 )   ; Negative Cache TTL
;
@       IN      NS      localhost.
@       IN      A       127.0.0.1
@       IN      AAAA    ::1
```

As explained earlier, the @ stands for the origin (the name of the zone), which is **localhost**, as specified in **named.conf**. The last three lines are the NS resource record that specifies the nameserver for the zone as **localhost**, the A resource record that specifies the IPv4 address of the host as 127.0.0.1, and the AAAA resource record that specifies the IPv6 address of the host as ::1.

db.127   The **db.127** zone file provides information about the 127.in-addr.arpa reverse lookup zone. It follows the same pattern as the **localhost** zone file, with one exception: Instead of the A resource record, this file has a PTR record that provides the name the zone associates with the IP address. The PTR resource record specifies the name 1.0.0, which equates the system at address 1.0.0 in the zone (127.in-addr.arpa) with the name **localhost**, which has an IP address of 127.0.0.1:

```
$ cat /etc/bind/db.127
;
; BIND reverse data file for local loopback interface
;
$TTL    604800
@       IN      SOA     localhost. root.localhost. (
                                1          ; Serial
                                604800     ; Refresh
                                86400      ; Retry
                                2419200    ; Expire
                                604800 )   ; Negative Cache TTL
;
@       IN      NS      localhost.
1.0.0   IN      PTR     localhost.
```

The other zone files perform similar functions as described under "Zone clauses" on page 802. Once **named** is started (page 796), you can use the tests described under "Troubleshooting" on page 810 to make sure the server is working.

DNS GLUE RECORDS

It is common practice to put the nameserver for a zone inside the zone it serves. For example, you might put the nameserver for the zone starting at site1.example.com

(Figure 24-3, page 787) in ns.site1.example.com. When a DNS cache tries to resolve www.site1.example.com, the authoritative server for example.com gives it the NS record pointing to ns.site1.example.com. In an attempt to resolve ns.site1.example.com, the DNS cache again queries the authoritative server for example.com, which points back to ns.site1.example.com. This loop does not allow ns.site1.example.com to be resolved.

The simplest solution to this problem is to prohibit any nameserver from residing inside the zone it points to. Because every zone is a child of the root zone, this solution means every domain would be served by the root server and would not scale at all.

A better solution is to use *glue* records. A glue record is an A record for a nameserver that is returned in addition to the NS record when an NS query is performed. Because the A record provides an IP address for the nameserver, it does not need to be resolved and does not create the problematic loop.

The nameserver setup for ubuntu.com illustrates the use of glue records. When you query for NS records for ubuntu.com, DNS returns three NS records. In addition, it returns three A records that provide the IP addresses for two of the hosts that the NS records point to (the AAAA record provides an IPv6 address):

```
$ dig -t NS ubuntu.com
...
;; QUESTION SECTION:
;ubuntu.com.                        IN      NS

;; ANSWER SECTION:
ubuntu.com.             10800   IN      NS      ns.ubuntu.com.
ubuntu.com.             10800   IN      NS      ns0.blackcatnetworks.co.uk.
ubuntu.com.             10800   IN      NS      ns1.blackcatnetworks.co.uk.

;; ADDITIONAL SECTION:
ns0.blackcatnetworks.co.uk. 160011 IN    A       193.201.200.34
ns0.blackcatnetworks.co.uk. 160011 IN    AAAA    2001:1b40:0:20::34
ns1.blackcatnetworks.co.uk. 160011 IN    A       69.55.225.40
```

You can create a glue record by providing an A record for the nameserver inside the delegating domain's zone file:

```
    site1.example.com              IN      NS      ns.site1.example.com
    ns.site1.example.com           IN      A       1.2.3.4
```

TSIGs: Transaction Signatures

Interaction between DNS components is based on the query–response model: One part queries another and receives a reply. Traditionally a server determines whether and how to reply to a query based on the client's IP address. *IP spoofing* (page 1115) is relatively easy to carry out, making this situation less than ideal.

Recent versions of BIND support transaction signatures (TSIGs), which allow two systems to establish a trust relationship by using a shared secret key.

TSIGs provide an additional layer of authentication between master and slave servers for a zone. When a slave server is located at a different site than the master server (as it should be), a malicious person operating a router between the sites can spoof the IP address of the master server and change the DNS data on the slave (a man-in-the-middle scenario). With TSIGs, this person would need to know the secret key to change the DNS data on the slave.

CREATING A SECRET KEY

A secret key is an encoded string of up to 512 bits. The dnssec-keygen utility, which is included with BIND, generates this key. The following command generates a 512-bit random key using MD5, a *one-way hash function* (page 1123):

```
$ /usr/sbin/dnssec-keygen -a hmac-md5 -b 512 -n HOST keyname
Kkeyname.+157+47586
```

In the preceding command, replace **keyname** with a string that is unique yet meaningful. This command creates a key in a file whose name is similar to the string **K*keyname*.+157+47586.private**, where **keyname** is replaced by the name of the key, **+157** indicates the algorithm used, and **+47586** is a hash of the key. If you run the same command again, the hash part will be different.

The key file is not used directly. Use cat with an argument of the private filename to display the algorithm and key information you will need in the next step:

```
$ cat Kkeyname.+157+47586.private
Private-key-format: v1.2
Algorithm: 157 (HMAC_MD5)
Key: uNPDouqVwR7fvo/zFyjkqKbQhcTd6Prm...
```

USING THE SHARED SECRET

The next step is to tell the nameservers about the shared secret by inserting the following code in the **/etc/named.conf** file on both servers. This code is a top-level clause; insert it at the end of the **named.conf.local** file (which is included in **named.conf**):

```
key keyname {
    algorithm "hmac-md5";
    secret "uNPDouqVwR7fvo/zFyjkqKbQhcTd6Prm...";
};
```

The **keyname** is the name of the key you created. The **algorithm** is the string that follows **algorithm** in the output of cat, above. The **secret** is the string that follows **secret** in the output of cat. You must enclose each string within double quotation marks. Be careful when you copy the key; although it is long, you must not break it into multiple lines.

Because key names are unique, you can insert any number of Keys clauses into **named.conf**. To keep the key a secret, make sure users other than **bind** cannot read it: Either give **named.conf.local** permissions such that no one except **bind** has access to it or put the key in a file that only **bind** can read and incorporate it in **named.conf.local** using an **include** statement.

Once both servers know about the key, use a **server** statement in **named.conf.local** to tell them when to use it:

```
server 1.2.3.4 {
# 1.2.3.4 is the IP address of the other server using this key
    keys {
        "keyname";
    };
};
```

Each server must have a Server clause, each containing the IP address of the other server. The servers will now communicate with each other only if they first authenticate each other using the secret key.

RUNNING BIND IN A chroot JAIL

To increase security, you can run BIND in a chroot jail. See page 450 for information about the security advantages of, and ways to set up, a chroot jail. The bind-chroot.sh shell script (below), which sets up BIND to run in a chroot jail, creates a directory named **/var/lib/named** that takes the place of the root directory (/) for all BIND files. The bind-chroot.sh shell installs the **bind9** package if it is not already installed and then runs the **bind9** init script to stop **named**. It then adds the **–t** option to the **named** options in **/etc/default/bind9** so **named** chroots to the **/var/lib/named** directory before it reads its configuration files. The **named** daemon is already set up to run as the user **bind** (**–u bind**).

After creating the necessary directories in **/var/lib/named**, the script moves the files from **/etc/bind** to **/var/lib/named**, creates a symbolic link from **/var/lib/named** back to **/etc/bind**, and creates and sets permissions on devices BIND may need. Next, bind-chroot.sh adds a line to the **syslogd** configuration file so messages from **named** that are not sent elsewhere go to the socket that **named** uses to send messages to **syslogd**. Finally, the script restarts **syslogd**, starts **named**, and displays the end of the **syslog** file.

```
$ cat bind-chroot.sh
#!/bin/bash

# install and stop bind
apt-get -y install bind9
/etc/init.d/bind9 stop

# add -t /var/lib/named to OPTIONS in /etc/default/bind9
sed -i 's:OPTIONS="\(.*\)":OPTIONS="\1\ -t /var/lib/named":' /etc/default/bind9
```

```
# make the chroot directories
mkdir -p /var/lib/named/{etc,dev,var/cache/bind,var/run/bind/run}

# move the configuration to the chroot and link back to /etc
mv /etc/bind /var/lib/named/etc
ln -s /var/lib/named/etc/bind /etc/bind

# create devices and set permissions
mknod /var/lib/named/dev/null c 1 3
mknod /var/lib/named/dev/random c 1 8
chmod 666 /var/lib/named/dev/{null,random}
chown -R bind:bind /var/lib/named/var/*
chown -R bind:bind /var/lib/named/etc/bind

# add -a /var/lib/named/dev/log to SYSLOGD in /etc/default/syslogd
# so messages go to the socket that named uses to send messages to syslogd
sed -i 's:^SYSLOGD="\(.*\)":SYSLOGD="\1\ -a /var/lib/named/dev/log":' /etc/default/syslogd

# restart syslogd and start bind
/etc/init.d/sysklogd restart
/etc/init.d/bind9 start

# check that everything started fine
tail /var/log/syslog
```

Following is the output of the execution of bind-chroot.sh. You must run this script while working with **root** privileges. You must also have execute permission to run the script. In the example, the **bind-chroot.sh** file is in the working directory.

```
$ sudo ./bind-chroot.sh
Reading package lists... Done
Building dependency tree
Reading state information... Done
bind9 is already the newest version.
0 upgraded, 0 newly installed, 0 to remove and 0 not upgraded.
 * Stopping domain name service... bind                              [ OK ]
 * Restarting system log daemon...                                   [ OK ]
 * Starting domain name service... bind                             [ OK ]
Apr 26 11:00:02 plum named[9301]: listening on IPv6 interfaces, port 53
Apr 26 11:00:02 plum named[9301]: listening on IPv4 interface lo, 127.0.0.1#53
Apr 26 11:00:02 plum named[9301]: listening on IPv4 interface eth0, 192.168.0.10#53
Apr 26 11:00:02 plum named[9301]: command channel listening on 127.0.0.1#953
Apr 26 11:00:02 plum named[9301]: command channel listening on ::1#953
Apr 26 11:00:02 plum named[9301]: zone 0.in-addr.arpa/IN: loaded serial 1
Apr 26 11:00:02 plum named[9301]: zone 127.in-addr.arpa/IN: loaded serial 1
Apr 26 11:00:02 plum named[9301]: zone 255.in-addr.arpa/IN: loaded serial 1
Apr 26 11:00:02 plum named[9301]: zone localhost/IN: loaded serial 1
Apr 26 11:00:02 plum named[9301]: running
```

After you run this script, all files that control BIND are located within this chroot jail and the filenames used in this chapter are symbolic links to the files in the chroot jail. See the command and output on the next page.

```
$ ls -l /etc/bind /var/lib/named/etc/bind
lrwxrwxrwx 1 root root    23 Apr 26 11:00 /etc/bind -> /var/lib/named/etc/bind

/var/lib/named/etc/bind:
total 44
-rw-r--r-- 1 bind bind  237 Feb 20 05:40 db.0
-rw-r--r-- 1 bind bind  271 Feb 20 05:40 db.127
-rw-r--r-- 1 bind bind  237 Feb 20 05:40 db.255
-rw-r--r-- 1 bind bind  353 Feb 20 05:40 db.empty
-rw-r--r-- 1 bind bind  256 Feb 20 05:40 db.local
-rw-r--r-- 1 bind bind 1507 Feb 20 05:40 db.root
-rw-r--r-- 1 bind bind 1611 Feb 20 05:40 named.conf
-rw-r--r-- 1 bind bind  165 Feb 20 05:40 named.conf.local
-rw-r--r-- 1 bind bind 1458 Feb 20 05:40 named.conf.options
-rw-r----- 1 bind bind   77 Apr 25 15:42 rndc.key
-rw-r--r-- 1 bind bind 1317 Feb 20 05:40 zones.rfc1918
```

BIND is running in a chroot jail in **/var/lib/named**. Because the **/etc/bind** directory is now a link to **/var/lib/named**, you can make changes to BIND from either location.

TROUBLESHOOTING

When you start a DNS cache, the **/var/log/syslog** file contains lines similar to the following. Other types of DNS servers display similar messages.

```
$ cat /var/log/syslog
...
Apr 26 11:00:02 plum named[9301]: starting BIND 9.3.4 -u bind
Apr 26 11:00:02 plum named[9301]: found 1 CPU, using 1 worker thread
Apr 26 11:00:02 plum named[9301]: loading configuration from '/etc/bind/named.conf'
Apr 26 11:00:02 plum named[9301]: listening on IPv6 interfaces, port 53
Apr 26 11:00:02 plum named[9301]: listening on IPv4 interface lo, 127.0.0.1#53
Apr 26 11:00:02 plum named[9301]: listening on IPv4 interface eth0, 192.168.0.10#53
Apr 26 11:00:02 plum named[9301]: command channel listening on 127.0.0.1#953
Apr 26 11:00:02 plum named[9301]: command channel listening on ::1#953
Apr 26 11:00:02 plum named[9301]: zone 0.in-addr.arpa/IN: loaded serial 1
Apr 26 11:00:02 plum named[9301]: zone 127.in-addr.arpa/IN: loaded serial 1
Apr 26 11:00:02 plum named[9301]: zone 255.in-addr.arpa/IN: loaded serial 1
Apr 26 11:00:02 plum named[9301]: zone localhost/IN: loaded serial 1
Apr 26 11:00:02 plum named[9301]: running
```

When you create or update DNS information, you can use dig or host to test whether the server works as planned. The most useful part of the output from dig is usually the answer section, which gives the nameserver's reply to your query:

```
$ dig example.com
...
;; ANSWER SECTION:
example.com.              72683   IN      A       192.0.34.166
...
```

The preceding output shows that the **example.com.** domain has a single A record that points to 192.0.34.166. The TTL of this record, which tells you how long the record can be held in cache, is 72,683 seconds (slightly less than one day). You can also use dig to query other record types by using the –t option followed by the type of record you want to query for (–t works with host, too):

```
$ dig -t MX ubuntu.com
...
;; ANSWER SECTION:
ubuntu.com.              3600     IN      MX       10 fiordland.ubuntu.com.
...
```

If you query for a domain that does not exist, dig returns the SOA record for the authority section of the highest-level domain in your query that does exist:

```
$ dig domaindoesnotexist.info
...
;; AUTHORITY SECTION:
info.    7200    IN    SOA    a9.info.afilias-nst.info. dns.afilias.info. ...
...
```

Because it tells you the last zone that was queried correctly, this information can be useful in tracing faults.

TSIGs   If two servers using TSIGs (page 806) fail to communicate, confirm that the time is the same on both servers. The TSIG authentication mechanism is dependent on the current time. If the clocks on the two servers are not synchronized, TSIG will fail. Consider setting up *NTP* (page 1123) on the servers to prevent this problem.

SETTING UP DIFFERENT TYPES OF DNS SERVERS

This section describes how to set up a full-functioned nameserver, a slave server, and a split-horizon server.

A FULL-FUNCTIONED NAMESERVER

Because the IP addresses used in this example are part of the *private address space* (page 1126), you can copy the example and run the server without affecting global DNS. Also, to prevent contamination of the global DNS, each zone has the **notify** option set to NO. When you build a nameserver that is integrated with the Internet, you will want to use IP addresses that are unique to your installation. You may want to change the settings of the **notify** statements.

named.conf   The **named.conf** file in this example limits the IP addresses that **named** answers queries from and sets up logging (next page).

```
$ cat /etc/bind/named.conf
options {
    directory "/etc/bind";
//  recursion NO;
    allow-query {127.0.0.1; 192.168.0.0/24;};
};

zone "." IN {
    type    hint;
    file    "db.root";
};

zone "0.168.192.in-addr.arpa" IN {
    type    master;
    file    "named.conf.local";
    notify  NO;
};

zone "sam.net" IN {
    type    master;
    file    "sam.net";
    notify  NO;
};
logging{
    channel "misc" {
        file "/var/log/bind/misc.log" versions 4 size 4m;
        print-time YES;
        print-severity YES;
        print-category YES;
    };
    channel "query" {
        file "/var/log/bind/query.log" versions 4 size 4m;
        print-time YES;
        print-severity NO;
        print-category NO;
    };
    category default {
        "misc";
    };
    category queries {
        "query";
    };
};
```

The **allow-query** statement in the Options clause specifies the IP addresses of systems the server answers queries from. You must include the local system as 127.0.0.1 if it will be querying the server. The server is authoritative for the zone **sam.net**; the zone file for **sam.net** is **/etc/bind/sam.net**.

Logging   Logging is turned on by the Logging clause. Logging is separate from **named** messages, which go to **syslogd**. The Logging clause in the preceding example opens two logging channels: one that logs information to **/var/log/bind/misc.log** and one that logs information to **/var/log/bind/query.log**. When either of these logs grows to 4 megabytes (**size 4m** in the file statement), it is renamed by appending **.1** to its file-name and a new log is started. The numbers at the ends of other, similarly named logs are incremented. Any log that would have a larger number than that specified by the **versions** keyword (**4** in the example) is removed. See logrotate (page 604) for another way to maintain log files.

The print statements determine whether the time, severity, and category of the information are sent to the log; specify each as YES or NO. The category determines what information is logged to the channel. In the previous example, default information is sent to the **misc** channel and queries are sent to the **query** channel. Refer to the **named.conf** man page for more choices.

named.conf.local The origin for the reverse zone file (**named.conf.local**) is 0.168.192.in-addr.arpa (as specified in the Zone clause that refers to this file in **named.conf**). Following the SOA and NS resource records, the first three PTR resource records equate address 1 in the subnet 0.168.192.in-addr.arpa (192.168.0.1) with the names **gw.sam.net.**, **www.sam.net.**, and **ftp.sam.net.**, respectively. The next three PTR records equate 192.168.0.3 with **mark.sam.net.**, 192.168.0.4 with **mail.sam.net.**, and 192.168.0.6 with **ns.sam.net.**.

```
$ cat /etc/bind/named.conf.local
$TTL    3D
@       IN      SOA     ns.sam.net. mgs@sobell.com. (
                                2007110501      ; serial
                                8H              ; refresh
                                2H              ; retry
                                4W              ; expire
                                1D)             ; minimum
        IN      NS      ns.sam.net.
1       IN      PTR     gw.sam.net.
1       IN      PTR     www.sam.net.
1       IN      PTR     ftp.sam.net.
3       IN      PTR     mark.sam.net.
4       IN      PTR     mail.sam.net.
6       IN      PTR     ns.sam.net.
```

sam.net The zone file for **sam.net** takes advantage of many BIND features and includes TXT (page 792), CNAME (page 790), and MX (page 790) resource records. When you query for resource records, **named** returns the TXT resource record along with the records you requested. The first of the two NS records specifies an unqualified name (**ns**) to which BIND appends the zone name (**sam.net**), yielding an FQDN of **ns.sam.net**. The second nameserver is specified with an FQDN name that BIND does not alter. The MX records specify mail servers in a similar manner and include a priority number at the start of the data field, where lower numbers indicate preferred servers.

```
$ cat sam.net
; zone "sam.net"
;
$TTL    3D
@       IN      SOA     ns.sam.net. mgs@sobell.com. (
                               200711051    ; serial
                               8H           ; refresh
                               2H           ; retry
                               4W           ; expire
                               1D )         ; minimum

                TXT     "Sobell Associates Inc."
                NS      ns          ; Nameserver address (unqualified)
                NS      ns.max.net.; Nameserver address (qualified)
                MX      10 mail     ; Mail exchange (primary/unqualified)
                MX      20 mail.max.net.; Mail exchange (2nd/qualified)

localhost IN    A       127.0.0.1

www     IN      CNAME   ns
ftp     IN      CNAME   ns

gw      IN      A       192.168.0.1
                TXT     "Router"

ns      IN      A       192.168.0.6
                MX      10 mail
                MX      20 mail.max.net.

mark    IN      A       192.168.0.3
                MX      10 mail
                MX      20 mail.max.net.
                TXT     "MGS"

mail    IN      A       192.168.0.4
                MX      10 mail
                MX      20 mail.max.net.
```

Some resource records have a value in the Name field; those without a name inherit the name from the previous resource record. In a similar manner, the previous resource record may have an inherited name value, and so on. The five resource records following the SOA resource record inherit the @, or zone name, from the SOA resource record. These resource records pertain to the zone as a whole. In the preceding example, the first TXT resource record inherits its name from the SOA resource record; it is the TXT resource record for the **sam.net** zone (give the command **host –t TXT sam.net** to display the TXT resource record).

Following these five resource records are resource records that pertain to a domain within the zone. For example, the MX resource records that follow the A resource record with the Name field set to **mark** are resource records for the **mark.sam.net.** domain.

The A resource record for **localhost** is followed by two CNAME resource records that specify www(.sam.net.) and ftp(.sam.net.) as aliases for the nameserver **ns.sam.net..** For example, a user connecting to ftp.sam.net will connect to 192.168.0.6. The resource records named **gw**, **ns**, **mark**, and **mail** are resource records for domains within the **sam.net** zone.

Log files Before restarting **named**, create the directory for the log files and give it permissions and ownership as shown below. If you are running **named** in a chroot jail, create the **bind** directory in **/var/lib/named/var/log**.

```
$ sudo mkdir /var/log/bind
$ sudo chown bind:bind /var/log/bind
$ ls -ld /var/log/bind
drwxr-xr-x 2 bind bind 4096 Apr 26 17:43 /var/log/bind
```

With the log directory in place, and the **named.conf, db.root, named.conf.local**, and **sam.net** zone files in **/etc/bind** (or in **/var/lib/named/etc/bind** if you are running **named** in a chroot jail), restart **named** and check the log files. The file **/var/log/syslog** should show something like the following (the example shows **named** started in a chroot jail):

```
# cat /var/log/syslog
...
Apr 26 18:05:19 plum named[22119]: starting BIND 9.3.4 -u bind -t /var/lib/named
Apr 26 18:05:19 plum named[22119]: found 1 CPU, using 1 worker thread
Apr 26 18:05:19 plum named[22119]: loading configuration from '/etc/bind/named.conf'
Apr 26 18:05:19 plum named[22119]: listening on IPv4 interface lo, 127.0.0.1#53
Apr 26 18:05:19 plum named[22119]: listening on IPv4 interface eth0, 192.168.0.10#53
Apr 26 18:05:19 plum named[22119]: command channel listening on 127.0.0.1#953
Apr 26 18:05:19 plum named[22119]: command channel listening on ::1#953
...
```

The **misc.log** file may show errors that do not appear in the **syslog** file:

```
# cat /var/log/bind/misc.log
... 01:05:19.932 general: info: zone 0.168.192.in-addr.arpa/IN: loaded serial 2007110501
... 01:05:19.933 general: info: zone sam.net/IN: loaded serial 200711051
... 01:05:19.933 general: notice: running
```

A Slave Server

To set up a slave server, copy the **/etc/bind/named.conf** file from the master server to the slave server, replacing the **type master** statement with **type slave** and adding a **masters { *1.2.3.4;* };** directive. Remove any zones the slave server will not be acting as a slave for, including the root (.) zone, if the slave server will not respond to recursive queries. If necessary, create the **/var/log/bind** directory for log files as explained at the end of the previous section.

notify statement Slave servers copy zone information from the primary master server or another slave server. The **notify** statement specifies whether you want a master server to notify slave servers when information on the master server changes. Set the (global) value of **notify** in the Options clause or set it within a Zone clause, which overrides a global setting for a given zone. The format is

> *notify YES | NO | EXPLICIT*

YES causes the master server to notify all slaves listed in NS resource records for the zone as well as servers at IP addresses listed in an **also-notify** statement. When you set **notify** to *EXPLICIT*, the server notifies servers listed in the **also-notify** statement only. *NO* turns off notification.

If you specify **notify YES** on the master server, the zone files on the slave server will be updated each time you change the serial field of the SOA resource record in a zone. You must manually distribute changes to **/etc/bind/named.conf** and included files.

A SPLIT HORIZON SERVER

Assume you want to set up a LAN that provides all of its systems and services to local users on internal systems, which may be behind a firewall, but only certain public services—such as Web, FTP, and mail—to Internet (public) users. A *split horizon* (also called *DMZ*) DNS server takes care of this situation by treating queries from internal systems differently from queries from public systems (systems on the Internet).

View clauses   BIND 9 introduced View clauses in **named.conf**. View clauses facilitate the implementation of a split DNS server. Each view provides a different perspective of the DNS namespace to a group of clients. When there is no View clause, all zones specified in **named.conf** are part of the implicit default view.

Assume that an office has several systems on a LAN and public Web, FTP, DNS, and mail servers. The single connection to the Internet is NATed (page 1121) so it is shared by the local systems and the servers. The system connected directly to the Internet is a router, firewall, and server. This scenario takes advantage of the View clauses in **named.conf** and supports separate secondary nameservers for local and public users. Although public users need access to the DNS server as the authority on the domain that supports the servers, they do not require the DNS server to support recursive queries. Not supporting recursion for public users limits the load on the DNS server and the Internet connection. For security reasons, public users must not have access to information about local systems other than the servers. Local users should have access to information about local systems and should be able to use the DNS server recursively.

Figure 24-6 shows that the server responds differently to queries from the LAN and from the Internet.

The firestarter (page 824) or iptables utility (page 836) controls which ports on which systems users on internal and external systems can access. DNS controls which systems are advertised to which users.

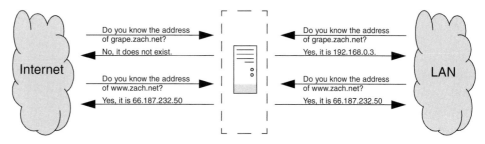

Figure 24-6   A split horizon DNS server

The **named.conf** file has four clauses: an Options clause, two View clauses, and a Logging clause. The Options clause specifies that the zone files be located in the **/etc/bind** directory. The View clauses specify the characteristics and zones that a resolver is given access to, which depend on the resolver's address. One zone is for use by the LAN/local users; the other is used by Internet/public users. The Logging clause sets up the **misc2.log** file for default messages.

There are several ways to specify which clients see a view. The following **named.conf** file uses **match-clients** statements:

```
$ cat /etc/bind/named.conf
options {
    directory "/etc/bind";
}; //end options


view "local" IN {                        // start local view
match-clients { 127.0.0.1; 192.168.0.0/24;};
recursion YES;


zone"zach.net" IN {
    type    master;
    file    "local.net";
    notify  YES;
};

zone "0.168.192.in-addr.arpa" IN {
    type    master;
    file    "named.local";
    notify  YES;
};

zone "." IN {
    type    hint;
    file    "named.ca";
};

};                  // end local view
```

```
view "public" IN {                      // start public view
match-clients { "all";};
recursion NO;

zone"zach.net" IN {
    type    master;
    file    "public.net";
    notify YES;
};

zone "0.168.192.in-addr.arpa" IN {
    type    master;
    file    "named.public";
    notify  YES;
};

zone "." IN {
    type    hint;
    file    "named.ca";
};

};                                       // end public view

logging{
    channel "misc" {
        file "/var/log/bind/misc2.log" versions 2 size 1m;
        print-time YES;
        print-severity YES;
        print-category YES;
    };
    category default {
        "misc";
    };
};                                       //end logging
```

The ordering of View clauses within **named.conf** is critical because the view that is presented to a client is the first view that the client matches. The preceding **named.conf** file holds two View clauses: one for local users and one for public users, in that order. Local users are defined to be those on the 192.168.0.0/24 subnet or **localhost** (127.0.0.1); public users are defined to be any users. If you reversed the order of the View clauses, all users—including local users—would get the view intended for the public and no users would see the local view.

Many statements from the Options clause can be used within View clauses, where they override statements in the (global) Options clause. The **recursion** statement, which can appear within an Options clause, appears in each View clause. This **named.conf** file sets up a server that provides recursive answers to queries that originate locally and iterative answers to queries from the public. This setup provides quick, complete answers to local users, limiting the network and processor bandwidth that is devoted to other users while continuing to provide authoritative name service for the local servers.

To make **named.conf** easier to understand and maintain, zones in different View clauses can have the same name but different zone files. Both the local and public View clauses in the example have zones named **zach.net**: The public **zach.net** zone file is named **public.net** and the local one is named **local.net**.

The Logging clause is described on page 812.

The zone files defining **zach.net** are similar to the ones in the previous examples; the public file is a subset of the local one. Following the SOA resource record in both files is a TXT, two NS, and two MX resource records. Next are three CNAME resource records that direct queries addressed to www.zach.net, ftp.zach.net, and mail.zach.net to the system named **ns.zach.net**. The next four resource records specify two nameserver addresses and two mail servers for the ns.zach.net domain.

The final four resource records appear in the local **zach.net** zone file and not in the public zone file; they are address (A) resource records for local systems. Instead of keeping this information in **/etc/hosts** files on each system, you can keep it on the DNS server, where it can be updated easily. When you use DNS instead of **/etc/hosts**, you must change the **hosts** line in **/etc/nsswitch.conf** (page 458) accordingly.

```
$ cat local.net
; zach.net local zone file
;
$TTL    3D
@       IN      SOA     ns.zach.net. mgs@sobell.com. (
                                200711118       ; serial
                                8H              ; refresh
                                2H              ; retry
                                4W              ; expire
                                1D )            ; minimum

        IN      TXT     "Sobell Associates Inc."
        IN      NS      ns              ; Nameserver address (unqualified)
        IN      NS      ns.speedy.net.; Nameserver address (qualified)
        IN      MX      10 mail    ; Mail exchange (primary/unqualified)
        IN      MX      20 mail.max.net.; Mail exchange (2nd/qualified)

www     IN      CNAME   ns
ftp     IN      CNAME   ns
mail    IN      CNAME   ns

ns      IN      A       192.168.0.1
        IN      A       192.168.0.6
        IN      MX      10 mail
        IN      MX      20 mail.max.net.

speedy  IN      A       192.168.0.1
grape   IN      A       192.168.0.3
potato  IN      A       192.168.0.4
peach   IN      A       192.168.0.6
```

The public version of the **zach.net** zone file follows:

```
$ cat public.net
; zach.net public zone file
;
$TTL    3D
@       IN      SOA     ns.zach.net. mgs@sobell.com. (
                                200711118       ; serial
                                8H              ; refresh
                                2H              ; retry
                                4W              ; expire
                                1D )            ; minimum

        IN      TXT     "Sobell Associates Inc."
        IN      NS      ns              ; Nameserver address (unqualified)
        IN      NS      ns.speedy.net.; Nameserver address (qualified)

        IN      MX      10 mail ; Mail exchange (primary/unqualified)
        IN      MX      20 mail.max.net.; Mail exchange (2nd/qualified)

www     IN      CNAME   ns
ftp     IN      CNAME   ns
mail    IN      CNAME   ns

ns      IN      A       192.168.0.1
        IN      A       192.168.0.6
        IN      MX      10 mail
        IN      MX      20 mail.max.net.
```

Here there are two reverse zone files, each of which starts with SOA and NS resource records, followed by PTR resource records for each of the names of the servers. The local version of this file also lists the names of the local systems:

```
$ cat named.local
;"0.168.192.in-addr.arpa" reverse zone file
;
$TTL    3D
@       IN      SOA     ns.zach.net. mgs@sobell.com. (
                                2007110501      ; serial
                                8H              ; refresh
                                2H              ; retry
                                4W              ; expire
                                1D)             ; minimum
        IN      NS      ns.zach.net.
        IN      NS      ns.speedy.net.
1       IN      PTR     gw.zach.net.
1       IN      PTR     www.zach.net.
1       IN      PTR     ftp.zach.net.
1       IN      PTR     mail.zach.net.
1       IN      PTR     speedy.zach.net.
3       IN      PTR     grape.zach.net.
4       IN      PTR     potato.zach.net.
6       IN      PTR     peach.zach.net.
```

CHAPTER SUMMARY

DNS maps domain names to IP addresses, and vice versa. It is implemented as a hierarchical, distributed, and replicated database on the Internet. You can improve the security of BIND, which implements DNS, by running it inside a chroot jail and using transaction signatures (TSIGs).

When a program on the local system needs to look up an IP address that corresponds to a domain name, it calls the resolver. The resolver queries the local DNS cache, if available, and then queries DNS servers on the LAN or Internet. There are two types of queries: iterative and recursive. When a server responds to an iterative query, it returns whatever information it has at hand; it does not query other servers. Recursive queries cause a server to query other servers if necessary to respond with an answer.

There are three types of servers. Master servers, which hold the master copy of zone data, are authoritative for a zone. Slave servers are also authoritative and copy their data from a master server or other slave servers. DNS caches are not authoritative and either answer queries from cache or forward queries to another server.

The DNS database holds resource records for domains. Many types of resource records exist, including A (address), MX (mail exchange), NS (nameserver), PTR (pointer for performing reverse name resolution), and SOA (start of authority, which describes the zone) records.

EXERCISES

1. What kind of server responds to recursive queries? How does this server work?

2. What kind of DNS record is likely to be returned when a Web browser tries to resolve the domain part of a URI?

3. What are MX resource records for?

4. How would you find the IP address of example.com from the command line?

5. How would you instruct a Linux system to use the local network's DNS cache, located at 192.168.1.254, or the ISP's DNS cache, located at 1.2.3.4, if the LAN nameserver is unavailable?

6. How would you instruct a DNS server to respond only to queries from the **137.44.*** IP range?

7. How might a resolver attempt to find the IP address of the **example** domain?

ADVANCED EXERCISES

8. How would you set up a private domain name hierarchy that does not include any of the official InterNIC-assigned domain names?

9. Which part of DNS is most vulnerable to an attack from a malicious user and why?

10. It is often irritating to have to wait for DNS records to update around the world when you change DNS entries. You could prevent this delay by setting the TTL to a small number. Why is setting the TTL to a small number a bad idea?

11. Outline a method by which DNS could be used to support encryption.

25

firestarter, ufw, AND iptables: SETTING UP A FIREWALL

The firestarter utility is a user-friendly, graphical front-end for iptables; iptables builds and manipulates network *packet filtering* (page 1123) rules in the Linux kernel. You can use firestarter, or iptables directly, to create a firewall that protects a system from malicious users and to set up *NAT* (Network Address Translation, page 1121), which can allow several systems to share a single Internet connection. In addition, firestarter can control a DHCP server.

The iptables utility is flexible and extensible, allowing you to set up both simple and complex network packet filtering solutions. It provides connection tracking (stateful packet filtering), allowing you to handle *packets* (page 1123) based on the state of their connection. For example, you can set up rules that reject inbound packets trying to open a new connection and accept inbound packets that are responses to locally initiated connections. Many features not included in the base **iptables** package are available as patches via the patch-o-matic program.

The firestarter utility is frequently sufficient to protect a single system or a small LAN but, because of its user-friendly nature, it does not provide access to the full complexity and power of iptables. Most of the concepts involving firestarter will probably be familiar, or easy to learn, for someone who is familiar with basic networking. Some of the concepts required to fully understand iptables are beyond the scope of this book. Although you can use iptables at different levels, this chapter presents only the fundamentals. There are, however, some sections of this chapter that delve into areas that may require additional understanding or explanation. If a concept is not clear, refer to one of the resources in "More Information" on page 839.

ufw   Ubuntu has added ufw (uncomplicated firewall) and its graphical interface gufw to its security arsenal. As these products mature, you may want to consider experimenting with and using them in place of firestarter. See page 834 for more information.

INTRODUCTION TO firestarter

The firestarter utility is a sophisticated, graphical tool for building and maintaining a firewall. Although it works with GTK and is designed to run under GNOME, it is equally at home under KDE. This utility enables a system to share an Internet connection with other systems on a LAN. It can also set up and control a DHCP (page 454) server. It provides a real-time view of intrusion and other events and allows you to tune ICMP (page 1113) parameters to help stop *DoS attacks* (page 1106). As installed, firestarter allows outbound connections and blocks and displays information about inbound connections that originate outside the system or LAN it is protecting (that is, connections that originate on the Internet). As you view these events, you can set up rules to allow them, facilitating firewall customization.

The firestarter utility can protect the single system it runs on (the firewall host) or it can protect the system it runs on as well as other client systems on a LAN that connect to the Internet through the firewall host. Figure 25-1 shows a typical setup where all network traffic to and from a LAN must pass through the firewall, enabling the firewall to control access between the Internet and the LAN (including the firewall host). In this setup the firewall host acts as a router (page 361).

NOTES

Terminology   This section explains what some of the words used to explain firestarter mean in this context. The terms *firewall* and firestarter are used interchangeably.

- **(Firewall) host (system)**—The system the firewall is running on.
- **Client systems**—Systems that are on the same LAN as the firewall host and whose packets to and from systems outside the LAN (specifically the Internet) pass through the firewall host.
- **Policy**—The set of rules that the firewall applies.

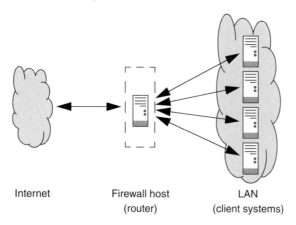

Figure 25-1   A typical firewall setup

- **Rule**—A statement that specifies what the firewall does with specific types of packets it receives from specific systems on its network interface(s).

- **Connection**—Under TCP, the path through which two systems exchange data. A client system opens a connection with a server system by sending it a SYN (synchronization) packet. The server sends an ACK (acknowledge) packet back to the client and the two systems exchange data. The client closes the connection with a SYN packet. Although UDP works differently because it has no concept of a connection, for the purposes of this discussion the concept of a UDP connection is appropriate.

- **Inbound connections**—Include connections that originate from the Internet and client systems with the firewall host as the destination.

- **Outbound connections**—Include connections that originate from the firewall host and client systems with the Internet as the destination.

Default policy   By default, firestarter implements a user-friendly policy that protects the firewall host and client systems. In general, it allows outbound traffic and blocks inbound traffic that is not sent in response to outbound traffic. Specifically, the default firestarter policy

- Blocks new inbound connections from the Internet that are destined for the firewall host or the client systems.

- Allows inbound packets that are sent in response to connections initiated by the firewall host or client systems to the Internet.

- Allows the firewall host to establish connections.

- Allows client systems to establish connections to the Internet.

- Does not allow client systems to establish connections to the firewall host.

After you set up firestarter with the Firewall Wizard, you can modify the default policy to meet your needs.

iptables and firestarter   Although firestarter is a front-end for iptables, it does not store its rules the way iptables does (using iptables-save [page 847]). Instead, it keeps configuration information in its own format in the **/etc/firestarter** directory hierarchy.

MORE INFORMATION

Web   www.fs-security.com

firestarter: SETTING UP AND MAINTAINING A FIREWALL

This section describes how to set up a firewall using the firestarter Firewall Wizard and how to maintain the firewall once it is set up.

PREREQUISITES

Install the following package:

- **firestarter**

- **dhcp3-server** (needed only if you want firestarter to run DHCP; page 456)

When you install the firestarter package, you must run the Firewall Wizard before firestarter will start (see the JumpStart section, next). After you configure it, firestarter starts running each time you boot the system. Although there is a firestarter init file, you never need to run it manually; use the firestarter GUI to turn the firewall on or off or to lock the system so no network traffic can enter or leave it. When you bring the system up, firestarter comes up in the state it was in when you shut the system down. The firestarter utility runs regardless of whether its GUI is displayed.

Figure 25-2   The Firewall Wizard: Welcome to Firestarter screen

JumpStart: Configuring a Firewall Using the firestarter Firewall Wizard

The Firewall Wizard and Firestarter windows (Figure 25-2 and Figure 25-6 on page 829) enable you to set up and control firestarter. To display this window, select **Main menu: System⇨Administration⇨firestarter** or give the command **gksudo firestarter** from a terminal emulator or Run Application window (ALT-F2).

When you run firestarter for the first time, it opens the Firewall Wizard (Figure 25-2), which helps you configure firestarter. You can rerun this wizard at any time by selecting **Firestarter menu: Firewall⇨Run Wizard**. The last step of the wizard allows you to start the firewall and display the Firestarter window.

Device setup   The first Firewall Wizard screen welcomes you to firestarter; click **Forward** to get started. The Firewall Wizard displays the Network device setup screen (Figure 25-3). In this screen you select the device that is connected to the Internet. You can also specify that you want the firewall to start when you dial out from the system (if you are using a modem to connect to the Internet) and/or that you want firestarter to use DHCP (page 454) to assign IP addresses and provide other network configuration information to the client systems.

From the drop-down list labeled **Detected device(s)**, select the device that is connected to the Internet. If the local system is functioning as a router, make sure to select the device that is connected to the Internet, not the device that is connected to the LAN. If the local system connects to the Internet using a modem only, put a tick in the check box labeled **Start the firewall on dial-out**.

DHCP   If you want to run DHCP, put a tick in the check box labeled **IP address is assigned via DHCP**. (You can also configure DHCP using **Firestarter menu: Edit⇨Preferences**.) If firestarter is going to control DHCP, you must install the DHCP package (page 826). Click **Forward**.

Figure 25-3   The Network device setup screen

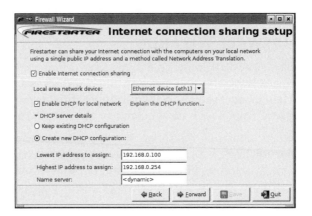

Figure 25-4   The Internet connection sharing setup screen

NAT (connection sharing)   The Internet connection sharing setup screen (Figure 25-4) allows you to set up *NAT* (page 1121) so systems on the LAN can share a single Internet connection. This window appears only if the system you are installing the firewall on has at least two network connections. Put a tick in the check box labeled **Enable Internet connection sharing** if the firewall host is to function as a router (Figure 25-1, page 825) and share an Internet connection; otherwise skip this screen. When you put a tick in this check box, firestarter enables you to select the device that is connected to the LAN (not the one that is connected to the Internet). Put a tick in the check box labeled **Enable DHCP for local network** to cause firestarter to run DHCP. When you put a tick in this check box, click the triangle adjacent to **DHCP server details** to choose whether to keep an existing DHCP configuration or create a new one. The Server name can be the IP address or name of the DHCP server. If you set the name to **<dynamic>**, firestarter determines the IP address of the DHCP server at runtime, which can be useful if the server is assigned an IP address using DHCP. Click **Forward**.

Starting the firewall   In the Ready to start your firewall screen (Figure 25-5), you can choose to start the firewall. The firewall starts in secure mode, which protects the LAN but may cause problems for some users and does not allow systems on the Internet to access servers behind the firewall. If you are configuring the firewall from a remote system, you will not be able to work with firestarter once you start the firewall. Put a tick in the check box labeled **Start firewall now** if you want to start the firewall immediately. Click **Save**.

MAINTAINING A FIREWALL USING firestarter

After you configure firestarter, you can make changes to the policy from the Firestarter window. After you run the Firewall Wizard, firestarter displays this window. You can display this window at any time by following the instruction at the start of the Jump-Start section on page 827. The firewall runs regardless of whether the Firestarter

Figure 25-5   The Ready to start your firewall screen

window is displayed. When you bring the system up, the firewall resumes the status it had (running, stopped, or locked) when you brought the system down.

THE STATUS TAB

The Firestarter window Status tab (Figure 25-6) displays an overview of the firewall. This tab can display active connections to the firewall. The toolbar allows you

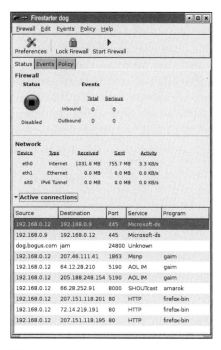

Figure 25-6   The Status tab with Active connections expanded

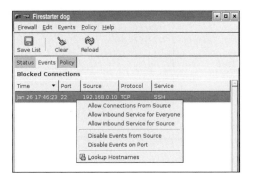

Figure 25-7   Events tab, right-click menu

to change the state of the firewall and specify preferences. The large round icon in the Firewall frame of the window indicates the status of the firewall:

- **Disabled**—The firewall is turned off—it is as though firestarter was not installed.

- **Active**—The firewall is up and running and implementing the policy you have set up (or the default policy).

- **Locked**—The firewall is up and running and blocking all packets. Nothing can get in or out of the firewall host over the network interfaces that firestarter controls.

Click the appropriate icon on the toolbar to change the state of the firewall.

Events   An *event* occurs when the firewall blocks a packet based on a rule. The Events columns in the Firewall frame list the number of inbound and outbound events the firewall has blocked and indicate how many of those were of a serious nature. Events are considered serious if they could have been attempts by malicious users to gain access to the system. For example, a blocked attempt to log in using ssh is a serious event; a blocked ping is not.

The Network frame shows the activity on each of the system's network connections.

When you click the small triangle to the left of **Active connections**, firestarter displays a scrollable list of active connections; lengthen the window to display more connections. Click on a line in this list to select it and then right-click and select **Lookup Hostnames** to change the value in the Source and Destination columns from IP addresses to hostnames. The Port column lists the port on the target host that the connection uses. The Service column indicates the service that is associated with the specified port. The Program column shows the name the program running the service if it is local and known to firestarter.

THE EVENTS TAB

The Firestarter window Events tab (Figure 25-7) is the key to modifying the default firewall policy. It displays a list of blocked connections. Each line in this list specifies an event that the firewall blocked based on a rule. Events displayed in black are attempts to connect to a random port and are typically not of concern. Events in gray are harmless, consisting mostly of broadcast traffic. Events in red are attempts

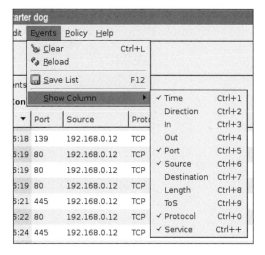

Figure 25-8   Selecting columns for the Blocked Connections list

to access a service that is not provided to the public and may indicate that a malicious user is attempting to gain access to the firewall host or a client system.

You can modify this list in several ways.

- To display a hostname in place of an IP address, highlight the entry you want to change, right-click, and select **Lookup Hostnames** (Figure 25-7).

- By default, the Blocked Connections list does not include redundant entries. To display redundant entries, remove the tick from the check box at **Firestarter menu: Edit⇨Preferences⇨Events⇨Skip redundant entries.**

- You can specify the columns that firestarter includes in the Blocked Connections list by selecting from the menu displayed by **Firestarter menu: Events⇨Show Column** (Figure 25-8).

As Figure 25-7 shows, the right-click menu also allows you to change the rule for the highlighted system and port (service). Inbound and outbound connections present different menus. The inbound menu includes the following selections:

- **Allow Connections from Source**—Enables the originating system on the Internet that the highlighted event blocked to make any type of connection to client systems or the firewall host. Set this rule only if you completely trust the source system.

- **Allow Inbound Service for Everyone**—Enables any system on the Internet to connect to the service (port) that the highlighted event blocked. Set this rule to allow the public to access servers behind the firewall.

- **Allow Inbound Service for Source**—Enables the originating system on the Internet to connect to the service (port) that the highlighted event blocked. The port protected by this rule is called a *stealth port* because it is invisible to all systems on the Internet except the specified system.

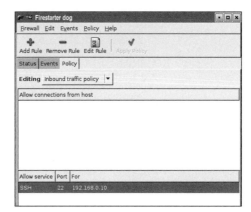

Figure 25-9   The Policy tab

The outbound menu includes the following selections:

- **Allow Connections to Destination**—Enables the firewall host and client systems to establish a connection with the destination system that the highlighted event blocked.

- **Allow Outbound Service for Everyone**—Enables the firewall host and client systems to establish a connection to the service (port) that the highlighted event blocked.

- **Allow Outbound Service for Source**—Enables the firewall host or a specific client that the event blocked to establish a connection to the service that the highlighted event blocked.

In addition, both menus include these two selections:

- **Disable Events from Source**—Prevents the highlighted originating system on the Internet from connecting to client systems or the firewall host.

- **Disable Events on Port**—Prevents any system on the Internet from connecting to the service (port) that the highlighted event blocked.

Events tab: ease of use

tip   It is easiest to set up rules from the Events tab and view them in the Policy tab. However, you cannot set up certain rules, such as forwarding rules, from the Events tab. Also, you cannot edit rules from the Events tab.

THE POLICY TAB

The Policy tab (Figure 25-9) displays the firewall rules and allows you to add, remove, and edit rules. The drop-down list labeled **Editing** allows you to select whether firestarter displays (and you can edit) inbound or outbound rules.

The Policy tab displays three frames each for inbound and outbound groups of rules. Right-click with the mouse pointer in a frame to display a context menu with these selections: Add Rule, Remove Rule, and Edit Rule. To use the last two selections, you must highlight a rule before right-clicking.

Applying changes By default, firestarter does not apply changes you make in this tab until you click **Apply Policy** at the top of the window. You can cause firestarter to apply changes immediately by selecting **Firestarter menu: Edit⇨Preferences⇨Policy** and putting a tick in the check box labeled **Apply policy changes immediately**.

INBOUND POLICY

The default inbound policy is to block all inbound connections except connections that are responding to outbound connections. When you select **Inbound traffic policy**, firestarter displays three frames that enable you to work with rules that are exceptions to the default policy:

- **Allow connections from host**—Specifies a host or network that firestarter accepts any incoming connection from. Make sure you trust this system or network completely.

- **Allow service**—Specifies a service (port) that firestarter accepts inbound connections on. You can specify that firestarter accept inbound connections on the specified port from anyone, all clients, or a specific host or network on the Internet.

- **Forward service**—Specifies a service (port) that firestarter will accept inbound connections on. The firestarter firewall forwards these connections to the client you specify on the port you specify. Forwarding a service is appropriate if you are running a server on a client system and want systems on the Internet to be able to connect to the server.

OUTBOUND POLICY

When you select **Outbound traffic policy**, firestarter displays two radio buttons that enable you to set the default outbound policy:

- **Permissive by default, blacklist traffic**—The default outbound policy. Allows all outbound connections that originate from the firewall host or clients. You must set up specific policies (a blacklist) to block outbound requests for specific services and/or requests from specific systems.

- **Restrictive by default, whitelist traffic**—Blocks all outbound traffic except connections that you set up rules to allow (a whitelist).

Permissive by default With the default policy of **Permissive by default,** firestarter displays three frames that enable you to deny connections and/or services:

- **Deny connections to host**—Specifies systems on the Internet that the firewall host and all client systems are not allowed to connect to.

- **Deny connections from LAN host**—Specifies client systems that are not allowed to connect to any system on the Internet.

- **Deny service**—Specifies a service and/or port that firestarter blocks outbound connections on. You can specify that firestarter block outbound connections on the specified port from anyone, clients, the firewall host, or a specific host or network on the Internet.

Restrictive by
default

With the **Restrictive by default** policy, firestarter displays three frames that enable you to allow connections and/or services:

- **Allow connections to host**—Specifies systems on the Internet that the firewall host and all client systems are allowed to connect to.

- **Allow connections from LAN host**—Specifies client systems that are allowed to connect to any system on the Internet.

- **Allow service**—Specifies a service and/or port that firestarter allows outbound connections on. You can specify that firestarter allow outbound connections on the specified port from anyone, clients, the firewall host, or a specific host or network on the Internet.

ufw: THE UNCOMPLICATED FIREWALL

The ufw (uncomplicated firewall) utility is a simple, easy-to-use, command-line interface to iptables. It is installed as part of the base system. The gufw (gufw.tuxfamily.org) utility is a graphical interface to ufw and is available in the **gufw** package.

As installed, ufw is turned off. The **status** command reports ufw is not loaded:

```
$ sudo ufw status
Status: not loaded
```

Use the **enable** command to turn ufw on (and use **disable** to turn it off). When you enable ufw, it starts each time you boot the system. By default, ufw starts with a default policy that blocks all inbound traffic (**ufw default deny**) and allows outbound traffic. If you want to allow all inbound traffic, give the command **ufw default allow**. If you are working from a remote system, you must open the port you are using to connect to the firewall system or you will not be able to reconnect to the system once you start the firewall and log off.

In the following example, first the **allow** command opens a port for ssh and then **enable** turns on ufw. Alternatively, you can specify the port number in the **allow** command (**ufw allow 22**). The **enable** command warns that turning on ufw may disconnect you from the system, asks whether you want to proceed, and reports that the firewall has been started and is set up to be enabled each time the system starts.

```
$ sudo ufw allow ssh
Rules updated

$ sudo ufw enable
Command may disrupt existing ssh connections. Proceed with operation (y|n)? y
Firewall started and enabled on system startup
```

Many services that are ufw-aware (e.g., Apache, CUPS, and OpenSSH) install a set of firewall rules in **/etc/ufw/applications.d**. The command **ufw app list** lists those services that have firewall rules installed on the local system.

```
$ sudo ufw app list
Available applications:
  CUPS
  OpenSSH
```

When you specify the name of a service (ssh in the preceding example) in a ufw command, ufw searches **/etc/services** to find the port number used by the service. When you specify the name of the application as listed by **ufw app list** (OpenSSH in the preceding list), ufw reads the rules from the file in **applications.d**. The difference between these techniques is important with services/applications that use multiple ports or a range of ports. The **/etc/services** file cannot represent this information; the rules in the files in **applications.d** can.

When you give a **status** command with an argument of **verbose**, it reports that ufw is loaded, logging is turned on, and the default policy is to deny incoming connections. With or without **verbose, status** reports that ufw allows connections on port 22 (the port ssh uses).

```
$ sudo ufw status verbose
Status: loaded
Logging: on
Default: deny
New profiles: skip

To                      Action  From
--                      ------  ----
22/tcp                  ALLOW   Anywhere
22/udp                  ALLOW   Anywhere
```

If you log in on the firewall system from one remote system only, you can make the firewall system more secure by limiting those systems you can log in from. The following **allow** command opens port 22 to connections from the system at 10.10.4.15 only:

```
$ sudo ufw allow from 10.10.4.15 port 22
Rule added
```

You remove a rule by giving the same command as you used to establish the rule, preceded by the word **delete**:

```
$ sudo ufw delete allow ssh
Rule deleted

$ sudo ufw status
Status: loaded

To                      Action  From
--                      ------  ----
Anywhere                ALLOW   10.10.4.15 22/tcp
Anywhere                ALLOW   10.10.4.15 22/udp
```

By default, logging is turned on (**ufw logging on**) and ufw sends messages about intrusion attempts to the **kern syslogd** facility (page 608). These messages go to the file named **/var/log/kern.log**. The same information is available from the dmesg utility (page 575).

```
$ sudo tail -1 /var/log/kern.log
Nov  1 15:52:19 fox4 kernel: [  905.965627] [UFW BLOCK INPUT]: IN=eth0 OUT= MAC=00:0c: ...
SRC=10.10.4.102 DST=10.10.4.91 LEN=60 TOS=0x00 PREC=0x00 TTL=64 ID=47101 DF PROTO=TCP
SPT=43494 DPT=22 WINDOW=5840 RES=0x00 SYN URGP=0
```

If you want to set up an Apache Web server that accepts requests on port 80 on the local system, you need to open port 80. The following commands open port 80 and verify the new rule:

```
$ sudo ufw allow 80
Rule added

$ sudo ufw status
...
80/tcp                        ALLOW    Anywhere
80/udp                        ALLOW    Anywhere
```

See the ufw man page for more information.

INTRODUCTION TO iptables

netfilter and iptables
The functionality referred to as iptables is composed of two components: **netfilter** and iptables. Running in *kernelspace* (page 1116), the **netfilter** component is a set of tables that hold rules that the kernel uses to control network packet filtering. Running in *userspace* (page 1139), the iptables utility sets up, maintains, and displays the rules stored by **netfilter**.

Rules, matches, targets, and chains
A *rule* comprises one or more criteria (*matches* or *classifiers*) and a single action (a *target*). If, when a rule is applied to a network packet, the packet matches all the criteria, the action is applied to the packet. Rules are stored in *chains*. Each rule in a chain is applied, in order, to a packet until a match is found. If there is no match, the chain's *policy*, or default action, is applied to the packet (page 842).

History
In the kernel, iptables replaces the earlier ipchains as a method of filtering network packets. It provides multiple chains for increased filtration flexibility. The iptables utility also provides stateful packet inspection (page 838).

Example rules
As an example of how rules work, assume a chain has two rules (Figure 25-10). The first rule tests whether a packet's destination is port 23 (TELNET) and drops the packet if it is. The second rule tests whether a packet was received from the IP address 192.168.1.1 and alters the packet's destination if it was. When a packet is processed by the example chain, the kernel applies the first rule in the chain to see whether the packet arrived on port 23. If the answer is yes, the packet is dropped and that is the end of processing for that packet. If the answer is no, the kernel applies the second rule in the chain to see whether the packet came from the specified IP address. If the answer is yes, the destination in the packet's header is changed and the modified packet is sent on its way. If the answer is no, the packet is sent on without being changed.

Chains are collected in three tables: Filter, NAT, and Mangle. Each of these tables has builtin chains (described next). You can create additional, user-defined chains in Filter, the default table.

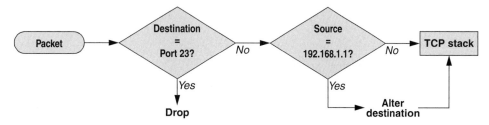

Figure 25-10   Example of how rules in a chain work

Filter table   The default table. This table is mostly used to DROP or ACCEPT packets based on their content; it does not alter packets. Builtin chains are INPUT, FORWARD, and OUTPUT. All user-defined chains go in this table.

NAT table   The Network Address Translation table. Packets that create new connections are routed through this table, which is used exclusively to translate the source or destination fields of packets. Builtin chains are PREROUTING, OUTPUT, and POSTROUTING. Use this table with DNAT, SNAT, and MASQUERADE targets only.

- **DNAT** (destination NAT) alters the destination IP address of the first inbound packet in a connection so it is rerouted to another host. Subsequent packets in the connection are automatically DNATed. DNAT is useful for redirecting packets from the Internet that are bound for a firewall or a NATed server (page 852).

- **SNAT** (source NAT) alters the source IP address of the first outbound packet in a connection so it appears to come from a fixed IP address— for example, a firewall or router. Subsequent packets in the connection are automatically SNATed. Replies to SNATed packets are automatically de-SNATed so they go back to the original sender. SNAT is useful for hiding LAN addresses from systems outside the LAN and using a single IP address to serve multiple local hosts.

- **MASQUERADE** differs from SNAT only in that it checks for an IP address to apply to each outbound packet, making it suitable for use with dynamic IP addresses such as those provided by DHCP (page 454). MASQUERADE is slightly slower than SNAT.

Mangle table   Used exclusively to alter the TOS (type of service), TTL (time to live), and MARK fields in a packet. Builtin chains are PREROUTING and OUTPUT.

Network packets   When a packet from the network enters the kernel's network protocol stack, it is given some basic sanity tests, including checksum verification. After passing these

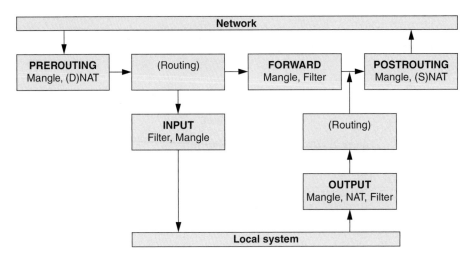

Figure 25-11   Filtering a packet in the kernel

tests, the packet goes through the PREROUTING chain, where its destination address may be changed (Figure 25-11).

Next the packet is routed based on its destination address. If it is bound for the local system, it first goes through the INPUT chain, where it can be filtered (accepted, dropped, or sent to another chain) or altered. If the packet is not addressed to the local system (the local system is forwarding the packet), it goes through the FOR-WARD and POSTROUTING chains, where it can again be filtered or altered.

Packets created locally pass through the OUTPUT and POSTROUTING chains, where they can be filtered or altered before being sent to the network.

State   The connection tracking machine (also called the state machine) provides informa-tion on the state of a packet, allowing you to define rules that match criteria based on the state of the connection the packet is part of. For example, when a connection is opened, the first packet is part of a NEW connection, whereas subsequent packets are part of an ESTABLISHED connection. Connection tracking is handled by the **conntrack** module.

The OUTPUT chain handles connection tracking for locally generated packets. The PREROUTING chain handles connection tracking for all other packets. For more information refer to "State" on page 845.

Before the advent of connection tracking, it was sometimes necessary to open many or all nonprivileged ports to make sure that the system accepted all RETURN and RELATED traffic. Because connection tracking allows you to identify these kinds of traffic, you can keep many more ports closed to general traffic, thereby increasing system security.

Jumps and targets A *jump* or *target* (page 846) specifies the action the kernel takes if a network packet matches all the match criteria (page 840) for the rule being processed.

MORE INFORMATION

Web Documentation, HOWTOs, FAQs, patch-o-matic, security information: www.netfilter.org
Tutorial: www.faqs.org/docs/iptables
Multicast DNS: www.multicastdns.org
Scripts and more: www.yourwebexperts.com/forum/viewforum.php?f=35

HOWTO *KernelAnalysis-HOWTO*
IP-Masquerade-HOWTO (contains useful scripts)
Netfilter Extensions HOWTO: www.netfilter.org
Netfilter Hacking-HOWTO: www.netfilter.org

Book *TCP/IP Illustrated* by W. Richard Stevens, Addison-Wesley, January 2002

PREREQUISITES

Installation Install the following package:

- **iptables**

iptables init script The **iptables** package does not include an init script because, under Ubuntu, it is generally called from firestarter. This chapter includes instructions for configuring and running iptables. You can save and reload iptables rules as explained in "Saving rules" below.

NOTES

Startup The iptables utility is a tool that manipulates rules in the kernel. It differs from daemons (servers) in its setup and use. Whereas Linux daemons such as Apache, **vsftpd**, and **sshd** read the data that controls their operation from a configuration file, you must provide iptables with a series of commands that build a set of packet filtering rules that are kept in the kernel.

Saving rules You can save and reload iptables rules as explained on page 847. Run iptables with the **–L** option to display the packet filtering rules the kernel is using. You can put a command to load iptables rules in **/etc/rc.local**. Or, if you want to start iptables earlier in the boot process, you can write a simple init script, put it in **/etc/init.d**, and use sysv-rc-conf (page 424) to tell **init** when to run it.

Resetting iptables If you encounter problems related to the firewall rules, you can return the packet processing rules in the kernel to their default state without rebooting by giving the following commands:

```
$ sudo iptables --flush && iptables --delete-chain
```

These commands flush all chains and delete any user-defined chains, leaving the system without a firewall.

ANATOMY OF AN iptables COMMAND

Command line   This section lists the components of an iptables command line that follow the name of the utility, iptables. Except as noted, the iptables utility is not sensitive to the positions of arguments on the command line. The examples in this chapter reflect a generally accepted syntax that allows commands to be easily read, understood, and maintained. Not all commands have all components.

Many tokens on an iptables command line have two forms: a short form, consisting of a single letter preceded by a single hyphen, and a long form, consisting of a word preceded by two hyphens. Most scripts use the short forms for brevity; lines using the long forms can get unwieldy. The following iptables command lines are equivalent and are used as examples in this section:

```
$ sudo iptables --append FORWARD --in-interface eth1 --out-interface eth0 --jump ACCEPT
$ sudo iptables -A FORWARD -i eth1 -o eth0 -j ACCEPT
```

Table   Specifies the name of the table the command operates on: Filter, NAT, or Mangle. You can specify a table name in any iptables command. When you do not specify a table name, the command operates on the Filter table. Most examples in this chapter do not specify table names and, therefore, work on the Filter table. Specify a table as **–t** *tablename* or **––table** *tablename*.

Command   Tells iptables what to do with the rest of the command line—for example, add or delete a rule, display rules, or add a chain. The example commands, **–A** and **––append**, append the rule specified by the command line to the specified table (defaults to Filter table) and chain. See page 841 for a list of commands.

Chain   Specifies the name of the chain that this rule belongs to or that this command works on. The chain is INPUT, OUTPUT, FORWARD, PREROUTING, POSTROUTING, or the name of a user-defined chain. Specify a chain by putting the name of the chain on the command line without any preceding hyphens. The examples at the beginning of this section work with the FORWARD chain.

Match criteria   There are two kinds of match criteria: *packet match* criteria, which match a network packet, and *rule match* criteria, which match an existing rule.

Packet match criteria/rule specifications   Packet match criteria identify network packets and implement rules that take action on packets that match the criteria. The combination of packet match criteria and an action is called a *rule specification*. Rule specifications form the basis for packet filtering. The first example at the beginning of this section uses the **––in-interface eth1 ––out-interface eth0** rule match criteria. The second example uses the short form of the same criteria: **–i eth1 –o eth0**. Both of these rules forward packets that come in on device **eth1** and go out on device **eth0**.

Rule match criteria   Rule match criteria identify existing rules. An iptables command can modify, remove, or position a new rule adjacent to a rule specified by a rule match criterion. There are two ways to identify an existing rule: You can use the same rule specification that was used to create the rule or you can use the rule's ordinal number, called a *rule number*. Rule numbers begin with 1, signifying the first rule in a chain, and can be displayed with **iptables –L** (or **––line-numbers**). The first command below deletes the rule listed at the beginning of this section; the second command replaces rule number 3 in the INPUT chain with a rule that rejects all packets from IP address 192.168.0.10:

```
$ sudo iptables --delete -A FORWARD -i eth1 -o eth0 -j ACCEPT
$ sudo iptables -R INPUT 3 --source 192.168.0.10 --jump REJECT
```

A jump or target specifies what action the kernel takes on packets that match all match criteria for a rule. Specify a jump or target as **–j** *target* or **––jump** *target*. The examples at the beginning of this section specify the ACCEPT target using the following commands: **––jump ACCEPT** and **–j ACCEPT**.

Jumps   A jump transfers control to a different chain within the same table. The following command adds (**––append**) a rule to the INPUT chain that transfers packets that use the TCP protocol (**––protocol tcp**) to a user-defined chain named **tcp_rules** (**––jump tcp_rules**):

```
$ sudo iptables --append INPUT --protocol tcp --jump tcp_rules
```

When the packet finishes traversing the **tcp_rules** chain, assuming it has not been dropped or rejected, it continues traversing the INPUT chain from the rule following the one it jumped from.

Targets   A target specifies an action the kernel takes on the packet; the simplest actions are ACCEPT, DROP, and REJECT. The following command adds a rule to the FORWARD chain that rejects packets coming from the FTP port (**/etc/services**, the file iptables consults to determine which port to use, shows that FTP uses port 21):

```
$ sudo iptables --append FORWARD --sport ftp --jump REJECT
```

Some targets, such as LOG, are *nonterminating*: Control passes to the next rule after the target is executed. See page 846 for information on how to use targets.

BUILDING A SET OF RULES USING iptables

To specify a table, it is common practice to put the table declaration on the command line immediately following **iptables**. For example, the following command flushes (deletes all the rules from) the NAT table:

```
$ sudo iptables -t NAT -F
```

COMMANDS

Following is a list of iptables commands:

––append   **–A** Adds rule(s) specified by *rule-specifications* to the end of *chain*. When a packet matches all of the *rule-specifications, target* processes it.

iptables –A chain rule-specifications ––jump target

--delete –D Removes one or more rules from *chain*, as specified by the *rule-numbers* or *rule-specifications*.

> *iptables –D chain rule-numbers | rule-specifications*

--insert –I Adds rule(s) specified by *rule-specifications* and *target* to the location in *chain* specified by *rule-number*. If you do not specify *rule-number,* it defaults to 1, the head of the chain.

> *iptables –I chain rule-number rule-specifications ––jump target*

--replace –R Replaces rule number *rule-number* in *chain* with *rule-specification* and *target*. The command fails if *rule-number* or *rule-specification* resolves to more than one address.

> *iptables –R chain rule-number rule-specification ––jump target*

--list –L Displays the rules in *chain*. Omit *chain* to display the rules for all chains. Use **––line-numbers** to display rule numbers or select other display criteria from the list on page 843.

> *iptables –L [chain] display-criteria*

--flush –F Deletes all rules from *chain*. Omit *chain* to delete all rules from all chains.

> *iptables –F [chain]*

--zero –Z Changes to zero the value of all packet and byte counters in *chain* or in all chains when you do not specify *chain*. Use with –L to display the counters before clearing them.

> *iptables –Z [–L] [chain]*

--delete-chain –X Removes the user-defined chain named *chain*. If you do not specify *chain*, removes all user-defined chains. You cannot delete a chain that a target points to.

> *iptables –X chain*

--policy –P Sets the default target or policy *builtin-target* for the builtin chain *builtin-chain*. This policy is applied to packets that do not match any rule in the chain. If a chain does not have a policy, unmatched packets are ACCEPTed.

> *iptables –P builtin-chain builtin-target*

--rename-chain –E Changes the name of the chain *old* to *new*.

> *iptables –E old new*

--help –h Displays a summary of the iptables command syntax.

> *iptables –h*

Follow a match extension protocol with **–h** to display options you can use with that protocol. For more information refer to "Help with extensions" on page 844.

PACKET MATCH CRITERIA

The following criteria match network packets. When you precede a criterion with an exclamation point (!), the rule matches packets that do not match the criterion.

--protocol [!] *proto*

–p   Matches if the packet uses the *proto* protocol. This criterion is a match extension (below).

--source [!] *address[/mask]*

–s or **--src**   Matches if the packet came from *address*. The *address* can be a name or IP address. See page 445 for formats of the optional *mask* (only with an IP address).

--destination [!] *address[/mask]*

–d or **--dst**   Matches if the packet is going to *address*. The *address* can be a name or IP address. See page 445 for formats of the optional *mask* (only with an IP address).

--in-interface [!] *iface[+]*

–i   For the INPUT, FORWARD, and PREROUTING chains, matches if *iface* is the name of the interface the packet was received from. Append a plus sign (+) to *iface* to match any interface whose name begins with *iface*. When you do not specify **in-interface**, the rule matches packets coming from any interface.

--out-interface [!] *iface[+]*

–o   For the OUTPUT, FORWARD, and POSTROUTING chains, matches if *iface* is the interface the packet will be sent to. Append a plus sign (+) to *iface* to match any interface whose name begins with *iface*. When you do not specify **out-interface**, the rule matches packets going to any interface.

[!] –fragment   **–f**   Matches the second and subsequent fragments of fragmented packets. Because these packets do not contain source or destination information, they do not match any other rules.

DISPLAY CRITERIA

The following criteria display information. All packets match these criteria.

--verbose   **–v**   Displays additional output.

--numeric   **–n**   Displays IP addresses and port numbers as numbers, not names.

--exact   **–x**   Use with **–L** to display exact packet and byte counts instead of rounded values.

--line-numbers   Displays line numbers when listing rules. These line numbers are also the rule numbers that you can use in rule match criteria (page 840).

MATCH EXTENSIONS

Rule specification (packet match criteria) extensions, called *match extensions*, add matches based on protocols and state to the matches described previously. Each of the protocol extensions is kept in a module that must be loaded before that match extension can be used. The command that loads the module must appear in the same rule specification as, and to the left of, the command that uses the module. There are two types of match extensions: implicit and explicit.

IMPLICIT MATCH EXTENSIONS

Help with
extensions

Implicit extensions are loaded (somewhat) automatically when you use a --**protocol** command (described below). Each protocol has its own extensions. Follow the protocol with –**h** to display extensions you can use with that protocol. For example, the following command displays TCP extensions *at the end* of the Help output:

```
$ iptables -p tcp -h
...
TCP v1.3.6 options:
  --tcp-flags [!] mask comp      match when TCP flags & mask == comp
                                 (Flags: SYN ACK FIN RST URG PSH ALL NONE)
  [!] --syn                      match when only SYN flag set
                                 (equivalent to --tcp-flags SYN,RST,ACK SYN)
  --source-port [!] port[:port]
  --sport ...
                                 match source port(s)
  --destination-port [!] port[:port]
  --dport ...
                                 match destination port(s)
  --tcp-option [!] number        match if TCP option set
```

This section does not describe all extensions. Use –**h**, as in the preceding example, to display a complete list.

--**protocol** [!] *proto*

–**p** Loads the *proto* module and matches if the packet uses the *proto* protocol. The *proto* can be a name or number from **/etc/protocols**, including **tcp**, **udp**, and **icmp** (page 1113). Specifying **all** or **0** (zero) matches all protocols and is the same as not including this match in a rule.

The following criteria load the TCP module and match TCP protocol packets coming from port 22 (ssh packets):

```
--protocol tcp --source-port 22
```

The following command expands the preceding match to cause the kernel to drop all incoming ssh packets. This command uses **ssh**, which iptables looks up in **/etc/services**, in place of **22**:

```
$ sudo iptables --protocol tcp --source-port ssh --jump DROP
```

TCP

The extensions in this section are loaded when you specify --**protocol tcp**.

--**destination-port** [!] [*port*][:*port*]]

--**dport** Matches a destination port number or service name (see **/etc/services**). You can also specify a range of port numbers. Specifically, *:port* specifies ports 0 through *port*, and *port:* specifies ports *port* through 65535.

--source-port [!] [*port*][:*port*]]

--**sport**   Matches a source port number or service name (see **/etc/services**). You can also specify a range of port numbers. Specifically, *:port* specifies ports 0 through *port,* and *port:* specifies ports *port* through 65535.

[!] --**syn**   Matches packets with the SYN bit set and the ACK and FIN bits cleared. This match extension is shorthand for --**tcp-flags SYN,RST,ACK SYN**.

--**tcp-flags** [!] *mask comp*

Defines which TCP flag settings constitute a match. Valid flags are SYN, ACK, FIN, RST, URG, PSH, ALL, and NONE. The *mask* is a comma-separated list of flags to be examined; *comp* is a comma-separated subset of *mask* that specifies the flags that must be set for a match to occur. Flags not specified in *mask* must be unset.

--**tcp-option** [!] *n*   Matches a TCP option with a decimal value of *n*.

UDP

When you specify --**protocol udp**, you can specify a source and/or destination port in the same manner as described under "TCP" on the preceding page.

ICMP

The extension in this section is loaded when you specify --**protocol icmp**. *ICMP* (page 1113) packets carry messages only.

--**icmp-type** [!] *name*

Matches when the packet is an ICMP packet of type *name*. The *name* can be a numeric ICMP type or one of the names returned by

```
$ iptables -p icmp -h
```

EXPLICIT MATCH EXTENSIONS

Explicit match extensions differ from implicit match extensions in that you must use a **–m** or --**match** option to specify a module before you can use the extension. Many explicit match extension modules are available; this section covers **state**, one of the most important.

STATE

The **state** extension matches criteria based on the state of the connection the packet is part of (page 838).

--**state** *state*   Matches a packet whose state is defined by *state*, a comma-separated list of states from the following list:

- **ESTABLISHED**—Any packet, within a specific connection, following the exchange of packets in both directions for that connection.

- **INVALID**—A stateless or unidentifiable packet.

- **NEW**—The first packet within a specific connection, typically a SYN packet.

- **RELATED**—Any packets exchanged in a connection spawned from an ESTABLISHED connection. For example, an FTP data connection might be related to the FTP control connection. (You need the **ip_conntrack_ftp** module for FTP connection tracking.)

The following command loads the **state** extension and establishes a rule that matches and drops both invalid packets and packets from new connections:

```
$ sudo iptables --match state --state INVALID,NEW --jump DROP
```

TARGETS

All targets are built in; there are no user-defined targets. This section lists some of the targets available with iptables. Applicable target options are listed following each target.

ACCEPT   Continues processing the packet.

DNAT   **Destination Network Address Translation**   Rewrites the destination address of the packet (page 837).

--to-destination *ip[-ip][:port-port]*
Same as SNAT with **to-source**, except that it changes the destination addresses of packets to the specified addresses and ports and is valid only in the PREROUTING or OUTPUT chains of the NAT table and any user-defined chains called from those chains. The following command adds to the PREROUTING chain of the NAT table a rule that changes the destination in the headers of TCP packets with a destination of 66.187.232.50 to 192.168.0.10:

```
$ sudo iptables -t NAT -A PREROUTING -p tcp -d 66.187.232.50 -j DNAT --to-destination 192.168.0.10
```

DROP   Ends the packet's life without notice.

LOG   Turns on logging for the packet being processed. The kernel uses **syslogd** (page 608) to process output generated by this target. LOG is a nonterminating target, so processing continues with the next rule. Use two rules to LOG packets that you REJECT or DROP, one each with the targets LOG and REJECT or DROP, with the same matching criteria.

--log-level *n*   Specifies logging level *n* as per **syslog.conf** (page 608).

--log-prefix *string*
Prefixes log entries with *string*, which can be a maximum of 14 characters long.

--log-tcp-options   Logs options from the TCP packet header.

--log-ip-options   Logs options from the IP packet header.

MASQUERADE   Similar to SNAT with **--to-source**, except that it grabs the IP information from the interface on the specified port. For use on systems with dynamically assigned IP addresses, such as those using DHCP, including most dial-up lines. Valid only in rules in the POSTROUTING chain of the NAT table.

––to-ports *port[-port]*
Specifies the port for the interface you want to masquerade. Forgets connections when the interface goes down, as is appropriate for dial-up lines. You must specify the TCP or UDP protocol (**––protocol tcp** or **udp**) with this target.

REJECT Similar to DROP, except that it notifies the sending system that the packet was blocked.

––reject-with *type* Returns the error *type* to the originating system. The *type* can be any of the following, all of which return the appropriate *ICMP* (page 1113) error: **icmp-net-unreachable, icmp-host-unreachable, icmp-port-unreachable, icmp-proto-unreachable, icmp-net-prohibited,** or **icmp-host-prohibited.** You can specify *type* as **echo-reply** from rules that require an ICMP ping (page 377) packet to return a ping reply. You can specify **tcp-reset** from rules in or called from the INPUT chain to return a TCP RST packet. This parameter is valid in the INPUT, FORWARD, and OUTPUT chains and user-defined chains called from these chains.

RETURN Stops traversing this chain and returns the packet to the calling chain.

SNAT **Source Network Address Translation** Rewrites the source address of the packet. Appropriate for hosts on a LAN that share an Internet connection.

––to-source *ip[-ip][:port-port]*
Alters the source IP address of an outbound packet, and the source IP addresses of all future packets in this connection, to *ip*. Skips additional rules, if any exist. Returning packets are automatically de-SNATed so they return to the originating host. Valid only in the POSTROUTING chain of the NAT table.

When you specify a range of IP addresses (*ip-ip*) or use multiple **to-source** targets, iptables assigns the addresses in a round-robin fashion, cycling through the addresses, one for each new connection.

When the rule specifies the TCP or UDP protocol (**–p tcp** or **–p udp**), you can specify a range of ports. When you do not specify a range of ports, the rule matches all ports. Every connection on a NATed subnet must have a unique IP address and port combination. If two systems on a NATed subnet try to use the same port, the kernel maps one of the ports to another (unused) port. Ports less than 512 are mapped to other ports less than 512, ports from 512 to 1024 are mapped to other ports from 512 to 1024, and ports above 1024 are mapped to other ports above 1024.

COPYING RULES TO AND FROM THE KERNEL

The iptables-save utility copies packet filtering rules from the kernel to standard output so you can save them in a file. The iptables-restore utility copies rules from standard input, as written by iptables-save, to the kernel. Sample output from iptables-save appears on the next page.

```
$ sudo iptables-save
# Generated by iptables-save v1.4.0 on Sat Jul 12 21:13:29 2008
*mangle
:PREROUTING ACCEPT [1720:889840]
:INPUT ACCEPT [1720:889840]
:FORWARD ACCEPT [0:0]
:OUTPUT ACCEPT [1391:111855]
:POSTROUTING ACCEPT [1391:111855]
COMMIT
# Completed on Sat Jul 12 21:13:29 2008
# Generated by iptables-save v1.3.6 on Sat Jul 12 21:13:29 2008
*filter
:INPUT DROP [1:44]
:FORWARD DROP [0:0]
:OUTPUT DROP [0:0]
:INBOUND - [0:0]
:LOG_FILTER - [0:0]
:LSI - [0:0]
:LSO - [0:0]
:OUTBOUND - [0:0]
-A INPUT -s 198.144.192.2 -p tcp -m tcp ! --tcp-flags FIN,SYN,RST,ACK SYN -j ACCEPT
-A INPUT -s 198.144.192.2 -p udp -j ACCEPT
-A INPUT -s 209.157.152.23 -p tcp -m tcp ! --tcp-flags FIN,SYN,RST,ACK SYN -j ACCEPT
-A INPUT -s 209.157.152.23 -p udp -j ACCEPT
-A INPUT -i lo -j ACCEPT
...
```

Most lines that iptables-save writes are iptables command lines without the **iptables** at the beginning. Lines that begin with a pound sign (#) are comments. Lines that begin with an asterisk (✽) are names of tables that the following commands work on; the first few commands in the preceding example work on the Mangle table, the rest work on the Filter table. The COMMIT line must appear at the end of all commands for a table; it executes the preceding commands. Lines that begin with colons specify chains in the following format:

> :*chain policy [packets:bytes]*

where *chain* is the name of the chain, *policy* is the policy (default target) for the chain, and *packets* and *bytes* are the packet and byte counters, respectively. The square brackets must appear in the line; they do not indicate optional parameters. Visit www.faqs.org/docs/iptables/iptables-save.html for more information.

SHARING AN INTERNET CONNECTION USING NAT

Many scripts that set up Internet connection sharing using iptables are available on the Internet. Each of these scripts boils down to the same few basic iptables commands, albeit with minor differences. This section discusses those few statements to explain how a connection can be shared. You can use the statements presented in this section or refer to the *Linux IP Masquerade HOWTO* for complete scripts.

The tldp.org/HOWTO/IP-Masquerade-HOWTO/firewall-examples.html Web page holds the simplest of these scripts.

There are two ways you can share a single connection to the Internet (one IP address), both of which involve setting up NAT to alter addresses in packets and then forward them. The first allows clients (browsers, mail readers, and so on) on several systems on a LAN to share a single IP address to connect to servers on the Internet. The second allows servers (mail, Web, FTP, and so on) on different systems on a LAN to provide their services over a single connection to the Internet. You can use iptables to set up one or both of these configurations. In both cases, you need to set up a system that is a router: It must have two network connections—one connected to the Internet and the other to the LAN.

For optimal security, use a dedicated system as a router. Because data transmission over a connection to the Internet—even over a broadband connection—is relatively slow, using a slower, older system as a router does not generally slow down a LAN. This setup also offers some defense against intrusion from the Internet. A workstation on the LAN can function as a router as well, but this setup means that you maintain data on a system that is directly connected to the Internet. The following sections discuss the security of each setup.

The examples in this section assume that the device named **eth0** connects to the Internet on 10.255.255.255 and that **eth1** connects to the LAN on 192.168.0.1. Substitute the devices and IP addresses that the local systems use. If you use a modem to connect to the Internet, you need to substitute **ppp0** (or another device) for **eth0** in the examples.

For the examples in this section to work, you must turn on IP forwarding. First give the following command and make sure everything is working:

```
$ sudo sysctl -w net.ipv4.conf.default.forwarding=1
net.ipv4.conf.default.forwarding = 1
```

If you want to forward IPv6 packets, give this command instead:

```
$ sudo sysctl -w net.ipv6.conf.default.forwarding=1
net.ipv6.conf.default.forwarding = 1
```

Once you know that iptables is working correctly, follow the instructions in **/etc/sysctl.conf** and uncomment one or both of the following assignments to make the kernel always perform IP forwarding for IPv4 and/or IPv6:

```
# Uncomment the next line to enable packet forwarding for IPv4
#net.ipv4.conf.default.forwarding=1

# Uncomment the next line to enable packet forwarding for IPv6
#net.ipv6.conf.default.forwarding=1
```

After making this change, give the command **/sbin/sysctl –p** to apply the change and to make sure that there are no typographical errors in the configuration file.

CONNECTING SEVERAL CLIENTS TO A SINGLE INTERNET CONNECTION

Configuring the kernel of the router system to allow clients on multiple local systems on the LAN to connect to the Internet requires you to set up *IP masquerading,* or *SNAT* (source NAT). IP masquerading translates the source and destination addresses in the headers of network packets that originate on local systems and the packets that remote servers send in response to those packets. These packets are part of connections that originate on a local system. The example in this section does nothing to packets that are part of connections that originate on the remote systems (on the Internet): These packets cannot get past the router system, which provides some degree of security.

The point of rewriting the packet headers is to allow systems with different local IP addresses to share a single IP address on the Internet. The router system translates the source or origin address of packets from the local systems to that of the Internet connection, so that all packets passing from the router to the Internet appear to come from a single system—10.255.255.255 in the example. All packets sent in response by remote systems on the Internet to the router system have the address of the Internet connection—10.255.255.255 in the example—as their destination address. The router system remembers each connection and alters the destination address of each response packet to that of the local, originating system.

The router system is established by four iptables commands, one of which sets up a log of masqueraded connections. The first command puts the first rule in the FORWARD chain of the Filter (default) table (**–A FORWARD**):

```
$ sudo iptables -A FORWARD -i eth0 -o eth1 -m state --state ESTABLISHED,RELATED -j ACCEPT
```

To match this rule, a packet must be

1. Received on **eth0** (coming in from the Internet): **–i eth0**.

2. Going to be sent out on **eth1** (going out to the LAN): **–o eth1**.

3. Part of an established connection or a connection that is related to an established connection: **––state ESTABLISHED,RELATED**.

The kernel accepts (**–j ACCEPT**) packets that meet these three criteria. Accepted packets pass to the next appropriate chain or table. Packets from the Internet that attempt to create a new connection are not matched and, therefore, are not accepted by this rule. Packets that are not accepted pass to the next rule in the FORWARD chain.

The second command puts the second rule in the FORWARD chain of the Filter table:

```
$ sudo iptables -A FORWARD -i eth1 -o eth0 -j ACCEPT
```

To match this rule, a packet must be

1. Received on **eth1** (coming in from the LAN): **–i eth1**.

2. Going to be sent out on **eth0** (going out to the Internet): **–o eth0**.

The kernel accepts packets that meet these two criteria, which means all packets that originate locally and are going to the Internet are accepted. Accepted packets pass to the next appropriate chain/table; packets that are not accepted pass to the next rule in the FORWARD chain.

The third command puts the third rule in the FORWARD chain of the Filter table:

```
$ sudo iptables -A FORWARD -j LOG
```

Because this rule has no match criteria, it acts on all packets it processes. This rule's action is to log packets—that is, it logs packets from the Internet that attempt to create a new connection.

Packets that reach the end of the FORWARD chain of the Filter table are done with the rules set up by iptables and are handled by the local TCP stack. Packets from the Internet that attempt to create a new connection on the router system are accepted or returned, depending on whether the service they are trying to connect to is available on the router system.

The fourth command puts the first rule in the POSTROUTING chain of the NAT table. Only packets that are establishing a new connection are passed to the NAT table. Once a connection has been set up for SNAT or MASQUERADE, the headers on all subsequent ESTABLISHED and RELATED packets are altered the same way as the header of the first packet. Packets sent in response to these packets automatically have their headers adjusted so that they return to the originating local system.

```
$ sudo iptables -t NAT -A POSTROUTING -o eth0 -j MASQUERADE
```

To match this rule, a packet must be

1. Establishing a new connection (otherwise it would not have come to the NAT table).

2. Going to be sent out on **eth0** (going out to the Internet): **–o eth0**.

The kernel MASQUERADEs all packets that meet these criteria. In other words, all locally originating packets that are establishing new connections have their source address changed to the address that is associated with **eth0** (10.255.255.255 in the example).

The following example shows all four commands together:

```
$ sudo iptables -A FORWARD -i eth0 -o eth1 -m state --state ESTABLISHED,RELATED -j ACCEPT
$ sudo iptables -A FORWARD -i eth1 -o eth0 -j ACCEPT
$ sudo iptables -A FORWARD -j LOG
$ sudo iptables -t NAT -A POSTROUTING -o eth0 -j MASQUERADE
```

See page 839 for instructions on how to save these rules so that the firewall comes up each time the system boots. To limit the local systems that can connect to the Internet, you can add a –s (source) match criterion to the last command:

```
$ sudo iptables -t NAT -A POSTROUTING -o eth0 -s 192.168.0.0-192.168.0.32 -j MASQUERADE
```

In the preceding command, **–s 192.168.0.0-192.168.0.32** causes only packets from an IP address in the specified range to be MASQUERADEd.

CONNECTING SEVERAL SERVERS TO A SINGLE INTERNET CONNECTION

DNAT (destination NAT) can set up rules that allow clients from the Internet to send packets to servers on the LAN. This example sets up an SMTP mail server on 192.168.1.33 and an Apache (Web) server on 192.168.1.34. Both protocols use TCP. SMTP uses port 25 and Apache uses port 80, so the rules match TCP packets with destination ports of 25 and 80. The example assumes that the mail server does not make outgoing connections and uses another server on the LAN for DNS and mail relaying. Both commands put rules in the PREROUTING chain of the NAT table (**–A PREROUTING –t NAT**):

```
$ sudo iptables -A PREROUTING -t NAT -p tcp --dport 25 --to-source 192.168.0.33:25 -j DNAT
$ sudo iptables -A PREROUTING -t NAT -p tcp --dport 80 --to-source 192.168.0.34:80 -j DNAT
```

To match these rules, the packet must use the TCP protocol (**–p tcp**) and have a destination port of either 25 (first rule, **––dport 25**) or 80 (second rule, **––dport 80**).

The **––to-source** is a target specific to the PREROUTING and OUTPUT chains of the NAT table; it alters the destination address and port of matched packets as specified. As with MASQUERADE and SNAT, subsequent packets in the same and related connections are altered the same way.

The fact that the servers cannot originate connections means that neither server can be exploited to participate in a *DDoS attack* (page 1104) on systems on the Internet, nor can they send private data from the local system back to a malicious user's system.

CHAPTER SUMMARY

A firewall, such as iptables or firestarter, is designed to prevent unauthorized access to a system or network. The firestarter utility is a sophisticated, graphical tool for building and maintaining a firewall. It can protect just the single system it runs on or it can protect the system it runs on plus other systems on a LAN that connect to the Internet through the system running firestarter.

An iptables command sets up or maintains in the kernel rules that control the flow of network packets; rules are stored in chains. Each rule includes a criteria part and an action part, called a target. When the criteria part matches a network packet, the kernel applies the action from the rule to the packet.

Chains are collected in three tables: Filter, NAT, and Mangle. Filter (the default table) DROPs or ACCEPTs packets based on their content. NAT (the Network Address Translation table) translates the source or destination field of packets. Mangle is used exclusively to alter the TOS (type of service), TTL (time to live), and MARK fields in a packet. The connection tracking machine, which is handled by the **conntrack** module, defines rules that match criteria based on the state of the connection a packet is part of.

EXERCISES

1. How would you remove all iptables rules and chains?

2. What is firestarter? How is it related to iptables?

3. What is the easiest way to set up a rule using firestarter?

4. How would you list all current iptables rules?

5. How is configuring iptables different from configuring most Linux services?

6. Define an iptables rule that will reject incoming connections on the TELNET port.

7. What does NAT stand for? What does the NAT table do?

ADVANCED EXERCISES

8. What does the **conntrack** module do?

9. What do rule match criteria do? What are they used for?

10. What do packet match criteria do? What are they used for?

11. Which utilities copy packet filtering rules to and from the kernel? How do they work?

12. Define a rule that will silently block incoming SMTP connections from **spmr.com**.

26

APACHE: SETTING UP A WEB SERVER

The World Wide Web (WWW or Web for short), is a collection of servers that hold material, called *content,* that Web browsers (or just browsers) can display. Each of the servers on the Web is connected to the Internet, a network of networks (an *internetwork*). Much of the content on the Web is coded in HTML (Hypertext Markup Language, page 1112). *Hypertext,* the links you click on a Web page, allows browsers to display and react to links that point to other Web pages on the Internet.

Apache is the most popular Web server on the Internet. It is both robust and extensible. The ease with which you can install, configure, and run it in the Linux environment makes it an obvious choice for publishing content on the World Wide Web. The Apache server and related projects are developed and maintained by the Apache Software Foundation (ASF), a not-for-profit corporation formed in June 1999. The ASF grew out of the Apache Group, which was established in 1995 to develop the Apache server.

This chapter starts by providing introductory information about Apache. Following this information is the JumpStart section, which describes the minimal steps needed to get Apache up and running. Next is "Filesystem Layout," which tells you where the various Apache files are located.

Configuration directives (referred to simply as directives) are a key part of Apache and are discussed starting on page 865. This section includes coverage of contexts and containers, two features/concepts that are critical to understanding Apache. The next section, which starts on page 888, explains the main Apache configuration file, **apache2.conf**, as distributed by Ubuntu. The final pages of the chapter cover virtual hosts, troubleshooting, and modules you can use with Apache, including CGI and SSL.

INTRODUCTION

Apache is a server that responds to requests from Web browsers, or *clients*, such as Firefox, Netscape, lynx, and Internet Explorer. When you enter the address of a Web page (a *URI*, page 1139) in a Web browser's location bar, the browser sends a request over the Internet to the (Apache) server at that address. In response, the server sends (serves) the requested content back to the browser. The browser then displays or plays the content, which might be a song, picture, video clip, or other information.

Content   Aside from add-on modules that can interact with the content, Apache looks only at the type of data it is sending so that it can specify the correct *MIME* (page 1120) type; otherwise it remains oblivious to the content itself. Server administration and content creation are two different aspects of bringing up a Web site. This chapter concentrates on setting up and running an Apache server; it spends little time discussing content creation.

Modules   Apache, like the Linux kernel, uses external modules to increase load-time flexibility and allow parts of its code to be recompiled without recompiling the whole program. Rather than being part of the Apache binary, modules are stored as separate files that can be loaded when Apache is started.

Apache uses external modules, called dynamic shared objects (DSOs), for basic and advanced functions; there is not much to Apache without these modules. Apache also uses modules to extend its functionality. For example, modules can process scripts written in Perl, PHP, Python, and other languages; use several different methods to authenticate users; facilitate publishing content; and process nontextual content, such as audio. The list of modules written by the ASF and third-party developers is constantly growing. For more information refer to "Modules" on page 897.

Setup   The Debian/Ubuntu Apache team provides one of the easiest-to-use Apache setups of any distribution. Most packages that provide a Web interface and that depend on Apache run as installed; typically you do not need to modify the configuration files.

For example, installing **phpmyadmin** (sourceforge.net/projects/phpmyadmin) makes it available to a browser as **/phpmyadmin**.

This section describes the packages you need to install and provides references for the programs covered in this chapter. The "Notes" section introduces terminology and other topics that may help you make better sense of this chapter. "JumpStart I" (page 859) gets Apache up and running as quickly as possible.

MORE INFORMATION

Local *Apache HTTP Server Version 2.2 Documentation*: With Apache running and **apache2-doc** installed, point a browser at *server*/**manual**, where *server* is **localhost** or the name or IP address of the Apache server.
Apache directives: *server*/**manual/mod/directives.html**
SSI directives: *server*/**manual/howto/ssi.html**

Web   Apache documentation: httpd.apache.org/docs/2.2
Apache directives: httpd.apache.org/docs/2.2/mod/directives.html
Apache Software Foundation (newsletters, mailing lists, projects, module registry, and more): www.apache.org
webalizer: www.mrunix.net/webalizer
awstats: awstats.sourceforge.net
libapache2-mod-perl2: perl.apache.org (**mod_perl**)
libapache2-mod-php5: www.php.net (**mod_php**)
libapache2-mod-python: www.modpython.org (**mod_python**)
SSL: www.modssl.org (**mod_ssl**)
MRTG: mrtg.hdl.com/mrtg
SNMP: net-snmp.sourceforge.net
SSI directives: httpd.apache.org/docs/2.2/howto/ssi.html

NOTES

Terms: Apache and **apache2**   Apache is the name of a server that serves HTTP and other content. The name of the Apache 2 daemon is **apache2**. This chapter uses Apache and **apache2** interchangeably.

Terms: server and process   An Apache *server* is the same thing as an Apache *process*. An Apache child process exists to handle incoming client requests; hence it is referred to as a server.

Firewall   An Apache server normally uses TCP port 80; a secure server uses TCP port 443. If the Apache server system is running or behind a firewall, you must open one or both of these ports. To get started, open port 80 (HTTP). Using firestarter (page 824), open these ports by setting a policy that allows service for HTTP and/or HTTPS.

Running with **root** privileges   Because Apache serves content on privileged ports, you must start it running with **root** privileges. For security reasons, Ubuntu sets up Apache to spawn processes that run as the user and group **www-data**.

Locale   The **apache2** daemon starts using the C locale by default. You can modify this behavior—for example, to use the configured system locale—by setting the LANG variable (in the line that starts with **ENV="env -i LANG=C** ...) in the **/etc/init.d/apache2** file.

Document root   The root of the directory hierarchy that Apache serves content from is called the *document root* and is controlled by the DocumentRoot directive (page 869). This directive defines a directory on the server that maps to **/**. This directory appears to users who are browsing a Web site as the root directory. As distributed by Ubuntu, the document root is **/var/www**.

Modifying content   With the default Ubuntu configuration of Apache, only a user working with **root** privileges (using sudo) can add or modify content in **/var/www**. To avoid having people work as **root** when they are manipulating content, create a group (**webwork**, for example), put people who need to work with Web content in this group, and make the directory hierarchy starting at **/var/www** (or another document root) writable by that group. In addition, if you give the directory hierarchy setgid permission, all new files created within this hierarchy will belong to the group, which facilitates sharing files. The first three commands below add the new group, change the mode of the document root to setgid, and change the group that the document root belongs to. The last command adds *username* to the **webwork** group; you must repeat this command for each user you want to add to the group.

```
$ sudo addgroup webwork
$ sudo chmod g+s /var/www
$ sudo chown :webwork /var/www

$ sudo usermod -aG webwork username
```

See page 580 for more information about working with groups.

Versions   Ubuntu runs Apache version 2.2.

RUNNING A WEB SERVER (APACHE)

This section explains how to install, test, and configure a basic Web server.

PREREQUISITES

Minimal installation   Install the following package:

• apache2

apache2 init script   When you install the **apache2** package, the **dpkg postinst** script starts the **apache2** daemon. After you configure Apache, call the **apache2** init script to restart the **apache2** daemon:

```
$ sudo /etc/init.d/apache2 restart
```

After changing the Apache configuration on an active server, use **reload** in place of **restart** to reload Apache configuration files without disturbing clients connected to the server.

Optional packages   The **mod_ssl** package is installed as part of the **apache2** package—you do not need to install it separately. You may want to install the following optional packages:

- **apache2-doc**—The Apache manual

- **webalizer**—Web server log analyzer (page 904)

- **awstats**—Web server log analyzer

- **libapache2-mod-perl2**—Embedded Perl scripting language (**mod_perl**)

- **libapache2-mod-python**—Metapackage that installs the embedded Python scripting language (**mod_python**)

- **libapache2-mod-php5**—Embedded PHP scripting language, including IMAP and LDAP support (**mod_php**)

- **mrtg**—MRTG traffic monitor (page 904)

The apache2ctl **utility and restarting Apache gracefully**

tip The **apache2** init script calls apache2ctl to start and stop Apache. The **reload** argument calls this utility with an argument of **graceful**, which does not disturb clients that are connected to the server. The **restart** and **force-reload** arguments call it with arguments of **stop** and then **start**; this pair of commands shuts down the server completely before restarting it.

JUMPSTART: GETTING APACHE UP AND RUNNING

To get Apache up and running, modify the **/etc/apache2/sites-available/default** configuration file as described in this section. "Directives I: Directives You May Want to Modify as You Get Started" on page 866 explains more about this file and explores other changes you may want to make to it.

MODIFYING THE CONFIGURATION FILES

Apache runs as installed, but it is a good idea to add the three lines described in this section to the **/etc/apache2/sites-available/default** configuration file. If you do not add these lines, Apache will assign values that may not work for you. After you modify this file, you must restart Apache (page 858).

The ServerName line establishes a name for the server. Add one of the following lines to **/etc/apache2/sites-available/default** to set the name of the server to the domain name of the server or, if you do not have a domain name, to the IP address of the server. Add the line just below the ServerAdmin line near the top of the file.

>   *ServerName* **example.com**

or

>   *ServerName* **IP_address**

where **example.com** is the domain name of the server and **IP_address** is the IP address of the server. If you are not connected to a network, you can use the **localhost** address, 127.0.0.1, so you can start the server and experiment with it. See page 890 for more information on the ServerName directive.

When a client has trouble getting information from a server, the server typically displays an error page that identifies the problem. For example, when Apache cannot find a requested page, it displays a page that says **Error 404: Not Found**. Each error page can include a **mailto:** link that the user can click to send mail to the server's administrator. The ServerSignature directive can specify that you want an email link on error pages. This link appears as the domain name the user called in the Browser. The ServerAdmin directive specifies the email address that the server sends mail to when a user clicks the link on an error page. Add these two lines to the file named **default**.

HARDY   Add each directive following the location at which the same directive is already defined (ServerSignature is near the end of the file).

INTREPID   Add both directives following the ServerAdmin directive (ServerSignature is not included).

> *ServerAdmin email_address*
>
> *ServerSignature EMail*

where *email_address* is the email address of the person who needs to know when people are having trouble using the server. Make sure that someone checks this email account frequently. But see the tip "ServerAdmin attracts spam" on page 868.

It can make system administration much easier if you use a role alias (for example, **webmaster@example.com**) instead of a specific username (e.g., **max@example.com**) as an *email_address*. See the discussion of email aliases on page 686.

After making the changes to the file named **default**, restart **apache2** as explained on page 858.

TESTING APACHE

Once you restart the **apache2** daemon, you can confirm that Apache is working correctly by pointing a browser on the local (server) system to **http://localhost/**. From a remote system, point a browser to **http://** followed by the ServerName you specified in the previous section. If you are displaying a page from a system other than the local one, the local system must know how to resolve the domain name you enter (e.g., by using DNS or the **/etc/hosts** file). For example, you might use either of these URI formats: **http://192.168.0.16** or **http://example.org**.

When you point a browser at a directory that holds a file named **index.html**, Apache causes the browser to display the contents of that file (otherwise it displays a directory listing). In response to your request, the browser should display the page stored at **/var/www/index.html** on the server. In this case, the browser should display **It works!**

If the server is behind a firewall, open TCP port 80 (page 857). If you are having problems getting Apache to work, see "Troubleshooting" on page 896.

PUTTING YOUR CONTENT IN PLACE

Place the content you want Apache to serve in **/var/www**. As shown previously, Apache automatically displays the file named **index.html** in this directory. Give the following command to create such a page, replacing the default page:

```
$ sudo tee /var/www/index.html
<html><body><p>This is <i>my</i> test page.</p></body></html>
<html><body><p>This is <i>my</i> test page.</p></body></html>
CONTROL-D
```

The tee utility (page 240) copies standard input (page 229) to the file you give as its argument and to standard output (page 229). Because of this redirection, tee repeats each line you type after you press RETURN. After you create this file, either refresh the page on the browser (if it is still running) or start it again and point it at the server. The browser should display the page you just created.

CONFIGURING APACHE

This section describes configuration tools you can use to make your job easier. It also tells you where you can find many of the files you may need to work with as you set up and modify an Apache server. Most of the configuration files are in the **/etc/apache2** hierarchy.

CONFIGURATION TOOLS

This section describes the utilities that manage some of the files in the **/etc/apache2** hierarchy. These utilities are part of the **apache2.2-common** package, which is installed as a dependency when you install **apache2**.

a2enmod and
a2dismod

The a2enmod (Apache 2 enable module) and a2dismod (Apache 2 disable module) utilities enable and disable an Apache module. The **/etc/apache2/mods-available** directory holds files that contain LoadModule directives (page 884) and options for modules that are installed on the local system. The **/etc/apache2/mods-enabled** directory holds symbolic links to the files in **mods-available**. Apache incorporates these links into its configuration files by using Include directives (next section). The **a2enmod** utility creates symbolic links in the **mods-enabled** directory from configuration files in the **mods-available** directory. It works on files whose basename is given as its argument.

```
$ sudo -i
# cd /etc/apache2
# ls mods-available/userdir*
mods-available/userdir.conf  mods-available/userdir.load
# ls mods-enabled/userdir*
ls: mods-enabled/userdir*: No such file or directory
# a2enmod userdir
Enabling module userdir.
Run '/etc/init.d/apache2 restart' to activate new configuration!
# ls mods-enabled/userdir*
mods-enabled/userdir.conf  mods-enabled/userdir.load
# exit
$
```

The **a2dismod** utility removes the symbolic links that **a2enmod** creates. You must reload Apache (page 858) after you give one or more of these commands before they will take effect.

The a2enmod and a2dismod utilities simplify Apache administration. Instead of adding or commenting out a LoadModule directive in the **httpd.conf** or **apache2.conf** file, you can use these programs to enable or disable a module. This setup enables APT or Synaptic, after it installs a package, to call a2enmod via a **dpkg postinst** script and then reload Apache so that the package is functional upon installation.

a2ensite and a2dissite   The a2ensite (Apache 2 enable site) and a2dissite (Apache 2 disable site) utilities enable and disable an Apache virtual host (page 893). These commands work similarly to the module commands described earlier. First you design a virtual host in a file in the **/etc/apache2/sites-available** directory. Then you call a2ensite with the name of the site as an argument to create a symbolic link in the **/etc/apache2/sites-enabled** directory. The a2dissite utility removes the symbolic link, disabling the virtual host.

INCLUDE DIRECTIVES

Under Ubuntu, the primary configuration file is **/etc/apache2/apache2.conf**. This file incorporates other files using Include directives (page 883):

```
$ grep '^Include' /etc/apache2/apache2.conf
Include /etc/apache2/mods-enabled/*.load
Include /etc/apache2/mods-enabled/*.conf
Include /etc/apache2/httpd.conf
Include /etc/apache2/ports.conf
Include /etc/apache2/conf.d/
Include /etc/apache2/sites-enabled/
```

apache2.conf   Typically, when you configure Apache, you do not make changes to **apache2.conf**; instead, you modify files that are specified in Include directives. You can also use the configuration tools described in the previous section. This setup allows updates to Apache to change **apache2.conf** without affecting the server.

When Apache reads its configuration files, if it finds more than one occurrence of the same directive, even in an Include file, it uses the value assigned by the last directive it encounters.

In the **apache2.conf** file, the Include directive for the **httpd.conf** file occurs after directives that set up the global environment, which includes various timeouts and limits as shown in Table 26-1. To change any of these directives, copy them to **httpd.conf** and make the changes there. You must change directives that appear after the Include httpd.conf directive in other included files as explained in this section.

The Include directive for **/etc/apache2/conf.d** (it includes all files in this directory) appears after the Include directive for **httpd.conf**, with only the Include directive for **/etc/apache2/ports.conf** separating them. This directory is a good place to put small configuration snippets, or break out parts of **httpd.conf** if it is growing too large.

Table 26-1   Directives that you can override in **httpd.conf**

AccessFileName	MaxRequestsPerChild
DefaultType	MaxSpareThreads
ErrorLog	MinSpareThreads
Group	PidFile
HostnameLookups	ServerRoot
KeepAlive	StartServers
KeepAliveTimeout	ThreadsPerChild
LockFile	Timeout
LogLevel	TypesConfig
MaxClients	User
MaxKeepAliveRequests	

Directives that control log formats, indexing options, MIME handling, and browser bug handling appear after the Include directive for **httpd.conf**, but before the Include directive for **/etc/apache2/sites-enabled**, which is the last line in **apache2.conf**. You can override these directives on a per-site basis by copying them to individual site files in the **sites-enabled** directory and modifying them there.

If you manage more than one Ubuntu Web server, it is nice to keep all the customized configuration code separate from the main configuration. That way you can use scp to copy the files to each new server. Or you can keep the custom code under a version control system and check it out to configure a new system. This technique is much easier than using diff to find out what you changed from system to system.

FILESYSTEM LAYOUT

This section lists the locations and uses of files you will work with to configure Apache and serve Web pages.

Binaries, scripts, and modules

The Apache server and related binary files are kept in several directories:

/usr/sbin/apache2—The Apache server (daemon).

/usr/sbin/apache2ctl—Starts and stops Apache. The **apache2** init script calls apachectl.

/usr/bin/htpasswd—Creates and maintains the password files used by the Apache authentication module (page 901).

/usr/sbin/rotatelogs—Rotates Apache log files so that these files do not get too large. See logrotate (page 604) for information about rotating log files.

/etc/apache2/mods-available—Holds files containing LoadModule directives (page 884) for their respective modules. The **alias.conf** file is kept in this directory and is enabled by default. Two of the most frequently used module binary files are **mod_perl** (part of the **libapache2-mod-perl2** package) and **mod_python** (part of the **libapache2-mod-python** metapackage). The *.load files in this directory load modules from the **/usr/lib/apache2/modules** directory (page 897). The *.conf files configure the modules for use. See page 861 for information on using a2enmod to enable a module.

/etc/apache2/mods-enabled—Holds links to files in **mods-available**. Use a2enmod to create links and a2dismod to remove links (page 861).

Configuration files   Apache configuration files are kept in the **/etc/apache2** hierarchy:

/etc/apache2/apache2.conf—Holds configuration directives. This file is the main Apache configuration file. You do not typically make changes to this file, but rather put any configuration directives in **httpd.conf** and other files.

/etc/apache2/envvars—Holds variables that modify the environment Apache runs in.

/etc/apache2/ports.conf—Holds the Listen directive (page 866), which controls which IP address(es) and port(s) Apache listens on.

/etc/apache2/sites-available—Holds files containing the code that describes virtual hosts. See page 862 for information on using a2ensite to enable a site.

/etc/apache2/sites-enabled—Holds links to files in **sites-available**. Use a2ensite to create links and a2dissite to remove links (page 862).

/etc/apache2/httpd.conf—Holds local configuration directives. This file augments the **apache2.conf** file in the same directory. The discussion of configuration directives starts on page 865.

/etc/apache2/conf.d—Holds configuration files.

Logs   Logs are kept in **/var/log/apache2**:

/var/log/apache2/access_log—Logs requests made to the server.

/var/log/apache2/error_log—Logs request and runtime server errors.

Web documents   Web documents (including the Web pages displayed by client browsers), custom error messages, and CGI scripts are kept in **/var/www** by default:

/usr/lib/cgi-bin—Holds CGI scripts (page 898). This directory is aliased to **/cgi-bin/**.

/usr/share/apache2/error—Holds default error documents. You can modify these documents to conform to the style of your Web site. This directory is aliased to **/error/**. See ErrorDocument (page 880).

/usr/share/apache2/icons—Holds icons used to display directory entries. This directory is aliased to **/icons/**.

/usr/share/doc/apache2-doc/manual/index.html—*Apache HTTP Server Version 2.2 Documentation.* With Apache running and **apache2-doc** installed, point a browser at *server*/**manual**, where *server* is **localhost** or the name or IP address of the Apache server.

Document root By default, the document root (page 858) is **/var/www**. You can change this location with the DocumentRoot directive (page 869). In addition to content for the Web pages that Apache serves, this directory can house the **webalizer** directory, which holds **webalizer** (page 904) output.

.htaccess files A **.htaccess** file contains configuration directives and can appear in any directory in the document root hierarchy. The location of a **.htaccess** file is critical: The directives in a **.htaccess** file apply to all files in the hierarchy rooted at the directory that holds the **.htaccess** file. The AllowOverride directive (page 886) controls whether Apache examines **.htaccess** files. Because the **default** site contains **AllowOverride None** directives, you must use an AllowOverride directive to cause Apache to examine **.htaccess** files and process directives in those files. This protection is duplicated and enhanced in the **apache2.conf** file distributed by Ubuntu, where a directive instructs Apache not to serve files whose names start with **.ht**. Because of this directive, Apache does not serve **.htaccess** files (nor does it serve **.htpassword** files).

CONFIGURATION DIRECTIVES

Configuration directives, or simply *directives,* are lines in a configuration file that control some aspect of how Apache functions. A configuration directive is composed of a keyword followed by one or more arguments (values) separated by SPACEs. For example, the following configuration directive sets **Timeout** to 300 (seconds):

```
Timeout 300
```

You must enclose arguments that contain SPACEs within double quotation marks. Keywords are not case sensitive, but arguments (pathnames, filenames, and so on) often are.

apache2.conf The main file that holds Apache configuration directives is, by default, **/etc/apache2/apache2.conf**. This file holds global directives that affect all content served by Apache. Include directives (pages 862 and 883) within **apache2.conf** incorporate the contents of other files as though they were part of **apache2.conf**.

.htaccess Local directives can appear in **.htaccess** files. A **.htaccess** file can appear in any directory within the document root hierarchy; it affects files in the directory hierarchy rooted at the directory it appears in.

Pathnames When you specify an absolute pathname in a configuration directive, the directive uses that pathname without modifying it. When you specify a relative pathname, such as a simple filename or the name of a directory, Apache prepends to that name the value specified by the ServerRoot (page 882) directive (**/etc/apache2** by default).

DIRECTIVES I: DIRECTIVES YOU MAY WANT TO MODIFY AS YOU GET STARTED

When it starts, Apache reads the **/etc/apache2/apache2.conf** configuration file (by default) for instructions governing every aspect of how Apache runs and serves content. The **apache2.conf** file shipped by Ubuntu is more than 600 lines long. As explained under **apache2.conf** on page 862, you do not normally make changes to this file.

This section details some directives you may want to add to the **/etc/apache2/httpd.conf** file, or change in one of the other configuration files, as you are getting started with Apache. You can use each of the following directives in **httpd.conf** to override the corresponding directive in **apache2.conf**. Or you can change the directive if it appears in another configuration file. In this chapter, the **Specify in** line near the end of each explanation tells you in which configuration file in the **/etc/apache2** hierarchy you typically specify that directive. If the directive already appears in a file, you must specify the new directive after the one you want to override. See **apache2.conf** (page 862) for more information. The **Context** line in each explanation tells you which locations the directives can appear in; contexts are explained on page 871. The section titled "Directives II: Advanced Directives" on page 875 describes more directives.

Listen   *Specifies the port(s) that Apache listens for requests on.*

*Listen [**IP-address:**]**portnumber***

where **IP-address** is the IP address that Apache listens on and **portnumber** is the number of the port that Apache listens on for the given **IP-address**. When **IP-address** is absent or is set to 0.0.0.0, Apache listens on all network interfaces. At least one Listen directive must appear in the configuration files or Apache will not work.

The following minimal directive from the **ports.conf** file listens for requests on all interfaces on port 80:

```
Listen 80
```

The next directive changes the port from the default value of 80 to 8080:

```
Listen 8080
```

When you specify a port other than 80, each request to the server must include a port number (as in **www.example.org:8080**) or the kernel will return a **Connection Refused** message. Use multiple Listen directives to have Apache listen on multiple IP addresses and ports. For example,

```
Listen 80
Listen 192.168.1.1:8080
Listen 192.168.1.2:443
```

accepts connections on all network interfaces on port 80, on 192.168.1.1 on port 8080, and on 192.168.1.2 on port 443.

Context: **server config**
Specify in **ports.conf**

Default: none (Apache will not start without this directive)
Ubuntu: Listen 80

Redirect *Tells the client to fetch a requested resource from a different, specified location.*

Redirect [status] requested-path [new-URI]

where *status* is the status that Apache returns along with the redirect. If you omit *status*, Apache assumes **temp**. The *status* can be an Apache error code in the range 300–399 or one of the following:

permanent	Returns status 301 (the resource has moved permanently)
temp	Returns status 302 (the resource has moved temporarily)
seeother	Returns status 303 (the resource has been replaced)
gone	Returns status 410 (the resource has been removed—does not take a *new-URI* argument

The *requested-path* is the absolute pathname of the ordinary file or directory that Apache is to redirect requests for. Apache redirects all requests that start with the absolute pathname specified by *requested-path*. (See the example below.) Use RedirectMatch (discussed next) if you want to use a regular expression in this argument.

The *new-URI* is the URI that Apache redirects requests to. If the *new-URI* starts with a slash (/) and not **http://**, **ftp://**, or a similar prefix, Apache uses the same prefix that it was called with. Most Redirect directives require a *new-URI* argument.

A request must match all segments of the *requested-path* argument. Assume the following directive:

```
Redirect /www.example.com/pictures http://pictures.example.com/
```

Apache will redirect a request for **http://www.example.com/pictures/mom.jpg** to **http://pictures.example.com/mom.jpg** but, because the final segment does not match, it will not redirect a request for **http://www.example.com/pictures_mom.jpg**.

Contexts: **server config, virtual host, directory, .htaccess**
Specify in **sites-available/***
Default: none
Ubuntu: none

RedirectMatch *Tells the client to fetch a requested resource from a different location specified by a regular expression.*

RedirectMatch [status] requested-path-re [new-URI]

This directive is the same as Redirect (discussed above), except that you can use a regular expression (Appendix A) in *requested-path-re*.

Contexts: **server config, virtual host, directory, .htaccess**
Specify in **sites-available/***
Default: none
Ubuntu: none

ServerAdmin   *Sets the email address used in **mailto:** links on error pages.*

*ServerAdmin **email-address***

where ***email-address*** is the email address of the person who is responsible for managing the Web content. Apache includes this address as a link on Apache-generated error pages. However, Ubuntu Linux sets ServerSignature (page 883) to **On**, which causes Apache to display information about the server—rather than a link to an email address—on error pages. If you want to display the link on error pages, set ServerSignature to **EMail**. Make sure ***email-address*** points to an email account that someone checks frequently. Users can use this address to get help with the Web site or to inform the administrator of problems. There is no default value for ServerAdmin; if you do not use this directive and ServerSignature is set to **EMail**, the **mailto:** link on error pages points to [**no address given**].

ServerAdmin attracts spam

security   The email address you put in ServerAdmin often attracts spam. Use a spam-guarded address such as **"mgs at sobell dot com"** (you must use the quotation marks) or use a custom error page to point to a Web page with a form for sending mail to the right person.

You can use a role alias such as **webmaster** at your domain and use a mail alias to forward mail that is sent to **webmaster** to the person who is responsible for maintaining the Web site. See the discussion of mail aliases on page 686.

Contexts: **server config, virtual host**
Specify in **sites-available/❖**
Default: none
Ubuntu: webmaster@localhost

ServerName   *Specifies the server's name and the port it listens on.*

*ServerName **FQDN** [:**port**]*

where ***FQDN*** is the fully qualified domain name or IP address of the server and ***port*** is the optional port number Apache listens on. The domain name of the server must be able to be resolved (by DNS or **/etc/hosts**) and may differ from the hostname of the system running the server. If you do not specify a ServerName, Apache performs a DNS reverse name resolution (page 793) on the system's IP address and assigns that value to ServerName. If the reverse lookup fails, Apache assigns the system's IP address to ServerName.

In the following example, substitute the FQDN or IP address of the server for **www.example.com**. Change the **80** to the port number Apache listens on (if it is not port 80).

```
ServerName www.example.com:80
```

The ports specified by ServerName and Listen (page 866) must be the same if you want the FQDN specified by ServerName to be tied to the IP address specified by the Listen directive.

Apache uses ServerName to construct a URI when it redirects a client (page 891). See also UseCanonicalName (page 878).

Contexts: **server config, virtual host**
Specify in **sites-available/***
Default: none
Ubuntu: none

DocumentRoot *Points to the root of the directory hierarchy that holds the server's content.*

*DocumentRoot **dirname***

where ***dirname*** is the absolute pathname of the directory at the root of the directory hierarchy that holds the content Apache serves. Do not use a trailing slash. You can put the document root wherever you like, as long as the user **www-data** has read access to the ordinary files and execute access to the directory files in the directory hierarchy. The FHS (page 199) specifies **/srv** as the top-level directory for this purpose. The following directive puts the document root at **/srv/www**:

```
DocumentRoot /srv/www
```

Contexts: **server config, virtual host**
Specify in **sites-available/***
Default: **/usr/local/apache/htdocs**
Ubuntu: **/var/www**

UserDir *Allows users to publish content from their home directories.*

*UserDir **dirname** | disabled | enabled **user-list***

where ***dirname*** is the name of a directory that, if it appears in a local user's home directory, Apache publishes to the Web. The ***disabled*** keyword prevents content from being published from users' home directories; ***enabled*** causes content to be published from the home directories of users specified in the SPACE-separated ***user-list***. When you do not specify a ***dirname***, Apache publishes content to ~/**public_html**.

Apache can combine the effects of multiple UserDir directives. Suppose you have the following directives:

```
UserDir disabled
UserDir enabled user1 user2 user3
UserDir web
```

The first directive turns off user publishing for all users. The second directive enables user publishing for three users. The third directive makes **web** the name of the directory that, if it appears in one of the specified users' home directories, Apache publishes to the Web.

To cause a browser to display the content published by a user, specify in the location bar the name of the Web site followed by a **/~** and the user's username. For example, if Sam published content in the **public_html** directory in his home directory and the URI of the Web site was **www.example.com**, you would enter **http://www.example.com/~sam**

to display Sam's Web page. To display a user's Web page, Apache must have execute permission (as user **www-data**) for the user's home directory and the directory holding the content, and read permission for the content files.

Ubuntu Linux provides the following configuration for user directories in the **/etc/apache2/mods-available/userdir.conf** file, which is disabled by default:

```
UserDir public_html
UserDir disabled root
```

Give the command **a2enmod userdir** to enable user directories.

Contexts: **server config, virtual host**
Specify in **mods-available/userdir.conf**
Default: none
Ubuntu: **public_html, disabled root**

DirectoryIndex   *Specifies which file Apache serves when a user requests a directory.*

*DirectoryIndex **filename** [**filename** ...]*

where ***filename*** is the name of the file that Apache serves.

This directive specifies a list of filenames. When a client requests a directory, Apache attempts to find a file in the specified directory whose name matches a file in the list. When Apache finds a match, it returns that file. When this directive is absent or when none of the files specified by this directive exists in the specified directory, Apache displays a directory listing as specified by the IndexOptions directive (page 880).

The following DirectoryIndex directive, which Ubuntu Linux provides in the **mods-enabled/dir.conf** file, is enabled by default:

```
DirectoryIndex index.html index.cgi index.pl index.php index.xhtml index.htm
```

This directive causes Apache to search the specified directory and return the file named **index.html**, **index.cgi**, **index.pl**, **index.php**, **index.xhtml**, or **index.htm**, where **index.html**, **index.htm**, and **index.xhtml** are the names of the standard, default HTML and XHTML documents; **index.cgi** is a CGI document; **index.pl** is a Perl document; and **index.php** is a PHP document. The name **index** is standard but arbitrary.

Using headers, a client can communicate a language preference to a server. If the server can handle the preference, it determines the best response from among its resources. The **.var** is an Ubuntu addition (a line in **apache2.conf**, **AddHandler type-map var,** makes the **.var** extension a type map, one of the forms of content negotiation; MultiViews is the other form). For more information refer to "Content Negotiation" on page 891.

Contexts: **server config, virtual host**
Specify in **mods-available/dir.conf**
Default: **index.html**
Ubuntu: **index.html index.cgi index.pl index.php index.xhtml index.htm**

CONTEXTS AND CONTAINERS

To make it flexible and easy to customize, Apache uses configuration directives, contexts, and containers. Configuration directives were covered in the previous section. This section discusses contexts and containers, which are critical to managing an Apache server.

CONTEXTS

Four locations, called *contexts*, define where configuration directives can appear. This chapter marks each configuration directive to indicate which context(s) it can appear in. Table 26-2 describes each of these contexts.

Table 26-2   Contexts

Context	Location(s) directives can appear in
server config	In **apache2.conf** or included files only, but not inside <VirtualHost> or <Directory> containers (next section) unless so marked
virtual host	Inside <VirtualHost> containers in **apache2.conf** or included files only
directory	Inside <Directory>, <Location>, and <Files> containers in **apache2.conf** or included files only
.htaccess	In **.htaccess** files (page 865) only

Directives in files incorporated by means of an Include directive (page 883) are part of the context they are included in and must be allowed in that context.

Putting a directive in the wrong context generates a configuration error and can cause Apache not to serve content correctly or not to start.

CONTAINERS

Containers, or *special directives*, are directives that group other directives. Containers are delimited by XML-style tags. Three examples are shown here:

```
<Directory> ... </Directory>

<Location> ... </Location>

<VirtualHost> ... </VirtualHost>
```

Look in **apache2.conf** and **sites-available/default** for examples of containers. Like other directives, containers are limited to use within specified contexts. This section describes some of the more frequently used containers.

<Directory> *Applies directives to all directories within the specified directory hierarchies.*

*<Directory **directory**> ... </Directory>*

where ***directory*** is an absolute pathname specifying the root of the directory hierarchy that holds the directories the directives in the container apply to. The ***directory*** can include wildcards; a * does not match a /.

A <Directory> container provides the same functionality as a **.htaccess** file. While an administrator can use a <Directory> container in Apache configuration files, regular users cannot. Regular users can use **.htaccess** files to control access to their own directories.

The directives in the <Directory> container shown in the following example apply to the **/var/www/html/corp** directory hierarchy. The Deny directive denies access to all clients, the Allow directive grants clients from the 192.168.10. subnet access, and the AllowOverride directive (page 886) enables Apache to process directives in **.htaccess** files in the hierarchy:

```
<Directory /var/www/html/corp>
    Deny from all
    Allow from 192.168.10.
    AllowOverride All
</Directory>
```

Contexts: **server config, virtual host**

<Files>   *Applies directives to specified ordinary files.*

*<Files **directory**> ... </Files>*

where **directory** is an absolute pathname specifying the root of the directory hierarchy that holds the ordinary files the directives in the container apply to. The **directory** can include wildcards; a * does not match a **/**. This container is similar to <Directory> but applies to ordinary files rather than to directories.

The following directive, from the Ubuntu **apache2.conf** file, denies access to all files whose filenames start with **.ht**, meaning that Apache will not serve these files. The tilde (~) changes how Apache interprets the following string. Without a tilde, the string is a simple shell match that interprets shell special characters (page 242). With a tilde, Apache interprets the string as a regular expression (page 1043):

```
<Files ~ "^\.ht">
    Order allow,deny
    Deny from all
</Files>
```

Contexts: **server config, virtual host, directory, .htaccess**

<IfModule>   *Applies directives if a specified module is loaded.*

*<IfModule [!]**module-name**> ... </IfModule>*

where **module-name** is the name of the module (page 897) that is tested for. Apache executes the directives in this container if **module-name** is loaded or with **!** if **module-name** is not loaded.

Apache will not start if you specify a configuration directive that is specific to a module that is not loaded.

The following <IfModule> container, which is located in the Ubuntu file named **mods-available/mime_magic.conf**, depends on the **mod_mime_magic.c** module being loaded. If this module is loaded, Apache runs the MIMEMagicFile directive, which tells the **mod_mime_magic.c** module where its hints file is located.

```
<IfModule mod_mime_magic.c>
    MIMEMagicFile /usr/share/file/magic.mime
</IfModule>
```

See page 889 for another example of an <IfModule> container.

Contexts: **server config, virtual host, directory, .htaccess**

<Limit> *Limits access-control directives to specified HTTP methods.*

*<Limit **method** [**method**] ... > ... </Limit>*

where **method** is an HTTP method. An HTTP method specifies which action is to be performed on a URI. The most frequently used methods are GET, PUT, POST, and OPTIONS; method names are case sensitive. GET (the default method) sends any data indicated by the URI. PUT stores data from the body section of the communication at the specified URI. POST creates a new document containing the body of the request at the specified URI. OPTIONS requests information about the capabilities of the server.

The <Limit> container binds a group of access-control directives to specified HTTP methods: Only methods named by this container are affected by this group of directives.

The following example disables HTTP uploads (PUTs) from systems that are not in a subdomain of **example.com**:

```
<Limit PUT>
order deny,allow
deny from all
allow from .example.com
</Limit>
```

Contexts: **server config, virtual host, directory, .htaccess**

Use <LimitExcept> instead of <Limit>

caution It is safer to use the <LimitExcept> container than to use the <Limit> container, as the former protects against arbitrary methods. When you use <Limit>, you must be careful to name explicitly all possible methods that the group of directives could affect.

It is safer still not to put access-control directives in any container.

<LimitExcept> *Limits access-control directives to all except specified HTTP methods.*

*<LimitExcept **method** [**method**] ... > ... </LimitExcept>*

where **method** is an HTTP method. See <Limit> for a discussion of methods.

This container causes a group of access-control directives *not* to be bound to specified HTTP methods. Thus methods *not* named in <LimitExcept> are affected by this group of directives.

The access-control directives within the following <LimitExcept> container affect HTTP methods other than GET, POST, and OPTIONS. You could put this container in a <Directory> container to limit its scope:

```
<LimitExcept GET POST OPTIONS>
        Order deny,allow
        Deny from all
    </LimitExcept>
```

Contexts: **server config, virtual host, directory, .htaccess**

<Location> *Applies directives to specified URIs.*

<Location URI> ... </Location>

where **URI** points to content; it specifies a file or the root of the directory hierarchy that the directives in the container apply to. While the <Directory> container points within the local filesystem, <Location> points outside the local filesystem. The **URI** can include wildcards; a * does not match a **/**.

The following <Location> container limits access to **http://*server*/pop** to clients from the **example.net** domain, where *server* is the FQDN of the server:

```
<Location /pop>
    Order deny,allow
    Deny from all
    Allow from .example.net
</Location>
```

Contexts: **server config, virtual host**

Use <Location> with care

caution Use this powerful container with care. Do not use it to replace the <Directory> container: When several URIs point to the same location in a filesystem, a client may be able to circumvent the desired access control by using a URI not specified by this container.

<LocationMatch> *Applies directives to URIs specified by a regular expression.*

<LocationMatch regexp> ... </LocationMatch>

where *regexp* is a regular expression that matches one or more URIs. This container works the same way as <Location>, except that it applies to any URIs that *regexp* matches.

Contexts: **server config, virtual host**

<VirtualHost> *Applies directives to a specified virtual host.*

<VirtualHost addr[:port] [addr[:port]] ... > ... </VirtualHost>

where ***addr*** is the IP address (or FQDN, although it is not recommended) of the virtual host (or * to represent all addresses) and ***port*** is the port that Apache listens on for the virtual host. This directive does not control which addresses and ports Apache listens on; use a Listen directive (page 866) for that purpose. This container holds commands that Apache applies to a virtual host. For more information see "NameVirtualHost" on page 876 and "Virtual Hosts" on page 893.

Context: **server config**

DIRECTIVES II: ADVANCED DIRECTIVES

This section discusses configuration directives that you may want to use after you have gained some experience with Apache.

DIRECTIVES THAT CONTROL PROCESSES

MaxClients   *Specifies the maximum number of child processes.*

MaxClients **num**

where **num** is the maximum number of child processes (servers) Apache runs at one time, including idle processes and processes that are serving requests. When Apache is running **num** processes and there are no idle processes, Apache issues **Server too busy** errors to new connections; it does not start new child processes. A value of 150 is usually sufficient, even for moderately busy sites.

Context: **server config**
Change in **httpd.conf**
Default: 256
Ubuntu: 150

MaxRequestsPerChild

Specifies the maximum number of requests a child process can serve.

MaxRequestsPerChild **num**

where **num** is the maximum number of requests a child process (server) can serve during its lifetime. After a child process serves **num** requests, it does not process any more requests but dies after it finishes processing its current requests. Apache can start another child process to replace the one that dies. Additional requests are processed by other processes from the server pool.

Set **num** to 0 to not set a limit on the number of requests a child can process, except for the effects of MinSpareServers. By limiting the lives of processes, this directive can prevent memory leaks from consuming too much system memory. However, setting MaxRequestsPerChild to a too-small value can hurt performance by causing Apache to create new child servers constantly.

Context: **server config**
Specify in **httpd.conf**
Default: 10000
Ubuntu: 0

MaxSpareServers   *Specifies the maximum number of idle processes.*

*MaxSpareServers **num***

where ***num*** is the maximum number of idle processes (servers) Apache keeps running to serve requests as they come in. Do not set this number too high, as each process consumes system resources.

Context: **server config**
Specify in **httpd.conf**
Default: 10
Ubuntu: 10

MinSpareServers   *Specifies the minimum number of idle processes.*

*MinSpareServers **num***

where ***num*** is the minimum number of idle processes (servers) Apache keeps running to serve requests as they come in. More idle processes occupy more computer resources; increase this value for busy sites only.

Context: **server config**
Specify in **httpd.conf**
Default: 5
Ubuntu: 5

NameVirtualHost

Specifies the address and port for a name-based (host-by-name) virtual host.

*NameVirtualHost **addr**[:**port**]*

where ***addr*** is the IP address (or FQDN, although it is not recommended) that Apache will use for serving a name-based virtual host and ***port*** is the port that Apache listens on for that virtual host. Specify ***addr*** as * to cause the server to process requests on all interfaces as name-based virtual hosts.

This directive does not control which addresses and ports Apache listens on; use a Listen directive (page 866) for that purpose. For more information see "<VirtualHost>" on page 874 and "Virtual Hosts" on page 893.

Context: **server config**
Specify in **sites-available/***
Default: none
Ubuntu: *

StartServers   *Specifies the number of child processes that Apache starts with.*

*StartServers **num***

where ***num*** is the number of child processes (servers) that Apache starts when it is brought up. This value is significant only when Apache starts; MinSpareServers and MaxSpareServers control the number of idle processes once Apache is up and running. Starting Apache with multiple servers ensures that a pool of servers is waiting to serve requests immediately.

Context: **server config**
Specify in **httpd.conf**
Default: 5
Ubuntu: 5 (**prefork** MPM) or 2 (**worker** MPM)

NETWORKING DIRECTIVES

HostnameLookups

Specifies whether Apache puts a client's hostname or its IP address in the logs.

HostnameLookups On | Off | Double

On: Performs DNS reverse name resolution (page 793) to determine the hostname of each client for logging purposes.

Off: Logs each client's IP address.

Double: To provide greater security, performs DNS reverse name resolution (page 793) to determine the hostname of each client, performs a forward DNS lookup to verify the original IP address, and logs the hostname. Denies access if it cannot verify the original IP address.

Contexts: **server config, virtual host, directory**
Specify in **httpd.conf**
Default: Off
Ubuntu: Off

Lookups can consume a lot of system resources

tip Use the **On** and **Double** options with caution: They can consume a lot of resources on a busy system. You can use a program such as logresolve to perform reverse name resolution offline for statistical purposes.

If you perform hostname resolution offline, you run the risk that the name may have changed; you usually want the name that was current at the time of the request. To minimize this problem, perform the hostname resolution as soon as possible after writing the log.

Timeout *Specifies the amount of time Apache waits for network operations to complete.*

Timeout num

where ***num*** is the number of seconds that Apache waits for network operations to finish. You can usually set this directive to a lower value; five minutes is a long time to wait on a busy server. The Apache documentation says that the default is not lower "because there may still be odd places in the code where the timer is not reset when a packet is sent."

Context: **server config**
Specify in **httpd.conf**
Default: 300
Ubuntu: 300

UseCanonicalName

Specifies the method the server uses to identify itself.

UseCanonicalName On | Off | DNS

On: Apache uses the value of the ServerName directive (page 868) as its identity.

Off: Apache uses the name and port from the incoming request as its identity.

DNS: Apache performs a DNS reverse name resolution (page 793) on the IP address from the incoming request and uses the result as its identity. Rarely used.

This directive is important when a server has more than one name and needs to perform a redirect. Ubuntu does not set this directive because it does not set the ServerName directive (page 868). Once you set ServerName, change UseCanonicalName to **On**. See page 891 for a discussion of redirects and this directive.

Contexts: **server config, virtual host, directory**
Specify in **sites-available/✱**
Default: Off
Ubuntu: none

Logging Directives

ErrorLog *Specifies where Apache sends error messages.*

ErrorLog filename | syslog[:facility]

where *filename* specifies the name of the file, relative to ServerRoot (page 882), that Apache sends error messages to. The *syslog* keyword specifies that Apache send errors to **syslogd** (page 608); *facility* specifies which **syslogd** facility to use. The default facility is **local7**.

Contexts: **server config, virtual host**
Specify in **httpd.conf** or **sites-available/✱**
Default: **logs/error_log**
Ubuntu: **/var/log/apache2/error.log**

LogLevel *Specifies the level of error messages that Apache logs.*

LogLevel level

where *level* specifies that Apache log errors of that level and higher (more urgent). Choose *level* from the following list, which is presented here in order of decreasing urgency and increasing verbosity:

emerg System unusable messages
alert Need for immediate action messages
crit Critical condition messages
error Error condition messages
warn Nonfatal warning messages

notice Normal but significant messages
info Operational messages and recommendations
debug Messages for finding and solving problems

Contexts: **server config, virtual host**
Specify in **httpd.conf** or **sites-available/***
Default: warn
Ubuntu: warn

DIRECTIVES THAT CONTROL CONTENT

AddHandler *Creates a mapping between filename extensions and a builtin Apache handler.*

*AddHandler **handler extension** [**extension**] ...*

where ***handler*** is the name of a builtin handler and ***extension*** is a filename extension that maps to the ***handler***. Handlers are actions that are built into Apache and are directly related to loaded modules. Apache uses a handler when a client requests a file with a specified filename extension.

For example, the following AddHandler directive causes Apache to process files that have a filename extension of **.cgi** with the **cgi-script** handler:

```
AddHandler cgi-script .cgi
```

See "Type Maps" on page 891 for another example of an AddHandler directive.

Contexts: **server config, virtual host, directory, .htaccess**
Specify in **httpd.conf**
Default: none
Ubuntu: type-map var

Alias *Maps a URI to a directory or file.*

*Alias **alias pathname***

where ***alias*** must match part of the URI that the client requested to invoke the alias. The ***pathname*** is the absolute pathname of the target of the alias, usually a directory.

For example, the following alias causes Apache to serve **/usr/local/pix/milk.jpg** when a client requests **http://www.example.com/pix/milk.jpg**:

```
Alias /pix /usr/local/pix
```

In some cases, you need to use a <Directory> container (page 871) to grant access to aliased content.

Contexts: **server config, virtual host**
Specify in **httpd.conf, sites-available/***, or **mods-available/alias.conf**
Default: None
Ubuntu: /icons/ /usr/share/apache2/icons/ and /doc/ /usr/share/doc/

ErrorDocument   *Specifies the action Apache takes when the specified error occurs.*

ErrorDocument **code action**

where **code** is the error code (page 904) that this directive defines a response for and **action** is one of the following:

string: Defines the message that Apache returns to the client.

absolute pathname: Points to a local script or other content that Apache redirects the client to.

URI: Points to an external script or other content that Apache redirects the client to.

When you do not specify this directive for a given error code, Apache returns a hardcoded error message when that error occurs.

Some examples of ErrorDocument directives follow:

```
ErrorDocument 403 "Sorry, access is forbidden."
ErrorDocument 403 /cgi-bin/uh-uh.pl
ErrorDocument 403 http://errors.example.com/not_allowed.html
```

Contexts: **server config, virtual host, directory, .htaccess**
Specify in **httpd.conf**
Default: none; Apache returns hardcoded error messages
Ubuntu: none (but see the comments in **apache2.conf**)

IndexOptions   *Specifies how Apache displays directory listings.*

IndexOptions [±]option [[±]option] ...

where **option** can be any combination of the following:

DescriptionWidth=*n*: Sets the width of the description column to *n* characters. Use ✳ in place of *n* to accommodate the widest description.

FancyIndexing: In directory listings, displays column headers that are links. When you click one of these links, Apache sorts the display based on the content of the column. Clicking the link a second time reverses the order.

FoldersFirst: Sorts the listing so that directories come before plain files. Use only with FancyIndexing.

HTMLTable: Displays a directory listing in a table.

IconsAreLinks: Makes the icons clickable. Use only with FancyIndexing.

IconHeight=*n*: Sets the height of icons to *n* pixels. Use only with IconWidth.

IconWidth=*n*: Sets the width of icons to *n* pixels. Use only with IconHeight.

IgnoreCase: Ignores case when sorting names.

IgnoreClient: Ignores options the client supplied in the URI.

NameWidth=*n*: Sets the width of the filename column to *n* characters. Use ✻ in place of *n* to accommodate the widest filename.

ScanHTMLTitles: Extracts and displays titles from HTML documents. Use only with FancyIndexing. Not normally used because it is CPU and disk intensive.

SuppressColumnSorting: Suppresses clickable column headings that can be used for sorting columns. Use only with FancyIndexing.

SuppressDescription: Suppresses file descriptions. Use only with FancyIndexing.

SuppressHTMLPreamble: Suppresses the contents of the file specified by the Header-Name directive, even if that file exists.

SuppressIcon: Suppresses icons. Use only with FancyIndexing.

SuppressLastModified: Suppresses the modification date. Use only with Fancy-Indexing.

SuppressRules: Suppresses horizontal lines. Use only with FancyIndexing.

SuppressSize: Suppresses file sizes. Use only with FancyIndexing.

VersionSort: Sorts version numbers (in filenames) in a natural way; character strings, except for substrings of digits, are not affected.

As an example, suppose a client requests a URI that points to a directory (such as **http://www.example.com/support/**) and none of the files specified by the Directory-Index directive (page 870) is present in that directory. If the directory hierarchy is controlled by a **.htaccess** file and AllowOverride (page 886) has been set to allow indexes, then Apache displays a directory listing according to the options specified by this directive.

When this directive appears more than once within a directory, Apache merges the options from the directives. Use **+** and **–** to merge IndexOptions options with options from higher-level directories. (Unless you use **+** or **–** with all options, Apache discards any options set in higher-level directories.) For example, the following directives and containers set the options for **/custsup/download** to Version-Sort; Apache discards FancyIndexing and IgnoreCase in the **download** directory because there is no **+** or **–** before VersionSort in the second <Directory> container:

```
<Directory /custsup>
    IndexOptions FancyIndexing
    IndexOptions IgnoreCase
</Directory>

<Directory /custsup/download>
    IndexOptions VersionSort
</Directory>
```

Because **+** appears before VersionSort, the directives and containers on the next page set the options for **/custsup/download** to FancyIndexing, IgnoreCase, and VersionSort.

```
<Directory /custsup>
    IndexOptions FancyIndexing
    IndexOptions IgnoreCase
</Directory>

<Directory /custsup/download>
    IndexOptions +VersionSort
</Directory>
```

Contexts: **server config, virtual host, directory, .htaccess**
Specify in **httpd.conf**
Default: none; lists only filenames
Ubuntu: FancyIndexing VersionSort HTMLTable NameWidth=✽
      DescriptionWidth=✽ Charset=UTF-8

ServerRoot *Specifies the root directory for server files (not content).*

ServerRoot **directory**

where **directory** specifies the pathname of the root directory for the files that make up the server. Apache prepends **directory** to relative pathnames in **httpd.conf**. This directive does not specify the location of the content that Apache serves; the DocumentRoot directive (page 869) performs that function. Do not change this value unless you move the server files.

Context: **server config**
Specify in **httpd.conf**
Default: **/usr/local/apache**
Ubuntu: **/etc/apache2**

ServerTokens *Specifies the server information that Apache returns to a client.*

ServerTokens Prod | Major | Minor | Min | OS | Full

Prod: Returns the product name: **Apache**. Also *ProductOnly.*

Major: Returns the major release number of the server: **Apache/2**.

Minor: Returns the major and minor release numbers of the server: **Apache/2.2**.

Min: Returns the complete version: **Apache/2.2.4**. Also *Minimal.*

OS: Returns the name of the operating system and the complete version: **Apache/2.2.4 (Ubuntu)**. Provides less information that might help a malicious user than *Full* does.

Full: Same as *OS*, except that *Full* also sends the names and versions of non-ASF modules: **Apache/2.2.4 (Ubuntu) PHP/5.1.2**.

Unless you want clients to know the details of the software you are running, set ServerTokens to reveal as little as possible.

Context: **server config**
Specify in **httpd.conf**
Default: **Full**
Ubuntu: **Full**

ServerSignature *Adds a line to server-generated pages.*

ServerSignature On | Off | EMail

On: Turns the signature line on. The signature line contains the server version as specified by the ServerTokens directive (discussed on the precedig page) and the name specified by the <VirtualHost> container (page 874).

Off: Turns the signature line off.

EMail: To the signature line, adds a **mailto:** link to the server email address. This option produces output that can attract spam. See ServerAdmin (page 868) for information on specifying an email address.

Contexts: **server config, virtual host, directory, .htaccess**
Specify in **httpd.conf** or **sites-available/***
Default: Off
Ubuntu: On

CONFIGURATION DIRECTIVES

Group *Sets the GID of the processes that run the servers.*

Group #groupid | groupname

where **groupid** is a GID value, preceded by **#**, and **groupname** is the name of a group. The processes (servers) that Apache spawns are run as the group specified by this directive. See the User directive (page 885) for more information.

Context: **server config**
Specify in **httpd.conf**
Default: #–1
Ubuntu: www-data

Include *Loads directives from files.*

Include filename | directory

where **filename** is the relative pathname of a file that contains directives. Apache prepends ServerRoot (page 882) to **filename**. The directives in **filename** are included in the file holding this directive at the location of the directive. Because **filename** can include wildcards, it can specify more than one file.

The **directory** is the relative pathname that specifies the root of a directory hierarchy that holds files containing directives. Apache prepends ServerRoot to **directory**. The directives in ordinary files in this hierarchy are included in the file holding this directive at the location of the directive. The **directory** can include wildcards.

Ubuntu Linux categorizes and splits Apache configuration information into files and directories related to virtual hosts, server configuration, ports, modules, and miscellaneous configuration options. These files are incorporated into the main **apache2.conf** file using Include directives; see page 862 for more information.

Contexts: **server config, virtual host, directory**
Specify anywhere
Default: none
Ubuntu:**/etc/apache2/mods-enabled/***.load
/etc/apache2/mods-enabled/*.conf
/etc/apache2/httpd.conf
/etc/apache2/ports.conf
/etc/apache2/conf.d/
/etc/apache2/sites-enabled/

LoadModule *Loads a module.*

*LoadModule **module filename***

where ***module*** is the name of an external DSO module and ***filename*** is the relative pathname of the named module. Apache prepends ServerRoot (page 882) to ***filename*** and loads the external module specified by this directive. Use a2enmod (page 861) to enable modules. For more information refer to "Modules" on page 897.

Context: **server config**
Specify in **mods-available/***.load
Default: none; nothing is loaded by default if this directive is omitted
Ubuntu: see the *.load files in the **mods-enabled** directory

Options *Controls server features by directory.*

*Options [±]**option** [[±]**option** ...]*

This directive controls which server features are enabled for a directory hierarchy. The directory hierarchy is specified by the container this directive appears in. A **+** or the absence of a **–** turns an option on, and a **–** turns it off.

The ***option*** may be one of the following:

None—None of the features this directive can control are enabled.

All—All of the features this directive can control are enabled, except for MultiViews, which you must explicitly enable.

ExecCGI—Apache can execute CGI scripts (page 898).

FollowSymLinks—Apache follows symbolic links.

Includes—Permits SSIs (server-side includes, page 899). SSIs are containers embedded in HTML pages that are evaluated on the server before the content is passed to the client.

IncludesNOEXEC—The same as Includes but disables the **#exec** and **#exec cgi** commands that are part of SSIs. Does *not* prevent the **#include** command from referencing CGI scripts.

Indexes—Generates a directory listing if DirectoryIndex (page 870) is not set.

MultiViews—Allows MultiViews (page 892).

SymLinksIfOwnerMatch—The same as FollowSymLinks but follows the link only if the file or directory being pointed to has the same owner as the link.

The following Options directive from the Ubuntu **sites-available/default** file sets the Indexes, FollowSymLinks, and MultiViews options and, because the <Directory> container specifies the **/var/www** directory hierarchy (the document root), affects all content:

```
<Directory /var/www/>
    Options Indexes FollowSymLinks MultiViews
...
```

Context: **directory**
Specify in **httpd.conf** or **sites-available/***
Default: All
Ubuntu: various

ScriptAlias   *Maps a URI to a directory or file and declares the target to be a server (CGI) script.*

ScriptAlias alias pathname

where *alias* must match part of the URI the client requested to invoke the ScriptAlias. The *pathname* is the absolute pathname of the target of the alias, usually a directory. Similar to the Alias directive, this directive specifies the target is a CGI script (page 898).

The following ScriptAlias directive from the Ubuntu **default** file maps client requests that include **/cgi-bin/** to the **/var/lib/cgi-bin** directory (and indicates that these requests will be treated as CGI requests):

```
ScriptAlias /cgi-bin/ "/usr/lib/cgi-bin/"
```

Contexts: **server config, virtual host**
Specify in **sites-available/***
Default: none
Ubuntu: **/cgi-bin/ /usr/lib/cgi-bin/**

User   *Sets the UID of the processes that run the servers.*

User #userid | username

where *userid* is a UID value, preceded by **#**, and *username* is the name of a local user. The processes that Apache spawns are run as the user specified by this directive.

Do not set User to **root** or **0**

security   For a more secure system, do not set User to **root** or **0** (zero) and do not allow the **www-data** user to have write access to the DocumentRoot directory hierarchy (except as needed for storing data), especially not to configuration files.

Apache must start with **root** privileges to listen on a privileged port. For reasons of security, Apache's child processes (servers) run as nonprivileged users. The default UID of –1 does not map to a user under Ubuntu Linux. Instead, Ubuntu's **apache2** package creates a user named **www-data** during installation and sets User to that user.

Context: **server config**
Specify in **httpd.conf**
Default: #–1
Ubuntu: www-data via the APACHE_RUN_USER variable (page 889)

SECURITY DIRECTIVES

Allow   *Specifies which clients can access specified content.*

Allow from All | host [host ...] | env=var [env=var ...]

This directive, which must be written as **Allow from**, grants access to a directory hierarchy to the specified clients. The directory hierarchy is specified by the container or **.htaccess** file this directive appears in.

All: Serves content to any client.

host: Serves content to the client(s) specified by *host*, which can take several forms: an FQDN, a partial domain name (such as **example.com**), an IP address, a partial IP address, or a network/netmask pair.

var: Serves content when the environment variable named *var* is set. You can set a variable with the SetEnvIf directive. See the Order directive (page 887) for an example.

Contexts: **directory, .htaccess**
Specify in **httpd.conf** or **sites-available/✷**
Default: none; default behavior depends on the Order directive
Ubuntu: various

AllowOverride   *Specifies whether Apache examines .htaccess files and which classes of directives in those files it processes.*

AllowOverride All | None | directive-class [directive-class ...]

This directive specifies whether Apache examines **.htaccess** files in the directory hierarchy specified by its container. If Apache does examine **.htaccess** files, this directive specifies which classes of directives within **.htaccess** files Apache processes.

All: Processes all classes of directives in **.htaccess** files.

None: Ignores directives in **.htaccess** files. However, Apache will still serve the content of **.htaccess** files, possibly exposing sensitive information. This choice does not affect **.htpasswrd** files. The example in the description of the <Files> container (page 872) shows how to prevent Apache from serving the content of files whose names begin with **.ht**.

The *directive-class* is one of the following directive class identifiers:

AuthConfig: Class of directives that control authorization (AuthName, AuthType, Require, and so on). This class is used mostly in **.htaccess** files to require a username and password to access the content. For more information refer to "Authentication Modules and **.htaccess**" on page 901.

FileInfo: Class of directives that controls document types (DefaultType, Error-Document, SetHandler, and so on).

Indexes: Class of directives relating to directory indexing (DirectoryIndex, Fancy-Indexing, IndexOptions, and so on).

Limit: Class of client-access directives (Allow, Deny, and Order).

Options: Class of directives controlling directory features.

Context: **directory**
Specify in **httpd.conf** or **sites-available/***
Default: All
Ubuntu: various

Deny *Specifies which clients are not allowed to access specified content.*

Deny from All | host [host ...] | env=var [env=var ...]

This directive, which must be written as **Deny from**, denies access to a directory hierarchy to the specified clients. The directory hierarchy is specified by the container or **.htaccess** file this directive appears in. See the Order directive (next) for an example.

All: Denies content to all clients.

host: Denies content to the client(s) specified by *host,* which can take several forms: an FQDN, a partial domain name (such as **example.com**), an IP address, a partial IP address, or a network/netmask pair.

var: Denies content when the environment variable named *var* is set. You can set a variable with the SetEnvIf directive.

Contexts: **directory, .htaccess**
Specify in **mods-available/proxy.conf, httpd.conf**, and **sites-available/***
Default: none
Ubuntu: All

Order *Specifies the default access and the order in which Allow and Deny directives are evaluated.*

Order Deny,Allow | Allow,Deny

Deny,Allow: Allows access by default; denies access only to clients specified in Deny directives. (First evaluates Deny directives, then evaluates Allow directives.)

Allow,Deny: Denies access by default; allows access only to clients specified in Allow directives. (First evaluates Allow directives, then evaluates Deny directives.)

There must not be SPACEs on either side of the comma. Access defaults to the second entry in the pair (Deny,Allow defaults to Allow) if there is no Allow from or Deny from directive that matches the client. If a single Allow from or Deny from directive matches the client, that directive overrides the default. If multiple Allow from and Deny from directives match the client, Apache evaluates the directives in the order specified by the Order directive; the last match takes precedence.

Access granted or denied by this directive applies to the directory hierarchy specified by the container or **.htaccess** file this directive appears in. Although Ubuntu Linux has a default of Allow,Deny, which denies access to all clients not specified by Allow directives, the next directive in **sites-available/default**, **Allow from all**, grants access to all clients:

```
Order allow,deny
Allow from all
```

You can restrict access by specifying Deny,Allow to deny all access and then specifying only those clients you want to grant access to in an Allow directive. The following directives grant access to clients from the **example.net** domain only and would typically appear within a <Directory> container (page 871):

```
Order deny,allow
Deny from all
Allow from .example.net
```

Contexts: **directory, .htaccess**
Specify in **httpd.conf** or **sites-available/***
Default: Deny,Allow
Ubuntu: Allow,Deny (for **/var/www**)

CONFIGURATION FILES

This section describes the **apache2.conf** and **default** configuration files.

THE UBUNTU apache2.conf FILE

This section highlights some of the important features of the Ubuntu version of the **/etc/apache2/apache2.conf** file, which is based on the **httpd.conf** file distributed by Apache. The version of this heavily commented file that is distributed by Apache is broken into three parts, of which Ubuntu uses the first (Section 1: Global Environment) as **apache2.conf**. Ubuntu distributes the contents of the other two sections among other configuration files, including the **sites-available/default** configuration file, which is described in the next section.

Include directives   See page 862 for information on Include directives in the **apache2.conf** file.

ServerRoot   The ServerRoot directive (page 882) is set to **/etc/apache2**, which is the pathname that Apache prepends to relative pathnames in the configuration files:

```
ServerRoot "/etc/apache2"
```

Do not modify apache2.conf

tip Typically, when you configure Apache, you do not make changes to **apache2.conf**; instead, you modify files that are specified in Include directives (page 862). You can also use the configuration tools described on page 861. This setup allows updates to Apache to change **apache2.conf** without affecting the server.

<IfModule> The <IfModule> containers (page 872) allow you to use the same **apache2.conf** file with different multiprocessing modules (MPMs, page 903). Apache executes the directives in an <IfModule> container only if the specified module is loaded. The **apache2.conf** file holds two <IfModule> containers that configure Apache differently, depending on which module—**prefork** or **worker**—is loaded. Ubuntu ships with the more efficient **worker** MPM loaded.

```
## Server-Pool Size Regulation (MPM specific)
...
<IfModule mpm_prefork_module>
    StartServers          5
    MinSpareServers       5
    MaxSpareServers      10
    MaxClients          150
    MaxRequestsPerChild   0
</IfModule>

<IfModule mpm_worker_module>
    StartServers          2
    MaxClients          150
    MinSpareThreads      25
    MaxSpareThreads      75
    ThreadsPerChild      25
    MaxRequestsPerChild   0
</IfModule>
```

For more information refer to "Multiprocessing Modules (MPMs)" on page 903.

User The User directive causes Apache to run as the user specified by the variable named APACHE_RUN_USER:

```
User ${APACHE_RUN_USER}
```

In the **/etc/apache2/envvars** file, the APACHE_RUN_USER variable is assigned a value of **www-data**:

```
export APACHE_RUN_USER=www-data
```

TypesConfig The TypesConfig directive specifies the file that defines the *MIME* (page 1120) types that Apache uses for content negotiation (page 891). It is used to match filename extensions with MIME types (e.g., **.png** with image/png).

```
TypesConfig /etc/mime.types
```

DefaultType Defines the content-type Apache sends if it cannot determine a type.

```
DefaultType text/plain
```

Modules   Instead of having a lot of LoadModule directives (page 884) in the **apache2.conf** file, Ubuntu puts the following Include directives in that file:

```
Include /etc/apache2/mods-enabled/*.load
Include /etc/apache2/mods-enabled/*.conf
```

These directives include all the ***.load** and ***.conf** files in the **mods-enabled** directory. For more information on how to enable modules, see the discussion of a2enmod on page 861.

There are many more directives in the **apache2.conf** file; the comments in the file provide a guide as to what they do. There is nothing here you need to change as you get started using Apache.

The Ubuntu default Configuration File

This section highlights some of the important features of the Ubuntu **default** configuration file, which is located in the **/etc/apache2/sites-available** directory.

ServerAdmin and   As Ubuntu Linux is shipped, the ServerAdmin directive is set to **webmaster@localhost**.
ServerName   Add a ServerName directive and change ServerAdmin to a useful value as suggested under ServerAdmin (page 868) and ServerName (page 868).

DocumentRoot   The DocumentRoot directive (page 869) appears as follows:

```
DocumentRoot /var/www/
```

Modify this directive only if you want to put content somewhere other than in the **/var/www** directory.

<Directory>   The following <Directory> container (page 871) sets up a restrictive environment for the entire local filesystem (specified by **/**):

```
<Directory />
    Options FollowSymLinks
    AllowOverride None
</Directory>
```

The Options directive (page 884) allows Apache to follow symbolic links but disallows many options. The AllowOverride directive (page 886) causes Apache not to process directives in **.htaccess** files. You must explicitly enable less restrictive options if you want them, but be aware that doing so can expose the root filesystem and compromise system security.

Next, another <Directory> container sets up less restrictive options for the Document-Root (**/var/www**). The code in **default** is interspersed with many comments. Without the comments it looks like this:

```
<Directory /var/www/>
    Options Indexes FollowSymLinks MultiViews
    AllowOverride None
    Order allow,deny
    allow from all
</Directory>
```

The Indexes option in the Options directive allows Apache to display directory listings. The Order (page 887) and Allow (page 886) directives combine to allow requests from all clients. This container is slightly less restrictive than the preceding one, although it still does not allow Apache to follow directives in **.htaccess** files.

ADVANCED CONFIGURATION

This section describes how to configure some advanced features of Apache.

REDIRECTS

Apache can respond to a request for a URI by asking the client to request a different URI. This response is called a *redirect*. A redirect works because redirection is part of the HTTP implementation: Apache sends the appropriate response code and the new URI, and a compliant browser requests the new location.

The Redirect directive can establish an explicit redirect that sends a client to a different page when a Web site is moved. Or, when a user enters the URI of a directory in a browser but leaves off the trailing slash, Apache can automatically redirect the client to the same URI terminated with a slash.

UseCanonicalName The ServerName directive (page 868), which establishes the name of the server, and the UseCanonicalName directive (page 878) are both important when a server has more than one name and needs to perform an automatic redirect. For example, assume the server with the name **zach.example.com** and the alias **www.example.com** has ServerName set to **www.example.com**. When a client specifies a URI of a directory but leaves off the trailing slash (**zach.example.com/dir**), Apache has to perform a redirect to determine the URI of the requested directory. When UseCanonicalName is set to On, Apache uses the value of ServerName and returns **www.example.com/dir/**. With UseCanonicalName set to Off, Apache uses the name from the incoming request and returns **zach.example.com/dir/**.

CONTENT NEGOTIATION

Apache can serve multiple versions of the same page, using a client's preference to determine which version to send. The process Apache uses to determine which version of a page (file) to send is called *content negotiation*. Apache supports two methods of content negotiation: MultiViews search and type maps, which can work together.

TYPE MAPS

The following AddHandler directive from **apache2.conf** tells Apache to use any filename ending in **.var** as a type map:

```
AddHandler type-map var
```

To see how type maps work, create the following files in **/var/www**:

```
$ cat /var/www/index.html.en
<html><body><h1>Hello</h1></body></html>

$ cat /var/www/index.html.fr
<html><body><h1>Bonjour</h1><body></html>

$ cat /var/www/index.html.var
URI: index.html.en
Content-Language: en
Content-type: text/html; charset=ISO-8859-1

URI: index.html.fr
Content-Language: fr
Content-type: text/html; charset=ISO-8859-1
```

If your browser's preferred language is set to English (**en**), it will display the **Hello** page when you browse to **http://localhost/index.html.var**. If your browser's preferred language is set to French (**fr**), it will display the **Bonjour** page. (With the MultiViews option turned on, as it is by default, the browser displays the correct page when you browse to **http://localhost**. See the next section.) You can change the default language in Firefox by selecting **Edit⇨Preferences** from the menubar, clicking the Advanced icon and then the General tab, and finally clicking **Choose** from the Languages frame. Select a language from the **Select a language to add** combo box, if necessary, and then move the preferred language to the top of the list. In the example, the **charset** assignments are not necessary. However, they would be helpful if you were sending pages using different encodings such as English, Russian, and Korean.

Type maps are used for more than selecting among different languages. Instead of matching **Content-Language** as in the preceding example, the map could match **Content-type** and send **jpeg** or **png** images depending on how the browser's preferences are set.

MultiViews

When you set the MultiViews option on a directory, Apache attempts to deliver the correct page when a requested resource does not exist. The following lines in the **sites-available/default** file set MultiViews for the document root (**/**):

```
<Directory /var/www/>
    Options Indexes FollowSymLinks MultiViews
...
```

To see how MultiViews work, remove the **/var/www/index.html.var** type map file that you created in the preceding section. Now browse to **http://localhost**. The proper language page is displayed, but why?

When a browser sends Apache a request for a directory, Apache looks for a file named **index.html** in that directory. In the example, Apache does not find the file. If MultiViews is enabled, as it is by default, Apache looks for files named **index.html.***.

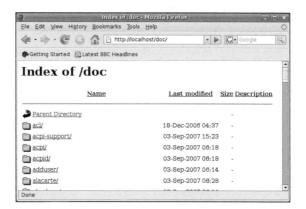

Figure 26-1 A server-generated directory listing

In the example it finds **index.html.en** and **index.html.fr**. Apache effectively creates a type map on the fly, mapping the **index.html.*** files to various languages, and sends its best guess as to the page you want.

MultiViews provides an easy way to serve multiple versions of the same file without having to create a type map. However if you require finer-grained control over which version of a resource should be sent, type maps are a better solution.

SERVER-GENERATED DIRECTORY LISTINGS (INDEXING)

When a client requests a directory, the Apache configuration determines what is returned to the client. Apache can return a file as specified by the DirectoryIndex directive (page 870), a directory listing if no file matches DirectoryIndex and the Options Indexes directive (page 884) is set, or an error message if no file matches Directory-Index and Options Indexes is not set. Figure 26-1 shows the server-generated directory listing that results from pointing a local browser at **http://localhost/doc/** (you must include the trailing slash) on the server system (assuming the default configuration).

VIRTUAL HOSTS

Apache supports *virtual hosts*, which means that one instance of Apache can respond to requests directed to multiple IP addresses or hostnames as though it were multiple servers. Each IP address or hostname can then provide different content and be configured differently.

SETTING UP A VIRTUAL HOST

To improve portability and make software upgrades easier, Ubuntu provides two directories that can hold the code to support virtual hosts. The **apache2.conf** file has an Include directive (page 862) that incorporates the files in the **/etc/apache2/sites-enabled** directory.

To create a new virtual host, you can create a file that defines the virtual host in **/etc/apache2/sites-available**. Then run a2ensite (page 862) with the name of the file you created as an argument and reload Apache. Running a2ensite enables the virtual host by creating a link in **/etc/apache2/sites-enabled**.

TYPES OF VIRTUAL HOSTS

There are two types of virtual hosts: *host-by-name* (also called *host-based*) and *host-by-IP*. Host-by-name relies on the FQDN the client uses in its request to Apache—for example, **www.example.com** versus **www2.example.com**. Host-by-IP examines the IP address the host resolves as and responds according to that match.

Host-by-name is handy if there is only one IP address, but Apache must support multiple FQDNs. Although you can use host-by-IP if a given Web server has aliases, Apache should serve the same content regardless of which name is used.

The VirtualHost container and the ServerName directive control which kind of virtual host you are running. The NameVirtualHost directive specifies which IP address supports host-by-name virtual hosting. You can specify many virtual hosts for a single instance of Apache.

THE default VIRTUAL HOST

Ubuntu ships with the host-by-name virtual host named **default** defined in **/etc/apache2/sites-available/default**. This virtual host displays a server-generated directory listing (page 893) of **/var/www**. This directory includes the **apache2-default** directory. When you click this directory, Apache serves the **index.html** file, which displays **It works!** If you uncomment the RewriteMatch directive in the **default** file, Apache serves the **apache2-default** directory in response to a request for **/** and automatically displays **It works!** Alternatively, if you put your content in **/var/www**, the default configuration will serve your site as you would expect. It is safe to remove the **apache2-default** directory.

EXAMPLES

The following examples of host-by-name virtual hosting use wildcards (*****) to remain as flexible as possible. You may want to replace the wildcards with the IP address of the server for more precise control when Apache is serving multiple virtual hosts.

The first <VirtualHost> container sets up host-by-name for the site named **example.com**. This virtual host handles requests that are directed to **example.com**. The ServerAlias directive allows it to also process requests directed to **www.example.com**.

```
<VirtualHost *>
    ServerName  example.com
    ServerAlias www.example.com
    ServerAdmin webmaster@example.com
    DocumentRoot /var/www/example.com
    CustomLog    /var/log/apache2/example.com.log combined
    ErrorLog     /var/lo, e2/example.com.err
</VirtualHost>
```

The next example is similar to the previous one. It adds a Directory directive that prevents remote users (users not coming from the 192.168. subnet) from accessing the Web site.

```
<VirtualHost *>
    ServerName intranet.example.com
    ServerAdmin webmaster@example.com
    DocumentRoot /var/www
    ErrorLog /var/log/apache2/intra.error_log
    CustomLog /var/log/apache2/example.com.log combined
    <Directory /var/www>
        Order deny,allow
        Deny from all
        Allow from 192.168.  # allow from private subnet only
    </Directory>
</VirtualHost>
```

The next example sets up two virtual hosts. The VirtualHost containers accept all traffic directed to the server by specifying *. The ServerName directives accept traffic for **sam.example.com** (or the alias **www.example.com/sam**) and **mail.example.com**. The first virtual host serves documents from Sam's **public_html** directory; the second is a Webmail server with its content at **/var/www/squirrelmail**. This example works because all three addresses resolve to the IP address of the server.

```
NameVirtualHost *:
<VirtualHost *>
    ServerName sam.example.com
    ServerAdmin webmaster@example.com
    DocumentRoot /home/sam/public_html
</VirtualHost>

<VirtualHost *:>
    ServerName mail.example.com
    ServerAdmin webmaster2@example.com
    DocumentRoot /var/www/squirrelmail
</VirtualHost>
```

If the user specifies an IP address and not a URI, that address may match more than one of the virtual hosts, as in the example. In this case, Apache serves the virtual host that best matches. If none of the virtual host addresses matches the IP address better than another, Apache serves the first virtual host. In the preceding example, both virtual hosts match an IP address the same way; neither is a better match, so Apache serves the first virtual host (**sam.example.com**). If **mail.example.com** was defined as <VirtualHost 192.168.1.102> and a user specified that IP address, Apache would serve **mail.example.com** because it is a better match for the IP address than the wildcard that the other virtual host specifies.

The next example shows VirtualHost containers for a host-by-IP server. The example assumes that 111.111.0.0 and 111.111.0.1 point to the local server. Here each virtual host has its own IP/port combination. The third virtual host is distinguished from the first by the port that a request comes in on.

```
<VirtualHost 111.111.0.0:80>
    DocumentRoot /var/www/www0
</VirtualHost>

<VirtualHost 111.111.0.1:80>
    DocumentRoot /var/www/www1
</VirtualHost>

<VirtualHost 111.111.0.0:8080>
    DocumentRoot /var/www/www2
    Listen 8080                    # this directive should go in ports.conf
</VirtualHost>
```

The final example sets up a virtual server for Webmail that can be accessed only over SSL. It would be appropriate to put the code for this example in a file named **/etc/apache2/sites-available/mail.example.com**. To use this example you must create an SSL certificate (page 899), enable the **ssl** module (included in the default Apache installation) with a2enmod (page 861), and enable the virtual domain using a2ensite (page 862).

```
<VirtualHost mail.example.com:80>
    Redirect permanent / https://mail.example.com/
</VirtualHost>
<VirtualHost mail.example.com:443>
    ServerName  mail.example.com
    ServerAdmin postmaster@example.com
    DocumentRoot /var/www/mail.example.com
    ErrorLog /var/log/apache2/mail.example.com.err
    CustomLog /var/log/apache2/mail.example.com.log combined
    SSLEngine On
    SSLCertificateFile /etc/apache2/ssl/apache.pem
</VirtualHost>
```

TROUBLESHOOTING

The **apache2** init script checks the syntax of the Apache configuration files and logs an error if there is a problem. You can also call apache2ctl directly to check the syntax:

```
$ apache2ctl configtest
Syntax OK
```

Once you start the **apache2** daemon, you can confirm that Apache is working correctly by pointing a browser on the local system at **http://localhost/**. From a remote system, use **http://***server*/, substituting the hostname of the server for *server*. In response, Apache displays a directory listing for **/var/www** unless you have added an index file or changed the default virtual host.

If the browser does not display the directory listing, it will display one of two errors: **Connection refused** or an error page. If you get a **Connection refused** error, make sure that port 80 is not blocked by a firewall (page 857) and check that the server is running:

```
$ ps -ef | grep apache2
max        3479 12869  0 16:55 pts/1    00:00:00 grep apache2
root       5031     1  0 Mar26 ?        00:00:00 /usr/sbin/apache2 -k start
www-data   5032  5031  0 Mar26 ?        00:00:00 /usr/sbin/apache2 -k start
www-data   5088  5031  0 Mar26 ?        00:00:00 /usr/sbin/apache2 -k start
www-data   5092  5031  0 Mar26 ?        00:00:00 /usr/sbin/apache2 -k start
```

If the server is running, confirm that you did not specify a port other than 80 in a Listen directive. If you did, the URI you specify in the browser must reflect this port number (**http://localhost:***port* specifies port *port*). Otherwise, check the error log (**/var/log/httpd/error_log**) for information about what is not working.

To verify that the browser is not at fault, use telnet to try to connect to port 80 of the server:

```
$ telnet www.example.com 80
Trying 192.0.34.166...
Connected to www.example.com.
Escape character is '^]'.
CONTROL-]
telnet> quit
Connection closed.
```

If telnet displays **Connection refused**, it means that the local system cannot connect to the server.

MODULES

Apache is a skeletal program that relies on external modules, called dynamic shared objects (DSOs), to provide most of its functionality. In addition to the modules included with Ubuntu Linux, many other modules are available. See httpd.apache.org/modules for more information. See a2enmod on page 861 for information on enabling modules.

Configuring modules

tip   You can configure some modules by editing their corresponding *.conf file in the **mods-available** directory.

The names of the files that hold modules start with the prefix **libapache2-mod-**. The following command displays a complete list of modules. You can pipe the list through grep to find the module you want. See page 512 for information on apt-cache.

```
$ apt-cache search libapache2-mod
libapache2-mod-auth-kerb - apache2 module for Kerberos authentication
libapache2-mod-auth-mysql - Apache 2 module for MySQL authentication
libapache2-mod-auth-pam - module for Apache2 which authenticate using PAM
libapache2-mod-auth-pgsql - Module for Apache2 which provides pgsql authentication
libapache2-mod-auth-plain - Module for Apache2 which provides plaintext authentication
libapache2-mod-auth-sys-group - Module for Apache2 which checks user against system group
libapache2-mod-macro - Create macros inside apache2 config files
libapache2-mod-perl2 - Integration of perl with the Apache2 web server
libapache2-mod-perl2-dev - Integration of perl with the Apache2 server - development files
libapache2-mod-perl2-doc - Integration of perl with the Apache2 web server - documentation
libapache2-mod-php5 - server-side, HTML-embedded scripting language (apache 2 module)
libapache2-mod-php5filter - server-side, HTML-embedded scripting language (apache 2...)
libapache2-mod-python - Apache 2 module that embeds Python within the server
...

$ apt-cache search libapache2-mod | grep ruby
libapache2-mod-ruby - Embedding Ruby in the Apache2 web server
```

mod_cgi and CGI Scripts

The CGI (Common Gateway Interface) allows external application programs to interface with Web servers. Any program can be a CGI program if it runs in real time (at the time of the request) and relays its output to the requesting client. Various kinds of scripts, including shell, Perl, Python, and PHP, are the most commonly encountered CGI programs because a script can call a program and reformat its output in HTML for a client.

Apache can handle requests for CGI programs in several different ways. The most common method is to put a CGI program in the **cgi-bin** directory and then enable its execution from that directory only. The location of the **cgi-bin** directory, as specified by the ScriptAlias directive (page 885), is **/usr/lib/cgi-bin**. Alternatively, an Add-Handler directive (page 879) can identify the filename extensions of scripts, such as **.cgi** or **.pl**, within the regular content (for example, **AddHandler cgi-script .cgi**). If you use AddHandler, you must also specify the ExecCGI option in an Options directive within the appropriate <Directory> container. The **mod_cgi** module must be loaded to access and execute CGI scripts.

The following Perl CGI script displays the Apache environment. This script should be used for debugging only because it presents a security risk if remote clients can access it:

```perl
#!/usr/bin/perl
##
##   printenv -- demo CGI program that prints its environment
##

print "Content-type: text/plain\n\n";
foreach $var (sort(keys(%ENV))) {
    $val = $ENV{$var};
    $val =~ s|\n|\\n|g;
    $val =~ s|"|\\"|g;
    print "${var}=\"${val}\"\n";
}
```

mod_ssl

SSL (Secure Sockets Layer), which is implemented by the **mod_ssl** module, has two functions: It allows a client to verify the identity of a server and it enables secure two-way communication between a client and a server. SSL is used on Web pages in conjunction with forms that require passwords, credit card numbers, or other sensitive data.

Apache uses the HTTPS protocol—not HTTP—for SSL communication. When Apache uses SSL, it listens on a second port (443 by default) for a connection and performs a handshaking sequence before sending the requested content to the client.

Server verification is critical for financial transactions. After all, you do not want to give your credit card number to a fraudulent Web site posing as a known company. SSL uses a certificate to positively identify a server. Over a public network such as the Internet, the identification is reliable only if the certificate contains a digital signature from an authoritative source such as VeriSign or Thawte. SSL Web pages are denoted by a URI beginning with **https://**.

Data encryption prevents malicious users from eavesdropping on Internet connections and copying personal information. To encrypt communication, SSL sits between the network and an application and encrypts communication between the server and the client.

SETTING UP mod_ssl

The **mod_ssl** package is installed as part of the **apache2** package—you do not need to install it separately. The **/etc/apache2/mods-available/ssl.conf** file configures **mod_ssl**; **ssl.load**, which is in the same directory, loads it. You must enable the module with the command **a2enmod ssl**. The first few directives in this file set various parameters for SSL operation.

You can set up a virtual host for SSL in the **sites-available** directory and enable it using a2ensite (page 862). As with any virtual host, a virtual host for SSL holds directives such as ServerName and ServerAdmin that need to be configured. In addition, it holds some SSL-related directives. See the example on page 896.

USING A SELF-SIGNED CERTIFICATE FOR ENCRYPTION

If you require SSL for encryption and not verification—that is, if the client already trusts the server—you can generate and use a self-signed certificate, bypassing the time and expense involved in obtaining a digitally signed certificate. Self-signed certificates generate a warning when you connect to the server: Most browsers display a dialog box that allows you to examine and accept the certificate. The **exim4** daemon also uses certificates (page 700).

The following example creates a self-signed certificate. (See the procedure at www.modssl.org/docs/2.8/ssl_faq.html#ToC28 if apache2-ssl-certificate is missing from the system. You do not need to send in the CSR for a self-signed certificate.)

```
$ sudo apache2-ssl-certificate
creating selfsigned certificate
replace it with one signed by a certification authority (CA)

enter your ServerName at the Common Name prompt

If you want your certificate to expire after x days call this program
with -days x
Generating a 1024 bit RSA private key
...................................................++++++
........++++++
writing new private key to '/etc/apache2/ssl/apache.pem'
-----
You are about to be asked to enter information that will be incorporated
into your certificate request.
What you are about to enter is what is called a Distinguished Name or a DN.
There are quite a few fields but you can leave some blank
For some fields there will be a default value,
If you enter '.', the field will be left blank.
-----
Country Name (2 letter code) [GB]:US
State or Province Name (full name) [Some-State]:California
Locality Name (eg, city) []:San Francisco
Organization Name (eg, company; recommended) []:Sobell Associates Inc.
Organizational Unit Name (eg, section) []:
server name (eg. ssl.domain.tld; required!!!) []:www.sobell.com
Email Address []:mgs@sobell.com
```

The answers to the first five questions are arbitrary: They can help clients identify a site when they examine the certificate. The answer to the sixth question (**server name**) is critical. Because certificates are tied to the name of the server, you must enter the server's FQDN accurately. If you mistype this information, the server name and the name of the certificate will not match. A browser will then generate a warning message each time a connection is made.

Now you must create an SSL-enabled virtual host in **/etc/apache2/sites-available**. Host-by-name virtual hosting will not work with SSL because the HTTP **Host** header sent by the client that Apache uses to differentiate between host-by-name virtual hosts is encrypted. You can use only one SSL certificate, matching one domain per IP address. You can have multiple virtual hosts on that IP address, but if they are accessed over HTTPS, the client will receive an error saying that the certificate does not match the domain name. After you enable the new virtual host and restart Apache, the new certificate will be in use.

Following is an example wildcard setup for **/etc/apache2/sites-available/ssl**. Enable it with **sudo a2ensite ssl**:

```
<VirtualHost *:80>
    Redirect permanent / https://www.sobell.com/
</VirtualHost>
```

```
<VirtualHost *:443>
    ServerName www.sobell.com
    SSLEngine On
    SSLCertificateFile /etc/apache2/ssl/apache.pem
    DocumentRoot /var/www
</VirtualHost>
```

This example directs all non-SSL traffic to the SSL site. You must add a **Listen 443** directive to **/etc/apache2/ports.conf** if you want Apache to listen on the default HTTPS port.

NOTES ON CERTIFICATES

- Although the server name is part of the certificate, the SSL connection is tied to the IP address of the server: You can have only one certificate per IP address. For multiple virtual hosts to have separate certificates, you must specify host-by-IP rather than host-by-name virtual hosts (page 893).

- As long as the server is identified by the name for which the certificate was issued, you can use the certificate on another server or IP address.

- A root certificate is the certificate that identifies the root certificate authority (root CA). Every browser contains a database of the public keys for the root certificates of the major signing authorities, including VeriSign and Thawte.

- It is possible to generate a root certificate and sign all your server certificates with this root CA. Regular clients can import the public key of the root CA so that they recognize every certificate signed by that root CA. This setup is convenient for a server with multiple SSL-enabled virtual hosts and no commercial certificates. For more information see www.modssl.org/docs/2.8/ssl_faq.html#ToC29.

- A self-signed certificate does not enable clients to verify the identity of the server.

AUTHENTICATION MODULES AND .htaccess

To restrict access to a Web page, Apache and third parties provide authentication modules and methods that can verify a user's credentials, such as a username and password. Some modules support authentication against various databases including *LDAP* (page 1116) and NIS (page 705).

User authentication directives are commonly placed in a **.htaccess** file. A basic **.htaccess** file that uses the Apache default authentication module (**mod_auth**) follows. Substitute appropriate values for the local server.

```
$ sudo cat .htaccess
AuthUserFile /var/www/.htpasswd
AuthGroupFile /dev/null
AuthName "Browser dialog box query"
AuthType Basic
require valid-user
```

The **/var/www/.htpasswd** is a typical absolute pathname of a **.htpasswd** file and **Browser dialog box query** is the string that the user will see as part of the dialog box that requests a username and password.

The second line of the preceding **.htaccess** file turns off the group function. The fourth line specifies the user authentication type **Basic,** which is implemented by the default **mod_auth** module. The last line tells Apache which users can access the protected directory. The entry **valid-user** grants access to the directory to any user whose username appears in the Apache password file and who enters the correct password.

You can put the Apache password file anywhere on the system, as long as Apache can read it. It is safe to put this file in the same directory as the **.htaccess** file because, by default, Apache will not answer any requests for files whose names start with **.ht.**

The following command creates a **.htpasswd** file in the working directory for Sam:

```
$ htpasswd -c .htpasswd sam
New password:
Re-type new password:
Adding password for user sam
```

The **default** virtual host includes an **AllowOverride None** directive (page 886) for **/var/www.** You must change this directive to at least **AllowOverride AuthConfig** in **sites-available/default** or remove it to enable Apache to process user authentication directives.

SCRIPTING MODULES

Apache can process content before serving it to a client. In earlier versions of Apache, only CGI scripts could process content. In the current version, *scripting modules* can work with scripts embedded in HTML documents.

Scripting modules manipulate content before Apache serves it to a client. Because they are built into Apache, scripting modules are fast. Scripting modules are especially efficient at working with external data sources such as relational databases. Clients can pass data to a scripting module that modifies the information that Apache serves.

Scripting modules stand in contrast to CGI scripts that are run externally to Apache. In particular, CGI scripts do not allow client interaction and are slow because they must make external calls.

Ubuntu provides packages that allow you to embed Perl (**mod_perl**), Python (**mod_python**), and PHP (**mod_php**) code in HTML content. Perl and Python, which are general-purpose scripting languages, are encapsulated for use directly in Apache and are available in the **libapache2-mod-perl2** and **libapache2-mod-python** packages, respectively.

PHP, which was developed for manipulating Web content, outputs HTML by default. Implemented in the **mod_php** module and available in **libapache2-mod-php5,** this language is easy to set up, has a syntax similar to that of Perl and C, and comes with a large number of Web-related functions.

MULTIPROCESSING MODULES (MPMs)

If Apache were to execute in only one process, every time a client requested a page, Apache would have to ignore other requests while it read that page from disk (or waited for a CGI script to generate it). After it read the page, it could send the page to the client and respond to the next request. With this setup, Apache could serve only one client at a time.

prefork MPM Apache 1.3 and earlier forked servers to respond to multiple clients. Apache 2 moved the forking behavior to the **prefork** multiprocessing module (MPM). MPMs introduced the ability to switch between various multiprocessing techniques.

The **prefork** MPM uses the **fork**() system call to create an exact copy of the running Apache process to serve each request. The MaxServers, MaxSpareServers, and similar directives control how many copies of Apache run at the same time. Because the operating system has to spend time context switching between Apache processes, and because each process has its own memory, the **prefork** MPM generates considerable overhead on a busy server.

worker MPM The **worker** MPM reduces this overhead by using **threads**. A thread is similar to a process in that it can execute independently of other threads or processes. Waiting for a read to complete in one thread does not stop (block) other threads from executing. The difference between threads and processes is that all the threads running under one process share the same memory, and the program—rather than the operating system—is responsible for managing the threads. The **worker** MPM maintains a pool of threads it can use to serve each request. Instead of the parent Apache process forking a child to serve each request for content as in **prefork**, the **worker** MPM uses threads to serve requests for content.

Threads Because all these threads run under the same process, they share the same memory. Code that is not *thread safe* (see *reentrant* on page 1128) can return inconsistent results. For example, some PHP library functions use the **strtok**() C function to convert a string to tokens. This function maintains internal variables. If it is called by multiple threads sharing the same memory, **strtok**()'s internal variables are put in an inconsistent state.

PHP If you want to use PHP, either you must use the **prefork** MPM or, if you want to use the **worker** MPM and PHP, you must remove **libapache2-mod-php5** and run PHP as a CGI script (page 898).

MPMs Available MPMs include

- **apache2-mpm-prefork**—Traditional MPM.

- **apache2-mpm-worker**—High-speed threaded MPM.

- **apache2-mpm-event**—Event driven MPM.

The **apache2-mpm-worker**, **apache2-mpm-event**, and **apache2-mpm-prefork** packages each supply the apache2 binary and conflict with one another. You cannot have more than one of these modules installed at the same time. When you install one of these packages, the installer automatically removes the existing MPM.

webalizer: ANALYZES WEB TRAFFIC

The **webalizer** package creates a directory at **/var/www/webalizer** and a cron file (page 588) at **/etc/cron.daily/webalizer**. Once a day, the cron file generates usage data and puts it in the **webalizer** directory; you can view this data by pointing a browser at **http://**server**/webalizer/**, where server is the hostname of the server.

The **/etc/webalizer/webalizer.conf** file controls the behavior of the webalizer utility. If you change the location of the DocumentRoot or log files, you must edit this file to reflect those changes. For more information on webalizer, refer to the webalizer man page and the sites listed under "More Information" on page 857.

MRTG: MONITORS TRAFFIC LOADS

Multi Router Traffic Grapher (MRTG; **mrtg** package) is an open-source application that graphs statistics available through SNMP (Simple Network Management Protocol). SNMP information is available on all high-end routers and switches as well as on some other networked equipment, such as printers and wireless access points.

Once MRTG is installed and running, you can view the reports at **http://**server**/mrtg**, where server is the hostname of the server. For more information see the mrtg man page and the sites listed under "More Information" on page 857.

ERROR CODES

Following is a list of Apache error codes:

100 Continue	404 Not Found
101 Switching Protocols	405 Method Not Allowed
200 OK	406 Not Acceptable
201 Created	407 Proxy Authentication Required
202 Accepted	408 Request Timed out
203 Non-Authoritative Info...	409 Conflict
204 No Content	410 Gone
205 Reset Content	411 Length Required
206 Partial Content	412 Precondition Failed
300 Multiple Choices	413 Request Entity Too Large
301 Moved Permanently	414 Request-URI Too Large

302 Moved Temporarily

303 See Other

304 Not Modified

305 Use Proxy

400 Bad Request

401 Unauthorized

402 Payment Required

403 Forbidden

415 Unsupported Media Type

500 Internal Server Error

501 Not Implemented

502 Bad Gateway

503 Service Unavailable

504 Gateway Time-out

505 HTTP Version Not Supported

CHAPTER SUMMARY

Apache is the most popular Web server on the Internet today. It is both robust and extensible. The **/etc/apache2/apache2.conf** configuration file controls many aspects of how Apache runs. This file, which is based on the first part of the **httpd.conf** file distributed by Apache, is heavily commented. Ubuntu also puts some configuration directives in the **/etc/apache2/sites-available/default** file.

Content to be served is typically placed in **/var/www**, called the document root. Apache automatically displays the file named **index.html** in this directory.

Configuration directives, or simply directives, are lines in a configuration file that control some aspect of how Apache functions. Four locations, called contexts, define where a configuration directive can appear: **server config**, **virtual host**, **directory**, and **.htaccess**. Containers, or special directives, are directives that group other directives.

To restrict access to a Web page, Apache and third parties provide authentication modules and methods that can verify a user's credentials, such as a username and password. Some modules enable authentication against various databases, including LDAP and NIS.

Apache can respond to a request for a URI by asking the client to request a different URI. This response is called a redirect. Apache can also process content before serving it to a client using scripting modules that work with scripts embedded in HTML documents.

Apache supports virtual hosts, which means that one instance of Apache can respond to requests directed to multiple IP addresses or hostnames as though it were multiple servers. Each IP address or hostname can provide different content and be configured differently.

The CGI (Common Gateway Interface) allows external application programs to interface with Web servers. Any program can be a CGI program if it runs in real time and relays its output to the requesting client.

SSL (Secure Sockets Layer) has two functions: It allows a client to verify the identity of a server and it enables secure two-way communication between a client and server.

EXERCISES

1. How would you tell Apache that your content is in **/usr/local/www**?

2. How would you instruct an Apache server to listen on port 81 instead of port 80?

3. How would you enable Sam to publish Web pages from his **~/website** directory but not allow anyone else to publish to the Web?

4. Apache must be started with **root** privileges. Why? Why does this action not present a security risk?

ADVANCED EXERCISES

5. If you are running Apache on a firewall system, perhaps to display a Web front-end for firewall configuration, how would you make sure that it is accessible only from inside the local network?

6. Why is it more efficient to run scripts using **mod_php** or **mod_perl** than to run them through CGI?

7. What two things does SSL provide and how does this situation differ if the certificate is self-signed?

8. Some Web sites generate content by retrieving data from a database and inserting it into a template using PHP or CGI each time the site is accessed. Why is this practice often a poor idea?

9. Assume you want to provide Webmail access for employees on the same server that hosts the corporate Web site. The Web site address is example.com, you want to use mail.example.com for Webmail, and the Webmail application is located in **/var/www/webmail**. Describe two ways you can set up this configuration.

10. Part of a Web site is a private intranet. Describe how you would prevent people outside the company's internal 192.168.0.0/16 network from accessing this site. The site is defined as follows:

```
<VirtualHost *>
  ServerName example.com
  DocumentRoot /var/www
  <Directory /var/www/intranet>
     AllowOverride AuthConfig
  </Directory>
</VirtualHost>
```

PART VI
PROGRAMMING TOOLS

27

PROGRAMMING THE BOURNE AGAIN SHELL

Chapter 7 introduced the shells and Chapter 9 went into detail about the Bourne Again Shell. This chapter introduces additional Bourne Again Shell commands, builtins, and concepts that carry shell programming to a point where it can be useful. Although you may make use of shell programming as a system administrator, you do not have to read this chapter to perform system administration tasks. Feel free to skip this chapter and come back to it if and when you like.

The first part of this chapter covers programming control structures, also called control flow constructs. These structures allow you to write scripts that can loop over command-line arguments, make decisions based on the value of a variable, set up menus, and more. The Bourne Again Shell uses the same constructs found in such high-level programming languages as C.

The next part of this chapter discusses parameters and variables, going into detail about array variables, local versus global variables, special parameters, and positional parameters. The exploration of builtin commands covers type, which displays information about a command, and read, which allows a shell

909

script to accept user input. The section on the exec builtin demonstrates how to use exec to execute a command efficiently by replacing a process and explains how to use exec to redirect input and output from within a script.

The next section covers the trap builtin, which provides a way to detect and respond to operating system signals (such as the signal generated when you press CONTROL-C). The discussion of builtins concludes with a discussion of kill, which can abort a process, and getopts, which makes it easy to parse options for a shell script. Table 27-6 on page 971 lists some of the more commonly used builtins.

Next the chapter examines arithmetic and logical expressions as well as the operators that work with them. The final section walks through the design and implementation of two major shell scripts.

This chapter contains many examples of shell programs. Although they illustrate certain concepts, most use information from earlier examples as well. This overlap not only reinforces your overall knowledge of shell programming but also demonstrates how you can combine commands to solve complex tasks. Running, modifying, and experimenting with the examples in this book is a good way to become comfortable with the underlying concepts.

Do not name a shell script test

tip   You can unwittingly create a problem if you give a shell script the name **test** because a Linux utility has the same name. Depending on how the **PATH** variable is set up and how you call the program, you may run either your script or the utility, leading to confusing results.

This chapter illustrates concepts with simple examples, which are followed by more complex ones in sections marked "Optional." The more complex scripts illustrate traditional shell programming practices and introduce some Linux utilities often used in scripts. You can skip these sections without loss of continuity. Return to them when you feel comfortable with the basic concepts.

CONTROL STRUCTURES

The *control flow* commands alter the order of execution of commands within a shell script. Control structures include the **if...then, for...in, while, until,** and **case** statements. In addition, the **break** and **continue** statements work in conjunction with the control structures to alter the order of execution of commands within a script.

if...then

The **if...then** control structure has the following syntax:

> *if test-command*
> > *then*
> > > *commands*
> *fi*

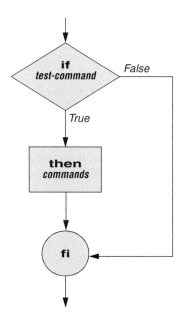

Figure 27-1 An **if...then** flowchart

The *bold* words in the syntax description are the items you supply to cause the structure to have the desired effect. The *nonbold* words are the keywords the shell uses to identify the control structure.

test builtin Figure 27-1 shows that the **if** statement tests the status returned by the ***test-command*** and transfers control based on this status. The end of the **if** structure is marked by a **fi** statement (*if* spelled backward). The following script prompts for two words, reads them, and then uses an **if** structure to execute commands based on the result returned by the test builtin when it compares the two words. (See the test info page for information on the test utility, which is similar to the test builtin.) The test builtin returns a status of *true* if the two words are the same and *false* if they are not. Double quotation marks around **$word1** and **$word2** make sure test works properly if you enter a string that contains a SPACE or other special character:

```
$ cat if1
echo -n "word 1: "
read word1
echo -n "word 2: "
read word2

if test "$word1" = "$word2"
    then
        echo "Match"
fi
echo "End of program."
```

```
$ ./if1
word 1: peach
word 2: peach
Match
End of program.
```

In the preceding example the *test-command* is **test** "**$word1**" = "**$word2**". The **test** builtin returns a *true* status if its first and third arguments have the relationship specified by its second argument. If this command returns a *true* status (= 0), the shell executes the commands between the **then** and **fi** statements. If the command returns a *false* status (not = 0), the shell passes control to the statement following **fi** without executing the statements between **then** and **fi**. The effect of this **if** statement is to display **Match** if the two words are the same. The script always displays **End of program.**

Builtins   In the Bourne Again Shell, **test** is a builtin—part of the shell. It is also a stand-alone utility kept in **/usr/bin/test**. This chapter discusses and demonstrates many Bourne Again Shell builtins. You typically use the builtin version if it is available and the utility if it is not. Each version of a command may vary slightly from one shell to the next and from the utility to any of the shell builtins. See page 958 for more information on shell builtins.

Checking arguments   The next program uses an **if** structure at the beginning of a script to confirm that you have supplied at least one argument on the command line. The **test –eq** operator compares two integers; the **$#** special parameter (page 953) takes on the value of the number of command-line arguments. This structure displays a message and exits from the script with an exit status of 1 if you do not supply at least one argument:

```
$ cat chkargs
if test $# -eq 0
    then
        echo "You must supply at least one argument."
        exit 1
fi
echo "Program running."
$ ./chkargs
You must supply at least one argument.
$ ./chkargs abc
Program running.
```

A test like the one shown in **chkargs** is a key component of any script that requires arguments. To prevent the user from receiving meaningless or confusing information from the script, the script needs to check whether the user has supplied the appropriate arguments. Some scripts simply test whether arguments exist (as in **chkargs**). Other scripts test for a specific number or specific kinds of arguments.

You can use **test** to verify the status of a file argument or the relationship between two file arguments. After verifying that at least one argument has been given on the command line, the following script tests whether the argument is the name of an ordinary file (not a directory or other type of file) in the working directory. The test builtin with the **–f** option and the first command-line argument (**$1**) check the file:

```
$ cat is_ordfile
if test $# -eq 0
    then
        echo "You must supply at least one argument."
        exit 1
fi
if test -f "$1"
    then
        echo "$1 is an ordinary file in the working directory"
    else
        echo "$1 is NOT an ordinary file in the working directory"
fi
```

You can test many other characteristics of a file using **test** options; see Table 27-1.

Table 27-1   Options to the **test** builtin

Option	Tests file to see if it
–d	Exists and is a directory file
–e	Exists
–f	Exists and is an ordinary file (not a directory)
–r	Exists and is readable
–s	Exists and has a size greater than 0 bytes
–w	Exists and is writable
–x	Exists and is executable

Other test options provide ways to test relationships between two files, such as whether one file is newer than another. Refer to later examples in this chapter for more information.

Always test the arguments

tip   To keep the examples in this book short and focused on specific concepts, the code to verify arguments is often omitted or abbreviated. It is good practice to test arguments in shell programs that other people will use. Doing so results in scripts that are easier to run and debug.

[ ] is a synonym for test   The following example—another version of **chkargs**—checks for arguments in a way that is more traditional for Linux shell scripts. This example uses the bracket ([]) synonym for **test**. Rather than using the word test in scripts, you can surround the arguments to test with brackets. The brackets must be surrounded by white-space (SPACEs or TABs).

```
$ cat chkargs2
if [ $# -eq 0 ]
    then
        echo "Usage: chkargs2 argument..." 1>&2
        exit 1
fi
echo "Program running."
exit 0
$ ./chkargs2
Usage: chkargs2 argument...
$ ./chkargs2 abc
Program running.
```

Usage messages   The error message that **chkargs2** displays is called a *usage message* and uses the **1>&2** notation to redirect its output to standard error (page 281). After issuing the usage message, **chkargs2** exits with an exit status of 1, indicating an error has occurred. The **exit 0** command at the end of the script causes **chkargs2** to exit with a 0 status after the program runs without an error. The Bourne Again Shell returns a 0 status if you omit the status code.

The usage message is commonly employed to specify the type and number of arguments the script takes. Many Linux utilities provide usage messages similar to the one in **chkargs2**. If you call a utility or other program with the wrong number or wrong kind of arguments, it will often display a usage message. Following is the usage message that cp displays when you call it without any arguments:

```
$ cp
cp: missing file operand
Try 'cp --help' for more information.
```

if...then...else

The introduction of an **else** statement turns the **if** structure into the two-way branch shown in Figure 27-2. The **if...then...else** control structure has the following syntax:

> *if test-command*
> > *then*
> > > *commands*
> > *else*
> > > *commands*
> *fi*

Because a semicolon (;) ends a command just as a NEWLINE does, you can place **then** on the same line as **if** by preceding it with a semicolon. (Because **if** and **then** are separate builtins, they require a command separator between them; a semicolon and NEWLINE work equally well [page 288].) Some people prefer this notation for aesthetic reasons; others like it because it saves space.

> *if test-command; then*
> > *commands*
> > *else*
> > > *commands*
> *fi*

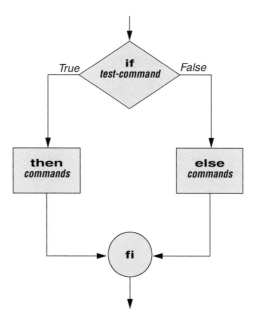

Figure 27-2 An **if...then...**else flowchart

If the *test-command* returns a *true* status, the **if** structure executes the commands between the **then** and **else** statements and then diverts control to the statement following **fi**. If the *test-command* returns a *false* status, the **if** structure executes the commands following the **else** statement.

When you run the **out** script with arguments that are filenames, it displays the files on the terminal. If the first argument is –**v** (called an option in this case), **out** uses less (page 148) to display the files one screen at a time. After determining that it was called with at least one argument, **out** tests its first argument to see whether it is –**v**. If the result of the test is *true* (the first argument is –**v**), **out** uses the shift builtin (page 954) to shift the arguments to get rid of the –**v** and displays the files using less. If the result of the test is *false* (the first argument is *not* –**v**), the script uses cat to display the files:

```
$ cat out
if [ $# -eq 0 ]
    then
        echo "Usage: out [-v] filenames..." 1>&2
        exit 1
fi

if [ "$1" = "-v" ]
    then
        shift
        less -- "$@"
    else
        cat -- "$@"
fi
```

optional In **out** the **– –** argument to cat and less tells these utilities that no more options follow on the command line and not to consider leading hyphens (–) in the following list as indicating options. Thus **– –** allows you to view a file with a name that starts with a hyphen. Although not common, filenames beginning with a hyphen do occasionally occur. (You can create such a file by using the command **cat > –fname.**) The **– –** argument works with all Linux utilities that use the getopts builtin (page 968) to parse their options; it does not work with more and a few other utilities. This argument is particularly useful when used in conjunction with rm to remove a file whose name starts with a hyphen (**rm – – –fname**), including any you create while experimenting with the **– –** argument.

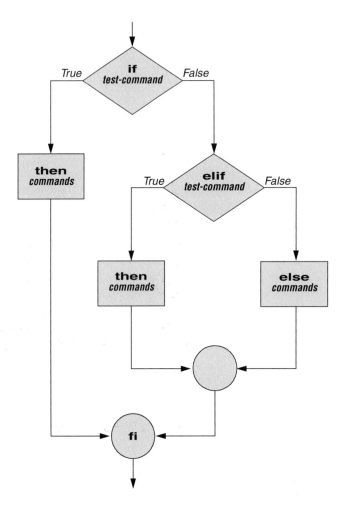

Figure 27-3 An **if...then...elif** flowchart

if...then...elif

The **if...then...elif** control structure (Figure 27-3) has the following syntax:

if test-command
   then
      commands
   elif test-command
     then
       commands

  . . .

   else
     commands
fi

The **elif** statement combines the **else** statement and the **if** statement and enables you to construct a nested set of **if...then...else** structures (Figure 27-3). The difference between the **else** statement and the **elif** statement is that each **else** statement must be paired with a **fi** statement, whereas multiple nested **elif** statements require only a single closing **fi** statement.

The following example shows an **if...then...elif** control structure. This shell script compares three words that the user enters. The first **if** statement uses the Boolean AND operator (**–a**) as an argument to test. The test builtin returns a *true* status only if the first and second logical comparisons are *true* (that is, **word1** matches **word2** and **word2** matches **word3**). If test returns a *true* status, the script executes the command following the next **then** statement, passes control to the statement following **fi**, and terminates:

```
$ cat if3
echo -n "word 1: "
read word1
echo -n "word 2: "
read word2
echo -n "word 3: "
read word3
if [ "$word1" = "$word2" -a "$word2" = "$word3" ]
    then
        echo "Match: words 1, 2, & 3"
    elif [ "$word1" = "$word2" ]
    then
        echo "Match: words 1 & 2"
    elif [ "$word1" = "$word3" ]
    then
        echo "Match: words 1 & 3"
    elif [ "$word2" = "$word3" ]
    then
        echo "Match: words 2 & 3"
    else
        echo "No match"
fi
```

```
$ ./if3
word 1: apple
word 2: orange
word 3: pear
No match
$ ./if3
word 1: apple
word 2: orange
word 3: apple
Match: words 1 & 3
$ ./if3
word 1: apple
word 2: apple
word 3: apple
Match: words 1, 2, & 3
```

If the three words are not the same, the structure passes control to the first **elif**, which begins a series of tests to see if any pair of words is the same. As the nesting continues, if any one of the **if** statements is satisfied, the structure passes control to the next **then** statement and subsequently to the statement following **fi**. Each time an **elif** statement is not satisfied, the structure passes control to the next **elif** statement. The double quotation marks around the arguments to echo that contain ampersands (&) prevent the shell from interpreting the ampersands as special characters.

optional   **THE lnks SCRIPT**

The following script, named **lnks**, demonstrates the **if...then** and **if...then...elif** control structures. This script finds hard links to its first argument, a filename. If you provide the name of a directory as the second argument, **lnks** searches for links in the directory hierarchy rooted at that directory. If you do not specify a directory, **lnks** searches the working directory and its subdirectories. This script does not locate symbolic links.

```
$ cat lnks
#!/bin/bash
# Identify links to a file
# Usage: lnks file [directory]

if [ $# -eq 0 -o $# -gt 2 ]; then
    echo "Usage: lnks file [directory]" 1>&2
    exit 1
fi
if [ -d "$1" ]; then
    echo "First argument cannot be a directory." 1>&2
    echo "Usage: lnks file [directory]" 1>&2
    exit 1
else
    file="$1"
fi
```

```
      if [ $# -eq 1 ]; then
          directory="."
      elif [ -d "$2" ]; then
          directory="$2"
      else
          echo "Optional second argument must be a directory." 1>&2
          echo "Usage: lnks file [directory]" 1>&2
          exit 1
fi

# Check that file exists and is an ordinary file
if [ ! -f "$file" ]; then
    echo "lnks: $file not found or special file" 1>&2
    exit 1
fi
# Check link count on file
set -- $(ls -l "$file")

linkcnt=$2
if [ "$linkcnt" -eq 1 ]; then
    echo "lnks: no other hard links to $file" 1>&2
    exit 0
fi

# Get the inode of the given file
set $(ls -i "$file")

inode=$1

# Find and print the files with that inode number
echo "lnks: using find to search for links..." 1>&2
find "$directory" -xdev -inum $inode -print
```

Max has a file named **letter** in his home directory. He wants to find links to this file in his and other users' home directory file trees. In the following example, Max calls **lnks** from his home directory to perform the search. The second argument to **lnks**, **/home**, is the pathname of the directory where he wants to start the search. The **lnks** script reports that **/home/max/letter** and **/home/zach/draft** are links to the same file:

```
$ ./lnks letter /home
lnks: using find to search for links...
/home/max/letter
/home/zach/draft
```

In addition to the **if...then...elif** control structure, **lnks** introduces other features that are commonly used in shell programs. The following discussion describes **lnks** section by section.

Specify the shell The first line of the **lnks** script uses **#!** (page 286) to specify the shell that will execute the script:

```
#!/bin/bash
```

In this chapter, the **#!** notation appears only in more complex examples. It ensures that the proper shell executes the script, even when the user is running a different shell or the script is called from a script running a different shell.

Comments   The second and third lines of **lnks** are comments; the shell ignores text follows a pound sign up to the next NEWLINE character. These comments in **lnks** briefly identify what the file does and explain how to use it:

```
# Identify links to a file
# Usage: lnks file [directory]
```

Usage messages   The first **if** statement tests whether **lnks** was called with zero arguments or more than two arguments:

```
if [ $# -eq 0 -o $# -gt 2 ]; then
    echo "Usage: lnks file [directory]" 1>&2
    exit 1
fi
```

If either of these conditions is *true*, **lnks** sends a usage message to standard error and exits with a status of 1. The double quotation marks around the usage message prevent the shell from interpreting the brackets as special characters. The brackets in the usage message indicate that the **directory** argument is optional.

The second **if** statement tests whether the first command-line argument (**$1**) is a directory (the **–d** argument to test returns *true* if the file exists and is a directory):

```
if [ -d "$1" ]; then
    echo "First argument cannot be a directory." 1>&2
    echo "Usage: lnks file [directory]" 1>&2
    exit 1
else
    file="$1"
fi
```

If the first argument is a directory, **lnks** displays a usage message and exits. If it is not a directory, **lnks** saves the value of **$1** in the **file** variable because later in the script set resets the command-line arguments. If the value of **$1** is not saved before the **set** command is issued, its value is lost.

Test the arguments   The next section of **lnks** is an **if...then...elif** statement:

```
if [ $# -eq 1 ]; then
        directory="."
    elif [ -d "$2" ]; then
        directory="$2"
    else
        echo "Optional second argument must be a directory." 1>&2
        echo "Usage: lnks file [directory]" 1>&2
        exit 1
fi
```

The first *test-command* determines whether the user specified a single argument on the command line. If the *test-command* returns 0 (*true*), the **directory** variable is assigned the value of the working directory (.). If the *test-command* returns *false*, the **elif** statement tests whether the second argument is a directory. If it is a directory, the **directory** variable is set equal to the second command-line argument, **$2**. If **$2** is not a directory, **lnks** sends a usage message to standard error and exits with a status of 1.

The next **if** statement in **lnks** tests whether **$file** does not exist. This test keeps **lnks** from wasting time looking for links to a nonexistent file. The **test** builtin, when called with the three arguments **!**, **–f**, and **$file**, evaluates to *true* if the file **$file** does *not* exist:

```
[ ! -f "$file" ]
```

The **!** operator preceding the **–f** argument to **test** negates its result, yielding *false* if the file **$file** *does* exist and is an ordinary file.

Next **lnks** uses **set** and **ls –l** to check the number of links **$file** has:

```
# Check link count on file
set -- $(ls -l "$file")

linkcnt=$2
if [ "$linkcnt" -eq 1 ]; then
    echo "lnks: no other hard links to $file" 1>&2
    exit 0
fi
```

The **set** builtin uses command substitution (page 346) to set the positional parameters to the output of **ls –l**. The second field in this output is the link count, so the user-created variable **linkcnt** is set equal to **$2**. The **--** used with **set** prevents **set** from interpreting as an option the first argument produced by **ls –l** (the first argument is the access permissions for the file and typically begins with –). The **if** statement checks whether **$linkcnt** is equal to 1; if it is, **lnks** displays a message and exits. Although this message is not truly an error message, it is redirected to standard error. The way **lnks** has been written, all informational messages are sent to standard error. Only the final product of **lnks**—the pathnames of links to the specified file—is sent to standard output, so you can redirect the output as you please.

If the link count is greater than 1, **lnks** goes on to identify the *inode* (page 1113) for **$file**. As explained on page 215, comparing the inodes associated with filenames is a good way to determine whether the filenames are links to the same file. The **lnks** script uses **set** to set the positional parameters to the output of **ls –i**. The first argument to **set** is the inode number for the file, so the user-created variable named **inode** is assigned the value of **$1**:

```
# Get the inode of the given file
set $(ls -i "$file")

inode=$1
```

Finally **lnks** uses the find utility to search for files having inode numbers that match **$inode**:

```
# Find and print the files with that inode number
echo "lnks: using find to search for links..." 1>&2
find "$directory" -xdev -inum $inode -print
```

The find utility searches the directory hierarchy rooted at the directory specified by its first argument (**$directory**) for files that meet the criteria specified by the remaining arguments. In this example, the remaining arguments send the names of files having inodes matching **$inode** to standard output. Because files in different filesystems can have the same inode number yet not be linked, find must search only directories in the same filesystem as **$directory**. The **–xdev** (cross-device) argument prevents find from searching directories on other filesystems. Refer to page 212 for more information about filesystems and links.

The echo command preceding the find command in **lnks**, which tells the user that find is running, is included because find can take a long time to run. Because **lnks** does not include a final exit statement, the exit status of **lnks** is that of the last command it runs, find.

DEBUGGING SHELL SCRIPTS

When you are writing a script such as **lnks**, it is easy to make mistakes. You can use the shell's **–x** option to help debug a script. This option causes the shell to display each command before it runs the command. Tracing a script's execution in this way can give you information about where a problem lies.

You can run **lnks** as in the previous example and cause the shell to display each command before it is executed. Either set the **–x** option for the current shell (**set –x**) so all scripts display commands as they are run or use the **–x** option to affect only the shell running the script called by the command line.

```
$ bash -x lnks letter /home
+ '[' 2 -eq 0 -o 2 -gt 2 ']'
+ '[' -d letter ']'
+ file=letter
+ '[' 2 -eq 1 ']'
+ '[' -d /home ']'
+ directory=/home
+ '[' '!' -f letter ']'
...
```

PS4   Each command the script executes is preceded by the value of the **PS4** variable—a plus sign (**+**) by default, so you can distinguish debugging output from script-produced output. You must export **PS4** if you set it in the shell that calls the script. The next command sets **PS4** to **>>>>** followed by a SPACE and exports it:

```
$ export PS4='>>>> '
```

You can also set the **–x** option of the shell running the script by putting the following set command near the beginning of the script:

```
set -x
```

Put **set –x** anywhere in the script you want to turn debugging on. Turn the debugging option off with a plus sign:

```
set +x
```

The **set –o xtrace** and **set +o xtrace** commands do the same things as **set –x** and **set +x**, respectively.

for...in

The **for...in** control structure has the following syntax:

for loop-index in argument-list
do
      commands
done

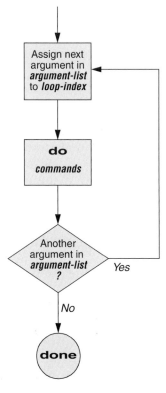

Figure 27-4 A **for...in** flowchart

The **for...in** structure (Figure 27-4, previous page) assigns the value of the first argument in the *argument-list* to the *loop-index* and executes the *commands* between the **do** and **done** statements. The **do** and **done** statements mark the beginning and end of the **for** loop.

After it passes control to the **done** statement, the structure assigns the value of the second argument in the *argument-list* to the *loop-index* and repeats the *commands*. It then repeats the *commands* between the **do** and **done** statements one time for each argument in the *argument-list*. When the structure exhausts the *argument-list*, it passes control to the statement following **done**.

The following **for...in** structure assigns **apples** to the user-created variable **fruit** and then displays the value of **fruit**, which is **apples**. Next the structure assigns **oranges** to **fruit** and repeats the process. When it exhausts the argument list, the structure transfers control to the statement following **done**, which displays a message.

```
$ cat fruit
for fruit in apples oranges pears bananas
do
    echo "$fruit"
done
echo "Task complete."

$ ./fruit
apples
oranges
pears
bananas
Task complete.
```

The next script lists the names of the directory files in the working directory by looping through the files in the working directory and using test to determine which are directory files:

```
$ cat dirfiles
for i in *
do
    if [ -d "$i" ]
        then
            echo "$i"
    fi
done
```

The ambiguous file reference character * matches the names of all files (except hidden files) in the working directory. Prior to executing the **for** loop, the shell expands the * and uses the resulting list to assign successive values to the index variable **i**.

for

The **for** control structure has the following syntax:

> *for loop-index*
> *do*
> > *commands*
> *done*

In the **for** structure, the *loop-index* takes on the value of each of the command-line arguments, one at a time. The **for** structure is the same as the **for...in** structure (Figure 27-4) except in terms of where it gets values for the *loop-index*. The **for** structure performs a sequence of commands, usually involving each argument in turn.

The following shell script shows a **for** structure displaying each command-line argument. The first line of the script, **for arg**, implies **for arg in "$@"**, where the shell expands **"$@"** into a list of quoted command-line arguments **"$1" "$2" "$3"** and so on. The balance of the script corresponds to the **for...in** structure.

```
$ cat for_test
for arg
do
    echo "$arg"
done
$ for_test candy gum chocolate
candy
gum
chocolate
```

optional **THE whos SCRIPT**

The following script, named **whos**, demonstrates the usefulness of the implied **"$@"** in the **for** structure. You give **whos** one or more users' full names or usernames as arguments, and **whos** displays information about the users. The **whos** script gets the information it displays from the first and fifth fields in the **/etc/passwd** file. The first field contains a username, and the fifth field typically contains the user's full name. You can provide a username as an argument to **whos** to identify the user's name or provide a name as an argument to identify the username. The **whos** script is similar to the finger utility, although **whos** delivers less information.

```
$ cat whos
#!/bin/bash

if [ $# -eq 0 ]
    then
        echo "Usage: whos id..." 1>&2
        exit 1
fi
for id
do
    mawk -F: '{print $1, $5}' /etc/passwd |
    grep -i "$id"
done
```

In the next example, **whos** identifies the user whose username is **chas** and the user whose name is **Marilou Smith**:

```
$ ./whos chas "Marilou Smith"
chas Charles Casey
msmith Marilou Smith
```

Use of "$@" The **whos** script uses a **for** statement to loop through the command-line arguments. In this script the implied use of **"$@"** in the **for** loop is particularly beneficial because it causes the **for** loop to treat an argument that contains a SPACE as a single argument. This example encloses **Marilou Smith** in quotation marks, which causes the shell to pass it to the script as a single argument. Then the implied **"$@"** in the **for** statement causes the shell to regenerate the quoted argument **Marilou Smith** so that it is again treated as a single argument.

mawk For each command-line argument, **whos** searches the **/etc/passwd** file. Inside the **for** loop, the **mawk** utility extracts the first (**$1**) and fifth (**$5**) fields from each line in **/etc/passwd**. The **–F:** option causes **mawk** to use a colon (**:**) as a field separator when it reads **/etc/passwd**, allowing it to break each line into fields. The **mawk** command sets and uses the **$1** and **$5** arguments; they are included within single quotation marks and are not interpreted by the shell. Do not confuse these arguments with positional parameters, which correspond to command-line arguments. The first and fifth fields are sent to **grep** (page 152) via a pipe. The **grep** utility searches for **$id** (to which the shell has assigned the value of a command-line argument) in its input. The **–i** option causes **grep** to ignore case as it searches; **grep** displays each line in its input that contains **$id**.

| at the end of a line An interesting syntactical exception that **bash** makes for the pipe symbol (**|**) appears on the line with the **mawk** command: You do not have to quote a NEWLINE that immediately follows a pipe symbol (that is, a pipe symbol that is the last character on a line) to keep the NEWLINE from executing a command. Try giving the command **who |** and pressing RETURN. The shell displays a secondary prompt. If you then enter **sort** followed by another RETURN, you see a sorted **who** list. The pipe works even though a NEWLINE follows the pipe symbol.

while

The **while** control structure has the following syntax:

while **test-command**
do
     commands
done

As long as the **test-command** (Figure 27-5) returns a *true* exit status, the **while** structure continues to execute the series of **commands** delimited by the **do** and **done** statements. Before each loop through the **commands**, the structure executes the **test-command**. When the exit status of the **test-command** is *false,* the structure passes control to the statement after the **done** statement.

test builtin The following shell script first initializes the **number** variable to zero. The **test** builtin then determines whether **number** is less than 10. The script uses **test** with the **–lt** argument to perform a numerical test. For numerical comparisons, you must use **–ne** (not equal), **–eq** (equal), **–gt** (greater than), **–ge** (greater than or equal to), **–lt** (less than), or **–le** (less than or equal to). For string comparisons, use **=** (equal) or **!=** (not equal) when you are working with **test**. In this example, **test** has an exit status of 0 (*true*) as long as **number** is less than 10. As long as **test** returns *true,* the structure

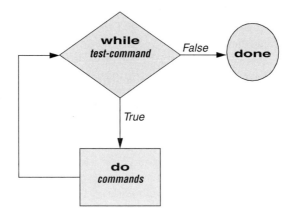

Figure 27-5   A **while** flowchart

executes the commands between the **do** and **done** statements. See page 911 for information on the test builtin.

```
$ cat count
#!/bin/bash
number=0
while [ "$number" -lt 10 ]
    do
        echo -n "$number"
        ((number +=1))
    done
echo
$ ./count
0123456789
$
```

The echo command following **do** displays **number**. The **–n** prevents echo from issuing a NEWLINE following its output. The next command uses arithmetic evaluation [((...)); page 972] to increment the value of **number** by 1. The **done** statement terminates the loop and returns control to the **while** statement to start the loop over again. The final echo causes **count** to send a NEWLINE character to standard output, so the next prompt occurs in the leftmost column on the display (rather than immediately following 9).

optional   THE spell_check **SCRIPT**

The aspell utility checks the words in a file against a dictionary of correctly spelled words. With the **list** command, aspell runs in list mode: Input comes from standard input and aspell sends each potentially misspelled word to standard output. The following command produces a list of possible misspellings in the file **letter.txt**:

```
$ aspell list < letter.txt
quikly
portible
frendly
```

The next shell script, named **spell_check**, shows another use of a **while** structure. To find the incorrect spellings in a file, **spell_check** calls aspell to check a file against a system dictionary. But it goes a step further: It enables you to specify a list of correctly spelled words and removes these words from the output of aspell. This script is useful for removing words that you use frequently, such as names and technical terms, that do not appear in a standard dictionary. Although you can duplicate the functionality of **spell_check** by using additional aspell dictionaries, the script is included here for its instructive value.

The **spell_check** script requires two filename arguments: the file containing the list of correctly spelled words and the file you want to check. The first **if** statement verifies that the user specified two arguments. The next two **if** statements verify that both arguments are readable files. (The exclamation point negates the sense of the following operator; the **–r** operator causes test to determine whether a file is readable. The result is a test that determines whether a file is *not readable*.)

```
$ cat spell_check
#!/bin/bash
# remove correct spellings from aspell output

if [ $# -ne 2 ]
    then
        echo "Usage: spell_check file1 file2" 1>&2
        echo "file1: list of correct spellings" 1>&2
        echo "file2: file to be checked" 1>&2
        exit 1
fi

if [ ! -r "$1" ]
    then
        echo "spell_check: $1 is not readable" 1>&2
        exit 1
fi

if [ ! -r "$2" ]
    then
        echo "spell_check: $2 is not readable" 1>&2
        exit 1
fi

aspell list < "$2" |
while read line
do
    if ! grep "^$line$" "$1" > /dev/null
        then
            echo $line
    fi
done
```

The **spell_check** script sends the output from aspell (with the **list** argument, so it produces a list of misspelled words on standard output) through a pipe to standard input of a **while** structure, which reads one line at a time (each line has one word on it) from standard input. The *test-command* (that is, **read line**) returns a *true* exit status as long as it receives a line from standard input.

Inside the **while** loop, an **if** statement[1] monitors the return value of grep, which determines whether the line that was read is in the user's list of correctly spelled words. The pattern grep searches for (the value of **$line**) is preceded and followed by special characters that specify the beginning and end of a line (**^** and **$**, respectively). These special characters ensure that grep finds a match only if the **$line** variable matches an entire line in the file of correctly spelled words. (Otherwise, grep would match a string, such as **paul**, in the output of aspell if the file of correctly spelled words contained the word **paulson**.) These special characters, together with the value of the **$line** variable, form a regular expression (Appendix A).

The output of grep is redirected to **/dev/null** (page 236) because the output is not needed; only the exit code is important. The **if** statement checks the negated exit status of grep (the leading exclamation point negates or changes the sense of the exit status—*true* becomes *false*, and vice versa), which is 0 or *true* (*false* when negated) when a matching line is found. If the exit status is *not* 0 or *false* (*true* when negated), the word was *not* in the file of correctly spelled words. The echo builtin sends a list of words that are not in the file of correctly spelled words to standard output.

Once it detects the EOF (end of file), the read builtin returns a *false* exit status, control passes out of the **while** structure, and the script terminates.

Before you use **spell_check**, create a file of correct spellings containing words you use frequently but that are not in a standard dictionary. For example, if you work for a company named **Blinkenship and Klimowski, Attorneys**, you would put **Blinkenship** and **Klimowski** in the file. The following example shows how **spell_check** checks the spelling in a file named **memo** and removes **Blinkenship** and **Klimowski** from the output list of incorrectly spelled words:

```
$ aspell list < memo
Blinkenship
Klimowski
targat
hte
$ cat word_list
Blinkenship
Klimowski
$ ./spell_check word_list memo
targat
hte
```

Refer to the aspell manual (in the **/usr/share/doc/aspell** directory or at aspell.net) for more information.

---

1. This **if** statement can also be written as

```
if ! grep -qw "$line" "$1"
```

The **–q** option suppresses the output from grep so it returns only an exit code. The **–w** option causes grep to match only a whole word.

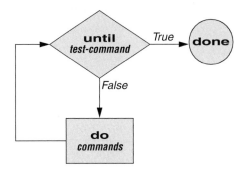

Figure 27-6   An **until** flowchart

until

The **until** and **while** structures are very similar, differing only in the sense of the test performed at the top of the loop. Figure 27-6 shows that **until** continues to loop *until* the *test-command* returns a *true* exit status. The **while** structure loops *while* the *test-command* continues to return a *true* or nonerror condition. The **until** control structure has the following syntax:

until **test-command**
do
   commands
done

The following script demonstrates an **until** structure that includes read. When the user enters the correct string of characters, the *test-command* is satisfied and the structure passes control out of the loop.

```
$ cat until1
secretname=zach
name=noname
echo "Try to guess the secret name!"
echo
until [ "$name" = "$secretname" ]
do
    echo -n "Your guess: "
    read name
done
echo "Very good."

$ ./until1
Try to guess the secret name!

Your guess: helen
Your guess: barbara
Your guess: rachael
Your guess: zach
Very good
```

The following **locktty** script is similar to the lock command on Berkeley UNIX and the **Lock Screen** menu selection in GNOME. The script prompts for a key (password) and uses an **until** control structure to lock the terminal. The **until** statement causes the system to ignore any characters typed at the keyboard until the user types the key followed by a RETURN on a line by itself, which unlocks the terminal. The **locktty** script can keep people from using your terminal while you are away from it for short periods of time. It saves you from having to log out if you are concerned about other users using your login.

```
$ cat locktty
#! /bin/bash

trap '' 1 2 3 18
stty -echo
echo -n "Key: "
read key_1
echo
echo -n "Again: "
read key_2
echo
key_3=
if [ "$key_1" = "$key_2" ]
    then
        tput clear
        until [ "$key_3" = "$key_2" ]
        do
            read key_3
        done
    else
        echo "locktty: keys do not match" 1>&2
fi
stty echo
```

Forget your password for **locktty**?

tip   If you forget your key (password), you will need to log in from another (virtual) terminal and kill the process running **locktty**.

trap builtin   The trap builtin (page 965) at the beginning of the **locktty** script stops a user from being able to terminate the script by sending it a signal (for example, by pressing the interrupt key). Trapping signal 18 means that no one can use CONTROL-Z (job control, a stop from a tty) to defeat the lock. Table 27-5 on page 965 provides a list of signals. The **stty –echo** command causes the terminal not to display characters typed at the keyboard, preventing the key the user enters from appearing on the screen. After turning off keyboard echo, the script prompts the user for a key, reads it into the user-created variable **key_1**, prompts the user to enter the same key again, and saves it in **key_2**. The statement **key_3=** creates a variable with a NULL value. If **key_1** and **key_2** match, **locktty** clears the screen (with the tput command)

and starts an **until** loop. The **until** loop keeps attempting to read from the terminal and assigning the input to the **key_3** variable. Once the user types a string that matches one of the original keys (**key_2**), the **until** loop terminates and keyboard echo is turned on again.

break **AND** continue

You can interrupt a **for, while,** or **until** loop by using a **break** or **continue** statement. The **break** statement transfers control to the statement after the **done** statement, thereby terminating execution of the loop. The **continue** command transfers control to the **done** statement, continuing execution of the loop.

The following script demonstrates the use of these two statements. The **for...in** structure loops through the values 1–10. The first **if** statement executes its commands when the value of the index is less than or equal to 3 (**$index –le 3**). The second **if** statement executes its commands when the value of the index is greater than or equal to 8 (**$index –ge 8**). In between the two **if**s, echo displays the value of the index. For all values up to and including 3, the first **if** statement displays **continue,** executes a **continue** statement that skips **echo $index** and the second **if** statement, and continues with the next **for** statement. For the value of 8, the second **if** statement displays **break** and executes a **break** statement that exits from the **for** loop.

```
$ cat brk
for index in 1 2 3 4 5 6 7 8 9 10
    do
        if [ $index -le 3 ] ; then
            echo "continue"
            continue
        fi
#
    echo $index
#
    if [ $index -ge 8 ] ; then
        echo "break"
        break
    fi
done

$ ./brk
continue
continue
continue
4
5
6
7
8
break
```

case

The **case** structure (Figure 27-7, next page) is a multiple-branch decision mechanism. The path taken through the structure depends on a match or lack of a match between the *test-string* and one of the *patterns*. The **case** control structure has the following syntax:

```
case test-string in
    pattern-1)
        commands-1
        ;;
    pattern-2)
        commands-2
        ;;
    pattern-3)
        commands-3
        ;;
    . . .
    esac
```

The following **case** structure examines the character the user enters as the *test-string*. This value is held in the variable **letter**. If the *test-string* has a value of **A**, the structure executes the command following the *pattern* **A**. The right parenthesis is part of the **case** control structure, not part of the *pattern*. If the *test-string* has a value of **B** or **C**, the structure executes the command following the matching *pattern*. The asterisk (*****) indicates *any string of characters* and serves as a catchall in case there is no match. If no *pattern* matches the *test-string* and if there is no catchall (*****) *pattern*, control passes to the command following the **esac** statement, without the **case** structure taking any action.

```
$ cat case1
echo -n "Enter A, B, or C: "
read letter
case "$letter" in
    A)
        echo "You entered A"
        ;;
    B)
        echo "You entered B"
        ;;
    C)
        echo "You entered C"
        ;;
    *)
        echo "You did not enter A, B, or C"
        ;;
esac

$ ./case1
Enter A, B, or C: B
You entered B
```

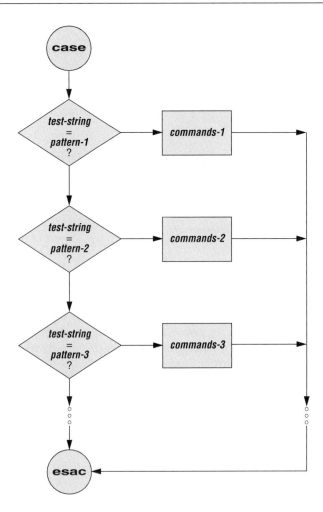

Figure 27-7   A case flowchart

The next execution of **case1** shows the user entering a lowercase **b**. Because the *test-string* **b** does not match the uppercase **B** *pattern* (or any other *pattern* in the **case** statement), the program executes the commands following the catchall *pattern* and displays a message:

```
$ ./case1
Enter A, B, or C: b
You did not enter A, B, or C
```

The *pattern* in the **case** structure is analogous to an ambiguous file reference. It can include any special characters and strings shown in Table 27-2.

The next script accepts both uppercase and lowercase letters:

```
$ cat case2
echo -n "Enter A, B, or C: "
read letter
case "$letter" in
    a|A)
        echo "You entered A"
        ;;
    b|B)
        echo "You entered B"
        ;;
    c|C)
        echo "You entered C"
        ;;
    *)
        echo "You did not enter A, B, or C"
        ;;
esac

$ ./case2
Enter A, B, or C: b
You entered B
```

Table 27-2   Patterns

Pattern	Function
*	Matches any string of characters. Use for the default case.
?	Matches any single character.
[...]	Defines a character class. Any characters enclosed within brackets are tried, one at a time, in an attempt to match a single character. A hyphen between two characters specifies a range of characters.
|	Separates alternative choices that satisfy a particular branch of the **case** structure.

optional   The following example shows how you can use the **case** structure to create a simple menu. The **command_menu** script uses echo to present menu items and prompt the user for a selection. (The **select** control structure [page 939] is a much easier way of coding a menu.) The **case** structure then executes the appropriate utility depending on the user's selection.

```
$ cat command_menu
#!/bin/bash
# menu interface to simple commands

echo -e "\n      COMMAND MENU\n"
echo "  a.  Current date and time"
echo "  b.  Users currently logged in"
echo "  c.  Name of the working directory"
echo -e "  d.  Contents of the working directory\n"
echo -n "Enter a, b, c, or d: "
read answer
echo
```

```
        #
        case "$answer" in
            a)
                    date
                    ;;
            b)
                    who
                    ;;
            c)
                    pwd
                    ;;
            d)
                    ls
                    ;;
            *)
                    echo "There is no selection: $answer"
                    ;;
        esac

        $ ./command_menu

                    COMMAND MENU

            a.   Current date and time
            b.   Users currently logged in
            c.   Name of the working directory
            d.   Contents of the working directory

        Enter a, b, c, or d: a

        Wed Jan  3 12:31:12 PST 2009
```

echo –e The –e option causes echo to interpret \n as a NEWLINE character. If you do not include this option, echo does not output the extra blank lines that make the menu easy to read but instead outputs the (literal) two-character sequence \n. The –e option causes echo to interpret several other backslash-quoted characters (Table 27-3). Remember to quote (i.e., place double quotation marks around the string) the backslash-quoted character so the shell does not interpret it but passes the backslash and the character to echo. See **xpg_echo** (page 339) for a way to avoid using the –e option.

Table 27-3 Special characters in echo (must use **–e**)

Quoted character	echo **displays**
\a	Alert (bell)
\b	BACKSPACE
\c	Suppress trailing NEWLINE
\f	FORMFEED
\n	NEWLINE
\r	RETURN

Table 27-3   Special characters in echo (must use **–e**) (continued)

Quoted character	echo **displays**
\t	Horizontal TAB
\v	Vertical TAB
\\	Backslash
nnn	The character with the ASCII octal code *nnn;* if *nnn* is not valid, echo displays the string literally

You can also use the **case** control structure to take various actions in a script, depending on how many arguments the script is called with. The following script, named **safedit**, uses a **case** structure that branches based on the number of command-line arguments (**$#**). It saves a backup copy of a file you are editing with vim.

```
$ cat safedit
#!/bin/bash

PATH=/bin:/usr/bin
script=$(basename $0)
case $# in

    0)
        vim
        exit 0
        ;;

    1)
        if [ ! -f "$1" ]
            then
                vim "$1"
                exit 0
            fi
        if [ ! -r "$1" -o ! -w "$1" ]
            then
                echo "$script: check permissions on $1" 1>&2
                exit 1
            else
                editfile=$1
            fi
        if [ ! -w "." ]
            then
                echo "$script: backup cannot be " \
                    "created in the working directory" 1>&2
                exit 1
            fi
        ;;
    *)
        echo "Usage: $script [file-to-edit]" 1>&2
        exit 1
        ;;
esac
```

```
        tempfile=/tmp/$$.$script
        cp $editfile $tempfile
        if vim $editfile
            then
                mv $tempfile bak.$(basename $editfile)
                echo "$script: backup file created"
            else
                mv $tempfile editerr
                echo "$script: edit error--copy of " \
                    "original file is in editerr" 1>&2
        fi
```

If you call **safedit** without any arguments, the **case** structure executes its first branch and calls vim without a filename argument. Because an existing file is not being edited, **safedit** does not create a backup file. If you call **safedit** with one argument, it runs the commands in the second branch of the **case** structure and verifies that the file specified by **$1** does not yet exist or is the name of a file for which the user has read and write permission. The **safedit** script also verifies that the user has write permission for the working directory. If the user calls **safedit** with more than one argument, the third branch of the **case** structure presents a usage message and exits with a status of 1.

Set **PATH**   In addition to using a **case** structure for branching based on the number of command-line arguments, the **safedit** script introduces several other features. At the beginning of the script, the **PATH** variable is set to search **/bin** and **/usr/bin**. Setting **PATH** in this way ensures that the commands executed by the script are standard utilities, which are kept in those directories. By setting this variable inside a script, you can avoid the problems that might occur if users have set **PATH** to search their own directories first and have scripts or programs with the same names as the utilities the script calls. You can also include absolute pathnames within a script to achieve this end, although this practice can make a script less portable.

Name of the program   The next line creates a variable named **script** and uses command substitution to assign the simple filename of the script to it:

```
        script=$(basename $0)
```

The basename utility sends the simple filename component of its argument to standard output, which is assigned to the **script** variable, using command substitution. The **$0** holds the command the script was called with (page 953). No matter which of the following commands the user calls the script with, the output of basename is the simple filename **safedit**:

```
$ /home/max/bin/safedit memo
$ ./safedit memo
$ safedit memo
```

After the **script** variable is set, it replaces the filename of the script in usage and error messages. By using a variable that is derived from the command that invoked the script rather than a filename that is hardcoded into the script, you can create links to the script or rename it, and the usage and error messages will still provide accurate information.

Naming temporary files Another feature of **safedit** relates to the use of the **$$** parameter in the name of a temporary file. The statement following the **esac** statement creates and assigns a value to the **tempfile** variable. This variable contains the name of a temporary file that is stored in the **/tmp** directory, as are many temporary files. The temporary filename begins with the PID number of the shell and ends with the name of the script. Using the PID number ensures that the filename is unique. Thus **safedit** will not attempt to overwrite an existing file, as might happen if two people were using **safedit** at the same time. The name of the script is appended so that, should the file be left in **/tmp** for some reason, you can figure out where it came from.

The PID number is used in front of—rather than after—**$script** in the filename because of the 14-character limit placed on filenames by some older versions of UNIX. Linux systems do not have this limitation. Because the PID number ensures the uniqueness of the filename, it is placed first so that it cannot be truncated. (If the **$script** component is truncated, the filename is still unique.) For the same reason, when a backup file is created inside the **if** control structure a few lines down in the script, the filename consists of the string **bak.** followed by the name of the file being edited. On an older system, if **bak** were used as a suffix rather than a prefix and the original filename were 14 characters long, **.bak** might be lost and the original file would be overwritten. The **basename** utility extracts the simple filename of **$editfile** before it is prefixed with **bak.**

The **safedit** script uses an unusual *test-command* in the **if** structure: **vim $editfile**. The *test-command* calls vim to edit **$editfile**. When you finish editing the file and exit from vim, vim returns an exit code. The **if** control structure uses that exit code to determine which branch to take. If the editing session completed successfully, vim returns 0 and the statements following the **then** statement are executed. If vim does not terminate normally (as would occur if the user killed [page 438] the vim process), vim returns a nonzero exit status and the script executes the statements following **else**.

select

The **select** control structure is based on the one found in the Korn Shell. It displays a menu, assigns a value to a variable based on the user's choice of items, and executes a series of commands. The **select** control structure has the following syntax:

> select *varname [in arg . . .]*
> do
>   *commands*
> done

The **select** structure displays a menu of the *arg* items. If you omit the keyword **in** and the list of arguments, **select** uses the positional parameters in place of the *arg* items. The menu is formatted with numbers before each item. For example, a **select** structure that begins with

```
select fruit in apple banana blueberry kiwi orange watermelon STOP
```

displays the following menu:

```
1) apple       3) blueberry   5) orange      7) STOP
2) banana      4) kiwi        6) watermelon
```

The **select** structure uses the values of the **LINES** and **COLUMNS** variables to specify the size of the display. (**LINES** has a default value of 24; **COLUMNS** has a default value of 80.) With **COLUMNS** set to 20, the menu looks like this:

```
1) apple
2) banana
3) blueberry
4) kiwi
5) orange
6) watermelon
7) STOP
```

PS3   After displaying the menu, **select** displays the value of **PS3**, the **select** prompt. The default value of **PS3** is ?#, but it is typically set to a more meaningful value. When you enter a valid number (one in the menu range) in response to the **PS3** prompt, **select** sets *varname* to the argument corresponding to the number you entered. An invalid entry causes the shell to set *varname* to null. Either way **select** stores your response in the keyword variable **REPLY** and then executes the *commands* between **do** and **done**. If you press RETURN without entering a choice, the shell redisplays the menu and the **PS3** prompt.

The **select** structure continues to issue the **PS3** prompt and execute the *commands* until something causes it to exit—typically a **break** or **exit** statement. A **break** statement exits from the loop and an **exit** statement exits from the script.

The following script illustrates the use of **select**:

```
$ cat fruit2
#!/bin/bash
PS3="Choose your favorite fruit from these possibilities: "
select FRUIT in apple banana blueberry kiwi orange watermelon STOP
do
    if [ "$FRUIT" == "" ]; then
        echo -e "Invalid entry.\n"
        continue
    elif [ $FRUIT = STOP ]; then
        echo "Thanks for playing!"
        break
    fi
echo "You chose $FRUIT as your favorite."
echo -e "That is choice number $REPLY.\n"
done
```

```
$ ./fruit2
1) apple      3) blueberry   5) orange     7) STOP
2) banana     4) kiwi        6) watermelon
Choose your favorite fruit from these possibilities: 3
You chose blueberry as your favorite.
That is choice number 3.

Choose your favorite fruit from these possibilities: 99
Invalid entry.

Choose your favorite fruit from these possibilities: 7
Thanks for playing!
```

After setting the **PS3** prompt and establishing the menu with the **select** statement, **fruit2** executes the *commands* between **do** and **done**. If the user submits an invalid entry, the shell sets *varname* (**$FRUIT**) to a null value. If **$FRUIT** is null, echo displays an error; **continue** then causes the shell to redisplay the **PS3** prompt. If the entry is valid, the script tests whether the user wants to stop. If so, echo displays a message and **break** exits from the **select** structure (and from the script). If the user enters a valid response and does not want to stop, the script displays the name and number of the user's response. (See page 936 for information about the echo –e option.)

HERE DOCUMENT

A Here document allows you to redirect input to a shell script from within the shell script itself. A Here document is so named because it is *here*—immediately accessible in the shell script—instead of *there*, perhaps in another file.

The following script, named **birthday**, contains a Here document. The two less than symbols (**<<**) in the first line indicate a Here document follows. One or more characters that delimit the Here document follow the less than symbols—this example uses a plus sign. Whereas the opening delimiter must appear adjacent to the less than symbols, the closing delimiter must be on a line by itself. The shell sends everything between the two delimiters to the process as standard input. In the example it is as though you have redirected standard input to grep from a file, except that the file is embedded in the shell script:

```
$ cat birthday
grep -i "$1" <<+
Max      June 22
Barbara  February 3
Darlene  May 8
Helen    March 13
Zach     January 23
Nancy    June 26
+
$ ./birthday Zach
Zach     January 23
$ ./birthday june
Max      June 22
Nancy    June 26
```

When you run **birthday**, it lists all the Here document lines that contain the argument you called it with. In this case the first time **birthday** is run, it displays Zach's birthday because it is called with an argument of **Zach**. The second run displays all the birthdays in June. The –i argument causes grep's search not to be case sensitive.

optional   The next script, named **bundle**,[2] includes a clever use of a Here document. The **bundle** script is an elegant example of a script that creates a shell archive (**shar**) file. The script creates a file that is itself a shell script containing several other files as well as the code to re-create the original files:

```
$ cat bundle
#!/bin/bash
# bundle:  group files into distribution package

echo "# To unbundle, bash this file"
for i
do
    echo "echo $i 1>&2"
    echo "cat >$i <<'End of $i'"
    cat $i
    echo "End of $i"
done
```

Just as the shell does not treat special characters that occur in standard input of a shell script as special, so the shell does not treat the special characters that occur between the delimiters in a Here document as special.

As the following example shows, the output of **bundle** is a shell script, which is redirected to a file named **bothfiles**. It contains the contents of each file given as an argument to **bundle** (**file1** and **file2** in this case) inside a Here document. To extract the original files from **bothfiles**, you simply give it as an argument to a bash command. Before each Here document is a cat command that causes the Here document to be written to a new file when **bothfiles** is run:

```
$ cat file1
This is a file.
It contains two lines.
$ cat file2
This is another file.
It contains
three lines.

$ ./bundle file1 file2 > bothfiles
$ cat bothfiles
# To unbundle, bash this file
echo file1 1>&2
cat >file1 <<'End of file1'
```

---

2. Thanks to Brian W. Kernighan and Rob Pike, *The Unix Programming Environment* (Englewood Cliffs, N.J.: Prentice-Hall, 1984), 98. Reprinted with permission.

```
        This is a file.
        It contains two lines.
        End of file1
        echo file2 1>&2
        cat >file2 <<'End of file2'
        This is another file.
        It contains
        three lines.
        End of file2
```

In the next example, **file1** and **file2** are removed before **bothfiles** is run. The **bothfiles** script echoes the names of the files it creates as it creates them. The ls command then shows that **bothfiles** has re-created **file1** and **file2**:

```
$ rm file1 file2
$ bash bothfiles
file1
file2
$ ls
bothfiles
file1
file2
```

FILE DESCRIPTORS

As discussed on page 281, before a process can read from or write to a file, it must open that file. When a process opens a file, Linux associates a number (called a *file descriptor*) with the file. A file descriptor is an index into the process's table of open files. Each process has its own set of open files and its own file descriptors. After opening a file, a process reads from and writes to that file by referring to its file descriptor. When it no longer needs the file, the process closes the file, freeing the file descriptor.

A typical Linux process starts with three open files: standard input (file descriptor 0), standard output (file descriptor 1), and standard error (file descriptor 2). Often these are the only files the process needs. Recall that you redirect standard output with the symbol **>** or the symbol **1>** and that you redirect standard error with the symbol **2>**. Although you can redirect other file descriptors, because file descriptors other than 0, 1, and 2 do not have any special conventional meaning, it is rarely useful to do so. The exception is in programs that you write yourself, in which case you control the meaning of the file descriptors and can take advantage of redirection.

Opening a file descriptor

The Bourne Again Shell opens files using the exec builtin as follows:

exec n> outfile
exec m< infile

The first line opens *outfile* for output and holds it open, associating it with file descriptor *n*. The second line opens *infile* for input and holds it open, associating it with file descriptor *m*.

Duplicating a
file descriptor

The **<&** token duplicates an input file descriptor; **>&** duplicates an output file descriptor. You can duplicate a file descriptor by making it refer to the same file as another open file descriptor, such as standard input or output. Use the following format to open or redirect file descriptor *n* as a duplicate of file descriptor *m*:

> *exec n<&m*

Once you have opened a file, you can use it for input and output in two ways. First, you can use I/O redirection on any command line, redirecting standard output to a file descriptor with **>&***n* or redirecting standard input from a file descriptor with **<&***n*. Second, you can use the read (page 959) and echo builtins. If you invoke other commands, including functions (page 333), they inherit these open files and file descriptors. When you have finished using a file, you can close it using

> *exec n<&–*

When you invoke the shell function in the next example, named **mycp**, with two arguments, it copies the file named by the first argument to the file named by the second argument. If you supply only one argument, the script copies the file named by the argument to standard output. If you invoke **mycp** with no arguments, it copies standard input to standard output.

A function is not a shell script

tip The **mycp** example is a shell function; it will not work as you expect if you execute it as a shell script. (It will work: The function will be created in a very short-lived subshell, which is probably of little use.) You can enter this function from the keyboard. If you put the function in a file, you can run it as an argument to the . (dot) builtin (page 280). You can also put the function in a startup file if you want it to be always available (page 335).

```
function mycp ()
{
case $# in
    0)
        # Zero arguments
        # File descriptor 3 duplicates standard input
        # File descriptor 4 duplicates standard output
        exec 3<&0 4<&1
        ;;
    1)
        # One argument
        # Open the file named by the argument for input
        # and associate it with file descriptor 3
        # File descriptor 4 duplicates standard output
        exec 3< $1 4<&1
        ;;
    2)
        # Two arguments
        # Open the file named by the first argument for input
        # and associate it with file descriptor 3
        # Open the file named by the second argument for output
        # and associate it with file descriptor 4
        exec 3< $1 4> $2
        ;;
```

```
    *)
        echo "Usage: mycp [source [dest]]"
        return 1
        ;;
esac

# Call cat with input coming from file descriptor 3
# and output going to file descriptor 4
cat <&3 >&4

# Close file descriptors 3 and 4
exec 3<&- 4<&-
}
```

The real work of this function is done in the line that begins with cat. The rest of the script arranges for file descriptors 3 and 4, which are the input and output of the cat command, to be associated with the appropriate files.

optional The next program takes two filenames on the command line, sorts both, and sends the output to temporary files. The program then merges the sorted files to standard output, preceding each line by a number that indicates which file it came from.

```
$ cat sortmerg
#!/bin/bash
usage ()
{
if [ $# -ne 2 ]; then
    echo "Usage: $0 file1 file2" 2>&1
    exit 1
    fi
}

# Default temporary directory
: ${TEMPDIR:=/tmp}

# Check argument count
usage "$@"

# Set up temporary files for sorting
file1=$TEMPDIR/$$.file1
file2=$TEMPDIR/$$.file2

# Sort
sort $1 > $file1
sort $2 > $file2

# Open $file1 and $file2 for reading. Use file descriptors 3 and 4.
exec 3<$file1
exec 4<$file2

# Read the first line from each file to figure out how to start.
read Line1 <&3
status1=$?
read Line2 <&4
status2=$?
```

```
# Strategy: while there is still input left in both files:
#   Output the line that should come first.
#   Read a new line from the file that line came from.
while [ $status1 -eq 0 -a $status2 -eq 0 ]
    do
        if [[ "$Line2" > "$Line1" ]]; then
            echo -e "1.\t$Line1"
            read -u3 Line1
            status1=$?
        else
            echo -e "2.\t$Line2"
            read -u4 Line2
            status2=$?
        fi
    done

# Now one of the files is at end-of-file.
# Read from each file until the end.
# First file1:
while [ $status1 -eq 0 ]
    do
        echo -e "1.\t$Line1"
        read Line1 <&3
        status1=$?
    done
# Next file2:
while [[ $status2 -eq 0 ]]
    do
        echo -e "2.\t$Line2"
        read Line2 <&4
        status2=$?
    done

# Close and remove both input files
exec 3<&- 4<&-
rm -f $file1 $file2
exit 0
```

PARAMETERS AND VARIABLES

Shell parameters and variables were introduced on page 296. This section adds to the previous coverage with a discussion of array variables, global versus local variables, special and positional parameters, and expansion of null and unset variables.

ARRAY VARIABLES

The Bourne Again Shell supports one-dimensional array variables. The subscripts are integers with zero-based indexing (i.e., the first element of the array has the subscript 0). The following format declares and assigns values to an array:

name=(element1 element2 ...)

The following example assigns four values to the array **NAMES**:

```
$ NAMES=(max helen sam zach)
```

You reference a single element of an array as follows:

```
$ echo ${NAMES[2]}
sam
```

The subscripts [*] and [@] both extract the entire array but work differently when used within double quotation marks. An @ produces an array that is a duplicate of the original array; an * produces a single element of an array (or a plain variable) that holds all the elements of the array separated by the first character in **IFS** (normally a SPACE). In the following example, the array **A** is filled with the elements of the **NAMES** variable using an *, and **B** is filled using an @. The declare builtin with the –a option displays the values of the arrays (and reminds you that bash uses zero-based indexing for arrays):

```
$ A=("${NAMES[*]}")
$ B=("${NAMES[@]}")

$ declare -a
declare -a A='([0]="max helen sam zach")'
declare -a B='([0]="max" [1]="helen" [2]="sam" [3]="zach")'
...
declare -a NAMES='([0]="max" [1]="helen" [2]="sam" [3]="zach")'
```

From the output of declare, you can see that **NAMES** and **B** have multiple elements. In contrast, **A**, which was assigned its value with an * within double quotation marks, has only one element: **A** has all its elements enclosed between double quotation marks.

In the next example, echo attempts to display element 1 of array **A**. Nothing is displayed because **A** has only one element and that element has an index of 0. Element 0 of array **A** holds all four names. Element 1 of **B** holds the second item in the array and element 0 holds the first item.

```
$ echo ${A[1]}

$ echo ${A[0]}
max helen sam zach
$ echo ${B[1]}
helen
$ echo ${B[0]}
max
```

You can apply the ${#*name*[*]} operator to array variables, returning the number of elements in the array:

```
$ echo ${#NAMES[*]}
4
```

The same operator, when given the index of an element of an array in place of *, returns the length of the element:

```
$ echo ${#NAMES[1]}
5
```

You can use subscripts on the left side of an assignment statement to replace selected elements of the array:

```
$ NAMES[1]=max
$ echo ${NAMES[*]}
max max sam zach
```

LOCALITY OF VARIABLES

By default variables are local to the process in which they are declared. Thus a shell script does not have access to variables declared in your login shell unless you explicitly make the variables available (global). Under bash, export makes a variable available to child processes.

export   Once you use the export builtin with a variable name as an argument, the shell places the value of the variable in the calling environment of child processes. This *call by value* gives each child process a copy of the variable for its own use.

The following **extest1** shell script assigns a value of **american** to the variable named **cheese** and then displays its filename (**extest1**) and the value of **cheese**. The **extest1** script then calls **subtest**, which attempts to display the same information. Next **subtest** declares a **cheese** variable and displays its value. When **subtest** finishes, it returns control to the parent process, which is executing **extest1**. At this point **extest1** again displays the value of the original **cheese** variable.

```
$ cat extest1
cheese=american
echo "extest1 1: $cheese"
subtest
echo "extest1 2: $cheese"
$ cat subtest
echo "subtest 1: $cheese"
cheese=swiss
echo "subtest 2: $cheese"
$ ./extest1
extest1 1: american
subtest 1:
subtest 2: swiss
extest1 2: american
```

The **subtest** script never receives the value of **cheese** from **extest1**, and **extest1** never loses the value. In bash—unlike in the real world—a child can never affect its parent's attributes. When a process attempts to display the value of a variable that has not been declared, as is the case with **subtest**, the process displays nothing; the value of an undeclared variable is that of a null string.

The following **extest2** script is the same as **extest1** except it uses export to make **cheese** available to the **subtest** script:

```
$ cat extest2
export cheese=american
echo "extest2 1: $cheese"
subtest
echo "extest2 2: $cheese"
$ ./extest2
extest2 1: american
subtest 1: american
subtest 2: swiss
extest2 2: american
```

Here the child process inherits the value of **cheese** as **american** and, after displaying this value, changes *its copy* to **swiss**. When control is returned to the parent, the parent's copy of **cheese** retains its original value: **american**.

An export builtin can optionally include an assignment:

```
export cheese=american
```

The preceding statement is equivalent to the following two statements:

```
cheese=american
export cheese
```

Although it is rarely done, you can export a variable before you assign a value to it. You do not need to export an already-exported variable a second time after you change its value.

FUNCTIONS

Because functions run in the same environment as the shell that calls them, variables are implicitly shared by a shell and a function it calls.

```
$ function nam () {
> echo $myname
> myname=zach
> }

$ myname=sam
$ nam
sam
$ echo $myname
zach
```

In the preceding example, the **myname** variable is set to **sam** in the interactive shell. The **nam** function then displays the value of **myname** (**sam**) and sets **myname** to **zach**. The final echo shows that, in the interactive shell, the value of **myname** has been changed to **zach**.

Function local
variables

Local variables are helpful in a function written for general use. Because the function is called by many scripts that may be written by different programmers, you need to make sure the names of the variables used within the function do not conflict with (i.e., duplicate) the names of the variables in the programs that call the function. Local variables eliminate this problem. When used within a function, the typeset builtin declares a variable to be local to the function it is defined in.

The next example shows the use of a local variable in a function. It features two variables named **count**. The first is declared and assigned a value of 10 in the interactive shell. Its value never changes, as echo verifies after **count_down** is run. The other **count** is declared, using typeset, to be local to the function. Its value, which is unknown outside the function, ranges from 4 to 1, as the echo command within the function confirms.

The example shows the function being entered from the keyboard; it is not a shell script. See the tip "A function is not a shell script" on page 944.

```
$ function count_down () {
> typeset count
> count=$1
> while [ $count -gt 0 ]
> do
> echo "$count..."
> ((count=count-1))
> sleep 1
> done
> echo "Blast Off."
> }
$ count=10
$ count_down 4
4...
3...
2...
1...
Blast Off.
$ echo $count
10
```

The ((**count=count–1**)) assignment is enclosed between double parentheses, which cause the shell to perform an arithmetic evaluation (page 972). Within the double parentheses you can reference shell variables without the leading dollar sign (**$**).

SPECIAL PARAMETERS

Special parameters enable you to access useful values pertaining to command-line arguments and the execution of shell commands. You reference a shell special parameter by preceding a special character with a dollar sign (**$**). As with positional parameters, it is not possible to modify the value of a special parameter by assignment.

$$: PID NUMBER

The shell stores in the **$$** parameter the PID number of the process that is executing it. In the following interaction, echo displays the value of this variable and the ps utility confirms its value. Both commands show that the shell has a PID number of 5209:

```
$ echo $$
5209
$ ps
  PID TTY          TIME CMD
 5209 pts/1    00:00:00 bash
 6015 pts/1    00:00:00 ps
```

Because echo is built into the shell, the shell does not create another process when you give an echo command. However, the results are the same whether echo is a builtin or not, because the shell substitutes the value of **$$** *before* it forks a new process to run a command. Try using the echo utility (**/bin/echo**), which is run by another process, and see what happens. In the following example, the shell substitutes the value of **$$** and passes that value to cp as a prefix for a filename:

```
$ echo $$
8232
$ cp memo $$.memo
$ ls
8232.memo memo
```

Incorporating a PID number in a filename is useful for creating unique filenames when the meanings of the names do not matter; this technique is often used in shell scripts for creating names of temporary files. When two people are running the same shell script, having unique filenames keeps the users from inadvertently sharing the same temporary file.

The following example demonstrates that the shell creates a new shell process when it runs a shell script. The **id2** script displays the PID number of the process running it (not the process that called it—the substitution for **$$** is performed by the shell that is forked to run **id2**):

```
$ cat id2
echo "$0 PID= $$"
$ echo $$
8232
$ id2
./id2 PID= 8362
$ echo $$
8232
```

The first echo displays the PID number of the interactive shell. Then **id2** displays its name (**$0**) and the PID number of the subshell that it is running in. The last echo shows that the PID number of the interactive shell has not changed.

$!   The shell stores the value of the PID number of the last process that ran in the background in $!. The following example executes sleep as a background task and uses echo to display the value of $!:

```
$ sleep 60 &
[1] 8376
$ echo $!
8376
```

$?: EXIT STATUS

When a process stops executing for any reason, it returns an *exit status* to its parent process. The exit status is also referred to as a *condition code* or a *return code*. The $? variable stores the exit status of the last command.

By convention a nonzero exit status represents a *false* value and means the command failed. A zero is *true* and indicates the command executed successfully. In the following example, the first ls command succeeds and the second fails, as demonstrated by the exit status:

```
$ ls es
es
$ echo $?
0
$ ls xxx
ls: xxx: No such file or directory
$ echo $?
1
```

You can specify the exit status that a shell script returns by using the exit builtin, followed by a number, to terminate the script. If you do not use exit with a number to terminate a script, the exit status of the script is that of the last command the script ran.

```
$ cat es
echo This program returns an exit status of 7.
exit 7
$ es
This program returns an exit status of 7.
$ echo $?
7
$ echo $?
0
```

The es shell script displays a message and terminates execution with an exit command that returns an exit status of 7, the user-defined exit status in this script. The first echo then displays the value of the exit status of es. The second echo displays the value of the exit status of the first echo. This value is 0, indicating the first echo was successful.

POSITIONAL PARAMETERS

Positional parameters comprise the command name and command-line arguments. These parameters are called *positional* because within a shell script, you refer to them by their position on the command line. Only the set builtin (page 954) allows you to change the values of positional parameters. However, you cannot change the value of the command name from within a script.

$#: NUMBER OF COMMAND-LINE ARGUMENTS

The $# parameter holds the number of arguments on the command line (positional parameters), not counting the command itself:

```
$ cat num_args
echo "This script was called with $# arguments."
$ ./num_args sam max zach
This script was called with 3 arguments.
```

$0: NAME OF THE CALLING PROGRAM

The shell stores the name of the command you used to call a program in parameter $0. This parameter is numbered zero because it appears before the first argument on the command line:

```
$ cat abc
echo "The command used to run this script is $0"
$ ./abc
The command used to run this script is ./abc
$ /home/sam/abc
The command used to run this script is /home/sam/abc
```

The preceding shell script uses echo to verify the name of the script you are executing. You can use the basename utility and command substitution to extract and display the simple filename of the command:

```
$ cat abc2
echo "The command used to run this script is $(basename $0)"
$ /home/sam/abc2
The command used to run this script is abc2
```

$1–$n: COMMAND-LINE ARGUMENTS

The first argument on the command line is represented by parameter $1, the second argument by $2, and so on up to $n. For values of n greater than 9, the number must be enclosed within braces. For example, the twelfth command-line argument is represented by ${12}. The following script displays positional parameters that hold command-line arguments:

```
$ cat display_5args
echo First 5 arguments are $1 $2 $3 $4 $5

$ ./display_5args zach max helen
First 5 arguments are zach max helen
```

The display_5args script displays the first five command-line arguments. The shell assigns a null value to each parameter that represents an argument that is not present on the command line. Thus the $4 and $5 parameters have null values in this example.

shift: Promotes Command-Line Arguments

The shift builtin promotes each command-line argument. The first argument (which was $1) is discarded. The second argument (which was $2) becomes the first argument (now $1), the third becomes the second, and so on. Because no "unshift" command exists, you cannot bring back arguments that have been discarded. An optional argument to shift specifies the number of positions to shift (and the number of arguments to discard); the default is 1.

The following **demo_shift** script is called with three arguments. Double quotation marks around the arguments to echo preserve the spacing of the output. The program displays the arguments and shifts them repeatedly until no more arguments are left to shift:

```
$ cat demo_shift
echo "arg1= $1     arg2= $2     arg3= $3"
shift
echo "arg1= $1     arg2= $2     arg3= $3"
shift
echo "arg1= $1     arg2= $2     arg3= $3"
shift
echo "arg1= $1     arg2= $2     arg3= $3"
shift
$ ./demo_shift alice helen zach
arg1= alice    arg2= helen    arg3= zach
arg1= helen    arg2= zach     arg3=
arg1= zach     arg2=          arg3=
arg1=          arg2=          arg3=
```

Repeatedly using shift is a convenient way to loop over all command-line arguments in shell scripts that expect an arbitrary number of arguments. See page 915 for a shell script that uses shift.

set: Initializes Command-Line Arguments

When you call the set builtin with one or more arguments, it assigns the values of the arguments to the positional parameters, starting with $1. The following script uses set to assign values to the positional parameters $1, $2, and $3:

```
$ cat set_it
set this is it
echo $3 $2 $1
$ ./set_it
it is this
```

Combining command substitution (page 346) with the set builtin is a convenient way to get standard output of a command in a form that can be easily manipulated in a shell script. The following script shows how to use date and set to provide the date in a useful format. The first command shows the output of date. Then cat displays the contents of the **dateset** script. The first command in this script uses command substitution to set the positional parameters to the output of the date utility. The next command, **echo $***, displays all positional parameters resulting from the previous set. Subsequent commands display the values of parameters **$1, $2, $3,** and **$6**. The final command displays the date in a format you can use in a letter or report:

```
$ date
Wed Aug 13 17:35:29 PDT 2008
$ cat dateset
set $(date)
echo $*
echo
echo "Argument 1: $1"
echo "Argument 2: $2"
echo "Argument 3: $3"
echo "Argument 6: $6"
echo
echo "$2 $3, $6"
$ ./dateset
Wed Aug 13 17:35:34 PDT 2008

Argument 1: Wed
Argument 2: Aug
Argument 3: 13
Argument 6: 2008

Aug 13, 2008
```

You can also use the +*format* argument to date to modify the format of its output.

When used without any arguments, set displays a list of the shell variables that are set, including user-created variables and keyword variables. Under bash, this list is the same as that displayed by declare and typeset when they are called without any arguments.

The set builtin also accepts options that let you customize the behavior of the shell. For more information refer to "set ±o: Turns Shell Features On and Off" on page 337.

$* AND $@: REPRESENT ALL COMMAND-LINE ARGUMENTS

The **$*** parameter represents all command-line arguments, as the **display_all** program demonstrates:

```
$ cat display_all
echo All arguments are $*

$ ./display_all a b c d e f g h i j k l m n o p
All arguments are a b c d e f g h i j k l m n o p
```

It is a good idea to enclose references to positional parameters between double quotation marks. The quotation marks are particularly important when you are using positional parameters as arguments to commands. Without double quotation marks, a positional parameter that is not set or that has a null value disappears:

```
$ cat showargs
echo "$0 was called with $# arguments, the first is :$1:."

$ ./showargs a b c
./showargs was called with 3 arguments, the first is :a:.
$ echo $xx

$ ./showargs $xx a b c
./showargs was called with 3 arguments, the first is :a:.
$ ./showargs "$xx" a b c
./showargs was called with 4 arguments, the first is ::.
```

The **showargs** script displays the number of arguments (**$#**) followed by the value of the first argument enclosed between colons. In the preceding example, **showargs** is initially called with three simple arguments. Next the echo command demonstrates that the **$xx** variable, which is not set, has a null value. In the final two calls to **showargs**, the first argument is **$xx**. In the first case the command line becomes **showargs a b c**; the shell passes **showargs** three arguments. In the second case the command line becomes **showargs "" a b c**, which results in calling **showargs** with four arguments. The difference in the two calls to **showargs** illustrates a subtle potential problem that you should keep in mind when using positional parameters that may not be set or that may have a null value.

"$*" versus "$@"   The **$*** and **$@** parameters work the same way except when they are enclosed within double quotation marks. Using "**$***" yields a single argument (with SPACEs or the value of the first character of **IFS** [page 307] between the positional parameters), whereas using "**$@**" produces a list wherein each positional parameter is a separate argument. This difference typically makes "**$@**" more useful than "**$***" in shell scripts.

The following scripts help explain the difference between these two special parameters. In the second line of both scripts, the single quotation marks keep the shell from interpreting the enclosed special characters so they are passed to echo and displayed as themselves. The **bb1** script shows that **set "$*"** assigns multiple arguments to the first command-line parameter:

```
$ cat bb1
set "$*"
echo $# parameters with '"$*"'
echo 1: $1
echo 2: $2
echo 3: $3
$ ./bb1 a b c
1 parameters with "$*"
1: a b c
2:
3:
```

The **bb2** script shows that **set "$@"** assigns each argument to a different command-line parameter:

```
$ cat bb2
set "$@"
echo $# parameters with '"$@"'
echo 1: $1
echo 2: $2
echo 3: $3

$ ./bb2 a b c
3 parameters with "$@"
1: a
2: b
3: c
```

EXPANDING NULL AND UNSET VARIABLES

The expression ${name} (or just $name if it is not ambiguous) expands to the value of the **name** variable. If **name** is null or not set, bash expands ${name} to a null string. The Bourne Again Shell provides the following alternatives to accepting the expanded null string as the value of the variable:

- Use a default value for the variable.
- Use a default value and assign that value to the variable.
- Display an error.

You can choose one of these alternatives by using a modifier with the variable name. In addition, you can use **set –o nounset** (page 339) to cause bash to display an error and exit from a script whenever an unset variable is referenced.

:– USES A DEFAULT VALUE

The :– modifier uses a default value in place of a null or unset variable while allowing a nonnull variable to represent itself:

    ${name:–default}

The shell interprets :– as "If *name* is null or unset, expand *default* and use the expanded value in place of *name;* else use *name.*" The following command lists the contents of the directory named by the **LIT** variable. If **LIT** is null or unset, it lists the contents of **/home/max/literature**:

    `$ ls ${LIT:-/home/max/literature}`

The default can itself have variable references that are expanded:

    `$ ls ${LIT:-$HOME/literature}`

:= ASSIGNS A DEFAULT VALUE

The :– modifier does not change the value of a variable. However, you can change the value of a null or unset variable to its default in a script by using the := modifier:

    ${name:=default}

The shell expands the expression *${name:=default}* in the same manner as it expands *${name:–default}* but also sets the value of *name* to the expanded value of *default*. If a script contains a line such as the following and **LIT** is unset or null at the time this line is executed, **LIT** is assigned the value **/home/max/literature**:

```
$ ls ${LIT:=/home/max/literature}
```

: (null) builtin   Shell scripts frequently start with the : (null) builtin followed on the same line by the := expansion modifier to set any variables that may be null or unset. The : builtin evaluates each token in the remainder of the command line but does not execute any commands. Without the leading colon (:), the shell evaluates and attempts to execute the "command" that results from the evaluation.

Use the following syntax to set a default for a null or unset variable in a shell script (a SPACE follows the first colon):

     :   *${name:=default}*

When a script needs a directory for temporary files and uses the value of **TEMPDIR** for the name of this directory, the following line assigns to **TEMPDIR** the value **/tmp** if **TEMPDIR** is null:

```
: ${TEMPDIR:=/tmp}
```

:? DISPLAYS AN ERROR MESSAGE

Sometimes a script needs the value of a variable but you cannot supply a reasonable default at the time you write the script. If the variable is null or unset, the **:?** modifier causes the script to display an error message and terminate with an exit status of 1:

     ${name:?message}

If you omit *message*, the shell displays the default error message (**parameter null or not set**). Interactive shells do not exit when you use **:?**. In the following command, **TESTDIR** is not set so the shell displays on standard error the expanded value of the string following **:?**. In this case the string includes command substitution for date with the **%T** format, followed by the string **error, variable not set**.

```
cd ${TESTDIR:?$(date +%T) error, variable not set.}
bash: TESTDIR: 16:16:14 error, variable not set.
```

BUILTIN COMMANDS

Builtin commands, which were introduced in Chapter 7, do not fork a new process when you execute them. This section discusses the type, read, exec, trap, kill, and getopts builtins. Table 27-6 on page 971 lists many bash builtin commands.

type: DISPLAYS INFORMATION ABOUT A COMMAND

The type builtin provides information about a command:

```
$ type cat echo who if lt
cat is hashed (/bin/cat)
echo is a shell builtin
who is /usr/bin/who
if is a shell keyword
lt is aliased to 'ls -ltrh | tail'
```

The preceding output shows the files that would be executed if you gave **cat** or **who** as a command. Because cat has already been called from the current shell, it is in the *hash table* (page 1111) and type reports that **cat is hashed**. The output also shows that a call to **echo** runs the echo builtin, **if** is a keyword, and **lt** is an alias.

read: ACCEPTS USER INPUT

One of the most common uses for user-created variables is storing information that a user enters in response to a prompt. Using read, scripts can accept input from the user and store that input in variables. The read builtin reads one line from standard input and assigns the words on the line to one or more variables:

```
$ cat read1
echo -n "Go ahead: "
read firstline
echo "You entered: $firstline"
$ ./read1
Go ahead: This is a line.
You entered: This is a line.
```

The first line of the **read1** script uses echo to prompt for a line of text. The **–n** option suppresses the following NEWLINE, allowing you to enter a line of text on the same line as the prompt. The second line reads the text into the variable **firstline**. The third line verifies the action of read by displaying the value of **firstline**. The variable is quoted (along with the text string) in this example because you, as the script writer, cannot anticipate which characters the user might enter in response to the prompt. Consider what would happen if the variable were not quoted and the user entered * in response to the prompt:

```
$ cat read1_no_quote
echo -n "Go ahead: "
read firstline
echo You entered: $firstline
$ ./read1_no_quote
Go ahead: *
You entered: read1 read1_no_quote script.1
$ ls
read1    read1_no_quote    script.1
```

The ls command lists the same words as the script, demonstrating that the shell expands the asterisk into a list of files in the working directory. When the variable $firstline is surrounded by double quotation marks, the shell does not expand the asterisk. Thus the read1 script behaves correctly:

```
$ ./read1
Go ahead: *
You entered: *
```

REPLY The read builtin includes several features that can make it easier to use. For example, when you do not specify a variable to receive read's input, bash puts the input into the variable named REPLY. You can use the –p option to prompt the user instead of using a separate echo command. The following read1a script performs exactly the same task as read1:

```
$ cat read1a
read -p "Go ahead: "
echo "You entered: $REPLY"
```

The read2 script prompts for a command line, reads the user's response, and assigns it to the variable cmd. The script then attempts to execute the command line that results from the expansion of the cmd variable:

```
$ cat read2
read -p "Enter a command: " cmd
$cmd
echo "Thanks"
```

In the following example, read2 reads a command line that calls the echo builtin. The shell executes the command and then displays **Thanks**. Next read2 reads a command line that executes the who utility:

```
$ ./read2
Enter a command: echo Please display this message.
Please display this message.
Thanks
$ ./read2
Enter a command: who
max      pts/4       Jun 17 07:50   (:0.0)
sam      pts/12      Jun 17 11:54   (bravo.example.com)
Thanks
```

If cmd does not expand into a valid command line, the shell issues an error message:

```
$ ./read2
Enter a command: xxx
./read2: line 2: xxx: command not found
Thanks
```

The read3 script reads values into three variables. The read builtin assigns one word (a sequence of nonblank characters) to each variable:

```
$ cat read3
read -p "Enter something: " word1 word2 word3
echo "Word 1 is: $word1"
echo "Word 2 is: $word2"
echo "Word 3 is: $word3"
```

```
$ ./read3
Enter something: this is something
Word 1 is: this
Word 2 is: is
Word 3 is: something
```

When you enter more words than read has variables, read assigns one word to each variable, assigning all leftover words to the last variable. Both **read1** and **read2** assigned the first word and all leftover words to the one variable the scripts each had to work with. In the following example, read assigns five words to three variables: It assigns the first word to the first variable, the second word to the second variable, and the third through fifth words to the third variable.

```
$ ./read3
Enter something: this is something else, really.
Word 1 is:  this
Word 2 is:  is
Word 3 is:  something else, really.
```

Table 27-4 lists some of the options supported by the read builtin.

Table 27-4 read options

Option	Function
–a *aname*	(array) Assigns each word of input to an element of array ***aname***.
–d *delim*	(delimiter) Uses ***delim*** to terminate the input instead of NEWLINE.
–e	(Readline) If input is coming from a keyboard, uses the Readline Library (page 324) to get input.
–n *num*	(number of characters) Reads ***num*** characters and returns. As soon as the user types ***num*** characters, read returns; there is no need to press RETURN.
–p *prompt*	(prompt) Displays ***prompt*** on standard error without a terminating NEWLINE before reading input. Displays ***prompt*** only when input comes from the keyboard.
–s	(silent) Does not echo characters.

–u *n*	(file descriptor) Uses the integer ***n*** as the file descriptor that read takes its input from. Thus
	
	    `read –u4 arg1 arg2`
	
	is equivalent to
	
	    `read arg1 arg2 <&4`
	
	See "File Descriptors" (page 943) for a discussion of redirection and file descriptors.

The read builtin returns an exit status of 0 if it successfully reads any data. It has a nonzero exit status when it reaches the EOF (end of file).

The following example runs a **while** loop from the command line. It takes its input from the **names** file and terminates after reading the last line from **names**.

```
$ cat names
Alice Jones
Robert Smith
Alice Paulson
John Q. Public

$ while read first rest
> do
> echo $rest, $first
> done < names
Jones, Alice
Smith, Robert
Paulson, Alice
Q. Public, John
$
```

The placement of the redirection symbol (<) for the **while** structure is critical. It is important that you place the redirection symbol at the **done** statement and not at the call to read.

optional Each time you redirect input, the shell opens the input file and repositions the read pointer at the start of the file:

```
$ read line1 < names; echo $line1; read line2 < names; echo $line2
Alice Jones
Alice Jones
```

Here each read opens **names** and starts at the beginning of the **names** file. In the following example, **names** is opened once, as standard input of the subshell created by the parentheses. Each read then reads successive lines of standard input:

```
$ (read line1; echo $line1; read line2; echo $line2) < names
Alice Jones
Robert Smith
```

Another way to get the same effect is to open the input file with **exec** and hold it open (refer to "File Descriptors" on page 943):

```
$ exec 3< names
$ read -u3 line1; echo $line1; read -u3 line2; echo $line2
Alice Jones
Robert Smith
$ exec 3<&-
```

exec: EXECUTES A COMMAND OR REDIRECTS FILE DESCRIPTORS

The exec builtin has two primary purposes: to run a command without creating a new process and to redirect a file descriptor—including standard input, output, or error—of a shell script from within the script (page 943). When the shell executes a command that is not built into the shell, it typically creates a new process. The new process inherits environment (global or exported) variables from its parent but does not inherit variables that are not exported by the parent. (For more information refer to "Locality of Variables" on page 948.) In contrast, exec executes a command in place of (overlays) the current process.

exec: EXECUTES A COMMAND

The exec builtin used for running a command has the following syntax:

exec command arguments

exec versus . (dot) Insofar as exec runs a command in the environment of the original process, it is similar to the . (dot) command (page 280). However, unlike the . command, which can run only shell scripts, exec can run both scripts and compiled programs. Also, whereas the . command returns control to the original script when it finishes running, exec does not. Finally, the . command gives the new program access to local variables, whereas exec does not.

exec does not return control Because the shell does not create a new process when you use exec, the command runs more quickly. However, because exec does not return control to the original program, it can be used only as the last command in a script. The following script shows that control is not returned to the script:

```
$ cat exec_demo
who
exec date
echo "This line is never displayed."

$ ./exec_demo
zach      pts/7     May 30   7:05 (bravo.example.com)
hls       pts/1     May 30   6:59 (:0.0)
Mon May 25 11:42:56 PDT 2009
```

The next example, a modified version of the **out** script (page 915), uses exec to execute the final command the script runs. Because **out** runs either cat or less and then terminates, the new version, named **out2**, uses exec with both cat and less:

```
$ cat out2
if [ $# -eq 0 ]
    then
        echo "Usage: out2 [-v] filenames" 1>&2
        exit 1
fi
if [ "$1" = "-v" ]
    then
        shift
        exec less "$@"
    else
        exec cat -- "$@"
fi
```

exec: REDIRECTS INPUT AND OUTPUT

The second major use of exec is to redirect a file descriptor—including standard input, output, or error—from within a script. The next command causes all subsequent input to a script that would have come from standard input to come from the file named **infile**:

```
exec < infile
```

Similarly the following command redirects standard output and standard error to **outfile** and **errfile**, respectively:

```
exec > outfile 2> errfile
```

When you use **exec** in this manner, the current process is not replaced with a new process, and **exec** can be followed by other commands in the script.

/dev/tty   When you redirect the output from a script to a file, you must make sure the user sees any prompts the script displays. The **/dev/tty** device is a pseudonym for the screen the user is working on; you can use this device to refer to the user's screen without knowing which device it is. (The tty utility displays the name of the device you are using.) By redirecting the output from a script to **/dev/tty**, you ensure that prompts and messages go to the user's terminal, regardless of which terminal the user is logged in on. Messages sent to **/dev/tty** are also not diverted if standard output and standard error from the script are redirected.

The **to_screen1** script sends output to three places: standard output, standard error, and the user's screen. When run with standard output and standard error redirected, **to_screen1** still displays the message sent to **/dev/tty** on the user's screen. The **out** and **err** files hold the output sent to standard output and standard error.

```
$ cat to_screen1
echo "message to standard output"
echo "message to standard error" 1>&2
echo "message to the user" > /dev/tty

$ ./to_screen1 > out 2> err
message to the user
$ cat out
message to standard output
$ cat err
message to standard error
```

The following command redirects the output from a script to the user's screen:

```
exec > /dev/tty
```

Putting this command at the beginning of the previous script changes where the output goes. In to_screen2, **exec** redirects standard output to the user's screen so the **> /dev/tty** is superfluous. Following the **exec** command, all output sent to standard output goes to **/dev/tty** (the screen). Output to standard error is not affected.

```
$ cat to_screen2
exec > /dev/tty
echo "message to standard output"
echo "message to standard error" 1>&2
echo "message to the user" > /dev/tty

$ ./to_screen2 > out 2> err
message to standard output
message to the user
```

One disadvantage of using **exec** to redirect the output to **/dev/tty** is that all subsequent output is redirected unless you use **exec** again in the script.

You can also redirect the input to read (standard input) so that it comes from **/dev/tty** (the keyboard):

```
read name < /dev/tty
```

or

```
exec < /dev/tty
```

trap: CATCHES A SIGNAL

A *signal* is a report to a process about a condition. Linux uses signals to report interrupts generated by the user (for example, pressing the interrupt key) as well as bad system calls, broken pipes, illegal instructions, and other conditions. The trap builtin catches (traps) one or more signals, allowing you to direct the actions a script takes when it receives a specified signal.

This discussion covers six signals that are significant when you work with shell scripts. Table 27-5 lists these signals, the signal numbers that systems often ascribe to them, and the conditions that usually generate each signal. Give the command **kill –l** (lowercase "ell"), **trap –l** (lowercase "ell"), or **man 7 signal** to display a list of all signal names.

Table 27-5 Signals

Type	Name	Number	Generating condition
Not a real signal	EXIT	0	Exit because of exit command or reaching the end of the program (not an actual signal but useful in trap)
Hang up	SIGHUP or HUP	1	Disconnect the line
Terminal interrupt	SIGINT or INT	2	Press the interrupt key (usually CONTROL-C)
Quit	SIGQUIT or QUIT	3	Press the quit key (usually CONTROL-SHIFT-| or CONTROL-SHIFT-\\)
Kill	SIGKILL or KILL	9	The kill builtin with the **–9** option (cannot be trapped; use only as a last resort)
Software termination	SIGTERM or TERM	15	Default of the kill command
Stop	SIGTSTP or TSTP	20	Press the suspend key (usually CONTROL-Z)
Debug	DEBUG		Executes **commands** specified in the trap statement after each command (not an actual signal but useful in trap)
Error	ERR		Executes **commands** specified in the trap statement after each command that returns a nonzero exit status (not an actual signal but useful in trap)

When it traps a signal, a script takes whatever action you specify: It can remove files or finish other processing as needed, display a message, terminate execution immediately, or ignore the signal. If you do not use trap in a script, any of the six actual signals listed in Table 27-5 (not EXIT, DEBUG, or ERR) will terminate the script. Because a process cannot trap a KILL signal, you can use kill –KILL (or kill –9) as a last resort to terminate a script or other process. (See page 968 for more information on kill.)

The trap command has the following syntax:

trap ['commands'] [signal]

The optional *commands* specifies the commands that the shell executes when it catches one of the signals specified by *signal*. The *signal* can be a signal name or number—for example, INT or 2. If *commands* is not present, trap resets the trap to its initial condition, which is usually to exit from the script.

Quotation marks   The trap builtin does not require single quotation marks around *commands* as shown in the preceding syntax, but it is a good practice to use them. The single quotation marks cause shell variables within the *commands* to be expanded when the signal occurs, rather than when the shell evaluates the arguments to trap. Even if you do not use any shell variables in the *commands*, you need to enclose any command that takes arguments within either single or double quotation marks. Quoting *commands* causes the shell to pass to trap the entire command as a single argument.

After executing the *commands*, the shell resumes executing the script where it left off. If you want trap to prevent a script from exiting when it receives a signal but not to run any commands explicitly, you can specify a null (empty) *commands* string, as shown in the **locktty** script (page 931). The following command traps signal number 15, after which the script continues:

```
trap '' 15
```

The following script demonstrates how the trap builtin can catch the terminal interrupt signal (2). You can use SIGINT, INT, or 2 to specify this signal. The script returns an exit status of 1:

```
$ cat inter
#!/bin/bash
trap 'echo PROGRAM INTERRUPTED; exit 1' INT
while true
do
    echo "Program running."
    sleep 1
done
$ ./inter
Program running.
Program running.
Program running.
CONTROL-C
PROGRAM INTERRUPTED
$
```

: (null) builtin   The second line of **inter** sets up a trap for the terminal interrupt signal using INT. When trap catches the signal, the shell executes the two commands between the single quotation marks in the trap command. The echo builtin displays the message **PROGRAM INTERRUPTED**, exit terminates the shell running the script, and the parent shell displays a prompt. If exit were not there, the shell would return control to the **while** loop after displaying the message. The **while** loop repeats continuously until the script receives a signal because the true utility always returns a *true* exit status. In place of true you can use the : (null) builtin, which is written as a colon and always returns a 0 (*true*) status.

The trap builtin frequently removes temporary files when a script is terminated prematurely, thereby ensuring the files are not left to clutter the filesystem. The following shell script, named **addbanner**, uses two traps to remove a temporary file when the script terminates normally or owing to a hangup, software interrupt, quit, or software termination signal:

```
$ cat addbanner
#!/bin/bash
script=$(basename $0)

if [ ! -r "$HOME/banner" ]
    then
        echo "$script: need readable $HOME/banner file" 1>&2
        exit 1
fi

trap 'exit 1' 1 2 3 15
trap 'rm /tmp/$$.$script 2> /dev/null' 0

for file
do
    if [ -r "$file" -a -w "$file" ]
        then
            cat $HOME/banner $file > /tmp/$$.$script
            cp /tmp/$$.$script $file
            echo "$script: banner added to $file" 1>&2
        else
            echo "$script: need read and write permission for $file" 1>&2
        fi
done
```

When called with one or more filename arguments, **addbanner** loops through the files, adding a header to the top of each. This script is useful when you use a standard format at the top of your documents, such as a standard layout for memos, or when you want to add a standard header to shell scripts. The header is kept in a file named ~/**banner**. Because **addbanner** uses the **HOME** variable, which contains the pathname of the user's home directory, the script can be used by several users without modification. If Max had written the script with **/home/max** in place of **$HOME** and then given the script to Zach, either Zach would have had to change it or **addbanner** would have used Max's **banner** file when Zach ran it (assuming Zach had read permission for the file).

The first trap in **addbanner** causes it to exit with a status of 1 when it receives a hangup, software interrupt (terminal interrupt or quit signal), or software termination signal. The second trap uses a 0 in place of **signal-number**, which causes trap to execute its command argument *whenever* the script exits because it receives an exit command or reaches its end. Together these traps remove a temporary file whether the script terminates normally or prematurely. Standard error of the second trap is sent to **/dev/null** whenever trap attempts to remove a nonexistent temporary file. In those cases rm sends an error message to standard error; because standard error is redirected, the user does not see the message.

See page 931 for another example that uses trap.

kill: ABORTS A PROCESS

The kill builtin sends a signal to a process or job. The kill command has the following syntax:

>   *kill [–signal] PID*

where *signal* is the signal name or number (for example, INT or 2) and *PID* is the process identification number of the process that is to receive the signal. You can specify a job number (page 240) as %*n* in place of *PID*. If you omit *signal*, kill sends a TERM (software termination, number 15) signal. For more information on signal names and numbers, see Table 27-5 on page 965.

The following command sends the TERM signal to job number 1, regardless of whether it is in the foreground (running) or in the background (running or stopped):

```
$ kill -TERM %1
```

Because TERM is the default signal for kill, you can also give this command as **kill %1**. Give the command **kill –l** (lowercase "l") to display a list of signal names.

A program that is interrupted can leave matters in an unpredictable state: Temporary files may be left behind (when they are normally removed), and permissions may be changed. A well-written application traps, or detects, signals and cleans up before exiting. Most carefully written applications trap the INT, QUIT, and TERM signals.

To terminate a program, first try INT (press CONTROL-C, if the job running is in the foreground). Because an application can be written to ignore these signals, you may need to use the KILL signal, which cannot be trapped or ignored; it is a "sure kill." For more information refer to "kill: Sends a Signal to a Process" on page 438.

getopts: PARSES OPTIONS

The getopts builtin parses command-line arguments, making it easier to write programs that follow the Linux argument conventions. The syntax for getopts is

>   *getopts optstring varname [arg ...]*

where *optstring* is a list of the valid option letters, *varname* is the variable that receives the options one at a time, and *arg* is the optional list of parameters to be processed. If *arg* is not present, getopts processes the command-line arguments. If *optstring* starts with a colon (:), the script must take care of generating error messages; otherwise, getopts generates error messages.

The getopts builtin uses the **OPTIND** (option index) and **OPTARG** (option argument) variables to track and store option-related values. When a shell script starts, the value of **OPTIND** is 1. Each time getopts is called and locates an argument, it increments **OPTIND** to the index of the next option to be processed. If the option takes an argument, bash assigns the value of the argument to **OPTARG**.

To indicate that an option takes an argument, follow the corresponding letter in *optstring* with a colon (:). The option string **dxo:lt:r** indicates that getopts should search for –d, –x, –o, –l, –t, and –r options and that the –o and –t options take arguments.

Using getopts as the ***test-command*** in a **while** control structure allows you to loop over the options one at a time. The getopts builtin checks the option list for options that are in *optstring*. Each time through the loop, getopts stores the option letter it finds in *varname*.

Suppose that you want to write a program that can take three options:

1. A –b option indicates that the program should ignore whitespace at the start of input lines.

2. A –t option followed by the name of a directory indicates that the program should store temporary files in that directory. Otherwise, it should use **/tmp**.

3. A –u option indicates that the program should translate all output to uppercase.

In addition, the program should ignore all other options and end option processing when it encounters two hyphens (––).

The problem is to write the portion of the program that determines which options the user has supplied. The following solution does not use getopts:

```
SKIPBLANKS=
TMPDIR=/tmp
CASE=lower
while [[ "$1" = -* ]] # [[ = ]] does pattern match
do
    case $1 in
        -b)     SKIPBLANKS=TRUE ;;
        -t)     if [ -d "$2" ]
                    then
                    TMPDIR=$2
                    shift
                else
                    echo "$0: -t takes a directory argument." >&2
                    exit 1
                fi ;;
        -u)     CASE=upper ;;
        --)     break   ;;      # Stop processing options
        *)      echo "$0: Invalid option $1 ignored." >&2 ;;
    esac
    shift
done
```

This program fragment uses a loop to check and shift arguments while the argument is not --. As long as the argument is not two hyphens, the program continues to loop through a **case** statement that checks for possible options. The -- **case** label breaks out of the **while** loop. The * **case** label recognizes any option; it appears as the last **case** label to catch any unknown options, displays an error message, and allows processing to continue. On each pass through the loop, the program uses shift to access the next argument. If an option takes an argument, the program uses an extra shift to get past that argument.

The following program fragment processes the same options, but uses getopts:

```
SKIPBLANKS=
TMPDIR=/tmp
CASE=lower

while getopts :bt:u arg
do
    case $arg in
        b)      SKIPBLANKS=TRUE ;;
        t)      if [ -d "$OPTARG" ]
                    then
                        TMPDIR=$OPTARG
                else
                    echo "$0: $OPTARG is not a directory." >&2
                    exit 1
                fi ;;
        u)      CASE=upper ;;
        :)      echo "$0: Must supply an argument to -$OPTARG." >&2
                exit 1 ;;
        \?)     echo "Invalid option -$OPTARG ignored." >&2 ;;
    esac
done
```

In this version of the code, the **while** structure evaluates the getopts builtin each time control transfers to the top of the loop. The getopts builtin uses the **OPTIND** variable to keep track of the index of the argument it is to process the next time it is called. There is no need to call shift in this example.

In the getopts version of the script, the **case** patterns do not start with a hyphen because the value of **arg** is just the option letter (getopts strips off the hyphen). Also, getopts recognizes -- as the end of the options, so you do not have to specify it explicitly, as in the **case** statement in the first example.

Because you tell getopts which options are valid and which require arguments, it can detect errors in the command line and handle them in two ways. This example uses a leading colon in *optstring* to specify that you check for and handle errors in your code; when getopts finds an invalid option, it sets *varname* to ? and **OPTARG** to the option letter. When it finds an option that is missing an argument, getopts sets *varname* to : and **OPTARG** to the option lacking an argument.

The \? **case** pattern specifies the action to take when getopts detects an invalid option. The : **case** pattern specifies the action to take when getopts detects a missing option argument. In both cases getopts does not write any error message but rather leaves that task to you.

If you omit the leading colon from *optstring*, both an invalid option and a missing option argument cause *varname* to be assigned the string ?. OPTARG is not set and getopts writes its own diagnostic message to standard error. Generally this method is less desirable because you have less control over what the user sees when an error occurs.

Using getopts will not necessarily make your programs shorter. Its principal advantages are that it provides a uniform programming interface and that it enforces standard option handling.

A PARTIAL LIST OF BUILTINS

Table 27-6 lists some of the bash builtins. You can use type (page 959) to see if a command runs a builtin. See "Listing bash builtins" on page 247 for instructions on how to display complete lists of builtins.

Table 27-6   bash builtins

Builtin	Function
:	Returns 0 or *true* (the null builtin; page 967)
. (dot)	Executes a shell script as part of the current process (page 280)
bg	Puts a suspended job in the background (page 293)
break	Exits from a looping control structure (page 932)
cd	Changes to another working directory (page 195)
continue	Starts with the next iteration of a looping control structure (page 932)
echo	Displays its arguments (page 157)
eval	Scans and evaluates the command line (page 335)
exec	Executes a shell script or program in place of the current process (page 962)
exit	Exits from the current shell (usually the same as CONTROL-D from an interactive shell; page 952)
export	Places the value of a variable in the calling environment (makes it global; page 948)
fg	Brings a job from the background into the foreground (page 292)
getopts	Parses arguments to a shell script (page 968)
jobs	Displays a list of background jobs (page 291)
kill	Sends a signal to a process or job (page 438)
pwd	Displays the name of the working directory (page 190)

Table 27-6   bash builtins (continued)

Builtin	Function
read	Reads a line from standard input (page 959)
readonly	Declares a variable to be readonly (page 301)
set	Sets shell flags or command-line argument variables; with no argument, lists all variables (pages 337 and 954)
shift	Promotes each command-line argument (page 954)
test	Compares arguments (page 911)
times	Displays total times for the current shell and its children
trap	Traps a signal (page 965)
type	Displays how each argument would be interpreted as a command (page 959)
umask	Returns the value of the file-creation mask (page 442)
unset	Removes a variable or function (page 300)
wait	Waits for a background process to terminate

EXPRESSIONS

An expression comprises constants, variables, and operators that the shell can process to return a value. This section covers arithmetic, logical, and conditional expressions as well as operators. Table 27-8 on page 975 lists the bash operators.

ARITHMETIC EVALUATION

The Bourne Again Shell can perform arithmetic assignments and evaluate many different types of arithmetic expressions, all using integers. The shell performs arithmetic assignments in a number of ways. One is with arguments to the let builtin:

```
$ let "VALUE=VALUE * 10 + NEW"
```

In the preceding example, the variables **VALUE** and **NEW** contain integer values. Within a let statement you do not need to use dollar signs ($) in front of variable names. Double quotation marks must enclose a single argument, or expression, that contains SPACEs. Because most expressions contain SPACEs and need to be quoted, bash accepts *((expression))* as a synonym for *let "expression"*, obviating the need for both quotation marks and dollar signs:

```
$ ((VALUE=VALUE * 10 + NEW))
```

You can use either form wherever a command is allowed and can remove the SPACEs if you like. In the following example, the asterisk (*) does not need to be quoted because the shell does not perform pathname expansion on the right side of an assignment (page 299):

```
$ let VALUE=VALUE*10+NEW
```

Because each argument to let is evaluated as a separate expression, you can assign values to more than one variable on a single line:

```
$ let "COUNT = COUNT + 1" VALUE=VALUE*10+NEW
```

You need to use commas to separate multiple assignments within a set of double parentheses:

```
$ ((COUNT = COUNT + 1, VALUE=VALUE*10+NEW))
```

Arithmetic evaluation versus arithmetic expansion

tip Arithmetic evaluation differs from arithmetic expansion. As explained on page 344, arithmetic expansion uses the syntax *$((expression))*, evaluates *expression*, and replaces *$((expression))* with the result. You can use arithmetic expansion to display the value of an expression or to assign that value to a variable.

Arithmetic evaluation uses the *let expression* or *((expression))* syntax, evaluates *expression*, and returns a status code. You can use arithmetic evaluation to perform a logical comparison or an assignment.

Logical expressions You can use the *((expression))* syntax for logical expressions, although that task is frequently left to *[[expression]]*. The next example expands the **age_check** script (page 344) to include logical arithmetic evaluation in addition to arithmetic expansion:

```
$ cat age2
#!/bin/bash
echo -n "How old are you? "
read age
if ((30 < age && age < 60)); then
        echo "Wow, in $((60-age)) years, you'll be 60!"
    else
        echo "You are too young or too old to play."
fi

$ ./age2
How old are you? 25
You are too young or too old to play.
```

The *test-statement* for the **if** structure evaluates two logical comparisons joined by a Boolean AND and returns 0 (*true*) if they are both *true* or 1 (*false*) otherwise.

LOGICAL EVALUATION (CONDITIONAL EXPRESSIONS)

The syntax of a conditional expression is

[[expression]]

where *expression* is a Boolean (logical) expression. You must precede a variable name with a dollar sign (**$**) within *expression*. The result of executing this builtin, as with the test builtin, is a return status. The *conditions* allowed within the brackets are almost a superset of those accepted by test (page 911). Where the test builtin uses **–a** as a Boolean AND operator, *[[expression]]* uses **&&**. Similarly, where test uses **–o** as a Boolean OR operator, *[[expression]]* uses **||**.

To see how conditional expressions work, replace the line that tests **age** in the **age2** script with the following conditional expression. You must surround the [[and]] tokens with whitespace or a command terminator, and place dollar signs before the variables:

```
if [[ 30 < $age && $age < 60 ]]; then
```

You can also use **test**'s relational operators **–gt**, **–ge**, **–lt**, **–le**, **–eq**, and **–ne**:

```
if [[ 30 -lt $age && $age -lt 60 ]]; then
```

String comparisons   The **test** builtin tests whether strings are equal. The *[[expression]]* syntax adds comparison tests for string operators. The > and < operators compare strings for order (for example, "aa" < "bbb"). The = operator tests for pattern match, not just equality: *[[string = pattern]]* is *true* if *string* matches *pattern*. This operator is not symmetrical; the *pattern* must appear on the right side of the equal sign. For example, [[**artist = a**∗]] is *true* (= 0), whereas [[**a**∗ **= artist**]] is *false* (= 1):

```
$ [[ artist = a* ]]
$ echo $?
0
$ [[ a* = artist ]]
$ echo $?
1
```

The next example uses a command list that starts with a compound condition. The condition tests that the directory **bin** and the file **src/myscript.bash** exist. If this is *true*, cp copies **src/myscript.bash** to **bin/myscript**. If the copy succeeds, chmod makes **myscript** executable. If any of these steps fails, echo displays a message.

```
$ [[ -d bin && -f src/myscript.bash ]] && cp src/myscript.bash \
bin/myscript && chmod +x bin/myscript || echo "Cannot make \
executable version of myscript"
```

STRING PATTERN MATCHING

The Bourne Again Shell provides string pattern-matching operators that can manipulate pathnames and other strings. These operators can delete from strings prefixes or suffixes that match patterns. Table 27-7 lists the four operators.

Table 27-7   String operators

Operator	Function
#	Removes minimal matching prefixes
##	Removes maximal matching prefixes
%	Removes minimal matching suffixes
%%	Removes maximal matching suffixes

The syntax for these operators is

${varname op pattern}

where *op* is one of the operators listed in Table 27-7 and *pattern* is a match pattern similar to that used for filename generation. These operators are commonly used to manipulate pathnames to extract or remove components or to change suffixes:

```
$ SOURCEFILE=/usr/local/src/prog.c
$ echo ${SOURCEFILE#/*/}
local/src/prog.c
$ echo ${SOURCEFILE##/*/}
prog.c
$ echo ${SOURCEFILE%/*}
/usr/local/src
$ echo ${SOURCEFILE%%/*}

$ echo ${SOURCEFILE%.c}
/usr/local/src/prog
$ CHOPFIRST=${SOURCEFILE#/*/}
$ echo $CHOPFIRST
local/src/prog.c
$ NEXT=${CHOPFIRST%%/*}
$ echo $NEXT
local
```

Here the string-length operator, ${#*name*}, is replaced by the number of characters in the value of **name**:

```
$ echo $SOURCEFILE
/usr/local/src/prog.c
$ echo ${#SOURCEFILE}
21
```

OPERATORS

Arithmetic expansion and arithmetic evaluation in bash use the same syntax, precedence, and associativity of expressions as in the C language. Table 27-8 lists operators in order of decreasing precedence (priority of evaluation); each group of operators has equal precedence. Within an expression you can use parentheses to change the order of evaluation.

Table 27-8 Operators

Type of operator/operator	Function
Post	
var++	Postincrement
var--	Postdecrement
Pre	
++*var*	Preincrement
--*var*	Predecrement

Table 27-8   Operators (continued)

Type of operator/operator	Function
Unary	
−	Unary minus
+	Unary plus
Negation	
!	Boolean NOT (logical negation)
~	Complement (bitwise negation)
Exponentiation	
**	Exponent
Multiplication, division, remainder	
*	Multiplication
/	Division
%	Remainder
Addition, subtraction	
−	Subtraction
+	Addition
Bitwise shifts	
<<	Left bitwise shift
>>	Right bitwise shift
Comparison	
<=	Less than or equal
>=	Greater than or equal
<	Less than
>	Greater than
Equality, inequality	
==	Equality
!=	Inequality
Bitwise	
&	Bitwise AND
^	Bitwise XOR (exclusive OR)
|	Bitwise OR

Table 27-8   Operators (continued)

Type of operator/operator	Function
Boolean (logical)	
&& Boolean AND	
|| Boolean OR	
Conditional evaluation	
? : Ternary operator	
Assignment	
=, ∗=, /=, %=, +=, −=, Assignment **<<=, >>=, &=, ^=, |=**	
Comma	
, Comma	

Pipe   The pipe token has higher precedence than operators. You can use pipes anywhere in a command that you can use simple commands. For example, the command line

```
$ cmd1 | cmd2 || cmd3 | cmd4 && cmd5 | cmd6
```

is interpreted as if you had typed

```
$ ((cmd1 | cmd2) || (cmd3 | cmd4)) && (cmd5 | cmd6)
```

Do not rely on rules of precedence: use parentheses

tip   Do not rely on the precedence rules when you use compound commands. Instead, use parentheses to explicitly state the order in which you want the shell to interpret the commands.

Increment and decrement   The postincrement, postdecrement, preincrement, and predecrement operators work with variables. The pre- operators, which appear in front of the variable name (as in **++COUNT** and **−−VALUE**), first change the value of the variable (**++** adds 1; **−−** subtracts 1) and then provide the result for use in the expression. The post- operators appear after the variable name (as in **COUNT++** and **VALUE−−**); they first provide the unchanged value of the variable for use in the expression and then change the value of the variable.

```
$ N=10
$ echo $N
10
$ echo $((--N+3))
12
$ echo $N
9
$ echo $((N++ - 3))
6
$ echo $N
10
```

Remainder   The remainder operator (%) yields the remainder when its first operand is divided by its second. For example, the expression **$((15%7))** has the value 1.

Boolean   The result of a Boolean operation is either 0 (*false*) or 1 (*true*).

The && (AND) and || (OR) Boolean operators are called *short-circuiting* operators. If the result of using one of these operators can be decided by looking only at the left operand, the right operand is not evaluated. The && operator causes the shell to test the exit status of the command preceding it. If the command succeeded, bash executes the next command; otherwise, it skips the remaining commands on the command line. You can use this construct to execute commands conditionally.

```
$ mkdir bkup && cp -r src bkup
```

This compound command creates the directory **bkup**. If mkdir succeeds, the contents of directory **src** is copied recursively to **bkup**.

The || separator also causes bash to test the exit status of the first command but has the opposite effect: The remaining command(s) are executed only if the first one failed (that is, exited with nonzero status).

```
$ mkdir bkup || echo "mkdir of bkup failed" >> /tmp/log
```

The exit status of a command list is the exit status of the last command in the list. You can group lists with parentheses. For example, you could combine the previous two examples as

```
$ (mkdir bkup && cp -r src bkup) || echo "mkdir failed" >> /tmp/log
```

In the absence of parentheses, && and || have equal precedence and are grouped from left to right. The following examples use the true and false utilities. These utilities do nothing and return *true* (0) and *false* (1) exit statuses, respectively:

```
$ false; echo $?
1
```

The **$?** variable holds the exit status of the preceding command (page 952). The next two commands yield an exit status of 1 (*false*):

```
$ true || false && false
$ echo $?
1
$ (true || false) && false
$ echo $?
1
```

Similarly the next two commands yield an exit status of 0 (*true*):

```
$ false && false || true
$ echo $?
0
$ (false && false) || true
$ echo $?
0
```

Because ǁ and && have equal precedence, the parentheses in the two preceding pairs of examples do not change the order of operations.

Because the expression on the right side of a short-circuiting operator may never be executed, you must be careful when placing assignment statements in that location. The following example demonstrates what can happen:

```
$ ((N=10,Z=0))
$ echo $((N || ((Z+=1)) ))
1
$ echo $Z
0
```

Because the value of **N** is nonzero, the result of the ǁ (OR) operation is 1 (*true*), no matter what the value of the right side is. As a consequence, ((**Z+=1**)) is never evaluated and **Z** is not incremented.

Ternary   The ternary operator, **? :**, decides which of two expressions should be evaluated, based on the value returned by a third expression:

> *expression1 ? expression2 : expression3*

If *expression1* produces a *false* (0) value, *expression3* is evaluated; otherwise, *expression2* is evaluated. The value of the entire expression is the value of *expression2* or *expression3*, depending on which is evaluated. If *expression1* is *true*, *expression3* is not evaluated. If *expression1* is *false*, *expression2* is not evaluated.

```
$ ((N=10,Z=0,COUNT=1))
$ ((T=N>COUNT?++Z:--Z))
$ echo $T
1
$ echo $Z
1
```

Assignment   The assignment operators, such as **+=**, are shorthand notations. For example, **N+=3** is the same as ((**N=N+3**)).

Other bases   The following commands use the syntax *base#n* to assign base 2 (binary) values. First **v1** is assigned a value of 0101 (5 decimal) and then **v2** is assigned a value of 0110 (6 decimal). The echo utility verifies the decimal values.

```
$ ((v1=2#0101))
$ ((v2=2#0110))
$ echo "$v1 and $v2"
5 and 6
```

Next the bitwise AND operator (**&**) selects the bits that are on in both 5 (0101 binary) and 6 (0110 binary). The result is binary 0100, which is 4 decimal.

```
$ echo $(( v1 & v2 ))
4
```

The Boolean AND operator (&&) produces a result of 1 if both of its operands are nonzero and a result of 0 otherwise. The bitwise inclusive OR operator (I) selects the bits that are on in either 0101 or 0110, resulting in 0111, which is 7 decimal. The Boolean OR operator (II) produces a result of 1 if either of its operands is nonzero and a result of 0 otherwise.

```
$ echo $(( v1 && v2 ))
1
$ echo $(( v1 | v2 ))
7
$ echo $(( v1 || v2 ))
1
```

Next the bitwise exclusive OR operator (^) selects the bits that are on in either, but not both, of the operands 0101 and 0110, yielding 0011, which is 3 decimal. The Boolean NOT operator (!) produces a result of 1 if its operand is 0 and a result of 0 otherwise. Because the exclamation point in $((! v1)) is enclosed within double parentheses, it does not need to be escaped to prevent the shell from interpreting the exclamation point as a history event. The comparison operators produce a result of 1 if the comparison is *true* and a result of 0 otherwise.

```
$ echo $(( v1 ^ v2 ))
3
$ echo $(( ! v1 ))
0
$ echo $(( v1 < v2 ))
1
$ echo $(( v1 > v2 ))
0
```

SHELL PROGRAMS

The Bourne Again Shell has many features that make it a good programming language. The structures that bash provides are not a random assortment, but rather have been chosen to provide most of the structural features that are found in other procedural languages, such as C or Perl. A procedural language provides the following abilities:

- Declare, assign, and manipulate variables and constant data. The Bourne Again Shell provides string variables, together with powerful string operators, and integer variables, along with a complete set of arithmetic operators.

- Break large problems into small ones by creating subprograms. The Bourne Again Shell allows you to create functions and call scripts from other scripts. Shell functions can be called recursively; that is, a Bourne Again Shell function can call itself. You may not need to use recursion often, but it may allow you to solve some apparently difficult problems with ease.

- Execute statements conditionally, using statements such as if.

- Execute statements iteratively, using statements such as while and for.

- Transfer data to and from the program, communicating with both data files and users.

Programming languages implement these capabilities in different ways but with the same ideas in mind. When you want to solve a problem by writing a program, you must first figure out a procedure that leads you to a solution—that is, an *algorithm*. Typically you can implement the same algorithm in roughly the same way in different programming languages, using the same kinds of constructs in each language.

Chapter 9 and this chapter have introduced numerous bash features, many of which are useful for both interactive use and shell programming. This section develops two complete shell programs, demonstrating how to combine some of these features effectively. The programs are presented as problems for you to solve, with sample solutions provided.

A Recursive Shell Script

A recursive construct is one that is defined in terms of itself. Alternatively, you might say that a recursive program is one that can call itself. This concept may seem circular, but it need not be. To avoid circularity, a recursive definition must have a special case that is not self-referential. Recursive ideas occur in everyday life. For example, you can define an ancestor as your mother, your father, or one of their ancestors. This definition is not circular; it specifies unambiguously who your ancestors are: your mother or your father, or your mother's mother or father or your father's mother or father, and so on.

A number of Linux system utilities can operate recursively. See the **–R** option to the chmod, chown, and cp utilities for examples.

Solve the following problem by using a recursive shell function:

Write a shell function named **makepath** that, given a pathname, creates all components in that pathname as directories. For example, the command **makepath a/b/c/d** should create directories **a**, **a/b**, **a/b/c**, and **a/b/c/d**. (The mkdir **–p** option creates directories in this manner. Solve the problem without using **mkdir –p**.)

One algorithm for a recursive solution follows:

1. Examine the path argument. If it is a null string or if it names an existing directory, do nothing and return.

2. If the path argument is a simple path component, create it (using mkdir) and return.

3. Otherwise, call **makepath** using the path prefix of the original argument. This step eventually creates all the directories up to the last component, which you can then create using mkdir.

In general, a recursive function must invoke itself with a simpler version of the problem than it was given until it is finally called with a simple case that does not need to call itself. Following is one possible solution based on this algorithm:

makepath
```
# This is a function
# Enter it at the keyboard, do not run it as a shell script
#
function makepath()
{
    if [[ ${#1} -eq 0 || -d "$1" ]]
        then
            return 0         # Do nothing
    fi
    if [[ "${1%/*}" = "$1" ]]
        then
            mkdir $1
            return $?
    fi
    makepath ${1%/*} || return 1
    mkdir $1
    return $?
}
```

In the test for a simple component (the **if** statement in the middle of the function), the left expression is the argument after the shortest suffix that starts with a **/** character has been stripped away (page 974). If there is no such character (for example, if **$1** is **max**), nothing is stripped off and the two sides are equal. If the argument is a simple filename preceded by a slash, such as **/usr**, the expression **${1%/*}** evaluates to a null string. To make the function work in this case, you must take two precautions: Put the left expression within quotation marks and ensure that the recursive function behaves sensibly when it is passed a null string as an argument. In general, good programs are robust: They should be prepared for borderline, invalid, or meaningless input and behave appropriately in such cases.

By giving the following command from the shell you are working in, you turn on debugging tracing so that you can watch the recursion work:

```
$ set -o xtrace
```

(Give the same command, but replace the hyphen with a plus sign (+) to turn debugging off.) With debugging turned on, the shell displays each line in its expanded form as it executes the line. A + precedes each line of debugging output.

In the following example, the first line that starts with + shows the shell calling **makepath**. The **makepath** function is initially called from the command line with arguments of **a/b/c**. It then calls itself with arguments of **a/b** and finally **a**. All the work is done (using mkdir) as each call to **makepath** returns.

```
$ ./makepath a/b/c
+ makepath a/b/c
+ [[ 5 -eq 0 ]]
+ [[ -d a/b/c ]]
+ [[ a/b = \a\/\b\/\c ]]
+ makepath a/b
+ [[ 3 -eq 0 ]]
+ [[ -d a/b ]]
+ [[ a = \a\/\b ]]
```

```
+ makepath a
+ [[ 1 -eq 0 ]]
+ [[ -d a ]]
+ [[ a = \a ]]
+ mkdir a
+ return 0
+ mkdir a/b
+ return 0
+ mkdir a/b/c
+ return 0
```

The function works its way down the recursive path and back up again.

It is instructive to invoke **makepath** with an invalid path and see what happens. The following example, which is run with debugging turned on, tries to create the path **/a/b**. Creating this path requires that you create directory **a** in the root directory. Unless you have permission to write to the root directory, you are not permitted to create this directory.

```
$ ./makepath /a/b
+ makepath /a/b
+ [[ 4 -eq 0 ]]
+ [[ -d /a/b ]]
+ [[ /a = \/\a\/\b ]]
+ makepath /a
+ [[ 2 -eq 0 ]]
+ [[ -d /a ]]
+ [[ '' = \/\a ]]
+ makepath
+ [[ 0 -eq 0 ]]
+ return 0
+ mkdir /a
mkdir: cannot create directory '/a': Permission denied
+ return 1
+ return 1
```

The recursion stops when **makepath** is denied permission to create the **/a** directory. The error returned is passed all the way back, so the original **makepath** exits with nonzero status.

Use local variables with recursive functions

tip   The preceding example glossed over a potential problem that you may encounter when you use a recursive function. During the execution of a recursive function, many separate instances of that function may be active simultaneously. All but one of them are waiting for their child invocation to complete.

Because functions run in the same environment as the shell that calls them, variables are implicitly shared by a shell and a function it calls. As a consequence, all instances of the function share a single copy of each variable. Sharing variables can give rise to side effects that are rarely what you want. As a rule, you should use typeset to make all variables of a recursive function be local variables. See page 949 for more information.

The quiz Shell Script

Solve the following problem using a bash script:

Write a generic multiple-choice quiz program. The program should get its questions from data files, present them to the user, and keep track of the number of correct and incorrect answers. The user must be able to exit from the program at any time and receive a summary of results to that point.

The detailed design of this program and even the detailed description of the problem depend on a number of choices: How will the program know which subjects are available for quizzes? How will the user choose a subject? How will the program know when the quiz is over? Should the program present the same questions (for a given subject) in the same order each time, or should it scramble them?

Of course, you can make many perfectly good choices that implement the specification of the problem. The following details narrow the problem specification:

- Each subject will correspond to a subdirectory of a master quiz directory. This directory will be named in the environment variable **QUIZDIR**, whose default will be **~/quiz**. For example, you could have the following directories correspond to the subjects engineering, art, and politics: **~/quiz/engineering**, **~/quiz/art**, and **~/quiz/politics**. Put the **quiz** directory in **/usr/games** if you want all users to have access to it (requires **root** privileges).

- Each subject can have several questions. Each question is represented by a file in its subject's directory.

- The first line of each file that represents a question holds the text of the question. If it takes more than one line, you must escape the NEWLINE with a backslash. (This setup makes it easy to read a single question with the read builtin.) The second line of the file is an integer that specifies the number of choices. The next lines are the choices themselves. The last line is the correct answer. Following is a sample question file:

      Who discovered the principle of the lever?
      4
      Euclid
      Archimedes
      Thomas Edison
      The Lever Brothers
      Archimedes

- The program presents all the questions in a subject directory. At any point the user can interrupt the quiz with CONTROL-C, whereupon the program will summarize the results so far and exit. If the user does not interrupt the program, the program summarizes the results and exits when it has asked all questions for the chosen subject.

- The program scrambles the questions in a subject before presenting them.

Following is a top-level design for this program:

1. Initialize. This involves a number of steps, such as setting the counts of the number of questions asked so far and the number of correct and wrong answers to zero. It also sets up the program to trap CONTROL-C.

2. Present the user with a choice of subjects and get the user's response.

3. Change to the corresponding subject directory.

4. Determine the questions to be asked (that is, the filenames in that directory). Arrange them in random order.

5. Repeatedly present questions and ask for answers until the quiz is over or is interrupted by the user.

6. Present the results and exit.

Clearly some of these steps (such as step 3) are simple, whereas others (such as step 4) are complex and worthy of analysis on their own. Use shell functions for any complex step, and use the trap builtin to handle a user interrupt.

Here is a skeleton version of the program with empty shell functions:

```
function initialize
{
# Initializes variables.
}

function choose_subj
{
# Writes choice to standard output.
}

function scramble
{
# Stores names of question files, scrambled,
# in an array variable named questions.
}

function ask
{
# Reads a question file, asks the question, and checks the
# answer. Returns 1 if the answer was correct, 0 otherwise. If it
# encounters an invalid question file, exit with status 2.
}

function summarize
{
# Presents the user's score.
}

# Main program
initialize                              # Step 1 in top-level design

subject=$(choose_subj)                  # Step 2
[[ $? -eq 0 ]] || exit 2                # If no valid choice, exit
```

```
cd $subject || exit 2            # Step 3
echo                             # Skip a line
scramble                         # Step 4

for ques in ${questions[*]}; do  # Step 5
    ask $ques
    result=$?
    (( num_ques=num_ques+1 ))
    if [[ $result == 1 ]]; then
        (( num_correct += 1 ))
    fi
    echo                         # Skip a line between questions
    sleep ${QUIZDELAY:=1}
done

summarize                        # Step 6
exit 0
```

To make reading the results a bit easier for the user, a sleep call appears inside the question loop. It delays **$QUIZDELAY** seconds (default = 1) between questions.

Now the task is to fill in the missing pieces of the program. In a sense this program is being written backward. The details (the shell functions) come first in the file but come last in the development process. This common programming practice is called top-down design. In top-down design you fill in the broad outline of the program first and supply the details later. In this way you break the problem up into smaller problems, each of which you can work on independently. Shell functions are a great help in using the top-down approach.

One way to write the **initialize** function follows. The cd command causes **QUIZDIR** to be the working directory for the rest of the script and defaults to **~/quiz** if **QUIZDIR** is not set.

```
function initialize ()
{
trap 'summarize ; exit 0' INT    # Handle user interrupts
num_ques=0                       # Number of questions asked so far
num_correct=0                    # Number answered correctly so far
first_time=true                  # true until first question is asked
cd ${QUIZDIR:=~/quiz} || exit 2
}
```

Be prepared for the cd command to fail. The directory may be unsearchable or conceivably another user may have removed it. The preceding function exits with a status code of 2 if cd fails.

The next function, **choose_subj**, is a bit more complicated. It displays a menu using a **select** statement:

```
function choose_subj ()
{
subjects=($(ls))
PS3="Choose a subject for the quiz from the preceding list: "
select Subject in ${subjects[*]}; do
    if [[ -z "$Subject" ]]; then
        echo "No subject chosen.  Bye." >&2
        exit 1
    fi
    echo $Subject
    return 0
done
}
```

The function first uses an ls command and command substitution to put a list of subject directories in the **subjects** array. Next the **select** structure (page 939) presents the user with a list of subjects (the directories found by ls) and assigns the chosen directory name to the **Subject** variable. Finally the function writes the name of the subject directory to standard output. The main program uses command substitution to assign this value to the **subject** variable [**subject=$(choose_subj)**].

The **scramble** function presents a number of difficulties. In this solution it uses an array variable (**questions**) to hold the names of the questions. It scrambles the entries in an array using the **RANDOM** variable (each time you reference **RANDOM**, it has the value of a [random] integer between 0 and 32767):

```
function scramble ()
{
typeset -i index quescount
questions=($(ls))
quescount=${#questions[*]}            # Number of elements
((index=quescount-1))
while [[ $index > 0 ]]; do
    ((target=RANDOM % index))
    exchange $target $index
    ((index -= 1))
done
}
```

This function initializes the array variable **questions** to the list of filenames (questions) in the working directory. The variable **quescount** is set to the number of such files. Then the following algorithm is used: Let the variable index count down from **quescount – 1** (the index of the last entry in the array variable). For each value of **index,** the function chooses a random value target between 0 and **index,** inclusive. The command

```
((target=RANDOM % index))
```

produces a random value between 0 and **index – 1** by taking the remainder (the % operator) when **$RANDOM** is divided by **index.** The function then exchanges the elements of **questions** at positions **target** and **index.** It is convenient to take care of this step in another function named **exchange:**

```
function exchange ()
{
temp_value=${questions[$1]}
questions[$1]=${questions[$2]}
questions[$2]=$temp_value
}
```

The **ask** function also uses the **select** structure. It reads the question file named in its argument and uses the contents of that file to present the question, accept the answer, and determine whether the answer is correct. (See the code that follows.)

The **ask** function uses file descriptor 3 to read successive lines from the question file, whose name was passed as an argument and is represented by **$1** in the function. It reads the question into the **ques** variable and the number of questions into **num_opts**. The function constructs the variable **choices** by initializing it to a null string and successively appending the next choice. Then it sets **PS3** to the value of **ques** and uses a **select** structure to prompt the user with **ques**. The **select** structure places the user's answer in **answer**, and the function then checks that response against the correct answer from the file.

The construction of the **choices** variable is done with an eye toward avoiding a potential problem. Suppose that one answer has some whitespace in it—then it might appear as two or more arguments in **choices**. To avoid this problem, make sure that **choices** is an array variable. The **select** statement does the rest of the work:

quiz
```
$ cat quiz
#!/bin/bash

# remove the # on the following line to turn on debugging
# set -o xtrace

#===================
function initialize ()
{
trap 'summarize ; exit 0' INT      # Handle user interrupts
num_ques=0                          # Number of questions asked so far
num_correct=0                       # Number answered correctly so far
first_time=true                     # true until first question is asked
cd ${QUIZDIR:=~/quiz} || exit 2
}

#===================
function choose_subj ()
{
subjects=($(ls))
PS3="Choose a subject for the quiz from the preceding list: "
select Subject in ${subjects[*]}; do
    if [[ -z "$Subject" ]]; then
        echo "No subject chosen.  Bye." >&2
        exit 1
    fi
    echo $Subject
    return 0
done
}
```

```
#==================
function exchange ()
{
temp_value=${questions[$1]}
questions[$1]=${questions[$2]}
questions[$2]=$temp_value
}


#==================
function scramble ()
{
typeset -i index quescount
questions=($(ls))
quescount=${#questions[*]}            # Number of elements
((index=quescount-1))
while [[ $index > 0 ]]; do
    ((target=RANDOM % index))
    exchange $target $index
    ((index -= 1))
done
}


#==================
function ask ()
{
exec 3<$1
read -u3 ques || exit 2
read -u3 num_opts || exit 2

index=0
choices=()
while (( index < num_opts )) ; do
    read -u3 next_choice || exit 2
    choices=("${choices[@]}" "$next_choice")
    ((index += 1))
done
read -u3 correct_answer || exit 2
exec 3<&-

if [[ $first_time = true ]]; then
    first_time=false
    echo -e "You may press the interrupt key at any time to quit.\n"
fi

PS3=$ques" "                          # Make $ques the prompt for select
                                      # and add some spaces for legibility.
select answer in "${choices[@]}"; do
    if [[ -z "$answer" ]]; then
            echo  Not a valid choice. Please choose again.
        elif [[ "$answer" = "$correct_answer" ]]; then
            echo "Correct!"
            return 1
        else
            echo "No, the answer is $correct_answer."
            return 0
    fi
done
}
```

```
#==================
function summarize ()
{
echo                                 # Skip a line
if (( num_ques == 0 )); then
    echo "You did not answer any questions"
    exit 0
fi

(( percent=num_correct*100/num_ques ))
echo "You answered $num_correct questions correctly, out of \
$num_ques total questions."
echo "Your score is $percent percent."
}

#==================
# Main program
initialize                           # Step 1 in top-level design

subject=$(choose_subj)               # Step 2
[[ $? -eq 0 ]] || exit 2             # If no valid choice, exit

cd $subject || exit 2                # Step 3
echo                                 # Skip a line
scramble                             # Step 4

for ques in ${questions[*]}; do      # Step 5
    ask $ques
    result=$?
    (( num_ques=num_ques+1 ))
    if [[ $result == 1 ]]; then
        (( num_correct += 1 ))
    fi
    echo                             # Skip a line between questions
    sleep ${QUIZDELAY:=1}
done

summarize                            # Step 6
exit 0
```

CHAPTER SUMMARY

The shell is a programming language. Programs written in this language are called shell scripts, or simply scripts. Shell scripts provide the decision and looping control structures present in high-level programming languages while allowing easy access to system utilities and user programs. Shell scripts can use functions to modularize and simplify complex tasks.

Control structures   The control structures that use decisions to select alternatives are **if...then, if...then...else,** and **if...then...elif.** The **case** control structure provides a multiway branch and can be used when you want to express alternatives using a simple pattern-matching syntax.

The looping control structures are **for...in, for, until,** and **while.** These structures perform one or more tasks repetitively.

The **break** and **continue** control structures alter control within loops: **break** transfers control out of a loop, and **continue** transfers control immediately to the top of a loop.

The Here document allows input to a command in a shell script to come from within the script itself.

File descriptors
The Bourne Again Shell provides the ability to manipulate file descriptors. Coupled with the read and echo builtins, file descriptors allow shell scripts to have as much control over input and output as do programs written in lower-level languages.

Variables
The typeset builtin assigns attributes, such as readonly, to bash variables. The Bourne Again Shell provides operators to perform pattern matching on variables, provide default values for variables, and evaluate the length of variables. This shell also supports array variables and local variables for functions and provides built-in integer arithmetic, using the let builtin and an expression syntax similar to that found in the C programming language.

Builtins
Bourne Again Shell builtins include type, read, exec, trap, kill, and getopts. The type builtin displays information about a command, including its location; read allows a script to accept user input.

The exec builtin executes a command without creating a new process. The new command overlays the current process, assuming the same environment and PID number of that process. This builtin executes user programs and other Linux commands when it is *not* necessary to return control to the calling process.

The trap builtin catches a signal sent by Linux to the process running the script and allows you to specify actions to be taken upon receipt of one or more signals. You can use this builtin to cause a script to ignore the signal that is sent when the user presses the interrupt key.

The kill builtin terminates a running program. The getopts builtin parses command-line arguments, making it easier to write programs that follow standard Linux conventions for command-line arguments and options.

Utilities in scripts
In addition to using control structures, builtins, and functions, shell scripts generally call Linux utilities. The find utility, for instance, is commonplace in shell scripts that search for files in the system hierarchy and can perform a vast range of tasks, from simple to complex.

Expressions
There are two basic types of expressions: arithmetic and logical. Arithmetic expressions allow you to do arithmetic on constants and variables, yielding a numeric result. Logical (Boolean) expressions compare expressions or strings, or test conditions to yield a *true* or *false* result. As with all decisions within Linux shell scripts, a *true* status is represented by the value zero; *false,* by any nonzero value.

Good programming practices
A well-written shell script adheres to standard programming practices, such as specifying the shell to execute the script on the first line of the script, verifying the number and type of arguments that the script is called with, displaying a standard usage message to report command-line errors, and redirecting all informational messages to standard error.

EXERCISES

1. Rewrite the **journal** script of Chapter 9 (exercise 5, page 352) by adding commands to verify that the user has write permission for a file named **journal-file** in the user's home directory, if such a file exists. The script should take appropriate actions if **journal-file** exists and the user does not have write permission to the file. Verify that the modified script works.

2. The special parameter "**$@**" is referenced twice in the **out** script (page 915). Explain what would be different if the parameter "**$∗**" was used in its place.

3. Write a filter that takes a list of files as input and outputs the basename (page 938) of each file in the list.

4. Write a function that takes a single filename as an argument and adds execute permission to the file for the user.

   a. When might such a function be useful?

   b. Revise the script so it takes one or more filenames as arguments and adds execute permission for the user for each file argument.

   c. What can you do to make the function available every time you log in?

   d. Suppose that, in addition to having the function available on subsequent login sessions, you want to make the function available in your current shell. How would you do so?

5. When might it be necessary or advisable to write a shell script instead of a shell function? Give as many reasons as you can think of.

6. Write a shell script that displays the names of all directory files, but no other types of files, in the working directory.

7. Write a script to display the time every 15 seconds. Read the date man page and display the time, using the **%r** field descriptor. Clear the window (using the clear command) each time before you display the time.

8. Enter the following script named **savefiles**, and give yourself execute permission to the file:

```
$ cat savefiles
#! /bin/bash
echo "Saving files in current directory in file savethem."
exec > savethem
for i in *
        do
        echo "==================================================="
        echo "File: $i"
        echo "==================================================="
        cat "$i"
        done
```

a. Which error message do you get when you execute this script? Rewrite the script so that the error does not occur, making sure the output still goes to **savethem**.

b. What might be a problem with running this script twice in the same directory? Discuss a solution to this problem.

9. Read the bash man or info page, try some experiments, and answer the following questions:

a. How do you export a function?

b. What does the hash builtin do?

c. What happens if the argument to exec is not executable?

10. Using the find utility, perform the following tasks:

a. List all files in the working directory and all subdirectories that have been modified within the last day.

b. List all files that you have read access to on the system that are larger than 1 megabyte.

c. Remove all files named **core** from the directory structure rooted at your home directory.

d. List the inode numbers of all files in the working directory whose filenames end in **.c**.

e. List all files that you have read access to on the root filesystem that have been modified in the last 30 days.

11. Write a short script that tells you whether the permissions for two files, whose names are given as arguments to the script, are identical. If the permissions for the two files are identical, output the common permission field. Otherwise, output each filename followed by its permission field. (*Hint:* Try using the cut utility.)

12. Write a script that takes the name of a directory as an argument and searches the file hierarchy rooted at that directory for zero-length files. Write the names of all zero-length files to standard output. If there is no option on the command line, have the script delete the file after displaying its name, asking the user for confirmation, and receiving positive confirmation. A **–f** (force) option on the command line indicates that the script should display the filename but not ask for confirmation before deleting the file.

ADVANCED EXERCISES

13. Write a script that takes a colon-separated list of items and outputs the items, one per line, to standard output (without the colons).

14. Generalize the script written in exercise 13 so that the character separating the list items is given as an argument to the function. If this argument is absent, the separator should default to a colon.

15. Write a function named **funload** that takes as its single argument the name of a file containing other functions. The purpose of **funload** is to make all functions in the named file available in the current shell; that is, **funload** loads the functions from the named file. To locate the file, **funload** searches the colon-separated list of directories given by the environment variable **FUNPATH**. Assume that the format of **FUNPATH** is the same as **PATH** and that searching **FUNPATH** is similar to the shell's search of the **PATH** variable.

16. Rewrite **bundle** (page 942) so the script it creates takes an optional list of filenames as arguments. If one or more filenames are given on the command line, only those files should be re-created; otherwise, all files in the shell archive should be re-created. For example, suppose all files with the filename extension **.c** are bundled into an archive named **srcshell**, and you want to unbundle just the files **test1.c** and **test2.c**. The following command will unbundle just these two files:

    ```
    $ bash srcshell test1.c test2.c
    ```

17. What kind of links will the **lnks** script (page 918) not find? Why?

18. In principle, recursion is never necessary. It can always be replaced by an iterative construct, such as **while** or **until**. Rewrite **makepath** (page 982) as a nonrecursive function. Which version do you prefer? Why?

19. Lists are commonly stored in environment variables by putting a colon (:) between each of the list elements. (The value of the **PATH** variable is an example.) You can add an element to such a list by catenating the new element to the front of the list, as in

    ```
    PATH=/opt/bin:$PATH
    ```

    If the element you add is already in the list, you now have two copies of it in the list. Write a shell function named **addenv** that takes two arguments: (1) the name of a shell variable and (2) a string to prepend to the list that is the value of the shell variable only if that string is not already an element of the list. For example, the call

    ```
    addenv PATH /opt/bin
    ```

would add **/opt/bin** to **PATH** only if that pathname is not already in **PATH**. Be sure that your solution works even if the shell variable starts out empty. Also make sure that you check the list elements carefully. If **/usr/opt/bin** is in **PATH** but **/opt/bin** is not, the example just given should still add **/opt/bin** to **PATH**. (*Hint:* You may find this exercise easier to complete if you first write a function **locate_field** that tells you whether a string is an element in the value of a variable.)

20. Write a function that takes a directory name as an argument and writes to standard output the maximum of the lengths of all filenames in that directory. If the function's argument is not a directory name, write an error message to standard output and exit with nonzero status.

21. Modify the function you wrote for exercise 20 to descend all subdirectories of the named directory recursively and to find the maximum length of any filename in that hierarchy.

22. Write a function that lists the number of ordinary files, directories, block special files, character special files, FIFOs, and symbolic links in the working directory. Do this in two different ways:

    a. Use the first letter of the output of **ls -l** to determine a file's type.

    b. Use the file type condition tests of the *[[expression]]* syntax to determine a file's type.

23. Modify the **quiz** program (page 988) so that the choices for a question are randomly arranged.

28

PERL

Larry Wall created the Perl (Practical Extraction and Report Language) programming language for working with text. Perl uses syntax and concepts from awk, sed, C, the Bourne Shell, Smalltalk, Lisp, and English. It was designed to scan and extract information from text files and generate reports based on that information. Since its introduction in 1987, Perl has expanded enormously—its documentation growing up with it. Today, in addition to text processing, Perl is used for system administration, software development, and general-purpose programming.

Perl code is portable because Perl has been implemented on many operating systems (see www.cpan.org/ports). It is also robust. Perl is an informal, practical, easy-to-use, efficient, and complete language. It is a down-and-dirty language that supports procedural and object-oriented programming. It is not necessarily elegant.

INTRODUCTION TO PERL

A couple of quotes from the manual shed light on Perl's philosophy:

> Many of Perl's syntactic elements are optional. Rather than requiring you to put parentheses around every function call and declare every variable, you can often leave such explicit elements off and Perl will frequently figure out what you meant. This is known as Do What I Mean, abbreviated DWIM. It allows programmers to be lazy and to code in a style with which they are comfortable.

> The Perl motto is "There's more than one way to do it." Divining how many more is left as an exercise to the reader.

One of Perl's biggest assets is its support by thousands of third-party modules. The Comprehensive Perl Archive Network (CPAN; www.cpan.org) is a repository for many of the modules and other information related to Perl. See page 1033 for information on downloading, installing, and using these modules in Perl programs.

Install perl-doc

tip   The **perl-doc** package holds a wealth of information. Install this package before you start using Perl; see page 999 for more information.

The best way to learn Perl is to work with it. Copy and modify the programs in this chapter until they make sense to you. Many system tools are written in Perl. The first line of most of these tools begins with **#!/usr/bin/perl**, which tells the shell to pass the program to Perl for execution. Most files that contain the string **/usr/bin/perl** are Perl programs. The following command uses grep to search the **/usr/bin** and **/usr/sbin** directories recursively (**–r**) for files containing the string **/usr/bin/perl**; it lists many local system tools written in Perl:

```
$ grep -r /usr/bin/perl /usr/bin /usr/sbin | head -4
/usr/bin/defoma-user:#! /usr/bin/perl -w
/usr/bin/pod2latex:#!/usr/bin/perl
/usr/bin/pod2latex:    eval 'exec /usr/bin/perl -S $0 ${1+"$@"}'
/usr/bin/splain:#!/usr/bin/perl
```

Review these programs—they demonstrate how Perl is used in the real world. Copy a system program to a directory you own before modifying it. Do not run a system program while running with **root** privileges unless you know what you are doing.

MORE INFORMATION

Local   man pages: See the perl and perltoc man pages for lists of Perl man pages

Web   Perl home page: www.perl.com
CPAN: www.cpan.org
blog: perlbuzz.com

perldoc

You must install the **perl-doc** package before you can use perldoc.

The perldoc utility locates and displays local Perl documentation. It is similar to man (page 122) but specific to Perl. It works with files that include lines of **pod** (plain old documentation), a clean and simple documentation language. When embedded in a Perl program, **pod** enables you to include documentation for the entire program, not just code-level comments, in a Perl program. Following is a simple Perl program that includes **pod**. The two lines following **=cut** are the program; the rest is **pod**-format documentation.

```
$ cat pod.ex1.pl
#!/usr/bin/perl

=head1 A Perl Program to Say I<Hi there.>

This simple Perl program includes documentation in B<pod> format.
The following B<=cut> command tells B<perldoc> that what follows
is not documentation.

=cut
# A Perl program
print "Hi there.\n";

=head1 pod Documentation Resumes with Any pod Command

See the B<perldoc.perl.org/perlpod.html> page for more information
on B<pod> and B<perldoc.perl.org> for complete Perl documentation.
```

You can use Perl to run the program:

```
$ perl pod.ex1.pl
Hi there.
```

Or you can use perldoc to display the documentation:

```
$ perldoc pod.ex1.pl
POD.EX1(1)          User Contributed Perl Documentation          POD.EX1(1)



A Perl Program to Say Hi there.
        This simple Perl program includes documentation in pod format.  The
        following =cut command tells perldoc that what follows is not documen-
        tation.

pod Documentation Resumes with Any pod Command
        See the perldoc.perl.org/perlpod.html page for more information on pod
        and perldoc.perl.org for complete Perl documentation.



perl v5.10.0                     2008-10-14                      POD.EX1(1)
```

Most publicly distributed modules and scripts, as well as Perl itself, include embedded **pod**-format documentation. For example, the following command displays information about the Perl **print** function:

```
$ perldoc -f print
    print FILEHANDLE LIST
    print LIST
    print   Prints a string or a list of strings. Returns true if success-
            ful.  FILEHANDLE may be a scalar variable name, in which case
            the variable contains the name of or a reference to the file-
            handle, thus introducing one level of indirection.  (NOTE: If
            FILEHANDLE is a variable and the next token is a term, it may
            ...
```

Once you have installed a module (page 1033), you can use perldoc to display documentation for that module. The following example shows perldoc displaying information on the locally installed **Timestamp::Simple** module:

```
$ perldoc Timestamp::Simple
Timestamp::Simple(3)   User Contributed Perl Documentation Timestamp::Simple(3)

NAME
      Timestamp::Simple - Simple methods for timestamping

SYNOPSIS
          use Timestamp::Simple qw(stamp);
          print stamp, "\n";
...
```

Give the command **man perldoc** or **perldoc perldoc** to display the perldoc man page and read more about this tool.

TERMINOLOGY

This section defines some of the terms used in this chapter.

Module   A Perl *module* is a self-contained chunk of Perl code, frequently containing several functions that work together. A module can be called from another module or from a Perl program. A module must have a unique name. To help ensure unique names, Perl provides a hierarchical *namespace* (page 1121) for modules, separating components of a name with double colons (::). Example module names are **Timestamp::Simple** and **WWW::Mechanize**.

Distribution   A Perl *distribution* is a set of one or more modules that perform a task. You can search for distributions and modules at search.cpan.org. Examples of distributions include **Timestamp-Simple** (the **Timestamp-Simple-1.01.tar.gz** archive file contains the **Timestamp::Simple** module only) and **WWW-Mechanize** (**WWW-Mechanize-1.34.tar.gz** contains the **WWW::Mechanize** module, plus supporting modules including **WWW::Mechanize::Link** and **WWW::Mechanize::Image**).

Package   A *package* defines a Perl namespace. For example, in the variable with the name **$WWW::Mechanize::ex**, **$ex** is a scalar variable in the **WWW::Mechanize** package, where "package" is used in the sense of a namespace. Using the same name, such as **WWW::Mechanize**, for a distribution, a package, and a module can be confusing.

Block
: A *block* is zero or more statements, delimited by curly braces ({}), that defines a scope. The shell control structure syntax explanations refer to these elements as *commands*. See the **if...then** control structure on page 910 for an example.

Package variable
: A *package variable* is defined within the package it appears in. Other packages can refer to package variables by using the variable's fully qualified name (for example, **$Text::Wrap::columns**). By default, variables are package variables unless you define them as lexical variables.

Lexical variable
: A *lexical variable,* which is defined by preceding the name of a variable with the keyword **my** (see the tip on page 1005), is defined only within the block or file it appears in. It is what other languages refer to as a local variable. When programming using **bash**, variables that are not exported (page 948) are local to the program they are used in. Because Perl 4 already used the keyword *local* with a different meaning, Perl 5 uses the term *lexical* in its place.

List
: A *list* is a series of zero or more scalars. The following list has three elements—two numbers and a string:

```
(2, 4, 'Zach')
```

Array
: An *array* is a variable that holds a list of elements in a defined order. Following, **@a** is an array. See page 1007 for more information about array variables.

```
@a = (2, 4, 'Zach')
```

Compound statement
: A *compound statement* is a statement made up of other statements. For example, the **if** compound statement (page 1012) incorporates an **if** statement and normally other statements within the block it controls.

RUNNING A PERL PROGRAM

There are several ways you can run a program written in Perl. Perl provides the **–e** option so you can enter a one-line program on the command line:

```
$ perl -e 'print "Hi there.\n"'
Hi there.
```

Using the **–e** option is good for testing Perl syntax and running brief, one-shot programs. This option requires that the Perl program appear as a single argument on the command line. The program must immediately follow this option—it is an argument to this option. An easy way to write this type of program is to enclose the program within single quotation marks.

Because Perl is a member of the class of utilities that take input from a file or standard input (page 234), you can give the command **perl** and enter the program terminated by CONTROL-D (end of file). Perl reads the program from standard input:

```
$ perl
print "Hi there.\n";
CONTROL-D
Hi there.
```

Neither of the preceding techniques is helpful for running more complex programs. Most of the time, a Perl program is stored in a text file. Although not required, the file typically has a filename extension of **.pl**. Following is the same simple program used in the previous examples stored in a file:

```
$ cat simp.pl
print "Hi there.\n";
```

You can run this program by specifying its name as an argument to Perl:

```
$ perl simp.pl
Hi there.
```

Most commonly and similarly to most shell scripts, the file containing the Perl program is executable. Following, chmod (page 284) makes the **simp2.pl** file executable. The **#!** (page 286) at the start of the first line of the file instructs the shell to pass the rest of the file to **/usr/bin/perl** for execution.

```
$ chmod 755 simp2.pl
$ cat simp2.pl
#!/usr/bin/perl -w
print "Hi there.\n";

$ ./simp2.pl
Hi there.
```

In this example, the **simp2.pl** program is executed as **./simp2.pl** because the working directory is not in the user's **PATH** (page 303). The **–w** option tells Perl to issue warning messages when it identifies potential errors in the code.

PERL VERSION 5.10

INTREPID Canonical introduced Perl version 5.10 in Ubuntu release 8.10 (Intrepid Ibex). All examples in this chapter were run under Perl 5.10. Give the following command to see which version of Perl the local system is running:

```
$ perl -v

This is perl, v5.10.0 built for i486-linux-gnu-thread-multi
...
```

Perl version 5.10 introduces many useful features. For example, the **say** function is new in 5.10. It works the same way as **print**, except it adds a NEWLINE (**\n**) at the end of each line it outputs. Some versions of Perl require you to tell Perl explicitly that you want to use version 5.10. The **use** function tells Perl to run the program using version 5.10. Try running this program without the **use** line to see if the local version of Perl requires it.

```
$ cat 510.pl
use v5.10;
say 'Output by say.';
print 'Output by print.';
say 'End.'
```

```
$ perl 510.pl
Output by say.
Output by print.End.
$
```

SYNTAX

This section describes the major components of a Perl program.

Statements A Perl program comprises one or more *statements,* each terminated by a semicolon. These statements are free-form with respect to *whitespace* (page 1140), except for whitespace within quoted strings.

Expressions The syntax of Perl expressions frequently corresponds to the syntax of C expressions, but is not always the same. Perl expressions are covered in examples throughout this chapter.

Quotation marks All character strings must be enclosed within single or double quotation marks. Perl differentiates between the two types of quotation marks in a manner similar to the way the shell does (page 298): Double quotation marks allow Perl to expand enclosed variables and interpret special characters such as \n (NEWLINE), whereas single quotation marks do not. Table 28-1 lists some of Perl's special characters.

Slash By default, regular expressions are delimited by slashes (/; page 1028).

Backslash Within a string enclosed between double quotation marks, a backslash escapes (quotes) another backslash. Thus Perl displays "\\n" as \n. Within a regular expression, Perl does not expand a metacharacter preceded by a backslash.

Comments As in the shell, a comment in Perl begins with a pound sign (#) and ends at the end of the line (just before the NEWLINE character).

Special characters Table 28-1 lists some of the characters that are special within strings. Perl expands these characters when they appear between double quotation marks but not when they appear between single quotation marks. Table 28-2 on page 1029 lists metacharacters, which are special within regular expressions.

Table 28-1   Some Perl special characters

Character	Within double quotation marks expands to
\0*xx* (zero)	The ASCII character whose octal value is ***xx***
\a	An alarm (bell or beep) character (ASCII 7)
\e	An ESCAPE character (ASCII 27)
\n	A NEWLINE character (ASCII 10)
\r	A RETURN character (ASCII 13)
\t	A TAB character (ASCII 9)
\x*yy*	The ASCII character whose octal value is ***yy***

PERL HELP

Perl is a forgiving language. As such, it is easy to write Perl code that runs but does not perform as you intended. Perl includes many tools that can help you find coding mistakes. The **–w** option and the **use warnings** statement can produce helpful diagnostic messages. The **use strict** statement (see the **perldebtut** man page) can impose order on a program by requiring, among other things, that you declare variables before you use them. When all else fails, you can use Perl's builtin debugger to step through a program. See the **perldebtut** and **perldebug** man pages for more information.

VARIABLES

Perl provides three types of variables: *scalar, array,* and *hash* (also called *associative arrays*). Perl identifies each type of variable by a special character preceding its name. The name of a scalar variable begins with a dollar sign (**$**), an array variable begins with an at sign (**@**), and a hash variable begins with a percent sign (**%**). As opposed to the way the shell identifies variables, Perl requires the leading character each time you reference a variable, including when you assign a value to the variable:

```
$ name="Zach" ; echo "$name"                    (bash)
Zach

$ perl -e '$name="Zach" ; print "$name\n";'  (perl)
Zach
```

Variable names, which are case sensitive, can include letters, digits, and the underscore character (_). A Perl variable is a package variable (page 1001) unless it is preceded by the keyword **my**, in which case it is a lexical variable (page 1001) which is defined only within the block or file it appears in. See "Subroutines" on page 1025 for a discussion of the locality of Perl variables.

Make Perl programs readable

tip   Although Perl has many shortcuts that are good for one-shot programming, the code in this chapter is written with the objective of being easy to understand and easy to maintain.

A Perl variable comes into existence when you assign a value to it—you do not need to define or initialize a variable, although it may make a program more understandable to do so. Include **use strict** to cause Perl to require variables to be declared before being assigned values. See the **perldebtut man** page for more information. Normally, Perl does not complain when you reference an uninitialized variable:

```
$ cat var1.pl
#!/usr/bin/perl
my $name = 'Sam';
print "Hello, $nam, how are you?\n"; # Typo, e left off of name
```

```
$ ./var1.pl
Hello, , how are you?
```

use strict   When you include **use strict** Perl displays an error message:

```
$ cat var1b.pl
#!/usr/bin/perl
use strict;
my $name = 'Sam';
print "Hello, $nam, how are you?\n"; # Typo, e left off of name

$ ./var1b.pl
Global symbol "$nam" requires explicit package name at ./var1b.pl line 4.
Execution of ./var1b.pl aborted due to compilation errors.
```

Using my: lexical versus package variables

tip   In **var1.pl**, **$name** is declared to be lexical by preceding its name with the keyword **my**; its name and value are known within the file **var1.pl** only. Declaring a variable to be lexical limits its scope to the block or file it is defined in. Although not necessary in this case, declaring variables to be lexical is good practice. This habit becomes especially useful when you write longer programs, subroutines, and packages, where it is harder to keep variable names unique. Declaring all variables to be lexical is mandatory when you write routines that will be used within code written by others. This practice allows those who work with your routines to use whichever variable names they like, without regard to which variable names you used in the code you wrote.

The shell and Perl scope variables differently. In the shell, if you do not **export** a variable, it is local to the routine it is used in (page 948). In Perl, if you do not use **my** to declare a variable to be lexical, it is defined for the package it appears in.

The **–w** option   The **–w** option causes Perl to generate an error message when it detects a syntax error. Following, Perl displays two warnings. The first tells you that you have used the variable named **$nam** once, on line 3, which probably indicates an error. This message is helpful when you mistype the name of a variable. In Perl 5.8, the second warning says you used an uninitialized value in line 3 of the program, but does not name the variable. This warning refers to the same problem as the first warning.

```
$ cat var1a.pl
#!/usr/bin/perl -w
my $name = 'Sam';
print "Hello, $nam, how are you?\n"; # Prints warning because of typo and -w

$ ./var1a.pl
Name "main::nam" used only once: possible typo at ./var1a.pl line 3.
Use of uninitialized value in concatenation (.) or string at ./var1a.pl line 3.
Hello, , how are you?
```

In Perl 5.10 (page 1002), the second warning specifies the name of the uninitialized variable. Although it is not hard to figure out which of the two variables is undefined in this simple program, doing so in a complex program can take a lot of time.

```
$ ./var1a.pl
Name "main::nam" used only once: possible typo at ./var1a.pl line 3.
Use of uninitialized value $nam in concatenation (.) or string at ./var1a.pl line 3.
Hello, , how are you?
```

You can also use **–w** on the command line. If you use **–e** as well, make sure the argument that follows it is the program you want to execute (e.g., **–e –w** does not work). See the tip on page 1028.

```
$ perl -w -e 'my $name = "Sam"; print "Hello, $nam, how are you?\n"'
Name "main::nam" used only once: possible typo at -e line 1.
Use of uninitialized value $nam in concatenation (.) or string at -e line 1.
Hello, , how are you?
```

undef and defined   An undefined variable has the special value **undef**, which evaluates to zero (0) in a numeric expression and expands to an empty string ("") when you print it. Ideally you will use the **defined** function to determine if a variable has been defined. The following example, which uses constructs explained later in this chapter, calls **defined** with an argument of **$name** and negates the result with an exclamation point (!). The result is that the **print** statement is executed if **$name** is *not* defined.

```
$ cat var2.pl
#!/usr/bin/perl
if (!defined($name)) {
print 'The variable $name is not defined.', "\n"
};
```

```
$ ./var2.pl
The variable $name is not defined.
```

Because the **–w** option causes Perl to warn you when you reference an undefined variable, using this option would generate a warning.

SCALAR VARIABLES

A scalar variable has a name that begins with a dollar sign ($) and holds a single string or number. Because Perl converts between the two when necessary, you can use strings and numbers interchangeably. The following example shows some uses of scalar variables. The first two lines of code (lines 3 and 4) assign the string **Sam** to **$name** and the numbers **5** and **2** to **$n1** and **$n2**, respectively. Because Perl is free-form with respect to whitespace, multiple statements can appear on a single line; Perl requires each statement to be terminated with a semicolon (;).

```
$ cat scal.pl
#!/usr/bin/perl -w

$name = "Sam";
$n1 = 5; $n2 = 2;

print "$name $n1 $n2\n";
print "$n1 + $n2\n";
print $n1 + $n2, " ", $n1 * $n2, "\n";
print $name + $n1, "\n";
```

```
$ ./scal.pl
Sam 5 2
5 + 2
7 10
Argument "Sam" isn't numeric in addition (+) at ./scal.pl line 9.
5
```

Double quotation marks The first **print** statement sends the string enclosed within double quotation marks to standard output (the screen unless you redirect it). Within double quotation marks, Perl expands variable names to the value of the named variable and replaces special characters (e.g., it replaces \n with a NEWLINE; see Table 28-1 on page 1003). Thus the first **print** statement displays the values of three variables, separated from one another by SPACEs, and terminates the line with a NEWLINE.

The second **print** statement includes a plus sign (+). Perl does not recognize operators such as + within either type of quotation marks. Thus Perl displays the plus sign between the values of the two variables. In the third **print** statement, the operators are not quoted, and Perl performs the addition and multiplication as specified. Without the quoted SPACE, Perl would catenate the two numbers (**710**). The last **print** statement attempts to add a string and a number; the –w option causes Perl to display an error message before displaying 5. The 5 results from adding **Sam**, which Perl evaluates as 0 in a numerical context, and the number 5 (0 + 5 = 5).

ARRAY VARIABLES

An array variable is an ordered container of scalars whose name begins with an at sign (@) and whose first element is numbered zero (zero-based indexing). An array can hold zero or more scalars. Arrays are ordered; hashes (page 1010) are unordered. In Perl, arrays grow as needed. If you reference an uninitialized element of an array, such as an element beyond the end of the array, Perl returns **undef**.

The first statement in the following program assigns the values of two numbers and a string to the array variable named **@avar**. By default, Perl uses zero-based indexing. Thus the second statement displays the value of the second element of the array (the element with the index 1).

```
$ cat avar1.pl
#!/usr/bin/perl -w
@avar = (8, 18, "Sam");
print @avar[1], "\n";

$ ./avar1.pl
Scalar value @avar[1] better written as $avar[1] at ./avar1.pl line 3.
18
```

When you include the –w option, Perl displays an interesting warning. Perl evaluates a one-element slice of an array variable (a list) as a scalar variable, so instead of writing the second element as **@avar[1]**, Perl suggest you write it as **$avar[1]**, which is an element of an array.

The next example shows a couple of ways to determine the length of an array and presents more information on using quotation marks within **print** statements. The first assignment statement in **avar2.pl** assigns values to the first six elements of the **@avar2** array. When used in a scalar context, Perl evaluates the name of an array as the length of the array. The second assignment statement assigns the number of elements in **@avar2** to the scalar variable **$num**.

```
$ cat avar2.pl
#!/usr/bin/perl -w
@avar2 = ("apple", "bird", 44, "Tike", "metal", "pike");

$num = @avar2;                       # number of elements in array
print "Elements: ", $num, "\n";      # two equivalent print statements
print "Elements: $num\n";

print "Last: $#avar2\n";             # index of last element in array

./avar2.pl
Elements: 6
Elements: 6
Last: 5
```

The first two **print** statements in **avar2.pl** display the string **Elements:**, a SPACE, the value of **$num**, and a NEWLINE, each using a different syntax. The first of these statements displays three values, using commas to separate them within the statement. The second print statement has one argument and demonstrates that Perl expands a variable (replaces the variable with its value) when the variable is enclosed within double quotation marks. If you replace the double quotation marks with single quotation marks, Perl displays the string within the quotation marks literally.

Use say in Perl 5.10

tip In Perl 5.10 (page 1002), you can replace a **print** statement that ends with **\n** with **say** (and omit the **\n**). For example, **avar2.pl** can rewritten as follows:

```
$ cat avar2b.pl
#!/usr/bin/perl -w
use v5.10;
@avar2 = ("apple", "bird", 44, "Tike", "metal", "pike");

$num = @avar2;                 # number of elements in array
say "Elements: ", $num;        # two equivalent print statements
say "Elements: $num";

say "Last: $#avar2";           # index of last element in array
```

$#*array* The final **print** statement in **avar2.pl** shows that Perl evaluates the variable **$#*array*** as the index of the last element in the array named *array*. Because Perl uses zero-based indexing by default, this variable evaluates to one less than the number of elements in the array.

The next example works with elements of an array and uses a dot (.; the string catenation operator). The first two lines assign values to four scalar variables. The third line shows that you can assign values to array elements using scalar variables, arithmetic, and catenated strings. The dot operator catenates strings, so Perl evaluates **$va . $vb** as **Sam** catenated with **uel**, or **Samuel** (see the output of the last **print** statement).

```
$ cat avar3.pl
#!/usr/bin/perl -w
$v1 = 5; $v2 = 8;
$va = "Sam"; $vb = "uel";
@avar3 = ($v1, $v1 * 2, $v1 * $v2, "Max", "Zach", $va . $vb);

print $avar3[2], "\n";          # one element of an array is a scalar
print @avar3[2,4], "\n";        # two elements of an array is a list
print @avar3[2..4], "\n\n";     # a slice

print "@avar3[2,4]", "\n";      # elements separated by SPACEs
print "@avar3[2..4]", "\n\n";   # slice, elements separated by SPACEs

print "@avar3\n";               # array with elements separated by SPACEs

$ ./avar3.pl
40
40Zach
40MaxZach

40 Zach
40 Max Zach

5 10 40 Max Zach Samuel
```

The first **print** statement in **avar3.pl** displays the third element (the element with an index of 2) of the **@avar3** array. This statement uses a **$** in place of **@** because it refers to a single element of the array. The subsequent **print** statements use **@** because they refer to more than one element. Within the brackets that specify an array subscript, two subscripts separated by a comma specify two elements of an array. The second **print** statement, for example, displays the third and fifth elements of the array.

array slice   When you separate two elements of an array with two dots (**..**; the range operator), Perl substitutes all elements between and including the two specified elements. A portion of an array comprising elements is called a *slice*. The third print statement in the preceding example displays the elements with indexes 2, 3, and 4 (the third, fourth, and fifth elements) as specified by **2..4**. Perl puts no SPACEs between the elements it displays.

Within a **print** statement, when you enclose an array variable, including its subscripts, within double quotation marks, Perl puts a SPACE between each of the elements. The fourth and fifth print statements in the preceding example illustrate this syntax. The last **print** statement displays the entire array, with elements separated by SPACEs.

shift, push, pop, and splice   The next example demonstrates several functions you can use to manipulate arrays. The example uses the **@colors** array, which is initialized to a list of seven colors. The **shift** function returns and removes the first element of an array, **push** adds an element to the end of an array, and **pop** returns and removes the last element of an array. The **splice** function replaces elements of an array with another array; in the example, **splice** inserts the **@ins** array starting at index 1 (the second element), replacing two elements of the array. See the **perlfunc** man page for more information on the functions described in this paragraph.

```perl
$ cat 10a.pl
#!/usr/bin/perl -w

@colors = ("red", "orange", "yellow", "green", "blue", "indigo", "violet");

print "colors: @colors\n";
print "shift1: ", shift (@colors), "\n";
print "shift2: @colors\n";

push (@colors, "WHITE");
print "  push: @colors\n";

print "  pop1: ", pop (@colors), "\n";
print "  pop2: @colors\n";

@ins = ("GREY", "FERN");
splice (@colors, 1, 2, @ins);
print "splice: @colors\n";

$ ./10a.pl
colors: red orange yellow green blue indigo violet
shift1: red
shift2: orange yellow green blue indigo violet
  push: orange yellow green blue indigo violet WHITE
  pop1: WHITE
  pop2: orange yellow green blue indigo violet
splice: orange GREY FERN blue indigo violet
```

HASH VARIABLES

A hash variable, sometimes called an associative array variable, is a data structure that holds an array of key–value pairs. It uses strings as keys (indexes) and is optimized to return a value quickly when given a key. Each key must be a unique scalar. Hashes are unordered; arrays (page 1007) are ordered. When you assign a hash to a list, the key–value pairs are preserved, but their order is not alphabetical nor the order in which they were inserted into the hash; the order is effectively random.

Perl provides two syntaxes to assign values to a hash. The first uses a single assignment statement for each key–value pair:

```perl
$ cat ha1.pl
#!/usr/bin/perl -w
$ha1{"boat"} = "tuna";
$ha1{"five"} = 5;
$ha1{4} = "fish";
```

```
@arrh1 = %ha1;
print "@arrh1\n";

$ ./ha1.pl
boat tuna 4 fish five 5
```

Within an assignment statement, the key is located within braces to the left of the equal sign; the value is on the right side of the equal sign. As illustrated in the preceding example, keys and values can take on either numeric or string values. This example also shows that you can display the keys and values held by a hash, each separated from the next by a SPACE, by assigning the hash to an array variable and then printing that variable enclosed within double quotation marks.

The next example shows the other way of assigning values to a hash and illustrates how to use the **keys** and **values** functions to extract keys and values from a hash. After assigning values to the **%ha2** hash, **ha2.pl** calls the **keys** function with an argument of **%ha2** and assigns the resulting list of keys to the **@arrh2k** array. The program then uses the **values** function to assign values to the **@arrh2v** array.

```
$ cat ha2.pl
#!/usr/bin/perl -w
%ha2 = (
    "boat" => "tuna",
    "number five" => 5,
    4 => "fish",
    );

@arrh2k = keys(%ha2);
print "  Keys: @arrh2k\n";

@arrh2v = values(%ha2);
print "Values: @arrh2v\n";

$ ./ha2.pl
  Keys: boat 4 number five
Values: tuna fish 5
```

Because Perl automatically quotes a single word to the left of the **=>** operator, you can remove the quotation marks that surround **boat** in the third line of this program:

```
boat => "tuna",
```

Removing the quotation marks from around **number five** would generate an error because the string contains a SPACE.

CONTROL STRUCTURES

Control flow statements alter the order of execution of statements within a Perl program. Starting on page 910, Chapter 27 discusses bash control structures in detail, including flow diagrams. Perl control structures perform the same functions as their bash counterparts, although the two languages use different syntaxes. The description of each control structure in this section references the discussion of the same control structure under bash.

In this section, the *bold italic* words in the syntax description are the items you supply to cause the structure to have the desired effect, the *nonbold italic* words are the keywords Perl uses to identify the control structure, and *{...}* represents a block (page 1001) of statements. Many of these structures use an expression, denoted as *expr*, to control their execution. See **if/unless** (next) for an example and explanation of a syntax description.

if/unless

The **if** and **unless** control structures are compound statements that have the following syntax:

> *if (expr) {...}*

> *unless (expr) {...}*

These structures differ only in the sense of the test they perform. The **if** structure executes the block of statements *if expr* evaluates to *true*; **unless** executes the block of statements *unless expr* evaluates to *true* (if *expr* is *false*).

The *if* appears in nonbold type because it is a keyword; it must appear exactly as shown. The *expr* is an expression; Perl evaluates the expression and executes the block (page 1001) of statements represented by *{...}* if the expression evaluates as required by the control structure.

The *expr* in the following example, **–r memo1**, uses the **–r** file test operator to determine if a file named **memo1** exists in the working directory and if the file is readable. Although this operator tests only whether you have read permission for the file, the file must exist for you to have read permission so it implicitly tests that the file is present. (Perl uses the same file test operators as bash; see Table 27-1 on page 913.) If this expression evaluates to *true*, Perl executes the block of statements (in this case one statement) between the braces. If the expression evaluates to *false*, Perl skips the block of statements. In either case, Perl then exits and returns control to the shell.

```
$ cat if1.pl
#!/usr/bin/perl -w
if (-r "memo1") {
    print "The file 'memo1' exists and is readable.\n";
    }

$ ./if1.pl
The file 'memo1' exists and is readable.
```

Following is the same program written using the postfix **if** syntax. Which syntax you use depends on which part of the statement is more important to someone reading the code.

```
$ cat if1a.pl
#!/usr/bin/perl -w
print "The file 'memo1' exists and is readable.\n" if (-r "memo1");
```

The next example uses a **print** statement to display a prompt on standard output and uses the statement **$entry = <>;** to read a line from standard input and assign the line to the variable **$entry**. Reading from standard input, working with other files, and use of the magic file handle (**<>**) for reading files specified on the command line are covered on page 1020. The expression in the **if** statement uses the **==** comparison operator to compare the value the user entered and **28**. This operator performs a numeric comparison, so the user can enter **28**, **28.0**, or **00028** and in all cases the result of the comparison will be *true*. Also, because the comparison is numeric, Perl ignores the whitespace around and NEWLINE following the user's entry. The **–w** option causes Perl to issue a warning if the user enters a nonnumeric value and the program uses that value in an arithmetic expression; without this option Perl silently evaluates the expression as *false*.

```
$ cat if2.pl
#!/usr/bin/perl -w
print "Enter 28: ";
$entry = <>;
if ($entry == 28) {                    # use == for a numeric comparison
    print "Thank you for entering 28.\n";
    }
print "End.\n";

$ ./if2.pl
Enter 28: 28.0
Thank you for entering 28.
End.
```

The next program is similar to the preceding one, except it tests for equality between two strings. The **chomp** function (page 1021) removes the trailing NEWLINE from the user's entry—without this function the strings in the comparison would never match. The **eq** comparison operator compares strings. In this example the result of the string comparison is *true* when the user enters the string **five**. Leading or trailing whitespace will yield a result of *false*, as would the string **5**, although none of these entries would generate a warning because they are legitimate strings.

```
$ cat if2a.pl
#!/usr/bin/perl -w
print "Enter the word 'five': ";
$entry = <>;
chomp ($entry);
if ($entry eq "five") {                # use eq for a string comparison
    print "Thank you for entering 'five'.\n";
    }
print "End.\n";

$ ./if2a.pl
Enter the word 'five': five
Thank you for entering 'five'.
End.
```

if...else

The **if...else** control structure is a compound statement that is similar to the bash **if...then...else** control structure (page 914). It implements a two-way branch using the following syntax:

if (expr) {...} else {...}

die   The next program prompts the user for two different numbers and stores those numbers in **$num1** and **$num2**. If the user enters the same number twice, an **if** structure executes a **die** function, which sends its argument to standard error and aborts program execution.

If the user enters different numbers, the **if...else** structure reports which number is larger. Because *expr* performs a numeric comparison, the program accepts numbers that include decimal points.

```
$ cat ifelse.pl
#!/usr/bin/perl -w
print "Enter a number: ";
$num1 = <>;
print "Enter another, different number: ";
$num2 = <>;

if ($num1 == $num2) {
    die ("Please enter two different numbers.\n");
    }
if ($num1 > $num2) {
    print "The first number is greater than the second number.\n";
    }
else {
    print "The first number is less than the second number.\n";
    }

$ ./ifelse.pl
Enter a number: 8
Enter another, different number: 8
Please enter two different numbers.

$ ./ifelse.pl
Enter a number: 5.5
Enter another, different number: 5
The first number is greater than the second number.
```

if...elsif...else

Similar to the bash **if...then...elif** control structure (page 917), the Perl **if...elsif...else** control structure is a compound statement that implements a nested set of **if...else** structures using the following syntax:

if (expr) {...} elsif {...} ... else {...}

The following program implements the functionality of the preceding **ifelse.pl** program using an **if...elsif...else** structure. A **print** statement replaces the **die** statement because the last statement in the program displays the error message; the program terminates after executing this statement anyway. You can use the STDERR handle (page 1020) to cause Perl to send this message to standard error instead of standard output.

```
$ cat ifelsif.pl
#!/usr/bin/perl -w
print "Enter a number: ";
$num1 = <>;
print "Enter another, different number: ";
$num2 = <>;

if ($num1 > $num2) {
        print "The first number is greater than the second number.\n";
        }
    elsif ($num1 < $num2) {
        print "The first number is less than the second number.\n";
        }
    else {
        print "Please enter two different numbers.\n";
        }
```

foreach/for

The Perl **foreach** and **for** keywords are synonyms; you can replace one with the other in any context. These structures are compound statements that have two syntaxes. Some programmers use one syntax with **foreach** and the other syntax with the **for**, although there is no need to do so. This book uses **foreach** with both syntaxes.

foreach: SYNTAX ONE

The first syntax for the **foreach** structure is similar to the shell's **for...in** structure (page 923):

foreach\for [var] (list) {...}

where *list* is a list of expressions or variables. Perl executes the block of statements once for each item in *list*, sequentially assigning to *var* the value of one item in *list* on each iteration, starting with the first item. If you do not specify *var*, Perl assigns values to $_ (page 1019).

The following program demonstrates a simple **foreach** structure. On the first pass through the loop, Perl assigns the string **Mo** to the variable $item and the **print** statement prints the value of this variable followed by a NEWLINE. On the second and third passes through the loop, $item is assigned the value of **Larry** and **Curly**. When there are no items left in the list, Perl continues with the statement following the **foreach** structure. In this case, the program terminates.

```
$ cat fore.pl
foreach $item ("Mo", "Larry", "Curly") {
    print "$item says hello.\n";
    }

$ perl fore.pl
Mo says hello.
Larry says hello.
Curly says hello.
```

Using $_ (page 1019), you can write this program as follows:

```
$ cat forea.pl
foreach ("Mo", "Larry", "Curly") {
    print "$_ says hello.\n";
    }
```

Or, using an array:

```
$ cat foreb.pl
@stooges = ("Mo", "Larry", "Curly");
foreach (@stooges) {
    print "$_ says hello.\n";
    }
```

Or, using the **foreach** postfix syntax:

```
$ cat forec.pl
@stooges = ("Mo", "Larry", "Curly");
print "$_ says hello.\n" foreach @stooges;
```

The loop variable (**$item** and **$_** in the preceding examples) references the elements in the list within the parentheses. When you modify the loop variable, you modify the element in the list. The **uc** function returns an upshifted version of its argument. The next example shows that modifying the loop variable **$stooge** modifies the **@stooges** array:

```
$ cat fored.pl
@stooges = ("Mo", "Larry", "Curly");
foreach $stooge (@stooges) {
    $stooge = uc $stooge;
    print "$stooge says hello.\n";
    }
print "$stooges[1] is uppercase\n"

$ perl fored.pl
MO says hello.
LARRY says hello.
CURLY says hello.
LARRY is uppercase
```

See page 1022 for an example that loops through command-line arguments.

foreach: SYNTAX TWO

The second syntax for the **foreach** structure is similar to the C **for** structure:

foreach\for (expr1; expr2; expr3) {...}

The *expr1* initializes the **foreach** loop; Perl evaluates *expr1* one time, before it executes the block of statements. The *expr2* is the termination condition; Perl evaluates it before each pass through the block of statements and executes the block of statements while *expr2* evaluates as *true*. Perl evaluates *expr3* after each pass through the block of statements—it typically increments a variable that is part of *expr2*.

In the next example, the **for1.pl** program prompts for three numbers; displays the first number; repeatedly increments this number by the second number, displaying each result until the result would be greater than the third number; and quits. See page 1020 for a discussion of the magic file handle (<>).

```
$ cat ./for1.pl
#!/usr/bin/perl -w

print "Enter starting number: ";
chomp ($start = <>);

print "Enter ending number: ";
$end = <>;

print "Enter increment: ";
$incr = <>;

if ($start >= $end || $incr < 1) {
    die ("The starting number must be less than the ending number\n",
    "and the increment must be greater than zero.\n");
    }

foreach ($count = $start; $count <= $end; $count += $incr) {
    print "$count\n";
    }

$ ./for1.pl
Enter starting number: 2
Enter ending number: 10
Enter increment: 3
2
5
8
```

After prompting for three numbers, the preceding program tests whether the starting number is greater than or equal to the ending number or if the increment is less than 1. The || is a Boolean OR operator; the expression within the parentheses following **if** evaluates to *true* if either the expression before or the expression following this operator evaluates to *true*.

while/until

The **while** (page 926) and **until** (page 930) control structures are compound statements that implement conditional loops using the following syntax:

*while (**expr**) {...}*

*until (**expr**) {...}*

These structures differ only in the sense of their termination conditions. The **while** structure repeatedly executes the block of statements *while expr* evaluates to *true*; **until** continues *until expr* evaluates to *true* (i.e., while *expr* is *false*).

The following example demonstrates one technique for reading and processing input until there is no more input. Although this example shows input coming from the user (standard input), the technique works the same way for input coming from a file (see the example on page 1022). The user enters CONTROL-D on a line by itself to signal the end of file.

In this example, *expr* is **$line = <>**. This statement uses the magic file handle (**<>**; page 1020) to read one line from standard input and assigns the string it reads to the **$line** variable. This statement evaluates to *true* as long as it reads data. When it reaches the end of file, the statement evaluates to *false*. The **while** loop continues to execute the block of statements (in this example, only one statement) as long as there is data to read.

```
$ cat while1.pl
#!/usr/bin/perl -w
$count = 0;
while ($line = <>) {
    print ++$count, ". $line";
    }
print "\n$count lines entered.\n";

$ ./while1.pl
Good Morning.
1. Good Morning.
Today is Monday.
2. Today is Monday.
CONTROL-D

2 lines entered.
```

In the preceding example, **$count** keeps track of the number of lines the user enters. Putting the **++** increment operator before a variable (**++$count**; called a preincrement operator) increments the variable before Perl evaluates it. You could write the program initializing **$count** to 1 and incrementing it with **$count++** (postincrement), but then in the final **print** statement **$count** would equal one more than the number of lines entered.

$. The **$.** variable keeps track of the number of lines of input a program has read. Using **$.** you can rewrite the previous example as follows:

```
$ cat while1a.pl
#!/usr/bin/perl -w
while ($line = <>) {
        print $., ". $line";
        }
print "\n$. lines entered.\n";
```

$_ Frequently you can simplify Perl code using the $_ variable. You can use $_ many places in a Perl program—think of $_ as meaning *it*, the object of what you are doing. It is the default operand for many operations. For example, the following section of code processes a line using the **$line** variable. It reads a line into **$line**, removes any trailing NEWLINE from **$line** using **chomp**, and checks whether a regular expression matches **$line**.

```
while (my $line = <>) {
    chomp $line;
    if ($line =~ /regex/) ...
}
```

You can rewrite this code using $_ in place of **$line**:

```
while (my $_ = <>) {
    chomp $_;
    if ($_ =~ /regex/) ...
}
```

Because $_ is the default operand in each of these instances, you can also omit $_ altogether:

```
while (<>) {          # read into $_
    chomp;            # chomp $_
    if (/regex/) ...  # if $_ matches regex
}
```

last **AND** next

Perl's **last** and **next** statements allow you to interrupt a loop; they are analogous to the Bourne Again Shell's **break** and **continue** statements (page 932). The **last** statement transfers control to the statement following the block of statements controlled by the loop structure, terminating execution of the loop. The **next** statement transfers control to the end of the block of statements, which continues execution of the loop with the next iteration.

The following program is similar to the preceding one, except it includes a **next** command. The **if** structure tests whether **$item** is equal to the string **two**; if it is, the structure executes the **next** command, which skips the **print** statement and continues with the next iteration of the loop. If you replaced **next** with **last**, Perl would exit from the loop and not display **three**.

```
$ cat fore1.pl
foreach $item ("one", "two", "three") {
    if ($item eq "two") {
        next;
        }
    print "$item\n";
    }

$ perl fore1.pl
one
three
```

WORKING WITH FILES

Opening a file and assigning a handle

As when you are working with the shell, the kernel automatically opens handles (they are referred to as file descriptors in the shell; page 943) for standard input (page 229), standard output (page 229), and standard error (page 281) before it runs a program. The kernel closes these descriptors after a program finishes running. The names for these handles are **STDIN**, **STDOUT**, and **STDERR**, respectively. You must manually open handles to read from or write to other files or processes. The syntax of an **open** statement is

> open (*file-handle*, ['*mode*',] "*file-ref*");

where *file-handle* is the name of the handle or a variable you will use in the program to refer to the file or process named by *file-ref*. If you omit *mode* or specify a *mode* of <, Perl opens the file for input (reading). Specify *mode* as > to truncate and write to a file or as >> to append to a file.

See page 1035 for a discussion of reading from and writing to processes.

Writing to a file

The **print** function writes output to a file or process. The syntax of a **print** statement is

> print [*file-handle*] "*text*";

where *file-handle* is the name of the handle you specified in an **open** statement and *text* is the information you want to output. The *file-handle* can also be **STDOUT** or **STDERR**, as explained earlier. You must specify a handle in a **print** statement, except when you send information to standard output. Do not place a comma after *file-handle*. Also, do not enclose arguments to **print** within parentheses because doing so can create problems in some cases.

Reading from a file

The following expression reads one line, including the NEWLINE (**\n**), from the file or process associated with *file-handle*:

> <*file-handle*>

This expression is typically used in a statement such as

> $line = <IN>;

which reads into the variable **$line** one line from the file or process identified by the handle **IN**.

Magic file handle (<>)

To facilitate reading from files named on the command line or from standard input, Perl provides the *magic file handle*. This book uses this file handle in most examples. In place of the preceding line, you can use

> $line = <>;

This file handle causes a Perl program to work like many Linux utilities: It reads from standard input unless the program is called with one or more arguments, in which case it reads from the files named by the arguments. See page 234 for an explanation of how this feature works with cat.

The **print** statement in the first line in the next example includes the optional handle **STDOUT**; subsequent **print** statements in this example omit this handle. The first **print** statement prompts the user to enter something. The string that this statement outputs is terminated with a SPACE, not a NEWLINE, so the user can enter information on the same line as the prompt. The second line uses a magic file handle to read one line from standard input, which it assigns to **$userline**. Because of the magic file handle, if you call **file1.pl** with an argument that is a filename, it reads one line from that file instead of standard input.

```
$ cat file1.pl
print STDOUT "Enter something: ";
$userline = <>;
print "1>>>$userline<<<\n";
chomp ($userline);
print "2>>>$userline<<<\n";
print STDERR "3. Error message.\n";

$ perl file1.pl 2> file1.err
Enter something: hi there
1>>>hi there
<<<
2>>>hi there<<<

$ cat file1.err
3. Error message.
```

chomp/chop The two **print** statements following the user input in **file1.pl** display the value of **$userline** immediately preceded by greater than signs (>) and followed by less than signs (<). The first of these statements demonstrates that **$userline** includes a NEWLINE: The less than signs following the string the user entered appear on the line following the string. The **chomp** function removes a trailing NEWLINE, if it exists, from a string. After **chomp** processes **$userline**, the **print** statement shows that this variable no longer contains a NEWLINE. (The **chop** function is similar to **chomp**, except it removes *any* trailing character from a string.)

The –l option The Perl **–l** option applies **chomp** to each line of input and places **\n** at the end of each line of output.

The next example shows how to read from a file. It uses an **open** statement to assign the lexical file handle **$infile** to the file **/usr/share/dict/words**. Each iteration of the **while** structure evaluates an expression that reads a line from the file represented by **$infile** and assigns the line to **$line**. When **while** reaches the end of file, the expression evaluates to *false*; control then passes out of the **while** structure. The block of one statement displays the line as it was read from the file, including the NEWLINE. This program copies **/usr/share/dict/words** to standard output. Using a pipe (|; page 156) to send the output through head (page 152) displays the first four lines of the file (the first line is blank).

```
$ cat file2.pl
open (my $infile, "/usr/share/dict/words") or die "Cannot open dictionary: $!\n";
while ($line = <$infile>) {
    print $line;
    }

$ perl file2.pl | head -4

A
A's
AOL
```

$!   The **$!** variable holds the last system error. In a numeric context, it holds the system error number; in a string context it holds the system error string. If the **words** file is not present on the system, **file2.pl** displays the following message:

```
Cannot open dictionary: No such file or directory
```

If you do not have read permission for the file, the program displays this message:

```
Cannot open dictionary: Permission denied
```

Displaying the value of **$!** gives the user more information about what went wrong than simply saying that the program could not open the file.

Always check for an error when opening a file

tip   When a Perl program's attempt to open a file fails, you will not get an error message unless you check whether **open** returned an error. In **file2.pl**, the **or** operator in the **open** statement causes Perl to execute **die** (page 1014) if the **open** fails. The **die** statement displays the string **Cannot open the dictionary** followed by the system error string and terminates the program.

@ARGV   The **@ARGV** array holds the arguments from the command line Perl was called with. When you call the following program with a list of filenames, it displays the first line from each file. If the program cannot read a file, **die** (page 1014) sends an error message to error output and quits. The **foreach** structure loops through the command-line arguments, as represented by **@ARGV**, assigning each argument in turn to **$filename**. The **foreach** block starts with an **open** statement. Perl executes the **open** statement that precedes the OR Boolean operator (**or**) or, if that fails, Perl executes the statement following the **or** operator (**die**). The result is that Perl either opens the file named by **$filename** and assigns **IN** as its handle or, if it cannot open that file, executes the **die** statement and quits. The **print** statement displays the name of the file followed by a colon and the first line of the file. When it accepts **$line = <IN>** as an argument to **print**, Perl displays the value of **$line** following the assignment.

```
$ cat file3.pl
foreach $filename (@ARGV) {
    open (IN, $filename) or die "Cannot open file '$filename': $!\n";
    print "$filename: ", $line = <IN>;
    close (IN);
    }
```

```
$ perl file3.pl f1 f2 f3 f4
f1: First line of file f1.
f2: First line of file f2.
Cannot open file 'f3': No such file or directory
```

The next example is similar to the preceding one, except it takes advantage of several Perl features that make the code simpler. It does not quit when it cannot read a file. Instead, Perl displays an error message and continues. The first line of the program uses **my** to declare **$filename** to be a lexical variable. Next, **while** uses the magic file handle to open and read each line of each file named by the command-line arguments; **$ARGV** holds the name of the file. When there are no more files to read, the **while** condition [(<>)] is *false,* **while** transfers control outside the **while** block, and the program terminates. Perl takes care of all file opening and closing operations; you do not have to write code to take care of these tasks. Perl also performs error checking.

The program prints the first line of each file named by a command-line argument. Each time through the **while** block, **while** reads another line. When it finishes with one file, it starts reading from the next file. Within the **while** block, **if** tests whether it is processing a new file. If it is, the **if** block displays the name of the file and the (first) line from the file and then assigns the new filename (**$ARGV**) to **$filename**.

```
$ cat file3a.pl
my $filename;
while (<>) {
    if ($ARGV ne $filename) {
        print "$ARGV: $_";
        $filename = $ARGV;
    }
}

$ perl file3a.pl f1 f2 f3 f4
f1: First line of file f1.
f2: First line of file f2.
Can't open f3: No such file or directory at file3a.pl line 3, <> line 6.
f4: First line of file f4.
```

SORT

reverse   The **sort** function returns elements of an array ordered numerically or alphabetically, based on the *locale* (page 1117) environment. The **reverse** function is not related to **sort**; it simply returns the elements of an array in reverse order.

The first two lines of the following program assign values to the **@colors** array and display these values. Each of the next two pairs of lines uses **sort** to put the values in the **@colors** array in order, assign the result to **@scolors**, and display **@scolors**. These sorts put uppercase letters before lowercase letters. Observe the positions of **Orange** and **Violet**, both of which begin with an uppercase letter, in the sorted output. The first assignment statement in these two pairs of lines uses the full sort syntax including the block {**$a cmp $b**} that tells Perl to use the **cmp** subroutine, which compares strings, and to put the result in ascending order. When you omit the block in a **sort** statement, as is the case in the second assignment statement, Perl also performs an ascending textual sort.

```
$ cat sort3.pl
@colors = ("red", "Orange", "yellow", "green", "blue", "indigo", "Violet");

print "@colors\n";

@scolors = sort {$a cmp $b} @colors;          # ascending sort with
print "@scolors\n";                           # an explicit block

@scolors = sort @colors;                      # ascending sort with
print "@scolors\n";                           # an implicit block

@scolors = sort {$b cmp $a} @colors;          # descending sort
print "@scolors\n";

@scolors = sort {lc($a) cmp lc($b)} @colors;  # ascending folded sort
print "@scolors\n";

$ perl sort3.pl
red Orange yellow green blue indigo Violet
Orange Violet blue green indigo red yellow
Orange Violet blue green indigo red yellow
yellow red indigo green blue Violet Orange
blue green indigo Orange red Violet yellow
```

The third sort in the preceding example reverses the positions of **$a** and **$b** in the block to specify a descending sort. The last sort forces the strings to lowercase before comparing them, providing a sort wherein the uppercase letters are folded into the lowercase letters, causing **Orange** and **Violet** to appear in alphabetical order.

To perform a numerical sort, specify the **<=>** subroutine in place of **cmp**. The following example demonstrates ascending and descending numerical sorts:

```
$ cat sort4.pl
@numbers = (22, 188, 44, 2, 12);

print "@numbers\n";

@snumbers = sort {$a <=> $b} @numbers;
print "@snumbers\n";

@snumbers = sort {$b <=> $a} @numbers;
print "@snumbers\n";

$ perl sort4.pl
22 188 44 2 12
2 12 22 44 188
188 44 22 12 2
```

SUBROUTINES

All variables are package variables (page 1001) unless you use the **my** keyword to define them to be lexical variables (page 1001). Lexical variables defined in a subroutine are local to that subroutine.

The following program includes a main part and a subroutine named **add()**. This program uses the variables named **$one**, **$two**, and **$ans**, all of which are package variables: They are available to both the main program and the subroutine. The call to the subroutine does not pass values to the subroutine and the subroutine returns no values. This setup is not typical; it demonstrates that all variables are package variables unless you use **my** to declare them to be lexical variables.

The **sub2.pl** program assigns values to two variables and calls a subroutine. The subroutine adds the values of the two variables and assigns the result to another variable. The main part of the program displays the result.

```
$ cat sub1.pl
$one = 1;
$two = 2;
add();
print "Answer is $ans\n";

sub add {
    $ans =$one + $two
    }
```

```
$ perl sub1.pl
Answer is 3
```

The next example is similar to the previous one, except the subroutine takes advantage of a **return** statement to return a value to the main program. The program assigns the value returned by the subroutine to the variable **$ans** and displays that value. Again, all variables are package variables.

```
$ cat sub2.pl
$one = 1;
$two = 2;
$ans = add();
print "Answer is $ans\n";

sub add {
    return ($one + $two)
    }
```

```
$ perl sub2.pl
Answer is 3
```

Keeping variables local to a subroutine is important in many cases. The subroutine in the next example changes the values of variables and insulates the calling program from these changes by declaring and using lexical variables. This setup is more typical.

@_ When you pass values in a call to a subroutine, Perl makes those values available in the array named **@_** in the subroutine. Although **@_** is local to the subroutine, its elements are aliases for the parameters the subroutine was called with. Changing a value in the **@_** array changes the value of the underlying variable, which may not be what you want. The next program avoids this pitfall by assigning the values passed to the subroutine to lexical variables.

The **sub3.pl** program calls the **addplusone**() subroutine with two variables as arguments and assigns the value returned by the subroutine to a variable. The first statement in the subroutine declares two lexical variables and assigns to them the values from the **@_** array. The keyword **my** declares these variables to be lexical. You can use **my** without assigning values to the declared variables, but the syntax in the example is commonly used. The next two statements increment the lexical variables **$lcl_one** and **$lcl_two**. The **print** statement displays the value of **$lcl_one** within the subroutine. The **return** statement returns the sum of the two incremented, lexical variables.

```
$ cat sub3.pl
$one = 1;
$two = 2;
$ans = addplusone($one, $two);
print "Answer is $ans\n";
print "Value of 'lcl_one' in main: $lcl_one\n";
print "Value of 'one' in main: $one\n";

sub addplusone {
    my ($lcl_one, $lcl_two) = @_;
    $lcl_one++;
    $lcl_two++;
    print "Value of 'lcl_one' in sub: $lcl_one\n";
    return ($lcl_one + $lcl_two)
    }

$ perl sub3.pl
Value of 'lcl_one' in sub: 2
Answer is 5
Value of 'lcl_one' in main:
Value of 'one' in main: 1
```

After displaying the result returned by the subroutine, the **print** statements in the main program demonstrate that **$lcl_one** is not defined in the main program (it is local to the subroutine) and that the value of **$one** has not changed.

The next example demonstrates another way to work with parameters passed to a subroutine. This subroutine does not use variables other than the **@_** array it was passed and it does not change the values of any elements of that array.

```
$ cat sub4.pl
$one = 1;
$two = 2;
$ans = addplusone($one, $two);
print "Answer is $ans\n";
```

```
sub addplusone {
    return ($_[0] + $_[1] + 2);
    }
```

```
$ perl sub4.pl
Answer is 5
```

The final example in this section presents a more typical Perl subroutine. The subroutine **max**() can be called with any number of numeric arguments and returns the value of the largest argument. It uses the **shift** function to assign to **$biggest** the value of the first argument the subroutine was called with and to shift the rest of the arguments. After using **shift**, argument number 2 becomes argument number 1 (**8**), argument 3 becomes argument 2 (**64**), and argument 4 becomes argument 3 (**2**). Next, **foreach** loops over the remaining arguments (@_). Each time through the **foreach** block, Perl assigns to **$_** the value of each of the arguments, in order. The **$biggest** variable is assigned the value of **$_** if **$_** is bigger than **$biggest**. When **max**() finishes going through its arguments, **$biggest** holds the maximum value, which **max**() returns.

```
$ cat sub5b.pl
$ans = max (16, 8, 64, 2);
print "Maximum value is $ans\n";

sub max {
    my $biggest = shift;  # Assign first and shift the rest of the arguments to max()
    foreach (@_) {        # Loop through remaining arguments
    $biggest = $_ if $_ > $biggest;
    }
return ($biggest);
}
```

```
$ perl sub5b.pl
Maximum value is 64
```

REGULAR EXPRESSIONS

Appendix A defines and discusses regular expressions as you can use them in many Linux utilities. All descriptions in Appendix A apply to Perl, except as noted. In addition to the facilities described in Appendix A, Perl offers regular expression features that allow you to perform more complex string processing. This section reviews some of the regular expressions covered in Appendix A and describes some of the additional features of regular expressions available in Perl. It also introduces the syntax Perl uses for working with regular expressions.

SYNTAX AND THE =~ OPERATOR

The –l and –e options The examples in this section use the Perl –l (page 1021) and –e (page 1001) options. The –l option causes Perl to remove trailing NEWLINEs from input and append NEWLINEs to output. Perl executes the program that follows the –e option on the command line. Because the program must be specified as a single argument, the examples enclose the Perl programs within single quotation marks. The shell interprets the quotation marks and does not pass them to Perl.

Using other options with –e

tip   When you use another option with **–e**, the program must immediately follow the **–e** on the command line. As with many other utilities, Perl allows you to combine options following a single hyphen; if **–e** is one of the combined options, it must appear last in the list of options. Thus you can use **perl –l –e** or **perl –le** but not **perl –e –l** or **perl –el**.

/ is the default delimiter   By default, Perl delimits a regular expression with slashes (**/**). The first program uses the **=~** operator to search for the pattern **ge** in the string **aged**. Or, using different terminology, the **=~** operator determines whether there is a match for the regular expression **ge** in the string **aged**. The regular expression in this example contains no special characters; the string **ge** is part of the string **aged** so the expression within the parentheses evaluates to *true* and Perl executes the **print** statement.

```
$ perl -le 'if ("aged" =~ /ge/) {print "true";}'
true
```

You can provide the same functionality using a postfix **if** statement:

```
$ perl -le 'print "true" if "aged" =~ /ge/'
true
```

The **!~** operator works in the opposite sense from the **=~** operator. The expression in the next example evaluates to *true* because the regular expression **xy** does *not* match any part of **aged**:

```
$ perl -le 'print "true" if ("aged" !~ /xy/)'
true
```

As explained on page 1045, a period within a regular expression matches any single character, so the regular expression **a..d** matches the string **aged**:

```
$ perl -le 'print "true" if ("aged" =~ /a..d/)'
true
```

You can use a variable to hold a regular expression. The following syntax quotes *string* as a regular expression:

qr/*string*/

The next example uses this syntax to assign the regular expression **/a..d/** (including the delimiters) to the variable **$re** and then uses that variable as the regular expression:

```
$ perl -le '$re = qr/a..d/; print "true" if ("aged" =~ $re)'
true
```

If you want to include the delimiter within a regular expression, you must quote it. In the next example, the default delimiter, a slash (**/**), appears in the regular expression. To keep Perl from interpreting the **/** in **/usr** as the end of the regular expression, the **/**

that is part of the regular expression is quoted by preceding it with a backslash (\). See page 1047 for more information on quoting characters in regular expressions.

```
$ perl -le 'print "true" if ("/usr/doc" =~ /\/usr/)'
true
```

Quoting several characters by preceding each one with a backslash can make a complex regular expression harder to read. Instead, you can precede a delimited regular expression with **m** and use a paired set of characters, such as {}, as the delimiters. In the following example, the caret (^) anchors the regular expression to the beginning of the line (page 1046):

```
$ perl -le 'print "true" if ("/usr/doc" =~ m{^/usr})'
true
```

You can use the same syntax when assigning a regular expression to a variable:

```
$ perl -le '$pn = qr{^/usr}; print "true" if ("/usr/doc" =~ $pn)'
true
```

Replacement string and assignment

Perl uses the syntax shown in the next example to substitute a string (the *replacement string*) for a matched regular expression. In the second line of the example, an s before the regular expression instructs Perl to substitute the string between the second and third slashes (**worst**; the replacement string) for a match of the regular expression between the first two slashes (**best**). Implicit in this syntax is the notion that the substitution is made in the string held in the variable on the left of the =~ operator.

```
$ cat re10a.pl
$stg = "This is the best!";
$stg =~ s/best/worst/;
print "$stg\n";

$ perl re10a.pl
This is the worst!
```

Table 28-2 list some of the characters, called metacharacters, that are considered special within Perl regular expressions. Give the command **perldoc perlre** for more information.

Table 28-2 Some Perl regular expression metacharacters

Character	Matches
^ (caret)	Anchors regular expression to the end of a line (page 1046)
$ (dollar sign)	Anchors regular expression to the beginning of a line (page 1046)
(...)	Brackets a regular expression (page 1031)
. (period)	Any single character except NEWLINE (\n; page 1045)
\\	A backslash (\)

Table 28-2   Some Perl regular expression metacharacters (continued)

Character	Matches
\b	A word boundary (zero-width match)
\B	A nonword boundary ([^\b])
\d	A single decimal digit ([0–9])
\D	A single nondecimal digit ([^0–9] or [^\d])
\s (lowercase)	A single whitespace character SPACE, NEWLINE, RETURN, TAB, FORMFEED
\S (uppercase)	A single nonwhitespace character ([^\s])
\w (lowercase)	A single word character (a letter or digit; [a–zA–Z0–9])
\W (uppercase)	A single nonword character ([^\w])

GREEDY MATCHES

By default, Perl performs *greedy matching*, which means a regular expression matches the longest string possible (page 1047). In the following example, the regular expression /{.*} / matches an opening brace followed by any string of characters, a closing brace, and a SPACE (**{remove me} may have two {keep me}**). Perl substitutes a null string (//) for this match.

```
$ cat 5ha.pl
$string = "A line {remove me} may have two {keep me} pairs of braces.";
$string =~ s/{.*} //;
print "$string\n";

$ perl 5ha.pl
A line pairs of braces.
```

Nongreedy matches   The next example shows the classic way of matching the shorter brace-enclosed string from the previous example. This type of match is called *nongreedy* or *parsimonious matching*. Here the regular expression matches

1. An opening brace followed by

2. A character belonging to the character class (page 1045) that includes all characters except a closing brace ([^}]) followed by

3. zero or more occurrences of the preceding character (*) followed by

4. a closing brace followed by

5. a SPACE.

(A caret as the first character of a character class specifies the class of all characters that do not match the following characters, so [^}] matches any character that is not a closing brace.)

```
$ cat re5b.pl
$string = "A line {remove me} may have two {keep me} pairs of braces.";
$string =~ s/{[^}]*} //;
print "$string\n";

$ perl re5b.pl
A line may have two {keep me} pairs of braces.
```

Perl provides a shortcut that allows you to specify a nongreedy match. In the following example, the question mark in {.*?} causes the regular expression to match the shortest string that starts with an opening brace followed by any string of characters followed by a closing brace.

```
$ cat re5c.pl
$string = "A line {remove me} may have two {keep me} pairs of braces.";
$string =~ s/{.*?} //;
print "$string\n";

$ perl re5c.pl
A line may have two {keep me} pairs of braces.
```

BRACKETING EXPRESSIONS

As explained on page 1048, you can bracket parts of a regular expression and recall those parts in the replacement string. Most Linux utilities use quoted parentheses [i.e., \(and \)] to bracket a regular expression. In Perl regular expressions, parentheses are special characters. Perl omits the backslashes and uses unquoted parentheses to bracket regular expressions. To specify a parenthesis as a regular character within a regular expression in Perl, you must quote it (page 1047).

The next example uses unquoted parentheses in a regular expression to bracket part of the expression. It then assigns the part of the string that the bracketed expression matched to the variable that held the string that Perl originally searched for the regular expression.

First the program assigns the string **My name is Sam** to $stg. The next statement looks for a match for the regular expression **/My name is (.*)/** in the string held by **$stg**. The part of the regular expression bracketed by parentheses matches **Sam**; the **$1** in the replacement string matches the first (and only in this case) matched bracketed portion of the regular expression. The result is that the string held in **$stg** is replaced by the string **Sam**.

```
$ cat re11.pl
$stg = "My name is Sam";
$stg =~ s/My name is (.*)/$1/;
print "Matched: $stg\n";

$ perl re11.pl
Matched: Sam
```

The next example uses regular expressions to parse a string for numbers. Two variables are initialized to hold a string that contains two numbers. The third line of the program uses a regular expression to isolate the first number in the string. The **\D***matches a string of zero or more characters that does not include a digit: The **\D** special character matches any single nondigit character. The trailing asterisk makes this part of the regular expression perform a greedy match that does not include a digit (it matches **What is**). The bracketed regular expression **\d+** matches a string of one or more digits. The parentheses do not affect what the regular expression matches; they allow the **$1** in the replacement string to match what the bracketed regular expression matched. The final **.*** matches the rest of the string. This line assigns the value of the first number in the string to **$string**.

The next line is similar but assigns the second number in the string to **$string2**. The **print** statements display the numbers and the result of subtracting the second number from the first.

```
$ cat re8.pl
$string = "What is 488 minus 78?";
$string2 = $string;
$string =~ s/\D*(\d+).*/$1/;
$string2 =~ s/\D*\d+\D*(\d+).*/$1/;

print "$string\n";
print "$string2\n";
print $string - $string2, "\n";

$ perl re8.pl
488
78
410
```

The next few programs show some of the pitfalls of using unquoted parentheses in regular expressions when you do not intend to bracket part of the regular expression. The first of these programs attempts to match parentheses in a string with unquoted parentheses in a regular expression and fails. The regular expression **ag(e** matches the same string as the regular expression **age** because the parenthesis is a special character. The regular expression does not match the string **ag(ed)**.

```
$ perl -le 'if ("ag(ed)" =~ /ag(ed)/) {print "true";} else {print "false";}'
false
```

The regular expression in the next example quotes the parentheses by preceding each with a backslash, causing Perl to interpret them as regular characters. The match is successful.

```
$ perl -le 'if ("ag(ed)" =~ /ag\(ed\)/) {print "true";} else {print "false";}'
true
```

Next, Perl finds an unmatched parenthesis in a regular expression:

```
$ perl -le 'if ("ag(ed)" =~ /ag(e/) {print "true";} else {print "false";}'
Unmatched ( in regex; marked by <-- HERE in m/ag( <-- HERE e/ at -e line 1.
```

When you quote the parenthesis, all is well and Perl finds a match:

```
$ perl -le 'if ("ag(ed)" =~ /ag\(e/) {print "true";} else {print "false";}'
true
```

CPAN MODULES

CPAN, the Comprehensive Perl Archive Network, provides Perl documentation, FAQs, modules (page 1000), and scripts on its Web site (www.cpan.org). It holds more than 16,000 distributions (page 1000) and also provides links, mailing lists, and versions of Perl compiled to run under various operating systems (ports of Perl). One way to locate a module is to visit search.cpan.org and use the search box or click one of the classes of modules listed on that page.

This section explains how to download a module from CPAN and how to install and run the module. Perl provides a hierarchical namespace for modules, separating components of a name with double colons (::). The example in this section uses the module named **Timestamp::Simple**, which you can read about and download from search.cpan.org/dist/Timestamp-Simple. The timestamp is the date and time in the format YYYYMMDDHHMMSS

To use a Perl module, you first download the file that holds the module. In the case of the example, the search.cpan.org/~shoop/Timestamp-Simple-1.01/Simple.pm Web page has a link on the right side labeled **Download**. Click this link and save the file to the directory you want to work in. You do not need to work as a privileged user until the last step of this procedure, when you install the module.

Most Perl modules come as compressed tar (page 162) files. With the downloaded file in the working directory, decompress the file:

```
$ tar xzvf Timestamp-Simple-1.01.tar.gz
Timestamp-Simple-1.01/
Timestamp-Simple-1.01/Simple.pm
Timestamp-Simple-1.01/Makefile.PL
Timestamp-Simple-1.01/README
Timestamp-Simple-1.01/test.pl
Timestamp-Simple-1.01/Changes
Timestamp-Simple-1.01/MANIFEST
Timestamp-Simple-1.01/ARTISTIC
Timestamp-Simple-1.01/GPL
Timestamp-Simple-1.01/META.yml
```

The **README** file in the newly created directory usually provides instructions for building and installing the module. Most modules follow the same steps.

```
$ cd Timestamp-Simple-1.01
$ perl Makefile.PL
Checking if your kit is complete...
Looks good
Writing Makefile for Timestamp::Simple
```

If the module you are building depends on other modules that are not installed on the local system, running **perl Makefile.PL** will display one or more warnings about prerequisites that are not found. This step writes out the makefile even if modules are missing. In this case the next step will fail, and you must build and install missing modules before continuing.

The next step is to run make on the makefile you just created. After you run **make**, run **make test** to be sure the module is working.

```
$ make
cp Simple.pm blib/lib/Timestamp/Simple.pm
Manifying blib/man3/Timestamp::Simple.3pm

$ make test
PERL_DL_NONLAZY=1 /usr/bin/perl "-Iblib/lib" "-Iblib/arch" test.pl
1..1
# Running under perl version 5.010000 for linux
# Current time local: Fri Sep  5 18:20:41 2008
# Current time GMT:   Sat Sep  6 01:20:41 2008
# Using Test.pm version 1.25
ok 1
ok 2
ok 3
```

Finally, running with **root** privileges, install the module:

```
$ sudo make install
Installing /usr/local/share/perl/5.10.0/Timestamp/Simple.pm
Installing /usr/local/man/man3/Timestamp::Simple.3pm
Writing /usr/local/lib/perl/5.10.0/auto/Timestamp/Simple/.packlist
Appending installation info to /usr/local/lib/perl/5.10.0/perllocal.pod
```

Once you have installed a module, you can use perldoc to display the documentation that tells you how to use the module. See page 999 for an example.

Some modules contain SYNOPSIS sections. If the module you installed has this section, you can test the module by putting the code from the SYNOPSIS section in a file and running it as a Perl program:

```
$ cat times.pl
use Timestamp::Simple qw(stamp);
print stamp, "\n";

$ perl times.pl
20080905182627
```

You can then incorporate the module in a Perl program. The following example uses the timestamp module to generate a unique filename:

```
$ cat fn.pl
use Timestamp::Simple qw(stamp);

# Save timestamp in a variable
$ts = stamp, "\n";
```

```
# Strip off the year
$ts =~ s/....(.*)/\1/;

# Create a unique filename
$fn = "myfile." . $ts;

# Open, write to, and close the file
open (OUTFILE, '>', "$fn");
print OUTFILE "Hi there.\n";
close (OUTFILE);
```

```
$ perl fn.pl
$ ls myf*
myfile.0905183010
```

substr You can use the **substr** function in place of the regular expression to strip off the year. To do so, replace the line that starts with **$ts =~** with the following line. Here, **substr** takes on the value of the string **$ts** starting at position 4 and continuing to the end of the string.

```
$ts = substr ($ts, 4);
```

EXAMPLES

This section provides some sample Perl programs. First try running these programs as is, and then modify them to learn more about programming with Perl.

The first example displays the list of groups that the user given as an argument is a member of. Without an argument, it displays the list of groups that the user running the program is a member of. In a Perl program, the **%ENV** hash holds the environment variables from the shell that called Perl. The keys in this hash are the names of environment variables. The values in this hash are the values of the corresponding variables. The first line of the program assigns a username to **$user**. The **shift** function (page 1010) takes on the value of the first command-line argument and shifts the rest of the arguments, if any remain. If the user runs the program with an argument, that argument is assigned to **$user**. If there was no argument on the command line, **shift** fails and Perl executes the statement following the Boolean OR (||). This statement extracts the value associated with the **USER** key in **%ENV**, which is the name of the user running the program.

Accepting output from a process
The third statement initializes the array **@list**. Although this statement is not required, it is good practice to include it to make the code easier to read. The next statement opens the **$fh** lexical handle. The trailing pipe symbol (|) in the *file-ref* (page 1020) portion of this **open** statement tells Perl to pass the command line preceding the pipe symbol to the shell for execution and to accept standard output from the command when the program reads from the file handle. In this case the command uses grep to filter the **/etc/group** file (page 474) for lines containing the username held in **$user**. The **die** statement displays an error message if Perl cannot open the handle.

```
$ cat groupfind.pl
$user = shift || $ENV{"USER"};
print "User $user belongs to these groups:\n";
@list = ();
open (my $fh, "grep $user /etc/group |") or die "Error: $!\n";
while ($group = <$fh>) {
    chomp $group;
    $group =~ s/(.*?):.*/$1/;
    push @list, $group;
}
close $fh;
@slist = sort @list;
print "@slist\n";

$ perl groupfind.pl
User sam belongs to these groups:
adm admin audio cdrom dialout dip floppy kvm lpadmin ...
```

The **while** structure in **groupfind.pl** reads lines from standard output of grep and terminates when grep finishes executing. The name of the group appears first on each line in **/etc/group**, followed by a colon and other information, including the names of the users who belong to the group. Following is a line from this file:

```
sam:x:1000:max,zach,helen
```

The line

```
$group =~ s/(.*?):.*/$1/;
```

uses a regular expression and substitution to remove everything except the name of the group from each line. The regular expression .*: would perform a greedy match of zero or more characters followed by a colon; putting a question mark after the asterisk causes the expression to perform a nongreedy match (page 1030). Putting parentheses around the part of the expression that matches the string the program needs to display enables Perl to use the string that the regular expression matches in the replacement string. The final .* matches the rest of the line. Perl replaces the **$1** in the replacement string with the string the bracketed portion of the regular expression (the part between the parentheses) matched and assigns this value (the name of the group) to **$group**.

The **chomp** statement removes the trailing NEWLINE (the regular expression did not match this character) and **push** adds the value of **$group** to the end of the **@list** array. Without **chomp**, each group would appear on a line by itself in the output. After the **while** structure finishes processing input from grep, **sort** orders **@list** and assigns the result to **@slist**. The final statement displays the sorted list of groups the user belongs to.

opendir and readdir   The next example introduces the **opendir** and **readdir** functions. The **opendir** function opens a directory in a manner similar to the way **open** opens an ordinary file. It takes two arguments: the name of the directory handle and the name of the directory to open. The **readdir** function reads the name of a file from an open directory.

In the example, **opendir** opens the working directory (specified by .) using the **$dir** lexical directory handle. If **opendir** fails, Perl executes the statement following the **or** operator: **die** sends an error message to standard error and terminates the program. With the directory opened, **while** loops through the files in the directory, assigning the filename that **readdir** returns to the lexical variable **$entry**. An **if** statement executes **print** only for those files that are directories (**–d**). The **print** function displays the name of the directory unless the directory is named . or .. When **readdir** has read all files in the working directory, it returns *false* and control passes to the statement following the **while** block. The **closedir** function closes the open directory and **print** displays a NEWLINE following the list of directories the program displayed.

```
$ cat dirs2a.pl
#!/usr/bin/perl
print "The working directory contains these directories:\n";

opendir my $dir, '.' or die "Could not open directory: $!\n";
while (my $entry = readdir $dir) {
    if (-d $entry) {
        print $entry, ' ' unless ($entry eq '.' || $entry eq '..');
    }
}
closedir $dir;
print "\n";

$ ./dirs2a.pl
The working directory contains these directories:
two one
```

split   The **split** function divides a string into substrings as specified by a delimiter. The syntax of a call to **split** is

split (/re/, string);

where *re* is the delimiter, which is a regular expression (frequently a single regular character), and *string* is the string that is to be divided. As the next example shows, you can assign the list that **split** returns to an array variable.

The next program lists the usernames of users with UIDs greater than or equal to 100 listed in the **/etc/passwd** (page 476) file. It uses a **while** structure to read lines from **passwd** into **$user**, and it uses **split** to break the line into substrings separated by colons. The line that begins with **@row** assigns each of these substrings to an element of the **@row** array. The expression the **if** statement evaluates is *true* if the third substring (the UID) is greater than or equal to 100. This expression uses the **>=** comparison operator because it compares two numbers; an alphabetic comparison would use the **ge** operator.

The **print** statement sends the UID number and the associated username to the **$sortout** file handle. The **open** statement for this handle establishes a pipe that sends its output to **sort –n**. Because the **sort** utility (page 154) does not display output until it finishes receiving input, **split3.pl** does not display output until it closes the **$sortout** handle, which it does when it finishes reading the **passwd** file.

```
$ cat split3.pl
#!/usr/bin/perl -w

open ($pass, "/etc/passwd");
open ($sortout, "| sort -n");
while ($user = <$pass>) {
    @row = split (/:/, $user);
    if ($row[2] >= 100) {
        print $sortout "$row[2] $row[0]\n";
        }
    }
close ($pass);
close ($sortout);

$ ./split3.pl
100 libuuid
101 syslog
102 klog
103 avahi-autoipd
104 pulse
...
```

The next example counts and displays the arguments it was called with, using **@ARGV** (page 1022). It uses a **foreach** structure that loops through the elements of the **@ARGV** array, which holds the command-line arguments. The **++** preincrement operator increments **$count** before it is displayed.

```
$ cat 10.pl
#!/usr/bin/perl -w

$count = 0;
$num = @ARGV;
print "You entered $num arguments on the command line:\n";
foreach $arg (@ARGV) {
    print ++$count, ". $arg\n";
    }

$ ./10.pl apple pear banana watermelon
You entered 4 arguments on the command line:
1. apple
2. pear
3. banana
4. watermelon
```

CHAPTER SUMMARY

Perl was written by Larry Wall in 1987. Since that time Perl has grown in size and functionality and is now a very popular language used for text processing, system administration, software development, and general-purpose programming. One of Perl's biggest assets is its support by thousands of third-party modules, many of which are stored in the CPAN repository.

The perldoc utility locates and displays local Perl documentation. It also allows you to document a Perl program by displaying lines of **pod** (plain old documentation) you include the program.

Perl provides three types of variables: scalar (begin with a **$**), array (begin with a **@**), and hash (also called associative arrays; begin with a **%**). Array and hash variables both hold lists, but arrays are ordered while hashes are unordered. Standard control flow statements allow you to alter the order of execution of statements within a Perl program. In addition, Perl programs can take advantage of subroutines which can include variables that are local to the subroutines (lexical variables).

Regular expressions are one of Perl's strong points. In addition to facilities that are available in many Linux utilities, Perl offers additional regular expression features that allow you to perform more complex string processing.

EXERCISES

1. What are two different ways to turn on warnings in Perl?

2. What is the difference between an array and a hash?

3. In each example, when would you use a hash and when would you use an array?

    a. Counting the number of occurrences of an IP address in a log file.

    b. Generating a list of users who are over disk quota for use in a report.

4. Write a regular expression to match a quoted string, such as

    ```
    He said, "Go get me the wrench," but I didn't hear him.
    ```

5. Write a regular expression to match an IP address in a log file.

6. Many configuration files contain many comments, including commented-out default configuration directives. Write a program to remove these comments from a configuration file.

ADVANCED EXERCISES

7. Write a program that removes ***.tmp** and ***~** files from a directory hierarchy. (*Hint:* Use the **File::Find** module.)

8. Describe a programming mistake that Perl's warnings do not report on.

9. Write a Perl program that counts the number of files in the working directory and the number of bytes in those files, by filename extension.

10. Describe the difference between quoting strings using single quotation marks and using double quotation marks.

11. Write a program that copies all the files with a **.ico** filename extension in a directory hierarchy to a directory named icons in your home directory. (*Hint:* Use the **File::Find** and **File::Copy** modules.)

12. Write a program that analyzes Apache logs. Display the number of bytes served by each path. Ignore unsuccessful page requests. If there are more than ten paths, display the first ten only.

    Following is a sample line from an Apache access log. The two numbers following the HTTP/1.1 are the response code and the byte count. A response code of 200 means the request was successful. A byte count of – means no data was transferred.

```
__DATA__
92.50.103.52 - - [19/Aug/2008:08:26:43 -0400] "GET /perl/automated-testing/next_active.gif
HTTP/1.1" 200 980 "http://example.com/perl/automated-testing/navigation_bar.htm"
"Mozilla/5.0 (X11; U; Linux x86_64; en-US; rv:1.8.1.6) Gecko/20061201 Firefox/3.0.0.6
(Ubuntu-feisty); Blazer/4.0"
```

PART VII

APPENDIXES

REGULAR EXPRESSIONS

A *regular expression* defines a set of one or more strings of characters. A simple string of characters is a regular expression that defines one string of characters: itself. A more complex regular expression uses letters, numbers, and special characters to define many different strings of characters. A regular expression is said to *match* any string it defines.

This appendix describes the regular expressions used by ed, vim, emacs, grep, mawk/gawk, sed, Perl, and many other utilities. Refer to page 1027 for more information on Perl regular expressions. The regular expressions used in shell ambiguous file references are different and are described in "Filename Generation/Pathname Expansion" on page 242.

CHARACTERS

As used in this appendix, a *character* is any character *except* a NEWLINE. Most characters represent themselves within a regular expression. A *special character,* also called a *metacharacter,* is one that does not represent itself. If you need to use a special character to represent itself, you must quote it as explained on page 1047.

DELIMITERS

A character called a *delimiter* usually marks the beginning and end of a regular expression. The delimiter is always a special character for the regular expression it delimits (that is, it does not represent itself but marks the beginning and end of the expression). Although vim permits the use of other characters as a delimiter and grep does not use delimiters at all, the regular expressions in this appendix use a forward slash (/) as a delimiter. In some unambiguous cases, the second delimiter is not required. For example, you can sometimes omit the second delimiter when it would be followed immediately by RETURN.

SIMPLE STRINGS

The most basic regular expression is a simple string that contains no special characters except the delimiters. A simple string matches only itself (Table A-1). In the examples in this appendix, the strings that are matched are underlined and look like this.

Table A-1   Simple strings

Regular expression	Matches	Examples
/ring/	ring	ring, spring, ringing, stringing
/Thursday/	Thursday	Thursday, Thursday's
/or not/	or not	or not, poor nothing

SPECIAL CHARACTERS

You can use special characters within a regular expression to cause the regular expression to match more than one string. A regular expression that includes a special character always matches the longest possible string, starting as far toward the beginning (left) of the line as possible.

PERIODS

A period (.) matches any character (Table A-2).

Table A-2 Periods

Regular expression	Matches	Examples
/ .alk/	All strings consisting of a SPACE followed by any character followed by alk	will talk, may balk
/.ing/	All strings consisting of any character preceding ing	sing song, ping, before inglenook

BRACKETS

Brackets ([]) define a *character class*[1] that matches any single character within the brackets (Table A-3). If the first character following the left bracket is a caret (^), the brackets define a character class that matches any single character not within the brackets. You can use a hyphen to indicate a range of characters. Within a character-class definition, backslashes and asterisks (described in the following sections) lose their special meanings. A right bracket (appearing as a member of the character class) can appear only as the first character following the left bracket. A caret is special only if it is the first character following the left bracket. A dollar sign is special only if it is followed immediately by the right bracket.

Table A-3 Brackets

Regular expression	Matches	Examples
/[bB]ill/	Member of the character class b and B followed by ill	bill, Bill, billed
/t[aeiou].k/	t followed by a lowercase vowel, any character, and a k	talkative, stink, teak, tanker
/# [6–9]/	# followed by a SPACE and a member of the character class 6 through 9	# 60, # 8:, get # 9
/[^a–zA–Z]/	Any character that is not a letter (ASCII character set only)	1, 7, @, ., }, Stop!

---

1. GNU documentation calls these List Operators and defines Character Class operators as expressions that match a predefined group of characters, such as all numbers (page 1100).

ASTERISKS

An asterisk can follow a regular expression that represents a single character (Table A-4). The asterisk represents *zero* or more occurrences of a match of the regular expression. An asterisk following a period matches any string of characters. (A period matches any character, and an asterisk matches zero or more occurrences of the preceding regular expression.) A character-class definition followed by an asterisk matches any string of characters that are members of the character class.

Table A-4   Asterisks

Regular expression	Matches	Examples
/ab*c/	<u>a</u> followed by zero or more <u>b</u>'s followed by a <u>c</u>	<u>ac</u>, <u>abc</u>, <u>abbc</u>, debbca<u>abbbc</u>
/ab.*c/	<u>ab</u> followed by zero or more characters followed by <u>c</u>	<u>abc</u>, <u>abxc</u>, <u>ab45c</u>, <u>xab 756.345 x c</u>at
/t.*ing/	<u>t</u> followed by zero or more characters followed by <u>ing</u>	<u>thing</u>, <u>ting</u>, I <u>thought of going</u>
/[a–zA–Z]*/	A string composed only of letters and SPACES	1. <u>any string without numbers or punctuation</u>!
/(.*)/	As long a string as possible between (and)	Get <u>(this) and (that)</u>;
/([^)]*)/	The shortest string possible that starts with (and ends with)	<u>(this)</u>, Get <u>(this and that)</u>

CARETS AND DOLLAR SIGNS

A regular expression that begins with a caret (^) can match a string only at the beginning of a line. In a similar manner, a dollar sign ($) at the end of a regular expression matches the end of a line. The caret and dollar sign are called anchors because they force (anchor) a match to the beginning or end of a line (Table A-5).

Table A-5   Carets and dollar signs

Regular expression	Matches	Examples
/^T/	A <u>T</u> at the beginning of a line	<u>T</u>his line..., <u>T</u>hat Time..., In Time
/^+[0–9]/	A plus sign followed by a digit at the beginning of a line	<u>+5</u> +45.72, <u>+7</u>59 Keep this...
/:$/	A colon that ends a line	...below<u>:</u>

QUOTING SPECIAL CHARACTERS

You can quote any special character (but not parentheses [except in Perl; page 1031] or a digit) by preceding it with a backslash (Table A-6). Quoting a special character makes it represent itself.

Table A-6 Quoted special characters

Regular expression	Matches	Examples
/end\./	All strings that contain end followed by a period	The end., send., pretend.mail
/ \\/	A single backslash	\
/ */	An asterisk	*.c, an asterisk (*)
/ \[5\]/	[5]	it was five [5]
/and\/or/	and/or	and/or

RULES

The following rules govern the application of regular expressions.

LONGEST MATCH POSSIBLE

A regular expression always matches the longest possible string, starting as far toward the beginning of the line as possible. Perl calls this type of mach a *greedy match* (page 1030). For example, given the string

```
This (rug) is not what it once was (a long time ago), is it?
```

the expression **/Th.*is/** matches

```
This (rug) is not what it once was (a long time ago), is
```

and **/(.*)/** matches

```
(rug) is not what it once was (a long time ago)
```

However, **/([^)]*)/** matches

```
(rug)
```

Given the string

```
singing songs, singing more and more
```

the expression **/s.*ing/** matches

```
singing songs, singing
```

and **/s.*ing song/** matches

```
singing song
```

EMPTY REGULAR EXPRESSIONS

Within some utilities, such as vim and less (but not grep), an empty regular expression represents the last regular expression that you used. For example, suppose you give vim the following Substitute command:

```
:s/mike/robert/
```

If you then want to make the same substitution again, you can use the following command:

```
:s//robert/
```

Alternatively, you can use the following commands to search for the string **mike** and then make the substitution

```
/mike/
:s//robert/
```

The empty regular expression (**//**) represents the last regular expression you used (**/mike/**).

BRACKETING EXPRESSIONS

You can use quoted parentheses, \(and \), to *bracket* a regular expression. (However, Perl uses unquoted parentheses to bracket regular expressions; page 1031.) The string that the bracketed regular expression matches can be recalled, as explained in "Quoted Digit." A regular expression does not attempt to match quoted parentheses. Thus a regular expression enclosed within quoted parentheses matches what the same regular expression without the parentheses would match. The expression /\(rexp\)/ matches what /rexp/ would match; /a\(b✳\)c/ matches what /ab✳c/ would match.

You can nest quoted parentheses. The bracketed expressions are identified only by the opening \(, so no ambiguity arises in identifying them. The expression /\([a–z]\([A–Z]✳\)x\)/ consists of two bracketed expressions, one nested within the other. In the string **3 t dMNORx7 l u**, the preceding regular expression matches **dMNORx**, with the first bracketed expression matching **dMNORx** and the second matching **MNOR**.

THE REPLACEMENT STRING

The vim and sed editors use regular expressions as search strings within Substitute commands. You can use the ampersand (**&**) and quoted digits (**\n**) special characters to represent the matched strings within the corresponding replacement string.

AMPERSAND

Within a replacement string, an ampersand (&) takes on the value of the string that the search string (regular expression) matched. For example, the following vim Substitute command surrounds a string of one or more digits with NN. The ampersand in the replacement string matches whatever string of digits the regular expression (search string) matched:

```
:s/[0-9][0-9]*/NN&NN/
```

Two character-class definitions are required because the regular expression [0–9]* matches *zero* or more occurrences of a digit, and *any* character string constitutes zero or more occurrences of a digit.

QUOTED DIGIT

Within the search string, a bracketed regular expression, \(**xxx**\) [(**xxx**) in Perl], matches what the regular expression would have matched without the quoted parentheses, **xxx**. Within the replacement string, a quoted digit, *n*, represents the string that the bracketed regular expression (portion of the search string) beginning with the *n*th \(matched. Perl accepts a quoted digit for this purpose, but the preferred style is to precede the digit with a dollar sign ($*n*; page 1031). For example, you can take a list of people in the form

```
last-name, first-name initial
```

and put it in the form

```
first-name initial last-name
```

with the following vim command:

```
:1,$s/\([^,]*\), \(.*\)/\2 \1/
```

This command addresses all the lines in the file (**1,$**). The Substitute command (**s**) uses a search string and a replacement string delimited by forward slashes. The first bracketed regular expression within the search string, \([^,]*\), matches what the same unbracketed regular expression, [^,]*, would match: zero or more characters not containing a comma (the **last-name**). Following the first bracketed regular expression are a comma and a SPACE that match themselves. The second bracketed expression, \(.*\), matches any string of characters (the **first-name** and **initial**).

The replacement string consists of what the second bracketed regular expression matched (\2), followed by a SPACE and what the first bracketed regular expression matched (\1).

EXTENDED REGULAR EXPRESSIONS

This section covers patterns that use an extended set of special characters. These patterns are called *full regular expressions* or *extended regular expressions*. In addition to ordinary regular expressions, Perl and vim provide extended regular expressions. The three utilities egrep, grep when run with the –E option (similar to egrep), and mawk/gawk provide all the special characters included in ordinary regular expressions, except for \(and \), as well those included in extended regular expressions.

Two of the additional special characters are the plus sign (+) and the question mark (?). They are similar to *, which matches *zero* or more occurrences of the previous character. The plus sign matches *one* or more occurrences of the previous character, whereas the question mark matches *zero* or *one* occurrence. You can use any one of the special characters *, +, and ? following parentheses, causing the special character to apply to the string surrounded by the parentheses. Unlike the parentheses in bracketed regular expressions, these parentheses are not quoted (Table A-7).

Table A-7   Extended regular expressions

Regular expression	Matches	Examples
/ab+c/	<u>a</u> followed by one or more <u>b</u>'s followed by a <u>c</u>	y<u>abc</u>w, <u>abbc</u>57
/ab?c/	<u>a</u> followed by zero or one <u>b</u> followed by <u>c</u>	b<u>ac</u>k, <u>abc</u>def
/(ab)+c/	One or more occurrences of the string <u>ab</u> followed by <u>c</u>	z<u>abc</u>d, <u>ababc</u>!
/(ab)?c/	Zero or one occurrence of the string <u>ab</u> followed by <u>c</u>	x<u>c</u>, <u>abc</u>c

In full regular expressions, the vertical bar (|) special character is a Boolean OR operator. Within vim, you must quote the vertical bar by preceding it with a backslash to make it special (\|). A vertical bar between two regular expressions causes a match with strings that match the first expression, the second expression, or both. You can use the vertical bar with parentheses to separate from the rest of the regular expression the two expressions that are being ORed (Table A-8).

Table A-8   Full regular expressions

Regular expression	Meaning	Examples
/ab|ac/	Either <u>ab</u> or <u>ac</u>	<u>ab</u>, <u>ac</u>, <u>abac</u> (***abac*** *is two matches of the regular expression*)
/^Exit|^Quit/	Lines that begin with <u>Exit</u> or <u>Quit</u>	<u>Exit</u>, <u>Quit</u>, No Exit
/(D|N)\. Jones/	<u>D. Jones</u> or <u>N. Jones</u>	P.<u>D. Jones</u>, <u>N. Jones</u>

APPENDIX SUMMARY

A regular expression defines a set of one or more strings of characters. A regular expression is said to match any string it defines.

In a regular expression, a special character is one that does not represent itself. Table A-9 lists special characters.

Table A-9   Special characters

Character	Meaning
.	Matches any single character
*	Matches zero or more occurrences of a match of the preceding character
^	Forces a match to the beginning of a line
$	A match to the end of a line
\	Quotes special characters
\<	Forces a match to the beginning of a word
\>	Forces a match to the end of a word

Table A-10 lists ways of representing character classes and bracketed regular expressions.

Table A-10   Character classes and bracketed regular expressions

Class	Defines
[xyz]	Defines a character class that matches x, y, or z
[^xyz]	Defines a character class that matches any character except x, y, or z
[x–z]	Defines a character class that matches any character x through z inclusive
\(xyz\)	Matches what xyz matches (a bracketed regular expression; not Perl)
(xyz)	Matches what xyz matches (a bracketed regular expression; Perl only)

In addition to the preceding special characters and strings (excluding quoted parentheses, except in vim), the characters in Table A-11 are special within full, or extended, regular expressions.

Table A-11   Extended regular expressions

Expression	Matches
+	Matches one or more occurrences of the preceding character
?	Matches zero or one occurrence of the preceding character

Table A-11   Extended regular expressions (continued)

Expression	Matches
(*xyz*)+	Matches one or more occurrences of what *xyz* matches
(*xyz*)?	Matches zero or one occurrence of what *xyz* matches
(*xyz*) *	Matches zero or more occurrences of what *xyz* matches
xyz|*abc*	Matches either what *xyz* or what *abc* matches (use \\| in vim)
(*xy*|*ab*)*c*	Matches either what *xyc* or what *abc* matches (use \\| in vim)

Table A-12 lists characters that are special within a replacement string in sed and vim.

Table A-12   Replacement strings

String	Represents
&	Represents what the regular expression (search string) matched
n	A quoted number, *n*, represents what the *n*th bracketed regular expression in the search string matched
$*n*	A number preceded by a dollar sign, *n*, represents what the *n*th bracketed regular expression in the search string matched (Perl only)

B

HELP

You need not be a user or system administrator in isolation. A large community of Linux experts is willing to assist you in learning about, helping you solve problems with, and getting the most out of a Linux system. Before you ask for help, however, make sure you have done everything you can to solve the problem yourself. No doubt, someone has experienced the same problem before you and the answer to your question exists somewhere on the Internet. Your job is to find it. This appendix lists resources and describes methods that can help you in that task.

SOLVING A PROBLEM

Following is a list of steps that can help you solve a problem without asking someone for help. Depending on your understanding of and experience with the hardware and software involved, these steps may lead to a solution.

1. Ubuntu Linux comes with extensive documentation. Read the documentation on the specific hardware or software you are having a problem with. If it is a GNU product, use info; otherwise, use man to find local information. Also look in **/usr/share/doc** for documentation on specific tools. For more information refer to "Where to Find Documentation" on page 121.

2. When the problem involves some type of error or other message, use a search engine, such as Google (www.google.com/linux) or Google Groups (groups.google.com), to look up the message on the Internet. If the message is long, pick a unique part of the message to search for; 10 to 20 characters should be enough. Enclose the search string within double quotation marks. See "Using the Internet to Get Help" on page 128 for an example of this kind of search.

3. Check whether the Linux Documentation Project (www.tldp.org) has a HOWTO or mini-HOWTO on the subject in question. Search its site for keywords that relate directly to the product and problem. Read the FAQs.

4. See Table B-1 for other sources of documentation.

5. Use Google or Google Groups to search on keywords that relate directly to the product and problem.

6. When all else fails (or perhaps before you try anything else), examine the system logs in **/var/log**. First look at the end of the **messages** file using the following command:

```
$ sudo tail -20 /var/log/messages
```

If **messages** contains nothing useful, run the following command. It displays the names of the log files in chronological order, with the most recently modified files appearing at the bottom of the list:

```
$ ls -ltr /var/log
```

Look at the files at the bottom of the list first. If the problem involves a network connection, review the **auth.log** file on the local and remote systems. Also look at **messages** on the remote system.

7. The **/var/spool** directory contains subdirectories with useful information: **cups** holds the print queues, **mail** or **exim4** holds the user's mail files, and so on.

If you are unable to solve a problem yourself, a thoughtful question to an appropriate newsgroup (page 1057) or mailing list (page 1057) can elicit useful information. When you send or post a question, make sure you describe the problem and identify the local system carefully. Include the version numbers of Ubuntu Linux and any software packages that relate to the problem. Describe the hardware, if appropriate. There is an etiquette to posting questions—see www.catb.org/~esr/faqs/smart-questions.html for a good paper by Eric S. Raymond and Rick Moen titled "How To Ask Questions the Smart Way."

The author's home page (www.sobell.com) contains corrections to this book, answers to selected chapter exercises, and pointers to other Linux sites.

FINDING LINUX-RELATED INFORMATION

Ubuntu Linux comes with reference pages stored online. You can read these documents by using the man or info (page 124) utility. You can read man and info pages to get more information about specific topics while reading this book or to determine which features are available with Linux. To search for topics, use apropos (see page 124 or give the command **man apropos**).

DOCUMENTATION

Good books are available on various aspects of using and managing UNIX systems in general and Linux systems in particular. In addition, you may find the sites listed in Table B-1 useful.[1]

Table B-1   Documentation

Site	About the site	URL
freedesktop.org	Creates standards for interoperability between open-source desktop environments.	freedesktop.org
GNOME	GNOME home page.	www.gnome.org
GNU Manuals	GNU manuals.	www.gnu.org/manual
info	Instructions for using the info utility.	www.gnu.org/software/texinfo/manual/info
Internet FAQ Archives	Searchable FAQ archives.	www.faqs.org

---

1. The right-hand columns of most of the tables in this appendix show Internet addresses (URLs). All sites have an implicit http:// prefix unless ftp:// or https:// is shown. Refer to "URLs (Web addresses)" on page 21.

Table B-1   Documentation (continued)

Site	About the site	URL
KDE Documentation	KDE documentation.	kde.org/documentation
KDE News	KDE news.	dot.kde.org
Linux Documentation Project	All things related to Linux documentation (in many languages): HOWTOs, guides, FAQs, man pages, and magazines. This is the best overall source for Linux documentation. Make sure to visit the Links page.	www.tldp.org
Ubuntu Documentation and Support	These URIs have links to many pages that provide documentation and support.	www.ubuntu.com/support help.ubuntu.com/community ubuntuforums.org
RFCs	Requests for comments; see *RFC* (page 1129).	www.rfc-editor.org
System Administrators Guild (SAGE)	SAGE is a group for system administrators.	www.sage.org

USEFUL LINUX SITES

Sometimes the sites listed in Table B-2 are so busy that you cannot connect to them. In this case, you are usually given a list of alternative, or *mirror*, sites to try.

Table B-2   Useful Linux sites

Site	About the site	URL
DistroWatch	A survey of many Linux distributions, including news, reviews, and articles.	distrowatch.com
GNU	GNU Project Web server.	www.gnu.org
Hardware compatibility	User-written hardware reviews for Ubuntu Linux.	www.ubuntuhcl.org
ibiblio	A large library and digital archive. Formerly Metalab; formerly Sunsite.	www.ibiblio.org www.ibiblio.org/pub/linux www.ibiblio.org/pub/historic-linux
Linux Standard Base (LSB)	A group dedicated to standardizing Linux.	www.linuxfoundation.org/en/LSB

Table B-2 Useful Linux sites (continued)

Site	About the site	URL
Sobell	The author's home page contains useful links, errata for this book, code for many of the examples in this book, and answers to selected exercises.	www.sobell.com
USENIX	A large, well-established UNIX group. This site has many links, including a list of conferences.	www.usenix.org
X.Org	The X Window System home.	www.x.org

LINUX NEWSGROUPS

One of the best ways of getting specific information is through a newsgroup (refer to "Usenet" on page 391). You can often find the answer to a question by reading postings to the newsgroup. Try using Google Groups (groups.google.com) to search through newsgroups to see whether the question has already been asked and answered. Or open a newsreader program and subscribe to appropriate newsgroups. If necessary, you can post a question for someone to answer. Before you do so, make sure you are posting to the correct group and that your question has not already been answered.

The newsgroup **comp.os.linux.answers** provides postings of solutions to common problems and periodic postings of the most up-to-date versions of FAQ and HOWTO documents. The **comp.os.linux.misc** newsgroup has answers to miscellaneous Linux-related questions.

MAILING LISTS

Subscribing to a mailing list (page 697) allows you to participate in an electronic discussion. With most lists, you can send and receive email dedicated to a specific topic to and from a group of users. Moderated lists do not tend to stray as much as unmoderated lists, assuming the list has a good moderator. The disadvantage of a moderated list is that some discussions may be cut off when they get interesting if the moderator deems that the discussion has gone on for too long. Mailing lists described as bulletins are strictly unidirectional: You cannot post information to these lists but can only receive periodic bulletins. If you have the subscription address for a mailing list but are not sure how to subscribe, put the word **help** in the body and/or header of email you send to the address. You will usually receive instructions via return email. Ubuntu hosts several mailing lists; go to lists.ubuntu.com for more information. You can also use a search engine to search for **mailing list linux**.

WORDS

Many dictionaries, thesauruses, and glossaries are available online. Table B-3 lists a few of them.

Table B-3   Looking up words

Site	About the site	URL
DICT.org	Multiple-database search for words	www.dict.org
Dictionary.com	Everything related to words	dictionary.reference.com
FOLDOC	The Free On-Line Dictionary of Computing	foldoc.org
GNOME Controls	Defines many GUI controls (widgets)	developer.gnome.org/projects/gup/hig/2.0/controls.html
The Jargon File	An online version of *The New Hacker's Dictionary*	www.catb.org/~esr/jargon
Merriam-Webster	English language	www.merriam-webster.com
OneLook	Multiple-site word search with a single query	www.onelook.com
Roget's Thesaurus	Thesaurus	humanities.uchicago.edu/forms_unrest/ROGET.html
Webopedia	Commercial technical dictionary	www.webopedia.com
Wikipedia	An open-source (user-contributed) encyclopedia project	wikipedia.org
Wordsmyth	Dictionary and thesaurus	www.wordsmyth.net
Yahoo Reference	Search multiple sources at the same time	education.yahoo.com/reference

SOFTWARE

There are many ways to learn about interesting software packages and their availability on the Internet. Table B-4 lists sites you can download software from. For security-related programs, refer to Table C-1 on page 1078. Another way to learn about software packages is through a newsgroup (page 1057).

Table B-4   Software

Site	About the site	URL
BitTorrent	BitTorrent efficiently distributes large amounts of static data	azureus.sourceforge.net help.ubuntu.com/community/BitTorrent
CVS	CVS (Concurrent Versions System) is a version control system	www.nongnu.org/cvs

Table B-4   Software (continued)

Site	About the site	URL
ddd	The ddd utility is a graphical front-end for command-line debuggers such as gdb	www.gnu.org/software/ddd
Firefox	Web browser	www.mozilla.com/firefox
Free Software Directory	Categorized, searchable lists of free software	directory.fsf.org
Freshmeat	A large index of UNIX and cross-platform software and themes	freshmeat.net
gdb	The gdb utility is a command-line debugger	www.gnu.org/software/gdb
GNOME Project	Links to all GNOME projects	www.gnome.org/projects
IceWALKERS	Categorized, searchable lists of free software	www.icewalkers.com
kdbg	The kdbg utility is a graphical user interface to gdb	freshmeat.net/projects/kdbg
Linux Software Map	A database of packages written for, ported to, or compiled for Linux	www.boutell.com/lsm
Mtools	A collection of utilities to access DOS floppy diskettes from Linux without mounting the diskettes	mtools.linux.lu
Network Calculators	Subnet mask calculator	www.subnetmask.info
NTFS driver	Driver that enables Linux to read from and write to Windows NTFS filesystems (available in the **ntfs-3g** package)	www.ntfs-3g.org
Savannah	Central point for development, distribution, and maintenance of free software	savannah.gnu.org
SourceForge	A development Web site with a large repository of open-source code and applications	sourceforge.net
strace	The strace utility is a system call trace debugging tool	http://sourceforge.net/
Thunderbird	Mail application	www.mozilla.com/thunderbird
ups	The ups utility is a graphical source-level debugger	ups.sourceforge.net

Office Suites and Word Processors

Several office suites and many word processors are available for Linux. Table B-5 lists a few of them. If you are exchanging documents with people using Windows, make sure the import from/export to MS Word functionality covers your needs.

Table B-5   Office suites and word processors

Product name	What it does	URL
AbiWord	Word processor	www.abisource.com
KOffice	Integrated suite of office applications, including the KWord word processing program	www.koffice.org
OpenOffice	A multiplatform and multilingual office suite	www.openoffice.org www.gnome.org/projects/ooo

Specifying a Terminal

Because vim, emacs, and other textual and pseudographical programs take advantage of features specific to various kinds of terminals and terminal emulators, you must tell these programs the name of the terminal you are using or the terminal your terminal emulator is emulating. Most of the time the terminal name is set for you. If the terminal name is not specified or is not specified correctly, the characters on the screen will be garbled or, when you start a program, the program will ask which type of terminal you are using.

Terminal names describe the functional characteristics of a terminal or terminal emulator to programs that require this information. Although terminal names are referred to as either Terminfo or Termcap names, the difference relates to the method each system uses to store the terminal characteristics internally—not to the manner in which you specify the name of a terminal. Terminal names that are often used with Linux terminal emulators and with graphical monitors while they are run in textual mode include **ansi**, **linux**, **vt100**, **vt102**, **vt220**, and **xterm**.

When you are running a terminal emulator, you can specify the type of terminal you want to emulate. Set the emulator to either **vt100** or **vt220**, and set **TERM** to the same value.

When you log in, you may be prompted to identify the type of terminal you are using:

```
TERM = (vt100)
```

You can respond to this prompt in one of two ways. First you can press RETURN to set your terminal type to the name in parentheses. If that name does not describe the terminal you are using, you can enter the correct name and then press RETURN.

```
TERM = (vt100) ansi
```

You may also receive the following prompt:

```
TERM = (unknown)
```

This prompt indicates that the system does not know which type of terminal you are using. If you plan to run programs that require this information, enter the name of the terminal or terminal emulator you are using before you press RETURN.

TERM If you do not receive a prompt, you can give the following command to display the value of the **TERM** variable and check whether the terminal type has been set:

```
$ echo $TERM
```

If the system responds with the wrong name, a blank line, or an error message, set or change the terminal name. From the Bourne Again Shell (bash), enter a command similar to the following to set the **TERM** variable so the system knows which type of terminal you are using:

export TERM=name

Replace *name* with the terminal name for the terminal you are using, making sure you do not put a SPACE before or after the equal sign. If you always use the same type of terminal, you can place this command in your **~/.bashrc** file (page 277), causing the shell to set the terminal type each time you log in. For example, give the following command to set your terminal name to **vt100**:

```
$ export TERM=vt100
```

LANG For some programs to display information correctly, you may need to set the **LANG** variable (page 310). Frequently you can set this variable to C. Under bash use the command

```
$ export LANG=C
```

C

SECURITY

Security is a major part of the foundation of any system that is not totally cut off from other machines and users. Some aspects of security have a place even on isolated machines. Examples of these measures include periodic system backups, BIOS or power-on passwords, and self-locking screensavers.

A system that is connected to the outside world requires other mechanisms to secure it: tools to check files (tripwire), audit tools (tiger/cops), secure access methods (kerberos/ssh), services that monitor logs and machine states (swatch/watcher), packet-filtering and routing tools (ipfwadm/iptables/firestarter), and more.

System security has many dimensions. The security of a system as a whole depends on the security of individual components, such as email, files, network, login, and remote access policies, as well as the physical security of the host itself. These dimensions frequently overlap, and their borders are not always static or clear. For instance, email security is affected by the security of both files and the network. If the medium (the network) over which you send and receive your email is not secure, then you must take extra steps to ensure the security of your messages. If you save your secure email in a file on the local system, then you rely on the filesystem and host access policies for file security. A failure in any one of these areas can start a domino effect, diminishing reliability and integrity in other areas and potentially compromising system security as a whole.

This short appendix cannot cover all facets of system security in depth, but provides an overview of the complexity of setting up and maintaining a secure system. This appendix offers some specifics, concepts, guidelines to consider, and many pointers to security resources (Table C-1 on page 1078).

Other sources of system security information

security Depending on how important system security is to you, you may want to purchase one or more books dedicated to system security, visit some of the Internet sites that are dedicated to security, or hire someone who is an expert in the field.

Do not rely on this appendix as your sole source of information on system security.

ENCRYPTION

One of the building blocks of security is *encryption,* which provides a means of scrambling data for secure transmission to other parties. In cryptographic terms, the data or message to be encrypted is referred to as *plaintext,* and the resulting encrypted block of text as *ciphertext.* Processes exist for converting plaintext into ciphertext through the use of *keys,* which are essentially random numbers of a specified length used to *lock* and *unlock* data. This conversion is achieved by applying the keys to the plaintext according to a set of mathematical instructions, referred to as the *encryption algorithm.*

Developing and analyzing strong encryption software is extremely difficult. Many nuances exist, many standards govern encryption algorithms, and a background in mathematics is requisite. Also, unless an algorithm has undergone public scrutiny for a significant period of time, it is generally not considered secure; it is often impossible to know that an algorithm is completely secure but possible to know that one is not secure. Ultimately time is the best test of any algorithm. Also, a solid algorithm does not guarantee an effective encryption mechanism because the fallibility of an encryption scheme frequently arises from problems with its implementation and distribution.

An encryption algorithm uses a key that is a certain number of bits long. Each bit added to the length of a key effectively doubles the *key space* (the number of combinations allowed by the number of bits in the key—2 to the power of the length of the key in bits[1]) and means it will take twice as long for an attacker to decrypt a message (assuming the scheme lacks any inherent weaknesses or vulnerabilities to

---

1. A 2-bit key would have a key space of 4 (2^2), a 3-bit key would have a key space of 8 (2^3), and so on.

exploit). However, it is a mistake to compare algorithms based only on the number of bits used. In some cases an algorithm that uses a 64-bit key can be more secure than an algorithm that uses a 128-bit key.

The two primary classifications of encryption schemes are *public key encryption* and *symmetric key encryption.* Public key encryption, also called *asymmetric encryption,* uses two keys: a public key and a private key. These keys are uniquely associated with a specific user. Public key encryption schemes are used mostly to exchange keys and signatures. Symmetric key encryption, also called *symmetric encryption* or *secret key encryption,* uses one key that you and the person you are communicating with (hereafter referred to as your *friend*) share as a secret. Symmetric key encryption is typically used to encrypt large amounts of data. Public key algorithm keys typically have a length of 512 bits to 2,048 bits, whereas symmetric key algorithms use keys in the range of 64 bits to 512 bits.

When you are choosing an encryption scheme, realize that security comes at a price. There is usually a tradeoff between resilience of the cryptosystem and ease of administration.

The practicality of a security solution is a far greater factor in encryption, and in security in general, than most people realize. With enough time and effort, nearly every algorithm can be broken. In fact, you can often unearth the mathematical instructions for a widely used algorithm by flipping through a cryptography book, reviewing a vendor's product specifications, or performing a quick search on the Internet. The challenge is to ensure the effort required to follow the twists and turns taken by an encryption algorithm and its resulting encryption solution outweighs the worth of the information it is protecting.

How much time and money should you spend on encryption?

tip When the cost of obtaining the information exceeds the value realized by its possession, the solution is an effective one.

PUBLIC KEY ENCRYPTION

To use public key encryption, you must generate two keys: a public key and a private key. You keep the private key for yourself and give the public key to the world. In a similar manner, each of your friends will generate a pair of keys and give you their public keys. Public key encryption is marked by two distinct features:

1. When you encrypt data with someone's public key, only that person's private key can decrypt it.

2. When you encrypt data with your private key, anyone can decrypt it with your public key.

You may wonder why the second point is useful: Why would you want everyone else to be able to decrypt something you just encrypted? The answer lies in the purpose of the encryption. Although encryption changes the original message into unreadable ciphertext, its purpose is to provide a *digital signature*. If the message can be properly decrypted with your public key, *only you* could have encrypted it with your private key, proving the message is authentic. Combining these two modes of operation yields privacy and authenticity. You can sign a message with your private key so it can be verified as authentic, and then you can encrypt it with your friend's public key so that only your friend can decrypt it.

Public key encryption has three major shortcomings:

1. Public key encryption algorithms are generally much slower than symmetric key algorithms and usually require a much larger key size and a way to generate large prime numbers to use as components of the key, making them more resource intensive.

2. The private key must be stored securely and its integrity safeguarded. If a person's private key is obtained by another party, that party can encrypt, decrypt, and sign messages while impersonating the original owner of the key. If the private key is lost or becomes corrupted, any messages previously encrypted with it are also lost, and a new keypair must be generated.

3. It is difficult to authenticate the origin of a key—that is, to prove whom it originally came from. This so-called key-distribution problem is the raison d'être for such companies as VeriSign (www.verisign.com).

Algorithms such as RSA, Diffie-Hellman, and El-Gamal implement public key encryption methodology. Today a 512-bit key is considered barely adequate for RSA encryption and offers marginal protection; 1,024-bit keys are expected to hold off determined attackers for several more years. Keys that are 2,048 bits long are now becoming commonplace and are rated as *espionage strength*. A mathematical paper published in late 2001 and reexamined in spring 2002 describes how a machine can be built—for a very large sum of money—that could break 1,024-bit RSA encryption in seconds to minutes (this point is debated in an article at www.schneier.com/crypto-gram-0203.html#6). Although the cost of such a machine exceeds the resources available to most individuals and smaller corporations, it is well within the reach of large corporations and governments.

SYMMETRIC KEY ENCRYPTION

Symmetric key encryption is generally fast and simple to deploy. First you and your friend agree on which algorithm to use and a key that you will share. Then either of you can decrypt or encrypt a file with the same key. Behind the scenes, symmetric key encryption algorithms are most often implemented as a network of black boxes, which can involve hardware components, software, or a combination of the two. Each box imposes a reversible transformation on the plaintext and passes it to the next box, where another reversible transformation further alters the data. The security of a symmetric key algorithm relies on the difficulty of determining which boxes were used and the number of times the data was fed through the set of boxes. A good algorithm will cycle the plaintext through a given set of boxes many times before yielding the result, and there will be no obvious mapping from plaintext to ciphertext.

The disadvantage of symmetric key encryption is that it depends heavily on the availability of a secure channel through which to send the key to your friend. For example, you would not use email to send your key; if your email is intercepted, a third party is in possession of your secret key, and your encryption is useless. You could relay the key over the phone, but your call could be intercepted if your phone were tapped or someone overheard your conversation.

Common implementations of symmetric key algorithms include DES (Data Encryption Standard), 3-DES (triple DES), IDEA, RC5, Blowfish, and AES (Advanced Encryption Standard). AES is the new Federal Information Processing Standard (FIPS-197) algorithm endorsed for governmental use and has been selected to replace DES as the de facto encryption algorithm. AES uses the Rijndael algorithm, chosen after a thorough evaluation of 15 candidate algorithms by the cryptographic research community.

None of the aforementioned algorithms has undergone more scrutiny than DES, which has been in use since the late 1970s. However, the use of DES has drawbacks and it is no longer considered secure because the weakness of its 56-bit key makes it unreasonably easy to break. Given the advances in computing power and speed since DES was developed, the small size of this algorithm's key renders it inadequate for operations requiring more than basic security for a relatively short period of time. For a few thousand dollars, you can link off-the-shelf computer systems so they can crack DES keys in a few hours.

The 3-DES application of DES is intended to combat its degenerating resilience by running the encryption three times; it is projected to be secure for years to come. DES is probably sufficient for such tasks as sending email to a friend when you need it to be confidential or secure for only a few days (for example, to send a notice of a meeting that will take place in a few hours). It is unlikely anyone is sufficiently interested in your email to invest the time and money to decrypt it. Because of 3-DES's wide availability and ease of use, it is advisable to use it instead of DES.

ENCRYPTION IMPLEMENTATION

Most of today's commercial software packages use both public and symmetric key encryption algorithms, taking advantage of the strengths of each and avoiding their weaknesses. The public key algorithm is used first, as a means of negotiating a randomly generated secret key and providing for message authenticity. Then a secret key algorithm, such as 3-DES, IDEA, AES, or Blowfish, encrypts and decrypts the data on both ends for speed. Finally a hash algorithm, such as DSA (Digital Signature Algorithm), generates a message digest that provides a signature that can alert you to tampering. The digest is digitally signed with the sender's private key.

GnuPG/PGP

The most popular personal encryption packages available today are GnuPG (GNU Privacy Guard, also called GPG; www.gnupg.org) and PGP (Pretty Good Privacy; www.pgp.com). GNU Privacy Guard was designed as a free replacement for PGP, a security tool that made its debut during the early 1990s. Phil Zimmerman developed PGP as a Public Key Infrastructure (PKI), featuring a convenient interface, ease of use and management, and the security of digital certificates. One critical characteristic set PGP apart from the majority of cryptosystems then available: PGP functions entirely without certification authorities (CAs). Until the introduction of PGP, PKI implementations were built around the concept of CAs and centralized key management controls.

Both PGP and GnuPG rely on the notion of a web of trust:[2] If you trust someone and that person trusts someone else, the person you trust can provide an introduction to the third party. When you trust someone, you perform an operation called *key signing*. By signing someone else's key, you verify that the person's public key is authentic and safe for you to use to send email. When you sign a key, you are asked whether you trust this person to introduce other keys to you. It is common practice to assign this trust based on several criteria, including your knowledge of a person's character or a lasting professional relationship with the person. The best practice is to sign someone's key only after you have met face to face to avert any chance of a man-in-the-middle[3] scenario. The disadvantage of this scheme is the lack of a central registry for associating with people you do not already know.

PGP is available without cost for personal use but its deployment in a commercial environment requires the purchase of a license. This was not always the case: Soon after its introduction, PGP was available on many bulletin board systems, and users could implement it in any manner they chose. PGP rapidly gained popularity in the networking community, which capitalized on its encryption and key management capabilities for secure transmission of email.

After a time, attention turned to RSA and IDEA, the two robust cryptographic algorithms that form an integral part of PGP's code. These algorithms are privately owned. The wide distribution of and growing user base for PGP sparked battles over patent violation and licenses, resulting in the eventual restriction of PGP's use.

Enter GnuPG, which supports most of the features and implementations made available by PGP and complies with the OpenPGP Message Format standard. Because GnuPG does not use the patented IDEA algorithm but rather relies on BUGS (Big and Useful Great Security; www.gnu.org/directory/bugs.html), you can use it almost without restriction: It is released under the GNU GPL (refer to "The Code Is Free" on page 6). PGP and GnuPG are considered to be interchangeable

---

2. For more information, see the section of *The GNU Privacy Handbook* (www.gnupg.org/documentation) titled "Validating Other Keys on Your Public Keyring."

3. Man-in-the-middle: If Max and Zach try to carry on a secure email exchange over a network, Max first sends Zach his public key. However, suppose Mr. X sits between Max and Zach on the network and intercepts Max's public key. Mr. X then sends *his* public key to Zach. Zach then sends his public key to Max, but once again Mr. X intercepts it and substitutes *his* public key and sends that to Max. Without some kind of active protection (a piece of shared information), Mr. X, the *man-in-the-middle,* can decrypt all traffic between Max and Zach, reencrypt it, and send it on to the other party.

and interoperable. The command sequences for and internal workings of these two tools are very similar.

The GnuPG system includes the gpg program

tip   GnuPG is frequently referred to as gpg, but gpg is actually the main program for the GnuPG system.

GNU offers a good introduction to privacy, *The GNU Privacy Handbook,* which is available in several languages and listed at www.gnupg.org (click **Documentation**⇨ **Guides**). Click **Documentation**⇨**HOWTOs** on the same Web page to view the *GNU Privacy Guard (GnuPG) Mini Howto,* which steps through the setup and use of gpg. And, of course, there is a gpg info page.

In addition to providing encryption, gpg is useful for authentication. For example, you can use it to verify that the person who signed a piece of email is the person who sent it.

FILE SECURITY

From an end user's perspective, file security is one of the most critical areas of security. Some file security is built into Linux: chmod (page 202) gives you basic security control. ACLs (Access Control Lists) allow more fine-grained control of file access permissions. ACLs are part of Solaris, Windows NT/2000/XP, VAX/VMS, and mainframe operating systems. Ubuntu Linux supports ACLs (page 207). Even these tools are insufficient, however, when your account is compromised (for example, by someone watching your fingers on the keyboard as you type your password). To provide maximum file security, you must encrypt your files. Then even someone who knows your password cannot read your files. (Of course, if someone knows your key, that person can decrypt your files if she can get to them.)

EMAIL SECURITY

Email security overlaps file security and, as discussed later, network security. GnuPG is the tool most frequently used for email security, although you can also use PGP. PEM (Privacy Enhanced Mail) is a standard rather than an algorithm and is used less frequently.

MTAS (MAIL TRANSFER AGENTS)

An increasingly commonplace MTA is STARTTLS (Start Transport Layer Security; www.sendmail.org/~ca/email/starttls.html). TLS itself usually refers to SSL (Secure Sockets Layer) and has become the de facto method for encrypting TCP/IP traffic on the Internet. The **sendmail** and **exim4** daemons can be built to support STARTTLS, and much documentation exists on how to do so. STARTTLS enhancements are also available for Qmail (page 679) and Postfix (page 679) and other popular MTAs. It is important to recognize that this capability provides encryption between two mail servers but not necessarily between your machine and the mail server. Also, the advantages of using TLS are negated if the email must pass through a relay that does not support TLS.

MUAs (Mail User Agents)

Many popular mail user agents, such as mutt, elm, Thunderbird, and emacs, include the ability to use PGP or GnuPG for encryption. Evolution, the default Ubuntu Linux MUA, has built-in GnuPG support. This approach has become the default way to exchange email securely.

Network Security

Network security is a vital component for ensuring the security of a computing site. However, without the right infrastructure, providing network security is difficult, if not impossible. For example, if you run a shared network topology,[4] such as Ethernet, and have in public locations jacks that allow anyone to plug in to the network at will, how can you prevent someone from plugging in a machine and capturing all the *packets* (page 1123) that traverse the network?[5] You cannot—so you have a potential security hole. Another common security hole relates to the use of telnet for logins. Because telnet sends and receives cleartext, anyone "listening in" on the line can easily capture usernames and passwords, compromising security.

Do not allow any unauthenticated PC (any PC that does not require users to supply a local name and password) on a network. With a Windows 9x PC, any user on the network is effectively working with **root** privileges for the following reasons:

- A PC does not recognize the concept of **root** privileges. All users, by default, have access to and can watch the network, capture packets, and send packets.

- On UNIX/Linux, only a user working with **root** privileges can put the network interface in promiscuous mode and collect packets. On UNIX and Linux, ports numbered less than 1024[6] are privileged—that is, normal user protocols cannot bind to these ports. This is an important but regrettable means of security for some protocols, such as NIS, NFS, RSH, and

---

4. Shared network topology: A network in which each packet may be seen by machines other than its destination. "Shared" means that the 100 megabits per second bandwidth is shared by all users.

5. Do not make the mistake of assuming that you have security just because you have a switch. Switches are designed to allocate bandwidth, not to guarantee security.

6. The term *port* has many meanings; here it is a number assigned to a program. This number links incoming data with a specific service. For example, port 21 is used by FTP traffic, and port 23 is used by TELNET.

LPD. Normally a data switch on a LAN automatically protects machines from people snooping on the network for data. In high-load situations, switches have been known to behave unpredictably, directing packets to the wrong ports. Certain programs can overload the switch tables that hold information about which machine is on which port. When these tables are overloaded, the switch becomes a repeater and broadcasts all packets to all ports. The attacker on the same switch as you can potentially see the traffic your system sends and receives.

NETWORK SECURITY SOLUTIONS

One solution to shared-network problems is to encrypt messages that travel between machines. IPSec (Internet Protocol Security Protocol) provides an appropriate technology. IPSec is commonly used to establish a secure point-to-point virtual network (*VPN*, page 1140) that allows two hosts to communicate securely over an unsecure channel, such as the Internet. This protocol provides integrity, confidentiality, authenticity, and flexibility of implementation that supports multiple vendors.

IPSec is an amalgamation of protocols (IPSec = AH + ESP + IPComp + IKE):

- **Authentication Header (AH)**—A cryptographically secure, irreversible *checksum* (page 1100) for an entire packet. AH guarantees that the packet is authentic.

- **Encapsulating Security Payload (ESP)**—Encrypts a packet to make the data unreadable.

- **IP Payload Compression (IPComp)**—Compresses a packet. Encryption can increase the size of a packet, and IPComp counteracts this increase in size.

- **Internet Key Exchange (IKE)**—Provides a way for the endpoints to negotiate a common key securely. For AH to work, both ends of the exchange must use the same key to prevent a "man-in-the-middle" (see footnote 3 on page 1068) from spoofing the connection.

While IPSec is an optional part of IPv4, IPv6 (page 371) mandates its use. It may be quite some time before IPv6 is widely implemented, however. See page 1088 for information about the implementation of IPSec in the Linux 2.6 kernel.

NETWORK SECURITY GUIDELINES

Some general guidelines for establishing and maintaining a secure system follow. This list is not complete but rather is meant as a guide.

- Fiberoptic cable is more secure than copper cable. Copper is subject to both active and passive eavesdropping. With access to copper cable, all a data thief needs to monitor your network traffic is a passive device for measuring magnetic fields. In contrast, it is much more difficult to tap a fiberoptic cable without interrupting the signal. Sites requiring top security keep fiberoptic cable in pressurized conduits, where a change in pressure signals that the physical security of the cable has been breached.

- Avoid leaving unused ports available in public areas. If a malicious user can plug a laptop into the network without being detected, you are at risk of a serious security problem. Network drops that will remain unused for extended periods should be disabled at the switch, preventing them from accepting or passing network traffic.

- Many network switches have provisions for binding a hardware address to a port for enhanced security. If someone unplugs one machine and plugs in another machine to capture traffic, chances are that the second machine will have a different hardware address. When it detects a device with a different hardware address, the switch can disable the port. Even this solution is no guarantee, however, as some programs enable you to change or mask the hardware address of a network interface.

Install a small kernel and run only the programs you need

security   Linux systems contain a huge number of programs that, although useful, significantly reduce the security of the host. Install the smallest operating system kernel that meets your needs. For Web and FTP servers, install only the needed components and do not install a graphical interface. Users may require additional packages.

- Do not allow NFS or NIS access outside the local network. Otherwise, it is a simple matter for a malicious user to steal the password map. Default NFS security is marginal to nonexistent (a common joke is that NFS stands for No File Security or Nightmare File System) so such access should not be allowed outside your network to machines that you do not trust. Experimental versions of NFS for Linux that support much better authentication algorithms are now becoming available. Use IPSec, NFSv4 (which includes improved authentication), or firewalls to provide access outside of your domain.

- Support for VPN configuration is often built into new firewalls or provided as a separate product, enabling your system to join securely with the systems of your customers or partners. If you must allow business partners, contractors, or other outside parties to access local files, consider using a secure filesystem, such as NFS with *Kerberos* (page 1116), secure NFS (encrypts authentication, not traffic), NFS over a VPN such as IPSec, or **cfs** (cryptographic filesystem).

- Specify **/usr** as readonly (**ro**) in **/etc/fstab**. Following is an example of such a configuration:

```
/dev/hda6      /usr      ext2      ro    0    0
```

This approach may make your machine difficult to update, so use this tactic with care.

- Mount filesystems other than **/** and **/usr nosuid** to prevent setuid programs from executing on this filesystem. For example:

```
/dev/hda4      /var       ext3    nosuid   0   0
/dev/hda5      /usr/local ext3    nosuid   0   0
```

- Use a barrier or firewall product between the local network and the Internet. Several valuable mailing lists cover firewalls, including the **comp.security.firewalls** newsgroup and the free firewalls Web site (www.freefire.org). Ubuntu Linux includes firestarter (page 824), ufw (page 834), and iptables (page 836), which allow you to implement a firewall.

HOST SECURITY

Your host must be secure. Simple security steps include preventing remote logins and leaving the **/etc/hosts.equiv** and individual users' **~/.rhosts** files empty (or not having them at all). Complex security steps include installing IPSec for VPNs between hosts. Many other security measures, some of which are discussed in this section, fall somewhere between these extremes. See Table C-1 on page 1078 for relevant URLs.

- Although potentially tricky to implement and manage, intrusion detection systems (IDSs) are an excellent way to keep an eye on the integrity of a device. An IDS can warn of possible attempts to subvert security on the host on which it runs. The great-granddaddy of intrusion detection systems is tripwire. This host-based system checks modification times and integrity of files by using strong algorithms (cryptographic checksums or signatures) that can detect even the most minor modifications. A commercial version of tripwire is also available. Another commercial IDS is DragonSquire. Other free, popular, and flexible IDSs include samhain and AIDE. The last two IDSs offer even more features and means of remaining invisible to users than tripwire does. Commercial IDSs that are popular in enterprise environments include Cisco Secure IDS (formerly NetRanger), Enterasys Dragon, and ISS RealSecure.

- Keep Ubuntu systems up-to-date by downloading and installing the latest updates. Use the Update Notifier to update the system regularly (page 99). You can set the system up to automatically install security updates using the Software Sources window, Updates tab (page 116).

- Complementing host-based IDSs are network-based IDSs. The latter programs monitor the network and nodes on the network and report suspicious occurrences (attack signatures) via user-defined alerts. These signatures can be matched based on known worms, overflow attacks against programs, or unauthorized scans of network ports. Such programs as snort, klaxon, and NFR are used in this capacity. Commercial programs, such as DragonSentry, also fill this role.

- Provided with Ubuntu Linux is PAM, which allows you to set up different methods and levels of authentication in many ways (page 461).

- Process accounting—a good supplement to system security—can provide a continuous record of user actions on your system. See the accton man page (part of the **acct** package) for more information.

- Emerging standards for such things as Role-Based Access Control (RBAC) allow tighter delegation of privileges along defined organizational boundaries. You can delegate a role or roles to each user as appropriate to the access required.

- General mailing lists and archives are useful repositories of security information, statistics, and papers. The most useful are the bugtraq mailing list and CERT.[7] The bugtraq site and email service offer immediate notifications about specific vulnerabilities, whereas CERT provides notice of widespread vulnerabilities and useful techniques to fix them, plus links to vendor patches.

- The **syslogd** facility can direct messages from system daemons to specific files such as those in **/var/log**. On larger groups of systems, you can send all important **syslogd** information to a secure host, where that host's only function is to store **syslogd** data so it cannot be tampered with. See page 389 and the **syslogd** man page for more information.

LOGIN SECURITY

Without a secure host, good login security cannot add much protection. Table C-1 on page 1078 lists some of the best login security tools, including replacement daemons for **telnetd**, **rlogind**, and **rshd**. Many sites use ssh, which comes as both freeware and a commercially supported package that works on UNIX/Linux, Windows, and Macintosh platforms.

The PAM facility (page 461) allows you to set up multiple authentication methods for users in series or in parallel. In-series PAM requires multiple methods of authentication for a user. In-parallel PAM uses any one of a number of methods for authentication.

Although not the most popular choice, you can configure a system to take advantage of one-time passwords. S/Key is the original implementation of one-time passwords by Bellcore. OPIE (one-time passwords in everything), which was developed by the U.S. Naval Research Labs, is an improvement over the original Bellcore system. In one permutation of one-time passwords, the user gets a piece of paper listing a set of one-time passwords. Each time a user logs in, she enters a password from the piece of paper. Once used, a password becomes obsolete, and the next password

---

7. CERT is slow but useful as a medium for coordination between sites. It acts as a tracking agency to document the spread of security problems.

in the list is the only one that will work. Even if a malicious user compromises the network and sees your password, this information will be of no use because the password can be used only once. This setup makes it very difficult for someone to log in as you but does nothing to protect the data you type at the keyboard. One-time passwords is a good solution if you are at a site where no encrypted login is available. A truly secure (or paranoid) site will combine one-time passwords and encrypted logins.

Another type of secure login that is becoming more common is facilitated by a token or a *smartcard*. Smartcards are credit-card-like devices that use a challenge–response method of authentication. Smartcard and token authentication rely on something you have (the card) and something you know (a pass phrase, user ID, or PIN). For example, you might enter your username in response to the login prompt and get a password prompt. You would then enter your PIN and the number displayed on the access token. The token has a unique serial number that is stored in a database on the authentication server. The token and the authentication server use this serial number as a means of computing a challenge every 30 to 60 seconds. If the PIN and token number you enter match what they should be as computed by the access server, you are granted access to the system.

REMOTE ACCESS SECURITY

Issues and solutions surrounding remote access security overlap with those pertaining to login and host security. Local logins may be secure with simply a username and password, whereas remote logins (and all remote access) should be made more secure. Many break-ins can be traced back to reusable passwords. It is a good idea to use an encrypted authentication client, such as ssh or kerberos. You can also use smartcards for remote access authentication.

Modem pools can also be an entry point into a system. Most people are aware of how easy it is to monitor a network line but they may take for granted the security of the public switched telephone network (PSTN, also known as POTS—plain old telephone service). You may want to set up an encrypted channel after dialing in to a modem pool. One way to do so is by running ssh over PPP.

There are ways to implement stringent modem authentication policies so unauthorized users cannot use local modems. The most common techniques are PAP (Password Authentication Protocol), CHAP (Challenge Handshake Authentication Protocol), and Radius. PAP and CHAP are relatively weak as compared to Radius, so the latter has rapidly gained in popularity. Cisco also provides a method of authentication called TACACS/TACACS+ (Terminal Access Controller Access Control System).

One or more of these authentication techniques are available in a RAS (remote access server—in a network, a computer that provides network access to remote users via modem). Before purchasing a RAS, check what kind of security it provides and decide whether that level of security meets your needs.

Two other techniques for remote access security can be built into a modem (or RAS if it has integrated modems). One is callback: After you dial in, you get a password prompt. Once you type your password, the modem hangs up and calls you back at a phone number it has stored internally. Unfortunately this technique is not fool-proof. Some modems have a built-in callback table that holds about ten entries, so this strategy works for small sites with only a few modems. If you use more modems, the RAS software must provide the callback.

The second technique is to use CLID (caller line ID) or ANI (automatic number identi-fication) to decide whether to answer the call. Depending on your wiring and the local phone company, you may or may not be able to use ANI. ANI information is provided before the call, whereas CLID information is provided in tandem with the call.

VIRUSES AND WORMS

Examples of UNIX/Linux viruses include the Bliss virus/worm released in 1997 and the RST.b virus discovered in December 2001. Both are discussed in detail in arti-cles on the Web. Viruses spread through systems by infecting executable files. In the cases of Bliss and RST.b, the Linux native executable format, ELF, was used as a propagation vector.

Just after 5 PM on November 2, 1988, Robert T. Morris, Jr., a graduate student at Cornell University, released the first big virus onto the Internet. Called an Internet worm, this virus was designed to propagate copies of itself over many machines on the Internet. The worm was a piece of code that exploited four vulnerabilities, including one in finger, to force a buffer to overflow on a system. Once the buffer overflowed, the code was able to get a shell and then recompile itself on the remote machine. The worm spread around the Internet very quickly and was not disabled, despite many people's efforts, for 36 hours.

The chief characteristic of any worm is propagation over a public network, such as the Internet. A virus propagates by infecting executables on the machine, whereas a worm tends to prefer exploiting known security holes in network servers to gain **root** access and then tries to infect other machines in the same way.

UNIX/Linux file permissions help to inoculate systems against many viruses. Win-dows NT is resistant for similar reasons. You can easily protect the local system against many viruses and worms by keeping its system patches up-to-date, not exe-cuting untrusted binaries from the Internet, limiting **PATH** (page 303) to include only necessary system directories, and doing as little as possible while working with **root** privileges. You can prevent a disaster in case a virus strikes by backing up your system frequently.

PHYSICAL SECURITY

Often overlooked as a defense against intrusion, physical security covers access to the computer itself and to the console or terminal attached to the machine. If the machine is unprotected in an unlocked room, there is very little hope for physical security. (A simple example of physical vulnerability is someone walking into the room where the computer is, removing the hard drive from the computer, taking it home, and analyzing it.) You can take certain steps to improve the physical security of a computer.

- Keep servers in a locked room with limited access. A key, a combination, or a swipe card should be required to gain access. Protect windows as well as doors. Maintain a single point of entry. (Safety codes may require multiple exits, but only one must be an entry.)

- For public machines, use a security system, such as a fiberoptic security system, that can secure a lab full of machines. With such a system, you run a fiberoptic cable through each machine such that the machine cannot be removed (or opened) without cutting the cable. When the cable is cut, an alarm goes off. Some machines—for example, PCs with plastic cases—are much more difficult to secure than others. Although it is not a perfect solution, a fiberoptic security system may improve local security enough to persuade a would-be thief to go somewhere else.

- Most modern PCs have a BIOS password. You can set the order in which a PC searches for a boot device, preventing the PC from being booted from a floppy disk or CD/DVD. Some BIOSs can prevent the machine from booting altogether without a proper password. The password protects the BIOS from unauthorized modification. Beware, however: Many BIOSs have well-known *back doors* (page 1096). Research this issue if the BIOS password is an important feature for you. In addition, you can blank the BIOS password by setting the clear-CMOS jumper on a PC motherboard; if you are relying on a BIOS password, lock the case.

- Run only fiberoptic cable between buildings. This strategy is not only more secure but also safer in the event of lightning strikes and is required by many commercial building codes.

- Maintain logs of who goes in and out of secure areas. Sign-in/out sheets are useful only if everyone uses them. Sometimes a guard is warranted. Often a simple proximity badge or smartcard can tell when anyone has entered or left an area and keep logs of these events, although these can be expensive to procure and install.

- Anyone who has access to the physical hardware has the keys to the palace. Someone with direct access to a computer system can do such things as swap components and insert boot media, all of which are security threats.

- Avoid having activated, unused network jacks in public places. Such jacks provide unnecessary risk.

- Many modern switches can lock a particular switch port so it accepts only traffic from an NIC (network interface card) with a particular hardware address and shuts down the port if another address is seen. However, commonly available programs can enable someone to reset this address.

- Make periodic security sweeps. Check doors for proper locking. If you must have windows, make sure they are locked or are permanently sealed.

- Waste receptacles are often a source of information for intruders. Have policies for containment and disposal of sensitive documents.

- Use a UPS (uninterruptable power supply). Without a clean source of power, your system is vulnerable to corruption.

SECURITY RESOURCES

Many free and commercial programs can enhance system security. Some of these are listed in Table C-1. Many of these sites have links to other, interesting sites that are worth looking at.

Table C-1   Security resources

Tool	What it does	Where to get it
AIDE	Advanced Intrusion Detection Environment. Similar to tripwire with extensible verification algorithms.	sourceforge.net/projects/aide
bugtraq	A moderated mailing list for the announcement and detailed discussion of all aspects of computer security vulnerabilities.	www.securityfocus.com/archive/1
CERT	Computer Emergency Response Team. A repository of papers and data about major security events and a list of security tools.	www.cert.org
chkrootkit	Checks for signs of a rootkit indicating that the machine has been compromised.	www.chkrootkit.org
dsniff	Sniffing and network audit tool suite. Free.	monkey.org/~dugsong/dsniff
freefire	Supplies free security solutions and supports developers of free security solutions.	www.freefire.org

Table C-1   Security resources (continued)

Tool	What it does	Where to get it
fwtk	Firewall toolkit. A set of proxies that can be used to construct a firewall.	www.fwtk.org
GIAC	A security certification and training Web site.	www.giac.org
hping	Multipurpose network auditing and packet analysis tool. Free.	www.hping.org
ISC^2	Educates and certifies industry professionals and practitioners under an international standard.	www.isc2.org
John	John the Ripper: a fast, flexible, weak password detector.	www.openwall.com/john
Kerberos	Complete, secure network authentication system.	web.mit.edu/kerberos/www
L6	Verifies file integrity; similar to **tripwire** (French and English).	www.pgci.ca/l6.html
Launchpad	Tracks Ubuntu Linux bugs.	bugs.launchpad.net/ubuntu
LIDS	Intrusion detection and active defense system.	www.lids.org
LinuxSecurity.com	A solid news site dedicated to Linux security issues.	www.linuxsecurity.com
LWN.net	Security alert database for all major Linux distributions.	lwn.net/Alerts
Microsoft Security	Microsoft security information.	www.microsoft.com/security
nessus	A plugin-based remote security scanner that can perform more than 370 security checks. Free.	www.nessus.org
netcat	Explores, tests, and diagnoses networks.	freshmeat.net/projects/netcat
nmap	Scans hosts to see which ports are available. It can perform stealth scans, determine operating system type, find open ports, and more.	nmap.org

Table C-1   Security resources (continued)

Tool	What it does	Where to get it
RBAC	Role-Based Access Control. Assigns roles and privileges associated with the roles.	csrc.nist.gov/rbac
SAINT	Security Administrator's Integrated Network Tool. Assesses and analyzes network vulnerabilities. This tool follows satan.	www.saintcorporation.com
samhain	A file integrity checker. Has a GUI configurator, client/server capability, and real-time reporting capability.	www.la-samhna.de
SANS	Security training and certification.	www.sans.org
SARA	The Security Auditor's Research Assistant security analysis tool.	www-arc.com/sara
Schneier, Bruce	Security visionary.	www.schneier.com
Secunia	Monitors a broad spectrum of vulnerabilities.	secunia.com
SecurityFocus	Home for security tools, mail lists, libraries, and cogent analysis.	www.securityfocus.com
snort	A flexible IDS.	www.snort.org
srp	Secure Remote Password. Upgrades common protocols, such as TELNET and FTP, to use secure password exchange.	srp.stanford.edu
ssh	A secure rsh, ftp, and rlogin replacement with encrypted sessions and other options. Supplied with Ubuntu Linux.	openssh.org www.ssh.com
swatch	A Perl-based log parser and analyzer.	swatch.sourceforge.net
Treachery	A collection of tools for security and auditing.	www.treachery.net/tools
tripwire	Checks for possible signs of intruder activity. Supplied with Ubuntu Linux.	www.tripwire.com
wireshark	Network protocol analyzer. Free.	www.wireshark.org

APPENDIX SUMMARY

Security is inversely proportional to usability. There must be a balance between users' requirements to get their work done and the amount of security that is implemented. It is often unnecessary to provide top security for a small business with only a few employees. By contrast, if you work for a government military contractor, you are bound to have extreme security constraints and an official audit policy to determine whether security policies are being implemented correctly.

Review your own security requirements periodically. Several of the tools mentioned in this appendix can help you monitor a system's security measures. Tools such as **nessus, samhain**, and SAINT, for example, provide auditing mechanisms.

Some companies specialize in security and auditing. Hiring one of them to examine your site can be costly but may yield specific recommendations for areas you may have overlooked in your initial setup. When you hire someone to audit your security, recognize you may be providing both physical and **root** access to local systems. Make sure the company that you hire has a good history, has been in business for several years, and has impeccable references. Check up on the company periodically: Things change over time. Avoid the temptation to hire former system crackers as consultants. Security consultants should have an irreproachable ethical background or you will always have doubts about their intentions.

Your total security package is based on your risk assessment of local vulnerabilities. Strengthen those areas that are most important for your business. For example, many sites rely on a firewall to protect them from the Internet, whereas internal hosts may receive little or no security attention. Crackers refer to this setup as "the crunchy outside surrounding the soft chewy middle." Yet this setup is entirely sufficient to protect some sites. Perform your own risk assessment and address your needs accordingly. If need be, hire a full-time security administrator whose job it is to design and audit local security policies.

D

THE FREE SOFTWARE DEFINITION[1]

We maintain this free software definition to show clearly what must be true about a particular software program for it to be considered free software.

"Free software" is a matter of liberty, not price. To understand the concept, you should think of "free" as in "free speech," not as in "free beer."

Free software is a matter of the users' freedom to run, copy, distribute, study, change and improve the software. More precisely, it refers to four kinds of freedom, for the users of the software:

- The freedom to run the program, for any purpose (freedom 0).

---

1. This material is at www.gnu.org/philosophy/free-sw.html on the GNU Web site. Because GNU requests a verbatim copy, links remain in place (underlined). View the document on the Web to ensure you are reading the latest copy and to follow the links.

- The freedom to study how the program works, and adapt it to your needs (freedom 1). Access to the source code is a precondition for this.

- The freedom to redistribute copies so you can help your neighbor (freedom 2).

- The freedom to improve the program, and release your improvements to the public, so that the whole community benefits (freedom 3). Access to the source code is a precondition for this.

A program is free software if users have all of these freedoms. Thus, you should be free to redistribute copies, either with or without modifications, either gratis or charging a fee for distribution, to <u>anyone anywhere</u>. Being free to do these things means (among other things) that you do not have to ask or pay for permission.

You should also have the freedom to make modifications and use them privately in your own work or play, without even mentioning that they exist. If you do publish your changes, you should not be required to notify anyone in particular, or in any particular way.

The freedom to use a program means the freedom for any kind of person or organization to use it on any kind of computer system, for any kind of overall job, and without being required to communicate subsequently with the developer or any other specific entity.

The freedom to redistribute copies must include binary or executable forms of the program, as well as source code, for both modified and unmodified versions. (Distributing programs in runnable form is necessary for conveniently installable free operating systems.) It is ok if there is no way to produce a binary or executable form for a certain program (since some languages don't support that feature), but you must have the freedom to redistribute such forms should you find or develop a way to make them.

In order for the freedoms to make changes, and to publish improved versions, to be meaningful, you must have access to the source code of the program. Therefore, accessibility of source code is a necessary condition for free software.

One important way to modify a program is by merging in available free subroutines and modules. If the program's license says that you cannot merge in an existing module, such as if it requires you to be the copyright holder of any code you add, then the license is too restrictive to qualify as free.

In order for these freedoms to be real, they must be irrevocable as long as you do nothing wrong; if the developer of the software has the power to revoke the license, without your doing anything to give cause, the software is not free.

However, certain kinds of rules about the manner of distributing free software are acceptable, when they don't conflict with the central freedoms. For example, copyleft (very simply stated) is the rule that when redistributing the program, you cannot add restrictions to deny other people the central freedoms. This rule does not conflict with the central freedoms; rather it protects them.

You may have paid money to get copies of free software, or you may have obtained copies at no charge. But regardless of how you got your copies, you always have the freedom to copy and change the software, even to <u>sell copies</u>.

"Free software" does not mean "non-commercial". A free program must be available for commercial use, commercial development, and commercial distribution. Commercial development of free software is no longer unusual; such free commercial software is very important.

Rules about how to package a modified version are acceptable, if they don't substantively block your freedom to release modified versions, or your freedom to make and use modified versions privately. Rules that "if you make your version available in this way, you must make it available in that way also" can be acceptable too, on the same condition. (Note that such a rule still leaves you the choice of whether to publish your version at all.) Rules that require release of source code to the users for versions that you put into public use are also acceptable. It is also acceptable for the license to require that, if you have distributed a modified version and a previous developer asks for a copy of it, you must send one, or that you identify yourself on your modifications.

In the GNU project, we use "<u>copyleft</u>" to protect these freedoms legally for everyone. But <u>non-copylefted free software</u> also exists. We believe there are important reasons why <u>it is better to use copyleft</u>, but if your program is non-copylefted free software, we can still use it.

See <u>Categories of Free Software</u> for a description of how "free software," "copylefted software" and other categories of software relate to each other.

Sometimes government <u>export control regulations</u> and trade sanctions can constrain your freedom to distribute copies of programs internationally. Software developers do not have the power to eliminate or override these restrictions, but what they can and must do is refuse to impose them as conditions of use of the program. In this way, the restrictions will not affect activities and people outside the jurisdictions of these governments.

Most free software licenses are based on copyright, and there are limits on what kinds of requirements can be imposed through copyright. If a copyright-based license respects freedom in the ways described above, it is unlikely to have some other sort of problem that we never anticipated (though this does happen occasionally). However, some free software licenses are based on contracts, and contracts can impose a much larger range of possible restrictions. That means there are many possible ways such a license could be unacceptably restrictive and non-free.

We can't possibly list all the ways that might happen. If a contract-based license restricts the user in an unusual way that copyright-based licenses cannot, and which isn't mentioned here as legitimate, we will have to think about it, and we will probably conclude it is non-free.

When talking about free software, it is best to avoid using terms like "give away" or "for free", because those terms imply that the issue is about price, not freedom. Some common terms such as "piracy" embody opinions we hope you won't endorse. See <u>Confusing Words and Phrases that are Worth Avoiding</u> for a discussion of these terms. We also have a list of <u>translations of "free software"</u> into various languages.

Finally, note that criteria such as those stated in this free software definition require careful thought for their interpretation. To decide whether a specific software license qualifies as a free software license, we judge it based on these criteria to determine whether it fits their spirit as well as the precise words. If a license includes unconscionable restrictions, we reject it, even if we did not anticipate the issue in these criteria. Sometimes a license requirement raises an issue that calls for extensive thought, including discussions with a lawyer, before we can decide if the requirement is acceptable. When we reach a conclusion about a new issue, we often update these criteria to make it easier to see why certain licenses do or don't qualify.

If you are interested in whether a specific license qualifies as a free software license, see our list of licenses. If the license you are concerned with is not listed there, you can ask us about it by sending us email at licensing@gnu.org.

If you are contemplating writing a new license, please contact the FSF by writing to that address. The proliferation of different free software licenses means increased work for users in understanding the licenses; we may be able to help you find an existing Free Software license that meets your needs.

If that isn't possible, if you really need a new license, with our help you can ensure that the license really is a Free Software license and avoid various practical problems.

Another group has started using the term "open source" to mean something close (but not identical) to "free software". We prefer the term "free software" because, once you have heard it refers to freedom rather than price, it calls to mind freedom. The word "open" never does that.

Other Texts to Read

Translations of this page:

[Català | Chinese (Simplified) | Chinese (Traditional) | Czech | Dansk | Deutsch | English | Español | Persian/Farsi | Français | Galego | Hebrew | Hrvatski | Bahasa Indonesia | Italiano | Japanese | Korean | Magyar | Nederlands | Norsk | Polski | Português | Româna | Russian | Slovinsko | Serbian | Tagalog | Türkçe]

Return to the GNU Project home page.

Please send FSF & GNU inquiries to gnu@gnu.org. There are also other ways to contact the FSF.

Please send broken links and other corrections (or suggestions) to webmasters@gnu.org

Please see the Translations README for information on coordinating and submitting translations of this article.

- Updated: $Date: 2005/11/26 13:16:40 $ $Author: rms $

E

THE LINUX 2.6 KERNEL

The Linux 2.6 kernel was released on December 17, 2003. A major release of a Linux kernel is not an everyday occurrence: The last kernel, Linux 2.4, was released in January 2001. This appendix lists features that are new to the 2.6 kernel.

Linux kernel revisions alternate between stable and unstable versions: 2.4 was the previous stable version, so 2.5 was the development branch, which later became 2.6. For each of the major revisions, there is a series of minor revisions. Usually, minor revisions do not contain major changes, although one minor revision to the 2.4 kernel replaced the entire virtual memory subsystem, a major part of the kernel.

See www.kniggit.net/wwol26.html if you want more information on the Linux 2.6 kernel than this appendix provides.

NATIVE POSIX THREAD LIBRARY (NPTL)

Classically programs start execution at the beginning of a series of instructions and execute them in sequence. While this technique works well for simple programs running on single CPU systems, it is often better to allow a program to execute different parts of itself simultaneously in parallel. Most programs with a GUI benefit from this functionality as it can prevent the user interface from freezing while the program performs computations.

The traditional way of writing parallel code under UNIX is to execute a **fork**() system call, which creates a copy of the running program in memory and starts it executing at the same point as the original. At the point **fork**() is called, the two copies of the program are indistinguishable, except for the fact that they receive different return values from their **fork**() call. One disadvantage of this approach is that each time **fork**() is called, the system must create a complete copy of the process. This copying takes a relatively long time and causes parallel applications to use a lot of memory. (This description is not quite accurate: Copy-on-write functionality in a modern operating system copies only those parts of memory that would be different.)

A more efficient solution to this problem is to allow a single process to run multiple threads. A thread exists in the same memory space as other threads and so has a much smaller overhead than a single program running multiple processes. The disadvantage of this strategy is that multithreaded applications must be designed more carefully and thus take more time to write than multiprocessor ones. Operating systems, such as Solaris, rely heavily on threads to provide scalability to very large SMP (symmetric multiprocessing) systems. The new threading support in the Linux 2.6 kernel uses the same industry standard POSIX APIs as Solaris for implementing threads and provides high-performance processing.

IPSECURITY (IPSEC)

IPSec is a network layer protocol suite that secures Internet connections by encrypting IP packets. IPSec is an optional part of IPv4 (page 1115) and a required part of IPv6 (page 1115). See page 1071 for more information on IPSec.

Kernel integration of IPSec means that any kernel module or application can use IPSec in the same way that it would use unsecured IP.

ASYNCHRONOUS I/O (AIO)

Without AIO, when an application needs to get data from a hardware device or a network connection, it can either poll the connection until the data becomes available or spawn a thread for the connection that waits for the data. Neither of these techniques is particularly efficient.

Asynchronous I/O allows the kernel to notify an application when it has data ready to be read. This feature is most useful to large servers but can provide moderate performance gains in almost any application.

O(1) SCHEDULER

One of the responsibilities of the kernel is to make sure that each execution thread gets a reasonable amount of time on the CPU(s). The scheduling algorithm used in the Linux 2.4 kernel gradually decreased performance as more processes were added and additional CPUs were brought online, making it hard to use Linux on large SMP systems. The 2.6 scheduling algorithm runs in O(1) time, a term that indicates that a process takes the same time to run under all conditions, making Linux better able to run large numbers of processes and scale to large systems.

OPROFILE

It is often said that a program spends 90 percent of its time executing 10 percent of the code. Programmers use profiling tools to identify bottlenecks in code and target this 10 percent for optimization. OProfile is an advanced profiling tool that identifies common programming inefficiencies. Thanks to its close relationship with the kernel, OProfile is able to identify hardware-specific efficiency problems, such as cache misses, which are often not possible to identify from source code.

kksymoops

When something goes wrong in the kernel, it generates an error message called an *OOPS*. This message is an in-joke from the Linux Kernel Mailing List, where developers would start bug reports with "Oops, we've found a bug in the kernel." An OOPS provides debugging information that can help kernel developers track down the offending code or indicate that the OOPS was caused by hardware failure.

The **kksymoops** functionality provides detailed debugging information, allowing a developer to determine the line of code in the kernel that caused the OOPS. While this feature does not directly benefit the end user, it allows developers to find kernel bugs more quickly, resulting in a more stable kernel.

REVERSE MAP VIRTUAL MEMORY (RMAP VM)

Virtual memory (VM) allows each process to exist in its own memory space. Every time a process attempts to access a portion of memory, the kernel translates the memory location from an address in the process's own address space to one in real memory. The reverse map enables the kernel to perform this process in reverse: Given a location in physical memory, the kernel can determine which process owns it. The reverse map allows pages to be unallocated quickly, giving the system more free memory, fewer page faults, and less overhead when quitting a program.

HugeTLBFS: Translation Look-Aside Buffer Filesystem

The kernel allocates memory in units of pages. Virtual memory uses these pages to map between the virtual and real memory address spaces. Older versions of the Linux kernel set the size of these pages to 4 kilobytes. In cases where a lot of virtual memory is used, such as in large database servers, this small size can place a heavy load on the VM subsystem. HugeTLBFS allows for much larger pages, which significantly improves performance under heavy VM load conditions.

remap_file_pages

When retrieving data from or writing data to a file, it is common practice to map the file on disk to an area of memory. The system then translates accesses to that area of memory directly into accesses to disk.

For additional flexibility, large database systems map different parts of a file to different parts of memory. Each mapping results in an additional load on the kernel and VM subsystems. The **remap_file_pages**() system call can perform a nonuniform mapping, meaning that a file needs to be mapped only once, which significantly improves the performance of large database servers.

2.6 Network Stack Features (IGMPv3, IPv6, and Others)

The Linux 2.6 kernel includes a large number of improvements in the area of networking, including support for IPv6 (page 1115) and enhanced multicast (page 1121) support. Although these features do not immediately benefit end users, they do permit the development and deployment of network services that will not require significant modification for integration with future technologies.

INTERNET PROTOCOL VIRTUAL SERVER (IPVS)

IPVS implements transport layer switching inside the kernel for load balancing. This feature enables a single machine to distribute connections to a server farm, allowing transparent load balancing.

ACCESS CONTROL LISTS (ACLs)

The traditional UNIX permission system allows three permissions to be assigned to each file: controlling access by the owner, by a single group, and by everyone else. ACLs provide much finer-grained access control. In theory, ACLs can increase security. However, they make setting correct permissions more complicated, which may encourage administrators to establish weaker controls than they should.

4GB-4GB MEMORY SPLIT: PHYSICAL ADDRESS EXTENSION (PAE)

The 32-bit CPUs are limited in that they can address only 2^{32} bytes (4 gigabytes) of memory. With the Pentium Pro, Intel introduced a work-around to this limitation called Physical Address Extension (PAE), which permits the operating system to address up to 64 gigabytes of memory. Because they are limited to addressing 4 gigabytes each, 32-bit programs cannot access this much memory. A Linux kernel from the main tree is able to allocate up to 1 gigabyte for the kernel and 3 gigabytes for each *userspace* (page 1139) process.

SCHEDULER SUPPORT FOR HYPERTHREADED CPUs

The Linux 2.6 kernel supports Intel's HyperThreading. The 2.6 kernel treats each virtual CPU as the equivalent of a physical CPU.

BLOCK I/O (BIO) BLOCK LAYER

The 2.6 kernel includes a completely redesigned interface to drivers for block devices (page 486). While this conveys a number of benefits, it also means that these device drivers need to be rewritten and tested.

SUPPORT FOR FILESYSTEMS LARGER THAN 2 TERABYTES

The Linux 2.6 kernel includes SGI's XFS journaling filesystem, which supports filesystems of up to 9 exabytes (9×2^{60} bytes).

NEW I/O ELEVATORS

I/O elevators control how long I/O requests can be queued to allow them to be reordered for optimal device performance. The Linux 2.6 kernel includes some additional settings that allow I/O elevators to be tuned for specific high-device-load situations.

INTERACTIVE SCHEDULER RESPONSE TUNING

The new scheduler in the Linux 2.6 kernel prioritizes I/O bound processes. Because most user interface processes spend most of their time waiting for input from the user, this tuning should result in a more responsive system under high system load.

GLOSSARY

All entries marked with ^{FOLDOC} are based on definitions in the Free On-line Dictionary of Computing (www.foldoc.org), Denis Howe, editor. Used with permission.

10.0.0.0   See *private address space* on page 1126.

172.16.0.0   See *private address space* on page 1126.

192.168.0.0   See *private address space* on page 1126.

802.11   A family of specifications developed by IEEE for wireless LAN technology, including 802.11 (1–2 megabits per second), 802.11a (54 megabits per second), 802.11b (11 megabits per second), and 802.11g (54 megabits per second).

absolute pathname   A pathname that starts with the root directory (represented by /). An absolute pathname locates a file without regard to the working directory.

access   In computer jargon, a verb meaning to use, read from, or write to. To access a file means to read from or write to the file.

Access Control List   See *ACL*.

access permissions   Permission to read from, write to, or execute a file. If you have write access permission to a file (usually just called *write permission*), you can write to the file. Also *access privilege*.

ACL   Access Control List. A system that performs a function similar to file permissions but with much finer-grain control.

active window   On a desktop, the window that receives the characters you type on the keyboard. Same as *focus, desktop* (page 1109).

address mask   See *subnet mask* on page 1135.

alias   A mechanism of a shell that enables you to define new commands.

alphanumeric character   One of the characters, either uppercase or lowercase, from A to Z and 0 to 9, inclusive.

ambiguous file reference   A reference to a file that does not necessarily specify any one file but can be used to specify a group of files. The shell expands an ambiguous file reference into a list of filenames. Special characters represent single characters (?), strings of zero or more characters (*), and character classes ([]) within ambiguous file references. An ambiguous file reference is a type of *regular expression* (page 1128).

angle bracket   A left angle bracket (<) and a right angle bracket (>). The shell uses < to redirect a command's standard input to come from a file and > to redirect the standard output. The shell uses the characters << to signify the start of a Here document and >> to append output to a file.

animate   When referring to a window action, means that the action is slowed down so the user can view it. For example, when you minimize a window, it can disappear all at once (not animated) or it can slowly telescope into the panel so you can get a visual feel for what is happening (animated).

anti-aliasing	Adding gray pixels at the edge of a diagonal line to get rid of the jagged appearance and thereby make the line look smoother. Anti-aliasing sometimes makes type on a screen look better and sometimes worse; it works best on small and large fonts and is less effective on fonts from 8 to 15 points. See also *subpixel hinting* (page 1135).
API	Application program interface. The interface (calling conventions) by which an application program accesses an operating system and other services. An API is defined at the source code level and provides a level of abstraction between the application and the kernel (or other privileged utilities) to ensure the portability of the code.^{FOLDOC}
append	To add something to the end of something else. To append text to a file means to add the text to the end of the file. The shell uses **>>** to append a command's output to a file.
applet	A small program that runs within a larger program. Examples are Java applets that run in a browser and panel applets that run from a desktop panel.
archive	A file that contains a group of smaller, typically related, files. Also, to create such a file. The tar and cpio utilities can create and read archives.
argument	A number, letter, filename, or another string that gives some information to a command and is passed to the command when it is called. A command-line argument is anything on a command line following the command name that is passed to the command. An option is a kind of argument.
arithmetic expression	A group of numbers, operators, and parentheses that can be evaluated. When you evaluate an arithmetic expression, you end up with a number. The Bourne Again Shell uses the expr command to evaluate arithmetic expressions; the TC Shell uses @, and the Z Shell uses let.
array	An arrangement of elements (numbers or strings of characters) in one or more dimensions. The Bourne Again, TC, and Z Shells and mawk/gawk can store and process arrays.
ASCII	American Standard Code for Information Interchange. A code that uses seven bits to represent both graphic (letters, numbers, and punctuation) and CONTROL characters. You can represent textual information, including program source code and English text, in ASCII code. Because ASCII is a standard, it is frequently used when exchanging information between computers. See the file **/usr/pub/ascii** or give the command **man ascii** to see a list of ASCII codes.
	Extensions of the ASCII character set use eight bits. The seven-bit set is common; the eight-bit extensions are still coming into popular use. The eighth bit is sometimes referred to as the metabit.
ASCII terminal	A textual terminal. Contrast with *graphical display* (page 1110).
ASP	Application service provider. A company that provides applications over the Internet.

asynchronous event
An event that does not occur regularly or synchronously with another event. Linux system signals are asynchronous; they can occur at any time because they can be initiated by any number of nonregular events.

attachment
A file that is attached to, but is not part of, a piece of email. Attachments are frequently opened by programs (including your Internet browser) that are called by your mail program so you may not be aware that they are not an integral part of an email message.

authentication
The verification of the identity of a person or process. In a communication system, authentication verifies that a message comes from its stated source. Methods of authentication on a Linux system include the **/etc/passwd** and **/etc/shadow** files, LDAP, Kerberos 5, and SMB authentication.ᶠᴼᴸᴰᴼᶜ

automatic mounting
A way of demand mounting directories from remote hosts without having them hard configured into **/etc/fstab**. Also called *automounting*.

avoided
An object, such as a panel, that should not normally be covered by another object, such as a window.

back door
A security hole deliberately left in place by the designers or maintainers of a system. The motivation for creating such holes is not always sinister; some operating systems, for example, come out of the box with privileged accounts intended for use by field service technicians or the vendor's maintenance programmers.

Ken Thompson's 1983 Turing Award lecture to the ACM revealed the existence, in early UNIX versions, of a back door that may be the most fiendishly clever security hack of all time. The C compiler contained code that would recognize when the **login** command was being recompiled and would insert some code recognizing a password chosen by Thompson, giving him entry to the system whether or not an account had been created for him.

Normally such a back door could be removed by removing it from the source code for the compiler and recompiling the compiler. But to recompile the compiler, you have to *use* the compiler, so Thompson arranged that the compiler would *recognize when it was compiling a version of itself*. It would insert into the recompiled compiler the code to insert into the recompiled **login** the code to allow Thompson entry, and, of course, the code to recognize itself and do the whole thing again the next time around. Having done this once, he was then able to recompile the compiler from the original sources; the hack perpetuated itself invisibly, leaving the back door in place and active but with no trace in the sources.

Sometimes called a wormhole. Also *trap door*.ᶠᴼᴸᴰᴼᶜ

background process
A process that is not run in the foreground. Also called a *detached process*, a background process is initiated by a command line that ends with an ampersand (**&**). You do not have to wait for a background process to run to completion before giving the shell additional commands. If you have job control, you can move background processes to the foreground, and vice versa.

basename	The name of a file that, in contrast with a pathname, does not mention any of the directories containing the file (and therefore does not contain any slashes [/]). For example, **hosts** is the basename of **/etc/hosts**.ᶠᴼᴸᴰᴼᶜ
baud	The maximum information-carrying capacity of a communication channel in symbols (state transitions or level transitions) per second. It coincides with bits per second only for two-level modulation with no framing or stop bits. A symbol is a unique state of the communication channel, distinguishable by the receiver from all other possible states. For example, it may be one of two voltage levels on a wire for a direct digital connection, or it might be the phase or frequency of a carrier.ᶠᴼᴸᴰᴼᶜ
	Baud is often mistakenly used as a synonym for bits per second.
baud rate	Transmission speed. Usually used to measure terminal or modem speed. Common baud rates range from 110 to 38,400 baud. See *baud*.
Berkeley UNIX	One of the two major versions of the UNIX operating system. Berkeley UNIX was developed at the University of California at Berkeley by the Computer Systems Research Group and is often referred to as *BSD* (Berkeley Software Distribution).
BIND	Berkeley Internet Name Domain. An implementation of a *DNS* (page 1105) server developed and distributed by the University of California at Berkeley.
BIOS	Basic Input/Output System. On PCs, *EEPROM*-based (page 1107) system software that provides the lowest-level interface to peripheral devices and controls the first stage of the *bootstrap* (page 1098) process, which loads the operating system. The BIOS can be stored in different types of memory. The memory must be nonvolatile so that it remembers the system settings even when the system is turned off. Also BIOS ROM. Refer to page 28 for instructions on how to open the BIOS screens for maintenance.
bit	The smallest piece of information a computer can handle. A *bit* is a binary digit: either 1 or 0 (*on* or *off*).
bit depth	Same as *color depth* (page 1101).
bit-mapped display	A graphical display device in which each pixel on the screen is controlled by an underlying representation of zeros and ones.
blank character	Either a SPACE or a TAB character, also called *whitespace* (page 1140). In some contexts, NEWLINEs are considered blank characters.
block	A section of a disk or tape (usually 1,024 bytes long but shorter or longer on some systems) that is written at one time.
block device	A disk or tape drive. A block device stores information in blocks of characters. A block device is represented by a block device (block special) file. Contrast with *character device* (page 1100).
block number	Disk and tape *blocks* are numbered so that Linux can keep track of the data on the device.

blocking factor	The number of logical blocks that make up a physical block on a tape or disk. When you write 1K logical blocks to a tape with a physical block size of 30K, the blocking factor is 30.
Boolean	The type of an expression with two possible values: *true* and *false*. Also, a variable of Boolean type or a function with Boolean arguments or result. The most common Boolean functions are AND, OR, and NOT._{FOLDOC}
boot	See *bootstrap*.
boot loader	A very small program that takes its place in the *bootstrap* process that brings a computer from off or reset to a fully functional state. See "grub: The Linux Boot Loader" on page 567.
bootstrap	Derived from "Pull oneself up by one's own bootstraps," the incremental process of loading an operating system kernel into memory and starting it running without any outside assistance. Frequently shortened to *boot*.
Bourne Again Shell	bash. GNU's command interpreter for UNIX, bash is a POSIX-compliant shell with full Bourne Shell syntax and some C Shell commands built in. The Bourne Again Shell supports emacs-style command-line editing, job control, functions, and online help._{FOLDOC}
Bourne Shell	sh. This UNIX command processor was developed by Steve Bourne at AT&T Bell Laboratories.
brace	A left brace ({) and a right brace (}). Braces have special meanings to the shell.
bracket	A *square bracket* (page 1134) or an *angle bracket* (page 1094).
branch	In a tree structure, a branch connects nodes, leaves, and the root. The Linux file-system hierarchy is often conceptualized as an upside-down tree. The branches connect files and directories. In a source code control system, such as SCCS or RCS, a branch occurs when a revision is made to a file and is not included in subsequent revisions to the file.
bridge	Typically a two-port device originally used for extending networks at layer 2 (data link) of the Internet Protocol model.
broadcast	A transmission to multiple, unspecified recipients. On Ethernet a broadcast packet is a special type of multicast packet that has a special address indicating that all devices that receive it should process it. Broadcast traffic exists at several layers of the network stack, including Ethernet and IP. Broadcast traffic has one source but indeterminate destinations (all hosts on the local network).
broadcast address	The last address on a subnet (usually 255), reserved as shorthand to mean all hosts.
broadcast network	A type of network, such as Ethernet, in which any system can transmit information at any time, and all systems receive every message.

BSD   See *Berkeley UNIX* on page 1097.

buffer   An area of memory that stores data until it can be used. When you write information to a file on a disk, Linux stores the information in a disk buffer until there is enough to write to the disk or until the disk is ready to receive the information.

bug   An unwanted and unintended program property, especially one that causes the program to malfunction.FOLDOC

builtin   A command that is built into a shell. Each of the three major shells—the Bourne
(command)   Again, TC, and Z Shells—has its own set of builtins. Refer to "Builtins" on page 247.

byte   A component in the machine data hierarchy, usually larger than a bit and smaller than a word; now most often eight bits and the smallest addressable unit of storage. A byte typically holds one character.FOLDOC

C   A modern systems language that has high-level features for efficient, modular pro-
programming   gramming as well as lower-level features that make it suitable for use as a systems
language   programming language. It is machine independent so that carefully written C programs can be easily transported to run on different machines. Most of the Linux operating system is written in C, and Linux provides an ideal environment for programming in C.

C Shell   csh. The C Shell command processor was developed by Bill Joy for BSD UNIX. It was named for the C programming language because its programming constructs are similar to those of C. See *shell* on page 1131.

cable modem   A type of modem that allows you to access the Internet by using your cable television connection.

cache   Holding recently accessed data, a small, fast memory designed to speed up subsequent access to the same data. Most often applied to processor-memory access but also used for a local copy of data accessible over a network, from a hard disk, and so on.FOLDOC

calling   A list of variables and their values that is made available to a called program. Refer
environment   to "Executing a Command" on page 314.

cascading   See *CSS* on page 1103.
stylesheet

cascading   An arrangement of windows such that they overlap, generally with at least part of
windows   the title bar visible. Opposite of *tiled windows* (page 1137).

case sensitive Able to distinguish between uppercase and lowercase characters. Unless you set the **ignorecase** parameter, vim performs case-sensitive searches. The grep utility performs case-sensitive searches unless you use the –i option.

catenate   To join sequentially, or end to end. The Linux cat utility catenates files: It displays them one after the other. Also *concatenate*.

chain loading	The technique used by a boot loader to load unsupported operating systems. Used for loading such operating systems as DOS or Windows, it works by loading another boot loader.
character-based	A program, utility, or interface that works only with *ASCII* (page 1095) characters. This set of characters includes some simple graphics, such as lines and corners, and can display colored characters. It cannot display true graphics. Contrast with *GUI* (page 1110).
character-based terminal	A terminal that displays only characters and very limited graphics. See *character-based*.
character class	In a regular expression, a group of characters that defines which characters can occupy a single character position. A character-class definition is usually surrounded by square brackets. The character class defined by [abcr] represents a character position that can be occupied by **a, b, c,** or **r.** Also *list operator*.
	In POSIX, used to refer to sets of characters with a common characteristic, denoted by the notation [:*class*:]; for example, [:upper:] denotes the set of uppercase letters.
	This book uses the term character class as explained under "Brackets" on page 1045.
character device	A terminal, printer, or modem. A character device stores or displays characters one at a time. A character device is represented by a character device (character special) file. Contrast with *block device* (page 1097).
check box	A GUI widget, usually the outline of a square box with an adjacent caption, that a user can click to display or remove a *tick* (page 1137). When the box holds a tick, the option described by the caption is on or true. Also *tick box*.
checksum	A computed value that depends on the contents of a block of data and is transmitted or stored along with the data to detect corruption of the data. The receiving system recomputes the checksum based on the received data and compares this value with the one sent with the data. If the two values are the same, the receiver has some confidence that the data was received correctly.
	The checksum may be 8, 16, or 32 bits, or some other size. It is computed by summing the bytes or words of the data block, ignoring overflow. The checksum may be negated so that the total of the data words plus the checksum is zero.
	Internet packets use a 32-bit checksum.<small>FOLDOC</small>
child process	A process that is created by another process, the parent process. Every process is a child process except for the first process, which is started when Linux begins execution. When you run a command from the shell, the shell spawns a child process to run the command. See *process* on page 1126.
CIDR	Classless Inter-Domain Routing. A scheme that allocates blocks of Internet addresses in a way that allows summarization into a smaller number of routing table entries. A CIDR block is a block of Internet addresses assigned to an ISP by the Internic. Refer to "CIDR: Classless Inter-Domain Routing" on page 370.<small>FOLDOC</small>

CIFS   Common Internet File System. An Internet filesystem protocol based on *SMB* (page 1132). CIFS runs on top of TCP/IP, uses DNS, and is optimized to support slower dial-up Internet connections. SMB and CIFS are used interchangeably.^{FOLDOC}

CIPE   Crypto IP *Encapsulation* (page 1107). This *protocol* (page 1126) *tunnels* (page 1138) IP packets within encrypted *UDP* (page 1138) packets, is lightweight and simple, and works over dynamic addresses, *NAT* (page 1121), and *SOCKS* (page 1133) *proxies* (page 1126).

cipher (cypher)   A cryptographic system that uses a key to transpose/substitute characters within a message, the key itself, or the message.

ciphertext   Text that is encrypted. Contrast with *plaintext* (page 1125). See also "Encryption" on page 1064.

Classless   See *CIDR* on page 1100.
Inter-Domain
Routing

cleartext   Text that is not encrypted. Also *plaintext*. Contrast with *ciphertext*. See also "Encryption" on page 1064.

CLI   Command-line interface. See also *character-based* (page 1100). Also *textual interface*.

client   A computer or program that requests one or more services from a server.

CODEC   Coder/decoder or compressor/decompressor. A hardware and/or software technology that codes and decodes data. MPEG is a popular CODEC for computer video.

color depth   The number of bits used to generate a pixel—usually 8, 16, 24, or 32. The color depth is directly related to the number of colors that can be generated. The number of colors that can be generated is 2 raised to the color-depth power. Thus a 24-bit video adapter can generate about 16.7 million colors.

color quality   See *color depth*.

combo box   A combination of a *drop-down list* (page 1106) and *text box* (page 1136). You can enter text in a combo box. Or, you can click a combo box, cause it to expand and display a static list of selections for you to choose from.

command   What you give the shell in response to a prompt. When you give the shell a command, it executes a utility, another program, a builtin command, or a shell script. Utilities are often referred to as commands. When you are using an interactive utility, such as vim or mail, you use commands that are appropriate to that utility.

command line   A line containing instructions and arguments that executes a command. This term usually refers to a line that you enter in response to a shell prompt on a character-based terminal or terminal emulator (page 111).

command   Replacing a command with its output. The shells perform command substitution
substitution   when you enclose a command between $(and) or between a pair of back ticks (` `), also called grave accent marks.

component architecture	A notion in object-oriented programming where "components" of a program are completely generic. Instead of having a specialized set of methods and fields, they have generic methods through which the component can advertise the functionality it supports to the system into which it is loaded. This strategy enables completely dynamic loading of objects. JavaBeans is an example of a component architecture.ᶠᴼᴸᴰᴼᶜ
concatenate	See *catenate* on page 1099.
condition code	See *exit status* on page 1107.
connection-oriented protocol	A type of transport layer data communication service that allows a host to send data in a continuous stream to another host. The transport service guarantees that all data will be delivered to the other end in the same order as sent and without duplication. Communication proceeds through three well-defined phases: connection establishment, data transfer, and connection release. The most common example is *TCP* (page 1136). Also called connection-based protocol and stream-oriented protocol. Contrast with *connectionless protocol* and *datagram* (page 1104).ᶠᴼᴸᴰᴼᶜ
connectionless protocol	The data communication method in which communication occurs between hosts with no previous setup. Packets sent between two hosts may take different routes. There is no guarantee that packets will arrive as transmitted or even that they will arrive at the destination at all. *UDP* (page 1138) is a connectionless protocol. Also called packet switching. Contrast with circuit switching and *connection-oriented protocol*.ᶠᴼᴸᴰᴼᶜ
console	The main system terminal, usually directly connected to the computer and the one that receives system error messages. Also *system console* and *console terminal*.
console terminal	See *console*.
control character	A character that is not a graphic character, such as a letter, number, or punctuation mark. Such characters are called control characters because they frequently act to control a peripheral device. RETURN and FORMFEED are control characters that control a terminal or printer. The word CONTROL is shown in this book in THIS FONT because it is a key that appears on most terminal keyboards. Control characters are represented by ASCII codes less than 32 (decimal). See also *nonprinting character* on page 1122.
control structure	A statement used to change the order of execution of commands in a shell script or other program. Each shell provides control structures (for example, **if** and **while**) as well as other commands that alter the order of execution (for example, **exec**). Also *control flow commands*.
cookie	Data stored on a client system by a server. The client system browser sends the cookie back to the server each time it accesses that server. For example, a catalog shopping service may store a cookie on your system when you place your first

order. When you return to the site, it knows who you are and can supply your name and address for subsequent orders. You may consider cookies to be an invasion of privacy.

CPU
Central processing unit. The part of a computer that controls all the other parts. The CPU includes the control unit and the arithmetic and logic unit (ALU). The control unit fetches instructions from memory and decodes them to produce signals that control the other parts of the computer. These signals can cause data to be transferred between memory and ALU or peripherals to perform input or output. A CPU that is housed on a single chip is called a microprocessor. Also *processor* and *central processor*.

cracker
An individual who attempts to gain unauthorized access to a computer system. These individuals are often malicious and have many means at their disposal for breaking into a system. Contrast with *hacker* (page 1110).FOLDOC

crash
The system suddenly and unexpectedly stops or fails. Derived from the action of the hard disk heads on the surface of the disk when the air gap between the two collapses.

cryptography
The practice and study of encryption and decryption—encoding data so that only a specific individual or machine can decode it. A system for encrypting and decrypting data is a cryptosystem. Such systems usually rely on an algorithm for combining the original data (plaintext) with one or more keys—numbers or strings of characters known only to the sender and/or recipient. The resulting output is called *ciphertext* (page 1101).

The security of a cryptosystem usually depends on the secrecy of keys rather than on the supposed secrecy of an algorithm. Because a strong cryptosystem has a large range of keys, it is not possible to try all of them. Ciphertext appears random to standard statistical tests and resists known methods for breaking codes.FOLDOC

.cshrc file
In your home directory, a file that the TC Shell executes each time you invoke a new TC Shell. You can use this file to establish variables and aliases.

CSS
Cascading stylesheet. Describes how documents are presented on screen and in print. Attaching a stylesheet to a structured document can affect the way it looks without adding new HTML (or other) tags and without giving up device independence. Also *stylesheet*.

current (process, line, character, directory, event, etc.)
The item that is immediately available, working, or being used. The current process is the program you are running, the current line or character is the one the cursor is on, and the current directory is the working directory.

cursor
A small lighted rectangle, underscore, or vertical bar that appears on a terminal screen and indicates where the next character will appear. Differs from the *mouse pointer* (page 1120).

daemon
: A program that is not invoked explicitly but lies dormant, waiting for some condition(s) to occur. The perpetrator of the condition need not be aware that a daemon is lurking (although often a program will commit an action only because it knows that it will implicitly invoke a daemon). From the mythological meaning, later rationalized as the acronym Disk And Execution MONitor. See Table 10-4 on page 386 for a list of daemons.^{FOLDOC}

data structure
: A particular format for storing, organizing, working with, and retrieving data. Frequently, data structures are designed to work with specific algorithms that facilitate these tasks. Common data structures include trees, files, records, tables, arrays, etc.

datagram
: A self-contained, independent entity of data carrying sufficient information to be routed from the source to the destination computer without reliance on earlier exchanges between this source and destination computer and the transporting network. *UDP* (page 1138) uses datagrams; *IP* (page 1114) uses *packets* (page 1123). Packets are indivisible at the network layer; datagrams are not.^{FOLDOC} See also *frame* (page 1109).

dataless
: A computer, usually a workstation, that uses a local disk to boot a copy of the operating system and access system files but does not use a local disk to store user files.

dbm
: A standard, simple database manager. Implemented as **gdbm** (GNU database manager), it uses hashes to speed searching. The most common versions of the **dbm** database are **dbm**, **ndbm**, and **gdbm**.

DDoS attack
: Distributed denial of service attack. A *DoS attack* (page 1106) from many systems that do not belong to the perpetrator of the attack.

debug
: To correct a program by removing its bugs (that is, errors).

default
: Something that is selected without being explicitly specified. For example, when used without an argument, ls displays a list of the files in the working directory by default.

delta
: A set of changes made to a file that has been encoded by the Source Code Control System (SCCS).

denial of service
: *See DoS attack* on page 1106.

dereference
: When speaking of symbolic links, follow the link rather than working with the reference to the link. For example, the –L or ––dereference option causes ls to list the entry that a symbolic link points to rather than the symbolic link (the reference) itself.

desktop
: A collection of windows, toolbars, icons, and buttons, some or all of which appear on your display. A desktop comprises one or more *workspaces* (page 1141). Refer to "A Tour of the Ubuntu Linux Desktop" on page 87.

desktop manager
: An icon- and menu-based user interface to system services that allows you to run applications and use the filesystem without using the system's command-line interface.

detached process	See *background process* on page 1096.
device	A disk drive, printer, terminal, plotter, or other input/output unit that can be attached to the computer. Short for *peripheral device*.
device driver	Part of the Linux kernel that controls a device, such as a terminal, disk drive, or printer.
device file	A file that represents a device. Also *special file*.
device filename	The pathname of a device file. All Linux systems have two kinds of device files: block and character device files. Linux also has FIFOs (named pipes) and sockets. Device files are traditionally located in the **/dev** directory.
device number	See *major device number* (page 1118) and *minor device number* (page 1120).
DHCP	Dynamic Host Configuration Protocol. A protocol that dynamically allocates IP addresses to computers on a LAN. Refer to "DHCP: Configures Network Interfaces" on page 454.ᶠᴼᴸᴰᴼᶜ
dialog box	In a GUI, a special window, usually without a titlebar, that displays information. Some dialog boxes accept a response from the user
directory	Short for *directory file*. A file that contains a list of other files.
directory hierarchy	A directory, called the root of the directory hierarchy, and all the directory and ordinary files below it (its children).
directory service	A structured repository of information on people and resources within an organization, facilitating management and communication.ᶠᴼᴸᴰᴼᶜ
disk partition	See *partition* on page 1124.
diskless	A computer, usually a workstation, that has no disk and must contact another computer (a server) to boot a copy of the operating system and access the necessary system files.
distributed computing	A style of computing in which tasks or services are performed by a network of cooperating systems, some of which may be specialized.
DMZ	Demilitarized zone. A host or small network that is a neutral zone between a LAN and the Internet. It can serve Web pages and other data to the Internet and allow local systems access to the Internet while preventing LAN access to unauthorized Internet users. Even if a DMZ is compromised, it holds no data that is private and none that cannot be easily reproduced.
DNS	Domain Name Service. A distributed service that manages the correspondence of full hostnames (those that include a domain name) to IP addresses and other system characteristics.
DNS domain name	See *domain name*.

document object model	See *DOM*.
DOM	Document Object Model. A platform-/language-independent interface that enables a program to update the content, structure, and style of a document dynamically. The changes can then be made part of the displayed document. Go to www.w3.org/DOM for more information.
domain name	A name associated with an organization, or part of an organization, to help identify systems uniquely. Technically, the part of the *FQDN* (page 1109) to the right of the leftmost period. Domain names are assigned hierarchically. The domain berkeley.edu refers to the University of California at Berkeley, for example; it is part of the top-level edu (education) domain. Also DNS domain name. Different than *NIS domain name* (page 1122).
Domain Name Service	See *DNS*.
door	An evolving filesystem-based *RPC* (page 1130) mechanism.
DoS attack	Denial of service attack. An attack that attempts to make the target host or network unusable by flooding it with spurious traffic.
DPMS	Display Power Management Signaling. A standard that can extend the life of CRT monitors and conserve energy. DPMS supports four modes for a monitor: Normal, Standby (power supply on, monitor ready to come to display images almost instantly), Suspend (power supply off, monitor takes up to ten seconds to display an image), and Off.
drag	The motion part of *drag-and-drop*.
drag-and-drop	To move an object from one position or application to another within a GUI. To drag an object, the user clicks a mouse button (typically the left one) while the mouse pointer *hovers* (page 1112) over the object. Then, without releasing the mouse button, the user drags the object, which stays attached to the mouse pointer, to a different location. The user can then drop the object at the new location by releasing the mouse button.
drop-down list	A *widget* (page 1140) that displays a static list for a user to choose from. When the list is not active, it appears as text in a box, displaying the single selected entry. When a user clicks the box, a list appears; the user can move the mouse cursor to select an entry from the list. Different from a *list box* (page 1117).
druid	In role-playing games, a character that represents a magical user. Red Hat uses the term *druid* at the ends of names of programs that guide you through a task-driven chain of steps. Other operating systems call these types of programs *wizards*.
DSA	Digital Signature Algorithm. A public key cipher used to generate digital signatures.

DSL	Digital Subscriber Line/Loop. Provides high-speed digital communication over a specialized, conditioned telephone line. See also *xDSL* (page 1142).
Dynamic Host Configuration Protocol	See *DHCP* on page 1105.
editor	A utility, such as vim or emacs, that creates and modifies text files.
EEPROM	Electrically erasable, programmable, readonly memory. A *PROM* (page 1126) that can be written to.
effective user ID	The user ID that a process appears to have; usually the same as the user ID. For example, while you are running a setuid program, the effective user ID of the process running the program is that of the owner of the program.
element	One thing; usually a basic part of a group of things. An element of a numeric array is one of the numbers stored in the array.
emoticon	See *smiley* on page 1132.
encapsulation	See *tunneling* on page 1138.
environment	See *calling environment* on page 1099.
EOF	End of file.
EPROM	Erasable programmable readonly memory. A *PROM* (page 1126) that can be written to by applying a higher than normal voltage.
escape	See *quote* on page 1127.
Ethernet	A type of *LAN* (page 1116) capable of transfer rates as high as 1,000 megabits per second. Refer to "Ethernet" on page 359.
event	An occurrence, or happening, of significance to a task or program—for example, the completion of an asynchronous input/output operation, such as a keypress or mouse click.^{FOLDOC}
exabyte	2^{60} bytes or about 10^{18} bytes. See also *large number* (page 1116).
exit status	The status returned by a process; either successful (usually 0) or unsuccessful (usually 1).
exploit	A security hole or an instance of taking advantage of a security hole.^{FOLDOC}
expression	See *logical expression* (page 1118) and *arithmetic expression* (page 1095).
extranet	A network extension for a subset of users (such as students at a particular school or engineers working for the same company). An extranet limits access to private information even though it travels on the public Internet.

failsafe session A session that allows you to log in on a minimal desktop in case your standard login does not work well enough to allow you to log in to fix a login problem.

FDDI Fiber Distributed Data Interface. A type of *LAN* (page 1116) designed to transport data at the rate of 100 million bits per second over fiberoptic cable.

file A collection of related information referred to with a *filename* and frequently stored on a disk. Text files typically contain memos, reports, messages, program source code, lists, or manuscripts. Binary or executable files contain utilities or programs that you can run. Refer to "Directory Files and Ordinary Files" on page 186.

filename The name of a file. A filename refers to a file.

filename completion Automatic completion of a filename after you specify a unique prefix.

filename extension The part of a filename following a period.

filename generation What occurs when the shell expands ambiguous file references. See *ambiguous file reference* on page 1094.

filesystem A *data structure* (page 1104) that usually resides on part of a disk. All Linux systems have a root filesystem, and many have other filesystems. Each filesystem is composed of some number of blocks, depending on the size of the disk partition that has been assigned to the filesystem. Each filesystem has a control block, named the superblock, that contains information about the filesystem. The other blocks in a filesystem are inodes, which contain control information about individual files, and data blocks, which contain the information in the files.

filling A variant of maximizing in which window edges are pushed out as far as they can go without overlapping another window.

filter A command that can take its input from standard input and send its output to standard output. A filter transforms the input stream of data and sends it to standard output. A pipe usually connects a filter's input to standard output of one command, and a second pipe connects the filter's output to standard input of another command. The grep and sort utilities are commonly used as filters.

firewall A device for policy-based traffic management used to keep a network secure. A firewall can be implemented in a single router that filters out unwanted packets, or it can rely on a combination of routers, proxy servers, and other devices. Firewalls are widely used to give users access to the Internet in a secure fashion and to separate a company's public WWW server from its internal network. They are also employed to keep internal network segments more secure.

Recently the term has come to be defined more loosely to include a simple packet filter running on an endpoint machine.

See also *proxy server* on page 1127.

firmware	Software built into a computer, often in *ROM* (page 1129). May be used as part of the *bootstrap* (page 1098) procedure.
focus, desktop	On a desktop, the window that is active. The window with the desktop focus receives the characters you type on the keyboard. Same as *active window* (page 1094).
footer	The part of a format that goes at the bottom (or foot) of a page. Contrast with *header* (page 1111).
foreground process	When you run a command in the foreground, the shell waits for the command to finish before giving you another prompt. You must wait for a foreground process to run to completion before you can give the shell another command. If you have job control, you can move background processes to the foreground, and vice versa. See *job control* on page 1115. Contrast with *background process* (page 1096).
fork	To create a process. When one process creates another process, it forks a process. Also *spawn*.
FQDN	Fully qualified domain name. The full name of a system, consisting of its hostname and its domain name, including the top-level domain. Technically the name that **gethostbyname**(2) returns for the host named by **gethostname**(2). For example, **speedy** is a hostname and **speedy.example.com** is an FQDN. An FQDN is sufficient to determine a unique Internet address for a machine on the Internet.^{FOLDOC}
frame	A data link layer packet that contains, in addition to data, the header and trailer information required by the physical medium. Network layer packets are encapsulated to become frames.^{FOLDOC} See also *datagram* (page 1104) and *packet* (page 1123).
free list	In a filesystem, the list of blocks that are available for use. Information about the free list is kept in the superblock of the filesystem.
free software	Refer to Appendix D, "The Free Software Definition."
free space	The portion of a hard disk that is not within a partition. A new hard disk has no partitions and contains all free space.
full duplex	The ability to receive and transmit data simultaneously. A *network switch* (page 1122) is typically a full-duplex device. Contrast with *half-duplex* (page 1110).
fully qualified domain name	See *FQDN*.
function	See *shell function* on page 1131.
gateway	A generic term for a computer or a special device connected to more than one dissimilar type of network to pass data between them. Unlike a router, a gateway often must convert the information into a different format before passing it on. The historical usage of gateway to designate a router is deprecated.

GCOS	See *GECOS*.
GECOS	General Electric Comprehensive Operating System. For historical reasons, the user information field in the **/etc/passwd** file is called the GECOS field. Also GCOS.
gibibyte	Giga binary byte. A unit of storage equal to 2^{30} bytes = 1,073,741,824 bytes = 1024 *mebibytes* (page 1119). Abbreviated as GiB. Contrast with *gigabyte*.
gigabyte	A unit of storage equal to 10^9 bytes. Sometimes used in place of *gibibyte*. Abbreviated as GB. See also *large number* on page 1116.
glyph	A symbol that communicates a specific piece of information nonverbally. A *smiley* (page 1132) is a glyph.
GMT	Greenwich Mean Time. See *UTC* on page 1139.
graphical display	A bitmapped monitor that can display graphical images. Contrast with *ASCII terminal* (page 1095).
graphical user interface	See *GUI*.
group (of users)	A collection of users. Groups are used as a basis for determining file access permissions. If you are not the owner of a file and you belong to the group the file is assigned to, you are subject to the group access permissions for the file. A user can simultaneously belong to several groups.
group (of windows)	A way to identify similar windows so they can be displayed and acted on similarly. Typically windows started by a given application belong to the same group.
group ID	A unique number that identifies a set of users. It is stored in the password and group databases (**/etc/passwd** and **/etc/group** files or their NIS equivalents). The group database associates group IDs with group names. Also *GID*.
GUI	Graphical user interface. A GUI provides a way to interact with a computer system by choosing items from menus or manipulating pictures drawn on a display screen instead of by typing command lines. Under Linux, the X Window System provides a graphical display and mouse/keyboard input. GNOME and KDE are two popular desktop managers that run under X. Contrast with *character-based* (page 1100).
hacker	A person who enjoys exploring the details of programmable systems and learning how to stretch their capabilities, as opposed to users, who prefer to learn only the minimum necessary. One who programs enthusiastically (even obsessively) or who enjoys programming rather than just theorizing about programming.[FOLDOC] Contrast with *cracker* (page 1103).
half-duplex	A half-duplex device can only receive or transmit at a given moment; it cannot do both. A *hub* (page 1112) is typically a half-duplex device. Contrast with *full duplex* (page 1109).

hard link	A directory entry that contains the filename and inode number for a file. The inode number identifies the location of control information for the file on the disk, which in turn identifies the location of the file's contents on the disk. Every file has at least one hard link, which locates the file in a directory. When you remove the last hard link to a file, you can no longer access the file. See *link* (page 1117) and *symbolic link* (page 1136).
hash	A string that is generated from another string. See *one-way hash function* on page 1123. When used for security, a hash can prove, almost to a certainty, that a message has not been tampered with during transmission: The sender generates a hash of a message, encrypts the message and hash, and sends the encrypted message and hash to the recipient. The recipient decrypts the message and hash, generates a second hash from the message, and compares the hash that the sender generated to the new hash. When they are the same, the message has probably not been tampered with. Hashed versions of passwords can be used to authenticate users. A hash can also be used to create an index called a *hash table*. Also *hash value*.
hash table	An index created from hashes of the items to be indexed. The hash function makes it highly unlikely that two items will create the same hash. To look up an item in the index, create a hash of the item and search for the hash. Because the hash is typically shorter than the item, the search is more efficient.
header	When you are formatting a document, the header goes at the top, or head, of a page. In electronic mail the header identifies who sent the message, when it was sent, what the subject of the message is, and so forth.
Here document	A shell script that takes its input from the file that contains the script.
hesiod	The nameserver of project Athena. Hesiod is a name service library that is derived from *BIND* (page 1097) and leverages a DNS infrastructure.
heterogeneous	Consisting of different parts. A heterogeneous network includes systems produced by different manufacturers and/or running different operating systems.
hexadecimal number	A base 16 number. Hexadecimal (or *hex*) numbers are composed of the hexadecimal digits 0–9 and A–F. See Table G-1, next page.
hidden filename	A filename that starts with a period. These filenames are called hidden because the ls utility does not normally list them. Use the –a option of ls to list all files, including those with hidden filenames. The shell does not expand a leading asterisk (*) in an ambiguous file reference to match files with hidden filenames. Also *hidden file*, *invisible file*.
hierarchy	An organization with a few things, or thing—one at the top—and with several things below each other thing. An inverted tree structure. Examples in computing include a file tree where each directory may contain files or other directories, a hierarchical network, and a class hierarchy in object-oriented programming.[FOLDOC] Refer to "The Hierarchical Filesystem" on page 186.

Table G-1   Decimal, octal, and hexadecimal numbers

Decimal	Octal	Hex	Decimal	Octal	Hex
1	1	1	17	21	11
2	2	2	18	22	12
3	3	3	19	23	13
4	4	4	20	24	14
5	5	5	21	25	15
6	6	6	31	37	1F
7	7	7	32	40	20
8	10	8	33	41	21
9	11	9	64	100	40
10	12	A	96	140	60
11	13	B	100	144	64
12	14	C	128	200	80
13	15	D	254	376	FE
14	16	E	255	377	FF
15	17	F	256	400	100
16	20	10	257	401	101

history   A shell mechanism that enables you to modify and reexecute recent commands.

home   The directory that is the working directory when you first log in. The pathname of
directory   this directory is stored in the **HOME** shell variable.

hover   To leave the mouse pointer stationary for a moment over an object. In many cases
                     hovering displays a *tooltip* (page 1137).

HTML   Hypertext Markup Language. A *hypertext* document format used on the World
                     Wide Web. Tags, which are embedded in the text, consist of a less than sign (<), a
                     directive, zero or more parameters, and a greater than sign (>). Matched pairs of
                     directives, such as <TITLE> and </TITLE>, delimit text that is to appear in a special
                     place or style.FOLDOC For more information on HTML, go to www.htmlhelp.com/faq/
                     html/all.html.

HTTP   Hypertext Transfer Protocol. The client/server TCP/IP protocol used on the World
                     Wide Web for the exchange of *HTML* documents.

hub   A multiport repeater. A hub rebroadcasts all packets it receives on all ports. This
                     term is frequently used to refer to small hubs and switches, regardless of the device's
                     intelligence. It is a generic term for a layer 2 shared-media networking device.
                     Today the term *hub* is sometimes used to refer to small intelligent devices, although
                     that was not its original meaning. Contrast with *network switch* (page 1122).

hypertext	A collection of documents/nodes containing (usually highlighted or underlined) cross-references or links, which, with the aid of an interactive browser program, allow the reader to move easily from one document to another.^{FOLDOC}
Hypertext Markup Language	See *HTML*.
Hypertext Transfer Protocol	See *HTTP*.
i/o device	Input/output device. See *device* on page 1105.
IANA	Internet Assigned Numbers Authority. A group that maintains a database of all permanent, registered system services (www.iana.org).
ICMP	Internet Control Message Protocol. A type of network packet that carries only messages, no data.
icon	In a GUI, a small picture representing a file, directory, action, program, and so on. When you click an icon, an action, such as opening a window and starting a program or displaying a directory or Web site, takes place. From miniature religious statues.^{FOLDOC}
iconify	The process of changing a window into an *icon*. Contrast with *restore* (page 1129).
ignored window	A state in which a window has no decoration and therefore no buttons or titlebar to control it with.
indentation	See *indention*.
indention	The blank space between the margin and the beginning of a line that is set in from the margin.
inode	A *data structure* (page 1104) that contains information about a file. An inode for a file contains the file's length, the times the file was last accessed and modified, the time the inode was last modified, owner and group IDs, access privileges, number of links, and pointers to the data blocks that contain the file itself. Each directory entry associates a filename with an inode. Although a single file may have several filenames (one for each link), it has only one inode.
input	Information that is fed to a program from a terminal or other file. See *standard input* on page 1134.
installation	A computer at a specific location. Some aspects of the Linux system are installation dependent. Also *site*.
interactive	A program that allows ongoing dialog with the user. When you give commands in response to shell prompts, you are using the shell interactively. Also, when you give commands to utilities, such as vim and mail, you are using the utilities interactively.

interface The meeting point of two subsystems. When two programs work together, their interface includes every aspect of either program that the other deals with. The *user interface* (page 1139) of a program includes every program aspect the user comes into contact with: the syntax and semantics involved in invoking the program, the input and output of the program, and its error and informational messages. The shell and each of the utilities and built-in commands have a user interface.

International Organization for Standardization See *ISO* on page 1115.

internet A large network that encompasses other, smaller networks.

Internet The largest internet in the world. The Internet (uppercase "I") is a multilevel hierarchy composed of backbone networks (ARPANET, NSFNET, MILNET, and others), midlevel networks, and stub networks. These include commercial (**.com** or **.co**), university (**.ac** or **.edu**), research (**.org** or **.net**), and military (**.mil**) networks and span many different physical networks around the world with various protocols, including the Internet Protocol (IP). Outside the United States, country code domains are popular (**.us**, **.es**, **.mx**, **.de**, and so forth), although you will see them used within the United States as well.

Internet Protocol See *IP*.

Internet service provider See *ISP*.

intranet An inhouse network designed to serve a group of people such as a corporation or school. The general public on the Internet does not have access to the intranet. See page 356.

invisible file See *hidden filename* on page 1111.

IP Internet Protocol. The network layer for TCP/IP. IP is a best-effort, packet-switching, *connectionless protocol* (page 1102) that provides packet routing, fragmentation, and reassembly through the data link layer. *IPv4* is slowly giving way to *IPv6*.FOLDOC

IP address Internet Protocol address. A four-part address associated with a particular network connection for a system using the Internet Protocol (IP). A system that is attached to multiple networks that use the IP will have a different IP address for each network interface.

IP multicast See *multicast* on page 1121.

IP spoofing   A technique used to gain unauthorized access to a computer. The would-be intruder sends messages to the target machine. These messages contain an IP address indicating that the messages are coming from a trusted host (page 375). The target machine responds to the messages, giving the intruder (privileged) access to the target.

IPC   Interprocess communication. A method to communicate specific information between programs.

IPv4   *IP* version 4. See *IP* and *IPv6*.

IPv6   *IP* version 6. The next generation of Internet Protocol, which provides a much larger address space (2^{128} bits versus 2^{32} bits for IPv4) that is designed to accommodate the rapidly growing number of Internet addressable devices. IPv6 also has built-in autoconfiguration, enhanced security, better multicast support, and many other features.

ISDN   Integrated Services Digital Network. A set of communications standards that allows a single pair of digital or standard telephone wires to carry voice, data, and video at a rate of 64 kilobits per second.

ISO   International Organization for Standardization. A voluntary, nontreaty organization founded in 1946. It is responsible for creating international standards in many areas, including computers and communications. Its members are the national standards organizations of 89 countries, including the American National Standards Institute.[FOLDOC]

ISO9660   The *ISO* standard defining a filesystem for CD-ROMs.

ISP   Internet service provider. Provides Internet access to its customers.

job control   A facility that enables you to move commands from the foreground to the background and vice versa. Job control enables you to stop commands temporarily.

journaling filesystem   A filesystem that maintains a noncached log file, or journal, which records all transactions involving the filesystem. When a transaction is complete, it is marked as complete in the log file.

               The log file results in greatly reduced time spent recovering a filesystem after a crash, making it particularly valuable in systems where high availability is an issue.

JPEG   Joint Photographic Experts Group. This committee designed the standard image-compression algorithm. JPEG is intended for compressing either full-color or gray-scale digital images of natural, real-world scenes and does not work as well on nonrealistic images, such as cartoons or line drawings. Filename extensions: **.jpg**, **.jpeg**.[FOLDOC]

justify   To expand a line of type in the process of formatting text. A justified line has even margins. A line is justified by increasing the space between words and sometimes between letters on the line.

Kerberos	An MIT-developed security system that authenticates users and machines. It does not provide authorization to services or databases; it establishes identity at logon, which is used throughout the session. Once you are authenticated, you can open as many terminals, windows, services, or other network accesses as you like until your session expires.
kernel	The part of the operating system that allocates machine resources, including memory, disk space, and *CPU* (page 1103) cycles, to all other programs that run on a computer. The kernel includes the low-level hardware interfaces (drivers) and manages *processes* (page 1126), the means by which Linux executes programs. The kernel is the part of the Linux system that Linus Torvalds originally wrote (see the beginning of Chapter 1).
kernelspace	The part of memory (RAM) where the kernel resides. Code running in kernelspace has full access to hardware and all other processes in memory. See the *KernelAnalysis-HOWTO*.
key binding	A *keyboard* key is said to be bound to the action that results from pressing it. Typically keys are bound to the letters that appear on the keycaps: When you press **A**, an **A** appears on the screen. Key binding usually refers to what happens when you press a combination of keys, one of which is CONTROL, ALT, META, or SHIFT, or when you press a series of keys, the first of which is typically ESCAPE.
keyboard	A hardware input device consisting of a number of mechanical buttons (keys) that the user presses to input characters to a computer. By default a keyboard is connected to standard input of a shell.^{FOLDOC}
kilo-	In the binary system, the prefix *kilo-* multiplies by 2^{10} (i.e., 1,024). Kilobit and kilobyte are common uses of this prefix. Abbreviated as *k*.
Korn Shell	ksh. A command processor, developed by David Korn at AT&T Bell Laboratories, that is compatible with the Bourne Shell but includes many extensions. See also *shell* on page 1131.
LAN	Local area network. A network that connects computers within a localized area (such as a single site, building, or department).
large number	Visit mathworld.wolfram.com/LargeNumber.html for a comprehensive list.
LDAP	Lightweight Directory Access Protocol. A simple protocol for accessing online directory services. LDAP is a lightweight alternative to the X.500 Directory Access Protocol (DAP). It can be used to access information about people, system users, network devices, email directories, and systems. In some cases, it can be used as an alternative for services such as NIS. Given a name, many mail clients can use LDAP to discover the corresponding email address. See *directory service* on page 1105.
leaf	In a tree structure, the end of a branch that cannot support other branches. When the Linux filesystem hierarchy is conceptualized as a tree, files that are not directories are leaves. See *node* on page 1122.

least privilege, concept of   Mistakes made by a user working with **root** privileges can be much more devastating than those made by an ordinary user. When you are working on the computer, especially when you are working as the system administrator, always perform any task using the least privilege possible. If you can perform a task logged in as an ordinary user, do so. If you must work with **root** privileges, do as much as you can as an ordinary user, log in as **root** or give an su or sudo command so you are working with **root** privileges, do as much of the task that has to be done with **root** privileges, and revert to being an ordinary user as soon as you can.

Because you are more likely to make a mistake when you are rushing, this concept becomes more important when you have less time to apply it.

Lightweight Directory Access Protocol   See *LDAP*.

link   A pointer to a file. Two kinds of links exist: *hard links* (page 1111) and *symbolic links* (page 1136) also called *soft links*. A hard link associates a filename with a place on the disk where the contents of the file is located. A symbolic link associates a filename with the pathname of a hard link to a file.

Linux-PAM   See *PAM* on page 1124.

Linux-Pluggable Authentication Modules   See *PAM* on page 1124.

list box   A *widget* (page 1140) that displays a static list for a user to choose from. The list appears as multiple lines with a *scrollbar* (page 1131) if needed. The user can scroll the list and select an entry. Different from a *drop-down list* (page 1106).

loadable kernel module   See *loadable module*.

loadable module   A portion of the operating system that controls a special device and that can be loaded automatically into a running kernel as needed to access that device. See "Using Loadable Kernel Modules" on page 564.

local area network   See *LAN* on page 1116.

locale   The language; date, time, and currency formats; character sets; and so forth that pertain to a geopolitical place or area. For example, en_US specifies English as spoken in the United States and dollars; en_UK specifies English as spoken in the United Kingdom and pounds. See the **locale** man page in section 5 of the system manual for more information. Also the locale utility.

log in   To gain access to a computer system by responding correctly to the **login:** and **Password:** prompts. Also *log on, login.*

log out   To end your session by exiting from your login shell. Also *log off.*

logical expression   A collection of strings separated by logical operators (>, >=, =, !=, <=, and <) that can be evaluated as *true* or *false.* Also *Boolean* (page 1098) *expression.*

.login file   A file in a user's home directory that the TC Shell executes when you log in. You can use this file to set environment variables and to run commands that you want executed at the beginning of each session.

login name   See *username* on page 1139.

login shell   The shell that you are using when you log in. The login shell can fork other processes that can run other shells, utilities, and programs.

.logout file   A file in a user's home directory that the TC Shell executes when you log out, assuming that the TC Shell is your login shell. You can put in the **.logout** file commands that you want run each time you log out.

MAC address   Media Access Control address. The unique hardware address of a device connected to a shared network medium. Each network adapter has a globally unique MAC address that it stores in ROM. MAC addresses are 6 bytes long, enabling 256^6 (about 300 trillion) possible addresses or 65,536 addresses for each possible IPv4 address.

A MAC address performs the same role for Ethernet that an IP address performs for TCP/IP: It provides a unique way to identify a host.

machine collating sequence   The sequence in which the computer orders characters. The machine collating sequence affects the outcome of sorts and other procedures that put lists in alphabetical order. Many computers use ASCII codes so their machine collating sequences correspond to the ordering of the ASCII codes for characters.

macro   A single instruction that a program replaces by several (usually more complex) instructions. The C compiler recognizes macros, which are defined using a #define instruction to the preprocessor.

magic number   A magic number, which occurs in the first 512 bytes of a binary file, is a 1-, 2-, or 4-byte numeric value or character string that uniquely identifies the type of file (much like a DOS 3-character filename extension). See **/usr/share/magic** and the **magic** man page for more information.

main memory   Random access memory (RAM), an integral part of the computer. Although disk storage is sometimes referred to as memory, it is never referred to as main memory.

major device number   A number assigned to a class of devices, such as terminals, printers, or disk drives. Using the ls utility with the –l option to list the contents of the **/dev** directory displays the major and minor device numbers of many devices (as major, minor).

MAN   Metropolitan area network. A network that connects computers and *LANs* (page 1116) at multiple sites in a small regional area, such as a city.

masquerade   To appear to come from one domain or IP address when actually coming from another. Said of a packet (iptables) or message (**exim4**). See also *NAT* on page 1121.

MD5   Message Digest 5. A *one-way hash function* (page 1123). The *SHA1* (page 1131) algorithm has supplanted MD5 in many applications.

MDA   Mail delivery agent. One of the three components of a mail system; the other two are the *MTA* (page 1120) and *MUA* (page 1120). An MDA accepts inbound mail from an MTA and delivers it to a local user.

mebibyte   Mega binary byte. A unit of storage equal to 2^{20} bytes = 1,048,576 bytes = 1,024 kibibytes. Abbreviated as MiB. Contrast with *megabyte*.

megabyte   A unit of storage equal to 10^6 bytes. Sometimes used in place of *mebibyte*. Abbreviated as MB.

memory   See *RAM* on page 1127.

menu   A list from which the user may select an operation to be performed. This selection is often made with a mouse or other pointing device under a GUI but may also be controlled from the keyboard. Very convenient for beginners, menus show which commands are available and facilitate experimenting with a new program, often reducing the need for user documentation. Experienced users usually prefer keyboard commands, especially for frequently used operations, because they are faster to use.FOLDOC

merge   To combine two ordered lists so that the resulting list is still in order. The sort utility can merge files.

META key   On the keyboard, a key that is labeled META or ALT. Use this key as you would the SHIFT key. While holding it down, press another key. The emacs editor makes extensive use of the META key.

metacharacter   A character that has a special meaning to the shell or another program in a particular context. Metacharacters are used in the ambiguous file references recognized by the shell and in the regular expressions recognized by several utilities. You must quote a metacharacter if you want to use it without invoking its special meaning. See *regular character* (page 1128) and *special character* (page 1133).

metadata   Data about data. In data processing, metadata is definitional data that provides information about, or documentation of, other data managed within an application or environment.

For example, metadata can document data about data elements or attributes (name, size, data type, and so on), records or *data structures* (page 1104) (length, fields, columns, and so on), and data itself (where it is located, how it is associated, who owns it, and so on). Metadata can include descriptive information about the context, quality and condition, or characteristics of the data.FOLDOC

metropolitan area network	See *MAN* on page 1119.
MIME	Multipurpose Internet Mail Extension. Originally used to describe how specific types of files that were attached to email were to be handled. Today MIME types describe how a file is to be opened or worked with, based on its contents, determined by its *magic number* (page 1118), and filename extension. An example of a MIME *type* is **image/jpeg**: The MIME *group* is **image** and the MIME *subtype* is **jpeg**. Many MIME groups exist, including application, audio, image, inode, message, text, and video.
minimize	See *iconify* on page 1113.
minor device number	A number assigned to a specific device within a class of devices. See *major device number* on page 1118.
modem	Modulator/demodulator. A peripheral device that modulates digital data into analog data for transmission over a voice-grade telephone line. Another modem demodulates the data at the other end.
module	See *loadable module* on page 1117.
mount	To make a filesystem accessible to system users. When a filesystem is not mounted, you cannot read from or write to files it contains.
mount point	A directory that you mount a local or remote filesystem on. See page 35.
mouse	A device you use to point to a particular location on a display screen, typically so you can choose a menu item, draw a line, or highlight some text. You control a pointer on the screen by sliding a mouse around on a flat surface; the position of the pointer moves relative to the movement of the mouse. You select items by pressing one or more buttons on the mouse.
mouse pointer	In a GUI, a marker that moves in correspondence with the mouse. It is usually a small black **x** with a white border or an arrow. Differs from the *cursor* (page 1103).
mouseover	The action of passing the mouse pointer over an object on the screen.
MTA	Mail transfer agent. One of the three components of a mail system; the other two are the *MDA* and *MUA*. An MTA accepts mail from users and MTAs.
MUA	Mail user agent. One of the three components of a mail system; the other two are the *MDA* (page 1119) and *MTA* (page 1120). An MUA is an end-user mail program such as KMail, mutt, or Outlook.
multiboot specification	Specifies an interface between a boot loader and an operating system. With compliant boot loaders and operating systems, any boot loader should be able to load any operating system. The object of this specification is to ensure that different operating systems will work on a single machine. For more information, go to odin-os.sourceforge.net/guides/multiboot.html.

multicast	A multicast packet has one source and multiple destinations. In multicast, source hosts register at a special address to transmit data. Destination hosts register at the same address to receive data. In contrast to *broadcast* (page 1098), which is LAN-based, multicast traffic is designed to work across routed networks on a subscription basis. Multicast reduces network traffic by transmitting a packet one time, with the router at the end of the path breaking it apart as needed for multiple recipients.
multitasking	A computer system that allows a user to run more than one job at a time. A multitasking system, such as Linux, allows you to run a job in the background while running a job in the foreground.
multiuser system	A computer system that can be used by more than one person at a time. Linux is a multiuser operating system. Contrast with *single-user system* (page 1132).
namespace	A set of names (identifiers) in which all names are unique.FOLDOC
NAT	Network Address Translation. A scheme that enables a LAN to use one set of IP addresses internally and a different set externally. The internal set is for LAN (private) use. The external set is typically used on the Internet and is Internet unique. NAT provides some privacy by hiding internal IP addresses and allows multiple internal addresses to connect to the Internet through a single external IP address. See also *masquerade* on page 1119.
NBT	NetBIOS over TCP/IP. A protocol that supports NetBIOS services in a TCP/IP environment. Also *NetBT*.
negative caching	Storing the knowledge that something does not exist. A cache normally stores information about something that exists. A negative cache stores the information that something, such as a record, does not exist.
NetBIOS	Network Basic Input/Output System. An *API* (page 1095) for writing network-aware applications.
netboot	To boot a computer over the network (as opposed to booting from a local disk).
netiquette	The conventions of etiquette—that is, polite behavior—recognized on Usenet and in mailing lists, such as not (cross-)posting to inappropriate groups and refraining from commercial advertising outside the business groups.

The most important rule of netiquette is "Think before you post." If what you intend to post will not make a positive contribution to the newsgroup and be of interest to several readers, do not post it. Personal messages to one or two individuals should not be posted to newsgroups; use private email instead.FOLDOC |
| **netmask** | A 32-bit mask (for IPv4), that shows how an Internet address is to be divided into network, subnet, and host parts. The netmask has ones in the bit positions in the 32-bit address that are to be used for the network and subnet parts and zeros for the host part. The mask should contain at least the standard network portion (as determined by the address class). The subnet field should be contiguous with the network portion.FOLDOC |

network address	The network portion (**netid**) of an IP address. For a class A network, it is the first byte, or segment, of the IP address; for a class B network, it is the first two bytes; and for a class C network, it is the first three bytes. In each case the balance of the IP address is the host address (**hostid**). Assigned network addresses are globally unique within the Internet. Also *network number*. See also "Host Address" on page 365.
Network Filesystem	See *NFS*.
Network Information Service	See *NIS*.
network number	See *network address*.
network segment	A part of an Ethernet or other network on which all message traffic is common to all nodes; that is, it is broadcast from one node on the segment and received by all others. This commonality normally occurs because the segment is a single continuous conductor. Communication between nodes on different segments is via one or more routers.^{FOLDOC}
network switch	A connecting device in networks. Switches are increasingly replacing shared media hubs in an effort to increase bandwidth. For example, a 16-port 10BaseT hub shares the total 10 megabits per second bandwidth with all 16 attached nodes. By replacing the hub with a switch, both sender and receiver can take advantage of the full 10 megabits per second capacity. Each port on the switch can give full bandwidth to a single server or client station or to a hub with several stations. Network switch refers to a device with intelligence. Contrast with *hub* (page 1112).
Network Time Protocol	See *NTP* on page 1123.
NFS	Network Filesystem. A remote filesystem designed by Sun Microsystems, available on computers from most UNIX system vendors.
NIC	Network interface card (or controller). An adapter circuit board installed in a computer to provide a physical connection to a network.^{FOLDOC}
NIS	Network Information Service. A distributed service built on a shared database to manage system-independent information (such as usernames and passwords).
NIS domain name	A name that describes a group of systems that share a set of NIS files. Different from *domain name* (page 1106).
NNTP	Network News Transfer Protocol. Refer to "Usenet" on page 391.
node	In a tree structure, the end of a branch that can support other branches. When the Linux filesystem hierarchy is conceptualized as a tree, directories are nodes. See *leaf* on page 1116.
nonprinting character	See *control character* on page 1102. Also *nonprintable character*.

nonvolatile storage	A storage device whose contents are preserved when its power is off. Also NVS and persistent storage. Some examples are CD-ROM, paper punch tape, hard disk, *ROM* (page 1129), *PROM* (page 1126), *EPROM* (page 1107), and *EEPROM* (page 1107). Contrast with *RAM* (page 1127).
NTP	Network Time Protocol. Built on top of TCP/IP, NTP maintains accurate local time by referring to known accurate clocks on the Internet.
null string	A string that could contain characters but does not. A string of zero length.
octal number	A base 8 number. Octal numbers are composed of the digits 0–7, inclusive. Refer to Table G-1 on page 1112.
one-way hash function	A one-way function that takes a variable-length message and produces a fixed-length hash. Given the hash, it is computationally infeasible to find a message with that hash; in fact, you cannot determine any usable information about a message with that hash. Also *message digest function*. See also *hash* (page 1111).
OpenSSH	A free version of the SSH (secure shell) protocol suite that replaces TELNET, rlogin, and more with secure programs that encrypt all communication—even passwords—over a network. Refer to "OpenSSH: Secure Network Communication" on page 627.
operating system	A control program for a computer that allocates computer resources, schedules tasks, and provides the user with a way to access resources.
option	A command-line argument that modifies the effects of a command. Options are usually preceded by hyphens on the command line and traditionally have single-character names (such as **–h** or **–n**). Some commands allow you to group options following a single hyphen (for example, **–hn**). GNU utilities frequently have two arguments that do the same thing: a single-character argument and a longer, more descriptive argument that is preceded by two hyphens (such as **––show-all** and **––invert-match**).
ordinary file	A file that is used to store a program, text, or other user data. See *directory* (page 1105) and *device file* (page 1105).
output	Information that a program sends to the terminal or another file. See *standard output* on page 1134.
P2P	Peer-to-Peer. A network that does not divide nodes into clients and servers. Each computer on a P2P network can fulfill the roles of client and server. In the context of a file-sharing network, this ability means that once a node has downloaded (part of) a file, it can act as a server. BitTorrent implements a P2P network.
packet	A unit of data sent across a network. *Packet* is a generic term used to describe a unit of data at any layer of the OSI protocol stack, but it is most correctly used to describe network or application layer (page 364) data units ("application protocol data unit," APDU).ᶠᴼᴸᴰᴼᶜ See also *frame* (page 1109) and *datagram* (page 1104).
packet filtering	A technique used to block network traffic based on specified criteria, such as the origin, destination, or type of each packet. See also *firewall* (page 1108).

packet sniffer A program or device that monitors packets on a network. See *sniff* on page 1133.

pager A utility that allows you to view a file one screen at a time (for example, less and more).

paging The process by which virtual memory is maintained by the operating system. The contents of process memory is moved (paged out) to the *swap space* (page 1135) as needed to make room for other processes.

PAM Linux-PAM or Linux-Pluggable Authentication Modules. These modules allow a system administrator to determine how various applications authenticate users. Refer to "PAM" on page 461.

parent process A process that forks other processes. See *process* (page 1126) and *child process* (page 1100).

partition A section of a (hard) disk that has a name so you can address it separately from other sections. A disk partition can hold a filesystem or another structure, such as the swap area. Under DOS and Windows, partitions (and sometimes whole disks) are labeled **C:**, **D:**, and so on. Also *disk partition* and *slice*.

passive FTP Allows FTP to work through a firewall by allowing the flow of data to be initiated and controlled by the client FTP program instead of the server. Also called PASV FTP because it uses the FTP PASV command.

passphrase A string of words and characters that you type in to authenticate yourself. A passphrase differs from a *password* only in length. A password is usually short—6 to 10 characters. A passphrase is usually much longer—up to 100 characters or more. The greater length makes a passphrase harder to guess or reproduce than a password and therefore more secure.FOLDOC

password To prevent unauthorized access to a user's account, an arbitrary string of characters chosen by the user or system administrator and used to authenticate the user when attempting to log in.FOLDOC See also *passphrase*.

PASV FTP See *passive FTP*.

pathname A list of directories separated by slashes (/) and ending with the name of a file, which can be a directory. A pathname is used to trace a path through the file structure to locate or identify a file.

pathname, last element of a The part of a pathname following the final /, or the whole filename if there is no /. A simple filename. Also *basename*.

pathname element One of the filenames that forms a pathname.

peripheral device See *device* on page 1105.

persistent Data that is stored on nonvolatile media, such as a hard disk.

phish	An attempt to trick users into revealing or sharing private information, especially passwords or financial information. The most common form is email purporting to be from a bank or vendor that requests that a user fill out a form to "update" an account on a phoney Web site disguised to appear legitimate. Generally sent as *spam* (page 1133).
physical device	A tangible device, such as a disk drive, that is physically separate from other, similar devices.
PID	Process identification, usually followed by the word *number*. Linux assigns a unique PID number as each process is initiated.
pipe	A connection between programs such that standard output of one program is connected to standard input of the next. Also *pipeline*.
pixel	The smallest element of a picture, typically a single dot on a display screen.
plaintext	Text that is not encrypted. Also *cleartext*. Contrast with *ciphertext* (page 1101). See also "Encryption" on page 1064.
Pluggable Authentication Modules	See *PAM* on page 1124.
point-to-point link	A connection limited to two endpoints, such as the connection between a pair of modems.
port	A logical channel or channel endpoint in a communications system. The *TCP* (page 1136) and *UDP* (page 1138) transport layer protocols used on Ethernet use port numbers to distinguish between different logical channels on the same network interface on the same computer.
	The **/etc/services** file (see the beginning of this file for more information) or the *NIS* (page 1122) **services** database specifies a unique port number for each application program. The number links incoming data to the correct service (program). Standard, well-known ports are used by everyone: Port 80 is used for HTTP (Web) traffic. Some protocols, such as TELNET and HTTP (which is a special form of TELNET), have default ports specified as mentioned earlier but can use other ports as well.ᶠᴼᴸᴰᴼᶜ
port forwarding	The process by which a network *port* on one computer is transparently connected to a port on another computer. If port X is forwarded from system A to system B, any data sent to port X on system A is sent to system B automatically. The connection can be between different ports on the two systems. See also *tunneling* (page 1138).
portmapper	A server that converts TCP/IP port numbers into *RPC* (page 1130) program numbers. See "RPC Network Services" on page 390.

printable character	One of the graphic characters: a letter, number, or punctuation mark. Contrast with a nonprintable, or CONTROL, character. Also *printing character*.
private address space	*IANA* (page 1113) has reserved three blocks of IP addresses for private internets or LANs:

```
10.0.0.0 - 10.255.255.255
172.16.0.0 - 172.31.255.255
192.168.0.0 - 192.168.255.255
```

You can use these addresses without coordinating with anyone outside of your LAN (you do not have to register the system name or address). Systems using these IP addresses cannot communicate directly with hosts using the global address space but must go through a gateway. Because private addresses have no global meaning, routing information is not stored by DNSs and most ISPs reject privately addressed packets. Make sure that your router is set up not to forward these packets onto the Internet.

privileged port	A *port* (page 1125) with a number less than 1024. On Linux and other UNIX-like systems, only a process running with **root** privileges can bind to a privileged port. Any user on Windows 98 and earlier Windows systems can bind to any port. Also *reserved port*.
procedure	A sequence of instructions for performing a particular task. Most programming languages, including machine languages, enable a programmer to define procedures that allow the procedure code to be called from multiple places. Also *subroutine*.ᶠᴼᴸᴰᴼᶜ
process	The execution of a command by Linux. See "Processes" on page 312.
.profile file	A startup file in a user's home directory that the Bourne Again or Z Shell executes when you log in. The TC Shell executes **.login** instead. You can use the **.profile** file to run commands, set variables, and define functions.
program	A sequence of executable computer instructions contained in a file. Linux utilities, applications, and shell scripts are all programs. Whenever you run a command that is not built into a shell, you are executing a program.
PROM	Programmable readonly memory. A kind of nonvolatile storage. *ROM* (page 1129) that can be written to using a PROM programmer.
prompt	A cue from a program, usually displayed on the screen, indicating that it is waiting for input. The shell displays a prompt, as do some of the interactive utilities, such as mail. By default the Bourne Again and Z Shells use a dollar sign ($) as a prompt, and the TC Shell uses a percent sign (%).
protocol	A set of formal rules describing how to transmit data, especially across a network. Low-level protocols define the electrical and physical standards, bit and byte ordering, and transmission, error detection, and correction of the bit stream. High-level protocols deal with data formatting, including message syntax, terminal-to-computer dialog, character sets, and sequencing of messages.ᶠᴼᴸᴰᴼᶜ
proxy	A service that is authorized to act for a system while not being part of that system. See also *proxy gateway* and *proxy server*.

proxy gateway   A computer that separates clients (such as browsers) from the Internet, working as a trusted agent that accesses the Internet on their behalf. A proxy gateway passes a request for data from an Internet service, such as HTTP from a browser/client, to a remote server. The data that the server returns goes back through the proxy gateway to the requesting service. A proxy gateway should be transparent to the user.

A proxy gateway often runs on a *firewall* (page 1108) system and acts as a barrier to malicious users. It hides the IP addresses of the local computers inside the firewall from Internet users outside the firewall.

You can configure browsers, such as Mozilla/Firefox and Netscape, to use a different proxy gateway or to use no proxy for each URL access method including FTP, netnews, SNMP, HTTPS, and HTTP. See also *proxy*.

proxy server   A *proxy gateway* that usually includes a *cache* (page 1099) that holds frequently used Web pages so that the next request for that page is available locally (and therefore more quickly). The terms proxy server and proxy gateway are frequently interchanged so that the use of cache does not rest exclusively with the proxy server. See also *proxy*.

Python   A simple, high-level, interpreted, object-oriented, interactive language that bridges the gap between C and shell programming. Suitable for rapid prototyping or as an extension language for C applications, Python supports packages, modules, classes, user-defined exceptions, a good C interface, and dynamic loading of C modules. It has no arbitrary restrictions. For more information, see www.python.org.^{FOLDOC}

quote   When you quote a character, you take away any special meaning that it has in the current context. You can quote a character by preceding it with a backslash. When you are interacting with the shell, you can also quote a character by surrounding it with single quotation marks. For example, the command **echo *** or **echo '*'** displays *. The command **echo *** displays a list of the files in the working directory. See *ambiguous file reference* (page 1094), *metacharacter* (page 1119), *regular character* (page 1128), *regular expression* (page 1128), and *special character* (page 1133). See also *escape* on page 1107.

radio button   In a GUI, one of a group of buttons similar to those used to select the station on a car radio. Radio buttons within a group are mutually exclusive; only one button can be selected at a time.

RAID   Redundant array of inexpensive/independent disks. Two or more (hard) disk drives used in combination to improve fault tolerance and performance. RAID can be implemented in hardware or software.

RAM   Random access memory. A kind of volatile storage. A data storage device for which the order of access to different locations does not affect the speed of access. Contrast with a hard disk or tape drive, which provides quicker access to sequential data because accessing a nonsequential location requires physical movement of the storage medium and/or read/write head rather than just electronic switching. Contrast with *nonvolatile storage* (page 1123). Also *memory*.^{FOLDOC}

RAM disk   *RAM* that is made to look like a floppy diskette or hard disk. A RAM disk is frequently used as part of the *boot* (page 1098) process.

RAS   Remote access server. In a network, a computer that provides access to remote users via analog modem or ISDN connections. RAS includes the dial-up protocols and access control (authentication). It may be a regular fileserver with remote access software or a proprietary system, such as Shiva's LANRover. The modems may be internal or external to the device.

RDF   Resource Description Framework. Being developed by W3C (the main standards body for the World Wide Web), a standard that specifies a mechanism for encoding and transferring *metadata* (page 1119). RDF does not specify what the metadata should or can be. It can integrate many kinds of applications and data, using XML as an interchange syntax. Examples of the data that can be integrated include library catalogs and worldwide directories; syndication and aggregation of news, software, and content; and collections of music and photographs. Go to www.w3.org/RDF for more information.

redirection   The process of directing standard input for a program to come from a file rather than from the keyboard. Also, directing standard output or standard error to go to a file rather than to the screen.

reentrant   Code that can have multiple simultaneous, interleaved, or nested invocations that do not interfere with one another. Noninterference is important for parallel processing, recursive programming, and interrupt handling.

It is usually easy to arrange for multiple invocations (that is, calls to a subroutine) to share one copy of the code and any readonly data. For the code to be reentrant, however, each invocation must use its own copy of any modifiable data (or synchronized access to shared data). This goal is most often achieved by using a stack and allocating local variables in a new stack frame for each invocation. Alternatively, the caller may pass in a pointer to a block of memory that that invocation can use (usually for output), or the code may allocate some memory on a heap, especially if the data must survive after the routine returns.

Reentrant code is often found in system software, such as operating systems and teleprocessing monitors. It is also a crucial component of multithreaded programs, where the term *thread-safe* is often used instead of reentrant.^{FOLDOC}

regular character   A character that always represents itself in an ambiguous file reference or another type of regular expression. Contrast with *special character*.

regular expression   A string—composed of letters, numbers, and special symbols—that defines one or more strings. See Appendix A.

relative pathname   A pathname that starts from the working directory. Contrast with *absolute pathname* (page 1094).

remote access server	See *RAS* on page 1128.
remote filesystem	A filesystem on a remote computer that has been set up so that you can access (usually over a network) its files as though they were stored on your local computer's disks. An example of a remote filesystem is NFS.
remote procedure call	See *RPC* on page 1130.
resolver	The TCP/IP library software that formats requests to be sent to the *DNS* (page 1105) for hostname-to-Internet address conversion.^{FOLDOC}
Resource Description Framework	See *RDF* on page 1128.
restore	The process of turning an icon into a window. Contrast with *iconify* (page 1113)
return code	See *exit status* on page 1107.
RFC	Request for comments. Begun in 1969, one of a series of numbered Internet informational documents and standards widely followed by commercial software and freeware in the Internet and UNIX/Linux communities. Few RFCs are standards but all Internet standards are recorded in RFCs. Perhaps the single most influential RFC has been RFC 822, the Internet electronic mail format standard.

The RFCs are unusual in that they are floated by technical experts acting on their own initiative and reviewed by the Internet at large rather than being formally promulgated through an institution such as ANSI. For this reason they remain known as RFCs, even after they are adopted as standards. The RFC tradition of pragmatic, experience-driven, after-the-fact standard writing done by individuals or small working groups has important advantages over the more formal, committee-driven process typical of ANSI or ISO. For a complete list of RFCs, go to www.rfc-editor.org.^{FOLDOC} |
| roam | To move a computer between *wireless access points* (page 1141) on a wireless network without the user or applications being aware of the transition. Moving between access points typically results in some packet loss, although this loss is transparent to programs that use TCP. |
| ROM | Readonly memory. A kind of nonvolatile storage. A data storage device that is manufactured with fixed contents. In general, ROM describes any storage system whose contents cannot be altered, such as a phonograph record or printed book. When used in reference to electronics and computers, ROM describes semiconductor integrated circuit memories, of which several types exist, and CD-ROM.

ROM is nonvolatile storage—it retains its contents even after power has been removed. ROM is often used to hold programs for embedded systems, as these usually have a fixed purpose. ROM is also used for storage of the *BIOS* (page 1097) in a computer. Contrast with *RAM* (page 1127).^{FOLDOC} |

root directory   The ancestor of all directories and the start of all absolute pathnames. The root directory has no name and is represented by **/** standing alone or at the left end of a pathname.

root filesystem   The filesystem that is available when the system is brought up in recovery mode. This filesystem is always represented by **/**. You cannot unmount or mount the root filesystem. You can remount root to change its mount options.

root login   Usually the username of *Superuser* (page 1135).

root (user)   Another name for *Superuser* (page 1135).

root window   Any place on the desktop not covered by a window, object, or panel.

rotate   When a file, such as a log file, gets indefinitely larger, you must keep it from taking up too much space on the disk. Because you may need to refer to the information in the log files in the near future, it is generally not a good idea to delete the contents of the file until it has aged. Instead you can periodically save the current log file under a new name and create a new, empty file as the current log file. You can keep a series of these files, renaming each as a new one is saved. You will then *rotate* the files. For example, you might remove **xyzlog.4**, **xyzlog.3**→**xyzlog.4**, **xyzlog.2**→**xyzlog.3**, **xyzlog.1**→**xyzlog.2**, **xyzlog**→**xyzlog.1**, and create a new **xyzlog** file. By the time you remove **xyzlog.4**, it will not contain any information more recent than you want to remove.

router   A device (often a computer) that is connected to more than one similar type of network to pass data between them. See *gateway* on page 1109.

RPC   Remote procedure call. A call to a *procedure* (page 1126) that acts transparently across a network. The procedure itself is responsible for accessing and using the network. The RPC libraries make sure that network access is transparent to the application. RPC runs on top of TCP/IP or UDP/IP.

RSA   A public key encryption (page 1065) technology that is based on the lack of an efficient way to factor very large numbers. Because of this lack, it takes an extraordinary amount of computer processing time and power to deduce an RSA key. The RSA algorithm is the de facto standard for data sent over the Internet.

run   To execute a program.

runlevel   Before the introduction of Upstart daemon, runlevels specified the state of the system, including single-user and multiuser. For more information refer to "Runlevel emulation" on page 418.

Samba   A free suite of programs that implement the Server Message Block (SMB) protocol. See *SMB* (page 1132).

schema   Within a GUI, a pattern that helps you see and interpret the information that is presented in a window, making it easier to understand new information that is presented using the same schema.

scroll	To move lines on a terminal or window up and down or left and right.
scrollbar	A *widget* (page 1140) found in graphical user interfaces that controls (scrolls) which part of a document is visible in the window. A window can have a horizontal scrollbar, a vertical scrollbar (more common), or both.ᶠᴼᴸᴰᴼᶜ
server	A powerful centralized computer (or program) designed to provide information to clients (smaller computers or programs) on request.
session	The lifetime of a process. For a desktop, it is the desktop session manager. For a character-based terminal, it is the user's login shell process. In KDE, it is launched by kdeinit. A session may also be the sequence of events between when you start using a program, such as an editor, and when you finish.
setgid	When you execute a file that has setgid (set group ID) permission, the process executing the file takes on the privileges of the group the file belongs to. The ls utility shows setgid permission as an **s** in the group's executable position. See also *setuid*.
setuid	When you execute a file that has setuid (set user ID) permission, the process executing the file takes on the privileges of the owner of the file. As an example, if you run a setuid program that removes all the files in a directory, you can remove files in any of the file owner's directories, even if you do not normally have permission to do so. When the program is owned by **root,** you can remove files in any directory that a user working with **root** privileges can remove files from. The ls utility shows setuid permission as an **s** in the owner's executable position. See also *setgid*.
sexillion	In the British system, 10^{36}. In the American system, this number is named *undecillion*. See also *large number* (page 1116).
SHA1	Secure Hash Algorithm 1. The SHA family is a set of cryptographic *hash* (page 1111) algorithms that were designed by the National Security Agency (NSA). The second member of this family is SHA1, a successor to *MD5* (page 1119). See also *cryptography* on page 1103.
share	A filesystem hierarchy that is shared with another system using *SMB* (page 1132). Also *Windows share* (page 1141).
shared network topology	A network, such as Ethernet, in which each packet may be seen by systems other than its destination system. *Shared* means that the network bandwidth is shared by all users.
shell	A Linux system command processor. The three major shells are the *Bourne Again Shell* (page 1098), the *TC Shell* (page 1136), and the *Z Shell* (page 1142).
shell function	A series of commands that the shell stores for execution at a later time. Shell functions are like shell scripts but run more quickly because they are stored in the computer's main memory rather than in files. Also, a shell function is run in the environment of the shell that calls it (unlike a shell script, which is typically run in a subshell).

shell script	An ASCII file containing shell commands. Also *shell program*.
signal	A very brief message that the UNIX system can send to a process, apart from the process's standard input. Refer to "trap: Catches a Signal" on page 965.
simple filename	A single filename containing no slashes (/). A simple filename is the simplest form of pathname. Also the last element of a pathname. Also *basename* (page 1097).
single-user system	A computer system that only one person can use at a time. Contrast with *multiuser system* (page 1121).
slider	A *widget* (page 1140) that allows a user to set a value by dragging an indicator along a line. Many sliders allow the user also to click on the line to move the indicator. Differs from a *scrollbar* (page 1131) in that moving the indicator does not change other parts of the display.
SMB	Server Message Block. Developed in the early 1980s by Intel, Microsoft, and IBM, SMB is a client/server protocol that is the native method of file and printer sharing for Windows. In addition, SMB can share serial ports and communications abstractions, such as named pipes and mail slots. SMB is similar to a remote procedure call (*RPC*, page 1130) that has been customized for filesystem access. Also *Microsoft Networking*.^{FOLDOC}
SMP	Symmetric multiprocessing. Two or more similar processors connected via a high-bandwidth link and managed by one operating system, where each processor has equal access to I/O devices. The processors are treated more or less equally, with application programs able to run on any or all processors interchangeably, at the discretion of the operating system.^{FOLDOC}
smiley	A character-based *glyph* (page 1110), typically used in email, that conveys an emotion. The characters :-) in a message portray a smiley face (look at it sideways). Because it can be difficult to tell when the writer of an electronic message is saying something in jest or in seriousness, email users often use :-) to indicate humor. The two original smileys, designed by Scott Fahlman, were :-) and :-(. Also *emoticon*, *smileys*, and *smilies*. For more information search on **smiley** on the Internet.
smilies	*See smiley.*
SMTP	Simple Mail Transfer Protocol. A protocol used to transfer electronic mail between computers. It is a server-to-server protocol, so other protocols are used to access the messages. The SMTP dialog usually happens in the background under the control of a message transport system such as **exim4**.^{FOLDOC}
snap (windows)	As you drag a window toward another window or edge of the workspace, it can move suddenly so that it is adjacent to the other window/edge. Thus the window *snaps* into position.
sneakernet	Using hand-carried magnetic media to transfer files between machines.

sniff	To monitor packets on a network. A system administrator can legitimately sniff packets and a malicious user can sniff packets to obtain information such as usernames and passwords. See also *packet sniffer* (page 1124).
SOCKS	A networking proxy protocol embodied in a SOCKS server, which performs the same functions as a *proxy gateway* (page 1127) or *proxy server* (page 1127). SOCKS works at the application level, requiring that an application be modified to work with the SOCKS protocol, whereas a *proxy* (page 1126) makes no demands on the application.
	SOCKSv4 does not support authentication or UDP proxy. SOCKSv5 supports a variety of authentication methods and UDP proxy.
sort	To put in a specified order, usually alphabetic or numeric.
SPACE **character**	A character that appears as the absence of a visible character. Even though you cannot see it, a SPACE is a printable character. It is represented by the ASCII code 32 (decimal). A SPACE character is considered a *blank* or *whitespace* (page 1140).
spam	Posting irrelevant or inappropriate messages to one or more Usenet newsgroups or mailing lists in deliberate or accidental violation of *netiquette* (page 1121). Also, sending large amounts of unsolicited email indiscriminately. This email usually promotes a product or service. Another common purpose of spam is to *phish* (page 1125). Spam is the electronic equivalent of junk mail. From the Monty Python "Spam" song.FOLDOC
sparse file	A file that is large but takes up little disk space. The data in a sparse file is not dense (thus its name). Examples of sparse files are core files and dbm files.
spawn	See *fork* on page 1109.
special character	A character that has a special meaning when it occurs in an ambiguous file reference or another type of regular expression, unless it is quoted. The special characters most commonly used with the shell are * and ?. Also *metacharacter* (page 1119) and *wildcard*.
special file	See *device file* on page 1105.
spin box	In a GUI, a type of *text box* (page 1136) that holds a number you can change by typing over it or using the up and down arrows at the end of the box. Also *spinner*.
spinner	See *spin box*.
spoofing	See *IP spoofing* on page 1115.
spool	To place items in a queue, each waiting its turn for some action. Often used when speaking about printers. Also used to describe the queue.
SQL	Structured Query Language. A language that provides a user interface to relational database management systems (RDBMS). SQL, the de facto standard, is also an ISO and ANSI standard and is often embedded in other programming languages.FOLDOC

square bracket   A left square bracket ([) or a right square bracket (]). These special characters define character classes in ambiguous file references and other regular expressions.

SSH Communications Security   The company that created the original SSH (secure shell) protocol suite (www.ssh.com). Linux uses *OpenSSH* (page 1123).

standard error   A file to which a program can send output. Usually only error messages are sent to this file. Unless you instruct the shell otherwise, it directs this output to the screen (that is, to the device file that represents the screen).

standard input   A file from which a program can receive input. Unless you instruct the shell otherwise, it directs this input so that it comes from the keyboard (that is, from the device file that represents the keyboard).

standard output   A file to which a program can send output. Unless you instruct the shell otherwise, it directs this output to the screen (that is, to the device file that represents the screen).

startup file   A file that the login shell runs when you log in. The Bourne Again and Z Shells run **.profile**, and the TC Shell runs **.login**. The TC Shell also runs **.cshrc** whenever a new TC Shell or a subshell is invoked. The Z Shell runs an analogous file whose name is identified by the **ENV** variable.

status line   The bottom (usually the twenty-fourth) line of the terminal. The vim editor uses the status line to display information about what is happening during an editing session.

sticky bit   An access permission bit that causes an executable program to remain on the swap area of the disk. It takes less time to load a program that has its sticky bit set than one that does not. Only a user with **root** privileges can set the sticky bit. If the sticky bit is set on a directory that is publicly writable, only the owner of a file in that directory can remove the file.

streaming tape   A tape that moves at a constant speed past the read/write heads rather than speeding up and slowing down, which can slow the process of writing to or reading from the tape. A proper blocking factor helps ensure that the tape device will be kept streaming.

streams   See *connection-oriented protocol* on page 1102.

string   A sequence of characters.

stylesheet   *See* CSS on page 1103.

subdirectory   A directory that is located within another directory. Every directory except the root directory is a subdirectory.

subnet   Subnetwork. A portion of a network, which may be a physically independent network segment, that shares a network address with other portions of the network and is distinguished by a subnet number. A subnet is to a network as a network is to an internet.FOLDOC

subnet address The subnet portion of an IP address. In a subnetted network, the host portion of an IP address is split into a subnet portion and a host portion using a subnet mask (also address mask). See also *subnet number.*

subnet mask A bit mask used to identify which bits in an IP address correspond to the network address and subnet portions of the address. Called a subnet mask because the network portion of the address is determined by the number of bits that are set in the mask. The subnet mask has ones in positions corresponding to the network and subnet numbers and zeros in the host number positions. Also *address mask.*

subnet number The subnet portion of an IP address. In a subnetted network, the host portion of an IP address is split into a subnet portion and a host portion using a *subnet mask.* Also *address mask.* See also *subnet address.*

subpixel hinting Similar to *anti-aliasing* (page 1095) but takes advantage of colors to do the anti-aliasing. Particularly useful on LCD screens.

subroutine See *procedure* on page 1126.

subshell A shell that is forked as a duplicate of its parent shell. When you run an executable file that contains a shell script by using its filename on the command line, the shell forks a subshell to run the script. Also, commands surrounded with parentheses are run in a subshell.

superblock A block that contains control information for a filesystem. The superblock contains housekeeping information, such as the number of inodes in the filesystem and free list information.

superserver The extended Internet services daemon. Refer to xinetd on page 389.

Superuser A user working with **root** privileges. This user has access to anything any other system user has access to and more. The system administrator must be able to become Superuser (work with **root** privileges) to establish new accounts, change passwords, and perform other administrative tasks. The username of Superuser is usually **root**. Also *root* or *root user.*

swap The operating system moving a process from main memory to a disk, or vice versa. Swapping a process to the disk allows another process to begin or continue execution. Refer to "swap" on page 480.

swap space An area of a disk (that is, a swap file) used to store the portion of a process's memory that has been paged out. Under a virtual memory system, the amount of swap space—rather than the amount of physical memory—determines the maximum size of a single process and the maximum total size of all active processes. Also *swap area* or *swapping area.*FOLDOC

switch See *network switch* on page 1122.

symbolic link	A directory entry that points to the pathname of another file. In most cases a symbolic link to a file can be used in the same ways a hard link can be used. Unlike a hard link, a symbolic link can span filesystems and can connect to a directory.
system administrator	The person responsible for the upkeep of the system. The system administrator has the ability to log in as **root** or use **sudo** to work with **root** privileges. See also *Superuser*.
system console	See *console* on page 1102.
system mode	The designation for the state of the system while it is doing system work. Some examples are making system calls, running NFS and autofs, processing network traffic, and performing kernel operations on behalf of the system. Contrast with *user mode* (page 1139).
System V	One of the two major versions of the UNIX system.
TC Shell	**tcsh**. An enhanced but completely compatible version of the BSD UNIX C shell, **csh**.
TCP	Transmission Control Protocol. The most common transport layer protocol used on the Internet. This connection-oriented protocol is built on top of *IP* (page 1114) and is nearly always seen in the combination TCP/IP (TCP over *IP*). TCP adds reliable communication, sequencing, and flow control and provides full-duplex, process-to-process connections. *UDP* (page 1138), although connectionless, is the other protocol that runs on top of *IP*.ꜰᴏʟᴅᴏᴄ
tera-	In the binary system, the prefix *tera-* multiplies by 2^{40} (1,099,511,627,776). Terabyte is a common use of this prefix. Abbreviated as *T*. See also *large number* on page 1116.
termcap	Terminal capability. The **/etc/termcap** file contains a list of various types of terminals and their characteristics. *System V* replaced the function of this file with the *terminfo* system.
terminal	Differentiated from a *workstation* (page 1141) by its lack of intelligence, a terminal connects to a computer that runs Linux. A workstation runs Linux on itself.
terminfo	Terminal information. The **/usr/lib/terminfo** directory contains many subdirectories, each containing several files. Each of those files is named for and holds a summary of the functional characteristics of a particular terminal. Visually oriented textual programs, such as vim, use these files. An alternative to the **termcap** file.
text box	A GUI *widget* (page 1140) that allows a user to enter text.
theme	Defined as an implicit or recurrent idea, *theme* is used in a GUI to describe a look that is consistent for all elements of a desktop. Go to themes.freshmeat.net for examples.
thicknet	A type of coaxial cable (thick) used for an Ethernet network. Devices are attached to thicknet by tapping the cable at fixed points.
thinnet	A type of coaxial cable (thin) used for an Ethernet network. Thinnet cable is smaller in diameter and more flexible than *thicknet* cable. Each device is typically attached

to two separate cable segments by using a T-shaped connector; one segment leads to the device ahead of it on the network and one to the device that follows it.

thread-safe   See *reentrant* on page 1128.

thumb   The movable button in the *scrollbar* (page 1131) that positions the image in the window. The size of the thumb reflects the amount of information in the buffer. Also *bubble*.

tick   A mark, usually in a *check box* (page 1100), that indicates a positive response. The mark can be a check mark (✔) or an **x**. Also *check mark* or *check*.

TIFF   Tagged Image File Format. A file format used for still-image bitmaps, stored in tagged fields. Application programs can use the tags to accept or ignore fields, depending on their capabilities.ᶠᵒˡᵈᵒᶜ

tiled windows   An arrangement of windows such that no window overlaps another. The opposite of *cascading windows* (page 1099).

time to live   See *TTL*.

toggle   To switch between one of two positions. For example, the ftp **glob** command toggles the **glob** feature: Give the command once, and it turns the feature on or off; give the command again, and it sets the feature back to its original state.

token   A basic, grammatically indivisible unit of a language, such as a keyword, operator, or identifier.ᶠᵒˡᵈᵒᶜ

token ring   A type of *LAN* (page 1116) in which computers are attached to a ring of cable. A token packet circulates continuously around the ring. A computer can transmit information only when it holds the token.

tooltip   A minicontext help system that a user activates by allowing the mouse pointer to *hover* (page 1112) over an object (such as those on a panel).

transient window A dialog or other window that is displayed for only a short time.

Transmission Control Protocol   See *TCP* on page 1136.

Trojan horse   A program that does something destructive or disruptive to your system. Its action is not documented, and the system administrator would not approve of it if she were aware of it. See "Avoiding a Trojan Horse" on page 436.

The term *Trojan horse* was coined by MIT-hacker-turned-NSA-spook Dan Edwards. It refers to a malicious security-breaking program that is disguised as something benign, such as a directory lister, archive utility, game, or (in one notorious 1990 case on the Mac) a program to find and destroy viruses. Similar to *back door* (page 1096).ᶠᵒˡᵈᵒᶜ

TTL   Time to live.

1. All DNS records specify how long they are good for—usually up to a week at most. This time is called the record's *time to live*. When a DNS server or an application stores this record in *cache* (page 1099), it decrements the TTL value and removes the record from cache when the value reaches zero. A DNS server passes a cached record to another server with the current (decremented) TTL guaranteeing the proper TTL, no matter how many servers the record passes through.

2. In the IP header, a field that indicates how many more hops the packet should be allowed to make before being discarded or returned.

TTY   Teletypewriter. The terminal device that UNIX was first run from. Today TTY refers to the screen (or window, in the case of a terminal emulator), keyboard, and mouse that are connected to a computer. This term appears in UNIX, and Linux has kept the term for the sake of consistency and tradition.

tunneling   Encapsulation of protocol A within packets carried by protocol B, such that A treats B as though it were a data link layer. Tunneling is used to transfer data between administrative domains that use a protocol not supported by the internet connecting those domains. It can also be used to encrypt data sent over a public internet, as when you use ssh to tunnel a protocol over the Internet.[FOLDOC] See also *VPN* (page 1140) and *port forwarding* (page 1125).

UDP   User Datagram Protocol. The Internet standard transport layer protocol that provides simple but unreliable datagram services. UDP is a *connectionless protocol* (page 1102) that, like *TCP* (page 1136), is layered on top of *IP* (page 1114).

Unlike *TCP*, UDP neither guarantees delivery nor requires a connection. As a result it is lightweight and efficient, but the application program must handle all error processing and retransmission. UDP is often used for sending time-sensitive data that is not particularly sensitive to minor loss, such as audio and video data.[FOLDOC]

UID   User ID. A number that the **passwd** database associates with a username.

undecillion   In the American system, 10^{36}. In the British system, this number is named *sexillion*. See also *large number* (page 1116).

unicast   A packet sent from one host to another host. Unicast means one source and one destination.

Unicode   A character encoding standard that was designed to cover all major modern written languages with each character having exactly one encoding and being represented by a fixed number of bits.

unmanaged   See *ignored window* on page 1113.
window

URI	Universal Resource Identifier. The generic set of all names and addresses that are short strings referring to objects (typically on the Internet). The most common kinds of URIs are *URLs*.ᶠᵒˡᵈᵒᶜ
URL	Uniform (was Universal) Resource Locator. A standard way of specifying the location of an object, typically a Web page, on the Internet. URLs are a subset of *URIs*.
usage message	A message displayed by a command when you call the command using incorrect command-line arguments.
User Datagram Protocol	See *UDP*.
User ID	See *UID*.
user interface	See *interface* on page 1114.
user mode	The designation for the state of the system while it is doing user work, such as running a user program (but not the system calls made by the program). Contrast with *system mode* (page 1136).
username	The name you enter in response to the **login:** prompt. Other users use your username when they send you mail or write to you. Each username has a corresponding user ID, which is the numeric identifier for the user. Both the username and the user ID are stored in the **passwd** database (**/etc/passwd** or the NIS equivalent). Also *login name*.
userspace	The part of memory (RAM) where applications reside. Code running in userspace cannot access hardware directly and cannot access memory allocated to other applications. Also *userland*. See the *KernelAnalysis-HOWTO*.
UTC	Coordinated Universal Time. UTC is the equivalent to the mean solar time at the prime meridian (0 degrees longitude). Also called Zulu time (Z stands for longitude zero) and GMT (Greenwich Mean Time).
UTF-8	An encoding that allows *Unicode* (page 1138) characters to be represented using sequences of 8-bit bytes.
utility	A program included as a standard part of Linux. You typically invoke a utility either by giving a command in response to a shell prompt or by calling it from within a shell script. Utilities are often referred to as commands. Contrast with *builtin (command)* (page 1099).
UUID	Universally Unique Identifier. A 128-bit number that uniquely identifies an object on the Internet. Frequently used on Linux systems to identify an **ext2** or **ext3** disk partition.

variable
A name and an associated value. The shell allows you to create variables and use them in shell scripts. Also, the shell inherits several variables when it is invoked, and it maintains those and other variables while it is running. Some shell variables establish characteristics of the shell environment; others have values that reflect different aspects of your ongoing interaction with the shell.

viewport
Same as *workspace* (page 1141).

virtual console
Additional consoles, or displays, that you can view on the system, or physical, console. See page 134 for more information.

virus
A *cracker* (page 1103) program that searches out other programs and "infects" them by embedding a copy of itself in them, so that they become *Trojan horses* (page 1137). When these programs are executed, the embedded virus is executed as well, propagating the "infection," usually without the user's knowledge. By analogy with biological viruses.FOLDOC

VLAN
Virtual LAN. A logical grouping of two or more nodes that are not necessarily on the same physical network segment but that share the same network number. A VLAN is often associated with switched Ethernet.FOLDOC

VPN
Virtual private network. A private network that exists on a public network, such as the Internet. A VPN is a less expensive substitute for company-owned/leased lines and uses encryption (page 1064) to ensure privacy. A nice side effect is that you can send non-Internet protocols, such as AppleTalk, IPX, or *NetBIOS* (page 1121), over the VPN connection by *tunneling* (page 1138) them through the VPN IP stream.

W2K
Windows 2000 Professional or Server.

W3C
World Wide Web Consortium (www.w3.org).

WAN
Wide area network. A network that interconnects *LANs* (page 1116) and *MANs* (page 1119), spanning a large geographic area (typically states or countries).

WAP
Wireless access point. A bridge or router between wired and wireless networks. WAPs typically support some form of access control to prevent unauthorized clients from connecting to the network.

Web ring
A collection of Web sites that provide information on a single topic or group of related topics. Each home page that is part of the Web ring has a series of links that let you go from site to site.

whitespace
A collective name for SPACEs and/or TABs and occasionally NEWLINEs. Also *white space*.

wide area network
See *WAN*.

widget
The basic objects of a graphical user interface. A button, *combo box* (page 1101), and *scrollbar* (page 1131) are examples of widgets.

wildcard
See *metacharacter* on page 1119.

Wi-Fi   Wireless Fidelity. A generic term that refers to any type of *802.11* (page 1094) wireless network.

window   On a display screen, a region that runs or is controlled by a particular program.

window manager   A program that controls how windows appear on a display screen and how you manipulate them.

Windows share   See *share* on page 1131.

WINS   Windows Internet Naming Service. The service responsible for mapping NetBIOS names to IP addresses. WINS has the same relationship to NetBIOS names that DNS has to Internet domain names.

WINS server   The program responsible for handling WINS requests. This program caches name information about hosts on a local network and resolves them to IP addresses.

wireless access point   See *WAP*.

word   A sequence of one or more nonblank characters separated from other words by TABs, SPACEs, or NEWLINEs. Used to refer to individual command-line arguments. In vim, a word is similar to a word in the English language—a string of one or more characters bounded by a punctuation mark, a numeral, a TAB, a SPACE, or a NEWLINE.

Work buffer   A location where vim stores text while it is being edited. The information in the Work buffer is not written to the file on the disk until you give the editor a command to write it.

working directory   The directory that you are associated with at any given time. The relative pathnames you use are *relative to* the working directory. Also *current directory*.

workspace   A subdivision of a *desktop* (page 1104) that occupies the entire display. See page 104.

workstation   A small computer, typically designed to fit in an office and be used by one person and usually equipped with a bit-mapped graphical display, keyboard, and mouse. Differentiated from a *terminal* (page 1136) by its intelligence. A workstation runs Linux on itself while a terminal connects to a computer that runs Linux.

worm   A program that propagates itself over a network, reproducing itself as it goes. Today the term has negative connotations, as it is assumed that only *crackers* (page 1103) write worms. Compare to *virus* (page 1140) and *Trojan horse* (page 1137). From **Tapeworm** in John Brunner's novel, *The Shockwave Rider*, Ballantine Books, 1990 (via XEROX PARC).FOLDOC

WYSIWYG   What You See Is What You Get. A graphical application, such as a word processor, whose display is similar to its printed output.

X server   The X server is the part of the *X Window System* that runs the mouse, keyboard, and display. (The application program is the client.)

X terminal   A graphics terminal designed to run the X Window System.

X Window System   A design and set of tools for writing flexible, portable windowing applications, created jointly by researchers at MIT and several leading computer manufacturers.

XDMCP   X Display Manager Control Protocol. XDMCP allows the login server to accept requests from network displays. XDMCP is built into many X terminals.

*x*DSL   Different types of *DSL* (page 1107) are identified by a prefix, for example, ADSL, HDSL, SDSL, and VDSL.

Xinerama   An extension to X.org. Xinerama allows window managers and applications to use the two or more physical displays as one large virtual display. Refer to the Xinerama-HOWTO.

XML   Extensible Markup Language. A universal format for structured documents and data on the Web. Developed by *W3C* (page 1140), XML is a pared-down version of SGML. See www.w3.org/XML and www.w3.org/XML/1999/XML-in-10-points.

XSM   X Session Manager. This program allows you to create a session that includes certain applications. While the session is running, you can perform a *checkpoint* (saves the application state) or a *shutdown* (saves the state and exits from the session). When you log back in, you can load your session so that everything in your session is running just as it was when you logged off.

Z Shell   zsh. A *shell* (page 1131) that incorporates many of the features of the *Bourne Again Shell* (page 1098), *Korn Shell* (page 1116), and *TC Shell* (page 1136), as well as many original features.

Zulu time   See *UTC* on page 1139.

JumpStart Index

FILE TREE INDEX

A light page number such as 456 indicates a brief mention.

Utility Index

A light page number such as 456 indicates a brief mention. Page numbers followed by the letter **t** refer to tables.

Main Index

An italic page number such as *123* indictes a definition. A light page number such as 456 indicates a brief mention. Page numbers followed by the letter t refer to tables. Only variables that must always appear with a leading dollar sign are indexed with a leading dollar sign. Other variables are indexed without a leading dollar sign.

NUMERICS

A

G

N

ALSO AVAILABLE FROM MARK G. SOBELL AND PRENTICE HALL

The Most Useful Linux Tutorial and Reference Ever, with Hundreds of High-Quality Examples Covering Every Linux Distribution!

To be truly productive with Linux, you need to thoroughly master the shells and the command line. Until now, you had to buy two books to gain that mastery: a tutorial on fundamental Linux concepts and techniques, plus a separate reference. Worse, most Linux references offer little more than prettied-up *man* pages. *Now, there's a far better solution.* Renowned Linux expert Mark G. Sobell has brought together comprehensive, insightful guidance on the tools system administrators, developers, and power users need most, and an outstanding day-to-day reference, *both in the same book.*

ISBN-13: 978-0-13-147823-7
©2006 · 1,008 pages

This book is 100 percent distribution and release agnostic: You can use it on any Linux system, now and for years to come. What's more, it's packed with *hundreds* of high-quality examples: better examples than you'll find in any other Linux guidebook. This is Linux from the ground up—the clearest explanations and most useful knowledge about everything from filesystems to shells, editors to utilities, and programming tools to regular expressions. And when you need instant answers, you'll constantly turn to Sobell's comprehensive command reference section—organized and tabbed for easy, fast access!

Don't settle for *yesterday's* Linux guidebook. Get the one book that meets today's challenges—and tomorrow's!

A Practical Guide to Linux® Commands, Editors, and Shell Programming is the most useful, most comprehensive Linux tutorial and reference you can find.

PRENTICE HALL

Visit us online for more information about this book and to read sample chapters.
www.informit.com/ph

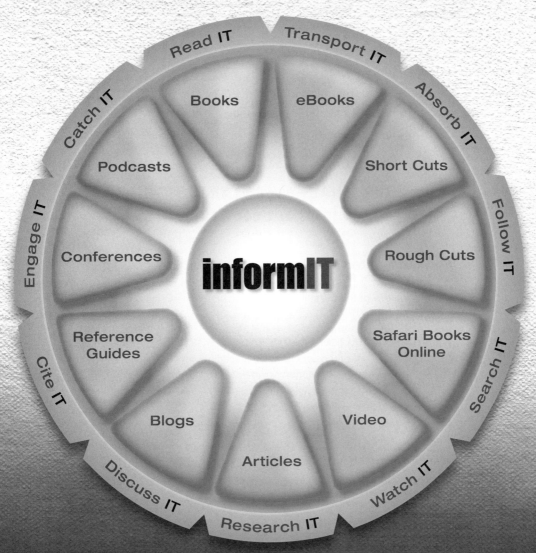

LearnIT at InformIT

Go Beyond the Book

informIT

Read IT · Books

Transport IT · eBooks

Absorb IT · Short Cuts

Catch IT · Podcasts

Follow IT · Rough Cuts

Engage IT · Conferences

Search IT · Safari Books Online

Cite IT · Reference Guides

Discuss IT · Blogs

Research IT · Articles

Watch IT · Video

11 WAYS TO LEARN IT at **www.informIT.com/learn**

The online portal of the information technology
publishing imprints of Pearson Education

DVD-ROM WARRANTY

Prentice Hall warrants the enclosed DVD-ROM to be free of defects in materials and faulty workmanship under normal use for a period of ninety days after purchase (when purchased new). If a defect is discovered in the DVD during this warranty period, a replacement DVD-ROM can be obtained at no charge by sending the defective DVD-ROM, postage prepaid, with proof of purchase to:

Disc Exchange
Prentice Hall
Pearson Technology Group
75 Arlington Street, Suite 300
Boston, MA 02116
Email: AWPro@aw.com

Prentice Hall makes no warranty or representation, either expressed or implied, with respect to this software, its quality, performance, merchantability, or fitness for a particular purpose. In no event will Prentice Hall, its distributors, or dealers be liable for direct, indirect, special, incidental, or consequential damages arising out of the use or inability to use the software. The exclusion of implied warranties is not permitted in some states. Therefore, the above exclusion may not apply to you. This warranty provides you with specific legal rights. There may be other rights that you may have that vary from state to state. The contents of this DVD-ROM are intended for personal use only.

More information and updates are available at informit.com/ph

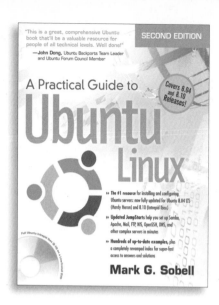

"This is a great, comprehensive Ubuntu book that'll be a valuable resource for people of all technical levels. Well done!"
—**John Dong**, Ubuntu Backports Team Leader and Ubuntu Forum Council Member

SECOND EDITION

A Practical Guide to

Ubuntu Linux

Covers 8.04 and 8.10 Releases!

» The #1 resource for installing and configuring Ubuntu servers: now fully updated for Ubuntu 8.04 LTS (Hardy Heron) and 8.10 (Intrepid Ibex)

» Updated JumpStarts help you set up Samba, Apache, Mail, FTP, NIS, OpenSSH, DNS, and other complex servers in minutes

» Hundreds of up-to-date examples, plus a completely revamped index for super-fast access to answers and solutions

Mark G. Sobell

FREE Online Edition

Your purchase of *A Practical Guide to Ubuntu Linux*®, *Second Edition,* includes access to a free online edition for 45 days through the Safari Books Online subscription service. Nearly every Prentice Hall book is available online through Safari Books Online, along with more than 5,000 other technical books and videos from publishers such as Addison-Wesley Professional, Cisco Press, Exam Cram, IBM Press, O'Reilly, Que, and Sams.

SAFARI BOOKS ONLINE allows you to search for a specific answer, cut and paste code, download chapters, and stay current with emerging technologies.

Activate your FREE Online Edition at www.informit.com/safarifree

> **STEP 1:** Enter the coupon code: YBTJIXA.

> **STEP 2:** New Safari users, complete the brief registration form.
> Safari subscribers, just log in.

If you have difficulty registering on Safari or accessing the online edition, please e-mail customer-service@safaribooksonline.com